# Nineteenth-Century Literature Criticism

# Guide to Gale Literary Criticism Series

**When you need to review criticism of literary works, these are the Gale series to use:**

**If the author's death date is:**

**You should turn to:**

After Dec. 31, 1959
(or author is still living)

### CONTEMPORARY LITERARY CRITICISM

for example: Jorge Luis Borges, Anthony Burgess,
William Faulkner, Mary Gordon,
Ernest Hemingway, Iris Murdoch

1900 through 1959

### TWENTIETH-CENTURY LITERARY CRITICISM

for example: Willa Cather, F. Scott Fitzgerald,
Henry James, Mark Twain, Virginia Woolf

1800 through 1899

### NINETEENTH-CENTURY LITERATURE CRITICISM

for example: Fedor Dostoevski, Nathaniel Hawthorne,
George Sand, William Wordsworth

1400 through 1799

### LITERATURE CRITICISM FROM 1400 TO 1800 (excluding Shakespeare)

for example: Anne Bradstreet, Daniel Defoe,
Alexander Pope, François Rabelais,
Jonathan Swift, Phillis Wheatley

### SHAKESPEAREAN CRITICISM

Shakespeare's plays and poetry

Antiquity through 1399

### CLASSICAL AND MEDIEVAL LITERATURE CRITICISM

for example: Dante, Homer, Plato, Sophocles, Vergil,
the Beowulf Poet

---

## Gale also publishes related criticism series:

### CHILDREN'S LITERATURE REVIEW

This series covers authors of all eras who have written for
the preschool through high school audience.

### SHORT STORY CRITICISM

This series covers the major short fiction writers of all nationalities
and periods of literary history.

ISSN 0732-1864

Volume 26

# Nineteenth-Century Literature Criticism

Excerpts from Criticism of the
Works of Novelists, Poets, Playwrights,
Short Story Writers, Philosophers, and Other
Creative Writers Who Died between 1800
and 1899, from the First Published Critical
Appraisals to Current Evaluations

**Janet Mullane**
**Robert Thomas Wilson**
Editors

**Cherie D. Abbey**
**Thomas Ligotti**
Associate Editors

 **Gale Research Inc.** · DETROIT · NEW YORK · LONDON

## STAFF

Janet Mullane, Robert Thomas Wilson, *Editors*

Cherie D. Abbey, Thomas Ligotti, *Associate Editors*

Christina Cramer, Michael W. Jones, Michelle L. McClellan, Ronald S. Nixon,
Debra A. Wells, *Assistant Editors*

Jeanne A. Gough, *Permissions & Production Manager*
Linda M. Pugliese, *Production Supervisor*
Jennifer E. Gale, David G. Oblender, Suzanne Powers, Maureen A. Puhl, Linda M. Ross, *Editorial Associates*
Donna Craft, *Editorial Assistant*

Victoria B. Cariappa, *Research Supervisor*
Karen D. Kaus, Eric Priehs, Maureen Richards, Mary D. Wise, *Editorial Associates*
H. Nelson Fields, Judy L. Gale, Jill M. Ohorodnik, Filomena Sgambati, *Editorial Assistants*

Sandra C. Davis, *Permissions Supervisor (Text)*
H. Diane Cooper, Kathy Grell, Josephine M. Keene,
Kimberly F. Smilay, *Permissions Associates*
Maria L. Franklin, Lisa M. Lantz, Camille Robinson, Shalice Shah, Denise M. Singleton,
*Permissions Assistants*

Patricia A. Seefelt, *Permissions Supervisor (Pictures)*
Margaret A. Chamberlain, *Permissions Associate*
Pamela A. Hayes, Lillian Quickley, *Permissions Assistants*

Mary Beth Trimper, *Production Manager*
Marilyn Jackman, *External Production Assistant*

Arthur Chartow, *Art Director*
C. J. Jonik, *Keyliner*

Laura Bryant, *Production Supervisor*
Louise Gagné, *Internal Production Associate*

Since this page cannot legibly accommodate all the copyright notices,
the acknowledgments constitute an extension of the copyright notice.

While every effort has been made to ensure the reliability of the information presented in this
publication, Gale Research Inc. does not guarantee the accuracy of the data contained herein.
Gale accepts no payment for listing; and inclusion in the publication of any organization,
agency, institution, publication, service, or individual does not imply endorsement of the
editors or publisher. Errors brought to the attention of the publisher and verified to the
satisfaction of the publisher will be corrected in future editions.

# Contents

# Preface

Since its inception in 1981, *Nineteenth-Century Literature Criticism* has been a valuable resource for students and librarians seeking critical commentary on writers of this transitional period in world history. Designated an "Outstanding Reference Source" by the American Library Association with the publication of its first volume, *NCLC* has since been purchased by over 6,000 school, public, and university libraries. With this edition, volume 26, the series has covered over 300 authors representing 22 nationalities and more than 15,000 titles. No other reference source has surveyed the critical reaction to nineteenth-century authors and literature as thoroughly as *NCLC*.

## Scope of the Series

*NCLC* is designed to serve as an introduction for students and advanced readers to the authors of the nineteenth century, and to the most significant interpretations of these authors' works. The great poets, novelists, short story writers, dramatists, and philosophers of this period are frequently studied in high school and college literature courses. By organizing and reprinting the enormous amount of commentary written on these authors, *NCLC* helps students develop valuable insight into literary history, promotes a better understanding of the texts, and sparks ideas for papers and assignments. Each entry in *NCLC* presents a comprehensive survey of an author's career or an individual work of literature and provides the user with a multiplicity of interpretations and assessments. Such variety allows students to pursue their own interests; furthermore, it fosters an awareness that literature is dynamic and responsive to many different opinions.

*NCLC* continues the survey of criticism of world literature begun by Gale's *Contemporary Literary Criticism (CLC)* and *Twentieth-Century Literary Criticism (TCLC),* both of which excerpt and reprint commentary on authors of the twentieth century. For additional information about *TCLC, CLC,* and Gale's other criticism series, users should consult the Guide to Gale Literary Criticism Series preceding the title page in this volume.

## Coverage

Each volume of *NCLC* is carefully compiled to present:

- criticism of authors who represent a variety of genres and nationalities

- both major and lesser-known writers of the period (such as non-Western authors increasingly read by today's students)

- 8 - 12 authors per volume

- individual entries that survey the critical response to each author's works, including early criticism to reflect initial reactions, later criticism to represent any rise or decline in the author's reputation, and current retrospective analyses. The length of each author entry also indicates an author's importance, reflecting the amount of critical attention he or she has received from critics writing in English, and from foreign criticism in translation.

An author may appear more than once in the series because of the great quantity of critical material available or because of a resurgence of criticism generated by such events as an author's centennial or anniversary celebration, the republication or posthumous publication of an author's works, or the publication of a new translation. Usually, one or more author entries in each volume of *NCLC* are devoted to individual works or groups of works by major authors who have appeared previously in the series. Only those works that have been the subjects of extensive criticism and are widely studied in literature courses are selected for this in-depth treatment.

## Organization of the Book

An author entry consists of the following elements: author heading, biographical and critical introduction, principal works, excerpts of criticism (each preceded by explanatory notes and followed by a bibliographical citation), and a bibliography of further reading.

- The **author heading** consists of the author's full name, followed by birth and death dates. The unbracketed portion of the name denotes the form under which the author most commonly wrote. If an author wrote consistently under a pseudonym, the pseudonym will be listed in the author heading and the real name given in parentheses on the first line of the biographical and critical introduction. Also located at the beginning of the introduction are any name variations under which an author wrote, including transliterated forms for authors whose languages use nonroman alphabets.

- A **portrait** of the author is included when available. Many entries also feature illustrations of materials pertinent to an author's career, including manuscript pages, letters, book illustrations, and representations of important people, places, and events in an author's life.

- The **biographical and critical introduction** contains background information that introduces the reader to an author and to the critical debate surrounding his or her work. When applicable, biographical and critical introductions are followed by references to additional entries on the author in other literary reference series published by Gale, including *Short Story Criticism, Dictionary of Literary Biography, Children's Literature Review,* and *Something about the Author.*

- The list of **principal works** is chronological by date of first book publication and identifies the genre of each work. In those instances where the first publication was in a language other than English, the title and date of the first English-language edition are given in brackets. Unless otherwise indicated, dramas are dated by the first performance, rather than first publication.

- **Criticism** is arranged chronologically in each author entry to provide a useful perspective on changes in critical evaluation over the years. All titles by the author featured in the critical entry are printed in boldface type to enable the user to ascertain without difficulty the works being discussed. Also for purposes of easier identification, the critic's name and the publication date of the essay are given at the beginning of each piece of criticism. Anonymous criticism is preceded by the title of the journal in which it appeared. Publication information (such as publisher names and book prices) and parenthetical numerical references (such as footnotes or page and line references to specific editions of works) have been deleted at the editors' discretion to provide smoother reading of the text.

- Critical excerpts are prefaced by **annotations** providing the reader with information about both the critic and the criticism that follows. Included are the critic's reputation, individual approach to literary criticism, and particular expertise in an author's works. Also noted are the relative importance of a work of criticism, the scope of the excerpt, and the growth of critical controversy or changes in critical trends regarding an author. In some cases, these notes include cross-references to excerpts by critics who discuss each other's commentary.

- A complete **bibliographic citation** designed to facilitate the location of the original essay or book follows each piece of criticism.

- An annotated bibliography of **further reading** appearing at the end of each author entry lists additional secondary sources on the author. In some cases it includes essays for which the editors could not obtain reprint rights.

## Cumulative Indexes

Each volume of *NCLC* includes a cumulative index listing all the authors who have appeared in *Contemporary Literary Criticism, Twentieth-Century Literary Criticism, Nineteenth-Century Literature Criticism, Literature Criticism from 1400 to 1800, Classical and Medieval Literature Criticism,* and *Short Story Criticism,* along with cross-references to the Gale series *Children's Literature Review, Authors in the News, Contemporary Authors, Contemporary Authors Autobiography Series, Dictionary of Literary Biography, Concise Dictionary of American Literary Biography, Something about the Author, Something about the Author Autobiography Series,* and *Yesterday's Authors of Books for Children.* Useful for locating an author within the various series, this index is particularly valuable for those authors who are identified with a certain period but who, because of their death dates, are placed in another, or for those authors whose careers span two periods. For example, Fyodor Dostoevsky is found in *NCLC,* yet Leo Tolstoy, another major nineteenth-century Russian novelist, is found in *TCLC* because he died after 1899.

Each new volume in Gale's Literary Criticism Series includes a cumulative topic index, which lists all literary topics treated in *NCLC, TCLC, LC 1400-1800,* and the *CLC Yearbook.* In addition, each volume of *NCLC* contains a cumulative nationality index in which authors' names are arranged alphabetically under their respective nationalities.

## Title Index

Each volume of *NCLC* also includes an index listing the titles of all literary works discussed in that volume. Foreign language titles that have been translated are followed by the titles of the translations—for example, *Notre-Dame de Paris (The Hunchback of Notre-Dame).* Page numbers following these translated titles refer to all pages on which any form of the title, either foreign language or translated, appears. Titles of novels, dramas, nonfiction books, and poetry, short story, or essay collections are printed in italics, while all individual poems, short stories, and essays are printed in roman type within quotation marks. The first volume of *NCLC* published each year contains a cumulative index to all titles discussed in the series since its inception. The last cumulative index appeared in *NCLC* in volume 25.

## Suggestions Are Welcome

In response to various suggestions, several features have been added to *NCLC* since the series began, including annotations to excerpted criticism, an index listing authors in all Gale literary criticism series, entries devoted to on a single work by a major author, more extensive illustrations, and an index to titles.

Readers who wish to suggest authors to appear in future volumes, or who have other comments regarding the series, are cordially invited to write the editors or call our toll-free number: 1-800-347-GALE.

# Authors to Be Featured in Forthcoming Volumes

Arthur Hugh Clough (English Poet)—Clough was a nineteenth-century poet whose works are considered a remarkable reflection of the moral and intellectual uncertainty of mid-Victorian England. Although his earlier poems, such as the popular *The Bothie of Toper-na-Fuosich,* were traditional and romantic, he is best known for two works written towards the end of his career: *Amours de Voyage,* an epistolary poem whose principal theme is the antithesis between reflection and action, and *Dipsychus,* a dialogue between a self-doubting man and the pernicious spirit that haunts him.

James Fenimore Cooper (American novelist, essayist, historian, travel writer, and satirist)—One of the earliest American writers of world stature, Cooper was a prolific novelist who is best known for his portrayal of the American wilderness as a colorful, mythological realm. The "Leatherstocking Tales," a series of five novels that focuses on the celebrated character Natty Bumppo, will be the subject of an entire entry in *NCLC.*

William Hazlitt (English critic and essayist)—Hazlitt was one of the most important and influential commentators during the Romantic age in England. In his literary criticism and miscellaneous prose he combined discerning judgment with strongly stated personal opinion, producing essays noted for their discursive style, evocative descriptions, and urbane wit.

Francis Jeffrey (Scottish journalist, critic, and essayist)—An influential literary critic, Jeffrey was also a founder and editor (1803-1829) of the prestigious *Edinburgh Review.* A liberal Whig, Jeffrey often allowed his political beliefs to color his critical opinions, and his commentary is judged the most characteristic example of "impressionistic" critical thought during the first half of the nineteenth century. Today, he is best remembered for his brutal attacks on the early Romantic poets, exemplified by the first sentence of a review of William Wordsworth's *Excursion:* "This will never do."

Immanuel Kant (German philosopher)—Considered perhaps the most important and influential philosopher of the Enlightenment, Kant developed a comprehensive philosophical system incorporating epistemology, ethics, aesthetic judgment, and political theory. In his masterpiece, *The Critique of Pure Reason,* Kant altered forever the course of Western thought by insisting on the distinction between sensible and intelligible knowledge, and between perceivable and nonperceivable reality. Kant is also well known for *The Critique of Practical Reason,* where he argued for the existence of a moral law based on purely rational precepts, and for *The Critique of Judgment,* where he investigated the basis of aesthetic discernment.

Charles-Marie-René Leconte de Lisle (French poet)—Leconte de Lisle was the leader of the Parnassians, a school of French poets that rejected the tenets of Romanticism in favor of emotional restraint, clarity of expression, and attention to artistic form. Inspired by the civilizations of ancient Greece, Scandinavia, and India, as well as by his love of nature, Leconte de Lisle's poetry has been described as impassive and pessimistic yet sensitive and acutely attuned to beauty.

Herman Melville (American novelist, novella and short story writer, and poet)—A major figure in American literature, Melville is recognized for his exploration of complex metaphysical and moral themes in his novels and short fiction. *NCLC* will devote an entry to his novella *Billy Budd,* a symbolic inquiry into the nature of good and evil, innocence and guilt.

John Henry Newman (English theologian and writer)—An influential theologian, Newman was a key figure in the Oxford movement, whose adherents advocated the independence of the Church of England from the state and sought to establish a doctrinal basis for Anglicanism in the Church's evolution from Catholicism. Newman's subsequent conversion to Roman Catholicism inspired his best-known work, *Apoligia pro vita sua,* an eloquent spiritual autobiography tracing the development of his beliefs.

Alexander (Sergeyevich) Pushkin (Russian poet, dramatist, short story writer, novelist, essayist, and critic)—Considered one of the greatest Russian writers of the nineteenth century, Pushkin elevated the Russian language to a new level of literary fluency. *Eugene Onegin,* a novel in verse that is considered his masterpiece, will be the subject of an entire entry in *NCLC.* A provocative study of the complex relationship between literature and life, *Eugene Onegin* also served to expose the aspirations and limitations of the Westernized Russian aristocracy to which Pushkin belonged.

# Acknowledgments

The editors wish to thank the copyright holders of the excerpted criticism included in this volume, the permissions managers of many book and magazine publishing companies for assisting us in securing reprint rights, and Anthony Bogucki for assistance with copyright research. We are also grateful to the staffs of the Detroit Public Library, the Library of Congress, the University of Detroit Library, Wayne State University Purdy/Kresge Library Complex, and University of Michigan Libraries for making their resources available to us. Following is a list of the copyright holders who have granted us permission to reprint material in this volume of *NCLC*. Every effort has been made to trace copyright, but if omissions have been made, please let us know.

## COPYRIGHTED EXCERPTS IN *NCLC*, VOLUME 26, WERE REPRINTED FROM THE FOLLOWING PERIODICALS:

*Dickens Studies Annual,* v. 2, 1972. Copyright © 1972 by Southern Illinois University Press. All rights reserved. Reprinted by permission of AMS Press, Inc.—*Eighteenth-Century Studies,* v. 7, Spring, 1974. © 1974 by The American Society for Eighteenth-Century Studies. Reprinted by permission of the publisher.—*ELH,* v. 48, Fall, 1981. Copyright © 1981 by The Johns Hopkins University Press. All rights reserved. Reprinted by permission of the publisher.—*Essays in Criticism,* v. X, January, 1960 for "The Hero's Guilt: The Case of 'Great Expectations' " by Julian Moynahan; v. XIII, October, 1963 for "Great Expectations" by Barbara Hardy; v. XV, July, 1965 for "The Ending of 'Great Expectations' " by Martin Meisel; v. XXIV, April, 1974 for "Beating and Cringing: 'Great Expectations' " by A. L. French. All reprinted by permission of the Editors of *Essays in Criticism* and the respective authors.—*Forum for Modern Language Studies,* v. VII, January, 1971 for "Illusions and Illusory Values in Fontane's Works" by E. F. George. Copyright © 1971 by *Forum for Modern Language Studies* and the author. Reprinted by permission of the publisher and the author.—*German Life & Letters,* n.s. v. 20, October, 1966. Reprinted by permission of the publisher.—*The Germanic Review,* v. 37, March, 1962 for "The Unreal in Fontane's Novels" by Lawrence O. Frye. Copyright 1962 by Helen Dwight Reid Educational Foundation. Reprinted by permission of the author.—*Harper's Magazine,* v. 183, June, 1941. Copyright 1941, renewed 1968 by *Harper's Magazine.* All rights reserved. Reprinted by special permission.—*The New York Review of Books,* v. XXXVI, October 12, 1989. Copyright © 1989 Nyrev, Inc. Reprinted with permission from *The New York Review of Books.*—*The New York Times Book Review,* November 25, 1979. Copyright © 1979 by The New York Times Company. Reprinted by permission of the publisher.—*Novel: A Forum on Fiction,* v. 14, Spring, 1981. Copyright © Novel Corp., 1981. Reprinted by permission of the publisher.—*The Sewanee Review,* v. LIV, January-March, 1946. Copyright 1946 by The University of the South. Renewed 1973 by Valerie Eliot.—*Southwest Review,* v. 61, Winter, 1976 for "Sentimental Songs in Antebellum America" by Ronald L. Davis. © 1976 the author. Reprinted by permission of the publisher.—*The Texas Quarterly,* v. XVIII, Winter, 1975 for "Hebrew or Hellene?: Religious Ambivalence in Renan" by Peter Heinegg. © 1975 by The University of Texas at Austin. Reprinted by permission of the author.

## COPYRIGHTED EXCERPTS IN *NCLC,* VOLUME 26, WERE REPRINTED FROM THE FOLLOWING BOOKS:

Baym, Nina. From *Woman's Fiction: A Guide to Novels by and About Women in America, 1820-1870.* Cornell University Press, 1978. Copyright © 1978 by Cornell University. All rights reserved. Used by permission of the publisher, Cornell University Press.—Belloc, Hilaire. From *A Conversation with an Angel and Other Essays.* Jonathan Cape, 1928. Copyright 1928 by Hilaire Belloc. Renewed 1956 by Eleanor Jebb. Reprinted by permission of Peters, Fraser & Dunlop Group Ltd.—Bode, Carl. From *The Anatomy of American Popular Culture: 1840-1861.* University of California Press, 1959. © 1959 by The Regents of the University of California. Renewed 1987 by Carl Bode. Reprinted by permission of the author.—Brown, Wallace Cable. From *The Triumph of Form: A Study of the Later Masters of the Heroic Couplet.* University of North Carolina Press, 1948. Copyright, 1948, by The University of North Carolina Press. Renewed 1976 by Mrs. Wallace C. Brown. Reprinted by permission of the publisher and the author.—Buchner, Georg. From *Complete Works and Letters.* Edited by Walter Hinderer and Henry J. Schmidt, translated by Henry J. Schmidt. Continuum Publishing Company, 1986. Copyright © 1986 by The Continuum Publishing Company. All rights reserved. Reprinted by permission of the publisher.—Canetti, Elias. From *The Conscience of Words.* Translated by Joachim Neugroschel. The Seabury Press, 1979. English translation copyright © 1979 by The Continuum Publishing Company. All rights reserved. Reprinted by permission of the publisher.—Chadbourne, Richard M. From *Ernest Renan as an Essayist.* Cornell University Press, 1957. © 1957 by Cornell University. Renewed 1985 by Richard M. Chadbourne. Reprinted by permission of the author.—Chase, Gilbert. From *America's Music: From the Pilgrims to the Present.* Revised edition. McGraw-Hill Book Company, 1966. Copyright © 1955, 1966, by Gilbert Chase. All rights reserved. Reproduced with permission.—Cockshut, A. O. J. From *The Imagination of Charles Dickens.* William Collins Sons & Co. Ltd., 1961. © A. O. J. Cockshut 1961. Reprinted by permission of William Collins Sons & Co. Ltd.—Colby, Vineta. From *Yesterday's Woman: Domestic Realism in the English Novel.* Princeton University Press, 1974. Copyright © 1974 by Princeton

# Georg (Karl) Büchner

## 1813-1837

German dramatist and novella writer.

Virtually unknown throughout most of the nineteenth century, Büchner has come to be regarded as one of the most important and influential authors in German literature. This belated renown is based on the few works he composed during his brief life: the novella *Lenz* and the plays *Dantons Tod* (*Danton's Death*), *Leonce und Lena* (*Leonce and Lena*), and *Woyzeck.* In these works Büchner rejected the idealism of the Romantic movement, which dominated German letters in the late eighteenth and early nineteenth centuries; instead, he sought to realistically depict what he saw as the hopelessness of life in a world where isolation, monotony, and suffering prevail and are perpetuated by deterministic historical forces. This pessimistic view of life, along with the innovative techniques he used to obtain a sense of realism, give Büchner a greater affinity with authors of the modern era than with those of the nineteenth century, and commentators have noted his influence on several later developments in the history of drama, among them Naturalism, the Theater of the Absurd, and Expressionism.

The eldest of six children, Büchner was born in Goddelau, Germany. When he was three, his family moved to nearby Darmstadt, the capital of the duchy of Hesse-Darmstadt. During Büchner's school years, his father, a physician, encouraged him to study the sciences; his mother, on the other hand, nurtured in him a love of literature and art. In 1831, he went to study medicine at the university in Strasbourg, France. At that time, Strasbourg was a refuge for German liberals seeking asylum from the widespread political repression in the German states following the Napoleonic Wars. In this environment, Büchner developed a harsh view of his country's government. Because of a law requiring all Hessian students to attend a native institution for at least two years in order to receive a degree, Büchner reluctantly returned to Hesse in 1833. He continued his studies at the university in Geissing and there became involved in radical politics. Early in 1834, he and some fellow students founded an underground revolutionary group, the *Gesellschaft der Menschenrechte* (Society for the Rights of Man), whose aim was to reform the Hessian government and social structure. Shortly thereafter, Büchner wrote a seditious pamphlet in collaboration with Friedrich Ludwig Weidig, an aging liberal devoted to revolutionary causes. The pamphlet, *Der Hessische Landbote* (*The Hessian Courier*), was distributed secretly among Hessian peasants by the Society; it urged the lower classes to violently uprise against the aristocracy, whose lives are described as "a long Sunday" compared with the miserable existence of the people, who "lie in front of them like manure in the fields." Later commentators have praised the *Hessian Courier* as one of the first revolutionary manifestos to be based exclusively on socioeconomic reasoning, but the pamphlet had very little effect on the Hessian peasantry, many of whom handed their copies over to the police.

After learning that several members of the Society had been arrested for distributing the *Hessian Courier,* Büchner returned to his parents' home in Darmstadt to hide while police

were conducting investigations. There, during late January and early February of 1835, he wrote his first play, *Danton's Death,* hoping to get it published to help finance his escape from Germany before his impending arrest. Büchner sent the manuscript to Karl Gutzkow, a young German man of letters, who was impressed with the work and soon succeeded in selling it to a publisher. However, Büchner was forced to flee the country before receiving payment. Subsequently, he renounced all revolutionary activity and resumed medical studies in Strasbourg, where, after writing a well-received dissertation, *Sur le système nervaux du barbeau* (On the Nervous System of the Barbel), he obtained his doctorate. To earn money during this time, Büchner translated into German two of Victor Hugo's dramas for the publisher of *Danton's Death;* he also composed *Leonce and Lena* for a romantic comedy contest, wrote *Lenz,* and began working on *Woyzeck* and possibly on *Pietro Aretino,* a play that has since been lost. In late 1836, he moved to Switzerland, where he taught at the University of Zurich. Early the following year, Büchner became ill with typhus. He died on 19 February 1837 at the age of twenty-four.

Following Büchner's death, his family would not allow his manuscripts in their possession to be published. Wilhelmine Jaegle, to whom Büchner was secretly engaged in Strasbourg, was initially cooperative with Gutzkow, sending him *Leonce and Lena* and *Lenz,* which he published in excerpted form in his periodical *Telegraf für Deutschland* (Telegraph for Germany), but she eventually became unwilling to surrender the other writings by Büchner that she owned, including a diary, many letters, and possibly a finished manuscript of *Pietro Aretino.* Moreover, she destroyed all of Büchner's writings in her possession before she died in 1880. Although Büchner's brother Ludwig published an incomplete collection of his works in 1850, the first significant and complete edition did not appear until 1879, when Karl Emil Franzos issued *Sämtliche Werke und handschriftelicher Nachlaß* after years of interviewing Büchner's acquaintances and collecting his manuscripts, letters, and papers. This edition led to increasing interest in Büchner's plays: in 1885 *Leonce and Lena* was first performed; in the late 1880s, the popular German dramatist Gerhart Hauptman enthusiastically praised Büchner; and in 1902 and 1913 respectively, *Danton's Death* and *Woyzeck* were given their first stage productions.

*Danton's Death* has often been called, in the words of Carl Richard Mueller, "the finest first play ever written." Frequently regarded as an expression of Büchner's disillusionment with radical politics, this work focuses on the last days of French Revolutionary leader Georges Jacques Danton, who, after the new régime had been established, became a proponent of peace and thus came into conflict with fellow insurrectionist Maximilien de Robespierre. Accusing Danton of trying to overthrow the government, Robespierre has him guillotined. Büchner depicts Danton as a passive hero who succumbs to the forces that oppose and torment him. These forces, palpably Robespierre and his adherents, are in the abstract a historical inevitability, what Büchner called in an often-quoted letter the "terrible fatalism of history." He added in this letter that he found "in human nature a horrifying sameness, in the human condition an inescapable force granted to all and to no one. The individual merely foam upon the waves, greatness sheer chance, the mastery of genius a puppet play, a ludicrous struggle against an iron law: to recognize it is our utmost achievement, to control it is impossible." While the dialogue of *Danton's Death* explicitly expresses the words of Büchner's letter, his later writings implicitly demonstrate this deterministic view. In the comedy *Leonce and Lena,* the title characters, the Prince of Popo and the Princess of Pepe, are the victims of an arranged marriage. They each attempt to escape their fate by running away, but they meet again, neither realizing the other's identity. Ultimately, they fall in love and, when their identities are revealed, marry. While seemingly a derivative and light romantic comedy, critics have detected in *Leonce and Lena* darker overtones of suicidal boredom, pessimism, and despair, themes that are emphasized in Büchner's last play, *Woyzeck.* Despite its unfinished state, this work is regarded as Büchner's masterpiece. The title character is a poor young army private who, driven to madness by jealousy and his vision of a wretched and futile existence, murders his girlfriend and then commits suicide. Regarded as one of the first plays to portray a lower-class hero, *Woyzeck* is often treated as a work of social criticism. On this level, the forces tormenting Woyzeck are represented by three characters from a higher social class: the Captain, who continually berates Woyzeck, the Drum Major, who is having an affair with Woyzeck's girlfriend, and the Doctor, who uses the private as a subject in an experiment in which he feeds him nothing but peas. On a philosophical level, however, the Captain, Drum Major, and Doctor are perceived by critics as grotesque figures who

are also victims of and thus motivated by the hopelessness and suffering that characterize the universe of Büchner's plays.

Büchner's philosophical outlook, particularly as evinced in *Danton's Death* and *Woyzeck,* is recognized as a forerunner to twentieth-century existentialism and the Theater of the Absurd. Equally advanced are the aesthetic concerns and techniques displayed in his works. From his first play, Büchner was an adherent of realism. All of his literary efforts except *Leonce and Lena,* which was written strictly to suit the requirements of a comedy competition, are based on fact. As he wrote in a letter to his parents, he believed that "the dramatic poet is . . . nothing but a writer of history; he is *superior* to the latter, however, in that he creates history a second time for us, and instead of telling us a dry story, he places us into the life of an era, giving us characters instead of characteristics and figures instead of descriptions. His greatest task is to come as close as possible to history as it actually happened." In *Danton's Death* and *Woyzeck,* Büchner chose to create a sense of realism by developing the dramatic action in a series of brief, episodic scenes that seem to mimic the sometimes trivial and random occurrences of everyday life. While each scene is apparently unconnected to those that precede or follow, collectively, they give the impression of a unified drama. Although traced by commentators to the works of William Shakespeare and the Sturm und Drang (Storm and Stress) playwrights, this use of episodic form is far more developed in Büchner's writings and, as such, is closely related to similar techniques employed by twentieth-century dramatists, particularly Bertolt Brecht.

Few studies of Büchner's techniques or aesthetic theories are undertaken without quoting from or discussing his novella fragment *Lenz.* Based on an episode in the life of Sturm und Drang dramatist Jakob Michael Reinhold Lenz, the story portrays the gradual deterioration of Lenz's mind until his total mental collapse. In an early part of the story, Lenz discusses his theories of art with Protestant clergyman Jean Frédéric Oberlin, whose diary account forms the basis of Büchner's novella. Attacking the idealism of the German Romantics, who were popular in both Lenz's and Büchner's time, Lenz states, "I demand of art that it be life. . . . Let them try just once to immerse themselves in the life of humble people and then reproduce this again in all its movements, its implications, in its subtle, scarcely discernible play of expressions." While some critics have argued that this merely summarizes Lenz's views on art, most critics accept it as the epitome of Büchner's aesthetic beliefs. To achieve realism in the story, he uses a complex technique of shifting viewpoints to render each subtle nuance of Lenz's situation. Within a given paragraph, for example, Büchner will often begin by describing a scene from the viewpoint of an objective third person narrator, then abruptly switch to Lenz's sensory and psychological perspective. Most commentators consider this method very effective.

Since the discovery of Büchner's works in the late nineteenth century, criticism has been for the most part positive. While some commentators have pointed to the discursive, unrefined quality of his writings, arguing that they lack the polish achieved by maturer artists, most contend that Büchner attained a remarkable artistic and philosophical sophistication during his brief life.

## PRINCIPAL WORKS

*Der Hessische Landbote* [with Friedrich Ludwig Weidig] (pamphlet) 1834
   [*The Hessian Courier* published in *Complete Plays and Prose,* 1963]
*Dantons Tod* [abridged edition] (drama) [first publication] 1835
   [*Danton's Death* published in *The Plays of Georg Büchner,* 1927]
*Leonce und Lena* [abridged edition] (drama) [first publication] 1838; published in the periodical *Telegraf für Deutschland*
   [*Leonce and Lena* published in *The Plays of Georg Büchner,* 1927]
*Lenz* (novella fragment) 1839; published in the periodical *Telegraf für Deutschland*
   [*Lenz* published in *Complete Plays and Prose,* 1963]
*Nachgelassene Schriften* (dramas and unfinished novella) 1850
*\*Sämtliche Werke und handschriftelicher Nachlaß* (dramas and unfinished novella) 1879
*Woyzeck* (unfinished drama) [first publication] 1879; published in *Sämtliche Werke und handschriftelicher Nachlaß*
   [*Woyzeck* published in *The Plays of Georg Büchner,* 1927]
*The Plays of Georg Büchner* (dramas) 1927
*Complete Plays and Prose* (pamphlet, dramas, and unfinished novella) 1963
*Sämtliche Werke und Briefe.* 2 vols. (pamphlet, dramas, unfinished novella, translations, and letters) 1967-71
*Georg Büchner: The Complete Collected Works* (pamphlet, dramas, unfinished novella, and letters) 1977; also published in revised form as *Complete Works and Letters,* 1986

\*This collection is the first complete and unabridged edition of Büchner's plays.

---

## GEORG BÜCHNER   (letter date 1835)

[*Writing to his parents, Büchner comments on* Danton's Death.]

I must say a few words about my drama [*Dantons Tod*]: first I must point out that my permission to make several changes was used to excess. Omissions and additions occur on almost every page, and almost always to the detriment of the whole. Sometimes the sense is completely distorted or missing entirely, replaced by almost sheer nonsense. Besides, the book is teeming with the most dreadful typographical errors. I received no *proofs.* The title is tasteless, and my name is under it, which I had explicitly forbidden; it was not on the title page of my manuscript. The editor has moreover credited me with several obscenities I never would have said in my life. I've read Gutzkow's splendid reviews and noticed, much to my pleasure, that I'm not inclined toward vanity. Regarding the so-called immorality of my book, I have the following to say: the dramatic poet is in my eyes nothing but a writer of history; he is *superior* to the latter, however, in that he creates

history a second time for us, and instead of telling us a dry story, he places us into the life of an era, giving us characters instead of characteristics and figures instead of descriptions. His greatest task is to come as close as possible to history as it actually happened. His book must be neither *more nor less moral* than *history itself;* but God didn't create history to be suitable reading matter for young ladies, and for that reason I can't be blamed if my drama is equally unsuitable. I can't make a Danton and the bandits of the Revolution into virtuous heroes! To show their dissoluteness I had to let them be dissolute, to show their godlessness I had to let them speak like atheists. Should you discover any improprieties, then think of the notoriously obscene language of that time; whatever my characters say is only a weak approximation of it. One might reproach me for choosing such material. But such a reproach has long been refuted. If one were to let it stand, then the greatest masterpieces of literature would have to be thrown out. The poet is not a teacher of morality, he invents and creates figures, he brings past times to life, and people can learn from that, just as well as from the study of history and from observation of what is going on around them. If you wished it *otherwise,* you shouldn't be permitted to study history at all, for it tells of many immoral acts; you'd have to walk blindfolded down the street, for you might see indecencies, and you'd have to cry out against a God who created a world in which so much dissoluteness occurs. If someone were to tell me that the poet shouldn't depict the world as it is but as it should be, then I answer that I don't want to make it better than God, who certainly made the world as it should be. As far as the so-called idealistic poets are concerned, I find that they have produced hardly anything besides marionettes with sky-blue noses and affected pathos, but not human beings of flesh and blood, whose sorrow and joy I share and whose actions fill me with loathing or admiration. In a word, I think much of Goethe or Shakespeare, but very little of Schiller. Moreover, it's obvious that highly unfavorable reviews will appear, for the governments must have their paid writers prove that their opponents are either idiots or immoral people. I do not in any way judge my work to be perfect and will accept any truly aesthetic criticism with thanks. (pp. 275-77)

> *Georg Büchner, in a letter to his parents on July 28, 1835, in his* Complete Works and Letters, *edited by Walter Hinderer and Henry J. Schmidt, translated by Henry J. Schmidt, The Continuum Publishing Company, 1986, pp. 275-77.*

## KARL GUTZKOW   (essay date 1837)

[*A German playwright, journalist, and novelist, Gutzkow was one of the leading Young Germans, a term describing young writers in early to mid-nineteenth-century Germany who rejected the conventions of idealism of the previous generation of Romantic writers in favor of political reform and sexual and religious freedom. In this excerpt from Büchner's obituary, Gutzkow records his own and his friends' impressions of* Danton's Death. *His remarks were first published in the newspaper the* Frankfurter Telgraf *in 1837.*]

During the last days of February 1835—a somewhat stormy year in the history of our modern literature—I had invited a congenial circle of friends of art and truth. . . . Just before the arrival of the expected guests I received a manuscript and a letter from Darmstadt. . . . The letter enticed me to read the manuscript immediately. It was a drama: *Danton's Death.* One could see from its appearance how hurriedly it had been thrown together. Its subject was arbitrarily chosen and overworked in its realization. Scenes and words followed each other rapidly, stormily. It was the frightened language of a pursued man who had to conclude something in haste and then find his safety in flight. Yet this haste did not hinder this genius from revealing his talent in short, sharp outlines, quickly, as in passing.

Every motif and elaboration in this loosely constructed drama grew out of his personality and talent. His personality did not allow his talent to develop itself broadly and at leisure, and his talent, on the other hand, prevented his personality from merely formulating feelings and hyperboles without at least a hasty attempt at smoothing out scenes and those bright and lively words flowing out of the most priceless spring of nature. *Danton's Death* was published. The first scenes I read secured him the gracious, friendly interest of the publisher Sauerländer on that same evening. A recitation of selected scenes aroused admiration for the talent of the youthful author, although now and then someone interrupted with the statement that this or that stood word for word in Thiers. (pp. 236-37)

I had great difficulty with . . . *Danton,* since such expressions as Büchner had permitted himself to cast about cannot be printed today. *Sansculotte* atmosphere pervaded the work; the Declaration of the Rights of Man roamed about in it, covered with roses, but naked. The symbol that held the whole work together was the red cap. Büchner studied medicine. His imagination played with that human misery which sickness incurs; indeed, the sicknesses of levity had to serve as the foil to his wit. The poetic vegetation of his book consisted of field blossoms and buds of mercury. His imagination disseminated the former, his cocky satire the latter. To deprive the censor of the pleasure of deleting, I assumed this office myself and pruned the drama's proliferating liberalism with the scissors of precensorship. I realized that the discarded parts, which had to be sacrificed to our customs and circumstances, were the best, the most individualistic and characteristic aspects of the whole. Long, off-color dialogues in the folk scenes, bubbling with wit and inspiration, had to be cut. Puns had to be blunted or bent awry, replaced by stupid figures of speech. Büchner's *true Danton* did *not* appear. What came of it was an impoverished remnant, the ruin of a devastation that caused me great reluctance. (pp. 237-38)

Karl Gutzkow, "Georg Büchner's Obituary," in Georg Büchner: The Complete Collected Works, *edited and translated by Henry J. Schmidt, Avon Books, 1977, pp. 236-40.*

### THE NATION, NEW YORK   (essay date 1881)

[*While judging Büchner's writings the work of a "powerful creative mind," this anonymous critic contends that they exhibit more promise than accomplishment.*]

[Büchner's writings] must be acknowledged to occupy a subordinate position, either with reference to himself as a man or to any very high standard of literary accomplishment. His first drama, *Danton's Death,* was produced in feverish haste under the most trying circumstances, and is decidedly lacking in artistic finish and form, though the portrayal of the characters is exceedingly vivid and real. Events and persons are painted with realistic fidelity by the aid of the most repulsive cynicism. Some critics have attributed this to coarseness in the moral fibre of the author. To us it appears to be merely

the result of artistic immaturity, of the want of sufficiently refined artistic taste. We are even somewhat reconciled to his excess of realism by the entire absence of that morbid sentimentalism which exhales like a miasma from the works of many poets contemporary with him, preachers of what they conceived to be a lofty idealism, but which was in reality only the evaporation of very common terrestrial mud. In Büchner's *Danton* his gloomy and pessimistic conception of history is poured forth with great intensity and vehemence. Though the subject can scarcely be called dramatic in its nature, the play is full of life and passion, and in spite of all its imperfections it bears the stamp of a powerful creative mind.

In the fragment of the novel entitled *Lenz* we find an entirely different manifestation of Büchner's poetic gift. It is a masterly delineation of the mental sufferings of the unhappy young poet of whom Goethe saw much during his residence in Strasbourg. Lenz fell in love with Goethe's Frederica, and became insane when he found that his love was not returned. The descriptions of nature in this fragment are truly poetical, and it is to be regretted that the work remained unfinished. *Leonce and Lena* is full of brilliant wit and drollery, while in *Woyzeck,* a fragmentary tragedy, the author dwells upon the dark and painful side of human nature, though the grotesque and the heroic are brought into close proximity. Büchner's strictly scientific and philosophical writings, highly spoken of at the time of their appearance, were bright indications of possible success in the severer departments of knowledge. Altogether, these works, few and fragmentary as they are, give abundant evidence of the many-sided genius of the man. Cut off at the very beginning of his career, at the age of twenty-three, what he actually accomplished can scarcely be regarded as more than a promise of future greatness. (p. 225)

"Georg Büchner," in The Nation, New York, *Vol. XXXII, No. 822, March 31, 1881, pp. 224-25.*

### JOSEPH KRESH   (essay date 1938)

[*Kresh contends that* Danton's Death *and* Woyzeck *show that Büchner did not abandon his revolutionary political ideals.*]

*Danton's Death* has often, especially of late, been interpreted as the result of Büchner's disillusionment with the revolutionary movement and as a symptom of his withdrawal from political activity due to the failure of the *Hessian Courier* to inspire the peasants to rebellion.

The facts seem to argue against this contention. [His friend August Becker] testified that Büchner often told him that in writing the *Hessian Courier* he sought to discover "to what extent the German people was inclined to take part in a revolution. . . . He wanted only to test the mood of the people and of the German revolutionaries." It is therefore clear that Büchner had no illusions when he wrote the *Courier* and could not have been disillusioned by the result it produced. To be sure, Becker continues, "When he heard later that the peasants had delivered most of the pamphlets which they found to the police, when he learned that the patriots, too, had spoken against his pamphlet, he gave up all his hopes of political change." But giving up hope of change need not mean abandonment of the desire for it. In this case it meant only that Büchner recognized that change was impossible at the time. . . . This contention is further borne out by a comparison of the following two passages. The first is from the beginning of the *Hessian Courier:*

The life of the rich is a long Sunday; they live in beautiful houses, they wear attractive clothes, they have fat faces and speak a language of their own; but the people lie before them like dung on a field. The peasant follows the plow, but the rich man follows the peasant and drives both him and his oxen, he takes the corn and leaves the stubble. The life of the peasant is a long work-day; strangers devour his fields before his eyes, his body is a single callous, his sweat the salt on the tables of the rich.

Compare this with the following passage from *Danton's Death:*

> FIRST CITIZEN. Yes, a knife, but not for the poor whore! What did she do? Nothing! Her hunger whores and begs. A knife for those who buy the flesh of our wives and daughters! Woe to them who whore with the daughters of the people! You have rumbles in your bodies, and they have distended bellies; you have holes in your jackets, and they have warm coats; you have callouses in your fists, and they have hands of satin. *Ergo* you work, and they do nothing; *ergo* you created it, and they stole it; *ergo* if you want a few pennies of what has been stolen from you, you must whore and beg; *ergo* they are rascals and they must be killed!
>
> THIRD CITIZEN. They have no blood in their veins but what they sucked out of ours. They told us: kill the aristocrats, they are wolves! We hanged the aristocrats to the lamp-posts. They said: the Veto is devouring your bread; we killed the Veto. They said: the Girondists are starving you; we guillotined the Girondists. But they stripped the dead, and we still run around with our legs bare and freeze. We'll strip the hide off them and make ourselves trousers, we'll render their fat and thicken our soup with it. Come! Kill anyone with no hole in his coat!

Even after *Danton's Death,* Büchner's opinion remained unchanged. From Strassburg, after his exile, Büchner wrote to [Karl] Gutzkow: "The *relationship between poor and rich* is the only revolutionary element in the world." There was absolutely no change in Büchner's point of view. Before the *Hessian Courier* he believed that only the action of the masses, impelled by their economic needs, could bring about a change. After the *Courier* he knew that action by the masses could not be expected at the time and that, as he had written to his family . . . , "all the activity and shouting of individuals is the vain work of fools." Therefore the only thing of which Büchner can be accused is that he withdrew from political activity. (pp. 19-20)

With this understanding of Büchner at the time he wrote *Danton's Death,* the meaning of the play becomes clearer. Although it was written under very unfavorable psychological conditions, in concealment from his father, he managed to complete it in a very short time, less than five weeks, he wrote to Gutzkow in submitting the drama to him. This referred, of course, to the actual composition, for since childhood Büchner had been interested in the French Revolution. Later in life Büchner pored over the many books on the subject in the Darmstadt library. The play gives evidence of these studies since it is full of historical incidents and in many cases employs the actual words attributed to the characters.

Büchner admits these resemblances and indeed intended the drama as a historical picture. To prepare his family for certain parts he wrote to them on May 5, 1835:

> I had to remain true to history and paint the men of the revolution as they were—bloody, dissolute, vigorous, cynical. I consider my drama a historical painting which must resemble its original.

He used the same argument against the changes which Sauerländer, the publisher, was compelled to make in order to pass the censor, and also against the criticism of the press.

> I can't make Sunday School heroes of Danton and the bandits of the revolution! If I wished to depict their lewdness I had to let them be lewd. If I wanted to show their ungodliness I had to let them speak like atheists.

The play takes place in those few days between Robespierre's decision that Danton must die and Danton's execution. The play is almost pure history, an account of what actually took place in those few days, with a psychological interpretation of the actions of the characters and a political explanation of why they were compelled to act so. The misinterpretation of *Danton's Death* is due chiefly to the fact that the play presents a conflict between Danton and Robespierre in which Büchner, while condemning both, seems to favor Danton. This is necessarily so, for even though *Danton's Death* is Büchner's first play, he was a great enough dramatist to present Danton's death as tragedy rather than as melodrama. As a tragic figure Danton must be drawn in a favorable light, a man with virtues as well as faults.

But although Büchner sympathizes with Danton, he is not entirely unfavorable to Robespierre. While he has not the same æsthetic and philosophical appeal for Büchner that Danton has, still Robespierre is presented as a far better leader of the revolution at the stage it had reached. He may have been a demagogue, but he sought no profit from the fact. He gave the people circuses, but he tried also to give them bread. Even Danton can find no reproach for him beyond his rectitude and asceticism.

The position of France at this time was critical. Büchner describes it quite accurately. Danton, having become a revolutionary only because, as he says, the people in power displeased him, has become bored now that they are overthrown, and wishes to end the revolution. Robespierre, on the other hand, recognized that the country was by no means safe. There remained a counter-revolutionary element in Paris as well as a determined opposition abroad. Even if Robespierre had no plan for establishing the republic firmly, the adoption of Danton's suggestion and the abolition of the Terror would have meant the immediate reestablishment of the pre-revolutionary state.

While Büchner favors Danton as a symbol of the intellectual in revolution, there can be no doubt that the Frenchman was a complete villain, even if an honest one. Robespierre has been condemned almost as universally as Danton, but there is still much to be said in his favor. . . . [Even] if we assume with Dareste that "Robespierre personified the Reign of Terror," we can still defend him. The Terror was not the result of sheer savagery on the part of the Revolution. It was a matter of practical necessity. (pp. 20-2)

The people of France were justified in their hatred of the aristocracy, and justified in using any means to prevent its return. Behind them lay centuries of starvation with which they had paid for the luxuries of their masters, and fresh memories of the year when the debauches of the nobles had continued while one-third of the population of France died of starvation. But then such things are of no importance beside the fact that the Terror in Paris killed almost two thousand prominent people, some of them common criminals. (pp. 22-3)

But as a matter of fact, Büchner does not side with Danton against Robespierre. He not only presents Danton as a self-confessed, debauched cynic, he shows that he has lost touch with the people and become politically unstable. In the first scene of the play one of Danton's friends says: "The Revolution has reached the stage of reorganization. The Revolution must stop and the Republic must begin." Danton makes no objection to this statement, but later, in another scene, he says: "The Revolution is not yet finished." Immediately after this follows the scene between Danton and Robespierre when Danton again shifts his position to accuse Robespierre, who insists that the Revolution must go on, of murder. It is this scene which underlies the belief that Büchner sides with Danton and is therefore disillusioned. But as a matter of fact Danton, who seems to have the better of the argument, is by no means the victor. Of the significance of this scene [Georg] Lukacs says:

> Danton refutes . . . the *political* views of Robespierre with not a single word. On the contrary, he avoids a political discussion. He has not a single argument against the political reproach, against Robespierre's political conception which . . . is essentially the conception of the poet [Büchner] himself. Danton turns the conversation into a discussion of the principles of morality and here, as a materialist, wins an easy victory over the Rousseauian moral principles of Robespierre. But this easy victory in discussion is no answer to the central question of the political situation, to the question of the contrast between poor and rich. Here Büchner shows himself a true-born great dramatist by embodying the great social contradiction, which is also the insoluble contradiction in his own emotions and thought, in two great historic figures— each with its necessary greatness and with its necessary narrow-mindedness.

This evasion of Danton's is no accident, but the very heart of his tragedy. Büchner makes Danton a great bourgeois revolutionist who can, however, by no means pass beyond the purely bourgeois goals of the revolution. He is an epicurean materialist, quite in the fashion of the eighteenth century, in the fashion of Holbach and Helvetius. This materialism is the highest and most consistent *ideological* form of pre-revolutionary France, the *Weltanschauung* of the ideological *preparation* for the revolution. Marx characterizes this philosophy as follows: "Holbach's theory is therefore the historically justified philosophical illusion of the rising bourgeoisie in France whose lust for exploitation could still be expressed as lust for the full development of the individual in intercourse liberated from the old feudal bonds. Liberation as seen by the bourgeoisie, competition, was, to be sure, the only way in which this new road for the free development could be opened to the individual in the eighteenth century."

But it is just when this revolution wins this victory over the king and the feudality, a victory in which Danton had a leading significance, that there arise in society those new contradictions to which Danton is strange and hostile, to which his *Weltanschauung* can give no answer. Robespierre and Saint Just want to continue the revolution, for Danton this

continuance is no longer *his* revolution. He fought for liberation from feudalism, the rescue of the poor from the yoke of capitalism has nothing in common with his goals. In a conversation immediately before the great discussion with Robespierre he says of the people: "It hates those who enjoy as a eunuch hates a man."

But essentially the Robespierre-Danton conflict is secondary. The real center of the play is the people of Paris who have been promised much from the Revolution and have received little. The conflict between Robespierre and Danton is only a reflection of this, for it is a conflict about the length to which the Revolution should go in redeeming its promises to the people. (pp. 23-4)

Danton, representing a higher stratum of the middle class, with pretensions to aristocracy and rich enough to be able to adopt a philosophy of leisure and sensuality, concludes that the Revolution is "accomplished" long before Robespierre, who represents the demands of a somewhat lower section of that class. Robespierre's group insists, therefore, upon carrying on the revolution even if it entails casting aside former allies. (p. 24)

[In a letter dated June 1833, Büchner proposed] the compelling necessities of the great mass as the motive force in history. These compelling necessities are disregarded by both Robespierre and Danton, and hence we have in the play the constant demands of the people, confused because they have won a revolution without attaining any real change. The revolutionary situation therefore continues to exist, for "the relationship between poor and rich . . . the only revolutionary element in the world" continues to exist. This Büchner makes clear in two scenes in which first Robespierre and then Danton are rejected by the people. In the first Robespierre appears while a commotion is going on in the streets.

> ROBESPIERRE. What's the matter, Citizens?
> THIRD CITIZEN. What should be the matter? The few drops of blood in August and September didn't make the people's cheeks red. The guillotine is too slow. We need a storm!
> FIRST CITIZEN. Our wives and children are crying for bread, we'll feed them aristocrat-meat. Hey! Kill anyone without a hole in his coat!
> ALL. Kill! Kill!
> ROBESPIERRE. In the name of the law!
> FIRST CITIZEN. What is the law?
> ROBESPIERRE. The will of the people.
> FIRST CITIZEN. We are the people and we want no law; *ergo* that will is the law, *ergo* in the name of the law there is no more law, *ergo* kill!

In this scene we see that despite his popularity Robespierre has not been able to solve the real problem of the Revolution, "the compelling necessities of the *great mass*." But, it may be argued, Büchner sides with Danton and hence it is to be expected that the people will be dissatisfied with Robespierre. But the last scene of Act III, the scene immediately after Danton's defense, answers this:

> FIRST CITIZEN. Who says Danton is a traitor?
> SECOND CITIZEN. Robespierre.
> FIRST CITIZEN. And Robespierre is a traitor!
> SECOND CITIZEN. Who says that?
> FIRST CITIZEN. Danton.
> SECOND CITIZEN. Danton has beautiful clothes, Danton has a beautiful house, Danton has a beautiful wife, he bathes in Burgundy, eats game from sil-

ver plates and sleeps with your wives and daughters
when he is drunk.—Danton was as poor as you.
Where did he get it all? . . .
ALL. Long live Robespierre! Down with Danton!
Down with the traitor!

The essential element is "the relationship between poor and
rich . . . the only revolutionary element in the world." Danton, even more obviously than Robespierre, has failed to
solve the problem of the Revolution.

This is the central theme of the play, in those grotesque mass
scenes with their ominous refrain. The bourgeoisie has won
the Revolution that the poor have made. The poor have nothing but their old hunger and the old holes in their coats. They
swing between Robespierre and Danton because they are embittered, resentful, bewildered, but as soon as the right note
is struck, "the relationship between poor and rich," they
know that they have been deceived.

Perhaps no play has ever been received with greater critical
acclaim than **Danton's Death.** From Gutzkow, the first critic
to read it, down to the present day, critic after critic has proclaimed it a work of genius. And it is that. . . . (pp. 24-6)

Büchner once more gave dramatic form to his political and
social ideas [in **Woyzeck**]. (p. 28)

Woyzeck works for a doctor and a captain, who represent the
liberal bourgeoisie. The former is the type of scientific charlatan who has reduced the world to pulse-counting and who believes he understands a thing if he can give it a polysyllabic
Latin name. He has discovered that the "*musculus constrictor
vesicae* is subject to the will," and therefore decides that man
is free. The captain is the same sort of character in another
field. He believes that he is likely to die of fear and borrows
his morals from his chaplain.

Woyzeck is going through a desperate crisis. He has just discovered that the woman he loves and with whom he lives, the
mother of his child, has been unfaithful to him. Faced with
this tragic situation, he must listen to his captain cant of morality while the doctor calls his attempts to find an answer to
the riddle of life "*Aberratio mentalis partialis,* second degree." Even Andres, his closest friend and constant companion, despite his attempts to be sympathetic, can suggest only
a powder in brandy as a remedy. The personal and political
isolation of the poor in a social system that neither understands nor considers them is an important element in this
play.

The captain, despite his inanity, is really kind-hearted and
well-meaning. He feels sorry for Woyzeck and often gives
him money. Indeed, he is even distressed by the fact that
horses must travel about on foot. The stupidity of his relationship to Woyzeck derives from his inability to "bridge the
chasm between educated and uneducated," between rich and
poor. Witness his lecture to Woyzeck on morality:

> Woyzeck, you are a good man—but [*with dignity*]
> Woyzeck, you have no morality! Morality, you un-
> derstand, means being moral. It's a good word.
> You have a child without benefit of clergy, as our
> most reverend chaplain says, without benefit of
> clergy; it's not my own phrase.

To which Woyzeck replies:

> We poor people—you see, Captain: money, money!
> Whoever has no money . . . We have flesh and

blood, too. After all, we're unhappy in this world
and the next. I think even if we went to heaven, we
would have to help make it thunder. . . . You see,
we common people, we haven't any virtue, we just
have nature; but if I were a gentleman and had a
hat and a watch and a monocle and could talk gen-
teely, then I'd be virtuous soon enough. There must
be something nice about virtue, Captain. But I'm
a poor devil.

Even more than a tragedy of individual isolation, **Woyzeck**
is a proletarian tragedy. Social injustice is the cause of Woyzeck's destruction. "Money! Money!" Woyzeck replies to the
captain's prattle of morality; and money, or rather the lack
of it, is the basis of the tragedy. Woyzeck, in order to support
Marie and their child, must work incessantly. He even permits the doctor to use him for his ridiculous experiments. Because of this he is left no time to devote to those he loves. The
situation is made clear in the passage where Woyzeck has just
come into Marie's room.

> WOYZECK: How the baby sleeps! Put your hand
> under his arm, the chair is pressing him. There are
> drops on his forhead; everything under the sun is
> work, sweat even in sleep. We poor people! Here is
> some more money, Marie; my pay and a little from
> the captain.
> MARIE: God reward it, Franz.
> WOYZECK: I must go. Tonight, Marie! Adieu!

Marie wants more from life than just work, and, not so much
for the sake of the earrings which the drum major gives her,
as for the entertainment which he can supply, she deceives
Woyzeck. In a larger sense, however, she is still faithful to
Woyzeck and immediately regrets her action. But Woyzeck
discovers her infidelity and kills her. The manuscript is unclear as to the end of the tragedy, but Woyzeck is either
drowned or captured by the police; either conclusion has the
same effect.

Büchner . . . once wrote: "The thought that for most people
even the most miserable pleasures and joys are unattainable
luxuries made me very bitter." Now in **Woyzeck** he makes
an unattainability of these pleasures the root of tragedy. Superficially the tragedy is motivated by jealousy, but essentially, like the occasion of the jealousy, it is motivated by economic injustice. We find, then, that Büchner has retained to
the end the convictions with which he started and which
dominated his life. The essential problem is poor against rich,
and the salvation of the poor is to be found only in themselves. Liberal intellectualism is, of course, better than brutal
and autocratic despotism, but in the end it is useless when it
attempts to improve society. **Woyzeck** is a ringing indictment
of an economic system that pampers the few at the expense
of the many. Büchner once more comes to grips with life; but
his opponent fades away before him. He has his problem, but
because Germany was not yet developed beyond the contradiction of poor and rich to the new contradiction of proletariat and capitalist, he can find no solution except death—and
death will not solve the problem of the proletariat, for, as
Woyzeck says, "even if we went to heaven, we would have
to help make it thunder." (pp. 28-30)

*Joseph Kresh, "Georg Büchner," in* Dialectics, *No.
7, 1938, pp. 19-31.*

**F. W. KAUFMANN** (essay date 1940)

[*Kaufmann views Büchner's works as expressions of despair at the futility of realizing one's social and political ideals through revolution.*]

The collapse of the idealistic faith and the process of reconciliation with the realities of their time is the characteristic crisis through which most of our nineteenth century dramatists had to pass. Almost the only variation in the crisis is the degree of intensity with which it is experienced. . . . Büchner's reaction might best be termed a rebellious resignation. His early death did not allow him to reach the stage of complete reconciliation with the world, and the three dramas he left behind are more the expression of his disillusionment. For he too came to doubt the idealistic claims which he ardently embraced with one side of his nature while rejecting them with equal determination with the other.

From his father he inherited a factual soberness and a stern objectivity, while his mother endowed him with romantic sensibility and an emotional devotion to things and people. His romantic turn of mind was responsible for his protest against the boring and pedantic treatment of the classics at the Gymnasium and his predilection for the private study of the works of Shakespeare, Goethe, Herder, and the romanticists. But his anti-illusionistic search for truth caused him to study with equal devotion the medical and natural sciences and critically to examine the systems of idealistic philosophy, so that we find him in his first drama in decided opposition to any idealistic interpretation of history and life.

Büchner regarded the reactionary Metternich régime with the eyes of a Late Romanticist. Late-Romantic political theory conceived a community of the people (*Volksgemeinschaft*), in which the state would express the inner life and integrate the will of its citizens. Büchner's personal experiences at Gieszen, however, where he finished his medical studies, made him despair of all bourgeois attempts at a national regeneration on the basis of the vague ideology of a liberal constitution, a united empire, and a German-Christian faith. The petty chicaneries of intimidated officials, the philistine resignation to the contemptible autocracy of the German princelings and their henchmen, the denunciation of one of his revolutionary accomplices, evoked in him a disgust for the "enervated modern society whose life consists only of attempts to dissipate the most horrible tedium, a society which, as far as I am concerned might as well die out, because that would be the only change which it is still possible for it to experience." His revolutionary attitude is not liberal, but socialistic, and is based on the reflection that it is never "the ideas of the educated classes, but only the needs of the masses which can bring about a change."

> Das Verhältnis zwischen Reichen und Armen ist das einzige revolutionäre Element in der Welt; der Hunger allein kann die Freiheitsgöttin, und nur ein Moses, der uns die ägyptischen Plagen auf den Hals schickte, könnte ein Messias werden.

But even the masses become immovable, he thinks, as soon as they have a chicken in the pot.

Büchner sees in the masses the degrading and retarding factor in history, but he sees in them also the only lever by which society can be raised to a higher plane. . . . [However], in his short dramatic career he does not come to a positive presentation of the idea. He hardly develops beyond a pessimistic attitude toward historical progress. Such a mood is despairingly expressed in a letter written during the spring of 1834, after he had studied the history of the French Revolution:

> Ich fühlte mich wie zernichtet unter dem gräszlichen Fatalismus der Geschichte. Ich finde in der Menschennatur eine entsetzliche Gleichheit, in den menschlichen Verhältnissen eine unabwendbare Gewalt, allen und keinem verliehen. Der einzelne nur Schaum auf der Welle, die Grösze ein bloszer Zufall, die Herrschaft des Genies ein Puppenspiel, ein lächerliches Ringen gegen ein ehernes Gesetz, es zu erkennen das Höchste, es zu beherrschen unmöglich. . . . Das Musz ist eins von den Verdammungsworten, womit der Mensch getauft worden.

Büchner, the revolutionary who had hoped to lead man to a higher level and who had seen his endeavors fail because of the pettiness and stupidity of his revolutionary comrades and his opponents, despairs of historical progress and of any possible upward evolution of mankind.

His opposition to the idealistic belief is complemented by his conception of man as a being essentially determined by instinct causality. Reason is for him, as it was for Schopenhauer, a power of secondary importance only, an instrument to stimulate the instincts and deceive them about their low and hideous nature. The surface of consciousness deludes man with the ideas of freedom, moral aims, and progress toward a better human order. Below this surface of pretense, in the stratum of the subconscious, the shining illusion fades away; the individual, like mankind in general, is apparently subject to blind fate and the causality of base instincts, a revelation which, at least for a time, causes Büchner to deny the value of all action and striving.

That is the inner despair from which Büchner suffered when he wrote his tragedy ***Dantons Tod.*** At the opening of the play, the first phase of the French Revolution is past, the phase which, in spite of all its brutality, demands our admiration as a revolt against an intolerable social and economic system. Now the revolution has entered the stage of personal revenge and ambition without any higher human aims, the stage of development which, historically, marks the transition to a military dictatorship and the degradation of liberty and equality to battlecries of international carnage. Danton, the courageous leader of the Revolution, has withdrawn from public activity; disillusioned and in despair of finding any sense in the historical process; he has yielded to the hypocritical, fanatic Robespierre, who cannot see in Danton's retirement anything but treason against the ideals of the Revolution and who has, therefore, selected him as the next sacrifice for the bloodthirsty mob. Danton could still be saved, if he would devote his entire energy to this purpose. But the consideration of the impossibility of leading the masses to a higher aim, and the consciousness that he himself has inaugurated this murderous fury by ordering the September massacre have driven him to fatalism and cynical resignation. After only a short rebellion, he prefers death on the guillotine to the continuation of an aimless and meaningless existence.

In the form of an historical drama, Büchner examines the postulates of idealism and the ideals proclaimed by the Revolution. Over against the classical ideas of God and a reasonable world order, he sets a metaphysical scepticism. Whereas the theologians and the philosophers writing under the influence of the Christian dogma deduced from the harmony and the order of the world the existence of a divine organizer,

Paine (III, 1) rejects the belief in a creator because of the intolerable imperfection of the world. If God existed, would he not have done better to leave the world uncreated than in such a state of imperfection? (pp. 103-05)

In a similar manner, Danton rejects the idea of moral freedom. At the beginning of the Revolution, he believed that the destruction of the aristocratic order would help to further the moral progress of mankind. The degeneration of the revolutionary idea in its practical application, however, demonstrated the idealist's dependence upon powers beyond his control, and thus drove him as political leader to involuntary brutalities. Now the will of man seems to Danton to be determined by instinct. All human striving is hedonistic, and, in the last analysis, the highest human desire is identical in motive with the basest sensuality, since the satisfaction of the instinct is the driving energy behind all human action. Again it is the murderers of the Robespierre party who consider themselves the representatives of virtue and who silence their conscience with moral platitudes. Robespierre's virtue partly consists in the petit bourgeois' resentment against the suppression of his own desires; he makes the fight against vice his revolutionary watchword because it is the safest way to further his selfish political aims; but he fights against vice only to the extent to which it serves his purpose, while he allows the masses to satisfy their immoral desires in the wildest orgies. Such a view of life, of course, deprives the idea of immortality of all meaning; Danton has only one fear, namely, that death might fail to obliterate *all* of his memories of life.

The revolutionary ideals seem to him just as futile as the classical postulates of God, moral freedom, and immortality, at least when the attempt is made to realize them in human society. Fraternity is replaced by murder from the basest motives of revenge, craving for sensation, greed, and ambition; only the word is retained as a propaganda slogan and as an ideological disguise for the real facts. Equality is maintained on the lowest level of society; anyone who has no holes in his sleeves and who does not wipe his nose with his fingers is an aristocrat and faces execution on the guillotine. The democratic ideal of freedom, too, is only for harlots and scoundrels; on the whole, the people are but the instrument of an imbecile leader whose tenure, in turn, depends upon compliance with the instincts and demands of the mob. Justice, finally, is degraded to a bloody farce; those who are to die are removed from the trial for contempt of court, when they try to defend themselves (II, 6), and he who shows any sign of fear thereby confesses his guilt (II, 7). (p. 107)

Büchner . . . despairs completely of the value and of the meaning of life. His Danton, to be sure, makes a last desperate effort to save his life; but it is the unconscious vital instinct which impels him to wage his battle of self-defense, while his conscious mind rejects life as not worth living. Man is essentially solitary and isolated from his most beloved friend by the fact that only the base sense organs are capable of leading him from his inner prison into the open (I, 1). Life is an eternal repetition of the same experience; a million times, millions of people do the same thing; and even such an exciting spectacle as the Revolution becomes a boring habit, one gets "tired of always playing the same string on an instrument which gives only one tone" (II, 1). So it is, according to Danton's opinion, hardly worth while to save one's life:

> ob sie nun an der Guillotine oder am Fieber oder
> am Alter sterben! . . . Es ist recht gut, wenn die

> Lebenszeit reduziert wird . . . das Leben ist nicht
> die Arbeit wert, die man sich macht, es zu erhalten.

*Danton's Tod* presents the tragedy of a leader who begins his revolutionary work believing in the idea and the possibility of its realization, later, however, recognizes that he has set in motion a chain of events which follow their own causality. Danton sees that the murders which he intended as a means of bringing about a better order become for the sensation-hunting mob a spectacle, and for the scoundrels among its leaders an instrument for entrenching their own power. He realizes the tragic dilemma of depending upon the masses for accomplishing change, and yet being forced to fight against them because they cannot understand higher aims and therefore degrade the noblest intentions to their own level. It is the tragedy of the idealist who sees his highest striving wrecked by the pettiness of his fellow men and who therefore begins to doubt the validity of the ideals themselves and to ask whether these ideals are not, after all, but a disguise for the sensual instincts. It is, finally, the tragedy which results from the problematic situation of life itself, of life which comes to consciousness in man; for by his consciousness he is impelled to ask whether his existence has a value and a meaning, but he is not capable of giving a definite and reassuring answer to the question, so that the same consciousness which raises him above other creatures also drives him to despair and death. It is the tragic paradox that the highest evolution of life in the human mind also becomes its greatest danger. Yet even this extremely pessimistic drama leaves one dim ray of hope; beneath the extreme resignation we can discover a postulate which might have led the author to a more conciliatory attitude towards life if only longer life had been granted to him. This postulate is indicated in the remark with which Danton justifies his withdrawal from the revolutionary movement:

> Ich habe es satt, wozu sollen wir Menschen
> miteinander kämpfen.

These words indicate the only remaining possibility for continuing to bear the burden of life: if life is hardly worth living, and yet is the only recognizable value, then man ought, on the basis of this universal and inescapable tragedy, to renounce all hatred and strife and live in mutual sympathy and tolerance. (pp. 108-09)

The comedy *Leonce und Lena* does not translate the author's *Weltschmerz* so vividly into dramatic symbol and lacks therefore the full artistic value of *Dantons Tod.* . . . He ridicules the German system of small states, the fatuity of the princelings and their courtiers, the romantic vagaries and the blasé pessimism of his younger contemporaries. As far as this is a genuine expression of the author's own state of mind, it had all been said with incomparably more dramatic force in *Dantons Tod.* The main complaint in the comedy, too, is that life is deprived of any worthwhile content, and that the attempt to escape tedium is the real impulse of man's activity. . . . With this reduction of all motives to one of escape from tedium, Büchner also destroys the basis for any differentiation of values. All types of man in this comedy suffer from the same ailment, from which there is but one relief, withdrawal from the world into eternal nothingness.

Human fate, imperfect and conditioned as it is by causality, is also the theme of the fragmentary tragedy *Woyzeck. Woyzeck,* too, expresses the same deep compassion with the tormented creature man, which inspired the author to dramatize the all-too-human decline of the French Revolution. Woyzeck is a sort of "everyman," the representative of his many companions in distress, who, poor and exploited, live their dull and meaningless existence. As a soldier he loves his brave companion Marie; he is the father of her child; but he is too poor to pay for the blessing of the church and to lead the regulated life of a middle class family. He would like to be as virtuous as his well-nourished captain, who is moved at the thought of his own goodness, would have him be. But there is no virtue without money, and so these poor creatures are condemned to misery in this world as well as in the next:

> Ich glaub', wenn wir in Himmel kämen, müszten
> wir noch donnern helfen.

The regimental surgeon uses him as a subject of his experiments. For a quarter of a year he has kept him on a diet of peas, and the students observe its effects on his pulse and his eyes. Marie, a strong and sensual woman, as good and as uncontrolled as an animal, drives him to despair by her relations with other men, and what she does not achieve by her faithlessness, her seducers achieve by their mockery. The thought of murdering her comes to Woyzeck first in ghostlike apparitions; like an animal sniffing the air, he has vague premonitions of some indefinite disaster; it torments him in his feverish dream in the guard-room. Thus, the actual murder does not strike us as a wicked deed, but as a catastrophe of nature which had to overtake any man so oppressed and inhibited within the fatal sphere of his most primitive desires. The somberness of the atmosphere is emphasized by naturalistic dialogue and the pregnancy of the scenes, in which a few words suffice to create an impressive vision of the whole environment,—as for example, the scene in the Jewish pedlar's store where Woyzeck buys the knife for the murder. When the words flow more abundantly, they serve to characterize the more pretentious and the better educated people who, because of their very education, are inferior to the more genuine and valuable naturalness of Woyzeck and even Marie. We feel a deep sympathy toward them, but there are doubts about the real human value of the virtuous captain, and we abhor the surgeon for whom human beings are mere objects of experiments and for whom other people's illnesses are a boon from heaven.

The fragment *Woyzeck* complements the heroic tragedy *Dantons Tod. Dantons Tod* presents the tragedy of the leader whose higher intentions have been frustrated by the degrading forces of the masses. *Woyzeck* examines the tragedy of the proletarian man himself, the causality of his animal behavior, the determinism of his environment, which prevents him from rising to the higher stage in humanity to which he is entitled by his natural goodness. Büchner expresses in *Woyzeck* his social belief, which we quoted from his letters, that human society cannot be reformed by the decrepit members of the educated class; that a reform must begin with the material distress of the proletariat. With these ideas, the author anticipates socialism. Such ideas are closely related to Büchner's conception of man as basically instinctive in nature, rooted in his environment, and barely capable of rising above his animal origin, however much his intellect may tempt him to consider himself the free master of his destiny. With this conception, Büchner comes rather close to the deterministic naturalism of the late nineteenth century. What distinguishes Büchner from naturalism is the idealistic point of departure. Inverted idealism remains with him in the negative form of disillusionment and fatalistic resignation, for

which he found further support in medical and scientific studies. (pp. 109-11)

*F. W. Kaufmann, "Georg Büchner," in his* German Dramatists of the 19th Century, *1940. Reprint by Russell & Russell, 1972, pp. 103-11.*

## A. H. J. KNIGHT (essay date 1951)

[*In the following excerpt from the first book-length study in English of Büchner, Knight examines the strengths and weaknesses of* Danton's Death, *concentrating on the portrayal of the two main characters, Danton and Robespierre.*]

*Dantons Tod* is a play in four acts, each act sub-divided into a considerable number of scenes (there are thirty-two scenes in all), written throughout in prose, in a realistic or naturalistic style of language, which will call for further discussion. The action is simple, straightforward, and fundamentally coherent, and though the conventional unities of time and place are not strictly observed, they are not altogether disregarded: . . . the events all take place in the same area, and occupy a period of only twelve days. The list of dramatis personae contains twenty-seven names (to which must be added an unspecified but considerable number of crowd-characters): but, of the twenty-seven, two, Danton and Robespierre, are on an altogether greater scale than the rest, while of these two Danton himself is obviously meant to be much the more conspicuous. Indeed, the title of the play is an exact description of its theme, though it may be remarked that Danton is portrayed not merely as an individual who comes to a tragic end, but also—it appears—as a representative, or symbol, both of a particular, recurrent revolutionary type of man and also of an allegedly universal human type. I shall return to the matter of character-drawing later on.

The perpetual changes of scene in *Dantons Tod,* which impose a severe and quite unnecessary burden on any producer and on the resources of any theatre, and reveal a not unnatural absence of practical dramatic sense in the young author, irresistibly remind one of [Goethe's] first version of *Götz von Berlichingen,* of which, no doubt, much in Büchner's play is a conscientious imitation: one or two scenes, such as III, 8, and IV, 1, are so short as to appear quite senseless. Yet, though some of the deficiencies of form are a result of inexperience, and some . . . are apparently ascribable to mere haste, it seems almost certain that Büchner, with immense boldness and originality, was deliberately aiming at an almost entirely new technical effect, something like that achieved in the as yet undiscovered *Urfaust* (and also, to some extent, in *Götz*), whereby the action is presented in a series of apparently, but not really, disconnected flashes, which ultimately, but only ultimately, form a picture that makes sense. Büchner was trying to show the men of the French Revolution as they actually were, and the milieu in which they lived as it was, to present, as background to his main character-theme, a series, one might say, of photographically realistic pictures of revolutionary Paris at one of the great crises of the Revolution: for this purpose a new technique, or, at any rate, a fuller use than had ever yet been made of a technique which had only occasionally been attempted, seemed promising: and so he evolved, partly from his Sturm-und-Drang predecessors, this disconnected, kaleidoscopic technique, which results in something rather like the scenario of a film, and foreshadows the Expressionist methods of eighty or ninety years later, though not so obviously as does *Woyzeck.* But not only does it anticipate the Expressionists; it anticipates the Naturalists too. Büchner would certainly not have subscribed to all of the specific theories of the Naturalist school, but this much is common to him and to them, the attempt, within the given, necessary (ultimately stultifying) limitations of dramatic form, to give a true, accurate, detailed, impartial picture of the setting against which the personal fate of his characters is played out. This completely realistic effect, he evidently thinks, can best be obtained by a technique of shots or flashes, which produce their result by means of contrast, by surprises, by juxtaposition of the serious and the frivolous, the political and the personal: they include a large number of real or apparent incoherencies and irrelevancies, which are apparently meant to enhance the realism of the picture, and actually do so. In fact (I think) Büchner is really quite right in adopting the technique which he does adopt, here and again in **Woyzeck,** in order to produce the effect of total realism; for, by an apparent paradox, of all dramatic methods the superficially disconnected, illogical, somewhat incoherent technique somehow manages to give the most convincing reproduction of reality, presumably because reality appears so, at any rate to an analytically-minded observer. The apparently inconsequent and jerky scenes and conversations (characters talking 'past' one another rather than 'to' one another) make, or can make, the most powerful and convincing impression; a point which is illustrated over and over again by a number of later 'realistic' plays by, for example, Ibsen, Strindberg, and Chekhov. I do not mean by this that Büchner, though he chose, or evolved, the right technique, always makes the best use of it: I do not think that he does, either in **Dantons Tod** or in **Woyzeck.** . . . But such occasional failures, after all, are almost inevitable, especially in a dramatist experimenting in this fashion for the first time: it is the fault of his *use* of the technique, not of the technique itself.

One of the means by which Büchner attempts to produce this effect of 'total' realism is the lavish use of obscenity. . . . Büchner altogether disclaimed the suggestion that he was, or might be, indulging in obscenity for its own sake, even to the extent of alleging that some of the obscene passages had been inserted by the compositor off his own bat [see letter dated 1835]: Gutzkow, on the other hand, evidently believed that Büchner's imagination naturally ran to such things, and apologetically insisted that his flowers of speech must be pruned. Büchner alleges that the obscenities are solely in the interest of historical accuracy: by no other means could the men of the French Revolution be depicted as they actually were. Up to a certain point, it is true, an impression of historical accuracy is produced by the obscenities as by other would-be realistic effects: but only up to a point, for in this respect, as in others, the realism is overdone, or clumsily managed: a good deal of the conversation in **Dantons Tod,** obscene and other, is mere long-winded nonsense, stuff which no actual human being could ever have uttered, nor any realistic dramatist of experience and ability put into his characters' mouths. (pp. 80-2)

The portrait of Danton, though 'realistic' and 'historical' in the senses discussed above, is no doubt partly a self-portrait. It is hardly possible to decide with any certainty to what extent this is so, and it appears to me that some commentators have exaggerated the matter. All the same, it is prima facie reasonable to argue that at this unhappy and frustrated period in his life Büchner saw a resemblance between himself and the fallen French leader, perhaps a resemblance in character as well as in situation. Actually the resemblance in character

was not very great: for example, Büchner was apparently an ascetic, in whose life there seems to have been no woman except Minna Jäglé, and he does not appear either to have possessed Danton's gifts of eloquence and of resolute leadership in emergencies or to have been liable to the extraordinary fits of lethargy and indolence which are the most striking thing about Danton as here portrayed, and which, from time to time, and notably at this critical time, occurred in the life of the historical Danton.

The real point of contact between Büchner, as he was at this point in his life, and Danton, is the disgust and satiety felt by them both. This comes out in most of Büchner's letters of this period (and, indeed, not only of this period), and in scene after scene of the play. Danton is inactive because he does not *want* to act, because he is tired of action and disgusted by the results of action, especially the September massacres: he has come to believe that there is no point in anything any more, certainly not in political activity, and he is dead tired. All these traits are historical, though to some extent Büchner simplifies and sharpens them for the purpose of his play: what is not historical is the matter of the motives from which Danton's enemies turn against him and destroy him. For in historical fact, the struggle between Danton and Robespierre was not a personal struggle, but a fighting out of the question which of two views should prevail, and prevail, it seems, rather as a matter of immediate practical expediency than as a matter of fundamental general principle. I refer, of course, to the clash between those who now wanted to stop the Revolution, to stabilize things in the position which they had now reached, and those who thought that revolution and reform should be carried further; that is, the clash between moderates and extremists, though extremists of a different style from the defeated and liquidated Hébert and his party. This clash is indeed one of the themes in Büchner's play; Danton does appear as a moderate and Robespierre as an uncompromising, would-be logical extremist: but the real clash is personal: Robespierre hates Danton, feels passionate jealousy against him, and is disgusted, like some prudish old woman, by Danton's private life and the whole doctrine of Epicurean pleasure and sensual gratification for which he stands. Along with this, it is clear, the clash takes place, and Danton is destroyed, because Büchner has come to believe that in revolutions things do happen in this way, and lead to dictatorship. The shadow of Napoleon Bonaparte is clearly visible in **Dantons Tod.**

This personal struggle between Danton, with his supporters, some of whom, like Camille Desmoulins, are individualized and differentiated, and Robespierre, with his supporters, of whom St. Just alone is depicted in any detail, is obviously a very important theme in the play, for it constitutes nearly all the action (of which, in fact, there is too little), and it affords Büchner the occasion for the delineation of his two main personages. One cannot reasonably doubt that, intentionally or not, **Dantons Tod** is a play of character, of these two characters, more than it is a political or social or philosophical play. It is all these other things too, but they are of secondary or incidental importance: the excellence of the work depends on the portrayal of Danton and Robespierre.

Now it seems to me that opinions may well differ considerably concerning the degree of success which Büchner has attained in drawing these two men, and that a reasonable case, up to a point, may be made out in favour of several diverse views. No doubt the depiction of character depends on, or ties up with, the whole matter of the motives which impelled Büchner to write, and the mental state he was in at the beginning of 1835: that is to say, the characters as we find them are a result of his study and interpretation of the history of the French Revolution, plus his convictions on the general nature of the world, plus the personal experiences which, following hard upon that study and upon the emergence of those convictions, seemed to confirm him in his gloomiest apprehensions. All these factors were reinforced by literary reading, above all, we can be pretty certain—for Büchner as good as tells us so—by reading Shakespeare and Goethe. Viëtor draws attention to striking resemblances between Danton and Hamlet, and it looks as if there are considerable resemblances, too, between Danton and Faust. For example, the contents of the famous monologue in the scene *Wald und Höhle* recur, as a rule in very different phraseology, in the mouth of Danton on more than one occasion; and it may be remarked, too, that the all-pervading, greatly overworked cynicism with which so many of Büchner's characters habitually express themselves, reminds one not only of Faust in his more sardonic moods, but even more strikingly of Mephistopheles.

The result of historical study, literary reading, and personal experience, Danton, as he actually appears in this play, is certainly very peculiar, and, as has been indicated above, it is a matter of arguable opinion whether or not the depiction of him comes off. First and foremost, he is a mixed, or, as Strindberg was to put it in 1888 apropos of the characters in his *Fröken Julie,* a 'characterless' character, full of the most patent and glaring contradictions, convincing and alive to anyone who can understand that kind of man, completely unreal to the many people who cannot. It seems to me that Büchner so depicted him partly because, from his reading of the sources, he concluded that the historical Danton really was such a man—which was no doubt true up to a point—partly because he believed that men in general are like that, and partly, too, because self-analysis seemed to reveal that he himself was. Danton is represented—as, indeed, we have seen in the scene-by-scene account of the play—as sensual, even promiscuous, yet tenderly, deeply, in love with his (recently-acquired) wife; as sensible and reasonable in his (recently-acquired) ideas on political moderation, yet as disillusioned, bored, utterly and fatally weary of politics; as intelligent yet stupid; as fatalistic, lazy, yet spasmodically energetic; as high-minded and low-minded; as a leader who cannot lead; as completely self-stultifying and totally, in the most literal sense suicidally, incompetent.

So represented, Danton seems to be the first 'unheroic hero' in German drama, with the possible, and probably irrelevant, exception of some of Grillparzer's characters; he is the sort of man whom Strindberg depicts with such extraordinary success, and whom the German Naturalists, doggedly pursuing the Swedish dramatist and never catching him, try to make convincing and never do. To-day, when the 'unheroic hero', the mixed character, the victim of circumstances, has become such an everyday figure, in ordinary life as well as in literature, it is difficult to realize how preternaturally original, even with Shakespeare before his eyes, Büchner was when he wrote his first play around a central figure of this type.

To say this, to commend the originality and boldness of Büchner's basic idea, is not necessarily to applaud all the details of its execution; and certainly, apart from certain faulty details, one almost inescapable weakness in the drama follows from this fundamental conception of Danton's personality, namely, that lack of action to which attention has already been drawn, and above all that lack of struggle, conflict, crisis, which has been justly criticized as detracting from the tragedy's dramatic qualities. I say 'almost inescapable'; for more experienced dramatists (Shakespeare in *Hamlet,* Strindberg in *Fröken Julie,* Ibsen in *Rosmersholm*) have used the same general type of central figure, but have created real conflict and crisis, such as we do not find here, where the outcome is certain from the very beginning, and where there is no possibility or indication of a reversal of the *predestined course of events.* But this last phrase makes one pause, for it is, in this connexion, especially significant, is indeed a sort of key to the whole depiction of character and of situation. Men, so Büchner believes, are the victims of the world-order, the 'fatalism of history' is everywhere at work, there is no such thing as greatness or genius, the individual is merely 'foam on the wave'; and in such a deterministically viewed universe there can be no genuine clashes or conflicts, and, to the clear-sighted observer, not even the appearance of them. (pp. 83-6)

Büchner did not altogether accept the deterministic view of life, or, at any rate, . . . his instincts were against doing so, that he was emotionally revolted by it. Moreover, it is men's universal experience that, though in strict logic it may appear that everything which happens is determined from the beginning, and that therefore there are no true choices or conflicts, this does not seem in practice, to any individual, to be so. Thus we find—and this is another factor contributing to the general impression of Danton's characterless character—that while, as a rule, he and the others express deterministic views, they do not *invariably* do this, and on occasions they certainly act as if they possessed real freedom of will and choice.

I believe that there is a real contradiction here, within the play itself, not merely an apparent one, and that this is revealed in what one can only call the dramatist's moral attitude. The word 'moral' is not used here in precisely the usual sense; that is, it does not imply that Büchner passes any normal judgments of right and wrong, good and evil. What is meant is, rather, that Büchner does, though unobtrusively, take sides in **Dantons Tod,** and that he appears to feel for his hero a degree of sympathy, even affection, which in strict logic is hardly compatible with the views expressed in [Büchner's letters]. . . . In other words, Büchner's determinism breaks down, at least partially, when it comes to the point; and the characters in **Dantons Tod,** even if originally conceived under the influence of a logical, omnipresent, hopeless, deterministic philosophy, may quite reasonably be criticized as if they had been created by a dramatist who believed in the freedom of the human will.

It must be emphasized that these remarks and arguments are to some extent speculative, that they are derived primarily from Büchner's apparent practice in **Dantons Tod,** not from his unambiguous statements in letters. There is, however, nothing inherently improbable in what has just been said, and nothing, so far as I can see, which contradicts the textual evidence of the play.

Büchner's sympathy, then, appears to be for the sensual, lazy, fatalistic, intelligent, disillusioned Danton, and against Danton's enemy Robespierre: but the character of Robespierre is also of great importance, and it is essential for Büchner to make us believe in him, if he is to achieve the proper tragic effect. I do not think he succeeds in this, and herein, it seems to me, lies the second considerable weakness of the play. Once more, it is mainly a matter of personal taste and opinion; and it may be said at once that in trying to make comprehensible the historical Robespierre, Büchner was very likely trying something foredoomed to failure from the start. It is no exaggeration to say that nobody has ever understood Robespierre, as history shows him to us, and that nobody has ever been able to believe that he was, in actual fact, as the accounts make him out to have been. And if the historical Robespierre is an incredible personality, it is difficult to criticize Büchner for not being able to explain him or put his character across, especially since Büchner regarded himself as bound by the known facts to so large an extent. Robespierre is altogether too simple, too stiff and pedantic, wooden and clumsy: one cannot, by any effort of the imagination, envisage him as a successful leader, or as a human being. He was, in actual fact, and is so shown in Büchner's play, an extremely effective controller of the Paris mob and of his own political following: but it does not here emerge, any more than it does from the historical documents, how this can have been so. The man who becomes intoxicated with his own virtues, his own eloquence, his belief in his own mission, is a figure sufficiently familiar to us, more familiar to us, indeed, than to Büchner and his contemporaries: and we know that Robespierre was one of those men, that he believed every word he said, and probably had the power of convincing himself, as he proceeded, by arguments which he was in the process of inventing as he went. Büchner, it is pretty clear, understood this, and wished to show, in Robespierre's character, how such men proceed, and how terribly dangerous they are, especially in times of disturbance and revolution. He seems to me to despise Robespierre, in one aspect, at any rate, despise him; that is to say, as a human being, though not as an effective force in affairs, and he appears also to hate him, but he cannot explain him.

There is, it is true, something which one might call an attempt at an explanation. It comes in the passage . . . in I, 6, *b*, in the speech in which Robespierre, soliloquizing, describes himself, and all men, as somnambulists: '. . . ist nicht unser Wachen ein hellerer Traum? sind wir nicht Nachtwandler? ist nicht unser Handeln wie das im Traum, nur deutlicher, bestimmter, durchgeführter? Wer will uns darum schelten? In einer Stunde verrichtet der Geist mehr Taten des Gedankens, als der träge Organismus unsres Leibes in Jahren nachzutun vermag. Die Sünde ist im Gedanken. Ob der Gedanke Tat wird, ob ihn der Körper nachspielt, das ist Zufall.'

That is to say, he, and all men, are merely the incorporation, half-unconscious, half-unwilling, of great historical forces, an instrument blindly executing the irresistible purpose, whatever that purpose may be, if, indeed, there is one, of the world-order, not understanding, save perhaps in the dimmest fashion, what it is all about, and incurring guilt not by their actions, but only by their thoughts.

Now, if Büchner meant these sentences in any way as an expression of his own ideas—and it is to be observed that they are sentences put into Robespierre's mouth, not derived from the historical sources—he seems to be approaching the question of free-will, responsibility, and determinism from another angle, and arriving at a very curious result. For, after all, what is plainly said here is that, though our actions may be determined, our thoughts are not. For them, then, we have responsibility, of a sort, and so for our characters, for these express their own nature in thoughts, which chance may convert into deeds, or again may not. It all seems highly illogical, and it may well be that Büchner did not realize, or did not intend to express as his own considered opinion, the ideas here put forward, but the point is at least worth noting.

The matter of motives, too, arises, not for the first time, in connexion with these utterances by Robespierre; indeed, in connexion with almost everything which Robespierre says or does in Büchner's play. Danton himself makes no secret of the motives which impel him to action or inaction: they are, indeed, all too obvious, often all too obviously discreditable in the eyes of poor, envious, bigoted, or over-righteous men. He is destroyed, as things turn out, in great part because he is not a dissembler. Robespierre, on the other hand, acts from one set of motives—that is, purely personal motives of jealousy, hate, prudery, even, one might say, prurient-mindedness—but makes out that he acts from totally different, even antithetical motives, the good of the state, the highest moral principles, the welfare of the poor, and so forth. Now it seems to me that, in acting thus, Robespierre, who in history is represented as a sincere man, if a monstrous self-deceiver, is indeed partly acting with deliberate hypocrisy, but not wholly, in fact, not primarily. He serves, in fact, to demonstrate, among other things, the nature of motive, and the difficulty of being sure or clear about it. For though, as I say, not absolutely sincere, he is meant to be regarded as self-deceived in this matter rather than as deliberately deceiving others: that is to say, Robespierre is portrayed as acting from motives other than those from which he believes himself to act; and therein he exemplifies a universal truth: that in nearly all the actions of nearly all human beings the real motives are hidden and unknown to the actors and their entourage, though they may be partly visible to the historian or the historical dramatist. The motives men allege for their actions are only skin-deep, and, sometimes at least, the persons who profess them, without knowing what their real motives are, will realize that their professed motives are more or less bogus. There is, in fact, a strong strain of humbug, deliberate or unintentional, about the human race: this is something which Büchner frequently emphasizes in his letters, especially those which deal with politics and public affairs, and it appears to be a major theme here. Men are driven by the force of circumstances, first and foremost through the mere necessity of satisfying their most primitive and elementary needs, which, the author thinks, so seldom are satisfied, in any men, or at any time. But, till these elementary needs, for food, warmth, clothing, and so on, have been satisfied, all the more elaborate ideals which men, and especially men's self-styled leaders, profess, and which they dress up in fine words, classical aspirations, aesthetic forms, are more or less bogus; *and so they are here.* There is no such thing as nobility or idealism, so the play tells us, no such thing as action from pure and properly comprehended motives, no such thing as freedom of action: it is easier to liberate destructive forces than to control them; it is impossible, in respect of one's deeds, though not, perhaps, of one's thoughts, to be 'right' or 'wrong': men long for things which they cannot achieve, and a Robespierre is more likely to dominate the scene than is a Danton.

***Dantons Tod*** is, in fact, not really a drama about politics or social problems, still less a drama in praise of the kind of revolutionary action which Büchner had so recently been endeavouring to bring about. This was realized at the time of its publication by the German authorities, who made no attempt to censor or suppress it; and it is only more recent readers, enthusiastic rather than clear-sighted, who have tried to

*A scene from a 1957 German production of* Danton's Death, *featuring (left to right) Robespierre, Danton and St. Just.*

interpret it as a call to action or a panegyric on 'radicalism'. *Dantons Tod* is a play about human beings and their situation in an unfriendly universe, an example drawn from recent history, with commentary and exegesis by the dramatist, of the tragic nature of existence and the hopelessness of all effort. Worst of all, a really diabolical refinement of a situation already bad enough, is the fact that human beings, in all their actual helplessness, are so constructed that they possess acute powers of suffering: this . . . is the argument used by Paine (but invented by Büchner, and put into Paine's mouth) in III, I, to disprove once for all the possibility that God exists. All the same, the opportunity for heroism does not seem to be excluded. Men are not free, but in some respects they act as if they were free, their feelings are not determined, even if their actions are; it is interesting, and may even be profitable, to analyse human character under stress, and to observe and note down the reactions of men in a given situation, especially a tragic or hopeless one. It seems to emerge from Büchner's drama that human efforts are futile—and how could they not be, given that things are as they are?—and that it is in the inevitable nature of human aims, struggles, and ideals to be mixed and compromised. But not always in the same way. The individual who asserts himself against the historical process (as Hebbel would have phrased it, and, after all, a great resemblance exists between Hebbel and Büchner) will be ruined by so doing; and in his ruin will reveal himself and his efforts and ideals as the mixed and puny things that they are: but some individuals will have the saving grace to go down in ruin as heroes, and the heroism of such men will be all the more heroic in proportion as they have previously shown themselves (as has Danton in all the earlier scenes of this play) to be human, all too human.

In fact, *Dantons Tod* is less a pro-revolutionary than an anti-revolutionary play or pamphlet. For though in a sense the 'crowd', the people of Revolutionary Paris, are one of its chief actors—and, so far as the German drama is concerned, this is an innovation of real importance, leading to [Gerhart Hauptmann's] *Die Weber* and other essentially modern works—no one could say that the revolutionary crowd is the hero of the play, or that the state of affairs depicted is in any way glorified or praised. The crowd are not so much hero as villain: they are inconstant, unreliable, easily swayed, foolish, comic, diseased, and dirty. They dominate the scene, it is true: it is because Robespierre and his party acquire a temporary ascendancy over them greater than Danton's that Robespierre wins. But this ascendancy is nothing for anyone to admire. The worse man and the worse party are the victors, and they are the victors because the Paris crowd are bloodthirsty and envious fools. Moreover, though it is nowhere very precisely stated, it is clear (and, in fact, it so happened) that Robespierre and his friends are only temporary victors: their turn will come next. And this total incalculability on the part of the people, and the consequent insecurity of the ground and of all the foundations of politics and state, are a necessary consequence of revolutions, which devour their children and lead, as Danton says, straight to dictatorship. On the other hand, though the crowd are represented with a kind of aristocratic contempt, very much as Shakespeare represents them in *Julius Caesar,* that appears very odd coming from the author of *Der Hessische Landbote,* the forerunner of Karl Marx, it is also clear that Büchner does not blame the proletariat for their nature and behaviour, nor in any way hold them morally responsible for it. They are as they are, a danger to all and sundry (not least to themselves), because they live in a perpetual condition of economic misery, which nobody does anything to alleviate. This is stressed again and again, very notably in I, 2. The two contending parties in the state, powerless to improve the material conditions of the mob, endeavour, each in its own way, to fob them off with political flattery and the destruction of alleged enemies, a process to which there can be no end but chaos and the emergence of a dictator, who will not be one of the revolutionary leaders: however, neither of the political parties which Büchner represents has anything genuine to offer the people, who, requiring bread, get, not even a stone, but the heads of their former political chiefs, and, from Robespierre at any rate, a series of interminable and barren tirades about rigid republican virtue. This, as *Der Hessische Landbote* and many other utterances of Büchner show, is in his eyes something that just will not do. Political harangues, programmes, speeches, resolutions, intrigues, are one and all worthless: the simplest problems are the most important, they are all economic problems, and the simplest of all is the most important of all, the mere provision of the necessities of life in sufficient abundance.

*Dantons Tod* has many weaknesses, some of them rather serious, and they are weaknesses which become not less but more obvious the more attention one gives to the work: but its merits, especially its vigour and vitality, the reality and force which transcend the manifestations of *Weltschmerz* and Romantic futility, raise it far above the general run of the German (or, so far as I know it, the European) drama of its day. Moreover, the weaknesses of the work largely arise, as is shown by their comparative insignificance in *Woyzeck,* from the fact above all others which makes *Dantons Tod* so extraordinary: that is to say, from the fact that it is its author's first play. For of all the first plays in the world's literature, *Dantons Tod* is surely the most remarkable. (pp. 86-92)

*A. H. J. Knight, in his* Georg Büchner, *Basil Blackwell, 1951, 181 p.*

**RONALD PEACOCK** (essay date 1957)

[*Peacock argues that Büchner's writings combine the thematic and stylistic tendencies of late Romanticism with an innovative form of social realism.*]

Reading Büchner's plays without special previous study one is struck quite especially by three features, the language, the tendency for feeling to be focused in flitting scenes of great poignancy, and a general mood of disillusion and futility, relieved here and there by moments of human tenderness. The language is a strong and supple dialogue prose, very alive, very near to spoken everyday idiom, often brutally direct, hard and spare, but often yielding to gentler sentiment and touched with vivid poetic images. The scenes that impress one so much are nearly always quite brief, intensively evocative of terror, despair, or anguish, and in consequence moving and beautiful. The general mood of pessimism includes feelings ranging from a coarse cynicism to a more dignified tragic despair. This mood can be rather futilely depressing, but it is sincere; it shows a genuine revulsion of feeling.

Having received these fresh impressions one is impelled, in the interests of a better understanding of *Dantons Tod* in particular, to look into Büchner's politics. At once the sky darkens. Too much happened, and too quickly, with Büchner's political activities; and then he died. No one can really know whether he had *Weltschmerz* because of his political views, or his particular politics because of his *Weltschmerz*. One turns, for instruction, to the literature of the subject, and though one finds much helpful information and illuminating comment, one remains aware of an oppressive, unresolved problem, seen most clearly in the way critical views, falling roughly into two groups, the metaphysical and the sociological, are too deliberately opposed to each other, too exclusive, too intent on a unitary system of thought in one direction or the other. Yet most critics, except the more cautious Knight [see excerpt dated 1951] and Sengle, manage to admire Büchner almost as though he were a sacred person.

Turning back to the plays one finds in them, especially in *Dantons Tod,* a good deal that is fundamentally unclarified, if one tries to make it fit into a neat, logical pattern in relation to his political activities and his declared opinions. But one is then, in my view, more than ever convinced of what makes his literary strength in the slender and fragmentary, but extremely moving, intermezzo that he contributed to German dramatic literature, and to which in fact both kinds of listeners, the sociologists and the metaphysically minded, may respond.

I think it helps with *Dantons Tod* if one faces up to the possibility of its being not a unified but a very un-unified work. We have Sengle's authority for saying that it is not a 'historical drama' in the traditional sense; that Büchner is using history to prove his own desperate view of men as the victims of the *Fatalismus* of history. Nevertheless it seems to me that there *is* a historical play in *Dantons Tod,* and one in which a true phase of the French Revolution can be made to yield a sym-

bolic meaning about the revolutionary process in general. In this part of the play there is a sketch for a grandiose tragedy of human effort. In the opposition between Danton's party and Robespierre's we see focused the moment in the Revolution where judgment is divided as to ends and means, success and failure. The advantages of the new order are not immediately gained, the promises not fulfilled. In the name of the same initial idealism some wish to call a halt, whilst others wish to go forward with still greater vigour. The picture is familiar enough to us now: the means of bloodshed and terror begin to negate the ends of social justice, and the original idealism of revolution is dissipated either in the rigid, Puritanical fanaticism of a Robespierre or a St. Just, or in the sense of futility, of human helplessness amidst forces unloosed and events set racing, focused in a Danton. It is the stage in revolution when the conflict of revolutionaries versus social enemy is transformed into that of revolutionary versus revolutionary. This aspect of the work, impressively stark in its insight and originality in the literature of Büchner's day, is one about which we can agree with sociological critics like Lukács without committing ourselves to doctrinaire views. It gives the play an appeal that becomes particularly effective at other periods of history where similar processes are at work. The Spender-Rees translation of *Dantons Tod* in 1939 shows how this happened in England in the 'thirties, the decade of ideological conflict, in which particularly the humane and liberal outlook was felt to be more and more helpless against the inherent power of massive social movements. There are instants, including the end of Act II and Act III, when *Dantons Tod* touches a grandeur that derives from the momentary vision of historical process and of the tragic in all revolutions.

But this is not Büchner's whole play; he would indeed have done better to devote himself whole-heartedly to this great subject. The conception just described is an abstraction from the play. Danton belongs to it, but not all of Danton. In this part Büchner uses Danton to focus disillusion and his own insight, gained from grievous experience, into the tangle of all human action, in which the forces outside men are seen as the decisive and true agents of events. But there is a more disturbing Danton than this symbolic figure. In the historical Danton the feature of paralysis of will, setting in somewhat unaccountably, was noted by the historians whom Büchner studied as his sources, and was taken over by him as an important motive in the action, such as it is, of his play. But this historical Danton's sudden weariness, his not wanting to go on shedding blood, not wanting to become simply a tyrant, is something very different from loathing and disgust with life, from reckless cynicism, from the denial of all ideals, meaning and value, and from the morbid reduction of things human and supra-human to senseless corruption. This Danton—the Danton of *Langeweile,* of the nihilistic world-chaos, the Danton who identifies the sensation of love with that of the grave, who seeks macabre images or exaggerative and defiantly cynical epitomizations to describe life—this is, in my view, not the same Danton, developed and made fuller and richer, but a different one, added to the play, and related to the other only as a caricature. This is Georg Büchner's private Danton. The language he speaks, the attitude he embodies, are not insincere, but they spoil the play. They bring in a pessimism of a lurid, brutish and sordid kind, making the work in some parts simply ugly and tedious.

No one, to my knowledge, has thus ventured to see two Dantons in Büchner's play. It is, however, on this very point of

Danton's *extreme* pessimism, that interpretations actually fall apart. This is where the play, for those who oppose the sociological view, offers decisive evidence of having a 'metaphysical' foundation, or a universalized human tragic note, or a 'religious' meaning, or of being a nihilistic gospel. I do not agree with these interpretations. They arise from the assumption, all too common, that poetic works express *a priori* a valid, finalized *Weltanschauung,* or perhaps also from the habit of taking scattered statements too absolutely and constructing from them logical and systematic schemes of thought. I do agree, however, that the feature of Danton's character under consideration makes the play less of a sociopolitical one; but it also, in my view, makes it a worse play, not a 'deeper', or more 'tragic', or more 'religious' one. I prefer to see here a disunity in the play that is a symptom both of Büchner's philosophical and of his poetic-dramatic immaturity.

His immaturity caused him to miss an opportunity; with greater and cooler mastery of architectonic form and of the development of dramatic scenes (he is rudimentary in this respect), with a greater sense of dramatic *art* supplementing his natural sense of dramatic event, he could have developed to perfection the noble play that never really bursts out of the shadows thrown by the sickening *Weltschmerz* of Danton. Lukács, with a sympathy proceeding from his political interests, spotted this; but he sees only the noble play and not the sordid one. In the former, Danton is still a heroic figure, in the latter only a mouthpiece for Büchner reviling man and nature in a phase of sullen desperation, which is not heroic at all. Danton's emotional outbursts in this mood are crude and unsightly; to glorify them as the profound expression of a cosmic despair is to lose the sense of the genuine poetic. It is common to suggest a kinship in Büchner with the *Geniezeit,* especially since the word *Genie* is felt to sum up his mental complexion in a quite special way. But the naked emotionalism, the frank violence of rebellious passions, the emphatic defiance, of the *Sturm und Drang,* distasteful as they are to a refined taste, rested on an ideal of nature and human fulfilment, and they were, however extravagant, a courageous protest against effete rationalism and stifling social conventions. Danton's 'protest' is by comparison morbid and decadent. Similarly, the comparison with the great philosophical pessimists and rebels breaks down. At the side of Schopenhauer, or Kierkegaard, or Nietzsche, Büchner's ideas are elementary and his emotional reactions those of a layman.

*Woyzeck* is a different matter. The reason seems to me simple; the gall has been forgotten and charity has taken its place, so that tragedy is achieved without a jarring note. The intense tragic effect, to which all respond, however they seek to explain it, derives from the presence of human compassion which only a faith makes possible. In **Dantons Tod** the potential tragedy of revolution is drowned in the negative unbelief of the ugly Danton; nihilism, even if it is only theoretical and verbal, excludes tragedy. In **Woyzeck** we have a great and moving compassion for a human being, and a vigorous and noble implicit protest against social failure.

This play, fragment though it is, has a unity absent in **Dantons Tod,** a unity, moreover, that embraces both the social and the general human sentiment. In fact, they cannot here be separated, and, far from being in conflict, reinforce each other. Woyzeck is a simple man of the people, living in poverty and ignorance, without any vestige, or chance, of civilized

living, a man dominated by the most elementary needs and feelings of nature, the tool of his superiors, physically unequal to his rival, helpless in his love and suffering. He represents vividly man in a condition of social deprivation. By nature man is only partly brutish; he is more so when kept poor and in servitude. When Woyzeck murders it is partly a failure in the nature of man, if he remains animal and savage, but partly a failure in society, when it fails to do what it can to humanize its own members. Yet Woyzeck is not simply a brute—what sympathy should we have for him otherwise?—but a human being with a loyal love and at least a remnant of pride. He is human because he loves and is faithful, because he aspires in his mute way to something higher, and because he is sinned against. This situation, however commonplace, is always tragic, and Büchner has presented it with a beautiful spareness and simplicity that make it moving. But it is rendered more interesting and enormously strengthened by the social implications. Woyzeck is persecuted by a society divided into haves and havenots. His helplessness, and the pity it evokes, are at once social and human. Many are unwilling to accept this view, because they feel that Woyzeck is a symbol of man's general solitude and stricken condition. He is not an interesting or complex enough character, however, to be such a representative. A valid spiritual despair, a genuine human accusation against God or the universe, can only be presented with the subtlest arguments of the soul, and never with the stammerings of the inarticulate. Moreover, apart from this general argument, it is entirely reasonable, in view of Büchner's political opinions and activities in Hessen, to give Woyzeck a social meaning. It makes better sense, too. Especially one understands more easily the harsh or patronizing parts played by the Doctor and the Captain, or such things as the introduction of the satirical scene about animal and social behaviour at the fairground, or the comment of the Polizist at the end: 'Ein guter Mord, ein echter Mord, ein schöner Mord.' The representative of the public order recognizes, from his superior bourgeois point of view, a crime that goes neatly into his categories, a perfect specimen of what one expects from the 'criminal classes'. Pity for the human condition, for the misery of life, is particularized here in relation to one of its forms, the social one. And because Büchner manages to express this without falling in any way into doctrinaire statements the play shows human and social tragedy conjoined. With his gaze on both man and society steadier, with his social philosophy unobtrusive but firm, Büchner's picture of tragedy is more convincing, more charitable and more moving. In its unity of vision and effect appears the greater maturity of **Woyzeck,** as compared with **Dantons Tod,** both in its philosophical tone and in its dramatic expression.

Just as the interpretation of Büchner's meanings tends to emphasize either a social vision or a tragic disillusion so also the interpretation of his style pendulates between the appreciation of a strong 'realism' and a poetic expression of 'Stimmungen'. And again, it seems to me, the error is to see these as mutually exclusive.

With regard to realism, there is a tendency for this term, used of Büchner, sometimes to mean the political thinker and sometimes to refer to his dramatic style. On the former score he was undoubtedly a realist by comparison with the political 'liberals' whose reformist zeal was sentimentally humane and idealistic. He has the distinction of being unusually aware for his time of the economic motive in society. His Hessian insurrectionism was directed against the 'rich', not merely against the feudal ruling class. He was one of the first to adopt an essentially two-level class analysis, anticipating a much later development.

How much has this to do with realism in his style? Something, but not everything. It accounts for the choice of Woyzeck as a subject; for the 'poor wretch' as hero and for the adoption of a true criminal case as his documentary foundation. It was a new realism of subject, showing Büchner taking a very decisive step beyond the classic-romantic era. A realist intention also informs his treatment of history in *Dantons Tod.* He subscribed to the view that the dramatist should be perfectly faithful to historical fact. Although it can be argued that he did in fact exercise choice in using his sources, he seems to have done so only within narrow limits. He certainly did not alter facts, and he quite deliberately avoided idealization in the manner of Schiller or in the interests of a 'universal' idea. The scenes with populace in both *Dantons Tod* and *Woyzeck* show his realism as a matter of sincerity and of taste.

The same anti-idealistic spirit informs his much quoted remarks in *Lenz* about simple truth to nature as the proper ideal for poets; the vitality of the created thing, its living quality, is the true criterion, and it doesn't matter whether it is beautiful or ugly. It is rare to find it, moreover; it meets us in Shakespeare, in folk poetry, sometimes in Goethe. In this famous passage, however, there are some remarks that are not usually quoted but are in my view crucial for the understanding of Büchner's ideal of style.

> Dieser Idealismus ist die schmählichste Verachtung der menschlichen Natur. Man versuche es einmal und senke sich in das Leben des Geringsten und gebe es wieder in den Zuckungen, den Andeutungen, dem ganzen feinen, kaum bemerkten Mienenspiel; er [i.e. Lenz] hätte dergleichen versucht im "Hofmeister" und den "Soldaten". Es sind die prosaischsten Menschen unter der Sonne; aber die Gefühlsader ist in fast allen Menschen gleich, nur ist die Hülle mehr oder weniger dicht, durch die sie brechen muss. Man muss nur Aug und Ohren dafür haben. Wie ich gestern neben am Tal hinaufging, sah ich auf einem Steine zwei Mädchen sitzen: die eine band ihre Haare auf, die andre half ihr; und das goldne Haar hing herab, und ein ernstes bleiches Gesicht, und doch so jung, und die schwarze Tracht, und die andre so sorgsam bemüht. Die schönsten, innigsten Bilder der altdeutschen Schule geben kaum eine Ahnung davon.

The ideal suggested here departs from realistic presentation proper and instead places the universals of *feeling* in the centre; it selects its pictures according to their manner of evoking responsive emotions. This is of great significance because it corresponds to what actually occurs in Büchner's execution of his dramatic scenes. It gives the clue to the rare quality in these scenes which makes them so poetically moving and raises them above the element of squalid truth that their realistic setting comprehends. This brings me back to what I said was one of the dominant impressions received from Büchner's work.

Büchner handles material that is fraught with drama, without following the convention—a good one, let us remind ourselves, though German critics underestimate its value, accepting too easily dramatic turbulence for dramatic art—of making a good plot. There is no plot, or only very little, in *Dantons Tod.* Danton and his friends are in danger, they are

arrested, they wait in dejection for their fate to be decided, and finally they are taken to the guillotine. There is no real dramatic development within the separate scenes; Büchner is almost innocent of the interlocking clash of purposes which is the working material of the dramatist. The basic conflict scarcely appears in the dialectic of scene and dialogue, but only from virtually monolithic statements on either side at different times, and even the one short scene between Danton and Robespierre is fundamentally similar—an opposition of statements rather than a passionate grappling of two wills and their actions. There are, moreover, too many characters, too many incidental persons without a sustained role, for dramatic clarity. Frequent change of scene suggests movement, yet the essential rhythm of a dramatic concatenation is missing. *Woyzeck* also has little plot. It is in effect a chronicle, a narrative sequence of scenes, given tension, however, by the simple jealousy story working up to the climax of murder.

But what is really original in Büchner is his mastery in framing the pregnant emotional or dramatic instant. These instants have a character quite their own. They are anything but 'short dramatic scenes' of vivid action or genre portraiture. In the latter category I would put, for example, the 'Bude' scene in *Woyzeck,* or the scene 'Eine Gasse' (Simon and his wife) in *Dantons Tod* Act I. They are good scenes, but Büchner becomes really remarkable with the kind that have for their purpose the focusing of intense phases of feeling and mood. At their best such scenes have a dramatic reference; they are the high points of a story, arranged in narrative sequence but with selective and concentrated dramatic significance. Two of the 'Mariens Kammer' scenes in *Woyzeck* are good examples. The first is where Marie has received gifts from her new lover, and Woyzeck finds her with them and gets his first fleeting suspicions. There is no attempt to develop a violent scene between them, to elaborate a conflict. On the contrary there is an agreement of feeling in the sense of poverty they both have, and the end of the short episode, its climax, is Marie's remorseful feeling of wickedness followed by the indifference of despair. The second example shows another pregnant moment when the light is focused for an instant on a phase of emotion. Marie is here with her bastard child and the Narr, a grotesque partner in the scene. She is driven to her Bible by the consciousness of her sin and faithlessness. She reads phrases about the woman taken in adultery and intersperses exclamations of remorse; the Narr repeats nonsensical bits from fairy stories and then is silent, holding the child. Wholly unconventional in technique, the dramatic significance of this scene lies in its presenting the moment of moral breakdown in Marie. The presence of the idiot gives something additional to the psychological drama, enlarging the scene to make it reflect a greater tragic discordance in life.

Büchner packs his dramatic excitements into scenes of this kind. But they do have a curiously ambiguous quality. It is no doubt a dramatic interest that isolates such highly charged instants, but they can sometimes have an effect more lyrical than dramatic; though it must also be added that the quality is not adequately described by the term 'Stimmung'. The scene of the murder in *Woyzeck,* for example, set with a maximum of 'atmosphere'—the forest, the pond, the cold night air, the blood-red moon—is given, beyond its meaning as action or climax of the story, the quality of a nightmare. It only comes to an end in a violent act; in itself it shows action suspended in Woyzeck's brooding and Marie's passive unknowingness. Often there is no action at all, or a minimum. The actual substance of many of Büchner's scenes is the pointed crystallization of emotion or mood in one of the principal persons, making a self-sufficient picture, by contrast with the more usual construction in which the criss-crossed lines of plot and action flow through every scene. His most beautiful and poetic moments are of this kind. One thinks of Danton and Julie in Act II, of the Lucile scenes at the end of the same play, of Julie taking poison, or of the great sadness of the Conciergerie scene in Act IV. Such scenes emerge, it is true enough, from a story or dramatic framework, but their nature is to be brief acted lyrics. Their predominant themes, moreover, are love, a wistful sense of nature and its moods, and the helplessness, solitude and terror of men.

In this, Büchner's strongest poetic vein, he was very much a late romantic. There is no need to feel that this contradicts his politics or such realism as he has, or that it reduces his status. His politics, like most progressive movements of the nineteenth century, derive ultimately from Rousseau's idealism, which was a political aspect of the romanticism that spread through Europe in the later eighteenth century and found varying literary expression as well. Democratic faiths and romantic moods went very well together in many writers of the eighteen-twenties and 'thirties. Büchner's moods of despair, cynicism, boredom, his motifs of death and corruption, his meaningless universe, his fatalism, his ear for a beautiful but also a sinister music in nature and the empty spaces, his glimpses into hallucination, nightmare and madness, all these are the common stock of much romantic literature. His conception of realism in art, meaning the simple natural truth of things and men, is also after all tinged with romanticism, just as poeticization by the use of *Volkslieder* is a romantic, not a realist, symptom. His hard-boiled political attitude, the atheism, the sober, unadorned scientific materialism, indicate perhaps an unromantic attitude that was to be possible in the future; in Büchner they are still a result of emotional reaction, not an entirely new, free beginning. From such attitudes there arose later in the century a characteristic realist style in literature. Büchner belongs to the period in which realist insights still jostled with romantic longings and above all with romantic poetic ideals. Even with a changing subject-matter the expression continued to reflect the romantic style. It is a mistake to be prejudiced one way or the other in Büchner's case, and see only half the picture. His finest scenes owe their character, their beauty, and their own original, rare quality to a romantic lyricism that flowers amidst intimations of a new, socially realistic subject. (pp. 189-97)

*Ronald Peacock, "A Note on Georg Büchner's Plays," in* German Life & Letters, *Vol. X, 1957, pp. 189-97.*

## WOLFGANG KAYSER (essay date 1957)

[*Kayser's 1957 study* The Grotesque in Art and Literature *was the earliest attempt to compose a critical history of the grotesque as a distinct category of aesthetics. Kayser traces the evolution of the term "grotesque" from its first application to an ornamental style in Roman architecture through its various manifestations in the works of nineteenth- and twentieth-century authors and artists, among them Edgar Allan Poe, Franz Kafka, and the Surrealist painters. Kayser defines the grotesque as "the estranged world." By choosing the modifier "estranged" Kayser intends to distinguish a merely non-naturalistic world, as in the traditional fairy tale, from one in which once familiar objects, characters, and situations are altered in some demonic and uncanny way. While Kayser man-*ages a precise description of the nature and function of the grotesque in art and literature, he concludes that its sources and ultimate meaning are unknown. The grotesque, he concludes, "is primarily the expression of our failure to orient ourselves in the physical universe," and the motive behind the artistic creation of the grotesque is the "attempt to invoke and subdue the demonic aspects of the world." In the following excerpt from this study, Kayser applauds Büchner's skillful handling of the grotesque in* Woyzeck.]

"What I look for in everything is life, the possibility of existence, and then I am satisfied. Then we must not ask whether life is beautiful or ugly. What truly matters is the awareness that life inheres in all created things, and that should be our sole esthetic criterion." With good reason one has taken these sentences, which are put into the mouth of Lenz in Büchner's novella [*Lenz*], to express Büchner's personal opinion, for Büchner's letters contain many similar observations. Equally faulty is the current interpretation of the fact that Büchner was rediscovered by the Naturalists and celebrated as their predecessor. This fact, indisputable in itself, does not confirm the strict realism of Büchner's writings but rather arouses doubt concerning the strict realism of the Naturalists. When read in context, passages like the above reveal that Büchner-Lenz was by no means inclined to regard the work of art as a mosaic composed of closely observed and painstakingly recorded bits of reality. Lenz expressly demands a penetration of the subject and a deeper understanding of the individual. This, however, presupposes a definite and consistent attitude on the part of the writer: "One has to love mankind if one wants to understand the particular nature of each individual; nobody must be too lowly or ugly for those who want to know him." The work of art, on the other hand, possesses certain qualities which are not found in reality: "I prefer the poet and artist who renders nature so real that I am moved by his creation." The task which is here assigned to the work of art—namely, that of affecting the audience in a special and analogous manner—appears to be connected with its being a structure (*Gebilde*). Büchner's esthetic admits the artificiality of art at least insofar as it recognizes the process of shaping, that is, unification, direction, selection, and limitation. The following sentence from a letter of 1 January 1836 shows a similar awareness of the limitations of a slavish copy: "I draw my figures as I find them appropriate to nature and history."

The aspect which prevails in the unifying process of artistic creation has to be one that also prevails in reality—such is the essence of Büchner's theory of art. The shaping from an extrinsic point of view, preferred by the Idealists (by Raphael, according to Lenz; by Schiller, according to Büchner's letters), is "a heinous defamation of human nature." This passage from Büchner's story echoes Lenz' authentic statement: "I esteem the characteristic, and even the caricatural, painter ten times more highly than the idealistic one." Lenz here empowers the artist to intensify and exaggerate "reality" from his "realistic" point of view. Lenz himself made ample use of this device, and so did Büchner, whose theory of the emphatic nature of art had given him the right to proceed in this manner. Only those who narrowly focus on the language used in the eclectic plays of the period can mistake the language of the lower-class characters in *Woyzeck* as being realistic, genuine, natural, naïve, or what other terms have been applied to it. Actually, it is as artificial as all artistic language:

"All earthly things are vain. Even gold rots. And my immortal soul reeks after brandy." "Heavens! Let's have a stud of drum majors. . . . " "Wish that our noses were two bottles of wine we could pour down each other's throats!"

If these expressions, selected at random from the speeches of the secondary characters in **Woyzeck,** remind one of anything, it is Shakespeare's language, the language of the poet whom Büchner enthusiastically admired, but hardly that of actual drum majors and journeymen such as one encounters in daily life.

What, however, is the point of view which Büchner adopted in his **Woyzeck** and which permits such artificiality? Let us collect some additional quotes from Büchner's letters: "I feel crushed by the abhorrent fatalism inherent in history. In human nature I discover a terrible equality, and in the human condition an ineluctable power bestowed on all and none. The individual but foam on top of the wave; greatness mere chance; the rule of genius a puppet show, a ridiculous struggle against the brazen law which we endeavor to know but cannot hope to control." "What in ourselves is it that lies, kills, and steals?" "Oh, we poor crying musicians! Our moaning on the rack, is its sole purpose to ascend through the spaces between the clouds, to sound on and on, and to die, a melodious breath, in heavenly ears?"

Such sentences express the fear of "fatalism," that is, of man's lack of freedom, his being determined and pushed, and his being afraid of dark, ominous, and mysterious forces that work through us but defy all human explanation. In his letters, Büchner employs a *topos* which appears also in the speech of several of his characters: the world as a puppet play. Some of the relevant sentences clearly betray Büchner's indebtedness to a wider historical context, although one cannot fail to see how much more bitter, harrassed, and tormented Büchner sounded when using the image. For an incomprehensible, meaningless, and anonymous force has replaced the God who wrote the parts and played the puppets. . . . The fear engendered by this overbearing impersonal force is increased by the awareness of the vanity of life and the aimlessness not only of man's action but also of his suffering. This feeling culminates in the burning question that is raised by Büchner's Danton, "Are we children who are crushed in the red-hot Moloch's arms of this world and tickled by light rays in order to amuse the gods by our laughter?" The satanic humorist Jean Paul would certainly have approved this definition of laughter as an expression of pain that pleases the gods. Büchner himself mentions another writer who portrayed such abysmal disillusionment and disorientation [E. T. A. Hoffmann]. In the letter in which he asks his fiancée whether our moanings sound like a melodic breath to heavenly ears he confesses: "I am afraid of my voice and my image in the mirror. I could have served as one of Callot-Hoffmann's models, couldn't I, my dear?" (pp. 89-92)

[We] must not forget that our quotes are taken from letters which Büchner addressed to specific individuals. Being such they are intensified, stylized, and colored by the artificiality characteristic of epistolary language—although it would be wrong to doubt the sincerity of Büchner's feelings. But there is still another Büchner, who is a fanatic student and teacher of the natural sciences, and the one who is more strongly convinced than Lenz of "the infinite beauty that constantly changes its form" and who knows "the inexpressible harmony which, in the more developed forms, communicates and feels with a greater number of organs and is, therefore, all the more deeply affected."

The other point of view, however, which, using Büchner's own words, we might call that of the puppet-play . . . , forms the central aspect under which the world of **Woyzeck** is created in a unified and deliberately exaggerated manner.

That the characters in this play are guided by an outside force like puppets is most easily shown in the figures of the Captain and the Doctor. Satiric intentions undoubtedly played a part in their creation, for they are caricatured representatives of the dominant society. But their caricatural aspect is not the exaggeration of traits proper to their class. The Captain, for instance, avows his idealism and his melancholic temper. He is "well-intentioned" toward Woyzeck because the latter is a *"guter Mensch"* (a decent fellow). The Captain talks a good deal about decent fellows. It is the essence of the man, and the crux of the matter, that he is obsessed by the formula *qua* formula without acting in accordance with it. For he has not acquired the notion of a decent fellow, and concepts like conviction, development, or personality can in no way be applied to him since he is a wooden puppet. He is never himself because he has no substance. The *idée fixe* which governs his speech and attitude is the stubborn belief in experiment for its own sake. Even the secondary characters are obsessed with preconceived ideas. Both in appearance and language the drum major is a sire of drum majors, while the journeyman is the incarnation of a soul reeking after brandy. The conception and execution of Woyzeck's plan to kill Marie, too, is imposed from the outside in the form of an *idée fixe.* It is the wire which sets him in motion and controls his limbs. Büchner's Lenz, too, is haunted by such notions, for this is what the narrator calls the manic urge which prompts him to attempt the resurrection of the dead child. When speaking of his intentions to give philosophical lectures, Büchner applied the formula even to himself. Once again one sees how a principle inherent in the puppet play and often instrumental in achieving purely comic effects is invested with deeper philosophical meaning and how, as a consequence, our smile is tinged by the fear of a world in which men are no longer themselves.

Büchner by far surpasses . . . [German Romantic dramatists] Klinger and Lenz in the stylistic unity he has given the characters of his **Woyzeck.** It is not true that, as one critic has maintained, "the middle-class characters are treated differently from the common people." The Captain and the Doctor are also ominous and terrifying and Woyzeck is ridiculous. Büchner makes no distinction between topically comic flights on one hand and high seriousness on the other, but the abysmal strangeness of tragicomedy is all-pervasive. The language of the Captain, the Doctor, and Woyzeck himself, seen in conjunction with Büchner's stage directions, clearly suggests that all three characters move in the eccentric manner of the *commedia dell'arte* figures: the Captain alarmingly phlegmatic, the Doctor with short-legged eagerness, Woyzeck with the haste of a fugitive. The conclusion of the scene "Street," which follows, offers one of the purest examples of the style of **Woyzeck,** in its language and action. At the end the Captain utters the summarizing, evaluative word at which our discussion aimed.

> WOYZECK. I am leaving. A lot can happen. The human being! A lot can happen.—Nice weather, Captain. Such a pretty, solid gray sky. Do you see? One is tempted to drive a log into it and hang oneself thereon, just because of the little hyphen between yes and yes again—and no. Captain, yes and no? Is the yes to blame for the no, or the no for the

yes? Let me think it over. (*Exits with long strides, at first slowly but then quickly increasing his speed.*)
DOCTOR (*Rushes after him*). Phenomenal! Woyzeck, I'll raise your pay.
CAPTAIN. These fellows make me dizzy. How fast they run! The tall one runs like the shadow of a spider's leg, and the short one, how it swerves! The tall one is the lightning and the short one the thunder. Haha! . . . Grotesque! grotesque!

Every word which the Captain uses to describe the scene hits home, and with each he further estranges the world of man by introducing that of animals as well as the neutral ("it swerves"), atmospheric, and extrahuman sphere.

In an earlier version of the play, Büchner had used the word "grotesque" in still another passage. After the barker in the scene "Public Square, Booths" has praised his astrological ass, the romantic horse, and the military ape, whose sensible beastliness considerably surpasses man's beastly foolishness; and after he has thoroughly confounded the various realms of being, Büchner puts the following synoptic interpretation into the mouth of one of the onlookers: "I am a friend of the grotesque." (The additional remark, "I am an atheist," is topped by another bystander's verbal grotesque, "I am a Christian dogmatic atheist. I must see the ass.")

The barker's speech is as idiosyncratic as many other varieties of language found in *Woyzeck* (numerous songs, the parodistic sermon of the journeyman, the biblical story of the adulteress, the fairy tale told by the fool and that told by the grandmother). The stylistic unity of the play ensues from the way in which the most diverse ingredients fit together and are integrated into a whole. This whole comprises the total isolation and helplessness of all things human expressed in the grandmother's tale, as well as the grotesque manner in which the barker presents his limited little world. The two aspects complement each other; and Büchner's stylistic genius has never been more strikingly revealed than in the way in which he harmonizes the grandmother's story of the lonely child with the total estrangement of the world: " . . . and when it finally reached the moon, it turned out to be a piece of rotten wood . . . and when it reached the sun, it was merely a withered sunflower . . . and when it reached the stars, they were little golden gnats affixed to the sky as the killer bird impales them on blackthorns. And when it wanted to return to the earth, the latter was an earthenware pot turned upside down. And then it was all by itself in the world and sat down and cried. And there it still sits all by itself." (pp. 92-5)

> Wolfgang Kayser, "The Grotesque in the Age of Romanticism," in his The Grotesque in Art and Literature, *translated by Ulrich Weisstein, Indiana University Press, 1963, pp. 48-99.*

## GEORGE STEINER  (essay date 1961)

[*Steiner is a French-born American critic, poet, and fiction writer. Though some commentators have faulted his occasionally exuberant prose style, he is generally regarded as a perceptive and erudite critic. In the following excerpt, Steiner recognizes Büchner as a tremendous influence on twentieth-century expressionist drama, especially noting his revolutionary use of language and defiance of classical dramatic conventions in* Woyzeck.]

[Büchner's] absurdly premature death is a symbol of waste more absolute than that of either of the two instances so often quoted in indictment of mortality, the deaths of Mozart and Keats. Not that one can usefully set Büchner's work beside theirs; but because the promise of genius in his writings is so large and explicit that what we have is like a mockery of that which was to come. There is some flagging in Keats's late poetry. Büchner was cut down in full and mounting career. One can scarcely foresee the directions in which might have matured a young boy who had already written *Dantons Tod, Leonce und Lena, Woyzeck,* and that massive torso of prose narrative, *Lenz.* At a comparable age, Shakespeare may have been the author of a few amorous lyrics.

Büchner's instantaneous ripeness staggers belief. The mastery is there from the outset. There is hardly an early letter or piece of political pamphleteering which does not bear the mark of originality and stylistic control. If we make exception of Rimbaud, there is no other writer who was so completely himself at so early an age. Usually passion or eloquence come long before style; in Büchner they were at once united. One marvels also at Büchner's range. In Marlowe, for example, there is a voice prematurely silenced, but already having defined its particular timbre. Büchner commits his powers to many different directions; all in his work is both accomplishment and experiment. *Dantons Tod* renews the possibilities of political drama. *Leonce und Lena* is a dream-play, a fusion of irony and heart's abandon that is still in advance of the modern theatre. *Woyzeck* is not only the historical source of "expressionism"; it poses in a new way the entire problem of modern tragedy. *Lenz* carries the devices of narrative to the verge of surrealism. I am mainly concerned with Büchner's dramatic prose and with his radical extension of the compass of tragedy. But every aspect of his genius reminds one that the progress of moral and aesthetic awareness often turns on the precarious pivot of a single life.

It turns also on trivial accidents. The manuscript of *Woyzeck* vanished from sight immediately after the death of Büchner in 1837. The faded, nearly illegible text was rediscovered and published in 1879, and it was not until the first World War and the 1920's that Büchner's dramas became widely known. They then exercised a tremendous influence on expressionist art and literature. Without Büchner there might have been no Brecht. But the long, fortuitous gap between the work and its recognition poses one of the most tantalizing questions in the history of drama. What would have happened in the theatre if *Woyzeck* had been recognized earlier for the revolutionary masterpiece it is? Would Ibsen and Strindberg have laboured over their unwieldy historical dramas if they had known *Dantons Tod?* In the late nineteenth century only Wedekind, that erratic, wildly gifted figure from the underworld of the legitimate theatre, knew and profited from Büchner's example. And had it not been for a minor Austrian novelist, Karl Emil Franzos, who rescued the manuscript, the very existence of *Woyzeck* might now be a disputed footnote to literary history.

Büchner knew the prose scene in *Faust* and cites one of Mephisto's derisive retorts in *Leonce und Lena.* He was familiar, also, with the energetic, though rather crude, uses of prose in Schiller's *Die Räuber.* But the style of *Woyzeck* is nearly autonomous; it is one of those rare feats whereby a writer adds a new voice to the means of language. Van Gogh has taught the eye to see the flame within the tree, and Schoenberg has brought to the ear new areas of possible delight. Büchner's work is of this order of enrichment. He revolutionized the language of the theatre and challenged definitions of tragedy which had been in force since Aeschylus. By one of those fortunate hazards which sometimes occur in the history of art, Büchner came at the right moment. There was crucial need of a new conception of tragic form, as neither the antique nor the Shakespearean seemed to accord with the great changes in modern outlook and social circumstance. *Woyzeck* filled that need. But it surpassed the historical occasion, and much of what it revealed is as yet unexplored. The most exact parallel is that of a contemporary of Büchner, the mathematician Galois. On the eve of his death in a ridiculous duel at the age of twenty, Galois laid down the foundations of topology. His fragmentary statements and proofs, great leaps beyond the bounds of classic theory, are still to be reckoned with in the vanguard of modern mathematics. Galois's notations, moreover, were preserved nearly by accident. So it is with *Woyzeck;* the play is incomplete and was nearly lost. Yet we know now that it is one of the hinges on which drama turned toward the future.

*Woyzeck* is the first real tragedy of low life. It repudiates an assumption implicit in Greek, Elizabethan, and neo-classic drama: the assumption that tragic suffering is the sombre privilege of those who are in high places. Ancient tragedy had touched the lower orders, but only in passing, as if a spark had been thrown off from the great conflagrations inside the royal palace. Into the dependent griefs of the menial classes, moreover, the tragic poets introduced a grotesque or comic note. The watchman in *Agamemnon* and the messenger in *Antigone* are lit by the fire of the tragic action, but they are meant to be laughed at. Indeed, the touch of comedy derives from the fact that they are inadequate, by virtue of social rank or understanding, to the great occasions on which they briefly perform. Shakespeare surrounds his principals with a rich following of lesser men. But their own griefs are merely a loyal echo to those of kings, as with the gardeners in *Richard II*, or a pause for humour, as in the Porter's scene in *Macbeth*. Only in *Lear* is the sense of tragic desolation so universal as to encompass all social conditions (and it is to *Lear* that *Woyzeck* is, in certain respects, indebted). Lillo, Lessing, and Diderot widened the notion of dramatic seriousness to include the fortunes of the middle class. But their plays are sentimental homilies in which there lurks the ancient aristocratic presumption that the miseries of servants are, at bottom, comical. Diderot, in particular, was that characteristic figure, the radical snob.

Büchner was the first who brought to bear on the lowest order of men the solemnity and compassion of tragedy. He has had successors: Tolstoy, Gorky, Synge, and Brecht. But none has equalled the nightmarish force of *Woyzeck.* Drama is language under such high pressure of feeling that the words carry a necessary and immediate connotation of gesture. It is in mounting this pressure that Büchner excels. He shaped a style more graphic than any since *Lear* and saw, as had Shakespeare, that in the extremity of suffering, the mind seeks to loosen the bonds of rational syntax. Woyzeck's powers of speech fall drastically short of the depth of his anguish. That is the crux of the play. Whereas so many personages in classic and Shakespearean tragedy seem to speak far better than they know, borne aloft by verse and rhetoric, Woyzeck's agonized spirit hammers in vain on the doors of language. The fluency of his tormentors, the Doctor and the Captain, is the more horrible because what they have to say should not be dignified with literate speech. Alban Berg's operatic version of *Woyzeck* is superb, both as music and drama. But it distorts Büchner's principal device. The music makes Woy-

zeck eloquent; a cunning orchestration gives speech to his soul. In the play, the soul is nearly mute and it is the lameness of Woyzeck's words which conveys his suffering. Yet the style has a fierce clarity. How is this achieved? By uses of prose which are undeniably related to *King Lear*. Set side by side, the two tragedies illuminate each other:

GLOUCESTER.  These late eclipses in the sun and moon portend no good to us. Though the wisdom of nature can reason it thus and thus, yet nature finds itself scourg'd by the sequent effects. Love cools, friendship falls off, brothers divide. In cities, mutinies; in countries, discord; in palaces, treason; and the bond crack'd twixt son and father. This villain of mine comes under the prediction; there's son against father; the King falls from bias of nature; there's father against child. We have seen the best of our time.

(I, ii)

WOYZECK.  Aber mit der Natur ist's was anders, sehn Sie; mit der Natur das is so was, wie soll ich doch sagen, zum Beispiel. . . .

(But with Nature, you see, it's something else again; with Nature it's like this, how shall I say, like. . . . )

. . . . .

Herr Doktor, haben Sie schon was von der doppelten Natur gesehn? Wenn die Sonn in Mittag steht und es ist, als ging' die Welt in Feuer auf, hat schon eine fürchterliche Stimme zu mir geredt!

(Herr Doktor, have you ever seen anything of compound Nature? When the sun is at midday and it feels as though the world might go up in flame, then a terrible voice has spoken to me!)

. . . . .

Die Schwämme, Herr Doktor, da, da steckt's. Haben Sie schon gesehn, in was für Figuren die Schwämme auf dem Boden wachsen? Wer das lesen könnt!

(In toadstools, Herr Doktor, there, there's where it lurks. Have you already observed in what configurations toadstools grow along the ground? He that could riddle that!)

("Beim Doktor")

LEAR.  Down from the waist they are Centaurs, though women all above; but to the girdle do the gods inherit, beneath in all the fiend's. There's hell, there's darkness, there's the sulphurous pit; burning, scalding, stench,

consumption. Fie, fie, fie! pah,
pah!

(IV, v)

WOYZECK.        Immer zu—immer zu! Immer
                zu, immer zu! Dreht euch, wälzt
                euch! Warum bläst Gott nicht
                die Sonn aus, dass alles in Un-
                zucht sich übereinander wälzt,
                Mann und Weib, Mensch und
                Vieh?! Tut's am hellen Tag, tut's
                einem auf den Händen wie die
                Mücken!—Weib! Das Weib is
                heiss, heiss! Immer zu, immer
                zu!

                (Ever and ever and ever and
                ever! Whirl around, wind
                around! Why does God not blow
                out the sun so that all may pile
                on top of one another in lechery,
                man upon woman, human upon
                beast?! They do it in broad day-
                light, they do it on your hands
                like gnats! Woman! Woman's
                hot, hot! Ever and ever!)

                ("Wirtshaus")

LEAR.           And when I have stolne upon
                these
                   son in lawes,
                Then kill, kill, kill, kill, kill, kill!

                (IV, v)

WOYZECK.        Hör ich's da auch?—Sagt's der
                Wind auch?—Hör ich's immer,
                immer zu: stich tot, tot!

                (Do I hear it here also?—Does
                the wind say it also?—Shall I
                hear it ever and ever: stick her
                dead, dead!)

                ("Freies Feld")

There are direct echoes. Lear calls upon the elements to
"crack nature's mould" at the sight of man's ingratitude;
Woyzeck wonders why God does not snuff out the sun. Both
Lear and Woyzeck are maddened with sexual loathing. Before their very eyes, men assume the shapes of lecherous
beasts: the polecat and the rutting horse in *Lear;* the gnats
coupling in broad daylight in **Woyzeck.** The mere thought of
woman touches their nerves like a hot iron: "there's the sulphurous pit; burning, scalding"; "Das Weib is heiss, heiss!"
A sense of all-pervading sexual corruption goads the old mad
king and the illiterate soldier to the same murderous frenzy:
"kill, kill"; "stich tot, tot!" (pp. 270-78)

But it is in their use of prose that the two plays stand nearest
to each other. Büchner is plainly in Shakespeare's debt. Prose
style is notoriously difficult to analyse, and there is a great
and obvious distance between post-romantic German and
Elizabethan English. Yet when we place the passages side by
side, the ear seizes on undeniable similarities. Words are organized in the same abrupt manner, and the underlying beat
works toward a comparable stress and release of feeling.
Read aloud, the prose in *Lear* and in **Woyzeck** carries with
it the same shortness of breath and unflagging drive. The
"shape" of the sentences is remarkably similar. In the
rhymed couplets of Racine there is a quality of poise and
roundedness nearly visible to the eye. But in the prose of *Lear*
as in **Woyzeck,** the impression is one of broken lines and

rough-edged groupings. Or, to paraphrase a conceit in *Timon
of Athens,* the words "ache at us."

Yet the psychological facts with which Shakespeare and
Büchner deal are diametrically opposed. The style of Lear's
agony marks a ruinous fall; that of Woyzeck, a desperate upward surge. Lear crumbles into prose, and fearing a total
eclipse of reason, he seeks to preserve within reach of his anguish the fragments of his former understanding. His prose
is made up of such fragments arrayed in some rough semblance of order. In place of rational connection, there is now
a binding hatred of the world. Woyzeck, on the contrary, is
driven by his torment toward an articulateness which is not
native to him. He tries to break out of silence and is continually drawn back because the words at his command are inadequate to the pressure and savagery of his feeling. The result
is a kind of terrible simplicity. Each word is used as if it had
just been given to human speech. It is new and full of uncon-
trollable meaning. That is the way children use words, holding them at arm's length because they have a natural apprehension of their power to build or destroy. And it is precisely
this childishness in Woyzeck which is relevant to Lear, for
in his decline of reason Lear returns to a child's innocence
and ferocity. In both texts, moreover, one important rhetorical device is that of a child—repetition: "kill, kill, kill";
"never, never, never"; "immer zu, immer zu!"; "stich tot,
tot!" as if saying a thing over and over could make it come
true.

Compulsive repetition and discontinuity belong not only to
the language of children, but also to that of nightmares. It is
the effect of nightmare which Büchner strives for. Woyzeck's
anguish crowds to the surface of speech, and there it is somehow arrested; only nervous, strident flashes break through.
So in black dreams the shout is turned back in our throats.
The words that would save us remain just beyond our grasp.
That is Woyzeck's tragedy, and it was an audacious thought
to make a spoken drama of it. It is as if a man had composed
a great opera on the theme of deafness.

One of the earliest and most enduring laments over the tragic
condition of man is Cassandra's outcry in the courtyard of
the house of Atreus. In the final, fragmentary scene of **Woyzeck** there are implications of grief no less universal. Woyzeck has committed murder and staggers about in a trance.
He meets an idiot and a child:

WOYZECK.        Christianchen, du bekommst ein
                Reuter, sa, sa: da, kauf dem Bub
                ein Reuter! Hop, hop! Ross!
KARL.           Hop, hop! Ross! Ross!

(WOYZECK.       Christianchen, you'll get a gee-
                gee, ho, ho: there, buy the lad a
                gee-gee! Giddy-up, giddy-up,
                horsey!
KARL.           Giddy-up, giddy-up! Horsey!
                Horsey!)

In both instances, language seems to revert to a communication of terror older than literate speech. Cassandra's cry is
like that of a sea bird, wild and without meaning. Woyzeck
throws words away like broken toys; they have betrayed him.

Büchner's was the most radical break with the linguistic and
social conventions of poetic tragedy. (pp. 279-81)

*George Steiner, in an excerpt from his* The Death of

Tragedy, *1961. Reprint by Oxford University Press, Inc., 1980, pp. 270-81.*

### CARL RICHARD MUELLER   (essay date 1962)

[*In the following excerpt, Mueller provides an overview of Büchner's works. His remarks were written in 1962.*]

[Büchner] wrote three plays, two of them so extraordinary that they have served as the impetus for literary movements down to the present day's Theatre of the Absurd. Theodore Hoffman has recently listed them as: Naturalism, Social Realism, Psychological Irrationalism, Expressionism, and Existential Theatre. He is the seemingly inexhaustible source of modern drama and has been universally extolled by the leaders of the aforementioned movements. And yet, though he was far ahead of his own time, and though he sank into virtual oblivion after his death, until his rediscovery by the first of the great Naturalist playwrights, Gerhart Hauptmann, he is still in advance of our own age. Only time will demonstrate what new movements he will father for future generations. (pp. xi-xii)

#### Danton's Death

In *Danton's Death* we have undoubtedly the finest first play ever written. It is powerful, relentless, inexorable, passionate, and personal—it is as bitter a philosophical statement as anyone since Sophocles has had the courage to put on a stage—and finally, despite much critical assertion that it lacks drama, it is dramatic in spite of itself.

*Danton's Death* is pervaded by one single concept, the leading obsession in all of Büchner's works, in his daily life and his correspondence; he is never tired of reiterating that there is no free will, that Man's destiny is determined. In *Danton* he takes the direct and easy way of declaring this doctrine: by preaching—but, after all, it was his first play; in *Leonce and Lena* it has been hidden beneath the deceptive surface of quite literary, derivative, but in the final analysis highly original, parody; and in *Woyzeck* it is ingeniously unstated, but always present in its implicit dramatic manifestation.

Man is not free—History is a relentless force which crushes Man—all action is futile—boredom with the sameness of existence is the universal curse. For so young a man as Büchner (he was twenty-one when he wrote *Danton*) these are somewhat explosive ideas to be toying with. And yet he came by them some years earlier as a result of research into the history of the French Revolution of 1789. According to Büchner's major German critic-editor Fritz Bergemann, the following letter to his fiancée was written possibly late in 1833, two years prior to the actual composition of *Danton's Death,* a task accomplished, as Büchner tells us, in a period of less than five weeks, for the sake of making money. These are his words:

> For several days now I have taken every opportunity of taking pen in hand, but have found it impossible to put down so much as a single word. I have been studying the history of the Revolution. I have felt as though crushed beneath the fatalism of History. I find in human nature a terrifying sameness, and in the human condition an inexorable force, granted to all and to none. The individual is no more than foam on the wave, greatness mere chance, the mastery of genius a puppet play, a ludicrous struggle against a brazen law, which to ac-

knowledge is the highest achievement, which to master, impossible. I no longer intend to bow down to the parade horses and the bystanders of History. I have grown accustomed to the sight of blood. But I am no guillotine blade. The word *must* is one of the curses with which Mankind is baptized. The saying: "It must needs be that offenses come; but woe to him by whom the offense cometh" is terrifying. What is it in us that lies, murders, steals? I no longer care to pursue this thought.

Here in brief is the core of *Danton's Death.* In fact, the same phrases occur in the play itself and reappear later in various forms in the other works. They served as inflexible guideposts for the remaining few years of his tragic life.

What precisely was it in this period of the French Revolution which most caught his attention? It was obviously the character of Georges Danton. The question here is not whether and to what extent Büchner remained faithful to his historical characters. The primary consideration is what they are in the play. In several instances Büchner defied history in so far as his characters are concerned, though they do conform to the over-all prospect he had of the historical period. And indeed he made his *Danton* characters reflections of that age, and in the figure of Georges Danton its proponent. Danton, indeed, is not merely the philosophical center of the play, he is as close as any dramatic author has ever come to putting himself into his own work. Almost every speech of Danton's can be traced to Büchner's letters or other personal statements. Danton is even endowed with his author's own ambivalence of attitude, a minor consideration, to be sure, but one no less significant for that.

*Danton's Death* has been severely criticized for the fact that it is a static play, that Danton is virtually nonexistent as a dramatic character in that he performs not a single plot-progressing action, that he is the most undramatic character ever conceived of by a playwright, that the play lacks any personal contact or exchange between characters. And every word of this indictment is true, true to the point of being painful—yet at the same time these very characteristics for which it is criticized are among the qualities that make the play something genuinely extraordinary.

Büchner was so much an artist, even at the time of the writing of *Danton,* that he knew one of the first precepts of art is not to force a plot or idea into an existing, acceptable, well-tried, and established form. If a work of art, and especially a literary work, and even more specifically a dramatic composition (lyric poetry and great drama being one) is even to approach perfection, then its form must be dictated by its content, the former must grow inevitably out of the latter. Aristotle said as much; and if I read him correctly he would have happily accepted Büchner's own version of tragedy, just as he would not have quarreled with Arthur Miller, for Woyzeck is the great-grandfather of Willy Loman.

Few works in the history of drama are so much a union of form and content as *Danton's Death.* This is true to the point of perhaps being a fault. Danton as the central figure is motivated by nothing: he is stationary, static, from the standpoint of action; he has one desire, an overwhelming longing for death as a result of disillusionment and ultimate boredom. It would be superfluous to remark that he is not the most ideal of central characters. And yet he is a most intriguing one.

What is it that makes him so? If not action, then something

else. The answer lies in the convenient title we must tab him with: *Passive Hero*. Strangely enough, he *is* a hero, pathetic, to be sure, but hero nonetheless. And this pathos springs from his attitude of mind, his—what shall we call it?—universal anguish. He is the only one in the entire play (save for his young comrade Camille, who has premonitions of it) who fully and tragically comprehends the human condition. Yes, Danton is a hero; not because he *does,* but because he *would do* if he knew that his doing would have any efficacy whatever. But life and all life's actions are futile, doomed to destruction, without meaning or reason. Each man exists in himself and is unable to break that impenetrable shell. Man is isolated. He knows no real communication with his fellow men. . . . Yet only Danton in the play is aware of this situation; the others *do,* they *act,* or *think they act,* blind to the fact, as Danton is not, that we are dragged along by the relentlessness of Fate or History, or call it what we will. We are crushed beneath it, as Büchner says in his letter. It is this knowledge on Danton's part that constitutes the greater part of his tragic condition. Were it not for this vision of the abyss which Danton must peer into and shudder at, he too would act. He acted once—but in the past; he was responsible for the September Massacre, the tenth of August, and the thirty-first of May—but then apparently he was naive in the ways of destiny. What possible reason has he to act now? His anguish is so great, as well as his desire to communicate, to experience real love and friendship, that we must see some part of him in his vision of the universal force (be it what it may be) when he says to himself on the night preceding his death on the guillotine:

> The stars are scattered through the night like glistening teardrops; what a terrible grief must be behind the eyes that dropped them.

Danton no more believes in God than did Büchner, yet he seems to imply that if there were God, how great His anguish and grief would have to be as He looked down on His bungled work, seeing the misery, the suffering and pain, to which His incompetent universal Artificer's craft gave being. But God does not exist, says Büchner in his play; if He did He could not endure the senseless pain and suffering to which Man is subject. Pain, then, is the foremost proof of the nonexistence of God. And if there is no God, then there is nothing to which to cling, there is no recourse. Woyzeck says it: "When God goes, everything goes."

> It is said [writes Büchner in February 1834] I am a ridiculer. True, I laugh a great deal; but my laughter is not at *how* a human being is, but rather at the fact *that* he is a human being; about which he can do nothing; and at the same time I laugh at myself because I must share in his fate.

This might have come from Danton, because in his reasoned passivity he surely sees the pitiable ludicrousness of the human condition.

Despite all this, both Büchner and Danton have an innate ambivalence. Büchner wrote to his parents: "It is my opinion that if anything in our time can help us, then it is force." And later:

> I will of course act moderately in regard to my principles, yet I have learned in recent years that only the urgent need of the majority is capable of bringing about change, and that all the excitement and screaming of individuals is only the idle work of fools. They write—but no one reads them; they cry

out—but no one hears; they act—but no one helps them.

And still later he wrote that he refrains from revolutionary activity neither because of scorn nor fear, but because at the time he regards every revolutionary movement as a vain enterprise.

And through the figure of Danton he says that force is ineffectual, and to act, futile. Yet Danton says in the prison scene just before his death that he and his friends may die, but it is possible that their bones, washed up by the flood of the Revolution, will be picked up by the people and be used to bash in the heads of the kings. A strangely optimistic note for Danton.

This duality makes him a most interesting character. At times he seems to himself two persons, each one different from the other. It is this facet which gives him greater interest and depth; it creates a tension, a mental struggle inside him, as when, after longing for death, he believes for a single moment that he would rather live despite life's torments, because not even death is desirable: death is not peace, not nothingness; even in death every atom of him would exist in torment. But again this duality is one of the mind; it never culminates in action.

Paradoxically, this Danton, the passive hero, is surrounded by much confusion and bustle, by crowd scenes and violence (the background rather than the substance of legitimate dramatic action), by people like Robespierre and his followers who believe their words communicate, but who only mouth empty and impersonal and formalistic oratory and rhetoric. As Lee Baxandall has recently pointed out [see Further Reading], the characters of *Danton's Death* do not speak *to,* but *past* one another; they speak not to elicit reply, but to convince; not even what has been called the "monologic lyricism" of Danton and of his followers is spoken to elicit reply. The most extreme example of this is the final "Conciergerie" scene which is scarcely more than a great fugal hymn to Nihilism, certainly one of the finest, though least dramatic, sections of the play. Such dialogue cannot be dramatic. It is instructive to read through the play omitting all speeches save those of Danton. Virtually every one is a philosophical comment or reminiscence of past actions, a descant on existing circumstances, the laments of a tormented mind. And yet the anguish in these statements, the bitterness, the pathos of them, makes Danton a truly remarkable figure. He *lives* his thoughts. He has made of his life the mirror of his mind. And so has Büchner made the form of his play the mirror of its philosophical core: form and content are successfully one, almost to the point of being a fault—and yet what an admirable fault it is.

> In the event that it comes to your hands [wrote Büchner to his parents concerning the first, mutilated, publication of *Danton's Death*], I beg you to consider, before you judge it, that I was compelled to be true to History and to show the men of the Revolution as they were; bloodthirsty, dissolute, vigorous, and cynical. I regard my play as an historical painting, which must be like its original. . . .

He was concerned with the crudities of language, of course; but he was more concerned with not covering over the real men and their motives with false idealism in the manner of a Schiller. It did not matter how terrible or embarrassing the picture presented, if only it was true. (pp. xii-xvii)

On July 28, 1835, [Büchner] set down in a letter to his parents what must be regarded as one of the most impressive and impeccable theories of dramatic art ever formulated [see letter dated 1835]. It is all the more remarkable considering the date of its composition, some fifty-four years before the official beginning of German Naturalism, the first performance of Gerhart Hauptmann's *Before Sunrise,* and fifty-six years prior to Hauptmann's *Weavers,* which might not have existed had it not been for the example of *Danton's Death.* And now, another half-century after the decline of Naturalism, Büchner's dictum concerning truth and the artist in relation to Nature is with us again in the guise of the New Drama, the Theatre of the Absurd.

In 1835 Büchner wrote:

> The dramatic poet is, in my eyes, nothing but a writer of history, except that he stands above the latter in that he creates history for the second time; he transplants us directly into the life of another time, instead of giving us a dry account of it; instead of characteristics, he gives us characters; instead of descriptions, he gives us living figures. His greatest task is to come as close as possible to history as it actually was. . . . As regards those so-called Idealist poets, I find that they have given us nothing more than marionettes with sky-blue noses and affected pathos, but not human beings of flesh and blood, who make us feel their joy and sorrow with them, and whose deeds and actions fill me with revulsion or admiration. In a word, I have great fondness for Goethe or Shakespeare, but very little for Schiller.

What there is of Schiller and Idealism in Büchner's work is parody, as in the high-flown language and declamation of the Simon scenes. From Goethe and Shakespeare he received truth and suggestions concerning form, but in the last analysis he transformed what he acquired into something wholly his own. *Danton* reminds one of *Götz* and Shakespeare's Roman plays, especially *Antony and Cleopatra* and *Coriolanus.* His fitful changes of scene may seem unnecessary, yet they are highly significant as regards his design and intention. What at first may seem chaotic and arbitrary actually achieves almost breathtaking relevance. Büchner's shrewd juxtaposition of scenes in *Danton* (so much a part of his theory of fidelity to Nature) evokes a mosaiclike pattern of restlessness and indecision. "The Open Field" scene in which Danton is almost flippant about his impending arrest is followed by "A Room. Night," in which he is tormented by memory and conscience, and doubts the validity of his former actions. It is the sort of scene with which Büchner punctuates his work. These moments are brief and fleeting, as in life itself, but they are the more poignant for that fact: their brevity points up their fragility. They are moments in which poetry and horror are firmly bound up with one another; moments in which we are shown the terrifying abyss which threatened Danton and Büchner.

Then suddenly, as though a knife had severed the fragile thread which balances one between life and the abyss, the scene changes rapidly to the "Street in Front of Danton's House," with its Shakespearean buffoonery, its parody of the "How goes the night" scene in Macbeth, and of Ancient Pistol's going off to the wars, as well as other typical Büchner crudities. To call such an arrangement chaos or even disorderly is to call *Antony,* that extreme example of Shakespeare's theatrical genius in the art of scenic arrangement, formless and confused. In *Danton's Death* Büchner is literally holding the mirror up to Nature, and in so doing he is fulfilling the precepts of his own dramatic theory.

### Leonce and Lena

What is it in *Leonce and Lena* that causes it to be so often dismissed by critics and producers? It may, of course, be less in stature than either *Danton's Death* or *Woyzeck,* but it is not what too many of Büchner's critics claim it to be, an unoriginal work. Relatively speaking, perhaps; but this ought not to be held against it. The play has been described as wholesale literary borrowing, as being a direct descendant of the *commedia dell'arte* tradition, as being weak in having caricatures rather than characters. In a sense each of these accusations is true. And yet each of them may have been intended by the author. The fact that it was written as an entry in a drama contest sponsored by a Stuttgart publisher, and that a comedy was needed, is of little significance.

If the play is more lightly passed over than the other works, it is because it is not so easily understandable, it is elusive, deceptive. Furthermore, it shows us a side of Büchner that is not so fully developed in *Danton* and *Woyzeck.* This side is simply that Büchner, for all his complaints against Schiller and Romanticism and Idealism, and his insistence on Naturalism, is nonetheless a Romantic. The important thing is that he is not what one would call a German Romanticist. A. H. J. Knight defined Büchner's position rather well when he said that he is unsentimental, but not unemotional or unromantic. Still, his Romantic elements are not those of Schiller and his school; they are straightforward and uncluttering. Where in *Leonce and Lena* he may seem to be following German Romanticism he is merely exaggerating so as to parody and consequently make nonsense of it. Again Knight would seem to be correct when he isolates this as a Heine-like element, and asserts that it is neither Romantic nor of the Young German Movement, but one of the play's most original elements.

Yes, *Leonce* is derivative. Its philosophical allusions are seemingly endless, its debts to Musset's *Fantasio,* to the image of Sancho Panza, to the monologues, as Hans Mayer points out, of Manfred, Childe Harold, and Don Juan, and to the tirades of the heroes of Tieck and Brentano, are obvious—but there is more to *Leonce and Lena* than this. It is as much a part of Büchner's work and thought as either *Danton* or *Woyzeck.* It is permeated with the same bitterness, even though this is seemingly softened by the so-called comic vision. *Leonce* is a severe attack on most of the injustices and stupidities prevalent in the Germany of Büchner's time. It rails against typical German Romanticism and its consequent ennui; it attacks Idealism; it is a diatribe against the sameness of the formalistic life; and finally, it is infused with the bitter fatalism of History, except that its characters *do* act, unlike Danton, because they do not realize their predicament; they exert what they wrongly take to be their free will. Both Leonce and Lena flee their separate kingdoms so as to avoid the preordained marriage to one another, even though they have never met. Still, they *do* meet, unknown to each other, fall in love, are married, ironically as proxies for the actual prince and princess, which is to say by Fate, and only then discover to their chagrin the truth of the matter.

All this is a gentler version of Danton's vision of the wild horse of the world set loose, dragging him with it, helpless, across the abyss. For all its dream-world atmosphere, **Leonce and Lena** is as real a world beneath its surface as **Danton** and **Woyzeck,** because this dream world is forever being intruded upon by the harshness and cruelty of pessimism and fatalism. The ironic apotheosis of this comic vision of the abyss comes during the two final speeches of the play. All having turned out "happily," Leonce says:

> And so, Lena, you see how our pockets are stuffed with puppets and playthings. What shall we do with them? Shall we make mustaches for them and hang broadswords about their waists? Or shall we dress them in frockcoats and let them practice infusorial politics and diplomacy, and sit here watching them through our microscopes? Or would you prefer a barrel-organ on which milk-white esthetic shrews flit about? Shall we build a theatre? [LENA *leans against him, shakes her head.*] Oh, but I know what it is you really want: we shall have all the clocks in the kingdom destroyed, forbid all calendars, and count off hours and months with the chronometer of the flowers, according to times of planting and times of harvest. And then we shall surround our tiny kingdom with burning glasses so that winter no longer exists, and in summer we shall rise up through a process of distillation as high as Ischia and Capri, and all year long live amidst roses and violets, surrounded with orange and laurel boughs.

And Valerio:

> And I'll be the Minister of State, and I'll issue a decree which reads: that anyone who works calluses on his hands will be placed in custody of a guardian; that anyone who works himself sick will be criminally prosecuted; that every man who prides himself on eating bread earned in the sweat of his brow will be declared insane and a hazard to human society. And then we shall lie in the shade and ask the Lord God for macaroni, melons, and figs, for voices soft as music, for bodies fine as classical heroes, and for a commodious religion!

### Woyzeck

What is it that constitutes Büchner's modernity almost a century and a quarter after his death, and that assures him an indisputable place in world literature? The answer lies deeper than his artistry; it has to do with more than the manner of his dialogue, the juxtaposition of his scenes, his delineation of character. The core of the matter lies in the scientific clarity of his vision and of his unfailing concern with the estate of Man.

**Woyzeck** is the first modern tragedy. It is the first *wholly* successful tragic representation of the common man on the stage, a representation which shows him capable of greatness of mind and soul and feeling, except he is kept from the realization of this by the millstone of environment hung about his neck.

**Woyzeck** is the great precursor of the Naturalist Movement, and its effect is with us again today in the Theatre of the Absurd. As a drama of social criticism **Woyzeck** has never been, and very likely never will be, superseded. Its power lies in the fact that its problems are, in addition to being specific, universal in time and place. Yet more is required of a great work than that it be an exposé of misery and social injustice. This may be the ultimate downfall of most of the works that con-

stitute the Theatre of the Absurd. For all their bitterness and social indignation, the greater number of these plays lack a vision of life that can serve as an apotheosis, that can transform them into works of the heart rather than of the groin. They lack an implicit moral center based on empirical evidence. The feeling that there might be such a center is always evident in Büchner. To write a sordid drama with social implications is only the first step. The apotheosis comes as a result of profound and overwhelming understanding of, and sympathy with, the estate of Man, with his suffering and struggle.

The basis of Büchner's vision is precisely that upon which the Theatre of the Absurd is founded. It is simply that the Absurd is that which is without purpose, futile, out of harmony with its surroundings. In short, the human condition is senseless. One play among all the modern works comes readily to mind, Beckett's *Waiting for Godot*. It is the logical successor to Büchner's vision. Its manner may be different on the surface, but its attitudes are one with Büchner's. Passivity is the universal disease. Man waits and waits (that is, if he has even only a remnant of hope) but nothing comes. Man acts, or thinks he acts, but all is futile. In *Godot* there is also greatness of mind, though not in the degree that we find it in Büchner, and this overwhelming sympathy with Man.

In both these plays this sympathy is never expressed, it is implicit. In *Godot* it is implied in the pathos engendered by the unrelenting sameness of life. In **Woyzeck** the method is different. In essence, Büchner's method in **Woyzeck** and **Danton** is the same: juxtaposition of scenes. (We may reasonably assume this, despite the fact that Büchner left the scenes of

*A scene from* Woyzeck *staged in Hamburg in 1953.*

*Woyzeck* unarranged at his death.) As in the Epic Theatre of Brecht, who owes his greatest debt to Büchner, each scene is virtually autonomous, yet when assembled they constitute a seemingly indissoluble whole. Each scene works with the others and comments implicitly upon them. Thus we understand the reasons for Woyzeck's state of mind and body, for his hallucinations, when we see him literally turned into a guinea pig by the Doctor's scientific observations and his injunction to eat "nothing but peas," as well as by the Captain's interminable prodding about his strangeness and his inability to keep Marie faithful to him.

Less a mosaic in structure than *Danton, Woyzeck* is more akin to a series of stained-glass windows in a medieval cathedral. In logical sequence one representation after another (each a self-contained unity) succeeds in telling the whole story. *Danton,* on the other hand, is more a gigantic panorama—a mosaic panorama, to be sure, since its individual pieces are not always inevitably positioned—which seems to show the whole story at a glance. *Danton* can be thought of *only* as a whole, *Woyzeck* both in that way and as individual scenes. In this way it is more akin to Epic Theatre than *Danton.*

The chief virtue of *Woyzeck*'s structure lies in its simplicity of development, in the uncluttered vision and lack of Germanic ponderousness. *Woyzeck* is clearly the product of a scientific mind. It is as dispassionate in any explicit way as a medical lecture. This clarity and sharpness of focus are due in great part to Büchner's practice of fully developing only his major character or characters. Only Woyzeck and Marie are fully rounded individuals. The others are boldly, succinctly, and incisively drawn, but they are shown in only one attitude. Woyzeck and Marie are seen in a whole range of attitudes; they are given to thinking about their state and condition, and to suffering pangs of conscience and despair. The others are utilized to set them off, to illustrate them in a gamut of situations. The fact that they are typical inventions may be seen in their being called simply Doctor, Captain, Drum Major, etc. They are there to *use* Woyzeck for their own ends; in short, to make a virtual animal of him, to point up the fact that Woyzeck in order to exist *must* hand himself over as a guinea pig to society. A properly organized society would not give rise to such a condition. If Woyzeck is to live, then he *must* do as he is *forced* to do by economic necessity. Büchner was one of the first to bring attention to the economic factor in society. When the Captain lectures him on virtue and morals, Woyzeck retorts:

> Yes, Captain, sir: Virtue. I haven't got much of that. You see, us common people, we haven't got virtue. That's the way it's got to be. But if I could be a gentleman, and if I could have a hat and a watch and a cane, and if I could talk refined, I'd want to be virtuous, all right. There must be something beautiful in virtue, Captain, sir.

And on the subject of morals:

> You see, Captain, sir . . . Money, money! Whoever hasn't got money . . . Well, who's got morals when he's bringing something like me into the world? We're flesh and blood, too. Our kind is miserable only once: in this world and in the next. I think if we ever got to Heaven we'd have to help with the thunder.

Danton asks that often-repeated question in Büchner's thought; it is the question to the answer which Woyzeck gives above. Asks Danton: "What is this in us that lies, whores, steals, and murders?" In the great metaphor which *Woyzeck* is, Büchner seems to answer: Society, Environment, Circumstance. And Danton says:

> What are we but puppets, manipulated on wires by unknown powers? We are nothing, nothing in ourselves: we are the swords that spirits fight with—except no one sees the hands—just as in fairy tales. . . .

### *Lenz* and *The Hessian Courier*

The composition of the *Lenz* fragment is positioned between the completion of *Danton's Death* and *Leonce and Lena,* and comprises Büchner's sole effort in the realm of nondramatic narrative prose. It is assumed that *Lenz* was to be a novel and that Büchner was never able to finish it, and yet it is relatively complete in itself as a picture of one segment in the life of the historical Jacob Michael Reinhold Lenz, born in 1751 in Livonia, who became an acquaintance of Goethe's, was known for his highly eccentric behavior, and finally died in obscurity, some say a beggar, near Moscow in 1792.

*Lenz* is by all standards one of the most remarkable pieces of German narrative prose ever composed. Its narrative style constitutes a category all its own, with its strange repetitions, its colloquial expressions, and its often maddening compressions. (pp. xviii-xxvi)

In addition to its eccentric and vigorous prose style (which, as in *Danton,* seems to be a perfect marriage of form and content), *Lenz* is also important for its long section devoted to a theory of art. . . . It seems valid . . . to accept it as Büchner's own, formulated, perhaps, under the influence of Lenz, for we find in that section ideas as well as phrases which turn up again and again in Büchner's work. The central idea is that art must remain faithful to nature. Lenz attacks Idealism and Romanticism with a bitterness worthy and characteristic of Büchner. God, he says, did not create the world only to have Man re-create it and try to make it better than it is.

> Let them [says Lenz, speaking of Idealist writers] try just once to immerse themselves in the life of humble people and then reproduce this again in all its movements, its implications, in its subtle, scarcely discernible play of expression . . .

Lenz's theory of Beauty is equally interesting and important in the light it throws on Büchner's own work. Lenz describes a walk into the mountains where he saw two girls seated on a rock, the one binding up her hair, the other helping her. It was so beautiful a picture that he wished to be able to preserve it by turning it into stone and calling the world to see it. But then—and this is the significant point—they rose and the picture dissolved, "the beautiful grouping was destroyed; but as they descended between the rocks they formed another picture." Lenz continues:

> The most beautiful pictures, the most swelling tones, form a group and then dissolve. Only one thing remains: an unending beauty which passes from one form to another, eternally revealed, eternally unchanged.

One has only to read through *Lenz* to see the application of this theory. One sees it, too, in the dramas, in the sudden coming together of events and characters which constitute moments, however brief, of extraordinary poignancy, only to dissolve again as quickly and as effortlessly as they formed, attesting, as it were, to the durable and indestructible fragility of Beauty.

The descriptions in **Lenz** are wholly Büchner's own. So much so, in fact, that the description of Lenz's passage through the mountains is a direct recollection of an excursion made by Büchner into the Vosges and celebrated in a letter to his family in the spring of 1833. . . . (pp. xxvi-xxvii)

If **Lenz** is a fragment of a projected longer work, I think it is not wholly wrong to suppose that Büchner, had he had the time to complete the work, would not have chosen to do so. The work is too eccentric, too intense, too impulsive, to have been carried to completion. As it stands now, its greatness and integrity strain the sensibilities of the reader. Perhaps Büchner realized that, too. Perhaps he felt that he was incapable of providing sufficient variety to render the projected work acceptable. Nonetheless, we must be grateful for even this small segment, which has exerted its own influence on succeeding generations of great German prose stylists.

Of **The Hessian Courier** there is little to say except that it is the first extended effort of the young socialist revolutionary. It can scarcely be regarded as a literary work in its own right, and yet it is not entirely devoid of such distinction. Its principal importance is to help the reader complete the portrait of Büchner which his works provide, especially since it is impossible to understand the man fully without an awareness of his political sympathies.

**The Hessian Courier** shows the work of a young, bitter, rebellious, and still naive, genius. It is obviously the product of his research into the French Revolution of 1789, which a year after **The Hessian Courier** gave rise to **Danton's Death.** In this work, a semisocialistic political pamphlet written and circulated in 1834, we find Büchner, intensely influenced by the Revolution, advocating a thoroughgoing revolt by the German people to overthrow their ruling class, their princes, their governmental institutions, everything, in order to help themselves to the freedom which is their right. He points out to them the mistakes made by the populace in the French Revolution and exhorts them against running aground in the same manner. His vision of Revolution, however, was still somewhat too naive to be practicable. Nonetheless, the pamphlet remains one of the most impressive political documents ever written, mainly by virtue of the passion and bitter sarcasm which are so much a part of it. It also gives some inkling of the writer still to come.

Büchner's intense and lifelong searching led only to nothingness, senselessness, and futility. History, morality, the arbitrary and needless course of events, were all without the slightest particle of meaning. He came to one conclusion: that Man is dirt, sand, and dung; this was for him the sole certainty. Had he lived to maturity he might well have transcended the entire body of German dramatists and drama, and his influence might have been even greater, if that were possible. At any rate it would have exerted itself far sooner than half a century after his death. Yet his pessimism, his determinism, his incurable sense of the futility and senselessness of the universe, however sincerely he might have searched, would only have deepened his belief in his conclusions and would have embittered him all the more, only to make of him as tragic a figure as the history of drama can boast of having nurtured.

The fact is, however, that he did *not* look for God, because he *knew* He could not exist; and if He were possible Büchner would only have challenged Him, as one critic has so aptly put it, to justify His brutality, His indifference, His invariable inhumanity toward Man.

Büchner was no fool. He could not postulate a God and proceed from there as so many others have done. He had to assume that God *is not* until he found Him. But, then, he knew the search was futile. It was not merely the senselessness and futility, the lack of direction and purpose in the world, that told him there is no God, or if there were then that He is a bungler; rather, the existence of pain, of suffering, was the only proof he needed to cement his convictions.

> Consider this, Anaxagoras [says Paine in **Danton's Death**]: Why do I suffer? That is the very bedrock of atheism. The least quiver of pain, in even the smallest of atoms, makes a rent in the curtain of your creation from top to bottom.

And again:

> One can deny evil, but not pain; only reasoning can prove God, feeling rebels against it.

Büchner's plays are a living testimonial to his life. And yet it is reported that in his last illness, shortly before death overtook him, he said:

> There is not too much suffering in our lives, there is too little, for it is through suffering that we reach God. We are death, dust, ashes, how should we complain?

A curious end to an even more curious life. (pp. xxvii-xxx)

> *Carl Richard Mueller, in an introduction to* Complete Plays and Prose *by Georg Büchner, translated by Carl Richard Mueller, Hill and Wang, 1963, pp. xi-xxx.*

### HERBERT LINDENBERGER    (essay date 1964)

[*Examining* Leonce and Lena, *Lindenberger argues that Büchner ostensibly sets the play up as a conventional romantic comedy but has the serious purpose of depicting the ultimate meaninglessness of life.*]

Of Büchner's four works, **Leonce and Lena** is the only one that takes its form from a recognizable generic tradition. It is a romantic comedy, and its roots are distantly in Shakespearean comedy, in the *commedia dell'arte,* in several comedies of the German Romantic Movement, and, most specifically, in the plays of Alfred de Musset. On the surface it looks like a fairly conventional romantic tale. A melancholy young prince is about to be forced to marry a princess whom he has never met. With the help of his servant Valerio he escapes the country and in a tavern accidentally meets the princess who, with the help of her governess, has also attempted to escape her fate. Neither knows who the other is, and they fall in love. Valerio brings them back to the prince's land and presents them, dressed as pasteboard effigies of themselves, to the court. The king marries them in effigy, their masks are removed, and prince and princess for the first time discover each other's true identity. At the end they seem about to live happily ever after. Or only seem to—for Büchner uses the conventions of romantic comedy only to confound them.

When one sets the play next to *As You Like It,* from which Büchner has drawn his epigraph for the first act, one is aware that in the course of imitating these conventions, Büchner has worked to undermine them. Prince Leonce, for example, turns out to be no more like a Shakespearean lover than Danton is like an Aristotelian tragic hero. He is less an Orlando than a Jacques who manages to amuse himself by assuming the manner of a Touchstone. The epigraph which Büchner chose—"O that I were a fool! / I am ambitious for a motley coat"—is, in fact, drawn from one of Jaques' speeches, in which the latter speaks of his meeting with Touchstone. Like the characters in Shakespeare's play Leonce escapes from an unsatisfactory everyday world into an ideal world, but the ideal world he chooses is nothing so substantial as the Forest of Arden; it is, rather, a private, inward world in which he seeks to distract himself with such activities as spitting on a stone 365 times in a row or trying to see the top of his head. The main representative of the real world in Büchner is not the tyrannical father of the *commedia dell'arte* tradition, but a bumbling, absurd king so lost in his own private world (a parody on Fichtean idealism) that he can hardly even remember the demand he makes on his son to get married. He consents to the marriage "in effigy" at the end only because he can justify it by his own absurd logic—"If you have a man hanged in effigy isn't that just as good as if he received a regulation hanging? . . . Now I have it. We'll celebrate the wedding in effigy."

The romance that takes place between the Prince of Popo and the Princess of Pipi (the names of the two kingdoms are affectionate slang terms, respectively, for *buttocks* and *urine*) is not precisely the romantic love out of which most comedies are made. The hero and heroine are never infatuated with one another in the usual way of comedies, nor is their relationship even based on their "being in love with love." If anything, their love seems to originate in a mutual feeling of compassion for each other's suffering. "I believe there are men who are unhappy, incurably so, merely because they exist," Lena says of Leonce, while the latter thinks himself moved by Lena's wistful plaint, "Is the way so long?" as she wearily enters the tavern. Leonce's declaration of love has none of the romantic enthusiasm one might expect, but is expressed in the most macabre imagery imaginable: "Then let me be your angel of death, let my lips swoop down upon your eyes like wings. [*He kisses her.*] Oh lovely dead body, you rest so charmingly on the black pall of night that Nature hates life and falls in love with death." After he has declared himself, instead of voicing his conviction that his love for her will last forever, he despairs of its ability to sustain itself and consequently decides to throw himself in a river. (Büchner does not, however, break the comic convention to the point of letting him go through with it, for Valerio immediately appears and talks him out of it.)

In Shakespearean romantic comedy and in the *commedia dell'arte* the youthful lovers are united in marriage at the end; the ideal world which they represent replaces a decadent or cruel "real" world; and we rest assured that they will live happily ever after. Büchner maneuvers his play at least formally through these steps, so shrewdly, in fact, that one of his finest critics [Karl Viëtor] was fooled into viewing the resolution as one of "serenity and joy, recognition and fulfillment." Certainly King Peter, about to retire permanently into his dogmatic slumbers with his philosophical advisers, hands the reins of government to the newly wedded couple. But the brave new world which they intend to set up is scarcely to be taken at face value: "Well, Lena, have you noticed yet that our pockets are full of toys and dolls? What shall we do with them? Shall we make moustaches for the dolls and hang sabres on them? Or shall we dress them in tail coats and

have them conduct miniature politics and diplomacy with us looking on through a microscope?"

Leonce, indeed, plans the same sort of absurd activities which he had engaged in—and quickly tired of—throughout the course of the play. And if Büchner needed to give us any further clues as to how seriously we should take Leonce's plans for a lotus land, he lets the ironic Valerio speak the last word:

> And I'll be Minister of State. And a decree will be issued that whoever gets calluses on his hands shall be placed under surveillance . . . whoever boasts that in the sweat of his brow he will eat bread shall be declared insane and dangerous to human society. And then we can lie in the shade and ask God for macaroni, melons, and figs, for musical throats, classic bodies, and a nice, çosy religion!

The irony that lurks behind the language in which both Leonce and Valerio sketch out their idyllic future is obvious even without the last line if one has noted the similarly ironic perspective in which Büchner has clothed their longings throughout the play. But Valerio's final words about a "nice, cosy religion" break down any illusions we may have about a "happily ever after." In the light of such irony one is tempted to view in a double perspective the words which the prince and princess speak after their marriage, when each discovers who the other really is:

> LENA. I've been deceived.
> LEONCE. *I've* been deceived.
> LENA. O chance!
> LEONCE. O Providence!

On the surface these words can all be taken as signs of a happy resolution; in this sense the couple was happily deceived, and chance and Providence were gracious to them. But if one remains aware of the normally negative meaning of *deceived,* chance and Providence may not have been so kind to them after all. The play, at any rate, leaves both possibilities open; the first supports the romantic conventions Büchner is using, the second his ironic questioning of these conventions.

Not that irony was missing from Shakespearean comedy. But the irony of a Touchstone or a Feste, by putting the romanticism of the various lovers to a test throughout the play, serves in the end to confirm the positive assertions toward which the play has been moving (Touchstone, in fact, himself gets married at the end). Valerio's irony, on the other hand, merely continues to break down whatever illusions we may have that the ending is a happy one. But Valerio's function throughout the play cannot be described simply as that of the ironic fool. Leonce, after all, has assumed this role for himself at times. What is basic to the Leonce-Valerio relationship is the fact that they assume opposing roles toward one another. Whenever Leonce waxes romantic—for instance, in his attempt at a love-death suicide—Valerio cuts him ironically down to size. But whenever Leonce plays the ironist, Valerio sets up a series of romantic pretensions to break down Leonce's ironic pretensions, for example, in their first encounter in the play:

> VALERIO. I shall lie on the greensward and let my nose blossom above the blades of grass and get romantic notions when bees and butterflies light on it. . . .
> LEONCE. Don't breathe so hard, my dear fellow, or the bees and butterflies will starve: the flowers

are their snuffbox, and you're taking great pinches of the snuff.
    VALERIO. Oh sir, how much feeling I have for
    Nature! . . .

The whole rhythm of the play, down to the final words, is
based on Büchner's setting up illusions and then systematically breaking them down. Though he goes through all the
motions of writing a romantic comedy—a genre which demands that romantic ideals eventually can become reality—
he has, at bottom, written an ironic comedy—one in which
ideals are shown up for the illusions they really are. It is as
if Shakespeare had used the plot and atmosphere of *As You
Like It* to create the mood and content of *Volpone.*

Although Büchner has rigorously kept up the forms of romantic comedy, the spirit of disillusionment which fills the
play is more closely related to that of Büchner's most immediate model, Musset's *Fantasio,* than it is to anything in
Shakespeare. Like **Leonce and Lena,** Musset's play has a sad
princess about to be forced into marriage with a distant
prince. The model for Leonce is not, however, the prince, but
a village melancholic, Fantasio, who complains of his ennui,
plans and rejects a multitude of activities, and finds a temporarily satisfying *métier* by disguising himself as a court jester.
He is more languid, though also less desperate than Leonce,
more sentimental and less incisively analytical about his
plight than his German counterpart.

Musset, too, borrows the conventions of romantic comedy,
but, quite in contrast to Büchner, he refuses to resolve the
play with the conventions he has used to shape it most of the
way through. Thus, after employing a number of charming
artifices—master and servant disguising as one another, the
hero knocking off the villain's wig—Musset is unwilling to
give us a happy ending. At the end the melancholy hero, recognizing he can never be happy in any occupation, refuses the
princess' offer of a permanent appointment as jester. He goes
his independent way, and the heroine, though he has saved
her from a marriage she dreaded, is left to brood alone. As
though he suddenly recognized the insincerity of his conventions, Musset—not only in *Fantasio,* but in the other two
plays from which Büchner borrowed, *Marianne's Whims* and
*One Shouldn't Trifle with Love*—at the last minute turns sincere and faces up to the problems of his characters as though
he were writing a realistic play. The effect of this change is
jarring, as if, after sitting through most of *As You Like It* or
a Marivaux comedy, we ended up with the last act of *A Doll's
House.* The surprise we experience at the end does not result
from any new insights which the author uncovers for us—as,
for instance, the surprises at the end of a Ionesco play do—
but is the surprise we feel at suddenly being let down; we feel
cheated, and wish that Musset had surprised us instead with
more and better artifices. *Fantasio,* of course, lives by the
charm of its language and atmosphere (charm is the word one
inevitably uses when speaking of Musset's plays), not by its
dramaturgy. And it is precisely in its dramaturgy that we see
the superiority of **Leonce and Lena.** For Büchner recognized
that a comedy is essentially a game, and that if he wished to
adjust his comedy to his more serious purposes, he must at
least pretend to abide by the rules of the game; the ironic undercurrent which runs through the play makes his serious
purposes amply clear, but it does not prevent the game from
moving to its logical conclusion.

Being a game, the comic form that Büchner employed provided him with an appropriate image for the activities that
his characters engage in: these characters do not live ordinary
lives, but instead keep themselves busy playing games with
life. And since a theater piece necessarily must express itself
in words, Büchner found an appropriate image for these
games in the punning and idle bantering in which his characters are constantly engaged. "O foul conception when you
were conceived!" Leonce shouts at Valerio at one point.
"Find yourself a better mode of expression or I'll give you an
impression of all the oppression that I . . . "—the translation, though it cannot be entirely literal, succeeds at least in
imitating the sort of word-play that goes on throughout the
comedy. Leonce is by no means angry at Valerio when he addresses him in this way; the word-game he plays here and
elsewhere becomes a sort of substitute for any real emotions
he might feel. Quite often he—and Valerio as well—gets so
lost in his verbal associations that these seem to have little if
any reference to any real situation. He finds himself lost not
only in words, but in images which he concocts in his mind.
At one point he announces: "I have the image and ideal of
a female in my head. I must go in quest of it. She is endlessly
beautiful and endlessly mindless. Her beauty is as helpless
and touching as a newborn infant's. Is the contrast not delightful—eyes both heavenly and dumb, a mouth both divine
and moronic . . . ?"

There is no reason we need take Leonce's search for the ideal
at all seriously; he is merely fascinated by the paradox suggested by his image, and he goes on to exploit this paradox
until he gets bored with it. Even in his love scene with Lena
language replaces relationship, for the contact between the
two is realized on a linguistic level only. "Träume sind selig"
(Dreams are blessed), says Lena, to which Leonce replies,
"So träume Dich selig und lass mich Dein seliger Traum
sein" (Then dream yourself blessed, and let me be your
blessed dream). Leonce's words, in the German at least, are
an exact repetition of Lena's words dreams and *blessed,* yet
by changing the syntactical functions of these words (*Träume*
is both a plural noun and an imperative verb, *selig* an adjective and an adverb), he gives the impression of a kind of miraculous transformation taking place. As one of Büchner's
best commentators, Gerhart Baumann, speaking of the play
as a whole, has put it, "In its most dream-like moments it is
the magic of the language that is working, while the characters become simply media." At various points in the play the
characters even resort to metaphors drawn from the vocabulary of linguistics. "When you bow, dear sir, your legs form
a beautiful parenthesis," Leonce tells the court tutor, and in
one of his verbal battles with Valerio, master accuses servant
of being "begotten by the five vowels," while the latter retorts, "And you, my prince, are a book with no words in it,
nothing but dashes."

If language can thus become a substitute for reality, the real
world, in turn, at least as it is shown in the play, has little sub-
stantiality of its own. It is represented, after all, by the ridiculous king, while the local folk whom we are shown—for example, the schoolmaster—display an absurdity totally un-
graced by wit. Valerio's description of one of the lands he and
Leonce pass through provides a suitable enough comment on
the real world that Leonce seeks to escape: "This country is
like an onion—nothing but skins. Or Chinese boxes—one inside the other—in the biggest, nothing but boxes, in the smallest, nothing at all."

Behind all the banter it gradually becomes clear to us that the
characters in the play are none too sure of their own identi-

ties. I mentioned earlier that Leonce and Valerio are constantly exchanging roles: when one of them plays the enthusiast, the other plays the ironist, and vice versa. Being uncertain who they are, they content themselves with the roles they assume; role-playing, moreover, helps kill time and diverts them from their real selves, whatever these may be. The traditional comic artifices which Büchner employs serve as ways of defining this theme. Thus, the fact that the lovers do not know each other's names is not only a convenient plot device, but it also suggests that such knowledge tells us very little about ourselves.

The knowledge that one must remain uncertain of his identity becomes a rather painful discovery in the context built up by the play. King Peter suggests the problem quite early in the text: "When I speak my thoughts aloud this way, I don't know who's speaking, myself or someone else. And this frightens me. [*After prolonged musing.*] I am I." But the king's attempt at self-assertion is obviously no solution to the problem. Valerio, when he removes a series of masks from his face, gives us a far more incisive answer. "Who are you?" the king asks him, and he replies "Do I know?" [*He slowly removes several masks, one after the other.*] Is this me? Or this? Or this? Shell the nut! Turn back the leaves! Really, I'm rather afraid I may peel myself completely away." The image in which he sees himself is essentially the onion or the Chinese boxes he had earlier used to describe the country he was passing through: behind the façade there is nothing at all. Leonce and Valerio find at least temporary diversions from this frightening discovery through the language games they play. But Lena, who is not so verbally endowed, must seek other means of escape; her solution is to identify herself with the vegetable world: "I should have been brought up in a pot like a plant, you know that. I need dew and night air, like flowers."

Büchner's most powerful suggestion about the true identities of his characters comes in the climactic scene, when Valerio leads in the lovers, disguised in pasteboard, whom he introduces as "The Two World-Famous Automata." In one sense the disguise is merely a part of the comic game, since after all it makes possible the marriage needed for a happy ending. But Valerio's speech describing the "automata" goes well beyond the exigencies of plot. Though wryly spoken, it presents an image of man reduced to something less than an animal, for he is totally devoid of will, yet fools himself into thinking he has chosen to cultivate moral ideals and civilized pleasures:

> Ladies and gentlemen, you see before you two persons of both the sexes, one little man and one little woman, a gentleman and a lady! It's all mechanism and art, all clock springs and pasteboard! Each of these two persons has a superfine ruby spring in his or her right foot just under the nail of his or her little toe, as the case may be. Give it a bit of a push, and the whole mechanism runs a full fifty years. . . . Take note of this, everyone, they have just come to a very interesting stage, at which stage a new mechanism manifests itself, the mechanism of love. The gentleman has carried the lady's shawl several times. The lady has averted her gaze several times and looked toward heaven. Both have more than once whispered: faith—love—hope. Both look very much as if an understanding had been arrived at. All that's lacking is the one very small word, Amen.

Through this, the longest single speech in the play, Leonce's earlier statements about the uselessness of all endeavor seem resoundingly confirmed, while his plans to lead an idyllic existence with Lena on an exotic Italian isle are set in an ironic perspective even before he can announce them.

For all its surface gaiety the play is centrally concerned with the exposure and analysis of Leonce's particular species of romantic agony. The most obvious manifestation of his disease is his boredom. "What people won't do out of boredom!" he soliloquizes in the opening scene. But his boredom is but one of many closely connected symptoms. Among other things he suffers from an intense self-consciousness which does not allow him to maintain any point of view without subjecting it to intense analysis and ultimately rejecting it. Though he identifies himself with Hamlet at one point (Act II, Scene 2), he is but one side of the real Hamlet: he is the introspective Hamlet which the nineteenth century often saw to the exclusion of other sides of Shakespeare's hero, an idle Hamlet, one might say, with absolutely no task to carry out. Valerio jokingly suggests a number of occupations to him—scientist, military hero, genius, being a "useful member of society"—but since he can see through them, he rejects them categorically; and he finds equal reason to reject the various preoccupations he flirts with in the course of the play—joker, drinker, romantic lover, or specialist in such pursuits as dissecting ants and counting the filaments of flowers. The only aim which he does not overtly reject is his dream of escape to a blissful southern never-never land, but within the context of the play we cannot believe he takes even this dream seriously.

He constantly maneuvers his thoughts into a vicious circle: he recognizes the emptiness of his existence ("my life yawns at me like a great white piece of a paper that I should cover all over with writing, and I don't get a word written"); he admits the reality of his sufferings; but he also goes to great lengths to convince himself that every possible solution to his ·dilemma will not work for him. He is so self-conscious about his emotions that when he comes to generalize about his dilemma he must introduce his remarks with the line, "Come on, Leonce, do me a monologue, I'll be a good listener," and conclude them with a still more histrionic gesture: "Bravo, Leonce, bravo! [*He claps.*] It really does me good to call out to myself like this." He is, in fact, two (or more) selves—enthusiast one moment, ironist the next, seeking an end to his dilemma, and yet not seeking it; and, as Valerio's image of the masks suggests, one is none too sure what ultimate self stands behind all the others.

Among the selves which Leonce tries out on occasion is the sadist. "Gentlemen, gentlemen, do *you* know what Caligula and Nero were like? *I* do," he desperately exclaims in his most histrionic monologue. As with the Roman emperors whom he invokes, the transition from feeling bored to being cruel comes to seem a wholly natural one to him. He puts on this self in an early scene, well before his meeting with Lena: he is about to play the lover with a girl named Rosetta, for whom he sets up a romantic atmosphere with candlelight, music and wine; but when the girl enters, his only response to her is a yawn. Büchner, of course, never allows the comic artifice to break down by letting us pity the girl. But at the same time he refuses to gloss over Leonce's cruelty. He resolves the dramatic problem by letting Rosetta leave the scene singing, her disappointment stylized by the sadness of the words she sings.

The emotional state which Leonce proclaims most frequently

is a feeling of indifference, an absence of real emotion. "To tired feet, every way is *too* long," he tells Lena, who soon after speaks of "spring on his cheeks, and winter in his heart." Words suggesting fatigue are used of and by him at innumerable points. Leonce, in short, is caught in a kind of living death. "The ticking of the death-watch beetle within our breasts is slow, every drop of our blood measures out its time, our life is a creeping fever"—these words of Leonce's might easily have come from *Danton's Death.* Amid the gaiety which Büchner keeps whipping up one almost fails to notice how often death is referred to; talk of death, in fact, is almost as dense in *Leonce and Lena* as in Büchner's earlier play. Valerio's description of the automata at the end of the play simply creates a memorable metaphor for the state of living death in which we have seen Leonce throughout. Büchner himself suggests a connection between the automaton image and the weary state of indifference he described in Leonce. In a letter written to his fiancée more than two years before . . . he speaks of the emptiness that overcame him after illness: "And now? And at other times? I do not feel even the ectasy of pain and yearning. Since crossing the bridge over the Rhine, I am as though annihilated within myself, not a single emotion rises in me. I am an automaton; my soul has been taken from me."

The sickness he portrays so vividly in Leonce was by no means a new phenomenon in literature at the time he wrote the play. Its literary roots go back at least to Rousseau and its basic symptoms fill the works of many German Romantics of a generation before, not to speak of contemporary French and English models, above all Musset. What separates Büchner from his predecessors is the thoroughness with which he has analyzed the disease and his refusal to sentimentalize it in any way. A passage such as the following, in which Musset's Fantasio (who otherwise has many symptoms in common with Leonce) romanticizes the simple life he had seen pictured in a Flemish painting, would be inconceivable in Büchner:

> A young woman on the threshold, the lighted fire which one sees at the back of the room, supper prepared, the children asleep; all the tranquility of the peaceful and contemplative life in a corner of the picture! And the man still short of breath but steady in the saddle. . . . The good woman follows him with her eyes for a minute and then, returning to her fire, utters that sublime blessing of the poor: "May God protect him!"

Leonce's corresponding dream is the southern idyll he plans with Lena at the end:

> We'll have all the clocks smashed and all the calendars suppressed, then we'll count the hours and the moons only by the flowers, by blossom and fruit. And then we'll surround our little country with burning lenses, so there'll be no more winter, and in summer the heat will shoot us clear up to Ischia and Capri by a process of distillation. And so we'll spend the whole year among roses and violets, oranges and laurel.

Leonce describes his longings with such outrageous extravagance that we view them critically even without the ironic perspective which Valerio introduces directly after. The rigor with which Büchner maintains the comic conventions works as a guarantee that the sentiments his characters express will maintain their proper distance from author and audience.

Through this very distance Büchner's approach to the sickness he describes has far less in common with that of his predecessors than with that of a writer such as Kierkegaard. Kierkegaard, who was Büchner's exact contemporary and no mean comic artist himself, did not begin writing until well after Büchner's death and was of course unaware of the German writer's work. Yet the affinities between the two writers, as Gustav Beckers has demonstrated with painstaking detail in his book-length study of *Leonce and Lena,* are considerable. For instance, Leonce, in his ambivalent attitude toward himself, his fascination for atmospheric effect, his constant search for distraction from boredom, his role-playing, his cruelty, his unwillingness to be burdened with any sort of commitment, is a model example of the phenomenon which Kierkegaard diagnosed as the "aesthetic" stage of life. Büchner, of course, does not postulate an "ethical" or a "religious" point of view through which to look at the aesthetic one; he does not, like Kierkegaard, create a larger dialectical system, but simply presents Leonce's dilemma with the characteristic tools of a comic dramatist. Indeed, it is through his success as a dramatist—in his unrelentingly ironic perspective, his manipulation of traditional comic devices—that this dilemma speaks to us with a contemporary relevance that we do not find in most other nineteenth-century accounts of the same phenomenon.

Leonce's view of life, one scarcely need add, in many respects re-echoes Danton's (as it, in turn, parallels that of such other Büchner characters as Lenz and the captain in *Woyzeck*). Yet Büchner creates far different dramatic contexts for Danton and Leonce, with the result that our attitudes toward their respective dilemmas are quite different. Danton's disillusionment is confirmed, as it were, by the inverted world of the Reign of Terror which surrounds and engulfs him; the irony with which he interprets this world is to a great degree, though not wholly, the point of view of the play. Leonce's irony, on the other hand, is constantly placed within other ironical perspectives, both by himself and by other characters; he serves at once as spokesman for the play and as comic butt. Above all, Büchner does not, in *Leonce and Lena,* struggle with the larger questions which give *Danton's Death* so vast a scope. He often enough suggests such questions in his comedy, for instance when Valerio, interrupting the court chaplain in the marriage ceremony, announces, "It was before the creation of the world . . . God was bored—." But these questions are kept carefully within comic bounds; the desperateness with which they are asked in the Conciergerie scenes of *Danton's Death* remains well outside the scope of the comedy. Although *Leonce and Lena,* then, does not strive to move us with the overwhelming force of the earlier play, the comic forms within which it works still provide a most appropriate vehicle for the attitudes which emerge from the text: by using comic routines which imply that nothing need be taken seriously Büchner found a way of expressing the painful discovery that nothing *can* be taken seriously. (pp. 54-67)

> *Herbert Lindenberger, in his* Georg Büchner, *Southern Illinois University Press, 1964, 162 p.*

## J. P. STERN   (essay date 1964)

*[In the following excerpt, Stern traces the theme of pain and suffering throughout Büchner's dramas.]*

The experience fundamental to Büchner's vision of human

character and destiny, and the unifying theme of his literary work, are the experience and the theme of the world under the aspect of suffering. The rudimentary and often discontinuous dramatic movement of his plays traces out a dialectic whose antitheses are formed by boredom and insensateness on the one hand and its conquest by feeling on the other. It is a movement from unreality, adumbrated as the all but incommunicable region of solipsism, unfeeling and isolation, to reality, experienced above all as encroachment, violation and ravage of the self by another. The grim fact of pain is seen, initially, as 'the bedrock of atheism', the irrefutable proof that an omnipotent, just and loving God does not exist. Yet the recognition that 'the least twinge of pain, and if it stir only an atom, rends creation from top to bottom' does not lead Büchner to the Hobbesian view that a man should put himself in a position where he can avoid pain, or to the Schopenhauerian view that he should regard it as illusory. On the contrary, in the visions which emerge from Büchner's work a man's capacity for suffering is his bedrock of reality, his one and only proof that he *is* and that the world *is*. Büchner's 'hero' is like a man waking from an anaesthetic or from a condition of total shock: the life and feeling that flow back into his limbs and flood his consciousness are the life and feeling of pain. The river of pain that flows through him yields the only proof he has of existing, but at the same time it is more than he can endure: the proof of his existence is also his undoing. Büchner's occasional use of the imagery of the dissecting table and of physiological experiments owes something to the laconic detachment and ribald humour of the medical student. But such images also indicate his view of men as specimens which are being 'prepared'—their every lethal spasm is watched—by a demiurge whose intentions remain hidden in sinister obscurity. The dialectic into which Büchner's characters are strung is not between good and evil, or fate and will, or hatred and love, but between feeling and unfeeling; and existence is manifest not yet in action but in endurance and suffering, not yet in pleasure but in pain. This far Büchner's work takes us, but no further; the 'not yet' belongs to our logic, not to his vision.

*Leonce und Lena,* Büchner's only comedy, is concerned mainly with the first half of the dialectic. The hero, Prince Leonce, is one of those 'who are unhappy, incurably, merely because they *are*'; and his escape from insensateness, which takes the form of an all but suicidal boredom, is effected by means of a fairy-tale device, convincing only in terms of a romantic convention of coincidences. At the same time the device is barely compatible with the emotion of boredom which casts a deadly chill on the harlequinade, or rather not with the emotion itself but with the intensity this emotion is given by the playwright. Knowing each other as the world knows them, a Prince and Princess in Never-neverland frustrate the world's—the silly King's—matchmaking intentions; intended for him by Polonius, Ophelia becomes the object of Hamlet's vicious scorn. But ignorant of each other's identity when they don the masks of the marionettes they 'really' are, Prince and Princess fall in love and marry. The curtain comes down on a happy Lena and a caustic Leonce wryly reconciled to the ambiguity of their union. And the meaning of this happy ending? As a goal to his search for reality and reassurance Leonce recognises it as ludicrously arbitrary. The only meaning of the conclusion is as a proof—and again he ironically recognises it as such—that an inescapable determinism governs men's destinies, that freedom, and thus purposeful actions, are wholly illusory. Determinism—that is, the rationalisation of arbitrary actions—is the intellectual correlative

of the emotion of boredom, and boredom is the soul's response to the void which encompasses it. Some of the most powerful lines of the play are devoted to characterisations of that emotion on the boundary of *Angst*. Just as boredom is interest without an object, a concern with nothing and over nothing, an encounter of the experiencing self with 'nothing in particular', so *Angst*, a negative boredom, is objectless fear, fear which fears 'nothing in particular' and thus everything; which fears existence itself as well as its end. Seeing in boredom not merely a trivial interlude between periods of meaningless action but a mode of life, a void which threatens all life, Büchner is writing out the experience of his post-Byronic, post-Napoleonic generation in Continental Europe everywhere. Lermontov and the Czech romantic poet K. H. Mácha, E. A. Poe, Leopardi, de Musset and, a little later, Baudelaire—they all speak of the atrophy of the heart and the dulling of the senses in a world where commerce and finance, the Civil Service and bourgeois orthodoxies have filled the place of heroism and adventure, and of faith. But taking this theme to its extreme point—the point of anguish of soul—Büchner upsets the precarious balance of comedy: . . .

> Come, Leonce, let's have a monologue, and I will listen. My life yawns up at me like a big white sheet of paper that I must fill with writing, but I can't produce a single letter. My head is an empty ballroom, a few withered roses and crumpled ribbons on the floor, broken violins in the corner, the last dancers have taken off their masks and are looking at each other with eyes weary unto death. I turn myself inside out like a glove twenty-four times a day. Oh, I know myself, I know what I shall be thinking and dreaming in a quarter of an hour, in a week's, in a year's time. God, what have I done that you should make me recite my lesson over and over again, like a schoolboy?—

In what follows the balance is not restored; the desolate anguish unleashed in the Prince, 'merely because he is', is stifled, not assuaged, by his subsequent happy fate.

In *Dantons Tod* the underlying emotion is substantially the same—the same region of soul is illuminated—but the emotion is rendered incomparably more intense because its proximate causes are intimated, its effects on the 'hero's' character more fully sustained, and because, above all, the dramatic situation is so much more commensurate with the emotion itself than it was in Büchner's romantic comedy. The drama opens on 24 March 1794; Danton is now on the point of complete disillusionment with the cause and development of the Revolution. He is haunted by nightmare visions of the September massacres in which he played a leading part. He now knows the sordid and trivial concerns, the greed and corruptness of 'the People' on whose behalf he conducted the massacres: he also knows the cowardice and cynicism and the hypocrisy (so strong as to be self-delusive) of his fellow-revolutionaries: and, having exhausted all physical pleasures, Danton has come to the end of experience, and knows himself to be alone. This is the end with which the play begins. He is like a man imprisoned in a maze, who knows the mechanism of every lock and of every guard's mind, yet who also knows that any door he may succeed in unlocking leads merely into another part of the maze. His knowledge is as complete as it is paralysing—the determinism, now projected on to a wide, historical plane, is reflected in boredom and *nausea vitae* which are almost suicidal. In this initial situation Danton is incapable of any meaningful human contact. Whatever happens outside him is unreal. 'They will not dare'—the phrase he repeats whenever his friends urge him to escape arrest by Robespierre's Revolutionary Tribunal—sums up his feelings, or rather unfeeling, about the world that surrounds him. Even to Julie, his wife, who tries to penetrate his insensate detachment with devotion and love, he can only speak of his isolation: . . .

> We know little of each other. We are thick-skinned creatures, we stretch out our hands to each other, but it is wasted effort, we are only rubbing our coarse hides together—we are very solitary.
> JULIE. You know me, Danton.
> DANTON. Yes, what passes for knowing. You have dark eyes and curly hair and a fine skin and you always call me 'dear George!' But (pointing to her forehead and her eyes) there, there, what lies behind there? It's no good, we have crude senses. Know each other? We should have to break open each other's skulls and drag the thoughts out of each other's brain-coils.—

Danton's and his friends' death under the guillotine is a foregone conclusion, the external action of the play leads towards it without being greatly modified by retarding events or by the stirring of a will to live. Danton's brilliant rhetorical victory before the Revolutionary Tribunal serves not to avert his fate, or even to delay it, but to demonstrate its arbitrariness: all rational argument, all personal and political action appear absurd. The dramatic movement that sustains the play is a movement of the ideas and emotions of men who are all caught up in the revolutionary situation. They are distinguished not by virtue of the political or moral principles they proclaim, but by the degrees of self-knowledge of which they are capable, where knowledge is the enemy of the will to survive. Thus the one quality which, even at the beginning of the play, distinguishes Danton from his enemies, and from Robespierre in particular, is his candid insight into the motives of political action, and his lack of hypocrisy. But this is no virtue in him, since his understanding of the truth about himself and about the Tribunal that will soon condemn him to the death to which he has condemned so many others, is a detached, cynical understanding. Furthermore, Danton has no decision to make, no active part to play any longer, and is thus in possession of a negative freedom: he cannot escape the 'dreadful fatalism of history', but he can choose to become its conscious victim rather than its blind instrument—'I'd rather be guillotined than guillotine. I've had enough. . . .' The sentient grasp of the truth of his guilt and his non-participation, his negative freedom, are the conditions from which a change proceeds: a change not of mind towards action but of soul towards suffering.

Imminent death appears to Danton not as punishment or retribution, but only as another kind of corruption, different from life merely by being less complicated. He now recognises, with all the anguish of one who has had enough of life, that the annihilation which death will bring is not total. What then does it amount to, this apparently wholly negative insight at which Danton arrives, the insight that 'nothing can turn to nothing'? Less than a positive assent to creation, and scarcely more than a hiatus in his nihilism, it is merely the recognition of the unending reality of 'something', of an object, a being, a resistance of some kind, against which life, flowing back into insensate limbs, into the soul, strikes: and, striking, wakens body and soul to pain. Fear—now no longer objectless anguish and nausea but the definite fear of an unending death—is indeed a strange 'value' to emerge at the point where Danton's false fearlessness (' . . . they will not

dare . . .') ends. Yet it *is* a rudimentary value when we compare it with the solipsistic insensateness with which the play opened. For Danton to fear death—to fear it for himself, but even more so for his friends—and to make his exit with the words (addressed to the executioner, who thrusts back Hérault as he tries to embrace Danton)— . . .

> Will you be more cruel than Death? Can you prevent our heads from kissing each other at the bottom of the basket?

—is to have undergone a change, a 'development' even: not towards any traditional morality (which to the end he rejects as a subtle kind of hedonism); nor towards heroism (which he ironically deprecates as a mere theatrical gesture); but towards the barest, the most rudimentary *apprehension* of reality through the capacity to feel it and to fear its endlessness. Danton dies at the point where, having freed himself from the negative infinity of unfeeling, he is exposed to—but does not enter—the positive infinity of creation. Yet it is a positive infinity: positive in relation to the other side of the dialectic, the insensate Nothing from which he awakens, and therefore also absolutely positive, in the sense that life, however terrible, is a condition, a *sine qua non,* no more than a bare foothold, of Grace. At this point the play—indeed Büchner's literary work—stops. The proof of Danton's existence is also his end as a living man.

The dialectic of pain is bodied forth, in **Dantons Tod** and everywhere in Büchner's work, not primarily by overt action and events, but by strange mosaics of words grouped in a series of individual scenes, their connections barely sustained yet never quite abandoned. The measure of Büchner's 'realism' is, formally speaking, his success in continuously conveying the discontinuity of experience, in making a rudimentary whole of his feeling for life as a thing fragmentary and incomplete. The strange mosaics of which the individual scenes of his plays consist are made up of two kinds of contrasting images, one grey and one scarlet. Insensateness and boredom are represented by an imagery, always forceful and sometimes obscene, which is related to the physical—the digestive and sexual—functions; the repetitiousness and tedium of the daily ritual of dressing, eating, the 'symbols of exhaustion' like discarded clothes, the smell of the grave, frozen ground and arid wastes, ashen skies and empty marshy landscapes, mechanical dolls, robots and marionettes—these are the images that give dramatic substance and poetic form to one side of the dialectic. In violent and dramatic contrast with these is the language of flesh and blood, of violence and of the Crucifixion.

No elaborate demonstration is needed to prove that this imagery owes much to Shakespeare; Macbeth's 'Life's but a walking shadow . . . a tale / Told by an idiot, full of sound and fury, / Signifying nothing'; Hamlet's 'Imperious Caesar, dead and turn'd to clay, / Might stop a hole to keep the wind away'; Lear's 'The wren goes to it, and the small gilded fly / Does lecher in my sight . . .', and countless other examples of this 'low' style spring to mind. The fundamental difference lies in the framework of the total vision to which this double imagery of feeling and unfeeling belongs. Shakespeare too is intimately familiar with the experience of life's meaninglessness and pain. But he contrasts it with invocations, as realistic as they are powerful, of the greatness and dignity of man, dramatically portrayed in a man's capacity for loyalty, love and courage; a capacity often unavailing but always real, that is, an element in the fashioning of a man's character and actions.

In Büchner the only contrast is between the scarlet and the grey, it lies within the double imagery itself; there is nothing outside or beyond it; the search for reality through the experience of pain and suffering makes up 'the whole', such as it is, of his work.

At this point, however, a vital question arises: what is it that makes the comparison with Shakespeare at all possible, that preserves Büchner's writings from the turgid pointlessness and horror-mongering of our 'Theatre of the Absurd'? What is it that preserves Büchner's ever-repeated variations on tedium from being tedious, on the pathos of the human situation from being merely 'pathetic', on the ghastly boredom of life from being ghastly and boring? In other words, what makes them into works of art? The answer lies in the paradox of all successful realism, which the naturalists (among them Büchner's imitators) have failed to heed. His world is like a giant battlefield, a pattern of livid greys and blood. Yet form—the manner in which these two kinds of images are presented—is peculiarly at odds with the apparent content. For while in speech after speech and scene after scene death and decay are invoked, the immense creative, poetic *energy* which informs each invocation—the living force of each image: the violence, for instance, of Danton's tedium—belie its overt meaning. And this energy—Aristotle's *sine qua non* of all drama—is present not only in the individual parts but also in the achieved whole of each work. **Dantons Tod** and **Woyzeck** both end on the same note, and leave the same total impression in our minds: that life *is,* that it is not a delusion (as insensateness is) but reality, and that its meaning is in pain. This far his vision takes us, and thus he attains to a rudimentary meaning which escapes the horror-mongers; but it takes us no further. The next step in the dramatic argument—the meaning of pain as a means to some end other than itself, as expiation to forgiveness and Grace, he does not express.

Danton's discussion with his friends in the Conciergerie (Act III, Scene 7), immediately before the opening of the Tribunal, provides an example of Büchner's technique of advancing his dramatic argument by means of a mosaic of images. Meaning and action, pressed together into the smallest conceivable grouping of words, are made to depend not upon the abstract opinion expressed, but upon the colours of the imagery and the tone of the speaker's voice. . . . To Phillippeau's question what there is left to hope for ['Was willst du denn?'] Danton replies, 'Peace.' *Phillippeau:* 'Peace is in God.' *Danton:* 'In Nothing. Immerse yourself in something more peaceful than Nothing, and if the greatest peace is God—then isn't Nothing God?' This is the *credo,* the ontological argument of nihilism. And Danton demolishes it in the next breath: 'But I am an atheist.' Here is no statement of fact but a cry of despair: a piece of cold logical deduction *and* a violent assertion of existence; and as such the sentence is as far as it could be from its overt lexical meaning. There is no God, and therefore no 'peace'; no peace, and therefore no Nothing: 'Oh, that accursed proposition, "Something cannot become Nothing"'. And I am something, that is the horror of it!' The something of creation is ubiquitous—'Creation has spread itself everywhere, nothing is empty, everything is crawling with it'—creation is the annihilation of peace: 'Nothingness has murdered itself, Creation is its wound, we are drops of its blood, the world is the grave where it lies rotting.'

All of which, as Danton adds, 'sounds mad'. And yet, in this assertion of the irreducible reality of existence, we have conveyed to us an experience less remote than Danton's enigmat-

ic negation may suggest. For what he asserts is as it were negative existence (in the same sense in which boredom is 'negative' interest)—it is life as it appears to the man awakening from shock. The vision which emerges from the double negation is the very opposite of Heidegger's *'Nichts das selbst nichtet'*—an empty, meaningless void . . . , which sucks in and silences all emotion and thought. It is the opposite, too, of Schopenhauer's disembodied 'Nirvana', his atheistic parallel to (and parody on) the Christian's 'Peace that passeth all understanding'. What emerges is something more familiar than these: it is the world encompassed by suffering, it is Being filled out with pain, sensate and throbbing with painful life. Peace—the Nothing—is desirable enough: it would indeed be an 'ideal' condition: *'das Nichts ist der zu gebärende Weltgott'*: 'Nothingness—*that* is the world's god that is yet to be born' (= that should be born). But peace *is* not, has no place in creation. Consequently (and here again the astonishing combination of cold logic and hot passion) absolute solitude too does not exist, is breached and violated by another. But just as the existence asserted through pain was a rudimentary, 'negative' existence, so the contact of two beings which is based on the violation of their solitudes (of their 'brainboxes') is a rudimentary, 'negative' contact: Danton's love for Julie is love in the face of death, Woyzeck's love for Marie is sealed by murder. And [Act III, Scene 7] ends, as it began, on a note of despair at the absence of Nothing, and now also of solitude: . . .

> O Julie, if I were to go alone! If she would leave me
> for long! And even if I could fall to pieces, utterly,
> dissolve entirely, yet I would be a handful of tor-
> mented dust, and every atom of me could only find
> peace with her.

But since there can be no death, no peace, what remains to be done? Before, in his state of boredom and heedless unfeeling, Danton had considered that nothing—no political action, no attempt to escape or survive, not even the cry of pain and anguish—was worth the effort it involved. Now this one thing only remains: the cry which will assert the *ne-plus-infra* of bare existence: . . .

> I cannot die, no, I cannot die. We must cry out—
> they must tear every drop of my life's blood out of
> my limbs.

To what end? Once again we come to the fragmentary, jagged open edge of the vision. There is no God because there is pain, which is the only, the terrible proof of existence: and if there is no God—no peace—is there thus no cessation of pain, no end to existence? Is existence pain into infinity? It is not so, D. H. Lawrence calls to us in his last poems, it cannot be so:

> And if there were not an absolute, utter forgetting
> and a ceasing to know, a perfect ceasing to know
> and a silent, sheer cessation of all awareness
> how terrible life would be!
> how terrible it would be to think and know, to have con-
> sciousness!
> But dipped, once dipped in dark oblivion
> the Soul has peace, inward and lovely peace.

But later still, on the very threshold of death, Lawrence adds that question which had tormented Danton; which leaves the vision open at the far end of life; and exposes all life—procreation and the enduring of joys and sorrows—to infinity:

> Oh lovely last, last lapse of death, into pure oblivion

at the end of the longest journey
peace, complete peace!

But can it be that also it is procreation?

Oh build your ship of death
oh build it!
Oh, nothing matters but the longest journey.

Which is it: the bad infinity of pain or the good infinity of Grace? It seems that in his hour of death Büchner was able to answer the question, to complete for himself the vision of the world under the aspect of pain. His last words, spoken to his friend and fellow-exile, Wilhelm Schulz, sum up poignantly the central experience of his short life and the theme of his literary work: . . .

　　　We do not suffer too much pain but too little, . . .

but to these words he adds the answer of faith which his writings do not contain, and thus gives to suffering the meaning which his creative imagination was not able to encompass: . . .

　　　for through pain we go home to God.

A singular progression is to be observed in the successive stages of Büchner's preoccupation with the problem of pain; like Danton's growing apprehension, it is the opposite of what ordinarily might be called a positive development. It is as if, from *Dantons Tod* through *Lenz* to *Woyzeck,* Büchner were trying to come ever closer to the experience and the problems it raises; as if, progressively discarding all that, from *its* point of view, appears as contingent, he were intent upon grasping the dialectic in its barest form. The complex and personal situation in which Danton is involved is seen as the outcome of the blind, anonymous forces of historical necessity. It is seen in this way by Büchner *and* by his hero, who understands his situation well enough to be able to expatiate on its absurdity. (And Danton's knowledge, as well as his eloquence, is shared in various degrees by his friends and fellow-prisoners.) Danton has no power—because he has no consistent desire: and no desire because no sustaining reason—to avert his execution, but at least he faces death with a distinct and highly articulated consciousness. Woyzeck has not even that. He is victim pure and simple—victim of his own birth and circumstances, of society, of his own dark nature. Or rather, he is as nearly a mere victim as it is possible—as we are made to accept as convincing—for a living man to be; not the least of the young dramatist's achievements is that he gives us an imaginative measure of that state. And in creating Woyzeck as the embodiment of a *ne-plus-infra* of the human condition, Büchner is wholly original. For the figure of this down-trodden simple soldier, passive and animal-like in his suffering, there is no literary precedent anywhere; in particular, not in Shakespeare, whose influence upon many details of characterisation in *Dantons Tod* is powerful and even, once or twice, overpowering. Here in *Woyzeck* it is as if, taking up such minor figures as Poor Tom or Private Feeble—'I'll ne'er bear a base mind: an 't be my destiny, so; an 't be not, so'—Büchner decided to enshrine a whole vision of life within the boundaries of the helpless victim's soul. Nor is his originality merely of historical interest. Creating situations in many ways similar to Woyzeck's, neither the Naturalists of the late nineteenth century nor the Expressionists of the early twentieth ever achieved a dramatic portrayal comparable in intensity and uncontrived pathos. Determinism, social indictment, the class-struggle—all these are implicit in the play,

but the vocabulary to which these terms belong is altogether too intellectualised, it describes a situation less primitive and fundamental than Woyzeck's. And since solitude, here too, is a part of the 'hero's' deprivation, it is still a single and distinct man, *an individual,* who occupies the stage (and thus appeals to our sympathy in the traditional manner). To think of a remedy for Woyzeck's situation—that is, to think of it socially—is to think of a different play.

He is, during the early part of the play, passive, a slave in body and mind. Words to him are strange, disconnected objects which he uses as one who had never used them before—falteringly, then again violently, hurling them at people: . . .

　　　I must go. Many things are possible. Humanity. Many things are possible. Fine weather we're having, Captain, Sir. Look, such a beautiful sky, all grey and hard. It almost makes you want to knock a hook in it and hang yourself on it, only because of the little dash between Yes and Yes again—and No. Captain, Sir: Yes and No? Is the No to blame for the Yes or the Yes for the No? I'll have to think about that . . .

Earlier in the scene the Captain whom he serves as a batman had insinuated that Marie, Woyzeck's mistress, had been unfaithful to him. Thus Woyzeck's 'Yea and Nay' is tied to the action by expressing the torment of his uncertainty; but his words are also an appeal to the biblical injunction—'Let your words be . . .'; and they are finally a cry of despair in the face of the eternal bedrock of guilt—'Scandal there must be, but woe to him from whom scandal cometh.' Her guilt? His own? He faces the question defenceless and alone.

Words, everywhere in Büchner's work, are such strange, isolated objects: now like gaudy beads of poison, now like knives quivering in the target, now like scalpels dissecting living limbs, now again like gory wounds. Büchner's style is 'dramatic' if by 'dramatic' we mean, not the coherence of sustained conflict recognisable to both parties and made meaningful by motivation, but annihilating tension and conflict compressed into momentary haphazard encounters. His tormented hero speaks without expectation of being understood or hope of being spared. He speaks, yet the world is silent to him—Woyzeck's tormenting doubt is silenced not by knowledge but by the irrational deed. . . . Is she guilty? 'Woman! . . . No, there would surely be some visible sign on you!' But would it be visible to him? 'Each person is an abyss. Giddiness takes you when you look down.' And yet: 'Could it be true? She walks like innocence itself.' But innocence has no visible sign, goodness is silent, only evil and pain call loudly from the void: 'Well, then, innocence, you have a sign on you. Do I know? Do I know? Who does know?'

His sentences are discontinuous as his self is isolated. He uses words the way Kaspar Hauser had done—the youth who, fully grown but with the mind of a savage or a child, had emerged from the dark woods into the blinding daylight of the world of men. Is not the first, the most 'obvious' thing we say of such an 'unaccommodated man' that he is defenceless? Do we not feel that the harm and injury that we know will come to him are somehow 'natural' and proper to his desolate situation? And yet, is there not, even in that bare and primitive condition of a Kaspar Hauser, of a Woyzeck, something that touches us with a recognition of ourselves? Is he not 'the thing itself', the very *a priori* of man? Man in this vision is not the glorious survivor of a process of natural selection but, on the contrary, a creature separate from all other creatures by virtue of the utter openness, exposedness, of the infinite vulnerability to which his organism and senses—his 'useless' sensibility—have condemned him. And his capacity for suffering, anguish and pain, is that not vastly in excess of, irrelevant and even hostile to, the process of 'natural' selection? (pp. 104-20)

Not all the speeches in **Woyzeck** are disconnected and incoherent. In contrast to Woyzeck's own violent and enigmatic utterances—as ashen grey stands in contrast to blood red—there is the fantastic coherence of rhetoric and rodomontade of the Doctor's physiological disquisitions, the Boothkeeper's exhibition of a calculating horse—

> ' . . . Yes indeed, ladies and gentlemen, here's no stupid beast, here is a person, a human being, an animal human being—and yet [the horse misbehaves] an animal, a beast . . . '

—or the parody of a teleological sermon by a drunken journeyman—

> ' . . . Why is man? Ah, why is man? Verily, verily I say unto you: what should the ploughman live on, the pargeter, the cobbler and the physician, if God had not created man?'

None of these speeches contains an ounce of truth or sympathy or insight, they are wordy lies against Woyzeck's inchoate truth. Their very rhetoric—the world's coherent discourse itself—is the harbinger of chaos, pain and death. To Woyzeck, crazed yet searching for reality, they are a meaningless rigmarole.

He is as solitary as any man can be in our world. The people around him rise up from the cracks in the earth's thin surface as in a dream or a delirium. They stand in certain simple social relations to the 'hero', yet they involve him in nothing like a substantial plot, in no give-and-take of opposing wills. The Doctor (perhaps a sketch of Büchner's father) is a harsh satire on the 'scientific', that is, the mercilessly curious mind; the Captain, a sketch of hypocrisy and inadequate sympathy; the Drum-Major—'what a man! like a tree!'—a portrayal of physical violence and sexuality. Yet these three—outlined with astonishing dramatic energy and in the briefest possible way—are not Woyzeck's opponents and tormentors so much as the inescapable and—since he is defenceless—necessarily hostile facts of his situation. How bare can a man, 'the thing itself', be? Love is not of his essence, it is not part of his irreducible self. Marie, Woyzeck's mistress, a victim of degrading indigence but also of her instincts, is not the object of his love so much as the one hold Woyzeck has on existence, on life itself; the only thing, in the threatening void outside his tormented mind, that tells him that he *is*. Hardening her heart against him, she returns the Drum-Major's embraces, and Woyzeck, a good man and a good father to their child, murders her. The deed is done in a fit of jealousy, but the jealousy itself reaches to a still more primitive and more fundamental emotion. His is an act of self-assertion: the act of a man who must 'make a bruise or break an exit for his life': who must carve a notch upon the tree of experience before he is himself crucified on it: a man who must do *this* deed since no other, more positive, lies within his power.

Yet although he stands before us in this state of all but complete deprivation, Woyzeck is an individual nevertheless, sharply outlined against all others. Not so much by a distinct consciousness as by the capacity for feeling which his wandering consciousness reflects. Again—more briefly but also

more powerfully than in **Dantons Tod**—the two contrasting imageries, of grey insensateness and of crimson pain—sustain and accompany the 'hero's' movement towards the reality of pain, the apprehension of which separates his hallucinative mind and injured heart from all around him. Andres, his fellow soldier, with his dull, mechanical reactions to everything—a mere human vegetable—provides a measure to Woyzeck's sentient soul. So does the Doctor with his laconic comments on the humiliating experiments he conducts on Woyzeck's body. But so too does Marie, whose last words before she succumbs to the Drum-Major are words of dead indifference. The Grandmother, a boothkeeper at the fair, a journeyman, a Jew who sells Woyzeck the knife he uses to murder his mistress, Marie's child which doesn't hear when told of its mother's death, a Policeman who sums up Woyzeck's passion, 'A good murder, a good honest murder, a lovely case. As nice a case as you could wish to see. We haven't had one like that in a long while . . . '—they all pass hurriedly before our eyes, figures in the icy void into which Woyzeck must reach, which he must somehow breach, and be it with a deed of violence: . . .

> (Woyzeck, alone, on the edge of the forest, near the pond): The knife? Where is the knife? This is where I left it. It will hang me! Closer, closer still! What place is this? What's that noise? Something moved. Sh! . . . closer at hand. Marie? Ha, Marie. Hush. It's so quiet. Why are you so pale, Marie? Why have you got that red cord round your neck? Who paid you with that necklace for your sins? You were black with sins, black! Have I made you white now? Why does your hair hang down so wild? Didn't you plait your hair this morning? . . . The knife, the knife! I've got it. Now. People! I hear them coming . . . there!

And the world, the empty void which engulfs Woyzeck? It is described in the scene immediately preceding the murder: in a fairy-tale the Grandmother tells the village children, the simplest and surely also the saddest fairy-tale ever told: . . .

> GRANDMOTHER. Come, you shrimps. Once upon a time there was a poor child that had no father and no mother, they were all dead, and there was no one left in the world. They were all dead, and so it set off and searched night and day. And as there was no one left on the earth it wanted to go up in the sky, and the moon seemed to have a friendly face. But when it came to the moon, it found it was a piece of rotten wood. So then it went to the sun, and when it came to the sun it was only a withered sunflower. And when it came to the stars they were little golden gnats, stuck on pins just as the shrike sticks them on the blackthorn. And when it wanted to go back to earth, the earth was just a pot that had been turned upside down. And it was all alone. So it sat down and cried, and it is still sitting there all alone.

(pp. 121-24)

*J. P. Stern, "A World of Suffering: Georg Büchner," in his Re-interpretations: Seven Studies in Nineteenth-Century German Literature, Thames & Hudson Ltd., 1964, pp. 78-155.*

**MICHAEL HAMBURGER** (essay date 1970)

[*Hamburger is a German-born English poet, translator, and critic. An accomplished lyric poet in his own right, Hamburger has been widely praised for his translations of several German poets previously unfamiliar to English readers, including Friedrich Hölderlin, Georg Trakl, and Hugo von Hofmannsthal. He has also written extensively on German literature. Here, Hamburger studies Büchner's theory of realism and the techniques he used to achieve it.*]

*Dantons Tod* was first performed in 1902, *Leonce und Lena* in 1911, *Woyzeck* in 1913. Büchner, in fact, was too "advanced" a dramatist to be acceptable even during the Naturalist eighteen-eighties and eighteen-nineties, when Ibsen, Hauptmann, and Sudermann dominated the German experimental theatres. Gerhart Hauptmann admired Büchner's works, editions of which had been published in 1850 and 1879; but it was not till after the experiments of Strindberg, Wedekind, and the first Expressionists that Büchner's plays established themselves on the stage. This very circumstance serves to confute the arguments of George Lukács and other critics of his school, who would like to persuade us that Büchner was an early practitioner of "Social Realism" of an art primarily directed toward social or political ends. For a time, undoubtedly, Büchner's preoccupation with human suffering caused him to seek relief in political action, for tyranny and injustice were two obvious causes of human suffering in his time; but only a very prejudiced reader of his works, from *Dantons Tod* to *Woyzeck,* can fail to see that Büchner's realism goes far deeper than that of the Naturalists and their successors, the Social Realists of this century. Büchner's view of life was a tragic one; his intense pity for the poor, the oppressed and the exploited was never alleviated by the comfortable belief that human suffering is due to no other causes than poverty, oppression, and exploitation. If Büchner had wished to glorify the French Revolution or the ideology behind it, he would have made Robespierre the hero of his play, not the irresolute and dissolute Danton; but Büchner's dominant passion was the passion for truth, for the whole truth; and even if the had taken Robespierre as the hero of his play, it would have been Robespierre at the moment of his fall, the victim of the same inhuman system that had brought about Danton's death. Büchner, in short, was never a party man; he was never purblind, as every party man must be, because he hated ideologies that enslave the minds of men as much as he hated the economic and social orders that enslave men bodily. As a scientist, he knew that body and mind are interdependent; he therefore revolted against the "idealistic" cant that denies or minimizes the extent to which material conditions affect us. Yet his true concern was with mental and spiritual suffering, Danton's vision of vanity and his fear of death, the religious torment of Lenz, the suicidal boredom of Leonce, the physical victimization of Woyzeck that leads to hallucination, paranoia, and murder. Büchner's realism was that of every great writer who seeks the truth about the human situation; a realism that is not incompatible with poetic vision. (pp. 173-74)

[In] the age of Hegelian dialectics, it was often the self-contradictions of a writer that revealed his vital preoccupations. Büchner, too, wrote out of a tragic tension between two conflicting views of life. What is so astonishing about his works is their consistency of purpose and achievement. One reason is that Büchner had no use at all for Hegel or for that idealistic German school from which Hegel derived. . . . Büchner had no patience with half-measures; like Schopenhauer, whom he resembled in his pessimism and in his pity, he based his thinking not on metaphysical premises, but on the bare condition of man, on the reality of suffering, our par-

ticipation in suffering not our own and our desire to relieve it. This basic existential preoccupation is at the root of all Büchner's works; but he was divided between a religious view of the human predicament and a cruelly deterministic view, brought home to him by his scientific studies and his reflections on history.

An early letter to his fiancée, written when he was twenty, contains a most poignant account of these conflicting views. The account is especially valuable because of its direct bearing on Büchner's first play, *Dantons Tod.* There can be no better introduction to it than Büchner's own reflections on the events with which it deals:

> I was studying the history of the French Revolution. I felt almost annihilated by the horrible fatalism of history. In human nature I discovered a terrifying sameness, in human institutions an incontrovertible power, granted to all and to none. The individual mere froth on the wave, greatness a mere accident, the sovereignty of genius a mere puppet play, a ludicrous struggle against an inalterable law; to recognize this law our supreme achievement, to control it impossible . . .

It was this experience of determinism that turned Büchner into a revolutionary of the most radical sort, as the same letter shows. It is the extremists of revolutionary politics, the Robespierres rather than the Dantons, who base their policies on the recognition of that "inalterable law." Yet the recognition ran counter to Büchner's nature and convictions, to his Christian sense of the value of the individual and his no less radical belief in free will. Hence the conflicting resolutions that follow:

> . . . Never again shall I feel obliged to bow to the parade horses and corner boys of History. I am accustoming my eyes to the sight of blood. But I am no guillotine blade. The word *must* is one of the curses pronounced at the baptism of men. The dictum: "for it must needs be that offences come; but woe to that man by whom the offence cometh!"—is terrible. What is it in us that lies, murders, steals? I can't bear to pursue this thought any further. But oh! if I could lay this cold and tormented heart on your breast!

The relevance of this passage to *Dantons Tod* would be obvious even if Büchner had not put much of it into Danton's own mouth in Act II of the play. The conflict between Robespierre and St. Just on the one hand, Danton and his friends on the other, is a conflict between two different views of political and historical necessity. Their dramatic conflict would be less convincing if Büchner had not been able to do full justice to both arguments. At one time, there can be no doubt, he would have identified himself with the party of Robespierre and St. Just. Not only Danton expresses thoughts that we know to have been Büchner's; St. Just's great speech in Act II is an apology for the very determinism that Büchner had come close to accepting:

> Nature calmly and irresistibly obeys her own laws; men are annihilated where they come into conflict with those laws. A change in the constitution of the air we breathe, a blazing up of the tellurian fire, a disturbance in the balance in a quantity of water, an epidemic, a volcanic eruption, a flood—each of these can cause the death of thousands. What is the result? An insignificant alteration of physical nature, hardly perceptible in the cosmos as a whole,

that would have left no trace to speak of but for the dead bodies left in its wake.

Now I ask you: should mental nature show more consideration in its revolutions than physical nature? Should not an idea have as much right as a physical law to destroy whatever opposes it? Indeed, should not any event that will change the entire constitution of moral nature, that is, of humanity, be permitted to attain its end by bloodshed? The World Spirit makes use of our arms in the mental sphere as it makes use of volcanoes and floods in the physical. What difference does it make whether men die of an epidemic or of a revolution?

The appeal to Hegel's "World Spirit" in this context may be an anachronism, but it is a significant one. Büchner was careful to grant both factions their fair share of religious, or pseudoreligious justification. Elsewhere Robespierre compares his mission to that of Christ:

He redeemed them with his blood, and I redeem them with their own. He made them sin, and I take this sin upon myself . . . And yet . . . Truly, the son of man is crucified in us all, we all sweat blood and writhe in the garden of Gethsemane, but no one redeems another with his wounds.

Dramatically, this passage serves to show that Robespierre too has scruples and affections, for he is moved to express these thoughts by Camille Desmoulins's desertion to Danton's party. Robespierre, who denies his scruples and affections in favor of impersonal ends, is no less deserving of pity than his victim, the individualist. But Büchner takes dramatic impartiality even further by throwing just a little shadow of doubt on the purity of Robespierre's motives, as indeed he suggests several possible explanations for the conduct of Danton himself. That is why *Dantons Tod* is a truly and profoundly tragic play; both Robespierre, who serves a certain ideal necessity, and Danton, who opposes it in the cause of individual freedom, are destroyed by the revolution, though Robespierre first destroys Danton for the Revolution's sake. The Revolution itself assumes a character akin to that of Fate in Greek tragedy; and the voice of the *people*—*vox populi, vox dei*—expresses a terrible indifference to the virtues and aspirations of both men. Yet amoral and brutish though they are, even the representatives of the people are not excluded from the pity that Büchner's play so powerfully evokes. (pp. 174-78)

•　•　•　•　•

[All] Büchner's heroes suffer from . . . a profound boredom that saps their willpower, sometimes their very desire to live. If this boredom were no more than a late variety of the Romantic *mal du siècle*, we might indeed regard it as the attribute of a single social class of a ruling class in decline. . . . The boredom of Leonce could easily pass for the mere languor of enforced idleness; and it is the seemingly innocent, pseudo-Romantic comedy *Leonce und Lena* that contains some of Büchner's most devastating political satire. "My Muse is a Samson in disguise," he wrote . . . ; but of all his works only *Leonce und Lena* makes its revolutionary impact by indirect means, by imitation and parody of current literary conventions. Since Leonce is a Prince, one might argue, and a particularly idle and useless one at that, Büchner used him to satirize the idleness and uselessness of the ruling class; and since boredom results from idleness and uselessness, Büchner saw to it that Leonce should be bored to the point of trying

to kill himself. This is the kind of argument put forward by the advocates of Social Realism; like most of their arguments, it is logical, but wholly specious.

Leonce himself is a rebel; his boredom is not the result of idleness and uselessness, but of his awareness that he is idle and useless. This awareness, as we shall see, has deeper implications than the social and political ones. Leonce not only questions his own function in the State—a function which, in any case, he is not prepared to perform—but doubts the value and purpose of human life itself. Romantic languor is the mood evoked at the beginning of his monologue in the first scene of the play; yet this languor soon gives way to reflections that have no place in the Romantic convention:

The bees cling so drowsily to the flowers, the sun's rays lie so lazily on the ground. A horrible idleness is spreading everywhere. Idleness is the root of every vice.—Just to think of all the things that people do out of boredom! They study out of boredom, they pray out of boredom, they fall in love out of boredom, marry and procreate out of boredom and finally die of it; what's more—and that's what makes the whole thing so funny—they do it all with such a solemn expression on their faces, not knowing why they do it, but attaching all sorts of weighty reasons to their pastimes. All these heroes, geniuses and blockheads, all these saints and sinners and family men are really nothing more than sophisticated idlers.—Why, of all people, do *I* have to know it? Why can't I become important to myself, dress the poor puppet in a morning coat and put an umbrella in its hand, so as to make it very righteous, very useful and very respectable?—

The allusion to a puppet in this passage—the significance of Büchner's obsession with puppets and robots has already been intimated—relates the boredom of Leonce to Büchner's own vision of vanity. Leonce thinks human endeavors vain because they are predetermined; he rebels against this determinism by refusing to marry the Princess for reasons of state, runs away from the kingdom, meets the same Princess without knowing it, falls in love with her and marries her of his own free will. . . . For all its whimsical humor, the implications of *Leonce und Lena* are no less terrifying than those of *Woyzeck* . . . ; both are cruel comments on the illusion of freedom and the pretensions of Homo sapiens. The boredom of Leonce, then, is more than his response to the rottenness of a social system; it is the aftereffect of that experience of the abyss in which all Büchner's principal characters participate.

Danton's boredom has the same origin; but in his case there can be no question of a mere indictment on social or political grounds. To understand his boredom, we should rather consider Baudelaire's "Ennui," which

ferait volontiers de la terre un débris
Et dans un bâillement avalerait le monde

and Yeats's bitter comment, true of more than his own time, that

The best lack all conviction, while the worst
Are full of passionate intensity.

In the case of Danton, boredom is not the result of idleness, but its cause; and behind this cause there is another, the demoralization induced by his experience of the abyss. In a certain sense one can say of his particular kind of boredom that it afflicts the best, because only those whose moral sense is highly developed are susceptible to demoralization from that cause; but, as Baudelaire knew, the cause does not excuse the effect. Danton is a morally ambiguous character because his boredom—the apathy that springs from despair—is itself a vice and the begetter of other vices.

Danton's apathy is bound up with an almost nihilistic skepticism about human motives. When, in the opening scene, his wife asks him whether he believes in her, he replies: "How can I tell? We know very little about one another. We are pachyderms, we reach out our hands towards others, but it's a wasted effort; all we rub off in that contact is a little of the callous hide;—we are very lonely." And again: "Know one another? Why, we should have to break open the other's cranium and pull his thoughts out of the fibres of his brain." Woyzeck's torment is even more extreme than Danton's; but it is out of the same experience that he says: "Every human being is an abyss; it makes you giddy to look down."

Danton's skepticism extends to his own motives. On the one hand he resists Robespierre's deterministic *"must"* in the cause of individual liberty; on the other, he questions his own free will in a speech that echoes Büchner's letter to his fiancée: "Puppets is what we are, puppets manipulated by unknown powers; nothing, nothing at all in ourselves; no more than the swords with which ghosts fight their battles—only one can't see their hands, as in fairy tales . . . " Danton is morally superior to his enemies when he says of himself that he "would sooner be guillotined than condemn another to be guillotined"; but, in his passion for the whole truth, Büchner makes Danton's friend Lacroix say that Danton "would sooner be guillotined than make a speech," thus putting a very different construction on Danton's failure to defend himself and his friends. Both the imputed motives are valid. Danton is morally superior to his opponents insofar as he has experienced the abyss and acts in accordance with that experience; insofar as, having recognized its futility, he refuses to set in motion the murderous revolutionary machine, even to save his own skin. He is morally inferior to Robespierre and St. Just insofar as he lacks all conviction and has fallen into an apathy that takes the form of promiscuous debauchery. Büchner himself doesn't tell us—and doesn't expect us to decide—how far Danton's attitude of laisser faire is due to genuine scruples, to remorse for his former part in the "liquidation" of others and to compassion with the people, who are fobbed off with severed heads and continue to go hungry; and how far it is due only to his *taedium vitae,* weariness and indifference. "I shall show them how to die bravely," he says to Camille; "That's easier than to go on living."

This *taedium vitae* comes out most clearly at the beginning of Act II. Camille tells Danton to hurry, for they can't afford to waste time; to which Danton replies:

> But time wastes us.
>
> Oh, it's very boring always to put on one's shirt first, and then pull one's trousers over it and go to bed at night and creep out of it in the morning and always be setting one foot before the other; there's simply no telling how this will ever change. It's very sad to think of it, and to think that millions have done it before you and that millions will do it again in exactly the same way, and that, moreover, we consist of two halves, both of which do the same thing, so that everything happens twice over—it's very sad . . .

Camille tells him not to be childish and reminds him that he is ruining not only himself, but his friends as well. Danton refuses to act. He is tired, he says, of being "a wretched instrument, each of whose strings only sounds on one note." He is even prepared to admit that Robespierre, "the dogma of the Revolution," as he calls him, may be indispensable, whereas he, Danton, is not. Danton has ceased to care; his experience of the abyss has stripped him of all but passive virtues and negative desires. "We should sit down one beside the other and have some peace. Something went wrong when we were created; there's something missing in us, I don't know what to call it—but we'll never pull it out of one another's entrails, so why rip open another fellow's belly to find it?"

Here Danton seems to point to something very much like original sin; but, if so, he doesn't recognize its corollary, free will. His tolerance rests on the denial of free will, just as much as Robespierre's intolerance does. The difference is one of emphasis. Robespierre is prepared to sacrifice any number of human beings to an ideal necessity, Danton to sacrifice every ideal to what he regards as the facts of the human condition. Danton's passive resistance to Robespierre's fanaticism would be heroic if Danton believed in heroism; as it is, he can only resist the tyranny of Robespierre's ideal necessity by appealing to a different necessity, based on the inborn corruption of human nature and its dependence on material factors. In the crowd scene of Act I, the citizen who defends an adulteress against her husband's anger speaks in the spirit of Danton: "A knife? True enough, but not for the poor whore. What has she done? It's her hunger that whores and begs . . . " Much more poignantly, Woyzeck resorts to the same argument in defending himself against the Captain's taunts: "As for virtue, sir, I haven't yet got the hang of it. You see, we common people haven't any virtue, we just let nature have its way; but if I was a gentleman and had a hat and a watch and a frock coat and could talk refined, I'd be virtuous in no time. It must be a fine thing—virtue, I mean, sir. But I'm a poor man."

Büchner would hardly have used this argument in two different plays if the moral problem had not concerned him personally; but, because of its very ambiguity, the conflict between Danton and Robespierre is more than a conflict between two political factions, two temperaments, or two views of life. It assumes the inevitability of a tragic dilemma, a dilemma that will recur as long as men disagree as to the relative value of ends and means; and since "there's something missing" in men, as Danton says, and they will always have to choose between one evil and another, **Dantons Tod** will never lose its appeal or its relevance.

It doesn't matter, therefore, that Büchner put his own conflicts, disillusionments, and sufferings into his plays. His magnificent impartiality saves all his works from being mere illustrations of this or that idea. From external evidence it would seem that Büchner would have taken Danton's side against Robespierre, whose fanatical insistence on abstract virtues was repellent to him; but the play both exposes and pardons both men. Büchner's impartiality made all the difference between the didactic realism of the Young Germany group and his own poetic realism. "I shall go my own way," he wrote . . . in 1836, "and continue to write a kind of drama that has nothing to do with all these controversial issues. I draw my characters in accordance with nature and history, as I see them, and laugh at the people who would like to make me responsible for the morality or immorality of those characters . . . " (pp. 179-85)

Büchner's passion for realism was such that he based three out of his four extant imaginative works on documentary evidence, much of which is quoted verbatim in his works. ***Dantons Tod*** was based on histories of the French Revolution by Thiers and Mignet, with other borrowings from a German work by Konrad Friedrich; ***Lenz*** on the diary of Pastor Oberlin, who looked after the poet and dramatist J. M. R. Lenz at the time of his mental breakdown in 1778; ***Woyzeck*** on reports of the trial and medical examination of a murderer of that name, who was almost reprieved on the grounds of insanity, but finally sentenced to death in 1824. But it would be quite wrong to regard these borrowings as a substitute for invention. What is so remarkable about all these works is their fusion of fact and imagination, verisimilitude, and passion, made possible by Büchner's extraordinary gift of empathy. His Lenz, for instance, expresses a view of art almost identical with Büchner's own when he says:

> Even the poets of whom we say that they reproduce reality have no conception of what reality is, but they're a great deal more bearable than those who wish to transform reality . . . I take it that God made the world as it should be and that we can hardly hope to scrawl or daub anything better; our only aspiration should be to re-create modestly in His manner . . . In all things, I demand life, the possibility of existence, and that's all; nor is it our business to ask whether it's beautiful, whether it's ugly. The feeling that there's life in the thing created is much more important than considerations of beauty and ugliness . . .

But Büchner was also expounding the views of the historical Lenz. He would never have chosen to write about Lenz at all, but for his deep affinity with this unhappy writer of the *Sturm und Drang*. Lenz himself had written: "But since the world has no bridges and we have to content ourselves with the things that are there, we do at least feel an accretion to our existence, happiness, by re-creating its Creation on a small scale." Like Lenz and other writers of the *Sturm und Drang*, Büchner claimed literary descent from Shakespeare; like them too, he was anticlassical and anti-idealistic. (pp. 186-87)

All Büchner's major characters resemble him in rejecting every idealistic, a priori explanation of life; and, with the exception only of Robespierre and St. Just, they are no less skeptical of rationalistic and mechanistic interpretations of nature, human and otherwise. This is the crux of Mercier's opposition to Robespierre's faction, and of Danton's too, if only Danton were not too demoralized to believe in his own assertion of the freedom to choose. Mercier says:

> Just pursue your cant for once to the point where it becomes concrete.—Just look around you and say: all this is what we've said; it's a mimed translation of your words. These wretches, their executioners and the guillotine are your speeches come to life. You built your systems as Bajazet built his pyramids, out of human heads.

On the same grounds, but in very cynical terms, Camille Desmoulins mocks Hérault for lapsing into noble rhetoric shortly before their execution:

> From the face he's making one would think it's going to be pertrified and excavated by posterity as an ancient work of art.
>
> Go on, then, distort your mouth into pretty shapes, lay on the rouge and talk with a good accent, if you

think it's worth the effort. I say we should take off our masks for once: as in a hall of mirrors, we'd see nothing anywhere but the primaeval, toothless, indestructible sheep's head—no more, no less. The distinctions don't really amount to much; we're all of us scoundrels and angels, asses and geniuses, and, what's more, we're all these things in one: there's room enough in the same body for all four, they aren't as big as one likes to think. Sleep, digest, conceive children—that's what we all do; as for the other things, they're only variations in different keys on the self-same theme. So there's no need to stand on tip-toe and pull faces, no need to be bashful in company!

What these two speeches have in common is the desire of both speakers to get down to the very rock bottom of human nature; and this, beyond doubt, was also Büchner's desire. The difficulty only comes with the next step. What are the positive convictions that sustained the humanism implicit in all Büchner's works?

An answer is provided in one of his scientific works, his lecture on the cranial nerves. Büchner introduces the subject by making a crucial distinction between two different approaches to the study of natural phenomena; these he calls the "teleological" and the "philosophical." To the teleological view, "every organism is a complex machine, provided with the most ingenious means of preserving itself up to a certain point. It sees the cranium as an artificial vault supported by buttresses, devised to protect its occupant, the brain,—cheeks, and lips as an apparatus for masticating and breathing,—the eye as an intricate glass,—the eye-lids and lashes as its curtains;—even tears are only the drops of water that keep the eye moist . . . " Büchner rejects this teleological view, and the scientific methods derived from it, as a vicious circle. His own view, the philosophical, as he calls it for lack of a better word, is that "nature does not act for specific ends, does not use itself up in an endless chain of cause and effect, each of which determines another; but in all its manifestations nature is immediately sufficient to itself. All that is, is for its own sake. To look for the law of this being is the aim of the view opposed to the teleological . . . All that the former sees as a cause, the latter sees as an effect. Where the teleological school is ready with an answer, the question only begins for the philosophical school." (pp. 189-90)

Büchner's dramatic realism . . . was closely connected with his preference for the "philosophical," as opposed to the "teleological," view of nature; and his rejection of all a priori explanations of the human condition accounts for the impartiality that characterizes his realism. In choosing to write his plays in prose—but a prose highly charged with imagery—Büchner linked his work to the *Sturm und Drang* and took sides in an issue that has divided German literature ever since the seventeen-seventies. Stendhal's names for the two conflicting principles, "Racine et Shakespeare," will do as well as any if we do not interpret them too narrowly in terms of literary schools; and we must not identify the battle cry of "Shakespeare" with the cause of Romanticism, an identification peculiar to France in the eighteen-twenties and eighteen-thirties. As far as Germany is concerned, "Shakespeare" stood for the principle of poetic realism; the German Romantics, philosophically and aesthetically, were idealists.

When the *Sturm und Drang* dramatists resorted to the medium of prose, they did so in order to combine the emotive power and flexibility of Shakespeare's blank verse with the realism of what Diderot called "le tragique domestique et bourgeois," as practiced in Germany by Lessing. (p. 195)

The diction of *Dantons Tod* is still close to that of Büchner's predecessors; if it shows little or no discrepancy between colloquialism and rhetoric, this is partly because all the chief characters, in any case, were politicians; partly because it was Büchner's crucial concern to strike just the right balance between public and private utterance. His rhythms, throughout the play, are the rhythms of prose; his imagery, much of which has the *Sturm und Drang* tendency toward extravagant, gruesome, and elaborately sustained trope, also serves to bear the dominant tension of the play, the conflict between determinism and freedom. (p. 197)

In *Woyzeck,* however, Büchner achieved a fusion of naturalism and intensity both unprecedented and unsurpassed. The play, as we know it, is nothing more than a number of short scenes and fragments of scenes, which Büchner's editors have pieced together in whatever sequence they thought most plausible. That so brief, so fragmentary, and even dubious a work has been acclaimed as a minor masterpiece, and rightly so, is one of the anomalies of modern literature. The plot is that of a vulgar melodrama, mere infidelity and revenge; and the extant scenes leave us in doubt as to its outcome. Yet to see or read *Woyzeck* is to gain an experience that no other play affords. Behind its bare diction and commonplace action there is a vision that removes this fragmentary melodrama from all the existing categories. The diction of *Woyzeck* is so perfectly adapted to its dramatic function that it draws the audience or reader into the very vortex of what it serves to express. It is a transparent diction, poetic not in itself, but despite itself, because it reveals what is essentially and timelessly human behind the semi-articulate utterings of vulgar persons, a murderer and a slut.

*Woyzeck* is the justification of Büchner's "philosophical" view, of his impartiality and compassion. Büchner's principal characters, unlike those of so many German dramatists, especially those that are made to speak in blank verse, do not stand for anything that can be specified with ease or with certainty. Even *Dantons Tod*—condemned as subversive both by the Imperial and the Nazi authorities—can be interpreted as a glorification or as a deadly indictment of the French Revolution. What was really intolerable about it was its refusal to strike any conventional attitude whatever, to worship any hero or do homage to power in any guise. The ruthless realism of Büchner had the effect of stripping human nature down to its constant essentials—to its lowest common denominator, many would say—and it is at this point of exposure that Büchner made his choice: the choice not to hate, despise, or give up this naked humanity at its worst, but to grant it his impartial compassion. The ultimate effect of his work is one of tragic affirmation; not because it contains a crypto-religious "message," but because it presents the naked truth about men and leaves the ultimate issues open. Büchner's impartiality, in itself, is an act of faith. There is a distinction between the impartiality of the truly imaginative writer, who does justice to all his characters, and that of the merely clever writer—common enough in our time—who does justice to none. If Büchner's realism was poetic, in spite of his medium, it was because his impartiality was of the former, much rarer, kind.

The narrative prose of *Lenz* is no less extraordinary than the dramatic prose of *Woyzeck.* Büchner relates the facts of Lenz's visit to Pastor Oberlin as he found them recorded in Oberlin's diary and in a French biography of Oberlin; but, from the first, he relates them from the point of view of Lenz himself, of a man suffering from religious mania and incipient schizophrenia. This feat of sympathetic penetration called for a new narrative style and technique; Büchner provided both and, in doing so, opened up new possibilities to writers of the twentieth century. The influence of *Lenz* is apparent in Hofmannsthal's prose, particularly in his masterly *Andreas* fragment. The dislocation of syntax in *Lenz* leads straight to the experimental prose of the Expressionists.

Büchner introduces Lenz as he crosses the mountains on foot, on his way to Oberlin's vicarage; he tells us nothing about Lenz or Oberlin, nothing about the purpose of the visit, nothing of what has gone before or is to happen. He introduces Lenz by making us see the mountain landscape through his eyes:

> . . . At first there was an urge, a movement inside him, when the stones and rocks bounded away, when the grey forest shook itself beneath him and the mist now blurred its outlines, now half unveiled the trees' gigantic limbs; there was an urge, a movement inside him, he looked for something, as though for lost dreams, but he found nothing. All seemed so small to him, so near, so wet. He would have liked to put the whole earth to dry behind the stove, he could not understand why so much time was needed to descend a steep slope, to reach a distant point; he thought that a few paces should be enough to cover any distance. Only from time to time, when the storm thrust clouds into the valley, and the mist rose in the forest, when the voices near the rocks awoke, now like thunder subsiding far away, now rushing back towards him as if in their wild rejoicing they desired to sing the praise of Earth, and the clouds like wild neighing horses galloped towards him, and the sunbeams penetrated in between them and came to draw a flashing sword against the snow-covered plains, so that a bright, dazzling light cut across the summits into the valleys; or when the gale drove the clouds downwards and hurled them into a pale-blue lake, and then the wind died down and from the depths of the ravines, from the crests of the pine-trees, drifted upwards, with a humming like that of lullabies and pealing bells, and a soft red hue mingled with the deep azure, and little clouds on silver wings passed across, and everywhere the mountain-tops, sharp and solid, shone and glittered for miles—then he felt a strain in his chest, he stood struggling for breath, heaving, his body bent forward, his eyes and mouth wide open; he thought that he must draw the storm into himself, contain it all within him, he stretched himself out and lay on the earth, dug his way into the All, it was an ecstasy that hurt him—or he rested, and laid his head into the moss and half-closed his eyes, and then it withdrew, away, far away from him, the earth receded from him, became small as a wandering star and dipped down into a roaring stream that moved its clear waters beneath him. But these were only moments; then, soberly, he would rise, resolute, calm, as though a mere phantasmagoria had passed before his eyes—he remembered nothing . . .

Büchner could not have achieved what he did achieve in his short life but for the creed implicit in all his works, a creed that combines an aesthetic doctrine with a new humanism. Lenz formulates this creed in the story:

One must love human nature in order to penetrate into the character of any individual; nobody, however insignificant, however ugly, should be despised; only then one can understand human nature as a whole.

(pp. 197-200)

*Michael Hamburger, "Georg Büchner," in his* Contraries: Studies in German Literature, *E. P. Dutton & Co., Inc., 1970, pp. 170-200.*

## JOHN SIMON (essay date 1971)

*[A Yugoslavian-born American film and drama critic, Simon has been both praised as a judicious reviewer and censured as a petty faultfinder. He believes that criticism should be subjective, and as Andrew Sinclair has observed: "He is as absolute and arrogant in his judgements as any dictator of culture, a rigidity that is his great strength and weakness." In the following excerpt, Simon first extols Büchner as a genius and then examines the style, subjects, and themes of* Danton's Death. *Simon's essay was originally published in 1971.]*

At a dinner party, W. H. Auden once expounded the idea that such is the wisdom of Divine Providence that people die when they have fulfilled themselves; that however short an artist's life may seem, he would not have added appreciably to his life's work by living on. James Merrill raised the name of Mozart, but Auden insisted that Mozart had nothing to add to his accomplishment. I ventured to name Georg Büchner, but to the best of my recollection Auden ignored the remark; perhaps, in the heat of discussion, he had not even heard it. That Georg Büchner should have died at the age of twenty-three is to me almost sufficient proof in itself of the nonexistence of God.

I can think of no greater loss to world drama, indeed to world literature, than this untimely decease. Think of what would have remained of Shakespeare had he died at twenty-three: probably not even the first part of *Henry VI.* Of Ibsen, only the melodramatic *Catiline* and *The Warrior's Barrow,* on the strength of which Ibsen himself would not remain. Shaw did not start to write plays till he was almost thirty. Brecht would have left behind unfinished versions of *Baal, Drums in the Night* and *In the Jungle of Cities,* three obviously gifted and equally obviously immature plays, as inferior to Büchner as they are plainly influenced by him. Pirandello came to the theater in middle life; O'Neill was twenty-four when he started out, in a sanitarium, on his first tentative little plays.

This is not intended as a brief for precocity; the play, not the date of its composition, is the thing. My point, in fact, is how unprecocious, how finished the writings of the young Büchner were. . . . (pp. 20-1)

To repeat, the point is not Büchner's precocity but his genius. Precocity and brilliance can perhaps replace existential experience, but only genius can triumph over total theatrical inexperience. Büchner could not even have *seen* much theater; his school was his politically and otherwise active life, and of course his reading. The influence on him of Shakespeare and Goethe is manifest, and he clearly knew the work of the gifted *Sturm und Drang* dramatist Lenz, about whom he wrote his one superb novelistic fragment. He may also have learned something from Victor Hugo, a brace of whose plays he ably translated, and something else (though this applies chiefly to his comedy, **Leonce and Lena**) from Musset. Yet these influences are already digested by the time Büchner writes his first

play at the age of twenty-one: **Danton's Death** is no more like one of Shakespeare's histories or tragedies than *Hamlet* is like *The Spanish Tragedy.*

In the case of Büchner, moreover, the negative influences, the works and ideas he did not allow to affect him, are probably as important as the positive ones. Thus he managed to ignore the powerful suasion of Kant and Schiller, and to eschew high-flown idealism, a puritanical sense of right and wrong, the somewhat facile elevated style couched in strictly metrical verse—models to be avoided if one was to create the theater of the future, which Büchner so spontaneously and unprogrammatically did.

The objections most often raised against **Danton's Death** are that it is much too sprawling and episodic a play; that its hero is a passive victim, doomed from the outset and accepting it without truly fighting back; that the play is one long, depressing downward movement without reversals to speak of; and that there is not even a major confrontation between Danton and Robespierre. To the first objection the answer is that the hero of the play is not so much Danton as humanity in a moment of eye-opening crisis, and that the broad canvas is the most suitable one. . . . Büchner does everything in his power to raise the action to the heights of timelessness and universality: Danton's predicament is manifestly not tied to revolutionary circumstances alone, and a protean despair, or at least clammy malaise, seems to envelop all the characters of the play except the crassest and vilest.

Indeed, the play is about human suffering and about the feverish, ludicrous, passionate ways in which people try to elude it, and about how all, whether gallant or ignoble, prove unsuccessful. Almost all the dramatis personae, certainly all the main ones, die in the course of the play, or are predictably not much longer for this world. But what makes the atmosphere so tragic lies elsewhere: in the pervasive sense of the vanity and sheer waste of it all. As Wolfgang Kayser expressed it (in *The Grotesque in Art and Literature*), there is an increasing awareness of "the aimlessness not only of man's action but also of his suffering" [see excerpt dated 1957]. A good part of tragedy, in life as on the stage, is mitigated by the sense of purification, redemption or furthering of the cause of humanity by the example set. To take an obvious instance, the ordeals of a Romeo and Juliet or the sufferings of a Hamlet have an ultimately beneficial effect on their respective societies, and even the heroic victims themselves may have a sense of tragic dignity, indeed exultation, as they rise to the loftiness of their deaths. But there is another kind of suffering—that of a Lear, for example—which does not purify, fulfill or improve anyone or anything. In fact, before Lear knew the meaning of suffering, which alone could teach him humanity, he was considerably better off. Acquaintance with injustice, grief and suffering makes him aware of the abundance of causes for suffering, open him up to it, invite suffering upon his head.

So, too, with Danton. He was once a great warrior for the cause, later a great butcher for it; now he has become conscious of the futility of it all, and life has become a burden to him. He can afford to be, he has to be, a passive hero, being a man who has been granted—or been punished with—a glimpse of the ultimate emptiness of the universe. Clearly he expresses the disillusion with politics and people of Büchner himself: for this sensitive, magnanimous young man to learn that you couldn't help the lower orders against their oppressors, not so much because of the political power of the latter

*A 1980 German production of* Danton's Death, *showing Danton (center) and wax figures of Danton, La Marseillaise, and Robespierre (left).*

as because of the moral weakness of the former, must have been a soul-shaking blow. Büchner's statement to August Becker that the masses were accessible by almost no other route than the purse, and his words to Gutzkow that there were only two levers for the large majority, material misery and religious fanaticism, are in part what is dramatized in **Danton's Death.** It must have struck Büchner as a significant coincidence that both Danton and he were named George, and this, along with the identical disenchantment in revolutionary activity (however different in scope and significance), must have encouraged Büchner to project himself into that much larger but coarser figure. And this is what makes the figure of Danton in the play less passive on closer inspection: his revulsion, fed by Büchner's youthful ardor, becomes cosmic; the wit, poetic passion and intemperateness with which he gives himself over to it add up to something almost like an affirmation.

Karl Viëtor is certainly right when he observes that "Danton's rejection of the world and life does not stem from a stoically resigned disposition. To damn so vehemently, one has to be a disappointed lover, a deceived friend . . . one who in all his inconsolable desperation feels that it is a pity about life." What also makes Danton's passivity less gray is the sense of something splendid being discarded, of the grandeur of this downfall even in its predictability. If there is no resounding final confrontation between Danton and Robespierre, it is because there was none in history, and because, in this play at least, the enemy is not so much Robespierre as the *condition humaine,* which Danton confronts throughout—with sardonic wit, with exquisite sadness, with brilliance of perception and utterance.

It is worth noting that the very first context in which we encounter Danton's existential dissatisfaction is the conjugal one. Julie, the simple, loving wife who gives evidence of supreme devotion and courage in the course of the action, clearly does not satisfy Danton. What lies behind her words of love? What hides beneath her beautiful exterior? The problem is both emotional and epistemological: can there be true love, and also can there be mutual understanding between two people? Our senses are too crude both for loving and for understanding. The superb and painful images in which these doubts are couched are enhanced by those two curious little "no's" with which two of Danton's most affectionate speeches to Julie begin: no's of impatience, restlessness, sheer exasperation. And the final image of Danton's loving Julie as he loves the grave magisterially compresses into itself all the themes of the play: the transience and inadequacy of life and love, the exhaustion from living and struggling, the maw of death gaping for these people basking in the last embers of their existence.

Danton is an exacerbated perfectionist. When Lacroix describes him as trying to piece together the Venus of Medici from the best features of the various grisettes of the Palais Royal, we are to understand that he is speaking the truth, for the next scene shows Danton precisely so engaged with the lovely Marion. We hear him bemoaning that he cannot encompass and absorb her entire beauty—which ironically echoes his complaint to his wife about not being able to possess her innermost thoughts. And yet he strives: "Danton, your lips have eyes," Marion tells him, for like eyes, his lips have been gliding over and enveloping her entire body. But if Danton is in pursuit of the Whole, so is Marion—another one of those wistful, shadowy female figures, like Rosetta in ***Leonce and Lena,*** whom Büchner drew so well. Marion, the girl of easy virtue, is a somewhat cruder replica of Danton: she reaches incessantly after all men, convinced that whoever enjoys the most prays the most. She embodies an uninterrupted yearning and clasping in much the same way Danton does, except that in her the hunger for quality is translated into an itch for quantity. We feel that Danton is after the "All," whereas Marion craves the "Every." Most remarkably, however, Marion starts her two first speeches to Danton, whom she momentarily loves, with the same intemperate no's with which Danton parried his wife's lovingly importunate questioning.

"Multiplicity of episode," Max Spalter writes (in *Brecht's Tradition*) in defense of the play's much-carped-at episodic structure, "allows Büchner to make the content of one scene footnote the content of another" [see Further Reading]. He observes that the playwright translates his realization "that all human activity is equally senseless" into "the very manner in which the drama unfolds. Robespierre pontificates, Danton philosophizes, and Simon curses—it all comes down to the same thing." By his episodism, Büchner not only sketches in a larger canvas of the Terror, but also does "his reporting in a context of meaningful cross-reference." Episodism "also makes for an exceedingly varied mixture of tonalities as Büchner alternates vulgar dialogue with political oratory as well as nihilistic lyricism." This is true enough but stops short of explaining how the scenes of the play interpenetrate and dramatically reinforce one another. The principal device is parody. Just as the major revolutionaries in their scenes earnestly emulate or ironically compare themselves to ancient Romans, so the little men in the street scenes consciously or unconsciously ape old and new heroes. But travesty can be nonpolitical too, like Marion's insatiability, which is a distortion and vulgarization of Danton's.

There are, to be sure, simple contrasts as well: the successful Moderates enjoying the fruits of *embourgeoisement* at the gaming table and in drawing-room badinage in Act I, Scene 1; in Scene 2 the impoverished masses venting their frustrations on daughters and wives reduced to whoring, or on some unlucky passer-by who for the mere possession of so aristocratic a luxury as a handkerchief is thought worthy of hanging. But consider now the two last scenes of Act III. In the first of these, Danton by his oratory manages to swing the spectators at his trial to his side. In the following scene the Second Citizen, vulgarizing oratory into mere demagoguery, makes the fickle crowd revert to Robespierre merely because he lives austerely, whereas Danton indulges in various pleasures. But Danton's hedonism at least has style; a few scenes before, Collot, Billaud and Barère evoked Clichy. There those among the Ultras who do not share Robespierre's asceticism revel in orgies that are a gross distortion of Danton's epicureanism.

For Danton is, above all, an epicurean. "There are only epicureans," he says, "either crude or refined. Christ was the most refined of all. That's the only difference I can discern among men." Later, awaiting execution at the Conciergerie, Danton reiterates this sentiment. In the hour of death Hérault declares, "Greeks and gods cried out, Romans and Stoics put on a heroic front." To which Danton replies, "But they were just as good epicureans as the Greeks. They worked out for themselves a very comfortable feeling of self-satisfaction." In that last, histrionic moment it is "not such

a bad idea to drape yourself in a toga and look around to see if you throw a long shadow." From life to death, from sinner to savior, the motive is epicureanism.

But this homage to the pleasure principle is not gratuitous self-indulgence on Danton's part. Rather it is a strategy in the all-out war on boredom (we find it again in ***Leonce and Lena,*** and even Marie's unfaithfulness in ***Woyzeck*** is largely motivated by it), a boredom which, as Michael Hamburger notes . . . , "is not the result of idleness, but its cause; and behind this cause there is another, the demoralization induced by the experience of the abyss" [see excerpt dated 1970]. We might call this a heroic epicureanism, a placebo to allay one's despair, to thwart the suicidal urge—thus not only a heroic but also a tragic epicureanism.

Corresponding to this bitter laughing all the way to the guillotine is the style, the language of most of the play. I say "most" because one-sixth, as Viëtor estimates, is taken over almost verbatim from Büchner's three historical sources. Such, however, is the young dramatist's artistry that quotations blend seamlessly into the fabric of his own poetic invention. Often it is almost disappointing to discover that a superb piece of dialogue (and not only, more predictably, the major political harangues) is transcribed from one of these sources. For example, Danton's remark that life is not worth the effort expended to maintain it ought really to be Büchner but is in fact Danton. Yet the slight tarnish this realization gives our pleasure is promptly swept away by our appreciation of how smoothly the passage fits into its context, which is from no other source than the wellspring of Büchner's imagination.

But to return to the correspondence of the style to the acrid, bittersweet, and finally wormwoodlike laughter that is the true subject, the dramatic vision of ***Danton's Death.*** To this underlying mood of gallows—or, in more up-to-date terms, black—humor the stylistic unit most appropriate is the epigram. Let us remember that "epigram" has two meanings, both of them relevant to the play's construction. ***Danton's Death*** is first epigrammatic in the sense of aphoristic, witty and compactly pregnant utterances. Characters, even some of the lowest, tend to express themselves in maxims, boutades, epigrams. This heightened, compressed wit—at times admittedly somewhat grating—is the nonobjective, the linguistic correlative of teetering on the brink, of trying to get off a good one before one topples, of feeling that every sentence may prove one's last and had better be memorable. Through such bons mots one keeps one's spirits up, one's fear or hopelessness amused. Yet these rounded, self-contained clevernesses are kept by their very rounding off, their smooth and hard sculpturedness, from fully latching onto and meshing with what the previous speaker said: there is something solipsistic about epigrams. They are part of what Spalter reminds us is the *Aneinandervorbeisprechen* ("talking past one another") that characterizes this play, which "is . . . Büchner's point, that most dialogue is really monologue."

But "epigram" has another meaning in classical prosody. The epigrams of the *Greek Anthology,* for example, are not necessarily witty; quite often they are simply lyrics characterized by concision and elegance. In this sense of a short, pithy poem, the epigram, or its prose-poetic equivalent, abounds in ***Danton's Death.*** Sometimes its lyricism approaches the laughter of the witty epigrams by its heightened, desperate cleverness; at other times it is the witty epigrams that become so fierce as to be a kind of savage poetry. But frequently the epigrams are sheer poignant lyricism. Let me give four examples of these shadings of the epigram and, to make the relationship and differences perspicuous, I choose them from among the specimens of the cosmic imagery that runs through the play and so powerfully contributes to lifting it above its time and place into transcendent poetry. "Nothingness has killed itself," says Danton. "Creation is its wound, we are its drops of blood, the world is the grave in which it rots." This is the witty epigram approaching the poetic one. The purely poetic is exemplified by Danton's *de profundis* as he looks at the night sky on the eve of his execution: "The stars are scattered over the sky like shimmering tears. There must be deep sorrow in the eye from which they trickled." The straight witty epigram appears in Danton's rebuke of Robespierre, set against a cosmic backdrop: "I'd be ashamed to walk around between heaven and earth for thirty years with that righteous face just for the miserable pleasure of finding others worse than I." Finally a poetic epigram, but with a wryness, a black nihilism that brings it back into the ambience of the bon mot: "The world is chaos. Nothingness is the world-god yet to be born." It should be noted that this image turns the first one in our series inside out. Why not? The play lurches and reverses itself, circles despairingly, guffawingly, weepingly, howlingly around that center that should be inhabited by the divine but remains empty—unless, worse yet, it is inhabited by the gods of *King Lear,* who kill us for their sport.

I said earlier that in **Danton's Death,** scene comments on scene, often by way of travesty. The Second Gentleman, who is afraid of puddles because he sees them as holes in the thin crust of the earth through which he might fall, crudely enacts the predicament of Danton and the Moderates, for whom the puddles of sensual indulgence, indolence and easy living prove indeed to be fatal holes through which they drop into their graves. But the grossly, bizarrely, vulgarly, even cruelly comic scenes involving the populace are meant as more than parodies: they are the unvarnished expression of Büchner's disenchantment with the masses. Still, even here there are not infrequent reversals, the mood flapping over into intense understanding, in the spirit of those beautiful lines from **Lenz:** "You must love mankind in order to penetrate into the essential identity of each individual; there must be no one too lowly, no one too unsightly, only then can you understand them all." It is this humaneness that acts as a softening echo of the shrill, anguished or sardonic, outcries of the play and lets them reverberate with softened edges, without however making the play less tragic—more tragic, in fact.

Michael Hamburger seems to me absolutely right when he says about Büchner's *oeuvre:* "What is so remarkable about all these works is their fusion of fact and imagination, verisimilitude, and passion made possible by Büchner's extraordinary gift of empathy." Very often it is this empathy that takes over in **Danton's Death,** displacing that much lesser artistic stance, sympathy. Büchner infiltrates all his characters; rather than feeling for them, he simply becomes Danton or Lucile or Simon or Marion, or even the contemptible yet fully apprehended and realized Laflotte. Even those ghoulish harridans, the *tricoteuses* of the Place de la Révolution, are so penetrated and comprehended by him that we cannot cast stones at them without hitting ourselves—or at least some ugly part within us. Having realized this, thanks to Büchner's empathy with them—and with other monsters, high and low, from Robespierre and St. Just to the venal carters—we may still cast those stones, but we cast them more in sorrow than in anger.

Finally there is the great, unalloyed beauty that weaves its way through the action in the figures of the two wives faithful unto death, Julie and Lucile—the former an out-and-out invention of Büchner's (the real wife was nothing like this), the latter a poetization of the historic Lucile. "The two feminine figures," writes Karl Viëtor, "are the poet's offering of thanks to the one pure happiness in his precarious, problematic existence." The reference is to Büchner's loving and forever true fiancée, who, without being fully able to understand his genius, remained faithful to his memory and never married another. This tribute to women—even to fallen ones, like Marion or Simon's daughter—is a strand of loveliness that becomes visible at crucial points of the play and makes its last scene almost unbearably moving. And with what terseness! In a few last words Büchner transports us to the summit of tragedy. That Lucile Desmoulins should have to cheer the king, the lord of misrule against whom she and her husband fought, in order to be able to buy herself the death that alone can unite her with her beloved husband Camille! Unite? Everything in the play denies the afterlife. And in whose name will she be slaughtered? "In the name of the Republic," that wise and righteous state for which she and Camille toiled and struggled. What a laugh! What horrible sadness!

Irony and sadness: a twenty-one-year-old youth writes a play from which he wants to make enough money to escape to political asylum, and has to leave before he can collect the measly honorarium. In exile he sees the play published, but with certain changes that deeply pain him. It is, needless to say, not performed during his lifetime—not until sixty-seven years after its publication. Yet it is a play that, along with its sister masterpiece **Woyzeck,** anticipates, as the literary historian Ernst Alker pointed out, the essential elements of realism, poetic realism, naturalism, impressionism, expressionism, *Sachlichkeit* and magic realism. And to these we might add black humor and the theater of the absurd.

Reviewing an unfortunate production of **Danton's Death** by the Lincoln Center Repertory Company, I wrote in *The Hudson Review* (Winter 1965-66) something about the language of the play that strikes me as worth repeating here: "The language, from the outset, catches hold of poetry, and, though dragged through the mire of history and morass of hopelessness, never lets go. There is, if anything, an overdose of poetry . . . simile, metaphor, symbol are not so much its utterance as its very breath; yet the imagery is handled with such integrity and tact that the personal flavor of each character is sovereignly preserved." Today, however, what might strike us as even more important about the play is its warning to young revolutionaries, not from an old fogy, but from an ex-revolutionary as young as, or younger than, most of today's radicals and, unlike them, a genius. The danger of a just revolution, runs the warning, is not only its failure; it is also its success. (pp. 21-31)

*John Simon, " 'Danton's Death',," in his* Singularities: Essays on the Theater, 1964-1973, *Random House, 1976, pp. 20-31.*

### ELIAS CANETTI   (lecture date 1972)

[*A Bulgarian-born man of letters and winner of the 1981 Nobel Prize in literature, Canetti is regarded as one of the most important intellectual figures of our era. Having fled Austria in 1938, he was deeply disturbed by the social climate in Europe before World War II, and eventually became concerned with "the conflict between culture and the mass mind." Canetti's sole novel,* Die Blendung *(1935;* Auto-da-Fé, *1946), is a socio-political satire exposing how the individual is both alienated from and victimized by the greed, cruelty, and intolerance of the mass mind. Often described as a companion piece to* Auto-da-Fé, Masse und Macht *(1962;* Crowds and Power, *1962) is considered his most influential work. This treatise on the psychology of the masses attempts to explain the origin, behavior, and significance of crowds as a force in society. In the following excerpt from a 1972 speech given in acceptance of the Georg Büchner Prize—the most prestigious German literary award, presented to writers whose works further the cultural heritage of Germany—Canetti offers a biographical interpretation of Büchner's writings.]*

Ladies and gentlemen, to express thanks for an honor that is given in Büchner's name strikes me as a foolhardy venture. For one thanks in words, and who would not have Büchner's in mind when his name is pronounced, and who could there be in any land on earth who had the right to place words of his own next to these words! (p. 192)

I am no connoisseur of critical writing on Büchner, and it is highly questionable whether I even have the right to say anything about him to you, who are probably all connoisseurs of that literature. If there is anything I could offer by way of apology, it is the fact that he changed my life as no other writer has done.

The true substance of a writer, that which appears unmistakable in him, forms, I think, in a few brief nights, which differ from all others in intensity and effulgence. It is those rare nights in which he is yet quite beset with himself, so very much that he is capable of losing himself totally in his completeness. The dark universe that he consists of, that he feels space for without being able to grasp what it contains, is suddenly penetrated by a different, an articulated world, and the clash is so violent that all matter floating, scattered and at its own devices within him will light up at one and the same time. It is the amount in which his inner stars notice each other across dreadful empty spaces. Now that they know they are there, everything is possible. Now the language of their signals can begin.

I lived through such a night in August 1931 when I first read *Woyzeck.* Throughout the entire previous year, I have lived in *Auto-da-Fé.* It was a retiring life, a kind of corvée, there was nothing outside of it, anything else happening in that year was repulsed. . . . I found myself burnt empty and blind in my self-created desert.

And so, one night, I opened up Büchner, and he opened himself up to me in *Woyzeck,* in the scene between Woyzeck and the doctor. I was thunderstruck, and it seems lamentable to put it so weakly. I read through all the scenes of the so-called fragment to be found in that volume, and since I could not admit that something like that existed, since I simply did not believe it, I reread them four or five times. I would not know of anything ever to affect me like that in my life, which was not poor in impressions. By dawn, I could not stand being alone with it anymore. Early in the morning, I went into Vienna, to the woman who was more than my wife, who also became my wife, and whom I would like to have among us today, now that she is no longer with us. She was far better read than I, *she* had read Büchner at twenty. Now I berated her for never, not even once, having mentioned *Woyzeck* to me, and there was hardly anything that we had not talked about. "Be glad you didn't know it," she said, "how could

you have written anything yourself! But now that it's happened, you could also finally read *Lenz.*"

Which I did, in her house, that same morning; and *Lenz* made *Auto-da-Fé,* which I *was* proud of, shrink down terribly, and I realized how decently she had behaved towards me.

This is my own sole legitimation for speaking to you today about Büchner.

I think about the stations of Büchner's life, Darmstadt, Strasbourg, Giessen, Darmstadt, Strasbourg, Zurich, and it strikes me how close they are to one another. Even for those days, it was quite neighborly. The extent to which people felt that in Darmstadt, at least about Strasbourg, is shown in his mother's last letter to Büchner. Despite her relief at his arrival in Zurich, she writes: "I feel that since you've left Strasbourg, you are really abroad; in Strasbourg, I always believed you nearby." Only Zurich, which is truly not far, seems like a foreign place to her. It is certainly characteristic of the elan in Büchner's work that one never thinks of these proximities. Other writers may not have gotten any further away; that seems proper for them; in Büchner, one is astonished. (pp. 192-94)

In Strasbourg, he learns to move about in French with complete ease, the one language is not displaced by the other. He makes friends, he gets to know Alsace quite well, and the Vosges. The new town, the new country are not such that one drowns in them. Two years in Paris would certainly have been quite different. The conspicuous thing about Büchner's life is that nothing is wasted. A nature that keeps its objects together, carefully distinguishing them, like individual people, like organs in a human being; playfulness does not become an end in itself, even dreams, even lightness have their sharp sides. A nature that is free despite the wealth of complexities, that views nothing as indissoluble and is thus, but only thus, very different from Lenz and quite reminiscent of Goethe.

No people or things are lost, and neither are any impulses that he has ever received: everything takes effect, he has no long deadlocks. It is amazing how swiftly and energetically he reacts to new circumstances. The return from Strasbourg and the narrow conditions of Darmstadt and Giessen torment him like a critical illness. But he makes his way out of the oppressive straits in the only way possible, by passing on the revolutionary impulses he has received, and without distinction as to person, unfalsified, in accordance with the essence—passing them on to people who are not after haughty separation. He founds the Society for Human Rights, the period of conspiracy begins, and with it his double life.

It can be shown in what form this double life continues after the failure of his action, how fruitful it is, how much he owes his oeuvre to it, how it leads to *Lenz* and even *Woyzeck.* The breadth of French conditions, which he experienced in Strasbourg, is brought home, to the confines of home; likewise, he takes along the most confining thing to threaten him, prison, on his escape from his homeland to Strasbourg, and he keeps the fear of it alive in him even after he succeeds in reaching the paradise of Zurich.

Büchner's fear, which never left him again, has a special character, because it is that of a man who has fought actively against danger. His daring behavior in front of the investigating judge, his efforts to free his friend Minnigerode from the prison, the replacement by his brother Wilhelm when he is subpoenaed, his letter to Gutzkow, finally the successful flight—all these things demonstrate a powerful character, which completely recognizes his situation and refuses to give in to it.

However, one views the matter too simply if one ignores **Danton's Death,** which he scrawled out during the month of preparing for his escape. Danton too is able to recognize his situation; in his talk with Robespierre, he actually does his best to worsen it. He wants it to be irreparable, he wants it to be acute; but when he is faced with a decision to save himself or flee, he *paralyzes* himself with a sentence that frequently recurs: "They won't dare!" It is the line in the play that seems most obsessive; the very first time, it makes the reader uneasy, and finally, after several repetitions, he feels it the way one would like to feel a slogan of the Revolution, but in reverse. It reveals the actual subject matter of the play, namely: should one save oneself? Danton wants to *remain:* there is a desire for persistence in him that is stronger than any danger. "Actually I have to laugh at the whole business," he says. "There is a feeling of remaining in me, which says tomorrow will be like today, and the day after tomorrow and so on and on, everything will be like now. That's empty noise, they want to frighten me, they will not dare!"

The figure of this man, who does not want to save himself, has to be set up by the author, who does want to save himself. It is his own danger, the Conciergerie and the *Arresthaus* in Darmstadt are one and the same. He writes in a fever, he has no choice, he cannot grant himself any peace and quiet until he has Danton under the guillotine. He says so to Wilhelm, his younger brother, his closest confidant during these weeks, and he also tells him that he has to flee. But various things hold him back: the thought of the falling-out with his father, the concern for friends in prison, the belief that the authorities cannot get at him, and the lack of money.

"The belief that the authorities cannot get him!" In Danton's mouth, that becomes, "They will not dare!" With this line of Danton's, Büchner tries to free himself from his own paralysis, it eggs him on to work against it. It strikes me as unquestionable that Büchner accepts Danton's fate, experiences it under a compulsion in order to escape his own.

Büchner's deeds adhere to him long after they are done, he looks back at them as if they were both undone and done. His flight, the central event in his existence, is outwardly successful, but the terror of the prison never fades from him again. He owes a debt to the friends he has left in Darmstadt, and he pays it by putting himself in their place. His letters from Strasbourg to his family are supposed to calm them and tell about his work and his prospects, but in reality they are filled with never ending disquiet. Refugees report to him about new arrests at home, and he passes all these items on to his family in detail. Although often better informed than they, he also expects their news about the same things. Nothing concerns him more, nothing interests him more. He, who is very aware of the value of freedom, whose work does everything to preserve it, as do his alertness and lucid appreciation of dangers—he feels as though he were also with his friends in prison. Their fear is his, one senses it when he writes about executions that have not even taken place. Ever since his second arrival in Strasbourg, one can speak about a new double life of his, which continues, albeit differently, his earlier life at home, in the time of conspiracy. The one life, external, factual, is the one he leads as an emigré, and he painstakingly tries to keep it free of any grounds for being extradited. The other

life is the one he leads in his mind and feelings at home, with his unfortunate friends. The necessity of flight is still constantly imminent, the month of preparing for it in Darmstadt has never ended.

It is the fate of the emigré that he would like to believe he is safe. He cannot be, for those he has left behind—the others—are not safe.

Two months after his arrival in Strasbourg, Gutzkow, in a letter to him, mentions "your novella **Lenz.**" Büchner, soon after his arrival, must have written to him about his plan for such a novella.

There would be much to say about the importance of his tale, about the things connecting Büchner to Lenz. Here, I would like to remark only one thing, which, measured by all that could be said, is certainly minor: the great extent to which the story is fed and colored by the flight. The Vosges were very familiar to Büchner, who had wandered through them with his friends; and he had also described them in a letter to his parents two years earlier. On the twentieth, when Lenz comes through the mountains, they are transformed into a landscape of angst. Lenz's condition, if it can at all be summed up in *one,* is a state of flight, which, however, falls apart into many, small, apparently senseless individual flights. No prison threatens him, but he is expelled, he is exiled from his homeland. His homeland, the only region in which he could breathe freely, was Goethe, and Goethe has banished him. Now he flees to places connected to Goethe, more or less remote; he comes, attaches himself, and tries to remain. But the exile, which is inside him and still in effect, forces him to destroy everything again. In small, befuddled motions, repeated over and over, he flees into water or out the window, to the next village, the church, a farmer's house, a dead child. He would have believed himself saved if he could have brought the child back to life.

In Lenz, Büchner found his own restlessness, the fear of flight which overcame him whenever he entered the prison to see his friends. He walked along a piece of his brittle road with Lenz, transformed into him and at the same time his companion, who saw him unswervingly from the outside as an Other. There was no end for it, no end for the expulsion, for the flight, there was only the same thing over and over again. "Thus he lived on." He wrote that last sentence and left him.

The Other, however, the man Büchner was known as in his milieu at the time, pursued a rigorous and tenacious scientific work on the nervous system of the barbels, thereby gaining the respect of natural scientists in Strasbourg and Zurich. He got his doctorate and went to Zurich for a test lecture.

In the Zurich period, which lasted no longer than four months, he succeeded in asserting and proving himself. He immediately became a docent, important men attended his lectures. A long letter to him testifies to his father's forgiveness. He likes Switzerland: "Friendly villages with lovely houses everywhere!" He praises the "healthy, strong people," and the "simple, good, purely republican government."

Right after that, in the same letter, the last extant letter to his family, written on November 20, 1836, the worst possible news flashes up like lightning: "Minnigerode is dead, as I am informed, that is to say, he was tortured to death for three years. Three years!" So close together: the salvation in the Zurich paradise and the mortal torment of the friend at home.

I think it was this news that led to the final manuscript of *Woyzeck.* Like no other work of his, it addresses the people at home. He may never have found out that the news was wrong. But in any event, it had its impact on him. Two years and four months have passed since Minnigerode's arrest; the fact that the time is prolonged into three years for him, who actually has always remained in Darmstadt, is not surprising. And yet this emphatic three recalls the imprisonment of another, that of the historical Woyzeck. Over three years passed between the murder of his mistress and his public execution. The case was known to Büchner, of course, from Court Councillor Clarus' report on the murderer Woyzeck.

Aside from the news of his friend's death in prison, aside from the acute memory of the oppressed and protesting friends at home, the conception of *Woyzeck* took in something else that would not necessarily occur to us: philosophy.

Part of Büchner's completeness is the fact that he confronted philosophy with grinding teeth. He has a faculty for it; Lüning, who met him as a student in Zurich, notices a "certain, utterly decided definiteness in making statements." Yet Büchner feels repelled by philosophical *language*. Very early, in a letter to his Alsatian friend August Stöber, he writes: "I am throwing myself with utter violence into philosophy. The artificial language is disgusting; I think that for human things one ought to find human expressions." And to Gutzkow, two years later, when he had already mastered this language: "I am becoming quite stupid in the study of philosophy, I am getting to know the poverty of the human mind from a new side." He delves into philosophy without becoming addicted, nor does he sacrifice a single grain of reality to it. He takes it seriously where it operates in the lowest, in Woyzeck, and he mocks it in those who feel superior to Woyzeck.

Woyzeck, a soldier, like the mountebank's monkey, "the lowest level of the human race," driven by voices and orders, a prisoner running around free, destined to be a prisoner, placed on prison fare, always the same, peas, degraded to an animal by the doctor, who dares to tell him: "Woyzeck, man is free; in man, individuality is transfigured into freedom," which only means that Woyzeck ought to be able to hold back his urine. Freedom to be resigned to any abuse of his human nature, freedom of enslavement for a few pennies, which he gets for feeding on peas. And then one is amazed to hear the doctor say: "Woyzeck, you are philosophizing again"—like the tribute paid by the booth-owner to the trained horse. But in the next sentence, the tribute is reduced to an "aberratio," and in the next, scientifically precise, to an "aberratio mentalis partialis," with a bonus.

The captain, however, the good, good man, who thinks he is good because things are good for him, who fears a fast shave like anything fast because of the tremendous time, because of eternity—the captain rebukes Woyzeck: "You think too much, that takes its toll, you always look so driven."

Büchner's study of individual philosophical doctrines affected *Woyzeck* in a different, a more hidden way. I am thinking of the frontal presentation of important characters, something that could be called their *self-denunciation.*

The assurance with which they exclude anything that is not they, the aggressive insistence on themselves, even in their choice of words, the heedless renunciation of the real world, in which, however, they strike about, powerfully and hatefully—all this has something of the offensive self-assertion of philosophers. These figures present themselves fully in their very first lines. The captain as well as the doctor and certainly the drum-major appear as proclaimers of their own persons. Mockingly or boastingly or enviously, they draw their borders, and they draw them against one and the same despised creature, whom they see under them and who is meant to serve them as an underling.

Woyzeck is the victim of all three. The doctor and the captain have learned their philosophy, and Woyzeck has real ideas to oppose them with. *His* philosophy is concrete, tied to fear and pain and contemplation. He is afraid when he thinks, and the voices driving him are more real than the captain's emotions at his coat, which hangs there, or the doctor's immortal pea experiments. In contrast to them, he is not presented frontally; from start to finish, he consists of live, often unexpected reactions. Since he is always exposed, he is always awake, and the words he finds in his alertness are words in a state of innocence. They are not ground up and misused, they are not coins, weapons, or stories, they are words, as though they had only just come into being. Even if he takes them over without understanding them, they go their own ways in him: the Freemasons hollow out the earth for him: "Hollow, do you hear? Everything hollow down there! The Freemasons!"

Into how many people is the world split up in *Woyzeck!* In *Danton's Death,* the characters still have much too much in common, they are all of a sweeping eloquence, and Danton is by no means the only man of wit among them. One can try to explain that with the fact that it is an eloquent time, and the spokesmen of the Revolution, among whom the drama takes place, have ultimately all attained prestige through the use of words. But then we remember Marion's story—it too is a summing-up, one could not conceive a more perfect one for her, and we must reluctantly resign ourselves to the idea that *Danton's Death* is a drama out of the school of rhetoric—to be sure, the most measureless of these schools: Shakespeare's.

It is distinguished from the plays of other disciples by its urgency and rapidity and by a special substance existing nowhere else in German literature and made up equally of fire and ice. It is a fire that forces one to run, and an ice in which everything appears transparent, and one runs to keep pace with the fire and tarries to peer into the ice.

Less than two years later, Büchner, with his *Woyzeck,* succeeded in performing the most perfect upset in literature: the discovery of the lowly. This discovery presupposes mercy; but only when the mercy is hidden, when it is dumb, when it does not articulate itself—only then is the lowly *intact.* The writer who gives himself airs with his feelings, who openly puffs up the lowly with his mercy, will sully and destroy it. Woyzeck is driven by voices and by other people's words, yet the driver has left him untouched. In this chastity regarding the lowly, there is no one comparable to Büchner even today.

In the last days of his life, Büchner is shaken with fever fantasies, today, little is known about their nature and content. These few items are in Caroline's Schulz's notes, in her own words. She writes:

"14th[February]. . . . Around eight o'clock, the delirium came back, and it was odd that he often spoke about his fantasies, judged them himself when we persuaded him they were not true. A recurrent fantasy was his imagining he had been extradited. . . .

"15th. . . . He spoke somewhat heavily when coming to his senses, but as soon as he was delirious, he spoke quite fluently. He told me a long coherent story: about his being brought out of the city yesterday, about first giving a speech in the marketplace, etc.

"16th. . . . The patient wanted to go out several times because he imagined he could be imprisoned or believed he already was imprisoned and wanted to escape."

I think if we had these fantasies in their true wording, we would be very close to Woyzeck: even in this report, which is reduced and mellowed by grief and love and which lacks the terror of a driven man, we can feel something of Woyzeck himself. Büchner still had Woyzeck in him when he died on the nineteenth.

It is not pointless to meditate over Büchner's possible later life, because it keeps one from looking for any sense in his death. It was as senseless as any death, but his death makes this senselessness particularly blatant. He was not fulfilled despite the weight and maturity of the works he left behind. It is part of his nature that he would never have been completed, not even later. He stands there as the pure exemplar of man who has to remain incomplete. His many abilities, alternately pinch-hitting for one another, testify to a nature that, in its inexhaustibility, demands an endless life. (pp. 195-202)

> Elias Canetti, "Georg Büchner: Speech at the Awarding of the Georg Büchner Prize," in his The Conscience of Words, translated by Joachim Neugroschel, The Seabury Press, 1979, pp. 192-202.

## RONALD HAUSER (essay date 1974)

[*Hauser explores some of the themes and narrative techniques of* Lenz.]

Büchner's **Lenz** has little in common with the novels and novellas dealing with the life and problems of the artist which were so much in vogue in Germany throughout the nineteenth century. It has even less in common with the sensationalism which, traditionally, dominated works exploring the question of insanity. In fact it would be difficult to categorize **Lenz** in any way, since it stands quite outside the German narrative tradition. (p. 51)

From the point of view of nineteenth-century literary concepts, the most striking feature of **Lenz** is its weak, almost nonexistent plot. Action is rarely the focal point; and even when it is treated in some detail, a feeling of nonchalance prevails. Events are reported in an undramatic, matter-of-fact, and often telegraphic style with a disregard for chronological and topical sequence. Frequently, the narrative only summarizes action; that is, instead of telling precisely what happens, the narrator offers only a brief sketch, as in the following passage: "Inside the huts there was lively activity: they thronged around Oberlin; he admonished, gave advice, consoled; everywhere trusting glances, prayer. The people told about dreams, premonitions. Then quickly, back to the practical life: Laying out roads, digging canals, going to school." A whole range of events is here concentrated into a few sentences. The language is cut to the bone, in an effort to achieve the greatest possible economy. Verbs and conjunctions are omitted, and hours are compressed into single phrases. Although not all action scenes are as abbreviated as this one,

it is characteristic for Büchner's studied inclination to minimize the importance of action.

Even more important to the structure of the narrative is the lack of connection between the various bits of "plot." Instead of giving a sense of continuity to the work, fragments of action tend rather to stress the often abrupt shifts in direction. Occasionally, such shifts even occur in the middle of a sentence, as in the following case: "Lenz went to his room pleased. He thought of a text for his sermon and lost himself in contemplation, and his nights became quiet." After a relatively detailed description of a conversation between Oberlin and Lenz, which precedes the quoted passage, a single sentence brings the evening's activities to an end and, with the interposition of a comma, lunges an unspecified number of days ahead. To be sure, the sentence does, in a way, connect two phases, but the connection does no more than underscore the gap by calling attention to it. (pp. 51-2)

The lack of continuity in the action is matched by an equally studied fragmentation in the realm of ideas. Theological, esthetic, and mystical notions are presented in the form of more or less extensive fragments of conversation, some of which are reported in detail. Yet they are scattered in such a way as to suggest anything but a systematic approach. To be sure, a feeling for Lenz's *Weltanschauung* develops, but Büchner is more concerned with keeping it from causing a distraction than with formulating clear concepts. Just like the action sequences, strings of ideas are sometimes abbreviated and cut off abruptly in order to reduce their weight:

> He [Lenz] expressed himself further. He said that each thing possessed its own inexpressible harmony . . . that higher forms with more organs were able to better choose, to express, to understand, and were therefore more deeply affected; and that lower forms were more repressed, more restricted, and therefore enjoyed a greater degree of tranquility. He pursued his line of thought further, but Oberlin put an end to it because it led him too far afield from his simple ideas.

Reminiscent of Goethe's biologically oriented philosophical speculations, Lenz here begins to develop a system of thought apparently aimed at relating certain psychological phenomena to the biological complexity of each organism. That such ideas touch close to the center of Büchner's intellectual interests can be seen from the fact that, in the heated attack upon the teleological approach to biology which serves as an introduction to his anatomical study, **"On the Cranial Nerves,"** he invokes much the same premise about the inner harmony of all living beings, in which he discerns the operation of a single fundamental law. The speculative extension of this life-governing law into the realm of psychology could certainly be expected to show some signs of deep personal involvement. Yet, despite the fact that the ideas have clearly captivated Lenz's imagination, they are left dangling in mid-air. Not only that; Büchner further underscores the relative lack of substantive importance in the arguments by adding the clause: "He pursued his line of thought further," thus, in effect, driving home the message that, while there is more to the argument, the whole thing is hardly worth reporting. A better way of undermining the ideas is hardly conceivable! (pp. 52-3)

That Büchner gives such seemingly indifferent treatment even to those ideas which lie close to the center of his own interests can only be explained as resulting from overriding esthetic considerations. His methodical refusal to buttress continuity either with action or with a systematic train of thought represents a radical departure from narrative traditions. The important questions, of course, are not *whether* the narrative represents a formal rebellion or even *how* it does so; they are, rather, *why* did Büchner strike out in new directions, and precisely *what* were his esthetic aims?

Fortunately, Büchner facilitates the search for answers to these questions by offering a number of direct hints about his artistic goals within the text. Indeed, his most formidable statement on the nature and purpose of art is contained in *Lenz.* Perhaps *concealed* would be a better term, for the substance of the dialogue which yields the crucial ideas also bears the narrator's usual tone of disdain for such matters. This dialogue, too, is left hanging in the air in such a way as to make it seem that the narrator had anything but a burning interest in it. (pp. 53-4)

Understated as they are, the contents of this dialogue are nevertheless described at sufficient length to offer at least a starting point for understanding the esthetic basis of the novel approach represented by *Lenz.* (p. 54)

The discussion takes place between Lenz and his friend Kaufmann, whose role is limited to that of a kind of straight man, that is, he represents common, rather philistine views against which Lenz then directs his attack. It is Kaufmann who raises the subject during a dinner conversation by declaring his adherence to the latest literary vogue:

> The period of idealism was then in fashion, and Kaufmann was its disciple. Lenz spoke violently against it. He said that those poets who claimed to represent reality hadn't even a conception of it; nonetheless they are more bearable than those who want to glorify reality. He said that the good Lord had indeed made the world as it should be, and we ought not to think ourselves capable of improving upon it; our sole endeavor should be to imitate Him a bit.

Lenz's two-pronged attack upon literary trends hits hardest against what is called the "period of idealism." The actual target is the esthetic tradition associated with Schiller (1759-1805). That point is clarified by [a letter written to his parents in] defense of *Danton,* where Büchner, using substantially the same argument, does not hesitate to call the devil by name [see letter dated 1835]. For the sake of at least a semblance of historical accuracy, Schiller could not be mentioned in *Lenz,* since he did not appear on the literary scene until several years after 1778. Yet the omission of the name can hardly obliterate the anachronism of the argument itself which, more properly, fits into Büchner's own time—a time that, as he might have expressed it, still suffered from the excessive weight of Schiller's influence.

The inclusion of such an attack on Schiller in *Lenz* runs directly counter to Büchner's conception of the poet as an historian who simply "creates history for the second time." In other words, the anachronism offered good reasons for hesitation. The fact that Büchner nevertheless included it shows that he must have considered it crucially important—so important, in fact, that he was willing to sacrifice one of his fundamental esthetic principles for it. (pp. 54-5)

In terms of the theme of *Lenz* (a young man's battle against madness), an attack upon idealism in literature, or any other esthetic argument, hardly seems crucial enough to warrant a compromise of principle. The previously discussed technique of de-emphasis in the realm of ideas, after all, shows that in terms of the theme, Büchner did not consider the episode to be exceptionally important. It therefore seems likely that with the Lenz-Kaufmann dialogue Büchner wanted to throw light not upon the content but upon the form of the work, and perhaps upon the relationship between form and content.

Actually, the previously quoted passage constitutes more than a mere attack upon idealism. Those who "claim to represent reality" but fail to do so are hardly spared. The important problem raised is the general failure of poets to come to terms with reality. (pp. 55-6)

If he wishes to come to terms with reality, the poet must absolutely restrict himself to the "sole endeavor" of imitating nature (God-made reality). This is the heart of the argument. Everything else is only an elaboration of this idea. Taken literally, it means that literature is limited to descriptive techniques which have the sole aim of reproducing the likeness of life. When he continues the discussion, Büchner-Lenz goes on to explain how he thinks the artist should proceed. Notably, there is no differentiation between the various media of art:

> I demand of art that it be life . . . nothing else matters; we then have no need to ask whether it is beautiful or ugly. . . . These people can't so much as draw a dog's kennel. They try to create ideal forms, but all I have seen of their work looks more like wooden dolls. Let them try just once to immerse themselves in the life of humble people and then reproduce this again in all its movements, its implications, in its subtle, scarcely discernible play of expressions.

"Life," as Büchner uses the term here, obviously does not mean biography. It refers to those inner forces which constitute the essence of being. What happens to people, where they go, and what they do, is of artistic importance only insofar as it represents an outward expression of these forces. Life reveals itself through the silent language of precisely such expressions—Büchner calls it "a scarcely discernible play of expression"—, and it should be the artist's exclusive aim to translate this language into poetry, painting, or sculpture. To accomplish this he must first immerse himself in the life of others, so that he will understand even the finest subtleties and nuances. Ordinary people are portrayed as the best models because their simple ways offer the most direct access to the essence of life which, as Büchner himself goes on to point out, is to be found in the "organs of feeling." These, he claims, "are the same in almost all men; the only difference is the thickness of the crust through which we must break."

Only when the artist has immersed himself in the life of the people, when he has broken through the crust and exposed the organs of feeling to view, and when he has learned to read the language of wordless expression, should he turn to the technical problem of reproduction; and Büchner also makes himself quite clear as to the guiding principle of this last step in the creative process. He circumscribes this principle by means of a symbol (Lenz is still speaking):

> As I walked in the valley yesterday I saw two girls sitting on a rock; one of them was binding up her hair, and the other helped her with it. Her golden hair hung down, her face serious and pale and young, her dress was black, and the other girl so at-

tentive to help her. . . . One might wish at times to be a Medusa's head, so as to be able to transform such a group into stone and summon the world to see it. Then they rose, and the beautiful grouping was destroyed; but as they descended between the rocks they formed another picture.

The Medusa's head, with its power to turn living beings into stone, obviously is meant as a symbol for the highest aspirations of the artist. Perfection in art is represented by an exact but frozen image of life. While this conception is primarily a somewhat amplified echo of the previously expressed demand for the faithful reproduction of reality, it is rich in overtones. Particularly striking is the heavy emphasis it places upon the static nature of art. Büchner wants to leave no doubt that the Medusa's head symbolizes perfection in all mimetic arts, including literature, when, a few sentences later, he has Lenz point out the difficulty of holding such "pictures" in the mind and transferring them to paper. The very fact, then, that Büchner chooses to symbolize the transformation of life into art by creating a completely static ideal strongly suggests that he considers any attempt to capture movement or action by means of literary techniques as superfluous and unrelated to the essential qualities of art. (pp. 56-8)

Büchner, of course, does not argue with the fact that poetry can simulate the fluidity of life. What he does suggest is that there is, at best, only very limited value in this power. The last sentence of the above quotation recognizes the fact that a series of "pictures" can produce the feeling of temporal continuity in art; but, at the same time, it puts forward the idea that these pictures should not be brought into close contact with one another. In fact, the stress is on their clear demarcation. The first image of the girls sitting in a group is "destroyed" before the next, completely different one takes shape. The action connecting the two petrified moments apparently reveals nothing essential about "life." The unmistakable implication is that the power to penetrate the "crust" and reveal those inner forces to which the artist owes his full allegiance is vested solely in the frozen image.

Even more important is the closely associated implication that life itself gives expression to its essence only in motionless pictures. Indeed, this must be considered the guiding principle of the emerging conception of artistic form, for it gives a truly functional meaning to the basic esthetic tenet that "art be life." Not only is the content of the work of art to be limited to the realistic representation of life, but the form—the vehicle of artistic expression—must be dictated by the manner in which the inner forces of man come to be expressed. In other words, art must communicate in the same way in which life communicates. (p. 58)

The literary form suggested by these considerations consists of static scenes or "pictures," each of which captures a revealing moment and then dissolves to make way for another. That such a chain of relatively independent images has no need for external unification is stressed once more when Lenz continues his argument: "The most beautiful pictures, the most swelling tones, form a group and then dissolve. Only one thing remains: an unending beauty which passes from one form to another, eternally revealed, eternally unchanged." The only necessary unifying force is the integrity of the individual scenes, for it is precisely the endless variation of the forms that unveils the eternally unchanging beauty inherent in the revelation of the inner spirit of man.

There can be no doubt that the narrative form of *Lenz* reflects

the esthetic ideals set forth within the text. To be sure, the argument does not represent anything that might be called a systematic approach—in a way, more problems are raised than solved by it—but it does point to a number of priorities which quite obviously guided Büchner. Moreover, the definition of artistic aims within the work, even on a highly abstract level, actually makes its form thematic. *Lenz* is not only meant as a work of art in its own right, but also as a kind of working model demonstrating specific literary theories. On the one hand, the theory illuminates the artistic aims of the work; while at the same time, the work constitutes a practical application of the theory. For example, if applied to *Lenz,* the theory would seem to demand anything but the story of a young man's experiences: Like any "true" work of art, it should strictly limit itself to the portrayal of the inner forces of life. The very last sentence of the work calls special attention to the importance of exactly this limitation, thereby underscoring Büchner's overall aim: "So (in this way) his life went on." In effect, this means: the portrait is complete, Lenz's "life" continues without change, regardless of where he goes or what happens to him; or, in terms of the theory, once the outer "crust" has been penetrated and the "organs of feeling" exposed, nothing else is of artistic significance. (pp. 58-9)

While the theory elucidates the goals of the work, the work, in turn, defines its implications as it applies specifically to literature. Central among the theoretical principles is the demand for a rather complex relationship between artist and subject. The necessity for the self-immersion of the artist in his subject is juxtaposed with the seemingly conflicting demand for the cold objectivity of the Medusa's head. In purely theoretical terms, this represents a somewhat disturbing dichotomy. On the one hand, the artist must enter into the world of the subject's feelings, while on the other, he is obliged to remain a distant and uninvolved observer in order to avoid the danger of falsification. Turning to the text would seem to offer the most direct approach to a possible resolution. How did Büchner actually satisfy both of these divergent demands in his work?

Besides helping to explain the theory, the answer to this question throws light on one of the thorniest problems in *Lenz.* The nature and urgency of this problem is revealed in one of the most recent interpretations of the work [*Georg Büchner* by Herbert Lindenberger] where the author-subject relationship is summed up in one sentence: "The story is told from Lenz's point of view; although it is in the third person, we view the events almost wholly (but not quite) as Lenz sees them, without direct comment from the author." Indeed, this is almost (but not quite) an accurate description of the point of view; but a fine distinction here means the difference between the success and the failure of Büchner's experiment. If Büchner really had wanted to tell the story from Lenz's point of view, he could hardly have chosen a less suitable vehicle than a straightforward third-person approach. It is fairly clear that the critic just quoted had certain misgivings about the apparent contradiction—between the first-person point of view and the third-person form—and rightly so. But there is yet another objection. A first-person point of view in the story would make the symbol of the Medusa's head into an empty slogan having no relation whatsoever to Büchner's own narrative style; to emulate the Medusa's head, the poet, at the very least, must keep his identity separate from that of his subject. Hence the question as to whether or not the story actually is told from Lenz's point of view is a crucial one, for if it is, the work would have to be condemned as clumsy and unsuccessful on at least two counts. Neither the choice of a fake third person nor the spinning of esthetic theories stressing the necessity for objectivity could be artistically justified. Yet, on a close reading of the text, it does almost seem as if the reader were seeing the world through Lenz's eyes. Almost, but not quite—and therein lies the vital, if hardly discernible, distinction. It is not that "we view the events almost wholly (but not quite) as Lenz sees them"; it is rather that the reader sees the events wholly from almost (but not quite) the same viewpoint as Lenz. Never does the author—or the reader—look at the world through the lenses of Lenz's eyes, but he repeatedly comes very close to doing that, so close, in fact, that, at times, only the relentless use of the third person form upholds the distinction.

To understand this distinction it is necessary to consider not only the point of view—that is, from what relative point the action is seen—but also the direction of the narrator's gaze. The Medusa's head directs its eyes toward the subject at all times, and never away, no matter how close to the subject it might be. Immersed in its subject, its eyes still would be directed toward the center and not toward the outside. This model defines quite precisely Büchner's relationship to his subject. Basically adopting a typical third-person narrative stance, he views Lenz from the outside. But frequently, after having given a picture of the outer reality, he immerses himself in Lenz's being. When he immerses himself in this way, he continues to direct his gaze toward the center of Lenz's inner world; he does not, so to speak, turn round and look back out through Lenz's eyes. To be sure, the outside world finds its reflection within—but only after the impressions have penetrated Lenz's consciousness, and have become part of his inner world. In other words, Büchner first describes Lenz and the people and objects around him as an outside observer might perceive them, and then he enters into Lenz's consciousness and records the latter's intellectual and emotional reactions to the aspects of reality he has described. Therefore, Lenz's actions are not seen in relation to his own, possibly erroneous and, in any case, subjective perceptions, but against a background of a reality as observed by the "objective" narrator.

Büchner's "pictures" of Lenz are, of course, not limited to visual impressions. Immersion in Lenz's inner world allows him to tune in on all sensations and feelings as well. The picture of this inner reality is no less objectively drawn than that of the outer realm. Büchner neither analyzes nor empathizes with his hero's mental responses; he simply describes them and allows them to communicate directly with the reader. The result is that the reader comes to understand and sympathize with Lenz but does not actually identify with him. Throughout the work, Lenz maintains his own clearly separate identity; he always remains a third person, not only in a grammatical, but also in a real, sense.

The opening passage of *Lenz* establishes just this kind of relationship between the reader and the protagonist. Büchner does not hesitate to use what might be called literary shock treatment to place the reader at the proper angle. Italics are used here to make the distinction between *inner* and outer reality graphically evident:

> On the twentieth of January Lenz went through the mountains. The peaks and the high regions white with snow, down the valleys: gray stone, green surfaces, boulders and fir trees. It was damp and cold;

the water rushed down the rocks and leaped over the road. The fir branches hung down heavily in the damp air. Gray clouds drifted across the sky, but everything so dense—and then the mist rose up from below and moved through the brush—so languidly, so heavily. *He walked on indifferently, the road meant nothing to him, sometimes uphill, then again downhill. He did not feel tired, only occasionally he regretted not being able to walk upside down.*

Both in time and in space, the first glimpse of Lenz comes from a distance. . . . The landscape is like a roughly sketched background in a painting; its functions are striking a mood and focusing attention upon the central subject. After the second sentence, the description proceeds beyond visual impressions. In remarkably few words, Büchner evokes all the feelings that make a mid-winter day a reality: coldness, dampness, oppressive closeness, languidness, heaviness of spirit. The scene is neither beautiful nor ugly. In fact, it is hardly a scene at all; it is more like a force impressing itself upon the reader's feelings, and as it presses in, the focus shifts to Lenz's inner reaction to that force. But the reader is in no way swept up in Lenz's feelings; he understands them, but does not share his response to the surroundings. Büchner creates a distance between his hero and the reader by eliciting an emotional response toward a winter mountain scene from the reader, a response that is totally different from that of his hero. Lenz feels indifferent toward the described landscape; he is only aware of the up and down of the road, but not of the snow and the water, the coldness and dampness, or the high peaks and the valleys below. Right from the beginning then, Büchner establishes for himself a clearly separate identity as a narrator who is aware of many things that escape the hero's notice. (pp. 59-63)

Though the focus is always upon Lenz, the point of view shifts freely from outside to inside. The author looks at Lenz from a distance, sees him in his environment, and then penetrates his emotional existence. There seem to be two separate, well-defined levels of reality which might be identified simply as outer and inner reality. Some other passages, however, present a more complex structure. In these, three levels can be distinguished. Between the outer level and the level of emotional or intellectual response, a third level, that of Lenz's perceptions, is interposed. The following is perhaps the most concentrated example; again the various levels are distinguished by the use of varying print:

> He went through the village. The lights shone through the windows, he looked in while passing: CHILDREN SITTING AT THE TABLE, OLD WOMEN, GIRLS, THEIR FACES CALM AND SERENE. *It seemed to him the light streamed from their faces; his spirit was lightened, he was almost at the parsonage in Waldbach.*

First, Lenz is seen from the outside as he walks through the little village. Lights shining through the windows are only peripherally visible. Just as in the opening passage, the observer or narrator keeps his eyes focused upon Lenz. But then the observer immerses himself within Lenz and describes those objects within the scene which Lenz perceives. Lenz sees much more detail because he is looking directly at the lighted windows while the observer was looking at Lenz walking past the houses. However, not everything that is there for Lenz to see, but only those details which strike his consciousness—the sitting children, the serene faces of the old women and the girls—are recorded. Finally, the perceptions are transformed into psychological responses; the observer now examines Lenz's emotions, which reflect not only his perceptions but also his intellect. Lenz knows that the lighted windows signal the proximity of his goal. The perceptions are interpreted in terms of this knowledge and translated into emotional reality: His spirit is lightened; he finds release from the anxieties that had previously plagued him.

The dimensions of Lenz's inner world are put in perspective by the juxtaposition of the various levels. In fact, it is this three-dimensional representation of reality which allows Büchner to dispense with explanations and analyses of his hero's thoughts and behavior, even though the central issue of the work is the psychology of madness. Again and again, the reader is confronted with a scene or event witnessed by both Lenz and the narrator, whose eyes never stray away from Lenz. The narrator then pursues the effect of the scene or event into the realm of Lenz's consciousness, where its perception and mental impact become matters of simple description. Sometimes the observer moves in and out several times in a single passage. While the process of shifting from one level to another gives a certain perspective of depth, it also necessitates the sacrifice of close chronological continuity both in the representation of actions and in the realm of ideas. Pursuing a complex series of actions through all three levels of reality would be laborious if not impossible. (pp. 64-5)

Of course, Büchner does not altogether dispense with the representation of actions, but he does limit strict chronological sequences to very short periods of time. An examination of precisely those passages which seem to be most oriented toward action offers perhaps the best method of demonstrating just how the concern for depth dominates his style, for it is in these that the maintenance of several levels creates the greatest technical problems. Without question, the most extensively detailed and vivid action sequence in the work is the following:

> Finally it was time to leave. Because the parsonage was too small, they took him across the road and gave him a room in the schoolhouse. He went upstairs. IT WAS COLD UP THERE; A WIDE ROOM THAT WAS EMPTY, WITH A HIGH BED IN THE BACKGROUND. He placed the lamp on the table and paced back and forth. *He thought again about the day just past, how he had come here, where he was. The room in the parsonage with its lights and dear faces seemed like a shadow now, like a dream, and he felt empty again, as on the mountain; but he could not fill this emptiness with anything.* The light was out, darkness swallowed up all things. *He felt gripped by an unnamable fear.* He leaped from bed, ran down the stairs to the front of the house; *but all in vain,* EVERYTHING WAS DARK, *nothing—he himself was a dream. Isolated thoughts rushed through his mind; he held fast to them. It seemed he should be always repeating the "Lord's Prayer." He was lost; an obscure instinct drove him to save himself.* He thrust himself against the stones, he tore himself with his nails; *the pain began, bringing him to his senses.* He threw himself into the fountain but the water wasn't deep, he splashed about.

Again, the observer initially views the subject from the outside. Although the individual images, even in the first few sentences, are too widely spaced to give the sequence real moment-to-moment fluidity, compared to other, far more static scenes, they do present a fairly smooth continuum of action

until the instant Lenz reaches his room. At that point, there is the first shift of levels. The room, presumably, is described as Lenz perceives it. Then, in rapid succession, there are a number of shifts from one level to another, the primary stress being, throughout, on the innermost one. Perception is translated into desperation and terror and ultimately expresses itself in renewed action. While there is an overall chronological integration, there is a certain loss of continuity at each level. For example, on the outer level, Lenz's pacing back and forth is followed by his jumping from the bed, leaving an obvious gap in the narrative sequence. (pp. 65-6)

Without doubt, Büchner's multi-leveled perspective tends to subdue even violent, relatively impulsive action. It clearly does not offer the best vehicle for capturing the sheer drama of human action, and, of course, that is hardly the aim of the few action sequences in *Lenz.* On the contrary, it seems to be Büchner's purpose to counteract sensationalism without going so far as to deny the existence of the sensational. By superimposing the inner world upon the outer, he brings the reader face to face with terror in such a way that it hardly terrorizes, and with the comic in such a way that it has little comic effect. Neither is the reader drawn emotionally into Lenz's existence (Lenz's fear, in the absence of a genuine external cause, inspires sympathy but not fear), nor is he alienated by the absurdities to which Lenz's life exposes him. A delicate balance keeps attention focused on the real problem. Even the action scenes are aimed at defining what Lenz is, not what he does.

In every detail *Lenz* is so structured as to force the reader's attention away from external appearances and toward the inner reality of existence. Büchner shows little interest in the ravings of a madman; what obviously intrigues him is the nature of madness. By means of his multi-leveled structure he attempts to show that insanity is not the moving force, but the effect of Lenz's condition. Rather than personal failings, the repeated mental crises are seen as relatively normal responses to the human condition. (pp. 67-8)

Perhaps the most fundamental stabilizing force in Lenz is his faith in God and love for the nature He created. Not only does his religious belief form the basis of his concepts of nature and art, but in his anguish he turns to it for comfort; reciting prayers or reading from the Bible. Yet he cannot still the doubts which come over him at crucial moments. . . . Upon the death of Friederike, a young girl in a neighboring village, he reacts with violent fury:

> He felt that he could raise a monstrous fist to the Heavens and tear God down and drag Him through His clouds; as if he could grind the world together with his teeth and spit it out into the Creator's face. . . . Lenz laughed loudly and with that laugh atheism took hold of him surely and calmly and firmly. . . . Everything was empty and hollow. . . .
>
> The following day he awoke horrified by his state on the previous day. He stood now at an abyss, and derived a mad delight from looking down into it and reliving his torment. Then his terror increased; he was faced with his sin against the Holy Ghost.

The cruelty of God's seeming indifference to human suffering is unbearable to Lenz. Yet atheism, the intellectual alternative, shakes the very foundation of his being. He is trapped in an irresolvable conflict. Facing the void of a Godless world is as impossible for him as is blind faith in a God who is capable of inflicting pain and suffering upon His creatures.

It is the desperation of this conflict which casts the darkest shadow over Lenz's life. His surroundings take on the appearance of the unreal. If there is no creator, how can there be a creation? This question, though it is not expressed in the text, always seems to hover over Lenz's most terrifying crises. The world seems to dissolve into a substanceless dream. The words *dream* and *dreamlike* appear with astonishing frequency to describe Lenz's perceptions, as, for example, in the following passage:

> As his surroundings grew darker in shadow, everything seemed dreamlike to him, repugnant; anxiety took hold of him like a child who must sleep in the dark; he felt as if he were blind. And now it grew, this mountain of madness shot up at his feet; the hopeless thought that everything was a dream spread itself out in front of him; he clung to all solid objects. Figures rapidly passed him by, he pressed toward them, they were shadows, life withdrew from him, his limbs were numb.
>
> (pp. 68-9)

Lenz is stimulated . . . by the severity of his doubt. As soon as he comes to his senses, he devotes all his energies to the restoration of the threatened superstructure. With fervor he throws himself into various acts of penitence, helps Oberlin with parish duties, prepares a sermon for the Sunday services, and visits the sick in the hope of allaying their suffering. But when his senses again become impeded, when darkness descends or when mists shroud the landscape, the superstructure begins to collapse anew, and the cycle begins again. Fear turns to panic, he feels himself slipping into a dream world, then come feverish, instinctive attempts to stimulate the senses (scratching himself, pounding his head against the ground, throwing himself into cold water, etc.), followed by penitence and a relatively peaceful period often dominated by religious fervor and the desire to help others.

Mainly due to the unique structure of *Lenz,* which allows the reader an objective view of the hero's inner life without losing sight of the outer world, a remarkable inversion of values is produced. If Lenz's actions were seen purely from the outside they would certainly appear as inexplicable ravings of a madman. While they might engender compassion for the sufferer, the reader would not feel personally addressed by the work. Much the same would be true if the story were told from the point of view of Lenz himself. The reader would be in a position to reject all association between Lenz's condition and his own, for he would be led to feel that the work represented the twisted conceptions of a diseased mind.

As it is, however, the reader cannot disassociate himself from Lenz's fate quite so readily. It is evident that Lenz's frenzied outbursts do not result from imaginary or even irrational fears. On the contrary, the fears are well founded in the human condition as Büchner sees it. They stem from questions which the mind is not equipped to resolve, questions which cast a shadow over all human endeavors. On the other hand, faith, whether it is in God, or in a universal order, or even faith in a world which lies beyond immediate perceptions, no matter how essential for survival, can be recognized as irrational response. In a moment of reflection Lenz himself gives expression to the idea that man actually invents his reality:

"Oh, this boredom! I scarcely know anymore what to say; I've drawn all kinds of figures on the walls." Oberlin told him to turn to God; this made Lenz laugh and say: "How I wish I were as fortunate as you to have so comfortable a pastime. One could very easily spend his time that way. Everything for idleness' sake. After all, most people pray out of boredom, others fall in love out of boredom, some are virtuous, some vicious, and I am nothing, absolutely nothing! I don't even want to take my own life: it would be too boring!"

Since the idea that all of man's actions result from his dread of boredom reappears almost verbatim in *Leonce and Lena,* it obviously embodies one of Büchner's central conceptions.

The clear and tragic implication is that man has invented an arbitrary *raison d'être* to give substance to his strivings. As long as he is unaware of the artificiality of this superstructure he can function "normally" in society. However, rational inquiry into the superstructure exposes the individual to great dangers. . . . [He] could suffer a total disenchantment and withdraw into a paralyzing cocoon of nihilism, or like Lenz he might panic at the sight of the dizzying abyss (a frequent Büchner symbol for the emptiness experienced by the nihilist) and become locked in a hopeless, often grotesque, struggle to buttress an undermined faith. The disquieting implication is that the whole question of sanity is a nebulous one indeed. Given the mind's limited capacity to recognize reality, who is more in tune with the real human condition, the so-called well-adjusted man who makes little effort to differentiate between reality and illusion, or the man whose mind cracks under the weight of doubts? (pp. 69-71)

> *Ronald Hauser, in his* Georg Büchner, Twayne *Publishers, Inc., 1974, 161 p.*

### DAVID G. RICHARDS   (essay date 1977)

[*Richards studies Büchner's use of the episodic form and repetitive words, phrases, themes, and images in* Woyzeck.]

No dramatist since Shakespeare has used the open or episodic form of drama with greater skill and effectiveness than Büchner does in *Woyzeck.* Büchner had as little use for the classical, Aristotelian dramatic form with its linear, causal plot development and its complex arrangement of independent parts according to principles of logic and rank, as he had sympathy for the idealistic, teleological, and hierarchical *Weltbild* which finds its proper medium in such a dramatic form. Unlike the idealists, who tend to view the moment in terms of the past and the future, Büchner considered each moment to be important in its own right; life consists of a series of such individual moments, each of which is complete in itself and its own reason for being. The succession of moments is not determined by a divine will or a rationally conceived world spirit, but by the laws of nature; life and history do not develop according to some grand scheme or design, which gives each event purpose and meaning, but according to the inherent physical, biological, and psychological patterns and processes, which are their own meaning and purpose. By representing such moments as they actually occurred or might have occurred, the author should attempt, in Büchner's opinion, to recreate the events he wishes to present and to capture the life of his figures and of the time in which they lived.

According to Büchner's Lenz the literary work of art should consist of a sequence of petrified moments or episodes from life. Of course the artist need not, and in a larger work cannot, present a sequence of contiguous moments. He must select those which are especially charged with meaning, tension, and action or those which effectively stretch beyond their own borders to imply what preceded and suggest what will follow, just as Büchner's Lenz sees an entire story in a painting, and not just the moment actually represented. Thus the episodic play demands the active participation of the spectator in filling in the background and connecting material from the hints and allusions contained in the various episodes.

In *Woyzeck* the paratactic structure is fully and consistently developed. This form is especially suitable for presenting a fragmented world, a world in which clearly defined relationships are lacking and in which the individual is isolated and alone. The play contains very few complex sentences, and only a small number of those involve subordinate relationships. Similarly, the speeches do not interlock and interconnect to form true dialogue or a "continuum of conversation." [Helmut Kropp, *Der Dialog bei Georg Büchner*]. The figures often strive to converse and communicate, but they seldom succeed in overcoming the distance which separates them.

In the first scene, for example, Woyzeck and his friend Andres talk to each other, but they do not communicate. Since Andres does not hear and see what Woyzeck does, he cannot understand what Woyzeck is trying to say. (Comparison of the finished scene with the first draft, in which Andres does hear the sounds, reveals that Büchner purposely reduced the amount of communication and community in the later version.) Andres even whistles and sings in order not to hear his friend's strange talk. Later, when Woyzeck is tortured by anguish and when he disposes of his possessions, Andres thinks he has a fever.

Likewise, in Woyzeck's first meeting with Marie . . ., Marie has the role of a spectator rather than a partner, as she merely responds to his account with her exclamations. As a further example of conversation with minimal communication and as an illustration of how dialogue is formed from the paratactic arrangement of distinct, loosely connected conversational units, the exchange immediately preceding the murder may be cited. Woyzeck's failure to visit Marie for two days has made her nervous and apprehensive; his sudden appearance after the Grandmother's tale and the peculiar manner in which he leads her away increase her fear and uncertainty:

> WOYZECK. Marie!
> MARIE (*startled*). What do you want?
> WOYZECK. Marie, let's go. It's time.
> MARIE. Where to?
> WOYZECK. How should I know?

The murder scene itself begins with Marie's observations: "So, the town's over that way. It's dark." The ominous tenor of Woyzeck's peculiar reply heightens the tension and increases Marie's apprehension. She cannot understand, as the spectator does, the hidden meaning of his statements, but she does sense from the peculiarity of his behavior and speech that he is severely disturbed and that she is threatened:

> WOYZECK. You must stay awhile. Come sit down.
> MARIE. But I have to go.
> WOYZECK. You won't get sore feet from walking.
> MARIE. What's gotten into you?!

The theme of the dialogue shifts several times, but the suggestion of impending disaster remains throughout as a unifying mood. A new unit begins when Woyzeck questions Marie about the past and future of their relationship:

> WOYZECK. Do you know how long it's been now, Marie?
> MARIE. Two years on Pentecost.
> WOYZECK. Do you also know how long it's going to be?
> MARIE. I must go make supper.

Woyzeck's monologic response to Marie's nervous reply constitutes a new unit:

> Are you freezing, Marie? And yet you're warm.
> How hot your lips are! Hot—hot whore's breath.
> But still I'd give heaven to kiss them once more.
>   When you're cold, you don't freeze any more.
> You won't freeze in the morning dew.

Two more short segments precede the murder, and the murder itself constitutes a final one.

The episodes in *Woyzeck* are basically of two types, those which form a part of the central action and those which contribute little or nothing to the development of the plot or to delineation of character, but which provide a new perspective, furnish some form of comment on the action, or add a universal dimension to the particular action of the central plot. To the latter category belong the carnival scene, the meeting between the Doctor and the Captain, the Grandmother's tale, the speeches of the Journeymen, and some of the songs. The poor orphan in the Grandmother's tale, for example, is analogous to Woyzeck and his child. Having lost its father and mother, the child looks all over the earth for human companionship, but everything is dead. The child extends its search for life into the universe, only to discover that the moon is nothing but a piece of rotten wood; the sun, a dead sunflower; and the stars, dead insects stuck on twigs. Upon its return to earth, it finds that the earth has become an overturned chamber pot: "And then it sat down and cried. And it sits there still and is all alone."

Büchner employs the form and conventions of the fairy tale to express hyperbolically one of the basic motifs of the play and of his works as a whole; in its loneliness and isolation the child represents not only Woyzeck and Woyzeck's child, but also Danton, Leonce, Lenz, and man in general. It learns what Woyzeck discovers at the inn and what Danton expresses at the beginning of *Danton's Death:* "We know little of each other. We are thick-skinned. We stretch out our hands toward each other, but the effort is futile. We only rub off the coarse leather against each other—*we are very lonely.*" (Italics added.) Where the fairy tale and the parable traditionally presuppose an ordered universe and a generally accepted, sacred system of beliefs, Büchner's inverted, nihilistic fairy tale presumes a chaotic and absurd world in which there are no positive values and no hope. In making a general statement about man and the world, this episode stands apart from the central action; but while it does not further the plot, it does contribute significantly to the mood of the play and to the intensification of its dramatic impact. When the silence that must follow the relating of such a tale is broken by Woyzeck, who has come to kill Marie, the expressiveness of their simple dialogue is so intensified by the context that a tension similar to that reached at the climax of a Greek tragedy is achieved.

Besides creating atmosphere, the carnival scene extends beyond the immediate plot to provide realistic criteria for judging or understanding the behavior of the figures of the play and of man in general. Like the carnival scene, the songs not only create atmosphere, but also provide comment on the action. And by relating the experiences of Marie and Woyzeck to the fundamental themes of folk songs, they also help to establish the play's universal validity. The position of the scenes or episodes of this type is not determined by their function in the development of the central action, but by their contribution to specific moments of that action.

Whether it be words in a sentence, sentences in a paragraph, or scenes in a play, the sequence of parts in a literary work is as much a determinant of meaning and effect as are the parts themselves. Thus, contrary to the claims of some critics and the practice of many directors, neither the position of the purely episodic scenes nor the sequence of scenes constituting the main action can be altered without changing the work's intended meaning and effect. In *Woyzeck* the sequence of events which begin with Woyzeck's suspicion of Marie's disloyalty and culminate in the murder constitute a basic framework in relation to which the other scenes fall naturally into place. Given with this sequence is a continual and dramatically effective increase of intensity and tension.

At the end of the first scene Andres hears the drumming which opens the second scene; and at the end of the latter Woyzeck stops on his way back from the field to talk briefly with Marie. In the final draft of the second scene Büchner omits Woyzeck's reference to the carnival, thus eliminating the only direct connection between the second and third scenes. The location of the carnival scene is nevertheless unequivocally determined by the sequence of Marie's increasing involvement with the Drum Major. In the second scene they greet each other; at the carnival the Drum Major gets another look at Marie and expresses the desire to mate with her; between the third and fourth scenes a meeting takes place in which Marie receives the earrings that arouse Woyzeck's suspicion in scene four.

While the scenes in which Woyzeck is with the Captain and the Doctor do not fit into any such scheme, one can recognize the structural and contextual reasons for their placement. Both of these episodes follow scenes in which Woyzeck's suspicion is aroused. By revealing after each step in the development of Marie's relationship with the Drum Major how the loyal Woyzeck drives himself and suffers humiliation in order to support his family, they provide ironic comment on those betrayal scenes and intensify their impact. (Woyzeck's mechanical responses and lack of attention in the first part of the scene with the Captain express his disturbed preoccupation with Marie's peculiar behavior.)

The only scene whose location cannot readily be determined by considering its relationship to its immediate surroundings and its function in the context of the whole is the one in which the Captain and the Doctor meet on the street. Perhaps its position can be explained by the author's penchant for using contrasts to set off important occurrences and to intensify dramatic effects. This scene provides a moment of pause and relaxed tension just before Woyzeck's suspicion becomes certainty.

As a relatively short literary form meant for performance, the drama must be extremely concentrated, and concentration demands unity of impression. The theoreticians of the neoclassical drama considered rigid adherence to the dramatic rules derived from Aristotle to be the *sine qua non* for creating such a unified impression. Of course the dogmatic appli-

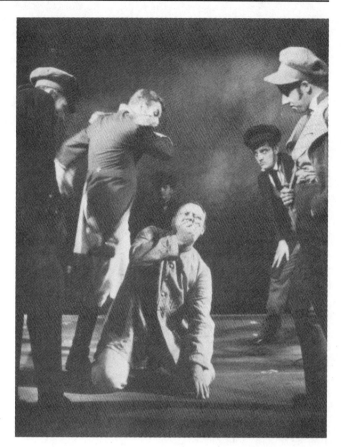

*Woyzeck and his tormentors in a 1953 production staged in Frankfurt am Main.*

cation of these rules may result in the creation of improbable and unbelievable situations and events, but their complete abandonment has revenged itself on many a would-be Shakespeare, for a play's effectiveness may indeed be enhanced by the judicious and reasonable observance of the unities of time, place, and especially action.

But there are subtler, more organic, and for the episodic play more effective ways of achieving unity of impression. Primary among these is the repetition and variation of words, phrases, images, themes, and rhythms. The interconnections and interrelations between motifs and motif-complexes bind the parts together into a unified whole. Through their recurrence, the motifs also extend the scope of their meaning and accumulate strength and intensity of expression.

Each major figure in the play can be associated with and characterized by specific motifs or motif-complexes. . . . Characteristic for the Captain's "complacent, conventional sentimentality" [Franz Heinrich Mautner in *Deutsche Vierteljahrsschrift* (1961)] is his repetition of the stock phrase "a good man," which occurs twelve times in two scenes. His melancholy lethargy and antipathy to haste and motion are expressed in his repeated admonitions to Woyzeck and the Doctor to slow down.

The repetition of words and motifs may also be used to demonstrate the compulsive nature of man's thoughts and behavior. That is clearly the case with the Doctor and the Captain, but also with Woyzeck, whose preoccupation or obsession is revealed by such words and phrases as "go on," "knife," and "stab dead" (or "stab"), and by such contrasting word pairs as "warm/cold," "hot/freezing," and "life/death." All of these relate to the sin/punishment motif associated with Woyzeck's visions. After Woyzeck discovers Marie's infidelity, he concludes that all life is lechery; and he considers the words with which Marie encourages the Drum Major to be a direct expression of the heat of her lechery: "That woman is hot, hot!—Go on, go on." But what is hot with sin will be made cold by the resulting punishment: the words which stand for Marie's lechery become transformed in Woyzeck's mind into the rhythmically similar phrase "stab dead." The relationships between these various motifs is clearly indicated in the speech that precedes the murder:

> Are you freezing, Marie? And yet you're warm.
> How hot your lips are! Hot—hot whore's breath.
> But still I'd give heaven to kiss them once more.
>     When you're cold, you don't freeze any more.
>     You won't freeze in the morning dew.

Following the murder, Woyzeck tells Kate that she is hot and that she too will become cold. At the same time he admits: "I'm hot, hot," thus indicating that he too has become guilty. That the heat of sin will be made cold by punishment is a compelling thought in Woyzeck's mind and may serve here as a foreshadowing of his own fate.

Closely associated with this complex are the motifs "red," and "blood." Red is the color of flesh and blood, and of sensuality and sin. Red also signifies beauty when used in reference to Marie's mouth: "and yet I have as red a mouth as the grandest ladies," Marie says. When looking for the blemish that he thinks should mar the beauty that has become sinful, Woyzeck also equates Marie's red mouth with beauty: "You have a red mouth, Marie. No blister on it? Farewell, Marie, you're as beautiful as sin. Can mortal sin be so beautiful?" The verse Woyzeck finds in his mother's Bible implies by association a connection between pain and suffering, blood, and the color red: "As your body, Lord, was red and sore [*wund*], / Let my heart be for evermore." The same complex of motifs recurs just prior to the murder: when Marie observes: "How red the moon is rising," Woyzeck associates the red color of the moon with blood and with the instrument for inflicting wounds that he is about to use: "Like a bloody knife."

"Red" and "blood" are connected again when Kate discovers blood on Woyzeck's hand: "Red! Blood!" and when Woyzeck returns to Marie's corpse: "What's that red string around your neck?" Once again he associates "red" and "blood" with sin, and perhaps also with the gift Marie received from the Drum Major: "Who gave you that necklace in payment for your sins?" Marie's sin exacts as retribution the very beauty and vitality that was its cause: "You were black from them [her sins], black! Have I made you white now?" Blood, beauty, suffering, and sin are all connected through the color red, and Marie loses them all when Woyzeck sheds her blood and makes her pale. But in assuming the role of judge and executioner, Woyzeck becomes bloody and guilty himself. There is no need for the author to present what is obvious, the fact, namely, that only death can free Woyzeck from the compulsive desire to cleanse himself from his own guilt. As the play ends, he is engaged in the futile attempt to wash off the bloody spots which mark and betray him.

Besides binding the parts together to create a unified impression, the recurring motifs also provide a means for achieving maximal concentration and force of expression. As words and phrases accumulate special nuances of meaning from the various contexts in which they occur, their capability of arousing specific emotional responses becomes heightened. Whenever Woyzeck repeats the phrase "go on," for example, we recall the circumstances in which he first heard it, and we realize that it obsesses him and that it is closely connected in his mind with the phrase "stab dead." This enrichment of key words and phrases allows the simple speech of Büchner's figures to become naively eloquent and ironic. By supercharging his language in this way, Büchner regains some of the poetic quality, concentration, and elevation that is typical of fine verse but rare in prose.

Where the language is simple and sometimes vague, nonverbal communication becomes all the more important. As the words, phrases, sentence fragments, and simple sentences emerge or explode from deep within the speakers, they demand and shape the clarifying accompaniment of gesture. Büchner occasionally uses stage instructions to describe the physical action which accompanies and complements the dialogue and fills the frequent pauses, but most often the requisite gestures and facial expressions are contained implicitly in the language itself.

Any passage which does not involve the Doctor and the Captain could be cited as an example of how Büchner achieves maximal expression from minimal means. Especially compact and dense is a short passage from the final inn scene, which recapitulates in scarcely more than a dozen words a number of the play's major motifs. The exchange begins when Kate asks Woyzeck, who has just come from the scene of the murder: "But what do you have on your hand?" Her tone of voice and physical reaction express astonishment accompanied by some degree of suspicion and accusation. This remark forces Woyzeck to become aware of the reality of his situation and to fear that his guilt will be discovered. Frightened bewilderment and self-incriminating defensiveness can be heard in his reply: "Me? Me?" The moment of discovery with its accompanying horror, accusation, disgust, and demand of an explanation is revealed in Kate's exclamation: "Red! Blood!" Still confused and baffled, Woyzeck turns her exclamation into a question, which is immediately followed by a verification: "Blood? Blood." Meanwhile a crowd has gathered; Kate's observation is affirmed and her reaction reinforced by the Innkeeper's response: "Uuh blood." Woyzeck collects himself enough to offer an explanation, but not enough to make it plausible. Seeing himself cornered and threatened, he covers his hasty escape with a frantic barrage of questions and exclamations: "Damn it, what do you want? It's none of your business! Make way! Or the first one—damn it! Do you think I killed someone? Am I a murderer? Why are you gaping? Look at yourselves! Make way there! (*He runs out.*)" Gesture, tone, and action are so clearly contained or suggested by Büchner's dialogue that specific stage instructions are unnecessary. This short exchange is no less effective than an eloquent monologue would be in providing insight into the state of Woyzeck's psyche.

Whether he attempts to philosophize, or whether he stammers in frightened confusion, Woyzeck's language always conveys far more than he is able to express consciously. Whether it is forced out with conscious effort, or whether it bursts forth on its own, it is always filled with life. It is language so charged with emotion and filled with meaning that it overcomes the artificial barriers that seem to separate the speaker from the spectator. Büchner accomplishes in his art what Danton considers to be impossible in life, but what Lenz demands of the artist: his love of mankind enables him to penetrate into the peculiar being of an individual and to share his insight and knowledge with the reader or spectator. (pp. 190-99)

> David G. Richards, in his Georg Büchner and the Birth of the Modern Drama, *State University of New York Press, 1977, 289 p.*

## MARTIN SWALES   (essay date 1977)

[*A Canadian educator and critic, Swales is the author of* The German "Novelle" *(1977) and* The German Bildungsroman *(1978). In this excerpt from the former work, Swales discusses Büchner's portrayal of madness in* Lenz.]

Büchner has been hailed as one of the seminal writers of the post-Romantic era: as a superbly tenacious realist, a man deeply aware of the extent to which history and society shape the fate of man; as a writer who constantly articulates the sense of a world bereft of any metaphysical anchorage; as a master of thoroughgoing psychological insight. In many of his works Büchner portrays the individual in the grip of forces (be they historical or psychological) that are outside his control. His one novelle *Lenz* is no exception. In this story Büchner concerns himself with a mind whose hold on reality becomes ever more precarious as the sparse events that constitute the plot unfold.

The story opens with a description of Lenz's journey through a mountainous landscape. The first mention of his reaction to this natural world is: "Indifferently, he walked on; the path he took, now ascending, now descending, did not matter to him. He felt no tiredness; only it occasionally irked him that he could not walk on his head." A few sentences later we read: "Everything struck him as so small, so near, so damp; he would have liked to stow the earth behind the stove. He did not understand that it should take so long to climb down a slope, to reach a distant point; he thought he should have been able to cover everything in a few steps." Both these statements serve to define Lenz's psychological condition at the beginning of the story. Two points should be noted: first, the dislocation and boredom, the indifference (*Gleichgültigkeit*); second, Lenz's wildly unfocused perception of the world around him, the sense of the closeness and smallness of everything—a sense that is contradicted by his actual experience of how long it takes him to get from one point to another. A further response to the natural world is suggested a few sentences later when we are told of moments when "he felt he must draw the storm to himself, take everything into him, he stretched himself out and lay over the earth, he bored his way into the All, it was a pleasure that hurt him." From such passages the reader gains a clear picture of the state of mind in which Lenz arrives at the house of Pastor Oberlin. It is a mind already unhinged, in the sense that there is no coherent and sustaining relationship to the world. Instead there are periods of utter indifference when the world becomes a small, indeed negligible entity, there are periods when it becomes a massive, physically assaulting experience. Lenz's mind moves uneasily within this spectrum of possible responses. This restless movement is symptomatic of his incipient madness, of his alienation from the world as binding reality. (pp. 99-100)

As a depiction of madness, *Lenz* is remarkable for the combination of structural control and imaginative empathy with which the subject matter is handled. The balance of intimacy

and detachment is central to the overall impact that the story makes, and it is mediated through the narrative perspective. Obviously, the fact that the story is a third-person narrative means that we, the readers, are made—at one level—to stand outside the protagonist, to view him thorugh the eyes of a dispassionate observer. Thus there is a curiously sober, factual register that recurs throughout the story. It allows us to know as facts the world through which Lenz moves, to see as facts the actions he performs. And, of course, much of the narrative is indebted to Oberlin's account of Lenz's behavior. Büchner remains close to this source material without attempting to play down the extent to which it is clear, sensible reportage. What Büchner adds to the Oberlin account is the whole depiction of the world as perceived through the distorting agency of Lenz's unhinged mind. At times this is achieved by the straightforward introduction of indirect speech, at times it is conveyed by means of a construction such as *"ihm war"* ("he felt"), at times it is attained by the use of *"erlebte Rede"* (free indirect speech) whereby the narrator simply adopts Lenz's perspective without comment. There is, then, a whole spectrum of narrative modes that allows the factual report to be colored by the protagonist's own highly charged response to the world around him—while never obliterating the register of sober reportage. At first sight, the net result might seem to be a curiously dislocated set of possible perspectives, but the overall import is anything but fragmented. We are never asked to forget that Lenz's is a mind unhinged, and this surely is central to Büchner's meaning; if madness is loss of relationship to the world, is alienation from the facts of experience, then the narrative must consistently intimate the binding presence of those facts upon which Lenz's hold becomes ever more tenuous. Furthermore, it must also intimate not simply the concrete reality of the objects present, but also the possibility of valuable and sustaining moral activity for human beings. In this sense, the real world that the narrator constantly acknowledges is affirmed both philosophically and ethically. Yet this is not all that Büchner wishes to convey. His analysis of the mad mind is anything but a simple case history, anything but an unproblematic assertion of the discrepancy between reality on the one hand and the individual capacity for psychological aberration on the other. The narrator does not choose to remain consistently outside the mad mind; hence, he will not allow his readers to remain outside that mind. In a feat of extraordinary imaginative empathy the narrative voice enters the mad mind and makes us share the devastating intensity of human response of which that mind is capable. It is an intensity that derives not from an exuberantly solipsistic fantasy, not from the endless creation of dream-worlds, but from a kind of helpless, unprotected exposure to certain kinds of—albeit dislocated—sense impression. Lenz's mind is defenseless before those sharp fragments of the world that pierce through his alienation. He is unable to hold what he perceives in any kind of perspective; distant things suddenly come up close, nearby things can withdraw into extinction. Yet what is involved here is both perception and interpretation. Because Lenz finds himself existing outside the perceptual framework of ordinary humanity, he is excluded from the normally interpreted, habitable universe. Once one admits the possibility that common human certainty rests on an interpretation of the facts that surround the individual mind, it follows that Lenz's perception becomes *another* interpretation, one that may reveal things that are normally obscured by accepted conventions. It is in this sense . . . that Büchner makes use of the mad mind to comment on the accepted universe, that Lenz's viewpoint acquires a kind of existential relevance. This is not, of course, to say that he is indulging in a simple inversion whereby the sane mind is mad and the mad sane. There is never any doubt in the story that Lenz *is* mad— and this leads to a powerful note of regret for the sheer human waste involved. Yet the mad mind is made to relativize the accepted human interpretations. Paradoxically, the mad or alienated mind is able to *see* precisely by virtue of its alienation, precisely because it does not have recourse to the prejudgments of the commonly accepted interpretation. The strangeness of Lenz's perception helps us, the readers, to see afresh. One is reminded of Brecht's aim of presenting an alienated image of the social world in order to peel away the "stamp of the familiar" from experience. One is also reminded of Aldous Huxley's comment on the perceptual gain—and the threatening implications—of the drug-taker's perspective: "The fear, as I analyze it in retrospect, was of being overwhelmed, of disintegrating under a pressure of reality greater than a mind accustomed to living most of the time in a cosy world of symbols could possibly bear." It is on these terms that the alienated mind matters to us; and in Büchner's story this is conveyed through the narrative presentation. Furthermore, if we ask by what stylistic means this story is able to intimate the relevance of the alienated mind, the answer must reside in the sheer imaginative and linguistic intensity with which Lenz's perception is presented to us. It is crucially important to note that Lenz's vision thereby acquires a *poetic* intensity and persuasiveness that is the deepest source of its significance. For this reason, the whole nature of artistic— and poetic—seeing and expression is one of the deepest concerns of this story (involving much more than the overt formulations of the *Kunstgespräch* section, the discussion about art).

The point can be made most clearly by specific analyses, and to this end I wish to look in some detail at two passages, both of which are concerned with description of the natural world. The first is taken from the first page or so of the story. The opening sentences are completely sober, laconically sketching in the necessary details: "On January 20 Lenz went through the mountains. The peaks and high mountain slopes snow-clad, down the valleys gray masses of stone, green patches, rocks and pine trees." We begin on a note of sparse reportage, with no particular stylistic intensity or pressure. However, the urgency soon enters the story as a personal note is struck and an emotive response to the landscape is hinted at: "It was wet cold, the water trickled down the rocks and bounded over the path. The boughs of the pines hung heavily down in the damp air. Gray clouds tracked across the sky, but everything so thick, and then the mist rose up as steam and moved slow and damp through the undergrowth, so lazy, so dull." Strangely, however, these sentences contain no explicit mention of Lenz himself; the emotive response—the sense of excessive heaviness, of oppressiveness in the landscape—would, then, appear to be attested to by the narrator. Syntactically, these are *his* observations. Hence, the first few sentences of the story establish the two registers within the narrative voice—that of sober reportage and that of emotive evaluation and response.

Almost immediately, the descriptive energy is intensified as we read: "At first his heart felt constricted when the stone broke away like that, when the gray forest shook under him and the mist now concealed outlines, now half-revealed mighty limbs." The construction here is important, because at the simplest level the syntax of the sentence suggests that

Lenz's reaction results from objective happenings in the natural world, that Lenz is not imposing his own responses onto—and thereby distorting—the natural world, but that his responses are *produced* by external facts. Of course, we are in uncertain territory here. We suspect that the narrator is—without admitting it—rendering Lenz's perception at this point. We may conjecture as much; but the fact remains that the narrator simply offers *his* description of those events that so oppress Lenz. The same is true of the enormous sentence that dominates the first page or so of the story:

> Only sometimes when the storm hurled the cloud masses into the valley and the steam rose up from the forest and the voices awoke and rebounded from the rocks, now like distant fading thunder, and then roaring mightily upward as though with their clamor they wanted to celebrate the earth in their wild tumult, and the clouds galloped toward him like wild neighing horses, and the sunshine came and went between them and passed its shining sword over the snow-covered slopes so that a bright, dazzling light cut its way over the peaks and into the valleys; or when the storm drove the cloud masses downward and tore open a light blue lake in them, and then the wind died away and from down below, from the chasms, from the tops of the pines sent its humming upward like a lullaby, like a peal of bells, and a gentle red climbed up the deep blue, and small clouds sailed along on silvery wings and all mountain peaks, sharp and clear, shone and sparkled far over the land, it tore at his heart, he stood, panting, his body bent forward, eyes and mouth wide open. . . .

Once again, the depiction of the natural landscape is given with the authority of what seems to be the narrator's perspective; Lenz's anguish is produced by certain phenomena that are described and evoked by the narrator. On the other hand, the sentence is only completed syntactically at the moment when it catalogues Lenz's reaction to the violence of the storm. It is, therefore, essentially concerned with the protagonist's responses, and we may therefore suspect that the seemingly objective cause-and-effect sequence is nowhere near so clear-cut as the narrator makes it appear. Yet we must remember that the narrator is prepared, elsewhere in the story, to enter Lenz's mind and to signal quite clearly the fact that he is writing not from his own but from the protagonist's perspective. Presumably, therefore, if he does not adopt this method in the opening section of the story, he chooses not to do so. It is almost as though he is prepared to allow his voice—and perception—to overlap with Lenz's but without ever getting to the point of forfeiting his own separate identity. Why should this be? The answer, in my view, lies in the crucial problem of the "poetic" relevance of Lenz's anguished vision. The narrator allows himself an imaginatively charged description of the storm to suggest the level at which—for all its hallucinations—Lenz's mind will matter to us, will be utterly and terribly relevant. The narrator in this story is not just a cataloguer of facts, an observer of what actually happens. He is also a poet who will attempt to interpret what he depicts, who will render not just actualities but the meaning facts acquire by becoming part of man's interpreted universe. The narrative voice—at its most poetic—reminds us of those passages that explicitly re-create the delusions that pass through Lenz's mind. For this reason, we find ourselves unable to keep the mad mind at a safe distance, we are forced to acknowledge our common ground with the hapless protagonist. Yet, of course, the narrator's description of the storm-filled landscape also intimates the difference between the poetic description of the world and the delusions of a madman. In the narrator's description of the storm one notices the recurrence of images, and in these images resides the creativity, the poetic power of the passage. Some of these images make explicit the introduction of analogues: "now like fading thunder," "as though with their clamor they wanted to celebrate the earth," "clouds like wild, neighing horses," "like a lullaby." Other images do not explicitly signal this analogizing process; they anchor it without comment in the very stuff of the experiences they evoke: "the voices awoke and rebounded," "when the sunshine passed its shining sword over the snow-covered slopes." Of course, none of this is in any way unfamiliar to us. We are perfectly used to this kind of writing, we have technical terms such as *simile* and *metaphor* that designate the figures of speech used. This is poetic language; but it is not only poetic language, it is also "our" language, human language. We are able to understand simile and metaphor when a poet uses them—for the quite simple reason that we use them ourselves, that we know of these resources from our own experience of language. For all the overlap, however, between the figurative use of language and the manic power of Lenz's visions, there is an important difference to be observed, a difference that is nonetheless valid for being one of degree and not one of kind. The narrator's images attempt to evoke the sheer animation of the scene he is describing, the analogues partake of and sustain the reality, whereas in Lenz's outbursts the analogues so take possession of the real that they tend to obliterate it to the point where we feel that mind and world are no longer interacting. Indeed, we feel that the mind has made reality the cipher for its present state: " 'Now I feel so confined, so confined, you see, it is sometimes as though my hands were knocking against the sky.' " Or again: "So he came to the top of the mountain, and the uncertain light spread down to where the white masses of stone lay, and the sky was a silly blue eye, and the moon stood quite ludicrously in it—stupid." Or again: " 'Do you hear nothing, do you not hear the terrible voice that screams round the whole horizon and that is normally called silence? Since I have been in this peaceful valley I hear it always.' "

All these perceptions of the world are not intrinsically foreign to our experience; we could be persuaded of them as a poetic truth about the world we all inhabit. Yet they have in common a certain radicalism, a forcing of the perception to the point where the link with our world is stretched to breaking point. The story forces us into an ambivalent situation with regard to such statements; it asks for both our assent and our rejection, for association and dissociation. In just the same way, the narrative perspective is ambivalent in its interpretative relationship to the protagonist. It can be dissociated in that it adopts the register of the factual report, viewing Lenz's behavior from the outside; it can be associated in that it allows itself a poetic rendering of the natural world whereby it comes close to the kind of linguistic vividness and stylistic intensity that characterize Lenz's anguished visions.

A brief discussion of a second passage—the closing paragraph of the story—can serve to summarize the points mentioned above:

> He sat, coldly resigned, in the carriage as they drove out of the valley toward the west. He was indifferent where they were taking him; several times when the coach threatened to overturn because of the poor surface, he remained calmly sitting as he

was. In this condition he traveled through the mountains. Toward evening they were in the Rhine valley. Gradually they left behind them the mountains, which now rose like a deep blue wave of crystal into the evening glow; on its warm tide the last red rays of the evening sun were playing; far over the plain at the foot of the mountain lay a shimmering bluish haze. It grew darker the closer they came to Strasbourg; a full moon high in the sky, all distant objects dark, only the mountain nearby formed a sharp outline, the earth was like a golden goblet over which the golden waves of the moon ran foaming. Lenz stared quietly out, no sense, no desire. Only a dull fear grew within him the more the objects were swallowed up in darkness. They had to find shelter for the night; then he made several attempts to take his life, but he was too closely watched. The following morning, in dull rainy weather, he arrived in Strasbourg. He seemed quite sensible and spoke with people. He did everything as the others did, but there was a terrible void within him. He felt no fear any more, no craving; his existence was a necessary burden to him. So he lived on.

This passage depicts the last flickerings of awareness—and fear—in Lenz before he succumbs to the ultimate emptiness. There is, as it were, very little of the mind left by now; there are no visions that the narrator needs to convey to us, no terrible premonitions, no livid perceptions. All we are given is the factual report of what Lenz did, of what happened to him on that final journey. Yet this is not all. The central section of the closing paragraph consists of the narrator's evocation of the sunset. For the last time in the story, the narrator's poetic register sounds as he conveys to us the sheer replete glory of the moonlit night. We notice the all-important presence of images. The narrator is not simply being factual here; he is interpreting the scene, he is giving it meaning by entering it imaginatively. The mountains are "like a deep blue wave of crystal," the earth is "like a golden goblet over which the golden waves of the moon ran foaming." The imaginative intensity of the narrator's description here would seem to contrast strangely with the spare, laconic account of Lenz's resignation and indifference. One asks oneself why the description is there, above all why the narrative should become so dramatically charged for these few sentences. Far from being an irrelevancy, a stylistic excrescence, this descriptive passage in my view unmistakably belongs to the argument of the story as a whole. At one level, it serves to heighten the poignancy of Lenz's utter emptiness. If madness in this story is shown as alienation from the real world, then the closing scene shows that splendor of which the protagonist is now irrevocably denied all knowledge. The sense of loss, of deprivation, is almost unbearable. At another level, the narrator's description reminds us for the last time of a thread that has been running through the whole story, of the theme of a poetic reworking of the world. Lenz, of course, is an artist; his loss of contact with the world is the measure of his loss of artistic creativity. The narrator's use of images to convey the glory of the sunset reminds us that we can be persuaded of the poetic truth of even the most idiosyncratic perceptions of the world, that we are not literal-minded to the point of being mere observers of facts. If we can be made to feel that the earth is a golden goblet, then *potentially* we can be persuaded of even the validity of Lenz's perceptions that the sky is a "silly blue eye," that silence is a voice screaming through an emptied world. Once we admit to ourselves that reality is not just objects present, but is something that partakes of—and indeed demands—a humanly interpreted context, then we admit the possible validity of poetic interpretations of the world. Then, on frequent, uncomfortable occasions, Lenz's madness feels like poetry.

The text itself constantly reminds us that the protagonist of Büchner's story is an artist. Indeed, the one lengthy discursive statement that Lenz makes in the whole work occurs in the famous *Kunstgespräch*, conversation on art, in which he gives us his artistic credo. The passage is not simply a piece of, as it were, *Sturm und Drang* local color. It has meaning in the story not only by virtue of the arguments it advances but above all because of the function of these arguments in a work where the artistic relationship to (and interpretation of) reality is one of the central themes. Lenz argues against any kind of idealist art, insisting: "The dear Lord has presumably made the world as it should be, and we therefore cannot put anything better together; our sole intention should be to copy the work of His hands. I demand in everything life, the possibility of being, and that is all; it is not our business to ask if it is beautiful or ugly, the feeling that what has been created has life takes precedence over these two qualities and is the only criterion in matters of art."

What Lenz asserts here is a kind of realistic principle behind artistic creation. Yet realism must not be understood as simply fidelity to facts and to external appearances. Rather, Lenz stresses the intense creativity of realistic art, a creativity that allows such art to satisfy the one criterion that ultimately matters: the end product shall be vibrantly, tinglingly alive. Indeed, Lenz throughout his remarks insists on the primacy of imaginative empathy; this is the one true aesthetic principle. At one point he makes it clear that no amount of factual details, of externals, will be able to bring the work of art alive. Realism is not to be equated with a simple allegiance to empirical facts; rather, it involves the recognition that man *creates* reality out of the dynamic interaction of the self and the world. The figures in a truly successful work of art, then, generate their living reality from within themselves: "One has to love humanity in order to be able to penetrate into the unique being of each person; nobody can be too humble, too ugly for us—only then can one understand mankind; the most insignificant face makes a deeper impression than the mere sense of the beautiful, and one can allow the characters to emerge out of themselves without slavishly copying externals where no life, no muscles, no pulse swell and throb toward us."

The crucial opposition here is that between externals (*"das Äussere"*) on the one hand and the living principle of an art that cherishes the outgoing creativity of the individual self (*"aus sich"*) on the other. Realism is concerned with a world whose every fact is alive with the dimension of human significance. This credo is implicit in the poetic intensity of the narrator's descriptive passages. Furthermore, Lenz's alienation from the world is intimated as precisely the inability to know and hold fast to the vital meaning of the created reality that man inhabits. Lenz finds either the hideous absence of this living agency—or the overwhelming presence of a power whose very intensity threatens to tear him asunder. Yet his anguish centers upon—and derives from—the desperate attempt to affirm the immanent poetry of the real. His anguish at his loss is anguish at the loss of human substance. Moreover, because his visions grope for the very stuff of poetry and art, they are related to—yet ultimately separate from—the narrator's capacity for poetic description.

Hence, the *Kunstgespräch*, the conversation on art, clarifies the fact that madness, because it is alienation from reality, involves also an alienation from the preconditions of artistic creativity. Moreover, the *Kunstgespräch* also serves to underpin the thematic significance of one whole strand within the narrator's stylistic handling of his material. If the story establishes the existential relevance of the mad mind, it does so by arguing this link through the narrative medium of artistic interpretation and expression. The narrative process becomes, then, part of the story's theme. No attempt is made to play down the precariousness of Lenz's mental state, to suggest that he is not "really" mad. Lenz is so radically distanced from our world that he exists at the very periphery of the commonly understood universe. Yet the story, through its all-important narrative perspective, is able to endow even the marginal mind of the protagonist with such an interpretative implication for us, the readers, that that mind acquires a nagging existential centrality. The disturbing mediations involved in this process are, in my view, characteristic of the novelle genre. Moreover, it is those mediations that make this particular story one of the great literary explorations of madness. (pp. 101-13)

> *Martin Swales, "Büchner: 'Lenz'," in his* The German "Novelle", *Princeton University Press, 1977, pp. 99-113.*

## REINHOLD GRIMM   (essay date 1985)

[*Grimm contends that love, both chaste and erotic, is as much a theme of* Danton's Death *as is revolution, a point he demonstrates by examining the play's three main female characters: Julie, Lucile, and Marion.*]

What the texts contain is clear—and clearly the critics, virtually without exception, have chosen to avert their eyes. Let us begin by simply listing what the reader encounters.

Two women commit suicide out of love for their men: one while in the grip of madness, the other through a conscious decision (decades before Wagner's *Tristan and Isolde*, she dies a veritable "love-death"). And there are men no less extreme in their passions: one drowns himself after having nearly strangled his lover; another attempts to take his own life in a similar manner—in a state of erotic intoxication, already anticipating ultimate fulfillment. A third, seized by blind despair, compulsively and methodically murders his woman, stabbing her to death in an almost ritualistic process of judgment and execution. All this in only three dramas, one of which is a sketchy fragment; dramas, moreover, teeming with true love and trollops, lovers and libertines, the most delicate tenderness and the most drastic lasciviousness, dramas in which flies mate on people's hands, curs couple in the streets, and we are confronted with the question: "Don't you feel like . . . tearing off your pants and copulating over someone's ass like dogs . . . ?"

I am speaking of **Danton's Death**, of **Leonce and Lena**, of **Woyzeck**. I am speaking of Georg Büchner. Of all the many dozens of studies, monographs, and dissertations that have been devoted to this writer, not a single one actually deals with love. . . . (pp. 79-80)

And yet, the very first scene of Büchner's first play begins with lines which unambiguously define the way this theme will be presented. A card game is in progress; and the figure who initiates the dialogue as well as the "love interest" is none other than Georg[es] Danton. He turns to his wife Julie and remarks: "Look at Madame over there—how sweetly she fingers her cards. She knows how, all right—they say her husband always gets the *cœur,* the others the *carreau.* You women could even make us fall in love with a lie." The symbolic implications of the card suits mentioned by Danton are unmistakable. This is true of the "cœur," the heart, which traditionally has expressed a concept of love containing both Amor and Caritas. It is equally true of the "carreau" or diamond: here Büchner sets up a frivolous, obscene counterpart to the heart, using a sign the shape of which is decidedly suggestive. . . . His friend Hérault develops and concretizes the reference when he takes the card names literally and declares that young ladies should not "play games like that. The kings and queens fall on top of each other so indecently and the jacks pop up right after." (pp. 80-1)

What the duality of "cœur" and "carreau" conjures up from the very beginning is the entire range of the erotic: from the purest, indeed most chaste, affection as expressed by that ancient emblem the heart, all the way to the crassest carnality, which is denoted by the red diamond. And the two areas are not kept separate from one another but are closely bound together, in however daring, unbourgeois, and unstable a manner. Their common denominator is love—but not love as a mere concept or some anemic "fundamental *idea,*" but rather as an all-embracing fundamental *experience,* an experience which is at once joyous and overwhelming. For let us not forget that Julie and Danton, whose gentleness and kindness toward each other ("dear heart," she calls him) culminate in Julie taking her own life for the sake of her beloved, exist alongside of Hérault and his promiscuous "queen of diamonds," a woman who can make a man fall in love with a lie. What is more, these two radically dissimilar couples are joined by Camille Desmoulins, who exhibits what is perhaps the most faithful and selfless love to be found in Büchner's works—yet it is precisely this figure who calls for the elemental "limb-loosening, wicked love" of Sappho, with "naked gods and bacchantes" and, again completely uneuphemistically, "Venus with the beautiful backside"! Unvarnished sexuality, the most tender affection, and a classical Greek sensuality which the declaration that Venus, along with Epicurus, is to become the "doorkeeper of the Republic" clearly endows with emancipatory and even utopian traits: all this is present in Büchner's images and allusions, as well as in his invocations of Renaissance licentiousness. Attentive readers cannot fail to note that in the opening scene of his first drama the playwright sketches out a full panorama of the world of Eros. . . . (pp. 81-2)

I wish to commit . . . [a] heresy by declaring that in [*Danton's Death*] the theme of love is no less central than that of revolution. Indeed, the two are inseparably intertwined. Even if we limit ourselves to the main characters, we see that this is true not only of Julie and Camille's wife, Lucile, but also of the "grisette" or "hetaera," Marion. All three of the leading female figures in *Danton's Death* contribute—each in her own way—to the exemplary unleashing of both the dialectic of revolution, with all its contradictions, and of love "in every form."

As has been indicated, Julie and Lucile belong together, even more so at the end of the play than in the early scenes. . . . [Something] that has hardly been noticed, let alone investigated, is the circular construction of *Danton's Death* and the concomitant function which is assigned to the two female fig-

ures as well as to love. This oversight is the more surprising since all these elements are particularly noticeable in Büchner's drama of revolution. One need only compare the first scene ("Danton on a footstool at Julie's feet") with the last scene where Lucile sits "on the steps of the guillotine":

> DANTON. No, Julie, I love you like the grave. . . . They say in the grave there is peace, and grave and peace are one. If that's so, then in your lap I'm already lying under the earth. You sweet grave—your lips are funeral bells, your voice my death knell, your breasts my burial mound, and your heart my coffin.
> LUCILE. (*enters* . . .) I'm sitting in your lap, you silent angel of death. . . . You dear cradle, you lulled my Camille to sleep, you strangled him under your roses. You death knell, you sang him to the grave with your sweet tongue.

The connection between these images, the cyclical way in which they anticipate and echo one another, can hardly be overlooked, especially since they are so boldly unusual. There can be no doubt that Büchner created this connection intentionally; the references to sweetness and love, peacefulness and silence, the correspondence established in both instances between a lap (*Schoß,* which can also mean "womb") and a grave—all this is simply too exact to be regarded as accidental. Even the cradle, which at first is missing from the opening scene, soon puts in an appearance. Before the next scene begins, we encounter the line, "having coffins for cradles," a phrase which clearly anticipates Lucile's speech at the end of the play; and, of course, the evocative rhyme of "womb" and "tomb," of "cave" and "grave," is something of which psychoanalysis has long been aware. In the programmatic writings of Norman O. Brown, to which I shall eventually return, one finds the laconic yet unambiguous words: "Birth, copulation, and death, equated." This is precisely what Büchner accomplishes: "cradle," "womb" (*Schoß*), and "grave" are—as Danton himself declares—"one and the same." When Lucile utters the phrase "dear cradle," she is addressing the dreaded guillotine, the killing machine she also refers to as an "angel of death" and a "death knell"; and when Julie reaches for the vial of poison from which she imbibes her love-death, she does so with the words: "Come, dearest priest, your amen makes us go to sleep." Both of these death scenes are love scenes, just as both figures are, above all else, women in love. True, it seems at first that Julie regards Danton's words as frivolous and shocking, for she turns away from him with an almost Kleistian "Oh." However, she quickly regains her composure, and with it her love for Danton, a love in which she henceforth abides with steadily increasing confidence and unreservedness until finally, with the words "sleep, sleep" on her lips, she follows Danton and the darkling world in to the "slumber" of death.

The same development can be discerned in Danton's much-cited loneliness: from his fatalistic and seemingly resigned declaration, "we are very lonely," to the fervent intimacy he shares with Julie in the aftermath of his agonizing nightmare. In the latter scene, which occurs in the second act, Danton is able to say, "Now I'm calm"—and are we not forced to envision him in his wife's arms, not just in her presence? "Completely calm, dear heart?" she asks, full of concern, and he replies: "Yes, Julie, come to bed." That all this is connected to various aspects of the play's concluding scenes—for example, to the revolutionary's fear of the loneliness of death, a fear which is so difficult to reconcile with the philosophy he manifests in other situations, and, above all, to Julie's actions and attitude, to the extraordinary love-sacrifice she offers—cannot be ignored. The correspondences extend even to specific words and phrases, something which is particularly evident in Danton's cry: "Oh Julie! If I had to go *alone!* If she would abandon me! And if I decomposed entirely, dissolved completely—I'd be a handful of tormented dust. Each of my atoms could find peace only with her. I can't die, no, I cannot die." As a comforting answer, Julie has a messenger carry a lock of her hair to the imprisoned Danton: "There, bring him that and tell him he won't go alone. He'll understand. Then come back quickly. I want to read his looks in your eyes." And, once again, Danton is freed from his agony. "I won't go alone," he says to himself as if he has been saved, "thank you, Julie." Now he is able to face the guillotine, composed and calm.

Julie's love-sacrifice is indeed extraordinary. What renders it even more extraordinary and even more indicative of the importance Büchner attached to love is the fact that it has absolutely no basis in historical reality. It did not at all occur to the real Julie (who was actually named Louise) to accompany her Georges in death. Not only did she survive him by decades, but she had also no compunctions about remarrying—although, admittedly, this did not happen until she had mourned Danton for a few chaste (or, at least, relatively chaste) years. The banality of these facts is sobering; yet it also serves to establish irrefutably that the heroic transfiguration effected by Büchner evinces his own concerns and conceptions. And then there is Lucile, who is presented as deriving a limpid, self-effacing happiness from the love she shares with Camille. Even with this character, Büchner departs from what he read in his history books. Instead of having her arrested, condemned, and executed on the basis of Laflotte's denunciation, which is what actually happened, he causes her to provide a second example of transfiguration achieved by means of a luminous love-sacrifice. Like Julie, Lucile is cloaked in radiance. Or, as Maurice B. Benn puts it: "Against the dark background [of the play, these] two pure figures . . . appear in an almost radiant light" [see Further Reading]. Of course, Julie chooses death without hesitation and in the full freedom of her spirit, while Lucile, like Ophelia, falls victim to madness and is able to return to herself only at the very end of the play. Yet this ending, one of the most moving and magnificent in all of world drama, not only presents, in the words of Benn, "a sudden return of lucidity" for Lucile; it also crowns and confirms the triumph, the limitless glorification of love in Büchner's drama of revolution. The passage in question is deceptively brief; it begins with the entrance of a militia patrol and then breaks off with Lucile being led away to her death:

> A CITIZEN. Hey—who's there?
> LUCILE. Long live the King!
> CITIZEN. In the name of the Republic! (*She is surrounded by the watch and led off.*)

These lines must be read with the utmost attentiveness and exactitude. On the one hand, they serve to close the circle of the play's "love interest" which begins at the gaming table with the bantering about "cœur" and "carreau"; on the other hand, in testifying to the power of love, they also provide a final manifestation, indeed a proclamation, of the republic, and with it, the revolution. The part of the play's action which is connected to the revolution is encompassed by the theme of love. Even the scene in which Danton and his followers are executed, a scene in which their severed heads kiss

"at the bottom of the basket," is framed by—and one might say, sublated into—this theme as it is developed in the two scenes devoted to Julie's and Lucile's acts of self-sacrifice and transfiguration. Yet, at the same time, the part of the play which deals with love is also subjected to a sublation. In that final scene, in which love shines forth one last time and reaches what could be termed its apotheosis, Lucile is, in a very literal manner, "surrounded" by the power of the revolution in its most concrete form.

The vividness of this action, which is truly theatrical in the best sense of the word, is no less striking than the imagery Büchner utilizes at the beginning and end of *Danton's Death,* or, for that matter, the basic circular structure of the play as a whole. Here, both themes are fused together in a relationship as inseparable as that of form and content. Comfort and hope, refuge from the present and assurances regarding the future, all are intertwined in Büchner's play. Truly, for individual human beings, love is all that remains. For humanity, however, there is the revolution. Although conservative critics would have us believe that the notion of progress and the linear movement of history is flatly rejected, and in its place a Spenglerian "circular movement of all history" is glorified, this conclusion cannot be substantiated, regardless of whether one concentrates exclusively on *Danton's Death* or examines the young writer's entire oeuvre and biography. Büchner was a man who despaired and yet continued to fight, a militant who founded the Society of Human Rights, wrote *The Hessian Messenger,* and yet admitted that he "felt as if [he] were crushed under the terrible fatalism of history." If ever anyone had a right to lay claim to that dictum of Gramsci, "pessimism of the intellect, optimism of the will," then it was surely Büchner, a revolutionary in that most reactionary of times, the German Vormärz period. However, what sets him apart from Gramsci, and even raises him above the Italian's paradox, is the fact that he was a great writer and, both as a writer and a revolutionary, a man who loved. Büchner wanted "life and love" among human beings to be "one and the same"; he wanted love to be life and "life [to be] love."

I believe that one can legitimately take these words, which come from a fragmentary scene not included in the final version of *Leonce and Lena,* and apply them in a general sense to Büchner's entire concept of love. For are they not equally true of Marion, the third major female figure in *Danton's Death?* Does not this "grisette," in an exemplary manner, live a life of love? In her existence, are not life and love in fact identical? Admittedly, this is yet another heresy, and one especially offensive to those who, while not necessarily conservative in their political views, are nonetheless rigorously moralistic. (pp. 85-90)

Unfortunately, there is not enough space here to quote the love scene between [Marion] and Danton in its entirety. I can only point to the naturalness, the lyrical-idyllic simplicity and yet eloquence with which Marion—sitting "at the feet" of Danton, according to a telling stage direction—narrates the story of her life, which is to say the story of her love. "My mother was a smart woman. She always said chastity was a nice virtue." Thus Büchner, taking a sly jab at bourgeois morality, has Marion begin her account: "When people came to the house and started talking about certain things, she told me to leave the room. When I asked what they wanted, she said I ought to be ashamed of myself. When she gave me a book to read, I almost always had to skip over a couple of pages." Marion goes on to recall how once, in springtime, while still a girl, she found herself "in a peculiar atmosphere," an atmosphere which "almost choked me." Luckily, a young man appeared who, though he often said "crazy things," was "good-looking." In time, Marion says, "we couldn't see why we might not just as well lie together between two sheets as sit next to each other in two chairs." Then, soon thereafter, she declares with calm frankness: "But I became like an ocean, swallowing everything and swirling deeper and deeper. For me there was only one opposite: all men melted into one body. That was my nature—who can escape it?"

When the young man, who believed Marion was his alone, learned of her activities, he kissed her as if he wanted—again that word—to "choke" her: his arms wrapped tight around her neck; she was "terribly afraid." But he released her and then went off and drowned himself. . . . "I had to cry," she admits, "that was the only break in my being." Since then she has lived in complete unity and harmony with herself:

> Other people have Sundays and working days, they work for six days and pray on the seventh; once a year, on their birthdays, they get sentimental, and every year on New Year's Day they reflect. I don't understand all that. For me there is no stopping, no changing. I'm always the same, an endless longing and seizing, a fire, a torrent. . . . It's all the same, whatever we enjoy: bodies, icons, flowers, or toys, it's all the same feeling. Whoever enjoys the most prays the most.

Marion's autobiographical account closes with this avowal, which clearly provides the philosophical, or ideological, highlight of the entire scene. Büchner was not, however, content to stop here. The ensuing dialogue between Marion and Danton provides yet another highlight—in this case, one which is lyrical-idyllic, even lyrical-utopian, in nature:

> DANTON. Why can't I contain your beauty in me completely, surround it entirely?
> MARION. Danton, your lips have eyes.
> DANTON. I wish I were a part of the atmosphere so that I could bathe you in my flood and break on every wave of your beautiful body.

It is at this point that Lacroix, loud-mouthed and vulgar, enters the scene. Accompanied by a pair of common whores, he fills the air with crude remarks; and thus the scene ends on a jarringly discordant note that tears apart the idyl briefly shared by the two lovers.

I would like to ask: Could a playwright possibly express more in a single scene? Could a scene be any more unambiguous? How can it be that Büchner has been so completely misunderstood here by so many experts, by virtually the entire corps of critics? . . . Critics' sensibilities—not to mention their senses—have failed to grasp this woman and her message even though, beginning with the very first scene and Camille's proclamation of Venus and Epicurus as the patron saints of the republic, it pervades the entire drama and stands inscribed as a secret motto over the events of the revolution. Of course, we also notice a marked heightening of the current of eroticism: Camille merely *demands* primal love and Greek sensuality, while Marion actually *manifests* these ideals, actually lives and proclaims them with her own flesh.

After Marion's scene, there can be no doubt that the erotic-utopian qualities which the play first presents in a purely theoretical manner or in broad outline, have now become elements of concrete praxis and thus must be recognized as a crucial dimension of the entire theme of revolution. And how could it be otherwise? Are not love and sensuality of every sort, as well as the achievement of full happiness in this life, integral and inalienable aspects of the complete and liberated human being, the *total* human being, and hence essential components of any full concept of revolution? If one draws on Camus, as does Benn, and speaks of Büchner's "threefold concept of revolution," which combines sociopolitical rebellion with metaphysical revolt and an overturning of established aesthetic norms—then why not also acknowledge Büchner's liberation of Eros, that is to say, his sexual revolt? Are we not forced to do so by what we encounter in his works? I can no longer ignore the testimony of these texts. (pp. 91-3)

However tempting it may be, one cannot connect Marion with Marie of the **Woyzeck** fragment; nor can one view the proletarian tragedy as a necessary continuation of **Danton's Death,** much less its recantation. This would presume, within Büchner's oeuvre, an evolution which has never been convincingly demonstrated. And if indeed one is willing to make the interpretative leap of associating the suicide of Marion's lover with the murder of Marie by the pond, why not link the young man's death with Leonce's loudly announced decision to plunge into the river and drown, a decision motivated not by despair, but rather by the ecstasy of love? In other words, one could just as easily concentrate on the laughable consequences of Marion's "terrible dangerousness" as on those which are somberly serious. Of course, it cannot be denied that she admits: "My mother died of grief, people point at me." But she adds: "That's silly"—a comment that Büchner meant to be taken seriously. Marion's mother, who is so ironically characterized as wise and moral, can hardly be regarded as tragic; if anything, she is to be pitied. And Marion's first lover is not only pitiable, he is comical. To say this obviously involves a degree of exaggeration—but is not the death brought on by grief a standard element of cheap melodrama? And does not the young man's impetuous suicide smack of a certain callow foolishness? The playwright, in any case, speaking through that incorrigible materialist, Valerio, describes such deeds as "lieutenants' romanticism." Even the phrase "a foolish thing" is supplied by Büchner himself. He refrains from condemning Marion morally—or, for that matter, in any way. She exists outside of the traditional value system which bases itself on Christian ethics and hence she cannot be defined in terms of its conception of morality. Marion does not have a faulty or corrupted conscience, she has no conscience at all. She is not an evildoer, not a sinner, not laden with guilt. In the final analysis, she is not even immoral. She can only be termed amoral. As both elemental nature and its utopian projection, she exists *before* as well as *after* and *above* all traditional, which is to say bourgeois, moral strictures and sexual mores. Marion is entirely natural and yet at the same time she presages a perfect utopia. The first of these aspects serves as an anticipatory manifestation, a poetic image, of the second aspect. (pp. 95-6)

It is only through an appreciation of such paradoxes that we are able to understand Marion, her relationship to Danton, and the function of her scene. On the one hand, she is nature in its purest form and yet, on the other, she is not at all natural. Actually, she is caught between two sets of constraints: she is acutely susceptible to those of nature and she finds herself a prey of those of society. Only gradually is she able to overcome the double disharmony caused by these forces and mechanisms. This is revealed to us twice—here Büchner is quite exact—in the oppressive feeling of suffocation or choking which is so vividly visited upon Marion before she finally is able to become herself. In the midst of spring's luxuriance, it symbolizes the powerful drives of nature; in the enraged embrace of her disappointed lover, it represents society's insistence upon possession. For Marion, both issues now belong to the past; life and love have long since become one and the same. When this feeling of suffocation recurs at the end of the scene, it is no longer associated with her but instead with Danton. Coming on the heels of his strained debate with Lacroix and Paris, it is symptomatic, both specifically and in a broad sense, of an external compulsion to "exertion" and "work," to purposeful "action" in general; symptomatic, moreover, of the individual's renunciation of pleasure and obsession with productive accomplishment, as well as of that sad state of affairs in which people mutually oppress one another. Referring to his friends, Danton might well have repeated his line from the opening scene: "Their politics [i.e., their plans, their appeals, their demands] are getting on my nerves." Marion, however, uses a different image in conveying this thought to Danton: "Your lips are cold, your words have stifled your kisses."

Even in her lament, Büchner's grisette manifests, as a utopian projection, precisely that which Büchner's revolutionary, who is trying to blaze a trail to utopia, would like to achieve in historical reality: the realm of untrammeled pleasure. Marion is actually able to live the existence Danton demands, impatient and audacious—and hence burdened with guilt. She is able to be what he can only long for. The playwright has allowed her to rise above all constraints and enter that much sought-after realm. As Ullmann points out, Marion has attained complete and unmutilated "humanness" (*Menschennatur*); she has managed to transcend all notions of private property, an achievement which allows her to possess the entire world. Moreover, she has dissolved her sense of self; thus her existence, while totally unfragmented, is marked by infinite multiplicity. However, such fulfillment can only exist as the projection of a possibility; this perfect unity of being can only reside on the periphery of history, where origin and goal flow into one another. For the revolutionary who lives in the midst of a bloody reality, all this is unattainable. Danton, entangled in history, thoroughly caught up in the developments of each new day, must remain in a state of inner disharmony from which he can escape only for a few moments at a time. His agonizingly acute consciousness, which constantly disturbs his peace of mind, and Marion's seamless, almost unconscious, happiness are discordantly juxtaposed, their compatibility and loving encounter notwithstanding. Büchner's grisette manifests a tangible utopia, a concrete praxis of erotic liberation; in Büchner's revolutionary, we see a concretization of utopia's dependence on history and its concomitant contradiction of reality.

Yet the difference between Danton and Marion is not presented simply as a painful disharmony, but instead primarily in terms of a reconciliation. For this is the central meaning of the brief, lyrical exchange that consummates the idyl shared by the two lovers. Does it not almost resemble a duet? While it seems to begin so abruptly, the dialogue actually is a logical continuation of what has already been said, a final, poetically terse evocation both of the undistorted nature that preceded man's descent into history and of the erotic utopia that lies somewhere in the future. These lines are not intended to provide contrast; instead, they represent a culmination.

What does it mean when Danton voices his ardent desire to enfold Marion "completely" inside himself and feels a need to become "part of the atmosphere" so that he might "bathe" his lover in his "flood" and "break on every wave" of her "beautiful body"? And what are we to make of that seemingly cryptic line in which Marion reproachfully tells Danton that his lips have eyes? Should we follow the lead of formalist criticism and conclude that this is nothing more than a bold image that anticipates Rimbaud and the Dadaist Hans Arp? Should we accept the judgment of the critic and poet Walter Höllerer and view it as "surreal estrangement"? But does not Hinderer offer a more convincing explanation when he speaks of a "metaphor for Danton's inability to turn off his consciousness"?

Yet even this interpretation, while establishing a persuasive connection between form and content, provides only half the answer. The other half can be found in a book which makes no reference to Büchner, a book which carries the trendy—and yet appropriate—title, *Love's Body.* Experiences of the sort described by Marion are, the author emphatically informs us, "polymorphous perversity, the translation of all our senses into one another, the interplay between the senses," which is to say "the metaphor, the free translation." And in truth, however suspicious we may be of faddish prophets and lecture-circuit revolutionaries, could we find a better description of Büchner's "new, previously unarticulated sensibility" than this passage by Norman O. Brown? Does not the concept of "polymorphous perversity," the interplay of all the senses, provide, if not *the,* at least *a* key to Danton's lips that have eyes? Or, to phrase the question differently, is not the "metaphor" also a sensual reality? This notion, among others, is elucidated as Brown, proceeding in his inimitably eclectic manner, issues a prophecy regarding an erotic utopia: "The human body would become polymorphously perverse, delighting in that full life of all the body which it now fears. The consciousness strong enough to endure full life would be no longer Apollonian but Dionysian— consciousness which does not observe the limit, but overflows, *consciousness which does not negate any more.*"

Does this not constitute a summation, and a rather detailed one at that, of both the dialogue and the relationship between Danton and Marion? Are they not, like the fervent disciple of Freud, though in a much more direct way, involved in the "complete abolition of repression" and the "resurrection of the body"? As if he were not only allowing Marion to reflect, but also seeking to outdo Danton's "laziness," Brown announces: "The riddle of history is not in Reason but in Desire; not in labor but in love." To be sure, Brown is indulging in extreme understatement when, in his earlier and better known book, *Life Against Death,* he refers to all this as "a little more Eros." . . . [In] Büchner's works we encounter a thoroughly modern view of revolution, one which is not just twofold but actually fourfold; indeed, I would go so far as to say that in his oeuvre every conceivable variety of revolt is not only present but is developed to its fullest extent. Both love and revolution are here in all their various forms; both possess central importance and, at the same time, are inseparable from each other. Nowhere is this more evident than in the female figures of **Danton's Death,** and most of all in Marion.

Thus it is no exaggeration to say that Marion, the embodiment of sexual liberation, can be viewed as the pleasure principle incarnate: a notion which—let me make this point one last time—involves absolutely no value judgment. (pp. 96-100)

In Büchner's works no clear distinction is made between carnal desire and spiritual love; hence it is entirely mistaken to draw a value-laden dichotomy between "love" on the one hand and "lust" on the other. . . . We must avoid tearing apart in dualistic fashion the realm of love as presented by Büchner. . . . Büchner's view of love is not typified by "cœur" or "carreau," but rather by "cœur" *and* "carreau." Throughout his works, love is consistently affirmed in both its aspects, in a virtually indivisible unity of the heart and the senses. (pp. 101-02)

> Reinhold Grimm, in his Love, Lust, and Rebellion: New Approaches to Georg Büchner, *The University of Wisconsin Press, 1985, 265 p.*

## WALTER HINDERER   (essay date 1986)

[*Hinderer finds social, religious, and economic reasons behind the title character's alienation in* Woyzeck.]

Büchner believed that idealism in art and philosophy was bound to lead to the mechanization of poetic representation and thought, [and] he consciously attempted to appeal to the "vein of sensitivity . . . alike in nearly all human beings." He felt the need to engage other aesthetic methods in order to break through the more or less thick shell, as he puts it in *Lenz.* To accomplish this, Büchner returned to Storm and Stress and folk-poetry aesthetics. Rather than idealize man, Büchner preferred to view him, to quote Prince Tandi in Lenz's *The New Menoza,* "as [he is], without gracefulness, rather than as if [he] emerged from the pointed quill of a pen." Human nature seemed to emerge only in its simple, elemental, and original form, without ideological dressing, but not in "genteel society." That is why, as Büchner wrote to Gutzkow in 1836, he wanted to "strive for the formation of a new mentality among the *people.*" In *Woyzeck,* Büchner follows the same aesthetic he had used in his novella *Lenz.* He immerses himself "in the life of the most insignificant person and reproduce[s] it, in the palpitations, intimations, the most subtle, scarcely perceptible gestures." (pp. 31-2)

Although the historical basis for *Woyzeck* is provided by the testimony in the well-documented case given by the physician Johann Christian August Clarus, a civil servant (*Hofrat* ) of the kingdom of Saxony, Büchner enriched Dr. Clarus's account with folk songs, verse quotations, and biblical references, which not only add a new dimension and perspective to the story, but also lend the case a representative quality. A comparison of the various stages of Büchner's play, however, reveals that the author only gradually became fully aware of the effectiveness the use of folk songs and biblical quotations possessed. They serve not just to enhance the commentary or merely to provide a thematic summary of the action, but to intensify the tragedy. It is astonishing to what extent the young playwright was able to achieve a maximum of expression with a minimum of vocabulary and with only the simplest aesthetic techniques. While *Woyzeck* exists only as a fragment and there are several rather problematic versions of the text, it has exerted a greater influence on later poets than any other of Büchner's works.

Büchner immediately indicates his attitude towards his material by giving names only to the poor people: Woyzeck, Marie, Andres, Margret, and the fool Karl, while the other characters only appear to be embodied functions: the captain, the doctor, and the drum major are the most important of these. Büchner reserves the most acerbic criticism for the two representatives of "higher" society. He mocks their "absurd superficiality called education" and the "dead stuff, learning," as he expresses it in a letter. He exposes their emptiness by pitting "arrogance against arrogance, ridicule against ridicule." Indirectly, Büchner's play refutes the materialistic-positivistic and idealistic theories that appropriated Woyzeck's case and submitted it to a scientific examination, but this was only a secondary effect. It was certainly Büchner's primary intention to depict the "suffering, oppressed being" who was powerless "not to become a criminal."

Woyzeck becomes an example, a representative case of human suffering. . . . Woyzeck experiences modern man's complete isolation from the world and even from himself. This experience of such extreme self-alienation for religious and social reasons is expressed in the fairy tale told by the grandmother, which is as succinct as it is powerful:

> Once upon a time there was a poor child with no father and no mother, everything was dead and no one was left in the whole world. Everything was dead, and it went and wept day and night. And since nobody was left on the earth, it wanted to go up to the heavens, and the moon was looking at it so friendly, and when it finally got to the moon, the moon was a piece of rotten wood and then it went to the sun and when it got there, the sun was a wilted sunflower and when it got to the stars, they were little golden flies stuck up there like the shrike sticks 'em on the blackthorn and when it wanted to go back down to the earth, the earth was an overturned pot and was all alone and it sat down and cried and there it sits to this day, all alone.

Although it cannot be said with certainty that Büchner intended to use the fairy tale in the final version, its content does illustrate at least one perspective of Marie's murder by Woyzeck: his increasing loneliness. When the drum major steals Marie from him, Woyzeck loses the last support the world could lend him. He despairs for Marie, himself, and the world, a process that, in the first version, Woyzeck gives voice to by saying: "Everyone's an abyss—you get dizzy when you look down into it." With this statement, Woyzeck anticipates modern self-perception as did not occur again until Franz Kafka, and like the metaphysical question of the connection between no and yes, which Büchner did not plan to use in the final version, for such thought would be above and beyond the horizon of the simple soldier. Thus, for similar reasons Büchner transposes the entire theme into a religious-apocalyptic vision: Woyzeck—and Marie—see their own destiny again and again as part of a world catastrophe. Woyzeck cries to the people dancing before him: "Why doesn't God blow out the sun so that everything can roll around in lust, man and woman, man and beast."

The first scene of the final version of *Woyzeck* establishes the referential nexus of "Sodom and Gomorrah, the whore of Babylon." The lines: "There's fire raging around the sky, and a noise is coming down like trumpets. It's coming closer! Let's go! Don't look back!" refer to Revelation 8:7 and Genesis 19:23-26. As Dr. Clarus noted, Woyzeck's vision anticipates his private fate with Marie, which, at that time, he could not have known and which assumes a metaphysical meaning through its apocalyptic undertone. But Marie, too, who scoffs at Woyzeck's visions and fears he's "going crazy with those thoughts of his," seems to have her own premonitions. For example, she tries to fend off an attack of remorse with the words: "Oh, what a world! Everything goes to hell anyhow, man and woman alike." To the drum major's question as to whether she has the devil in her eyes, Marie answers defiantly: "For all I care. What does it matter?"

Marie's infidelity, which Woyzeck declares a "mortal sin," leads him to despair. But she, too, is finally tormented by her guilt and the thought of her child's father. While the biblical quotations about Maria Magdalena allude to Marie's situation, Woyzeck's state of being is characterized by the verses . . . about suffering as devotion and an imitation of Christ. In both passages, the general situation is individualized, differentiated, and intensified by additional commentary. Marie beats her breast, as the stage directions read, and cries in despair: "It's all dead! Savior, Savior, I wish I could anoint your feet." Woyzeck, who pointedly gives away his few personal belongings to Andres, comments on the verses about "suffering," saying: "My mother can only feel the sun shining on her hands now. That doesn't matter." In both cases, the same extreme feeling of abandonment that the grandmother's fairy tale expresses is predominant.

In spite of the religious conceptual framework, neither Marie nor Woyzeck is to be understood as religious in the ecclesiastical sense. . . . [They] refer to Christ as a model of suffering, yet without sharing the others' rebellious attitude toward God. In contrast to Marie, the "haunted" and "insane" Woyzeck is driven by the idea of plumbing the depth of things. "The toadstools," he fantasizes in the scene with the doctor. "There—that's where it is. Have you seen how they grow in patterns? If only someone could read that." Woyzeck's fixed ideas are . . . projections of his own insecurity and despair. . . . Woyzeck reflects, whereas Marie gives her senses free rein. For this reason, he appears broken, hunted, and persecuted, whereas she, with the exception of her moral scruples, seems at one with herself. . . . (pp. 32-5)

The characters of Marie and Woyzeck . . . [sound] the familiar opposition of spirituality and sensuality. As Marie stands before the mirror judging herself in a sort of erotic competition with the "great ladies," the only difference she is able to acknowledge between rich and poor are her little room, her little piece of mirror—and the fact that the "handsome lords . . . kiss their hands." Woyzeck, however, perceives that the difference between the "common people" and the members of higher society is money. In his simple way, he sees how all notions of virtue and morality—in Marxian terms, the superstructure—derive from economic conditions, or the base. With hidden irony, he tells the captain, "Virtue must be nice, Cap'n. But I'm just a poor guy."

In this famous scene, Büchner confronts the two socially and economically determined ways of thinking and of life of the time, issues with which he had grappled before in *The Hessian Messenger.* The captain prattles on about virtue and morality and feigns respect for the "Reverend Chaplain." Woyzeck, on the other hand, speaks with remarkable accuracy about money, nature, flesh and blood, and defends his "poor little kid," who did not have the blessing of the church, with a corresponding reference to Christ's words. It is important to note that the scene is not dominated by the representative of educated society, who so effectively controls his drives that he automatically suppresses his desire for the owners of the "white stockings as they go tripping down the street." Instead, it is the representative of the poor people who dominates the scene, who, according to the Captain, thinks "too much"—and thought "upsets" one.

The antinomies of bourgeois society that were evident in Büchner's day are all included in his portrait of the Captain, which is a composite of melancholy, boredom, hypochondria, existential fear, and *Weltschmerz.* In his bourgeois way, the Captain also senses the abyss that Woyzeck traces back at one point to the Freemasons, at another to the imminent judgment day. The vertigo that grips the Captain becomes grotesque in the scene with the doctor, whereas for Woyzeck it is apocalyptic. Woyzeck is forced to run himself into the ground in order to provide the bare minimum necessary for the survival of Marie, the child, and himself, but the blissfully ignorant Captain always feels obliged to try to calm and slow him down. Ironically, the Captain, who apparently has all the leisure time in the world at his disposal, recommends that Woyzeck try "activity," although he already has more to do than he can bear. This indicates precisely that essential difference in whether one seeks something to do, like the Captain, in order to avoid the thought of eternity, or if, like Woyzeck, one must sell oneself at the doctor's to earn a couple of extra pennies just in order to eke out a scanty livelihood.

In the scene between the doctor and Woyzeck . . . the opposition of bourgeois virtue or morality and nature comes to the fore, this time, though, with a different emphasis. Philosophical-scientific idealism is called in question here by Woyzeck's nature, or more precisely, by the *musculus constrictor vesicae.* This evidently violates Woyzeck's agreement with the doctor who is paying the soldier to be a guinea pig so that he can prove that "in man alone is individuality exalted to freedom." The lapses in the Captain's and the doctor's ability to control their own emotions prove how shallow this autonomy of the individual and of the will really is. The Captain insists on morality and virtue, the doctor on health and science. When Woyzeck mentions his visions and begins to philosophize about "double nature," the doctor diagnoses "a marvelous *aberratio mentalis partialis,*" an "obsession with a generally rational condition." The Captain is "quite worn out" by the end of his conversation with Woyzeck, but the doctor still maintains rational control, which he achieves by encompassing Woyzeck's interpretation and perspective of the world in established concepts and thus minimizing them.

During this scene, a sentence from Büchner's first lecture (**"On Cranial Nerves"**) comes unbidden to mind: "The question begins for the philosophical school where the teleological school claims to have found an answer." While the doctor transforms Woyzeck into a "complicated machine," or a mere abstraction (*aberratio mentalis partialis*), which for Büchner were the same thing, in an earlier version Woyzeck represents the "unspoiled nature" that shames "human society." What the doctor and the Captain take to be the human *specifica differentia* is nothing more than the product of social conditioning, roles that are imposed and sanctioned by society, but which Büchner divulges in all their empty functionality through the anonymity of those who play them. In the first version, the Barker derides the "progress of civilization. Everything progresses," he cries, "—a horse, a monkey, a cannery-bird. The monkey is already a soldier—that's not much, it's the lowest level of the human race!" This sentiment overlaps with the drunken apprentice's sermon in the eleventh scene of the last version, in which he asks: "Why does man exist? Why does man exist?" The reply ridicules the materialistic viewpoint in the same way that the scene with the doctor satirizes the idealistic perspective. Man exists so that the farmer, the cooper, the shoemaker, and the doctor have work and can make a living. Woyzeck identifies money as the root of his material and psychological destitution and the apprentice proves the vanity of money by indulging in the enjoyment of its exchange value: "My soul, my soul it stinks of booze.—Even money eventually decays." (pp. 35-7)

Büchner differentiates the themes [of *Woyzeck*] by mirroring them from various perspectives. Thus, the frivolous *memento mori* of the apprentice is set in contrast to Woyzeck's "terrible" presentiments and his almost sectarian philosophical-metaphysical questions; the sensualistic, vital world view shared by Marie and the Drum Major are juxtaposed to the morality and virtue of the educated bourgeoisie, and the conceptual apparatus of the scholar clashes with the contradictions of human nature. But all of these perspectives meet at a single point: the example of Woyzeck. He appears as the damned, exiled man, fallen into a veritable state of servitude. He tells the melancholic Captain that "the likes of us [poor people] are wretched in this world and in the next; I guess if we ever got to Heaven, we'd have to help with the thunder." He pursues this damning judgment and discovers the abysses in society, in mankind, in himself. Certainly, he is persecuted by voices and he is sometimes a victim of his own visions, but in the last version the possibility of a choice does occur. Woyzeck asks before the murder: "Should I? Must I?" Thematically, this points to the connection between freedom and historical necessity that Büchner had treated in *Danton's Death*. In *Woyzeck,* however, historical necessity has become eschatological necessity. Like Robespierre, who saw the original of all evil in the excesses of the Dantonists and sought to purge all evil by liquidating them, when Woyzeck murders Marie, he is simultaneously aiming at the more general promiscuity of "man and woman, man and beast."

At the end of the play the question of redemption remains unresolved. In a way, Robespierre had already answered it representatively for . . . [Marie] and Woyzeck when he said: "Why do we always look only toward Him? Truly the Son of Man is crucified in each of us, we all struggle in bloody sweat in the Garden of Gethsemane, but not one of us redeems the other with his wounds." Redemption does not occur in Woyzeck's case either, only suffering, pain, and loneliness remain. Thus, a parallel can undoubtedly be drawn between *Woyzeck* and the tragedy of the German baroque which, as martyr drama, reveals history as a reenactment of the Passion. The significant difference exists in that it is not a sovereign who represents "human nature" and history, but rather what is embodied is "the life of the most insignificant person," a representative of the "poor people," and of "unspoiled nature." (pp. 37-8)

> *Walter Hinderer, in an introduction to* Georg Büchner: Complete Works and Letters, *edited by Walter Hinderer and Henry J. Schmidt, translated by Henry J. Schmidt, The Continuum Publishing Company, 1986, pp. 1-38.*

## JAN KOTT (essay date 1989)

[*Considered one of the most original and influential Polish critics, Kott is best known for his* Szkice o Szekspirze (1961; Shakespeare: Our Contemporary, 1964). *In the following excerpt, he reveals affinities between Büchner's tragic view of history in* Danton's Death *and that of Shakespeare in* Julius Caesar.]

*Julius Caesar* is certainly one of the most shocking of all Shakespeare's tragedies. Caesar is murdered at the height of his triumphs. A moment before his death, before the last words of his final speech, he compares himself to the northern star "of whose true-fix'd and resting quality / There is no fellow in the firmament," and now he is lying bleeding on the steps of the Capitol pierced by the daggers of the Roman senators. Shakespeare saw with the utmost clarity that Caesar's death is a twofold exemplum, of both history and tragedy, and that it would be played all over again on the steps of many capitols and on the stages of many theaters " . . . be acted over / In [states] unborn and accents yet unknown!" (p. 40)

For the twenty-two-year-old Georg Büchner *Julius Caesar* was the model of historical tragedy; or perhaps it would be better to say that for Büchner *Julius Caesar* was the model not of historical tragedy, but of the tragedy of history. And for that reason Büchner could undertake his own version of *Julius Caesar,* transposing it, in *Danton's Death,* into the drama of revolution. At a midnight meeting of the conspirators Brutus says:

> Let's be sacrificers, but not butchers, Caius.
> We all stand up against the spirit of Caesar,
> And in the spirit of men there is no blood.
>       . . . . .
> Let's carve him as a dish fit for the gods,
> Not hew him as a carcass fit for hounds;
>       . . . .
> . . .to the common eyes,
> We shall be call'd purgers, not murderers.

Brutus wants to put Caesar's body on the altar of the Republic, to change murder into a ritual in which the sacrificial lamb is offered up to save Rome. "Let's be sacrificers, but not butchers." The spirit has no blood, but the sacrificial lamb bleeds. Shakespeare knows that ritual is still murder. The same pure Brutus who, one hour before sunrise on the day of the murder, had talked about Caesar's death as an act of cleansing, the way a surgeon wearing antiseptic gloves talks about an operation, now, when the deed is done, lifts his bloody hands over Caesar's body. After the murder, a new Brutus is born—an ideologue.

> And let us bathe our hands in Caesar's blood
> Up to the elbows, and besmear our swords;
> Then walk we forth, even to the market-place . . .

In *Danton's Death* Saint-Just is the deputy who speaks first, when he urges Robespierre to take part in the murder of their fellow revolutionaries, Danton and his circle. He repeats almost exactly Brutus' words, which Shakespeare took from Plutarch: "We must bury the great corpse with proper decorum, like priests, not murderers. We dare not chop it up, all its limbs must fall with it." When Robespierre interrupts him—"Speak more clearly"—Saint-Just becomes the counterpart of Cassius, who demanded that Antony be done away with along with Caesar. "We must bury him in full armor and slaughter his horses and slaves on his burial ground."

Shakespeare's Brutus calls Caesar's murders "the purgers." In the first act of *Danton's Death* Robespierre and Saint-Just draw up the list of names for the great purge of the Terror. One after the other they put down the names of the deputies of the Convention, the Jacobins, the old comrades, including Camille Desmoulins, the legendary editor of the *Vieux Cordelier* and Robespierre's schoolmate and friend: he had dared to call the "Incorruptible," Robespierre, the "Messiah of Blood." "Then quickly, tomorrow," says the new Brutus of the Revolution. "No long death agony! I've become sensitive lately. Quickly!" And Büchner adds, in the spirit of Macbeth: "Only the dead do not return," an ill-fated prophecy.

Büchner was not the first to show how the French Revolution wore the costume of republican Rome. But more penetratingly and more sharply than Marx, for instance, Büchner revealed for what sort of masquerade and for what purpose that costume, and the Roman names and gestures, were intended. In Act I, scene two of *Danton's Death,* as in Shakespeare, the action takes place in the streets. A drunken theater prompter mercilessly beats his wife while he is reciting some fragments from *Hamlet* and shouting at the passers-by: "A knife, give me a knife, Romans!" He calls his wife alternately a whore and Baucis. His daughter, Lucretia, is standing on the corner. "Would you have a pair of pants to pull *up,*" the new Baucis asks her husband, "if the young gentlemen didn't pull theirs *down* with her?"

In the street scene of *Julius Caesar* the Roman rabble, enraged by Caesar's murder, attacks Cinna the poet instead of the conspirator bearing the same name. In the street scene of *Danton's Death* the citizens drag to the lamppost a passer-by who happens to have a handkerchief around his neck. "Our wives and children cry out for bread. We want to feed them with the flesh of aristocrats. Hey! Kill anyone without a hole in his coat!"

Less than a year before writing *Danton's Death* Büchner founded . . . "The Society for the Rights of Man," an organization intended to prepare the ground for the "revolution," and in *The Hessian Messenger* (*Der Hessiche Landbote*), of which he was the publisher, he declared, "Freedom for the huts! Wars to the palaces!" Now, with all the bitterness of defeat, convinced of the implacable fatalism of history and abandoning Schiller for Shakespeare, Büchner did not forget that people were hungry. It was the same in Hesse, which was ruled by feudal princes, as it had been in Paris during the Revolution. Instead of bread, Revolution could offer only heads falling into the basket from the guillotine.

"The weapon of the Republic is terror, the power of the Republic is virtue," says Robespierre. "Virtue, for without it terror is corruptible. Terror, for without it, virtue is powerless." Büchner extracted from Robespierre's speeches their essence—a corrosive essence, one might say. In *Danton's Death* Büchner, one hundred years before Orwell, was one of the first writers to reveal the newspeak of terror.

> Terror is an outgrowth of virtue. . . .
> The revolutionary government is the despotism of
> freedom against the tyranny of Kings.

In this chilling semantic system words can be inverted at will. Kindness turns into crime and crime into kindness. "To punish the oppressors of mankind is kindness—to pardon them is barbarity." The despotism of freedom differs from the despotism of kings only in the different heads that fell from the guillotine, just as the difference between "internationalism" and "cosmopolitanism" can be measured by the thousands who perished in Lubyanka prison or rotted in the labor camps. It is quite possible that Büchner found this appalling semantics not only in the words of Robespierre but also in those of Shakespeare's Brutus. Consider Brutus' speech over Caesar's body:

> . . . then is death a benefit;

So are we Caesar's friends, that have abridg'd
His time of fearing death.

The horror of this stupefying sentence, which must be breathtaking when delivered by a great actor, became clear to me only when Büchner's Robespierre says, "To punish the oppressors of mankind is kindness." But Büchner unveiled in Robespierre's speeches not only the semantics of terror but also its deadly logic. "The internal enemies of the Republic consist of two factions, like two armies." The relentless repetitious quality of this logic seems to define the terror. "One of the factions," Robespierre continues,

> no longer exists. In its presumptuous insanity it tried to throw aside the most proven patriots as worn-out weaklings in order to rob the Republic of its strongest arms. It declared war on God and property in order to create a division on behalf of the kings. It parodied the illustrious drama of the Revolution in order to compromise it through premeditated excesses. Hébert's triumph would have turned the Republic into chaos, and despotism would have been satisfied. The sword of judgment has struck the traitor down.

It is not necessary to bring Robespierre's logic up to date; it is already modern enough. Two factions, two deviations, both enemies of the people. The other faction, Robespierre goes on, "is the opposite of the first. It leads us to weakness; its battle cry is: mercy!" After the Trotskyites we have Zinoviev and the followers of Bukharin; after Hébert and the Hébertistes we have Danton.

There is then a brief exchange which also needs no updating. We have heard it all too often.

> ROBESPIERRE. Whoever said that an innocent person was struck down?
> DANTON. Do you hear that Fabricius? No innocent person was killed!

The twenty-two-year-old Büchner shows not only the logic of terror, but the face of the Incorruptible as well. Here again one thinks of Büchner's apprenticeship with Shakespeare. Sleep has abandoned Robespierre, just as it did Brutus that night full of "figures and fantasies" before the murder of Caesar or Macbeth after killing the king. Robespierre looks out the window at Paris.

> I can't tell what part of me is deceiving the other. Night snores over the earth and wallows in wild dreams. . . . Aren't we sleepwalkers?

At that moment, enter Saint-Just, the archangel of terror. A maid brings a lighted candelabra. Death sentences are soon being signed. Even the closest friends must perish. Robespierre is once more left alone. A new day breaks. The guillotine erected at the Place de la Révolution can be seen from the window. "They're all leaving me—all is desolate and empty—I am alone." Robespierre brushes off his jacket. From early childhood he has hated dirt. His face is almost white. He has powdered it again. He smiles. And one thinks not only of dozens of portraits of Robespierre but of a famous smile in [*Hamlet*]: "O villain, villain, smiling, damned villain!"

In *Danton's Death* the guillotine appears on the stage only at the denouement, but its presence can be felt throughout the play. If I were to stage *Danton's Death,* the guillotine would always be there, looming over the actors and the spectators alike, since in this kind of a theater the spectators become the actors.

In Act I, scene one, the conversations take place as cards are being shuffled and fall on a card table. "Did it rain while they were guillotining or did you get a bad seat and not see anything?" But who guillotined whom? "They" did, but who are "they"? At the card table Hérault-Séchelles talks with Camille Desmoulins and Philippeau. Danton sits nearby. All three are deputies to the Convention. So who are "they"—the guilliotiners or the guillotined? The game is being played with cards falling on the table like the severed heads that fell in the Place de la Révolution during the first week of April 1794. In Büchner's play, as in Shakespeare's histories, time passes at variable speeds, only the hours of the day or night are given precisely. But the precise historical dates are important to the play. In October 1793, during the trial of Marie Antoinette, Hébert heaped abuse upon the queen and demanded her immediate execution. Six months later, in the fourth week of March 1794—and therefore no more than a week before the card game we see—Danton sent Hébert to the guillotine. Only a few days after the rainy morning when Philippeau got a bad seat at the Place de la Révolution and had difficulty seeing the guillotining, he was himself executed along with Danton, Camille Desmoulins, and Hérault-Séchelles, at the same hour, the difference being that now it was easier to see.

The spectators, those sending others to the guillotine, and the guillotined, change rapidly at the Place de la Révolution. The guillotine was called "the great widow." "She has had at least a half-dozen husbands," Desmoulins wrote at an unguarded moment, "and she had to bury them all." *"On couche avec, on ne la féconde pas,"* wrote Victor Hugo in his novel *93.* ("Men lie with her, but she does not become pregnant.") On days when it stood idle, the guillotine was covered with a white sheet. Like an altar. "The Revolution," Büchner's Saint-Just says in a speech to the Convention,

> is like the daughters of Pelias: it cuts humanity in pieces to rejuvenate it. Humanity will rise up with mighty limbs out of this cauldron of blood, like the earth out of the waters of the Flood, as if it had been newly created.

At this point the deputies give Saint-Just a long, standing ovation. At the same meeting of the Convention Saint-Just asks for Danton's head.

That same night, or perhaps it was the night before, neither Robespierre nor Danton was able to sleep. In this sudden dramatic kinship between Danton and Robespierre, we can sense the shadow of Shakespeare's Brutus, with his nightly specters. Now it is Danton's turn to stand at the window looking out at Paris. And he hears voices coming from outside, or perhaps he hears them within himself: *"September, September!"* During the first days of September 1792, the sansculottes massacred thousands of prisoners in Paris and the provinces.

> JULIE. The Kings [of the invading countries] were just forty hours from Paris . . .
> DANTON. We killed them. That was not murder, that was internal war.
> JULIE. You saved the country.

"The guillotine is an instrument of division," writes the contemporary French historian François Furet, "separating the good from the bad." It should be added that by means of this instrument of division the good would invariably turn into the bad, and patriots into traitors. In this theater of revolution, we and "they"—spectators, those sending others to the guillotine and the guillotined—all change places, sometimes during a single week. In *Danton's Death* the guillotine cuts off Danton's head; in actual history, less than six months after Danton's execution, it cuts off Robespierre's head. In Büchner's play the guillotine, along with Danton and Robespierre, is the third protagonist of the drama. It destroyed the Revolution that it was supposed to save. The fearsome widow has two faces: that of a savior and that of an executioner.

In the last scene of *Danton's Death,* the day after the execution, the widow of Camille Desmoulins, who was executed along with Danton, sits on the steps of the guillotine:

> LUCILLE. (Reflectively, then suddenly as if reaching a decision) Long Live the King!
> CITIZEN. In the name of the Republic! (She is surrounded by the watch and is led off.)

Historical tragedy depends on the choice of historical sequence. In *Danton's Death* the action starts a week, or perhaps even only a few days, before his execution, but the decisive historical dates that stand behind the play are recited by Saint-Just: "the 14th of July, the 10th of August, the 31st of May"—the storming of the Bastille, the dethroning of Louis XVI, the seizure of power by the Jacobins. Lucille's suicidal scream ends Act IV, and *Danton's Death* has no Act V. In the entire history of the theater, starting with Greek tragedy which is divided into five episodes, through the Renaissance and up to the German and French romantics, I know of no other instance of a drama in four acts that still works on the stage. There always have been either three acts or five acts. What happened to Act V in Büchner's play?

Roman Jacobson calls the absence of a foot or a part of it at the end of a line of verse a zero sign—a sign signifying an absence. Barthes has written about how "nonpresence" can be a sign of presence—the letter that does not arrive, the telephone that does not ring. In a theatrical performance, an unwritten Act V goes on existing as an expectation. In historical drama, it is history still open, also as though suspended.

In *Danton's Death* Robespierre's execution is foreshadowed, or, rather, foretold. During the final night before his own execution Danton says to his fellow prisoners: "Freedom will now respectably prostitute herself in the marriage bed of the lawyer of Arras [Robespierre]. But I imagine she'll play Clytemnestra to him. I don't give him six months. I'm dragging him down with me."

The nonexistent Act V could have turned on Robespierre's execution. The piece of history being reenacted would have started with the destruction of the Bastille, or at least with the September massacres, and would have ended with Thermidor. *Danton's Death* then could have had an ending comparable to the denouement of *Julius Caesar.* "Take away the corpses and let soldiers pitch their tents at the Place de la Révolution," the future first consul could say, still wearing his general's uniform with its white, tightly fitting trousers and the three-cornered hat of the revolutionary army. But he has already put his hand over his breast in celebration of his first victory [as in *Julius Caesar*].

> So call the field to rest, and let's away,
> To part the glories of this happy day.

In the nonexistent Act V of *Danton's Death,* history continues to move ahead, constantly digging like Shakespeare's "old mole"—"A worthy pioneer!" (*Hamlet*), but its real conclusion would not be Thermidor, the end of the Reign of Terror and the beginning of Caesarism. For Büchner the time of the Terror did not end with Robespierre's beheading. In that unwritten Act V of **Danton's Death,** the bitter chapter of history would continue, but when would it end? With what sort of new defeat after what kind of new revolution? For the first readers of **Danton's Death** in the mid-1830s, and even for its first spectators in Berlin in 1902, Lucile's suicidal scream on the steps of the scaffold had a sinister irony. Kings were already reigning "in the name of the Republic." And Act V goes on still, *"le temps des assassins,"* the time of uninterrupted terror. (pp. 40-2)

> Jan Kott, "Caesar at the Bastille," translated by Jadwiga Kosicka, in The New York Review of Books, *Vol. XXXVI, No. 15, October 12, 1989, pp. 40-2.*

---

# FURTHER READING

Baxandall, Lee. "Georg Büchner's *Danton's Death.*" *The Tulane Drama Review* 6, No. 3 (March 1962): 136-49.
Investigates the style and themes of Büchner's first play, considering it one of the earliest dramatic expressions of social alienation.

Bell, Gerda E. "Windows: A Study of a Symbol in Georg Büchner's Work." *The Germanic Review* XLVII, Vol. 2 (March 1972): 95-108.
Argues that Büchner uses windows as a symbol of existential despair.

Benn, Maurice B. *The Drama of Revolt: A Critical Study of Georg Büchner.* Cambridge, England: Cambridge University Press, 1976, 321 p.
Examines Büchner as a rebel in politics, aesthetics, drama, and philosophy.

Closs, August. "Nihilism and Modern German Drama: Grabbe and Büchner." In his *Medusa's Mirror: Studies in German Literature,* pp. 147-63. London: The Cresset Press, 1957.
Traces the development of nihilism in the works of various German writers, including Johann Wolfgang von Goethe, Christian Dietrich Grabbe, and Büchner.

Cowen, Roy C. "Grabbe's *Don Juan und Faust* and Büchner's *Dantons Tod:* Epicureanism and *Weltschmerz.*" *PMLA* LXXXII, No. 5 (October 1967): 342-52.
A comparison of Grabbe's and Buchner's plays noting how each dramatist similarly treats the themes of Epicureanism and *Weltschmerz.*

——. "Identity and Conscience in Büchner's Works." *The Germanic Review* XLIII, No. 4 (November 1968): 258-66.
Concludes that in Büchner's writings "conscience, guilt and pain form the necessary foundation for man's unending defence of his identity and intrinsic worth."

Dunlop, Geoffrey. Introduction to *The Plays of Georg Büchner,* by Georg Büchner, translated by Geoffrey Dunlop, pp. 7-64. 1927. Reprint. London: Vision Press, 1952.
A biographical introduction to the first English translation of Büchner's works.

Fleissner, E. M. "Revolution as Theatre: *Danton's Death* and

*Marat/Sade.*" *The Massachusetts Review* VII, No. 3 (Summer 1966): 543-56.
Considers revolt a central issue in *Danton's Death,* marking "the beginning of revolution as theatre," and compares Büchner's play with Peter Weiss's *Marat/Sade,* which he regards as the leading example of revolt in the modern theater.

Furness, N. A. "Georg Büchner's Translations of Victor Hugo." *The Modern Language Review* LI, No. 1 (January 1956): 49-54.
A comparison of Büchner's German translations of Hugo's dramas *Lucrèce Borgia* and *Marie Tudor* with the French originals, revealing that Büchner was not a faithful translator.

Hauch, Edward Franklin. "The Reviviscence of Georg Büchner." *PMLA* XLIV, No. 3 (September 1929): 892-900.
Provides reasons for the delayed recognition of Büchner's works. Hauch concludes, "The truth of the whole matter is that he was notably in advance of his age. Fortunately there were now and then a few who caught some inkling of his significance, but this significance was not fully realized until recently when a new generation of kindred minds had . . . caught up with him."

Hilton, Julian. *Georg Büchner.* New York: Grove Press, 1982, 167 p.
A biographical and critical introduction. Hilton also offers his ideas on staging the plays.

Jacobs, Margaret. Introduction to *"Dantons Tod" and "Woyzeck",* by Georg Büchner, ix-xxxii. Manchester: Manchester University Press, 1954.
An interpretation of *Dantons Tod* and *Woyzeck,* including a brief note on ordering the scenes of the latter.

James, Dorothy. *Georg Büchner's "Dantons Tod": A Reappraisal.* Texts and Dissertations, edited by H. B. Nisbet, vol. 16. London: Modern Humanities Research Association, 1982, 138 p.
Analyzes *Danton's Death,* taking into account Büchner's views of history, science, and art.

King, Janet K. "Lenz Viewed Sane." *The Germanic Review* XLIX, No. 2 (March 1974): 146-53.
A reaction to critics who view *Lenz* as an artistic study of madness. King argues instead that the narrative focuses on societal conditions that either support or stifle artistic creativity.

Lukens, Nancy. *Büchner's Valerio and the Theatrical Fool Tradition.* Stuttgarter Arbeiten zur Germanistik, edited by Ulrich Müller, Franz Hundsnurscher and Cornelius Sommer, no. 37. Stuttgart: Akademischer Verlag Hans-Dieter Heinz, 1977, 221 p.
Finds that Büchner's Valerio in *Leonce and Lena* transcends the "theatrical fool tradition."

McCarthy, John A. "Some Aspects of Imagery in Büchner's *Woyzeck.*" *Modern Language Notes* 91, No. 3 (April 1976): 543-51.
Explores images in *Woyzeck* in order to show that "as much, if not more, importance is to be attached to the images and symbols, as to the economic and social indictment in an evaluation of the work."

Mac Ewen, Leslie. *The Narren-motifs in the Works of Georg Büchner.* Bern: Verlag Herbert Lang, 1968, 49 p.
Traces the development of the fool as a dramatic figure from its first recorded appearance in the Hebrew Scriptures to its use in Büchner's works.

Majut, Rudolf. "Georg Büchner and Some English Thinkers." *The Modern Language Review* XLVIII, No. 3 (July 1953): 310-22.
Studies the relationship between Büchner's beliefs and those of several English thinkers and scientists, including Thomas Carlyle and Thomas Hobbes.

——. "Some Literary Affiliations of Georg Büchner with England." *The Modern Language Review* L, No. 1 (January 1955): 30-43.

A companion piece to the above article examining Büchner's ideological affinities with English poets and novelists, including Geoffrey Chaucer, William Shakespeare, and Charles Dickens.

Otten, Terry. "*Woyzeck* and *Othello:* The Dimensions of Melodrama." *Comparative Drama* 12, No. 2 (Summer 1978): 123-36.
A comparative study of *Woyzeck* and Shakespeare's *Othello* pointing out similarities in plot, style, and technique.

Pascal, Roy. "Georg Büchner: *Lenz.*" In his *The Dual Voice,* pp. 60-6. Manchester: Manchester University Press, 1977.
Uses *Lenz* as one of several illustrations of "free indirect speech," a technique in which narrative is related from a particular character's viewpoint.

Price, Victor. Introduction to *The Plays of Georg Büchner,* by Georg Büchner, translated by Victor Price, pp. vii-xix. London: Oxford University Press, 1971.
A brief discussion of Büchner's life and writings, including a stage history of his plays and reflections on the difficulties of translating them.

Reeve, William C. *Georg Büchner.* New York: Frederick Ungar Publishing Co., 1979, 186 p.
A general overview of Büchner's life, works, and critical reputation.

Rosenberg, Ralph P. "Georg Büchner's Early Reception in America." *The Journal of English and Germanic Philology* XLIV, No. 3 (July 1945): 270-73.

Provides an American publication history of Büchner's writings.

Schmidt, Henry J. *Satire, Caricature and Perspectivism in the Works of Georg Büchner.* Stanford Studies in Germanics and Slavics, edited by Edgar Lohner, C. H. Van Schooneveld, and F. W. Strothmann, vol. VIII. The Hague: Mouton, 1970, 119 p.
Studies the relationship between the primary and secondary characters of Büchner's dramas, finding that the environment in which the dramatist places his main characters is significant in grasping the whole meaning of a play.

Shaw, Leroy R. "Symbolism of Time in Büchner's *Leonce und Lena.*" *Monatshefte* XLVIII, No. 4 (March-April 1956): 221-30.
Contends that the language of *Leonce and Lena* reflects Büchner's dissatisfaction with the age in which he lived.

Spalter, Max. "Georg Büchner." In his *Brecht's Tradition,* pp. 75-111. Baltimore: Johns Hopkins Press, 1967.
A perceptive exploration of Büchner as a precursor of Bertolt Brecht.

White, John S. "Georg Büchner; or, The Suffering through the Father." *The American Imago* 9, No. 3-4 (Fall-Winter 1952): 365-427.
A psychoanalytic character study of Büchner claiming that his premature death "has a deeper root than its definite physiological cause. It is the self-inflicted result of a morbid pathological temperament which, through its defective attitude toward mental and physical health, undermined and sapped the vitality of the organism into which it was born."

# George Crabbe

## 1754-1832

English poet.

Crabbe is considered a key figure in the shift from Augustan to Romantic modes in English poetry. While many critics regard him as a traditional poet for his reliance on the heroic couplet and penchant for satire, both trademarks of the Augustan age, his clear, graphic descriptions of rural life and natural scenery and his interest in the psychology of human nature are regarded as innovative for his time. Crabbe's best-known work is *The Village,* a sordid, detailed portrait of the English countryside and its humble inhabitants that countered the sentimentalism of the eighteenth-century pastoral with a new sense of realism. However, his extended narrative poems—most notably *The Borough, Tales,* and *Tales of the Hall,* in which Crabbe developed the art of storytelling through the creation of incisive character portraits—have ultimately received greater critical attention. Although Crabbe is not widely read today, his works continue to be studied for their contribution to the genre of narrative poetry and for their unique insights into the social conditions of eighteenth-century rural England.

The eldest of six children, Crabbe was born in 1754 in the Suffolk town of Aldeborough. His father, a minor customs official who supplemented his small income through part ownership of a fishing business, proved to be a decisive, if contradictory, influence on the poet's personality. On the one hand, his habitual drunkenness and violent temper frightened the young Crabbe and fostered a severe, pessimistic outlook on life; on the other hand, his readings from such authors as John Milton and Edward Young instilled a love of English literature in his son from an early age. The environs of Aldeborough also had a profound effect on the boy's developing sensibilities: the dramatic spectacle of the sea, the flat, melancholy landscape of the surrounding countryside, and the difficult yet colorful life of the villagers would become dominant themes of Crabbe's poetry.

Although Crabbe's family was poor, his father determined that his eldest son should go away to school. He was sent at an early age to Bungay, near Norfolk, though he soon returned home, spending much of his time reading in his father's library, where he developed an interest in adventure stories. In 1766, Crabbe was again sent away to school, this time to Stowmarket. It was there that Crabbe began his first experiments in verse, penning satirical observations of his fellow students in the manner of Alexander Pope. Crabbe's formal education ended in late 1767, and the following year he was apprenticed to an apothecary at Wickham Brooke in Suffolk, where he was forced to spend much of his time in manual work. In 1771, he became apprenticed to a surgeon and apothecary at Woodbridge, a situation he found far more congenial. During this time he was able to work on his poetry, and also met his future wife, Sarah Elmy, whom he later referred to in his works as "Mira." Her family, descended from minor land owners and manufacturers, provided Crabbe with a more stimulating intellectual and social life, and he intensified his efforts to improve his poetry. In 1772, the *Lady's Magazine* agreed to publish five of his poems, one

of which, entitled "Hope," received a prize from the publisher. Three years later, near the end of his long apprenticeship, he published his first major poem, *Inebriety,* but it was not a critical or financial success, and Crabbe returned to Aldeborough, where he discovered that his father's alcoholism had driven his family to poverty. Obliged to assist, he became for a short time a common laborer on the quay at Aldeborough. In September 1775, he purchased an apothecary business on credit, hoping to use it as a basis to establish a medical practice; within two years, however, he was ruined by rival practitioners. Beset by continuing family problems and poverty, Crabbe resolved to go to London and pursue a literary career. He arrived there in April 1780, and later that year convinced a small publisher to issue in a limited printing his poem *The Candidate,* yet like his first production, this too was a failure. With no source of income, Crabbe's position rapidly became desperate. He wrote an appeal to the prime minister, Lord North, for financial assistance, but was rebuffed. Crabbe made a final appeal to the statesman Edmund Burke, sending him a highly emotional letter together with unfinished drafts of *The Library* and *The Village.* Impressed by Crabbe's forthrightness and poetic powers, Burke agreed to pay his debts and advance funds for further work, and was instrumental in having *The Library* published in 1781. A didactic poem that addressed the relation of poetry to knowledge, *The Library* was the first of Crabbe's efforts to receive significant critical attention.

Although Crabbe's literary career was beginning to prosper, he expressed a desire to enter the church in order to obtain a steady income, relying on Burke's influence to secure him a position. He was ordained a deacon by the Bishop of Norwich in November 1781, and through Burke's recommendation was appointed private chaplain to the Duke of Rutland in 1782, which required him to move to Belvoir Castle, where he remained for three years. Through Burke and Rutland, Crabbe became acquainted with fashionable London society, meeting such figures as Sir Joshua Reynolds and Samuel Johnson during a visit to the capital in 1782. In the meantime, he continued writing, publishing his most famous poem, *The Village,* to widespread critical and popular acclaim in May 1783. Rutland left Belvoir in 1784 when he was appointed lord-lieutenant of Ireland, but Crabbe chose to stay in England, where for the next two years he divided his time between parish duties and various occupations at the duke's country seat. 1785 saw the appearance of *The Newspaper,* a satire on the political machinations of the English press. Apparently chastened by critical reaction to *The Newspaper* and increasingly isolated due to the deaths of his patrons (Johnson, 1784; Rutland, 1787; Burke, 1797), Crabbe ceased publishing for twenty-two years, though he continued writing. His career in the church kept him well occupied, however, as he was obliged to move frequently to the various parishes to which he was assigned.

During a trip to Suffolk in 1790, Crabbe experienced an attack of light-headedness, for which he took opium as a cure; scholars attribute the surrealistic aspect of his work composed around this time to a possibly chronic addiction to the drug. The 1790s were also marked by the loss of Crabbe's two youngest children, a tragedy that severely affected his wife, whose behavior became increasingly irrational. In 1805, Crabbe returned to the parish of Muston, Leicestershire, where he had been rector in 1789, for an extended stay. His new collection, *Poems,* appeared in 1807 and was an immediate critical and popular success. Two volumes of narrative verse followed and were similarly well received: *The Borough,* describing the period of his youth in Aldeborough, appeared in 1810, *Tales,* a series of character portraits, in 1812. In 1813, Crabbe's wife died, and in the following year, he moved for the last time, to Trowbridge, Wiltshire, where he worked on his final volume of poetry, *Tales of the Hall.* Also a narrative series, it appeared in 1819 to a somewhat reserved critical reception, though Crabbe received the then fabulous sum of three thousand pounds for the copyrights. Crabbe's remaining years at Trowbridge were pleasant ones, spent in close proximity to his two surviving children. His company continued to be sought by the local aristocracy and by literary society, and in 1822, he travelled to Edinburgh to meet Sir Walter Scott, who greatly admired his work. On 27 January 1832, Crabbe was suddenly struck by illness when he experienced a violent headache and a high fever. He remained in a state of half-conscious delirium for four days, dying on 3 February 1832.

Crabbe's career is classified by most critics into three distinct phases. The first includes the topical poems published in the 1770s and 1780s, the second those shorter, innovative compositions collected in *Poems,* and the third the lengthy narrative compositions that began to appear in 1810 with *The Borough.* Of the first group, only *The Village* is considered of great critical importance. The poem first set forth Crabbe's poetic credo of delineating the life of rural society with accuracy and unrelenting candor, although its gloomy social view was mitigated by vivid descriptions of nature. Crabbe eschewed the prevailing sentimentalism about rural life, implicitly attacking both Oliver Goldsmith and Thomas Grey for falsely glorifying that subject in their works *The Deserted Village* (1770) and *Elegy Written in a Country Churchyard* (1751). But if *The Village* broke new ground thematically, Crabbe's use of the heroic couplet, which he would continue in his later work, ties him to Pope and the conservative norms of Augustan taste. *Poems* introduced new themes for Crabbe. "The Parish Register," one of the principal pieces in the collection, is a three-part composition featuring a village clergyman who narrates his parishioners' lives, as suggested to him by his register of baptisms, marriages, and burials. The work continues the stark realism of *The Village* in its portrayal of rural life, but also includes picturesque descriptions of the English countryside in the manner of Goldsmith and Grey. Critics consider another prominent poem in the collection, "Sir Eustace Grey," to be highly original for its depiction of a disturbed inmate of a madhouse. The poem's atmospheric, sensual depictions of nature and hallucinatory rendering of its subject's mental delirium were highly unusual for Crabbe, and for this reason are frequently attributed to his concurrent use of opium. The third phase of Crabbe's poetic career, now considered his most important, is exclusively narrative in conception. Crabbe continued to use the provincial English town or village as his principal subject, deriving as much inspiration from his experiences in various country parishes as from his memories of Aldeborough. *The Borough* begins with the depiction of the physical and social characteristics of a town like Aldeborough, but gradually evolves into a series of related narratives, some of which address such general subjects as the Church, law, and the trades, while others examine variations in human character with great psychological insight. "Peter Grimes," a vivid analysis of a young man's spiritual and moral collapse, is considered by many critics to be one of Crabbe's finest dramatic compositions. Like its predecessor, *Tales* does not contain a unifying narrative, but presents a series of individual portraits that suggest a social tableau of provincial society. Although the poem has been faulted for its lack of structural unity, critics agree that it is superior to *The Borough* stylistically for its more dignified language, refined versification, and skillfully handled dialogue, as well as thematically for its clear enunciation of commonsense ethical priorities. Crabbe's last published work, *Tales of the Hall,* asserts a strong narrative structure, as its series of character portraits are told by two brothers who meet after a lengthy separation. However, in contrast to *The Borough* or *Tales,* its subjects are drawn from what Crabbe called "the superior classes," including squires and clergymen, thus enlarging the scope of Crabbe's social analysis. Although commentators agree that the volume shows less dramatic power than his earlier work, they acknowledge that many of the tales effectively portray the results of human error and weakness, thus invoking the strong moral lessons of his earlier narrative poems.

In order to understand the first few decades of critical reaction to Crabbe's poetry, it is essential to recognize that the greater part of his work appeared during the Romantic revolution in English poetry (1780-1820). His earlier works, such as *The Village,* were topical poems whose themes were frequently controversial, but which conformed stylistically to Augustan ideas of objectivity, balance, and restraint, and were thus well received until the Romantic sensibility began to become influential around 1800. After this date, responses to Crabbe's poetry shifted dramatically. Generally speaking, the leading Romantic poets, particularly Samuel Taylor Coleridge, held his work in disdain, asserting its lack of poetic vision and deficiency in feeling, a viewpoint shared by many other prominent critics, including William Hazlitt. However, those critics who opposed the aesthetic credo of the Romantics, such as Francis Jeffrey, applauded Crabbe's straightforward realism, citing his skill in depicting individual characters within particular social environments. Late nineteenth-century commentators were just as divided in their opinions. Some critics praised Crabbe's stylistic competence and interest in vernacular subjects, but many reiterated the objections raised during the Romantic epoch; George Saintsbury, for instance, claimed that in Crabbe's poetry "there is no music." With the anti-Victorian reaction of the early twentieth century, however, the prevailing critical attitude towards Crabbe's poetry essentially reversed. Such influential proponents of Modernism as T. S. Eliot and Ezra Pound praised Crabbe's poetry for its objective, rational qualities, while other critics took interest in the psychological aspects of such tales as "Peter Grimes." Critics after 1945 have expanded the scope of early modern criticism, often focusing on narrative structures in Crabbe's later writings and paying particular attention to his dramatic handling of the couplet form. Others have concentrated on his work's stylistic provenance, attempting to determine the extent to which Crabbe must be seen as an eighteenth- rather than as a nineteenth-century poet, or have examined previously ignored aspects of his work, such as the meaning and function of his nature descriptions. Given this sustained and complex history of critical opinion, future interest in Crabbe's poetry seems assured.

## PRINCIPAL WORKS

*Inebriety* (poetry) 1775
*The Candidate: A Poetical Epistle to the Authors of the "Monthly Review"* (poetry) 1780
*The Library* (poetry) 1781
*The Village* (poetry) 1783
*The News-paper* (poetry) 1785
*Poems* (poetry) 1807
*The Borough* (poetry) 1810
*Tales* (poetry) 1812
*Tales of the Hall* (poetry) 1819
*The Poetical Works* (poetry) 1822
*\*The Poetical Works of the Rev. George Crabbe; with His Letters and Journals and His Life* (poetry, letters, and journals) 1834
*Poems.* 3 vols. (poetry) 1905-07
*New Poems* (poetry) 1960

*This work contains a biography of Crabbe written by his son.

---

### THE CRITICAL REVIEW (essay date 1780)

[*In the following review of* The Candidate, *the critic censures Crabbe's diction and grammar.*]

The anonymous author of this Poetical Epistle [*The Candi-*

date] is, it seems, an unfortunate gentleman, who having long laboured under a *cacoethes scribendi,* humbly requests the advice and assistance of Dr. G—, and his brethren of the faculty, concerned in the *Monthly Review.* The patient, it is observable, takes no notice of us Critical Reviewers, though we have been pretty famous for eradicating disorders of this kind. When the disease, however, increases, as it probably will, there is no doubt but we shall be called in. In the mean time, though we have received no fee, we shall (like the noble-minded physician to a certain news-paper) give our advice *gratis.* Temperance in this, as in almost every other case, is the grand specific, we shall confine our prescription, therefore, in a very few words; viz. *Abstinè à plumâ & atramento;* a safe, an easy, and we will venture to add, an infallible remedy. For the too visible symptoms of this poor man's malady, we refer our readers to the poem, where he says,

> We write enraptur'd, and we write in haste,
> Dream idle dreams, and call them things of taste;
> Are seldom cautious, all advice detest,
> And ever think our own opinions best.

If these are not marks of what we call the incurable METROMANIA, we know not what are. He then breaks out into the following mad questions:

> Say, shall my name, to future song prefix'd,
> Be with the meanest of the tuneful mix'd?
> Shall my soft strains the modest maid engage,
> My graver numbers move the silver'd sage,
> My tender themes delight the lover's heart,
> And comfort to the poor my solemn songs impart?

To which we answer, No, no, no.—I grant it true, says our distracted bard,

>           that others better tell
> Of mighty Wolfe, who conquer'd as he fell,
> Of heroes born their threaten'd realms to save,
> Whom fame *anoints,* and *envy tends whose grave.*

Instead of, Whose grave envy tends. This, we are afraid, is a bold ungrammatical transposition, which even the *licentia poetica* can never excuse, any more than it can the following, where he says, others can better tell,

> How Spanish bombast blusters—they were beat,
> And French politeness dulcifies defeat.

When he was young, he informs us,

>           No envy entrance found,
> Nor flattry's *silver'd* tale, nor sorrow's *sage.*

*Sage,* we suppose, is meant for another epithet for *Tale,* but surely this is a strange kind of *subintelligitur,* and our author, we believe, has no authority for it. Pretty early one morning, the Muse tells us,

> The vivid dew hung trembling on the thorn,
> And mists, like *creeping rocks,* arose to meet the morn.

How *mists* can be like *rocks,* and what is meant by *creeping* ones, in particular, we cannot comprehend. Still less are we pleased with the unintelligible expressions of *shrouds well shrouded,* and *Hermes's own Cheapside;* nor are we fond of such compound epithets as, *woe-taught, fate-lop'd, song-invited, pine-prest, virtue-scorn'd, croud-beffitting,* &c. Whatever this writer may plead in his own behalf, we cannot entirely acquit him of pride, when he says,

> My song

Shall please the sons of taste, and please them long.

Though he is afterwards modest enough to add (speaking of himself ),

Faults he must own, tho' hard for him to find.

Hard, however, as it is for *him*, faults may possibly be found by *others* in this poem. For our own parts, we cannot but be of opinion, that if this *Candidate* (which we suppose is his intention) sets up for the borough of Parnassus, he will most probably lose his election, as he does not seem to be possessed of a foot of land in that county. (pp. 233-34)

> *A review of "The Candidate," in* The Critical Review, *London, Vol. L, September, 1780, pp. 233-34.*

### THE CRITICAL REVIEW   (essay date 1781)

[*In the following excerpt, the critic addresses stylistic and thematic aspects of* The Library.]

A vein of good sense and philosophical reflection runs through this little performance [**The Library**] which distinguishes it from most modern poems, though the subject is not sufficiently interesting to recommend it to general attention. The rhymes are correct, and the versification smooth and harmonious. The author ranges his books scientifically, and carries us through natural philosophy, physic, romance, history, &c.—What he says of physical writers is not less true than severe; their aim, says he, is glorious.

> But man, who knows no good unmix'd and pure,
> Oft finds a poison where he sought a cure;
> For grave deceivers lodge their labours here,
> And cloud the science they pretend to clear:
> Scourges for sin the solemn tribe are sent;
> Like fire and storms, they call us to repent;
> But storms subside, and fires forget to rage;
> These are eternal scourges of the age:
> 'Tis not enough that each terrific hand
> Spreads desolation round a guilty land;
> But, train'd to ill, and harden'd by its crimes,
> Their pen relentless kills through future times.

These lines are manly, nervous, and poetical. We were still more pleased with the . . . description of romance, which is full of fancy and spirit. (pp. 148-49)

The reader will meet with many other passages in this poem that will give him pleasure in the perusal. It is observable, that the author in his account of all the numerous volumes in every science, has never characterised or entered into the merits of any particular writer in either of them, though he had so fair an opportunity, from the nature of his subject; this, however, for reasons best known to himself, he has studiously avoided. (p. 150)

> *A review of "The Library," in* The Critical Review, *London, Vol. LII, August, 1781, pp. 148-50.*

### SAMUEL JOHNSON   (letter date 1783)

[*A critic, essayist, poet, and lexicographer, Johnson was one of the principal English literary figures of the eighteenth century. His* Dictionary of the English Language *(1755) helped standardize English spelling, while his moralistic criticism strongly influenced the literary taste of his time. His analytical writings, which are characterized by sound judgment, generally promote his theory that a work of literature should be evaluated chiefly on its ability to please and instruct the reader. In the following letter to Sir Joshua Reynolds, Johnson comments favorably on the stylistic attributes of* The Village.]

I have sent you back Mr. Crabbe's poem [**The Village**], which I read with great delight. It is original, vigorous, and elegant. The alterations which I have made, I do not require him to adopt; for my lines are, perhaps, not often better than his own: but he may take mine and his own together, and, perhaps, between them, produce something better than either. . . . His dedication will be least liked: it were better to contract it into a short sprightly address. I do not doubt of Mr. Crabbe's success.

> *Samuel Johnson, in a letter to Joshua Reynolds on March 4, 1783, in* Crabbe: The Critical Heritage, *edited by Arthur Pollard, Routledge & Kegan Paul, 1972, p. 41.*

### THE CRITICAL REVIEW   (essay date 1783)

[*In the following excerpt from a review of* The Village, *the critic comments favorably on Crabbe's realistic and emotive portrayal of the rural laboring class.*]

Though this gentleman seems to have taken the hint of his poem [**The Village**] from Goldsmith's *Deserted Village*, he does not represent it, like that writer 'as the seat of indolence and ease,' but describes it with more justice, and almost an equal warmth of colouring, as too commonly the abode of toil, misery, and vice. He begins with ridiculing the idea of shepherds, who

> in alternate verse,
> Their country's beauty, or their nymphs' rehearse;
> Yet still for these we frame the tender strain,
> Still in our lays fond Corydons complain,
> And shepherds' boys their amorous pains reveal,
> The only pains, alas! they never feel.
> On Mincio's banks, in Cæsar's bounteous reign,
> If Tityrus found the golden age again,
> Must sleepy bards the flattering dream prolong,
> Mechanic echos of the Mantuan song?

Our pastorals are certainly in general unnatural and absurd. Neither are Virgil's exempt from censure on the same account. They but little agree with the Roman manners in his time, which in no respect coincided with those fancied ones of 'the golden age.' Theocritus alone, whom he copied, adhered to nature, and the prevailing customs of the country, and succeeded accordingly. The misery of the poor worn-out labourer and his family is thus described:

> Ye gentle souls, who dream of rural ease,
> Whom the smooth stream and smoother sonnet please;
> Go! if the peaceful cot your praises share,
> Go look within, and ask if peace be there:
> If peace be his—that drooping weary fire,
> Or their's, that offspring round their feeble fire,
> Or her's, that matron pale, whose trembling hand
> Turns on the wretched hearth th' expiring brand.
> Nor yet can time itself obtain for these
> Life's latest comforts, due respect and ease;
> For yonder see that hoary swain, whose age
> Can with no cares except its own engage;
> Who, propt on that rude staff, looks up to see
> The bare arms broken from the withering tree;
> On which, a boy, he climb'd the loftiest bough,
> Then his first joy, but his sad emblem now.
> He once was chief in all the rustic trade,

His steady hand the straitest furrow made;
Full many a prize he won, and still is proud
To find the triumphs of his youth allow'd;
A transient pleasure sparkles in his eyes,
He hears and smiles, then thinks again and sighs:
For now he journeys to his grave in pain;
The rich disdain him; nay, the poor disdain;
Alternate masters now their slave command,
And urge the efforts of his feeble hand;
Who, when his age attempts its task in vain,
With ruthless taunts of lazy poor complain.
Oft may you see him when he tends the sheep,
His winter charge, beneath the hillock weep;
Oft hear him murmur to the winds that blow
O'er his white locks, and bury them in snow;
When rouz'd by rage and muttering in the morn,
He mends the broken hedge with icy thorn.

The subsequent account of his sickness, death, &c. is, we fear, too true a picture. (pp. 60-1)

This poem deserves much approbation, both for language and sentiment. The subject is broken off rather abruptly towards the conclusion, where we meet with a long encomium on the Duke of Rutland, and the hon. Capt. Manners, who was killed in that memorable action in the West Indies, when the French fleet was defeated, and their admiral taken prisoner. (p. 61)

*A review of "The Village," in* The Critical Review, *London, Vol. LVI, July, 1783, pp. 60-1.*

## [EDMUND CARTWRIGHT]   (essay date 1783)

[*In the following excerpt from a review of* The Village, *Cartwright argues that the pessimistic view of rural life presented in the first part of the poem is not corroborated in the second part.*]

It has long been objected to the Pastoral Muse, that her principal employment is to delineate scenes that never existed, and to cheat the imagination by descriptions of pleasure that never can be enjoyed. Sensible of her deviation from Nature and propriety, the Author of the present poem [*The Village*] has endeavoured to bring her back into the sober paths of truth and reality. It is not, however, improbable that he may have erred as much as those whom he condemns. For it may be questioned whether he, who represents a peasant's life as a life of unremitting labour and remediless anxiety; who describes his best years as embittered by insult and oppression, and his old age as squalid, comfortless, and destitute, gives a juster representation of rural enjoyments than they, who, running into a contrary extreme, paint the face of the country as wearing a perpetual smile, and its inhabitants as passing away their hours in uninterrupted pleasure, and unvaried tranquillity; such as are supposed to have prevailed in those fabled æras of existence,

When youth was extacy, and age repose.

Mr. Crabbe divides his poem into two parts. In the first he principally confines himself to an enumeration of the miseries, which, he supposes, are peculiar to the poor villager. In this part there is a great deal of painting that is truly characteristic; and had not that indispensible rule, which both painters and poets should equally attend to, been reversed, namely, to form their individuals from ideas of general nature, it would have been unexceptionable. (p. 418)

In the second part the Author's good sense compels him to acknowledge, contrary to the tenor of what had gone before, that the poor have no reason to envy their superiors; that neither virtue nor vice, happiness nor misery, depend on either rank or station; that the peasant is frequently as vicious as the peer; and that the peer feels distress as poignantly as the peasant. He then points out to the latter a source of consolation, which, it is to be feared, would avail very little in the hour of affliction:

Oh! if in life one noble chief appears,
Great in his name, while blooming in his years;
Born to enjoy whate'er delights mankind,
And yet to all you feel or fear resign'd;
Who gave up pleasures you could never share,
For pain which you are seldom doom'd to bear;
If such there be, then let your murmurs cease,
Think; think of him, and take your lot in peace.
And such there was:—oh grief! that checks our pride,
Weeping we say there was, for MANNERS died.

With a warm, though merited, panegyric on this gallant officer, and some consolatory compliments to his noble brother, the poem concludes. Considered as a whole, its most strenuous advocates must acknowledge it to be defective. The first part asserts as a general proposition what can only be affirmed of individuals; and the second part contradicts the assertion of the first. The chain of argument is illogical, and it is carried on, for the most part, without any apparently determinate object. It must not, however, be denied, that the poem contains many splendid lines, many descriptions that are picturesque and original, and such as will do credit to the ingenious Author of *The Library.* (pp. 420-21)

*[Edmund Cartwright ], in a review of "The Village," in* The Monthly Review, *Vol. LXIX, November, 1783, pp. 418-21.*

## *THE ANTI-JACOBIN REVIEW AND MAGAZINE*   (essay date 1807)

[*In the following excerpt from a review of* Poems, *the critic assesses Crabbe's overall literary achievement, focusing on the integration of naturalistic and poetic description and treatment of religious issues in "The Parish Register," while indicating problems in diction and punctuation in* The Village *and other poems.*]

In our younger days we read Mr. Crabbe's admirable poems, *The Library* and *The Village,* with enthusiastic delight; and long endeavoured, but in vain, to procure *The Newspaper.* It was, therefore, with that kind of pleasure, which men experience on seeing an old friend after a long interval of absence, that we opened the volume before us; most happy, indeed, to renew our acquaintance with a companion at once so amusing, so interesting, and so instructive. After an attentive perusal of these *Poems,* we find our first opinion of the author's genius and merit strongly confirmed. We regard him, indeed, as fully entitled to rank with the first moral poets of the present age, nor would those of the past be injured by a comparison with him. In addition to the *Village,* the *Library,* and the *Newspaper,* this volume contains, "The Parish Register;" "The Birth of Flattery," a moral poem, without a title; "Sir Eustace Grey;" "The Hall of Justice;" and "Woman." The "Parish Register" is the longest of these; it forms a supplement to the *Village;* and is divided into three parts; 1. "Baptisms"; 2. "Marriages"; 3. "Burials". But the author's own description of this poem will convey the best idea of it.

> In the **"PARISH REGISTER,"** he (the reader) will find an endeavour once more to describe village manners, not by adopting the notion of pastoral simplicity, or assuming ideas of rustic barbarity, but by more natural views of the peasantry, considered as a mixed body of persons, sober or profligate, and from hence, in a great measure, contented or miserable. To this more general description are added, the various characters which occur in the three parts of a register: baptisms, marriages, and burials."

In this endeavour Mr. Crabbe has most completely succeeded; his characters are ably drawn; his descriptions are highly poetical; and the moral reflections with which they are interspersed are excellent. Few poems are better calculated to interest the feelings, to meliorate the heart, and to inform the mind. They do great credit to the author's talents, while they reflect honour on his principles. (pp. 337-38)

He may most truly be called the poet of nature who best delineates natural characters and natural scenes; and certainly no one displays more skill, in this kind of delineation, than Mr. Crabbe. All his scenes, and all his characters, are, indeed, taken from common life, and chiefly from rural life; they are such as every man *may* meet with, and such as most men, who live in the country, *do* meet with; but they are presented in a manner which heightens their natural effect, and are marked by many of those delicate touches which none but the hand of a master can give to a picture. (p. 340)

[The] last portion of the **"Register"** . . . contains a dismal catalogue of departed Christians, and affords an ample field for moral reflections, and for the impression of salutary admonitions. . . . (p. 342)

We much fear that more Christian pastors than Mr. Crabbe have to deplore the dearth of that true Christian knowledge, and the want of that true Christian spirit, which can alone entitle men to expect the advantages of the Christian covenant. The enthusiastic cant of those ignorant preachers whom the Methodists send forth in swarms, more destructive to the inhabitants than locusts would be to the fruits of the land, have materially tended to poison the source of true knowledge, and to substitute the fountain of presumption in its stead: and until our legislature shall adopt some effectual means for the preservation of Christianity against both the insidious and the open attacks of those mischievous assailants (who know little of Christianity but the name), the evil will continue to increase with additional rapidity, and will, at no remote period, spread over the whole kingdom.

There is much good satire well applied in the **Newspaper.** . . . We could wish, however, that the author had enlarged this poem, as a considerable revolution has occurred in the management of newspapers since it was written, which would have afforded him ample food for satire, and which, indeed, call loudly for the satirical lash. Of the smaller poems we think **"Sir Eustace Grey"** and the **"Hall of Justice"** unquestionably the best, and the **"Birth of Flattery"** the least pleasing; but it is fair to add, that our dislike to allegorical poems in general may possibly influence our opinion. Of the **Library** and the **Village** too much cannot be said in their praise; it may, however, perhaps be objected to the latter, that if Goldsmith has fallen into one extreme in his delineation of village manners, Mr. Crabbe has here fallen into the other; and that Goldsmith's is the most pleasing delusion of the two. Still it must be acknowledged that there is much truth and

nature even in the most disgusting scenes which Mr. C. exhibits. We are happy to see the apologetical note at the end of the **Village,** for it always appeared to us that the censure which the passage there alluded to conveyed on the clergy, was, in its *general* application, both severe and unjust. Mr. C. writes nupt*u*al for nupt*i*al, and *i*ndure for *e*ndure, for which there is, we believe, no authority, and which indeed no authority could justify. He also uses *projection* as synonymous with *project,* which though strictly *defensible,* is nevertheless extremely awkward and dissonant. The punctuation, too, throughout the volume, is extremely defective; whence we are led to suspect, that a point so essential was left entirely to the management of the printer. (pp. 344-45)

*A review of "Poems," in* The Anti-Jacobin Review and Magazine, *Vol. XXVIII, No. CXIV, December, 1807, pp. 337-47.*

## [FRANCIS JEFFREY]   (essay date 1808)

*[Jeffrey was a founder and editor of the* Edinburgh Review, *one of the most influential magazines in early nineteenth-century England. A liberal Whig, Jeffrey often allowed his political beliefs to color his critical opinions. In the following review of* Poems, *Jeffrey upholds Crabbe's literary reputation, focusing on his unaffected depiction of rural English society in* The Village *and "The Village Register" (usually referred to as "The Parish Register"). He compares Crabbe's work favorably to the less natural pastoral poetry of Oliver Goldsmith and William Wordsworth.]*

We receive the proofs of Mr Crabbe's poetical existence, which are contained in this volume [**Poems**], with the same sort of feeling that would be excited by tidings of an antient friend, whom we no longer expected to hear of in this world. We rejoice in his resurrection; both for his sake, and for our own: but we feel also a certain movement of self-condemnation, for having been remiss in our inquiries after him, and somewhat too negligent of the honours which ought at any rate to have been paid to his memory.

It is now we are afraid, upwards of twenty years since we were first struck with the vigour, originality, and truth of description of **The Village;** and since we regretted that an author, who could write so well, should have written so little. From that time to the present, we have heard little of Mr Crabbe; and fear that he has been in a great measure lost sight of by the public, as well as by us. With a singular, and scarcely pardonable indifference to fame, he has remained, during this long interval, in patient or indolent repose; and, without making a single movement to maintain or advance the reputation he had acquired, has permitted others to usurp the attention which he was sure of commanding, and allowed himself to be nearly forgotten by a public, which reckons upon being reminded of all the claims which the living have on its favour. His former publications, though of distinguished merit, were perhaps too small in volume to remain long the objects of general attention, and seem, by some accident, to have been jostled aside in the crowd of more clamorous competitors.

Yet, though the name of Crabbe has not hitherto been very common in the mouths of our poetical critics, we believe there are few real lovers of poetry to whom some of his sentiments and descriptions are not secretly familiar. There is a truth and a force in many of his delineations of rustic life, which is calculated to sink deep into the memory; and, being confirmed by daily observation, they are recalled upon innumerable occasions,—when the ideal pictures of more fanciful authors have lost all their interest. For ourselves at least, we profess to be indebted to Mr Crabbe for many of these strong impressions; and have known more than one of our unpoetical acquaintances, who declared they could never pass by a parish workhouse, without thinking of the description of it they had read at school in the Poetical Extracts. The volume before us will renew, we trust, and extend many such impressions. It contains all the former productions of the author, with about double their bulk of new matter; most of it in the same taste and manner of composition with the former, and some of a kind, of which we have had no previous example in this author. The whole, however, is of no ordinary merit, and will be found, we have little doubt, a sufficient warrant for Mr Crabbe to take his place as one of the most original, nervous, and pathetic poets of the present century.

His characteristic, certainly, is force, and truth of description, joined for the most part to great selection and condensation of expression;—that kind of strength and originality which we meet with in Cowper, and that sort of diction and versification which we admire in Goldsmith. If he can be said to have imitated the manner of any author, it is Goldsmith, indeed, who has been the object of his imitation; and yet his general train of thinking, and his views of society are so extremely opposite, that when *The Village* was first published, it was commonly considered as an antidote or answer to the more captivating representations of *The Deserted Village*. Compared with this celebrated author, he will be found, we think, to have more vigour and less delicacy; and, while he must be admitted to be inferior in the fine finish and uniform beauty of his composition, we cannot help considering him as superior, both in the variety and the truth of his pictures. Instead of that uniform tint of pensive tenderness which overspreads the whole poetry of Goldsmith, we find in Mr Crabbe many gleams of gaiety and humour. Though his habitual views of life are more gloomy than those of his rival, his poetical temperament seems far more cheerful; and when the occasions of sorrow and rebuke are gone by, he can collect himself for sarcastic pleasantry, or unbend in innocent playfulness. His diction, though generally pure and powerful, is sometimes harsh, and sometimes quaint; and he has occasionally admitted a couplet or two in a state so unfinished, as to give a character of inelegance to the passages in which they occur. With a taste less disciplined and less fastidious than that of Goldsmith, he has, in our apprehension, a keener eye for observation, and a readier hand for the delineation of what he has observed. There is less poetical keeping in his whole performance; but the groups of which it consists, are conceived, we think, with equal genius, and drawn with greater spirit as well as greater fidelity.

It is not quite fair, perhaps, thus to draw a detailed parallel between a living poet, and one whose reputation has been sealed by death, and by the immutable sentence of a surviving generation. Yet there are so few of his contemporaries to whom Mr Crabbe bears any resemblance, that we can scarcely explain our opinion of his merit, without comparing him to some of his predecessors. There is one set of writers, indeed, from whose works those of Mr Crabbe might receive all that elucidation which results from contrast, and from an entire opposition in all points of taste and opinion. We allude now to the Wordsworths, and the Southeys, and Coleridges, and all that misguided fraternity, that, with good intentions and extraordinary talents, are labouring to bring back our po-

etry to the fantastical oddity and puling childishness of Withers, Quarles, or Marvel. These gentlemen write a great deal about rustic life, as well as Mr Crabbe; and they even agree with him in dwelling much on its discomforts; but nothing can be more opposite than the views they take of the subject, or the manner in which they execute their representation of them.

Mr Crabbe exhibits the common people of England pretty much as they are, and as they must appear to every one who will take the trouble of examining into their condition; at the same time that he renders his sketches in a very high degree interesting and beautiful,—by selecting what is most fit for description,—by grouping them into such forms as must catch the attention or awake the memory,—and by scattering over the whole, such traits of moral sensibility, of sarcasm, and of useful reflection, as every one must feel to be natural, and own to be powerful. The gentlemen of the new school, on the other hand, scarcely ever condescend to take their subjects from any description of persons that are at all known to the common inhabitants of the world; but invent for themselves certain whimsical and unheard of beings, to whom they impute some fantastical combination of feelings, and labour to excite our sympathy for them, either by placing them in incredible situations, or by some strained and exaggerated moralization of a vague and tragical description. Mr Crabbe, in short, shows us something which we have all seen, or may see, in real life; and draws from it such feelings and such reflections as every human being must acknowledge that it is calculated to excite. He delights us by the truth, and vivid and picturesque beauty of his representations, and by the force and pathos of the sensations with which we feel that they ought to be connected. Mr Wordsworth and his associates show us something that mere observation never yet suggested to any one. They introduce us to beings whose existence was not previously suspected by the acutest observers of nature; and excite an interest for them, more by an eloquent and refined analysis of their own capricious feelings, than by any obvious or very intelligible ground of sympathy in their situation. The common sympathies of our nature, and our general knowledge of human character, do not enable us either to understand, or to enter into the feelings of their characters. They are unique specimens and varieties of our kind, and must be studied under a separate classification. (pp. 131-34)

Those who are acquainted with the *Lyrical Ballads,* or the more recent publication of Mr Wordsworth, will scarcely deny the justice of this representation; but in order to vindicate it to such as do not enjoy that inestimable advantage, we must beg leave to make a few hasty references to the former, and by far the least exceptionable of these productions.

A village schoolmaster, for instance, is a pretty common poetical character. Goldsmith has drawn him inimitably; so has Shenstone, with the slight change of sex; and Mr Crabbe, in two passages, has followed their footsteps. Now, Mr Wordsworth has a village schoolmaster also—a personage who makes no small figure in three or four of his poems. But by what traits is this worthy old gentleman delineated by the new poet? No pedantry—no innocent vanity of learning—no mixture of indulgence with the pride of power, and of poverty with the consciousness of rare acquirements. Every feature which belongs to the situation, or marks the character in common apprehension, is scornfully discarded by Mr Wordsworth, who represents this grey-haired rustic pedagogue as a sort of half crazy, sentimental person, overrun with fine feelings, constitutional merriment, and a most humorous melancholy. Here are the two stanzas in which this consistent and intelligible character is pourtrayed. The diction is at least as new as the conception.

> The sighs which Mathew heard were sighs
> Of one tired out with *fear* and *madness;*
> The tears which came to Mathew's eyes
> Were tears of light—*the oil of gladness.*
>
> Yet sometimes, when the secret cup
> Of still and serious thought went round,
> He seemed as if he *drank it up,*
> He felt with spirit so profound.
> Thou *soul,* of God's best *earthly mould,* &c.

(pp. 134-35)

From these childish and absurd affectations, we turn with pleasure to the manly sense and correct picturing of Mr Crabbe; and, after being dazzled and made giddy with the elaborate raptures and obscure originalities of these new artists, it is refreshing to meet again with the nature and spirit of our old masters, in the nervous pages of the author now before us.

The poem that stands first in the volume [*The Village*], is that to which we have already alluded as having been first given to the public upwards of twenty years ago. (pp. 137-38)

The scope of the poem is to show, that the villagers of real life have no resemblance to the villagers of poetry; that poverty, in sober truth, is very uncomfortable; and vice by no means confined to the opulent. (p. 139)

The following exhibits a fair specimen of the strokes of sarcasm, which the author, perhaps not very judiciously, intermingles with his description. He is speaking of the stern Justice who keeps the parish in awe.

> To him with anger or with shame repair
> The injur'd peasant and deluded fair.
> Lo! at his throne the silent nymph appears,
> Frail by her shape, but modest in her tears;
> And while she stands abash'd, with conscious eye,
> Some favourite female of her judge glides by;
> Who views with scornful glance the strumpet's fate,
> And thanks the stars that made her keeper great:
> Near her the swain, about to bear for life
> One certain evil, doubts 'twixt war and wife;
> But, while the faltering damsel takes her oath,
> Consents to wed, and so secures them both.

We shall only give one other extract from this poem; and we select the following fine description of that peculiar sort of barrenness which prevails along the sandy and thinly inhabited shores of the channel.

> Lo! where the heath, with withering brake grown o'er,
> Lends the light turf that warms the neighbouring poor;
> From thence a length of burning sand appears,
> Where the thin harvest waves its wither'd ears;
> There thistles stretch their prickly arms afar,
> And to the ragged infant threaten war;
> There poppies nodding, mock the hope of toil,
> There the blue bugloss paints the sterile soil:
> Hardy and high, above the slender sheaf,
> The slimy mallow waves her silky leaf,
> O'er the young shoot the charlock throws a shade,
> And clasping tares cling round the sickly blade;
> With mingled tints the rocky coasts abound,
> And a sad splendour vainly shines around.

The next poem, and the longest in the volume, is now presented for the first time to the public. It is dedicated, like the former, to the delineation of rural life and characters, and is entitled, **"The Village Register;"** and, upon a very simple but singular plan, is divided into three parts, viz. Baptisms, Marriages, and Burials. After an introductory and general view of village manners, the Reverend author proceeds to present his readers with an account of all the remarkable baptisms, marriages and funerals, that appear on his register for the preceding year, with a sketch of the character and behaviour of the respective parties, and such reflections and exhortations as are suggested by the subject. The poem consists, therefore, of a series of portraits taken from the middling and lower ranks of rustic life, and delineated on occasions at once more common and more interesting, than any other that could well be imagined. They are selected, we think, with great judgment, and drawn with inimitable accuracy and strength of colouring. They are finished with much more minuteness and detail, indeed, than the more general pictures in **The Village;** and, on this account, may appear occasionally deficient in comprehension, or in dignity. They are, no doubt, executed in some instances with a Chinese accuracy; and enter into details which many readers may pronounce tedious and unnecessary. Yet, there is a justness and force in the representation which is entitled to something more than indulgence; and though several of the groups are confessedly composed of low and disagreeable subjects, still, we think that some allowance is to be made for the author's plan of giving a full and exact view of village life, which could not possibly be accomplished without including those baser varieties. He aims at an important moral effect by this exhibition; and must not be defrauded either of that, or of the praise which is due to the coarser efforts of his pen, out of deference to the sickly delicacy of his more fastidious readers. We admit, however, that there is more carelessness, as well as more quaintness in this poem than in the other; and that he has now and then apparently heaped up circumstances rather to gratify his own taste for detail and accumulation, than to give any additional effect to his description. (pp. 140-41)

We think this the most important of the new pieces in the volume; and have extended our account of it so much, that we can afford to say but little of the others. *The Library* and the *Newspaper* are republications. They are written with a good deal of terseness, sarcasm, and beauty; but the subjects are not very interesting, and they will rather be approved, we think, than admired or delighted in. We are not much taken either with the **"Birth of Flattery."** With many nervous lines and ingenious allusions, it has something of the languor which seems inseparable from an allegory which exceeds the length of an epigram.

**"Sir Eustace Grey"** is quite unlike any of the preceding compositions. It is written in a sort of lyric measure, and is intended to represent the perturbed fancies of the most terrible insanity settling by degrees into a sort of devotional enthusiasm. The opening stanza, spoken by a visitor in the madhouse, is very striking.

> I'll know no more;—the heart is torn
> By views of woe we cannot heal;
> Long shall I see these things forlorn,
> And oft again their griefs shall feel,
> As each upon the mind shall steal;
> That wan projector's mystic style,
> That lumpish idiot leering by,
> That peevish idler's ceaseless wile,

And that poor maiden's half-form'd smile,
While struggling for the full-drawn sigh!—
I'll know no more.

There is great force, both of language and conception, in the wild narrative Sir Eustace gives of his frenzy; though we are not sure whether there is not something too elaborate, and too much worked up, in the picture. We give only one image, which we think is original. He supposed himself hurried along by two tormenting demons—

Through lands we fled, o'er seas we flew,
And halted on a boundless plain;
Where nothing fed, nor breath'd, nor grew,
But silence rul'd the still domain.

Upon that boundless plain, below,
The setting sun's last rays were shed,
And gave a mild and sober glow,
Where all were still, asleep or dead;
Vast ruins in the midst were spread,
Pillars and pediments sublime,
Where the grey moss had form'd a bed,
And cloth'd the crumbling spoils of Time.

There was I fix'd, I know not how,
Condemn'd for untold years to stay;
Yet years were not;—one dreadful *now,*
Endur'd no change of night or day;
The same mild evening's sleeping ray,
Shone softly-solemn and serene,
And all that time, I gaz'd away,
The setting sun's sad rays were seen.

**"The Hall of Justice,"** or the story of the Gypsy Convict, is another experiment of Mr Crabbe's. It is very nervous—very shocking—and very powerfully represented. (pp. 148-49)

[**"The Hall of Justice"**] certainly is not pleasing reading; but it is written with very unusual power of language, and shows Mr Crabbe to have great mastery over the tragic passions of pity and horror. The volume closes with some verses of no great value in praise of Women.

We part with regret from Mr Crabbe; but we hope to meet with him again. If his muse, to be sure, is prolific only once in twenty-four years, we can scarcely expect to live long enough to pass our judgment on the progeny; but we trust, that a larger portion of public favour than has hitherto been dealt to him, will encourage him to greater efforts; and that he will soon appear again among the worthy supporters of the old poetical establishment, and come in time to surpass the revolutionists in fast firing as well as in weight of metal. (pp. 150-51)

[*Francis Jeffrey*], *in a review of "Poems," in* The Edinburgh Review, *Vol. XII, No. XXIII, April, 1808, pp. 131-51.*

## WILLIAM WORDSWORTH   (letter date 1808)

[*Wordsworth is considered by many scholars to be the greatest and most influential English Romantic poet. Wordsworth's literary criticism reflects his belief that neither the language nor the content of poetry should be stylized or elaborate and that the aim of a poet is to feel and express the relation between humankind and nature. In the following excerpt from a letter to the poet Samuel Rogers, Wordsworth criticizes "The Parish Register," questioning the accuracy and consistency of its characterizations as well as the poetic virtues of its insistent realism.*]

I am happy to find that we coincide in opinion about Crabbe's verses, for poetry in no sense can they be called. Sharp is also of the same opinion. I remember that I mentioned in my last that there was nothing in the last publication [**"The Parish Register"**] so good as the description of the parish workhouse, apothecary, &c. This is true, and it is no less true that the passage which I commended is of no great merit, because the description, at the best of no high order, is, in the instance of the apothecary, inconsistent—that is, false. It no doubt sometimes happens, but, as far as my experience goes, very rarely, that country practitioners neglect and brutally treat their patients; but what kind of men are they who do so?—not apothecaries like Crabbe's professional pragmatical coxcombs, "all pride, generally neat, business, bustle, and conceit"—no, but drunken reprobates, frequenters of boxing-matches, cock-fightings, and horse-races. These are the men who are hard-hearted with their patients, but any man who attaches so much importance to his profession as to have strongly caught, in his dress and manner, the outward formalities of it may easily indeed be much occupied with himself, but he will not behave towards his "victims," as Mr. Crabbe calls them, in the manner he has chosen to describe. After all, if the picture were true to nature, what claim would it have to be called poetry? At the best, it is the meanest kind of satire, except the merely personal. The sum of all is, that nineteen out of twenty of Crabbe's pictures are mere matters of fact, with which the Muses have just about as much to do as they have with a collection of medical reports or of law cases. (pp. 49-50)

*William Wordsworth, in a letter to Samuel Rogers on September 29, 1808, in* Rogers and His Contemporaries, *Vol. I by P. W. Clayden, Smith, Elder, & Co., 1889, pp. 48-50.*

## LORD BYRON   (poem date 1809)

[*Byron was an English poet and dramatist who is now considered one of the most important poets of the nineteenth century. Because of the satiric nature of much of his work, Byron is difficult to place within the Romantic movement. His most notable contribution to Romanticism is the Byronic hero: a melancholy man, often with a dark past, who eschews societal and religious structures, seeking truth and happiness in an apparently meaningless universe. In the following excerpt from the satirical poem* English Bards and Scotch Reviewers *(1809), Byron contrasts the "strain'd invention" of contemporary poetry with Crabbe's realism.*]

There be who say, in these enlighten'd days,
That splendid lies are all the poet's praise;
That strain'd invention, ever on the wing,
Alone impels the modern bard to sing.
'T is true that all who rhyme—nay, all who write,
Shrink from that fatal word to genius—trite;
Yet Truth sometimes will lend her noblest fires,
And decorate the verse herself inspires:
This fact in Virtue's name let Crabbe attest;
Though nature's sternest painter, yet her best.

*Lord Byron, in an excerpt in* Poet to Poet: A Treasury of Golden Criticism, *edited by Houston Peterson and William S. Lynch, Prentice-Hall, Inc., 1945, p. 188.*

## [ROBERT GRANT]   (essay date 1810)

[*In the following excerpt from a review of* The Borough, *Grant finds fault with Crabbe's overtly pessimistic realism, arguing that aesthetic faults arise from his rejection of the traditional definition of poetry, which emphasizes the instrumental role of the imagination.*]

The history of Mr. Crabbe as an author has been somewhat singular. He first appeared in that character in the year 1783, and was received in such a manner as might have warranted the hope that his second appearance would not be long delayed. But, too indolent or too unambitious, Mr. Crabbe sunk back into privacy; and five and twenty years elapsed before he renewed his claims on the public notice. His increased success on this second occasion does not strike us as matter of surprise. We had become sick of the luscious monotony of Muses who seemed to have been fed only on flowers; and were therefore prepared to receive with indulgence even the rude efforts of a more firm and manly genius. At the same time it must be confessed, that the candidate was in no want of illustrious friends to bring him down (like the *deductores* of old) to the place of canvas, and to secure, by their influence, the favourable suffrages of his countrymen. Criticism itself could not refuse a smile to the verse which had early obtained the praise of Burke and Johnson [see letter dated 1783], and more recently cheered the dying bed of Fox.

The first glow of admiration, however, is now gone; and sufficient time has since passed to allow of our ascertaining, pretty accurately, the final judgment of the public respecting the merits of Mr. Crabbe. It is, if we are not mistaken, that he has greatly misapplied great powers; and that, although an able, he is not a pleasing poet. In this judgment we entirely acquiesce.

The peculiarity of this author is, that he wishes to discard everything like illusion from poetry. He is the poet of reality, and of reality in low life. His opinions on this subject were announced in the opening of his first poem, **The Village** and will be best explained by extracting from that work some lines which contain a general enunciation of his system.

> The village life, and ev'ry care that reigns
> O'er youthful peasants and declining swains;
> What labour yields, and what, that labour past,
> Age in its hour of languor finds at last;
> What form the real picture of the poor,
> Demand a song—the Muse can give no more.

> . . . . .

> On Mincio's banks, in Cæsar's bounteous reign,
> If Tityrus found the golden age again,
> Must sleepy bards the flatt'ring dreams prolong?
> Mechanic echoes of the Mantuan song?
> From Truth and Nature shall we widely stray
> Where Virgil, not where Fancy, leads the way?
> Yes, thus the Muses sing of happy swains,
> Because the Muses never knew their pains.—

> . . . . .

> Then shall I dare these real ills to hide
> In tinsel trappings of poetic pride?

> . . . . .

> By such examples taught, I paint the cot
> As Truth will paint it, and as bards will not.—

From these extracts, as well as from the constant tenor of his writings, it is clear, that Mr. Crabbe condemns the common representations of rural life and manners as fictitious; that he

is determined in his own sketches of them to confine himself, with more than ordinary rigour, to truth and nature;—to draw only 'the real picture of the poor,' which, be it remembered, must necessarily, according to his opinion, be a picture of sorrow and depravity. Now all this tends greatly to circumscribe, if not completely to destroy, the operation of illusion in poetry; and proceeds on what we conceive to be an entire misconception of the principles on which the pleasure of poetic reading depends. Notwithstanding the saving clause in favour of the privileges of Fancy, which is inserted in one of the preceding extracts, the doctrines of Mr. Crabbe appear to us essentially hostile to the highest exercise of the imagination, and we cannot therefore help regarding them with considerable doubt and jealousy.

To talk of binding down poetry to dry representations of the world as it is, seems idle; because it is precisely in order to escape from the world as it is, that we fly to poetry. We turn to it, not that we may see and feel what we see and feel in our daily experience, but that we may be refreshed by other emotions and fairer prospects—that we may take shelter from the realities of life in the paradise of fancy. To spread out a theatre on which this separate and intellectual kind of existence might be enjoyed, has in all ages been the great business of the speculative powers of the species. For this end new worlds have been framed, or the old embel'ished; imaginary joys and sorrows have been excited; the elements have been peopled with ideal beings. To this moral necessity, the divinities of ancient mythology owed their popularity, if not their birth; and when that visionary creation was dissolved, the same powerful instinct supplied the void with the fays and genii and enchantments of modern romance.

Poetry then, if it would answer the end of its being, must flatter the imagination. It must win the mind to the exercise of its contemplative faculties by striking out pictures on which it may dwell with complacency and delight. It does not follow that these pictures should be exclusively of a gay and smiling nature. The mind is notoriously so constituted as to enjoy, within certain limits, the fictitious representations of sad or terrible things.

But why, it is said, does poetry realize that which has no existence in nature? It is, at least, some answer to the question to observe, that, in this respect, poetry only does for us more perfectly what, without its assistance, we every day do for ourselves. It is to illusions, whether excited by the art of the poet, or by the secret magic of association, that life owes one of its first charms; and in both cases they give rise to feelings the same in their nature and in their practical effect. The pleasures of memory, for example, are great in exact proportion to the ardour with which the mind embraces this sort of self-deception. When we remember a past event in a very lively manner, what is it but to realize that which has no existence;—and this, not only according to the popular mode of stating the fact, but in strict metaphysical truth. Such, too, is, in a striking degree, the case, when a portrait or some other memorial vividly affects us with the imagined presence of a deceased friend; or when we are presented with the prospect of scenes resembling those to which we are attached by interesting recollections, especially if they meet us in a foreign climate. (pp. 281-83)

Some of the emigrants from the north of Scotland to America have, it is said, chosen for their residence situations similar to those which they left; and have even given to the principal features of their new country the names by which the corresponding objects of the old were distinguished. This is only one instance of that desire to encourage illusions which so universally prevails, and which continually leads us to surround ourselves, if the expression may be allowed, with hints and suggestions of the distant or the past.

If, in common life, such artifices may innocently be employed to steal the mind from itself, it is not easy to perceive why they become objectionable in works of taste; and we must therefore be allowed still to number them among the legitimate stratagems of the poetic art. (pp. 283-84)

The preceding observations relate generally to the principle of confining poetry to the realities of life; but they are peculiarly relevant, when that principle is applied to the realities of *low life,* because these, are of all others, the most disgusting. If therefore the poet choose to illustrate the department of low life, it is peculiarly incumbent on him to select such of its features, as may at least be inoffensive. Should it be replied, that there is no room for such selection; then it follows, that he must altogether refrain from treating the subject, as utterly unworthy of his art. The truth however is, that there *is* room for selection. No department of life, however darkened by vice or sorrow, is without some brighter points on which the imagination may rest with complacency; and this is especially true, where rural scenes make part of the picture. We are not so absurd as to deny, that the country furnishes abundant examples of misery and depravity; but we deny, that it furnishes none of a different kind. In common life every man instinctively acquires the habit of diverting his attention from unpleasing objects, and fixing it on those that are more agreeable; and all we ask is, that this practical rule should be adopted in poetry. The face of Nature under its daily and periodical varieties, the honest gaiety of rustic mirth, the flow of health and spirits which is inspired by the county, the delights which it brings to every sense—such are the pleasing topics which strike the most superficial observer. But a closer inspection will open to us more sacred gratifications. Wherever the relations of civilized society exist, particularly where a high standard of morals, however imperfectly acted upon, is yet publicly recognized, a ground-work is laid for the exercise of all the charities social and domestic. In the midst of profligacy and corruption, some trace of those charities still lingers; there is some spot which shelters domestic happiness; some undiscovered cleft, in which the seeds of the best affections have been cherished and are bearing fruit in silence. Poverty, however blighting in general, has graces which are peculiarly its own. The highest order of virtues can be developed only in a state of habitual suffering.

These are the realities which it is the duty of the poet to select for exhibition; and these, as they have nothing of illusion in themselves, it is not necessary to recommend by the magic of a richly-painted diction. Even presented to us in language the most precise and unadorned, they cannot fail to please; and please perhaps then most surely, when told in words of an almost abstract simplicity; words so limpid and colourless, that they seem only to discover to us the ideas, not to convey them, still less to lend them any additional sweetness or strength. Every reader will recollect some passages in our best authors which answer to this character; yet we cannot resist the temptation of exemplifying our position by an instance from Mr. Crabbe himself. What can be more *unfanciful,* and yet what more affecting, or more sublime, than his representation of a young woman watching over the gradual decay of her lover?

Still long she nurs'd him; tender thoughts meantime
Were interchang'd, and hopes and views sublime.
To her he came to die, and every day
She took some portion of the dread away;
With him she pray'd, to him his Bible read,
Sooth'd the faint heart, and held the aching head:
She came with smiles the hour of pain to cheer;
Apart she sigh'd; alone, she shed the tear.

(pp. 288-89)

It must then be acknowledged that even the meanest station is not perfectly barren of interesting subjects; but the writer, who covets the praise of being a faithful transcriber rather than a generous interpreter of Nature, may be allowed to descend a step lower in the scale of exact delineation. There is a class of 'real pictures,' which is connected with no peculiar associations; and which may therefore, as far as the imagination is concerned, be called neutral. Of this nature are minute descriptions of agricultural pursuits, of ingenious mechanism, of the construction of buildings, of the implements of husbandry. Such descriptions are, in a long work, necessary, for the sake of variety; and are, at all times, if happily executed, grateful to the understanding, as specimens of intellectual skill and dexterity. But it is indispensable, that they should be strictly neutral. On this head much misconception has arisen from a confused apprehension of the analogy between poetry and painting. Because in painting, low and even offensive subjects are admitted; it is taken for granted that poetry also ought to have its Dutch school.

Without entering at length into this discussion, it may not be improperly suggested, that, even in painting, there is a limit, beyond which no prudent artist would venture to try the indulgence of the spectator. A variety of performances might be specified, in which the highest powers are in vain tasked to their utmost, to atone for the vulgarity and grossness of the subjects.

It may be suggested farther, that the Dutch school is indebted for its celebrity, not in any part to the nature of its subjects, but exclusively to its happiness of execution. It professes to address only the eye; and its failings are lost and overlooked in the perfection of its mechanical excellence; in its grouping, and management of light and shade; in the harmony and radiance of its tones, and the luxuriance of its manner. The success of its productions is signally the triumph of colouring and composition. The subject, in a word, is the least part of these paintings. Poetry, on the other hand, is destitute of means to fascinate the external senses, and appeals to the mind alone. It is indeed popularly said, that words are the colours of poetry. But if this metaphor were just, it would, in the present case, be inapplicable. The new system which Mr. Crabbe patronizes, and to which therefore our remarks primarily refer, disclaims the attempt to disguise its *studies from Nature* under glowing and ornamental language.

We have hitherto considered the great principle on which our author proceeds. But this principle is not with him merely theoretical. Its impression visibly affects the character and impairs the merit of his writings.

The minute accuracy of relation which it inculcates, however favourable to the display of his uncommon powers of research, has a tendency to throw an air of littleness and technical precision over his performances. His description is frittered down, till instead of a spirited sketch, it becomes a tame detail. We will not say that he is incapable of large and comprehensive views; but he is surely somewhat slow to indulge in them. Thus his knowledge of man is never exhibited on a grand scale. It is clear and exact, but statistical rather than geographic; a knowledge of the individual rather than of the species. In his pictures there is little keeping; his figures, though singly admirable, are carelessly and clumsily grouped; and the whole drawing, while it abounds in free and masterly strokes, is yet deficient in depth and roundness.

The characteristic of Mr. Crabbe's writings is force; and this is the quality of which he most affects the praise. The finer parts of genius he neglects as useless or despises as weak. What he sees strongly, he makes a point of conscience to describe fearlessly. Occasionally perhaps this ambition of vigour drives him into unintentional vulgarity. Yet it cannot be disguised that the more commonly sins without this excuse: he admits coarseness on system. It is the original principle still operating. His sagacity in the discovery, and his ardour in the pursuit of offensive images are sometimes astonishing. His imagination never shrinks from the irksome task of threading the detail of vice and wretchedness.

The habit of anatomically tracing and recording the deformities of his fellow-creatures, has communicated to some of his descriptions an appearance of harshness and invective which, we are persuaded, has no counterpart in his feelings. He is evidently a man of great benevolence, but is apt to indulge in a caustic raillery which may be mistaken for ill-nature. In his pity there seems to be more of contempt than of tenderness, and the objects of his compassion are at the same time the objects of his satire. In the same manner he is jealous of giving his reader unmixed gratification; and even when his subject is inevitably pleasing, too often contrives, by the dexterous intervention of some less agreeable image, to dash the pleasure which he may have unwillingly inspired.

To the effect of his favourite doctrines also, we are disposed to ascribe it, that his perception of the beauties of nature has so little of inspiration about it. Living on the verge of fields, and groves, and streams, and breathing the very air which fans them, he is never tempted to forget himself in the contemplation of such scenes. A prospect of the country never thrills him as with the sudden consciousness of a new sense. We do not recollect that in any part of his writings he mentions the singing of birds, except

> ————the tuneless cry
> Of fishing Gull or clanging Golden-eye.

(pp. 290-92)

It is consistent with this habit of mind that our author should evince little relish for the sentimental. From that whole class of intellectual pleasures he is not less averse in principle than in practice. He lives, if we may be allowed the expression, without an atmosphere. Every object is seen in its true situation and dimensions;—there is neither colour nor refraction. No poet was ever less of a visionary.

We are inclined to think that Mr. Crabbe's taste is not equal to his other powers; and this deficiency we attribute, partly indeed to the original constitution of his genius, but much more to the operation of local circumstances. A life of retirement is, perhaps, in no case, very favourable to the cultivation of taste. Unless the mind be sustained in its just position by the intercourse and encounter of living opinions, it is apt to be carried away by the current of some particular system, and contracts in science, as well as in morals, a spirit of favouritism and bigotry. The love of simplicity especially, which is natural to an intellect of strong and masculine proportions,

is peculiarly liable to degenerate into a toleration of coarseness. Mr. Crabbe, however, seems to have been exposed to an influence doubly ungenial—that of solitude, in his hours of study; and in his hours of relaxation, that of the society with which his professional duties probably obliged him to become familiar. Even on a judgment the most happily tempered and vigilantly guarded, an intimate acquaintance with such a society, must have operated fatally; either by deadening its tact altogether, or by polishing it to an unnatural keenness; and its influence will be still greater on a mind naturally little fastidious, and predisposed perhaps to prefer strength to elegance.

The impression which results from a general view of our author's compositions, is such as we have stated. There are detached passages, however, in which he appears under a more engaging character. When he escapes from his favourite topics of vulgarity and misery,

> Cœtusque vulgares et udam
> Spernit humum,

he throws off his defects, and purifies himself as he ascends into a purer region. Some of the most pleasing are also among the happiest of his efforts. The few sketches which he has condescended to give of rural life are distinguished not more for their truth, than for their sobriety and chasteness of manner. His love of circumstantial information is likely, in ordinary cases, to confound rather than inform, by inducing him to present us with a collection of unconnected and equally prominent facts, of which no arrangement is made, because there is no reason why one should have the precedence of another. But when the feelings are to be questioned, and the heart is to be laid bare, the same principle leads him closely to follow up nature; and thus we are conducted, step by step, to the highest point of interest. In the struggle of the passions, we delight to trace the workings of the soul; we love to mark the swell of every vein, and the throb of every pulse; every stroke that searches a new source of pity and terror we pursue with a busy and inquisitive sympathy. It is from this cause that Mr. Crabbe's delineations of the passions are so just—so touching of the gentle, and of the awful so tremendous. Remorse and madness have been rarely pourtrayed by a more powerful hand. For feeling, imagery, and agitation of thoughts, the lines in which Sir Eustace Grey tells the story of his insanity, are second to few modern productions. The contrast between the state of the madman, and the evening scene on which he was condemned to gaze, gives a tone of penetrating anguish to the following verses:—

> Upon that boundless plain below
> The setting Sun's last rays were shed;
> And gave a mild and sober glow,
> Where all were still, asleep, or dead.
>
> There was I fix'd, I know not how,
> Condemn'd for untold years to stay;
> Yet years were not—one dreadful Now
> Endur'd no change of night or day.
> The same mild evening's sleeping ray
> Shone softly solemn and serene;
> And all that time, I gaz'd away,
> The setting Sun's sad rays were seen.

It may be remarked, that the emphatical expression, one dreadful *Now* is to be found in Cowley's "Davideis."

There is great force in these two lines—

I've dreaded all the guilty dread,
And done what they would fear to do.

But that which gives the last finish to this vision of despair is contained in these words—

And then, my dreams were such as nought
Could yield, but my unhappy case.

Our author is no less successful, when he wishes to excite a milder interest, when he describes the calm of a virtuous old age, the cheerfulness of pious resignation, the sympathies of innocent love. His paintings of this nature are done in his best style; and though we perceive in them something of his usual dry and harsh manner, yet this peculiarity is now no longer a blemish, because it accords with the unpretending plainness of his subject.

It is, after all, on this portion of his works that he must build the fairest part of his reputation. The poetry, which speaks to the understanding alone, cannot permanently attract the mass of mankind; while that, which moves the passions and the heart, has already received the talisman of fame, and may securely commit itself to the affections of every coming age. It is very pleasing to perceive, that, in his best passages, Mr. Crabbe is, practically at least, a convert to the good old principle of paying some regard to fancy and taste in poetry. In these passages he works expressly for the imagination; not perhaps awakening its loftiest exertions, yet studiously courting its assistance, and conciliating its good will. He now accommodates himself to the more delicate sympathies of our nature, and flatters our prejudices by attaching to his pictures agreeable and interesting associations. Thus it is that, for his best success, he is indebted to something more than ungarnished reality. He is the Paladin, who on the day of decisive combat, laid aside his mortal arms, and took only the magic lance.

The remarks which we have made apply so generally to Mr. Crabbe's writings, that little more remains for us now to do, than to exemplify them by extracts from the work to which they immediately owe their origin.

The *Borough* contains a description in twenty-four letters of a sea-port, under the following heads:

General Description—The Church—The Vicar, the Curate, &c.—Sects and Professions in Religion—Elections—Professions, Law, Physic—Trades—Amusements—Clubs and Social Meetings—Inns—Players—The Alms-House and Trustees—Inhabitants of the Alms-House, Blaney, Clelia, Benbow—The Hospital and Governors—the Poor and their Dwellings—The Poor of the Borough, the Parish Clerk, Ellen Orford, Abel Keene, Peter Grimes—Prisons—Schools.

A glance at the preceding table is sufficient to prove that our author is far from having abjured the system of delineating in verse subjects little grateful to poetry. No themes surely can be more untunable than those to which he has here attempered his lyre. It is observable too, that they are sought in a class of society yet lower than that which he has hitherto represented. The impurities of a rural hamlet were sufficiently repulsive;—what then must be those of a maritime borough? This gradual sinking in the scale of realities seems to us a direct consequence of that principle of Mr. Crabbe, on which we have, in a former part of this article, hazarded some strictures. The *Borough* is purely the creature of that principle; the legitimate successor of the *Village* and the **"Parish Register."**—Indeed, if the checks of fancy and taste be re-

moved from poetry, and admission be granted to images, of whatever description, provided they have the passport of reality, it is not easy to tell at what point the line of exclusion should be drawn, or why it should be drawn at all. No image of depravity, so long as it answers to some archetype in nature or art, can be refused the benefit of the general rule. The mind which has acquired a relish for such strong painting, is not likely to be made fastidious by indulgence. When it has exhausted one department of life, it will look for fresh materials in that which is more highly rather than in that which is more faintly coloured. From the haunts of rustic debauchery, the transition is natural to the purlieus of Wapping.

By the choice of this subject, Mr. Crabbe has besides exposed himself to another inconvenience. It was the misfortune of his former poems that they were restricted to a narrow range. They treated of a particular class of men and manners, and therefore precluded those representations of general nature, which, it scarcely needs the authority of Johnson to convince us, are the only things that 'can please many and please long.'—But, with respect to the present poem, this circumstance prevails to a much greater degree. In the inhabitants of a sea-port there are obviously but few generic traces of nature to be detected. The mixed character of their pursuits, and their amphibious sort of life, throw their manners and customs into a striking cast of singularity, and make them almost a separate variety of the human race. Among the existing modifications of society, it may be questioned if there be one which is more distinctly specified, we might say individualized.

The volume before us [*The Borough*] exhibits all the characteristic qualities of its author; a genius of no common order, but impaired by system—a contempt for the *bienséances* of life, and a rage for its realities. The only 'imaginary personage' (as Mr. Crabbe is pleased to style him) introduced into this poem, is 'a residing burgess in a large sea-port;' and this 'ideal friend' is brought in for the purpose of describing the 'Borough' to the inhabitant of a village in the centre of the kingdom.' In other respects, the poem inherits the beauties and defects of its predecessors; but while the defects are more aggravated as well as more thickly sown, the beauties, though not less scantily doled out, are unquestionably touched with a more affecting grace and softness. Although, therefore, the effect of the whole may be far from lively, yet in the strength and pathos of single passages the *Borough* will not have many rivals.

It is not perhaps from detached extracts so much as from a general acquaintance with our author's works, that a correct impression of the principal defects of his composition can be obtained. We shall merely collect a few passages for the satisfaction of those amongst our readers who may not be tempted to travel through the *Borough* themselves; premising however that our quotations must, for obvious reasons, be limited to those specimens which are the least objectionable in their respective kinds.

It will perhaps appear surprising that, under this privileged class, we should reckon the spirited, but not very fastidious, representation of sailors assembled to pass the evening at the 'Anchor.'

The *Anchor* too affords the Seaman Joys
In small smok'd Room, all Clamour, Crowd, and Noise;
Where a curv'd Settle half surrounds the Fire,
Where fifty Voices Purl and Punch require:
They come for Pleasure in their leisure Hour,

And they enjoy it to their utmost Power;
Standing they drink, they swearing smoke, while all
Call or make ready for a second Call;
There is no time for trifling—"Do ye see?
We drink and drub the French extempore."

See! round the Room, on every Beam and Balk,
Are mingled Scrolls of hieroglyphic Chalk;
Yet nothing heeded—would one Stroke suffice,
To blot out all here Honour is too nice,—
"Let knavish Landsmen think such dirty things,
We're British Tars, and British Tars are Kings."

In the following description there is more fineness of execution. But, in spite of its singular accuracy and clearness, it is one of those unpleasing pictures, which are condemned alike by taste and by feeling.

Say, wilt thou more of Scenes so sordid know?
Then will I lead thee down the dusty Row;
By the warm Alley and the long close Lane,—
There mark the fractur'd Door and paper'd Pane,
Where flags the noon-tide Air, and as we pass,
We fear to breathe the putrifying Mass:
But fearless yonder Matron; she disdains
To sigh for Zephyrs from ambrosial Plains;
But mends her Meshes torn, and pours her Lay
All in the stifling Fervour of the Day.

Her naked Children round the Alley run,
And roll'd in Dust, are bronz'd beneath the Sun;
Or gamble round the Dame, who, loosely drest,
Woos the coy Breeze to fan the open Breast:
She, once an Handmaid, strove by decent art
To charm her Sailor's Eye and touch his Heart;
Her Bosom then was veil'd in Kerchief clean,
And Fancy left to form the Charms unseen.

But when a Wife, she lost her former Care,
Nor thought on Charms, nor time for dress could spare;
Careless she found her Friends who dwelt beside,
No rival Beauty kept alive her Pride:
Still in her bosom Virtue keeps her place,
But Decency is gone, the Virtue's Guard and Grace.

The 'long boarded building,' which serves as a common receptacle for profligates and outcasts, 'an asylum for deceit and guilt,' is still less likely to be regarded with complacency.

In this vast Room, each Place by habit fixt,
Are Sexes, Families, and Ages mixt,—
To union forc'd by Crime, by Fear, by Need,
And all in Morals and in Modes agreed;
Some ruin'd Men, who from Mankind remove,
Some ruin'd Females, who yet talk of Love,
And some grown old in Idleness—the prey
To vicious Spleen, still railing through the Day;
And Need and Misery, Vice and Danger bind
In sad Alliance each degraded Mind.

The lines that follow those which we have just quoted, are among the most successful of Mr. Crabbe's performances in the minute style; yet they develop a scene of such detailed guilt and wretchedness as no skill of execution can render palatable. This indeed, it must be confessed, is the case with no small part of the present volume. The characters of Thompson, Blaney, Clelia, and Benbow, excellently as they are in many particulars drawn, afford exhibitions of a depravity which can excite no emotions but those of disgust. Thus also the five letters on 'the Poor,' (Letter 18—22) contain a series of stories which successively rise above each other in horror.

In point of style our author is extremely negligent. Some of his better and more laboured parts are indeed distinguished by much vigour and compactness of expression; but he is too apt to write hastily, and of course writes diffusely. His best passages are sometimes injured by this namby-pamby feebleness; as in the case of the following ingenious, though not very intelligible, comparison, which is a counterpart to a celebrated simile on the *Essay on Man*.

Though mild Benevolence our Priest possess'd,
Twas but by wishes or by words express'd:
Circles in water as they wider flow
The less conspicuous in their progress grow;
And when at last they touch upon the shore,
Distinction ceases, and they're view'd no more:
His Love, like that last Circle, all embrac'd,
But with effect that never could be trac'd.

There is too a want of refinement, if we may so express it, about the *air* of his poetry; we do not here mean about its moral or intellectual parts, but about what may be termed its manners—its external deportment. The *costume* of his ideas is slovenly and ungraceful. He is indeed always at ease; but it is the ease of confident carelessness rather than of good breeding. Thus the letter on Elections begins—

Yes! our election's past; and we've been free,
Somewhat as madmen without keepers be.

The substitution of *be* for *are* occurs more than once in our author; but, though it may be justified by the authority of Dryden, it can scarcely be reconciled to the rules of polished speech.

He thus describes a lady renouncing a cold and uncertain lover—

The wondering Girl, no prude, but something nice,
At length was chill'd by his unmelting ice;
She found her tortoise held such sluggish pace,
That she must turn and meet him in the chace:
This not approving, she withdrew till one
Came who appear'd with livelier hope to run.

Of a man whom the acquisition of wealth inspired with ambition for heraldic honours, we are told—

he then conceiv'd the thought
To *fish* for pedigree, but never *caught*.

We constantly meet with such phrases as *'he's pros'd,' 'who're maids,' 'he'd* now the power,' for *he had;* 'feeling *he's* none,' for *he has* none. In one place occur these rhymes:

pray'rs and *alms*
Will soon suppress these idly rais'd *alarms*.

In another—

intent on *cards,*
Oft he amus'd with riddles and *charardes*—for charades.

His humour, though at times peculiarly good, yet frequently trenches on buffoonery; and is sometimes unintentionally, we are convinced, carried to the verge of profaneness. Of these qualities we shall not give any examples, but offer in their place a few puns—

From Law to Physic stepping at our ease,
We find a way to finish—by *degrees*.
With the same Parts and Prospects, one a *Seat*
Builds for himself; one finds it in the Fleet.

The character of a tradesman, who, having contributed by unkindness to the death of a brother, relieves his remorse by active charity, is thus concluded—

> And if he wrong'd one Brother,—Heav'n forgive
> The Man by whom so many *Brethren* live!

Some of his efforts are more happy. There is true epigrammatic point in the account of an old toper celebrating the former companions of his debaucheries.

> Each Hero's Worth with much delight he paints,
> Martyrs they were, and he would make them Saints.

But we have been too long detained by these specimens, and are impatient to gratify our readers with some of a different nature. And here we shall cordially agree with the most devoted of Mr. Crabbe's admirers.—Whatever may be our opinion on other points, we are ready to maintain, that few excellencies in poetry are beyond the reach of his nervous and versatile genius; a position which, if our limits allowed it, we should not despair to make good by a reference only to the work before us.

Our first extract shall be of the class which we have in a former place called neutral. It sets the object before us in the most vivid manner; but at the same time neither irritates nor pleases the imagination.

> Lo! yonder Shed; observe its Garden-Ground,
> Which that low Paling, form'd of wreck, surround!
> There dwells a fisher; if you view his Boat,
> With Bed and Barrel—'tis his House afloat;
> Look at his House, where Ropes, Nets, Blocks, abound,
> Tar, Pitch, and Oakum—'tis his Boat aground:
> That Space enclos'd, but little he regards,
> Spread o'er with relicks of Mats, Sails, and Yards:
> Fish by the Wall, on Spit of Elder, rest
> Of all his Food, the cheapest and the best,
> By his own Labour caught, for his own Hunger drest.
>                                        (pp. 292-300)

The following sketch is truly in Mr. Crabbe's style. Without the romantic mellowness which envelopes the landscape of Goldsmith, or the freshness and hilarity of colouring which breathe in that of Graham, it is perhaps superior to both in distinctness, animation, and firmness of touch; and to these is added a peculiar air of facility and freedom.

> Thy Walks are ever pleasant; every Scene
> Is rich in beauty, lively, or serene—
> Rich—is that varied View with Woods around,
> Seen from the Seat, within the Shrubb'ry bound;
> Where shines the distant Lake, and where appear
> From Ruins bolting, unmolested Deer:
> Lively—the Village-Green, the Inn, the Place,
> Where the good Widow schools her Infant-Race.
> Shops, whence are heard, the Hammer and the Saw,
> And Village-Pleasures unreprov'd by Law;
> Then how serene! when in your favourite Room,
> Gales from your Jasmines soothe the Evening Gloom;
> When from your upland Paddock you look down,
> And just perceive the Smoke which hides the Town;
> When weary Peasants at the close of Day
> Walk to their Cots, and part upon the way;
> When Cattle slowly cross the shallow Brook,
> And Shepherds pen their Folds, and rest upon their
>     Crook.

As a contrast to this inland scene, we shall give an evening view on the sea-shore. The topics which it embraces have never, as far as we recollect, been so distinctly treated of in

poetry; they are here recorded too in very appropriate numbers. The versification of the latter part of the passage particularly, is brilliant and *éveillée,* and has something of the pleasing restlessness of the ocean itself.

> Now is it pleasant in the Summer-Eve,
> When a broad Shore retiring Waters leave,
> Awhile to wait upon the firm fair Sand,
> When all is calm at Sea, all still at Land;
> And there the Ocean's produce to explore,
> As floating by, or rolling on the Shore;
> Those living Jellies which the Flesh inflame,
> Fierce as a Nettle, and from that its Name;
> Some in huge masses, some that you may bring
> In the small compass of a Lady's ring;
> Figur'd by Hand divine—there's not a Gem
> Wrought by man's Art to be compar'd to them;
> Soft, brilliant, tender, through the Wave they glow,
> And make the Moon-beam brighter where they flow.
>
> See as they float along th' entangled Weeds
> Slowly approach, upborn on bladdery Beads;
> Wait till they land, and you shall then behold
> The fiery Sparks those tangled Frons' infold,
> Myriads of living Points; th' unaided Eye
> Can but the Fire and not the Form descry.
> And now your view upon the Ocean turn,
> And there the Splendour of the Waves discern;
> Cast but a Stone, or strike them with an Oar,
> And you shall Flames within the Deep explore;
> Or Scoop the Stream phosphoric as you stand,
> And the cold Flame shall flash along your Hand;
> When lost in wonder, you shall walk and gaze
> On Weeds that sparkle and on Waves that blaze.
>                                        (pp. 303-04)

We have already adverted to the talent which Mr. Crabbe possesses of delineating despair. That talent he has in this work exercised with a daring prodigality. There are no less than three very prominent representations of this kind; distinguished indeed from each other by varieties of circumstance and crime, but all bearing marks of the same dark and terrible pencil.

The first instance is that of a parish-clerk, a man strictly, but ostentatiously virtuous; who is at length seized with a spirit of avarice, which leads him to secure to himself a part of the sacramental collections. After a course of successful villany, he is detected; and the disgrace, awakening remorse, drives him to melancholy.

> In each lone place, dejected and dismay'd,
> Shrinking from view, his wasting Form he laid;
> Or to the restless Sea and roaring Wind,
> Gave the strong Yearnings of a ruin'd Mind:
> On the broad Beach, the silent Summer-day,
> Stretch'd on some Wreck, he wore his Life away;
> Or where the River mingles with the Sea,
> Or on the Mud-bank by the Elder-tree,
> Or by the bounding Marsh-dyke, there was he:
> And when unable to forsake the Town,
> In the blind Courts he sate desponding down—
> Always alone; then feebly would he crawl
> The Church-way Walk, and lean upon the Wall.

To this may be opposed the representation of the feelings of one who, at an advanced age, became a libertine, but was finally deserted by the world, and reduced to poverty.

> And now we saw him on the Beach reclin'd,
> Or causeless walking in the wintry Wind;
> And when it rais'd a loud and angry Sea,

He stood and gaz'd, in wretched reverie:
He heeded not the Frost, the Rain, the Snow,
Close by the Sea he walked alone and slow:
Sometimes his Frame through many an hour he spread
Upon a Tomb-Stone, moveless as the dead;
And was there found a sad and silent place,
There would he creep with slow and measur'd pace;
Then would he wander by the River side,
And fix his eyes upon the falling Tide;
The deep dry Ditch, the Rushes in the Fen,
And mossy Crag-Pits were his Lodgings then:
There, to his discontented Thoughts a prey,
The melancholy Mortal pin'd away.

The third victim is of a quite distinct character. 'The mind here exhibited,' says our author in his preface, 'is one untouched by pity, unstung by remorse, and uncorrected by shame: yet is this hardihood of temper and spirit broken by want, disease, solitude and disappointment, and he becomes the victim of a distempered and horror-stricken fancy.' (pp. 306-07)

From these specimens our readers will receive a very favourable impression of the poetical talent of Mr. Crabbe; and of this impression we are now content to leave them to the uninterrupted indulgence. That it should be the tendency of the former part of our criticism, to excite somewhat different feelings, would be to us a matter of much self-reproach, if we were not convinced that, in commenting on a writer at once of such powers and such celebrity, a frank exposition of our sentiments was due both to him and to ourselves. Should these imperfect strictures be fortunate enough to meet the eye of Mr. Crabbe, we have so much reliance on his candour as to believe that he will forgive their freedom. If however we are mistaken in this conjecture, we can only express our hope that he may speedily revenge himself, as he is well able, by the production of some work which shall compel our unqualified praise. (p. 312)

> [*Robert Grant*], *in a review of "The Borough," in* The Quarterly Review, *Vol. IV, No. VIII, November, 1810, pp. 281-312.*

### THE BRITISH CRITIC  (essay date 1811)

[*In the following excerpt from a review of* The Borough, *the critic praises the poem's overall style and approach to its subject, focusing on characterization, versification, and language.*]

We promised ourselves great satisfaction, and we may promise the same to our readers, in the examination and reporting of this poem. It cannot, in the nature of things, be an ordinary occurrence to meet with a poem which stands much above the common class of compositions; we must not expect to live on literary luxuries, and the daily bread of the press certainly has no resemblance to Mr. Crabbe's ***Borough.***

The talent of this author for accurate and lively delineation of character, is already known and acknowledged; and we are inclined to think that it is here displayed with more vigour and liveliness, than even in his former works. He has the art, a truly poetic quality, of rendering even the most trivial objects and events interesting; of placing them exactly before the eyes of his reader; and of pointing out those characteristics which every one must acknowledge to belong to them, and yet no one perhaps before had marked with such precision. As it is in the very conclusion of his poem that he speaks of his own general design in writing poetry, we shall, without

scruple, go to that part for our first specimen. He has drawn in it, and evidently meant to draw his own character, which will therefore complete our description of him.

> For this the poet looks the world around,
> Where form and life and reasoning man are found;
> He loves the mind, in all its modes, to trace,
> And all the manners of the changing race;
> Silent he walks the road of life along,
> And views the aims of its tumultuous throng:
> He finds what shapes the proteus-passions take,
> And what strange waste of life and joy they make,
> And loves to shew them in their varied ways,
> With honest blame or with unflattering praise:
> 'Tis good to know, 'tis pleasant to impart,
> These turns and movements of the human heart;
> The stronger features of the soul to paint,
> And make distinct the latent and the faint;
> Man as he is, to place in all men's view,
> Yet none with rancour, none with scorn pursue:
> Nor be it ever of my portraits told—
> 'Here the strong lines of malice we behold.'

He adds a wish, which we think descriptive of the actual effect of his compositions.

> This let me hope, that when in public view
> I bring my pictures, men may feel them true;
> 'This is a likeness,' may they all declare,
> 'And I have seen him, but I know not where:'
> For I should mourn the mischief I had done,
> If as the likeness all would fix on one.

It does indeed appear to us, that he is as clear from the imputation of particular satire, as he is strong in his description of characters, which from their accuracy *might* be real. We only lament that in one or two instances he has drawn atrocious pictures of vice, which whoever believes to be natural, cannot but sigh for that nature which is capable of such depravity. That it is so must, we fear, be owned; but we cannot but a little wonder at the taste which dwells by preference on such representations. This observation, however, applies to a very small part of the poem: and chiefly to such characters as those of Blaney and Peter Grimes, which having once read, we never wish to see again. The more they have of truth and probability, the more curious but the more disgusting they must be felt. Mr. Crabbe's versification is well suited to his subjects; easy and flowing; sometimes apparently negligent; at others pointed and neat. The reader, as he proceeds, is neither fatigued by constant exertion, nor satiated by uniformity of style; he can read the letters with as much ease as if they were prose, with the frequently recurring stimulus of poetical effect, both in the thought and in the expressions. Comparing the present volume with the former poems of the author, we think it in general composed with more care; and if not always pointed with more felicity, yet certainly not often inferior.

***The Borough,*** which the poet has undertaken to describe, is, like his human characters, not easily fixed to any one in particular. It is supposed to be situated on the sea coast, but that is all which can be ascertained; and as the author, by his own account, inhabits "a village in the centre of the kingdom," there are no means of guessing to which coast his footsteps would be turned, when he went to make poetical observations at a distance from home. It is likely indeed that his observations were made at various times, and in various excursions, through a long course of years. The subject, however, has enabled him to quit his usual scope of description, and to introduce new objects and new persons. Accustomed habits of thought have indeed led him to give a disproportionate share of his attention to the lowest classes of society; and it may be objected, not entirely without reason, that, out of twenty-four letters, nearly one half are given to the alms-house and other objects on a level with it. The only excuse for this fault, if it be a fault, will be found in the liveliness and originality of the descriptions and narratives which it produces. (pp. 236-38)

So much do these letters abound with passages of strong and original effect, that we feel no danger but that of extending our specimens to an unreasonable length. The letters on the sects, on trades, and professions, have all their various merits.—The letter on amusements (9) is concluded by an incident so natural and so well described, of a party of pleasure overtaken by the tide on a small islet, that nothing but its length, after the many passages we have produced, deters us from inserting it. The style of the author is often varied; sometimes he is even sportive in his descriptions, and with good success. In few passages more successful than in his picture of a flourishing inn, contrasted afterwards by one fallen into decay. We give a part of the former:

> The ample yards on either side contain
> Buildings where order and distinction reign;—
> The splendid carriage of the wealthier guest,
> The ready chaise and driver smartly drest;
> Whiskeys and gigs and curricles are there.

*Facsimile of the first letter addressed by Crabbe to Edmund Burke.*

> And high fed prancers many a raw bon'd pair.
> On all without a lordly host sustains
> The care of empire, and observant reigns;
> The parting guest beholds him at his side,
> With pomp obsequious, bending in his pride;
> Round all the place his eyes all objects meet,
> Attentive, silent, civil and discreet.
> O'er all within the lady hostess rules,
> Her bar she governs, and her kitchen schools;
> To every guest th' appropriate speech is made,
> And every duty with distinction paid;
> Respectful, easy, pleasant and polite—
> 'Your honour's servant—*Mister Smith,* good night.'

The accuracy as well as humour of the concluding lines cannot require to be pointed out to those who have ever travelled or observed. It is time, however, to conclude, and for the sake of literature, we will conclude with the author's view of the delights of study, which he paints, not only with true feeling, but in the third paragraph, with an artifice of construction which only those who are used to composition will completely estimate.

> Books cannot always please, however good;
> Minds are not ever craving for their food;
> But sleep will soon the weary soul prepare
> For cares to-morrow, that were this day's care;
> For forms, for feasts, that sundry times have past,
> And formal feasts that will for ever last.
>
> 'But then from study will no comforts rise?'
> Yes! such as studious minds alone can prize;
> Comforts, yea!—joys ineffable they find,
> Who seek the prouder pleasures of the mind:
> The soul, collected in those happy hours,
> Then makes her efforts, then enjoys her powers;
> And in those seasons feels herself repaid,
> For labours past and honours long delay'd.
>
> 'No! 'tis not worldly gain, although by chance
> The sons of learning may to wealth advance;
> Nor station high, though in some favouring hour
> The sons of learning may arrive at power;
> Nor is it glory, though the public voice
> Of honest praise will make the heart rejoice:
> But 'tis the mind's own feelings give the joy,
> Pleasures the gathers in her own employ—
> Pleasures that gain or praise cannot bestow,
> Yet can dilate and raise them when they flow.

(pp. 245-46)

*A review of "The Borough," in* The British Critic, *Vol. XXXVII, March, 1811, pp. 236-47.*

## GEORGE CRABBE   (essay date 1812)

[*In the following excerpt from Crabbe's preface to* Tales, *first published in 1812, the poet explains his general theory of poetry, defending the logic behind his conception of narrative style as well as the poetic character of his work.*]

Reproof and advice, it is probable, every author will receive, if we except those who merit so much of the former, that the latter is contemptuously denied them; now, of these, reproof, though it may cause more temporary uneasiness, will in many cases create less difficulty, since errors may be corrected when opportunity occurs: but advice, I repeat, may be of such nature, that it will be painful to reject and yet impossible to follow it; and in this predicament I conceive myself to be placed. There has been recommended to me, and from authority which neither inclination nor prudence leads me to resist, in any new work I might undertake, an unity of subject, and that arrangement of my materials which connects the whole and gives additional interest to every part; in fact, if not an Epic Poem, strictly so denominated, yet such composition as would possess a regular succession of events, and a catastrophe to which every incident should be subservient, and which every character, in a greater or less degree, should conspire to accomplish.

In a Poem of this nature, the principal and inferior characters in some degree resemble a general and his army, where no one pursues his peculiar objects and adventures, or pursues them in unison with the movements and grand purposes of the whole body; where there is a community of interests and a subordination of actors: and it was upon this view of the subject, and of the necessity for such distribution of persons and events, that I found myself obliged to relinquish an undertaking, for which the characters I could command, and the adventures I could describe, were altogether unfitted.

But if these characters which seemed to be at my disposal were not such as would coalesce into one body, nor were of a nature to be commanded by one mind, so neither on examination did they appear as an unconnected multitude, accidentally collected, to be suddenly dispersed; but rather beings of whom might be formed groups and smaller societies, the relations of whose adventures and pursuits might bear that kind of similitude to an Heroic Poem, which these minor associations of men (as pilgrims on the way to their saint, or parties in search of amusement, travellers excited by curiosity, or adventurers in pursuit of gain) have in points of connection and importance with a regular and disciplined army.

Allowing this comparison, it is manifest that, while much is lost for want of unity of subject and grandeur of design, something is gained by greater variety of incident and more minute display of character, by accuracy of description and diversity of scene: in these narratives we pass from gay to grave, from lively to severe, not only without impropriety, but with manifest advantage. In one continued and connected poem, the reader is, in general, highly gratified or severely disappointed; by many independent narratives, he has the renovation of hope, although he has been dissatisfied, and a prospect of reiterated pleasure, should he find himself entertained.

I mean not, however, to compare these different modes of writing as if I were balancing their advantages and defects before I could give preference to either; with me the way I take is not a matter of choice, but of necessity: I present not my *Tales* to the reader as if I had chosen the best method of ensuring his approbation, but as using the only means I possessed of engaging his attention.

It may probably be remarked, that Tales, however dissimilar, might have been connected by some associating circumstance to which the whole number might bear equal affinity, and that examples of such union are to be found in Chaucer, in Boccace, and other collectors and inventors of Tales, which, considered in themselves, are altogether independent; and to this idea I gave so much consideration as convinced me that I could not avail myself of the benefit of such artificial mode of affinity. To imitate the English poet, characters must be found adapted to their several relations, and this is a point of great difficulty and hazard: much allowance seems to be required even for Chaucer himself; since it is difficult to conceive that on any occasion the devout and delicate Prioress, the courtly and valiant Knight, and "the poure good Man the

persone of a Towne," would be the voluntary companions of the drunken Miller, the licentious Sompnour, and "the Wanton Wife of Bath," and enter into that colloquial and travelling intimacy which, if a common pilgrimage to the shrine of St. Thomas may be said to excuse, I know nothing beside (and certainly nothing in these times) that would produce such effect. Boccace, it is true, avoids all difficulty of this kind, by not assigning to the ten relators of his hundred Tales [the *Decamoran*] any marked or peculiar characters; nor, though there are male and female in company, can the sex of the narrator be distinguished in the narration. To have followed the method of Chaucer might have been of use, but could scarcely be adopted, from its difficulty; and to have taken that of the Italian writer would have been perfectly easy, but could be of no service: the attempt at union, therefore, has been relinquished, and these relations are submitted to the public, connected by no other circumstance than their being the productions of the same author, and devoted to the same purpose, the entertainment of his readers.

It has been already acknowledged, that these compositions have no pretensions to be estimated with the more lofty and heroic kind of poems; but I feel great reluctance in admitting, that they have not a fair and legitimate claim to the poetic character: in vulgar estimation, indeed, all that is not prose passes for poetry; but I have not ambition of so humble a kind as to be satisfied with a concession which requires nothing in the poet, except his ability for counting syllables; and I trust something more of the poetic character will be allowed to the succeeding pages, than what the heroes of the *Dunciad* might share with the author: nor was I aware that, by describing, as faithfully as I could, men, manners, and things, I was forfeiting a just title to a name which has been freely granted to many, whom to equal, and even to excel, is but very stinted commendation.

In this case it appears, that the usual comparison between Poetry and Painting entirely fails: the artist who takes an accurate likeness of individuals, or a faithful representation of scenery, may not rank so high in the public estimation as one who paints an historical event, or an heroic action; but he is nevertheless a painter, and his accuracy is so far from diminishing his reputation, that it procures for him in general both fame and emolument: nor is it perhaps with strict justice determined that the credit and reputation of those verses which strongly and faithfully delineate character and manners, should be lessened in the opinion of the public by the very accuracy which gives value and distinction to the productions of the pencil.

Nevertheless, it must be granted that the pretensions of any composition to be regarded as poetry will depend upon that definition of the poetic character which he who undertakes to determine the question has considered as decisive; and it is confessed also, that one of great authority may be adopted, by which the verses now before the reader, and many others which have probably amused and delighted him, must be excluded: a definition like this will be found in the words which the greatest of poets, not divinely inspired, has given to the most noble and valiant Duke of Athens—

> The poet's eye, in a fine frenzy rolling,
> Doth glance from heaven to earth, from earth to heaven;
> And as Imagination bodies forth
> The forms of things unknown, the poet's pen
> Turns them to shapes, and gives to airy nothing
> A local habitation, and a name.

Hence we observe the Poet is one who, in the excursions of his fancy between heaven and earth, lights upon a kind of fairy-land, in which he places a creation of his own, where he embodies shapes, and gives action and adventure to his ideal offspring: taking captive the imagination of his readers, he elevates them above the grossness of actual being, into the soothing and pleasant atmosphere of supramundane existence: there he obtains for his visionary inhabitants the interest that engages a reader's attention without ruffling his feelings, and excites that moderate kind of sympathy which the realities of nature oftentimes fail to produce, either because they are so familiar and insignificant that they excite no determinate emotion, or are so harsh and powerful that the feelings excited are grating and distasteful.

Be it then granted that (as Duke Theseus observes) "such tricks hath strong Imagination," and that such poets "are of imagination all compact;" let it be further conceded, that theirs is a higher and more dignified kind of composition, nay, the only kind that has pretensions to inspiration; still, that these poets should so entirely engross the title as to exclude those who address their productions to the plain sense and sober judgment of their readers, rather than to their fancy and imagination, I must repeat that I am unwilling to admit—because I conceive that, by granting such right of exclusion, a vast deal of what has been hitherto received as genuine poetry would no longer be entitled to that appellation.

All that kind of satire wherein character is skilfully delineated must (this criterion being allowed) no longer be esteemed as genuine poetry; and for the same reason many affecting narratives which are founded on real events, and borrow no aid whatever from the imagination of the writer, must likewise be rejected: a considerable part of the poems, as they have hitherto been denominated, of Chaucer, are of this naked and unveiled character: and there are in his Tales many pages of coarse, accurate, and minute, but very striking description. Many small poems in a subsequent age, of most impressive kind, are adapted and addressed to the common sense of the reader, and prevail by the strong language of truth and nature: they amused our ancestors, and they continue to engage our interest, and excite our feelings, by the same powerful appeals to the heart and affections. In times less remote, Dryden has given us much of this poetry, in which the force of expression and accuracy of description have neither needed nor obtained assistance from the fancy of the writer; the characters in his *Absalom and Achitophel* are instances of this, and more especially those of Doeg and Og in the second part: these, with all their grossness, and almost offensive accuracy are found to possess that strength and spirit which has preserved from utter annihilation the dead bodies of Tate, to whom they were inhumanly bound, happily with a fate the reverse of that caused by the cruelty of Mezentius; for there the living perished in the putrefaction of the dead, and here the dead are preserved by the vitality of the living. And, to bring forward one other example, it will be found that Pope himself has no small portion of this actuality of relation, this nudity of description, and poetry without an atmosphere; the lines beginning, "In the worst inn's worst room," are an example, and many others may be seen in his Satires, Imitations, and above all in his *Dunciad:* the frequent absence of those "Sports of Fancy," and "Tricks of strong imagination," have been so much observed, that some have ventured to question whether even this writer were a poet; and though, as Dr. Johnson has remarked, it would be difficult to form a definition of one in which Pope should not

be admitted, yet they who doubted his claim had, it is likely, provided for his exclusion by forming that kind of character for their Poet, in which this elegant versifier, for so he must be then named, should not be comprehended.

These things considered, an author will find comfort in his expulsion from the rank and society of Poets, by reflecting that men much his superiors were likewise shut out, and more especially when he finds also that men not much his superiors are entitled to admission.

But, in whatever degree I may venture to differ from any others in my notions of the qualifications and character of the true Poet, I most cordially assent to their opinion who assert, that his principal exertions must be made to engage the attention of his readers; and further, I must allow that the effect of poetry should be to lift the mind from the painful realities of actual existence, from its everyday concerns, and its perpetually-occurring vexations, and to give it repose by substituting objects in their place which it may contemplate with some degree of interest and satisfaction: but, what is there in all this, which may not be effected by a fair representation of existing character? nay, by a faithful delineation of those painful realities, those every-day concerns, and those perpetually-occurring vexations themselves, provided they be not (which is hardly to be supposed) the very concerns and distresses of the reader? for when it is admitted that they have no particular relation to him, but are the troubles and anxieties of other men, they excite and interest his feelings as the imaginary exploits, adventures, and perils of romance;—they soothe his mind, and keep his curiosity pleasantly awake; they appear to have enough of reality to engage his sympathy, but possess not interest sufficient to create painful sensations. Fiction itself, we know, and every work of fancy, must for a time have the effect of realities; nay, the very enchanters, spirits, and monsters of Ariosto and Spenser must be present in the mind of the reader while he is engaged by their operations, or they would be as the objects and incidents of a nursery tale to a rational understanding, altogether despised and neglected in truth, I can but consider this pleasant effect upon the mind of a reader, as depending neither upon the events related (whether they be actual or imaginary), nor upon the characters introduced (whether taken from life or fancy), but upon the manner in which the poem itself is conducted; let that be judiciously managed, and the occurrences actually copied from life will have the same happy effect as the inventions of a creative fancy;—while, on the other hand, the imaginary persons and incidents to which the poet has given "a local habitation and a name," will make upon the concurring feelings of the reader the same impressions with those taken from truth and nature, because they will appear to be derived from that source, and therefore of necessity will have a similar effect.

Having thus far presumed to claim for the ensuing pages the rank and title of poetry, I attempt no more, nor venture to class or compare them with any other kinds of poetical composition; their place will doubtless be found for them.

A principal view and wish of the poet must be to engage the mind of his readers, as, failing in that point, he will scarcely succeed in any other. I therefore willingly confess that much of my time and assiduity has been devoted to this purpose; that, to the ambition of pleasing, no other sacrifices have, I trust, been made, than of my own labour and care. Nothing will be found that militates against the rules of propriety and good manners, nothing that offends against the more important precepts of morality and religion; and with this negative kind of merit, I commit my book to the judgment and taste of the reader—not being willing to provoke his vigilance by professions of accuracy, nor to solicit his indulgence by apologies for mistakes. (pp. 136-49)

> *George Crabbe, in a preface in* The Poetical Works *of the Rev. George Crabbe: With His Letters and Journal and His Life, Vol. I, edited by George Crabbe, Jr., John Murray, 1838, pp. 128-49.*

## *THE CRITICAL REVIEW,* LONDON   (essay date 1812)

[*In the following excerpt from a review of* Tales, *the critic evaluates negative and positive reactions to Crabbe's realism, focusing on the poet's depiction of local environments and use of characterization.*]

The names of Voltaire and Crebillon never divided the critics of Paris into contrary parties more effectually than this world of ours is now set at variance by the disputed merits of Mr. Crabbe. It is not unusual at the present day to find one's self in a society of which one half is loud in extolling him as *a poet* in the truest sense of the word—as the *inventor* or *creator* . . . of a new field for the exercise of the imagination—and on that account worthy of a comparison with the greatest original geniuses of antiquity—while the other is roused to indignation by the bare idea of what appears to them so exaggerated and almost blasphemous an elevation, and, running headlong to the contrary extreme, refuses him even the name of a poet, and all pretensions to the alleged qualifications of poetry, to the high honours of invention and imagination, whatever. The most remarkable feature in the present controversy is, that both parties are right, at least in their premises, whatever may be the consequence as to the conclusions they respectively draw from them. Mr. Crabbe is absolutely and indubitably a poet in the sense which his admirers annex to the term; and, although in the other and more popular acceptation of the phrase, we cannot admit in the full extent which is sometimes contended for, his want of all pretension to the dignity demanded by him, yet we must confess that his general style and disposition are such as in a great degree to bear out his objectors in their refusal. On examining the subject more in detail, we find ourselves also compelled to admit the justice of almost every censure and of almost every praise that he has received; and, to reconcile these apparent contradictions, and try both praise and censure by the test afforded us in his most recent publication, will be the principal object of our present article.

On the appearance of his last work, *the Borough,* he received from some of his warmest panegyrists a piece of advice which we thought at the time rather misplaced, and which we are not at all sorry to find was lost upon its object. Mr. Crabbe was recommended, as we recollect, to turn his thoughts thenceforward to the construction of some interesting and connected story. Now we never imagined that Pope would have made any thing of his intended epic on the conquest of this island by Brute the Trojan; and it is surely no ill compliment to Mr. Crabbe to suppose that he also would have failed where Pope was not qualified to succeed. A resemblance has before been remarked in the genius of these two poets; and we think that a strong resemblance certainly does exist, and that it consists in a happy perception of strong individual traits of character, and a peculiar power of delineating them, which go far towards constituting the whole excellence of sa-

tirical and didactic poetry, but a very small way in exciting dramatic or epic interest. In many of the qualities which are necessary to these far different purposes, we conceive Mr. Crabbe to be altogether deficient; and of this a stronger proof can scarcely be afforded than by his present publication, which, though he has chosen to give to it the title of *Tales,* consists rather of insulated descriptions of character and manners than of that species of narrative to which the denomination of fable properly applies. Out of the twenty-one separate pieces with which we are here presented, by far the greater number, at least, such as **"The Dumb Orators," "The Gentleman Farmer," "The Frank Courtship," "The Widow's Tale," "Arabella," "The Lover's Journey," "Edward Shore," "The precipitate Choice," "The Struggles of Conscience," "The Convert," "The Learned Boy,"** and others, wear much more the appearance of characters to be inserted in some description or satirical essay than of separate historical narrations, which demand the interest of incident as well as of character to support them; and (although we are little disposed on our own parts to quarrel with mere names, which are in themselves indifferent), we think that many of the objections which will be made to the present publication, might probably have been avoided, if some such title as that of 'Characteristic Sketches of Life,' had been given to it, instead of that which the author has assumed.

In order to complete the catalogue of pieces which the volume contains, and at the same time to divide them into the three classes, which we think may be fairly instituted to receive them, we will now enumerate the titles in the following order. Those which appear to us to contain the largest portion of Mr. Crabbe's peculiar and acknowledged beauties, and to have afforded the widest scope to the exercise of his powers, are **"The parting Hour," "The Patron," "The Lover's Journey," "Edward Shore;"** to which we would perhaps add **"The Confidant,"** and **"Resentment."** In those which follow, **"The Dumb Orators," "The Gentleman Farmer," "Procrastination," "The Frank Courtship," "The Widow's Tale," "The Mother," "Arabella," "Jesse and Colin," "The Wager," "The Convert,"** and **"The Brothers,"** either his faults and his beauties have been so equally dealt, or his powers have been so much cramped by the defect of the subject, that they may be fairly set down in a middling or neutral class—but **"The Struggles of Conscience," "Squire Thomas, or the precipitate Choice," "Advice, or the Squire and the Priest,"** and **"The Learned Boy,"** and performances which deserve a much smaller share of indulgence, and must therefore be set down among the decidedly bad. Not but in the very best there are unfortunate blemishes, by the aid of which Mr. Crabbe's detractors may turn the whole into ridicule; while in the very worst there are traces of genius and talent, which in the opinion of his admirers may, perhaps, redeem all their defects; and as for those which we have classed as neutrals, they may, (we think) very fairly be admitted into the higher, or degraded to the lower rank, according to the general inclination of the reader in favour of the author or otherwise.

The excellencies of Mr. Crabbe have thus been summed up by some of his most devoted lovers—force and truth of description—selection and condensation of expression. He is said to possess the strength and originality of Cowper. His versification is compared to that of Goldsmith. His language is commended for its strength and purity. His taste for the talents of selecting and grouping his objects. His descriptions for their minute resemblance and 'Chinese' accuracy. His reflections for their moral sensibility, and their alternate tone of sarcasm and pathos. With regard to the subjects he has chosen, the interest excited by humble life is said to be general, profound, and lasting. The most popular passages even of Shakspeare himself are of this nature; and if there is often no intrinsic beauty in the objects which he describes, the truth of nature nevertheless demands the description of them. Nay, the poet, as the painter, of low life *must* descend to particulars which in other subjects would be impertinent and obtrusive. A 'distinct locality and imaginary reality' must be given to his pictures. His objects must be distinguished with 'a minute and anatomical precision.' Thus, in the judgment of these writers, much of what at first sight and unconnected with the general design of his works, would necessarily be condemned as vulgar, bald, or prosaïc, is in fact necessary to the completion of that design, and therefore to be ranked in the class of beauties rather than of defects.

In our opinion, Mr. Crabbe amply deserves every commendation which has thus been bestowed upon him; and, before we proceed to contemplate the other side of the picture, we shall present to our readers a few out of the many specimens which we might select from the volume now before us, in justification of our opinion. Our first extracts shall be from the **"Lover's Journey,"** which, considered not as a tale, but (as we before denominated it) a sketch of character, merits every praise which it is possible for the warmest friends of the author to bestow upon it.

> It is the soul that sees; the outward eyes
> Present the object, but the mind descries;
> And thence delight, disgust, or cool indiff'rence rise;
> When minds are joyful, then we look around,
> And what is seen is all on fairy ground;
> Again they sicken, and on every view
> Cast their own dull and melancholy hue;
> Or, if absorbed by their peculiar cares,
> The vacant eye on viewless matter glares.
> Our feelings still upon our views attend,
> And their own natures to the objects lend;
> Sorrow and joy are in their influence sure,
> Loug as the passion reigns th' effects endure;
> But love in minds his various changes makes,
> And clothes each object with the change he takes;
> His light and shade on every view he throws,
> And on each object, what he feels bestows.

The exemplification of these just and beautiful sentiments immediately follows,

> Fair was the morning, and the month was June,

when the lover set out early on the delightful errand of visiting the object of his affections. His day's ride conducted him through a great variety of country of what would be ordinarily deemed the gloomiest or most uninteresting description; but the cheerful and happy tone of his mind reflects a gaiety on all that he sees, which the poet has contrived to colour with all the force and brilliancy of the lover's own imagination. (pp. 561-65)

The merits of this beautiful poem are too obvious to require any further illustration . . . ; and we shall only advert to one of its minor excellencies, which might otherwise escape the reader's attention, that which we may venture to call its geographical precision and accuracy. Various as are the descriptions of natural scenery which it embraces, it is easy to believe that the whole may fall within the compass of a twenty miles' ride on the eastern coast of the island; and there is a truth,

and (to adopt the expression of some former critics) a 'distinct locality' about it, which almost persuades us that Mr. Crabbe has himself (we will not say on a similar occasion) taken the very ride which he here describes, and that his pictures are neither drawn from imagination, nor strung together by the fancy, but taken from reality in the very succession in which he has placed them. (pp. 568-69)

Without disputing any more than is necessary about words, for which, (as words merely,) we again repeat, we have no value, it does appear to us an extremely childish perversion of language to deny the praise of poetry to such passages as those we have now had the pleasure of laying before our readers. But we are told that Mr. Crabbe is only the poet of reality, whose wish and aim it is to discard every thing like illusion; that, on the contrary, men fly to poetry for the express purpose of getting rid of reality; that the office of poetry is to flatter the imagination merely; that the pleasures of poetry depend entirely on illusion, &c.&c. all which, with great submission, appears to us the most absurd and inconsiderate jargon; the meaning of which, (if any meaning whatever can be collected from it) is, not simply that Mr. Crabbe is no poet, but that all didactic and all descriptive writers of all ages are equally to be excluded from that denomination; that Pope is a mere stringer of verses—nay, more, that (with the exception of a few flights of imagination which we find scattered in their works,) Homer and Shakspeare are equally undeserving of the title; and, moreover, that there is no writer past or present among all those, whom the common consent of the world has classed among the poets, who is not improperly so classed, with the saving (perhaps) of Mr. Southey alone. But Mr. Crabbe does not stand in need of the poor defence of hyperbole against a charge so very hyperbolic. (pp. 573-74)

But although the defence of Mr. Crabbe is easy . . . against a censure so indiscriminate and extravagant, there is no writer who enjoys a similar degree of reputation with himself, equally obnoxious to fair and honest criticism on points with regard to which his own rules of poetry will afford him no justification. It is true that we feel no *actual* pain in what does not concern ourselves; but Mr. Crabbe will not pretend to say that the imagination may not be painfully affected by the mere relation of what does not immediately concern the individual; and if the manner in which the imagination is affected be *merely* painful, we presume he will not attempt to deny that the means by which that effect is produced are contrary to the true end and purpose of poetry. It is most truly remarked that distress, in order to be interesting, must be unattended with disgust; that there is 'a degree of depravity which counteracts our sympathy with suffering, and of insignificance which extinguishes our interest in guilt.' It has also been observed, and that by no unfriendly critic, that no poet has ever sinned so deeply in violation of this rule as the author now before us. The present volume contains much less of what is strictly obnoxious to this censure than either of his former works. The subjects of which it treats are raised one step higher in the scale of humanity. The 'depraved, abject, diseased, and neglected poor,' are no longer the objects which he employs his pencil to pourtray; and, in a less abject view of society, that of our yeomanry, our mechanics, little tradesmen, and inferior gentry, there rarely presents itself to our view any picture of unmixed disgust and uninteresting depravity. Yet such characters as those which are designed in **"the Mother," "Squire Thomas," "the Learned Boy,"** and perhaps some few more of these pieces, can hardly be considered as entirely free from the objection to which we now refer.

We have one further remark to make as to the class of subjects which he has now chosen for the exercise of his talents; and that is, that while it tends, in a great degree, to exempt him from the force of the objection which has been so frequently made to his former writings, it has an equal tendency to diminish one of the principal sources of the gratification which his readers have hitherto derived from him. The characters and habits, the vices and sufferings of the poor, possessed much of that interest which is attached to novelty—to the description of scenes which, though familiar as to the sort of sympathy which they are intended to excite, are nevertheless, not *personally* familiar, or of constant and every-day occurrence to the generality of readers. Every step which the poet advances in the rank of his subjects, approaches them nearer to that of his readers; the charm of novelty is altogether wanting to the description of scenes which resemble those of our own fire-sides; and it is in treating of the characters and habits of the middle ranks of society, that the relief of fable and incident to diversify the narrative becomes more than ever indispensable.

Another topic of censure to which this poet has exposed himself, the force of which, the present volume is rather calculated to augment than to obviate, is his indiscriminate love of minute detail, of unnecessary, uninteresting, *prosing* circumstance. We do not agree with those who deny the closeness of the analogy which has been generally conceived to exist between the arts of poetry and painting, and, without going to China for our illustration, shall be content to acquiesce in the strong resemblance which has been pointed out between the style of Crabbe's descriptive poetry and that of what is called the Dutch school of painting. But the best masters of that school are at least as remarkable for the force, brilliancy, and (to employ a metaphor which the subject seems to justify,) the *terseness* of their execution, as for the minuteness of detail which is their most prominent quality; and the poet, who forgetting this important ingredient, squanders himself away in tedious and flat circumstantiality, may indeed resemble *the school* to which he is assimilated in the eyes of the superficial and tasteless observer, but will never be ranked by the connoisseur or the critic on the same level with Teniers, Ostade, or Vandevelde. It is not his love of minuteness and detail which ought to be objected to Mr. Crabbe, but his want of taste and discrimination in rendering those qualities subservient to the general effect of his picture. The '*distinct locality and imaginary reality*' which this faculty of particularizing is said to confer, may be obtained at too great an expence of the time and patience of the reader. At all events, what possible advantage is gained to the interest of, for instance, the **"Lover's Journey,"** by his telling us in measured prose that the gentleman whom he calls Orlando, was really christened John, and that his mistress's appellation in the parish register was not Laura, but Susan; and that the more poetical names of Orlando and Laura were conferred on them not by their god-fathers and god-mothers, but by those ideal worthies, love and fancy? Of what possible importance is it that the contested election which gave rise to the connection, the consequences of which are so feelingly and exquisitely pourtrayed in the tale of **"The Patron,"** was carried on between Sir Godfrey Ball and Lord Frederick Damer, the son of the Earl of Fitzdonnel? And a thousand other the like insignificant and impertinent pieces of newspaper information?

There is an easy familiarity which, when kept within decent bounds, is a peculiarly fit vehicle for the introduction of a long narration; and Dryden may, in this particular, have served Mr. Crabbe for a model worthy of imitation. But vulgarity is far removed from that frank good-humoured air which tends to ingratiate the reader at the outset, and to give him precisely that complacent impression with which it is the poet's interest that he should proceed. The impression which Mr. Crabbe's blunt ploughman-like familiarity is calculated to produce is very different, and if he had displayed the same disgusting and repulsive coarseness in the introductions to his earlier works, that he has since suffered to grow upon him, bold indeed must have been the man who could have ventured to explore the hidden treasures of so unpromising a superficies. The commencement of almost every tale in this collection is in this perverted taste:

> Gwynn was a farmer, whom the farmers all,
> Who dwelt around, the *gentleman* would call.

> A borough bailiff, who to law was train'd,
> A wife and sons in decent state maintain'd.

> Grave Jonas Kindred, Sybil Kindred's sire,
> Was six feet high, and look'd six inches higher.

> To farmer Moss, in Laugar Vale, came down
> His only daughter, from her school in town—

> Of a fair town, where Dr. Rack was guide, &c.

> 'Squire Thomas flatter'd long a wealthy aunt, &c.

> A serious toyman in the city dwelt,
> Who much concern for his religion felt.

> Than' old George Fletcher, on the British coast
> Dwelt not a seaman who had more to boast.
> Kind, simple, and sincere,—he seldom spoke,
> But sometimes sang and chorus'd *"Hearts of Oak!"*

> An honest man was farmer Jones, and true,
> He did by all, as all by him should do.

What reader, unacquainted with Mr. Crabbe's previous reputation, would think of reading a single line more of an author who forces himself into his notice with such vulgar effrontery, and who thinks to gain by repelling him, like the beggar at the corner of the street who thrusts his stump of an arm into the passenger's face, in order to compel his attention and extort his alms? Who does not turn from the obtrusive mendicant in disgust, and escape his importunities if the swiftness of his feet will only enable him to elude them?

We forbear to instance any of the passages in which the same offensive vulgarity arrests or startles us in almost every page of some, and occasionally even in his best and most interesting pieces. Another observation to which he is fairly liable, is that his very virtues are often pushed to such an excess as to become glaring and capital defects. For instance, he has been commended for his force and compression, his sententious brevity and manly strength of language. It is singular enough that in the same author such admirable qualities as those which we have just cited, and their very opposites, of tame languid diffuseness, and 'namby-pamby feebleness,' should be found co-existent. Yet so it certainly is with Mr. Crabbe. We have now, however, only to do with the former, and to say that he sometimes pushes those very excellencies for which he has been justly admired, to their vicious extremes of abrupt conciseness, quaint mannerism, and antithetical jingle. They even carry him so low as to the mean pedestrian vice of punning; and that species of *wit* which is habitually condemned, even in the freedom of conversation, is thus, (we believe,) for the first time, introduced into the regions of serious, descriptive, or didactic, poetry.

It has been remarked that he is always at ease, but that his ease is rather that of confident carelessness than of good breeding. This reflection is too general, and by no means universally applicable. We are quite sure that many passages of all his works have been deeply studied, and (if we mistake not) some have been many times written and re-written before they were committed to the press. Nevertheless, he is very often, we may perhaps say most generally, careless both of his thoughts and language to an extent that we have seldom seen paralleled in any writer who has so much value for his reputation as Mr. Crabbe undoubtedly possesses.

All these defects, however, when collected together, cannot counterbalance the many claims which Mr. Crabbe possesses upon our admiration and gratitude. The worst perhaps is that they are so glaringly obvious to the whole world, while his beauties are of a nature which few, comparatively speaking, know how properly to estimate. His style is more apt to provoke the dangerous ridicule of parody than that of any poet of the present day. The very best of poets, may be and have been parodied, but not till long after their merits have been sufficiently understood and established, to bear the severest test of ridicule. Mr. Crabbe only irresistably incites the reader to the exercise of this species of wit, even while he is fresh from the first perusal of him. The disadvantage attending the excitement of such a propensity is obvious. Thousands are endowed with a sense of ridicule, while a hundred only possess a refined and intelligent taste; and out of that more select number, perhaps there are very few who are able to resist the influence of ridicule when once excited. Ridicule is not, nor ever ought to be made, the test either of moral or of political truth—nevertheless no man should be so confident either in his virtue or his talents as to venture wantonly to incur its hostility. (pp. 574-79)

> *A review of "Tales," in* The Critical Review, *London, n.s. Vol. II, No. VI, December, 1812, pp. 561-79.*

## JAMES SMITH (poem date 1812)

[*Smith was a comedic poet who collaborated with his brother Horace on two notable works,* Rejected Addresses *(1812), a collection of humorous poems that parodied the works of leading contemporary poets, and* Horace in London *(1813), an imitation of selected odes by the Latin poet Horace. In the following poem from* Rejected Addresses, *entitled "The Theatre," Smith employs the heroic couplet and creates a humorous montage of classical and vernacular elements in order to satirize Crabbe's style. It was in "A Preface of Apologies" to this piece that Smith coined for Crabbe the famous epithet "Pope in worsted stockings."*]

Tis sweet to view, from half-past five to six,
Our long wax-candles, with short cotton wicks,
Touch'd by the lamplighter's Promethean art,
Start into light and make the lighter start;
To see red Phoebus through the gallery pane
Tinge with his beam the beams of Drury-Lane
While gradual parties fill our widen'd pit,
And gape, and gaze, and wonder, ere they sit.
At first, while vacant seats give choice and ease;
Distant or near, they settle where they please;
But when the multitude contracts the span,
And seats are rare, they settle where they can.
Now the full benches, to late comers, doom

No room for standing, miscall'd *standing room.*

Hark! the check-taker moody silence breaks,
And bawling 'Pit full,' gives the check he takes;
Yet onward still the gathering numbers cram,
Contending crowders should the frequent damn,
And all is bustle, squeeze, row, jabbering, and jam.

See to their desks Apollo's sons repair;
Swift rides the rosin o'er the horse's hair;
In unison their various tones to tune
Murmurs the hautboy, growls the hoarse bassoon;
In soft vibration sighs the whispering lute,
Tang goes the harpsichord, too-too the flute,
Brays the loud trumpet, squeaks the fiddle sharp,
Winds the French-horn, and twangs the tingling harp;
Till, like great Jove, the leader, figuring in,
Attunes to order the chaotic din.
Now all seems hush'd—but no, one fiddle will
Give, half-ashamed, a tiny flourish still;
Foil'd in his crash, the leader of the clan
Reproves with frowns the dilatory man;
Then on his candlestick three taps his bow,
Nods a new signal, and away they go.

Perchance, while pit and gallery cry, 'Hats off,'
And awed Consumption checks his chided cough,
Some giggling daughter of the Queen of Love
Drops, reft of pin, her play-bill from above;
Like Icarus, while laughing galleries clap,
Soars, ducks, and dives in air the printed scrap;
But, wiser far than he, combustion fears,
And, as it flies, eludes the chandeliers;
Till sinking gradual, with repeated twirl,
It settles, curling, on a fiddler's curl;
Who from his powder'd pate the intruder strikes,
And, for mere malice, sticks it on the spikes.

Say, why these Babel strains from Babel tongues?
Who's that calls 'Silence' with such leathern lungs?
He, who, in quest of quiet, 'silence' hoots,
Is apt to make the hubbub he imputes.

What various swains our motley walls contain!
Fashion from Moorfields, honour from Chick Lane;
Bankers from Paper Buildings here resort,
Bankrupts from Golden Square and Riches Court;
From the Haymarket canting rogues in grain,
Gulls from the Poultry, sots from Water Lane;
The lottery cormorant, the auction shark,
The full-price master, and the half-price clerk;
Boys who long linger at the gallery door,
With pence twice five, they want but two-pence more,
Till some Samaritan the two-pence spares,
And sends them jumping up the gallery stairs.

Critics we boast who ne'er their malice balk,
But talk their minds, we wish they'd mind their talk;
Big-worded bullies, who by quarrels live,
Who give the lie, and tell the lie they give;
Jews from St. Mary Axe, for jobs so wary,
That for old clothes they'd even axe St. Mary;
And bucks with pockets empty as their pate,
Lax in their gaiters, laxer in their gait,
Who oft, when we our house lock up, carouse
With tippling tipstaves in a lock-up house.

Yet here, as elsewhere, chance can joy bestow,
Where scowling Fortune seem'd to threaten woe.

John Richard William Alexander Dwyer
Was footman to Justinian Stubbs, Esquire;
But when John Dwyer listed in the Blues,
Emanuel Jennings polish'd Stubbs's shoes.

Emanuel Jennings brought his youngest boy
Up as a corn-cutter, a safe employ;
In Holywell Street, St. Pancras, he was bred
(At number twenty-seven, it is said),
Facing the pump, and near the Granby's Head:
He would have bound him to some shop in town,
But with a premium he could not come down;
Pat was the urchin's name, a red hair'd youth,
Fonder of purl and skittle-grounds than truth.

Silence, ye gods! to keep your tongues in awe,
The muse shall tell an accident she saw.

Pat Jennings in the upper gallery sat,
But, leaning forward, Jennings lost his hat;
Down from the gallery the beaver flew,
And spurn'd the one to settle in the two.
How shall he act? Pay at the gallery door
Two shillings for what cost, when new, but four?
Or till half-price, to save his shilling, wait,
And gain his hat again at half-past eight?
Now, while his fears anticipate a thief,
John Mullins whispers, Take my handkerchief.
Thank you, cries Pat, but one won't make a line;
Take mine, cried Wilson, and cried Stokes, take mine.
A motley cable soon Pat Jennings ties,
Where Spital-fields with real India vies.
Like Iris' bow, down darts the painted hue,
Starr'd, striped, and spotted, yellow, red, and blue,
Old calico, torn silk, and muslin new.
George Green below, with palpitating hand,
Loops the last 'kerchief to the beaver's band.
Upsoars the prize; the youth, with joy unfeign'd,
Regain'd the felt, and felt what he regain'd,
While to the applauding galleries grateful Pat
Made a low bow, and touch'd the ransom'd hat.

(pp. 202-05)

> *James Smith, in an excerpt in* Crabbe: The Critical
> Heritage, *edited by Arthur Pollard, Routledge &
> Kegan Paul, 1972, pp. 202-05.*

## THOMAS CARLYLE    (letter date 1816)

[*A noted nineteenth-century essayist, critic, and social commentator, Carlyle was a central figure of the Victorian age in
England and Scotland. In his writings, Carlyle advocated a
Christian work ethic and stressed the importance of order,
piety, and spiritual fulfillment. Known to his contemporaries
as the "Sage of Chelsea," Carlyle exerted a powerful moral influence in an era of rapidly shifting values. In the following excerpt from a letter to Robert Mitchell, Carlyle praises Crabbe's
poetry for its exacting descriptions while deprecating its stylistic
flatness.*]

I cannot well say what I have been about since I wrote to you
last. Out of a considerable quantity of garbage which I have
allowed myself, at different intertervals, to devour, I have
only to mention Crabbe's Poems as worthy of being read. In
addition to great powers of correct description, he possesses
all the sagacity of an anatomist in searching into the stormy
passions of the human heart—and all the apathy of an anatomist in describing them.

> *Thomas Carlyle, in a letter to Robert Mitchell in
> 1816, in* Early Letters of Thomas Carlyle: 1814-
> 1821, Vol. I, *edited by Charles Eliot Norton, 1886.
> Reprint by Milford House, 1973, pp. 75-8.*

## [FRANCIS JEFFREY]    (essay date 1819)

[*In the following excerpt from a review of* Tales of the Hall,
*Jeffrey lauds Crabbe's critical approach to his subject matter
before analyzing his dramatic handling of romantic relationships in* Tales.]

Mr Crabbe is the greatest *mannerist,* perhaps, of all our living
poets; and it is rather unfortunate that the most prominent
features of his mannerism are not the most pleasing. The
homely, quaint, and prosaic style—the flat, and often broken
and jingling versification—the eternal full-lengths of low and
worthless characters,—with their accustomed garnishings of
sly jokes and familiar moralizing—are all on the surface of
his writings; and are almost unavoidably the things by which
we are first reminded of him, when we take up any of his new
productions. Yet they are not the things that truly constitute
his peculiar manner, or give that character by which he will,
and ought to be, remembered with future generations. It is
plain, indeed, that they are things that will make nobody remembered—and can never, therefore, be really characteristic
of some of the most original and powerful poetry that the
world ever saw.

Mr C., accordingly, has other gifts; and those not less peculiar or less strongly marked than the blemishes with which
they are contrasted—an unrivalled and almost magical
power of observation, resulting in descriptions so true to nature as to strike us rather as transcripts than imitations—an
anatomy of character and feeling not less exquisite and
searching—an occasional touch of matchless tenderness—
and a deep and dreadful pathetic, interspersed by fits, and
strangely interwoven with the most minute and humble of his
details. Add to all this the sure and profound sagacity of the
remarks with which he every now and then startles us in the
midst of very unambitious discussions;—and the weight and
terseness of the maxims which he drops, like oracular responses, on occasions that give no promise of such a revelation;—and last, though not least, that sweet and seldom
sounded chord of lyrical inspiration, the lightest touch of
which instantly charms away all harshness from his numbers,
and all lowness from his themes—and at once exalts him to
a level with the most energetic and inventive poets of his age.

These, we think, are the true characteristics of the genius of
this great writer; and it is in their mixture with the oddities
and defects to which we have already alluded, that the peculiarity of his manner seems to us substantially to consist. The
ingredients may all of them be found, we suppose, in other
writers; but their combination—in such proportions at least
as occur in this instance—may safely be pronounced to be
original.

Extraordinary, however, as this combination must appear, it
does not seem very difficult to conceive in what way it may
have arisen; and, so far from regarding it as a proof of singular humorousness, caprice or affectation in the individual, we
are rather inclined to hold that something approaching to it
must be the natural result of a long habit of observation in
a man of genius, possessed of that temper and disposition
which is the usual accompaniment of such a habit; and that
the same strangely compounded and apparently incongruous
assemblage of themes and sentiments would be frequently
produced under such circumstances—if authors had oftener
the courage to write from their own impressions, and had less
fear of the laugh or wonder of the more shallow and barren
part of their readers.

A great talent for observation, and a delight in the exercise of it—the power and the practice of dissecting and disentangling that subtle and complicated tissue of habit, and self-love, and affection, which constitute human character—seems to us, in all cases, to imply a contemplative, rather than an active disposition. It can only exist, indeed, where there is a good deal of social sympathy; for, without this, the occupation could excite no interest, and afford no satisfaction—but only such a measure and sort of sympathy as is gratified by being a spectator, and not an actor on the great theatre of life—and leads its possessor rather to look on with eagerness on the feats and the fortunes of others, than to take a share for himself in the game that is played before him. Some stirring and vigorous spirits there are, no doubt, in which this taste and talent is combined with a more thorough and effective sympathy; and leads to the study of men's characters by an actual and hearty participation in their various passions and pursuits;—though it is to be remarked, that when such persons embody their observations in writing, they will generally be found to show their characters in action, rather than to describe them in the abstract; and to let their various personages disclose themselves and their peculiarities, as it were spontaneously, and without help or preparation, in their ordinary conduct and speech—of all which we have a very splendid and striking example in the Tales of My Landlord, and the other pieces of that extraordinary writer. In the common case, however, a great observer, we believe, will be found, pretty certainly, to be a person of a shy and retiring temper,—who does not mingle enough with the people he surveys, to be heated with their passions, or infected with their delusions—and who has usually been led, indeed, to take up the office of a looker on, from some little infirmity of nerves, or weakness of spirits, which has unfitted him from playing a more active part on the busy scene of existence.

Now, it is very obvious, we think, that this contemplative turn, and this alienation from the vulgar pursuits of mankind, must, in the first place, produce a great contempt for most of those pursuits, and the objects they seek to obtain—a levelling of the factitious distinctions which human pride and vanity have established in the world, and a mingled scorn and compassion for the lofty pretensions under which men so often disguise the nothingness of their chosen occupations. When the many-coloured scene of life, with all its petty agitations, its shifting pomps, and perishable passions, is surveyed by one who does not mix in its business, it is impossible that it should not appear a very pitiable and almost ridiculous affair; or that the heart should not echo back the brief and emphatic exclamation of the mighty dramatist,

> Life's a poor player,
> Who frets and struts his hour upon the stage,
> And then is heard no more.—
>
> (pp. 118-20)

This is the more solemn view of the subject:—but the first fruits of observation are most commonly found to issue in Satire—the unmasking the vain pretenders to wisdom and worth and happiness with whom society is infested, and holding up to the derision of mankind those meannesses of the great, those miseries of the fortunate, and those

> Fears of the brave, and follies of the wise,

which the eye of a dispassionate observer so quickly detects under the glittering exterior by which they would fain be disguised—and which bring pretty much to a level the intellect and morals and enjoyments of the great mass of mankind.

This misanthropic end has unquestionably been by far the most common result of a habit of observation, and that in which its effects have most generally terminated:—Yet we cannot bring ourselves to think that it is their just or natural termination. Something, no doubt, will depend on the temper of the individual, and the proportions in which the gall and the milk of human kindness have been originally mingled in his composition.—Yet satirists, we think, have not in general been ill-natured persons—and we are inclined rather to ascribe this limited and uncharitable application of their powers of observation to their love of fame and popularity,—which are well known to be best secured by successful ridicule or invective—or quite as probably, indeed, to the narrowness and insufficiency of their observations themselves, and the imperfection of their talents for their due conduct and extension.—It is certain, at least, we think, that the satirist makes use but of half the discoveries of the observer; and teaches but half—and the worser half—of the lessons which may be deduced from his occupation.—He puts down, indeed, the proud pretensions of the great and arrogant, and levels the vain distinctions which human ambition has established among the brethren of mankind—he

> Bares the mean heart that lurks beneath a Star,

—and destroys the illusions which would limit our sympathy to the forward and figuring persons of this world—the favourites of fame and fortune.—But the true result of observation should be not so much to cast down the proud, as to raise up the lowly—not so much to extinguish our sympathy with the powerful and renowned, as to extend it to all those who, in humbler conditions, have the same claims on our esteem or affection.—It is not surely the natural consequence of learning to judge truly of the characters of men, that we should despise or be indifferent about them all;—and though we have learned to see through the false glare which plays round the envied summits of existence, and to know how little dignity, or happiness, or worth, or wisdom, may sometimes belong to the possessors of power and fortune and learning and renown,—it does not follow, by any means, that we should look upon the whole of human life as a mere deceit and imposture, or think the concerns of our species fit subjects only for scorn and derision. Our promptitude to admire and to envy will indeed be corrected, our enthusiasm abated, and our distrust of appearances increased;—but the sympathies and affections of our nature will continue, and be better directed—our love of our kind will not be diminished—and our indulgence for their faults and follies, if we read our lesson aright, will be signally strengthened and confirmed. The true and proper effect, therefore, of a habit of observation, and a thorough and penetrating knowledge of human character, will be, not to extinguish our sympathy but to extend it—to turn, no doubt, many a throb of admiration, and many a sigh of love into a smile of derision or of pity, but at the same time to reveal much that commands our homage and excites our affection in those humble and unexplored regions of the heart and understanding which never engage the attention of the incurious,—and to bring the whole family of mankind nearer to a level, by finding out latent merits as well as latent defects in all its members, and compensating the flaws that are detected in the boasted ornaments of life, by bringing to light the richness and the lustre that sleep in the mines beneath its surface.

We are afraid some of our readers may not at once perceive

the application of these profound remarks to the subject immediately before us. But there are others, we doubt not, who do not need to be told, that they are intended to explain how Mr Crabbe, and other persons with the same gift of observation, should so often busy themselves with what may be considered as low and vulgar characters; and, declining all dealings with heroes and heroic topics, should not only venture to seek for an interest in the concerns of ordinary mortals, but actually intersperse small pieces of ridicule with their undignified pathos, and endeavour to make their readers look on their books with the same mingled feelings of compassion and amusement, with which—unnatural as it may appear to the readers of poetry—they, and all judicious observers, actually look upon human life and human nature. This, we are persuaded, is the true key to the greater part of the peculiarities of the author before us; and though we have disserted upon it a little longer than was necessary, we really think it may enable our readers to comprehend him, and our remarks on him, something better than they could have done without it.

There is, as everybody must have felt, a strange mixture of satire and sympathy in all his productions—a great kindliness and compassion for the errors and sufferings of our poor human nature—but a strong distrust of its heroic virtues and high pretensions. His heart is always open to pity, and all the milder emotions—but there is little aspiration after the grand and sublime of character, nor very much encouragement for raptures and ecstacies of any description. These, he seems to think, are things rather too fine for the said poor human nature—and that, in our low and erring condition, it is a little ridiculous to pretend, either to very exalted and immaculate virtue, or very pure and exquisite happiness. He not only never meddles, therefore, with the delicate distresses and noble fires of the heroes and heroines of tragic and epic fable, but may generally be detected indulging in a lurking sneer at the pomp and vanity of all such superfine imaginations—and turning to draw men in their true postures and dimensions, and with all the imperfections that actually belong to their condition:—the prosperous and happy overshadowed with passing clouds of *ennui,* and disturbed with little flaws of bad humour and discontent—the great and wise beset at times with strange weaknesses and meannesses and paltry vexations—and even the most virtuous and enlightened falling far below the standard of poetical perfection—and stooping every now and then to paltry jealousies and prejudices—or sinking into shabby sensualities,—or meditating on their own excellence and importance, with a ludicrous and lamentable anxiety.

This is one side of the picture; and characterizes sufficiently the satirical vein of our author: But the other is the most extensive and important. In rejecting the vulgar sources of interest in poetical narratives, and reducing his ideal persons to the standard of reality, Mr C. does by no means seek to extinguish the sparks of human sympathy within us, or to throw any damp on the curiosity with which we naturally explore the characters of each other. On the contrary, he has afforded new and more wholesome food for all those propensities—and, by placing before us those details which our pride or fastidiousness is so apt to overlook, has disclosed, in all their truth and simplicity, the native and unadulterated workings of those affections which are at the bottom of all social interest, and are really rendered less touching by the exaggerations of more ambitious artists—while he exhibits, with admirable force and endless variety, all those combinations of passions and opinions, and all that cross-play of self-

ishness and vanity, and indolence and ambition, and habit and reason, which make up the intellectual character of individuals, and present to every one an instructive picture of his neighbour or himself. Seeing, by the perfection of his art, the master passions in their springs, and the high capacities in their rudiments—and having acquired the gift of tracing all the propensities and marking tendencies of our plastic nature, in their first slight indications, or from the very disguises they so often love to assume, he does not need, in order to draw out his characters in all their life and distinctness, the vulgar demonstration of those striking and decided actions by which their maturity is proclaimed even to the careless and inattentive;—but delights to point out to his readers, the seeds or tender filaments of those talents and feelings and singularities which wait only for occasion and opportunity to burst out and astonish the world—and to accustom them to trace, in characters and actions apparently of the most ordinary description, the self-same attributes that, under other circumstances, would attract universal attention, and furnish themes for the most popular and impassioned descriptions.

That he should not be guided in the choice of his subject by any regard to the rank or condition which his persons hold in society, may easily be imagined; and, with a view to the ends he aims at, might readily be forgiven. But we fear that his passion for observation, and the delight he takes in tracing out and analyzing all the little traits that indicate character, and all the little circumstances that influence it, have sometimes led him to be careless about his selection of the instances in which it was to be exhibited, or at least to select them upon principles very different from those which give them an interest in the eyes of ordinary readers. For the purposes of mere anatomy, beauty of form or complexion are things quite indifferent; and the physiologist, who examines plants only to study their internal structure, and to make himself master of all the contrivances by which their various functions are performed, pays no regard to the brilliancy of their hues, the sweetness of their odours, or the graces of their form. Those who come to him for the sole purpose of acquiring knowledge, may participate perhaps in this indifference; but the world at large will wonder at them—and he will engage fewer pupils to listen to his instructions, than if he had condescended in some degree to consult their predilections in the beginning. It is the same case, we think, in many respects, with Mr Crabbe. Relying for the interest he is to produce, on the curious expositions he is to make of the elements of human character; or at least finding his own chief gratification in those subtle investigations, he seems to care very little upon what particular individuals he pitches for the purpose of these demonstrations. Almost every human mind, he seems to think, may serve to display that fine and mysterious mechanism which it is his delight to explore and explain;—and almost every condition, and every history of life, afford occasions to show how it may be put into action, and pass through its various combinations. It seems, therefore, almost as if he had caught up the first dozen or two of persons that came across him in the ordinary walks of life,—and then opening up his little window in their breasts,—and applying his tests and instruments of observation, had set himself about such a minute and curious scrutiny of their whole habits, history, adventures and dispositions, as he thought must ultimately create not only a familiarity, but an interest, which the first aspect of the subject was far enough from leading any one to expect. That he succeeds more frequently than could have been anticipated, we are very willing to allow. But we cannot help feeling also, that a little more pains bestowed in the selection of his characters, would have made his power of observation and description tell with tenfold effect; and that, in spite of the exquisite truth of his delineations, and the fineness of the perceptions by which he was enabled to make them, it is impossible to take any considerable interest in many of his personages, or to avoid feeling some degree of fatigue at the minute and patient exposition that is made of all that belongs to them.

These remarks are a little too general, we believe—and are not introduced with strict propriety at the head of our *fourth* article on Mr Crabbe's productions. They have drawn out, however, to such a length, that we can afford to say but little of the work immediately before us. It is marked with all the characteristics that we have noticed, either now or formerly, as distinctive of his poetry. On the whole, however, it has certainly fewer of the grosser faults—and fewer too, perhaps, of the more exquisite passages which occur in his former publications. There is nothing at least that has struck us, in going over [*Tales of the Hall*], as equal in elegance to "Phoebe Dawson" in the Register, or in pathetic effect to the "Convict's Dream," or "Edward Shore," or the "Parting Hour," or the "Sailor" dying beside his sweetheart. On the other hand, there is far less that is horrible, and nothing that can be said to be absolutely disgusting; and the picture which is afforded of society and human nature is, on the whole, much less painful and degrading. There is both less misery and less guilt; and, while the same searching and unsparing glance is sent into all the dark caverns of the breast, and the truth brought forth with the same stern impartiality, the result is more comfortable and cheering. The greater part of the characters are rather more elevated in station, and milder and more amiable in disposition; while the accidents of life are more mercifully managed, and fortunate circumstances more liberally allowed. It is rather remarkable, too, that Mr C. seems to become more amorous as he grows older,—the interest of almost all the stories in this collection turning on the tender passion—and many of them on its most romantic varieties. (pp. 121-26)

One of the best managed of all the tales, is that entitled "Delay has Danger"—which contains a very full, true, and particular account of the way in which a weakish, but well meaning young man, engaged on his own suit to a very amiable girl, may be suduced, during her unlucky absence, to entangle himself with a far inferior person, whose chief seduction is her apparent humility and devotion to him. The introduction to this story is in Mr Crabbe's best style of concise and minute description.

> Three weeks had past, and Richard rambles now
> Far as the dinners of the day allow;
> He rode to Farley Grange and Finley Mere,
> That house so ancient, and that lake so clear:
> He rode to Ripley through that river gay,
> Where in the shallow stream the loaches play,
> And stony fragments stay the winding stream,
> And gilded pebbles at the bottom gleam,
> Giving their yellow surface to the sun,
> And making proud the waters as they run:
> It is a lovely place, and at the side
> Rises a mountain-rock in rugged pride;
> And in that rock are shapes of shells, and forms
> Of creatures in old worlds, of nameless worms,
> Whose generations lived and died ere man,
> A worm of other class, to crawl began.

(p. 141)

"The Natural Death of Love" is perhaps the best written of all the pieces before us. It consists of a very spirited dialogue between a married pair, upon the causes of the difference between the days of marriage and those of courtship;—in which the errors and faults of both parties, and the petulance, impatience, and provoking acuteness of the lady, with the more reasonable and reflecting, but somewhat insulting manner of the gentleman, are all exhibited to the life, and with more uniform delicacy and *finesse* than is usual with the author.

"Gretna Green" is a strong picture of the happiness that may be expected from a premature marriage between a silly mercenary girl, and a brutal selfwilled boy. (p. 143)

We shall be abused by our political and fastidious readers for the length of this article. But we cannot repent of it. It will give as much pleasure, we believe, and do as much good, as many of the articles that are meant for their gratification; and, if it appear absurd to quote so largely from a popular and accessible work, it should be remembered, that no work of this magnitude passes into circulation with half the rapidity of our Journal—and that Mr Crabbe is so unequal a writer, and at times so unattractive, as to require, more than any other of his degree, some explanation of his system, and some specimens of his powers, from those experienced and intrepid readers whose business it is to pioneer for the lazier sort, and to give some account of what they are to meet with on their journey. To be sure, all this is less necessary now than it was on Mr Crabbe's first reappearance nine or ten years ago; and though it may not be altogether without its use even at present, it may be as well to confess, that we have rather consulted our own gratification than our readers' improvement, in what we have now said of him; and hope they will forgive us. (p. 148)

[*Francis Jeffrey*], *in a review of "Tales of the Hall,"
in* The Edinburgh Review, *Vol. XXXII, No. LXIII,
July, 1819, pp. 118-48.*

## WILLIAM HAZLITT   (essay date 1825)

[*One of the most important commentators of the Romantic age, Hazlitt was an English critic and journalist. He is best known for his descriptive criticism, in which he stressed that no motives beyond judgment and analysis are necessary on the part of the critic. In the following excerpt from a comparative review of the poetry of Thomas Campbell and Crabbe, Hazlitt attacks the style and content of Crabbe's poetry.*]

Mr. Crabbe presents an entire contrast to [Thomas] Campbell:—the one is the most ambitious and aspiring of living poets, the other the most humble and prosaic. If the poetry of the one is like the arch of the rainbow, spanning and adorning the earth, that of the other is like a dull, leaden cloud hanging over it. Mr. Crabbe's style might be cited as an answer to Audrey's question—"Is poetry a true thing?" There are here no ornaments, no flights of fancy, no illusions of sentiment, no tinsel of words. His song is one sad reality, one unraised, unvaried note of unavailing woe. Literal fidelity serves him in the place of invention; he assumes importance by a number of petty details; he rivets attention by being tedious. He not only deals in incessant matters of fact, but in matters of fact of the most familiar, the least animating, and the most unpleasant kind; but he relies for the effect of novelty on the microscopic minuteness with which he dissects the most trivial objects—and for the interest he excites, on the unshrinking determination with which he handles the most painful. His poetry has an official and professional air. He is called in to cases of difficult births, of fractured limbs, or breaches of the peace; and makes out a parochial list of accidents and offences. He takes the most trite, the most gross and obvious and revolting part of nature, for the subject of his elaborate descriptions; but it is Nature still, and Nature is a great and mighty Goddess! It is well for the Reverend Author that it is so. Individuality is, in his theory, the only definition of poetry. Whatever *is,* he hitches into rhyme Whoever makes an exact image of any thing on the earth, how ever deformed or insignificant, according to him, must succeed—and he himself has succeeded. Mr. Crabbe is one of the most popular and admired of our living authors. That he is so, can be accounted for on no other principle than the strong ties that bind us to the world about us, and our involuntary yearnings after whatever in any manner powerfully and directly reminds us of it. His Muse is not one of *the Daughters of Memory,* but the old toothless, mumbling, dame herself, doling out the gossip and scandal of the neighbourhood, recounting *totidem verbis et literis,* what happens in every place of the kingdom every hour in the year, and fastening always on the worst as the most palatable morsels. But she is a circumstantial old lady, communicative, scrupulous, leaving nothing to the imagination, harping on the smallest grievances, a village oracle and critic, most veritable, most identical, bringing us acquainted with persons and things just as they chanced to exist, and giving us a local interest in all she knows and tells Mr. Crabbe's Helicon is choked up with weeds and corruption; it reflects no light from heaven, it emits no cheerful sound: no flowers of love, of hope, or joy spring up near it, or they bloom only to wither in a moment. Our poet's verse does not put a spirit of youth in every thing, but a spirit of fear, despondency and decay: it is not an electric spark to kindle or expand, but acts like the torpedo's touch to deaden or contract. It lends no dazzling tints to fancy, it aids no soothing feelings in the heart, it gladdens no prospect, it stirs no wish; in its view the current of life runs slow, dull, cold, dispirited, half under ground, muddy, and clogged with all creeping things. The world is one vast infirmary; the hill of Parnassus is a penitentiary, of which our author is the overseer: to read him is a penance, yet we read on! Mr. Crabbe, it must be confessed, is a repulsive writer. He contrives to "turn diseases to commodities," and makes a virtue of necessity. He puts us out of conceit with this world, which perhaps a severe divine should do; yet does not, as a charitable divine ought, point to another. His morbid feelings droop and cling to the earth, grovel where they should soar; and throw a dead weight on every aspiration of the soul after the good or beautiful. By degrees we submit, and are reconciled to our fate, like patients to the physician, or prisoners in the condemned cell. We can only explain this by saying, as we said before, that Mr. Crabbe gives us one part of nature, the mean, the little, the disgusting, the distressing; that he does this thoroughly and like a master, and we forgive all the rest.

Mr. Crabbe's first poems were published so long ago as the year 1782, and received the approbation of Dr. Johnson only a little before he died [see letter dated 1783]. This was a testimony from an enemy; for Dr. Johnson was not an admirer of the simple in style or minute in description. Still he was an acute, strong-minded man, and could see truth when it was presented to him, even through the mist of his prejudices and his foibles. There was something in Mr. Crabbe's intricate points that did not, after all, so ill accord with the Doc-

tor's purblind vision; and he knew quite enough of the petty ills of life to judge of the merit of our poet's descriptions, though he himself chose to slur them over in high-sounding dogmas or general invectives. Mr. Crabbe's earliest poem of the *Village* was recommended to the notice of Dr. Johnson by Sir Joshua Reynolds; and we cannot help thinking that a taste for that sort of poetry, which leans for support on the truth and fidelity of its imitations of nature, began to display itself much about that time, and, in a good measure, in consequence of the direction of the public taste to the subject of painting. Book-learning, the accumulation of wordy common-places, the gaudy pretensions of poetical fiction, had enfeebled and perverted our eye for nature. The study of the fine arts, which came into fashion about forty years ago, and was then first considered as a polite accomplishment, would tend imperceptibly to restore it. Painting is essentially an imitative art; it cannot subsist for a moment on empty generalities: the critic, therefore who had been used to this sort of substantial entertainment, would be disposed to read poetry with the eye of a connoisseur, would be little captivated with smooth, polished, unmeaning periods, and would turn with double eagerness and relish to the force and precision of individual details, transferred, as it were, to the page from the canvas. Thus an admirer of Teniers or Hobbima might think little of the pastoral sketches of Pope or Goldsmith; even Thomson describes not so much the naked object as what he sees in his mind's eye, surrounded and glowing with the mild, bland, genial vapours of his brain:—but the adept in Dutch interiors, hovels, and pig-styes must find in Mr. Crabbe a man after his own heart. He is the very thing itself; he paints in words, instead of colours: there is no other difference. As Mr. Crabbe is not a painter, only because he does not use a brush and colours, so he is for the most part a poet, only because he writes in lines of ten syllables. All the rest might be found in a newspaper, an old magazine, or a county-register. Our author is himself a little jealous of the prudish fidelity of his homely Muse, and tries to justify himself by precedents. He brings as a parallel instance of merely literal description, Pope's lines on the gay Duke of Buckingham, beginning "In the worst inn's worst room see Villiers lies!" [see excerpt dated 1812] But surely nothing can be more dissimilar. Pope describes what is striking. Crabbe would have described merely what was there. The objects in Pope stand out to the fancy from the mixture of the mean with the gaudy, from the contrast of the scene and the character. There is an appeal to the imagination; you see what is passing in poetical point of view. In Crabbe there is no foil, no contrast, no impulse given to the mind. It is all on a level and of a piece. In fact, there is so little connection between the subject-matter of Mr. Crabbe's lines and the ornament of rhyme which is tacked to them, that many of his verses read like serious burlesque, and the parodies which have been made upon them are hardly so quaint as the originals.

Mr. Crabbe's great fault is certainly that he is a sickly, a querulous, a uniformly dissatisfied poet. He sings the country; and he sings it in a pitiful tone. He chooses this subject only to take the charm out of it, and to dispel the illusion, the glory, and the dream, which had hovered over it in golden verse from Theocritus to Cowper. He sets out with professing to overturn the theory which had hallowed a shepherd's life, and made the names of grove and valley music to our ears, in order to give us truth in its stead, but why not lay aside the fool's cap and bells at once? Why not insist on the unwelcome reality in plain prose? If our author is a poet, why trouble himself with statistics? If he is a statistic writer, why set his ill news to harsh and grating verse? The philosopher in painting the dark side of human nature may have reason on his side, and a moral lesson or remedy in view. The tragic poet, who shows the sad vicissitudes of things and the disappointments of the passions, at least strengthens our yearnings after imaginary good, and lends wings to our desires, by which we, "at one bound, high overleap all bound" of actual suffering. But Mr. Crabbe does neither. He gives us discoloured paintings of life; helpless, repining, unprofitable, unedifying distress. He is not a philosopher, but a sophist, a misanthrope in verse; a *namby-pamby* Mandeville, a Malthus turned metrical romancer. He professes historical fidelity; but his vein is not dramatic; nor does he give us the *pros* and *cons* of that versatile gipsy, Nature. He does not indulge his fancy or sympathise with us, or tell us how the poor feel; but how he should feel in their situation, which we do not want to know. He does not weave the web of their lives of a mingled yarn, good and ill together, but clothes them all in the same dingy linsey-woolsey, or tinges them with a green and yellow melancholy. He blocks out all possibility of good, cancels the hope, or even the wish for it as a weakness; check-mates Tityrus and Virgil at the game of pastoral cross-purposes, disables all his adversary's white pieces, and leaves none but black ones on the board. The situation of a country clergyman is not necessarily favourable to the cultivation of the Muse. He is set down, perhaps, as he thinks, in a small curacy for life, and he takes his revenge by imprisoning the reader's imagination in luckless verse. Shut out from social converse, from learned colleges and halls, where he passed his youth, he has no cordial fellow-feeling with the unlettered manners of the *Village* or the *Borough;* and he describes his neighbors as more uncomfortable and discontented than himself. All this while he dedicates successive volumes to rising generations of noble patrons; and while he desolates a line of coast with sterile, blighting lines, the only leaf of his books where honour, beauty, worth, or pleasure bloom, is that inscribed to the Rutland family! We might adduce instances of what we have said from every page of his works: let one suffice—

Thus by himself compelled to live each day,
To wait for certain hours the tide's delay;
At the same times the same dull views to see,
The bounding marsh-bank and the blighted tree;
The water only when the tides were high,
When low, the mud half-covered and half-dry;
The sun-burnt tar that blisters on the planks,
And bank-side stakes in their uneven ranks;
Heaps of entangled weeds that slowly float,
As the tide rolls by the impeded boat.
When tides were neap, and in the sultry day,
Through the tall bounding mud-banks made their way,
Which on each side rose swelling, and below
The dark warm flood ran silently and slow;
There anchoring, Peter chose from man to hide,
There hang his head, and view the lazy tide
In its hot slimy channel slowly glide;
Where the small eels, that left the deeper way
For the warm shore, within the shallows play;
Where gaping muscles, left upon the mud,
Slope their slow passage to the fall'n flood:
Here dull and hopeless he'd lie down and trace
How side-long crabs had crawled their crooked race;
Or sadly listen to the tuneless cry
Of fishing gull or clanging golden-eye;
What time the sea-birds to the marsh would come,
And the loud bittern from the bull-rush home,
Gave from the salt-ditch-side the bellowing boom:
He nursed the feelings these dull scenes produce

And loved to stop beside the opening sluice;
Where the small stream, confined in narrow bound,
Ran with a dull, unvaried, saddening sound;
Where all, presented to the eye or ear,
Oppressed the soul with misery, grief, and fear.

This is an exact *fac-simile* of some of the most unlovely parts of the creation. Indeed the whole of Mr. Crabbe's *Borough,* from which the above passage is taken, is done so to the life, that it seems almost like some sea-monster, crawled out of the neighbouring slime, and harbouring a breed of strange vermin, with a strong local scent of tar and bulge-water. Mr. Crabbe's *Tales* are more readable than his *Poems;* but in proportion as the interest increases, they become more oppressive. They turn, one and all, upon the same sort of teazing, helpless, mechanical, unimaginative distress;—and though it is not easy to lay them down, you never wish to take them up again. Still in this way, they are highly finished, striking, and original portraits, worked out with an eye to nature, and an intimate knowledge of the small and intricate folds of the human heart. Some of the best are the **"Confidant,"** the story of **"Silly Shore,"** the **"Young Poet,"** the **"Painter."** The episode of **"Phoebe Dawson"** in the *Village,* is one of the most tender and pensive; and the character of the methodist parson who persecutes the sailor's widow with his godly, selfish love is one of the most profound. In a word, if Mr. Crabbe's writings do not add greatly to the store of entertaining and delightful fiction, yet they will remain, "as a thorn in the side of poetry," perhaps for a century to come! (pp. 238-44)

*William Hazlitt, "Mr. Campbell and Mr. Crabbe," in his* The Spirit of the Age; or, Contemporary Portraits, *J. B. Lippincott Company, 1825, pp. 231-44.*

**WILLIAM WORDSWORTH** (letter date 1834)

[*In the following excerpt from a letter to George Crabbe, the poet's son, Wordsworth questions the sociological accuracy of* The Village *while affirming the lasting value of the poet's works.*]

I first became acquainted with Mr Crabbe's Works in the same way, and about the same time, as did Sir Walter Scott, as appears from his letter in the prospectus; and the extracts made such an impression upon me, that *I* can also repeat them. The two lines [from *The Village*]

Far the happiest they
The moping idiot and the madman gay

struck my youthful feelings particularly—tho' facts, as far as they had then come under my knowledge, did not support the description; inasmuch as idiots and lunatics among the humbler Classes of society were not to be found in Workhouses—in the parts of the North where I was brought up,—but were mostly at large, and too often the butt of thoughtless Children. Any testimony from me to the merit of your revered Father's Works would I feel be superfluous, if not impertinent. They will last, from their combined merits as Poetry and Truth full as long as any thing that has been expressed in Verse since they first made their appearance. (pp. 1376-77)

*William Wordsworth, in a letter to George Crabbe, Jr., in February, 1834, in* The Letters of William and Dorothy Wordsworth: The Later Years, 1841-50, Vol. III, *edited by Ernest De Selincourt, Oxford at the Clarendon Press, 1939, pp. 1376-77.*

## SAMUEL TAYLOR COLERIDGE　(conversation date 1834)

[*Coleridge was central to the English Romantic movement as both a poet and critic. His most important critical contributions include his formulation of Romantic theory, his introduction of the ideas of the German Romantics to England, and his Shakespearean criticism, which focused on Shakespeare as a masterful portrayer of human character, overthrowing the last remnants of the neoclassical approach to the author. In the following excerpt from a conversation, Coleridge compares Robert Southey's poetry with Crabbe's.*]

I think Crabbe and Southey are something alike; but Crabbe's poems are founded on observation and real life—Southey's on fancy and books. In facility they are equal, though Crabbe's English is of course not upon a level with Southey's, which is next door to faultless. But in Crabbe there is an absolute defect of the high imagination; he gives me little or no pleasure: yet, no doubt, he has much power of a certain kind, and it is good to cultivate, even at some pains, a catholic taste in literature. I read all sorts of books with some pleasure except modern sermons and treatises on political economy. (pp. 432-33)

> *Samuel Taylor Coleridge, in a conversation on March 5, 1834, in his* Coleridge's Miscellaneous Criticism, *edited by Thomas Middleton Raysor, 1936. Reprint by The Folcroft Press, Inc., 1969, pp. 432-33.*

## FREDERICK SHELDON　(essay date 1872)

[*In the following excerpt from a review of* The Poetical Works of the Rev. George Crabbe, *Sheldon affirms the value of Crabbe's poetry as a whole, commenting on thematic issues but focusing on such stylistic concerns as versification and language and the poet's preference for highly detailed descriptive passages. Sheldon concludes with a comparison between Crabbe's realism and the eclectic and didactic modes of Victorian verse.*]

[Crabbe] was a bard with but one string to his lyre; he sang the same tune throughout his long life. *The Tales of the Hall,* published in 1822, and a volume of *Posthumous Tales,* present the same minute sketches of low character and the same peculiarities of style. The impression made upon his mind by the misery of his early surroundings was never effaced. It was not the imaginary and almost maudlin misery of Dickens when he spoke of his month or two in the blacking business, but an indelible scar left upon his brain by the suffering of his youth. Even in his London days, when smiles, flattery, and good dinners were offered him daily, those Aldborough scenes would revisit him in his dreams; "asleep all was misery and degradation." As his Muse was truly the daughter of Memory, when he describes a village, his mind always reverted to those two unpaved streets running between mean and scrambling houses, the homes of squalid, commonplace want. In his sketches of scenery he is never vivid, except when he paints the ocean and the open sandy commons, the sterile half-cultivated farms, and the dreary marshes of Aldborough. The half-savage men who spent their days in cheerless toil and their nights in drunkenness are always present in his pages. He found others more or less like them in his country parish, and opportunity as well as inclination led him to study their achromatic existence, made up of shop, table, and bed, with a dark background of almshouse and prison. It has been said of him that he handled human nature so as to take the bloom off; but it was rather that he selected for a subject human nature that had lost its bloom.

Crabbe had probably less imagination that any man who ever wrote verses after the age of twenty; he confessed with his usual honesty that he had no taste for music, art, or architecture. His mind was like a camera, receiving every impression, and rendering it exactly. Those "painted clouds that beautify our days" were seldom seen in his sky; the bright ideal side of human nature that redeems "man's life from being cheap as beasts' " was beyond his ken. Like Lucian's Menippus, when Mercury points out to him in Hades, Leda, Helen of Troy, and other celebrated fair ones, he could see nothing but skulls and bones naked of flesh. Hence his pictures are photographs in their accuracy and in their want of color. His realism is complete and unmitigated, not like the spiritualized realism of the Pre-Raphaelite school. The **"Dead Stone-Breaker"** is painted to the last button like Crabbe's pauper in the village workhouse; but the body of the stone-breaker is transfigured by "a light that knows no waning." We feel that the tears have been wiped away forever from the poor weary eyes. Crabbe's pauper lies upon the bier, a grim, ghastly, emaciated corpse.

This is his dreariest vein. In his more cheerful sketches he is frequently harsh and coarse. He has often been called the Hogarth of poetry, and indeed no better illustrator could be found for Crabbe than Hogarth. Bedlam, the Tavern, the Prison in the "Rake's Progress," Bridewell, the garret, and the gin-shop in "Industry and Idleness," might be bound up with his works. His tales often leave an after-taste of disgust in the mind like Hogarth's plates.

Crabbe was born a naturalist, with a strong bias for writing in verse. A keen botanist and entomologist, one might have expected from him a poem like **"The Loves of the Plants,"** chanting the emotions of the "love-sick violet," the "virgin lily," "the jealous cowslip," and "the enamored woodbine"; but he liked to examine the motives of mankind even better than pistils and stamens. And as in science he devoted himself principally to common herbs and garden insects, so in character his speciality was peasants and village tradespeople,—

> Fixed like a plant on their peculiar spot,
> To draw nutrition, propagate, and rot.

He picked up a Simon or a Phebe, put them under his microscope,—an almost perfect instrument,—classed them in genus *homo insipiens,* species *rusticus communis;* prepared them, and placed them in his collection. As you turn over his works you find a new specimen preserved on every page. He described their habitat and habits in a cool, scientific way. He had little more sympathy with them than with his beetles. But he is always accurate and true. He never tries to make a beetle a butterfly. One may thank him for that.

In spite of his profession, the duties of which he fulfilled most conscientiously, Crabbe was a looker-on in the world rather than an actor. He was kind-hearted, charitable; in individual cases, no sympathy was like his; but he was with his flock, not of them. Their failings lay bare before him. He looked down upon the struggling creatures about him, each one wrapped in its own petty interests with a good-natured indulgence; much as a farmer looks upon the cattle and the corn he expects to harvest. They were his crop; as Heine says, "his fool crop, all his own." He never shows much feeling of any kind, except when he describes jacobinical radicals,

Who call the wants of knaves the rights of man,

or noisy dissenters, like his "serious toyman" who trod pretty often upon his clerical toes. He was not a satirist. A satirist has an object in his attack. Crabbe had none. He studied mankind; the particular specimen might be mean, ridiculous, wicked: it was indifferent to him.

There is little or no plot in Crabbe's stories, and a very moderate allowance of incident. Not a character ever stepped out of them into daily life, to become a household acquaintance. There is no grace of thought, no play of fancy. Even the few similes he used did not spring up spontaneously in his mind when heated by his subject. One can see the seams where he has patched them on. Jeffrey noticed this [see excerpt dated 1819], and Crabbe admitted it in his simple, straightforward way. "My usual method," he said, "has been to think of such illustrations and insert them after finishing a tale." He told Mrs. Leadbeater that all his characters were drawn from life; "there is not one of whom I had not in my mind the original." "Indeed I do not know that I could paint merely from my own fancy; and there is no cause why we should. Is there not diversity sufficient in society? And who can go even but a little into the assemblies of our fellow-wanderers from the way of perfect rectitude, and not find characters so varied and so pointed that he need not call upon his imagination?"

Pope was his model in versification, but he never attained Pope's exquisite polish. In Crabbe one can always see the marks of the tools. James Smith, whose parody of Crabbe in the *Rejected Addresses* is one of the best ever written [see poem dated 1812], called him, "Pope in worsted stockings." He has a profusion of antithesis, and a tiresome fondness for alliteration and plays upon words, often mere puns. His metre is frequently rough and jolting, and his style a "little word-bound," as Addison expressed it. The verse does not flow smoothly, there is a perceptible effort; he evidently does not sing because he cannot help it.

In all his volumes, one can hardly find a hundred lines containing that subtle indefinable essence that constitutes poetry. On the other hand, very many are the merest prose run into the mould of Pope, simple to puerility, like these:—

> Grave Jonas Kindred, Sybil Kindred's sire,
> Was six feet high, and looked six inches higher.

And these:—

> And I was asked and authorized to go
> To seek the firm of Clutterbuck & Co.

Others read like the rhymed rules for wise conduct of the Poor Richard school:—

> Who would by law regain his plundered store,
> Would pick up fallen mercury from the floor.

> We find too late, by stooping to deceit,
> It is ourselves, and not the world we cheat.

And occasionally he is guilty of a line that is not even verse, like this one:—

> I for your perfect acquiescence call.

The *naïveté* of his prefaces and notes, and his scruples lest by accident he should offend somebody or misrepresent something, are delightful. The

> Brick-floored parlor which the butcher lets,

"is so mentioned," he tells the reader, "because the lodger is vain." "I shall be sorry if by any I am supposed to treat the wants and infirmities of men with derision and disdain." In another note, he deprecates the wrath of the legal profession: "I entertain the strongest, because the most reasonable hope, that no liberal practitioner in the law will be offended by the notice taken of dishonest and crafty attorneys." And he is careful of the feelings even of his arch-enemies, the dissenters. He had used the word "saints" in describing them; at the foot of the page he adds: "This appellation is here used, not ironically nor with malignity, but it is taken merely to designate a morosely devout people, with peculiar austerity of manners."

And yet, in spite of his puerility, and his makeshift rawboned verses, Crabbe could please Burke and Johnson [see letter dated 1783]; he amused Charles Fox. Lockhart says that Walter Scott used to call for his Bible and his Crabbe; and he was a general favorite with a generation that had Byron, Coleridge, Shelley, and Wordsworth writing for them. One reason of his good fortune was that he struck a new vein in literature. Cowper looked at external nature through the windows of a comfortable countryhouse. His human nature is in easy circumstances and of a domestic turn. It drops the curtains to keep out cold draughts, wheels the sofa in front of a good fire, drinks tea, and knits or reads the London paper. But Crabbe exhibits the common people of England as they were, and describes their homes and habits, too often cheerless and wretched, as they had never been painted before. It was something quite original in the language. He first introduced into literature the real laboring man, ignorant, narrow-minded, overworked, rough in his manners, surly in his temper, dirty in his attire. He sketched from the life, and not from the conventional lay-figure. Before his time, peasants and paupers were introduced in fiction, like the chorus in an opera, dressed poorly but neatly, to echo with becoming humility the sentiments of the well-born and the rich. Crabbe showed the reading class (there was a property qualification in culture in those days) what George Stephenson, the engineer, announced more coarsely afterward, "Strip us and we are all pretty much alike." We must throw ourselves back some eighty or a hundred years in imagination to feel what a revelation this must have been to ordinary minds. In Crabbe's youth rank in England was as well defined as caste in India. Society, as Fielding said in *Tom Jones,* was divided into those who were born to enjoy the blessings of life and those who were born to furnish them. "The rude and unpolished masses" were almost a different race; with a certain claim on the rich for alms when they were starving, but with hardly any other. They were taught, as we can read in the "Prayer Book," "to order themselves lowly and reverently before all their betters," and "to be contented in that state of life unto which it had pleased God to call them." Time and steam and universal suffrage and other forms of progress have changed all that. Enough is left of the old order of society to enable us to understand it, and not much more. And theoretically, as Mr. Proudhon remarked in his peculiar style, we have *dansé plus vîte que les violons*. We have kept faster time even than the music. The ethical writers of the eighteenth century liked to attribute to the "noble savage" all the sense and goodness they thought their contemporaries deficient in. We have given up the "noble savage"; we know too well what he is. In place of him we have taken the laboring man as our type of civic and of moral excellence. That sounding and empty phrase of the first French Revolution, "the virtue and intelligence of the people," has lost a portion of its merit. The whole people is now too aristocratic. It is considered necessary to restrict the signification of the word "people" to its lowest class, and of "work" to its least intelligent form. We have centred all the virtues in the laboring man, made an idol of him, as the Hindoos have of the tiger, and bow down to him for the same reason as they, because we are afraid of him.

To novelty of subject Crabbe added freshness of treatment. His anatomy of character of the commonplace sort, the sort he studied, extends to the smallest moral fibre. He is the La Bruyère of the lower middle and lower classes. No detail of dress, decoration, or furniture in a cottage was lost upon him, and he noted with equal exactness the daily thoughts, habits, and feelings of the dwellers in the cottage. Nothing escaped him but the ethereal part. Crabbe's power of minute observation has never been surpassed; it was a kind of genius, it stood him instead of imagination. We get constant peeps behind the scenes of human nature, and often very pleasant ones. (pp. 55-61)

As no man can write verses all his life without occasionally rising into poetry, Crabbe now and then accomplished it, especially in his descriptions of the sea, and in some tender little touches of human feeling that reach every heart. Age mellowed him: he was milder without growing weaker. Some of his best passages are in the **Posthumous Tales.** A sly humor and a shrewd way of saying things, good sense and sagacity that never fail him, make his stories pleasant reading to this day; and if he limped in numbers, and lacks grace, he has vigor, and could attain a power of epigrammatic expression not surpassed by Pope or by Dryden. Crabbe's quaint, homely style is utterly dissimilar from any other author. With all its awkwardness and mannerism, it has an agreeable flavor of the soil about it like *vin du pays.* He is as English as Chaucer; all his roots are in English ground: and if Cowper is to have a monument at Barkhampstead, there should be one erected to Crabbe at Aldborough.

We recommend Crabbe as an alterative to those who have read too much of the poetry of our day. His hard realism is a capital tonic for minds surfeited with the vaporing verse of the nineteenth century, curiously compounded as it is of mysticism and metaphysics, fault-finding and sensuality. It is refreshing to turn from the discordant obscurity of Browning, from Tennyson's feminine prettiness, from the chaotic licentiousness and affectations of Swinburne and Rossetti, and the neat, nicely combed and curled little plaints of Matthew Arnold, to plain, robust, keen old Crabbe. He at least was equal to his times. The world, with its trials and its mysteries, was good enough for him. He "saw it whole" and had a contented and healthy appreciation of it as it was; not a paradise, by any means, but he had never heard of "world sorrow" or of "longings," nor did he think it a merit to "sit apart" from his fellow-men, impatient and disgusted with them and with their doings. (pp. 62-3)

*Frederick Sheldon, in a review of "The Poetical Works of the Rev. George Crabbe," in* The North American Review, *Vol. CXV, No. CCXXXVI, July, 1872, pp. 48-65.*

### G. E. WOODBERRY (essay date 1880)

[*In the following excerpt, Woodberry appraises the historic and literary value of Crabbe's narrative poetry, stressing the virtues of his "physical vision" of English life.*]

We have done with Crabbe. His tales have failed to interest us. Burke and his friends, as we all know, held a different opinion from ours; and their praise is not likely to have been ill founded. The cultivated taste of Holland House, thirty years later, is also against our decision. (p. 624)

Crabbe is a story-teller. He describes the life he saw,—common, homely life, sometimes wretched, not infrequently

*Belvoir Castle, English country seat of Crabbe's patron, the Duke of Rutland, about 1700.*

criminal; the life of the country poor, with occasional light and shadow from the life of the gentlefolk above them. He had been born into it, in a village on the Suffolk coast, amid stern and cheerless natural scenes: landward, the bramble-overgrowth heath encompassing crowded and mean houses; eastward,

> Stakes and sea-weed withering on the mud.

Here he had passed his boyhood, in the midst of human life equally barren and stricken with the ugliness of poverty, among surly and sordid fishers given to hard labor and rough brawl,—

> A joyless, wild, amphibious race,
> With sullen woe displayed in every face,—

and the sight had been a burden to him. The desire to throw off this twofold oppression of mean nature and humanity must have counted for much in determining him on that long-remembered December day, when, as the bleak twilight came down, darkening the marshy pool on the heath where he stood, he took his resolve to go up to London and seek poetical fame; and glad at heart he must have been, that morning of early spring, when he left all this ugliness behind him, ignorant of the struggle and distress he was to meet where he was going.

In that early poem which Johnson praised [*The Village;* see letter dated 1783] he described this village life with the vigor of a youth who had escaped out of its dreary imprisonment, and without a touch of that tenderness for early associations which softened Goldsmith's retrospect of the scenes of his early days. Crabbe told of exhausting labor leading on to prematurely useless and neglected age; of storms sweeping away the shelter of the poor; of smugglers, poachers, wreckers, tavern debauchery, and, worst of all, the poor-house,—a terrible picture, perhaps the best known of all his drawing,—with its deserted inmates cut off from all human care except that of the heedless physician and the heartless parson; a miserable tale, but too much of it only what his own eyes had seen. We do not know the contents of those piles of manuscripts which he wrote during his twenty years of silence, and—not much to the world's loss, some think—made bonfires of to amuse his children; but his first poem after that long interval was the same story, the experience of those whose names appeared in the year's parish register of births, marriages, and deaths, and was a sorrowful survey of seduction, desertion, crime, discontent, and folly. In his later tales he dealt less in unrelieved gloom and bitter misery, and at times made a trial at humor. There are glimpses of pleasant English life and character, but these are only glimpses; the ground of his painting is shadow,—the shadow that rested on the life of the English poor in his generation.

I do not know where else one would turn for an adequate description of that life, or would gain so direct an insight into the social sources and conditions of the Methodist revival or into the motives and convictions of reformers like Mary Wollstonecraft; or where one would obtain so keen a sense of the vast change which has taken place in the conditions of humble human life within this century. Leslie Stephen, in that essay which is so good-humored but so unsuccessful an attempt to appreciate Crabbe [see Further Reading], mentions the few illustrations in modern literature of the life Crabbe described; it is seen in Charlotte Brontë's Yorkshiremen, and George Eliot's millers, and in a few other characters, "but," he says, "to get a realistic picture of country life as Crabbe saw it, we must go back to Squire Western, or to some of the roughly-hewn masses of flesh who sat to Hogarth." The setting of Crabbe's tales has this special historic interest. The schools, houses, books, habits, occupations, and all the external characteristics of the tales belong to the time: the press-gang comes to carry off the lover just before his wedding-day, and leaves the bride to nurse an unfathered child, to receive the courtship of a canting and carnal preacher, and to find a refuge from him, and from the father who favors him, in suicide; orphan boys are bound over to brutal task-masters; pictures of the sects (from the pen of a respectable clergyman of the established church, it is true) recall the beginnings of Methodism with a vividness only to be equaled by the books and pamphlets of the early converts' own writing. This historic value of the tales, however, great as it is to the student of manners, is secondary to their poetic value, which lies in the sentiment, feeling, and pathos with which the experience of life embodied in them, the workings of simple human nature, in however debased surroundings, is set forth. It is an experience which results usually from the interplay of low and selfish motives, and of ignoble or weak passions; it is, too, often, the course of brutal appetite, thoughtless or heartless folly, avarice, sensuality, and vice, relieved too seldom by amiable character, sympathy, charity, self-sacrifice, or even by the charm of natural beauty. Yet if all the seventy tales be taken into account, they contain nearly all varieties of character and circumstance among the country poor; and, though the darker side may seem to be more frequently insisted upon, it is because the nature of his subject made it necessary, because he let his light, as Moore said,

> Through life's low, dark interior fall,
> Opening the whole, severely bright,

rather than because he had any lack of cheerfulness of temper.

Crabbe does not, in a true sense, give expression to the life of the poor; he merely narrates it. There are here and there, throughout the poems, episodes written out of his own life; but usually he is concerned with the experience of other men, which he had observed, rather than with what his own heart had felt. A description of life is of course vastly inferior to an utterance of it, such as was given to us by Burns, who dealt with the life of the poor so much more powerfully than Crabbe; and a realistic description has less poetic value than an imaginative one, such as was given to us by Wordsworth when at his best. Crabbe's description is perhaps the most nakedly realistic of any in English poetry, but it is an uncommonly good one. Realism has a narrow compass, and Crabbe's powers were confined strictly within it; but he had the best virtues of a realist. His physical vision—his sight of what presents itself to the eye—was almost perfect; he saw every object, and saw it as it was. Perhaps the minuteness with which he saw was not altogether an advantage, for he does not seem to have taken in the landscape as a whole, but only as a mosaic of separate objects. He never gives general effects of beauty or grandeur; indeed, he seldom saw the beauty of a single object; he did little more than catalogue the things before him, and employ in writing poetry the same faculty in the same way as in pursuing his favorite studies of botany and entomology. Yet, with these limitations, what realist in painting could exceed in truthfulness and carefulness of detail this picture of a fall morning?—

> It was a fair and mild autumnal sky,
> And earth's ripe treasures met th' admiring eye;

The wet and heavy grass where feet had strayed,
Not yet erect, the wanderer's way betrayed;
Showers of the night had swelled the deep'ning rill,
The morning breeze had urged the quick'ning mill;
Long yellow leaves, from osiers strewed around,
Choked the small stream and hushed the feeble sound.

Or this sketch of light in a decayed warehouse turned into a tenement for the poor?—

That window view! oiled paper and old glass
Stain the strong rays, which, though impeded, pass,
And give a dusty warmth to that huge room,
The conquered sunshine's melancholy gloom;
When all those western rays, without so bright,
Within become a ghastly glimmering light,
As pale and faint upon the floor they fall,
Or feebly gleam on the opposing wall.

Nor is this carefulness of detail a trick, such as is sometimes employed, to give the appearance of reality to unreal human life. Crabbe's mental vision, his sight into the workings of the passions and the feelings, although not so perfect as his physical vision, was yet at its best very keen and clear; the sentiments, moods, reflections, and actions of his characters are seldom out of nature. (pp. 624-27)

[Qualities] of fine, true physical and mental vision are the essential qualities for valuable realistic work; if there be room for regret in Crabbe's share of them, it is because their range is contracted. I have mentioned the limitations of his physical vision; in respect to his mental vision Crabbe saw only a few and comparatively simple operations of human nature,—the workings of country-bred minds, not finely or complexly organized, but slow-motioned, and perplexed, if perplexed at all, not from the difficulty of the problem, but from their own dullness. Yet within these limits his characters are often pathetic, sometimes tragic, or even terrible, in their energy of evil passion or remorse.

One other quality, without which clear mental and physical vision would be ineffective, is essential to realism like Crabbe's,—transparency, the quality by virtue of which life is seen through another plainly and without distortion; and this is the quality which Crabbe possessed in most perfection. He not only saw the object as it was; he presented it as it was. He neither added nor took away; he did not unconsciously darken or heighten color, soften or harden line. Whatever was before his mind—the conversation of a gossip, the brutality of a ruffian, the cant of a convert—he reproduced truthfully; whatever was the character of his story, mean or tragic, trivial or pathetic, he did not modify it. There was no veil of fancy, no glamour of amiable deception or dimness of charitable tears, to obscure his view: if he found nudity and dirt, they reappeared in his work mere nudity and dirt still; if he found courage and patience, he dealt the same even-handed justice. His distinction is that he told a true story.

It was because he was thus able to present accurately and faithfully the human life which he saw so clearly, I have no doubt, that he won such admiration from Scott; for Scott had the welcome of genius for any new glimpse of humanity, and he knew how rare, and consequently how valuable, is the gift of simple and direct narration of what one sees. I am not so sure of Fox's discrimination; but Fox had great sensibility and tenderness of heart, and Crabbe presented the lot of the poor so vividly, so lucidly, so immediately, that he stirred in Fox the same feelings with which a better poet would have so charged his verses that natures not so finely endowed as

Fox would have been compelled to feel them too. Scott and Fox knew what a valuable acquisition this realistic sketch of humble life in their generation was, so faithful, minute, and trustworthy; they felt that their experience was enlarged, that real humanity had been brought home to them, and in the sway of those emotions, which Crabbe did not infuse into his work, but which his work quickens in sympathetic hearts, they could forgive him his tediousness, his frequent commonplace, his not unusual absurdity of phrase, his low level of flight with its occasional feebleness of wing.

In their minds, too, his style must have had more influence than we are apt to think,—the style of the great school which died with him, the form and versification which they had been taught to believe almost essential to the best poetry, and from a traditional respect for which they could hardly free their minds as easily as ourselves. Crabbe used the old heroic rhymed couplet, that simplest form of English verse music, which could rise, nevertheless, to the almost lyric loftiness of the last lines of the *Dunciad;* so supple and flexible; made for easy simile and compact metaphor; lending itself so perfectly to the sudden flash of wit or turn of humor; the natural shell of an epigram; compelling the poet to practice all the virtues of brevity; checking the wandering fancy, and repressing the secondary thought; requiring in a masterly use of it the employment of more mental powers than any other metrical form; despised and neglected, yet the best verse form which intelligence, as distinct from poetical feeling, can employ. Crabbe did not handle it in any masterly way; he was careless, and sometimes slipshod; but when he chose he could employ it well, and should have credit for it. (pp. 627-28)

But Wordsworth said Crabbe was unpoetical; he condemned him for "his unpoetical mode of considering human nature and society;" and, after all, the world has agreed with Wordsworth, and disagreed with Scott and Fox. Wordsworth told Scott an anecdote in illustration of his meaning. Sir George Beaumont, sitting with himself and Crabbe one day, blew out the candle which he had used in sealing a letter. Sir George and Wordsworth, with proper taste, sat watching the smoke rise from the wick in beautiful curves; but Crabbe seeing—or rather smelling—the object, and not seeing the beauty of it, put on the extinguisher. Therefore, said Wordsworth, Crabbe is unpoetical,—as fine a bit of æsthetic priggishness as is often met with. Scott's opinion was not much affected by the anecdote, and Wordsworth was on the wrong track. It is true, however, that Crabbe was unpoetical in Wordsworth's sense. Crabbe had no imaginative vision,—no such vision as is shown in that stormy landscape of Shelley's, in the opening of *Laon and Cythna,* which lacks the truth of actuality, but possesses the higher imaginative truth, like Turner's painting, or as is shown in that other storm in Pippa Passes. Crabbe saw sword-grass and saltwort and fen, but he had no secret of the imagination by which he could mingle them into harmonious beauty; there is loveliness in a salt marsh, but Crabbe could not present it, nor even see it for himself. The couplet of Arnold,

Say, has some wet, bird-haunted English lawn
Lent it the music of its trees at dawn?

has more poetical feeling in it than the whole description of the fall morning which has been quoted, and in the concluding lines of Sohrab and Rustum there is such imaginative vision as is worth all Crabbe's natural scenes. As in landscape, so in life: Goldsmith was untrue to the actual Auburn, but he was faithful to a far more precious truth, the truth of remembered childhood, and he revealed with the utmost beauty the effect of the subtlest working of the spirit of man on practical fact; it is his fidelity to this psychological and spiritual truth which makes Auburn the "loveliest village of the plain." Crabbe exhibited nothing of this imaginative transformation of the familiar and the commonplace, perhaps saw nothing of it; he described the fishing village of Aldborough as any one with good powers of perception, who took the trouble, might see it. Through these defects of his powers he loses in poetic value; his poetry is, as he called it, poetry without an atmosphere; it is a reflection, almost mirror-like, of plain fact.

Men go to poetry too often with a preconceived notion of what the poet ought to give, instead of with open minds for whatever he has to give. Too much is not to be expected from Crabbe. He was only a simple country clergyman, half educated, with no burning ideals, or beautiful reveries, or passionate dreams; his mind did not rise out of the capabilities and virtues of respectability. His life was as little poetical, in Wordsworth's sense, as his poetry. Yet his gift was not an empty one. Moore, Scott, and Byron were story-tellers who were poetical, in Wordsworth's sense; but is Crabbe's true description of humble life less valuable than Scott's romantic tradition, or Moore's melting, sensuous Oriental dream, or Byron's sentimental, falsely-heroic adventure, or even, in our own day, than Morris's indolent, smooth-flowing lotus-land fable? It is far more valuable, because there is more of the human heart in it; because it contains actual suffering and joy of fellow-men;' because it is humanity, and calls for hospitality in our sympathies and charities. Unpoetical? Yes; but it is something to have real life brought home to our tears and laughter, although it be presented barely, and the poet has trusted to the rightness and tenderness of our hearts for those feelings the absence of which in his verse led Wordsworth to call these tales unpoetical. Yet, it must be confessed, all of Crabbe is not to be read; it is only when he is at his best that his verse has this extraordinary power over the heart; but he is often at his best. Would that in this revival of the eighteenth century, when so much of its driftweed and wreck seems flooding back to burden life a generation longer, some one who knows Crabbe well would gather up the best of his work, and so save it from an otherwise inevitable forgetfulness, and give our generation knowledge of a pleasure it is missing! (pp. 628-29)

*G. E. Woodberry, "A Neglected Poet," in* The Atlantic Monthly, *Vol. XLV, No. 271, May, 1880, pp. 624-29.*

**EDWARD FITZGERALD**  (essay date 1882)

[*Fitzgerald was a nineteenth-century English writer who is best known as the translator of the* Rubáiyát of Omar Khayyám. *In the following excerpt from an essay on Crabbe that originally served as an introduction to an 1882 edition of* Tales of the Hall, *Fitzgerald comments on the shift in that work towards lighter subjects and more varied characterization. He also assesses nineteenth-century critical opinions of Crabbe, defending his importance as a poet.*]

The plan and nature of [*Tales of the Hall*] are . . . described by the author himself in a letter written to his old friend, Mary Leadbetter, and dated October 30, 1817:

> I know not how to describe the new, and probably (most probably) the last work I shall publish.

> Though a village is the scene of meeting between my two principal characters, and gives occasion to other characters and relations in general, yet I no more describe the manners of village inhabitants. My people are of superior classes, though not the most elevated; and, with a few exceptions, are of educated and cultivated minds and habits. I do not know, on a general view, whether my tragic or lighter Tales, etc., are most in number. Of those equally well executed, the tragic will, I suppose, make the greater impression; but I know not that it requires more attention.

(p. 461)

The scene has also changed with Drama and Dramatis Personæ: no longer now the squalid purlieus of old, inhabited by paupers and ruffians, with the sea on one side, and as barren a heath on the other; in place of that, a village, with its tidy homestead and well-to-do tenant, scattered about an ancient Hall, in a well-wooded, well-watered, well-cultivated country, within easy reach of a thriving country town, and

> West of the waves, and just beyond the sound,

of that old familiar sea, which (with all its sad associations) the Poet never liked to leave far behind him.

When he wrote the letter above quoted (two years before the publication of his book) he knew not whether his tragic exceeded the lighter stories in quantity, though he supposed they would leave the deeper impression on the reader. In the completed work I find the tragic stories fewer in number, and, to my thinking, assuredly not more impressive than such as are composed of that mingled yarn of grave and gay of which the kind of life he treats of is, I suppose, generally made up. "Nature's sternest Painter" [see poem by Byron dated 1809] may have mellowed with a prosperous old age, and, from a comfortable grand-climacteric, liked to contemplate and represent a brighter aspect of humanity than his earlier life afforded him. Anyhow, he has here selected a subject whose character and circumstance require a lighter touch and shadow less dark than such as he formerly delineated.

Those who now tell their own as well as their neighbours' stories are much of the Poet's own age as well as condition of life, and look back (as he may have looked) with what Sir Walter Scott calls a kind of humorous retrospect over their own lives, cheerfully extending to others the same-kindly indulgence which they solicit for themselves. The book, if I mistake not, deals rather with the follies than with the vices of men, with the comedy rather than the tragedy of life. Assuredly there is scarce anything of that brutal or sordid villainy of which one has more than enough in the Poet's earlier work. And even the more sombre subjects of the book are relieved by the colloquial intercourse of the narrators, which twines about every story, and, letting in occasional glimpses of the country round, encircles them all with something of dramatic unity and interest; insomuch that of all the Poet's works this one alone does not leave a more or less melancholy impression upon me; and, as I am myself more than old enough to love the sunny side of the wall, is on that account, I do not say the best, but certainly that which best I like, of all his numerous offspring.

Such, however, is not the case, I think, with Crabbe's few readers, who, like Lord Byron, chiefly remember him by the sterner realities of his earlier work. Nay, quite recently Mr. Leslie Stephen [see Further Reading], in that one of his admirable essays which analyses the Poet's peculiar genius, says:

The more humorous portions of these performances may be briefly dismissed. Crabbe possessed the faculty, but not in any eminent degree; his tramp is a little heavy, and one must remember that Mr. Tovell and his like were of the race who require to have a joke driven into their heads by a sledgehammer. Sometimes, indeed, we come upon a sketch which may help to explain Miss Austen's admiration. There is an old maid devoted to china, and rejoicing in stuffed parrots and puppies, who might have been another Emma Woodhouse; and a Parson who might have suited the Eltons admirably.

The spinster of the stuffed parrot indicates, I suppose, the heroine of **"Procrastination"** in another series of tales. But Miss Austen, I think, might also have admired another, although more sensible, spinster in these, who tells of her girlish and only love while living with the grandmother who maintained her gentility in the little town she lived in at the cost of such little economies as "would scarce a parrot keep;" and the story of the romantic friend who, having proved the vanity of human bliss by the supposed death of a young lover, has devoted herself to his memory; insomuch that as she is one fine autumnal day protesting in her garden that, were he to be restored to her in all his youthful beauty, she would renounce the real rather than surrender the ideal Hero awaiting her elsewhere—behold him advancing toward her in the person of a prosperous, portly merchant, who reclaims, and, after some little hesitation on her part, retains her hand.

There is also an old Bachelor whom Miss Austen might have liked to hear recounting the matrimonial attempts which have resulted in the full enjoyment of single blessedness. . . . (pp. 466-69)

If **"Love's Delay"** be of a graver complexion, is there not some even graceful comedy in **"Love's Natural Death;"** some broad comedy—too true to be farce—in **"William Bailey's"** old housekeeper; and up and down the book surely many passages of gayer or graver humour; such as the Squire's satire on his own house and farm; his brother's account of the Vicar, whose daughter he married; the gallery of portraits in the **"Cathedral Walk,"** besides many a shrewd remark so tersely put that I should call them epigram did not Mr. Stephen think the Poet incapable of such; others so covertly implied as to remind one of old John Murray's remark on Mr. Crabbe's conversation—that he said uncommon things in so common a way as to escape notice; though assuredly not the notice of so shrewd an observer as Mr. Stephen if he cared to listen, or to read.

Nevertheless, with all my own partiality for this book, I must acknowledge that, while it shares with the Poet's other works in his characteristic disregard of form and diction—of all indeed that is now called "Art"—it is yet more chargeable with diffuseness, and even with some inconsistency of character and circumstance, for which the large canvas he had taken to work on, and perhaps some weariness in filling it up, may be in some measure accountable. So that, for one reason or another, but very few of Crabbe's few readers care to encounter the book. (pp. 470-71)

Mr. Stephen has said—and surely said well—that, with all its short- and long-comings, Crabbe's better work leaves its mark on the reader's mind and memory as only the work of genius can, while so many a more splendid vision of the fancy slips away, leaving scarce a wrack behind. If this abiding impression result (as perhaps in the case of Richardson or Wordsworth) from being, as it were, soaked in through the longer process by which the man's peculiar genius works, any abridgment, whether of omission or epitome, will diminish from the effect of the whole. But, on the other hand, it may serve, as I have said, to attract a reader to an original which, as appears in this case, scarce anybody now cares to venture upon in its integrity.

I feel bound to make all apology for thus dealing with a Poet whose works are ignored, even if his name be known, by the readers and writers of the present generation. "Pope in worsted stockings" he once was called [see James Smith excerpt dated 1812]; and those stockings, it must be admitted, often down at heel, and begrimed by many a visit among the dreary resorts of *"pauvre et triste humanité."* And if Pope, in his silken court suit, scarcely finds admittance to the modern Parnassus, how shall Crabbe with his homely gear and awkwarder gait? Why had he not kept to level prose, more suitable, some think, to the subject he treats of, and to his own genius? As to subject, Pope, who said that Man was man's proper study, treated of finer folks indeed, but not a whit more or less than men and women, nor the more life-like for the compliment or satire with which he set them off. And, for the manner, he and Horace in his Epistles and Satires, and the comedy-writers of Greece, Rome, Spain, and France, availed themselves of Verse, through which (and especially when clenched with rhyme) the condensed expression, according to Montaigne, rings out as breath through a trumpet. I do not say that Comedy (whose Dramatic form Crabbe never aimed at) was in any wise his special vocation, though its shrewder—not to say, saturnine—element runs through all except his earliest work, and somewhat of its lighter humour is revealed in his last. And, if Verse has been the chosen organ of Comedy proper, it assuredly cannot be less suitable for the expression of those more serious passions of which this Poet most generally treats, and which are nowhere more absolutely developed than amid the classes of men with which he had been so largely interested. And whatever one may think Crabbe makes of it, verse was the mode of utterance to which his genius led him from first to last (his attempt at prose having failed); and if we are to have him at all, we must take him in his own way.

Is he then, whatever shape he may take, worth making room for in our overcrowded heads and libraries? If the verdict of such critics as Jeffrey [see excerpts dated 1808 and 1819] and Wilson be set down to contemporary partiality or inferior "culture," there is Miss Austen, who is now so great an authority in the representation of genteel humanity, so unaccountably smitten with Crabbe in his worsted hose that she is said to have pleasantly declared he was the only man whom she would care to marry. If Sir Walter Scott and Byron are but unæsthetic judges of the Poet, there is Wordsworth, who was sufficiently exclusive in admitting any to the sacred brotherhood in which he still reigns, and far too honest to make any exception out of compliment to anyone on any occasion—he did, nevertheless, thus write to the Poet's son and biographer in 1834: "Any testimony to the merit of your revered father's works would, I feel, be superfluous, if not impertinent. They will last, from their combined merits as poetry and truth, full as long as anything that has been expressed in verse since they first made their appearance" [see excerpt above]—a period which, be it noted, includes all Wordsworth's own volumes except "Yarrow Revisited," "The Prelude," and "The Borderers." And Wordsworth's living successor to the laurel no less participates with him in his appreciation of their forgotten brother. Almost the last time I met him he was quoting from memory that fine passage in **"Delay has Danger,"** where the late autumn landscape seems to borrow from the conscience-stricken lover who gazes on it the gloom which it reflects upon him; and in the course of further conversation on the subject, Mr. Tennyson added, "Crabbe has a world of his own;" by virtue of that original genius, I suppose, which is said to entitle, and carry, the possessor to what we call Immortality. (pp. 474-77)

> Edward Fitzgerald, "Crabbe's 'Tales of the Hall',"
> in his Works of Edward Fitzgerald, Vol. I, Houghton, Mifflin & Co., 1887, pp. 461-77.

## GEORGE SAINTSBURY    (essay date 1889)

[*Saintsbury was an English literary historian and critic of the late nineteenth and early twentieth centuries. A prolific writer, he composed several histories of English and European literature as well as numerous critical works on individual authors, styles, and periods. In the following excerpt from a general overview of Crabbe's life and literary accomplishments, Saintsbury compares the early and late phases of Crabbe's poetry, analyzing his use of diction and characterization, as well as the thematic approach to human nature that unifies his writings. Saintsbury concludes with an appraisal of the poetic character of Crabbe's work, considering the opinions of such critics as William Hazlitt on this issue.*]

Crabbe, though by no means always at his best, is one of the most curiously equal of verse writers. *Inebriety* and such other very youthful things are not to be counted; but between **The Village** of 1783 and the **Posthumous Tales** of more than fifty years later the difference is surprisingly small. Such as it is, it rather reverses ordinary experience, for the later poems exhibit the greater play of fancy, the earlier the exacter graces of form and expression. Yet there is nothing really wonderful in this, for Crabbe's earliest poems were published under severe surveillance of himself and others, and at a time which still thought nothing of such value in literature as correctness, while his later were written under no particular censorship, and when the romantic revival had already for better or worse emancipated the world. The change was in Crabbe's case not wholly for the better. He does not in his later verse become more prosaic, but he becomes considerably less intelligible. There is a passage in **"The Old Bachelor"** too long to quote but worth referring to, which, though it may be easy enough to understand it with a little goodwill, I defy anybody to understand in its literal and grammatical meaning. Such welters of words are very common in Crabbe, and Johnson saved him from one of them in the very first lines of **The Village** by an emendation which Mr. Kebbel seems not quite to understand. Yet Johnson could never have written the passages which earned Crabbe his fame. The great lexicographer knew man in general much better than Crabbe did; but he nowhere shows anything like Crabbe's power of seizing and reproducing man in particular. Crabbe is one of the first and certainly one of the greatest of the "realists" who exactly reversing the old philosophical signification of the word, devote themselves to the particular only. Yet of the three small volumes by which he, after his introduction to Burke, made his reputation and on which he lived for a quarter of a century, the first and the last display comparatively little of this peculiar quality. **The Library** and **The Newspaper** are characteristic pieces of the school of Pope, but not characteristic of their author. The first catalogues books as folio, quarto, octavo,

and so forth, and then cross-catalogues them as law, physic, divinity, and the rest, but is otherwise written very much "in the air". **The Newspaper** suited Crabbe a little better, because he pretty obviously took a particular newspaper and went through its contents—scandal, news, reviews, advertisements—in his own special fashion, but still the subject did not appeal to him. In **The Village,** on the other hand, contemporaries and successors alike have agreed to recognize Crabbe in his true vein. The two famous passages which attracted the suffrages of judges so different as Scott and Wordsworth [see letter dated 1834], are still, after more than a hundred years, fresh, distinct, and striking. Here they are once more.

> There is yon House that holds the parish poor,
> Whose walls of mud scarce bear the broken door;
> Thee, where the putrid vapours, flagging, play,
> And the dull wheel hums doleful through the day;—
> There children dwell who know no parents' care;
> Parents who know no children's love dwell there!
> Heart-broken matrons on their joyless bed,
> Forsaken wives, and mothers never wed;
> Dejected widows, with unheeded tears,
> And crippled age with more than childhood fears;
> The lame, the blind, and, far the happiest they!
> The moping idiot and the madman gay.
>
> Anon, a figure enters, quaintly neat,
> All pride and business, bustle and conceit;
> With looks unaltered by these scenes of woe,
> With speed that, entering, speaks his haste to go,
> He bids the gazing throng around him fly,
> And carries fate and physic in his eye:
> A potent quack, long versed in human ills,
> Who first insults the victim whom he kills;
> Whose murderous hand a drowsy Bench protect,
> And whose most tender mercy is neglect.
> Paid by the parish for attendance here,
> He wears contempt upon his sapient sneer;
> In haste he seeks the bed where Misery lies,
> Impatience marked in his averted eyes;
> And some habitual queries hurried o'er,
> Without reply he rushes on the door:
> His drooping patient, long inured to pain,
> And long unheeded, knows remonstrance vain,
> He ceases now the feeble help to crave
> Of man; and silent, sinks into the grave.

The poet executed endless variations on this class of theme, but he never quite succeeded in discovering a new one, though in process of time he brought his narrow study of the Aldborough fishermen and townsfolk down still more narrowly to individuals. His landscape is always marvellously exact, the strokes selected with extraordinary skill so as to show autumn rather than spring, failure rather than hope, the riddle of the painful earth rather than any joy of living. Attempts have been made to vindicate Crabbe from the charge of being a gloomy poet, but I cannot think them successful; I can hardly think that they have been quite serious. Crabbe, our chief realistic poet, has an altogether astonishing likeness to the chief prose realist of France, Gustave Flaubert, so far as his manner of view goes, for in point of style the two have small resemblance. One of the most striking things in Crabbe's biography is his remembrance of the gradual disillusion of a day of pleasure which as a child he enjoyed in a new boat of his father's. We all of us, except those who are gifted or cursed with the proverbial "duck's back", have these experiences and these remembrances of them. But most men either simply grin and bear it, or carrying the grin a little farther, console themselves by regarding their own disappointments from the ironic and humorous point of view. Crabbe, though not destitute of humour, does not seem to have been able or to have been disposed to employ it in this way. Perhaps he never quite got over the terrible and for the most part unrecorded year in London: perhaps the difference between the Mira of promise and the Mira of possession—the "happiness denied"—had something to do with it: perhaps it was a question of natural disposition with him. But when, years afterwards, as a prosperous middle-aged man, he began his series of published poems once more with *The Parish Register,* the same manner of seeing is evident, though the minute elaboration of the views themselves is almost infinitely greater. Nor did he ever succeed in altering this manner, if he ever tried to do so.

With the exception of his few Lyrics, the most important of which, **"Sir Eustace Grey"** (one of his very best things), is itself a tale in different metre, and a few other occasional pieces of little importance, the entire work of Crabbe, voluminous as it is, is framed upon a single pattern, the vignettes of *The Village* being merely enlarged in size and altered in frame in the later books. The three parts of *The Parish Register,* the twenty-four Letters of *The Borough,* some of which have single and others grouped subjects, and the sixty or seventy pieces which make up the three divisions of *Tales,* consist almost exclusively of heroic couplets, shorter measures very rarely intervening. They are also almost wholly devoted to narratives, partly satirical, partly pathetic, of the lives of individuals of the lower and middle class chiefly. Jeffrey, who was a great champion of Crabbe and allotted several essays to him, takes delight in analysing the plots or stories of these tales; but it is a little amusing to notice that he does it for the most part exactly as if he were criticizing a novelist or a dramatist. 'The object,' says he, in one place, 'is to show that a man's fluency of speech depends very much upon his confidence in the approbation of his auditors': 'In Squire Thomas we have the history of a mean domineering spirit,' and so forth. Gifford in one place actually discusses Crabbe as a novelist. I shall make some further reference to this curious attitude of Crabbe's admiring critics. For the moment I shall only remark that the singularly mean character of so much of Crabbe's style, the 'style of drab stucco,' as it has been unkindly called, which is familiar from the wicked wit that told how the youth at the theatre

Regained the felt and felt what he regained,

is by no means universal. The most powerful of all his pieces, the history of **"Peter Grimes,"** the tyrant of apprentices, is almost entirely free from it, and so are a few others. But it is common enough to be a very serious stumbling block. In nine tales out of ten this is the staple:

Of a fair town where Dr. Rack was guide,
His only daughter was the boast and pride.

Now that is unexceptionable verse enough, but what is the good of putting it in verse at all? Here again:

For he who makes me thus on business wait,
Is not for business in a proper state.

It is obvious that you cannot trust a man who, unless he is intending a burlesque, can bring himself to write like that. Crabbe not only brings himself to it, but rejoices and luxuriates in the style. The tale from which that last luckless distich is taken, **"The Elder Brother"**, is full of pathos and about equally full of false notes. If we turn to a far different subject,

the very vigorously conceived **"Natural Death of Love"**, we find a piece of strong and true satire, the best thing of its kind in the author, which is kept up throughout. Although, like all satire, it belongs at best but to the outer courts of poetry, it is so good that none can complain. Then the page is turned and one reads:

"I met," said Richard, when returned to dine,
"In my excursion with a friend of mine."

It may be childish, it may be uncritical, but I own that such verse as that excites in me an irritation which destroys all power of enjoyment, except the enjoyment of ridicule. Nor let any one say that pedestrian passages of the kind are inseparable from ordinary narrative in verse and from the adaptation of verse to miscellaneous themes. If it were so the argument would be fatal to such adaptation, but it is not. Pope seldom indulges in such passages, though he does sometimes: Dryden never does. He can praise, abuse, argue, tell stories, make questionable jests, do anything, in verse that is still poetry, that has a throb and a quiver and a swell in it, and is not merely limp, rhythmed prose. In Crabbe, save in a few passages of feeling and a great many of mere description—the last an excellent setting for poetry but not necessarily poetical—this rhythmed prose is everywhere. The matter which it serves to convey is, with the limitations above given, varied, and it is excellent. No one except the greatest prose novelists has such a gallery of distinct, sharply etched characters, such another gallery of equally distinct scenes and manner-pieces, to set before the reader. Exasperating as Crabbe's style sometimes is he seldom bores—never indeed except in his rare passages of digressive reflection. It has, I think, been observed, and if not the observation is obvious, that he has done with the pen for the neighbourhood of Aldborough and Glemham what Crome and Cotman have done for the neighbourhood of Norwich with the pencil. His observation of human nature, so far as it goes, is not less careful, true, and vivid. His pictures of manners, to those who read them at all, are perfectly fresh and in no respect grotesque or faded, dead as the manners themselves are. His pictures of motives and of facts, of vice and virtue, never can fade, because the subjects are perennial and are truly caught. Even his plays on words, which horrified Jeffrey,—

Alas! your reverence, wanton thoughts I grant
Were once my motive, now the thoughts of want,

and the like,—are not worse than Milton's jokes on the guns. He has immense talent, and he has the originality which sets talent to work in a way not tried by others, and may thus be very fairly said to turn it into genius. His is all this and more. But despite the warnings of a certain precedent, I cannot help stating the case which we have discussed in the old form, and asking, was Crabbe a poet?

And thus putting the question, we may try to sum up. It is the gracious habit of a summing up to introduce, if possible, a dictum of the famous men our fathers that were before us, a habit which by me shall ever be honoured. [In reference] . . . to Hazlitt's criticism on Crabbe in *The Spirit of the Age",* . . . I need not, here at least, repeat at very great length the cautions which are always necessary in considering any judgment of Hazlitt's [see excerpt dated 1825]. Much that he says even in the brief space of six or eight pages which he allots to Crabbe is unjust; much is explicably, and not too creditably, unjust. Crabbe was a successful man, and Hazlitt did not like successful men: he was a clergyman of the

Church of England, and Hazlitt did not love clergymen of the Church of England: he had been a duke's chaplain, and Hazlitt loathed dukes: he had been a Radical, and was still (though Hazlitt does not seem to have thought him so) a Liberal, but his Liberalism had been Torified into a tame variety. Again, Crabbe, though by no means squeamish, is the most unvoluptuous and dispassionate of all describers of inconvenient things; and Hazlitt was the author of "Liber Amoris". Accordingly there is much that is untrue in the tissue of denunciation which the critic devotes to the poet. But there are two passages in this tirade which alone might show how great a critic Hazlitt himself was. Here in a couple of lines ("they turn, one and all, on the same sort of teasing, helpless, unimaginative distress") is the germ of one of the most famous and certainly of the best passages of the late Mr. Arnold; and here again is one of those critical taps of the finger which shivers by a touch of the weakest part a whole Rupert's drop of misapprehension. Crabbe justified himself by Pope's example. "Nothing", says Hazlitt, "can be more dissimilar. Pope describes what is striking: Crabbe would have described merely what was there. . . . In Pope there was an appeal to the imagination, you see what was passing *in a poetical point of view.*"

Even here (and I have not been able to quote the whole passage) there is one of the flaws, which Hazlitt rarely avoided, in the use of the word "striking"; for, Heaven knows, Crabbe is often striking enough. But the description of Pope as showing things "in a poetical point of view" hits the white at once, wounds Crabbe mortally, and demolishes "realism", as we have been pleased to understand it for the last generation or two. Hazlitt, it is true, has not followed up the attack, as I shall hope to show in an instant; but he has indicated the right line of it. As far as mere treatment goes, the fault of Crabbe is that he is pictorial rather than poetic, and photographic rather than pictorial. He sees his subject steadily, and even in a way he sees it whole; but he does not see it in the poetical way. You are bound in the shallows and the miseries of the individual; never do you reach the large freedom of the poet who looks at the universal. The absence of selection, of the discarding of details that are not wanted, has no doubt a great deal to do with this—Hazlitt seems to have thought that it had everything to do. I do not quite agree with him there. Dante, I think, was sometimes quite as minute as Crabbe; and I do not know that any one less hardy than Hazlitt himself would single out, as Hazlitt expressly does, the death-bed scene of Buckingham as a conquering instance in Pope to compare with Crabbe. We know that the bard of Twickenham grossly exaggerated this. But suppose he had not? Would it have been worse verse? I think not. Although the faculty of selecting instead of giving all, as Hazlitt himself justly contends, is one of the things which make *poesis non ut pictura,* it is not all, and I think myself that a poet, if he is a poet, could be almost absolutely literal. Shakespeare is so in the picture of Gloucester's corpse. Is that not poetry?

The defect of Crabbe, as it seems to me, is best indicated by reference to one of the truest of all dicta on poetry, the famous maxim of Joubert—that the lyre is a winged instrument and must transport. There is no wing in Crabbe, there is no transport, because, as I hold (and this is where I go beyond Hazlitt), there is no music. In all poetry, the very highest as well as the very lowest that is still poetry, there is something which transports, and that something in my view is always the music of the verse, of the words, of the cadence, of the rhythm, of the sounds superadded to the meaning. When you

get the best music married to the best meaning, then you get, say, Shakespeare: when you get some music married to even moderate meaning, you get, say, Moore. Wordsworth can, as everybody but Wordsworthians holds, and as some even of Wordsworthians admit, write the most detestable doggerel and platitude. But when any one who knows what poetry is reads,

> Our noisy years seem moments in the being
> Of the eternal silence,

he sees that, quite independently of the meaning, which disturbs the soul of no less a person than Mr. John Morley, there is one note added to the articulate music of the world—a note that never will leave off resounding till the eternal silence itself gulfs it. He leaves Wordsworth, he goes straight into the middle of the eighteenth century, and he sees Thomson with his hands in his dressing-gown pockets biting at the peaches, and hears him between the mouthfuls murmuring,

> So when the shepherd of the Hebrid Isles,
> Placed far amid the melancholy main,

and there is another note, as different as possible in kind yet still alike, struck for ever. Yet again, to take example still from the less romantic poets, and in this case from a poet, whom Mr. Kebbel specially and disadvantageously contrasts with Crabbe, when we read the old schoolboy's favourite,

> When the British warrior queen,
> Bleeding from the Roman rods,

we hear the same quality of music informing words though again in a kind somewhat lower, commoner, and less. In this matter, as in all matters that are worth handling at all, we come of course *ad mysterium.* Why certain combinations of letters, sounds, cadences, should almost without the aid of meaning though no doubt immensely assisted by meaning, produce this effect of poetry on men no man can say. But they do; and the chief merit of criticism is that it enables us by much study of different times and different languages to recognize something like the laws, though not the ultimate causes, of the production.

Now I can only say that Crabbe does not produce, or only in the rarest instances produces, this effect on me, and what is more, that on ceasing to be a patient in search of poetical stimulant and becoming merely a gelid critic, I do not discover even in Crabbe's warmest admirers any evidence that he produced this effect on them. Both in the eulogies which Mr. Kebbel quotes and in those that he does not quote I observe that the eulogists either discreetly avoid saying what they mean by poetry, or specify for praise something in Crabbe that is not distinctly poetical. Cardinal Newman says that Crabbe "pleased and touched him at thirty years' interval", and pleads that this answers to the "accidental definition of a classic". Most certainly; but not necessarily to that of a poetical classic. Jeffrey thought him "original and powerful". Granted; but there are plenty of original and powerful writers who are not poets. Wilson gave him the superlative for "original and vivid painting". Perhaps; but is Hogarth a poet? Jane Austen "thought she could have married him". She had not read his biography; but even if she had would that prove him to be a poet? Lord Tennyson is said to single out the following passage, which is certainly one of Crabbe's best, if not his very best.

> Early he rose, and looked with many a sigh
> On the red light that filled the eastern sky;

Oft had he stood before, alert and gay,
To hail the glories of the new-born day;
But now dejected, languid, listless, low,
He saw the wind upon the water blow,
And the cold stream curled onward as the gale
From the pine-hill blew harshly down the vale;
On the right side the youth a wood surveyed,
With all its dark intensity of shade;
Where the rough wind alone was heard to move
In this, the pause of nature and of love
When now the young are reared, and when the old,
Lost to the tie, grow negligent and cold':
Far to the left he saw the huts of men,
Half hid in mist that hung upon the fen:
Before him swallows gathering for the sea,
Took their short flights and twittered o'er the lea;
And near the bean-sheaf stood, the harvest done,
And slowly blackened in the sickly sun:
All these were sad in nature, or they took
Sadness from him, the likeness of his look
And of his mind—he pondered for a while,
Then met his Fanny with a borrowed smile.

It is good: it is extraordinarily good: it could not be better of its kind. It is as nearly poetry as anything that Crabbe ever did—but is it quite? If it is (and I am not careful to deny it) the reason as it seems to me is that the verbal and rhythmical music here, with its special effect of "transporting" of "making the common as if it were uncommon", is infinitely better than is usual with Crabbe, that in fact there is music as well as meaning. Hardly anywhere else, not even in the best passages of the story of **"Peter Grimes,"** shall we find such music; and in its absence it may be said of Crabbe much more truly than of Dryden (who carries the true if not the finest poetical under-tone with him even into the rant of Almanzor and Maximin, into the interminable arguments of "Religio Laici" and "The Hind and the Panther") that he is a classic of our prose.

Yet the qualities which are so noteworthy in him are all qualities which are valuable to the poet, and which for the most part are present in good poets. And I cannot help thinking that this was what actually deceived some of his contemporaries and made others content for the most part to acquiesce in an exaggerated estimate of his poetical merits. It must be remembered that even the latest generation which, as a whole and unhesitatingly, admired Crabbe, had been brought up on the poets of the eighteenth century, in the very best of whom the qualities which Crabbe lacks had been but sparingly and not eminently present. It must be remembered, too, that from the great vice of the poetry of the eighteenth century, its artificiality and convention, Crabbe is conspicuously free. The return to nature was not the only secret of the return to poetry; but it was part of it, and that Crabbe returned to nature no one could doubt. Moreover he came just between the school of prose fiction which practically ended with *Evelina* and the school of prose fiction which opened its different branches with *Waverley* and *Sense and Sensibility*. His contemporaries found nowhere else the narrative power, the faculty of character drawing, the genius for description of places and manners which they found in Crabbe; and they knew that in almost all, if not in all the great poets there is narrative power, faculty of character-drawing, genius for description. Yet again, Crabbe put these gifts into verse which at its best was excellent in its own way, and at its worst was a blessed contrast to Darwin or to Hayley. Some readers may have had an uncomfortable though only half conscious feeling that if they

had not a poet in Crabbe they had not a poet at all. At all events they made up their minds that they had a poet in him.

But are we bound to follow their example? I think not. You could play on Crabbe that odd trick which used, it is said, to be actually played on some mediæval verse chroniclers and unrhyme him—that is to say, put him into prose with the least possible changes—and his merits would, save in rare instances, remain very much as they are now. You could put other words in the place of his words, keeping the verse, and it would not as a rule be much the worse. You cannot do either of these things with poets who are poets. Therefore I shall conclude that save at the rarest moments, moments of some sudden gust of emotion, some happy accident, some special grace of the Muses to reward long and blameless toil in their service, Crabbe was not a poet. But I have not the least intention of denying that he was great, and all but of the greatest, among English writers. (pp. 104-10)

*George Saintsbury, "George Crabbe," in* Macmillan's Magazine, *Vol. LX, No. 356, June, 1889, pp. 99-110.*

## PAUL ELMER MORE    (essay date 1901)

[*More was an American critic who, along with Irving Babbitt, formulated the doctrines of New Humanism in early twentieth-century American thought. The New Humanists were strict moralists who adhered to traditional conservative values in reaction to an age of scientific and artistic self-expression. Regarding literature, they believed that a work's reflection of classical ethical norms was as important as its aesthetic qualities. More was particularly opposed to Naturalism, which he believed accentuated the animal nature of humans, and to any literature, such as Romanticism, that broke with established classical tradition. He is especially esteemed for the philosophical and literary erudition of his multi-volumed* Shelburne Essays. *In the following excerpt from a review of* The Life and Poetical Works of George Crabbe, *More addresses the fusion of natural description and human sentiment in* The Borough *and* Tales of the Hall.]

It would be a pleasure to suppose that the new edition of Crabbe in a single volume [***The Life and Poetical Works of George Crabbe***] would at last bring to him that popularity which his lover, FitzGerald, labored so insistently to create [see excerpt dated 1882], but any such hope is bound to be frustrate. Here is, in fact, one of the curiosities of literature: that a poet who has been admired so extravagantly by the wisest of England's readers should fail, I do not say of popularity, but even of recognition among critics and historians. For certainly no one would call Crabbe popular, and to realize the neglect of the critics we need only turn to the most sympathetic study of the poet in recent years and read Mr. Woodberry's opening words: "We have done with Crabbe" Yet to Byron this was "the first of living poets;" and Byron's epigram, "Nature's sternest painter, yet the best,"— commonly misquoted, by the way,—is on the lips of a host of readers who have never so much as opened a volume of Crabbe's works [see poem dated 1809]. Nor was Byron alone among the great men of that period to reverence what we have elected to forget. On his deathbed Fox called for Crabbe's poems, and in the sorrows of Phœbe Dawson found consolation while his life was ebbing away. And of Scott we are told that these same poems were at all times more frequently in his hands than any other work except Shakespeare, and that during his last days at Abbots-ford the only books he asked to be read aloud to him were his Bible and his Crabbe. But the true worshiper of our poet's genius was that gentle cynic and recluse, Edward FitzGerald. There is something really pathetic in FitzGerald's constant lamentation that no one reads his "eternal Crabbe." Our English Omar at least is popular, and it looks as if the Suffolk poet were to attain a kind of spurious fame from the way his name is imbedded in the letters of the "Suffold dreamer."

Now it is superfluous to say that a writer who has been so lauded by the greatest poet, the most ardent orator, the most honored novelist, and the most refined letter-writer of England in a century must himself have possessed extraordinary qualities. Yet it remains true that Crabbe is not read, is not even likely to be much read for many years to come; and the reason of this is perfectly simple: his excellencies lie in a direction apart from the trend of modern thought and sentiment, while his faults are such as must strongly repel modern taste.

As for the faults of Crabbe, it is enough to say that he is an avowed imitator of Pope in all formal matters, and that the antithetic style of the master too often descends in his to a grotesque flaccidity. It would not be impossible to quote a dozen lines almost as absurd as the parody in *Rejected Addresses:* [see poem dated 1812]:—

"Regained the felt, and felt what he regained."

But even where his style is wrought with nervous energy, it fails to attract an audience who have tasted the rapturous liberties of Shelley and Keats, and who love to take their sentiment copiously in unrestrained draughts. They do not see that the despised heroic couplet permits the narrative poet to condense into a pair of verses the insignificant joinings of a tale which in any other form would occupy a paragraph; nor does it interest them that in the hands of a moral poet the couplet is like a keen two-edged sword to strike this way and that. They are only offended by what seems to them the monotonous seesaw of the rhythm; and a style which constantly opposes an effort of the judicial understanding at every pause in the flow of sentiment repels those who think wit (in the old sense of the word) a poor substitute for celestial inspiration. It is partly a matter of psychology, partly a matter of inscrutable taste, that a generation of readers who are attracted by the slipshod rhythms of Epipsychidion or Endymion should find the close-knit periods of Crabbe unendurable.

To me personally there is no tedium, but only endless delight, in these mated rhymes which seem to pervade and harmonize the whole rhythm. And withal they help to create the artistic illusion, that wonderful atmosphere, I may call it, which envelops Crabbe's world. No one, not even the most skeptical of Crabbe's genius, can deny that he has succeeded in giving to his work a tone or atmosphere peculiarly and consistently his own. It would be curious to study this question of atmosphere in literature, and determine the elements that go to compose it. Why are the works of Dickens or Smollett or Spenser, to choose almost at random, so marked by a distinctive atmosphere, while in a greater writer, in Shakespeare for example, it may be less observable? Something of bulk is necessary to its existence, for it can hardly be created by a single book or a single poem. A certain consistency of tone is needed, and a unity of effect. It cannot exist without perfect sincerity in the writer; and, above all, there is required some idiosyncrasy of genius, some peculiar emotional or intellectual process in the author's mind, which imposes itself on us so powerfully that when we arise from his works the life of the world no longer seems quite the same to us; for we have learned to see the quiet fields of nature and the thronging activities of mankind through a new medium.

All these qualities, and more particularly this individuality of vision, pervade Crabbe's descriptive passages and his portraits of men. They color all his painting of inanimate things, but they are most evident, perhaps, in his pictures of the sea, whose varied aspects, whether sublime or intimate, seem to have become a part of his sensitive faculties through early associations. He has caught the real life of the sea, its calm and tempest or sudden change, as few poets in English have done. Especially he loves the quiet scenes, the beach when the tide retires; when all is calm at sea and on land, and the wonders of the shore lie glittering in the sunlight or the softer light of the moon. Even more characteristic are his pictures of the muddy, oozing shallows, as in that passage where the dull terrors of such a waste are employed to heighten the most tragic of his *Tales:*—

> When tides were neap, and, in the sultry day,
> Through the tall bounding mud-banks made their way,
> Which on each side rose swelling, and below
> The dark warm flood ran silently and slow;
> There anchoring, Peter chose from man to hide,
> There hang his head, and view the lazy tide
> In its hot slimy channel slowly glide;
> Where the small eels that left the deeper way
> For the warm shore, within the shallows play;
> Where graping mussels, left upon the mud,
> Slope their slow passage to the fallen flood;—
> Here dull and hopeless he'd lie down and trace
> How sidelong crabs had scrawled their crooked race,
> Or sadly listen to the tuneless cry
> Of fishing gull or clanging golden-eye;
> What time the sea-birds to the marsh would come,
> And the loud bittern, from the bull-rush home,
> Gave from the salt ditch side the bellowing boom:
> He nursed the feelings these dull scenes produce,
> And loved to stop beside the opening sluice;
> Where the small stream, confined in narrow bound,
> Ran with a dull, unvaried, sadd'ning sound;
> Where all, presented to the eye or ear,
> Oppressed the soul with misery, grief, and fear.

There, if anywhere in English, is the artist's vision, the power to concentrate the mind upon a single scene until every detail in its composition is corroded on the memory, and the skill, no less important, to select and arrange these details to a clearly conceived end.

These lines may serve to exemplify another trait of Crabbe's genius, the rare union of scientific detail with pervading human interest. He was, in fact, all his life a curious and exact student of botany and geology. Even in his old age he kept up these scientific pursuits, and his son, in the excellent biography, tells how the old man on his visits would leave the house every morning, rain or shine, and go alone to the quarries to search for fossils and to pick up rare herbs on the wayside. "The dirty fossils," says the dutiful son, "were placed in our best bedroom, to the great diversion of the female part of my family; the herbs stuck in the borders, among my choice flowers, that he might see them when he came again. I never displaced one of them,"—a pretty picture of busy eld. Of this inanimate lore of plants and rocks Crabbe is most prodigal in his verse, but, by some true gift of the Muses, it never for a moment obscures the human interest of the narrative. After all, it was the man, and the moral springs in man, that really concerned him. As he himself says, the best description of sea or river is incomplete.

> But when a happier theme succeeds, and when
> Men are our subjects and the deeds of men;
> Then may we find the Muse in happier style,
> And we may sometimes sigh and sometimes smile.

Even when he submits his art to minute descriptions, as for instance to a study of the growth of lichens, there still lurks this human ethical instinct behind the scientific eye. Read in their proper place, the following lines are but a little lesson to set forth the associations of mortal antiquity:—

> Seeds, to our eyes invisible, will find
> On the rude rock the bed that fits their kind;
> There, in the rugged soil, they safely dwell,
> Till showers and snows the subtle atoms swell,
> And spread the enduring foliage;—then we trace
> *The freckled flower upon the flinty base;*
> These all increase, till in unnoticed years
> The stony tower as gray with age appears;
> With coats of vegetation, thinly spread,
> Coat above coat, the living on the dead:
> These then dissolve to dust, and make a way
> For bolder foliage, nursed by their decay;
> The long-enduring Ferns in time will all
> Die and depose their dust upon the wall;
> Where the winged seed may rest, till many a flower
> Show Flora's triumph o'er the falling tower.

I choose these lines for citation because they form, perhaps, the most purely descriptive passage in Crabbe; and even here it is really the associations of generations of mankind with an ancient house of worship that stir the poet's feelings. For pieces of greater scope one should go to such pictures as the ocean tempest in *The Borough,* which I would not spoil by quoting incomplete. In his study of the Roman decadent poets, M. Nisard has instituted a careful comparison of the storm scenes in the Odyssey, the Æneid, and the Pharsalia, showing the regular increase from Homer down of descriptive matter added for merely picturesque effect, apart from its connection with the human action involved. It would not be easy to find a better example of extended description completely fused with human interest than this tempest in *The Borough.* Every detail of that animated picture is interpreted through human activity and emotion. This does not mean that Crabbe's attitude toward nature is that of an emotional pantheism which uses the outer world as a mere symbol of the soul. Very far from that: the human emotions are in this passage the direct outcome of a sharply defined natural occurrence. In another scene, one that has achieved a kind of fame among critics, he tells the story, in his quiet, satirical manner, of a lover who goes a journey to meet his beloved. The lover's way leads him over a barren heath and a sandy road, but, in his state of exalted expectation, everything that meets his eye is charged with loveliness. At last he arrives only to find his mistress has gone away,—gone, as he thinks, to see a rival. He follows her, and now his way takes him

> by a river's side,
> Inland and winding, smooth, and full, and wide,
> That rolled majestic on, in one soft-flowing tide;
> The bottom gravel, flowery were the banks,
> Tall willows waving in their broken ranks;
> The road, now near, now distant, winding led
> By lovely meadows which the waters fed.

But all is hideous to his jealous eye. "I hate these scenes!" he cries:—

> I hate these long green lanes; there's nothing seen
> In this vile country but eternal green.

All this is the furthest possible remove from vague reverie; it is a bit of amusing psychology, tending to distinguish more sharply between man and nature rather than to blend them in any haze of symbolism.

It may be imagined from Crabbe's power over details that he should excel in another sort of description, in scenes of still life, which come even closer to the affairs of humanity; and, indeed, there are scattered through his poems little genre pictures that for minuteness and accuracy can be likened only to the masterpieces of Dutch art in that kind. The *locus classicus* (if such a term may be used of so unfamiliar of poet) of this genre writing is the section of *The Borough* that describes the dwellings of the poor. I cannot refrain from quoting a few of the introductory lines to show how skillfully he prepares the mind for the picture that is to succeed:—

> There, fed by food they love, to rankest size,
> Around the dwellings docks and wormwood rise;
> Here the strong mallow strikes her slimy root,
> Here the dull nightshade hangs her deadly fruit;
> On hills of dust the henbane's faded green,
> And penciled flower of sickly scent is seen.

And this is the poet who has been censured for lack of descriptive powers! Of the scene that follows,—the "long boarded building," with one vast room, where the degraded families of the outcast are huddled together,—no selection can convey anything but the most inadequate impression; it must be read intact, and once read it will cling to the memory forever. Here, at least, is a bit that is as vivid as a picture by Van Ostade or Teniers:—

> On swinging shelf are things incongrous stored,—
> Scraps of their food,—the cards and cribbage-board,—
> With pipes and pouches; while on peg below,
> Hang a lost member's fiddle and its bow;
> That still reminds them how he'd dance and play,
> Ere sent untimely to the Convicts' Bay.

It must be clear even from these imperfect selections that Crabbe was able to envelop his inanimate world with an atmosphere peculiar to his own genius. As for the human beings that move through his scenes, if one were given to comparisons, he would probably liken them to the people of Dickens. The comparison is apt both for its accuracy and its limitations. The world of Crabbe is on the surface much like that of Dickens, but examined more closely it is seen to be less pervaded with humor, and more with wit; its pathos, too, is less pungent and firmer, and its moral tone is quite diverse. Save in his later *Tales of the Hall,*—which, after all, are scarcely an exception to the rule,—the characters in Crabbe's poems are taken from the ranks of the humble and poor; they are in external appearance the London folk of Dickens transferred to the country. But they rarely ever descend, like Dickens's portraits, into caricature, for the reason that their divergencies grow more from some inner guiding moral trait, and are less the mere outward distinctions of trick and manner. They are, too, more directly the outcome of divergent individual will; they are, for this reason, more perfectly rounded out in their personality, and they bear with them more complete a sense of moral responsibility for their associations.

We are carried to the green lanes and sandy shores of England, but it is not the land of old poetic illusions. Here are no scenes of idyllic peace, no Corydons murmuring liquid love to Phyllis or Neæra in the shade. I do not mean to imply that the orthodox pastoral dreams are without justification, for that would be to condemn the central theme of *Paradise Lost,* not to mention a host of minor poems justly beloved. But certainly these dreams lie perilously near to mawkishness and insincerity, and if for no other reason we could admire Crabbe for his manly resistance to their easy allurements. It seems that he set himself deliberately to ridicule and rebuke the common vapidities of that facile school. In those introductory lines to **The Village,** notable chiefly because they were tampered with by Dr. Johnson [see letter dated 1783], he directly satirizes the poets—and his master, Pope, was in youth one of the worst sinners in this respect—who imitate Virgil rather than nature. He too had sought the sweet peace and smiling resignation of rural life, but instead he had found only the cry of universal labor and contention:—

> Here, wandering long, amid these frowning fields,
> I sought the simple life that Nature yields;
> Rapine and Wrong and Fear usurped her place,
> And a bold, artful, surly, savage race.

An atmosphere of gloom is, indeed, over Crabbe's human world; not moroseness or morbid sentimentality, but a note of stern judicial pity for the frailties and vices of the men he knew and portrayed. His own early life in a miserable fishing hamlet on the Suffolk coast, under a hard father, his hard years of literary apprenticeship in London, and then for a time the salt bread of dependency as private chaplain to the Duke of Rutland, gave him a knowledge of many sorrows which years of comparative prosperity could not entirely obliterate. He is at bottom a true Calvinist, showing that peculiar form of fatalism which still finds it possible to magnify the free will, and to avoid the limp surrender of determinism. Mankind as a body lies under a fatal burden of suffering and toil, because as a boy men are depraved and turn from righteousness; but to the individual man there always remains open a path up from darkness into light, a way out of condemnation into serene peace. And it is with this mixture of judicial aloofness and hungering sympathy that Crabbe dwells on the sadness of long and hopeless waiting, the grief of broken love, the remorse of wasted opportunities, the burden of poverty, the solitude of failure, which run like dark threads through most of his Tales. And in one poem, at least, he has attained the full tragic style with an intensity and singleness of effect that rank him among the few master poets of human passion. The story of **"Peter Grimes"**—his abuse of his old father, his ill treatment of the workhouse lads bought from London, and his final madness and death—is the most powerful tragedy of remorse in the English language. (pp. 850-55)

But if the atmosphere of these poems is sombre, that does not mean they are without brighter glimpses of joy. As he himself expresses it, they are relieved by "gleams of transient mirth and hours of sweet repose." In fact, Crabbe has contrived to include a vast number of human interests and passions in these simple Tales. There are pages of literary satire on the Gothic romances of the day, more neatly executed even than Northanger Abbey. There are poems, like the second letter of **The Borough,** overflowing with tender sentiment; tales such as **"Phoebe Dawson,"** where the pathos is almost too painful to be easily supported. There are stories of quaint playfulness, like **"The Frank Courtship."** Humor, too, is not wanting, and now and then comes a stroke of memorable wit. Jealousy, ambition, pride, vanity, despair, and all the petty tyrannies of conceit are set off with marvelous acuteness.

Even abounding joy is not absent. I do not know but the sense of charm, of homely intimate life, of tranquil resignation, is, for all their dark colors, the final impression of these Tales. And everywhere they show the delightful gift of the story-teller. Each separate poem is a miniature novel wrought out with unflagging zest and almost impeccable art. The story of the younger brother in **Tales of the Hall** glows again with "the sober certainty of waking bliss;" and the older brother's history begins with a rapturous tide of romantic dreaming that fairly sings and pulses with beauty. The whole of this second story is, in fact, a literary masterpiece, for its scenes of joy, followed by despondency and heroic forbearance, controlled throughout by the unerring psychological instinct of the poet.

But this unerring instinct is not confined to any one tale; it guides the poet in the creation of all his multitudinous characters. At first, perhaps, as we see the ethical motives that underlie a character so clearly defined, it seems the poet is dealing merely with a moral type; but suddenly some little limitation is thrown in, some modification of motive, which changes the character from a cold abstraction to a living and unmistakable personality. Crabbe has been called a realist; and in one sense the term is appropriate, but in the meaning commonly given to the word it is singularly inept. The inner moral springs of character are what first interested him, and his keen perception of manners and environment only serves to save him from the coldness of eighteenth-century abstractions.

I have dwelt at length on these phases of Crabbe's work which would strike even a casual reader, for the sufficient reason that the casual reader in his case scarcely exists. The real problem, as I have already intimated, is to explain why a poet of such great, almost supreme powers should fail to preserve a place in the memory of critics, not to mention his lack of a popular audience. His failure is due in part, no doubt, to the use of a metrical form which we choose to contemn, but chiefly it is due to the fact that he is at once of us and not of us. His presentation of the world is in spirit essentially modern, so that we do not grant him the indulgence unconsciously allowed to poets who describe a difference form of society, and whose appeal to us is impersonal and general; while at the same time he ignores or even derides what has become the primary emotion we desire in our literary favorites. Since the advent of Shelley and Wordsworth and the other great contemporaries of Crabbe our attitude toward nature has altered profoundly. We demand of the poet a minute, almost a scientific acquaintance with the obscurer beasts and flowers; but still more we demand, if the poet is to receive our deeper admiration, a certain note of mysticism, a feeling of some vast and indefinable presence beyond the finite forms described, a lurking sense of pantheism by which the personality of the observer seems to melt into what he observes or is swallowed up in a vague reverie. When we think of the great nature passages of the century, we are apt to recall the solemn mysteries of Wordsworth's "Tintern Abbey" or Shelley's "Ode to the West Wind." Even in poets who are not frankly of the romantic school, and who are imbued with the classical spirit, the same undercurrent of reverie is heard. Matthew Arnold's verse is full of these subtle echoes. It may be caused by a tide of reminiscence which dulls the sharpness of present impressions, as in so simple a line as this:—

> Lone Daulis and the high Cephissian vale;

or it may be present because the words are overfreighted with reflection, as in the closing lines of The Future:—

> As the pale waste widens around him,
> As the banks fade dimmer away,
> As the stars come out, and the night-wind
> Brings up the stream
> Murmurs and scents of the infinite sea;

but everywhere this note of reverie runs through the greater modern poets. Now of science Crabbe owned more than a necessary share, but for reverie, for symbolism, for mystic longings toward the infinite, he had no sense whatever. It is quite true, as Goethe declared, that a "sense of infinitude" is the mark of high poetry, and I firmly believe that the absence of this sense is the one thing that shuts Crabbe out of the company of the few divinely inspired singers,—the few who bring to us gleanings from their "commerce with the skies," to use old Ovid's phrase. But it is also true that this sense of infinitude as it speaks in Homer and Shakespeare is something far more sober and rational than the musings of the modern spirit,—something radically different from the brooding rhapsodies of Shelley's *Prometheus Unbound;* and Crabbe's very limitations lend to his verse a brave manliness, a clean good sense, that tone up the mind of the reader like a strong cordial.

And there is the same difference in Crabbe's treatment of humanity. Wordsworth, feeling this difference, was led to speak slightingly of Crabbe's "unpoetical mode of considering human nature and society." His repulsion may be attributed in part to Crabbe's constant use of a form of analysis which checks the unconstrained flow of the emotions; but the chasm between the two is deeper than that. Wordsworth was ready to ridicule the sham idyllic poetry as freely as Crabbe or any other; but, at bottom, are not Michael and the leech-gatherer, and a host of others that move through Wordsworth's scenes, the true successors of the Corydons and Damons that dance under the trees on the old idyllic swards? In place of pastoral dreams of peace we hear now "the still, sad music of humanity." Yet it is the same humanity considered as a whole; humanity betrayed by circumstances and corrupted by luxury, but needing only the freedom of the hills and likes to develop its native virtues; humanity caught up in some tremulous vision of harmony with the universal world; it is, in short, the vague aspiration of what we have called humanitarianism, and have endowed with the solemnities of a religion. If this is necessary to poetry, Crabbe is undoubtedly "unpoetical." In him there is no thought of a perfect race made corrupt by luxury, no vision of idyllic peace, no musing on humanity as an abstraction, but always a sturdy understanding of the individual man reaping the fruits of his own evil doing or righteousness; his interest is in the individual will, never in the problem of classes. His sharply defined sense of man's personal responsibility coincides with his lack of reverent enthusiasm toward nature as an abstract idea, and goes to create that unusual atmosphere about his works which repels the modern sentimentalist. So it happens, we think, that he can appeal strongly to only a few readers of peculiar culture; for it is just the province of culture or right education—is it not?—that it shall train the mind to breathe easily an atmosphere foreign to its native habit. (pp. 855-57)

*Paul Elmer More, "A Plea for Crabbe," in* The Atlantic Monthly, *Vol. LXXXVIII, No. DXXX, December, 1901, pp. 850-57.*

## OLIVER ELTON   (essay date 1909)

[*In the following excerpt, Elton contrasts elements of realism and romanticism in Crabbe's poetry, tracing the thematic and stylistic progress of his work from* The Village *to* Tales of the Hall.]

[Crabbe's] first work of any character, **The Village,** came out in 1783, in the same decade as Blake's *Poetical Sketches,* Burns's Kilmarnock poems, and Cowper's "Task." For this Crabbe is miscalled a pioneer, though he really stands at the close of a literary age. If he is a pioneer at all, it is more in the history of fiction than in that of poetry. His style and verse, with some exceptions, are of the old school. His aims are those of the preacher and the photographic satirist, not those of the makers of romance. Hence his vogue and its long eclipse. Burke launched him and Johnson greeted him; he was thinking in their own spirit; he chronicled realities of their own time in a cadence which they knew and sanctioned; he tacked a homespun moral to a concrete anecdote in a familiar rhyme which disconcerted nobody. If he wrote to show up Goldsmith's idyllic picture of Auburn he did so only in a modification of that classical style and rhetoric, of which Goldsmith had used another modification. Later, the arch-reviewers Jeffrey and Gifford, who briefed themselves against Wordsworth and his fellows, poured their praise on Crabbe [for commentary by Jeffrey see excerpts dated 1808 and 1819], and indeed rated him more truly than a later age, if with some extravagance. Crabbe was priceless to them; he showed what could be done in the old poetic manner which they officially upheld, as distinct from the new poetic manner which they were vainly committed to obstructing. But their praises perished with their rule, to the detriment of Crabbe's glory, which dwindled, although Scott honoured him, and Byron, in a famous line, spoke to his "sternness" and veracity [see poem dated 1809]. Wordsworth's appreciation is of note, being unwittingly a tribute to the "classical" school which he detested [see letter dated 1834]. Crabbe's works, he said, "will last, from their combined merits as Poetry and Truth, full as long as anything that has been expressed in verse since they first made their appearance." He especially admired the sketch of the poorhouse in **The Village,** no doubt for its "truth"; but the "poetry," which is in the minute style of Pope when Pope drew the deathbed of Zimri Duke of Buckingham, Wordsworth might at best have been expected to tolerate—

> Theirs is yon House that holds the parish poor,
> Whose walls of mud scarce bear the broken door;
> There, where the putrid vapours, flagging, play,
> And the dull wheel hums doleful throught the day;—
> There children dwell who know no parents' care;
> Parents, who know no children's love, dwell there!
> Heart-broken matrons on their joyless bed,
> Forsaken wives, and mothers never wed. . . . .

As the more winged kind of poetry triumphed, this sort of excellence went out of vogue, and Crabbe with it, to be defended from time to time by connoisseurs like Edward FitzGerald [see excerpt dated 1882]. But the reason why Crabbe is little read lies deeper than the advent of Keats and Tennyson, or than his own undeniable gift for being lengthy and obvious. His scene is too like that of life as we know it really to be; and most of us, so far from rejoicing in that scene, go to poetry and fiction in order to forget it and to be charmed out of all necessity for reckoning with it. But there is a minority. Crabbe's stories, like those of the late George Gissing, must retain a small yet stubborn public, who do not mind being made to wince by the representation of life as they know it to be, even though the tones of the recital be hard, grim, and didactic. The chronicles of Aldborough at the close of the eighteenth century, and of New Grub Street at the end of the nineteenth, do they not endure like hammered ironwork? Why should they be pleasant? (pp. 78-9)

The rare sallies of Crabbe into romantic verse are remarkable. They are not in the fashion of "Marmion" or "Lara," but in that of the *Lyrical Ballads,* whose occasional influence upon him is manifest though never a vowed. **"Sir Eustace Grey,"** **"The World of Dreams,"** and **"The Hall of Justice,"** none of them printed earlier than 1805, are in fact "lyrical ballads," not novelettes in heroic couplet. The author has read Coleridge and Wordsworth, but rises to a high, nervous, passionate note of his own, which, had it failed and flagged less often, would have raised him nearer to their province. One example may serve. **"Sir Eustace Grey,"** who is in a madhouse, after telling, in a sane and dispiriting style enough, the story of his wife's elopement, suddenly startles us by reciting how the "ill-favoured Ones," the demons of his delirium, bore his dispossessed spirit along sea and land, through fen and over precipice, and by the salt scents of the foreshore. Some of the stanzas are the finests in this peculiar orders between "The Ancient Mariner" and "Ravelston"—

> At length a moment's sleep stole on,—
> Again came my commission'd foes;
> Again through sea and land we're gone,
> No peace, no respite, no response:
> Above the dark broad sea we rose,
> We ran through bleak and frozen land;
> I had no strength their strength t' oppose,
> An infant in a giant's hand.
> They placed me where those streamers play,
> Those nimble beams of brilliant light;
> It would the stoutest heart dismay,
> To see, to feel, that dreadful sight:
> So swift, so pure, so cold, so bright,
> They pierced my frame with icy wound;
> And, all that half-year's polar night,
> Those dancing streamers wrapp'd me round.

Here then, in a way quite foreign to his habit, and somewhat in the way of Coleridge, Crabbe lets himself go. But the regular tissue of his tales is quite different, as a chance passage from **"The Sisters"** shows—

> Jane laugh'd at all their visits and parade,
> And call'd it friendship in a hot-house made;
> A style of friendship suited to his taste,
> Brought on and ripen'd, like his grapes, in haste;
> She saw the wants that wealth in vain would hide,
> And all the tricks and littleness of pride:
> On all the wealth would creep the vulgar stain,
> And grandeur strove to look itself in vain.

The contrast shows in what opposite fashion romance and realism work when a tale has to be told. The romantic imagination of Coleridge or Keats, or of Crabbe in these few pieces, evolves itself in a series of liberating touches. It is like a new butterfly or young bird which begins with weak gentle flights, but goes further and higher every moment, and at last is out of sight of the ground where it could only crawl or struggle one way. We are left with the sense of freedom and release, and, even if the subject be painful or tragic, of expansion and joy. We are bound by no laws but those of beauty and coherence and fidelity to the spirit of the dream, and the effect may be won by the intimation of limitless space and movement—

> And all that half-year's polar night
> Those dancing streamers wrapp'd me round.

But this is not the normal way of the imagination in writers like Crabbe. *They* are bound to the fatalities of this earth, to the chainwork of real cause and effect, to expressiveness and not to beauty. Their fancy works by exclusion, not by expansion. They shut one door upon charm, and another upon freedom. Their scenery is hueless and exact—

> The few dull flowers that o'er the place are spread
> Partake the nature of their fenny bed;
> Here on its wiry stem, in rigid bloom,
> Grows the salt lavender that lacks perfume;
> Here the dwarf sallows creep, the septfoil harsh,
> And the soft slimy mallow of the marsh.

This is a tolerable allegory of the garden of Crabbe's own fancy. He relates his passages of the human comedy in much the same tone. He enjoys tracing frustrate lives and the slow degeneration of the soul. He notes the outward obstructions and inward faintings of ordinary men or women, who at last appear to us, in Hamlet's phrase, either as *lapsed in time and passion,* like half the persons over fifty whom we encounter, or as winning, at the utmost, some such tempered grey happiness or relative success as fall to the lot of the other half. Most of his tales are of this complexion; they are such as we hear every day, and they leave in the memory that sediment of regret without surprise which of all feelings is the least accessible and the most exasperating to youth. For youth, or for a young forward-looking epoch—for his own epoch—Crabbe did not write. In 1820, he had become a stranger, save in his rarer moods, and a chance survivor; and that is why, beside Byron or Coleridge, he and his style are so instructive. Both orders of style are good, and art and thought are incomplete without them both. Indeed, they are apt to recur in a curious rhythm, one overlapping the other, and of this rhythm a great deal of inventive literature is made up; as we see by confronting the first part of the *Romance of the Rose* with the second, or *The Winter's Tale* with *The Alchemist.* We have to denote these contrasting modes of art by such rough terms as romantic and realistic. But, while both are good, the after-world, which is always young and not middle-aged, finds a nobler nourishment in the freer and happier kind of creation; which is therefore safe, and needs no rescuing; while criticism has always to be rescuing the other kind, of which Crabbe is a master, and to be pleading that this also is of the kingdom.

Crabbe's art has a definite progress of its own. He forced his way out of the empty, rancid invective of the school of Churchill. He advanced from the general to the concrete, from tirades like *Inebriety,* to descriptions like those of *The Village.* But in *The Village* he is trying to depict real life in half-real language. The Poor and the Great, Sloth and Danger, the finny tribe, the deluded fair, and the stout churl with his teeming mate, are still queerly obtrusive amidst the literal, thudding diction which Crabbe was to retain and shape so aptly. But he can already draw a scene or a silhouette; and the excellent sketch of his hunting parson, who fights shy of pauper deathbeds, is possibly provoked by Goldsmith's idyl. But he cannot yet model a portrait, or invent a situation, or tell a story; and at this point he pauses for twenty-four years, improving his art in silence, curbing the desire to publish, burnishing and rejecting. When he produced **"The Parish Register"** and *The Borough,* it was plain that he had not altered but only bettered his methods, and that he was still doing an eighteenth century thing in an eighteenth century way. The tune was finer, but it was played on the old instrument. His portraits are now those of a master, but they are of the type already made classical by Dryden and Pope; only the social scene is changed, and people are called by their names. Instead of Shimei and Chloe, Jacob Holmes and Peter Grimes. In the preface to the *Tales,* Crabbe appeals formally to the shades of his poetic ancestors to warrant this method—the "fair representation of existing character"—and expresses his willingness "to find some comfort in his expulsion from the rank and society of Poets, by reflecting that men much his superiors are likewise cut out." But he can now exhibit a situation and a scene, as well as draw a "character." He has begun to find his ultimate and characteristic form of the Tale, which is sometimes a mere anecdote, but in its fullest development is a foreshortened and dramatic life-history. He has even gone further, and tried to brace his tales together into a larger unity by some "associating circumstance," after the manner of Chaucer and Boccaccio. But this last effort he found a strain. **"The Parish Register"** is artificially assorted under births, marriages, and deaths; and in *The Borough* the wish to be doggedly exhaustive hurts the performance. It is a survey of Aldborough, done from memory, with trades, clubs, alms-houses, inns, and elections all painfully gazetted. He describes jelly-fish, and the "various tribes and species of marine vermes," in verse which Gifford hailed as "pleasing and *éveillé,*" but which is as glossy and repugnant as Erasmus Darwin's. Also he discourses on preparatory schools, and on the "mode of paying the borough minister." For these misdeeds his excuse is their "variety"; yet it is only a variety of tedium. Crabbe has dropped the tedium of rhetoric, only to inflict the tedium of fact. But in both poems there are wonderful acrid landscapes, and little tragic biographies, and raking satire as of old, and of dramatic action and suspense not a little. The easy, lazy, popular vicar is sketched with a distant, half-scornful good-temper, if not very grammatically—

> Mothers approved a safe contented guest,
> And daughters one who backed each small request:
> In him his flock found nothing to condemn;
> Him sectaries liked—he never troubled them;
> No trifles failed his yielding mind to please,
> And all his passions sunk in early ease;
> Nor one so old has left this world of sin
> More like the being that he enter'd in.

But when Crabbe comes to the chronicle of **"Peter Grimes,"** the murderer of his prentices, or of Clelia the coquette, who ends her days in the alms-house, he is on his final ground; and his power of working out the slow fatal mutations of ordinary character approves him as by far the greatest novelist between Sterne and Scott. He favours the old scheme of tragedy, which Dante describes as beginning cheerfully, while its ending is *foetida et horribilis.* He enjoys his own vigour and rancour in developing such a scheme. He likes, too, the form of the "Progress," as practised by Hogarth or Lillo in the preceding age. The "Progress" is a tragical tract in artistic form, showing in definite stages the punishment, or self-punishment, of a vice or a foible. The decline of Clelia is demonstrated at halting-points of ten years, which affect us like a Hogarthian series. No one can sum them up more aptly than Jeffrey, whose notes on Crabbe are amongst the best things that he did, and are almost amongst the best things ever written on Crabbe—

> She began life as a sprightly, talking, flirting girl,
> who passed for a wit and a beauty in the half-bred
> circle of the *Borough,* and who, in laying herself out

to entrap a youth of distinction, unfortunately fell a victim to his superior art, and forfeited her place in society. She then became the smart mistress of a dashing attorney—then tried to teach a school—lived as the favourite of an innkeeper—let lodgings—wrote novels—set up a toyshop—and, finally, was admitted into the Alms-house. There is nothing very interesting, perhaps, in such a story; but the details of it show the wonderful accuracy of the author's observation of character.

In his studies of crime, of which Crabbe is a keen observer, this curious habit of marking out uniform stages or milestones of life is carried into detail. It is unlike the free, continuous style of Balzac or the great dramatists, but it is very lucid. Jachin, the parish clerk, who is nervous at first, but soons robs the offertory regularly, seems to slip one stair downward to Avernus with each succeeding couplet—

> But custom sooth'd him-ere a single year
> All this was done without restraint or fear:
> Cool and collected, easy and composed,
> He was correct till all the service closed;
> Then to his home, without a groan or sigh,
> Gravely he went, and laid his treasure by.

Jachin is found out but not prosecuted; he is dismissed, and wastes in a remorse of which all the phases are sharply marked; and the mud-bank and the marsh-dyke are the right background for "the strong yearnings of a ruin'd mind." Crabbe here dwells with gusto upon the successful onset of mean temptation; in **"Peter Grimes"** he is engrossed with the gradual breakdown of the brain under the delirium of fruitless repentance. The spirits of the slaughtered boys rise up before Grimes, each at the fatal spot in the river. They call him with "weak, sad voices," and amidst them stands his own father, whom he had one day struck down though not actually knifed:—

> He cried for mercy, which I kindly gave,
> But he has no compassion in his grave.

This couplet, singled out by Ruskin, shows a higher reach of Crabbe's art than his usual symmetrical analysis. Now and then, not often, he has the Jacobean power of tragic thrust. (pp. 80-4)

Such are a few of Crabbe's narratives. Their variety, which cannot further be illustrated here, is somewhat concealed by the style in which they are told. The history of that style, which is not so monotonous as it seems at first, is straightforward enough. Allowing for a few excursions, he remained throughout "classical" in his form. He slowly escaped from the fetters of the classical verbiage. He never, indeed, quite escaped, but then he never had been quite enslaved. From the first he has a habit of swinging his moralist's ferule vaguely in the air, and then suddenly letting it whistle down on a concrete pair of shoulders—

> Bland adulation! other pleasures pall
> On the sick taste, and transient are they all;
> But this one sweet has such enchanting power,
> The more we take, the faster we devour:
> Nauseous to those who must the dose apply,
> And most disgusting to the standersby.

This might have been written by anybody of Crabbe's generation, but his peculiar, clumsy, efficient stroke is heard at once—

> Yet in all companies will Laughton feed,

Nor care how grossly men perform the deed.

It was not, however, for his acres of declamation that Crabbe was mocked in *Rejected Addresses,* but for the dead prosaic minuteness, of which there are acres also [see poem by James Smith dated 1812]. It is needless to quote James or Horace Smith, for Crabbe is often his own parodist. He was always ready to write "meanly," in a kind of rhyming prose,—if the phrase is allowable,—in which not the prose but the rhyme seems to be the intruder. He could write—

> Mamma look'd on with thoughts to these allied;
> She felt the pleasure of reflected pride;

or even thus—

> But how will Bloomer act
> When he becomes acquainted with the fact?

Much of the meanness of such passages is due to their thick and lumbering rhymes. *Act, fact; all, scrawl; aunt, grant; flood, mud!* The whole weight of a couplet lies upon its rhymes, and Crabbe does not mind making the worst of them. In defence of such practices, and of his general fen-like level, he might have said that his business was to reproduce the flat encumbered talk of common folk, and that to have quitted verse for prose would have been to resign half his power. Such a plea does not make the passages more lively. But after all he is an artist. FitzGerald and other admirers, distressed by his inequalities, have tried to make anthologies. But his work that is worth keeping would fill a big anthology, and it is better to take him wholesale. Without essentially altering his narrative style, he cleared and purged it. He stretched and adjusted the familiar couplet with singular address to his chosen purpose, nor has it ever again been used so well for that purpose. Our bourgeois fiction has been written in prose instead, not wholly to its gain. It is not clear that *Middlemarch,* cast into form like his, would have had a better chance of permanence. The narratives in blank verse of *The Excursion* are more liable to be dull than Crabbe's heroics, to which dialogue and monologue are much better fitted. The motion is sometimes that of a springless cart, but the ground is covered quicker than might be feared. After a time the sensation is pleasant, and we can watch the life of the roadside and the inn-parlour.

The hardest task of Crabbe was to manage the speeches of his prosaic *dramatis personæ* in a medium so full of rhetorical associations. We can trace the increase of his skill. In *The Village* he resembles a professional letter-writer who puts fine language into the mouths of the inarticulate. His old shepherd, for example, perorates most disastrously, like somebody in Dryden's heroic plays—

> I, like yon wither'd leaf, remain behind,
> Nipt by the frost, and shivering in the wind;
> There it abides till younger buds come on;
> As I, now all my fellow-swains are gone.
> Then, from the rising generation thrust,
> It falls, like me, unnoticed in the dust.

After a while this kind of talk gives way to another one, much more subtly modulated to the tones of actual prosaic speech, and yet not out of place in rhyme. In the scathing story of **"The Brothers,"** Isaac, the elder, under the pressure of a stingy wife, edges the younger one, an old sailor who is down in the world, into the worst room of the house, and finally begs him to "go upon the loft." The effect is aided by the poet's great care in the detail of punctuation and printing.

> 'Ah, brother Isaac!— What! I'm in the way!'
> 'No, on my credit, look ye, No! but I
> Am fond of peace, and my repose must buy
> On any terms—in short, we must comply:
> My spouse had money—she must have her will—
> Ah! Brother—marriage is a bitter pill!'
> George tried the lady—'Sister, I offend.'
> 'Me?' she replied—'Oh no! you may depend
> On my regard—but watch your Brother's way,
> Whom I, like you, must study and obey.'

Crabbe's versification likewise grew in freedom, though he remained faithful to his distich. In his handling of it, he remembers the finish and balance of Pope, but aspires to the nobler sweep of Dryden, freely using the triple rhymes and alexandrines. His lines are more continuous than Pope's, and in their overrunning and interlacing come to resemble what Johnson, speaking of "The Hind and Panther," calls Dryden's "deliberate and ultimate scheme" of verse. Only, Crabbe goes further still, since he has to forge a rhythm that accords with natural domestic talk. He is therefore the last great writer of the couplet in its "classical" form. Its later used by Keats and William Morris for romantic narrative are coloured by memories of the Jacobeans and of Chaucer. Nothing could be more skillful technically, or better done, than some lines from **"Procrastination."** Dinah has waited many years for her absent lover Rupert, but has become meanwhile rich, avaricious, and sanctimonious. He returns, poor as he went, to claim her, and she rebuffs him.

> She ceased;—with steady glance, as if to see
> The very root of this hypocrisy,—
> He her small fingers moulded in his hard
> And bronzed broad hand; then told her his regard,
> His best respect were gone, but love had still
> Hold in his heart, and govern'd yet the will—
> Or he would curse her:—saying this, he threw
> The hand in scorn away, and bade adieu
> To every lingering hope, with every care in view:

A plain style, but inimitable; the verse follows every wave of the wanderer's disgust and chagrin. Now and then, in higher mood, Crabbe escapes still more thoroughly from the bonds of his metrical tradition; and we could almost believe that some lines he wrote in 1817 or 1818 were shaped after reading Keats, whose *Endymion* came out in the spring of the latter year.

> He chose his native village, and the hill
> He climb'd a boy had its attraction still;
> With that small brook beneath, where he would stand
> And scooping fill the hollow of his hand
> To quench th' impatient thirst—then stop awhile
> To see the sun upon the waters smile,
> In that sweet weariness, when, long denied,
> We drink and view the fountain that supplied
> The sparkling bliss, and feel, if not express,
> Our perfect ease in that sweet weariness.

Crabbe is so little read, that to quote him is not the same sort of impertinence as quoting Byron or Shelley. He is one of the poets whose day has declined and who is spoken of with distant respect. But his day may ripen again "into a steady morning." He did not always see why poetry should be pleasant; but he did want poetry to be a means of representing life, and his verse beats into us the impression of life and of his own faithful and brooding spirit. (pp. 88-90)

*Oliver Elton, "Crabbe," in* Blackwood's Magazine,

*Vol. CLXXXV, No. MCXIX, January, 1909, pp. 78-90.*

### EZRA POUND (essay date 1917)

[*An American poet, translator, essayist, and critic, Pound was "the principal inventor of modern poetry," according to Archibald MacLeish. He is chiefly renowned for his poetic masterpiece, the* Cantos, *which he revised and enlarged throughout much of his life. These poems are noted for their lyrical intensity, metrical experimentation, literary allusions, varied subject matter and verse forms, and incorporation of phrases from foreign languages. History and politics also greatly interested Pound, and many of his poems and critical writings reflect his attempt to synthesize his aesthetic vision with his political, economic, and cultural ideals. In the following excerpt from a 1917 essay, Pound provides a general assessment of Crabbe's poetry, defending his unequivocally realistic outlook.*]

'Since the death of Laurence Sterne or thereabouts, there has been neither in England nor America any sufficient sense of the value of realism in literature, of the value of writing words that conform precisley with fact, of free speech without evasions and circumlocutions.'

I had forgotten, when I wrote this, the Rev. Crabbe, LL.B.

Think of the slobber that Wordsworth would have made over the illegitimate infant whom Crabbe dismisses with: *'There smiles your Bride, there sprawls your new-born Son.'* (p. 276)

The worst that should be said of Crabbe is that he still clings to a few of Pope's tricks, and that he is not utterly free from the habit of moralizing. What is, in actuality, usually said of him is that he is 'unpoetic', or, patronizingly, 'that you can't call this really great poetry.'

Pope is sometimes an excellent writer, Crabbe is never absolute slush, nonsense or bombast. That admission should satisfy the multitudinous reader, but it will not.

If the nineteenth century had built itself on Crabbe? Ah, if! But no; they wanted confections.

Crabbe has no variety of metric, but he shows no inconsiderable skill in the use of his one habitual metre, to save the same from monotony.

I admit that he makes vague generalities about 'Vice', 'Villainy and Crime', etc., but these paragraphs are hardly more than short cuts between one passage of poetry and another.

He does not bore you, he does not disgust you, he does not bring on that feeling of nausea which we have when we realize that we are listening to an idiot who occasionally makes beautiful (or ornamental) verses.

Browning at his best went on with Crabbe's method. He expressed an adoration of Shelley, and he might have learned more from Crabbe, but he was nevertheless the soundest of all the Victorians. Crabbe will perhaps keep better than Browning, he will have a savour of freshness; of course his is *not* 'the greater poet' of the two, but then he gives us such sound satisfaction in his best moments. And those moments are precisely the moments when he draws his ***Borough*** with the greatest exactness, and when he refrains from commenting. They are the moments 'when he lets himself go', when he is neither 'The Rev.' nor the 'LL.B.' but just good, sensible Crabbe, as at the end of **"Inns"**, or reporting conversations in **"Amusements"**, **"Blaney"**, **"Clelia"**, and the people re-

membered by **"Benbow"**. If Englishmen had known how to select the best out of Crabbe they would have less need of consulting French stylists. Et pourtant—

> Then liv'd the good Squire Asquill-what a change
> Has Death and Fashion shown us at the Grange?
> He bravely thought it best became his rank,
> That all his Tennants and his Tradesmen drank;
>
> He was delighted from his favourite Room
> To see them 'cross the Park go daily home,
> Praising aloud the Liquor and the Host,
> And striving who should venerate him most
>
> . . . . .
>
> Along his valleys in the Evening-Hours
> The Borough Damsels stray'd to gather Flowers
> Or by the Brakes and Brushwood of the Park
> To take their pleasant rambles in the dark.
>
> Some Prudes, of rigid kind, forbore to call
> On the kind Females—Favourites at the Hall;
> But better natures saw, with much delight,
> The different orders of mankind unite;
> 'Twas schooling Pride to see the Footman wait,
> Smile on his sister and receive her plate.

Or Sir Denys admitting Clelia to the alms-house—

> 'With all her faults,' he said, 'the woman knew
> How to distinguish—had a manner too;
> And, as they say, she is allied to some
> In decent station—let the creature come.

Oh, well! Byron enjoyed him. And the people liked Byron. They liked him for being 'romantic'. They adored Mrs Hemans. And some day when Arthur's tomb is no longer an object for metrical research, and when the Albert Memorial is no longer regilded, Crabbe's people will still remain vivid. People will read Miss Austen because of her knowledge of the human heart, and not solely for her refinement.

His, Crabbe's, realism is not the hurried realism of ignorance, he describes an inn called 'The Boar'; in his day there was no 'Maison Tellier' to serve for a paradigm:

> There dwells a kind old aunt, and there you'll see
> Some kind young nieces in her company:
>
> . . . . .
>
> What though it may some cool observers strike,
> That such fair sisters should be so unlike;
> And still another and another comes,
> And at the Matron's table smiles and blooms;
>
> . . . . .
>
> A pious friend who with the ancient Dame
> At sober cribbage takes an Evening-Game;
> His cup beside him, through their play he quaffs
>
> . . . . .
>
> Or growing serious to the Text resorts,
> And from the Sunday-Sermon makes reports, . . .
>
> (pp. 277-79)

*Ezra Pound, "The Rev. G. Crabbe, LL.B.," in his* Literary Essays of Ezra Pound, *edited by T. S. Eliot, New Directions Publishing Corporation, 1968, pp. 276-79.*

### F. R. LEAVIS  (essay date 1936)

[*An influential English critic and teacher, Leavis articulated his views in his lectures, in his many critical works, and in* Scrutiny, *a quarterly that he cofounded and edited from 1932 to 1953. His methodology combines close textual analysis, predominantly moral and social concerns, and emphasis on the development of "the individual sensibility." Leavis believed that the artist should strive to eliminate "ego-centered distortion and all impure motives" in order to be able to explore the proper place of persons in society. Although Leavis's advocacy of a cultural elite and the occasional vagueness of his moral assumptions were sometimes criticized, his writings remain an important, if controversial, force in literary criticism. In the following excerpt from a study of aesthetic developments in English poetry from the seventeenth century to the Romantic period, Leavis argues that the Augustan character of Crabbe's verse complements his abbreviated narrative form.*]

It is unfortunate that Crabbe should be left to students of literature, and that he should in the student's memoranda be represented mainly by the titles of early works. **The Village,** we know, is to be compared (or contrasted) with Goldsmith's poem, and **The Borough** and **"The Parish Register"** illustrate the growing interest in realism and the poor. Of the later work we know that we may find in it traces of Romantic influence. Actually, it is in the later work, the Tales of the various collections, that he is (or ought to be—for who reads him?) a living classic, because it is in this work that he develops to the full his peculiarly eighteenth-century strength. His strength is that of a novelist and of an eighteenth-century poet who is positively in sympathy with the Augustan tradition, and it is one strength. The Augustan form, as he adapts it, is perfectly suited to his matter and to his outlook—matter and outlook that have close affinities with Jane Austen's, though he has a range and a generous masculine strength that bring out by contrast her spinsterly limitations (we remember D. H. Lawrence's excessively unsympathetic allusions to her).

Not that Crabbe produced any work of art of the order of her novels: his art is that of the short-story writer, and of this he is a master. To this art the verse-form, favouring concentration and point, lends itself peculiarly well. 'Pope in worsted stockings' is a description that is far from having the felicity commonly attributed to it, and the parody in *Rejected Addresses* conveys a false impression [see poem by James Smith dated 1812]. Crabbe handles the couplet in his own way, adapting it to an admirable use of dialogue:

> "I must be loved," said Sybil; "I must see
> The man in terrors who aspires to me;
> At my forbidding frown, his heart must ache,
> His tongue must falter, and his frame must shake:
> And if I grant him at my feet to kneel,
> What trembling, fearful pleasure must he feel;
> Nay, such the raptures that my smiles inspire,
> That reason's self must for a time retire."
> "Alas! for good Josiah," said the dame,
> "These wicked thoughts would fill his soul with shame;
> He kneel and tremble at a thing of dust!
> He cannot, child":—the child replied, "He must."

That is not clumsy or provincial Pope, nor does the Augustan form represent an awkward elegance clothing an incongruous matter. It represents, one might say, 'reason's self,' a 'reason' the authority of which Crabbe's matter recognizes as naturally as Sybil recognizes it in the passage quoted. And the last line illustrates the kind of point to which 'wit' in Crabbe so appropriately runs.

*Muston Church, where Crabbe was rector for many years after 1805.*

What we recognize locally as wit is, as a matter of fact, the art of the short story. . . . (pp. 124-26)

This is the end of **"Procrastination"** a tale of slow moral decay and of disillusionment, theme and effect being such as are commonly sought by modern practitioners of the 'art of the short-story':

> But Dinah moves—she had observed before
> The pensive Rupert at an humble door:
> Some thoughts of pity raised by his distress,
> Some feeling touch of ancient tenderness;
> Religion, duty urged the maid to speak
> In terms of kindness to a man so weak:
> But pride forbad, and to return would prove
> She felt the shame of his neglected love;
> Nor wrapp'd in silence could she pass, afraid
> Each eye should see her, and each heart upbraid;
> One way remain'd—the way the Levite took,
> Who without mercy could on misery look;
> (A way perceived by craft, approved by pride),
> She cross'd, and pass'd him on the other side.

But since the unit of his art is truly the tale, the art cannot be fairly represented by quotations. It is with assertion that Crabbe must be left: the assertion (easily tested—see for example **"The Lover's Journey"**) that in the use of description, of nature and the environment generally, for emotional purposes he surpasses any Romantic.

Crabbe, however, was hardly at the fine point of consciousness in his time. His sensibility belongs to an order that those who were most alive to the age—who had the most sensitive antennae—had ceased to find sympathetic. For them the work of Wordsworth and Coleridge provided the impulse and showed the way to congenial idioms and forms. (pp. 127-28)

*F. R. Leavis, "The Augustan Tradition," in his* Re-valuation: Tradition and Development in English Poetry, *Chatto & Windus, 1936, pp. 101-29.*

## T. S. ELIOT (essay date 1946)

[*Eliot, an American-born English poet, essayist, and critic, is regarded as one of the most influential literary figures of the first half of the twentieth century. As a poet, he is closely identified with many of the qualities denoted by the term Modernism, including experimentation, formal complexity, artistic and intellectual eclecticism, and a classical sense of distance from one's artistic creation. As a critic, Eliot's rejection of extratextual criteria and emphasis on imagery, symbolism, and meaning helped to establish the theories of New Criticism. Eliot, who converted to the Anglican Church in 1928, also stressed the importance of tradition, religion, and morality in literature. In the following excerpt, Eliot assesses Crabbe's stature as a minor poet, upholding the inherent virtues of his realistic style.*]

When we talk about Poetry, with a capital P, we are apt to think only of the more intense emotion or the more magical phrase: but there are a great many casements in poetry which are not magic, and which do not open on the foam of perilous seas, but are perfectly good windows for all that. I think that the Revd. George Crabbe was a very good poet, but you do not go to him for magic: if you like realistic accounts of village life in Suffolk a hundred and twenty years ago, in verse so well written that it convinces you that the same thing could not be said in prose, you will like Crabbe. Crabbe is a poet who has to be read in large chunks, if at all; so if you find him dull you must just glance and pass by. But it is worth while to know of his existence, in case he might be to your liking, and also because that will tell you something about the people who do like him. (p. 14)

*T. S. Eliot, "What Is Minor Poetry?" in* The Sewanee Review, *Vol. LIV, No. 1, January-March, 1946, pp. 1-18.*

## HERBERT J. C. GRIERSON AND J. C. SMITH (essay date 1947)

[*In the following excerpt, Grierson and Smith defend Crabbe's poetry against the negative criticism of nineteenth-century reviewers, particularly William Hazlitt and George Saintsbury (for commentary by Hazlitt and Sainstbury on Crabbe, see excerpts dated 1825 and 1889).*]

Writing in 1825, Hazlitt could describe Crabbe as "one of the most popular and admired of all living authors". Saintsbury, writing some sixty or more years later (1889) [see excerpt above], contrasts the popularity which Hazlitt records, a popularity that included such names among his admirers as Scott, Lockhart, Byron, Jeffrey, Wilson, with the fact of "the almost total forgetfulness of his works"; and Canon Ainger in 1903 endorses Saintsbury's pronouncement: "As Crabbe is practically unknown to the readers of the present day, **"Sir Eustace Gray"** will be hardly even a name to them".

It has, however, been the fate of more than one poet, as of some musicians, to suffer a long period of neglect after greater or less contemporary recognition. What was known of Donne's poetry between Dryden and Coleridge? The appeal that a poet makes will depend largely on the temper of the time, and there are not wanting signs that Crabbe has still readers and that in an increasing number. It would be strange indeed if the present reaction from the romantics and taste for realism both in poetry and fiction should not revive an interest in Crabbe's poetry. It is more important to define as clearly as possible the character of Crabbe's realism, his attitude towards his own stories.

Where Hazlitt is unjust to Crabbe is in declaring that there are in the poet's survey of life no flowers of hope or love or joy [see excerpt dated 1825]. Not so great a poet as the author of *Ecclesiastes,* his philosophy is much the same, supplemented by an at least intellectual acceptance of a Christian doctrine of immortality. There is none of Hardy's incessant arraignments of Providence, nothing like "the President of the Immortals had finished his sport with Tess". Crabbe was not like Cowper a Calvinist, a believer in the doctrines of predestination, election, conversion, salvation by the grace of God and that alone, which is the theme of the poem *Truth* in Cowper's first volume. What Crabbe thought of these doctrines in the abstract is not clear. He leaned for his own faith on the historical rather than the theological. What he did dislike was the manner in which the doctrine of conversion and grace seemed to him to work in practice, as he shows in the story of Abel Keene in **The Borough.** For Cowper the sinner,

> The worn-out nuisance of the public streets,

was in a happier condition for grace to work upon than the moral man, and this is what the "good man" tells Abel:

> "Once thou wert simply honest, just and pure,
> Whole as thou thoughtst, and never wished a cure:
> Now thou hast plung'd in folly, shame, disgrace;
> Now thou'rt an object meet for healing grace;
> No merit thine, no virtue, hope, belief,
> Nothing hast thou but misery, sin and grief,
> The best, the only titles of relief."
>
> "What must I do," I said, "my soul to free?"
> "Do nothing, man; it will be done for thee."
> "But must I not, my reverend guide, believe?"
> "If thou art call'd, thou wilt the faith receive."

The result of such waiting was for Abel—as for Cowper incidentally—despair. In belief as in other things, Crabbe thinks men must use their will, doing the best they can. Unbelief is most often the consequence of shallow vanity, and he gives some examples, as of the Gentleman Farmer. The nearest Crabbe comes to any comment on the course of events is in the closing lines in the story of Ruth:

> Well had it still remain'd a world unseen.

In the last resort, however, it is not a poet's choice of subject, his being a realist or a romantic, that makes him a poet, but the manner in which he treats his subject, the charm which he lends to it by depth of feeling, beauty of language, music of verse. The most serious charges which have been brought against Crabbe are that his treatment is didactic rather than poetic, and that his verse is wanting in music.

But to say that Crabbe is didactic is simply to say that he was an eighteenth-century poet, for every poet of that century thought it his duty to be didactic. Yet the effect of a tale by Crabbe is not in the end didactic. It is not the lesson, the warning, that one remembers, but the inevitability of what has been related. Such is human nature; so man will act and so in consequence he will suffer; or such are men's hopes, and so are they too often disappointed. Virtue itself is no guarantee of happiness. "Consider the work of God, for who can make that straight which he has made crooked? . . . there is a righteous man that perishes in his righteousness, and there is a wicked man that prolongeth his life in evil-doing." That is the burden of the *Book of Job,* of Johnson's *Rasselas* and *Vanity of Human Wishes,* and it is the burden of Crabbe's stories, told dramatically in his dry yet for that reason effective manner, the story left to speak for itself. But for Crabbe, as for the author of *Ecclesiastes,* there are good things in life—love, affection, kindness, pity, the beauty of Nature, wisdom. Nor have all his tales a didactic intention. What lesson is taught by **"The Parting Hour?"** Pity is the dominant mood in all Crabbe's most serious pictures of life from **The Village** onwards. "What made Crabbe a new force in English poetry", Canon Ainger justly wrote, "was that in his verse Pity appears, after a long oblivion, as the true antidote to sentimentalism . . . if Crabbe is our first great realist he uses his realism in the cause of a true humanity, *facit indignatio versus.*"

By the complaint that Crabbe does not envisage his subject poetically, Saintsbury had doubtless in view, as well as the didactic tone, the matter-of-fact style in which he describes his scenes, characters, and incidents, and the occasional flatness of his diction and verse. Wordsworth's criticism, when he invites comparison with Crabbe, of his own tales of peasant's life and suffering in *The Excursion* is Saintsbury's but with a difference. Crabbe does not invest, as Wordsworth endeavours to do, his story with an atmosphere which suggests that there is more than pathos in the tale, that there is something that helps us to transcend or sublimate the sadness, to discover:

> Sorrow that is not sorrow but delight,
> And miserable love that is not pain
> To hear of, for the glory that redounds
> Therefrom to human kind and what we are.

But the sheer truthfulness of Crabbe's tales has a power which any attempt to interpret or adorn might easily mar. Is there nothing of the miserable love that is not pain to hear of in **"The Parting Hour"** or **"Ruth?"** Crabbe had passed through the bitter experiences of life as Wordsworth had not. For his purpose the matter-of-fact style,—"poetry without an atmosphere", as he himself calls it—even the occasional descents—and he had not so far to descend as Milton and Wordsworth—are better suited than a more decorative style, a more swelling verse. But it is the verse on which Saintsbury based his final summing-up against Crabbe, the want of variety in his music; and this is not to be altogether denied. Yet his style and verse are the fitting garb of his feeling and themes, nor is his style always flat, his verse always monotonous. When deeply moved, as in the account of the condemned man's last night or the story of Ruth, there is both moving description and adequate rhythm. Where he is least successful is in the satirical, half-humorous tales, where he wants the art of Chaucer, the more sinuous movement of his verse. (pp. 259-62)

> *Herbert J. C. Grierson and J. C. Smith, "Crabbe," in their* A Critical History of English Poetry, *second edition, 1947. Reprint by Chatto & Windus, 1965, pp. 246-62.*

## E. M. FORSTER    (lecture date 1948)

[*Forster was a prominent English novelist, critic, and essayist whose works reflect his liberal humanism. His most celebrated novel,* A Passage to India *(1924), is a complex examination of personal relationships amid the conflicts of the modern world. Although some of Forster's critical essays are considered naive in their literary assessments, his* Aspects of the Novel *(1927), a discussion of the techniques of novel writing, is regarded as a minor classic in literary criticism. In the following excerpt from a lecture given at the Aldeborough music festival in 1948, Forster discusses autobiographical elements and psychological and moral themes in "Peter Grimes."*]

Crabbe's antipathy to his birthplace was to play an essential part in the creation of **"Peter Grimes."** It was not a straight-forward antipathy. It was connected with a profound attraction. He might leave Aldeburgh with his body, but he never emigrated spiritually; here on the plane of creation was his home and he could not have found a better one. This Borough made him a poet, through it he understood Suffolk, and through East Anglia he approached England. He remains here, however far he seems to travel, whatever he says to the contrary. His best work describes the place directly—the *Village,* the **"Parish Register,"** the *Borough*—and its atmosphere follows him when he attempts other themes.

> The few dull flowers that o'er the place are spread
> Partake the nature of their fenny bed;
> Here on its wiry stem with rigid bloom
> Grows the salt lavender that lacks perfume;
> Here the dwarf sallows creep, the septfoil harsh
> And the soft slimy mallow of the marsh.
> Low on the ear the distant billows sound
> And just in view appears their stony bound
> No hedge nor tree conceals the glowing sun. . . .

Dull, harsh, stony, wiry, soft, slimy—what disobliging epithets, and yet he is in love with the scene. And the love becomes explicit in a prose footnote which he appends to the passage.

> Such is the vegetation of the fen when it is at a small distance from the ocean; and in this case, there arise from it effluvia strong and peculiar, half saline, half putrid, which would be considered by most people as offensive and by some as dangerous; but there are others to whom singularity of taste or association of ideas has rendered it agreeable and pleasant.

The sights and the sounds are not beautiful, the smells are putrid, yet through the singularity of his taste and the associations they bring to him he loves them and cannot help loving them. For he had the great good luck to belong to a particular part of England and to belong to it all his life.

This attraction for the Aldeburgh district, combined with that strong repulsion from it, is characteristic of Crabbe's uncomfortable mind. Outwardly he did well for himself, married money and ended up as a west country pluralist. Inwardly he remained uneasy, and out of that uneasiness came his most powerful poems. It is natural to remember Wordsworth in connection with him. They were contemporaries, and they had this in common, that they were regional and that their earliest impressions were the most durable. But there the resemblance between them ends. Wordsworth—his superior genius apart—had a power of harmonising his experiences which was denied to Crabbe. He could encircle them with the sky, he could overawe them with tremendous mountains. Crabbe remains down amongst them on the flat, amongst pebbles and weeds and mud and driftwood, and within ear-shot of a sea which is no divine ocean. Thus based, he is capable of considerable achievements, and the contradictory impulses possessing him generated **"Peter Grimes."**

We know how this sombre masterpiece originated. When Crabbe was trying to be a doctor he came across an old fisherman who had had a succession of apprentices from London and a sum of money with each. The apprentices tended to disappear and the fisherman was warned he would be charged with murder next time. That is the meagre material upon which a poet's imagination worked. According to Edward FitzGerald—who was a persistent student of Crabbe—the fisherman's name was Tom Brown. Anyhow, he is transformed into Peter Grimes.

The poem occurs in the series of *The Borough,* which was written for the most part away from Aldeburgh, and finished there in 1809. As a narrative, it is one of the best of the series, and it is prefaced by quotations from *Macbeth* and *Richard III* which fix the emotional atmosphere and warn us that the murdered apprentices will live again. It opens with a father-motive; like Crabbe himself, Peter Grimes hates his own father—a pious old fisherman who makes him go to church—and breaks away from him abusively, on one occasion striking him on the head and felling him. Murder is not done, but the wish to murder has been born.

> The father groan'd. "If thou art old," said he,
> "And hast a son, thou wilt remember me."

Peter was indeed to beget sons, though not in the flesh. For the present he gets drunk, and when his father passes away, indulges in maudlin grief. It is a prelude to the main tragedy.

Freed from control, the young fisherman proposes to enjoy life—"the life itself" he has called it exultantly—and gambles and drinks. But money is required for such joys, so he develops into a poacher and trespasser, a rustic Ishmael. Then come the sadistic lines:

> But no success could please his cruel soul
> He wish'd for one to trouble and control;
> He wanted some obedient boy to stand
> And bear the blow of his outrageous hand;
> And hoped to find in some propitious hour
> A feeling creature subject to his power,

and the first of the apprentices arrives, a product of the eighteenth-century workhouse system. Everyone knows he is being mishandled and starved, no one protects him,

> and some on hearing cries
> Said calmly "Grimes is at his exercise"—

The second apprentice follows, also with premium, and he too dies. Peter's explanation is that he was playing on the main mast at night, fell into the well where the catch was kept and hit his head. The jury exonerate him. The third apprentice is a delicate well-mannered child, who rouses the townsfolk to pity and charity and whom Peter dares not beat too hard. He disappears during a voyage at sea. Peter had his fish and wanted to sell it in the London market. They encountered a storm, the boat leaked, the boy fell ill and before Peter could make harbour both the fish and the boy had died. Such anyhow was Peter's account. But

> The pitying women raised a clamour round
> And weeping said "Thou hast thy prentice drown'd."

The mayor forbade him to hire any more apprentices (as in the opening of the opera) and none of his neighbours would help him, so henceforward he carried on his trade alone, and melancholy invades him.

Now begin the depths, and I would add the flats of the poem—using "flat" in no derogatory sense, but to indicate the glassy or muddy surface upon which the action now proceeds and through which at any moment something unexpected may emerge. Nothing is more remarkable, in the best work of Crabbe, than the absence of elevation. As a preacher, he may lift up his eyes to the hills. As a poet he was fascinated by

> The bounding marsh-bank and the blighted tree;
> The water only, when the tides were high,
> When low, the mud half-cover'd and half dry;
> The sun-burnt tar that blisters on the planks,
> And bank-side stakes in their uneven ranks;
> Heaps of entangled weeds that slowly float,
> As the tide rolls by the impeded boat.

That is what attracts him—flatness—and upon it the most tragic of his poems deploys. The idea of regeneration, so congenial to Wordsworth and the Lake District, does not appeal to this son of the estuary. Those who sin on the lines of Peter Grimes must sink and sink—incapable ever of remorse, though not of fear, incapable of realising the sun except as a blistering heat, and incapable of observing the stars.

> When tides were neap, and, in the sultry day,
> Through the tall bounding mud banks made their way,
> There anchoring, Peter chose from man to hide,
> There hang his head . . .
> Here dull and hopeless he'd lie down and trace
> How sidelong crabs had scrawl'd their crooked race
> Or sadly listen to the tuneless cry
> Of fishing gull or clanging golden-eye . . .
> He nursed the feelings these dull scenes produce,
> And loved to stop beside the opening sluice . . .

The hanging of the head, the dullness, the nursing of dullness, the lying down motionless in a motionless boat, the dreary contemplation of nature in her trickling exhaustion, the slow downward bending paralysis of the once active man—they present what the poet too had experienced and the clergyman had combated or ignored. They spring from the attraction and from the repulsion exercised on Crabbe by the surrounding scenery, from the dual feeling which I analysed earlier.

We must consider Crabbe's sensitiveness to dreams in a moment—we are not quite in the world of dreams yet. Peter is still sane and awake. The only sign of abnormality is that he avoids three particular places in the estuary of the Alde; when near them he rows away whistling until they are out of sight. It would seem that here and there the surface of the water is thinner than elsewhere, more liable to be broken from below. He becomes a solitary, seeks men and curses them, and they curse him and he retires to his boat. For a whole winter no one sees him. Next summer, he is afloat as before, but no longer fishing. He is gazing, hypnotised by the three places in the stream. "Dost thou repent?" he is asked. The words have a crystallising effect and shatter him. Quitting his boat, he goes raving mad, rushes over the countryside and is caught and carried to the parish infirmary. Here, half nightmare, half vision, the story culminates. Grimes himself takes up the tale in the sedate eighteenth-century couplets and the formal diction which Crabbe could not and perhaps did not desire to forgo. (pp. 174-79)

Crabbe is explicit on the character of Peter Grimes, and appends an interesting note. "The mind here exhibited is one untouched by pity, unstung by remorse and uncorrected by shame." And he shrewdly observed that "no feeble vision, no half-visible ghost, not the momentary glance of an unbodied being nor the half-audible voice of an invisible one would be created by the continual workings of distress on a mind so depraved and flinty." Grimes is tough, hard and dull, and the poet must be tough with him, tougher than Shakespeare had to be with Macbeth, who possessed imagination. He must smash him up physically with penury, disease and solitude, and then place indubitable spectres in his path. Physical sufferings have their effect on any nature:

> and the harder that nature is, and the longer time required upon it, so much the more strong and indelible is the impression. This is all the reason I am able to give why a man of feeling so dull should yet become insane, and why the visions of his distempered brain should be of so horrible a nature.

The poet sees his literary problem very clearly. A sensitive Grimes would mean a different poem. He must make him a lout, normally impervious to suffering, though once suffering starts it is likely to take a strange form.

Grimes in a normal state would be inarticulate. He can only address us effectively through nightmares, and skilful use is made, at the close, of that dream state with which Crabbe was himself too familiar for his own happiness. He recognised its value for his work. He once told Lady Scott, Sir Walter's wife, "I should have lost many a good bit, had I not set down at once things that occurred in my dreams," and he kept a lamp and writing material by his bedside in order to record them before they were forgotten. Many of them were unpleasant. He suffered himself from a recurrent one, induced perhaps by opium. He would dream that he was teased by boys who were made of leather so that when he beat them they felt nothing. "The leather lads have been at me again," he would remark in fatigued tones at the rectory breakfast table. Dreams of all types occur in his work. **"The World of Dreams"** and **"Sir Eustace Grey"** are terrifying. There is a poignant one at the close of **"The Parting Hour"** where a desolate man dreams that his wife and children are with him in an enchanting tropical land. And there is a nightmare, rivalling Grimes' in terror and exceeding it in subtlety, where an imprisoned highwayman, condemned to death for murder, dreams that he is innocent and is walking in exquisite weather down to the sea with the girl he loves, and with his sister. The three young people pass through the lanes and over the sheep walk, "Where the lamb browses by the linnet's bed," cross the brook and behold

> The ocean smiling to the fervid sun—
> The waves that faintly fall and slowly run—
> The ship at distance and the boats at hand:
> And now they walk upon the sea-side sand,
> Counting the number and what kind they be,
> Ships softly sinking in the sleepy sea.

On it flows, with a gentleness and sensuousness unusual with Crabbe, in order that the awakening may be the more terrible. They admire

> those bright red pebbles that the sun
> Through the small waves so softly shines upon:
> And those live lucid jellies which the eye
> Delights to trace as they swim glittering by;
> Pearl-shells and rubied starfish they admire,

> And will arrange above the parlour-fire—
> Tokens of bliss—

Then the nightmare asserts itself, the surface is broken:

> Oh! horrible! a wave
> Roars as it rises—save me, Edward! save!
> She cries:—Alas! the watchman on his way
> Calls, and lets in—truth, terror, and the day!

This famous passage is more dramatic and more sensitive than anything in Grimes. More human values are involved, so there is more to lose, the sudden reversal in fortune is only too typical of sleep, and the wave joins the horrors of imagination to those of fact. We are back in the prison which we had forgotten. Truth re-establishes itself, the more relentless for its withdrawal when the criminal walked with those he had loved and lost.

As for Peter Grimes. He has gone to hell and there is no doubt about it. No possibility of mercy intervenes. A simple rough fisherman over whom some would have sentimentalised, he is none the less damned, the treacherous flatness of the estuary has opened at last. He will sink into the fire and the blood, the only torments he can appreciate. His father has brought him to disaster—that is his explanation, and the father-motive which preluded the tragedy has re-emerged. To push the motive too hard is to rupture the fabric of the poem and to turn it into a pathological tract, but stressed gently it helps our understanding. The interpretations of Freud miss the values of art as infallibly as do those of Marx. They cannot explain values to us, they cannot show us why a work of art is good or how it became good. But they have their subsidiary use: they can indicate the condition of the artist's mind while he was creating, and it is clear that while he was writing **"Peter Grimes"** Crabbe was obsessed by the notion of two generations of males being unkind to one another and vicariously punishing unkindness. It is the grandsire-grandson alliance against the tortured adult.

The other motive—also to be stressed cautiously—is the attraction-repulsion one. Peter tries to escape from certain places on the stream, but he cannot, he is always drifting back to them. Crabbe is always drifting back in the spirit to Aldeburgh. The poet and his creation share the same inner tension, the same desire for what repels them. Such parallels can often be found between the experiences of a writer, and the experiences of a character in his books, but the parallels must be drawn lightly by the critic, for the experiences have usually been transformed out of recognition and the moral climate changed. To say that Crabbe is Peter Grimes would make that prosperous clergyman indignant and would be false. To say that Crabbe and Grimes share certain psychological tensions might also make him indignant, but it would be true. (pp. 181-84)

> *E. M. Forster, "George Crabbe and 'Peter Grimes',"
> in his* Two Cheers for Democracy, *Harcourt Brace
> Jovanovich, Inc., 1951, pp. 171-87.*

## WALLACE CABLE BROWN (essay date 1948)

[*In the following excerpt, Brown analyzes Crabbe's method of adapting the heroic couplet to narrative form, discussing his treatment of syntax, dramatic structure, and characterization, primarily in* Tales *and* Tales of the Hall.]

The reputation of George Crabbe today owes most of its lingering vitality to one poem. In his standard anthology piece, *The Village,* he is usually accorded the faint praise of having written, in traditional couplets, a grim and realistic rejoinder to Goldsmith. As for Crabbe's later work, it "may be looked upon as little more than an expansion" of *The Village.* The adequacy of this assertion by the editors of the Oxford edition of Crabbe we can at least test; and in so doing we shall be dealing with a poet who was, in a very real sense, the last of the Augustans. It is common knowledge that Crabbe wrote wholly in the neo-classic tradition, but that he added anything to the tradition perhaps requires demonstration. What he added was a masterful adaptation of the heroic couplet to narrative. This achievement not only places Crabbe among the great storytellers in verse—it also reveals the vitality of the heroic couplet almost two hundred years after Waller's earliest use of it in 1623.

In Crabbe's earlier and better known poems there are numerous anticipations of his later major work; but none of these completely fulfills the formula for the "tale" as he developed it. In *The Village,* for example, appear the creation of atmosphere through description and the creation of character by means of the type portrait. Thus described is the village's depressing background:

> There thistles stretch their prickly arms afar,
> And to the ragged infant threaten war;
> There poppies, nodding, mock the hope of toil;
> There the blue bugloss points the sterile soil;
> Hardy and high, above the slender sheaf,
> The slimy mallow waves her silky leaf;
> O'er the young shoot the charlock throws a shade,
> And clasping tares cling round the sickly blade;
> With mingled tints the rocky coasts abound,
> And a sad splendour vainly shines around.

Here the modifiers, of which Crabbe was always in danger of using too many, add effectively to the total picture: "ragged infant," "sterile soil," "slimy mallow," "sickly blade," "sad splendour," "vainly shines," etc.

As portraiture, we may consider the following lines about an old man:

> Oft may you see him, when he tends the sheep,
> His winter-charge, beneath the hillock weep;
> Oft hear him murmur to the winds that blow
> O'er his white locks and bury them in snow,
> When, roused by rage and muttering in the morn,
> He mends the broken hedge with icy thorn:—
> "Why do I live, when I desire to be
> At once from life and life's long labour free?"

And his soliloquy continues for eighteen more lines. In this passage and throughout the whole portrait, the details create a typical old man who is a model of virtue unrewarded because he is poor. Furthermore, the device of having the old man speak foreshadows the action through dialogue in the later tales.

In **"The Parish Register"** we approach more closely to the full-fledged tale. This poem is a kind of "Spoon-River Anthology," consisting of a series of portraits drawn from the lower levels of rural life. Through the device of describing the births, marriages, and deaths of the past year, the poet in the person of the village rector proceeds from the baptism of the illegitimate child of Lucy, the proud miller's daughter, at the beginning to the burial of old Ralph Dibble at the end.

Some of the portraits are that and nothing more, but many

of them go beyond the status of a static picture and become sketches of the life and fortunes of a particular character. The account of Phoebe Dawson is one of these. It tells the kind of story usually associated with Crabbe—the story of a beautiful innocent country girl, who is too weak to resist temptation. She falls and is forsaken by her lover soon after they are married. The account of Lucy Collins is another sketch of the same kind, although it is told with more concentration and economy. Indeed the end is foreshadowed in the opening couplet:

> For Lucy Collins happier days had been,
> Had Footman Daniel scorn'd his native green.

Both sketches are straightforward narrative that makes no use of dialogue.

But not all the sketches in **"The Parish Register"** are sordid and tragic. A few of them are light and humorously satiric, anticipating similar kinds of tales later. Thus when a foundling is left in the parish, the "village sires" solemnly meet to give it a name, a difficult problem,

> For he who lent it to a babe unknown,
> Censorious men might take it for his own:
> They look'd about, they gravely spoke to all,
> And not one Richard answer'd to the call.
> Next they inquired the day, when, passing by,
> Th' unlucky peasant heard the stranger's cry:
> This known, how food and raiment they might give,
> Was next debated—for the rogue would live;
> At last, with all their words and work content,
> Back to their homes the prudent vestry went,
> And Richard Monday to the workhouse sent.

In the end Richard Monday, neglected and mistreated in the poorhouse, makes his way in the world so successfully that he dies rich—

> But, to his native place severely just,
> He left a pittance bound in rigid trust,

that is both an embarrassment and humiliation to the parish.

Finally, the experiment with dialogue begins in some of the sketches. In one, Roger Cuff, who has been forty years at sea, returns disguised to test the hospitality of his nephews and niece:

> Then the gay Niece the seeming pauper press'd:—
> "Turn, Nancy, turn, and view this form distress'd;
> Akin to thine is this declining frame,
> And this poor beggar claims an Uncle's name."
> "Avaunt! begone!" the courteous maiden said,
> "Thou vile impostor! Uncle Roger's dead:
> I hate thee, beast; thy look my spirit shocks;
> Oh! that I saw thee starving in the stocks!"
> "My gentle niece!" he said—and sought the wood.

This is somewhat flamboyant, but the author's restrained irony (in "the *courteous* maiden said" and "My *gentle* niece!"—italics mine) counterbalances the rhetorical excesses of the dialogue.

In *The Borough* Crabbe moves still closer to the tale as he finally developed it. In this series of twenty-four "letters" his materials are "the sea, and the country in the immediate vicinity; the dwellings, and the inhabitants; some incidents and characters, with an exhibition of morals and manners. . . ." In his treatment of them, Crabbe makes the incidents and characters stand out more independently; they are structurally more complete in themselves; and technically the couplets become more flexible and generally appropriate for narration and dialogue. It is noteworthy too that the sketches become progressively better and that the account of **"Peter Grimes"** in Letter XXII is probably the best of them all.

Although it lacks the subtlety and finish of the later tales at their best, **"Peter Grimes"** contains most of the ingredients of the typical Crabbe story. (pp. 161-65)

Foreshadowing to create suspense appears early in the story, where, for example, young Peter turns savagely on his father,

> And while old Peter in amazement stood,
> Gave the hot spirit to his boiling blood;—
> How he, with oath and furious speech, began
> To prove his freedom and assert the man;
> And when the parent check'd his impious rage,
> How he had cursed the tyranny of age . . .

And later we are told about Peter that "no success could please his cruel soul, He wish'd for one to trouble and control." Suspense is maintained in other ways, one of which makes use of grim humorous understatement. At one point, just before the first apprentice dies, Peter is beating him—

>        . . . and some, on hearing cries,
> Said calmly, "Grimes is at his exercise."

The creation of atmosphere adds greatly to the total effect of the story, especially the kind that is a favorite with Crabbe. He often describes the natural background of human actions in such a way that nature powerfully reflects the human situation. Thus when the reaction to Grimes's cruelty sets in, he is ostracized by society and begins to suffer from his own conscience, all of which is implied symbolically in nature itself:

> When tides were neap, and, in the sultry day,
> Through the tall bounding mud-banks made their way,
> Which on each side rose swelling, and below
> The dark warm flood ran silently and slow:
> There anchoring, Peter chose from man to hide,
> There hang his head, and view the lazy tide
> In its hot slimy channel slowly glide;
>
>         . . . . .
>
> He nursed the feelings these dull scenes produce,
> And loved to stop beside the opening sluice;
> Where the small stream, confined in narrow bound,
> Ran with a dull, unvaried, sadd'ning sound;
> Where all presented to the eye or ear
> Oppress'd the soul with misery, grief, and fear.

A great deal of dialogue appears in this story, particularly in the third part where it reinforces the dramatic situation of Grimes's hallucinations. The dialogue in couplets tends, however, to be rather stiff and mechanical, although there are exceptions, as in Grimes's account of the three ghosts that plague him:

> To hear and mark them daily was my doom,
> And "Come," they said, with weak, sad voices, "come."
> To row away with all my strength I try'd;
> But there were they, hard by me in the tide,
> The three unbodied forms—and "Come," still "come,"
>     they cried.

Technically the couplets are not exceptional; they are for the most part traditional and, like the dialogue, are too often stiff and mechanical.

Although **"Peter Grimes"** is well constructed and contains

some powerful scenes, it is on the whole too sensational and melodramatic to rank among Crabbe's best stories. Compared to them, it is like a Gothic novel in relationship to one by Fielding or Thackeray. It does, however, point the way to Crabbe's full poetic achievement in narrative, which first appeared two years later—in the *Tales*—and was continued in his last work, *Tales of the Hall.*

In these poems Crabbe's use of the heroic couplet for narrative is the most interesting and successful of any since Dryden. In Crabbe's hands, however, the couplet itself does not attain that mastery of form that it does in the work of Churchill, Johnson, and Pope. Like Goldsmith's and Cowper's, Crabbe's couplet is more relaxed. The most obvious sign of this relaxing is his regular use of the triplet and alexandrine, a practice that he shares with Dryden. These exceptions to the couplet form Crabbe employs for definite purposes: to secure variety, emphasis, and structural demarcation in the development of the story. Thus in **"The Mother,"** thirty of the poem's 360 lines are grouped into ten triplets, of which nine have a hexameter and one a pentameter third line. The triplets are spaced evenly throughout the poem, and six are used simply as variations. The remaining four mark points of emphasis and structural change—uses that are similar to one function of the couplet in Elizabethan drama, that of pointing up and concluding blank verse scenes.

Crabbe's adaptation of the couplet form to short narrative is in itself a brilliant achievement. As he uses it, the end-stopped couplet adds point and concentration to the narrative. In **"The Mother"** note, for example, how the couplets give a tone of sharp finality to the following ideas:

> Hope, ease, delight, the thoughts of dying gave,
> Till Lucy spoke with fondness of the grave;
> She smiled with wasted form, but spirit firm,
> And said, she left but little for the worm.

This passage also contains a grimly humorous shock that is in a sense "metaphysical"—an effect that the couplets contribute to and that F. R. Leavis would call the operation of a kind of "wit" [see excerpt dated 1936]. The touch of this wit, pointed up by the couplet form and often making excellent use of dialogue, appears throughout the *Tales.* Another instance occurs in the story of **"Jesse and Colin,"** a pair of lovers who, after much difficulty, are brought together:

> The youth embolden'd, yet abash'd, now told
> His fondest wish, nor found the maiden cold;
> The mother smiling whisper'd—"Let him go
> And seek the license!" Jesse answer'd, "No":
> But Colin went . . .

And we find, as often happens in Crabbe, that the maiden's "no" means "yes."

Although Crabbe's mature style is not epigrammatic, he could write in this manner, both seriously and humorously; and when he does so, the effect is a heightening of summary and emphasis in the narrative. Thus in **"Arabella"** the beautiful bluestocking heroine is applauded by the mothers of the town as a model for their daughters; Crabbe comments on the results:

> From such applause disdain and anger rise,
> And envy lives where emulation dies.

The same Arabella is subtly ridiculed after she "becomes the wonder of the town":

And strangers, coming, all were taught t' admire
The learned lady, and the lofty spire.

From *Tales of the Hall* consider the ironic question put by the disillusioned lover ("**The Elder Brother**") to his faithless Rosabella:

"My faith must childish in your sight appear,
Who have been faithful—to how many, dear?"

Or, in "**The Maid's Story**," the old maid's concise summary of a supposed frailty among women:

"Secrets with girls, like loaded guns with boys,
Are never valued till they make a noise."

And, finally, the Old Bachelor's epigrammatic expression of the inappropriateness of loving a young girl at his age—"When it was almost treason to be kind."

Special syntactic constructions characteristic of the heroic couplet also add their special effects to Crabbe's handling of narrative. Among these, as we noted in the work of earlier poets, are the uses of word order which give balance and antithesis, as well as unexpected variations of them. The simplest is of course the balanced line of two similarly constructed elements, separated by a preposition or a conjunction:

The scatter'd hovels on the barren green.
                    ("**The Lover's Journey**")

He reached the mansion, and he saw the maid.
                    ("**The Lover's Journey**")

To cause some wonder or excite some fear.
                    ("**The Dumb Orators**")

Such lines usually contain four stresses, with the middle accent suppressed.

In the balanced construction expectation is always rewarded. Just as often, however, Crabbe introduces elements that are out of balance or makes the balance one between unequal parts; the result is an unexpected structural development:

Yet few there were who needed less the art
To hide an error, or a grace impart.
                    ("**Lady Barbara**")

In the first half of the second line the normal word order ("to hide an error") leads us to expect the same order in the second half; instead we are surprised by the inversion: "or a grace impart." Similarly in the line,

She saw the wonders, she the mercies felt,
                    ("**The Mother**")

the verb-object inversion in the second half creates an imbalance within the otherwise perfectly balanced line. When the two parts are unequal, the element that makes them so becomes conspicuous. Thus in the line,

He rich and proud—I very proud and poor,
                    ("**The Hall**")

the balanced elements are "He rich and proud—I . . . proud and poor"; the adverb "very" therefore provides the inequality and attracts our attention. There is also the contrast in meaning between rich and poor at the beginning and end of the line. In the following line,

"She will be kind, and I again be blest,"
                    ("**The Lover's Journey**")

the word "again" makes the balance unequal. Finally, there is the kind of partial balance that involves the repetition of words as well as special uses of word order:

There went the nymph, and made her strong complaints,
Painting her woe as injured feeling paints.
                    ("**The Widow's Tale**")

Now weak, now lively, changing with the day,
These were his feelings, and he felt his way.
                    ("**The Convert**")

Sometimes whole passages will be united by balance and contrast, as in the following lines about two types of women:

Those are like wax—apply them to the fire,
Melting, they take th' impression you desire;
Easy to mould, and fashion as you please,
And again moulded with an equal ease;
Like melted iron these the forms retain,
But once impress'd will never melt again.
                    ("**Resentment**")

The two types are introduced by balanced elements—"Those are like wax . . . Like melted iron these"; but within them the word order is reversed, and "those" contrasts with "these." In addition to rhyme, the lines of the second couplet are held together by the partial repetition of "Easy to mould" and "Again moulded"; and the whole passage is united by the repetition of the ideas of melting and taking an impression. All of these qualities appear in single lines, couplets, and groups of couplets; but for narrative they are most significant when they control a whole verse paragraph, as in the following from "**The Frank Courtship**":

Peace in the sober house of Jonas dwelt,
Where each his duty and his station felt:
Yet not that peace some favour'd mortals find,
In equal views and harmony of mind;
Not the soft peace that blesses those who love,
Where all with one consent in union move;
But it was that which one superior will
Commands, by making all inferiors still;
Who bids all murmurs, all objections cease,
And with imperious voice announces—Peace!

In these ten lines the most obvious unifying device is the repetition of the word "peace": it not only encloses the passage at the beginning and end, but holds everything together by reappearing in the third and fifth lines as well. In terms of thought and syntax, the paragraph is also effectively and characteristically unified. The first couplet, ending with a colon, asserts the peace that reigns in the house. The next two couplets, introduced by "yet not," define the kind of peace by contrasts; and the last two couplets, beginning with "but," complete the definition by a positive description. Structurally, therefore, the passage is divided into three parts: the first couplet, the next two, and the last two; and in thought and syntax the conclusion takes us back to the beginning.

This passage appears early in the introduction of "**The Frank Courtship**," where its function is to characterize the home atmosphere in which the heroine grew up. The precise structure, the syntactic balance and repetition, parallel and reinforce the qualities of precision, order, and control which the father, Jonas, imposes on his wife and daughter. In an impressive way, therefore, not only the sound but also the syntax is made to echo the sense of the entire passage.

Contrary to expectation, Crabbe manages dialogue in the relatively rigid couplet with surprising ease and flexibility.

Technically, of course, the very rigidity of the couplet allows greater variation without destroying the pattern than would otherwise be possible. We can readily illustrate how Crabbe takes advantage of this situation. In **"The Sisters,"** Jane and Lucy are opposites in temperament, as the dialogue of their reactions to news of an absconding banker shows:

> "The odious villain!" Jane in wrath began;
> "In pity Lucy," The unhappy man!
> When time and reason our affliction heal,
> How will the author of our sufferings feel?
> And let him feel, my sister—let the woes
> That he creates be bane to his repose!"

In this passage two points are note worthy: the natural division of the couplet at every other line is used to mark the change from one speaker to another, and in one instance the speakers change within the couplet itself. In **"The Learned Boy,"** widower Farmer Jones is being pursued by a widow with matrimonial intent:

> "Three girls," the widow cried, "a lively three
> To govern well—indeed it cannot be."
> "Yes," he replied, "it calls for pains and care;
> But I must bear it."—"Sir, you cannot bear;
> Your son is weak, and asks a mother's eye."—
> "That, my kind friend, a father's may supply."—
> "Such growing griefs your very soul will tease."—
> "To grieve another would not give me ease;
> I have a mother"—"She, poor ancient soul!
> Can she the spirits of the young control?"

Here the dialogue changes at an even faster pace—not only between and within couplets, but within individual lines as well.

The foregoing characteristics reveal Crabbe's adaptation of the heroic couplet to narrative. His management of content and structure was equally successful. Criticism of the *Tales* and *Tales of the Hall* has usually taken the form of criticism of Crabbe as a didactic storyteller. Little has therefore been said about his skill as a master of the short narrative. In the first place, although they do contain didactic interpolations, Crabbe's tales always make a strong appeal to the emotions, for they were intended primarily as entertainment. Thus the opening of **"The Confidant"** presents a strongly sympathetic picture of the heroine:

> Anna was young and lovely—in her eye
> The glance of beauty, in her cheek the dye;
> Her shape was slender, and her features small,
> But graceful, easy, unaffected all.
> The liveliest tints her youthful face disclosed;
> There beauty sparkled, and there health reposed;
> For the pure blood that flush'd that rosy cheek
> Spoke what the heart forbad the tongue to speak.

And the following view of nature is charged with emotions that reflect those of the weak young hero in **"Delay Has Danger"**:

> But now dejected, languid, listless, low,
> He saw the wind upon the water blow,
> And the cold stream curl'd onward as the gale
> From the pine-hill blew harshly down the dale.
> On the right side the youth a wood survey'd,
> With all its dark intensity of shade;
> Where the rough wind alone was heard to move,
> In this, the pause of nature and of love.

In the context of the whole story, the sixth line ("With all its dark intensity of shade") is particularly successful.

Secondly, Crabbe understood and put into practice many of the structural techniques of the short story. Most of his tales concentrate on a single climactic situation. In **"Resentment,"** for example, a stubborn obtuse woman carries revenge too far. Step by step, we follow her machinations until she finally relents—too late: her husband, the object of her revenge, is dead. The foreshortening of incidental materials to heighten the total effect is another structural device that Crabbe often makes use of. A somewhat extreme example appears in **"The Widow's Tale."** The widow, who has survived a loveless marriage, tells of the earlier tragedy of her real love. In search of fortune, the young man goes to sea, pursues his new career, and returns a failure—all in four lines!

> "From the rough ocean we beheld a gleam
> Of joy, as transient as the joys we dream;
> By lying hopes deceived, my friend retired,
> And sail'd—was wounded—reach'd us—and expired!"

The heightening of interest through foreshadowing is also a regular occurrence in the mature tales. Sometimes it is an obvious warning to the reader, as in **"The Confidant,"** where the heroine, Anna, has confided the secret of her illegitimate child to her friend Eliza:

> The infant died; the face resumed each charm,
> And reason now brought trouble and alarm:
> "Should her Eliza—no! she was too just,
> Too good and kind—but ah! too young to trust."

At other times the foreshadowing is more subtle. In **"The Mother,"** for example, a young parson is courting the daughter, Lucy, against her mother's wishes. She succeeds in creating the following situation, in which the last line hints at Lucy's subsequent disappointment and tragedy:

> Whate'er he wrote, he saw unread return'd,
> And he, indignant, the dishonour spurn'd;
> Nay, fix'd suspicion where he might confide,
> And sacrificed his passion to his pride.

The development of conflict through contrasts in character and situation is still another structural method used by Crabbe. Thus in **"Advice, or The Squire and the Priest"** a domineering worldly squire selects his young nephew as the rector of his village church on the assumption that he will be wholly compliant. The nephew's character is of course diametrically opposed to that of the uncle. In the end the young priest not only rejects the squire's "advice," but successfully challenges his authority. Contrasts in setting may be illustrated in **"The Lover's Journey."** The young lover, on his way to an assignation, rides through scenes of squalor and ugliness, seeing in them nothing but beauty because he is happy; then, when the girl fails to meet him, he rides on through contrasting scenes of actual beauty, which now seem to him ugly and repulsive because he sees them with a jaundiced eye. There is in this situation an ingeniously worked out double contrast, psychologically in the young man and objectively in nature around him; and each side of the one is juxtaposed with the opposite side of the other.

A third way in which Crabbe's mastery of the short narrative reveals itself in the tales is in their emphasis upon character realistically interpreted. It is often Crabbe's practice to bring a character, with traits already indicated, into a crucial situation which dramatizes these traits. Thus in **"The Brothers"** we first learn of their contrasting natures:

> George was a bold, intrepid, careless lad,

With just the failings that his father had;
Isaac was weak, attentive, slow, exact,
With just the virtues that his father lack'd.

As the story proceeds, these characteristics slowly flower in the lives of the two men. George, a sailor carelessly generous, aids his brother time and time again. Isaac, accepting this aid, selfishly gives nothing but advice in return. Then comes the crucial situation. George loses his leg at sea, but confidently looks to Isaac, now rich and happily married, to take him in. This test Isaac fails to meet, thus revealing his true character or lack of it.

Like **"The Brothers,"** the majority of Crabbe's tales are studies of character placed in situations which reveal strength or weakness. One of the best of these is **"Procrastination,"** a study of the disintegrating effects of delay on character and on love. The subject seems to have interested Crabbe greatly, for he used it again as one of the *Tales of the Hall,* **"Delay Has Danger,"** in which the delay reveals the weakness of the man in succumbing to the charms of another woman. In **"Procrastination,"** however, the delay involves the girl, Dinah, who, separated from her lover Rupert, gradually succumbs to her wealthy aunt's love of riches and finery. (pp. 165-77)

[**"Procrastination"**] succeeds as narrative fiction because its people are never merely symbols of moral abstractions. Their world is not the black-and-white world of right and wrong: it is the actual world with infinite mixtures of the two, in which these people live as complex human beings. Although he is more sinned against than sinning, Rupert is weak; he partially forfeits our sympathy by his failures before going abroad and by his oversimplified demands on his return.Dinah, although acting despicably at the end, nevertheless feels "Some thought of pity raised by his distress, Some feeling touch of ancient tenderness." There is a genuine struggle within her, finally resolved in favor of the baser side of her nature, the growth of which has been the theme of the story. But of the three elements of this baser nature—pride, fear, and shame—the last two reveal the operation of a guilty conscience.

Not all of Crabbe's successful tales emphasize character as strongly as does **"Procastination."** Again like the short story, some of them depend primarily upon situation. Of these **"The Frank Courtship"** is an excellent example. Unlike the tales of pathos and grim reality commonly associated with Crabbe, **"The Frank Courtship"** is almost Chaucerian in its humorous vitality. And as is usual with Crabbe at his best, the structure and dialogue in couplet form are precise and sure. (pp. 181-82)

In **"The Frank Courtship,"** as in **"Procastination,"** we are in the real world of lights and shades. The character of Sybil is extremely complex, as revealed particularly in the scenes with her lover and her father at the end. Even Josiah, who appears late in the story, is made thoroughly human by a number of quick insights into his character—such as his response to the father's advice that he dominate the forthcoming interview with Sybil:

A sober smile return'd the youth, and said,
"Can I cause fear, who am myself afraid?"

And old imperious Jonas himself becomes sympathetic and likable when he meets his match in his versatile and talented daughter.

There are not many today who would echo a critic's recent comment on Crabbe, "that he is (or ought to be—for who reads him?) a living classic [see excerpt by Leavis dated 1936]. The decline of Crabbe's reputation in the nineteenth century is of course understandable. Far more genuinely than Byron, he defended the Augustan tradition by precept and practice at a time when Shelley and Keats were doing some of their best work. Yet the archromantic Scott was one of Crabbe's most enthusiastic admirers, and Charles Lamb dramatized one of his *Tales* ("The Confidant")! Unquestionably Crabbe had something to offer which transcended these labels. For us today that something lies both in the fact that he was the last of the Augustans and that, in his best work, he brilliantly adapted the heroic couplet to the art of narrative. (pp. 186-87)

> *Wallace Cable Brown, "Crabbe: Neo-Classic Narrative," in his* The Triumph of Form: A Study of the Later Masters of the Heroic Couplet, *The University of North Carolina Press, 1948, pp. 161-87.*

**ARTHUR SALE**   (essay date 1952)

> [*In the following excerpt, Sale appraises the development of narrative technique in Crabbe's poetry from* The Village *to* Tales of the Hall, *arguing that Crabbe is one of the most distinguished practitioners of the "realistic short story in English verse."*]

Instead of his assiduous summarizing, which was simple but unnecessary, Jeffrey should have traced the development of Crabbe's narrative art, which would have been a simple and worthwhile task of a kind in which he excelled. That development was itself simple, but as it was sidelong—for Crabbe's conscious goal was description—it continued for a generation or so before he fully realized what he was about. But as not only the gait but also the recurrent crises between inner growth and outward form are cancerian nature, it is more sensible to observe the race than to regret its crookedness.

But what is regrettable is that Crabbe should be known to the Common Reader only by his first discarded carapace—*The Village.* Lord Jeffrey, collecting his old reviews of Crabbe about a decade after the latter had died full of fame, oddly attributed their inordinate length not to its effective cause—his gratuitous summarizing of contents—but to his conviction that the poet had never received his due of popularity. What is still odder, but far less creditable, than that conviction is the present paradox that now he is unknown, Crabbe should be known of for his least characteristic poem. The effective (but not the first) cause is that curry-combing of the eighteenth century for larvae of Romanticism which was until recently part of the regimen of literary history. The latter knows him as a signpost pointing back to the City and, over its shoulder, to the Lakes, and leaning protectively over a few huts huddled round a large workhouse. This prevailing notion is not derived exclusively from those derivative Histories of Literature which are, in Crabbe's words, 'Attendants fix'd at learning's lower gate,' and read by those who do not, unless perforce, read the writers they read about: such an accredited commissionaire to the the inner ring as the Oxford *Crabbe* declares that his life work ended with *The Village,* and the rest—seven volumes of it—is merely the comment. Yet that poem, which has no narration and not even a character study, gives no indication whatever that Crabbe is almost the only, and almost the greatest, practitioner of the realistic short story in English verse. Chaucer is, of course, the greatest, but even his rippling joyous realism is lavished rather on the *fabliau* or the *exemplum* than on the true story which is the basis of every Cancerian tale; Crabbe's habitual and total immersion in the life around him is, in fact, unique in our poetry. But any temptation this scarcity value may have for the literary historian has been sacrificed to his stern sense of duty towards Romanticism. Even so, a just view of the situation will observe Crabbe's pre-Romanticism to have been in the fashion rather than in the van.

Two other half-truths have attached themselves by epigrammatic hooks to the popular memory, which has, indeed, improved one of them from 'nature's sternest painter, but the best' into 'nature's sternest painter, but her best', and been given enduring sanction by the memorial marble in Trowbridge parish church. Belief in the first half of Byron's line has accompanied incredulity towards the second, and has blinkered even the best short study of Crabbe, that by Paul Elmer More in the second volume of *Shelburne Essays*. Yet it was effectively discredited as early as 1834:

> The vulgar impression that Crabbe is throughout a gloomy author, we attribute to the choice of certain specimens of his earliest poetry in the 'Elegant Extracts'—the only specimens of him that had been at all generally known at the time when most of those who have criticized his later works were young. That exquisitely-finished but heart-sickening description, in particular, of the poorhouse in *The Village,* fixed itself on every imagination: and when the **"Register"** and *Borough* came out, the reviewers, unconscious perhaps of the early prejudice that was influencing them, selected quotations mainly of the same class.

Jane Austen's remark that she would not half mind being Mrs Crabbe shows that this 'vulgar impression' was not quite universal, but its persistence justifies the selection of quotation in the following pages which is, to redress the balance, mainly of the opposite class. Actually, Crabbe's best work—**"The Confidant"** and **"Procrastination"** are examples—shows a willing co-operation of Austenity with austerity that is peculiarly Cancerian.

Of the burr which the Brothers Smith, in *Rejected Addresses,* attached with self-conscious casualness to Crabbe's nether garments, all that can be said here is that 'Pope in worsted stockings' is a generic rather than an individual description [see poem dated 1812]. Crabbe's manner is often satiric and so, inevitably, owes, among others, to Pope, but the mere existence of his narrative medium and sober realism, equally inevitably, reveal that debt as of incidental occurrence; categoric differences alone preclude identity. An early satire, *The Newspaper,* shows how little interest Crabbe as a coarse facsimile of Pope would have for us.

Another distorted stress set up by the impossible locating of *The Village* as the hub of Crabbe's poetry is in the insistence that 'sympathy with the poor' is a major theme of that poetry. Crabbe was a sympathetic and generous man, and probably not entirely convinced of Wordsworth's belief that rural poverty was a condition of the right growth of character, but the picture of Crabbe brooding in a pebbly nest over seven volumes of the wrongs of the poor belongs to fantasy rather than to literary history. Even in *The Village,* the Aldburghers (who had no use for their prophet as either 'pothecary or priest) are 'a bold, artful, surly, savage race . . . only skilled

to take the finny tribe, The yearly dinner or septennial bribe' (or the contraband bottle or the enticed wreck), and the second part of the poem might have been written by a hack hired to confute the thesis of the first, for, it declares, the complaints of the poor should be awed into silence by the thought that the miseries of the great are greater. The near-political tone of some passages probably took its courage if not its conviction from the louder indignation of Langhorne's *The Country Justice,* which, being nearly a decade earlier, and also popular, might be thought to deserve the credit for pioneering mistakenly given to *The Village,* had not the whole thing been nutshelled still another twenty years earlier in a generously open order to

> reward
> The poor man's toil, whence all your riches spring

If it is too disruptive to trace back the succession to such a rock of revolution as Robert Dodsley, honour is satisfied if the point be accepted that the thoughts to which a successful publisher commits himself are not usually dangerous ones. (pp. 480-82)

I still remember the shock of delight which **"the Widow Goe"** gave me when, years ago, I came across her in an anthology. The shock may have been intensified by the fact that she was the first adventure I had encountered in what was unadventurous even for a school anthology but, allowing for the unexpectedness, it is perhaps worth recording that my immediate response to her distinctiveness preceded both the recognition of the tradition of charactery to which she obviously belonged, and the recognition of her author.

> Next died *the Widow Goe,* an active dame,
> Famed ten miles round, and worthy all her fame;
> She lost her husband when their loves were young,
> But kept her farm, her credit, and her tongue . . .
> She match'd both sons and daughters to her mind,
> And lent them eyes, for Love, she heard, was blind. . . .
> 'Bless me! I die, and not a warning giv'n—
> With *much* to do on Earth, and ALL for Heav'n!—
> No reparation for my soul's affairs,
> No leave petition'd for the barn's repairs . . .
> A lawyer haste, and in your way, a priest. . . .'
> She spake, and, trembling, dropp'd upon her knees,
> Heaven in her eye and in her hand her keys . . .
> Then fell and died!—In haste her sons drew near,
> And dropp'd, in haste, the tributary tear,
> Then from th' adhering clasp the keys unbound,
> And consolation for their sorrows found.

Even these *disjecta membra* of an articulated but not very rounded form may be enough to suggest the difference in tendency from the characteries of Dryden and Pope. In them, incident is directed inwards towards character: in Crabbe, character is directed outwards towards incident. He may, of course, be merely reverting to the shouldering bustle of the Roman satirists, but there is still this difference of direction, that in Juvenal incidents are *exempla* of forcible convictions, whereas in **"The Parish Register"**, though strictly related to character, they exist in their own right and any general truth they are meant to illustrate is subdued unto their quality. The unequal tug in the widow between love of temporal and fear of spiritual power produces strong contrasts rather than strong denunciation, and the only rubbing in of the moral is a typographical ('*much*—ALL') indication (in reverse) of the lady's own relative emphasis of tone. This loading of every rift of character with fictional ore is Crabbe's extension, in **"The Parish Register"**, of the Augustan character study, but what is equally notable is the tart freshness he can give to a tradition of reduction to contrast that had been in constant use for a century and a half, and that he relies on in every line of the quotation, for even the second line has a double contrast implicit in its straight use of the Goldsmithian mock heroic and in its ironic use of the Goldsmithian affection.

The best example of the kind, though from a later poem, is in place here as more characteristic of **"The Parish Register"** (1807) than of *The Borough* (1810). Sir Denys Brand's virtues are first presented in their public aspect and then denied in their private aspect. His humility and asceticism are traced to their source:

> . . . the sleek rogues [his servants] with one consent declare
> They would not live upon his honour's fare;
> He daily took but one half-hour to dine,
> On one poor dish and some three sips of wine;
> Then he'd abuse them for their sumptuous feasts . . .
> 'Learn to be temperate'.—Had they dar'd t'obey,
> He would have praised, and turn'd them all away . . .
> An old grey pony 'twas his will to ride . . .
> A five-pound purchase, but so fat and sleek,
> His very plenty made the creature weak.
> "Sir Denys Brand! and on so poor a steed!"
> "Poor! it may be—such things I never heed."
> And who that youth behind, of pleasant mien,
> Equipp'd as one who wishes to be seen . . .
> "A handsome youth, Sir Denys; and a horse
> Of finer figure never trod the course—
> Yours, without question?"—"Yes! I think a groom
> Bought me the beast; I cannot say the sum:
> I ride him not; it is a foolish pride
> Men have in cattle—but my people ride;
> The boy is—hark ye sirrah! What's your name?
> Ay, Jacob, yes! I recollect—the same;
> As I bethink me now, a tenant's son—
> I think a tenant—is your father one?"

The whole study runs to about a hundred and fifty lines: its leisureliness, elaboration, and profusion of detail might seem in the abstract a diffusion and relaxation, rather than an extension, of the intensely centripetal white-knuckled norm of Pope's charactery or the few careless words of Dryden which are so little compressed as to seem as large as the total situation they contain. But apart from the debating point that 'He would have praised, and turn'd them all away' is a success of the latter kind comparable with 'He had his jest, and they had his estate', there are obvious concrete gains if one thinks of narration rather than of portraiture. Even the metrical pedestrianism, apparently so inferior to the Popeian dance, is in part required by realistic narration, where Pope's highly concentrated manner is at a disadvantage. A final semi-narrative use of servants rounds off the study: an idle boy who had 'found his master's humble spirit out' found also favour by running off in ostentatious awe whenever he saw Sir Denys. This triple use of servants is integral; the poet needs them for contrast as much as their master did.

As the priest turns over his register of baptisms, marriages and burials, it is only natural that reminiscence and moralizing suggest themselves. What does not suggest itself is what later came to be the natural to Crabbe—the verse narration. Despite the frequent dialogue, the anecdote, the potted biography, it seems that Crabbe still regarded himself as a descriptive poet. **"Phoebe Dawson"** is even an exercise in the antithetical structure that later shaped so many of his tales, but it is largely a pictorial contrast, which might easily hang

on the wall as a 'pair', to which the painter supplies his own reiterated text—

> Ah! fly temptation, youth; refrain! refrain!
> Each yielding maid and each presuming swain!

Yet an occasional reversionary passage reminds us that it is description of a very different order from that of *The Village:* the Lady of the Hall is blamed for absenteeism in life—

> Her oaks or acres, why with care explore;
> Why learn the wants, the sufferings of the poor—

and for magnificence in death—

> And shake their sables in the wearied eye,
> That turns disgusted from the pompous scene,
> Proud without grandeur, with profusion mean . . .
> When woes are feign'd, how ill such forms appear,
> And oh! how needless, when the wo's sincere . . .
> A Village-father look'd disdain and said:
> 'Away, my friends! why take such pains to know
> What some brave marble soon in church shall show? . . .
> What groans we uttered and what tears we shed;
> Tears, true as those, which in the sleepy eyes
> Of weeping cherubs on the stone shall rise;
> Tears, true as those which, ere she found her grave,
> The noble lady to our sorrows gave.'

It is surely curious that Crabbe should be known for this archaistic mixture of Gray, Goldsmith and Johnson, rather than for the Widow Goe and Sir Denys Brand. But even from these gloomy echoes the new Cancerian humour, which might later have reminded him that he too was an absentee landlord of spiritual halls, is not completely excluded, for one of 'the dismal Sons of Darkness' is granted a descent from periphrasis into a mere undertaker's pleasure

> . . . that our rustic men and maids behold
> His plate like silver, and his studs like gold.

If Crabbe's new manner, which may be defined negatively as an attempt, no doubt intuitive, to discard the outgrown carapaces of rhetorics which prevent the right growth of realistic narration, does owe anything to others it is, oddly enough, to the same poet on whose social indignation he drew in *The Village.* There is one passage in **"The Country Justice"** which he must have marked as the road to pastures new, though he did not follow it for over thirty years:

> The parson's maid—sore cause had she to rue
> The gipsy's tongue; the parson's daughter too.
> Long had that anxious daughter sighed to know
> What Vellum's sprucy clerk, the valley's beau,
> Meant by those glances which at church he stole,
> Her father nodding to the psalm's slow drawl.
> Long had she sigh'd: at length a prophet came,
> By many a sure prediction known to fame,
> To Marion known, and all she told, for true:
> She knew the future, for the past she knew.

Its context shows that this passage, in turn, derives from Gay's *The Shepherd's Week,* which cannot be the most acceptable of ancestors for Nature's sternest painter.

An important indication of a change of direction in **"The Parish Register"** is Crabbe's natural resort to dialogue. At this stage it is usually monologue, and usually assigned only to the hero of the moment, but already it often has the clinching close of a period which Mr F. R. Leavis has praised in Crabbe [see excerpt dated 1936]. Sometimes it is a dramatic monologue and once, in the account of Nathan Kirk's marriage, even anticipates the 'cousins' of Andrea del Sarto's mistress. And the poem ends with a neat inlay of dialogue that foreshadows the Chinese-box recessions of *Tales of the Hall* (1819):

> My Record ends:—But hark! e'en now I hear
> The bell of death, and know not whose to fear. . . .
> 'Go; of my Sexton seek, whose days are sped?—
> What! he himself!—and is old *Dibble* dead?' . . .
> His masters lost, he'd oft in turn deplore,
> And kindly add—"Heaven grant, I lose no more!"
> Yet, while he spake, a sly and pleasant glance
> Appear'd at variance with his complaisance:
> For, as he told their fate and varying worth,
> He archly look'd—'I yet may bear thee forth'.
>
> (pp. 483-87)

*The Borough* (1810) shows the fictional bent gradually proclaiming itself as inevitable. The poem begins with a sectarian account of the religious sects of the town but ends, a volume or so later, with a series of unattached fictions which differ from the *Tales* of 1812 chiefly in being still monograph and monologue. Crabbe's vocation naturally plays little part in his narrative development—though his too-automatic allocation of responsibilities does limit his stature—and all there is to say about his sectarianism here is that once or twice—as in his comic treatment of it in **"The Parish-Clerk"** (*The Borough*), and in his objective view of it in **"Advice"** (*Tales*)—he makes a virtue of it. But not often enough does he turn it to such good account as he does electioneering of a different kind in the Letter (IV) which follows those on Religion:

> Election-friends are worse than any foes;
> The party-curse is with the canvass past,
> But party-friendship, for your grief, will last . . .
> One enters hungry—not to be denied,
> And takes his place and jokes—'We're of a side' . . .
> Then comes there one, and tells in friendly way
> What the opponents in their anger say . . .
> And having through your own offences run,
> Adds (as appendage) what your friends have done.
> Has any female cousin made a trip
> To Gretna Green, or more vexatious slip? . . .
> and the while
> You silent sit, and practise for a smile.

The poke in the vulnerable social middle of political conventions no doubt accounts for Jeffrey's disapproval of this wry Letter.

The social observation in the descriptive parts of *The Borough* is midway between the extremes of generalizing in *The Village* and of particularizing in the realistic tales. It is, in short, typical.

> There dwells a kind old Aunt, and there you see
> Some kind young nieces in her company . . .
> What though it may some cool observers strike,
> That such fair sisters should be so unlike;
> That still another and another comes . . .
> Yet let Suspicion hide her odious head . . .
> A pious friend, who with the ancient dame
> At sober cribbage takes an evening game . . .
> A grave protector and a powerful friend:
> But Slander says, who indistinctly sees,
> Once he was caught with Sylvia on his knees;—
> A cautious burgess with a careful wife
> To be so caught!—'tis false upon my life.

This passage of type-observation from the account of the inns (*Letter* XI) still shows the satirist's withdrawal of the fellow-feeling with which Crabbe's later humour is instinct: other passages show the obverse—the facile pathos which he always possessed and by which he is usually represented in such anthologizing as ventures outside *The Village.*

> 'Sir, I protest, were Job himself at play,
> He'd rave to see you throw your cards away;
> Not that I care a button—not a pin
> For what I lose; but we had cards to win . . .'
> 'I scorn suspicion, ma'am; but while you stand
> Behind that lady, pray, keep down your hand' . . .
> 'There, there's your money; but, while I have life,
> I'll never more sit down with man and wife.'

Crabbe shows an ear for typical conversation in recording (above) the eternal acerbity of whist drives, and (later in *Letter* X) the fuddlement of the smoke-room:

> 'Well, very well—then freely as I drink,
> I spoke my thought—you take me—what I think . . .'
> 'Ay, there you posed him: I respect the Chair,
> But man is man, although the man's a Mayor . . .'
> 'I'll speak my mind, for here are none but friends:
> They're all contending for their private ends;
> No public spirit . . .'

But these tritical and polite conversations are only five-finger exercises, tinklings preliminary to the gradual emergence from the compendious length of *The Borough* of the independent narrations which that poem throws up towards its end like the pebble ridge on Aldeburgh beach. Except that they are still in the form of monograph and monologue, **"The Parish-Clerk"** (*Letter* XIX) and **"Peter Grimes,"** both of which have focal situations (in each case, a striking monologue), might belong to the *Tales* of 1812. But the norm of the Borough tales is still potted biography and, so, without situations. Even so, one of them has an arbitrary attempt at structure: the long descent of Clelia is reviewed by decades, and although she is a lady of too many situations to provide *a* situation, by explicitly contrasting her last stage with her first, Crabbe anticipates, as **"Phoebe Dawson"** had done but only pictorially—'Look here upon this picture, then on this'—that contrast which, being basic to the Augustan conception of art, determined the structure of its verse, its prose, and, now, its verse narration . . . **"Peter Grimes"** (*Letter* XXII) has a key situation (Grimes's death-bed 'part confession and the rest defence'): a form of contrast (this apologia at once corroborates the brisk narration of his suspected crimes and contrasts in treatment with it): and a minute description of scenery that chimes or clashes with the hero's state of mind and that forms the transition between the brisk narration and the final brooding dramatic monologue. To these familiar elements is added a fourth—the macabre. **"Sir Eustace Grey"** is usually chosen to illustrate this new element, no doubt because it is easier to claim that poem for Romanticism. But if only because it is but one element in **"Grimes"**, and the only one in **"Grey"**, it is more effective, and less of an indulgence, in the former. . . . Mr F. C. Brown, in an appreciative chapter on Crabbe in *The Triumph of Form,* calls **"Peter Grimes"** 'Gothic' [see excerpt dated 1948]. The story is likely enough (as Mr G. G. Carter shows in *Forgotten Ports of England),* the treatment realistic, the scenery dull; there is a faint echo of that 'correct' Gothic elegy—*Eloisa to Abelard*—but nothing at all of the 'Gothic' Romance, not even in the sensationalism of the confession, which is more like Hood's *Eugene Aram* than like Gothic horrors, and has, in any case, already been offset by the laconic narration of the events which caused Peter's visions:

The boat grew leaky and the wind was strong,
Rough was the passage and the time was long,
His liquor fail'd and Peter's wrath arose . . .

Peter says, he 'spied
The stripling's danger and for harbour tried;
Meantime the fish, and then th' apprentice died.'

"Peter Grimes" is, in fact, realistic fiction, with a theme which, when not handled with Crabbe's restraint and sense, can produce an ineptitude like Browning's *Halbert and Hob*. Realism of Crabbe's kind is neither as easy nor as obvious as it looks. And it is as much a product of character as the more patently subjective forms of verse.

In the *Tales* of 1812, the framed portrait and the undichotomous line of narration are usually discarded in favour of a nucleus of situation, or a polarity of situations, and an interaction of character. **"The Dumb Orators,"** the first of the *Tales*, which Jeffrey thought a poor opener, is at any rate so useful a diagram of their narrative form that it asks for a pause, at the expense of better things to come. In structure it is simply a see-saw. Justice Bolt, a local dictator of opinions, longing to show his prowess in a town he visits, attends a meeting at which, finding himself alone in his views, he is too scared to say a word. Years later, the chief speaker finds himself in the same situation at a gathering of Bolt and his friends. Bolt takes his revenge. Jeffrey found the subject lacking in universal interest, but it is precisely its universality that preserves it from mere anecdotage. Not so much the characters as their plight is the centre of interest, and *that* is universal enough. Disconcerted at having noticed Bolt amongst his prospective audience, Hammond the Jacobin deist looks round the dining table:

Hammond look'd round again; but none was near,
With friendly smile to still his growing fear;
But all above him seem'd a sullen row
Of priests and deacons, so they seem'd below;
He wonder'd who his right-hand man might be—
Vicar of Holt cum Uppingham was he;
And who the man of that dark frown possess'd—
Rector of Bradley and of Barton-west;
"A pluralist", he growl'd—but check'd the word.

The mock-grandiose use of his own calling conveniently introduces the related point—that Crabbe's concern with morality, however professional, is not that of the cautionary tale. The simple structure involves no undue simplification of experience: it is a convenience for intensification and complication of effect, not a crudity. Potential blacks and whites are actual blends. He accepts Bolt's views but not Bolt: and the latter's defeat of the godless, so far from being a victory for the right, is actually a retrogression, both for the chastening of spirit caused by his former cowardice, and for his long-reprieved audience, whose renewal of suffering, as once more he 'dwelt all night on politics and laws', joins the end of the tale to its beginning. So does the next tale, **"The Parting Hour"**, the second situation of which contrasts with the one indicated by the title. The hero, leaving his betrothed in order to make a fortune for her abroad, returns on a similar evening, forty years later, to claim her not as his wife but as sympathetic audience for his feverish memories of the wife and family he has had to abandon in South America. The dry realism, the very awkwardness of the unsentimentality, are a good antidote to the overcharged nobilities and intimacies of **"Enoch Arden"**. Tennyson's admiration for Crabbe did not avail: Browning's bungling of a Cancerian theme has been noted. That only prose writers could succeed Crabbe is, however disheartening for verse, some measure of his achievement: Jane Austen's verse tales are impossible to imagine, and Hardy's just impossible. (pp. 487-92)

Obsession is the centre of **"Procrastination"**, but that tale is not, as **"Catherine Lloyd"** was, a monograph. The aunt, a Jane Austen figure, has a decisive impact Jane Austen refuses her comic aunts or allows, and then only in retrospect, only to a serious agent like Lady Russell.

Upon her anxious looks the widow smiled,
And bade her wait, "for she was yet a child".
The dame was sick, and when the youth applied
For her consent, she groan'd, and cough'd, and cried,

and was pleased when Rupert (now thirty) is invited to work abroad:

'You now are young, and for this brief delay,
And Dinah's care, what I bequeath will pay.
All will be yours: nay love, suppress that sigh;
The kind must suffer and the best must die'.
Then came the cough, and strong the signs it gave
Of holding long contention with the grave . . .
She wonder'd much why one so happy sigh'd:
Then bade her see how her poor aunt sustain'd
The ills of life, nor murmur'd nor complain'd.

But although the comic widow, the scandalous spinsters, and the comic servant all help to keep the story within the field of social comedy, and so to distinguish it from **"The Parting Hour"**, of the two it is **"Procrastination"** which has the painful ending. In the interests of a conventional happy ending, Jane Austen rectifies Emma's character and Anne's mistake: Crabbe's conception perhaps rectifies Jane's. **"The Frank Courtship"** (*Tale* VI) is, however, pure comedy, all situation and no incident, and the contrast is merely between

'He kneel and tremble at a thing of dust!
He cannot, child:'—the Child replied, 'He must'.

and

'Dear child! in three plain words thy mind express—
Wilt thou have this good youth?'—'Dear father! yes.'

**"The Widow's Tale"** (*Tale* VII) has a similar victory of sense over sensibility but the disarmingly obvious moral is Edgeworth rather than Austen. Arabella (*Tale* IX), who rejects her lover on the highest principles, later refuses, on the highest principles, to reject another lover accused of the same sin. After seriously, and in parts movingly, defending the reversal, Crabbe quietly draws attention to the element of rationalizing in all 'interested' reasoning by allowing his heroine to make this defence her own:

'We may be too nice
And lose a soul in our contempt of vice;
If false the charge, I then shall show regard
For a good man, and be his just reward:
And what for virtue can I better do
Then to reclaim him if the charge be true?'
She spoke, nor more her holy work delay'd;
'Twas time to lend an erring mortal aid.

But it is an amused and kindly exposure, and the simple contrasts in the tale once more justify themselves as a natural human pattern. What is at once pointed and unobtrusive in Crabbe is too pointed and too obtrusive in Hardy's *Satires of Circumstance*, where similar contrast is often a falsification of the human condition. The accent of quiet unvindictive wisdom in

> And steals from virtue her asperities
>
> ("Arabella")

and

> It might some wonder in a stranger move
> How these together could have talk'd of love
>
> ("Procrastination")

and

> Oft he was forced his reasons to repeat
> Ere he could kneel in quiet at his seat
>
> ("The Parish-Clerk")

is absent from the narrations of the spirits of Pity and Irony. (pp. 493-94)

**"The Confidant"** (*Tale* XVI) has an attention to presentation very rare in Crabbe. The heroine, a companion, seems as innocent as she is lovely but what her suitor, a cultured yeoman, does not know is that at fifteen she had a child, the only witness of which was a friend—which was unlucky, for the child died but the friend lived on to be dreaded. Anna's reaction to her first legal offspring is given with Crabbe's usual concern for contrast in similarity:

> To her fond breast the wife her infant strain'd,
> Some feelings utter'd, some were not explain'd;
> And she enraptured with her treasure grew.
> The sight familiar, but the pleasure new. . . .

Structurally, the tale has a threefold indirectness. Anna, the first centre of interest, is presented as in a state of innocence and we are gradually led *back* to her fall. Eliza, the second motivator, is revealed almost entirely through her letters and through Stafford's eyes. But when it is his turn to motivate, his eyes are concealed and his discovery is revealed only through the Eastern analogue. The brief bland account of the Caliph's victory over himself is a radiantly effective and extremely economical method of presenting Stafford's own crisis. The simple device of arousing suspense and mystification by apparent disconnectedness: e.g. 'For once he fled to measures indirect. One day the Friends were seated in that room', and 'They parted thus, and Anna went her way. To shed her secret sorrows, and to pray. Stafford, amused with books, and fond of home, By reading oft dispell'd the evening gloom'; and the use of prolonged repetition (the description of Eliza's room) to clinch a point—all this concern for art is so well rewarded that one regrets it was only 'for once' that Crabbe 'fled to measures indirect'.

In *Tales of the Hall* (1819) there is, perhaps in accordance with their post-prandial circumstances, a relaxation of the norm of contrast and cross-reference. Their contribution to Crabbe's art is warmth, which, not itself structural, affects structure in that it loosens the narrative fibres by interpenetration. This quiet strength of feeling, already manifest in Stafford, is distinct from the warm exhortations to virtue which sometimes do duty for love in Crabbe's work, and has been attributed to his reading of the Romantic poets. But though the narrator's emotion is sometimes more important than the narration, as in Wordsworth's tale of Margaret in *The Excursion,* there is no need to go for a source outside the nostalgia natural in an aging poet recounting the reminiscences of two brothers who wander about the landscape of their boyhood. Any technical development is in the adumbration of a novel of sense and sensibility in their colloquy and conduct. It is not carried very far and there is reason to believe that Crabbe's power of organization would have been inadequate for such a project (his son George remembers its inadequacy in the burnt prose novels of the generation of silence), but the specimen leaves we have show a recognition of the difference in scale and pace between novel and short story.

The best example of the last stage in Crabbe's art is not, as it happens, a Tale of the Hall, but the posthumous **"Tale of Silford Hall,"** in which a quaint little country boy is shown round a ducal mansion, and which has a Chaucerian freshness of appreciation and tenderness of humour that makes a study in the old shrewd sarcastic vein such as that of the much-married lady in Book XVII of *Tales of the Hall* seem anachronistic, a return to the eighteenth century. Although the occasion is largely autobiographical, the posthumous tale gains in detachment by eschewing the self-conscious and sometimes rhetorical first person of the fraternal autobiographies in *Tales of the Hall.* Crabbe's art may safely be left at this last triumph of his last development, in which the momentousness of the occasion for the boy (the sub-title is **"The Happy Day"**) is radiantly there for the reader too, either despite or because of the absence of narrative excitement. The series of posthumous tales, *"Farewell and Return,"* are indeed a farewell to these tales of feeling and a return, bald, schematic, perfunctory, to the use of contrast (the returned native is told the history of his remembered friends, from the point where his memories cease), and the only point of mentioning them here is as a retrospective warning against any implication that there is an equation between the use of a device and the worth of what is devised. (pp. 495-98)

*Arthur Sale, "The Development of Crabbe's Narrative Art," in* The Cambridge Journal, *Vol. V, No. 8, May, 1952, pp. 480-98.*

**IAN GREGOR** (essay date 1955)

[*In the following excerpt, Gregor focuses on the disparity between thematic and stylistic aspects of* The Village, *highlighting the tension between Crabbe's unrestrained realism and his concessions to Augustan literary norms.*]

There is a consensus of critical opinion that a consideration of Crabbe must involve a discussion of his realism. 'Nature's sternest painter, yet her best', Byron's comment on Crabbe could conveniently serve as an epigraph for a study of the critical attention he has received [see excerpt dated 1809]. (p. 38)

By far the most important poem that Crabbe wrote during the first period of his work was *The Village,* a piece intended partly as a retort to the sentimentalism of Goldsmith's *The Deserted Village* (1770). Begun in 1780 and completed two years later, Crabbe's poem is, for the most part, a sustained exercise in poetic 'realism', accomplished by exploring the horrors that were overtaking English rural life at the end of the eighteenth century. More often referred to than read, *The Village* has served as a quarry both for the social historian looking for 'literary evidence' about the agrarian revolution, and for the literary historian tracing out the decline and fall of the eighteenth-century pastoral convention. As the poem presents a more interesting 'case' than either historian would suggest it is useful to preface a brief analysis with a word about the pastoral convention itself.

The persistence of the pastoral convention in European literature suggests that it cannot be described in purely literary terms. Its most interesting implications are sociological. In any society with strong class divisions, it is necessary for there to be certain channels of inter-communication if its stability and poise are to be maintained. Mr. Eliot reminds us, 'Neither a classless society, nor a society of strict and impenetrable social barriers is good; . . . they should all have a community of culture with each other which will give them something in common, more fundamental than each class has with its counterpart in another society.' In a keenly differentiated society like the eighteenth century, one of the ways in which the more sophisticated imagined they maintained 'a community of culture' with those that were less so, was through pastoral literature. In the drama of the swain it saw the values it assumed stripped to their bare essentials, and confirmed in a way pleasing and flattering to its expectations. A hierarchical social structure was affirmed in terms of extreme social simplicity; for 'the court' Arcadia had become a place for vicarious pleasure. Obviously, this account is much too compressed to be satisfactory, and many other factors, such as the classical origins of the pastoral, are brought into play, but basically the pastoral convention supplied a protective class-function, linking the 'natural' with the 'sophisticated', and by doing so in imaginative terms, revealed criteria by which the sophisticated reader was to achieve a detached appraisal of his own attitudes and those of society in general. The wide popularity of such mock pastorals as *The Beggar's Opera* and *The Shepherd's Week* do not indicate the death of a convention, but simply a variation within it. 'Rejection' only becomes possible when the relationship between 'society' and 'the poor' is seen to involve questions of social justice. The interest of *The Village* is that for the first time these questions begin to vibrate beneath the surface, and then are elaborately stilled.

The poem opens strongly with its celebrated attack on the pastoral convention; the reasons are practical, 'down-to-earth', and 'the discrepancies' between 'the poet's rapture' and 'the peasant's care' are well pointed. 'What forms the real picture of the poor / Demands a song'—such is the proposed theme, and the opening salvo concludes with the couplet:

> Then shall I dare these real ills to hide
> In tinsel trappings of poetic pride?

With this emphasis on 'the real' the poem broadens out and the remainder of Book I is composed of three main elements—'the poor, barbarous natives of the place', 'the bold, artful, surly, savage race', and as background to both 'the famish'd land'. To say 'background' is misleading in that it gives inadequate stress to the way in which Crabbe uses it as an integral part of the poem. Indeed, the poverty of the bleak Suffolk coastline serves him in a way not unlike that of the Landes region for M. Mauriac, as a means of amplifying and enforcing the spiritual unrest of the inhabitants. Crabbe's attitude to Nature was not visionary; it was that of a botanist, and of 'a man', as Leslie Stephen once remarked, 'never really at home beyond the tide-marks' [see Further Reading]. Poverty and desiccation he can portray with unerring accuracy:

> The thin harvest waves its wither'd ears.

The harvest, usually a symbol of 'ripeness' and 'bounty', is in *The Village* the result of 'nature's niggard hand'; the inversion parallels the human theme, the pastoral swain turned village labourer.

Before the first part of the poem is concluded, there are signs that the intention so firmly announced at the beginning is responding to some undercurrent. For a poem so firmly 'propagandist' in purpose, it is surprising that such emphasis should be placed on 'Rapine, Wrong, Fear' as they exist in the village. It might be said that Crabbe, intent on realistic portrayal, was not going to exclude any element, even if its inclusion meant off-setting some of the sympathy his main theme was intended to arouse. The second book suggests, however, that the reason is not so much obedience to the demands of realism within the poem, as realism about the expectations of his reading public. The second book concludes with a long threnody on Lord Robert Manners, the brother of Crabbe's patron the Duke of Rutland, who was killed in a naval engagement in 1782. This conclusion to the poem has often been regarded as something simply 'tacked on', but its presence completely transforms the *kind* of poem that *The Village* is, so that Dr. Johnson was moved to call it not simply 'original' but 'elegant' [see excerpt dated 1783]. The elegance that Johnson found arises from the fact that Crabbe having come desperately near to overturning the pastoral convention, alters aim in the second half, quietly asserts the traditional 'reader-swain' relationship,

> Yet still, *ye humbler friends,* enjoy your hour,
> *This is your position,* yet unclaimed of power,

sees in Manners' death a link between the distresses of the great and those of the poor, both being involved in a 'universal woe', and so succeeds in making the poem a striking variation of a well-recognized 'kind'—the elegiac pastoral. The elegiac sentiments with which the poem concludes are an artistic sleight-of-hand, by means of which the defined miseries of a particular social class are made to take their place among the truisms applicable to any society at any time. The 'labourer falling unnoticed to the dust', 'the forsaken wives and the mothers never wed', 'the moping idiot and the madman gay' become lost in 'the still sad music of humanity', and the image of the irresistible river which brings the poem to a conclusion, 'still it flows on and shall forever flow', enforces the inevitability of human suffering brought about by agencies beyond man's control. The threnody on Manners places the poem within a traditional frame, the 'realism' is seen, in retrospect, to be a new blending of colour and not, as the first brush strokes suggested, a new way of painting.

*The Village* shows the kind of deflexion that Crabbe's poetry made from the Augustan norm. It was a deflexion encouraged by personal circumstances. He had known domestic misery and poverty, he had grown up in a bleak, unprepossessing country; to present such an environment 'as Truth will have it, And Bards will not', was a task which engaged his full artistic attention. Then, dramatically, came the introduction to Burke and within a matter of months Crabbe enjoyed a Cinderella-like transformation. From extreme poverty and social isolation, he was taken into the best literary society of the day, and through Burke's ministrations he found himself a ducal chaplain. The literary background to this dramatic period in Crabbe's life was the writing of *The Village.* The opening of the poem was written when he was an unknown, the conclusion a year or two later when he was 'a made man'; the pressure of biographical circumstances goes far to explain the curious ambivalence of the poem. Reviewing the theme which best 'tapped' his poetic inspiration, Crabbe found it containing strong social overtones, which to record 'realistically' would be disturbing to readers' expectations. It is important not to mistake the emphasis here. To bring out the inconsistencies in the poem and suggest their significance, I have had to attribute to Crabbe a degree of artistic and social self-consciousness which he clearly didn't possess. An air of artistic and social discomfort is all that is overtly present in the poem, and it would be as foolish to think of Crabbe deliberately muting his poem, as to suggest that he was a social reformer *manqué*. Nevertheless, the uneasiness that is present in the poem seems of a kind to invite and support the analysis I have attempted, and the conclusions derive from what is implicit in the poem, rather than what is consciously attempted. Accounting for the impoverished condition of poetry in the mid-eighteenth century, Mr. Eliot remarked that the poets were second rate because 'they were incompetent to find a style of writing for themselves suited to the matter they wanted to talk about and the way in which they apprehended that matter'. Alone among poets in the closing decades of the eighteenth century, Crabbe found 'matter' perfectly suited to his style of writing, and in exploring, particularly in his later verse, the world of a carefully limited social group, he succeeded in restoring vitality to the couplet, and rescuing it from the nervous, irresolute click to which it had fallen victim. (pp. 38-42)

> Ian Gregor, *"The Last Augustan: Some Observations on the Poetry of George Crabbe (1755-1832),"* in The Dublin Review, *Vol. 229, No. 467, first quarter, 1955, pp. 37-50.*

## OLIVER F. SIGWORTH  (essay date 1965)

[*In the following excerpt from his full-length critical study on Crabbe, Sigworth discusses the meaning and function of nature description in Crabbe's poetry, arguing that in his handling of the natural world, Crabbe essentially continues the classical tradition of the eighteenth century.*]

The use of natural description in poetry is a peculiar characteristic of neither the eighteenth nor the early nineteenth centuries—unless we continue to insist that Thomson and Collins were really born before their time—and in certain respects Crabbe's use of nature allies him with both. In other and more important respects, however, it allies him with neither.

The Biographer remarks at one point that his father" . . . had no real love for painting, or music, or architecture, or for what a painter's eye considers as the beauties of landscape. But he had a passion for science of the human mind, first;—then, that of nature in general; and, lastly, that of abstract quantities" [see Crabbe entry in Further Reading]. The son very possibly had in mind the landscapes of the school of Constable, and, the biography being written in the early 1830's, it is not remarkable that the poet's deficiency in the appreciation of "the beauties of landscape" should at that time be pointed out as a defect of his taste, even though the modern reader may not worry about the lack of "landscapes" in Crabbe's poetry. Whether a "real love" for the "proper objects of taste" would have remedied the ineptitude in "the conduct of the whole" which the Biographer noted as a major fault of his father's poetry is a question open to dispute. Certainly in the best of the *Tales* and in the more memorable letters of *The Borough* this fault is not an obtrusive one, and it is just these in which the reader is most aware of Crabbe's "passion for science": precisely those first two of the "sciences" which his son mentions. But it is not "nature in gener-

al"—whatever the biographer meant by that phrase—which we remember when we have laid the book aside, just as it is not mankind "in general" which is commonly the explicit subject of Crabbe's writing.

Only once, in the preface to the *Tales,* does Crabbe make any considerable pronouncement as to his own literary practice [see excerpt dated 1812]. In this preface he is primarily concerned to defend himself against the charges . . . by Jeffrey and, principally, by Gifford that in his meticulously accurate presentation of some of the more sordid levels of life in *The Borough,* he had offended against poetic decorum and even sacrificed the right to be called a poet. He points to the examples of Chaucer, Dryden, and Pope, and says that if the standards of his critics are to prevail, "an author will find comfort in his expulsion from the rank and society of poets, by reflection that men much his superiors were likewise shut out, and more especially when he finds also that men much his superiors are entitled to admission." He goes on to say, " . . . I must allow that the effect of poetry should be to lift the mind from the painful realities of actual existence . . . by substituting objects in their place which it may contemplate with some degree of interest and satisfaction; but what is there in this which may not be effected by a faithful delineation of existing character?" Fiction, he later points out, must have the effect of reality, and this reality depends not upon the incidents related nor the characters introduced, but upon the "Manner in which the poem itself is conducted."

We note here what we could easily deduce from Crabbe's works, that the poet makes no pretense to being a lyric, an inspirational, or any kind of poet other than a teller of tales. This is not precisely accurate, since in his first three major works he included only incidental narrative; but we may easily perceive the narrative element absorbing more and more of his interest, until, in the last letters of *The Borough*, it has for the most part overtaken whatever other intentions he may have had. By the time of the *Tales,* he was clearly a narrative poet, and with the exception of such incidental verse as **"The**

*Rendering of Aldeborough, "The Borough."*

Flowers" in *New Poems* and the remarkable **"World of Dreams"**—and even that is a tale of sorts—he wrote only narratives thereafter. Even his earlier, "descriptive," poems are, however, not in an important sense descriptive of natural objects, but, rather, of the manners and characters of men and of local institutions. They are "descriptive" in a sense which might, in common use, be applied to Pope's or Johnson's verse rather than to Thomson's *Winter* or Collins' *Ode to Evening*. As a matter of fact, as early as 1779 Crabbe had explicitly renounced Thomson:

> Nor shares my Soul the soft enchanting Stream,
> The lambent Blaze, that [Thomson] knew to blend
> With his Creation; when he led the Eye
> Through the [year's Verdant] Gate, the budding Spring;
> And from the Willow o'er the tuneless Stream,
> And from the [Aspen] Rind, ere yet her Leaf
> Unfolding flicker'd, and from limpid rills
> Unmantled, cull'd Simplicity and Grace.

This poem is, incidentally, apparently Crabbe's only essay in blank verse until 1822, when he attempted, fairly successfully, narrative blank verse in **"In a Neat Cottage,"** now published in **New Poems**. However, **"Midnight"** is interesting not only for this reason, but also because it combines with an experiment in "graveyard" poetry such early indications as the following of what was to be some of Crabbe's best and most characteristic material:

> The Sea-Bird sleeps upon yon hoary Cliff,
> Unconscious of the Surge that Grates below
> The frozen Shore; and Icy Friendship binds,
> As Danger Wretches Destitute of Soul,
> The wave-worn pebbles, which the ebbing Tide,
> Left with the Salt-Flood shining; dark is now
> The awfull Deep, and O'er the Seaman's Grave
> Rolls pouring, and forbids the lucid Stream,
> That silvers oft the way, a shining Beast,
> Spring from the scaly people's putrid Dead,
> Hanging unhers'd upon the Coral Bough . . .

Ten lines of Crabbe's sampling of one poetic taste of his day is quite enough; certainly no one will be sorry that he rejected this mode. It was almost thirty years before he found his artistic métier in the poetic tale, but in the meantime he had written almost all of those poems by which he is commonly remembered today. However, even though Crabbe did not make extensive use of nature in his three most important non-narrative poems—nor in his later poetry either for that matter—the relationships which he bears to the age of Johnson on the one hand, and to some of the "romantics," particularly Wordsworth, on the other, become more apparent when we consider the rôle of nature in his works.

With Wordsworth Crabbe did have in common his use of the more humble levels of society as subjects for sympathetic poetic treatment, but the similarity, for our present purposes, ends there. Not only did Wordsworth draw his characters from pastoral life as opposed to Crabbe's use of those from a seaport village, but in his most memorable poems he placed those characters, frequently, in a setting of sympathetic nature—a nature which seems actively to influence them, or from which they somehow derive spiritual strength. Crabbe's use of nature is almost neutral in this respect; or else, as in **"The Lover's Journey,"** it is precisely the opposite of Wordsworth's practice. That is, Crabbe shows how the states of mind of his characters change, for them, the aspects of nature.

Another way in which Crabbe's use of nature is distinct from Wordsworth's, and distinct at the same time from a great deal of eighteenth-century writing about nature, is his common avoidance in the first place of "the sublime," and in the second, of organized landscapes or "prospects." Of the latter he no doubt could have provided more examples had he had many occasions to do so; so far as "the sublime" is concerned, he seems consciously to have avoided it. His only efforts to describe any of the larger aspects of nature concern the sea, and even then he does not feel entirely comfortable:

> Turn to the watery world!—but who to thee
> (A wonder yet unview'd) shall paint—the sea?

> (pp. 88-92)

The sea had a particular fascination for Crabbe. He speaks of it as "that first great Object of my Admiration and indeed the first of my Notice. I was an Infant Worshipper of its Glory. . . ." We then need not be surprised that he should portray it, as Mr. Spingarn says, "with a distinction that a Turner might envy." It is only surprising that he does not do so more often. The storm which follows the passage just quoted is a real one, and conveys, as aptly as so few words could do, the force and majesty of a turbulent sea. We can imagine how Wordsworth or Thomson would have concluded the passage. The description would probably have led them somehow to a series of reflections upon man and the universe. Not so Crabbe. The human troubles—a shipwreck—appear in his poem, but not until the reactions of birds have first been described, and the only moral reflection with which he favors us is contained in the lines:

> And lo! the sailors homeward take their way;
> Man must endure—let us submit and pray.

On at least three other occasions Crabbe had use for ocean storms, but then he only sketched them in the roughest outlines.

A suspicion that Crabbe prefers the more intimates, less "sublime" faces of nature is confirmed as a fact by a further examination of his passages descriptive of natural scenes. He almost invariably describes not a "prospect" but a selection of details which he never unites, or else he limits himself to portraying the smallest possible area. "Seek, then, thy garden's shrubby bound . . ." he writes, and in another passage:

> To dream these dreams I chose a woody scene,
> My guardian-shade, the world and me between;
> A green inclosure, where beside its bound
> A thorny fence beset its beauties round,
> Save where some creature's force had made a way
> For me to pass, and in my kingdom stray.
> Here then I stray'd then sat me down to call,
> Just as I will'd, my shadowy subjects all!

Notice that it is a "guardian shade, the world and me between" to which the Elder Brother retreats for his dreaming, not a hill with a wide view, or a heath, or the seashore, any one of which might have been the preferred dreaming-place of another poet. This is, to be sure, a part of the Elder Brother's fictional character, but it is nevertheless significant that, for dreaming purposes, he was placed by the author in a particular situation which contained none of those more majestic or awful aspects of nature which conventionally inspired so many of Crabbe's 1819 contemporaries and their followers and which, to them, would have been more appropriate to the Elder Brother's "romantic" temperament.

This abstention from the "sublime" and preference for that within reach of his hand probably bears some relationship to Crabbe's own scientific turn of mind. He had a lifelong interest in botany and entomology, and, in his later years, was fascinated by fossils. . . . The result of this scientific interest is sometimes almost too readily apparent in his verse:

> Eager he looks, and soon, to glad his eyes,
> From the sweet bower, by nature form'd arise
> Bright troops of virgin moths and fresh-born butterflies,
> Who broke that morning from their half-year's sleep,
> To fly o'er flow'rs where they were wont to creep.
> Above the sovereign oak a sovereign skims
> The purple Emp'ror, strong in wing and limbs:
> There fair Camilla takes her flight serene,
> Adonis blue, and Paphia, silver queen;
> With every filmy fly from mead or bower,
> And hungry Sphinx, who threads the honey'd flower;
> She o'er the Larkspur's bed, where sweets abound,
> Views ev'ry bell, and hums th'approving sound;
> Poised on her busy plumes, with feeling nice
> She draws from every flower, nor tries a floret twice.

This is charmingly done and in itself is pleasant enough, but it is versified entomology, and is not very skillfully worked into a letter entitled **"Trades."**

His preference for nature at close range is further exhibited, and an interesting question raised, by the following quotation:

> He rode to Ripley through that river gay,
> Where in the shallow stream the loaches play,
> And stony fragments stay the winding stream,
> And gilded pebblers at the bottom gleam,
> Giving their yellow surface to the sun,
> And making proud the waters as they run.
> It is a lovely place, and at the side
> Rises a mountain-rock in rugged pride;
> And in the rock are shapes of shells, and forms
> Of creatures in old worlds, of nameless worms,
> Whose generations lived and died ere man,
> A worm of other class, to crawl began.

Edmund Blunden's comment on this passage is worth quoting:

> All our memories of the brooks in Anglia, making "washes" across the sandy cartways, are brought to their brightest in the first part of the passage, and we may well suppose that another sort of fancy or personality would have gone on with the delightfulness of that little river; but Crabbe the geologist (and obviously the geologist cares nothing for the parson) cannot be long excluded. . . . He is true to himself and he records his train of thought, ending with his ambiguous definition—is it satirical, is it merely scientific?—of the human being. And is this, in an artistic consideration, a false note? Those who live with Crabbe as he remains in his book will be less inclined to think so.

Agreeing to the delightfulness of the passage, we may still wonder about the definition. If it is satirical, it is just a little *gauche,* for it does not represent Crabbe's working viewpoint of man; if it is merely scientific, it does seem artistically out of place, for as a generalization it is neither very original nor striking. It shows, at any rate, how this scientific interest-for whether the definition is intended to be a scientific observation or not, it certainly had its inception in Crabbe's interest in science— can sometimes play the poet false. But we must also give this turn of mind credit for the minute and vital ob-

servation of the "gilded pebbles" in the water, which gives the passage its appeal.

It is clearly impossible to make any reasonable assessment of the role his scientific mind played in contributing to or detracting from the artistic success of Crabbe's poetry, because it is impossible to imagine any other kind of mind writing the poetry Crabbe's produced. It is not "science" which was responsible for the peculiarly refreshing quality of the butterfly passage itself, depending as it does upon the euphonious scientific names—yet also, we must notice, poetic and imaginative names—of the insects. The lambent dulness of Erasmus Darwin is never present in Crabbe; the moments when he is most like his unfortunate predecessor in the versification of science, are also frequently the moments when he is most readable. So far as I know, for another example, no other poet has celebrated the beauties of a jellyfish, yet Crabbe does so twice, and each time entrancingly:

> Now is it pleasant in the summer-eve,
> When a broad shore retiring waters leave,
> Awhile to wait upon the firm fair sand,
> When all is calm at sea, all still at land;
> And there the ocean's produce to explore,
> As floating by, or rolling on the shore;
> Those living jellies which the flesh inflame,
> Fierce as a nettle, and from that its name;
> Some in huge masses, some that you may bring
> In the small compass of a lady's ring;
> Figured by hand divine—there's not a gem
> Wrought by man's art to be compared to them;
> Soft, brilliant tender, through the wave they glow,
> And make the moonbeam brighter where they flow.

We remember these passages as among Crabbe's best not only because of their own intrinsic quality but also because of the contrast in subject-matter with the greater body of his verse, which deals with quite other affairs. They are not the most significant use Crabbe makes of nature, as Paul Elmer More was aware when he wrote: "Of this inanimate lore of plants and rocks Crabbe is most prodigal in his verse, but, by some true gift of the Muses, it never for a moment obscures the human interest of the narrative. After all, it was man, and the moral springs in man, that really concerned him" [see excerpt dated 1901]."

As in a discussion of any other aspect of Crabbe's work, it is to man and his moral springs that we must turn eventually to see the relationship of that aspect to the whole. As I have pointed out in another connection, Crabbe's descriptive passages never exist exclusively for themselves, for his world is peopled, and it is the people who are his chief concern.

In all of *The Village,* for example, there is only one short passage which makes an extensive use of nature imagery:

> Lo! where the heath, with withering brake grown o'er,
> Lends the light turf that warms the neighbouring poor;
> From thence a length of burning sand appears,
> Where the thin harvest waves its wither'd ears;
> Rank weeds, that every art and care defy,
> Reign o'er the land, and rob the blighted rye;
> Where thistles stretch their prickly arms afar,
> And to the ragged infant threaten war;
> There poppies, nodding, mock the hope of toil;
> There the blue bugloss paints the sterile soil;
> Hardy and high, above the slender sheaf,
> The slimy mallow waves her silky leaf;
> O'er the young shoot the charlock throws a shade,
> And clasping tares cling round the sickly blade;

With mingled tints the rocky coasts abound,
And a sad splendour vainly shines around.

This passage is striking and memorable (and it was possibly more striking to the reader of 1783 than to us today), and, indeed, it must be so, for it forms a sort of scenic back-drop for the tableaux which Crabbe is to present. Holme refers to Crabbe's "constant choice of the less pleasing parts of a landscape for minute treatment," and, even though it is clearly not true that Crabbe's choice of these parts of the landscape is "constant," particularly in the later works, it is an attestation of the force of a few descriptions such as this that he should remember them as being practically omnipresent in the poetry. The back-drop remains throughout the performance, although it is pointed out to us only at curtain-time.

That the back-drop in this case, as through most parts of the three earlier important poems, is a gloomy one cannot be disputed. "Withering," "burning," "thin," "blighted," "prickly," "ragged," "sterile," "slim'"—adjective after adjective drives home to the reader the picture Crabbe wants him to keep in mind. The only flowers blooming are those that "mock the hope of toil"; the only plant "hardy and high" is the mallow, and the "young shoot" is shaded by wild mustard. The splendor is vain and sad. It is completely beside the point that, as Woodberry, with his late Victorian prejudices as to the nature of beauty, remarked, "there is loveliness in a salt marsh," and probably untrue that "Crabbe could not present it, nor even see it for himself" [see excerpt dated 1880]. Woodberry happened to be referring to a description in **"Peter Grimes,"** but for our purposes the situation is the same: if Crabbe does not in this instance present the loveliness of the scene, it is because that loveliness is not to his artistic purpose. The details he presents are carefully selected with the tone and subject of the poem and its effect upon the reader in mind. In other words, to carry on with our mid-twentieth century prejudices as to the nature of beauty, by his selection of these particular details Crabbe is not only setting the scene for the entire poem, but subtly inducing the reader to adopt a mental "set" from which to approach the remainder of what he has to present. The poet has completed his introduction—the prologue to the succeeding tableaux—in which he has stated that he paints "the Cot / As Truth will paint it, and as Bards will not," and now he presents us with the first and most plainly visible truth, the natural surroundings of the village—the stage back-drop, which hints to us what we may expect from the remainder of the performance.

The question of some sort of interaction between "nature" and the other elements of the poem does not become prominent in **The Village,** nor, indeed, in **"The Parish Register."** Crabbe uses a few lines at intervals throughout the poem to recall the initial picture of the natural surroundings to our minds, but these surroundings are, in themselves, not the subject of his discussion, and he gives us no clear indication of what part he thinks external nature plays in the lives and thoughts of the characters he introduces, beyond the obvious implication that because here "Nature's niggard hand / Gave a spare portion to the famished land" the people inhabiting that "frowning coast" will suffer for Nature's niggardliness.

The first letter of **The Borough** bears almost the same relationship to the whole of that poem as the lines we have been discussing bear to **The Village.** It is, however, more than a poetical back-drop, since actual incident, and interaction between men and nature, occurs in the lines devoted to a storm and shipwreck. The background is, however, only in part the

sea, even though it is in writing of it in this letter that Crabbe, as we have seen, produces some of his best description. The lines from line 163 to the end of the letter are probably among the most memorable pictures of the sea in English literature, but that element does not play quite the important part in the ensuing poem which this first "General Description of The Borough" would lead us to expect. The fault is not a very important one, but it is a small example of the "deficiency in the conduct of the whole" of which the Biographer speaks.

The technique of presenting the natural setting at the very beginning of the poem is a simple and not very subtle one, and since Crabbe uses it only seldom in poems after **The Borough** it is pleasant to believe that he outgrew it, if it was ever an essential part of his technical apparatus. Crabbe's subjects do not in general require a natural background and, as a matter of fact, his method of describing natural scenery does not readily lend itself to use in providing one. This is true because he very seldom presents us an entire, organized scene; he does not as a rule write "landscape" poetry.

The question of "landscape" poetry as such is, I think, one which need not long detain us. The fact that Crabbe did not in this respect follow the footsteps of Thomson, Dyer, and others in in him neither a singularity nor necessarily a deficiency. When he wants to present a scene organized pictorially he does so very effectively, but he ordinarily had no occasion for such pictures, and made his nature passages serve quite different purposes.

If one has the impression of a "landscape" after reading the lines quoted from **The Village,** it is because he has himself organized the objects presented into a coherent scene. We have at least a heath, apparently in the foreground, and a length of "burning sand" "where the thin harvest waves its wither'd ears," but the "rocky coasts" are in a completely unspecified relationship to these. The poet has almost entirely confined his attention to the sickly plants, indeed, to specific species. These plants the reader can see clearly, but not in any organized way as growing upon a heath (or upon the "length of burning sand"—we do not know positively where we are looking through most of the passage). The description is one which gives us, rather than a literally pictorial back-drop for the tableaux—if we may revert to our earlier metaphor—an *impressionistic* one such as scenic designers for the modern ballet frequently provide. Since Crabbe presents no coherent scene which can be grasped in its entirety, it is the mood and attitude conveyed to us by the description of these unhappy vegetables which are important to the poem. The same situation prevails in his other works. In the use of nature to prepare his scene or to illuminate the occurences thereon, Crabbe is a master, giving just the proper touches, emphasizing precisely the detail which we recall later as important for his purposes, yet never allowing an obviously genuine pleasure in writing of nature to divert him from his main design.

Crabbe was too much concerned with human beings and their tragedies and comedies, and too little considered any cosmic significance these dramas might have had, to have devoted very much effort to thinking through a "theory of nature." Not being a Deist, he would be naturally disinclined to accept the idea that nature is in itself a revelation of divine attributes, and he had none of the enthusiasm for the act of contemplating nature, displayed by Thomson, which might have led him to evolve an original theory. But there is what we could call a theory of perception underlying many of Crabbe's nature passages, a theory generally only implied, but stated at least once, and made then the chief matter of one of his tales:

> It is the soul that sees; the outward eyes
> Present the object, but the mind descries;
> And thence delight, disgust, or cool indiff 'rence rise:
> When minds are joyful, then we look around,
> And what is seen is all on fairy ground;
> Again they sicken, and on every view
> Cast their own dull and melancholy hue . . .
>
> (pp. 93-103)

This view of the perception of nature as a reflection of a state of mind might easily have been expanded into a full-blown psychology, and it has obvious relationships with the empirical philosophy of the late eighteenth century, but the country parson was not a philosopher, and with him it was a matter-of-fact result of his artistic concern with the observation of people rather than with ideas or things. It is in relation to this view that almost all the nature passages in the later poetry appear . . . Crabbe occasionally indulges (one almost says "indulges himself ") in a kind of purely objective description which is unusual because it is not closely integrated with the matter of the tale he is telling. But . . . in [*Tales of the Hall*] we find this passage:

> Early he rose, and look'd with many a sigh
> On the red light that fill'd the eastern sky;
> Oft had he stood before, alert and gay,
> To hail the glories of the new-born day;
> But now dejected, languid, listless, low,
> He saw the wind upon the water blow,
> And the cold stream curl'd onward as the gale
> From the pine-hill blew harshly down the dale.
> On the right side the youth a wood survey'd,
> With all its dark intensity of shade;
> Where the rough wind alone was heard to move,
> In this, the pause of nature and of love,
> When new the young are rear'd, and when the old,
> Lost to the tie, grow negligent and cold—
> Far to the left he saw the huts of men,
> Half hid in mist, that hung upon the fen;
> Before him swallows, gathering for the sea,
> Took their short flights, and twitter'd on the lea;
> And near the bean-sheaf stood, the harvest done,
> And slowly blacken'd in the sickly sun;
> All these were sad in nature, or they took
> Sadness from him, the likeness of his look,
> And of his mind—he ponder'd for awhile,
> Then met his Fanny with a borrow'd smile.

This description has been quoted before in essays on Crabbe; it is surely one for which no English poet would need to apologize. We might analyze it as a "prospect"—one of the very few which Crabbe wrote—for certainly the fact that the scene is organized for us may contribute something to its high quality; but it is more interesting still to observe how the scene, at least so far as the tone and mood are concerned, is not, and is explicitly pointed out not to be, a representation of whatever might actually have been there. It is in this sense a fabrication of the character's mind. (pp. 105-06)

There is very little variation in the quality of Crabbe's nature-writing throughout his career. We may think to find a more relaxed, reflective tone in the later passages, and it is possible that he chose in the later years to describe more pleasant aspects of the natural scene than had earlier been his wont; but on the whole he not only continues to use nature with about the same infrequency, but his manner of writing about it remains almost constant once he has found the tradition within which he was to work.

It is to that classic-realistic tradition which we have discussed that we must ultimately turn if we are to see Crabbe's nature-writing in its proper perspective, for the men of the eighteenth century whose shadows glide wherever we look in Crabbe's poetry would all, to some extent at least, have agreed with Johnson's remark that "a blade of grass is always a blade of grass whether in one country or another. . . . Men and women are my subjects of inquiry." To this attitude is certainly to be attributed the fact that Crabbe, who wrote nature poetry very well, wrote so little of it. Here also may we look to account for the fact that, as Paul Elmer More remarked, he "tends to distinguish . . . sharply between men and nature rather than to blend them in any haze of symbolism." Crabbe may draw instructive lessons by a parallel with nature, but he neither tries to learn from nature nor in any way identifies himself, as the poet, with nature. He has not the slightest inclination either to deistic transcendentalism or toward the pantheistic belief in immanence which so many men of the nineteenth century shared. Nature existed for him as apart from, though influencing, man; as an object for pleasant contemplation, but not in and for itself a fit object for art.

In respect to his use of nature, then, Crabbe did work outside two important poetic tendencies of his time. He can be identified neither with the writers of "prospect poems" such as *Grongar Hill,* nor with poets such as Thomson and, later, Wordsworth, who used nature as a medium for the expression of philosophical ideas. Although his delight in certain aspects of nature is occasionally reflected in his poetry, we can point to no single passage in his verse with the assurance that in those lines we have the quintessential expression of that delight. Crabbe is by no means a "nature poet," even if, as Mr. Leavis remarks, "in the use of description, of nature, and the environment generally, for emotional purposes he surpasses any Romantic" [see excerpt dated 1936]. Mr. Leavis has his own predispositions, but even he would hardly dispute that not only are Crabbe's nature passages few, but when he introduces a passage embodying a description of external nature, that passage is subordinate, and clearly subordinate, to the "manner in which the poem itself is conducted."

A literary "if " is even more futile than an historical one, but the critic may find amusement in his fancies. It is not too much to say that *if* Crabbe had not been so much a part of the eighteenth-century "realistic" tradition, he could have been a nature poet in the commonly accepted sense of the word, for he had the requisite powers had he chosen to use them. The fact that he was not a nature poet may cast an illuminating glow, if only faintly, upon some of the puzzling ways in which neo-classical poetry operates. The mind of attuned to the world as it is (however it may be), the mind of the "realist" in art, prefers to deal with the world on its own terms, not on terms imposed upon it by an imaginative, or creative, extension of the artist's own sensibilities. All art in the twentieth century has, either in its very creation or at least in its interpretation, been subjected to this "romantic" egocentricity. Such an operation may lead to richer and more complex art (though I think not necessarily so, for classical art is rich and complex as the artist sees richness and complexity in the world he deals with, not merely as he imposes the convolutions of his own spirit upon not always tractable material), but it is not the mode of Dryden, Pope, or Johnson. Nor, as we have seen, is it the mode of Crabbe, whose interest finds its full expression in his narrative verse. He was not really happy writing descriptions, for nature was to him important in poetry only in its relation to the primary fact of the world in which man lives—man himself. (pp. 111-13)

> *Oliver F. Sigworth, in his* Nature's Sternest Painter: Five Essays on the Poetry of George Crabbe, *The University of Arizona Press, 1965, 191 p.*

## RONALD B. HATCH   (essay date 1974)

[*The following excerpt is from an article that originally appeared in* Eighteenth-Century Studies *with full documentation and explanatory notes not included here. Hatch focuses on* The Village, *commenting on the thematic significance of the disparity between the unconventional, anti-pastoral realism of the first part and the invocation of classical poetic ideas in the second part through the introduction of Robert Manners.*]

The poet George Crabbe is typical of many of the post-Augustan writers, such as Thomson, Shenstone, Goldsmith, and even Johnson, in that his work embodies alternate or antithetic visions of the world which result from a conflict between consciously held ideas and those created under the pressure of creative practice. (p. 274)

Crabbe's growing awareness of the problems implicit in the choice of an appropriate perspective can be seen in his early poems loosely grouped together by Sir Adolphus Ward as "juvenilia" in the three-volume Cambridge edition of his [works]. In **"Midnight,"** written around 1779, Crabbe is already grappling with the problem of finding a "voice" for his view of the world. A partial imitation of the graveyard school, the poem permits Crabbe to use as his narrator a man of vision set aside from his fellowmen. Acutely aware of his skimpy formal education and his lower-class origins, Crabbe recognizes that he cannot write in the same tradition as that of most previous poets. Respectfully the young poet asks the men of learning to forgive him for tampering with their subjects, but in the seeming humility of this address to the "Wise" lies a Socratic irony. Quite obviously Crabbe has no faith in their type of wisdom:

> Forgive me then, ye Wise, who seem awake,
> A Midnight Song, and let your Censure sleep.

Since the Wise only "seem" to be awake, their "wisdom" can be a knowledge only of other times and other places. Crabbe implies that the situation has changed, and that acknowledged men of letters are no longer competent to deal with new conditions. The great poets of the past—Homer, Virgil, Milton—all dealt with grand and beautiful themes; Crabbe feels the modern age needs poets to describe man's disappointments in everyday life. As he says, theirs was a "blest Task, a gloomier task is mine." Akenside, for instance, Crabbe feels, "let the soul thro' Nature, and display'd / Imagination's Pleasures to the Eye." While recognizing the value of Akenside's themes, Crabbe feels that his own experience of the bleak Suffolk coast, and his continual struggle to earn enough to feed and clothe himself, have ill-equipped him to write poetry in the same grand style. (p. 275)

Crabbe wants to turn away from the grand and marvelous to detail the minute. As a consequence, he believes that he must begin a new style of poetry:

> He, tyed to some poor Spot, where e'en the rill
> That owns him Lord untasted steals away,

Hallows a Clod, and spurns Immensity.

Not only are the themes and forms of the past insufficient to handle the new situations, they are obstacles to a clear presentation of the new problems.

In **"Midnight,"** the youthful Crabbe had humbly requested his audience to permit his new perspective; by 1783, the time of *The Village,* Crabbe is adamant about life in the country had strayed widely from the truth, he feels, because the poets themselves had been unacquainted with village life and had consequently looked to models from the past for their inspiration. By turning to authority or by relying on the "Muses" for their inspiration instead of referring to the empirical world for their evidence, the poets had distorted their descriptions. Crabbe notes:

> . . . the Muses sing of happy swains,
> Because the Muses never knew their pains.

Since the Muses, or the traditional sources of poetic inspiration, have nothing to say about the contemporary world, Crabbe takes upon himself to "paint the Cot, / As Truth will paint it, and as Bards will not." In part Crabbe is claiming that complete verisimilitude to the ordinary facts of the world is antithetical to the more traditional concerns of poetry which had relied upon the Muses' divine inspiration. But also he is suggesting that communication between the divine and the human, where it has been attempted, has led to misleading interpretations about the material world. Crabbe, it should be noted, is not running the risk of Thamyris, the Thracian bard who was deprived of sight when he boasted himself the equal of the Muses, since Crabbe is not competing with the Muses. Whereas in Homer and Hesiod, the Muses, around the altar of Zeus, had glorified the deeds of gods and heroes, Crabbe wishes to take over a new province of poetry that the Muses had never claimed; he is not inspired to write of divine harmony, but will attempt to deal with evidence manifest to the five senses.

Crabbe in a curious way resembles Keats in that both had a strong desire for concrete perception. In reading Keats one feels that man is rediscovering his body; and in reading Crabbe one feels as if man is rediscovering his social world. Of course the differences between Crabbe's approach and that of the Romantic poets are almost total. Whereas Crabbe was attempting to discover *the* correct perspective from which man's condition could be viewed, the Romantic poets were interested in showing that any given perspective of the world, no matter how powerfully rooted, was a product of man's making. For Crabbe in *The Village* there exist "weighty griefs" and "real ills" which he scorns to hide "In tinsel trappings of poetic pride." In order to impress upon his readers that his descriptions of hardship were not merely poetic effusions, Crabbe felt it necessary, in later editions of *The Village,* to add a footnote to this passage explaining the circumstances of the peasant. The social evils described in the poem were to be read as documentaries, not poetic constructs. For Crabbe, a dangerous schism has grown up between the imaginative arts and the real world.

If Crabbe intended to give "the real picture" then there must also have been a false picture. This false picture, largely but not entirely a literary creation, rested on the assumption that a pastoral life of ease and pleasure existed in England. Crabbe's first job was to demolish this pastoral myth. And just as Ralegh answered Marlowe's "The Passionate Shepherd to his Love" by having the nymph reply to the shepherd in his own style, so does Crabbe ensure that his criticism of the classical pastoral is formulated in a classical manner:

> In fairer scenes, where peaceful pleasures spring,
> Tityrus, the pride of Mantuan swains, might sing:
> But charmed by him, or smitten with his views,
> Shall modern poets court the Mantuan muse?
> From Truth and Nature shall we widely stray,
> Where Fancy leads, or Virgil led the way?

Written in the formal style, with classical allusions, these lines appealed greatly to the Augustan sensibility, and led Johnson, to whom *The Village* was shown in manuscript [see letter dated 1783], to interest himself in a rewording which Crabbe accepted. But the point is that in spite of their classical appearance, they are a repudiation of the classical aesthetic as practiced in the eighteenth century. Crabbe is claiming that Roman models will cause English poets to stray from the truth of English life. But it should also be noted that in claiming the Muses cannot give a better picture than that of the truthful documentary, Crabbe is consciously creating a parallel between his guiding model—empirical observation—and the inspiration of the nine Muses. Thus is he attempting to strike out a new path for poetry without appearing to overthrow traditional patterns. He has created for himself what could be called the "tenth muse."

Also worthy of note is that Johnson's revision, the lines now read, partially obscure Crabbe's intention. Where Johnson declares that the poet would go astray if he followed Virgil and not his "Fancy," in the original Crabbe had said that the poet would be mistaken if he followed either Virgil or his "Fancy." Obviously what Crabbe wanted was poetry which incorporated direct observation, and which did not attempt either "fanciful" or Virgilian commentary. (pp. 276-79)

However, Crabbe's main argument is not with classical poetry per se, but with the inclusion of classical subject matter in descriptions of English country life. Crabbe no doubt realized as well as we do that the landscape of the traditional pastoral was meant to symbolize a state of innocence, and not to represent a physical environment. Yet the pastoral underwent some extremely curious changes in the eighteenth century, first when Pope altered the tradition by including "the best side only of a shepherd's life," and later when poets such as William Shenstone and his friend Richard Jago introduced classical shepherds into their poems of topographic description. The result, a curious mixture of myth and geography, was neither symbolic nor naturalistic. It is this eighteenth-century development of the pastoral which Crabbe is denouncing.

Because *The Village* describes the harsh and unjust life of the villagers it has often been assumed that Crabbe was appealing primarily for the reader's sympathy. Yet this is to misunderstand the tradition in which Crabbe was writing, for if he had simply asked his readers to pity the poor, he would not have been offering anything new, and he would not have been giving a faithful account of the "real picture." To understand Crabbe's attitude one should recognize that *The Village* was written in protest against a particularly obnoxious version of sentimentalized humanitarianism which was rife in the period 1740-1790. Very often throughout the century when the poor were discussed the emphasis fell not on the condition of the poor, but on the feelings of the observer. This can be seen in Richard Steele's comment on the paupers of London: "Such miserable Objects affect the compassionate Beholder with dismal Ideas, discompose the Chearfulness of his Mind,

and deprive him of the Pleasure that he might otherwise take in surveying the Grandeur of our Metropolis." One sees immediately that Steele is interested as much in the effect of poverty on the mind of the beholder as he is in poverty itself.

Had Crabbe made a simple plea for the reader's sympathy toward the poor, he would inevitably have fallen into a series of those stock epithets which one finds attributed to any member of the leisured class claiming to fulfill Shaftesbury's ideal of the man of taste, humanity, and culture. It was standard procedure to include in poems as widely different as Pomfret's *The Choice,* John Philip's *Cyder,* and James Thomson's *Winter* and acknowledgement that the true gentleman and humanitarian remembered and pitied the poor. (pp. 279-80)

One can understand better Crabbe's vehement dislike of pastoral when it is realized that as a result of the emphasis placed on the feelings of the philanthropist, the poor were no longer described as distressed people, but pastoral shepherds idling in a green and merry land. Since poets wished to emphasize the beauty of the act of charity, they found it necessary to describe beautiful surroundings and not empty commons. (p. 281)

Once one sees the connection between the pastoral and humanitarian poetry, Crabbe's attack on "sleepy bards" should be all the more understandable and his purpose in *The Village* easier to define. He is not developing the idea that the poor should be helped (the humanitarians had made this theme appear trite), but rather that one must learn to recognize the poor and their conditions before attempting to help them. In many ways, Crabbe's *The Village* is anti-humanitarian, because in the 1780s "humanitarian" entailed a sentimental attitude to the poor. I am not saying that no genuine humanitarian poetry was written before Crabbe's time. Obviously sections of Pope's *Moral Essays* and Thomson's *The Seasons,* Johnson's *London* and Langhorne's *The Country Justice* show a genuine concern for the poor. The point which needs stressing, however, is that the great mass of humanitarian verse, especially from 1740 to 1780, tended to organize the facts of the material world to create a warmth in the observer. In order to avoid the dangers of a trite humanitarian appeal to the conscience of the rich, Crabbe decided that a true account of the state of the poor was required. Opinions can be easily disregarded; a statement of fact almost always stirs the conscience.

In attempting to distinguish the difference between Crabbe's treatment of the poor in *The Village* and that of earlier eighteenth-century poets, one is often driven to say that Crabbe's portraits are "realistic" or "naturalistic." Indeed, the demands by writers such as Johnson and Crabbe for a reformulation of the literary account of English country life can be seen exemplified in the "rise of the novel" as opposed to the old "romance." Yet terms such as "realism and naturalism" have become overused in recent years; what is required is an explication of Crabbe's technique of portrayal. The most obvious point is Crabbe's choice of his native Aldborough for his setting. The importance of this lies not so much in the way the features of Aldborough differ from, say Farnham in Sussex, but in the way the topographic details of a particular place give the poem a locus outside the customary poetic backgrounds. Beginning with the particular, and not with the universal or generic, Crabbe was creating his own world and its own values. In choosing to emphasize certain features of his own area, and thus giving them universal significance,

Crabbe was one of the first of a long line of artists such as Thomas Hardy and Robert Frost who created their distinctive world from the particularized details of the surrounding countryside.

The choice of Aldborough as his setting supplied Crabbe with a host of details that could not easily be accommodated to the normal eighteenth-century picture of the world. Just as late eighteenth-century botanists were discovering vast numbers of new plants with new properties that were finally to overthrow their classification system and call into doubt the idea of special creation with each plant embodying its God-given logical essence, so Crabbe's introduction of plants such as the blue bugloss and the slimy mallow forced him (or perhaps "allowed" is a better choice of terminology) to offer an alternative structuring of the world from that ordinarily accepted at the time. In contrast to most eighteenth-century poetry of natural description where the background is meant to suggest benevolence and harmony, the setting of *The Village* creates a sense of inherent tragedy. Crabbe explains how he was born, not on an ordinary coast, but on a "frowning coast" where the countryside is filled with Manichean forces ready to thwart man's efforts:

> Lo! where the heath, with withering brake grown o'er,
> Lends the light turf that warms the neighbouring poor;
> From thence a length of burning sand appears,
> Where the thin harvest waves its wither'd ears;
> Rank weeds, that every art and care defy,
> Reign o'er the land, and rob the blighted rye:
> There thistles stretch their prickly arms afar,
> And to the ragged infant threaten war;
> There poppies, nodding, mock the hope of toil;
> There the blue bugloss paints the sterile soil;
> Hardy and high, above the slender sheaf,
> The slimy mallows waves her silky leaf;
> O'er the young shoot the charlock throws a shade,
> And clasping tares cling round the sickly blade;
> With mingled tints the rocky coasts abound,
> And a sad splendour vainly shines around.

Endowed with human feelings, the threatening landscape is a good example of what Ruskin derisively termed the pathetic fallacy. Mrs. Haddakin has said: "The function of the passage as a whole is to demonstrate that if you look closely enough into a picturesque landscape you are led, by way of agricultural problems, to consider the welfare of human beings" [see Further Reading]. But even more than this, Crabbe's description of "rank weeds" reigning over the land and defying all man's efforts to cultivate anything but the scantest garden for pleasure and use creates the terms by which man inhabits the world. Images such as "clasping tares," and the "slimy mallow" waving its "silky leaf," have been carefully chosen to convey the impression that, on the most primeval terms, man has to combat forces of destruction. The inhabitants of the village do not live in a "Happy Valley" where the design of nature is ordered to help man, but on a coast where the sea is swallowing the homes built upon the loose shingle.

The weeds may look splendid to the "sleepy bards" who do not see clearly, but they are a sad sight to the villager attempting to earn a living from the "thin harvest." Crabbe's own viewpoint is interesting, for unlike the laborers who can see only the sadness of the weeds and the sleepy bards who see only the splendor, Crabbe can see both sides. These weeds grow among the sustaining corn, and threaten it, but the principle of growth is there in both weed and corn. The thistles

are noble in a way; the poppies are narcotics as well as pretty; the colors are striking; the leaves are "silky." Everything is involved with its opposite: beauty and wastefulness, use and want. "Sad splendour" sums it up.

Crabbe of course is himself open to the same sort of criticism that he gave of the earlier "pastoral" poets; for just as they created an ethical universe in which man lives in harmony with nature, so Crabbe has created a universe in which an amoral force involves everything with its opposite to create "sad splendour." But every artist (indeed everyone) must have some organizing principle of selection: what matters is how well the principle accounts for the observed facts and how successful it is in predicting as yet unobserved phenomena. Part of what gives the early parts of *The Village* so much power is the way the organizing principle that Crabbe posits in nature carries over into the people, or, to put it another way, the way the people are rooted in their milieu.

The transition between the landscape and the people is made with devastating understatement. Like the weeds, the people have a sturdy and unruly vigor. But they are not civilized, and in their wild actions they threaten to overcome the conventions and arts of society. The central notion of "sad splendour" evoked by the setting is seen to have a direct corollary in the people:

> So looks the nymph whom wretched arts adorn,
> Betray'd by man, then left for man to scorn;
> Whose cheek in vain assumes the mimic rose,
> While her sad eyes the troubled breast disclose;
> Whose outward splendour is but folly's dress,
> Exposing most, when most it gilds distress.

Crabbe was never greatly influenced by theories of the natural goodness of man, so that having once established in *The Village* the idea that man as a part of nature is moved by a principle of growth which has little respect for ends, he does not hesitate to draw the conclusion that the people of the village are rude and lawless.

Critics such as René Huchon have made much of the way Crabbe, in Book II, shows his villagers to be brawling drunkards, as if this controverted the intention of Book I [see Further Reading]. But Crabbe's wish to show the real picture of the poor by no means implies that he wanted to show the good villagers living in harsh surroundings; rather he shows how the villagers reflect their environment:

> Here joyless roam a wild amphibious race,
> With sullen wo display'd in every face;
> Who far from civil arts and social fly,
> And scowl at strangers with suspicious eye.

The village then is preeminently a place of hostility in which man's role is no different from that of other living things. Man's misery and his viciousness are explained as the counterparts of environment.

In choosing to describe villagers who live "far from civil arts and social," and showing them as a part of nature which has vigor and splendor, but which is amoral, Crabbe developed a view of man and nature which has little in common with the optimism of mid-century poets. Many eighteenth-century writers believed that the new science offered proof that one could see aspects of God through his harmonious and beautiful world. Thomson wrote of Isaac Newton:

> All intellectual eye, our solar round
> First gazing thro', he by the blended power

Of *gravitation* and *projection* saw
The whole in silent harmony revolve.

An amateur scientist himself, Crabbe valued the principle of classification which Thomson praises so highly, but as Crabbe said in **"Midnight,"** his was a "horizontal Eye" that saw "all things grey." Whereas Thomson believed that Newton's "intellectual eye" gave man insight into the hierarchial laws by which God harmonizes the universe, Crabbe's "horizontal Eye" led to empirical observations that did not assume a moral universe. Thomson began with the assumption that Newton had been able to give a reason for everything, including, in his words, "the yellow waste of idle sands." This traditional view in which man was seen as a unique creation with an immortal soul participating in an ethically organized universe is implicitly challenged by Crabbe's "scientific" method, where he begins by describing the particular, the barren soil of Aldborough, and from this particular attempts to draw conclusions. The difference is crucial and it should be no surprise to find that Crabbe draws the conclusion that man, like all other living things, has to battle in order to live. As an amateur scientist, Crabbe has offered a picture of man in terms of his observed outward actions with no mention of the usual moral and spiritual dimensions. He is explained in terms of natural phenomena.

Crabbe's use of environment serves yet another purpose, for nature, if it is an active force resisting man's attempts to sustain himself, must be a conditioning factor as well. Crabbe explains how he too had once lived in the village. But realizing that circumstances would defeat him if he remained, he seized the "favouring hour" and fled. Looking back at the neighbors he left behind, he holds out little hope for their welfare: "Ah! hapless they who still remain." In Crabbe's view, the people are helpless, because the ocean will sooner or later swallow them by sweeping "the low hut and all it holds away." When this happens, as Crabbe feels it inevitable, the only alternative for the poor villager is to weep from door to door and beg "a poor protection from the poor."

Crabbe is here in the process of formulating a tentative theory of the influence of environment on man, where man is not free to make himself what he wants to be, but is molded into the person he is by the physical and social forces around him. Nature and society force upon him a life of "Rapine and Wrong and Fear," about which he can do little.

The question then arises why Crabbe should want to add to his "real" descriptions of the early part of the poem his famous or rather infamous threnody on Robert Manners. . . . In *The Village* the introduction of Robert Manners comes exactly at the point when Crabbe is face to face with the consequences of his empirical world. Significantly, Crabbe introduces Manners, not to show that he helped the poor, but because Manners' way of life demonstrates that "Life is not measured by the time we live." In this respect *The Village* resembles Wordsworth's *Resolution and Independence.* Both poems are concerned with the seeming futility of man's life and the way in which meaning can be found or given. Where Wordsworth speaks of the "cold, pain and labour" of a totally secular life, Crabbe speaks of "Narrow views and paltry fears." And just as the old leech-gatherer gives Wordsworth new resolution so does Robert Manners provide Crabbe with hope. Manners is the noble "chief" who has accepted the fallen world, while still managing to experience joy.

Crabbe tells the poor that if such great men exist "then let

your murmurs cease, / Think, think of him, and take your lot in peace." Caution is necessary at this point since at first sight it is unclear why the poor should cease complaining because one noble man has been found. But assume the opposite to be the case; suppose it had proved impossible to find such a man. The conclusion would be that nothing anyone could do would have meaning. In rejecting the pastoral world in which man lives in harmony with nature, Crabbe developed a world in which nature is either indifferent or hostile to man. Such a "naturalistic" world places man on the same plane as other animals, and seems to make him the slave of his passions and instincts. In his early and very fine parody, *Inebriety,* Crabbe had already described a world in which men and women both descended to the level of brutes. In *The Village* when Crabbe looked closely at the "simple life that Nature yields" he found a Hobbesian world of "Rapine and Wrong and Fear." Instead of simple shepherds, he found poor villagers and villainous employers; in the place of harmony, he found class conflict. . . . Whereas, at the end of Book I, the reader was moved to pity the poor worker, and feel that he should receive more aid, by the end of this vision of universal corruption in Book II, Crabbe has constructed a situation in which there seems no hope for anyone.

One might object that Crabbe's naturalism ignores man in society and holds true only for a small number of unrepresentative villagers on the Suffolk coast living in a Hobbesian state of nature. But this is to miss the main thrust of Crabbe's argument. Although *The Village* has as its foundation the amoral force of nature, Crabbe widens the poem to scenes "more fair in view" to show how the same type of existence is apparent there. In the more prosperous counties, nature is no longer so hostile, but the people who have tamed the countryside are themselves untamed. Laborers are still just as poor. And the reason is that they are now coerced by yet another unfriendly agent, employers. . . . If on the "frowning coast" poverty was the "fault" of nature, then inland, where the country is rich, the blame must be placed on the unequal division of property. Here Crabbe introduces the idea that poverty is the result of exploitation by the landed class. As slaves dig the golden ore for their masters, so the English peasants till the fields of golden corn for the landlords. Crabbe is implying that an invidious type of slavery, economic slavery, as unjust as the physical slavery of the West Indies, could be found in England.

Although Crabbe admits the existence of some who, with "manly pride" attempt to hide the "fainting heart," eventually all are beaten down. Man's drive for existence—which Pope had correctly termed self-love—nowhere shows evidence of a metamorphosis into social love. Crabbe introduces Goldsmith's priest, but he is no longer described as a selfless man seeking to aid others; he is very much the selfish individual performing public acts for personal benefit. Nor is Crabbe so naive as to claim that the world imagined by the pastoralists is completely false. Undoubtedly there exist houses for the care of the poor. The Statute 43 Eliz. c. 2 established that "every poor, old, blind, lame, and impotent person, or other person not able to work" was entitled to relief. What Crabbe does is to point out the implications of including within a single room

> The lame, the blind, and, far the happiest they!
> The moping idiot and the madman gay.

By questioning the motives behind such "benevolence," he reorganizes the accepted "facts." Moreover the poor themselves are not sentimentalized; they are no better than their "betters." The old man caught up in the "roundsman system" has children who should help to care for him, but they refuse. The entire community is built upon the amoral energy that characterizes the natural world.

The poem, beginning with thistles and tares, widens to encompass the poor, and then expands further to apply to all men. The relation between rich and poor is evidenced when Crabbe describes how the brutal poverty of the poor implies a poverty of mind in the farmers. The laborers enjoy their day of rest, not because of, but in spite of, the efforts of the middle and upper classes. The "careful masters" would like to see Sunday outlawed so that the laborers could work every day of the week:

> Thus, as their hours glide on, with pleasure fraught,
> Their careful masters brood the painful thought;
> Much in their mind they murmur and lament,
> That one fair day should be so idly spent;
> And think that Heaven deals hard, to tithe their store
> And tax their time for preachers and the poor.

It should be emphasized that Crabbe is not saying that the rich cause the poverty of the poor; he is not blaming the rich. Rather he seems to be pointing out the much more subtle implication that the existence of brutal servants necessitates the existence of brutal masters. Physical poverty in one class is inevitably linked to moral and spiritual poverty in other classes.

It is against this background that Crabbe's introduction of Robert Manners with his Christ-like associations should be viewed. In a world of self-interest, Manners, the one noble man, brings everyone of the village—rich and poor alike—the evidence that man can rise above himself. Manners, it should be stressed, is necessary not simply because he was generous or happy, or even virtuous, but because he did not bow down to circumstances. He chose to die for the cause he believed in. Thus Manners' may of death offers proof that man is not merely the product of outside forces, but can himself shape his own destiny. But the introduction of Robert Manners also signals that Crabbe is not interpreting the Hobbesian world of the earlier part of the poem in terms of the Christian view of history where man is in a fallen state to be saved only by the intercession of a man-god. It will be recalled that many writers since the time of Pascal have been motivated to a belief in God because a Godless world seemed so unbearable. Christ is not actually introduced into *The Village,* but Robert Manners is clearly an analogue. Crabbe's difficulty in managing the transition is seen most clearly in his imagery. While he does not forsake the nature imagery of the first part of the poem—Manners is likened to a "tall oak"—nature is no longer amoral, but ethical and protective. The "tall oak" is the "guard and glory" of the trees below.

Although this Christ-like figure, so suddenly and preposterously introduced, strikes almost all modern readers as vestigial, one can see how Crabbe's concern with "the real," which generated a description of the man's condition extraordinarily similar to that of the Christian view of fallen man, left him with only the Christian solution as a means of escape from the labyrinth of Hobbes' world. Crabbe has posited a static world where man and society do not change, where in fact man's behavior can be described in terms of unchanging natural phenomena. Under such conditions, the artist can describe man only as he was and always will be. (pp. 281-91)

It would be . . . well to point out that in terms of the situation Crabbe created in *The Village,* he did not actually have to choose the Christ-like figure of Robert Manners as the solution to his "realist" dilemma. After all, as narrator, Crabbe himself escaped and changed, and his work presumably will help to further the changes already in motion. But Crabbe does not press this point; instead, he assumes the static world of his eighteenth-century forebears, which because it is now without value, is meaningless.

In his later work Crabbe often pursues this line of thought by describing in great detail the lack of meaning and emotional color in everyday life. Many of his later characters flee this type of life with its banal mediocrity by resorting to neurotic aberration—a technique used by many twentieth-century authors. In poems such as **"Peter Grimes,"** Crabbe, in a very Kafka-like way, is able to show how the typical details of everyday life, emptied of meaning, have a spectral character which evokes the sense of a disintegrating personality. Yet in a few of his later poems, such as **"The Frank Courtship"** and **"The Natural Death of Love,"** Crabbe does permit a modicum of change in his characters, and thereby creates some of his finest comic poems. In his dream poems, moreover, Crabbe does go on to explore the possibility of an earthly paradise as a counterpart to man's fallen estate, but although intrigued, his inability to conceive of the material and political exertion necessary to effect the change leads him to conclude with unsatisfactory repudiations. In *The Village* Crabbe refuses to accept the imaginative logic of his environmentally described world, and since he does not introduce a sense of historical dynamic, he is left with the factitious Robert Manners in the abstract-idealist mode of thought to dispel the poem's oppression.

Although the figure of Manners does not resolve the poem's questions in the same empirical mode in which they are asked, his introduction carries its own poetic logic, and is by no means totally out of order. Ian Gregor has pointed out that the ending of Book II converts the poem into "a striking variation of a well-recognized 'kind'—the elegiac pastoral" [see excerpt dated 1955]. It clearly resembles the ending of such poems as John Philips' *Cyder* where Philips encourages the young Harcourt to return to England to follow his father's example: "See! how the Cause / Of Widows, and of Orphans He asserts / With winning Rhetoric, and well-argu'd Law!" I would suggest that the classical elegy in Book II affords a counterpart to the classical opening of Book I. It will be recalled that Crabbe opened the poem in the classical style; in Book II he closes singing of the "pure stream" which still flows on, " and shall for ever flow." In effect the classical eulogy of the great man rounds out and completes the classical opening of the poem.

Yet since Crabbe employed the classical form at the beginning of *The Village* as an ironic device to contain anticlassical ideas, the classical ending coming as it does after so much abjuration of the classical also partakes of this ironic mode. Irony demands two points of view in conflict, and usually deliberate irony results when the author holds one of the views to be correct and the other false. What happens in *The Village* is that Crabbe introduces a conventional viewpoint—for instance, the "sweet repose" of the villager—pretends for a moment to argue its validity, and then turns round to show its falsity. From the beginning of Book II, versions of pastoral are suggested, and then rejected. At the end, the theme of the "great man" sweeps in and overwhelms the poem. Obviously the "great man" is a variant of pastoral just as was the "sweet repose" of the villager, but Crabbe bows to the inevitable, and permits himself a "pastoral" solution. (pp. 292-93)

Thus *The Village* combines Crabbe's perceptions of an empirically based world with his belief in man's ability to find values and goals. Fitting in with Crabbe's sense of things in his own life and concluding the classical manner of the poem, the elegiac ending informs the poem with those transcendent ideals for which Crabbe could find no place in the world of the village. (p. 294)

> *Ronald B. Hatch, "George Crabbe and the Tenth Muse," in* Eighteenth-Century Studies, *Vol. 7, No. 3, Spring, 1974, pp. 274-94.*

### JEROME J. McGANN   (essay date 1981)

[*In the following excerpt, McGann assesses the Romantic perception of Crabbe as an anachronism; comparing his theoretical and poetic principles with those of Samuel Taylor Coleridge and William Wordsworth, he emphasizes the originality of Crabbe's empirical realism.*]

Hazlitt's revulsion from Crabbe's poetry epitomizes the attitude of most English Romantics—Byron only, as usual, excepted. Leavis said later, correctly, that "Crabbe . . . was hardly at the fine point of consciousness of his time," and we see what he meant when we read remarks like the following from Coleridge and Wordsworth [for further commentary by Coleridge and Wordsworth see conversation dated 1834 and letters dated 1808 and 1834]:

> in Crabbe there is an absolute defect of the high imagination.

> I am happy to find that we coincide in opinion about Crabbe's *verses;* for *poetry* in no sense can they be called. . . . After all, if the Picture [given in his work] were true to nature, what claim would it have to be called Poetry? . . . The sum of all is, that nineteen out of twenty of Crabbe's Pictures are mere matters of fact. . . .

These Romantic judgments upon Crabbe eventually became normative, not merely for those who agreed with their assessment of Crabbe's *value,* but even for those who—like Leavis himself—saw Crabbe as "a living classic." It is a commonplace of criticism to say of Crabbe that he was "the last of the Augustans." Leavis himself reproduced such a view when he said that Crabbe's "sensibility belongs to an order that those who were most alive to the age . . . had ceased to find sympathetic" [see excerpt dated 1936]. In short, Crabbe was an anachronism, and was recognized as such by the most advanced of his contemporaries.

We may obtain a sharper understanding of these critical judgments, however, if we place them in a more generous historical context. We must see, first of all, that the Romantic judgment was part of a more general ideological struggle in which various parties engaged. Coleridge's and Wordsworth's views corresponded to those set forth in, for example, the *Quarterly Review,* but they were vigorously contested by many others—most notably in the series of articles on Crabbe written for the *Edinburgh Review* by Jeffrey [see excerpts dated 1808 and 1819]. Indeed, Jeffrey's hostility to Wordsworth and the Lake School, and his approbation of Crabbe, constitute one of the most important local manifestations of the various cultural struggles which marked the entire period. We may glimpse

the complexity of these struggles if we simply recall that Hazlitt—no champion of Crabbe's work—had reluctantly to grant not only his artistic power, but his surpassing originality among the poets of the early nineteenth century [see excerpt dated 1825].

Coleridge's and Wordsworth's judgments, then, must be seen for what they are: part of a polemic on behalf of certain poetical criteria. The fact that their programs largely prevailed—we now call the period which nurtured Jane Austen and Crabbe The Romantic Age—establishes the proper measure of the truth of their judgments: that is to say, they measure a relative truth, a partisan view.

From our present perspective, however, the Romantic judgment upon Crabbe's poetry must be forced to yield up its specific historical shape. We may begin to define precisely what the Romantics took their stand upon by turning to Crabbe himself, who contested, in a most illuminating way, the very issues which his own work has raised into view.

In his "Preface" to the *Tales* [see excerpt dated 1812] Crabbe shows himself well aware of the charges brought against his work (its matter-of-fact and anti-imaginative qualities, its gloomy and even depressing effect). More than this, Crabbe understands that these specific issues represent a more fundamental argument over the nature of poetry.

> Nevertheless, it must be granted that the pretensions of any composition to be regarded as poetry will depend upon that definition of the poetic character which he who undertakes to determine the question has considered as decisive.

Crabbe then begins his counter-argument with an ironic attack upon Romantic premises and authorities. His antagonists found their "definition of the poetic character" upon "the words which the greatest of poets, not divinely inspired, has given to the most noble and valiant Duke of Athens." Crabbe quotes the relevant passage from *A Midsummer Night's Dream* (V,i) and explicates the Romantic concept of Imagination. The visionary poet captivates

> the imagination of his readers, he elevates them above the grossness of actual being, into the soothing and pleasant atmosphere of supra-mundane existence: there he obtains for his visionary inhabitants the interest that engages a reader's attention without ruffling his feelings, and excites that moderate kind of sympathy which the realities of nature oftentimes fail to produce, either because they are so familiar and insignificant that they excite no determinate emotion, or are so harsh and powerful that the feelings excited are grating and distasteful.

Crabbe's argument is empirical and quietly ironic. In the first place, he attacks the Romantic "definition" by exposing its lack of inclusiveness. The received facts of the matter belie the definition, which necessarily excludes "a vast deal of what has been hitherto received as genuine poetry." Chaucer, Dryden, and Pope are Crabbe's most prominent instances, but his most trenchant and subtle is Shakespeare himself. Indeed, Crabbe's use of Shakespeare constitutes a brilliant piece of ironical argumentation. Though the author of one of the most famous statements on behalf of the inspirational theory of poetry, Shakespeare is "not divinely inspired." Far from being a visionary poet, Shakespeare is the creator of an array of human creatures some of whom—like Duke Theseus—believe that poets are "of imagination all compact." But

Crabbe's Shakespeare overlooks the opinions of his various fictional creatures.

Crabbe's ironic point, then, is not merely that the world displays many different sorts of poets and poetry—some of them "divinely inspired" in the Romantic sense—but that the *measure* of what constitutes poetry is human, social, and historical rather than divine, inspired, and transcendent. Crabbe's prime exemplar of the "poetic character" is Shakespeare, who is at once "the greatest of poets" (as all agree), but who is also "not divinely inspired," and who does not measure poetry in inspirational terms. Shakespeare's fictional Duke proposes such a measure, and in so doing he aligns himself with a particular theoretical tradition; but Crabbe, following Shakespeare, argues the limited nature of such a view.

Crabbe's position follows upon his different "definition of the poetic character." According to Coleridge, for example, the immediate object of poetry is "pleasure, not truth," but its ultimate object is "a species of Revelation" akin to a religious experience. In its balance and reconciliation of opposite and discordant qualities, poetry elevates the human mind into contact with the whole truth of existence: with the transcendent Idea, the Truth of the One Life. This definition of poetry derives from the general tradition of Christian Humanism epitomized earlier in Sidney. It ultimately connects with the classical idea that poetry should teach and delight, but it changes the pragmatic and operational character of those ancient concepts into philosophic categories (pleasure and truth). This alteration follows directly on the method of Kantian aesthetics as it was set forth in the third *Critique*.

Rather than dealing with poetry in terms of pleasure and truth, however, Crabbe's definition is based upon functional notions much more akin to the ancient classical concepts. In the "Preface" to ***Tales of the Hall*** he speaks of "the entertainment or the instruction" which poetry produces, and of the author's obligation "to please or to instruct" the audience. This formulation in fact supports Crabbe's own poetic practise, which does not aim for a Kantian/Coleridgean aesthesis, and does not aspire to the revelation of a final Truth. Rather, Crabbe's field of poetic "pleasure" contains a variety of less totalizing pleasures: it gratifies, entertains, and pleases (in many different local and particular ways). As for its "truth" content, once again Crabbe takes a human, non-transcendent approach. Crabbe wants to teach and to instruct, not to deliver a new (or old) revelation.

In all these respects Crabbe obviously differs sharply from Coleridge, but the ways he differs from Wordsworth are perhaps even more instructive. (pp. 555-58)

Crabbe, Wordsworth, and Coleridge all agree that"man and the objects that surround him [are] acting and re-acting on each other," but whereas this systematic complex is a benevolent One Life to the Romantics, it is a circumstantial field to Crabbe, who sees in it endless eventual possibilities, most of which will be hurtful and destructive rather than benevolent precisely because the eventualities—being unforeseeable—will rudely interrupt our projects and plans.

The difference between Wordsworth and Crabbe is interesting since both men wrote a number of narratives which deal with similar subjects. What Wordsworth represents in, for example, "The Brothers" or "Michael" or "The Ruined Cottage" has much in common with the typical Crabbe narrative. "The Ruined Cottage" is especially pertinent here, first, because the grim features of the story are so comparable to

Crabbe's tales of woe; and second, because those very similarities serve to highlight the final and decisive differences. The fact that Wordsworth's is a framed narrative—with the author presenting himself as a dramatic figure in the story, and the reader's surrogate for the poem's moral lesson—reveals an important difference between a typical Wordsworthian narrative and Crabbe's characteristically non-subjective method of tale-telling. Wordsworth wants, and proposes to deliver, a solution to the problem of evil in the world. (p. 559)

Wordsworth's Nature "upholds and cherishes" suffering humanity "first and last and midst and without end." Ecological nature is Wordsworth's fundamental sign and symbol of his transcendent Nature because the objective natural world—the field of chemistry, physics, biology—contains for human beings, whose more immediate lives are lived in social and historical fields, the images of permanence which they need. Like Coleridge, however, Wordsworth translates those ecological forms into theological realities: nature as Nature, the Active Universe and manifest form of the One Life. When Wordsworth writes framed tales, then—his famous retrospective narratives—he uses a poetic form which itself represents the prevenient existence of that something far more deeply interfused. Benevolence and consolation arrive when they are discovered, when we see that their authority has always been present, though unseen. When M. H. Abrams describes the "Natural Super-naturalism" of Romanticism, with its characteristic "circuitous journeys," this is the pattern he details for us.

The pattern is not Crabbe's, whose orderly couplets marshall, paradoxically, a world "Sad as realities, and wild as dreams" (**"The Parting Hour."**) Whereas Wordsworth's symbolical method constantly offers the reader an anticipatory narrative—a tale whose benevolent ending is hidden in its beginning—Crabbe's method is to move inexorably from point to point, couplet to couplet, building its features of grimness as "sorrow takes new sadness from surprise" (**"The Parting Hour."**) Like Wordsworth, Crabbe knows that human beings are subject to unforeseeable events and circumstances; unlike Wordsworth, Crabbe does not see that a system of divine benevolence—to which both men gave official assent—provided anything more than an ideological solution to problems which were fundamentally social, psychological, and economic. Crabbe's tale of **"Ellen Orford"**—so comparable to Wordsworth's tale of Margaret—gives us a woman who has undergone intolerable sufferings, and who has yet remained in the end "true" to her religion and the social structures she was born to.

> And as my mind looks cheerful to my end,
> I love mankind and call my GOD my friend.

These final lines in the poem, which in Wordsworth would be consoling, are in Crabbe perfectly shocking because nothing in the narrative justifies them. Ellen Orford's final testament of faith comes to us as one last item in an empirical and seriatim narrative. God and mankind have not protected Ellen Orford from her miseries—on the contrary, in fact—but then she, quite rightly, does not look for such protection. Wordsworth too does not look directly to God or society for protection from misery, but tells us to trust to the "humanized" (Wordsworthian) imagination, which can generate tales and poetic devices which themselves create the consolations and the solutions which human beings need. "The Ruined Cottage" is the answer to the problems it raises up for us out of the world beyond the tale itself.

Crabbe's story of **"Ellen Orford,"** however, vigorously forbids any solution that is grounded in the Romantic Imagination. Indeed, the poem is largely an indictment of such solutions via its attack upon those popular romantic narratives of Crabbe's day which built up tales of woe only to afford a final deliverance from their machineries of terror:

> Till some strange means afford a sudden view
> Of some vile plot, and every wo adieu!

Wordsworth's stories do not reveal "some vile plot"; they involve, as it were, the apocalypse of "some kind scheme" which displaces the misery in a benevolent spiritual field. Crabbe's tales, however, involve neither vile plot nor benevolent scheme; rather they demonstrate what he called "realities." Ellen Orford is both subject to and aware of such "realities," but in terms of a functional knowledge she remains in darkest ignorance. Indeed, when Crabbe presents her, in the end, as helpless and literally blind, he gives the reader an objective correlative for the state of her human understanding. What "Ellen Orford knows"—*all* that she knows—is "That we should humbly take what Heaven bestows." Though he honors such piety, Crabbe is well aware how sadly inadequate it is to the whole of her case. Still, his sympathetic presentation of such piteous and fragile creatures contains the secret to the appalling power of his narratives, which are at once full of pity, yet (finally) pitiless.

When Ellen Orford calmly narrates her terrible story she calls her life "A common case" because it is, as she unprotestingly knows, typical of people who live in certain social and economic circumstances. Readers of her story, then as well as now, find her narrative peculiarly shocking for this very reason: she records a detailed history which the more comfortable reader, alienated from her social "realities," must acknowledge to be a generic story rather than a special case. In Crabbe's handling of such realities, no adequate preventions can be expected from God or society or imagination, which at best can promise to displace them within various ideological transformations. But the method of a Crabbe narrative resists a final displacement, and especially disallows that famous Romantic displacement we recognize in the Wordsworthian mode. Crabbe's couplets serve at once to fix our attention on specific matters, on a series of particular facts and ideas and events, and at the same time to accumulate their data in an additive scheme.

This additive method results in a poetry of truths rather than a poetry of Truth. In contrast to Wordsworth's and Coleridge's efforts to establish " general" Truth through their poetry, and to argue, in their criticism, for the centrality of "universal" and trans-historical Truth, Crabbe's work is deeply time and place specific: in Wordsworth's terms, "individual and local." Each of his famous characters focus, as it were, a case-history of some important sort. Ellen Orford, Peter Grimes, Edward Shore: all are what Lukacs would later call "typical" characters, and their stories are illustrative instances. Most emphatically are they not "types and symbols" in either the Neo-Platonic or the Romantic sense. The problems they illuminate are social, psychological, and historical, which is why a Crabbe narrative must operate with "individual and local" matters—with specific details, and highly particularized representations of time, place, circumstance.

For the Romantics, Crabbe's work was a peculiarly depressing form of art. Written in the face of the same severe realities which Crabbe saw, Romantic poetry attempted to formulate a positive and, above all, a final solution to the recurrent problems of human change and suffering. Reading Crabbe, however, we clearly see that the Romantic solution—which Wordsworth and Coleridge call Imagination—is regarded as no more than *yet another* final solution; indeed, under the circumstances, is regarded as something worse, as a sort of final or grand illusion. The sign of Crabbe's attitude is to be traced in his "figures of imagination": in every case these are desperate and incapable figures, lost souls whose final place of refuge is with fantasm, pathetic dreams and memories, or mere nightmare visions.

The Romantic revulsion from Crabbe's poetry is entirely understandable, then, since the truths to which he is devoted institute a devastating critique upon the Truth which the Romantics sought to sustain. Crabbe's poetry takes up its traditional human materials but delivers them to us under the sign not of Imagination but of Science. He accumulates his material, he distinguishes it into various parts, he particularizes. Furthermore, he adds that last, crucial scientific dimension by historicizing his materials at all points. Finality, in the philosophic sense, does not govern Crabbe's tales, which emphasize relative creatures, human time, and a continuous movement of accumulation that marks out not a Romantic form of process but a scientific form of addition.

Thus Crabbe's is a poetry of science in a very particular sense: his work illustrates a modern scientific method not in its synthetic or theoretical phase, but at its fundamental inductive and critical stage, when the necessary data are being collected. "The Muses have just about as much to do [with Crabbe's poetry] as they have with a Collection of medical reports, or of Law cases," said Wordsworth when he dismissed Crabbe's "verses." The critique accurately reports the method of many of Crabbe's poems; what may be disputed, then as now, is the comparative value of Crabbe's method.

Crabbe and his contemporary defenders represented his "value" under two principal headings. First, his work dealt with the "truth" of certain important human "realities" which poetry did not normally examine. It was therefore important not merely for the *facts* of its content but for the originality of its subject matter. Second, Crabbe's poetry offers the reader the pleasure of coming to such knowledge—the pleasure of learning new "realities"—rather than the pleasure of an imaginative aesthesis.

Because this last distinction is crucial for understanding Crabbe's work, I must expand upon it in some detail. The Romantic—prototypically Coleridgean—concept of poetic pleasure is a philosophic category of human Being. Though a subjective experience, it is metaphysically transcendent; indeed, the individual's experience of such an aesthetic pleasure is a felt apprehension (rather than an understood cognition) of the persistent reality of that transcendent Form of Being. Poetry is a vehicle which induces the experience of such pleasure, thereby reaffirming the reality of the ultimate Form of Pleasure in the act of reading the poem. What Crabbe called, in the "Preface" to the *Tales,* the "painful realities" of existence are revealed, through Romantic Imagination, to be "passing shows" and temporal illusions. Romantic Imagination creates a "world elsewhere" which corresponds to whatever the heart desires; it substitutes an Eden of Imagination for the lost Edens of the past.

Crabbe does not undertake to offer such acts of final substitution. His poetic pleasures deal with more limited values in a world which, to Crabbe's experience, seems more various, complex, and unknown than is often realized by himself or his middle and upper class readers. He is especially interested in the "Painful realities of actual existence" among which he includes—indeed, emphasizes—the realities of the Romantic Imagination. His work endeavors to create, via the illusion of art, a peculiar place of disinterested "repose by substituting [for our "perpetually-occurring vexations" of life] objects in their place which [the mind] may contemplate with some degree of interest and satisfaction":

> for when it is admitted that they have no particular relation to him, but are the troubles and anxieties of other men, they excite and interest his feelings as the imaginary exploits, adventures, and perils of romance;—they soothe his mind, and keep his curiosity pleasantly awake; they appear to have enough of reality to engage his sympathy, but possess not interest sufficient to create painful sensations. Fiction itself, we know, and every work of fancy, must for a time have the effect of realities.

What is important about Crabbe's proposal is that the "pleasant effect upon the mind of the reader" which his poetry offers is conceived in very limited terms ("some degree of interest and satisfaction"). Crabbe's pleasure is a moment of repose whose local and particular character is defines by the systems of "painful realities" which his poetry uncovers. Crabbe speaks of "those every-day concerns . . . and vexations" of life, but he treats poetry in precisely similar terms, as if it too were an every-day matter, only a pleasant one. The pleasure we are to derive from his poems, then, is not conceived as "moments in the being of the eternal silence" so much as moments in the being of recurrent bedlam.

To understand this interesting (and unromantic) theory of poetic pleasure we must grasp the importance which Crabbe attaches to his particularities. The "every-day concerns . . . and vexations" may nevertheless "lift the mind [of the reader] from the painful realities of actual existence" because the stories are "not [in literal fact] the very concerns and distresses of the reader." We sympathize with the characters and their stories because they detail commonplaces with which we are familiar; but we are distanced from the stories because the experiences are not, *in their particulars,* our own (something, as Crabbe says, "hardly to be supposed"). This apparently pedantic and fussy distinction points toward the crucial importance which matters-of-fact play in Crabbe's work. Indeed, it shows us the fundamentally scientific (rather than metaphysical) bent of Crabbe's mind. Distinctions for him can be made both categorically and empirically. Furthermore, empirical distinctions—the fact that Edward Shore's best friend was a certain age, or the fact that Dinah's aunt ( in **"Procrastination"**) lived longer than expected—may focus differences which, from a human (social and psychological) point of view, are every bit as important as any "fundamental" distinction in metaphysics, ethics, or epistemology. In the world of human experience it may be just these "insignificant" empirical differences which make *all* the difference in the lives of individuals, social groups, even kingdoms. Ultimately, then, Crabbe's method subjects all higher-order syntheses, whether cognitive (philosophic) or non-cognitive (poetic), to an existential critique.

The empirical distinction Crabbe draws in the passage I have been discussing represents no small matter for him. The entire issue of poetic distance and sympathy for Crabbe rests on the differences that poems draw between particular readers

and particular subject matters. These are, literally, differences in fact which signal important differences in (subsequent) poetic effects. By establishing the separation of the reader from the poem on this empirical basis, Crabbe emphasizes the very terms under which a reading of his work will take place. The "pleasure" of a Crabbe poem is not a matter of "seeing into the life of things," of experiencing a sense of the One Life or the "One Spirit's plastic stress"; it is rather the pleasure of a particular experience wherein the mind becomes an observer within a manifold of fascinating, highly specified details and differentials. Crabbe's reader is lifted above the poetic materials the way an observer gains distance on the objects brought before his view.

From this elevated vantage Crabbe fashions his critique of the Idealistic traditions of poetry and criticism. This argument is explicitly made not only in the "Preface" to the 1812 *Tales;* it appears in earlier works as well. *The Village* is famous for its attack upon idealized representations of country life, but a similar assault is mounted in the opening Letter of *The Borough.* The basis for the attack lies in Crabbe's insistence upon factual accuracy in verse, a criterion which demands that poetic details be presented in contexts that are time and place specific. Such contexts, because they are empirically structured and elaborated, deliver poetry from the grip of abstract and idealized modes of perception.

In addition to this critique, however, Crabbe's method opens up an entirely new poetic world. His verse is at once critique and revelation, for its novel subject matter represents the discovery that no subject lies outside the province of verse. This definitive break with a traditional (and increasingly threatened) rule of poetic decorum represents a far more important theoretical advance than has often been realized. In his new subject matter Crabbe defined the significance of his new aesthetic: that his was a poetry of discovery and investigation, of empirical research whose initial limits would be set in scientific rather than in ideological terms.

Crabbe's method, then, is to train his readers in critical and exploratory observation. A concrete and "material" vantage is adopted because it alone provides an escape from received conceptions (and hence perceptions) of the world. Empiricism is, for Crabbe and his epoch, a sharp critical differential from received methods and categories of religious and philosophic thought. This materialist differential operates in *The Village,* as we know, but it loses none of its force or relevance in the later poetry, where it undermines that latest appearance of Idealistic ideology, Romantic displacement.

Crabbe's poetic "originality," then, which was universally acknowledged by his contemporaries (and which is generally forgotten by us), is a function of an aesthetic that made a fundamental break with traditional approaches. When twentieth-century scholars classify him as an Augustan or Neo-Classical throwback, a reactionary figure who somehow lived on to write verse in the proto-modern Romantic Age, some crucial distortions are being allowed to enter the analysis. *The Village* is a critique of Neo-Classical poetic standards as they were embodied in the traditional methods of pastoral verse. But the poetry which Crabbe wrote after *Lyrical Ballads,* precisely because it was published *when it was* (1807-19), has —shifted the focus of Crabbe's attack from Neo-Classical ideas to the new Romantic ones. Crabbe's "preface" to the 1812 *Tales* shows us quite clearly that he was aware of his new set of opponents; indeed, the remarks on Crabbe made by so many of the period's leading Romantic figures, like Wordsworth, Coleridge, and Hazlitt, reinforce our sense of the gulf which divides Crabbe's work from theirs. (pp. 560-67)

In the historical triumph of Romantic ideology, later commentators found it convenient to treat Crabbe as a Neo-Classical anachronism in a Romantic age. Anti-Romantic Modernists, like Pound [see excerpt dated 1917] and Leavis, sought to "save" Crabbe from his age by calling him an Augustan, whereas Neo-Romantic critics merely ignored Crabbe as an insignificant glacial deposit. Both of these views, however, are seriously inadequate, as we may now begin to see. More than that, however, we may also begin to see how later historical imperatives transform our sense of the place of certain writers. A critical view of Romantic ideology in our day inevitably makes Crabbe seem not an Augustan throwback but a writer whose true historical period has yet to arrive. (pp. 570-71)

> Jerome J. McGann, "The Anachronism of George Crabbe," in ELH, Vol. 48, No. 3, Fall, 1981, pp. 555-72.

————————

## FURTHER READING

Abrams, Meyer Howard. *The Milk of Paradise: The Effect of Opium Visions on the Works of DeQuincey, Crabbe, Francis Thompson, and Coleridge.* Harvard Honors Theses in English, No. 7. Cambridge: Harvard University Press, 1934, 85 p.
    A study of the influence of opium on early nineteenth-century English literature that assesses the effects of opium use on Crabbe's poetry.

Ainger, Alfred. *Crabbe.* English Men of Letters, edited by John Morley. New York: Macmillan Co., 1903, 210 p.
    A biographical study of Crabbe that reviews several of his major works.

Bareham, Terence. *George Crabbe.* New York: Barnes & Noble, 1977, 245 p.
    A thematic study of Crabbe's poetry that focuses on the political and religious context of his work.

————, and Gatrell, S. *A Bibliography of George Crabbe.* Kent, England: Wm. Dawson & Sons, 1978, 194 p.
    An annotated list of primary and secondary sources.

Blackburne, Neville. *The Restless Ocean: The Story of George Crabbe, The Aldeburgh Poet, 1754-1832.* Lavenham, Suffolk: Terence Dalton, 1972, 236 p.
    An illustrated biographical study that contains a bibliography of Crabbe criticism.

Brett, R. L. *George Crabbe.* Writers and Their Work, edited by Bonamy Dobrée, no. 75. London: Longmans, Green & Co., 1956, 42 p.
    A short biographical and critical study that refutes earlier critical objections to Crabbe's work, asserting that Crabbe's imagination is capable of attaining "a sublimity that belongs only to the greatest of tragic artists."

Browman, Walter E. "Factors in Crabbe's Eminence in the Early Nineteenth Century." *Modern Philology* LI, No. 1 (August 1953): 42-9.
    Reviews critical reactions to Crabbe during the Romantic period, claiming that he was not an anachronism of the Augustan age but must be considered "as much an integral part of the trends in early nineteenth-century literature as Scott or Byron."

Chamberlain, Robert L. *George Crabbe.* Twayne's English Authors Series, edited by Sylvia E. Bowman, No. 18. New York: Twayne Publishers, 1965, 188 p.
    A biographical and critical study of Crabbe that contains an annotated bibliography of secondary sources.

Crabbe, George, Jr. *The Life of George Crabbe by His Son.* The Cresset Library, edited by John Hayward. London: Cresset Press, 1947, 286 p.
    Considered the standard account of Crabbe's life. The volume features detailed anecdotes concerning Crabbe's career and social life.

Cruttwell, Patrick. "The Last Augustan." *The Hudson Review* VII, No. 4 (Winter 1955): 533-54.
    Discusses the Augustan authors that influenced Crabbe's approach to poetry.

Evans, J. H. *The Poems of George Crabbe: A Literary and Historical Study.* London: Sheldon Press, 1933, 208 p.
    A biographical study, interspersed with critical remarks, emphasizing the role of Crabbe's various patrons in his life.

Haddakin, Lilian. *The Poetry of Crabbe.* London: Chatto & Windus, 1955, 175 p.
    A critical account of Crabbe's poetry that addresses a wide range of thematic issues and seeks to restore his literary status.

Hatch, Ronald B. *Crabbe's Arabesque: Social Drama in the Poetry of George Crabbe.* Montreal: McGill—Queen's University Press, 1976, 284 p.
    A study concentrating on Crabbe's dramatic handling of social issues in his poetry.

Hodgart, Patricia, and Redpath, Theodore, eds. "George Crabbe (1754-1832)." In their *Romantic Perspectives: The Work of Crabbe, Blake, Wordsworth, and Coleridge as Seen by Their Contemporaries and by Themselves,* pp. 85-124. London: George G. Harrap & Co., 1964.
    Reprints important early nineteenth-century criticism on Crabbe.

Hsia, C. T. "Crabbe's Poetry: Its Limitations." *Tamkang Review* I, No. 1 (April 1970): 61-77.
    Reviews the history of Crabbe criticism, focusing on his stylistic limitations.

Huchon, René. *George Crabbe and His Times, 1754-1832: A Critical and Biographical Study.* Translated by Frederick Clarke. London: John Murray, 1907, 561 p.
    An important early account of Crabbe's life and writings containing extended critical commentary on Crabbe's major works and a detailed bibliography.

Ker, W. P. "George Crabbe." In *On Modern Literature: Lectures and Addresses,* edited by Terence Spencer and James Sutherland, pp. 62-77. 1936. Reprint. St. Clair Shores, Mi.: Scholarly Press, 1971.
    A biographical and critical appraisal of Crabbe that disputes William Hazlitt's claim that Crabbe was a shallow realist, arguing that in the naturalness and variety of his style he succeeded in "restoring the heroic couplet as a form of narrative verse."

Lang, Varley. "Crabbe and the Eighteenth Century." *ELH* 5, No. 4 (December 1938): 305-33.
    Analyzes the extent to which Crabbe's verse was influenced by neoclassical rules and conventions.

Looker, Samuel J. "In Praise of Crabbe." *The Nineteenth Century and After* 110, No. DCLVI (October 1931): 489-502.
    In a chronological survey of Crabbe's poetic career, argues that his realism and psychological interests demonstrate that "in temper he was a modern."

Mills, Howard. Introduction to *Tales, 1812 and Other Selected Poems,* by George Crabbe, pp. xi-xxvi. Cambridge: Cambridge University Press, 1967.

Traces the development of Crabbe's poetry from *The Village* to *Tales,* focusing on the shifts in his social and moral perspective and on the relationship between linguistic patterns and character analysis.

New, Peter. *George Crabbe's Poetry.* London: Macmillan Press, 1976, 248 p.

A critical study that focuses on the place of Crabbe's poetry in England's literary and social traditions.

Pollard, Arthur, ed. *Crabbe: The Critical Heritage.* The Critical Heritage Series, edited by B. C. Southam. London: Routledge & Kegan Paul, 1972, 495 p.

Contains a representative sample of important criticism on Crabbe from the eighteenth and nineteenth centuries as well as a select bibliography.

Spiegelman, Willard. "Peter Grimes: The Development of a Hero." *Studies in Romanticism* 25, No. 4 (Winter 1986): 541-60.

In a comparative analysis of the eponymous hero of Benjamin Britten's 1945 opera and the character of "Peter Grimes" from *The Borough,* argues that the romantic aspects of Crabbe's character are more "Wordsworthian" than "Byronic."

Stephen, Leslie. "Crabbe's Poetry." *The Cornhill Magazine* XXX (July-September 1874): 454-73.

Assesses the thematic integrity and stylistic competence of Crabbe's poetry, arguing that Crabbe deserves a minor but significant place in English literature.

Thomas, W. K. "Crabbe's Borough: The Process of Montage." *University of Toronto Quarterly* XXXVI, No. 2 (January 1967): 181-92.

Speculates on the process of montage used by Crabbe in his depiction of the physical environment of the seaside town of Aldeborough in *The Borough.*

———. "George Crabbe: Not Quite the Sternest." *Studies in Romanticism* VII, No. 3 (Spring 1968): 166-75.

Argues that Crabbe was neither the first English poet to present an unvarnished account of rural conditions nor unjustly severe in his depiction of the English peasantry.

Unwin, Rayner. "George Crabbe: The Real Picture of the Poor." In his *The Rural Muse: Studies in the Peasant Poetry of England,* pp. 110-20. London: George Allen and Unwin, 1954.

Asserts that despite Crabbe's aloofness from the peasant class, he succeeded as a poet because he chose to portray rural conditions in a realistic rather than in a "generalized or imaginative" fashion.

Wecter, Dixon. "Four Letters from George Crabbe to Edmund Burke." *The Review of English Studies* XIV, No. 55 (July 1938): 298-309.

Presents four previously unpublished letters from Crabbe to Edmund Burke that shed light on the latter's role as patron and critic of Crabbe's early poetry.

Whitby, Charles. "A Student of Humanity." *Poetry Review* XII, No. 5 (September-October 1921): 251-59.

Attests to the "sober beauty" of Crabbe's work and his penetrating insights into the life and character of the common people.

[Wilson, John]. Review of *Tales of the Hall,* by George Crabbe. *Blackwood's Edinburgh Magazine* V, No. XXVIII (July 1819): 469-83.

A positive assessment of Crabbe's *Tales of the Hall,* emphasizing his poetic insights into human character.

Wilson, P. B. "Crabbe's Narrative World." *Durham University Journal* n.s. XXXVII, No. 2 (June 1976): 135-43.

Assesses the various narrative techniques used by Crabbe to formally accomodate the continual presence of an omniscient narrator, focusing on *The Borough* and *Tales.*

Woolf, Virginia. "Crabbe." In her *The Captain's Death Bed and Other Essays,* pp. 28-30. New York: Harcourt, Brace and Co., 1950.

A short, anecdotal portrait of Crabbe, emphasizing his eccentricities.

# Charles Dickens

## 1812-1870

(Also wrote under the pseudonym Boz) English novelist, short story writer, dramatist, poet, and essayist.

The following entry presents criticism of Dickens's novel *Great Expectations* (1861). For criticism focusing on Dickens's novels *Bleak House* (1853) and *The Mystery of Edwin Drood* (1870), see *NCLC*, Vols. 8 and 18, respectively. For information on Dickens's complete career, see *NCLC,* Vol. 3.

Dickens's *Great Expectations* is one of the most acclaimed and best loved nineteenth-century English novels. Though it received mixed appraisals from contemporary reviewers, *Great Expectations* is now considered an artistic triumph for Dickens, combining a concision unrivaled by his longer novels with his skill of intricately blending plot, form, theme, and imagery. Regarded as both a work of social criticism and a telling and complex study of personal guilt and self-discovery, *Great Expectations* has confounded critics in search of decisive interpretations. Part of its complexity and interest involves two fully written endings that seem antithetical and that have sparked controversy over which one more appropriately conveys Dickens's intended meaning. While debate goes on, *Great Expectations* continues to be admired as one of Dickens's and English literature's finest novels.

Dickens was at the height of his popularity and artistic powers when he began writing *Great Expectations* in late 1860. Originally planning the novel for twenty monthly parts, his preferred method of publication, he felt compelled to quickly rework it into a weekly format for his magazine *All the Year Round,* the sales of which were declining rapidly as a result of unfavorable public reaction to the magazine's lead serial novel, Irish author Charles Lever's *A Day's Ride: A Life's Romance.* The first installment of *Great Expectations* appeared on the opening pages of *All the Year Round* on 1 December, relegating Lever's work to a secondary position, and the magazine's sales soon rebounded. Dickens liked his new novel, as he wrote on 28 December 1860 to his friend Mary Boyle: "Pray read *Great Expectations.* I think it is very droll." Writing the novel was a physical strain for Dickens, however; in a letter to another friend, the actor and theatrical manager William C. Macready, on 11 June 1861, he revealed, "I have just finished my book of *Great Expectations,* and am the worse for wear. . . . But I hope that the book is a good book, and I have no doubt of very soon throwing off the little damage it has done me." Yet Dickens was to resume work on the novel, rewriting its conclusion at the suggestion of friend and fellow novelist Edward Bulwer-Lytton before the last installment was published on 3 August 1861.

Narrated by the main character, Philip Pirrup (self-named "Pip"), the novel opens in a village cemetery where the young Pip contemplates his parents' gravestones. He is suddenly accosted by an escaped convict, Abel Magwitch, who forces him to steal food and a file. Pip obtains these items and brings them to Magwitch, who is soon recaptured and transported to Australia. Later in his youth, Pip is invited by a wealthy, half-insane recluse, Miss Havisham, to visit her home, Satis House, where he provides company for her and her adopted

daughter, Estella. Pip eventually falls in love with Estella and becomes ashamed of his own modest existence in the village, where he lives with his abusive sister and her gentle, childlike husband, Joe Gargery, the village blacksmith and Pip's good friend. Pip is later informed that an anonymous benefactor is going to educate and support him as a gentleman in London. Wrongly assuming that his patron is Miss Havisham and that she intends to groom him to wed Estella, Pip leaves the village for London, where, neglecting his education and his friends, he lives prodigally on his new money and dreams of marrying Estella. His dreams vanish, however, when Magwitch, who has become an extremely successful sheep farmer in Australia, illegally returns to England and reveals himself as Pip's benefactor. Another devastating discovery follows as Pip learns that Estella is engaged to Pip's vicious arch-rival, Bentley Drummle. Pip later tries to help Magwitch escape, but the attempt fails. The convict dies in prison, and Pip then leaves England to work in Egypt. Several years later, chastened by the realization that he had abandoned friendship in pursuit of wealth and social stature, Pip returns to see Joe. He also decides to visit Satis House one last time and unexpectedly meets Estella, now a widow. The novel ends with Pip and Estella leaving Satis House hand in hand.

*Great Expectations* was extremely popular with the general

reading public, but contemporary critical reaction varied. For example, while reviewer Henry Fothergill Chorley extolled the novel, arguing that its brevity was the only objection that could be raised, Margaret Oliphant saw no merit in the work, describing it as "feeble, fatigued, and colourless." Most reviewers, however, were between these two extremes; despite objections that some of the characters were exaggerated and that the plot relied on too many incredible coincidences, they recommended the novel and compared it favorably with Dickens's previous works, noting particularly its many humorous scenes and characters, among them Mr. Wopsle, Trabb's boy, and Wemmick.

In 1874, Dickens's friend and biographer John Forster published Dickens's discarded conclusion to *Great Expectations* in his *The Life of Charles Dickens* (1872-74), an event that had a significant impact on criticism of the novel. In the discarded ending, Pip accidentally meets Estella after visiting Joe, and they converse briefly and part forever. Forster and many subsequent critics have deemed this version artistically and thematically superior to the revision, which some have considered a concession to the public's desire for a happy ending. Advocates of the original conclusion believe that the alteration conflicts with what they view as the pessimistic tone of *Great Expectations* and the novel's logical outcome: although Pip learns from his experience and expiates his guilt, he was meant to be sadder at the end. Opponents of this view contend that Pip has indeed become both wiser and sadder in the revised conclusion, which is somberly cast; moreover, they maintain that the added element of hope expressed in Pip's leaving Satis House while holding hands with Estella harmonizes perfectly with his moral improvement. On the arguable question of Pip's future with Estella, whether they marry or remain friends, the text of the revision remains silent, and critics continue to speculate on Dickens's intentions. Owing to the ongoing controversy over the novel's different endings, recent editions of the work often provide both conclusions.

In addition to examining its conclusion, critics of *Great Expectations* have often focused on its social message and exploration of guilt. Many commentators have seen the novel as an assault on false class distinctions. George Bernard Shaw and Edgar Johnson, for example, both contend that in his novels prior to and including *David Copperfield* (1850), Dickens had given tacit approval to such distinctions, but came to reject them as he developed intellectually. Thus, whereas in *David Copperfield*, Dickens seemingly condones David's shame at being thrust into the humble occupation of labelling wine bottles, he condemns Pip for repudiating his lower-class origins as a blacksmith's apprentice upon assuming the role of a London gentleman. Other critics, however, including Humphry House, have opposed the view that Dickens completely rejected notions of social stratification in *Great Expectations,* arguing instead that he directs his attack more at social snobbery and the corrupting power of money than at the class structure itself. In examining the psychological and moral aspects of *Great Expectations,* critics frequently note the related themes of Pip's guilt and his moral education. Most commentators argue that Pip's guilt results from his placing false importance on wealth and social status and ignoring the value of love and friendship. Critics generally agree that Pip is ultimately absolved of his guilt by renouncing his selfish, acquisitive desires and learning instead generosity, love, and friendship.

While the social perspective of *Great Expectations* and the development of Pip's conscience have often dominated commentary on the novel, numerous other aspects of the work have been the subject of critical inquiry, including such specific characters as Miss Havisham, Joe, and Mr. Jaggers, the poetic qualities of its narrative, and its autobiographical implications. Noting the diversity of opinion on *Great Expectations,* K. J. Fielding has pointed out that "one of the merits of the novel is that it allows the reader a teasing variety of interpretations." Indeed, some have argued that the novel evinces an artistic depth and complexity of characterization, language, structure, imagery, and theme that forms an autonomous world where contradictory actions and feelings, as in the real world, are possible, thus making decisive interpretation difficult. In the last two decades, commentators have applied a wide range of critical methods to the novel, providing, for example, psychoanalytical and deconstructionist analyses of the work. Despite its complexity, the length of *Great Expectations,* which is about half the size of most of Dickens's other novels, has made it a favorite among teachers introducing Dickens to high school students. This enduring popularity, combined with the critical interest the novel continues to generate, attests to the status of *Great Expectations* as a masterpiece of construction and psychological insight that remains one of the greatest novels in the English language.

(See also *Something about the Author,* Vol. 15, and *Dictionary of Literary Biography,* Vol. 21: *Victorian Novelists before 1885;* Vol. 55: *Victorian Prose Writers before 1867;* and Vol. 70: *British Mystery Writers, 1860-1919.*)

---

**CHARLES DICKENS**  (letter date 1861)

[*Writing to his friend John Forster, Dickens briefly mentions the altered ending of* Great Expectations.]

You will be surprised to hear that I have changed the end of *Great Expectations* from and after Pip's return to Joe's, and finding his little likeness there.

Bulwer (who has been, as I think I told you, extraordinarily taken by the book), so strongly urged it upon me, after reading the proofs, and supported his views with such good reasons, that I resolved to make the change. You shall have it when you come back to town. I have put in a very pretty piece of writing, and I have no doubt the story will be more acceptable through the alteration. (p. 167)

> *Charles Dickens, in a letter to John Forster on July 1, 1861, in* The Letters of Charles Dickens: 1857-1870, Vol. II, *edited by Georgina Hogarth and Mary Dickens, Charles Scribner's Sons, 1879, pp. 167-69.*

**[H. F. CHORLEY]**  (essay date 1861)

[*Chorley extols* Great Expectations, *asserting that the novel "can be charged with only one fault;—that of being too short."*]

Whether the library of English fiction contains a romance comparable with *Great Expectations* is a matter which admits of doubt—because with the breathless interest of a tale of mystery and adventure, with descriptions in which familiar and tame scenery is wrought up so as to exceed in picturesqueness the Apennine landscapes of a Radcliffe, or the deep-sea storms of a Fenimore Cooper, are combined such variety of humour, such deep and tender knowledge of the secrets of a yearning human heart, as belong to a novel of the highest order. Grant the two leading inventions of the tale as romantic, but not impossible; grant a certain exaggeration, so artfully distributed over the whole work as to amount to nothing more than a high tone of colour, and *Great Expectations* can be charged with only one fault;—that of being too short. It stands the test of collection, too, as few tales published in its fragmentary fashion can. Every week almost, as it came out, we were artfully stopped at some juncture which made Suspense count the days till the next number appeared,—again to be baulked, and anew to count.—Yet, on reading through the romance as a whole, there is no feeling of shock or spasm, still less any impression of "dropped stitches," but a sense that we have to do with a work of Art arranged from the first moment of conception with power, progress, and a minuteness consistent with the widest apparent freedom. Trying Mr. Dickens by himself, we find in this his last tale as much force as in the most forcible portions of *Oliver Twist,*—as much delicacy as in the most delicate passages of *David Copperfield,*—as much quaint humour as in *Pickwick.* In short, that this is the creation of a great artist in his prime we have felt from the very first moment of its appearance, and can deliberately sign and seal the conviction, even though the catastrophe is before us, and though we have been just devouring the solution of *Great Expectations.*

It is not lost time, neither a case of "painting the lily," to insist on certain details and characteristics of a tale already in thousands of hands.—No scenery could be imagined less romantic than the marshes in which the romance begins and ends; the soaking flat country, with its pollards,—with its "broads," in the furthest of which lie moored the convict-hulks, the old churchyard on the verge of this district, the sluices, and the limekiln.—But out of such common materials a Cuyp, or a Ruysdael, or a Hobbima makes a poetical landscape; and so with his pen does Mr. Dickens. The scene holds the reader from the first; the boy, born to be tormented by his "great expectations," is as much a dreamer, in right of his natural surroundings, as if he had been born at the feet of the Jungfrau, or bred in that Paradise of heaven, earth and sea, "the Golden Shell" of Palermo.—That Nature has influences apart from her sublimities, and that these speak to all who have ears to hear, is told with the decision of a key-note clearly touched, in the very first lines of this strong story. The return to the key, from time to time, is masterly, in the fullest sense of the word, because never monotonous.

The hero of the tale,—a dreaming, ambitious boy, with a grain of genius in him, and flung out by Fate into a narrow and cramping existence, which in no respect contents his yearnings,—may interest few people; and yet he is true to a life with which many have struggled, and to dreams which have put right, or put wrong, many a better man than himself. His shrewish guardian sister, with her perpetual apron (a household ephod of self-defence and assertion), and her sycophants, may be, we trust, more shrewish than are the sisters of many child-dreamers; but how admirably is her bitterness and vulgarity (fed by parasites) balanced by the sweet, truthful nature of Joe, with his dull wits and his meandering speech, and his huge hands like two forge hammers, and his tender, loving heart. (pp. 43-4)

Most admirable is the manner in which the plot of the tale

winds round the wretched hunted jail-bird. Those who from the first understood the delusion of the boy's great expectations,—who felt or saw that they had nothing to do with the ghastly recluse in the deserted house, and her brooding revengeful sense of the wicked wrong which had laid her woman's life waste—were, therefore, all the more terribly held in thrall by the knowledge that the convict would return some day, and the air-castle be blown into fragments as by a whirlwind.—It is much to say, that the suspense so strongly excited is followed by a catastrophe as fearfully and forcibly outdoing expectation as if it had not been foreseen. There is nothing in English fiction, not even "the print of the man's foot in the sand" in *Robinson Crusoe,* fuller of engrossing and legitimate terror than the night scene of the convict's return, dogged from its first moment by Death.—From this point to its close, the interest of the romance increases with a resistless and steady power never before attained by Mr. Dickens. Nor has he ever used his own language with such poignant muscular force as here. Not an epithet is lost; not a touch is laid on carelessly; not a sentence is mannered. Adventure follows adventure—each one more riveting than the last—each one, too, adding some softening and redeeming light to the character of the poor hunted "warmint," without making the close of his sad story maudlin or sentimental. Everything is as it should be, great and small;—from the tremendous murder-scene in the limekiln down to Wemmick's lamentation over "the portable property."

There are those who will say that Miss Havisham's strange mad life is overdrawn; but such have not been conversant with the freaks and eccentricities which a haughty spirit in agony can assume: nor the manner in which a resolution once taken becomes a law never to be broken. We have no doubt, that, even now, in remote places of England, rich old mansions might be found as strangely peopled as the deserted brewery—with its spectre in white. Satis House, with its dank and weed-grown garden and the mouldering bridal feast, is as real, to us, as the lonely church on the marshes,—or as the wonderful estate in Walworth, with its works of art and ingenuity—the original of which, by the way, we have heard claimed for half-a-dozen different localities.

One word more. In no late fiction has Mr. Dickens been so happy in his group of what may be called accessory characters. Mr. Jaggers, with his handkerchief; Mr. Wopsle, with his dramatic instincts,—the greedy, sycophantish seedsman,—that wonderful thorn in everyone's side, Trabb's boy—are all capital. We fancy that at the outset he may have meant to make more of Mr. and Mrs. Matthew Pocket,—but they are not missed—Herbert is as fresh and genial an *Horatio* as a hero could desire; and most particularly are we grateful for the uncertainty in which the tale closes, as we interpret it. We do not believe that Pip *did* marry Estella, though there are two opinions on the subject.

We part from this tale with as much reluctance as if we had never before known the dear delight of reading a romance. So strong a sensation of pleasure is too rarely received in this wilderness of dubious literature of ours. *Great Expectations,* we are satisfied, will add to Mr. Dickens's reputation, and is the imaginative book of the year. (pp. 44-5)

[*H. F. Chorley*], in a review of "Great Expectations," in The Athenaeum, No. 1759, July 13, 1861, pp. 43-5.

*THE SATURDAY REVIEW,* LONDON   (essay date 1861)

[*In this mixed evaluation of* Great Expectations, *the reviewer praises the story as original and often powerfully written, but faults the work for its extremely rapid pace and frequently exaggerated comic scenes and characters.*]

Mr. Dickens may be reasonably proud of [*Great Expectations*]. After the long series of his varied works—after passing under the cloud of *Little Dorrit* and *Bleak House*—he has written a story that is new, original, powerful, and very entertaining. It has its weaknesses, as most compositions have, but it is astonishing that a writer who has written so much should still have so much novelty to offer us. He does not serve up the hashes of his old entertainments, and live on repeated resuscitations of his defunct creation. He does not bring in David Copperfield at every stage of his life, and David Copperfield's sons and granddaughters. He thinks of new characters, makes new jokes, contrives new incidents. He ought to have the thanks of the wearied public, and the admiration of those who know how hard it is to observe when the first zest of observation is passed away, and how much courage and resolution it demands to note the comic in life and manners amid the tragedy and farce of declining years. *Great Expectations* restores Mr. Dickens and his readers to the old level. It is in his best vein, and although unfortunately it is too slight, and bears many traces of hasty writing, it is quite worthy to stand beside *Martin Chuzzlewit* and *David Copperfield.* It has characters in it that will become part of common talk, and live even in the mouths of those who do not read novels. Wemmick strikes us as the great creation of the book, and his marriage as the funniest incident. How often will future jokers observe, "Halloa, here's a church; let's have a wedding." It is impossible not to regret that a book so good should not have been better. Probably the form in which it was first published may have had something to do with its faults. The plot ends before it ought to do. The heroine is married, reclaimed from harshness to gentleness, widowed, made love to, and remarried, in a page or two. This is too stiff a pace for the emotions of readers to live up to. We do not like to go beyond a canter through the moral restoration of a young lady. Characters, too, are entirely altered, in order to make the story end rapidly. Herbert, one of the most pleasing characters Mr. Dickens ever drew, starts as an amiable dreamy creature, incapable of business, and living on the vaguest hopes. But at the close of the tale it becomes necessary to provide for the hero. So Herbert comes out all at once as a shrewd, successful Levant merchant, and takes the hero into partnership. Villains, again, are sketched in and then smeared out again. Old Orlick, the gigantic lout of a blacksmith, commits every kind of atrocity, from breaking the skull of his mistress to purposing to burn the hero in a limekiln, and yet all we hear of him at the end is, that he is taken up for a burglary which forms no part of the story. These are little things, but they might have been avoided. There appears to be no reason why *Great Expectations* should fall below any of Mr. Dickens' works, and yet it undoubtedly does. It is rather a story with excellent things in it than an excellent story.

Mr. Dickens has always had one great fault, and it was not to be supposed that he would suddenly shake this fault off. *Great Expectations* is strongly marked with it. This fault is that of exaggerating one particular set of facts, a comic side in a character, or a comic turn of expression, until all reality fades away, and the person who is the centre of the extravagance becomes a mere peg or clothes-horse on which the rags of comedy hang loosely and flutter backwards and forwards. Miss Havisham is one of Mr. Dickens' regular pieces of melodramatic exaggeration. She is represented as having lived for a quarter of a century in a room never dusted or cleaned, and always lighted with candles. During all this time she has worn her bridal dress, and everything on her and in the room has remained exactly the same and exactly in the same position for this enormous length of time. Human life cannot go on in this way. We cannot, indeed, prove a negative. We cannot show that no woman ever lived in this manner. But even if it were possible, the manner of living would be too exceptional, too nearly bordering on the monstrous and loathsome, to be appropriately introduced in the midst of a story of ordinary English life. Pumblechook, again, is an instance of the personages in Mr. Dickens' novels who only exist to say one set of things, and who do say it, and persist in saying it, until they are equally wearisome and unreal. He is a wordy humbug, who claims, without the slightest reason, to have made the hero's fortunes. This claim he urges with the pertinacity with which Carker shows his teeth and Mr. Turveytop advocates deportment. Sometimes, in the midst of this artificial exaggeration and uniformity of the general type, Mr. Dickens, as in Pecksniff, introduces such a variety of incident and expression that we are amused in spite of the unreality. But in the minor characters, who appear only to introduce the exaggeration, the disagreeable effect is unrelieved, and we get tired before we become interested. Mrs. Pocket, too, is even less like a possible woman than Pumblechook is like a possible man. She is the mother of seven or eight children, but she has never learned how to hold a baby, because her whole time is taken up in reading the Peerage and Baronetage. She cannot talk to any one or perform any household task, because her thoughts and eyes instantly wander to her beloved volumes. That there are silly women in England, who give up much more time than is wise to thinking of grand people with whom they have nothing to do, is very true, and the folly is a very fit, though rather a small subject for satire; but when satire represents a mother of eight children as prevented by the Baronetage from knowing how to hold a baby without bumping its head against a table, we get away from the follies of flesh and blood to the oddities of puppets and to the kind of fun that lights up the pages of *Charivari.*

But if this new tale is marked with the faults of its predecessors, it appears to us to surpass them in one point. There are passages and conceptions in it which indicate a more profound study of the general nature of human character than Mr. Dickens usually betrays. The hero writes an autobiography of his own life, tells the story of his childhood, of his struggles with poverty, and of his gradual rise in the world until he attains what, in Mr. Dickens' novels, is the very vague position of a gentleman. Every one is a gentleman there who is not a comic servant or labourer or tradesman on the one hand, or a bloated aristocrat on the other. The adventures of Pip, therefore, threaten to trespass very closely on the adventures of David Copperfield, and the power of novel creation which Mr. Dickens possesses is shown in nothing more than that he should have succeeded in keeping two stories of a boy's childhood so wholly distinct. The method he has adopted to create the distinction lies not only in the contrivance of an entirely different set of incidents, but also in making Pip a much more thorough study of character than David Copperfield was. Pip is elated, spoilt, made conceited and mean by his good fortune; but he always remains a good fellow, with a desire to do right, and with warm feelings. The best of all the scenes to which these conflicting elements of character give rise is one where Pip revisits the poor home in which he has been brought up, and has a friendly talk with Biddy, who had been very much inclined to love him when he was her equal. He is melted by the sight of old scenes and old faces, and resolves that the pleasures and occupations of wealth shall not again make him forget his early friends. He tells Biddy that in future he will often revisit his home. She is wise enough to disbelieve him, and tells him that she does not and cannot deceive herself. She knows that his feelings and resolutions are transient, and that the gentleman could not really bear the quiet and homely life of the cottage. The way in which Pip answers her is admirable. He takes a very high line of moral condescension. He explains to Biddy, as if he were a philosophic apostle, that this distrust of him shows something wrong in her own feelings, and he advises her to examine herself, and to check these evil thoughts in the bud. It is needless to say that Biddy was quite right, and that next morning the philosopher is very glad to get away. The same knowledge of character is displayed on a smaller scale in the very amusing scene in which Pip and Herbert make up their accounts, and seem to themselves to be almost paying off their debts by the rigid and businesslike way in which they schedule the amounts and docket the bills. When the accounts are ended, Pip instructs Herbert that the right thing is to leave what he calls a margin. This means that they should state the sum total of debt in round figures exceeding the known amount, so as to provide against all contingencies. They thus seem to have a new stock of unappropriated money, and hasten at once to spend it, and to bring their debts up to the round figure.

There are also many passages of powerful writing, and many incidents that are new to novel readers, and very effective. The whole framework of the story is new. A convict meets the hero in a churchyard, and, under the coercion of the most frightful threats, makes the little boy steal a file and some food for him. This the hero does, and the convict is profoundly grateful. Being retaken and transported, he makes a fortune in Australia, and as his heart is always full of the thought of the little boy that has been so kind to him, he determines that he will make this boy a gentleman. Without disclosing where the money comes from, he manages to get Pip taught and provided with ample means. Pip has "great expectations," and lives accordingly. At last the convict comes home, as his desire to see the object of his benevolence and love overpowers all the considerations of prudence. He discloses himself to Pip, and then for the first time Pip, who believes the eccentric Miss Havisham has been his friend, learns that his old acquaintance, the terrible convict, is the author of his grandeur. This plot affords many openings for effective writing. There is a description of the convict on one of the lonely and gloomy marshes that border the Thames, of the pursuit of the officials, and of the chase, which is as interesting as that kind of description can be. The uncertainty, also, in which not only Pip but the reader remains as to the source from which Pip's money comes, is contrived so as to keep expectation continually alive. But the best part of the whole is the scene in which the convict discloses himself to Pip. The contrast between the embarrassment of the created gentleman and the ease of the creating felon is very amusing. The convict has no other wish than simply to please his Pip. He once raps out an oath or two, and then he bethinks himself that this is unworthy of their mutual position, and he cannot help continually recurring to his transgression, and entreating the "dear boy" to forgive him for being "low." The simplicity of the convict, his perfect indifference to life, his con-

tempt of danger, and his anxiety not only to please, but to win the esteem of Pip, make up a character that attracts us equally by its originality and its naturalness. (pp. 69-70)

*A review of "Great Expectations," in* The Saturday Review, *London, Vol. 12, No. 299, July 20, 1861, pp. 69-70.*

[E. S. DALLAS] (essay date 1861)

[*Although he faults* Great Expectations *for having an improbable plot and for evincing what he calls "some of Dicken's worst mannerisms," Dallas considers the novel "well worth reading" for its humor.*]

Mr. Dickens has good-naturedly granted to his hosts of readers the desire of their hearts. They have been complaining that in his later works he has adopted a new style, to the neglect of that old manner which first won our admiration. Give us back the old **Pickwick** style, they cried, with its contempt of art, its loose story, its jumbled characters, and all its jesting that made us laugh so lustily; give us back Sam Weller and Mrs. Gamp and Bob Sawyer, and Mrs. Nickleby, Pecksniff, Bumble, and the rest, and we are willing to sacrifice serious purpose, consistent plot, finished writing, and all else. Without calling upon his readers for any alarming sacrifices, Mr. Dickens has in the present work given us more of his earlier fancies than we have had for years. **Great Expectations** is not, indeed, his best work, but it is to be ranked among his happiest. There is that flowing humour in it which disarms criticism, and which is all the more enjoyable because it defies criticism. Faults there are in abundance, but who is going to find fault when the very essence of the fun is to commit faults? Does the reader who, after feasting on the **Pickwick Papers** for the fifth time, begins to get fastidious suppose that Mr. Dickens is not fully alive to all the absurdities which he has committed in that work? In foregoing, to some extent, the correct and highly proper style of his more recent productions, and in falling back upon the jovial extravagancies of his younger days, is it to be supposed that so masterly a writer is not quite aware of what he has done, and has not deliberately chosen his path? A wild story, odd characters, absurd situations, whimsical descriptions—it is easy to make a long catalogue of such crimes. To do so, however, were merely to give the body without the soul,—to hang, draw, and quarter the body, and to present its dead fragments as specimens of the living man. Lord Chesterfield advised his son not to laugh, because laughter disfigures the countenance. All comedy is liable to the same objection. If the comical element predominates in a story, it is impossible to avoid some distortion of feature, and for the sake of a good laugh most readers are prepared to tolerate a good many violations of symmetry in plot, passion, and character.

The method of publishing an important work of fiction in monthly instalments was considered a hazardous experiment, which could not fail to set its mark upon the novel as a whole. Mr. Dickens led the way in making the experiment, and his enterprise was crowned with such success that most of the good novels now find their way to the public in the form of a monthly dole. We cannot say that we have ever met with a man who would confess to having read a tale regularly month by month, and who, if asked how he liked Dickens's or Thackeray's last number, did not instantly insist upon the impossibility of his getting through a story piecemeal. Nevertheless, the monthly publication succeeds, and thousands of a novel are sold in minute doses, where only hundreds would have been disposed of in the lump. . . .

But what are we to say to the new experiment which is now being tried of publishing good novels week by week? Hitherto the weekly issue of fiction has been connected with publications of the lowest class—small penny and halfpenny serials that found in the multitude some compensation for the degradation of their readers. . . . Mr. Dickens has tried another experiment. The periodical which he conducts is addressed to a much higher class of readers than any which the penny journals would reach, and he has spread before them novel after novel specially adapted to their tastes. The first of these fictions which achieved a decided success was that of Mr. Wilkie Collins—*The Woman in White.* It was read with avidity by hosts of weekly readers, and the momentum which it acquired when published in fragments carried it through several large editions when published as a whole. The novel was most successful, but if we are from it to form a judgment of the sort of story which succeeds in a weekly issue our estimate will not be very high. Everything is sacrificed to the plot—character, dialogue, passion, description; and the plot, when we come to examine it, is not merely improbable—it is impossible. We are fascinated with a first reading of the tale, but, having once had our curiosity appeased, we never wish to take it up again. After Mr. Wilkie Collins's tale, the next great hit was this story of Mr. Dickens's to which we invite the attention of our readers. It is quite equal to *The Woman in White* in the management of the plot, but, perhaps, this is not saying much when we have to add that the story, though not impossible like Mr. Wilkie Collins's, is very improbable. If Mr. Dickens, however, chose to keep the common herd of readers together by the marvels of an improbable story, he attracted the better class of readers by his fancy, his fun, and his sentiment. Altogether, his success was so great as to warrant the conclusion, which four goodly editions already justify, that the weekly form of publication is not incompatible with a very high order of fiction. . . .

*Great Expectations* is republished as a three-volume novel. Mr. Dickens, we believe, only once before published a three-volume tale—*Oliver Twist.* We mention the fact because the resemblance between the two tales is not merely the superficial one that they are both in the same number of volumes, but is also one of subject very much and of treatment. The hero of the present tale, Pip, is a sort of Oliver. He is lowborn, fatherless and motherless, and he rises out of the cheerless degradation of his childhood into quite another sphere. The thieves got a hold of Oliver, tried to make him a pickpocket, and were succeeded in their friendly intentions by Mr. Brownlow, who thought that he could manage better for the lad. Pip's life is not less mixed up with the ways of convicts. He befriends a convict in his need, and henceforth his destiny is involved in that of the prisoner. The convict in the new story takes the place of Mr. Brownlow in the old, and supplies Master Pip with every luxury. In either tale, through some unaccountable caprice of fortune, the puny son of poverty suddenly finds himself the child of affluence. If we are asked which of the tales we like best, the reply must be that the earlier one is the more fresh in style, and rich in detail, but that the later one is the more free in handling, and the more powerful in effect. It is so, even though we have to acknowledge in the work some of Mr. Dickens's worst mannerisms. For example, it is a mere mannerism that in all his tales there should be introduced some one—generally a woman—who has been confined indoors for years, and who, either

from compulsion or from settled purpose, should live in dirt and gloom, never breathing the fresh air and enjoying the sunshine. A lady who has a whim of this sort is here, as in most of Mr. Dickens's tales, the blind of the story. Making every allowance, however, for repetitions, the tale is really worthy of its author's reputation, and is well worth reading. . . .

In the course of this story several characters are introduced which will take rank with some of Mr. Dickens's best, such as Joe the blacksmith, Pumblechook the corndealer, and Wemmick the lawyer's clerk. To enjoy these characters, the story itself must be read; and here we contine ourselves to a few extracts illustrative of Mr. Dickens's manner. His description of Joe is very characteristic:—"Joe was a fair man, with curls of flaxen hair on each side of his smooth face, and with eyes of such a very undecided blue that they seemed to have somehow got mixed with their own whites." . . . Another of Mr. Dickens's fancies is this—"I think the Romans must have aggravated one another very much with their noses. Perhaps they became the restless people they were in consequence. Anyhow, Mr. Wopsle's Roman nose so aggravated me that I should have liked to pull it until he howled." Wopsle was the parish clerk. "The church not being 'thrown open,' he was, as I have said, our clerk. But he punished the Amens tremendously, and when he gave out the psalm—always giving the whole verse—he looked all round the congregation first, as much as to say, 'You have heard my friend overhead; oblige me with your opinion of this style.'" The following is a little boy's opinion of the shop of Pumblechook, the corndealer:—"It appeared to me that he must be a very happy man indeed, to have so many little drawers in his shop." The owner of this shop one day at dinner made a profound remark:—"Pork—*regarded as biled*—is rich too, aint it?" After this neat specimen of the art by which pompous and homely phraseology may be united together, we are a few pages further on instructed how to answer "Halloa!"—"Halloa being a general observation which I have usually observed to be best answered by itself, I said 'Halloa.'" . . . Wopsle makes his appearance again, no longer a clerk, but an actor. "I don't know what he looked like, except a funeral; with the addition of a large Danish sun or star hanging round his neck by a blue riband, that had given him the appearance of being insured in some extraordinary fire-office." As an actor, Wopsle entertained immense schemes for the improvement of the drama. "I forget in detail what they were, but I have a general recollection that he was to begin with reviving the drama and to end with crushing it; inasmuch as his decease would leave it utterly bereft and without a chance or hope."

These few quotations are taken from the first two volumes. When Mr. Dickens gets into the third he is driven along by the exigencies of the story, and he can no longer afford to play with his subject. The interest is still sustained, but it is of a different kind. We might quote whole pages of eloquent writing and passionate dialogue, but readers, we dare say, will be better pleased with the sort of extracts we have given. The public insist upon seeing in Mr. Dickens chiefly the humourist; and, however great he may be in other directions, they count all as nothing beside his rare faculty of humour. To those who may not be satisfied with a work of this author's unless humour superabounds most we can heartily commend *Great Expectations.*

*[E. S. Dallas], in a review of "Great Expectations," in* The Times, *London, October 17, 1861, p. 6.*

## [HANNAH LAWRANCE]   (essay date 1862)

*[In the following excerpt from a review of Dickens's collected works, Lawrance rates* Great Expectations *highly.]*

[*Great Expectations*] may fairly rank among Dickens' most powerful works. We should have been well pleased had the story been less sombre in character, and some of the incidents less unnatural; but to its great merit in delineation of character, and its careful construction, we willingly bear testimony. The hero, to whom we wish a better name than Pip had been given, is most naturally drawn; and the story of his boyhood may well stand beside David Copperfield's. The convict, with whose fortunes he becomes so mysteriously linked, will rank high in Mr. Dickens' gallery of portraits. There is nothing melodramatic about him; he is the fierce, ignorant outcast, accustomed to find every man's hand against him, and for that very reason more likely to remember with gratitude the little boy who came out over the marshes that cold, misty Christmas morning, to bring the food for which he was starving, and the file without which he could not escape. Even the great fortune which he makes, and which he lavishes with such reckless generosity on his young benefactor, is not an unnatural incident, when we remember the well-authenticated tales told of convicts some forty or fifty years ago. And then, when the returned convict makes his startling appearance at Pip's elegant chambers, and slowly finds out that there can be little real sympathy between them, we almost pity the poor lifer who has incurred so terrible a risk, only to find that in making his boy 'a gentleman' he has placed an insurmountable bar between them. The progress of the story here is very admirable. Pip, gradually awakening to the sense of what he owes the poor outcast—although until then believing his good fortune to have arisen from a very different source; and then, while determinately refusing to receive his gifts, striving so devotedly to effect his escape; and all the incidents of that escape too—the delays, the obstacles, the unforeseen disappointments, how admirably are they drawn—and the last scenes, where the convict sinks into death, with Pip keeping gentle watch by his side; invest the poor hunted outcast with a lasting interest.

Far less natural is the character of disappointed, half-crazed Miss Havisham. That under the shock of a sudden disappointment, the room where the bridal-feast was laid should have been shut up, is a fact that has really occurred; but a woman never seeing the light of day for twenty years is too extravagant for any one but a complete lunatic; while her constant wearing, through the same long period, the white satin dress, and the bridal veil, is an obvious impossibility; two or three years constant wear would reduce both lace and satin to the veriest rags. We wish the story could have been managed without the intervention of either Miss Havisham or Estella, or that their characters had been softened. Both are most unpleasing; the latter especially, cold and cruel through mere waywardness. Indeed, the child of convicts, and the adopted daughter of so implacable a woman, we greatly doubt if the mere discipline of a brutal husband for some five or six years could have availed to tame Estella sufficiently to make her a suitable wife for Pip. After his disappointments and strivings, we think he deserved a better fate. But then what an admirable character is Joe Gargery, the blacksmith—one of the finest Dickens has ever drawn, al-

though one of the most amusing—making such extravagant blunders in words, but never in deeds; so simple, truthful, upright; the very husband for poor Biddy, simple, upright, kindhearted as he. Jaggers, the Old Bailey lawyer, looks like a portrait, but a very repulsive one. Wemmick, his clerk, is scarcely natural,—ruralising at his 'castle' at Walworth, and tending his aged father with such affectionate care, and yet the adviser of thieves and murderers during all his working hours; the contrast is too great. On the whole, *Great Expectations* is a most powerful story; and though we could have wished for a little more sunshine, still the marvellous force with which the darker scenes are painted place it very high among Dickens' works. (pp. 154-55)

*[Hannah Lawrance], in a review of "The Collected Works of Charles Dickens," in* The British Quarterly Review, *Vol. XXXV, January, 1862, pp. 135-59.*

## [MARGARET OLIPHANT]   (essay date 1862)

*[A prolific nineteenth-century Scottish novelist, critic, biographer, and historian, Oliphant published nearly one hundred novels. Many of them were tales of Scottish and English provincial life, including her most popular work, a series of novels called the* Chronicles of Carlingford *(1863-76). She was also a regular contributor to* Blackwood's Magazine, *from which this excerpted review of* Great Expectations *is taken. Censuring its plot as implausible and its characters as eccentric and lifeless, Oliphant considers the novel "feeble, fatigued, and colourless" in comparison with Dickens's earlier works.]*

Mr. Dickens was one of the first popular writers who brought pictures of what is called common life into fashion. It is he who has been mainly instrumental in leading the present generation of authors to disregard to a great extent the pictorial advantages of life on the upper levels of society, and to find a counter-picturesqueness in the experiences of the poor. But while this is the case, it is equally certain that Mr. Dickens, for his own part, has never ventured to depend for his special effects upon the common incidents of life. He has shifted the fashionable ground, and sought his heroes among penniless clerks and adventurers, as little beholden to their ancestors as to fortune. He has made washerwomen as interesting as duchesses, and found domestic angels among the vagabonds of a circus, on the very edge between lawlessness and crime; but whenever he has aimed at a scene, he has hurried aside into regions of exaggeration, and shown his own distrust of the common and usual by fantastic eccentricities, and accumulations of every description of high-strained oddity. The characters upon which he depends are not individual only, with a due recognisable difference to distinguish them from their fellows, but always peculiar, and set forth with a quaintly exaggerated distortion, by which we identify in a moment, not the character described, but the author who has made it, and of whom these oddities are characteristic. If it were possible to quicken these curious originals into life, what an odd crowd of ragamuffins and monsters would that be which should pursue this Frankenstein through the world! In the flush of fresh life and invention, when Sam Wellers and Mark Tapleys led the throng, we all awaited with impatience and received with delight the new oddities with which the great novelist filled his pages; but it is impossible to deny that nowadays that fertile fulness has failed, and that the persistent devotion to the eccentric which has distinguished Mr. Dickens through all his literary life, does now no longer produce fruits such as earn him our forgiveness for all the daring steps he takes beyond the modesty of nature. In his last work, [**Great Expectations**], symptoms of a dangerous adherence to, and departure from his old habitudes, will strike most of his faithful readers. The oddity remains, but much of the character has evaporated. The personages in **Great Expectations** are less out of the way, and the circumstances more so. Strange situations and fantastic predicaments have very much taken the place of those quaint and overstrained but still lifelike phases of humanity in which the author used to delight. He now carves his furniture grotesquely, and makes quaint masks upon his friezes; but he has no longer patience to keep up the strain so long as is necessary for the perfection of a character. After an indication of what he means this and that figure to be, he goes on with his story, too indifferent about it, one could suppose, to enter into the old elaboration. The book reminds us of a painter's rapid memoranda of some picture, in which he uses his pencil to help his memory. After he has dashed in the outline and composition, he scribbles a hasty "carmine" or "ultramarine" where those colours come. So the reds and blues of Mr. Dickens's picture are only written in. He means us to fill in the glow of the natural hue from the feeble symbol of the word which represents it, or perhaps to go back in our own memory to those forcible and abundant days when he wrought out his own odd conceptions minutely as if he loved them. Perhaps it was not at any time the wholesomest kind of art, but it was certainly much more satisfactory and piquant than now. (pp. 574-75)

[As] one of the series of Mr. Dickens's works, it is feeble, fatigued, and colourless. One feels that he must have got tired of it as the work went on, and that the creatures he had called into being, but who are no longer the lively men and women they used to be, must have bored him unspeakably before it was time to cut short their career, and throw a hasty and impatient hint of their future to stop the tiresome public appetite. Joe Gargery the blacksmith alone represents the ancient mood of the author. He is as good, as true, patient, and affectionate, as ungrammatical and confused in his faculty of speech, as could be desired; and shields the poor little Pip when he is a child on his hands, and forgives him when he is a man too grand for the blacksmith, with all that affecting tenderness and refinement of affection with which Mr. Dickens has the faculty of making his poor blacksmiths and fishermen much more interesting than anything he has ever produced in the condition of gentleman. Near Joe's abode, however, dwells a lady who is intended to have much more influence upon the fortunes of the hero than his humble protector. Here is the first sight of Miss Havisham and her surroundings, as they are disclosed to little Pip and to the reader:

> I entered, and found myself in a pretty large room, well lighted with wax candles. No glimpse of daylight was to be seen in it. It was a dressingroom, as I supposed from the furniture, though much of it was of forms and uses then quite unknown to me. . . . In an arm-chair, with an elbow resting on the table, and her head leaning on that hand, sat the strangest lady I have ever seen, or shall ever see.
>
> She was dressed in rich materials—satins and laces and silks—all of white. Her shoes were white, and she had a long white veil dependent from her hair, and she had bridal flowers in her hair; but her hair was white. Some bright jewels sparkled on her neck and on her hands, and some other jewels lay sparkling on the table. Dresses less splendid than the dress she wore, and half-packed trunks, were scattered about. She had not quite finished dressing, for

she had but one shoe on—the other was on the table near her hand; her veil was but half arranged; her watch and chain were not put on, and some lace for her bosom lay with those trinkets, and with her handkerchief and gloves and some flowers, and a prayer-book, all confusedly heaped about the looking-glass. It was not in the first moment that I saw all these things, though I saw more of them in the first moments than might be supposed. But I saw that everything within my view which ought to be white, had been white long ago, and had lost its lustre, and was faded and yellow. I saw that the bride within the bridal dress had withered like the dress and like the flowers, and had no brightness left but the brightness of her sunken eyes. I saw that the dress had been put upon the rounded figure of a young woman, and that the figure upon which it now hung loose had shrunk to skin and bone.

(pp. 575-76)

This is fancy run mad. As the story progresses, we learn that this poor lady, who is perfectly sane, much as appearances are against her, has lived in this miraculous condition for five-and-twenty years. Not very long ago we heard an eminent Scotch divine pause in the middle of his exposition to assure his hearers that it was not necessary to believe that the garments of the children of Israel were literally preserved from the wear and tear of the forty years in the wilderness, but simply that God provided them with clothing as well as food. We should like to know what the reverend gentleman would say to that wedding-dress of Miss Havisham's, which, in five-and-twenty years, had only grown yellow and faded, but was still, it appears, extant in all its integrity, no tatters being so much as inferred, except on the shoeless foot, the silk stocking on which "had been trodden ragged." In this ghastly company lived a pretty young girl called Estella, whom Miss Havisham had reared with the avowed intention of avenging her own wrongs against men in general by breaking as many hearts as possible. The unlucky little Pip is the first victim selected. He is brought there to be operated upon in the special hope that he may learn to love Estella, and by her means have his heart broken—though the unfortunate little individual in question has no connection whatever with the breaking of Miss Havisham's heart, nor any other title to be considered as a representative of male humanity. If startling effects were to be produced by any combination of circumstances or arrangement of still life, here, surely, was the very scene for a sensation. But somehow the sensation does not come. The wretched old heroine of this masquerade is, after all, notwithstanding her dire intentions of revenge upon the world, a very harmless and rather amiable old woman, totally incapable of any such determined folly. Estella grows up everything she ought not to grow up, but breaks nobody's heart but Pip's, so far as there is any evidence, and instead of carrying out the benevolent intentions of her benefactress, only fulfils a vulgar fate by marrying a man without any heart to be broken, and being miserable herself instead. . . . With the most fantastic exaggeration of means, here is no result at all achieved, and no sensation produced upon the composed intelligence of the reader. The shut-up house does not deceive that wary and experienced observer: he waits to see what comes of the bridal dress of twenty-five years' standing, and its poor old occupant; and as nothing in the least startling comes of either the one or the other, declines to be excited on the subject. The whole of this scene, and of the other scenes which follow in this house, and the entire connection between Miss Havisham, Pip, and Estella, is a failure. It is a mere piece of masquerading which deceives nobody, and carries to the utmost bounds of uninteresting extravagance that love of the odd and eccentric which has already brought Mr. Dickens to occasional misfortune in his long and well-deserved round of success.

Very different, however, is the darker side of the story. The appearance of the escaped convict in the squalid and dismal solitude of the marsh—the melancholy landscape with that one wretched figure embodying the forlorn and desolate sentiment of the scene—is perhaps as vivid and effective a sketch as Mr. Dickens ever drew. It is made in fewer words than usual, done at a breath, as if the author felt what he was saying this time, and saw the scene too vividly himself to think a full development of every detail necessary to enable his reader to see it also. Here is the apparition and the scene:—

> A fearful man, all in coarse grey, with a great iron on his leg. A man with no hat, and with broken shoes, and with an old rag tied round his head. A man who had been soaked in water, and smothered in mud, and lamed by stones, and cut by flints, and stung by nettles, and torn by briars; who limped, and shivered, and glared, and growled, and whose teeth chattered in his head as he seized me by the chin. . . . When he came to the low church-wall, he got over it like a man whose legs were numb and stiff, and then turned round to look for me. When I saw him turning, I set my face towards home, and made the best use of my legs. But presently I looked over my shoulder, and saw him going on towards the river, still hugging himself in both arms, and picking his way with his sore feet among the great stones dropped into the marshes here and there for stepping-places when the rains were heavy or the tide was in.
>
> (pp. 576-77)

After another very vivid picture of the same marshes under the wild torchlight of a convict-hunt, this horrible figure disappears out of the book, and only comes to life again at the end of the second volume, when, as Pip's unknown benefactor, the mysterious secret friend who has made the young blacksmith a gentleman, he re-emerges, humanized and horribly affectionate, out of the darkness. The young fellow's utter despair when he finds himself held fast in the clutches of this man's gratitude and bounty—compelled to be grateful in his turn while loathing the very thought of the obligation which he has been unwittingly incurring—is very powerfully drawn, and the predicament perhaps as strange and frightful as could be conceived. The terrible benefactor appears without the slightest warning in the young man's chambers, startling his harmless youthful life into the rudest, yet most intense tragedy; for his convict patron is a "Lifer," and the penalty of his return, if found out, is death. The sudden change which thus clouds over a hitherto harmless and aimless existence; the precautions necessary to keep the stranger safe; the gradual concentration of all interests into this one; the way in which, when hunted and in danger, the unfortunate young hero grows first tolerant, then anxious, and at last affectionate, to his strange and uncongenial friend,—is carefully done, and contains all that there is of interest and excitement in the book. It is a struggle against an unseen enemy—always an exciting spectacle; and the fact that it is not the imperilled criminal himself for whom we are principally concerned, but the generous young men who have devoted themselves to save him, refines the contest, and gives it an interest less coarsely tragical. Through the whole, he, the man specially in danger,

is acquiescent, passive; while the unlucky object of his bounty contrives and plots for him, accepting the bond between them with hearty youthful generosity as soon as his dreadful patron is in trouble. The narrative is close and rapid, and told without much unnecessary detail; but notwithstanding its undeniable effectiveness as a whole, it must be admitted that neither its successive incidents nor even its crisis strikes sharp upon the course of the story, or stands out with any distinctness from its general level. We watch the second boat stealing out upon the river without any sudden thrill of interest. We see the two convicts go down together into the water churned by the agitating passage of the great steamer which lowers over them like a castle in the water, but we draw our breath as calm as before. The means, in short, are superabundant, and full of all the natural elements of wonder, pity, and terror, but the effect is *not* produced. Perhaps most readers will make sure of what is going to happen to Abel Magwitch before they retire to their peaceful pillows, but once there, the returned convict will not haunt them. He will neither interfere with their sleep, nor startle their leisure with any uncomfortable consciousness of his own lurking, clandestine figure. At first, when he was out on the marsh, there seemed some likelihood that he might—but he has died, so far as his faculty of exciting a sensation goes, for long before he dies in prison. By means almost as exciting as those which, in the case of Bill Sykes, made the reading world hold its breath, and invested with all the dark grandeur of tragedy the vulgar fate of a brutal wretch, too debased for sympathy, Mr. Dickens has this time made nothing but a narrative, powerful, indeed, but not pictorial, and from which we cannot quote any one incident sufficiently vivid and distinct to concentrate the attention of the reader. The following deathbed sketch, however, is full of a subdued pathos and tenderness, without exaggeration or overdoing, dismissing in pity and charity, but without any attempt to make him a wonder either of remorse or reformation, the lawless soul who has been the overshadowing terror of the book:—

> The kind of submission or resignation that he showed was that of a man who was tired out. I sometimes derived an impression from his manner, or from a whispered word or two which escaped him, that he pondered over the question whether he might have been a better man under better circumstances. But he never justified himself by a hint tending that way, or tried to bend the past out of its eternal shape. . . .
>
> The number of the days had risen to ten, when I saw a greater change on him than I had yet seen. His eyes were turned towards the door and lighted up as I entered.
>
> "Dear boy," he said, as I sat down by his bed, "I thought you was late. But I knowed you couldn't be that."
>
> "It is just the time," said I; "I waited for it at the gate."
>
> "You always waits at the gate; don't you, dear boy?"
>
> "Yes. Not to lose a minute of the time."
>
> "Thank'ee, dear boy, thank'ee—God bless you! You've never deserted me, dear boy."
>
> I pressed his hand in silence, for I could not forget that I had once meant to desert him. . . .

"Are you in much pain to-day?"

"I don't complain of none, dear boy."

He had spoken his last words. He smiled, and I understood his touch to mean that he wished to lift my hand and lay it on his breast. I laid it there, and he smiled again, and laid both his hands upon it.

This picture is affecting in its simplicity and composure. The man has been a criminal, but he is not remorseful, or even affected by the solemn agitation and thrill of expectancy which we naturally associate with the approach of death. He is only weary and worn out, as most people are when they come to that inevitable hour, unsusceptible of impression. . . . The convict dies with a certain subdued halo of patience and gentleness about him; yet he has been a troublesome ruffian enough as long as he had any opportunities that way, and very shortly before the end of his life has exhibited towards his persecutor sentiments which were anything but Christian. But notwithstanding these drawbacks, Abel Magwitch makes, on the whole, an edifying end; and Mr. Dickens seizes the opportunity to note with delicate skill that pathetic gratification in the affection shown them, which is common to the old and weak of all classes. The tender pride with which the dying man dwells on the fact that his "dear boy" always waits at the gate for the hour of entrance is a touch as true to nature as it is affecting in itself.

The secondary persons of this book, however—almost entirely separated as they are from the main action, which is connected only in the very slightest way with the rest of the story—are, so far as they possess any individual character at all, specimens of oddity run mad. The incredible ghost, in the wedding-dress which has lasted for five-and-twenty years, is scarcely more *outré* than the ridiculous Mrs. Pocket, whom the hero finds seated in her garden, oblivious of everything that is going on around her, absorbed in a book which it is natural to suppose must be a novel—for popular superstition still believes in the existence of individuals capable of abandoning all the duties of life for the superior charms of fiction. But it is not a novel, but a Red book, which wraps the lady in an ideal world. Of the same description is the ingenious Mr. Wemmick, the lawyer's clerk, who lives in a little castle at Walworth, and calls his old father the Aged, and exclaims, "Hulloa! here's a church—let's go in!" when he is going to be married. Is this fun? Mr. Dickens ought to be an authority in that respect, seeing he has made more honest laughter in his day than any man living, and called forth as many honest tears; but we confess it looks exceedingly dull pleasantry to us, and that we are slow to accept Mr. Wemmick's carpentry as a substitute for all the homely wit and wisdom in which Mr. Dickens's privileged humorists used to abound. Besides all this heavy sport, there is a sensation episode of a still heavier description, for the introduction of which we are totally unable to discover any motive, except that of filling a few additional pages—unless, perhaps, it might be a desperate expedient on the part of the author to rouse his own languid interest in the conduct of the piece. Otherwise, why Pip should be seduced into the clutches of the senseless brute Orlick, and made to endure all the agonies of death for nothing, is a mystery quite beyond our powers of guessing. And again Mr. Dickens misses fire—he rouses himself up, indeed, and bethinks himself of his old arts of word and composition, and does his best to galvanise his figures into momentary life. But it is plain to see all along that he means nothing by it; we are as sure that help will come at the right moment, as if we saw

it approaching all the time; and the whole affair is the most arbitrary and causeless stoppage in the story—perhaps acceptable to weekly readers, as a prick of meretricious excitement on the languid road, perhaps a little stimulant to the mind of the writer, who was bored with his own production—but as a part of a narrative totally uncalled for, an interruption and encumbrance, interfering with the legitimate interest of the story, which is never so strong as to bear much trifling with. . . . The most popular of writers would do well to pause before he yawns and flings his careless essay at the public, and to consider that the reputation which makes everything he produces externally successful is itself mortal, and requires a sustenance more substantial than a languid owner can be expected to give. (pp. 577-80)

[*Margaret Oliphant*], *"Sensation Novels," in* Blackwood's Edinburgh Magazine, *Vol. DLIX, No. XCI, May, 1862, pp. 564-84.*

## JOHN FORSTER (essay date 1874)

[*Forster was a Victorian biographer, historian, and critic who became Dickens's lifelong friend and literary advisor. Forster's* The Life of Charles Dickens (1872-74), *from which the following excerpt is drawn, is considered one of the greatest biographies of a literary figure in the English language. To complement his discussion of* Great Expectations, *Forster offers some personal reminiscences on the topography and composition of the novel. Forster's comments were first published in 1874.*]

It may be doubted if Dickens could better have established his right to the front rank among novelists claimed for him, than by the ease and mastery with which, in . . . **Copperfield** and **Great Expectations,** he kept perfectly distinct the two stories of a boy's childhood, both told in the form of autobiography. A subtle penetration into character marks the unlikeness in the likeness; there is enough at once of resemblance and of difference in the position and surroundings of each to account for the divergences of character that arise; both children are good-hearted, and both have the advantage of association with models of tender simplicity and oddity, perfect in their truth and quite distinct from each other; but a sudden tumble into distress steadies Peggotty's little friend, and as unexpected a stroke of good fortune turns the head of the small protégé of Joe Gargery. What a deal of spoiling nevertheless, a nature that is really good at the bottom of it will stand without permanent damage, is nicely shown in Pip; and the way he reconciles his determination to act very shabbily to his early friends, with a conceited notion that he is setting them a moral example, is part of the shading of a character drawn with extraordinary skill. His greatest trial comes out of his good luck; and the foundations of both are laid at the opening of the tale, in a churchyard down by the Thames, as it winds past desolate marshes twenty miles to the sea, of which a masterly picture in half a dozen lines will give only average example of the descriptive writing that is everywhere one of the charms of the book. It is strange, as I transcribe the words, with what wonderful vividness they bring back the very spot on which we stood when he said he meant to make it the scene of the opening of his story—Cooling Castle ruins and the desolate church, lying out among the marshes seven miles from Gadshill!

My first most vivid and broad impression . . . on a memorable raw afternoon towards evening . . . was . . . that this bleak place, overgrown with nettles, was the churchyard, and that the dark flat wilderness beyond the churchyard, intersected with dykes and mounds and gates, with scattered cattle feeding on it, was the marshes; and that the low leaden line beyond, was the river; and that the distant savage lair from which the wind was rushing, was the sea. . . . On the edge of the river . . . only two black things in all the prospect seemed to be standing upright . . . one, the beacon by which the sailors steered, like an unhooped cask upon a pole, an ugly thing when you were near it; the other, a gibbet with some chains hanging to it which had once held a pirate.

Here Magwitch, an escaped convict from Chatham, terrifies the child Pip into stealing for him food and a file; and though recaptured and transported, he carries with him to Australia such a grateful heart for the small creature's service, that on making a fortune there he resolves to make his little friend a gentleman. This requires circumspection; and is so done, through the Old Bailey attorney who has defended Magwitch at his trial (a character of surprising novelty and truth), that Pip imagines his present gifts and "great expectations" to have come from the supposed rich lady of the story (whose eccentricities are the unattractive part of it, and have yet a weird character that somehow fits in with the kind of wrong she has suffered). When therefore the closing scenes bring back Magwitch himself, who risks his life to gratify his longing to see the gentleman he has made, it is an unspeakable horror to the youth to discover his benefactor in the convicted felon. If anyone doubts Dickens's power of so drawing a character as to get to the heart of it, seeing beyond surface peculiarities into the moving springs of the human being himself, let him narrowly examine those scenes. There is not a grain of substitution of mere sentiment, or circumstance, for the inner and absolute reality of the position in which these two creatures find themselves. Pip's loathing of what had built up his fortune, and his horror of the uncouth architect, are apparent in even his most generous efforts to protect him from exposure and sentence. Magwitch's convict habits strangely blend themselves with his wild pride in, and love for, the youth whom his money has turned into a gentleman. He has a craving for his good opinion; dreads to offend him by his "heavy grubbing," or by the oaths he lets fall now and then; and pathetically hopes his Pip, his dear boy, won't think him "low"; but, upon a chum of Pip's appearing unexpectedly while they are together, he pulls out a jack-knife by way of hint he can defend himself, and produces afterwards a greasy little clasped black Testament on which the startled new-comer, being found to have no hostile intention, is sworn to secrecy. At the opening of the story there had been an exciting scene of the wretched man's chase and recapture among the marshes, and this has its parallel at the close in his chase and recapture on the river while poor Pip is helping to get him off. To make himself sure of the actual course of a boat in such circumstances, and what possible incidents the adventure might have, Dickens hired a steamer for the day from Blackwall to Southend. Eight or nine friends and three or four members of his family were on board, and he seemed to have no care, the whole of that summer day (22 May, 1861), except to enjoy their enjoyment and entertain them with his own in shape of a thousand whims and fancies; but his sleepless observation was at work all the time, and nothing had escaped his keen vision on either side of the river. The fifteenth chapter of the third volume is a masterpiece.

The characters generally afford the same evidence as those two that Dickens's humour, not less than his creative power,

*Illustration by Frederic W. Pailthorpe depicting Magwitch and Pip's first encounter.*

was at its best in this book. The Old Bailey attorney Jaggers, and his clerk Wemmick (both excellent, and the last one of the oddities that live in everybody's liking for the good-heartedness of its comic surprises), are as good as his earliest efforts in that line; the Pumblechooks and Wopsles are as perfect as bits of *Nickleby* fresh from the mint; and the scene in which Pip, and Pip's chum Herbert, make up their accounts and schedule their debts and obligations, is original and delightful as Micawber himself. It is the art of living upon nothing and making the best of it, in its most pleasing form. Herbert's intentions to trade east and west, and get himself into business transactions of a magnificent extent and variety, are as perfectly warranted to us, in his way of putting them, by merely "being in a counting-house and looking about you," as Pip's means of paying his debts are lightened and made easy by his method of simply adding them up with a margin. "The time comes," says Herbert, "when you see your opening. And you go in, and you swoop upon it, and you make your capital, and then there you are! When you have once made your capital you have nothing to do but employ it." In like manner Pip tells us, "Suppose your debts to be one hundred and sixty-four pounds four and two-pence, I would say, leave a margin and put them down at two hundred; or suppose them to be four times as much, leave a margin and put them down at seven hundred." He is sufficiently candid to add, that, while he has the highest opinion of the wisdom and prudence of the margin, its dangers are that in the sense of freedom and solvency it imparts there is a tendency to run into new debt. But the satire that thus enforces the old warning against living upon vague hopes, and paying ancient debts by contracting new ones, never presented itself in more amusing or kindly shape. A word should be added of the father of the girl that Herbert marries, Bill Barley, ex-ship's-purser, a gouty, bed-ridden, drunken old rascal, who lies on his back in an upper floor on Mill Pond Bank, by Chinks's Basin, where he keeps, weighs, and serves out the family stores or provisions, according to old professional practice, with one eye at a telescope which is fitted on his bed for the convenience of sweeping the river. This is one of those sketches, slight in itself but made rich with a wealth of comic observation, in which Dickens's humour took especial delight; and to all this part of the story there is a quaint riverside flavour that gives it amusing reality and relish.

Sending the chapters that contain it, which open the third division of the tale, he wrote thus:

> It is a pity that the third portion cannot be read all at once, because its purpose would be much more apparent; and the pity is the greater, because the general turn and tone of the working out and winding up, will be away from all such things as they conventionally go. But what must be, must be. As to the planning out from week to week, nobody can imagine what the difficulty is, without trying. But, as in all such cases, when it is overcome the pleasure is proportionate. Two months more will see me through it, I trust. All the iron is in the fire, and I have 'only' to beat it out.

One other letter throws light upon an objection taken not unfairly to the too great speed with which the heroine, after being married, reclaimed, and widowed, is in a page or two again made love to, and remarried by the hero. This summary proceeding was not originally intended. But, over and above its popular acceptance, the book had interested some whose opinions Dickens specially valued (Carlyle among them, I remember); and upon Bulwer Lytton objecting to a close that should leave Pip a solitary man, Dickens substituted what now stands. "You will be surprised," he wrote, "to hear that I have changed the end of *Great Expectations* from and after Pip's return to Joe's, and finding his little likeness there. . . . I have no doubt the story will be more acceptable through the alteration [see excerpt dated 1861]. This turned out to be the case; but the first ending nevertheless seems to be more consistent with the drift, as well as natural working out, of the tale. (pp. 285-89)

*John Forster, in his* The Life of Charles Dickens, *Vol. 2, second edition, J. M. Dent & Sons Ltd., 1966, 480 p.*

## ROBERT LOUIS STEVENSON   (letter date 1883)

[*A famed Scottish novelist and essayist, Stevenson wrote some of the nineteenth-century's most beloved novels, including* Treasure Island, Dr. Jekyll and Mr. Hyde, *and* Kidnapped. *His novels are considered classics for their fast-paced action, strong plots, and well-drawn characters. In the following excerpt from a letter to his father dated 17 March 1883, Stevenson comments on the success of* Great Expectations *while discussing the possibility of adapting the novel for the theater—an idea that he never brought to fruition.*]

We have both re-read [*Great Expectations*] this winter, and I, in a manner, twice. The object being a play; the play, in its rough outline, I now see: and it is extraordinary how much of Dickens had to be discarded as unhuman, impossible, and ineffective: all that really remains is the loan of a file (but from a grown-up young man who knows what he was doing, and to a convict who, although he does not know it is his father—the father knows it is his son), and the fact of the convict-

father's return and disclosure of himself to the son whom he has made rich. Everything else has been thrown aside; and the position has had to be explained by a prologue which is pretty strong. I have great hopes of this piece, which is very amiable and, in places, very strong indeed: but it was curious how Dickens had to be rolled away; he had made his story turn on such improbabilities, such fantastic trifles, not on a good human basis, such as I recognised. . . . The only really well *executed* scenes are the riverside ones; the escape in particular is excellent; and I may add, the capture of the two convicts at the beginning. Miss Havisham is, probably, the worst thing in human fiction. But Wemmick I like; and I like Trabb's boy; and Mr. Wopsle as Hamlet is splendid. (pp. 126-27)

*Robert Louis Stevenson, in a letter to Thomas Stevenson on March 17, 1883, in* The Letters of Robert Louis Stevenson: 1880-1887, Vol. II, *edited by Sidney Colvin, Charles Scribner's Sons, 1911, pp. 126-28.*

## CHARLES DICKENS, JR.   (essay date 1896?)

[*Dickens's eldest child, Charles Dickens, Jr., worked on his father's weekly* All the Year Round *and eventually inherited it. Here, he remarks upon the altered ending of* Great Expectations *and provides some real-life locations for scenes in the book. Due to a lack of information as to when these comments were written, the date given is the year of the younger Dickens's death.*]

It has been objected to *Great Expectations* that its conclusion is faulty and inartistic: firstly, because the whole intention and plan of the book are to a very great extent spoilt by the marriage of Pip and Estella; and, secondly, because, in any case, her widowhood and second marriage are disposed of with a rapidity and a kind of nonchalance which really come upon the reader as a shock, as disagreeable as it is sudden. There is undoubted truth in this objection, and the best evidence of the soundness of the general judgment on the point lies in the fact that the published conclusion is not that which was originally devised by Charles Dickens, but one which he was persuaded into adopting by Bulwer. "You will be surprised," Charles Dickens wrote to Mr. Forster, "to hear that I have changed the end of *Great Expectations* from and after Pip's return to Joe's, and finding his little likeness there. Bulwer, who has been, as I think you know, extraordinarily taken by the book, so strongly urged it upon me, after reading the proofs, and supported his view with such good reasons that I resolved to make the change. . . . I have put in as pretty a little piece of writing as I could, and I have no doubt the story will be more acceptable through the alteration" [see excerpt dated 1861]. More acceptable it was, probably, to those readers who are never satisfied without "a happy ending," but it is certain that the only really natural as well as artistic conclusion to the story was that which was originally intended by Charles Dickens, and which kept Pip and Estella apart.

There was to be yet another alteration, although not one of great importance, in the closing words of the book. These, in *All the Year Round* and in the three-volume reprint, ran, "I saw the shadow of no parting from her." In later editions they read, "I saw no shadow of another parting from her."

It has occasionally happened that controversies of quite a heated kind have sprung up over questions as to what particular places or people Charles Dickens may have had in his mind when he described certain scenes or invented certain characters. There can be no such difficulty in regard to *Great Expectations.* The description of the marsh country about Joe Gargery's forge is so vivid that there would have been no difficulty in identifying it as the neighbourhood of Cooling, near Rochester, even if Charles Dickens had not testified to the fact; while Satis House requires very little alteration to make it a portrait of the old Restoration House in Rochester itself. (pp. xi-xii)

> *Charles Dickens, Jr., in an introduction to* Great Expectations and Hard Times *by Charles Dickens, Macmillan and Co., Limited, 1904, pp. ix-xvii.*

## GEORGE GISSING   (essay date 1898)

[*An English novelist, critic, and essayist whose works exemplify the changes that mark the transition from Victorian to modern literature, Gissing is best remembered for the harsh realism of such novels as* New Grub Street (*1891*) *and* Born in Exile (*1892*). *He is also known for his* Charles Dickens: A Critical Study (*1898*), *one of the earliest and most comprehensive studies of Dickens's writings. In this excerpt from that work, Gissing briefly discusses* Great Expectations.]

[*Great Expectations*] would be nearly perfect in its mechanism but for the unhappy deference to Lord Lytton's judgment, which caused the end to be altered. Dickens meant to have left Pip a lonely man, and of course rightly so; by the irony of fate he was induced to spoil his work through a brother novelist's desire for a happy ending—a strange thing, indeed, to befall Dickens. Observe how finely the narrative is kept in one key. It begins with a mournful impression—the foggy marshes spreading drearily by the seaward Thames— and throughout recurs this effect of cold and damp and dreariness; in that kind Dickens never did anything so good. Despite the subject, we have no stage fire—except around the person of Mr. Wopsle, a charming bit of satire, recalling and contrasting with the far-off days of *Nickleby.* The one unsatisfactory feature is the part concerned with Miss Havisham and Estella. Here the old Dickens survives in unhappy fashion; unable to resist the lure of eccentricity, but no longer presenting it with the gusto which was wont to be more than an excuse. Passing this, one can hardly overpraise the workmanship. No story in the first person was ever better told. (p. 66)

> *George Gissing, in his* Charles Dickens: A Critical Study, *1898. Reprint by Scholarly Press, Inc., 1972, 293 p.*

## ALGERNON CHARLES SWINBURNE   (essay date 1902)

[*Swinburne was an English poet, dramatist, and critic. Though he was renowned in his lifetime for his lyric poetry, he is remembered today for his rejection of Victorian mores. His explicitly sensual themes shocked his contemporaries: while they demanded that poetry reflect and uphold current moral standards, Swinburne's only goal, implicit in his poetry and explicit in his critical writings, was to express beauty. In the following excerpt from a survey of Dickens's career, Swinburne lauds* Great Expectations *for its characters and for its story, which he regards as possibly the greatest in English fiction.*]

Among the highest landmarks of success ever reared for immortality by the triumphant genius of Dickens, the story of *Great Expectations* must for ever stand eminent beside that of *David Copperfield.* These are his great twin masterpieces. Great as they are, there is nothing in them greater than the very best things in some of his other books: there is certainly no person preferable and there is possibly no person comparable to Samuel Weller or to Sarah Gamp. Of the two childish and boyish autobiographers, David is the better little fellow though not the more lifelike little friend; but of all first chapters is there any comparable for impression and for fusion of humour and terror and pity and fancy and truth to that which confronts the child with the convict on the marshes in the twilight? And the story is incomparably the finer story of the two; there can be none superior, if there be any equal to it, in the whole range of English fiction. And except in *Vanity Fair* and *The Newcomes,* if even they may claim exception, there can surely be found no equal or nearly equal number of living and everliving figures. The tragedy and the comedy, the realism and the dreamery of life, are fused or mingled together with little less than Shakesperean strength and skill of hand. To have created Abel Magwitch is to be a god indeed among the creators of deathless men. Pumblechook is actually better and droller and truer to imaginative life than Pecksniff: Joe Gargery is worthy to have been praised and loved at once by Fielding and by Sterne: Mr Jaggers and his clients, Mr Wemmick and his parent and his bride, are such figures as Shakespeare, when dropping out of poetry, might have created, if his lot had been cast in a later century. Can as much be said for the creatures of any other man or god? The ghastly tragedy of Miss Havisham could only have been made at once credible and endurable by Dickens; he alone could have reconciled the strange and sordid horror with the noble and pathetic survival of possible emotion and repentance. And he alone could have eluded condemnation for so gross an oversight as the escape from retribution of so important a criminal as the 'double murderer and monster' whose baffled or inadequate attempts are enough to make Bill Sikes seem comparatively the gentlest and Jonas Chuzzlewit the most amiable of men. I remember no such flaw in any other story I ever read. But in this story it may well have been allowed to pass unrebuked and unobserved; which yet I think it should not.

Among all the minor and momentary figures which flash into eternity across the stage of Dickens, there is one to which I have never yet seen the tribute of grateful homage adequately or even decently paid. The sonorous claims of old Bill Barley on the reader's affectionate and respectful interest have not remained without response; but the landlord's Jack has never yet, as far as I am aware, been fully recognised as great among the greatest of the gods of comic fiction. We are introduced to this lifelong friend in a waterside public-house as a 'grizzled male creature, the "Jack" of the little causeway, who was as slimy and smeary as if he had been low watermark too.' It is but for a moment that we meet him: but eternity is in that moment. (pp. 31-3)

This was the author's last great work: the defects in it are as nearly imperceptible as spots on the sun or shadows on a sunlit sea. (p. 34)

> *Algernon Charles Swinburne, "Charles Dickens," in* The Quarterly Review, *Vol. CXCVI, No. CCCXCI, July, 1902, pp. 20-39.*

## G. K. CHESTERTON   (essay date 1907)

[*Chesterton was one of England's most prominent and colorful men of letters during the early twentieth century. Although he is best known today as a detective novelist and essayist, he was also an eminent literary critic. Chesterton's works are charac-*

*terized by their humor, frequent use of paradox, and chatty, rambling style. In the following excerpt, first published as part of an introduction to a 1907 edition of* Great Expectations, *Chesterton distinguishes the novel from Dickens's other works, pointing out that it is his only novel without a hero; nonetheless, he asserts that, despite the lack of a heroic figure in* Great Expectations, *Dickens maintains his powerful ability to portray humanity.*]

**Great Expectations,** which was written in the afternoon of Dickens's life and fame, has a quality of serene irony and even sadness, which puts it quite alone among his other works. At no time could Dickens possibly be called cynical, he had too much vitality; but relatively to the other books this book is cynical; but it has the soft and gentle cynicism of old age, not the hard cynicism of youth. To be a young cynic is to be a young brute; but Dickens, who had been so perfectly romantic and sentimental in his youth, could afford to admit this touch of doubt into the mixed experience of his middle age. At no time could any books by Dickens have been called Thackerayan. Both of the two men were too great for that. But relatively to the other Dickensian productions this book may be called Thackerayan. It is a study in human weakness and the slow human surrender. It describes how easily a free lad of fresh and decent instincts can be made to care more for rank and pride and the degrees of our stratified society than for old affection and for honour. It is an extra chapter to *The Book of Snobs.*

The best way of stating the change which this book marks in Dickens can be put in one phrase. In this book for the first time the hero disappears. The hero had descended to Dickens by a long line which begins with the gods, nay, perhaps if one may say so, which begins with God. First comes Deity and then the image of Deity; first comes the god and then the demi-god, the Hercules who labours and conquers before he receives his heavenly crown. That idea, with continual mystery and modification, has continued behind all romantic tales; the demi-god became the hero of paganism; the hero of paganism became the knight-errant of Christianity; the knight-errant who wandered and was foiled before he triumphed became the hero of the later prose romance, the romance in which the hero had to fight a duel with the villain but always survived, in which the hero drove desperate horses through the night in order to rescue the heroine, but always rescued her.

This heroic modern hero, this demi-god in a top-hat, may be said to reach his supreme moment and typical example about the time when Dickens was writing that thundering and thrilling and highly unlikely scene in **Nicholas Nickleby,** the scene where Nicholas hopelessly denounces the atrocious Gride in his hour of grinning triumph, and a thud upon the floor above tells them that the heroine's tyrannical father has died just in time to set her free. That is the apotheosis of the pure heroic as Dickens found it, and as Dickens in some sense continued it. . . . But **Great Expectations** may be called, like *Vanity Fair,* a novel without a hero. Almost all Thackeray's novels except *Esmond* are novels without a hero, but only one of Dickens's novels can be so described. I do not mean that it is a novel without a *jeune premier,* a young man to make love; **Pickwick** is that and **Oliver Twist,** and, perhaps, **The Old Curiosity Shop.** I mean that it is a novel without a hero in the same far deeper and more deadly sense in which *Pendennis* is also a novel without a hero. I mean that it is a novel which aims chiefly at showing that the hero is unheroic.

All such phrases as these must appear of course to overstate the case. Pip is a much more delightful person than Nicholas Nickleby. Or to take a stronger case for the purpose of our argument, Pip is a much more delightful person than Sydney Carton. Still the fact remains. Most of Nicholas Nickleby's personal actions are meant to show that he is heroic. Most of Pip's actions are meant to show that he is not heroic. The study of Sydney Carton is meant to indicate that with all his vices Sydney Carton was a hero. The study of Pip is meant to indicate that with all his virtues Pip was a snob. The motive of the literary explanation is different. Pip and Pendennis are meant to show how circumstances can corrupt men. Sam Weller and Hercules are meant to show how heroes can subdue circumstances.

This is the preliminary view of the book which is necessary if we are to regard it as a real and separate fact in the life of Dickens. Dickens had many moods because he was an artist; but he had one great mood, because he was a great artist. Any real difference therefore from the general drift, or rather (I apologise to Dickens) the general drive of his creation is very important. This is the one place in his work in which he does, I will not say feel like Thackeray, far less think like Thackeray, less still write like Thackeray, but this is the one of his works in which he understands Thackeray. He puts himself in some sense in the same place; he considers mankind at somewhat the same angle as mankind is considered in one of the sociable and sarcastic novels of Thackeray. When he deals with Pip he sets out not to show his strength like the strength of Hercules, but to show his weakness like the weakness of Pendennis. When he sets out to describe Pip's great expectation he does not set out, as in a fairy tale, with the idea that these great expectations will be fulfilled; he sets out from the first with the idea that these great expectations will be disappointing. We might very well . . . apply to all Dickens's books the title **Great Expectations.** All his books are full of an airy and yet ardent expectation of everything; of the next person who shall happen to speak, of the next chimney that shall happen to smoke, of the next event, of the next ecstasy; of the next fulfilment of any eager human fancy. All his books might be called **Great Expectations.** But the only book to which he gave the name of **Great Expectations** was the only book in which the expectation was never realised. It was so with the whole of that splendid and unconscious generation to which he belonged. The whole glory of that old English middle class was that it was unconscious; its excellence was entirely in that, that it was the culture of the nation, and that it did not know it. If Dickens had ever known that he was optimistic, he would have ceased to be happy.

It is necessary to make this first point clear: that in **Great Expectations** Dickens was really trying to be a quiet, a detached, and even a cynical observer of human life. Dickens was trying to be Thackeray. And the final and startling triumph of Dickens is this: that even to this moderate and modern story, he gives an incomparable energy which is not moderate and which is not modern. He is trying to be reasonable; but in spite of himself he is inspired. He is trying to be detailed, but in spite of himself he is gigantic. Compared to the rest of Dickens this is Thackeray; but compared to the whole of Thackeray we can only say in supreme praise of it that it is Dickens.

Take, for example, the one question of snobbishness. Dickens has achieved admirably the description of the doubts and vanities of the wretched Pip as he walks down the street in his new gentlemanly clothes, the clothes of which he is so proud and so ashamed. Nothing could be so exquisitely human, nothing especially could be so exquisitely masculine as that combination of self-love and self-assertion and even insolence with a naked and helpless sensibility to the slightest breath of ridicule. Pip thinks himself better than every one else, and yet anybody can snub him; that is the everlasting male, and perhaps the everlasting gentleman. Dickens has described perfectly this quivering and defenceless dignity. Dickens has described perfectly how ill-armed it is against the coarse humour of real humanity—the real humanity which Dickens loved, but which idealists and philanthropists do not love, the humanity of cabmen and costermongers and men singing in a third-class carriage; the humanity of Trabb's boy. In describing Pip's weakness Dickens is as true and as delicate as Thackeray. But Thackeray might have been easily as true and as delicate as Dickens. This quick and quiet eye for the tremors of mankind is a thing which Dickens possessed, but which others possessed also. George Eliot or Thackeray could have described the weakness of Pip. Exactly what George Eliot and Thackeray could not have described was the vigour of Trabb's boy. . . . It is the real unconquerable rush and energy in a character which was the supreme and quite indescribable greatness of Dickens. He conquered by rushes; he attacked in masses; he carried things at the spear point in a charge of spears; he was the Rupert of Fiction. The thing about any figure of Dickens, about Sam Weller or Dick Swiveller, or Micawber, or Bagstock, or Trabb's boy,—the thing about each one of these persons is that he cannot be exhausted. A Dickens character hits you first on the nose and then in the waistcoat, and then in the eye and then in the waistcoat again, with the blinding rapidity of some battering engine. The scene in which Trabb's boy continually overtakes Pip in order to reel and stagger as at a first encounter is a thing quite within the real competence of such a character; it might have been suggested by Thackeray, or George Eliot, or any realist. But the point with Dickens is that there is a rush in the boy's rushings; the writer and the reader rush with him. They start with him, they stare with him, they stagger with him, they share an inexpressible vitality in the air which emanates from this violent and capering satirist. Trabb's boy is among other things a boy; he has a physical rapture in hurling himself like a boomerang and in bouncing to the sky like a ball. It is just exactly in describing this quality that Dickens is Dickens and that no one else comes near him. No one feels in his bones that Felix Holt was strong as he feels in his bones that little Quilp was strong. No one can feel that even Rawdon Crawley's splendid smack across the face of Lord Steyne is quite so living and life-giving as the "kick after kick" which old Mr. Weller dealt the dancing and quivering Stiggins as he drove him towards the trough. This quality, whether expressed intellectually or physically, is the profoundly popular and eternal quality in Dickens; it is the thing that no one else could do. This quality is the quality which has always given its continuous power and poetry to the common people everywhere. It is life; it is the joy of life felt by those who have nothing else but life. It is the thing that all aristocrats have always hated and dreaded in the people. And it is the thing which poor Pip really hates and dreads in Trabb's boy.

A great man of letters or any great artist is symbolic without knowing it. The things he describes are types because they are truths. . . . Hence it is unavoidable in speaking of a fine book like *Great Expectations* that we should give even to its unpretentious and realistic figures a certain massive mysticism. Pip is Pip, but he is also the well-meaning snob. And

this is even more true of those two great figures in the tale which stand for the English democracy. For, indeed, the first and last word upon the English democracy is said in Joe Gargery and Trabb's boy. The actual English populace, as distinct from the French populace or the Scotch or Irish populace, may be said to lie between those two types. The first is the poor man who does not assert himself at all, and the second is the poor man who asserts himself entirely with the weapon of sarcasm. The only way in which the English now ever rise in revolution is under the symbol and leadership of Trabb's boy. What pikes and shillelahs were to the Irish populace, what guns and barricades were to the French populace, that chaff is to the English populace. It is their weapon, the use of which they really understand. It is the one way in which they can make a rich man feel uncomfortable, and they use it very justifiably for all it is worth. (pp. 197-205)

Of the other type of democracy it is far more difficult to speak. It is always hard to speak of good things or good people, for in satisfying the soul they take away a certain spur to speech. Dickens was often called a sentimentalist. In one sense he sometimes was a sentimentalist. But if sentimentalism be held to mean something artifical or theatrical, then in the core and reality of his character Dickens was the very reverse of a sentimentalist. He seriously and definitely loved goodness. To see sincerity and charity satisfied him like a meal. What some critics call his love of sweet stuff is really his love of plain beef and bread. Sometimes one is tempted to wish that in the long Dickens dinner the sweet courses could be left out; but this does not make the whole banquet other than a banquet singularly solid and simple. The critics complain of the sweet things, but not because they are so strong as to like simple things. They complain of the sweet things because they are so sophisticated as to like sour things; their tongues are tainted with the bitterness of absinthe. Yet because of the very simplicity of Dickens's moral tastes it is impossible to speak adequately of them; and Joe Gargery must stand as he stands in the book, a thing too obvious to be understood. But this may be said of him in one of his minor aspects, that he stands for a certain long-suffering in the English poor, a certain weary patience and politeness which almost breaks the heart. One cannot help wondering whether that great mass of silent virtue will ever achieve anything on this earth. (pp. 205-06)

> G. K. Chesterton, " 'Great Expectations'," in his Appreciations and Criticisms of the Works of Charles Dickens, E. P. Dutton & Co., 1911, pp. 197-206.

## ERNEST A. BAKER (essay date 1936)

[*In the following excerpt, Baker comments on the plot, characters, and style of* Great Expectations.]

Any misgivings engendered by the hardness of *Hard Times,* the inequality of *Little Dorrit,* and the grandiose artifice of *A Tale of Two Cities,* that the creative energy and humour of Dickens were on the wane, must have been put to rest by *Great Expectations,* in which the freshness and spontaneity of his previous autobiographical novel [*David Copperfield*] came to life again. . . . In the first two pages, an indelible picture is flung upon the mind's eye of the bleak and desolate marshes environing the tiny churchyard, where the orphaned Pip is crying to himself and weaving fancies over the graves of his parents and brothers and sisters. It is the first glimpse of a stage on which some fearful scenes are to be enacted; and with the lift of the curtain the drama begins. "Hold your noise!" cries a terrible voice, as a man starts up among the graves. "Keep still, you little devil, or I'll cut your throat!" It is the runaway convict, with the iron still on his leg, who years later is to be the arbiter of the boy's destinies. He sends the terror-stricken lad to get him food and a file.

Dickens never hit upon a finer opening. Here begins the first act in a drama that reaches its logical conclusion on the final page, when years have elapsed, and a number of people have been implicated in the web of fate connecting Pip and the strange fugitive. The earlier autobiography, *David Copperfield,* had been a straightforward history of childhood and young manhood, with a plot loosely tacked on. This time the plot is fundamental. That other had been in the main a domestic story, with more stirring episodes coming in, as they often do into the most commonplace life. *Great Expectations* is a novel of adventure, the sort of adventure that might well happen to a person who got himself mixed up with questionable characters, in such a spot as this, close to the convict-ships, or in what really were in those days the wilds of London. Pip has narrow escapes, and goes through many racking experiences; he has to be prepared for acts of violence, and before the end his manhood is put to the proof in a way unusual in a novel by Dickens. All this is related with a force and terseness equal to that of the initial scene. On the present occasion, Dickens had calculated his effects beforehand, and he secured them without beating about the bush, only once or twice having to fall back upon his regular expedient, barefaced coincidence. The drama has, moreover, what had been a rarity if not quite unexampled in Dickens, an inner side, in the effect of the great expectations and the subsequent contacts with people and events upon the character of Pip. He grows and changes and develops, which cannot be said without many qualifications of any single one in the previous novels. True, David Copperfield also grew up, and learned from experience how to face a complicated world. But in *David Copperfield* it was a sensitive boy's impressions of a crowd of extraordinary fellow-beings that were so absorbing; David himself left a pleasant but not a very memorable impression.

In *Great Expectations,* those Pip meets with are hardly less wonderful; but Pip himself is interesting, and still more interesting are the ordeals through which he arrives at self-knowledge, realizes the value of what he has slighted in Joe Gargery and Biddy, and puts himself right at last with those faithful friends. It is Dickens's one serious study of the growth of personality; and, though he lets Pip tell the story, he manages with great skill to bring out the true significance and the humour of the strange situations, without showing his own hand, and, notably, without the heavy moralizing which Thackeray put in the mouth of his imaginary autobiographer in *Lovel the Widower* . . . [the critic adds in a footnote that ". . . Some misguided people would make out *Great Expectations* to be a didactic story, whilst others regard it as a satire on snobbishness, in Pip's pretences and uppishness and subsequent humiliations. A moral can, of course, be extracted from almost any story that is tolerably true to life. But Dickens kept clear more than usual here of the temptation to moralize."]. There was much of the same vein of comedy in the tale of David's change of circumstances. Both boys are rescued from poverty, and find themselves in unfamiliar spheres. Both have their troubles with manners and deportment. Sitting side by side with the nice boys at Dr Strong's school, David cannot forget that his recent associates were the street

urchins, Mick Walker and Mealy Potatoes; and, when years later he writes his reminiscences, he can see the humour of his shyness and confusion at the visit to the Steerforths, how he blushed when the chambermaid brought him his hot water, and was a mere worm in the presence of Littimer, that superfine gentleman's gentleman. But Pip's agonies are much more trying. All the old friends and townsfolk who knew him as the poor boy in the blacksmith's shop have to be duly impressed with the fact that he is now a young gentleman with expectations. He has to flabbergast the old humbug Pumblechook, and show an imperturbable face to the scurrilous Trabb's boy's chaff.

> Words cannot state the amount of aggravation and injury wreaked upon me by Trabb's boy, when, passing abreast of me, he pulled up his shirt-collar, twined his side-hair, stuck an arm akimbo, and smirked extravagantly by, wriggling his elbows and body, and drawling to his attendants, "Don't know yah, don't know yah, pon my soul don't know yah!"

And Pip is not David. His airs of dignity and condescension make him an easier prey to ridicule, and are the cause of untold anguish when he discovers the odious source of all his great expectations.

At this point the comedy grows serious; and Pip has the shock of his life to find that the rich benefactor is none other than the returned convict, whom he has been patronizing in his genteel chambers and lecturing with priggish superiority. Happily, Magwitch is not over-sensitive, and Pip fights down his abhorrence, comes gradually even to sympathize with the hunted wretch, and at last, cheerfully and with no thought of himself, faces considerable risk in trying to get him out of the country. Nothing Dickens had previously written showed him capable of revealing with such accuracy and delicacy all that went on in Pip's mind, from that midnight interview when Magwitch made himself known, to the terrible moment when Pip and the rest of the boat's crew are flung into the water, and presently he finds himself seated beside the recaptured man, who is on the way back to prison and the gallows.

> For now my repugnance to him had all melted away, and in the hunted, wounded, shackled creature who held my hand in his, I only saw a man who had meant to be my benefactor, and who had felt affectionately, gratefully, and generously, towards me with great constancy through a series of years. I only saw in him a much better man than I had been to Joe.

For Pip is not yet out of his predicaments. He still has to put himself right with Joe Gargery and Biddy. The great expectations have melted away, and left him resigned; but he cannot rest till he has wiped out his disloyalty to the old friend whose simple-heartedness and greatness of spirit have never even been conscious of it. The end Dickens had in mind for a story in which comedy and tragedy were so closely mixed was not the "happy ever after" which he was persuaded to substitute by Bulwer-Lytton. Pip and Joe were to be the same frank and loving old friends again, as the child and man had been at the beginning, and Pip was to be reconciled to his baffled hopes and to the lot he had earned. That was the right note. Marrying him to Estella after all was a conclusion for which Dickens had not prepared, by the lucid baring of motive which he applied to the other chief characters.

It is remarkable how the characters in *Great Expectations*

seem to fall into two divisions, according to their attitude towards Pip: the malignant and the friendly. It is further evidence of Dickens's careful dramatic planning. On the one side, the two half-realized fantasies, Miss Havisham and Estella, stand at the head. It would be rash to pronounce them impossible; Dickens may even have known two such anomalous beings. But he failed to explain and make them credible; they might not have looked so unreal had he gone a little deeper. The difficulty in accepting Miss Havisham is that the blow which unhinged her mind is so lightly and casually intimated. . . . And Estella, whom she formed to avenge her on the other sex, is just as artificial—a new sort of minx, as impenetrable to the reader as to the unfortunate Pip.

Among the other thorns in the flesh to Pip are that violent governing female, his sister, Mrs Joe; "bullying old Pumblechook," last avatar of the soul of Pecksniff and Chadband, who poses as the boy's deeply injured patron; Mr Wopsle, playing George Barnwell, and identifying Pip with that "ferocious and maudlin" scapegrace; Sarah Pocket, and the rest of the snobs who rage at the boy's elevation; Drummle the "Spider"; and, last not least, his relentless persecutor, Trabb's boy. Orlick and Compeyson, the two murderous ruffians, are enemies of a more fearful brand. All the others who matter much go into the opposite corps. Joe and Biddy come first, from every point of view, and then the unfortunate Magwitch, as chief agent in the strange complication of destinies. Magwitch, it should be noted, in spite of some discrepancies, is no mere automaton; as a study of the operations of a primitive mind he is not inferior to Joe Gargery. The men of law are the next in importance. Jaggers is a powerful creation; as Wemmick says, "There's only one Jaggers." His terrible clairvoyance! The way he turns you inside out!

> If anybody wouldn't make an admission, he said, "I'll have it out of you!" and if anybody made an admission, he said, "Now I have got you!" The magistrates shivered under a single bite of his finger. Thieves and thief-takers hung in dread rapture on his words, and shrank when a hair of his eyebrows turned in their direction.

It is as daring a figure as Dickens ever imagined, but, like the rest, justified by results. The fault with Wemmick is that he is made too deliberately quaint; he is almost a museum specimen, with his everlasting injunction, "Get hold of portable property"; the little castellated mansion where he lives with his Aged P., and the famous "Halloa! Here's a church! Let's go in!" "Here's Miss Skiffins! Let's have a wedding." Of the other dramatis personae, hardly one is a mere supernumerary; certainly not that hopeful young fellow, Herbert Pocket, who makes such a practical job of turning Pip into a gentleman; nor the charming Clara, whom he marries. Her father, old Bill Barley, is neutral, an invisible though a very audible character, in his room upstairs, his grog ready mixed in a little tub on the table, and his voice heard at intervals hoarsely growling the refrain, in which Pip says, "I substitute good wishes for something quite the reverse":

> "Ahoy! Bless your eyes, here's old Bill Barley . . . old Bill Barley on the flat of his back, by the Lord. Lying on the flat of his back, like a drifting old dead flounder, here's your old Bill Barley, bless your eyes. Ahoy! Bless you."

But the best of the lot, and the one who would have redeemed a duller story than Dickens ever wrote, is the man with the innocent soul of a child, Joe Gargery, that "worthy, worthy man," as Biddy calls him. Dickens loved integrity and reverenced the beauty of unselfishness and good-will, and was sometimes wise enough to see that to pay them due honour was better than any formal poetic justice. Never was there a truer example of what has been called a "Nature's gentleman." There is a veritable sublimity in such goodness of heart and utter selflessness, such sweetness of disposition, and humility combined with a proud self-respect. It sounds superhuman. But Joe is credible; the man lives.

> "Pip, dear old chap, life is made of ever so many partings welded together, as I may say, and one man's a blacksmith, and one's a whitesmith, and one's a goldsmith, and one's a coppersmith. Divisions among such must come, and must be met as they come. If there's been any fault to-day at all, it's mine. You and me is not two figures to be together in London; nor yet anywheres else but what is private, and beknown, and understood among friends. It ain't that I am proud, but that I want to be right, as you shall never see me no more in these clothes. I'm wrong out of the forge, the kitchen, or off th' meshes. You won't find half so much fault in me if, supposing as you should ever wish to see me, you come and put your head in at the forge window and see Joe the blacksmith, there, at the old anvil, in the old burnt apron, sticking to the old work. I'm awful dull, but I hope I've beat out something nigh the rights of this at last. And so GOD bless you, dear old Pip, old chap, GOD bless you!"

> I had not been mistaken in my fancy that there was a simple dignity in him. The fashion of his dress could no more come in its way when he spoke these words, than it could come in its way in Heaven. He touched me gently on the forehead, and went out. As soon as I could recover myself sufficiently, I hurried out after him and looked for him in the neighbouring streets; but he was gone.

This is not quoted as an example of Joe's gift of simple English, so elemental that it seems to consist of things rather than mere words. It is his one long-winded speech, but it happens to express his homely philosophy. *Great Expectations,* in comparison with Dickens's besetting carelessness, is a masterpiece of verbal art, whether in narrative and description or in the dialogue. It is not more than half as long as his average novel; and whatever else this thriftiness indicates, it is a sign that Dickens kept his characters in their place, and did not let them display themselves for the sake of display, as was too often his wont, in [his next novel, *Our Mutual Friend* ], for instance. He evidently saw his ending from the very first, and from time to time put in little hints of what was in store; as when Pip tells Miss Havisham that he only knows how to play beggar my neighbour, and she bids Estella, "Beggar him." It is almost as clear a warning as the later injunction, "Love her, love her, love her!" which is again as ominous as the notice Pip receives when there are other dangers about, "Don't go home!" The presentiments and intuitions, for instance, which somehow convince Pip that Jaggers's housekeeper is Estella's mother, and that her father is Magwitch, are among the links scattered all over the story which hold it firmly together. One thing they make clear and definite, that Estella was meant to be his bane and not his blessing: the altered ending falsified everything. (pp. 306-13)

*Ernest A. Baker, "Dickens—II. Novels of Plot," in his The History of the English Novel: The Age of Dickens and Thackeray, H. F. & G. Witherby Ltd., 1936, pp. 279-331.*

## BERNARD SHAW (essay date 1937)

*[Shaw is generally considered the greatest and best-known dramatist to write in the English language since Shakespeare. He is closely identified with the intellectual revival of the British theater, and in his dramatic theory he advocates eliminating romantic conventions in favor of a theater of ideas, grounded in realism. During the late nineteenth century, Shaw was a prominent literary, art, music, and drama critic, and his reviews were known for their biting wit and brilliance. In this excerpt from his preface to an edition of* Great Expectations *that retains the original ending, Shaw explains why he prefers it to the second version and suggests reasons why Dickens decided to change it.]*

*Great Expectations* is the last of the three full-length stories written by Dickens in the form of an autobiography. Of the three, *Bleak House,* as the autobiography of Miss Esther Summerson, is naturally the least personal; for Esther is not only a woman but a maddening prig, though we are forced to admit that such paragons exist and are perhaps worthy of the reverent admiration with which Dickens regarded them. Ruling her out, we have *David Copperfield* and *Great Expectations.* David was, for a time at least, Dickens's favorite child, perhaps because he had used him to express the bitterness of that episode in his own experience which had wounded his boyish self-respect most deeply. For Dickens, in spite of his exuberance, was a deeply reserved man: the exuberance was imagination and acting (his imagination was ceaseless, and his outward life a feat of acting from beginning to end); and we shall never know whether in that immensely broadened outlook and knowledge of the world which began with **Hard Times** and **Little Dorrit,** and left all his earlier works behind, he may not have come to see that making his living by sticking labels on blacking bottles and rubbing shoulders with boys who were not gentlemen, was as little shameful as being the genteel apprentice in the office of Mr Spenlow, or the shorthand writer recording the unending twaddle of the House of Commons and its overflow of electioneering bunk on the hustings of all the Eatanswills in the country.

That there was a tragic change in his valuations can be shewn by contrasting Micawber with William Dorrit. Beside Dorrit Micawber suddenly becomes a mere marionette pantaloon with a funny bag of tricks which he repeats until we can bear no more of him, and Dorrit a ruthless study of what snobbish gentility can make of reasonably decent human material. Now turn to *Great Expectations,* and, comparing David Copperfield with Pip, believe, if you can, that there was no revision of his estimate of the favorite child David as a work of art and even as a vehicle of experience. The adult David fades into what stage managers call a walking gentleman. The reappearance of Mr Dickens in the character of a black-smith's boy may be regarded as an apology to Mealy Potatoes.

Dickens did in fact know that *Great Expectations* was his most compactly perfect book. In all the other books, there are episodes of wild extravagance, extraordinarily funny if they catch you at the right age, but recklessly grotesque as nature studies. Even in *Little Dorrit,* Dickens's masterpiece among many masterpieces, it is impossible to believe that the perfectly authentic Mr Pancks really stopped the equally authentic Mr Casby in a crowded street in London and cut his hair; and though Mr F's aunt is a first-rate clinical study of senile deficiency in a shrewd old woman, her collisions with Arthur Clennam are too funny to be taken seriously. (pp. v-vi)

In *Great Expectations* we have Wopsle and Trabb's boy; but they have their part and purpose in the story and do not overstep the immodesty of nature. It is hardly decent to compare Mr F's aunt with Miss Havisham; but as contrasted studies of mad-women they make you shudder at the thought of what Dickens might have made of Miss Havisham if he had seen her as a comic personage. For life is no laughing matter in *Great Expectations:* the book is all-of-one piece and consistently truthful as none of the other books are, not even the compact *Tale of Two Cities,* which is pure sentimental melodrama from beginning to end, and shockingly wanting in any philosophy of history in its view of the French Revolution. (p. vi)

I will not go so far as to say that Dickens's novels are full of melancholy intentions which he shrank from carrying through to their unhappy conclusions; but he gave us no vitally happy heroes and heroines after Pickwick (begun, like Don Quixote, as a contemptible butt). Their happy endings are manufactured to make the books pleasant. Nobody who has endured the novels of our twentieth-century emancipated women, enormously cleverer and better informed than the novels of Dickens, and ruthlessly calculated to leave their readers hopelessly discouraged and miserable, will quarrel with Dickens for speeding his parting guests with happy faces by turning from the world of destiny to the world of imaginary good luck; but as our minds grow stronger and sterner some of his consolations become unnecessary and even irritating. And it happens that it is with just such a consolation that *Great Expectations* ends.

It did not always end so. In the *Clarion* of May 16, 1902, the late Hugh Mann, known to *Clarion* readers as Slender, quoted a different ending as the original, and raised the question whether an author has any right to commit what the editor (Mr Robert Blatchford) had called "literary infanticide" by discarding his inspired version of a story and substituting a changeling under external pressure. . . . [In his *Life of Dickens,* Foster quoted a letter from Dickens (see excerpt dated 1874)] declaring "I have no doubt the story will be more acceptable for the alteration". The alteration was urged on him by Bulwer Lytton. Forster then goes on to say "This turned out to be the case; but the first ending nevertheless seems to me more consistent with the drift as well as the natural working out of the tale. . . ." (pp. xiv-xvi)

Then I butted in and muddled matters by declaring that in my childhood I had read *Great Expectations* in its first form in *All the Year Round,* and that it was so much better that if ever I edited the book I should unhesitatingly restore the original ending. The result of this was a demand for such an edition. . . . (p. xvi)

[The] second ending, though psychologically wrong, is artistically much more congruous than the original. The scene, the hour, the atmosphere are beautifully touching and exactly right. Only at the end of the very last line did Dickens allow himself to say that between Pip and Estella there was "no shadow of parting". If I ever indulge in the luxury of a copy of *Great Expectations* made all for myself, Pip shall end by saying "Since that parting I have been able to think of her without the old unhappiness; but I have never tried to see her again, and I know I never shall". That would be the perfect ending.

But it would not have satisfied Bulwer Lytton. In his day there was a convention called a happy ending. It did not mean a happy ending: it meant that the lovers were married in the last chapter. Byron complained that "romances paint at full length people's wooings but only give a bust of marriages". Early in the present century the late St John Hankin published a volume entitled *Three Plays with Happy Endings.* In none of them did the lovers marry: they all had very happy escapes. That made us more critical of happiness and of marriage, and incidentally made us less tolerant of the convention that a marriage between Pip and Estella had any prospect of happiness for either of them, or indeed was not the most unhappy ending that could possibly be devised.

The discarded ending was, in fact, the true happy ending. . . . [With the original ending, the book's] atmosphere is a change which only the English climate could produce from the melancholy marshes where Magwitch starved and shivered in the winter dusk, with the guns of the horrible prison hulks booming their sullen hue and cry in the distance, to Piccadilly in spring. And the Shropshire doctor seems almost unbearably eupeptic in the procession of morbid or unhappy or dislikeable creatures who make the book so tragic. In fact, this ending is too happy if we may assume that Bentley Drummle had really thrashed the malicious complex out of Estella, and been himself well hammered by the doctor, who, being able to thrash both of them, was capable of living happily for ever after even with Estella. It is quite a healthy ending and a possible one; but it somehow does not belong to the tale. And the other ending belongs to the tale, but falsifies it at the last moment. I really think my own ending is the right one because I recollected it so in spite of that fatal phrase, and a child's wisdom is to be respected; but as Dickens is the final authority I am afraid the Bulwer Lytton version must stand for all editions beyond this very special one.

Note, by the way, that the passing carriage in the Piccadilly ending was unconsciously borrowed from *A Day's Ride: A Life's Romance,* the novel by Charles Lever which was so unpopular that Dickens had to write *Great Expectations* to replace it in *All the Year Round.* But in Lever's story it is the man who stops the carriage, only to be cut dead by the lady. That also, was the happiest possible ending both for Potts and Katinka, though the humiliation of Potts makes it painful for the moment. Lever was shewing Dickens the way; and Dickens instinctively took it until Lytton moidered him by fears for its effect on the sales.

Estella is a curious addition to the gallery of unamiable women painted by Dickens. In my youth it was commonly said that Dickens could not draw women. The people who said this were thinking of Agnes Wickfield and Esther Summerson, of Little Dorrit and Florence Dombey, and thinking of them as ridiculous idealizations of their sex. Gissing stopped that by asking whether shrews like Mrs Raddle, Mrs Macstinger, Mrs Gargery, featherheads like Mrs Nickleby and Flora Finching, warped spinsters like Rosa Dartle and Miss Wade, were not masterpieces of woman drawing. And they are all unamiable. But for Betsy Trotwood, who is a very lovable fairy godmother and yet a genuine nature study, and an old dear like Mrs Boffin, one would be tempted to ask whether Dickens had ever in his life met an amiable female. The transformation of Dora into Flora is diabolical, but frightfully true to nature. Of course Dickens with his imagination could invent amiable women by the dozen; but somehow he could not or would not bring them to life as he brought the others. We doubt whether he ever knew a little Dorrit; but Fanny Dorrit is from the life unmistakably. So is Estella. She is a much more elaborate study than Fanny, and, I should guess, a recent one.

Dickens, when he let himself go in *Great Expectations,* was separated from his wife and free to make more intimate acquaintances with women than a domesticated man can. I know nothing of his adventures in this phase of his career, though I daresay a good deal of it will be dug out by the little sect of anti-Dickensites whose fanaticism has been provoked by the Dickens Fellowships, and threatens to become as pathological as Bacon-Shakespear. It is not necessary to suggest a love affair; for Dickens could get from a passing glance a hint which he could expand into a full-grown character. Estella is a born tormentor. She torments Pip all through for the fun of it; and in the little we hear of her intercourse with others there is no suggestion of a moment of kindness: in fact her tormenting of Pip is almost affectionate in contrast to the cold disdain of her attitude towards the people who were not worth tormenting. It is not surprising that the unfortunate Bentley Drummle, whom she marries in the stupidity of sheer perversity, is obliged to defend himself from her clever malice with his fists: a consolation to us for Pip's broken heart, but not altogether a credible one; for the real Estellas can usually intimidate the real Bentley Drummles. At all events the final sugary suggestion of Estella redeemed by Bentley's thrashings and waste of her money, and living happily with Pip for ever after, provoked even Dickens's eldest son to rebel against it, most justly [see excerpt by Charles Dickens, Jr., dated 1896]. And yet Pip never loses his sense of "the indescribable majesty and indescribable charm" of her beauty. She still forces us to accept her as a superior creature who never learnt how to live in the real vulgar world. That is entirely true to nature.

Save for the last words the story is the most perfect of Dickens's works. In it he does not muddle himself with the ridiculous plots that appear like vestiges of the stone age in many of his books, from *Oliver Twist* to the end. The story is built round a single and simple catastrophe: the revelation to Pip of the source of his great expectations. There is, it is true, a trace of the old plot superstition in Estella turning out to be Magwitch's daughter; but it provides a touchingly happy ending for that heroic Warmint. Who could have the heart to grudge it to him?

As our social conscience expands and makes the intense class snobbery of the nineteenth century seem less natural to us, the tragedy of *Great Expectations* will lose some of its appeal. I have already wondered whether Dickens himself ever came to see that his agonizing sensitiveness about the blacking bottles and his resentment of his mother's opposition to his escape from them was not too snobbish to deserve all the sympathy he claimed for it. Compare the case of Mr H. G. Wells, who is our twentieth century Dickens. Mr Wells hated being a draper's assistant as much as Dickens hated being a warehouse boy; but he is not in the least ashamed of it, and never blamed his mother for regarding it as the summit of her ambition for him. Fate having imposed on that engaging cricketer Mr Wells's father an incongruous means of livelihood in the shape of a small shop, shopkeeping did not present itself to the young Wells as beneath him, whereas to the genteel Dickens being a warehouse boy was an unbearable comedown. Still, I cannot help speculating on whether if Dickens had not killed himself prematurely to pile up money for that excessive family of his, he might not have reached a stage at which he could have got as much fun out of the blacking bottles as Mr Wells has got out of his abhorred draper's counter.

Dickens never reached that stage; and there is no prevision of it in *Great Expectations,* in which he never raises the question why Pip should refuse Magwitch's endowment and shrink from him with such inhuman loathing. Magwitch no doubt was a Warmint from the point of view of the genteel Dickens family and even from his own; but Victor Hugo would have made him a magnificent hero, another Valjean. Inspired by an altogether noble fixed idea, he had lifted himself out of his rut of crime, and honestly made a fortune for the child who had fed him when he was starving. If Pip had no objection to be a parasite instead of an honest blacksmith, at least he had a better claim to be a parasite on Magwitch's earnings than, as he imagined, on Miss Havisham's property. It is curious that this should not have occurred to Dickens; for nothing could exceed the bitterness of his exposure of the futility of Pip's parasitism. If all that came of spunging on Miss Havisham (as Pip thought) was the privilege of being one of the Finches of the Grove, he need not have felt his dependence on Magwitch to be incompatible with his entirely baseless self-respect. But Pip—and I am afraid Pip must be to this extent identified with Dickens—could not see Magwitch as an animal of the same species as himself or Miss Havisham. His feeling is true to the nature of snobbery; but his creator says no word in criticism of that ephemeral limitation.

The basic truth of the situation is that Pip, like his creator, has no culture and no religion. Joe Gargery, when Pip tells a monstrous string of lies about Miss Havisham, advises him to say a repentant word about it in his prayers; but Pip never prays; and church means nothing to him but Mr Wopsle's orotundity. In this he resembles David Copperfield, who has gentility but neither culture nor religion. Pip's world is therefore a very melancholy place, and his conduct, good or bad, always helpless. This is why Dickens worked against so black a background after he was roused from his ignorant middle class cheery optimism by Carlyle. When he lost his belief in bourgeois society and with it his lightness of heart he had neither an economic Utopia nor a credible religion to hitch on to. His world becomes a world of great expectations cruelly disappointed. Mr Wells's world is a world of greater and greater expectations continually being fulfilled. That is a huge improvement. Dickens never had time to form a philosophy or define a faith; and his later and greater books are saddened by the evil that is done under the sun; but at least he preserved his intellectual innocence sufficiently to escape the dismal pseudo-scientific fatalism that was descending on the world in his latter days, founded on the preposterous error as to causation in which the future is determined by the present, which has been determined by the past. Mere accident apart, the true dynamic causation is always the incessant irresistible attraction of the evolutionary future. (pp. xvi-xxii)

> *Bernard Shaw, in a preface to* Great Expectations *by Charles Dickens, R. & R. Clark, Limited, 1937, pp. v-xxii.*

## T. A. JACKSON  (essay date 1938)

[*Jackson suggests that Dickens intended in* Great Expectations *to demonstrate that mid-Victorian English society's expectations of future prosperity—wealth whose source would be* the "labour of the depressed and exploited masses"—*were foolish and destructive.*]

[In contrast to Dickens's previous novels, the plot of *Great Expectations*] is comparatively simple. The tendency of his earlier days to let the sub-plot grow to the over-shadowing of the main plot, Dickens had, by now, brought well under control. . . . [The] subplots are so closely interwoven with the main plot that together they form a perfectly compacted whole. There is, of course, a big use made of dramatic surprise: in fact, the whole plot turns upon such an unexpected revelation. But instead of this making the plot "mysterious" it has the reverse effect.

Interest from the first is concentrated on the central character and his "great expectations." The other characters, leading and secondary, group themselves around this central theme with only a minimum of complication and diversion of interest. Not that the novel lacks diversity; on the contrary it contains as much diversity and variety as most of Dickens' novels. But the diversity is so well subordinated to the unity of the whole that the prevailing tone is grey upon grey, deepening into sombre gloom—and such, too, is the moral of the work as a whole.

If Dickens had not allowed himself to be overpersuaded by Bulwer Lytton, he would have achieved, for once, a novel with a positively "unhappy" ending. Even with its point somewhat self-blunted it remains an exercise on the theme of Frustration—of "great expectations" destroyed and punished by pitiless Reality. (pp. 188-89)

It is clear that the logical consequence of Pip's delusion about his "great expectations" was not only the shock of disillusionment—and the loss of his fortune along with his real benefactor—but also the frustration of all his love expectations. And this, all the more, since, in his infatuated belief that Estella was intended for him, he had been blind to the affection, as well as the good qualities, of the girl Biddy, who instead marries Pip's widowed brother-in-law, Joe Gargery. It is no less clear that the logical consequence of such an upbringing as that in which Estella's disposition was formed, would be to unfit her for any sort of marriage. It is clear, too, in the third place, that Dickens, setting to work to build a novel in which the folly of living in a fool's paradise is demonstrated by making the lure of "great expectations" lead to nothing but disaster, was in a mood, for once, to cut out the conventional wedding bells, and finish on a note of failure and grey disillusionment.

Thus interpreted the net effect of the novel would be to demonstrate . . . that Dickens saw in existing society and its whole crop of "great expectations" (it was the period of the most lurid mid-Victorian optimism, remember) nothing but folly and a headlong rush towards disaster.

The class bias of *Great Expectations* is so evident as almost to be underscored. Miss Havisham is a fine lady, who has been cruelly deceived and robbed. But it was by fine gentlemen that she was deceived and robbed—gentlemen of authentic "gentility," even though both finished their days as "swell mobsmen." And Miss Havisham's plan of revenge is, if possible, even more heartless and cruel than was the injury done to her. To fill the account full a select company of relatives are forever on the prowl round Miss Havisham, hating each other, and scheming and counter-scheming to oust each other from "expectations" under her will. So far the gentlefolks pass scrutiny very badly. There is a partial exception in the case of one of Miss Havisham's relatives, Matthew Pocket, who is the only one who never makes fawning visits to her. He is represented as a good sort, who has to work hard as a tutor, lecturer and writer, to keep a considerable family and an expensive wife—who spends her time lolling about and studying the Peerage. All the other characters in the book are either hard-working professionals, like the lawyer, Jaggers, and Wemmick his clerk; shopkeepers, like the egregious humbug Pumblechook; sea captains, like the drunken and outrageous Bill Barley; commercial men, like Herbert Pocket, son of Matthew; craftsmen like the blacksmith Joe Gargery, Pip's brother-in-law; wage-earners, like the blackguard, Orlick; plain "varmints" like the convict Magwitch. Thus such class-antagonism as there is in *Great Expectations* is not that between aristocrats (as such) and common people, but that between, on the one side, the "gentlemen" (who are for one reason or another either crazily vengeful or callously cold-hearted and corrupt) and with them their sycophants and attendant slum-hooligans and on the other, the honest, working section of the population.

By far the most attractive characters in the book are the blacksmith, Joe Gargery, and Biddy, the self-taught schoolmistress, who becomes his second wife. Pip himself begins as a proletarian and after his spell of prosperity is proletarianized again—except so far as his superior education equates him with the petit-bourgeoisie.

The two legal characters, Jaggers and his clerk Wemmick, are decisive in this regard. Both are exceedingly well-drawn, and each is quite different from the other. But they have this in common—they are different men, when at work in their Old Bailey practice, from what they are, secretly, in their private lives. They are inverted hypocrites. In business cold, unsentimental, calculating and ruthless; each, in private, is capable of deep affection, sympathy and compassion. It is impossible not to see in these two characters—especially when the care with which they have been drawn is taken into account—Dickens' deepening sense that success in business in the bourgeois world can be won only at the expense of everything nobly generous, elevating, sympathetic and humane. And as though to force this upon the reader's notice, Dickens endows Jaggers with the special characteristic that, invariably, after doing some more than usually dirty piece of work, he carefully washes his hands—with *scented soap.*

There is, significantly, no trace whatever in *Great Expectations* of the "Cheeryble" illusion—the notion that the world will be put right by the large-hearted benevolence of the employing class. Instead of Mr. Pickwick, the Cheeryble brothers, the elder Martin Chuzzlewit in his final, benevolent phase, John Jarndyce, or Jervis Lorry (the Cheeryble-illusion died hard!) we have the convict Magwitch; victim of an evil state of society; a neglected and ill-treated outcast from birth; savagely treated by law; tricked, exploited, and victimized by the gentleman swindler and forger, Compayson. After all this he shows, notwithstanding, a finely-human and pathetic capacity for unstinted gratitude; and a profoundly human desire for a generously impersonal revenge on the official society which has been his enemy all his life long.

In the character of Magwitch, and in his relation to Pip's "great expectations"—he was Estella's father!—the moral of the novel is clearly indicated.

Self-satisfied, mid-Victorian, British society buoyed itself up with as great "expectations" of future wealth and glory as did poor, deluded, Pip. If it had but known, its means of ostentation came from a source (the labour of the depressed and exploited masses) to which it would have been as shocked to acknowledge indebtedness as Pip was to find he owed all his acquired gentility to the patronage of a transported felon. Magwitch differed little from the uncouth monster which respectable society envisaged to itself as the typical "labouring man." And in literal truth, good, respectable society owed as much to these working men, and was as little aware of it, as was Pip of the source of his advantages. And respectable society is as little grateful as Pip, whenever the truth is revealed.

*Great Expectations* shows Dickens in the trough of the wave, his optimism shattered, and his Radicalism nonplussed in consequence. He had not reached a conception of any revolutionary role open to the proletariat. But, if the bourgeoisie is, after all, made up of nothing but Bentley Drummles, Compaysons, Pumblechooks and their like, even another September 1792, and another Reign of the Guillotine, would be preferable to the continuance of their rule in perpetuity. No inference but this is possible from a novel which preaches so clearly the folly and worse of a refusal to face the ugly actualities of life.

And as though to prove that just this conclusion and none other is the one Dickens is resolved we shall reach, his next novel [*Our Mutual Friend*] takes as its theme just these ugly actualities, and has as its chief "villain" the egregious Podsnap, who "abolishes" with a wave of the hand everything which doesn't fit in with his smug, self-satisfied optimism.

The development of Pip's character bears no other interpretation.

Like *David Copperfield* the story is told in the first person, and the earlier chapters recount Pip's childhood experiences. It was a bold thing in Dickens to thus challenge a comparison with his own masterpiece; but, although many find Pip a much less admirable and likeable character than David, the later work stands the test of comparison well.

Nothing could be finer than the child-psychology of the earlier chapters of *Great Expectations*—nothing in Dickens even, betters the delineation of Pip, his irascible and spiteful sister, Mrs. Gargery, and her splendidly simple and good-hearted husband, Joe. And the highwater mark of a masterly performance—whose lowest level exceeds the best of any other English writer in this vein—is the description of Pip's mental agonies during the Christmas dinner, racked by frightful apprehensions of the inevitable discovery of the depredations he had worked upon the larder for the relief of the hunted convict starving in the fog on the marshes outside.

Another masterly passage is Pip's lapse into romantic lying when called upon to give an account of what had happened on his first summons to visit Miss Havisham. The actual reality was so weirdly uncanny to a sensitive child that Pip simply could not bring himself to disclose the truth. Hence, child-like, he grabs at every suggestion from the stupidly greedy and unimaginative Uncle Pumblechook, and makes it an ingredient in a marvellous romance. Dickens' profundity of grasp of child-psychology was never better shown; nor, for that matter, his grasp of adult-psychology, since his audience, led by Pumblechook, swallows the fiction much more readily than they would have accepted the pathetically-morbid truth. Joe Gargery—to whom in private, Pip at once admits he has been lying—is quite upset; and not so much at Pip's lying as at having to part with a genuine gorgeous real-life romance.

No less masterly is Dickens' delineation of Pip's turning—in his days of prosperous expectation—into an appalling little snob: his shameful turning-away from, and growing ashamed of, Joe Gargery and Biddy, the devoted friends of his pre-prosperity years. In fact, these scenes are too well done for the novel to be popular with readers who "take" novels as a "dope." They are so true, and so shrewd, that they strike home to the streak of snobbery in every one of us; and so give, not pleasure, but acute pain.

It is not possible to read the pathetically-painful story of Pip's cruel awakening in the midst of his snobbery without realizing that here is the pith and marrow of the author's purpose—that Pip . . . stands for Everyman. (pp. 194-200)

*T. A. Jackson, in his* Charles Dickens: The Progress of a Radical, *International Publishers, 1938, 303 p.*

## HUMPHRY HOUSE    (essay date 1942)

[*A respected English scholar, House is best remembered for his seminal work of Dickens criticism* The Dickens World *(1941). In the following excerpt from the second edition of that work, first published in 1942, House examines class issues in Dickens's novels, contending that* Great Expectations *is not a denunciation of social stratification but rather a study of both the good and bad effects of money on the individual.*]

A great deal has been written and said about Dickens as a writer for 'the people'. Yet his chief public was among the middle and lower-middle classes, rather than among the proletarian mass. His mood and idiom were those of the class from which he came, and his morality throve upon class distinctions even when it claimed to supersede them. He belonged to the generation which first used the phrase 'the great unwashed' and provided a Chadwick to scrub the people clean. (p. 152)

Many misunderstandings have been caused by the fact that Dickens himself so often and in so many voices proclaimed the gospel that class distinctions do not matter so much as common humanity, nor rank so much as virtue. . . . In one speech (1844) he quoted 'the words of a great living poet, who is one of us, and who uses his great gifts, as he holds them in trust, for the general welfare—

Howe'er it be, it seems to me,
'Tis only noble to be good.
True hearts are more than coronets,
And simple faith than Norman blood.

But that he *could* make such quotations, as he did, to audiences of working men, without the slightest trace of self-consciousness or condescension, only shows the confidence he had in his own class position. In the same speech in which he made the Tennyson quotation he also said: 'Differences of wealth, of rank, of intellect, we know there must be, and we respect them.' Sentiments like that of Tennyson, so frequent in Victorian literature, have their origin more in the assertion by the bourgeois of his essential similarity to the aristocrat than in any levelling denial of all differences everywhere. The English aristocracy, for centuries recruited from the middle classes, was forced into still closer cultural and social contact with them in the generation after 1832: only then began those interminable controversies about what a gentleman is, and the countless jokes about snobs. Compared with Thackeray and most of the *Punch* circle, for instance, Dickens steered through these dangers handsomely.

The snob problem was not acute before the 'forties. In Dickens's earlier books the strata of class are different from those of the later. . . . Mr. Pickwick thought of himself as a gentleman, but he slides quite easily up and down a considerable distance on the social scale: he would gladly have met the Cheerybles, who did not think of themselves as gentlemen, on equal terms, without needing to exploit his benevolence. The important thing is that people like Pickwick, Mr. Garland, and the Cheerybles in the positively good camp, others like Nupkins, Slammer, and Benjamin Allen among the neutrals, though not without class-consciousness, are quite without class pedantry. . . . (pp. 153-54)

The general vagueness about class distinctions in these books has sometimes been attributed to a supposed deficiency in young Dickens's knowledge of the world; but Dickens's 18 was most men's 25, and in his work in Doctors' Commons and Parliament and in miscellaneous reporting all over the country he must have had unusually good opportunities of observing all the details of social difference; and *David Copperfield* is reason enough for supposing that he did observe them. But why were they not used till 1849-50? The answer seems to be that the social atmosphere of the 'forties led him to revise his pattern of interpretation; and that as the shifting and mingling of classes became more *apparent* in the habits of London society he was better able to understand the implications of what he had observed in earlier years. In his own work this shifting is first plain in *Dombey and Son.*

Dombey himself is the first full-length Dickens business-man to be solemnly self-conscious about his 'station and its duties', and a good deal of his pride is class-pride. 'I beg,' he says to Edith, 'that Mrs. Granger's very different experiences may now come to the instruction of Mrs. Dombey.' He plays his wealth against Granger's family and speaks of Edith's 'worldly advancement' in her second marriage. He differs from business-men like Pickwick, Brownlow, the Cheerybles, and the Chuzzlewits not only in living far more expensively, but in the importance he attaches to doing so. . . . Dickens originally set himself in Dombey a problem in personal psychology: he did not make it very interesting; but in proportion as he failed to make convincing the workings of Dombey's mind he gave more attention to the money-class context in which they were expressed. The effectiveness of his later portraits of middle-class snobs—Merdles, Podsnaps, Veneerings, and the rest—is largely achieved by the deliberate identification of the whole personality with the context.

Dickens was attempting to define within the middle classes some such boundary as he had already accepted in the lower between the respectable and the low. In the last resort he shared Magwitch's belief that money and education can make a 'gentleman', that birth and tradition count for little or nothing in the formation of style. The final wonder of *Great Expectations* is that in spite of all Pip's neglect of Joe and coldness towards Biddy and all the remorse and self-recrimination that they caused him, he is made to appear at the end of it all a really better person than he was at the beginning. It is a remarkable achievement to have kept the reader's sympathy throughout a snob's progress. The book is the clearest artistic triumph of the Victorian bourgeoisie on its own special ground. The expectations lose their greatness, and Pip is saved from the grosser dangers of wealth; but by the end he has gained a wider and deeper knowledge of life, he is less rough, better spoken, better read, better mannered; he has friends as various as Herbert Pocket, Jaggers, and

Wemmick; he has earned in his business abroad enough to pay his debts, he has become third partner in a firm that 'had a good name, and worked for its profits, and did very well'. Who is to say that these are not advantages? Certainly not Dickens. But he shirks the implications of the reconciliation with Joe and Biddy: there is one emotional scene with friendliness all round, which shows that in spite of his new accent and new manners Pip is the same decent little fellow after all: but what if he had had no Herbert to fall back on, and had been forced to build his fortunes again from scratch in the old village with Gargerys and Wopsles? Dickens does not face this: he takes Pip's new class position as established, and whisks him off to the East, where gentlemen grow like mushrooms. Yet we do not feel that this is artistically wrong, as the final marriage to Estella is wrong: for the book is the sincere, uncritical expression of a time when the whole class-drift was upwards and there was no reason to suppose that it would ever stop being so. The social ideals of Pip and Magwitch differ only in taste. Though Pip has shuddered at the convict for being coarse and low, he consoles him on his death-bed with the very thought that first fired and then kept alive his own love for Estella: 'You had a child. . . . She is a lady and very beautiful.'

Here is the story allegorized by Mr. Jackson, writing as a Marxist [see excerpt dated 1938]:

> Self-satisfied, mid-Victorian, British society buoyed itself up with as great 'expectations' of future wealth and glory as did poor, deluded Pip. If it had but known, its means of ostentation came from a source (the labour of the depressed and exploited masses) to which it would have been as shocked to acknowledge indebtedness as Pip was to find he owed all his acquired gentility to the patronage of a transported felon. Magwitch differed little from the uncouth monster which respectable society envisaged to itself as the typical 'labouring man'. And in literal truth, good, respectable society owed as much to these working men, and was as little aware of it, as was Pip of the source of his advantages. And respectable society is as little grateful as Pip, whenever the truth is revealed.

This would be very plausible if only the rest of the class distinctions in the novel were what Mr. Jackson makes them out to be:

> Such class-antagonism as there is in *Great Expectations* is not that between aristocrats (as such) and common people, but that between, on the one side, the 'gentlemen' (who are for one reason or another either crazily vengeful or callously cold-hearted and corrupt) and with them their sycophants and attendant slum-hooligans and on the other, the honest, working section of the population.

Applied in detail this means Bentley Drummle, Compeyson, and Pumblechook on one side, with Joe, Biddy, Matthew and Herbert Pocket, Jaggers, and Wemmick all lumped together on the other. This is virtually to say that in the end class distinctions are identical with moral distinctions, without even being particularly nice about morals; it is to ignore all the facts of class difference that Dickens was so subtly analysing. It is in things like Estella's early treatment of Pip, Pip's first weeks with Herbert, Jaggers's treatment of Estella's mother, and the behaviour of Trabb's boy, that these real differences are to be found.

Chesterton professed to find in Trabb's boy the last word

upon the triumphant revolutionary sarcasm of the English democracy [see excerpt dated 1907]; you might almost as well find the ultimate English democrat in old Orlick, the soured 'hand' turning to crime because of his inferior status, whom Mr. Jackson just leaves as a 'blackguard'—a man who in another novel might well have been the leader of a no-Popery mob or of physical-force Chartists. The assault of Trabb's boy, which brings Pip's class-consciousness to a head, is more personal than political: Dickens doesn't mean that good clothes are worse than bad or that they are intrinsically funny and that the class that wears them is doomed to die of jeers. . . . As things were he was a good pin to prick Pip's conceit; but if he himself had come into a fortune, he would have been just as nasty about it as Pip in his own way; and his way might have been worse.

*Great Expectations* is the perfect expression of a phase of English society: it is a statement, to be taken as it stands, of what money can do, good and bad; of how it can change and make distinctions of class; how it can pervert virtue, sweeten manners, open up new fields of enjoyment and suspicion. The mood of the book belongs not to the imaginary date of its plot, but to the time in which it was written; for the unquestioned assumptions that Pip can be transformed by money and the minor graces it can buy, and that the loss of one fortune can be repaired on the strength of incidental gains in voice and friends, were only possible in a country secure in its internal economy, with expanding markets abroad: this

*An 1861 caricature of Dickens that originally appeared with the caption, "From whom we have great expectations."*

could hardly be said of England in the 'twenties and 'thirties. (pp. 154-59)

*Humphry House, in his* The Dickens World, *second edition, Oxford University Press, London, 1942, 232 p.*

## EDGAR JOHNSON (essay date 1952)

[*Johnson is a major Dickens scholar whose* Charles Dickens: His Tragedy and Triumph *is considered the definitive biography of the novelist. In the following excerpt from that work, Johnson combines a biographical interpretation of* Great Expectations *with an examination of its dominant social themes.*]

With *Great Expectations* Dickens returned to familiar scenes. The village where Joe Gargery had his forge is the tiny village of Cooling, a few miles north of Gad's Hill, and the small lozenge-shaped gravestones in a row beside the two parent stones, which Pip describes as those of his father and mother and little brothers, are to be found in Cooling Churchyard. The gray neighboring marshes across which Magwitch limps, shivering, with his fettered limbs, are those of the surrounding countryside sinking muddily to the winding river. The black prison hulk lying out in the stream "like a wicked Noah's ark" is one of the convict ships Dickens had known in the Chatham of his boyhood. The near-by country town is Rochester, the Blue Boar is the Bull, Uncle Pumblechook's house an ancient half-timbered structure in the High Street, and Satis House, where Miss Havisham lives, is really Restoration House, the Elizabethan mansion south of Rochester Cathedral, across the Vines.

The impulse that sent Dickens back to this world of his childhood, now the landscape of his daily walks, was more, however, than the desire to have an appropriate setting for his story. It rose from some deeper need to explore once again, more profoundly even than he had been able to do in *David Copperfield,* his formative years and the bent they had given him, to weigh the nature of his response to them and discover what it revealed. In the intervening years he had written *Bleak House, Hard Times,* and *Little Dorrit;* there were crucial ways in which he had developed tremendously beyond the man he had been. *Great Expectations* shows no trace of *David Copperfield* 's self-pity. It pierces fathoms down in self-understanding. It is relentless in self-judgment.

Though the story is told as an autobiographical narrative, Pip, its hero, is much less literally a portrayal of Dickens than David Copperfield was, and the outward events of his life have no resemblance to those in the career of his creator. But, with an emblematic significance, they are so shaped as to enable Dickens to plumb those youthful humiliations and griefs whose wounds even in maturity he buried from all the world. Of his grandfather, the butler at Crewe, he breathed never a syllable, and his grandmother, the housekeeper, peeps out only as Mrs. Rouncewell, down at Chesney Wold in *Bleak House.* Of the debtors' prison and the blacking warehouse he could not bear to tell his own children. Subtly disguised, but now seen in a new light, these shames recur as central themes in *Great Expectations.* (pp. 982-83)

[The] entire drift of the story reveals how clearly Dickens had at last "come to see that making his living by sticking labels on blacking bottles and rubbing shoulders with boys who were not gentlemen, was as little shameful as being the genteel apprentice in the office of Mr. Spenlow, or the shorthand

writer recording the unending twaddle of the House of Commons and its overflow of electioneering bunk on the hustings of all the Eatanswills in the country." (p. 988)

*Great Expectations* is Dickens's penance for his subservience to false values. The blacksmith and "the taint of prison and crime" which have so mortified Pip, and of which he comes to feel a remorseful humiliation at ever having been ashamed, are both more humbling to genteel thought than the blacking warehouse and the debtors' prison. "The reappearance of Mr. Dickens in the character of a blacksmith's boy," as Shaw remarks, "may be regarded as an apology to Mealy Potatoes" [see excerpt dated 1937].

There is a layer of criticism, however, in *Great Expectations* still deeper than this personal triumph over false social values. It pierces to the very core of the leisure-class ideal that lurks in the heart of a pecuniary society. This is symbolized in Pip's dream of becoming a gentleman living in decorative grandeur on money he has done nothing to earn, supported entirely by the labors of others. It was the dream of nineteenth-century society, willing to base its hopes of comfort and ostentation on the toil of the laboring classes. Pip's "great expectations" were the great expectations of Victorian society, visions of a parasitic opulence of future wealth and glory, a materialistic paradise of walnut, plush, gilt mirrors, and heavy dinners. The aim of the fashionable world was an external and luxurious ease, the goal of the middle-class businessman to retire to a surburban villa on a fortune.

Although Dickens never expected to be exempt from work himself, and worked hard all his life, earlier in his career he had accepted this ideal. There is no suggestion that Mr. Winkle, Mr. Tupman, or Mr. Snodgrass need ever think of doing anything for a living. Mr. Brownlow and Mr. Grimwig have no occupations. At the close of *Nicholas Nickleby,* Nicholas retires to a country villa and lives upon his share from the profits of the Cheeryble business which others carry on. Little Nell's grandfather sounds the first warning note against the false dream of gaining a luxury one has not earned. Martin Chuzzlewit, after a few abortive efforts to make a living, returns to living on his grandfather. Mr. Dombey leaves to Mr. Carker and a host of subordinates almost all the management of the enterprise from which he derives his wealth. Even the benevolent Mr. Jarndyee seems to be merely a man of property, although Richard Carstone now strikes another warning note against depending upon "expectations" instead of making oneself of use to the world. Stephen Blackpool in *Hard Times,* and Arthur Clennam in *Little Dorrit,* represent the emergence of a new kind of hero in Dickens's novels: the earnest, sober, industrious worker who contributes his share to the efforts of the world.

But Pip has no occupation and no ideal save that of an empty good form. He and the "Finches of the Grove," the club of young men of leisure to which he belongs, do nothing but spend money, play cards, drink toasts, buy elaborate wardrobes, drive horses, and go to the theater. They have no culture, no interest in the arts, in music, in the world of reflective thought. Pip "reads" with his tutor and has books on his shelves, but we never learn what he reads or perceive that it has had any effect on him. He has no philosophy, only a set of conventions. The virtues that ultimately save him are mainly those that he unconsciously absorbed from Joe in his childhood. His return to a life of modest usefulness is a repudiation of the ideal of living by the sweat of someone else's brow. And Dickens's analysis of the frivolity, falseness, emptiness, loss of honor, loss of manhood, and sense of futility that the acceptance of that ideal imposed upon Pip is a measure of the rottenness and corruption he now found in a society dominated by it. The system of that society and its grandiose material dreams, he realizes, involve a cheapening, a distortion, a denial of human values.

From another angle, in the portrayal of the lawyer Jaggers, *Great Expectations* conveys the same judgment. It is impossible not to see in him, T. A. Jackson points out, "Dickens' deepening sense that success in business in the bourgeois world can be won only at the expense of everything nobly generous, elevating, sympathetic, and humane" [see excerpt dated 1938]. Mr. Jaggers specializes in representing accused criminals, whose unsavory cases he handles with the most unscrupulous and triumphant skill. But with the departure of every felonious visitor he goes to a closet and cleans his hands with scented soap, as if he were washing off the client. On one occasion, Pip remarks, "he seemed to have been engaged on a case of a darker complexion than usual, for we found him with his head butted into this closet, not only washing his hands, but laving his face and gargling his throat. And even when he had done all that, and had gone all round the jacktowel, he took out his penknife and scraped the case out of his nails before he put his coat on." Though Mr. Jaggers is a highly successful and respected professional man, his own sense of the necessities his life imposes on him is one of degradation and pollution. Could there be a clearer symbolic suggestion that much of the business of such a society is dirty business?

Its consequence is almost to force upon a man of any sensitivity a dual personality, a division and antagonism between the selfish-acquisitive and all that is warmly human. Mr. Jaggers's clerk Wemmick dwells in the kindest domestic affection at Walworth with his deaf and ancient father, "the aged parent," in a little wooden villa with a narrow moat, a plank drawbridge, a miniature cannon which he fires at night, and a small Gothic entrance door. But all this feeling and imagination he keeps for his home; in the office his mouth is a dry slit like a mailbox, he is dead against Pip's desire to serve his friend Herbert, and harps on the dominant necessity of acquiring "portable property." Only at home will he tell Pip, "This is devilish good of of you." "Walworth is one place," he says, "and this office is another."

Both for Wemmick and for Mr. Jaggers, then, their office in Little Britain is a kind of prison in which they lock up their better selves and subdue them to the world of venality. Thus the symbolism of *Great Expectations* develops that of *Little Dorrit* and of *A Tale of Two Cities.* The Marshalsea and Mrs. Clennam in the dark house of greed and Mr. Merdle in the glittering mansion of speculation and the world of "society" are all immured in the same vast outer dungeon of imprisoning ideas. Darnay and Carton are the jailed victims of revenge for past deeds of exploitation and cruelty, and Dr. Manette is driven mad in the Bastille, broken and goaded to a destroying curse by that past injustice. Now, in this last story of the three, Jaggers, Wemmick, Magwitch, Pip, are under like shadows of prison walls; and Miss Havisham, her heart broken by a rapacious adventurer, creates in Estella a living curse, and, surrounded by greedy relatives, wanders self-incarcerated in her dark, decaying house. And intertwined like an iron chain with all of these is Pip's despairing and disillusioned obsession with Estella, the darkest emotional imprisonment of them all.

It is inevitable that we should associate Pip's helpless enslavement to Estella with Dickens's desperate passion for Ellen Lawless Ternan. The very name "Estella" seems a kind of lawless anagram upon some of the syllables and initials of Ellen's name. The tone of Dickens's unhappy letters to Collins and Forster during all the time between the last night of *The Frozen Deep* and the time of the separation discloses an entirely new intensity of personal misery far exceeding the restlessness of years before. His insistence that since that last night he had "never known a moment's peace or content" centers his distress unmistakably not on the "domestic unhappiness" alone but on a person: "never was a man so seized and rended by one Spirit." His allusion in a letter to Mrs. Watson to "the princess I adore—you have no idea how intensely I love her!" points in the same direction, like the desire he there expresses to go "climbing after her, sword in hand," and either win her "or be killed." The words are a kind of desperate playing with his frustration, a half unveiling disguised in ambiguity. And later still there is the black mingling of fear and bitterness and rage in his outburst about the policeman endeavoring to enact the role of a go-between in Berners Street.

With these things must be seen the unprecedently somber hues in which Dickens depicts Pip's feeling for Estella. Never before had he portrayed a man's love for a woman with such emotional depth or revealed its desperation of compulsive suffering. Dolly Varden's capriciousness is a childish coquetry beside Estella's cold obduracy. The unhappiness that breathes in Dickens's youthful letters to Maria Beadnell is the suffering of a boy, whereas Pip's is the stark misery of a man. David Copperfield's heartache for Dora Spenlow is an iridescent dream-grief to this agonized nightmare-reality. Only with Philip Carey's dreadful servitude to the pallid indifference of the sluttish Mildred, in *Of Human Bondage,* or, in Proust's masterpiece, with Swann's craving for Odette, is there anything like Pip's subjection to Estella's queenly and torturing disregard. Pip's love is without tenderness, without illusion; it reveals no desire to confer happiness upon the beloved; it is all self-absorbed need. Where in all his past career as a novelist had Dickens painted such passions and in what abyss of personal agony had he learned them?

In love, too, then, Pip's "great expectations," like Dickens's own, have been disappointed and deceived, and ideally the story should have ended on that loss, as Dickens originally planned. Pip's desire for Estella is as selfish as his desire to be a gentleman, not at all the desire to give, only the desire to receive. It is the culminating symbol and the crowning indictment of a society dedicated to selfish ends. It is a bitter revelation of the emptiness of its values and of the distortions they inflict upon all generous feeling, even upon the need to love and to be loved. Pip is not all selfish; he is capable both of generosity and of love. Indeed, at the end he has learned from his experience, learned to work, learned to love, learned to think for others.

Both as art and as psychology it was poor counsel that Lytton gave in urging that the shaping of a lifetime in Estella be miraculously undone. Save for this, though, *Great Expectations* is the most perfectly constructed and perfectly written of all Dickens's works. It should close with that misty moonlight scene in Miss Havisham's ruined garden, but, as Shaw suggests, with Pip and Estella then bidding each other a chastened farewell and Pip saying, "Since that parting I have been able to think of her without the old unhappiness; but I have never tried to see her again, and I know I never shall."

In spite of its theme of disillusion *Great Expectations* is not in its pervading atmosphere a melancholy book. Not merely does it move to an ending of serene and twilight peace, but there are many scenes of high-spirited enjoyment and of the comic gusto Dickens had always been able to command even in the midst of his deepest despair. There is the child Pip's flight into a series of fantastic whoppers when Uncle Pumblechook is badgering him to tell what happened at his first visit to Miss Havisham's and he invents a picture of Miss Havisham sitting in a black velvet coach having cake and wine on gold plates while they feed veal cutlets from a silver basket to four large dogs, wave flags, and shout hurrahs. There is Mr. Wopsle's famous performance of *Hamlet,* with the Danish nobility represented by "a noble boy in the wash-leather boots of a gigantic ancestor, a venerable Peer with a dirty face, who seemed to have risen from the people late in life, and the Danish chivalry with a comb in its hair and a pair of white silk legs presenting on the whole a feminine appearance," and the church in the graveyard scene resembling a "small ecclesiastical wash-house." There is Trabb's boy imitating Pip's progress down the High Street by pulling up his shirt collar, twining his side hair, sticking an arm akimbo, smirking extravagantly, and drawling, "Don't know yah, don't know yah, 'pon my soul don't know yah!" There is Joe's description of how the robbers looted Pumblechook's shop: "and they drinked his wine, and they partook of his wittles, and they slapped his face, and they pulled his nose, and they tied him up to his bedpust, and they giv' him a dozen, and they stuffed his mouth full of flowering annuals to perwent his crying out."

But these joyous moments do not undermine the predominant seriousness of *Great Expectations* and its theme. As Pip and Estella, with linked hands, leave that misty and forlorn garden of their childhood they are reminiscent of the parents of humanity exiled, but not utterly without hope, from another Garden:

> The world was all before them, where to choose
> Their place of rest, and Providence their guide.
> They hand in hand, with wandering steps and slow,
> Through Eden took their solitary way.
>
> [John Milton, *Paradise Lost* ]
>
> (pp. 988-94)

*Edgar Johnson, in his* Charles Dickens: His Tragedy and Triumph, *2 Vols., Simon and Schuster, 1952, 1158 p.*

**DOROTHY VAN GHENT** (essay date 1953)

[*Van Ghent examines the images and techniques that Dickens uses in* Great Expectations *to develop the themes of personal and social guilt and of redemption through love.*]

"The distinguishing quality of Dickens's people," says V. S. Pritchett,

> is that they are solitaries. They are people caught living in a world of their own. They soliloquize in it. They do not talk to one another; they talk to themselves. The pressure of society has created fits of twitching in mind and speech, and fantasies in the soul . . . The solitariness of people is paralleled by the solitariness of things. Fog operates as a sepa-

rate presence, houses quietly rot or boisterously prosper on their own . . . Cloisterham believes itself more important than the world at large, the Law sports like some stale and dilapidated circus across human lives. Philanthropy attacks people like a humor or an observable germ. The people and the things of Dickens are all out of touch and out of hearing of each other, each conducting its own inner monologue, grandiloquent or dismaying. By this dissociation Dickens brings to us something of the fright of childhood. . . .

Some of the most wonderful scenes in *Great Expectations* are those in which people, presumably in the act of conversation, raptly soliloquize; and Dickens' technique, in these cases, is usually to give the soliloquizer a fantastic private language as unadapted to mutual understanding as a species of pig Latin. Witness Mr. Jaggers' interview with Joe Gargery, in which the dignified lawyer attempts to compensate Joe financially for his part in Pip's upbringing, and Joe swings on him with unintelligible pugilistic jargon.

> "Which I meantersay . . . that if you come into my place bull-baiting and badgering me, come out! Which I meantersay as sech if you're a man, come on! Which I meantersay that what I say, I meantersay and stand or fall by!"

Or Miss Havisham's interview with Joe over the question of Pip's wages; for each question she asks him, Joe persists in addressing his reply to Pip rather than herself, and his replies have not the remotest relation to the questions. Sometimes, by sheer repetition of a phrase, the words a character uses will assume the frenzied rotary unintelligibility of an idiot's obsession, as does Mrs. Joe's "Be grateful to them which brought you up by hand," or Pumblechook's mincing "May I?—May I?" The minimal uses of language as an instrument of communication and intellectual development are symbolized by Pip's progress in the school kept by Mr. Wopsle's great-aunt, where the summit of his education consists in his copying a large Old-English "D," which he assumes to be the design for a belt buckle; and by Joe's pleasure in the art of reading, which enables him to find three "J's" and three "O's" and three "J-O, Joes" in a piece of script.

> "Give me [he says] a good book, or a good newspaper, and sit me down afore a good fire, and I ask no better. Lord! when you *do* come to a J and a O, and says you, 'Here, at last, is a J-O, Joe,' how interesting reading is!"

There is, perhaps, no purer expression of solipsism in literature. The cultivation of the peculiar Dickensian values of language reaches its apogee when the convict Magwitch, with a benefactor's proud delight, asks Pip to read to him from a book in a foreign language, of which he understands no syllable. (pp. 125-26)

Language as a means of communication is a provision for social and spiritual order. You cannot make "order" with an integer, one thing alone, for order is definitively a relationship among things. Absolute noncommunication is an unthinkable madness for it negates all relationship and therefore all order, and even an ordinary madman has to create a kind of order for himself by illusions of communication. Dickens' soliloquizing characters, for all their funniness (aloneness is inexorably funny, like the aloneness of the man who slips on a banana peel, seen from the point of view of togetherness), suggest a world of isolated integers, terrifyingly alone and un-related.

The book opens with a child's first conscious experience of his aloneness. Immediately an abrupt encounter occurs—Magwitch suddenly comes from behind a gravestone, seizes Pip by the heels, and suspends him upside down.

> "Hold your noise!" cried a terrible voice, as a man started up from among the graves at the side of the church porch. "Keep still, you little devil, or I'll cut your throat!"

Perhaps, if one could fix on two of the most personal aspects of Dickens' technique, one would speak of the strange languages he concocts for the solitariness of the soul, and the abruptness of his tempo. His human fragments suddenly shock against one another in collisions like those of Democritus' atoms or of the charged particles of modern physics. Soldiers, holding out handcuffs, burst into the blacksmith's house during Christmas dinner at the moment when Pip is clinging to a table leg in an agony of apprehension over his theft of the pork pie. A weird old woman clothed in decayed satin, jewels and spider webs, and with one shoe off, shoots out her finger at the bewildered child, with the command: "Play!" A pale young gentleman appears out of a wilderness of cucumber frames, and daintily kicking up his legs and slapping his hands together, dips his head and butts Pip in the stomach. These sudden confrontations between persons whose ways of life have no habitual or logical continuity with each other suggest the utmost incohesion in the stuff of experience.

Technique is vision. Dickens' technique is an index of a vision of life that sees human separatedness as the ordinary condition, where speech is speech *to* nobody and where human encounter is mere collision. But the vision goes much further. Our minds are so constituted that they insist on seeking in the use of language an exchange function, a delivery and a passing on of perceptions from soul to soul and generation to generation, binding them in some kind of order; and they insist on finding cause and effect, or *motivation,* in the displacements and encounters of persons or things. Without these primary patterns of perception we would not have what we call minds. And when these patterns are confused or abrogated by our experience, we are forced, in order to preserve some kind of psychic equilibrium, to seek them in extraordinary explanations—explanations again in terms of mutual exchange and cause and effect. Dickens saw his world patently all in pieces, and as a child's vision would offer some reasonable explanation of why such a world was that way—and, by the act of explanation, would make that world yield up a principle of order, however obscure or fantastic—so, with a child's literalism of imagination, he discovered organization among his fragments.

Dickens lived in a time and an environment in which a full-scale demolition of traditional values was going on, correlatively with the uprooting and dehumanization of men, women, and children by the millions—a process brought about by industrialization, colonial imperialism, and the exploitation of the human being as a "thing" or an engine or a part of an engine capable of being used for profit. This was the "century of progress" which ornamented its steam engines with iron arabesques of foliage as elaborate as the antimacassars and aspidistras and crystal or cut-glass chandeliers and bed-and-feather portieres of its drawing rooms, while the

human engines of its welfare groveled and bred in the fox-holes described by Marx in his *Capital.* (Hauntingly we see this discordance in the scene in *Great Expectations* where Miss Havisham, sitting in her satin and floral decay in the house called Satis, points her finger at the child and outrageously tells him to "play." For though the scene is a potent symbol of childish experience of adult obtuseness and sadism, it has also another dimension as a social symbol of those economically determined situations in which the human soul is used as a means for satisfactions not its own, under the gross and transparent lie that its activity is its happiness, its welfare and fun and "play"—a publicity instrument that is the favorite of manufacturers and insurance agencies, as well as of totalitarian strategists, with their common formula, "We're just a happy family.") The heir of the "century of progress" is the twentieth-century concentration camp, which makes no bones about people being "things."

Dickens' intuition alarmingly saw this process in motion, a process which abrogated the primary demands of human feeling and rationality, and he sought an extraordinary explanation for it. People were becoming things, and things (the things that money can buy or that are the means for making money or for exalting prestige in the abstract) were becoming more important than people. People were being de-animated, robbed of their souls, and things were usurping the prerogatives of animate creatures—governing the lives of their owners in the most literal sense. This picture, in which the qualities of things and people were reversed, was a picture of a daemonically motivated world, a world in which "dark" or occult forces or energies operate not only in people (as modern psychoanalytic psychology observes) but also in things: for if people turn themselves or are turned into things, metaphysical order can be established only if we think of things as turning themselves into people, acting under a "dark" drive similar to that which motivates the human aberration.

There is an old belief that it takes a demon to recognize a demon, and the saying illustrates the malicious sensibility with which things, in Dickens, have felt out and imitated, in their relationship with each other and with people, the secret of the human arrangement. A four-poster bed in an inn, where Pip goes to spend the night, is a despotic monster that straddles over the whole room,

> putting one of his arbitrary legs into the fireplace, and another into the doorway, and squeezing the wretched little washing-stand in quite a Divinely Righteous manner.

Houses, looking down through the skylight of Jaggers' office in London, twist themselves in order to spy on Pip like police agents who presuppose guilt. Even a meek little muffin has to be "confined with the utmost precaution under a strong iron cover," and a hat, set on a mantelpiece, demands constant attention and the greatest quickness of eye and hand to catch it neatly as it tumbles off, but its ingenuity is such that it finally manages to fall into the slop basin. The animation of inanimate objects suggests both the quaint gaiety of a forbidden life and an aggressiveness that has got out of control—an aggressiveness that they have borrowed from the human economy and an irresponsibility native to but glossed and disguised by that economy.

Dickens' fairly constant use of the pathetic fallacy (the projection of human impulses and feelings upon the nonhuman, as upon beds and houses and muffins and hats) might be considered as incidental stylistic embellishment if his description of people did not show a reciprocal metaphor: people are described by nonhuman attributes, or by such an exaggeration of or emphasis on one part of their appearance that they seem to be reduced wholly to that part, with an effect of having become "thinged" into one of their own bodily members or into an article of their clothing or into some inanimate object of which they have made a fetish. Dickens' devices for producing this transposition of attributes are various. To his friend and biographer, Forster, he said that he was always losing sight of a man in his diversion by the mechanical play of some part of the man's face, which "would acquire a sudden ludicrous life of its own." Many of what we shall call the "signatures" of Dickens' people—that special exaggerated feature or gesture or mannerism which comes to stand for the whole person—are such dissociated parts of the body, like Jaggers' huge forefinger which he bites and then plunges menacingly at the accused, or Wemmick's post-office mouth, or the clockwork apparatus in Magwitch's throat that clicks as if it were going to strike. The device is not used arbitrarily or capriciously. In this book, whose subject is the etiology of guilt and of atonement, Jaggers is the representative not only of civil law but of universal Law, which is profoundly mysterious in a world of dissociated and apparently lawless fragments; and his huge forefinger, into which he is virtually transformed and which seems to act like an "it" in its own right rather than like a member of a man, is the Law's mystery in all its fearful impersonality. Wemmick's mouth is not a post-office when he is at home in his castle but only when he is at work in Jaggers' London office, where a mechanical appearance of smiling is required of him. And as Wemmick's job has mechanized him into a grinning slot, so oppression and fear have given the convict Magwitch a clockwork apparatus for vocal chords.

Or this general principle of reciprocal changes, by which things have become as it were daemonically animated and people have been reduced to thing-like characteristics—as if, by a law of conservation of energy, the humanity of which people have become incapable had leaked out into the external environment—may work symbolically in the association of some object with a person so that the object assumes his essence and his "meaning." Mrs. Joe wears a large apron, "having a square impregnable bib in front, that was stuck full of pins and needles"—she has no reason to wear it, and she never takes it off a day in her life. Jaggers flourishes a large white handkerchief—a napkin that is the mysterious complement of his blood-smeared engagements. Estella—who is the star and jewel of Pip's great expectations—wears jewels in her hair and on her breast; "I and the jewels," she says, as if they were interchangeable. This device of association is a familiar one in fiction; what distinguishes Dickens' use of it is that the associated object acts not merely to *illustrate* a person's qualities symbolically—as novelists usually use it—but that it has a necessary metaphysical function in Dickens' universe: in this universe objects actually usurp human essences; beginning as fetishes, they tend to—and sometimes quite literally do—devour and take over the powers of the fetish-worshiper.

The process of conversion of spirit into matter that operates in the Dickens world is shown working out with savage simplicity in the case of Miss Havisham. Miss Havisham has been guilty of aggression against life in using the two children, Pip and Estella, as inanimate instruments of revenge for her broken heart—using them, that is, as if they were not

human but things—and she is being changed retributively into a fungus. The decayed cake on the banquet table acts, as it were, by homeopathic magic—like a burning effigy or a doll stuck with pins; its decay parallels the necrosis in the human agent. "When the ruin is complete," Miss Havisham says, pointing to the cake but referring to herself, she will be laid out on the same table and her relatives will be invited to "feast on" her corpse. But this is not the only conversion. The "little quickened hearts" of the mice behind the panels have been quickened by what was Miss Havisham, carried off crumb by crumb.

The principle of reciprocal changes, between the human and the nonhuman, bears on the characteristic lack of complex "inner life" on the part of Dickens' people—their lack of a personally complex psychology. It is inconceivable that the fungoid Miss Havisham should have a complex inner life, in the moral sense. But in the *art* of Dickens (distinguishing that moral dialectic that arises not solely from the "characters" in a novel but from all the elements in the aesthetic structure) there is a great deal of "inner life," transposed to other forms than that of human character: partially transposed in this scene, for instance, to the symbolic activity of the speckle-legged spiders with blotchy bodies and to the gropings and pausings of the black beetles on Miss Havisham's hearth. Without benefit of Freud or Jung, Dickens saw the human soul reduced literally to the images occupying its "inner life."

Through the changes that have come about in the human, as humanity has leaked out of it, the atoms of the physical universe have become subtly impregnated with daemonic aptitude. Pip, standing waiting for Estella in the neighborhood of Newgate, and beginning dimly to be aware of his implication in the guilt for which that establishment stands—for his "great expectations" have already begun to make him a collaborator in the generic crime of using people as means to personal ends—has the sensation of a deadly dust clinging to him, rubbed off on him from the environs, and he tries to beat it out of his clothes. Smithfield, that "shameful place," "all asmear with filth and fat and blood and foam," seems to "stick to him" when he enters it on his way to the prison. The nettles and brambles of the graveyard where Magwitch first appears "stretch up cautiously" out of the graves in an effort to get a twist on the branded man's ankles and pull him in. The river has a malignant potentiality that impregnates everything upon it—discolored copper, rotten wood, honeycombed stone, green dank deposit. The river is perhaps the most constant and effective symbol in Dickens, because it establishes itself so readily to the imagination as a daemonic element, drowning people as if by intent, disgorging unforeseen evidence, chemically or physically changing all it touches, and because not only does it act as an occult "force" in itself but it is the common passage and actual flowing element that unites individuals and classes, public persons and private persons, deeds and the results of deeds, however fragmentized and separated. Upon the river, one cannot escape its action; it may throw the murderer and his victim in an embrace. At the end of *Great Expectations,* it swallows Compeyson, while, with its own obscure daemonic motivation, though it fatally injures Magwitch, it leaves him to fulfill the more subtle spiritual destiny upon which he has begun to enter. The river scene in this section, closely and apprehensively observed, is one of the most memorable in Dickens.

It is necessary to view Dickens' "coincidences" under the aspect of this wholesale change in the aptitudes of external nature. Coincidence is the violent connection of the unconnected. Life is full of violent connections of this sort, but one of the most rigorous conventions of fictional and dramatic art is that events should make a logically sequential pattern; for art is the discovery of order. Critics have frequently deplored Dickens' use of coincidences in his plots. But in a universe that is nervous throughout, a universe in which nervous ganglia stretch through both people and their external environment, so that a change in the human can infect the currents of the air and the sea, events and confrontations that seem to abrogate the laws of physical mechanics can logically be brought about. In this sense, the apparent coincidences in Dickens actually obey a causal order—not of physical mechanics but of moral dynamics.

> What connection can there be [Dickens asks in another novel] between many people in the innumerable histories of this world, who, from opposite sides of great gulfs, have, nevertheless, been very curiously brought together!

What brings the convict Magwitch to the child Pip, in the graveyard, is more than the convict's hunger; Pip (or let us say simply "the child," for Pip is an Everyman) carries the convict inside him, as the negative potential of his "great expectations"—Magwitch is the concretion of his potential guilt. What brings Magwitch across the "great gulfs" of the Atlantic to Pip again, at the moment of revelation in the story, is their profoundly implicit compact of guilt, as binding as the convict's leg iron which is its recurrent symbol. The multiplying likenesses in the street as Magwitch draws nearer, coming over the sea, the mysterious warnings of his approach on the night of his reappearance, are moral projections as "real" as the storm outside the windows and as the crouched form of the vicious Orlick on the dark stairs. The conception of what brings people together "coincidentally" in their seemingly uncaused encounters and collisions—the total change in the texture of experience that follows upon any act, public or private, external or in thought, the concreteness of the effect of the act not only upon the conceiving heart but upon the atoms of physical matter, so that blind nature collaborates daemonically in the drama of reprisal—is deep and valid in this book.

In a finely lucid atmosphere of fairy tale, Dickens uses a kind of montage in *Great Expectations,* a superimposing of one image upon another with an immediate effect of hallucination, that is but one more way of representing his vision of a purely nervous and moral organization of reality. An instance is the scene in which Estella walks the casks in the old brewery. Estella's walking the casks is an enchanting ritual dance of childhood (like walking fence rails or railroad ties), but inexplicably present in the tableau is the suicidal figure of Miss Havisham hanging by her neck from a brewery beam. Accompanying each appearance of Estella—the star and the jewel of Pip's expectations—is a similarly disturbing ghost, an image of an unformed dread. When Pip thinks of her, though he is sitting in a warm room with a friend, he shudders as if in a wind from over the marshes. Her slender knitting fingers are suddenly horribly displaced by the marred wrists of a murderess. The technique of montage is that of dreams, which know with awful precision the affinities between the guilt of our desires and the commonplaces of our immediate perceptions.

This device, of doubling one image over another, is paralleled in the handling of character. In the sense that one implies the other, the glittering frosty girl Estella, and the decayed and false old woman, Miss Havisham, are not two characters but a single one, or a single essence with dual aspects, as if composed by montage—a spiritual continuum, so to speak. For inevitably wrought into the fascinating jewel-likeness of Pip's great expectations, as represented by Estella, is the falsehood and degeneracy represented by Miss Havisham, the soilure on the unpurchased good. The boy Pip and the criminal Magwitch form another such continuum. Magwitch, from a metaphysical point of view, is not outside Pip but inside him, and his apparition is that of Pip's own unwrought deeds: Pip, having adopted "great expectations," will live by making people into Magwitches, into means for his ends. The relationship between Joe Gargery, saintly simpleton of the folk, and Orlick, dark beast of the Teutonic marshes (who comes "from the ooze"), has a somewhat different dynamics, though they too form a spiritual continuum. Joe and Orlick are related not as two aspects of a single moral identity, but as the opposed extremes of spiritual possibility—the one unqualified love, the other unqualified hate—and they form a frame within which the actions of the others have their ultimate meaning. A commonplace of criticism is that, as Edmund Wilson puts it, Dickens was usually unable to "get the good and bad together in one character." The criticism might be valid if Dickens' were a naturalistic world, but it is not very relevant to Dickens' daemonically organized world. In a naturalistic world, obeying mechanical laws, each character is organically discrete from every other, and presumably each contains a representative mixture of "the good and bad." But in Dickens' thoroughly nervous world, that does not know the laws of mechanics but knows only spiritual law, one simple or "flat" character can be superimposed upon another so that together they form the representative human complexity of good-in-evil and evil-in-good.

Two kinds of crime form Dickens' two chief themes, the crime of parent against child, and the calculated social crime. They are formally analogous, their form being the treatment of persons as things; but they are also inherent in each other, whether the private will of the parent is to be considered as depraved by the operation of a public institution, or the social institution is to be considered as a bold concert of the depravities of individual "fathers." In *Great Expectations* the private crime against the child is Mrs. Joe's and Pumblechook's and Wopsle's, all "foster parents" either by necessity or self-conceit; while the social crime is the public treatment of Magwitch. That the two kinds of crime are inherent in each other we are made aware of as we are led to identify Magwitch's childhood with Pip's; the brutality exercised toward both children was the same brutality, though the "parents" in the one case were private persons, and in the other, society itself. Complicating the meaning of "the crime" still further, Magwitch also has taken upon himself the role of foster parent to Pip, and whether, as parent, he acts in charity or impiousness, or both, is a major ambiguity which the drama sets out to resolve.

"The crime," in Dickens, is evidently a permutation of multiple motivations and acts, both public and private, but always with the same tendency to convert people into things, and always implying either symbolically or directly a child-parent situation. The child-parent situation has been disnatured, corrupted, with the rest of nature; or rather, since the child-parent situation is the dynamic core of the Dickens world, the radical disnaturing here is what has corrupted the rest. His plots seldom serve to canalize, with the resolution of the particular set of plotted circumstances, the hysteria submerged in his vision of a nature gone thoroughly wrong; the permutations of the crimes are too many, and their ultimate cause or root is evasive, unless one would resort to some dramatically unmanageable rationale such as original sin. The Dickens world requires an act of redemption. A symbolic act of this kind is again and again indicated in his novels, in the charity of the uncherished and sinned-against child for the inadequate or criminal father—what might be called the theme of the prodigal father, Dickens' usual modification of the prodigal son theme. But the redemptive act should be such that it should redeem not only the individual "fathers," but society at large. One might almost say—thinking of Dickens' caricatures of the living dead, with their necrotic members and organs, their identifications of themselves with inanimate objects—that it should be such as to redeem the dead. *Great Expectations* is an exception among his novels in that here the redemptive act is adequate to and structural for both bodies of thematic material—the sins of individuals and the sins of society.

Pip first becomes aware of the "identity of things" as he is held suspended heels over head by the convict; that is, in a world literally turned upside down. Thenceforth Pip's interior landscape is inverted by his guilty knowledge of this man "who had been soaked in water, and smothered in mud, and lamed by stones, and cut by flints, and stung by nettles, and torn by briars." The apparition is that of all suffering that the earth can inflict, and that the apparition presents itself to a child is as much as to say that every child, whatever his innocence, inherits guilt (as the potential of his acts) for the condition of man. The inversion of natural order begins here with first self-consciousness: the child is heir to the sins of the "fathers." Thus the crime that is always pervasive in the Dickens universe is identified in a new way—not primarily as that of the "father," nor as that of some public institution, but as that of the child—the original individual who must necessarily take upon himself responsibility for not only what is to be done in the present and the future, but what has been done in the past, inasmuch as the past is part and parcel of the present and the future. The child is the criminal, and it is for this reason that he is able to redeem his world; for the world's guilt is his guilt, and he can expiate it in his own acts.

The guilt of the child is realized on several levels. Pip experiences the psychological *form* (or feeling) of guilt before he is capable of voluntary evil; he is treated by adults—Mrs. Joe and Pumblechook and Wopsle—as if he were a felon, a young George Barnwell (a character in the play which Wopsle reads on the night when Mrs. Joe is attacked) wanting only to murder his nearest relative, as George Barnwell murdered his uncle. This is the usual nightmare of the child in Dickens, a vision of imminent incarceration, fetters like sausages, lurid accusatory texts. He is treated, that is, as if he were a thing, manipulable by adults for the extraction of certain sensations: by making him feel guilty and diminished, they are able to feel virtuous and great. But the psychological *form* of guilt acquires spiritual *content* when Pip himself conceives the tainted wish—the wish to be like the most powerful adult and to treat others as things. At the literal level, Pip's guilt is that of snobbery toward Joe Gargery, and snobbery is a denial of the human value of others. Symbolically, however, Pip's guilt is that of murder; for he steals the file with which the convict rids himself of his leg iron, and it is this leg iron, picked up on the marshes, with which Orlick attacks Mrs. Joe; so that the child does inevitably overtake his destiny, which was, like

George Barnwell, to murder his nearest relative. But the "relative" whom Pip, adopting the venerable criminality of society, is, in the widest symbolic scope of intention, destined to murder is not Mrs. Joe but his "father," Magwitch—to murder in the socially chronic fashion of the Dickens world, which consists in the dehumanization of the weak, or in moral acquiescence to such murder. Pip is, after all, the ordinary mixed human being, one more Everyman in the long succession of them that literature has represented, but we see this Everyman as he develops from a child; and his destiny is directed by the ideals of his world—toward "great expectations" which involve the making of Magwitches—which involve, that is, murder. These are the possibilities that are projected in the opening scene of the book, when the young child, left with a burden on his soul, watches the convict limping off under an angry red sky, toward the black marshes, the gibbet, and the savage lair of the sea, in a still rotating landscape.

In Dickens' modification of the folk pattern of the fairy wishing, Magwitch is Pip's "fairy godfather" who changes the pumpkin into a coach. Like all the "fathers," he uses the child as a thing in order to obtain through him vicarious sensations of grandeur. In relation to society, however, Magwitch is the child, and society the prodigal father; from the time he was first taken for stealing turnips, the convict's career has duplicated brutally and in public the pathos of the ordinary child. Again, in relation to Pip, Magwitch is still the child; for, spiritually committed by his "great expectations" to that irresponsibility which has accounted for the Magwitches, Pip is projectively, at least, answerable for Magwitch's existence and for his brutalization. Pip carries his criminal father within him; he is, so to speak, the father of his father. The ambiguities of each term of the relationship are such that each is both child and father, making a fourfold relationship; and the act of love between them at the end is thus reinforced fourfold, and the redemption by love is a fourfold redemption: that is to say, it is symbolically infinite, for it serves for all the meanings Dickens finds it possible to attach to the central child-father situation, the most profound and embracing relationship that, in Dickens' work, obtains among men.

As the child's original alienation from "natural" order is essentially mysterious, a guilty inheritance from the fathers which invades first awareness, so the redemptive act is also a mysterious one. The mysterious nature of the act is first indicated, in the manner of a motif, when Mrs. Joe, in imbecile pantomime, tries to propitiate her attacker, the bestial Orlick. In Orlick is concretized all the undefined evil of the Dickens world, that has nourished itself underground and crept along walls, like the ancient stains on the house of Atreus. He is the lawlessness implied in the unnatural conversions of the human into the nonhuman, the retributive death that invades those who have grown lean in life and who have exercised the powers of death over others. He is the instinct of aggression and destruction, the daemonism of sheer external Matter as such; he is pure "thingness" emerging without warning from the ooze where he has been unconsciously cultivated. As Orlick is one form of spiritual excess—unmotivated hate—Joe Gargery is the opposed form—love without reservation. Given these terms of the spiritual framework, the redemptive act itself could scarcely be anything but grotesque—and it is by a grotesque gesture, one of the most profoundly intuitive symbols in Dickens, that Mrs. Joe is redeemed. What is implied by her humble propitiation of the beast Orlick is a recognition of personal guilt in the guilt of others, and of its dialectical relationship with love. The motif reappears in the moment of major illumination in the book. Pip "bows down," not to Joe Gargery, toward whom he has been privately and literally guilty, but to the wounded, hunted, shackled man, Magwitch, who has been guilty toward himself. It is in this way that the manifold organic relationships among men are revealed, and that the Dickens world—founded in fragmentariness and disintegration—is made whole. (pp. 126-38)

*Dorothy Van Ghent, "On 'Great Expectations'," in her* The English Novel: Form and Function, *Holt, Rinehart and Winston, 1953, pp. 125-38.*

### G. ROBERT STANGE   (essay date 1954)

[*Analyzing* Great Expectations *as a moral fable, Stange touches upon several aspects of the novel, including character, theme, and narrative technique.*]

*Great Expectations* is a peculiarly satisfying and impressive novel. It is unusual to find in Dickens' work so rigorous a control of detail, so simple and organic a pattern. In this very late novel the usual features of his art—proliferating subplots, legions of minor grotesques—are almost entirely absent. The simplicity is that of an art form that belongs to an ancient type and concentrates on permanently significant issues. *Great Expectations* is conceived as a moral fable; it is the story of a young man's development from the moment of his first self-awareness, to that of his mature acceptance of the human condition.

So natural a theme imposes an elemental form on the novel: the over-all pattern is defined by the process of growth, and Dickens employs many of the motifs of folklore. The story of Pip falls into three phases which clearly display a dialectic progression. We see the boy first in his natural condition in the country, responding and acting instinctively and therefore virtuously. The second stage of his career involves a negation of child-like simplicity; Pip acquires his "expectations," renounces his origins, and moves to the city. He rises in society, but since he acts through calculation rather than through instinctive charity, his moral values deteriorate as his social graces improve. This middle phase of his career culminates in a sudden fall, the beginning of a redemptive suffering which is dramatically concluded by an attack of brain fever leading to a long coma. It is not too fanciful to regard this illness as a symbolic death; Pip rises from it regenerate and percipient. In the final stage of growth he returns to his birthplace, abandons his false expectations, accepts the limitations of his condition, and achieves a partial synthesis of the virtue of his innocent youth and the melancholy insight of his later experience.

Variants of such a narrative are found in the myths of many heroes. In Dickens' novel the legend has the advantage of providing an action which appeals to the great primary human affections and serves as unifying center for the richly conceived minor themes and images which form the body of the novel. It is a signal virtue of this simple structure that it saves *Great Expectations* from some of the startling weaknesses of such excellent but inconsistently developed novels as *Martin Chuzzlewit* or *Our Mutual Friend.*

The particular fable that Dickens elaborates is as interesting for its historical as for its timeless aspects. In its particulars the story of Pip is the classic legend of the nineteenth century: *Great Expectations* belongs to that class of education or development-novels which describe the young man of talents

who progresses from the country to the city, ascends in the social hierarchy, and moves from innocence to experience. Stendhal in *Le Rouge et le Noir,* Balzac in *Le Père Goriot* and *Les Illusions perdues,* use the plot as a means of dissecting the post-Napoleonic world and exposing its moral poverty. This novelistic form reflects the lives of the successful children of the century, and usually expresses the mixed attitudes of its artists. Dickens, Stendhal, Balzac communicate their horror of a materialist society, but they are not without admiration for the possibilities of the new social mobility; *la carrière ouverte aux talents* had a personal meaning for all three of these energetic men.

Pip, then, must be considered in the highly competitive company of Julien Sorel, Rubempré, and Eugène de Rastignac. Dickens' tale of lost illusions, however, is very different from the French novelists'; *Great Expectations* is not more profound than other development-novels, but it is more mysterious. The recurrent themes of the genre are all there: city is posed against country, experience against innocence; there is a search for the true father; there is the exposure to crime and the acceptance of guilt and expiation. What Dickens' novel lacks is the clarity and, one is tempted to say, the essential tolerance of the French. He could not command either the saving ironic vision of Stendhal or the disenchanted practicality and secure Catholicism of Balzac. For Dickens, always the Victorian protestant, the issues of a young man's rise or fall are conceived as a drama of the individual conscience; enlightenment (partial at best) is to be found only in the agony of personal guilt.

With these considerations and possible comparisons in mind I should like to comment on some of the conspicuous features of *Great Expectations.* The novel is interesting for many reasons: it demonstrates the subtlety of Dickens' art; it displays a consistent control of narrative, imagery, and theme which gives meaning to the stark outline of the fable, and symbolic weight to every character and detail. It proves Dickens' ability (which has frequently been denied) to combine his genius for comedy with his fictional presentation of some of the most serious and permanently interesting of human concerns.

The principal themes are announced and the mood of the whole novel established in the opening pages of *Great Expectations.* The first scene with the boy Pip in the graveyard is one of the best of the superbly energetic beginnings found in almost all Dickens' mature novels. In less than a page we are given a character, his background, and his setting; within a few paragraphs more we are immersed in a decisive action. Young Pip is first seen against the background of his parents' gravestones—monuments which communicate to him no clear knowledge either of his parentage or of his position in the world. He is an orphan who must search for a father and define his own condition. The moment of this opening scene, we learn, is that at which the hero has first realized his individuality and gained his "first most vivid and broad impression of the identity of things." This information given the reader, the violent meeting between Pip and the escaped convict abruptly takes place.

The impression of the identity of things that Pip is supposed to have received is highly equivocal. The convict rises up like a ghost from among the graves, seizes the boy suddenly, threatens to kill him, holds him upside down through most of their conversation, and ends by forcing the boy to steal food for him. The children of Dickens' novels always receive rather strange impressions of things, but Pip's epiphany is the

oddest of all, and in some ways the most ingenious. This encounter in the graveyard is the germinal scene of the novel.
While he is held by the convict, Pip sees his world upside
down; in the course of Dickens' fable the reader is invited to
try the same view. This particular change of viewpoint is an
ancient device of irony, but an excellent one: Dickens' satire
asks us to try reversing the accepted senses of innocence and
guilt, success and failure, to think of the world's goods as the
world's evils.

A number of ironic reversals and ambiguous situations develop out of the first scene. The convict, Magwitch, is permanently grateful to Pip for having brought him food and a file
with which to take off his leg-iron. Years later he expresses
his gratitude by assuming in secrecy an economic parenthood; with the money he has made in Australia he will, unbe-
knownst to Pip, make "his boy" a gentleman. But the money
the convict furnishes him makes Pip not a true gentleman,
but a cad. He lives as a *flâneur* in London, and when he later
discovers the disreputable source of his income is snobbishly
horrified.

Pip's career is a parable which illustrates several religious
paradoxes: he can gain only by losing all he has; only by being
defiled can he be cleansed. Magwitch returns to claim his gentleman, and finally the convict's devotion and suffering
arouse Pip's charity; by the time Magwitch has been captured
and is dying Pip has accepted him and come to love him as
a true father. The relationship is the most important one in
the novel: in sympathizing with Magwitch Pip assumes the
criminal's guilt; in suffering with and finally loving the despised and rejected man he finds his own real self.

Magwitch did not have to learn to love Pip. He was naturally
devoted to "the small bundle of shivers," the outcast boy who
brought him the stolen food and the file in the misty graveyard. There is a natural bond, Dickens suggests, between the
child and the criminal; they are alike in their helplessness;
both are repressed and tortured by established society, and
both rebel against its incomprehensible authority. In the first
scene Magwitch forces Pip to commit his first "criminal" act,
to steal the file and food from his sister's house. Though this
theft produces agonies of guilt in Pip, we are led to see it not
as a sin but as an instinctive act of mercy. Magwitch, much
later, tells Pip: "I first become aware of myself, down in
Essex, a thieving turnips for my living." Dickens would have
us, in some obscure way, conceive the illicit act as the means
of self-realization.

In the opening section of the novel the view moves back and
forth between the escaped criminal on the marshes and the
harsh life in the house of Pip's sister, Mrs. Joe Gargery. The
"criminality" of Pip and the convict is contrasted with the
socially approved cruelty and injustice of Mrs. Joe and her
respectable friends. The elders who come to the Christmas
feast at the Gargerys' are pleased to describe Pip as a criminal: the young are, according to Mr. Hubble, "naterally wicious." During this most bleak of Christmas dinners the child
is treated not only as outlaw, but as animal. In Mrs. Joe's first
speech Pip is called a "young monkey"; then, as the spirits
of the revellers rise, more and more comparisons are made
between boys and animals. (pp. 9-12)

This identification of animal and human is continually repeated in the opening chapters of the novel, and we catch its
resonance throughout the book. When the two convicts—
Pip's "friend" and the other fugitive, Magwitch's ancient

enemy—are captured, we experience the horror of official justice, which treats the prisoners as if they were less than
human: "No one seemed surprised to see him, or interested
in seeing him, or glad to see him, or sorry to see him, or spoke
a word, except that somebody in the boat growled as if to
dogs, 'Give way, you!' " And the prison ship, lying beyond
the mud of the shore, looked to Pip "like a wicked Noah's
ark."

The theme of this first section of the novel—which concludes
with the capture of Magwitch and his return to the prison
ship—might be called "the several meanings of humanity."
Only the three characters who are in some way social outcasts—Pip, Magwitch, and Joe Gargery the child-like blacksmith—act in charity and respect the humanity of others. To
Magwitch Pip is distinctly not an animal, and not capable of
adult wickedness: "You'd be but a fierce young hound indeed, if at your time of life you could help to hunt a wretched
warmint." And when, after he is taken, the convict shields
Pip by confessing to have stolen the Gargerys' pork pie, Joe's
absolution affirms the dignity of man:

> "God knows you're welcome to it—so far as it was
> ever mine," returned Joe, with a saving remem-
> brance of Mrs. Joe. "We don't know what you have
> done, but we wouldn't have you starved to death
> for it, poor miserable fellow-creatur.—Would us,
> Pip?"

The next section of the narrative is less tightly conceived than
the introductory action. Time is handled loosely; Pip goes to
school, and becomes acquainted with Miss Havisham of Satis
House and the beautiful Estella. The section concludes when
Pip has reached early manhood, been told of his expectations,
and has prepared to leave for London. These episodes develop, with variations, the theme of childhood betrayed. Pip
himself renounces his childhood by coming to accept the false
social values of middle-class society. His perverse development is expressed by persistent images of the opposition between the human and the non-human, the living and the
dead.

On his way to visit Miss Havisham for the first time, Pip
spends the night with Mr. Pumblechook, the corn-chandler,
in his lodgings behind his shop. The contrast between the
aridity of this old hypocrite's spirit and the viability of his
wares is a type of the conflict between natural growth and social form. Pip looks at all the shop-keeper's little drawers
filled with bulbs and seed packets and wonders "whether the
flower-seeds and bulbs ever wanted of a fine day to break out
of those jails and bloom." The imagery of life repressed is developed further in the descriptions of Miss Havisham and
Satis House. The first detail Pip notices is the abandoned
brewery where the once active ferment has ceased; no germ
of life is to be found in Satis House or in its occupants:

> . . . there were no pigeons in the dove-cot, no
> horses in the stable, no pigs in the sty, no malt in
> the storehouse, no smells of grains and beer in the
> copper or the vat. All the uses and scents of the
> brewery might have evaporated with its last reek of
> smoke. In a by-yard, there was a wilderness of
> empty casks. . . .

On top of these casks Estella dances with solitary concentration, and behind her, in a dark corner of the building, Pip fancies that he sees a figure hanging by the neck from a wooden
beam, "a figure all in yellow white, with but one shoe to the
feet; and it hung so, that I could see that the faded trimmings

of the dress were like earthy paper, and that the face was Miss Havisham's."

Miss Havisham *is* death. From his visits to Satis House Pip acquires his false admiration for the genteel; he falls in love with Estella and fails to see that she is the cold instrument of Miss Havisham's revenge on human passion and on life itself. When Pip learns he may expect a large inheritance from an unknown source he immediately assumes (incorrectly) that Miss Havisham is his benefactor; she does not undeceive him. Money, which is also death, is appropriately connected with the old lady rotting away in her darkened room.

Conflicting values in Pip's life are also expressed by the opposed imagery of stars and fire. Estella is by name a star, and throughout the novel stars are conceived as pitiless: "And then I looked at the stars, and considered how awful it would be for a man to turn his face up to them as he froze to death, and see no help or pity in all the glittering multitude." Estella and her light are described as coming down the dark passage of Satis House "like a star," and when she has become a woman she is constantly surrounded by the bright glitter of jewelry.

Joe Gargery, on the other hand, is associated with the warm fire of the hearth or forge. It was his habit to sit and rake the fire between the lower bars of the kitchen grate, and his workday was spent at the forge. The extent to which Dickens intended the contrast between the warm and the cold lights—the vitality of Joe and the frigid glitter of Estella—is indicated in a passage that describes the beginnings of Pip's disillusionment with his expectations:

> When I woke up in the night . . . I used to think, with a weariness on my spirits, that I should have been happier and better if I had never seen Miss Havisham's face, and had risen to manhood content to be partners with Joe in the honest old forge. Many a time of an evening, when I sat alone looking at the fire, I thought, after all, there was no fire like the forge fire and the kitchen fire at home.
>
> Yet Estella was so inseparable from all my restlessness and disquiet of mind, that I really fell into confusion as to the limits of my own part in its production.

At the end of the novel Pip finds the true light on the homely hearth, and in a last twist of the father-son theme, Joe emerges as a true parent—the only kind of parent that Dickens could ever fully approve, one that remains a child. The moral of this return to Joe sharply contradicts the accepted picture of Dickens as a radical critic of society: Joe is a humble countryman who is content with the place in the social order he has been appointed to fulfill. He fills it "well and with respect"; Pip learns that he can do no better than to emulate him.

The second stage of Pip's three-phased story is set in London, and the moral issues of the fiction are modulated accordingly. Instead of the opposition between custom and the instinctive life, the novelist treats the conflict between man and his social institutions. The topics and themes are specific, and the satire, some of it wonderfully deft, is more social than moral. Not all Dickens' social message is presented by means that seem adequate. By satirizing Pip and his leisure class friends (The Finches of the Grove, they call themselves) the novelist would have us realize that idle young men will come to a bad end. Dickens is here expressing the Victorian Doctrine of

Work—a pervasive notion that both inspired and reassured his industrious contemporaries.

The difficulty for the modern reader, who is unmoved by the objects of Victorian piety, is that the doctrine appears to be the result, not of moral insight, but of didactic intent; it is presented as statement, rather than as experience or dramatized perception, and consequently it never modifies the course of fictional action or the formation of character. The distinction is crucial: it is between the Dickens who *sees* and the Dickens who *professes;* often between the good and the bad sides of his art.

The novelist is on surer ground when he comes to define the nature of wealth in a mercantile society. Instead of moralistic condemnation we have a technique that resembles parable. Pip eventually learns that his ornamental life is supported, not by Miss Havisham, but by the labor and suffering of the convict Magwitch:

> "I swore arterwards, sure as ever I spec'lated and got rich, you should get rich. I lived rough, that you should live smooth; I worked hard that you should be above work. What odds, dear boy? Do I tell it fur you to feel a obligation? Not a bit. I tell it, fur you to know as that there dunghill dog wot you kep like in, got his head so high that he could make a gentleman—and, Pip, you're him!"

The convict would not only make a gentleman but own him. The blood horses of the colonists might fling up the dust over him as he was walking, but, "I says to myself, 'If I ain't a gentleman, nor yet ain't got no learning, I'm the owner of such. All on you owns stock and land; which on you owns a brought-up London gentleman?'"

In this action Dickens has subtly led us to speculate on the connections between a gentleman and his money, on the dark origins of even the most respectable fortunes. We find Magwitch guilty of trying to own another human being, but we ask whether his actions are any more sinful than those of the wealthy *bourgeois.* There is a deeper moral in the fact that Magwitch's fortune at first destroyed the natural gentleman in Pip, but that after it was lost (it had to be forfeited to the state when Magwitch was finally captured) the "dung-hill dog" did actually make Pip a gentleman by evoking his finer feelings. This ironic distinction between "gentility" and what the father of English poetry meant by "gentilesse" is traditional in our literature and our mythology. In ***Great Expectations*** it arises out of the action and language of the fiction; consequently it moves and persuades us as literal statement never can.

The middle sections of the novel are dominated by the solid yet mysterious figure of Mr. Jaggers, Pip's legal guardian. Though Jaggers is not one of Dickens' greatest characters he is heavy with implication; he is so much at the center of this fable that we are challenged to interpret him—only to find that his meaning is ambiguous. On his first appearance Jaggers strikes a characteristic note of sinister authority:

> He was a burly man of an exceedingly dark complexion, with an exceedingly large head and a correspondingly large hand. He took my chin in his large hand and turned up my face to have a look at me by the light of the candle. . . . His eyes were set very deep in his head, and were disagreeably sharp and suspicious. . . .
>
> "How do *you* come here?"

"Miss Havisham sent for me, sir," I explained.

"Well! Behave yourself. I have a pretty large experience of boys, and you're a bad set of fellows. Now mind!" said he, biting the side of his great forefinger, as he frowned at me, "you behave yourself."

Pip wonders at first if Jaggers is a doctor. It is soon explained that he is a lawyer—what we now ambiguously call a *criminal* lawyer—but he is like a physician who treats moral malignancy, with the doctor's necessary detachment from individual suffering. Jaggers is interested not in the social operations of the law, but in the varieties of criminality. He exudes an antiseptic smell of soap and is described as washing his clients off as if he were a surgeon or a dentist.

Pip finds that Jaggers has "an air of authority not to be disputed . . . with a manner expressive of knowing something secret about every one of us that would effectually do for each individual if he chose to disclose it." When Pip and his friends go to dinner at Jaggers' house Pip observes that he "wrenched the weakest parts of our dispositions out of us." After the party his guardian tells Pip that he particularly liked the sullen young man they called Spider: " 'Keep as clear of him as you can. But I like the fellow, Pip; he is one of the true sort. Why if I was a fortune-teller. . . . But I am not a fortune-teller,' he said. . . . 'You know what I am don't you?' " This question is repeated when Pip is being shown through Newgate Prison by Jaggers' assistant, Wemmick. The turnkey says of Pip: "Why then . . . he knows what Mr. Jaggers is."

But neither Pip nor the reader ever fully knows what Mr. Jaggers is. We learn, along with Pip, that Jaggers has manipulated the events which have shaped the lives of most of the characters in the novel; he has, in the case of Estella and her mother, dispensed a merciful but entirely personal justice; he is the only character who knows the web of secret relationships that are finally revealed to Pip. He dominates by the strength of his knowledge the world of guilt and sin—called *Little Britain*—of which his office is the center. He has, in brief, the powers that an artist exerts over the creatures of his fictional world, and that a god exerts over his creation.

As surrogate of the artist, Jaggers displays qualities of mind—complete impassibility, all-seeing unfeelingness—which are the opposite of Dickens', but of a sort that Dickens may at times have desired. Jaggers can be considered a fantasy figure created by a novelist who is forced by his intense sensibility to re-live the sufferings of his fellow men and who feels their agonies too deeply.

In both the poetry and fiction of the nineteenth century there are examples of a persistent desire of the artist *not to care*. The mood, which is perhaps an inevitable concomitant of Romanticism, is expressed in Balzac's ambivalence toward his great character Vautrin. As arch-criminal and Rousseauistic man, Vautrin represents all the attitudes that Balzac the churchman and monarchist ostensibly rejects, yet is presented as a kind of artist-hero, above the law, who sees through the social system with an almost noble cynicism.

Related attitudes are expressed in the theories of art developed by such different writers as Flaubert and Yeats. While—perhaps because—Flaubert himself suffered from hyperaesthesia, he conceived the ideal novelist as coldly detached, performing his examination with the deft impassivity of the surgeon. Yeats, the "last Romantic," found the construction of

a mask or anti-self necessary to poetic creation, and insisted that the anti-self be cold and hard—all that he as poet and feeling man was not.

Dickens' evocation of this complex of attitudes is less political than Balzac's, less philosophical than Flaubert's or Yeats'. Jaggers has a complete understanding of human evil but, unlike the living artist, can wash his hands of it. He is above ordinary institutions; like a god he dispenses justice, and like a god displays infinite mercy through unrelenting severity:

"Mind you, Mr. Pip," said Wemmick, gravely in my ear, as he took my arm to be more confidential; "I don't know that Mr. Jaggers does a better thing than the way in which he keeps himself so high. He's always so high. His constant height is of a piece with his immense abilities. That Colonel durst no more take leave of *him,* than that turnkey durst ask him his intentions respecting a case. Then between his height and them, he slips in his subordinate—don't you see?—and so he has 'em soul and body."

Pip merely wishes that he had "some other guardian of minor abilities."

The final moral vision of *Great Expectations* has to do with the nature of sin and guilt. After visiting Newgate Pip, still complacent and self-deceived, thinks how strange it was that he should be encompassed by the taint of prison and crime. He tries to beat the prison dust off his feet and to exhale its air from his lungs; he is going to meet Estella, who must not be contaminated by the smell of crime. Later it is revealed that Estella, the pure, is the bastard child of Magwitch and a murderess. Newgate is figuratively described as a greenhouse, and the prisoners as plants carefully tended by Wemmick, assistant to Mr. Jaggers. These disturbing metaphors suggest that criminality is the condition of life. Dickens would distinguish between the native, inherent sinfulness from which men can be redeemed, and that evil which destroys life: the sin of the hypocrite or oppressor, the smothering wickedness of corrupt institutions. The last stage of Pip's progression is reached when he learns to love the criminal and to accept his own implication in the common guilt.

Though Dickens' interpretation is theologically heterodox, he deals conventionally with the ancient question of free will and predestination. In one dramatic paragraph Pip's "fall" is compared with the descent of the rock slab on the sleeping victim in the *Arabian Nights* tale: Slowly, slowly, "all the work, near and afar, that tended to the end, had been accomplished; and in an instant the blow was struck, and the roof of my stronghold dropped upon me." Pip's fall was the result of a chain of predetermined events but he was, nevertheless, responsible for his own actions; toward the end of the novel Miss Havisham gravely informs him: "You have made your own snares. *I* never made them."

The patterns of culpability in *Great Expectations* are so intricate that the whole world of the novel is eventually caught in a single web of awful responsibility. The leg-iron, for example, which the convict removed with the file Pip stole for him is found by Orlick and used as a weapon to brain Mrs. Joe. By this fearsome chain of circumstance Pip shares the guilt for his sister's death.

Profound and suggestive as is Dickens' treatment of guilt and expiation in this novel, to trace its remoter implications is to find something excessive and idiosyncratic. A few years after he wrote *Great Expectations* Dickens remarked to a friend that he felt always as if he were wanted by the police—"irretrievably tainted." Compared to most of the writers of his time the Dickens of the later novels seems to be obsessed with guilt. The way in which his development-novel differs from those of his French compeers emphasizes an important quality of Dickens' art. The young heroes of *Le Rouge et le Noir* and *Le Père Goriot* proceed from innocence, through suffering to learning. They are surrounded by evil, and they can be destroyed by it. But Stendhal, writing in a rationalist tradition, and Balzac displaying the worldliness that only a Catholic novelist can command, seem astonishingly cool, even callous, beside Dickens. *Great Expectations* is outside either Cartesian or Catholic rationalism; profound as only an elementally simple book can be, it finds its analogues not in the novels of Dickens' English or French contemporaries, but in the writings of that other irretrievably tainted artist, Fyodor Dostoevski. (pp. 12-17)

> G. Robert Stange, "Expectations Well Lost: Dickens' Fable for His Time," in College English, Vol. 16, No. 1, October, 1954, pp. 9-17.

## J. HILLIS MILLER   (essay date 1958)

[*An American critic, Miller is associated with the "Yale critics," a group that includes Harold Bloom, Paul de Man, and Geoffrey Hartman. Throughout his career Miller has successfully applied several critical methods to literature, including New Criticism, the existential phenomenology of Georges Poulet, and deconstructionism. Here, he closely studies the themes and characters of* Great Expectations, *considering it the clearest and most representative expression of Dickens's worldview.*]

*Great Expectations* is the most unified and concentrated expression of Dickens' abiding sense of the world, and Pip might be called the archetypal Dickens hero. In *Great Expectations* Dickens' particular view of things is expressed with a concreteness and symbolic intensity he never surpassed. Perhaps the restrictions of shorter length and of weekly rather than monthly publication led Dickens to present his story more in symbolic than in discursive form. The result is not a narrowing and rarefying of meaning, but rather a large increase in intensity and complexity. . . .[In] following Pip's adventures we perhaps come closest to the intimate center of Dickens' apprehension of the world and of his mode of existence within it. *Great Expectations* makes available, as does no other of Dickens' novels, the central experiences of the universal Dickensian hero. (pp. 247-50)

*Great Expectations,* like most of Dickens' novels, does not begin with a description of the perfect bliss of childhood, the period when the world and the self are identified, and the parents are seen as benign gods whose care and whose overlooking judgment protect and justify the child. Like Oedipus, who, as a newborn baby, was put out in the fields to die, Dickens' heroes and heroines have never experienced this perfect security. Each becomes aware of himself as isolated from all that is outside of himself. The Dickensian hero is separated from nature. The world appears to him as cold and unfriendly, as a "wilderness" or a graveyard. . . . The Dickensian hero is also alienated from the human community. He has no familial tie. He is an orphan, or illegitimate, or both. He has no status in the community, no inherited role which he can accept with dignity. He is characterized by desire, rather than

by possession. His spiritual state is one of an expectation founded on a present consciousness of lack, of deprivation. He is, in Wallace Stevens' phrase, "an emptiness that would be filled."

Furthermore, the Dickensian hero becomes aware of himself as guilty. His very existence is a matter of reproach and a shameful thing. . . . Pip says of himself: "I was always treated as if I had insisted on being born in opposition to the dictates of reason, religion, and morality, and against the dissuading arguments of my best friends." It is mere accident that he is alive at all, and is not buried beside his brothers in the lonely churchyard by the sea. "As to you," says Joe of his first glimpse of the infant Pip, "if you could have been aware how small and flabby and mean you was, dear me, you'd have formed the most contemptible opinions of yourself!" And Mrs. Joe recalls "all the times she had wished [Pip] in [his] grave, and [he] had contumaciously refused to go there." The typical Dickens hero, like Pip, feels guilty because he has no given status or relation to family, to nature, or to the community. He is, in everyone's eyes, in the way, superfluous. He is either ignored by society altogether, thrown into the streets to beg or starve, or he is taken care of by the state or by his foster parents in an impersonal way which deprives him of any real identity. To submit to this "care" is to be transformed into an object. He may, alternatively, accept a job as a functionary in the vast system of money-getting which dominates urban society. This will as effectively dehumanize him as going to the poorhouse. (pp. 251-52)

Since the Dickensian hero has initially no real role, any status he attains in the world will be the result of his own efforts. He will be totally responsible, himself, for any identity he achieves, and thus "guilty" in the sense of being the source of his own values. He has no hope of ever being justified by any external approval. He will be, whatever he does, a "self-made man," a man who has made himself his own goal and end. This will be true in spite of any efforts on his part to escape his superfluity. The world has simply refused to give him any assigned place, and any place he gets will have to be seized. (pp. 252-53)

[Dickens' characters] seek some way out that will make possible the achievement of true selfhood, while not necessitating the extreme of anarchic individualism. These protagonists try various ways, some proper, some improper, of attaining the reconciliation of freedom and security. The single great development in Dickens' world view is the change in the kinds of expedients which are deemed to be proper or possible. *Great Expectations* is the novel in which the various alternatives are most clearly presented and opposed.

In a world where the only possible relation to other people seems to be that of oppressor to oppressed, or oppressed to oppressor, those who are born into oppression may try to seize the role of oppressor. . . . Only those who are born members of the upper class can rule guiltlessly, by "divine right," as it were, and the outcast knows that neither God nor the collective approval of society will justify any open attempts on his part to reverse the role, and to become oppressor rather than oppressed. So he tries various ways to attain the same movement up in the social scale without incurring guilt for it.

He may simply dominate those beneath him in the social chain of being, as Wemmick, himself a victim of the great

*Dickens in 1861 as rendered by Rudolph Lehmann.*

legal organization, treats those beneath him, Jaggers' clients, condemned jailbirds, as though they were the plants in his flower garden, or as Abel Magwitch, escaped convict, at the extreme point of his exclusion from society, coerces Pip into feeding him. He is "beneath" everyone in the world except Pip, whom he seizes and turns upside down, as though to reverse their roles. Much later in the novel, when Pip is being browbeaten by Jaggers (surely "master" rather than "slave" in the world of the novel), he says: "I felt at a disadvantage, which reminded me of that old time when I had been put upon a tombstone."

The inadequacies of this expedient are obvious. The "exploiter" cannot hide from himself the fact that he has unjustifiably seized power over another human being.

But two other more surreptitious ways are attempted by characters in *Great Expectations.* In the first case, one person manipulates another not as his victim, but as the agent of his revenge on society. In one way or another several characters in *Great Expectations* try to "make" other characters. They do not try to make them into mere dehumanized tools, but to make them into members of the upper class who will have all the prerogatives of justified exploitation which they themselves lack. Thus Magwitch boasts that Pip is "the gentleman what I made." If he cannot himself ever be anything but a transported felon, "hunted dunghill dog," perhaps he can secretly create a gentleman through whom he will vicariously enjoy all the powers he could never attain himself: "I says to myself, 'If I ain't a gentleman, nor yet ain't got no learning,

I'm the owner of such. All on you owns stock and land; which on you owns a brought-up London gentleman?'" Magwitch is a nightmare permutation of Mr. Brownlow and Mr. Jarndyce. He is the benevolent guardian, secretly manipulating the fortunes of the hero and protecting him, turned into a condemned felon who, like a horrible old dog, gloats over his victim.

There is at least one comic parody of this theme: Pumblechook boasts that he is the "founder" of Pip's fortune, and he shakes Pip's hand again and again on the day his great expectations are announced. Pumblechook's action is an ominous anticipation of Magwitch's symbolic gesture of appropriation when he appears at Pip's door, and grasps his hands. (pp. 253-55)

But Miss Havisham is a more important parallel to Magwitch. Her heart has been broken by Compeyson, the archvillain who lies behind all the evil in the story. She has withdrawn forever from the world, and has renounced all attempts to act in her own person. Miss Havisham has attempted to stop time at the moment she received the news that her bridegroom-to-be had deceived and deserted her. She does not try to stop time at the moment *before* she heard the news. No, she does not want to escape the harsh reality of her betrayal, and return to the time when she was living in an illusory world of innocence, security, and, as she thought, reciprocal love. She wants, rather, to crystallize her grief and bereavement into an eternal moment of shock and sorrow. . . . (pp. 255-56)

Miss Havisham has two motives for her attempt to freeze time. She wants to make certain that her betrayal will be the whole meaning of her life, that nothing more will happen to change her destiny as it existed at the moment of betrayal. She does not want it to be possible for her to stop suffering, to forget, to turn her attention to other things and other people, and so cease to be the Miss Havisham who was cruelly abandoned on the day of her wedding. If she allows herself to change at all that self may become a thing of the past, a matter of history, a self she no longer is. She may slip back into time, which means to slip back into a human existence which is conditioned in its essence by temporality. And to be essentially conditioned by time means never to reach a stopping place in one's life, to be "ever more about to be," to be not yet what one is going to be, and never finally what one is. . . . Miss Havisham's attempt is doomed to failure. For in willing to freeze her life at the moment the annihilating blow came from the outside, she changes her abandonment from a "cruel fate" to a chosen role. It is Miss Havisham herself who chooses to make her betrayal the central event and meaning of her life. And in so choosing she makes herself responsible for it. She tries to flee forever out of the realm of freedom, unpredictability, and change, but she only succeeds in making herself responsible for ruining her own life, and for nearly ruining Estella's and Pip's.

Miss Havisham's second motive for attempting to freeze time at the moment of her betrayal is the motive of revenge. She had loved Compeyson with a love she herself defines as "blind devotion, unquestioning self-humiliation, utter submission, trust and belief against yourself and against the whole world, giving up your whole heart and soul to the smiter. . . ." "There is no doubt," says Herbert Pocket, "that she perfectly idolised him." Miss Havisham tries to carry the same kind of all or nothing quality into her new life. Her revenge is to make her betrayal into the very meaning of her life, and to make her resulting death-in-life a curse on her heartless lover. . . . (pp. 256-57)

Miss Havisham's other method of revenge is Estella. ". . . with my praises, and with my jewels, and with my teachings, and with this figure of myself always before her," says Miss Havisham of Estella, ". . . I stole her heart away and put ice in its place." Just as Magwitch, another victim of Compeyson, creates in Pip an "instrument" of his revenge on society, so Miss Havisham "mould[s] [Estella] into the form that her wild resentment, spurned affection, and wounded pride, found vengeance in." Estella will draw men as a candle attracts moths, but, being without a heart, she will treat them as Compeyson treated Miss Havisham: "How does she use you, Pip, how does she use you?" asks Miss Havisham. She had deluded herself into thinking she is taking no direct revenge on mankind, but only letting her state of abandonment be a punishment. Through Estella she will take an indirect and therefore guiltless revenge, and break a hundred hearts for her own one heart that was broken.

This transformation of the master-slave relation is apparently a reconciliation of irreconcilables. Miss Havisham and Magwitch hope to attain vicariously all that they lack. They will enjoy the power of the oppressor without being guilty of having unjustifiably seized that power. No one will be able to blame Magwitch for the arrogance of Pip the gentleman, and no one will blame Miss Havisham for the cruelties Estella practices on her suitors. Since the low origin of his great expectations is hidden from Pip, he will have the sense of "divine right" that is enjoyed by a gentleman born. His transformation from "common" blacksmith's boy to London gentleman will seem to him like a "destiny," something at any rate for which he is not guiltily responsible. And Estella will be brought up to feel that men are her natural enemies. She will experience no remorse for breaking their hearts because she will have no heart herself. She will be like a superhuman goddess, unable to understand the sorrows of mere mortals.

This attempt to transcend isolation without guilt, by paradoxically both being and not being another person whom one has created, in both cases fails. (pp. 258-59)

Miss Havisham imagines that she can escape the uncertainty of all authentic human relationships if she takes a young girl, before her personality has been formed, and brings her up to look only to her guardian for protection and love. She wants Estella to love her only, so that in the dark, airless confines of Satis House they may dwell safe from all the world, and be sufficient to one another. Miss Havisham succeeds in making Estella wholly her "creation," but, at the same time, she destroys any possibility of a return of her love. The kind of relation Miss Havisham wants cannot be achieved without risk, without an acceptance of the unpredictability and insecurity of all real human relations. At the very moment Miss Havisham makes sure of Estella, Estella will, paradoxically, reverse roles and become Miss Havisham's master: " 'But to be proud and hard to *me!*' Miss Havisham quite shrieked, as she stretched out her arms. 'Estella, Estella, Estella, to be proud and hard to *me!*' "

In the same way Magwitch cannot resist the temptation to return from New South Wales, even at the risk of his life, to see with his own eyes the gentleman he has made: "I've come to the old country fur to see my gentleman spend his money *like* a gentleman. That'll be *my* pleasure. *My* pleasure 'ull be fur to see him do it. And blast you all! . . . blast you every

one, from the judge in his wig, to the colonist a stirring up the dust, I'll show a better gentleman than the whole kit on you put together!" Magwitch has returned to let Pip know the real source of his transformation into a gentleman. His project cannot succeed because Pip must both know and not know that Magwitch has "made" him. He must not know, in order to remain a true gentleman, conscious of enjoying his status by right. He must know in order really to be Magwitch's representative, the creature he has manufactured to wreak his vengeance on society: "Once more he took me by both hands and surveyed me with an air of admiring proprietorship. . . ." Magwitch wants to enjoy directly his sense of power, and he wants Pip to know that all his acts are as the vicar of Magwitch. But of course as soon as Pip knows the source of his great expectations he no longer thinks of himself as a gentleman. Rather he repudiates with horror his connection with Magwitch, and looks upon himself as Magwitch's dupe, manipulated, as Magwitch was by Compeyson, for his criminal assault upon society. (pp. 259-61)

Neither way out of alienation will work, neither the attempt to become an oppressor of those below even while being oppressed from above, nor the attempt to endow someone else with the power to be an oppressor while one remains innocently passive oneself. One other way remains, a way that even more subtly than the others hides its radical defect: The disinherited one may accept "great expectations." . . . Pip's acceptance of great expectations does not mean seizing recognition of his usefulness by force. It means believing that he will be miraculously given a place in society as though it were his natural right, as though the world had for some unaccountable reason conspired to keep his real place hidden, only to bestow it at last as a free gift. Such are Pip's hopes. He believes that Estella and all the privileges possessed by a gentleman are destined for him by Miss Havisham. He will not need to dirty his hands with the crime of appropriating a place among the oppressors. He will suddenly be transformed from the class of the exploited to the class of the exploiters. There will be an absolute discontinuity between his initial given condition of alienation and isolation, and the suddenly attained possession of a secure place in society. The new man will be both free (cannot Pip buy anything he wants?), and at the same time wholly consecrated in his new role by the approval of society. (pp. 261-62)

Pip might have moved beyond awareness that the family and the social order are based on the notion that there are two distinct kinds of being. He might have rejected the whole structure. But no; he accepts the situation, and simply "expects" to move from one status to the other. When Jaggers announces the great expectations, he tells Pip what he has been hoping for all along: his benefactor wishes "that he be immediately removed from his present sphere of life and from this place, and be brought up as a gentleman—in a word, as a young fellow of great expectations." When Joe and Biddy express "wonder" at the notion of Pip as a gentleman, he doesn't "half like it." To him the good fortune is merely the recognition of the true Pip, the Pip who has heretofore by accident been hidden from view. (pp. 262-63)

It is at first difficult to see why Pip's great expectations do not seem to him another form of the degrading manipulation by society, another subtler form of alienation. They do appear that way to Joe and Biddy, who accept their status with the proud independence of the lower class. When Pip suggests to Biddy that he might "remove Joe into a higher sphere" (a parody of what Jaggers said when he announced the great expectations), she says, "He may be too proud to let any one take him out of a place that he is competent to fill, and fills well and with respect." Why then does Pip accept so readily a change in status which to Joe seems an affront to his pride and independence? It is a very different thing to have as one's given place in society the status of a gentleman rather than the status of a blacksmith. It approaches the reconciliation of freedom and security which Pip seeks. Moreover, the circumstances of mystery which surround the great expectations make it possible to manipulate their meaning ambiguously. Pip thinks they come from Miss Havisham, but he is not certain, and this uncertainty allows him to interpret them as at once a willful choice on someone's part to change his place in society, or as a reward for faithful service, or as recognition that he has too noble a nature to be a blacksmith. Because of the mystery about the gift Pip can look upon his great expectations as at once earned and gratuitously bestowed. The more pleasant interpretation is the one which makes them the recognition by society of what his inmost nature has been all along. (pp. 263-64)

Pip's first visit to Miss Havisham's determines everything which follows in his life, because it determines the way he reacts to everything which happens to him thereafter: "That was a memorable day to me, for it made great changes in me. But it is the same with any life. Imagine one selected day struck out of it, and think how different its course would have been. Pause you who read this, and think for a moment of the long chain of iron or gold, of thorns or flowers, that would never have bound you, but for the formation of the first link on one memorable day." Pip is "bound" by his reaction to the experiences of this day, as firmly as he is bound apprentice to Joe, and as firmly as the captured Magwitch is bound by his fetters. On this day he makes the original choice of a desired self, and binds his destiny inextricably to Estella. Pip is able to understand this only much later, on the day when, aware that he has lost Estella, he first confesses his love for her: "You are part of my existence, part of myself. You have been in every line I have ever read, since I first came here, the rough common boy whose poor heart you wounded even then. . . ." Pip's desire to possess Estella, in spite of his recognition of her nature, is identified with his deepest project of selfhood. It is, he says, "the clue by which I am to be followed into my poor labyrinth," "the innermost life of my life." In choosing Estella, Pip alters and defines the entire world, and gives it a permanent structure pervaded by her presence. He is true to the determining choice of his life, the choice that was made when, "humiliated, hurt, spurned, offended, angry, sorry," he reacted to the taunts of Estella not by hating and rejecting her, but by accepting her judgment of him, and by spontaneously rejecting all the pieties of the forge. Before he went to Satis House the forge had been sacred. . . . Now all that is changed. The old gods have been rejected, and Pip is ashamed of home: "Within a single year all this was changed. Now, it was all coarse and common, and I would not have had Miss Havisham and Estella see it on any account." It is only in response to his acceptance of Estella's judgment of him that Pip's great expectations come into existence. It is only because Estella has become part of "every prospect" that Pip makes the otherwise unlikely mistake of assuming Miss Havisham is the source of his great expectations and intends Estella for him. Just as he has rejected as far as possible his relation to Magwitch—being "on secret terms of conspiracy with convicts" is to Pip a "guiltily coarse and common thing," "a feature in [his] low career that [he]

had previously forgotten"—so he interprets everything that happens to him in terms of Estella and Miss Havisham. He is not fooled; he fools himself: "All other swindlers upon earth are nothing to the self-swindlers, and with such pretences did I cheat myself."

Pip's love of Estella is by its very nature a self-deception, because it is a love which is based on its own impossibility. It depends in its intimate nature on the fact that it can never be satisfied. On the one hand, Pip says, ". . . I loved her against reason, against promise, against peace, against hope, against happiness, against all discouragement that could be," and, on the other hand, he can say, "Then, a burst of gratitude came upon me, that she should be destined for me, once the blacksmith's boy." From the beginning Estella is the judge who scornfully labels Pip "a common labouring-boy," who looks down on him from a great height like a cold star, and fixes everything eternally in its place, as everything seems eternally immobilized under the winter stars. To Pip, Estella seems always "immeasurably above [him]," and treats him "as insolently as if [he] were a dog in disgrace." But he does not wish to escape from this relationship to Estella, any more than he wishes to escape from his submission to society in those "wretched hankerings after money and gentility" which cannot be dissociated from "her presence." Rather, he imagines that when Estella is given to him as his wife he will succeed in possessing his judge. She is "destined" for him, and therefore he expects to bring down his star from the sky, to have in Estella at once judge and submissive wife.

Pip has succeeded through Estella, if not in escaping his initial state, then at least in defining himself as the lack of something particular. His essence is defined entirely by negations (he lacks the education, language, manners, and fine clothes of a gentleman; he fails to possess Estella—she is "inaccessible"), but even a definition in terms of what he is not is better than no definition at all. Pip in his relation to Estella achieves the only kind of definiteness, it may be, which is available to man: the definition of a desired future self. In spite of her infinite distance and inaccessibility, and in a way because of them, Estella is the source of all the meaning and coherence of Pip's life. To Pip it is a great relief to be judged. . . . Pip never hesitates a moment to accept Estella's judgment of him, even though it means accepting a much less admirable self than he is in the eyes of Biddy. To Biddy he is an honest blacksmith's apprentice faithful to his duty. But to accept Biddy's judgment rather than Estella's means accepting the role which has become identified for Pip with his initial state of isolation and subjection. On the other hand, Estella's judgment that he is coarse and common implies a very definite self which he fails to be, and which would transcend his first state if he could reach it. It is no wonder that he repudiates Herbert's suggestion that he give her up because she will never make him happy. To give up Estella would be to give up the very meaning of his life. Pip can abandon this relationship to Estella only when the entire structure of his world has been destroyed by the return of Magwitch.

But why did Dickens choose to have his hero enchanted by such a person as Miss Havisham? What is the relation between Pip and Miss Havisham? And why should Estella be identified with the desolation of Satis House? Satis House is an elaborate example of a figurative technique constantly employed by Dickens: the use of houses to symbolize states of soul. Again and again in Dickens' novels we find houses which are the mirror images of their masters or mistresses.

But Satis House expresses far more than merely Miss Havisham's nature. Miss Havisham and her house are the images of a fixed social order, the power which can judge Pip at first as coarse and common, and later as a gentleman. The name "Satis House," as Estella tells Pip, "meant, when it was given, that whoever had this house, could want nothing else." That Pip becomes fascinated by such a vision of the upper class and of its norms is all the stronger testimony to the falsity of his desire to be a gentleman. Miss Havisham's house of darkness, decay, and frozen time is a symbol of the upper class, paralyzed in its codified mores and prejudices, as much as it is a symbol of the spiritual condition of Miss Havisham. When Pip sees in "the stopped clock, . . . the withered articles of bridal dress upon the table and the ground, . . . in the falls of the cobwebs from the centre-piece, in the crawlings of the spiders on the cloth," "in everything the construction that [his] mind [has] come to, repeated and thrown back to [him]," he is confessing to the effect of his infatuation with the idea of being a gentleman as much as to the effect of his submission to Miss Havisham or to Estella as persons. Pip in London, living in the eternally unsatisfied pursuit of Estella and of the "pleasure" of London high society, is as much the victim of his desire to be a gentleman as he is of his love for Estella, or of his "enchantment" by Miss Havisham. Miss Havisham and her house, then, are the concrete symbols of that place in the upper class Pip has been led to want by Estella's judgment of him. They express his fatuity as no abstract analysis could do. Pip is willing to barter all the spontaneity and charity of his relations to Joe for the coldness, formality, and decay of Miss Havisham's house, and for the life as a gentleman he thinks she has given him.

But Pip finds that being a gentleman is no escape from uncertainty and guilt. One of the conditions of his great expectations is that he shall still go by the name of Pip, the name he gave himself in his early childhood. This is a symbol of the fact that he cannot make a full break with the past, and in a way hints of the terrible revelation which will shatter his expectations. But even when he has received his expectations, is living as a gentleman in London, and has not received the blow which will destroy his hopes, he is not at peace: "I cannot tell you how dependent and uncertain I feel, and how exposed to hundreds of chances"; "I lived in a state of chronic uneasiness respecting my behaviour to Joe"; ". . . a weariness on my spirits"; ". . . restlessness and disquiet of mind." This is partly, no doubt, because of Pip's uncertainty about Estella, but it is also part of the very condition of being a gentleman—as Dickens showed in his other portraits of idle and uneasy aristocrats (such as Eugene Wrayburn or Henry Gowan). These young gentlemen all suffer from ennui, and from an inability to choose a course of action. Paralysis of will seizes them precisely because they have unlimited possibilities. There are so many courses open to them that they are wholly unable to choose one. Far from realizing the peace of a reconciliation of freedom and security, Pip's transformation into a gentleman only plunges him into deeper disquietude and weariness of spirits—deeper because he is even further than ever away from the discovery of some externally imposed duty which will tell him what to do and who he is.

There comes a moment, then, when Pip discovers the futility and hollowness of his expectations. Already he has discovered that the mere unlimited possession of money is not "enough." When he is learning to be a gentleman in London with Herbert Pocket he gets further and further into debt, and his device of projecting the debt limit further and further by leaving a "margin" is an effective dramatization of the ever-receding character of his attempt to achieve peace and stability through money. Each time he runs into debt immediately "to the full extent of the margin, and sometimes, in the sense of freedom and solvency it impart[s], [gets] pretty far on into another margin." The more money Pip spends, the more he needs, and the goal of satisfaction recedes further and further, like the end of the rainbow. The actual possession of the tangible evidence of his great expectations leaves him what he has always been: "restless aspiring discontented me." Dickens is dramatizing here his recognition of the bankruptcy of the idea of the gentleman, who rules by inherited right, but owes protection and help to those beneath. Since society has ceased, in Dickens' view, to be an organic structure, being a gentleman means chiefly having the money to buy education and luxuries. It no more means being part of a community than does being sent to the hulks, like Magwitch, or being bound apprentice, like Pip. Pip the gentleman, spending money in London, enjoying the frivolities of his club, the Finches of the Grove, has no authentic relation to anybody. Instead of improving his condition, he has substituted for a dehumanizing relation to society no relation at all.

Moreover, Pip discovers when he at last openly admits his love for Estella that she cannot at the same time be both distant judge, and possessed and enjoyed as a wife. As transcendent judge she is not really human at all, but a superhuman goddess, and as a woman she could not play the role of judge. It is not until Pip learns that Estella is not "destined" for him that he really faces the fact that she has no heart, and cannot love him. Until then he has believed, in the *hubris* of his great expectations, that she would be able to combine the two incompatible roles. (pp. 264-70)

Finally, Pip discovers the emptiness of his hope of being given a justified place in the ruling class. He discovers that his real benefactor is not Miss Havisham, the representative of society, but the pariah Magwitch, "hunted dunghill dog." This discovery is really a discovery of the self-deception of his great expectations, his recognition that they were based on an irreconcilable contradiction. Pip has been climbing slowly toward Estella and toward the freedom and security of gentility. Now the ladder has collapsed, and he finds himself back at his origin again, back where he was at the opening of the story. Then he had received his "first most vivid and broad impression of the identity of things," including himself, on the day he stole food from his home to feed an escaped convict. Now he has discovered that the source of his "expectations" is not Miss Havisham, but that same convict. Moreover, he has discovered that Estella, the star of his expectations and the symbol of his desire for gentility, is really the daughter of Magwitch. All that he thought was taking him further and further from his shameful beginning has only been bringing him inexorably back to his starting point. He is like a man lost in the woods who struggles for hours to find his way out, only to discover suddenly that he has returned by a circuitous route to the exact spot where he first realized that he did not know where he was.

But Pip's return is to an origin which has been transformed into its opposite. Then the tie to Magwitch was repudiated as sinful, as the guilty secret of a crime against home, as a shameful bond to the dregs of society, and as the pain of moral isolation. Now that same tie is about to be revalued. As Pip starts down the Thames on the desperate attempt to save the life of the convict who has broken parole to return to him, "a veil [seems] to be drawn from the river, and millions of sparkles burst out upon its waters," and "[f]rom [Pip], too, a veil [seems] to be drawn." The mists that rose from the marshes as he started off for London have been dissipated at last, and Pip stands ready to face the truth which lies at the very center of **Great Expectations:** all the claims made by wealth, social rank, and culture to endow the individual with true selfhood are absolutely false. However far he apparently travels from his origin he will still be akin to the mud and briars of the marshes and to the terrible man he met there on the day he became aware of himself as Pip, the Pip who has named himself because there is no person and no institution that cares enough for him to give him a name. And, at the same time, Pip discovers that he himself has initiated the series of events which he believed were descending on him from the outside through a mysterious grace. He it was who committed the act of aggression against his family, stole for the convict, did not give him up to the soldiers, and formed the secret "taint of prison and crime" which has stuck to him all his life. He it is who is himself the source of all that has happened to him, all that he has believed was not his responsibility. The appearance of Magwitch to claim the "gentleman what he has made" reveals to the horrified Pip that he has not been free, that he has been secretly manipulated as though he were a passive tool, or puppet, or a mechanical man created for Magwitch's revenge on society. But it also reminds him that he has himself been guilty of the act of kindness, outside the bounds of all socially approved morality, which formed his tie to the convict. Moreover, he has also been Miss Havisham's "tool." She has not been secretly planning to bestow on him Estella and her jewels as a reward for his intrinsic nobility of character. No, she has rather been using him as something for Estella to practice her techniques of heart-breaking on. Pip's voyage, his attempt to sustain himself above all coercion and determination, and yet not to accept any responsibility for this, has ended in utter shipwreck. . . . (pp. 270-72)

Pip's life as a gentleman turns out to have combined the worst possible aspects of both sides of the human condition: its unjustifiable freedom, and its imprisonment in a given situation. On the one hand, Pip's life as a gentleman has been a fraud practiced on society. He has in effect pushed and elbowed his way into a place in the upper class—gratuitously and under false pretenses. He must experience the bad conscience of the social climber, the parvenu. Pip is thrown back, therefore, on his initial isolation. There is nothing outside himself that judges, approves, consecrates his existence. On the other hand, Pip discovers that his life as a gentleman has been unwittingly a return to the life of a manipulated object he had so hated when he was a child being brought up "by hand." He is returned to his alienation, and to his submission to what is imposed on him by force from the outside, and determines his actions, his place in the world, and even his nature. . . . He is, in fact, even more disinherited than he was at the beginning, for now he knows the full meaning of his state, and he is able to compare this realization that he is nothing except what he has made himself with the self-deceiving hope of the great expectations he has so recently lost. At "the end of the second stage of [his] expectations," Pip is at the deepest point of his wretchedness: ". . . it was not until I began to think," he says, "that I began fully to know how wrecked I was, and how the ship in which I had sailed was gone to pieces."

The third part of "Pip's Expectations" traces the slow rise of the hero's fortunes. He moves out of the depths of despair in which he finds himself at the end of the second part. Love is the cause of this reversal of fortune. For Dickens, as for the general tradition of ethical thought, love is the only successful escape from the unhappiness of singularity, the unhappiness of being this unique and isolated person, Pip.

For Dickens, as for generations of Christian moralists, love means sacrifice. Pip must abandon all the proud hopes which have formed the secret core of his life. He must abandon forever his project of being a gentleman, the belief that somewhere there is a place for him which he can possess by right. He must accept the fact that he can in no way transcend the gap between "the small bundle of shivers growing afraid of it all and beginning to cry" and the wind, sea, sky, and marshland, the alien universe—in no way, that is, but by willingly accepting this separation. And to accept this means to accept Magwitch, who springs up with "a terrible voice" from the marshes at the moment Pip becomes aware of his separateness.

Pip learns about love, then, not through Estella, but through the slow change in his relation to Magwitch. Only this change makes possible a transformation of his relation to Estella. Otherwise, Pip would have remained, even if he had possessed Estella, the submissive worshiper of a cold and distant authority. Just as Mrs. Joe atones for her cruelties to Pip and Joe by bowing down to Orlick, so Pip can escape from despair, from the total loss of his great expectations, only by a change in his attitude toward Magwitch. His acceptance of Magwitch is not only the relinquishment of his great expectations; it is also the replacement of these by a positive assertion that he, Pip alone, will be the source of the meaning of his own life, Pip finally accepts as the foundation of his life the guilt which has always haunted him: his secret and gratuitous act of charity to the escaped convict. Pip slowly realizes that if he betrays Magwitch . . . it will be to betray himself, to betray the possible foundation of himself by self-denial, by the abandonment of his egoistic expectations. (pp. 272-74)

[It] is only slowly that Pip realizes what his faithfulness means. It means facing the fact that he and Magwitch are in the same position of isolation. If they do not help one another, no one will. It means discovering that each can help the other by offering himself as the foundation of the other's selfhood, Pip by sacrificing all his hopes, Magwitch by his change from a fierce desire to "make" a gentleman for revenge, to the desire to help Pip be a gentleman for Pip's own sake: "For now my repugnance to him had all melted away, and in the hunted wounded shackled creature who held my hand in his, I only saw a man who had meant to be my benefactor, and who had felt affectionately, gratefully, and generously, towards me with great constancy through a series of years." Magwitch's handclasp, originally a symbolic appropriation of Pip as his creation and possession, now becomes the symbol of their mutual love, and of their willingness to sacrifice all for one another. This transformation is complete after the unsuccessful attempt to get Magwitch safely out of the country. Thereafter, Magwitch thinks only of Pip, and not at all of the "society" he had so hated, and Pip thinks only of Magwitch. (pp. 275-76)

Once Pip has established his new relationship to Magwitch he is able at last to win Estella. Pip's final love for Estella is a single complex relation which is both identification with the loved person (he is no longer conscious of a lack, a void of unfulfilled desire), and separation (he is still aware of himself as a self, as a separate identity; he does not melt into the loved person, and lose himself altogether). (p. 277)

Pip and Estella have experienced before their union their most complete separation, Pip in the agony of his discovery that Estella is not destined for him and that Magwitch is his real benefactor, and Estella in her unhappy marriage to Bentley Drummle, who has "used her with great cruelty," just as Pip has been "used" by Estella. These experiences have transformed them both. It is only when Estella has been tamed by the cruelty of her bad husband that she and Pip can enter into a wholly different relationship. Only when Estella's proud, cold glance is transformed into "the saddened softened light of the once proud eyes" can she and Pip transform the fettering of slave by master into the handclasp of love. Estella too must suffer the slave's loss of selfhood in order to be herself transformed. Both have come back from a kind of death to meet and join in the moonlight in Miss Havisham's ruined garden. The second ending is, in my opinion, the best. Not only was it, after all, the one Dickens published (would he really have acceded to Mrs. Grundy in the mask of Bulwer-Lytton without reasons of his own?), but, it seems to me, the second ending, in joining Pip and Estella, is much truer to the real direction of the story. The paragraphs which, in the second version of the ending, close the novel remind us, in their echo of Milton, that Estella and Pip are accepting their exile from the garden of false hopes. Now that the mists of infatuation have cleared away Pip and Estella are different persons. They go forth from the ruined garden into a fallen world. In this world their lives will be given meaning only by their own acts and by their dependence on one another. Pip now has all that he wanted, Estella and her jewels, but what he has is altogether different from what he expected. Rather than possessing the impossible reconciliation of freedom and security he had sought in Estella and in gentility, he now loves and is loved by another fallible and imperfect being like himself. . . . (pp. 277-78)

> *J. Hillis Miller, in his* Charles Dickens: The World of His Novels, *1958. Reprint by Indiana University Press, 1969, 346 p.*

## JULIAN MOYNAHAN   (essay date 1960)

[*In the following excerpt, Moynahan argues that Pip's feelings of guilt have a concrete psychological foundation in his ambitious desires and that Dickens intended his readers to view his narrator's shortcomings from a severer moral perspective than Pip himself.*]

Two recent essays on *Great Expectations* have stressed guilt as the dominant theme. They are Dorothy Van Ghent's 'On Great Expectations' and G. R. Stange's 'Dickens's Fable for his Time' [see excerpts dated 1953 and 1954]. . . . Pip has certainly one of the guiltiest consciences in literature. He not only suffers *agenbite of inwit* for his sin of snobbish ingratitude toward Joe and Biddy, but also suffers through much of the novel from what can only be called a conviction of criminal guilt. Whereas he expiates his sins of snobbery and ingratitude by ultimately accepting the convict Magwitch's unspoken claim for his protection and help, by willingly renouncing his great expectations, and by returning in a chastened mood to Joe and Biddy, he cannot expiate—or exorcise—his conviction of criminality, because it does not seem to correspond with any real criminal acts or intentions.

Snobbery is not a crime. Why should Pip feel like a criminal?

Perhaps the novel is saying that snobbery of the sort practiced by Pip in the second stage of his career is not very different from certain types of criminal behaviour. For instance, a severe moralist might point out that snobbery and murder are alike in that they are both offences against persons rather than property, and both involve the culpable wish to repudiate or deny the existence of other human beings. On this view, Pip reaches the height of moral insight at the start of the trip down the river, when he looks at Magwitch and sees in him only 'a much better man than I had been to Joe'. By changing places with the convict here, he apparently defines his neglectful behaviour toward Joe as criminal. Does this moment of vision objectify Pip's sense of criminality and prepare the way for expiation? (pp. 60-1)

Without question, Pip . . . interprets the frequent manifestations in his experience of criminal elements—the runaway prisoner on the marshes, the man with the two pound notes, the reappearance of the same man in chains on the coach going down into the marsh country, the reappearance of Magwitch's leg iron as the weapon which fells Mrs. Joe, the accident making the criminal lawyer Jaggers, whose office is beside Newgate prison, the financial agent of his unknown patron—as signs that indicate some deep affinity between him and a world of criminal violence. But a question that the reader must face here and elsewhere in the novel is whether to accept Pip's interpretation. If we conclude that Pip is in fact tainted with criminality, we must rest our conclusion on a kind of symbolic reading of the coincidences of the plot. Through these coincidences and recurrences, which violate all ordinary notions of probability, Dickens, so this argument must go, weaves together a net in whose meshes his hero is entrapped. Regardless of the fact that Pip's association with crimes and criminals is purely adventitious and that he evidently bears no responsibility for any act or intention of criminal violence, he must be condemned on the principle of guilt by association. (p. 62)

Both Mr. Stange and Miss Van Ghent present readings of the guilt theme which are an attempt to validate this principle. Mr. Stange decides that 'the last stage of Pip's progression is reached when he learns to love the criminal and to accept his own implication in the common guilt'. He believes that one of Dickens's major points is that 'criminality is the condition of life'. Pip, therefore, feels criminal guilt because he is criminal as we are all criminal. Along similar lines, Miss Van Ghent remarks, 'Pip . . . carries the convict inside him, as the negative potential of his 'great expectations'—Magwitch is the concretion of his potential guilt.' The appearance of Magwitch at Pip's apartment in the Temple is 'from a metaphysical point of view . . . that of Pip's own unwrought deeds'. Finally, she maintains that Pip bows down before Magwitch, who has been guilty towards him, instead of bowing down before Joe, toward whom Pip has been guilty. In so doing Pip reveals by a symbolic act that he takes the guilt of the world on his shoulders. . . . This is shown particularly by the fact that Pip assumes culpability in a relationship where he is, in fact, the innocent party. (pp. 62-3)

Miss Van Ghent's and Mr. Stange's efforts to demonstrate Pip's metaphysical involvement in the criminal milieu of *Great Expectations* are dictated, rightly enough, by their concern for the unifying and inclusive significance of the guilt theme. Their readings provide a means of bridging the gulf between Pip's social sins and the more drastic phenomena of criminality presented in the novel—attempts to moralise the melodrama, as it were, attempts to make the complete narrative presentation revolve around the crucial question of Pip's moral nature. Sensitive readers of the novel will sympathise with this effort, but I do not believe they will agree that the gulf *is* bridged by making criminal guilt a universal condition and by insisting that this is what Pip comes to understand by the time his story is told.

In my opinion, Pip's relation to the criminal milieu of ***Great Expectations*** is not that of an Everyman to a universal condition. It is rather a more concrete and particularised relation than the metaphysical approach would indicate, although the novel defines that relation obliquely and associatively, not through discursive analysis. Miss Van Ghent has suggested a metaphoric connection between Magwitch and Pip. Her proposal of such implicit relations between character and character, even though they do not become rationalised anywhere, is an illuminating insight into the artistic method of the mature Dickens. But her principle can be applied differently and yield rather different results.

I would suggest that Orlick rather than Magwitch is the figure from the criminal milieu of the novel whose relations to him come to define Pip's implicit participation in the acts of violence with which the novel abounds. Considered by himself, Orlick is a figure of melodrama. He is unmotivated, his origins are shrouded in mystery, his violence is unqualified by regret. In this last respect he is the exact opposite of Pip, who is, of course, filled with regret whenever he remembers how he has neglected his old friends at the forge.

On the other hand, if we consider Orlick in his connections with Pip, some rather different observations can be made. In the first place, there is a peculiar parallel between the careers of the two characters. We first encounter Orlick as he works side by side with Pip at the forge. Circumstances also cause them to be associated in the assault on Mrs. Joe. Orlick strikes the blow, but Pip feels, with some justification, that he supplied the assault weapon. Pip begins to develop his sense of alienation from the village after he has been employed by Miss Havisham to entertain her in her house, but Orlick too turns up later on working for Miss Havisham as gatekeeper. Finally, after Pip has become a partisan of the convict, it turns out that Orlick also has become a partisan of an ex-convict, Compeyson, who is Magwitch's bitter enemy.

Up to a point, Orlick seems not only to dog Pip's footsteps, but also to present a parody of Pip's upward progress through the novel, as though he were in competitive pursuit of some obscene great expectations of his own. Just as Pip centres his hopes successively on the forge, Satis House, and London, so Orlick moves his base of operations successively from the forge, to Satis House, and to London. From Pip's point of view, Orlick has no right to interest himself in any of the people with whom Pip has developed close ties. For instance, he is appalled when he discovers that his tender feeling for Biddy is given a distorted echo by Orlick's obviously lecherous interest in the same girl. And when he discovers that Orlick has the right of entry into Satis House he warns Jaggers to advise Miss Havisham to get rid of him. But somehow he cannot keep Orlick out of his affairs. When Magwitch appears at Pip's London lodging half-way through the novel, Orlick is crouching in darkness on the landing below Pip's apartment. And when Pip is about to launch the escape attempt down the Thames, his plans are frustrated by the trick which brings him down to the marshes to face Orlick in the hut by the limekiln. Its lurid melodrama and the awkwardness of its integration with the surrounding narrative has made many readers dismiss this scene as a piece of popular writing aimed at the less intelligent members of Dickens's audience. But the confrontation of Orlick and Pip on the marshes is crucial for an understanding of the problem I am discussing, because it is the scene in which Dickens comes closest to making explicit the analogy between the hero and the novel's principal villain and criminal.

Orlick inveigles Pip to the limepit not only to kill him but to overwhelm him with accusations. Addressing Pip over and over again as 'Wolf', an epithet he might more readily apply to himself, he complains that Pip has cost him his place, come between him and a young woman in whom he was interested, tried to drive him out of the country, and been a perpetual obstacle in the path of his own uncouth ambitions. But the charge he makes with the greatest force and conviction is that Pip bears the final responsibility for the assault on Mrs. Joe:

> 'I tell you it was your doing—I tell you it was done through you,' he retorted, catching up the gun and making a blow with the stock at the vacant air between us. 'I come upon her from behind, as I come upon you to-night. I giv' it to her! I left her for dead, and if there had been a limekiln as nigh her as there is now nigh you, she shouldn't have come to life again. But it warn't old Orlick as did it; it was you. You was favoured, and he was bullied and beat. Old Orlick bullied and beat, eh? Now you pays for it. You done it; now you pays for it.'

The entire scene was a nightmare quality. This is at least partly due to the weird reversal of rôles, by which the innocent figure is made the accused and the guilty one the accuser. As in a dream the situation is absurd, yet like a dream it may contain hidden truth. On the one hand Orlick, in interpreting Pip's character, seems only to succeed in describing himself—ambitious, treacherous, murderous, and without compunction. On the other hand, several of Orlick's charges are justified, and it is only in the assumption that Pip's motives are as black as his own that he goes wrong. We know, after all, that Pip is ambitious, and that he has repudiated his early associates as obstacles to the fulfilment of his genteel aspirations. Another interesting observation can be made about Orlick's charge that it was you as did for your shrew sister'. Here Orlick presents Pip as the responsible agent, himself merely as the weapon. But this is an exact reversal of Pip's former assumptions about the affair. All in all, Orlick confronts the hero in this scene, not merely as would-be murderer, but also as a distorted and darkened mirror-image. In fact, he presents himself as a monstrous caricature of the tenderminded hero, insisting that they are two of a kind with the same ends, pursued through similarly predatory and criminal means. This is what his wild accusations come down to.

Is Orlick mistaken in representing himself in this scene as a sort of double, *alter ego,* or shadow of Pip? Is he merely projecting his own qualities upon him, or do Orlick's accusations, in any sense, constitute a partially or wholly valid comment on Pip's actions? In order to answer these questions we shall have to begin by analysing the fantasy of great expectations which gives the book so much of its universal appeal. This fantasy, so the psychologists tell us, is a well-nigh universal imaginative flight of childhood. By creating for himself a fiction wherein the world is made to conform to his desire and will, the child succeeds in compensating himself for the fact that his real position is without power and that the quantity of love and nurture to which he believes himself entitled is greatly in excess of the amount he actually receives. Out of this unbalance between an unbounded demand and a limited supply of love and power proceed the fairy godmothers as well as the vicious step-parents and bad giants in which world legend abounds. The fantasy element *Great Expectations* shares with such stories as *Cinderella* and *Jack and the Beanstalk* contains, then, two implicit motives: the drive for power and the drive for more mother-love. However, of the two, the power motive, since it involves the aggressive wish to push beyond the authoritarian figures who hold the child powerless, is apt to be more productive of guilt and, consequently, is likely to be expressed with a certain amount of concealment. (pp. 64-7)

In *Great Expectations,* the second motive is clearly represented in the early stages of Pip's career. His early experiences follow the fairy-tale pattern. Circumstances magically conspire to rescue him from the spartan rigours of Mrs. Joe. In taking him up, Miss Havisham plays the rôle of fairy godmother, and later permits him to continue in his belief that she is also the sponsor of his luxury in London—until he is brought up short by the rough figure of Magwitch. Until the real world breaks in on him, Pip allows himself to be pushed along, never challenging the requirement that he must not look too closely into the sources of his good fortune. Likewise, he is passive in his longing for Estella, who, in her metaphoric associations with precious jewels and lofty stars, comes to symbolise to him the final goal of his dreams of love, luxury, and high position. Instead of trying to capture her through an aggressive courtship he simply pines, assuming on very little evidence that one day she will be bestowed upon him by Miss Havisham as everything else has been.

Upon the return of Magwitch, Pip is forced to wake up and recognise that life is not, after all, a fairy tale. He learns that his own wealth comes from a criminal, that even the magical figures of Satis House, Miss Havisham and Estella have criminal connections, and, as we have seen, that his callous treatment of Joe Gargery was essentially criminal. This linking up of the criminal milieu and the milieu of wealth and high position is a way of drawing the strongest possible contrast between Pip's regressive fantasy-world, where wealth and good luck have seemed unremitting and uncompromised, and a real world where the dominant moral colouring is at best a dirty grey.

In terms of what we have called the love-motive, then, Dickens has shown fantasy in collision with reality. Pip learns that the world is not a vast mammary gland from which he can draw rich nourishment with moral impunity. He finds that he must hunger and struggle like all the rest. Furthermore, he must accept the unhappy fact that his participation in the old dream of great expectations has hurt real people. With his awakening to reality he develops a capacity for active, self-bestowing love. But the mature tough-minded perspective from which the hero's development is viewed does not permit him to move on into happiness and fulfilment. In the final chapters of *Great Expectations* Pip wants to give himself, but there is no longer anyone in a position to accept his gift. Magwitch's fate is upon him; the circumstance of marriage has carried both Biddy and Estella beyond his reach. In bestowing himself upon the family of Herbert Pocket, Pip comes to rest in a kind of limbo. The book seems to imply that Pip is doomed to a lifetime of vicarious experience, because he lingered too long in his condition of alienation from the real.

This is not a complete account of Dickens's critique of the great expectations fantasy, that dream of huge and easy success which has always haunted the imagination of children and also haunted the imaginations of adults in the increasingly commercial and industrial society of nineteenth-century England. In *Great Expectations,* as in its legendary prototypes, the theme of ambition is treated under the two aspects of desire and will, the search for a superabundance of love and the drive for power. And it is in his presentation of the theme in the latter aspect that Dickens makes the more profound analysis of the immoral and criminal elements in his hero's (and the century's) favourite dream.

But Pip's ambition is passive. He only becomes active and aggressive after he has ceased to be ambitious. How then does *Great Expectations* treat the theme of ambition in terms that are relevant to the total action of which Pip is the centre? I have already begun to suggest an answer to the question. Ambition as the instinct of aggression, as the pitiless drive for power directed against what we have called authority-figures is both coalesced and disguised in the figure of Orlick. And Orlick is bound to be the hero by ties of analogy as double, *alter ego* and dark mirror-image. We are dealing here with an art which simultaneously disguises and reveals its deepest implications of meaning, with a method which apparently dissociates its thematic materials and its subject matter into moral fable-*cum*-melodramatic accompaniment, yet simultaneously presents through patterns of analogy a dramatic perspective in which the apparent opposites are unified. In *Great Expectations* criminality is displaced from the hero on to a melodramatic villain. But on closer inspection that villain becomes part of a complex unity—we might call it Pip-Orlick—in which all aspects of the problem of guilt become interpenetrant and co-operative. The only clue to this unity which is given at the surface level of the narrative is Pip's obsession of criminal guilt. Pip tells us over and over again that he feels contaminated by crime. But we do not find the objective correlative of that conviction until we recognise in the insensate and compunctionless Orlick a shadow image of the tender-minded and yet monstrously ambitious young hero. (pp. 68-70)

The meaning remains submerged and is communicated to the reader through other channels than the agonised confession of a first-person narrator. Indeed, the profoundest irony of the novel is not reached until the reader realises he must see Pip in a much harsher moral perspective than Pip ever saw himself.

Recognition that Pip's ambition is definable under the aspect of aggression as well as in terms of the regressive desire for passive enjoyment of life's bounty depends upon the reader's willingness to work his way into the narrative from a different angle than the narrator's. The evidence for the hero's power-drive against the authority-figures, the evidence of his 'viciousness' if you will, is embodied in the story in a number of ways, but a clear pattern of meaning only emerges after the reader has correlated materials which are dispersed and nominally unrelated in the story *as told*. Orlick, thus far, has been the figure whose implicit relations to the hero have constituted the chief clue to the darker meaning of Pip's career. He continues to be important in any attempt to set forth the complete case, but there are also some significant correlations to be made in which he does not figure. (pp. 70-1)

We might begin with the apparently cynical remark that Pip, judged on the basis of what happens to many of the characters closely associated with him, is a very dangerous young man. He is not accident-prone, but a great number of people who move into his orbit decidedly are. Mrs. Joe is bludgeoned, Miss Havisham goes up in flames, Estella is exposed through her rash marriage to vaguely specified tortures at the hands of her brutal husband, Drummle. Pumblechook has his house looted and his mouth stuffed with flowering annuals by a gang of thieves led by Orlick. All of these characters, with the exception of Estella, stand at one time or another in the relation of patron, patroness, or authority-figure to Pip the boy or Pip the man. (Pumblechook is, of course, a parody patron, and his comic chastisement is one of the most satisfying things in the book.) Furthermore, all of these characters, including Estella, have hurt, humiliated, or thwarted Pip in some important way. All in some way have stood between him and the attainment of the full measure of his desires. All are punished.

Let us group these individual instances. Mrs. Joe, the cruel foster-mother, and Pumblechook, her approving and hypocritical relation by marriage, receive their punishment from the hands of Orlick. Mrs. Joe hurts Pip and is hurt in turn by Orlick. Pip has the motive of revenge—a lifetime of brutal beatings and scrubbings inflicted by his sister—but Orlick, a journeyman who does not even lodge with the Gargerys, bludgeons Mrs. Joe after she has provoked a quarrel between him and his master. If we put together his relative lack of motive with his previously quoted remarks at the limekiln and add to these Pip's report of his own extraordinary reaction upon first hearing of the attack—

> With my head full of George Barnwell, I was at first disposed to believe that *I* must have had some hand in the attack upon my sister, or at all events that as her near relation, popularly known to be under obligations to her, I was a more legitimate object of suspicion than anyone else—

we arrive at an anomalous situation which can best be resolved on the assumption that Orlick acts merely as Pip's punitive instrument or weapon.

With regard to Pumblechook's chastisement, the most striking feature is not that Orlick should break into a house, but that he should break into Pumblechook's house. Why not Trabb's? One answer might be that Trabb has never stood in Pip's light. Pumblechook's punishment is nicely proportioned to his nuisance value for Pip. Since he has never succeeded in doing him any great harm with his petty slanders, he escapes with a relatively light wound. Although we are told near the end of the novel that Orlick was caught and jailed after the burglary, we are never told that Pip reported Orlick's murderous assault on him or his confessions of his assault on Mrs. Joe to the police. Despite the fact that there is enough accumulated evidence to hang him, Orlick's end is missing from the book. Actually, it seems that Orlick simply evaporates into thin air after his punitive rôle has been performed. His case needs no final disposition because he has only existed, essentially, as an aspect of the hero's own far more problematic case.

Estella receives her chastisement at the hands of Bentley Drummle. How does this fit into the pattern we have been exploring? In the first place, it can be shown that Drummle stands in precisely the same analogical relationship to Pip as Orlick does. Drummle is a reduplication of Orlick at a point higher on the social-economic scale up which Pip moves with such rapidity through the first three-quarters of the novel.

Drummle, like Orlick, is a criminal psychopath. At Jaggers's dinner party the host, a connoisseur of criminal types, treats Drummle as 'one of the true sort', and Drummle demonstrates how deserving he is of this distinction when he tries to brain the harmless Startop with a heavy tumbler.

But the most impressive evidence that Orlick and Drummle are functional equivalents is supplied by the concrete particulars of their description. To an extraordinary degree, these two physically powerful, inarticulate, and dark-complexioned villains are presented to the reader in terms more often identical than similar. Orlick, again and again, is one who lurks and lounges, Drummle is one who lolls and lurks. When Pip, Startop, and Drummle go out rowing, the last 'would always creep in-shore like some uncomfortable amphibious creature, even when the tide would have sent him fast on his way; and I always think of him as coming after us in the dark or by the back-water, when our own two boats were breaking the sunset or the moonlight in mid-stream'. . . . The other creeper, follower and amphibian of *Great Expectations* is Orlick, whose natural habitat is the salt marsh, who creeps his way to the dark landing below Pip's apartment to witness the return of Magwitch from abroad, who creeps behind Biddy and Pip as they walk conversing on the marshes and overhears Pip say he will do anything to drive Orlick from the neighbourhood, who appears out of the darkness near the turnpike house on the night Pip returns from Pumblechook's to discover that his sister has been assaulted, and who, finally, creeps his way so far into Pip's private business that he ends by acting as agent for Compeyson, Magwitch's—and Pip's—shadowy antagonist.

Like Orlick, Drummle is removed from the action suddenly; Pip is given no opportunity to settle old and bitter scores with him. In the last chapter we hear that he is dead 'from an accident consequent on ill-treating a horse'. This is the appropriate end for a sadist whose crimes obviously included wife-beating. But more important to the present argument is our recognition that Drummle has been employed to break a woman who had, in the trite phrase, broken Pip's heart. Once he has performed his function as Pip's vengeful surrogate he can be assigned to the fate he so richly deserves.

Mrs. Joe beats and scrubs Pip until she is struck down by heavy blows on the head and spine. Pumblechook speaks his lies about him until his mouth is stuffed with flowers. Estella treats his affections with cold contempt until her icy pride is broken by a brutal husband. In this series Orlick and Drummle behave far more like instruments of vengeance than like three-dimensional characters with understandable grudges of their own. In terms of my complete argument, they enact an aggressive potential that the novel defines, through patterns of analogy and linked resemblances, as belonging in the end to Pip and to his unconscionably ambitious hopes.

When Miss Havisham bursts into flames, there is no Orlick or Drummle in the vicinity to be accused of having set a match to her. In the long series of violence which runs through *Great Expectations* from the beginning to end, this is one climax of violence that can be construed as nothing more than accidental. And yet it is an accident which Pip, on two occasions, has foreseen. Before Miss Havisham burns under the eye of the horror-struck hero, she has already come to a violent end twice in his hallucinated fantasies—in Pip's visionary experiences in the abandoned brewery, where he sees Miss Havisham hanging by the neck from a beam. He has this vision once as a child, on the occasion of his first visit to Satis House, and once as an adult, on the occasion on his last visit, just a few minutes before Miss Havisham's accident occurs. What are we to make, if anything, of these peculiar hallucinatory presentiments and of the coincidence by which they come true?

The child first sees his patroness hanging from a beam after his first hour of service with her. At this point the novel dwells at length on his keen awareness that he has been cruelly treated, generalises on the extreme sensitiveness of children to injustice, and describes how Pip in utter frustration vents his injured feelings by kicking a wall and twisting his own hair. In these passages it seems to me that the reader is being prepared to interpret Pip's immediately ensuing hallucination as the child's further attempt to discharge his anger and grief against his adult tormenter. In fantasy Pip punishes a woman whom in fact he cannot disturb in any way, and, by hanging her, attempts to destroy the threat to his peace and security which she represents. This interpretation excludes the possibility of a supernatural element in the experience; the novel provides abundant evidence that the imagination of a child operating under a great stress of emotion is possessed of a hallucinatory power. When Pip carries stolen provisions to Magwitch on the marshes, his guilt-ridden imagination effects a transformation of the countryside through which he passes, until even gates, dykes, banks, cattle and a signpost seem to him to be pursuing him and crying out his guilt. Pip's hallucination, then, is an imaginative fantasy which both projects and disguises the boy's desire to punish his employer and to destroy her baleful power over him.

Pip experiences no recurrence of the hallucination during the long years of an association with Miss Havisham based on his mistaken assumption that she is the sole author of his good fortunes. The fantasy returns only after his eyes have been opened to the fact that nothing has come to him from Miss Havisham except unhappiness. On that last visit to Satis House he learns definitely of Estella's marriage. With this information the last link between him and his former employer snaps. The false fairy godmother kneels to ask forgiveness for her crimes against him, and the duped hero offers forgiveness sincerely, if sadly. Nevertheless, as Pip strolls through the ruins of the estate he is not able to refrain from brooding over Miss Havisham's 'profound unfitness for this earth', and when he walks into the chilly, twilit brewery building he is not able to prevent the return of the old hallucination of Miss Havisham hanging from the beam. We are told that this was owing to the revival of a childish association. But surely the episode represents more than a curious psychological detail. It is profoundly right that the fantasy should return at a time when he can see in complete clarity and detail how his connection with Miss Havisham has hurt him. It is profoundly right that he should forgive the false patroness and yet not forgive her, behave generously toward her and yet feel deeply that she has no right to live, treat her with some degree of melancholy affection, yet hate her also in the depths of his being. (pp. 71-6)

Pip's ambivalence is embodied dramatically. It must be known not as it is talked about, but as enacted. A man forgives a woman, then hallucinates her death by hanging. A man watches a woman burst into flames, then leaps bravely to her rescue, but in the course of describing this rescue is forced to remark, 'We were on the ground struggling like desperate enemies.'

How do these hallucinations, the second followed immediately by Miss Havisham's fatal accident, add to the burden of the hero's guilt? The answer is obvious. Because Pip's destructive fantasy comes true in reality, he experiences the equivalent of a murderer's guilt. As though he had the evil eye, or as though there were more than a psychological truth in the old cliché, 'if looks could kill', Pip moves from the brewery, where he has seen Miss Havisham hanging, to the door of her room, where he gives her one long, last look—until she is consumed by fire. But here the psychological truth suffices to establish imaginative proof that Pip can no more escape untainted from his relationship to the former patroness than he can escape untainted from any of his relationships to characters who have held and used the power to destroy or hamper his ambitious struggles. In all these relationships the hero becomes implicated in violence. With Estella, Pumblechook, and Mrs. Joe, the aggressive drive is enacted by surrogates linked to the hero himself by ties of analogy. With Miss Havisham the surrogate is missing. Miss Havisham falls victim to the purely accidental. But the 'impurity' of Pip's motivation, as it is revealed through the device of the recurrent hallucination, suggests an analogy between that part of Pip which wants Miss Havisham at least punished, at most removed from this earth for which she is so profoundly unfit, and the destroying fire itself.

In this essay I have argued that Dickens's novel defines its hero's dream of great expectations and the consequences stemming from indulgence in that dream under the two aspects of desire and will, of regressive longing for an excess of love and of violent aggressiveness. In the unfolding of the action these two dramas are not presented separately. Instead they are combined into Dickens's most complex representation of character in action. Pip is Dickens's most complicated hero, demonstrating at once the traits of criminal and gull, of victimiser and victim. He is victimised by his dream and the dream itself, by virtue of its profoundly anti-social and unethical nature, forces him into relation with a world in which other human beings fall victim to his drive for power. He is, in short, a hero sinned against and sinning: sinned against because in the first place the dream was thrust upon the helpless child by powerful and corrupt figures from the adult world; a sinner because in accepting for himself a goal in life based upon unbridled individualism and indifference to others he takes up a career which *Great Expectations* repeatedly, through a variety of artistic means, portrays as essentially criminal.

After Magwitch's death, Pip falls a prey to brain fever. During his weeks of delirium it seems to me that his hallucinations articulate the division in his character between helpless passivity and demonic aggressiveness. Pip tells us he dreamed

> that I was a brick in the house wall, and yet entreating to be released from the giddy place where the builders had set me; that I was a steel beam of a vast engine clashing and whirling over a great gulf, yet that I implored in my own person to have the engine stopped, and my part in it hammered off.

It is tempting to read these images as dream logic. The hero-victim cries for release from his unsought position of height and power, but cannot help himself from functioning as a moving part of a monstrous apparatus which seems to sustain itself from a plunge into the abyss only through the continuous expenditure of destructive force. In the narrative's full context this vast engine can be taken to represent at one and the same time the demonic side of the hero's career and a society that maintains its power intact by the continuous destruction of the hopes and lives of its weaker members. In the latter connection we can think of Magwitch's account of his childhood and youth, and of the judge who passed a death sentence on thirty-two men and women, while the sun struck in through the courtroom windows making a 'broad shaft of light between the two-and-thirty and the judge, linking them both together'. But to think of the engine as a symbol of society is still to think of Pip. For Pip's career enacts his society's condition of being—its guilt, its sinfulness, and in the end, its helplessness to cleanse itself of a taint 'of prison and crime'.

When Pip wakes up from his delirium he finds himself a child again, safe in the arms of the angelic Joe Gargery. But the guilt of great expectations remains inexpiable, and the cruelly beautiful original ending of the novel remains the only possible 'true' ending. Estella and Pip face each other across the insurmountable barrier of lost innocence. The novel dramatises the loss of innocence, and does not glibly present the hope of a redemptory second birth for either its guilty hero or the guilty society which shaped him. I have already said that Pip's fantasy of superabundant love brings him at last to a point of alienation from the real world. And similarly Pip's fantasy of power brings him finally to a point where withdrawal is the only positive moral response left to him.

The brick is taken down from its giddy place, a part of the engine is hammered off. Pip cannot redeem his world. In no conceivable sense a leader, he can only lead himself into a sort of exile from his society's power centres. Living abroad as the partner of a small, unambitious firm, he is to devote his remaining life to doing the least possible harm to the smallest number of people, so earning a visitor's privileges in the lost paradise where Biddy and Joe, the genuine innocents of the novel, flourish in thoughtless content. (pp. 76-9)

> *Julian Moynahan, "The Hero's Guilt: The Case of 'Great Expectations',"* in Essays in Criticism, Vol. *X, No. 1, January, 1960, pp. 60-79.*

## A. O. J. COCKSHUT   (essay date 1961)

[*Cockshut is an English critic who specializes in the study of Victorian thought and literature. Here, he discusses the themes of parasitism, alienation, and reverence of wealth in* Great Expectations, *arguing that the novel's ambiguity frustrates all attempts to reach a conclusive interpretation of Dickens's moral purpose.*]

**Great Expectations** suffers a little from over-correction of the characteristic failings of the early Dickens. He was determined to create a coherent unity at last; and perhaps a bit concerned also to prove to his critics that he could do so. It was natural for him to conceive unity partly in terms of harmonising images, and partly in terms of a neat plot. In the first he succeeded; the marshes, the hulks, the wedding-cake and many other images coalesce into an impression of decay and deceit and uncertainty, as subtle and satisfying as any the English novel can show. But a neat plot, in the hands of Dickens, even a mature Dickens, will never be quite free from melodrama. So we have a curious contrast at times between the book's tone, reminiscent, psychologically inquiring, morally penetrating, and some of its events which seem to belong to the world of the thriller. The whole conception of Orlick, for instance, seems out of keeping, and particularly the scene in which he lures Pip into an obvious trap, and allows a rescue, as so many murderers have done in detective stories

since, by his endless explanations. [The critic adds in a footnote that a "valuable article by Julian Moynahan (see excerpt dated 1960) suggests that there is a transference of Pip's guilt on to Orlick, and that his function in the novel is psychologically important. Mr. Moynahan makes out a good case, but if it is accepted it would not invalidate the point made in the text."]

Similarly, the fact that Pip's wealth comes from the convict, and its consequent connection with crime and brutality, is too obviously stressed in Chapter 32, when Wemmick takes Pip to see the prison, and the criminals among whom Jaggers works, and: "I consumed the whole time in thinking how strange it was that I should be encompassed by all this taint of prison and crime; that in my childhood out on our lonely marshes I should have first encountered it; that it should have reappeared on two occasions, starting out like a stain that was faded but not gone. . . ." The trouble here, of course, is the familiar one of the point of view. The narrator, who at this time has no idea that the convict will return and reveal himself as the founder of Pip's fortunes, cannot credibly be made to think all that the author wants said.

The unlikely bones of the story show through too, when Estella turns out exactly as Miss Havisham intended, and then blames her patron for her own lack of feeling. Estella speaks here rather in the style of a lawyer putting a case against Miss Havisham. But it is scarcely credible that she should bitterly lament the absence of feelings she has never had. In any case, would not this gloomy and solitary upbringing rather tend to encourage dreaming, a willingness to love, and even romantic illusions?

But there is another and more important sense in which the book represents a conscious correction of the author's past. Edgar Johnson says that **Great Expectations** is Dickens's penance for subservience to false values [see excerpt dated 1952]; and though the question may be more complicated than he allows, there is clearly a good deal of truth in this. When we recall Dickens's earlier assaults on rank and wealth, we are struck both by the subtlety and by the ambiguity of the satirical light cast upon them here. It is remarkable that no one in **Great Expectations** is free from the taint of servility towards rank and wealth. . . . [Everybody], including the kindhearted Herbert sees wealth through a romantic haze; even honest Joe's humble acceptance of Pip's sudden rise contains an unhealthy element of confusion between worth and fortune: "Which," he says, "you have that growed and that swelled, and that gentle-folked, as, to be sure, you are a honour to your king and country." At the same time, Magwitch, in his reckless generosity, curiously combines the almost accidental possession of great wealth with a servile admiration of the "gentlemanly" qualities he imagines it can bring to others.

All this suggests that we have here something a little different from a penance. For this protean admiration of wealth does not appear as an error to be repudiated, but as a universal and unexplained blight affecting good and bad men in different ways. The technique of story-telling, too, is better suited to the posing of ambiguous moral problems than to providing clear solutions to them. Pip tells his own story, and combines and at times confuses in a single narrative what he felt at the time, what he ought to have felt, and what later reflection made him feel. It is as if the author wished a little ambiguity to remain.

Why should this be? In part it fits well enough into the pattern of the author's mature development. He had become more aware of the mixture of human motives, of the unexpectedness of consequences. But Dickens was still capable of wielding sharp satirical blades; we look for another explanation of the faintness of moral condemnation, and we notice that Pip is almost alone among Dickens's characters in showing how things may appear in the eyes of the rich. Pip is, for instance, worried and bullied by his servant. He is irritable, bored and neurotic. His discontent excites sympathy even when he is being most contemptuous of others. There may be many reasons for this, but one is so very obvious that we may be inclined to overlook it altogether. Dickens was, after all, a very rich man in 1860, and he had no intention of ever being anything else. What may be called the mythical side of the story—the side that suggests by means of Magwitch that the wealth of society comes from tainted sources—is beautifully lucid. The past in which Pip's changing motives are weighed and judged is subtle and fascinating, but also elusive and ultimately inconclusive. In the person of Pip, Dickens was indeed striking at himself, as Edgar Johnson says, but he took good care not to strike too hard. He provided Pip (and himself) with many excuses, and allowed him to shelter behind the amiable failings of such fine fellows as Herbert and Joe Gargery.

In view of the deadly seriousness of the theme, it is hard not to feel, that at times things are a bit too jolly. Wemmick's castle and aged parent, schematically, seem to represent the divorce between business and private life, the tendency of the cash nexus to drive anyone possessing strong human sympathies into a futile longing for an imaginary past. There is a mournful, even tragic, pre-Raphaelite latent in the conception of Wemmick's character. But this interesting figure is never released. Wemmick's story is actually treated more in the style of *Nicholas Nickleby.* The innocent arm creeping round the waist of his beloved, his "Here's a church, let's get married" are amusing, but they really belong to a phase of Dickens's development that he could no longer recapture with full conviction. They belong to a past period when the laws of time and space and the limitations of human nature seemed like putty in the hands of a young genius of abounding energy and huge popularity.

But the main symbolical framework, which came into being at a deeper level of the mind than Wemmick's castle, is splendidly pervasive and never too obtrusive. The two leading

*Dickens's home, Gad's Hill Place, where he wrote* Great Expectations.

ideas would seem to be parasitism and rejection from society. Living on unearned income is, of course, seen as parasitism; and it is reflected in a series of controlled echoes and parallels. Miss Havisham, after her disappointment, has developed into a kind of emotional *voyeur,* feeding upon the passions and illusions of the young, because they alone can persuade her that she is still capable of feeling—in its negative forms of revenge, deceit and frustration. Her enjoyment of Pip's mistake about the source of his money is essentially parasitic. She is not even capable now of active deceit. Pumblechook and the local tailor, bowing down before Pip's new greatness are going through the motions of a parasitism that cannot even feed. For Pip is himself a parasite, and will, in any case, give them nothing. Pip's social success is likewise unreal; he does not even achieve full acceptance as one of the "Finches of the Grove." And the Finches themselves are only copying without purpose the external formulas of Parliamentary procedure. Into this pattern details fit with beautiful naturalness. A very minor character, Jack at the Ship, has his interest in the recovery of Compeyson's body from the river "much heightened when he heard it had stockings on. Probably it took about a dozen drowned men to fit him out completely; and that may have been the reason why the different articles of his dress are in various stages of decay." Decay— parasitism and decay inevitably go together, and decay is at the centre of the symbolic structure, corresponding to the parasitic moral situation just outlined. Rot is by nature slow, pervasive and undramatic. It needs to be presented in many different guises to take full imaginative effect. The marsh, the rotting hulks, the Thames waterside, the wedding cake— none of them seems otiose or repetitive.

To carry the idea of exclusion from society there are two contrasted figures, Magwitch and Miss Havisham. One is the apparent and the other the real source of Pip's fortune; one is the guardian and the other the real father of the girl he loves. One is, in Pip's eyes, a delicate, awe-inspiring high-class female, the other is a despised ruffian, who admires Pip and is despised by him. But these contrasts serve also to draw our attention to deep similarities. Each lives outside normal society. Miss Havisham has rejected society, and entered a voluntary imprisonment. Magwitch is excluded from society by crime, by legal imprisonment, and then by transportation. The difficulty of returning to society, for Miss Havisham, is psychological; and the stubbornness of this barrier of feeling is suggested by the fact that when at last she begins to show normal feelings she undergoes an ordeal by fire, and narrowly escapes death. Magwitch can only return to society at the risk of incurring a sentence of death. All this is meant to show that the voluntary and the involuntary prisoner are bound by fetters of equal strength. To drive this home there is the melodramatic dual link with Compeyson.

The value of all this begins to become clear when we see how oblivious Pip is to the likeness. The grotesque paraphernalia of the Havisham mansion does not repel or alarm him. He feels that Miss Havisham, being rich or upper class (the two ideas are hardly separate in his mind), has a right to her eccentricities. So the shock of Magwitch's revelation does not merely consist in learning that there is a social gulf between himself and the Havisham-Estella household; the trouble is that Magwitch's theory of wealth is only a slightly cruder version of Pip's own. Pip has worshipped Miss Havisham's insolent use of wealth; and now the despised convict is asking him to use it with a similar insolence. And Magwitch wants him to do what he has always intended to do, to live as a fine gentleman on someone else's money. So Pip is forced to realise that his horror of Magwitch is irrational; and hence to question everything he had taken for granted. But nothing positive replaces the shattered dream; and his renunciation is deeply ironical. For he renounces his wealth and position, with much conscious nobility, but he does so on snobbish principles. For Magwitch's Australian fortune has been fairly earned. The inadequacy of his change of heart is conveyed with fine symbolic appropriateness when pathetically he tries to repay his debt to Magwitch, not yet knowing him to be the cause of all his wealth: "He [the messenger] came faithfully, and he brought me the two one-pound notes. I was a poor boy then, as you know, and to a poor boy they were a little fortune. But like you, I have done well since, and you must let me pay them back. You can put them to some other poor boy's use." Pip can be seen as the image of the philanthropy of the rich, not really giving, but repaying a tiny part of what they have received.

Suggested parallels of this kind throughout the book are at once indefinite and pervasive. More than anything else they prevent the image of parasitism from becoming a merely limiting factor. From the brief analysis of this image offered above, it might be supposed that the book was only about a sort of respectable underworld of shady and greedy money-worshippers. But the book as a whole, on the contrary, gives an irresistible impression of portraying society as a whole. ***Great Expectations*** is not, like ***David Copperfield*** and like so many English and French novels of the nineteenth century, the story of a young man growing up and gradually shedding illusions and being assimilated to society's ways. Society fawns on him. Pumblechook recognises his superiority. Even Joe shares some of his illusions. There seems to be a conspiracy to treat money as an independent self-created entity, worthy of reverence. Hardly anyone in the book works productively. Magwitch's fortune was made by work, certainly; but far away, by methods unknown to the reader. So the solitary exception that counts is Joe Gargery. His forge is the only reminder of the necessity of work, of the connection between skill and wealth. In a book full of soft, hazy images, of mists and marshes, and full also of hazy mental processes, Joe's forge is a hard fact, represented by iron and fire.

Pip's erratic fortunes begin and end with Joe, who gives up the advantage of having Pip as an apprentice, and finally pays off the debts which are all that remain of Pip's wealth and expectations. The forge is indeed a moving image of the dignity of work. But Joe, too, as we have seen is in his innocent, unselfish way a snob. Even Joe is on the fringe of the conspiracy to regard money as sacred.

It is at this point, it seems to me, that we reach a fascinating and intractable dilemma of criticism. Are we to say that Dickens in the end faltered before the devastating satirical demands that the book's plan should have imposed? The symbolic suggestiveness of Pip's position in society (for instance, the meaning of his utterly inadequate offer or repayment to Magwitch, mentioned above) is unwontedly vague. And the vagueness is reflected in another uncertainty of a technical character. From what point of view is the story told? Ostensibly it comes from the mature, disillusioned Pip. But this is hardly satisfactory. The neat, comfortable and moderately lucrative business position, which is Pip's haven when the storms of expectation are over, is scarcely a suitable place from which to adjudicate on a capitalist society's attitude to money and class. And Pip's own final attitude is never clear. Does he reject all unearned wealth? Does he come to realise

his own inconsistency about the excellence of accepting money from Miss Havisham and the degradation of accepting it from Magwitch? Pip can indeed comprehend his past mistakes, but he cannot in retrospect effectively judge the society in which he had lived.

This line of argument, which tends to show that the book, for all its brilliance, in the end stifles unworthily the moral problems it raises, might receive powerful support from the ending. The fact that the "unhappy ending" was altered at an outsider's request is perhaps not very important. I agree, myself, with those who regard the "happy" ending actually published as representing best the author's intentions and the book's own logic. It is fitting that Pip should frustrate Miss Havisham's designs on Estella just as he has frustrated Magwitch's plans to make him rich. But it is still a most ambiguous ending. What is Pip really getting in the person of Estella? Mr. Hillis Miller [see excerpt dated 1958] makes this interesting comment: "Pip now has all that he wanted, Estella and her jewels, but what he has is altogether different from what he expected. Rather than possessing the impossible reconciliation of freedom and security he had sought in Estella and gentility, he now loves and is loved by another fallible and imperfect human being like himself." This would seem to be good summary of what Dickens intended. But Mr. Miller makes no allowance for the artistic failure which must surely be involved if this interpretation is right. For how are we to believe that Estella has changed enough to be worth having?

The book ends with a characteristically ambiguous amalgam of mist and light. "I took her hand in mine, and we went out of the ruined place; and, as the morning mists had risen long ago when I first left the forge, so, the evening mists were rising now, and in all the broad expanse of tranquil light they showed to me, I saw no shadow of another parting from her." It is an ending which leaves many questions open. It does not rule out the possibility that Pip has yet another terrible disillusionment in store. Is this ambiguity also a sign of a new timidity in Dickens, and of a faltering grasp?

Such a line of criticism may seem strong or weak to different people. But it is, in any case, not conclusive. It could be argued that all this vagueness and ambiguity is perfectly appropriate; moreover, that it is implicit in the book's whole plan, as the persistent images of mist and marsh, the persistent weariness and decay clearly show. It would then follow that Dickens was not here timid or muddled. Practised craftsman that he had now become, he merely understood the necessary limits of satire. Satire can attack the vices of society, but it cannot effectively attack society itself. If it makes the attempt, it must degenerate into a mere tirade, a fictionalised pamphlet. (A study of some of Zola's failures would be instructive here.) Dickens, the argument would run, was now humble enough to realise that he, too, was a man and a member of society; that there was no easy solution to the moral problems raised by money; that even palpable injustices could seldom be fairly blamed on any individual. Moreover, in this way, the theme of alienation from society could acquire an additional force. According to the book's own logic the satirist who rejects and condemns society utterly is not the brave and shining rebel he is so often represented as being. He is, ultimately, of the same party as Magwitch and Miss Havisham. His intentions may be excellent; but he is a dying limb cut from the body. On this view, then, Dickens went as far as was reasonably possible in exposing the unreality of dreams of wealth, but he wisely showed the question complete with all the mysterious ambiguity it actually assumes in life.

Personally, I cannot see that either of these lines of argument has the power to refute the other. The study of this great novel ends with a question mark. (pp. 159-69)

> *A. O. J. Cockshut, in his* The Imagination of Charles Dickens, *1961. Reprint by New York University Press, 1962, 192 p.*

## BARBARA HARDY (essay date 1963)

[*Hardy studies the ceremonial aspects of meals in* Great Expectations, *arguing that the manner in which they are served reflects the moral values of the characters serving them. Hardy's commentary was first published in 1963.*]

We all know that food has a special place in the novels of Dickens. He loves feasts and scorns fasts. His celebration of the feast is not that of the glutton or the gourmet: eating and drinking are valued by him as proofs of sociability and gusto, but more important still, as ceremonies of love. The conversion of Scrooge is marked by his present of a goose to Bob Cratchit and his reunion at his nephew's table: both the giving and the participation show his newly found ability to love. The Christmas dinner and the geniality of the English pub are not sentimentalized as isolated institutions of goodwill, conveniently cut off from the poverty and hunger outside the window. Good housekeeping is proved by nourishing and well-ordered meals, and Mrs Jellyby cannot feed her family properly; but the same is true of the bleak housekeeping of England, which cannot feed Jo or the brickmasters. Chadband's superfluous feasts are put beside Jo's hunger and Guster's loving crust to qualify the approval of good appetite. The social emphasis in *Great Expectations* is rather different from that of *Bleak House,* but in both novels, and elsewhere, the same moral values are attached to meals—to the giving, receiving, eating, and serving of food. These values might be summed up as good appetite without greed, hospitality without show, and ceremony without pride or condescension. Pip's deterioration and change of heart are shown in terms of these values.

All these values are shown, positively and negatively, in the meals in *Great Expectations.* Food is used to define various aspects of love, pride, social ambition, and gratitude, and the meals are often carefully placed in order to underline and explain motivation and development. Dickens's attitude to food has no doubt considerable biographical interest. Dickens—deprived child, food-lover, great talker, oral type—juxtaposes Mrs Joe's pincushion breast and her dispensation of bread, and this may well be his grimmest attack on the maternal image. But in spite of this grotesque instance, I believe that the generalized association of food and love in Dickens strikes us less by its neurotic fantasy than by its use of what we all feel to be the natural appropriateness of the metaphor 'hunger' when it is used of love. I do not call the meals in *Great Expectations* symbols: their affirmation of value seems to involve no conceptual transference and little heightening. It is our awareness of the Last Supper which often tempts us to describe this kind of significant meal as symbolic (the meal shared by Bartle Massey and Adam Bede in the upper room is a good example) but the Last Supper (like the Passover and other ritual feasts) became an effective symbol, in part at least, because it tapped the significance of ordinary commu-

nion—the eating, giving, and receiving, in public, amongst friends and associates. The meals in Dickens convey no more, I suggest, than the elementary implications of natural domestic and social order, given particularity by the context of the novel. The generalizations which the meals in *Great Expectations* carry involve none of the transference associated with symbolism, nothing of the movement from a first term to a second which is involved in our reading of the symbol of the wild waves, the fog, or the prison. There is certainly an accumulation of significance in *Great Expectations,* and we may come to expect that when characters sit down to eat there will be more than a furtherance of action, local colour, or comic play. We come to expect some extension or qualification of the moral significance already correlated with the meals. This is an extension of the particular definition of character, a way of emphasizing the connections and distances between different characters or different events, showing the irony and necessity of the internal moral pattern. The meals themselves are charged with no more than the moral significances of everyday life. . . . (pp. 139-41)

The first meal in *Great Expectations* is *demanded* in the first chapter. Magwitch in desperate hunger terrifies Pip into stealing food: 'You know what wittles is . . . you get me wittles.' In the third chapter Pip brings the food, and Magwitch makes the first response of gratitude which begins the long chain of obligation, illusion, pride, and love. It is necessary to see what moves his gratitude: it is not the mere provision of food, important though this is. Pip is doing more than satisfy the physical need, he is allowing nature more than nature needs. Magwitch is eating like a beast but Pip treats him as a guest and makes him respond as a guest:

> He was already handing mincemeat down his throat in the most curious manner—more like a man who was putting it away somewhere in a violent hurry, than a man who was eating it—but he left off to take some of the liquor. He shivered all the while so violently, that it was quite as much as he could do to keep the neck of the bottle between his teeth, without biting it off . . .

> He was gobbling mincemeat, meat bone, bread, cheese, and pork pie, all at once: staring distrustfully while he did so at the mist all round us, and often stopping—even stopping his jaws—to listen.

This is a grotesque table, spread in the wilderness of mist and marshes for a man who is wolfing down the food out of fear. Pip is no more in the conventional position of host than Magwitch is in the conventional position of guest, but the very lack of ceremony moves Pip to do more than steal and give in terror and in minimal satisfaction of need. Pity moves him to sauce the meat with ceremony and turn it into something more than Lady Macbeth's 'bare meeting'. Just as Lady Macbeth's rebuke has special point because it is made at a great feast to the host who is a guest-murderer, so Pip's ceremony has special point in this bare rough meeting where the guest is desperate and the host terrorized:

> Pitying his desolation . . . I made bold to say, 'I am
> glad you enjoy it'.
> 'Did you speak?'
> 'I said, I am glad you enjoyed it.'
> 'Thankee, my boy. I do.'

The child's civility and pity take no offence from his guest's table-manners. These are carefully observed, without revulsion:

I had often watched a large dog of ours eating his food; and now I noticed a decided similarity between the dog's way of eating, and the man's. The man took strong sharp sudden bites, just like the dog. He swallowed, or rather snapped up, every mouthful, too soon and too fast; and he looked sideways here and there while he ate, as if he thought there was danger in every direction of somebody's coming to take the pie away. He was altogether too unsettled in his mind over it, to appreciate it comfortably, I thought, or to have anybody to dine with him, without making a chop with his jaws at the visitor. In all of which particulars he was very like the dog.

The detached account makes the politeness more marked. It is apparent that Pip's naïve comparisons, to the dog and to more comfortable meals, imply no sense of social superiority, though the social implications are plain to the reader. Pip is not repelled by the resemblance to the dog, but is sorry for it, and instead of treating the man like a dog, gives with love. The 'I am glad you enjoy it' and the 'Thankee' turn the rudest meal in the novel into an introductory model of ceremony. What makes the ceremony is love, generosity, and gratitude. I need not labour the attachment of this scene to the main themes of the novel.

This meal acts as a model of ceremony, and controls our response to the many related descriptions of meals which succeed it. The gratitude and compassionate love are both present in chapter v, when Magwitch lies about stealing the food, to protect Pip, and is answered by Joe: 'God knows you're welcome to it—so far as it was ever mine. . . . We don't know what you have done, but we wouldn't have you starved to death for it, poor miserable fellow-creatur.—Would us, Pip?'

This in its turn evokes another response of gratitude—an inarticulate working of the throat—from Magwitch. The first small links are forged in Pip's chain 'of iron or gold, of thorns or flowers'.

It is not until much later, in chapter xxxviii, that Pip sees that this is where his chain really begins, 'before I knew that the world held Estella'. The actual image is narrowed down, in the next chapter, to the 'wretched gold and silver chains' with which Magwitch has loaded him. When the image of the chain first appears (in the singular) it has no connection with the convict for Pip sees its beginning in his encounter with Miss Havisham and Estella, in Satis House. The beginning of his illusory great expectations, like the beginning of the real ones, is marked by a significant meal. Estella is the hostess, Pip the guest. The meal is less grotesque than the meal with Magwitch but it too lacks the ceremonious cover of a roof, for Estella tells Pip to wait in the yard:

> She came back, with some bread and meat and a little mug of beer. She put the mug down on the stones of the yard, and gave me the bread and meat without looking at me, as insolently as if I were a dog in disgrace. I was so humiliated, hurt, spurned, offended, angry, sorry—I cannot hit upon the right name for the smart—God knows what its name was—that tears started to my eyes. (ch. viii)

The contrast is clinched by the comparison with the dog. Pip's full wants are not satisfied, even though this is the hospitality of Satis House, but in terms of physical need he is given enough. He is treated like a dog, given no more than nature needs, but he does not lose his appetite, any more than

Magwitch, treated with courtesy, stops eating like a dog. Dickens makes this distinction unsentimentally and truthfully, merely allowing Pip to observe that 'the bread and food were acceptable, and the beer was warming and tingling, and I was soon in spirits to look about me'. Like Magwitch, and for similar reasons of protective love, Pip lies about this meal. His sense of humiliation and his desire to protect Estella from 'the contemplation of Mrs Joe' makes him elaborate the marvellous childish fantasy about the 'cake and wine on gold plates', which Pumblechook and Joe and Mrs Joe, in their social innocence, accept. Pip invents a meal appropriate to Satis House, and hides his shame, but he preserves both the hierarchy and the bizarre quality of his encounter by placing the meal in a coach, and saying that he 'got up behind the coach to eat mine, because she told me to'. Even the dog comes back, magnified into 'four immense dogs' who come off rather better than Pip did since they fight 'for veal-cutlets out of a silver basket'. On his next visit to Satis House we return briefly to the dog: 'I was taken into the yard to be fed in the former dog-like manner.' The two meals respond in perfect antithesis.

The first ceremony of love finds another responsive scene when Magwitch discloses his responsibility and motivation to Pip. We are carefully reminded of the first meal on the marshes: 'I drops my knife many a time in that hut when I was a eating my dinner or my supper, and I says, "Here's the boy again, a looking at me whiles I eats and drinks!"' (ch. xxxix).

It is to this actual memory of the meal that he attaches his plan to 'make that boy a gentleman' but when the gentleman serves him with a meal he does not look at him as the boy did:

> He ate in a ravenous manner that was very disagreeable, and all his actions were uncouth, noisy, and greedy. Some of his teeth had failed him since I saw him eat on the marshes, and as he turned his food in his mouth, and turned his head sideways to bring his strongest fangs to bear upon it, he looked terribly like a hungry old dog.

> If I had begun with any appetite, he would have taken it away, and I should have sat much as I did—repelled from him by an insurmountable aversion, and gloomily looking at the cloth. (ch. xl)

The uncouth eating, the hunger, the sideways movement, and the comparison with the dog are repetitions from the early scene which emphasize the distance between the child and the man. This time the observation is full of revulsion, the food is not sauced with ceremony. But if the host has changed, the guest has not, and he apologizes for his doglike eating with undoglike courtesy:

> 'I'm a heavy grubber, dear boy,' he said, as a polite kind of apology when he had made an end of his meal, 'but I always was. If it had been in my constitution to be a lighter grubber, I might ha' got into lighter trouble.'

The apology is made without shame or self-pity on the part of Magwitch, and provokes no sympathy on the part of Pip. In the early scene the child's pity was impulsive and provoked simply by the desperate eating and panic. In the later scenes, Pip is in a position to see the connection between the heavy grubbing and the heavy trouble, but describes without pity the roughness and greed: 'there was Prisoner, Felon, Bondsman, plain as plain could be'.

The next meal is described without emphasis. We are told that Magwitch wipes his knife on his leg, but by now Pip is too concerned to hear the convict's history to have room for shame and revulsion. The very last meal described—supper on the night before the attempted escape—contains no comment on manners or response: 'It was a dirty place enough . . . but there was a good fire in the kitchen, and there were eggs and bacon to eat, and various liquors to drink' (ch. liv).

By now Pip's pride has been entirely subdued to the need for action. The quiet disappearance of comment testifies to the naturalness and literalness of the scenes of eating and drinking: a series of related scenes has been established, bringing out the moral significance of needs and hospitality and good manners, but it is brought to no formal climax. There is no explicit comment on the irrelevance of good manners in the crisis of need, no reminiscence of the fellowship of the first meal and the first occasion when Pip helped Magwitch to escape his pursuers, nothing of the climactic recognition of symbolism which we find in James's dove, or Lawrence's rainbow, or Dickens's own wild waves. The meals are only tapped for their moral significance on occasions when men need food desperately or when there is scope for hospitality: towards the end of the story the meals are inartificially subordinated to other features of the action. I do not make this distinction in order to decry the more contrived symbolism in other novels, but merely in order to bring out Dickens's unheightened and sober reliance on everyday moral and social facts. There is, I think, no question of an unconscious moral pattern, for the repetition of details makes the control quite plain, but Dickens is content to subdue this significant series of meals to the proportions and emphases of his story.

With the same almost unobtrusive reflection of ordinary moral fact, the meals with Estella are also described without schematic arrangement. They scarcely develop into a pattern, and Dickens can allow himself to describe a meal without relating it to earlier significances. When Estella and Pip have tea together in the hotel, or when Pip does eventually dine with some ceremony inside Satis House, no moral emphasis is present: on the first occasion Dickens is concerned to develop aspects of the relationship to which need and ceremony are irrelevant; on the second he is concerned with the tense understatement of Jaggers's observation of Estella. But although some of the meals in this novel make no moral definition, it is true that nearly all the characters and families are given, at some point, their significant ceremony of food. Magwitch tells Pip and Herbert how his heavy grubbing explains his troubled career and begins his life-story with the little boy who stole turnips and who was always driven by the need 'to put something into his stomach'. Pip as a child is not physically deprived in this way, but although he is given enough to eat, he is not given his food with love. In Chapter ii, between Magwitch's demand for food and Pip's generous response, we are given a glimpse of Mrs Joe's 'bringing up by hand'. She is an unloving mother-surrogate who feeds her family unceremoniously:

> My sister had a trenchant way of cutting our bread-and-butter for us, that never varied. First, with her left hand she jammed the loaf hard and fast against her bib—where it sometimes got a pin into it, and sometimes a needle, which we afterwards got into

our mouths. Then she took some butter (not too much) on a knife and spread it on the loaf, in an apothecary kind of way, as if she were making a plaister—using both sides of the knife with a slapping dexterity, and trimming and moulding the butter off round the crust. Then, she gave the knife a final smart wipe on the edge of the plaister . . .

The pins and needles have already been mentioned as characteristic of this unmotherly breast: 'She was tall and bony, and almost always wore a coarse apron, fastened over her figure behind with two loops, and having a square impregnable bib in front, that was stuck full of pins and needles.'

Some of the implications of this juxtaposition are terrifying, but the Gargery household is treated with comedy rather than with the harsh violence which is the medium for the Murdstones. But both the comic mode and the grim seem at times to draw freely on Dickens's fantasy. The moral implications within the novel are plain: Mrs Joe gives unlovingly, to put it mildly, taking most pleasure in the administration of Tar-Water and fasts, while Joe shares the wedges of bread in love and play, and tries to make up for Pip's sufferings at the Christmas dinner with spoonfulls of gravy.

The cold comfort of Mrs Joe's meals, like her uncomfortable cleanliness, makes her an ancestress of Mrs Ogmore-Pritchard, though Dickens inflicts a terrible revenge on her in the action. She has the front-parlour mentality, and the only ceremony in the Gargery household, apart from the rough meals shared by Pip and Joe, is the false ceremony of hospitality. Her showing-off at the dinner-party contrasts rudely with her earlier words to Joe and Pip: 'I ain't a going to have no formal cramming and busting and washing-up now', and they have their slices served out as if they 'were two thousand troops on a forced march instead of a man and boy at home'. I need not dwell on the Christmas dinner, with Mr Wopsle's theatrical declamation of grace, with the adjurations to Pip to be grateful 'to them which brought you up by hand', with Pumblechook's immodest generosity and gluttony and the comic nemesis when he chokes on the Tar-Water. The contrast between the ceremony of love and the false ceremony is there, together with the rebuke of starvation. For Magwitch has eaten the pie and drunk the brandy. This is underlined when Pip observes Pumblechook's possessive appropriation of the wine he has given to Mrs Joe and his generous treating of the flattering sergeant. The false giving and receiving are put in the context of the first meal with Magwitch when Pip comments, 'I thought what terrible good sauce for a dinner my fugitive friend on the marshes was.'

Pip's humiliation by Estella is also put into a larger context when he explains that his susceptibility to injustice and shame was attributable to the unloving home. Joe makes even the hacked bread and superfluous gravy the food of love, but Estella sharpens the sense of false ceremony, in part by denying ceremony, and Pip becomes less conscious of love's seasoning than of good manners. He continues in fantasy, and eventually moves from the back of the coach. The actual social significance of eating habits becomes emphatic in a novel about snobbery and aspiration, and there are other meals which raise the question of love and ceremony. When Pip has his first meal with Herbert Pocket, a difficult social situation is eased by Herbert's friendly delicacy, and he gives both the strawberries and the lessons in etiquette with true ceremony. This is a scene which establishes both the importance of good manners and the importance of love. It contrasts strongly with the second meal with Magwitch, where Pip is the bad host, and is paralleled by the first, when Pip is the true host. It is closest of all to another scene, where Herbert and Pip are entertaining Joe to breakfast. Joe is 'stiff from head to foot', cannot say outright that he prefers tea to coffee, and is as self-conscious in his politeness as Magwitch is unself-conscious in his roughness:

> Then he fell into such unaccountable fits of medita-
> tion, with his fork midway between his plate and
> his mouth; had his eyes attracted in such strange
> directions; was afflicted with such remarkable
> coughs; sat so far from the table, and dropped so
> much more than he ate, and pretended he hadn't
> dropped it; that I was heartily glad when Herbert
> left us for the city. (ch. xxvii)

This failure in hospitality—'I had neither the good sense nor the good feeling to know that this was all my fault'—prepares us for the greater failure, the greater social gulf, and the greater shame, when Magwitch returns and Pip makes a first false, but healthy, comparison between his shame for Joe and his shame before the convict, for whom he had deserted Joe.

There are other scenes, more or less emphatic, in which the social values of eating are defined. There is the false show, lightly touched on, in the last celebratory supper at the forge before Pip leaves home, when he sits ashamed in his splendour for their delight and they are all 'very low' despite roast fowl and flip. This contrasts with another kind of false show, in the same chapter, when Mr Pumblechook flatters and celebrates in a travesty of the love-feast. He toasts Pip in extravagant mock-abasement when he toasts Pip—'May I?—*may I?*'—and elaborately deprecates the chicken and tongue—'one or two little things had round from the Boar, that I hope you may not despise'—and apostrophizes the fowl—'Ah! poultry, poultry! You little thought . . . when you was a young fledgling, what was in store for you' (ch. xix). At the other social extreme from this exhibition of hospitable abasement, but close to it morally, is Pip's little fantasy, at the beginning of the same chapter, of feasting the villagers, 'bestowing a dinner of roast-beef and plum-pudding, a pint of ale, and a gallon of condescension'. There are many other details which might be mentioned: the funeral repast after Mrs Joe's death, Jaggers's good food and ruthless hospitality, the geniality of the pub, Pip's susceptibility to wine on one or two occasions, the lavishness of his housekeeping with Herbert, and the ordered, warm, and unpretentious hospitality of Wemmick.

Almost all characters and groups are given moral and social definition by their attitudes to food and hospitality. Old Barley keeps the provisions in his room, and provides Clara with bread and cheese while he has mutton-chops, potatoes, and split pease stewed up in butter; he roars and bangs for his grog and growls in pain while trying to cut through a Double Gloucester with his gouty hand. The ill-fed children are the unloved children. The baby Pocket, like Pip, is endangered by being fed on pins, though in his case the inappropriate food is the result of neglect and disorder not of an aggressive display of good housekeeping. The disorder, bad economy, and inadequate meals of the Pocket family are another version of the neglected Jellybys in **Bleak House,** and just as Mrs Jellyby is ironically exposed as a model of displaced charity, so Mrs Pocket is shown in her disorder as another qualification of class-distinction and great expectations. Her delusions of grandeur lead to the disregard of proper ceremony. Al-

though each bad mother is attached to the special theme of each novel, the basic moral failure is the same. It is a failure in love.

I have not yet mentioned one of the most prominent failures in love in **Great Expectations.** This is Miss Havisham's failure. Her love-feast is preserved in its decay to make the most conspicuous contribution to the themes of love and nature. Nothing remains of the expectations of Satis House but a gruesome parody of ceremony:

> The most prominent object was a long table with
> a tablecloth spread on it, as if a feast had been in
> preparation when the house and the clocks all
> stopped together. An *épergne* or centre-piece of
> some kind was in the middle of this cloth; it was so
> heavily overhung with cobwebs that its form was
> quite undistinguishable; and as I looked along the
> yellow expanse out of which I remember its seem-
> ing to grow, like a black fungus, I saw speckled-
> legged spiders with blotchy bodies running home to
> it . . . (ch. xi)

Miss Havisham makes a symbolic correlation between the mouldering wedding-breakfast and her own life. She has been gnawed by pain as the food has been gnawed by mice, she has worn away with the meal, and when she is dead she too will be laid out on that table, where she has allocated the places for her predatory family to sit and 'feast upon' her. The betrayal of love and the hypocritical greedy show of love are both bracketed as false ceremony in this grisly image of transubstantiation. The ghastly conceit stands out from Dickens's other significant correlations of love and food as a product of a diseased fancy and an impossible attempt to pervert nature. Jaggers makes explicit the other implications of the stasis and decay which relate this meal to the pattern of normal routine and relationship:

> He asked me how often I had seen Miss Havisham
> eat and drink . . .
>
> I considered, and said, 'Never'. 'And never will,
> Pip,' he retorted, with a frowning smile. 'She has
> never allowed herself to be seen doing either, since
> she lived this present life of hers. She wanders
> about in the night, and then lays hands on such
> food as she takes.' (ch. xxix)

Miss Havisham's rejection of ordinary public meals is like her attempt to shut out the daylight. Food in **Great Expectations,** as in *Macbeth,* is part of the public order, and the meals testify to human need and dependence, and distinguish false ceremony from the ceremony of love. They are not literary symbols but natural demonstrations. Pip's change of heart is a change from the unconditioned act of love to this contaminated false ceremony and back again to the Dickensian natural man. Like Scrooge, he demonstrates the vulnerable virtue by loss and gain. (pp. 141-55)

> *Barbara Hardy, " 'Great Expectations', " in her* The
> Moral Art of Dickens: Essays, *Oxford University
> Press, Inc., 1970, pp. 139-55.*

**MARTIN MEISEL**   (essay date 1965)

[*Expanding the debate over the most appropriate ending for* Great Expectations, *Meisel contends that both the original and revised conclusions are equally suitable postcripts to what he considers the novel's true ending: the meeting between Pip and the child of Joe and Biddy.*]

Since Forster's *Life of Dickens* and his account of how Bulwer Lytton persuaded Dickens to change the ending of *Great Expectations,* for the worse, the main stream of perceptive comment on the novel has agreed with Forster and regretted the change [see excerpt dated 1874]. The regret, however, has had a peculiarly pharisaical quality, as if it beheld a moral as well as artistic lapse. Tempted by Bulwer, Dickens fell; and in place of an austere ending consistent with the theme of vanished expectations, an ending in which Jack hath not Jill, he concocted an eleventh-hour union to indulge the popular appetite. Until recently even apologists have had to plead as mitigation the primitiveness of the artistic conscience for fiction in pre-George Eliot circles, or Dickens' special and intense relation to his audience. Recently, however, the second ending has found defenders on intrinsic grounds. With its chastened, scarred, no longer youthful couple who join hands and depart from the ruined garden, it is shown to culminate the essential tale of Paradise Lost [see excerpt by J. Hillis Miller dated 1958].

That either ending works very well indeed, once we set aside fashions and prejudices on endings, ought to be enough to vindicate Dickens' artistry. But morality contemplates not just the deed but the intention. And by the puritanical standards of modern artistic morality, there is no defense, even artistic, for Dickens' evident willingness to tinker so casually, not just with any passage, but with the end of his novel, that moment which fixes literary characters in their permanent states of bliss or misery like the Last Judgment itself. There is no defense for his evident willingness to juggle with poetic justice to accommodate an importunate friend and a weak-minded public.

Yet there is a defense, even in such a court, though Dickens seems to have done his best to hang himself. (He wrote to Forster with a coy and philistine smugness, 'I have put in as pretty a little piece of writing as I could, and I have no doubt the story will be more acceptable through the alteration'). The defense is that in the total architecture of the novel neither ending is very important. Each gives a similar graceful accent to a more or less completed structure. Dickens was willing to be accommodating, but only on non-essentials; on a genuine matter of conscience he was like a rock. He begins his confession to Forster [see letter by Dickens dated 1861], 'You will be surprised to hear that I have changed the end of *Great Expectations* from and after Pip's return to Joe's, and finding his little likeness there'. That scene, the return to Joe's and the finding of little Pip, remains practically unchanged, and it is the true ending of *Great Expectations.*

The effect of the true ending on the narrative line is to bring it full circle, to transform what potentially is infinitely extensible into a closed form. The weight of the scene thematically is to give final definition to issues of redemption and penalty, natural innocence and natural depravity.

'The novel dramatises the loss of innocence,' writes Julian Moynihan, 'and does not glibly present the hope of a redemptory second birth for either its guilty hero or the guilty society which shaped him' [see essay dated 1960]. That this formulation is true at least where it concerns the hero in his own person is urged upon us by the episode of Pip's illness following hard upon the death of Magwitch. For a while, however, the episode seems to suggest an opposite conclusion. The fever itself with its nightmare crisis recapitulates Pip's life of expectation and the subsequent harrowing of his body and soul, and through it he returns to a physical and spiritual infancy.

The crisis of the fever distinctly resembles the crisis of a second birth. Pip's delusions are dreams of imprisonment and desperation to escape, in imagery that suggests the womb of his shaping past and the great social machine in which he had been caught up. That he survives, escapes, and is in some sense reborn is the difference between what he makes of his actual harrowing and what Miss Havisham made of hers. He imagines *her* in the matrix of 'a closed iron furnace in a dark corner of the room, and a voice had called out over and over again that Miss Havisham was consuming within it'.

That Pip has successfully recovered his lost innocence through a redemptory second birth seems to be confirmed as he emerges into awareness and finds himself once more in the care of Joe, 'and I fancied I was little Pip again'. He is 'like a child in [Joe's] hands. He would sit and talk to me in the old confidence, and with the old simplicity, and in the old unassertive protecting way, so that I would half believe that all my life since the days of the old kitchen was one of the mental troubles of the fever that was gone'. Born again, Pip seems to have recovered the lost paradise of Joe's love. Pip's narrative harps on this return to the perfection of the relationship before Pip's knowledge of guilt began the course of his alienation. Together they look forward to Pip's first venture outdoors 'as we had once looked forward to the day of my apprenticeship'. When the day comes, Joe wraps him up, carries him down in his arms, and puts him in an open carriage 'as if I were still the small helpless creature to whom he had so abundantly given of the wealth of his great nature'. Pip is overwhelmed by the early summer loveliness and its evidence of natural fulfilment, by the 'mere remembrance' of his fever and the evidence of his salvation; and he lays his head on Joe's shoulder 'as I had laid it long ago when he had taken me to the Fair or where not, and it was too much for my young senses'. But when they return, and Joe lifts and carries him across the court and up the stairs, Pip thinks 'of that eventful Christmas Day' when the change had begun, 'when he had carried me over the marshes'.

Pip's recovery quickly recapitulates his early growth. He inexorably gets well, and inevitably the formality and protective distance of later days reappears. The return to his childhood is a symbolic event that transcends time; but the return—and this is the culminating point of the episode—must in the nature of things be temporary. The symbolism which transcends time, the symbolism of grace and reprobation, of ultimate spiritual states, gives way in the novel to the symbolism of act and consequence and to the sterner realities of the temporal process. The past is real, and its consequences, regretted and as nearly as possible paid for, must still be lived with.

Throughout Pip's convalescence, he tells us, a second thought has been taking shape, and it emerges on Joe's departure as the 'settled purpose' of marrying Biddy. She loved and comforted him once 'in my first unhappy time'. He wants her to receive him now 'with all my faults and disappointments on my head'; to receive him 'like a forgiven child (and indeed I am as sorry, Biddy, and have as much need of a hushing voice and a soothing hand)'. But chastened and forgiven as he is, Pip is not permitted to go back to Biddy any more than to Joe. He can neither regain nor remake any stage of the past. The perfect mother, teacher, and comforter now marries the at least perfectly loving father, and what has been called Pip's 'second chance'—for indeed there is one—is in the next generation. Bereft of 'this last baffled hope' for himself, Pip yet hopes that Joe and Biddy will have children to love, and in particular 'that some little fellow will sit in this chimney corner of a winter night, who may remind you of another little fellow gone out of it for ever'. And if Pip is excessively sorry for himself here, he also recognises the finality of his exile, the slimness of his deserts, and his subjection to time.

When Pip returns once more to the blacksmith's cottage after years spent in the East, he finds Joe 'in the old place by the kitchen firelight . . . and there, fenced into the corner with Joe's leg, and sitting on my own little stool looking at the fire, was—I again!' The child's name is Pip—'we hoped he might grow a little bit like you, and we think he do'—and he and Pip talk the next day 'immensely, understanding one another to perfection'. Everything is the same as in the opening scenes, but in everything there is a difference. Joe's leg is no longer a fence against Joe's wife. Pip the visitor makes a point of *not* rumpling little Pip's hair 'which from my earliest remembrance, as already hinted, I have in my soul denied the right of any fellow-creature to do'. And when Biddy touches first her little girl (a second chance for Pip requires a second chance for Estella) and then her old friend Pip with 'her good matronly hand', Pip finds something in the action and 'in the light pressure of Biddy's wedding-ring, that had a very pretty eloquence in it'. It is the eloquence of contrast with 'the ridgy effect of a wedding-ring, passing unsympathetically over the human countenance', on which Pip, brought up by another kind of hand, was the greatest living authority.

As Biddy and Joe replace the parents who failed the first Pip, first through death, then through harshness and helplessness, so Pip replaces Magwitch as spiritual father to the child christened with his name. 'Biddy,' he announces the second evening of his visit, 'you must give Pip to me, one of these days; or lend him, at all events.' Earlier in the day he has taken young Pip to the churchyard on the marshes. The older Pip had been in his seventh year, at the dawn of responsibility and self knowledge, the point at which the infant becomes the catechumen, when he had found himself in the marsh church on Christmas Eve, and there met his demon godfather. He had been in the very act of discovering 'for certain' who he was and where he was, when Magwitch turned him upside down and sat him 'on a high tombstone' from which Pip showed him the grave of his parents and on which he bent Pip to his will. The younger Pip is also about seven (the years of Pip's absence from England are in no version less than eight); the visit also takes place in December; and in the churchyard Pip sets young Pip 'on a certain tombstone there, and he showed me from that elevation which stone was sacred to the memory of Philip Pirrip, late of this Parish, and Also Georgiana, Wife of the Above'.

There is a deliberate ceremony in Pip's return to his own beginnings in the company of little Pip. By this act he confirms himself as godfather, in place of Magwitch, and commits himself, by sameness, to the difference in the world of little Pip. By it he also accepts his declension from the centre of the stage—something Pip in his hopes of Biddy had not yet been ready to do. For the first time Pip casts himself in an adult if subsidiary role. The ceremony is a formal installation of the young Pip, as the focus of promise and expectation, and a formal abdication of the old.

The novel has come full circle, and the end is a new beginning. The end is an acceptance of irredeemable loss, but it establishes a continuing and perhaps inexhaustible possibility

of individual and social redemption, in the children. The seed continues good, despite the losses of earlier generations, despite the blighting legacy of their crimes and follies, despite the universal subjection to time which makes renewal possible as well as loss inevitable. The end in a new beginning does not mean the vanity of an eternal return for Dickens. The continuing possibility of redemption lies precisely in that the future need not be the same as the past. Second Pip need not go the way of first Pip, for as the first declares in wishing Joe and Biddy a child that reminds them of himself, 'only tell him . . . that, as your child, I said it would be natural to him to grow up a much better man than I did'. And such indeed is the case in a world no longer governed by the captious tyranny of Mrs. Joe, a world where Joe's love is effectual, where Pumblechook has his mouth stuffed, and Pip's benevolence has replaced Magwitch's terror.

The last two paragraphs of the novel as originally written are a reinforcing postscript to the conclusion proper. While walking along Picadilly with little Pip, Pip meets Estella, and the encounter allows the novelist to carry out his obligation of tying up loose ends. Pip learns that Estella too has been harrowed and taught by suffering. She has been widowed, and has remarried. She takes little Pip to be Pip's own child. Pip's possibilities are concluded, his sufferings are confirmed as past, and his future is acknowledged as the little boy.

The substituted passage is longer, more elaborate; but it remains a tidying postscript to the ending proper. Pip's ceremonial visit to the site of the old house complements his visit to the churchyard as a return to his beginnings. He meets Estella in the old garden, and points the structural moral: 'After so many years, it is strange that we should thus meet again, Estella, here where our first meeting was!' They meet in sadness, and in moonlit ruin, like pale ghosts of themselves, full of the knowledge of their loss and the knowledge that comes through suffering. Their departure at nightfall from the ruined garden is no new joint venture in possibility, but a departure whose rising evening mists, in pointed contrast to 'the morning mists [that] had risen long ago when I first left the forge', and whose revealed 'expanse of tranquil light' without a shadow suggest an afterworld without colour, sound, or warmth, a world of pale companionship, sad serenity, and of disembodied contemplation of life by those who have left it for ever. (pp. 326-31)

> *Martin Meisel, "The Ending of 'Great Expectations'," in* Essays in Criticism, *Vol. XV, No. 3, July, 1965, pp. 326-31.*

## HARVEY PETER SUCKSMITH   (essay date 1970)

[*By comparing three real-life models for the character of Miss Havisham with her depiction in the novel, Sucksmith reveals some of the techniques that Dickens used to create complex tragic and ironic effects in his fiction.*]

Although much scholarship, including a whole book by Edwin Pugh, has been devoted to the task of identifying the Dickens 'originals', the critical study of how Dickens treats his 'originals' has been rather neglected. Yet such a study promises to throw some light on Dickens's methods of composition and his craftsmanship.

A good illustration is provided by the material Dickens used in creating Miss Havisham of *Great Expectations.* This material shows that three separate ideas went to the making of the character. Thus, the idea of the upper-class female recluse is to be found in a letter of 1856 from Dickens to Forster:

> The murder over the way (the third or fourth event of that nature in the Champs Elysées since we have been here) seems to disclose the strangest state of things. The Duchess who is murdered lived alone in a great house which was always shut up, and passed her time entirely in the dark. In a little lodge outside lived a coachman (the murderer), and there had been a long succession of coachmen who had been unable to stay there, and upon whom, whenever they asked for their wages, she plunged out with an immense knife, by way of an immediate settlement. The coachman never had anything to do, for the coach hadn't been driven out for years; neither would she ever allow the horses to be taken out for exercise. Between the lodge and the house, is a miserable bit of garden, all overgrown with long rank grass, weeds, and nettles; and in this, the horses used to be taken out to swim—in a dead green vegetable sea, up to their haunches. On the day of the murder, there was a great crowd, of course; and in the midst of it up comes the Duke her husband (from whom she was separated), and rings at the gate. The police open the gate. "C'est vrai donc," says the Duke, "que Madame la Duchesse n'est plus?"—"C'est trop vrai, Monseigneur."—"Tant mieux," says the Duke, and walks off deliberately, to the great satisfaction of the assemblage.

As Dickens himself says, what interested him about this episode were the odd facts of human behaviour it revealed. He does succeed in communicating this interest and the stress tends to remain upon facts. . . . As for effect, there is no attempt to involve the reader emotionally with any of the characters. Even the victim is not allowed one jot of sympathy; on the contrary, both alive and dead she appears slightly funny. There is a certain grim humour about her manner of settling accounts with her coachmen and about her husband's satisfaction with the news that she is well and truly disposed of. Yet it is not quite true to say the whole incident is passed off as a black joke. Although it is surprising to find that, for all his fascination with murder, Dickens does not mention any details of the crime, yet he cannot resist dwelling on one or two bizarre details connected with the affair: that touch, for example, about the Duchess's spending all her time in the dark or his description of the horses appearing to swim up to the haunches in the dead green sea of overgrown grass and weeds. Far from there being any effort to unify the impression created by the passage, the effect is allowed to wander back and forth between the curiosity evoked by odd behaviour, the relish excited by scandal, the amusing and the bizarre. This is as it should be here. It gives an impression of life recorded directly—unedited and disorderly.

In a second anecdote sent by Dickens to Forster some time during the spring of 1856, there is a hint for the motivation of Miss Havisham. Since this anecdote is cited by Forster immediately after the account of the Duchess's murder and is used to illustrate the same general point, both anecdotes may have been taken from the same letter; if so, they would have been closely associated in Dickens's mind. The relevant part of the second anecdote is as follows:

> The Squire had married a woman of the town from whom he was now separated, but by whom he had a daughter. The mother, to spite the father, had bred the daughter in every conceivable vice.

Daughter, then 13, came from school once a month. Intensely coarse in talk, and always drunk. As they drove about the country in two open carriages, the drunken mistress would be perpetually tumbling out of one, and the drunken daughter perpetually tumbling out of the other. At last the drunken mistress drank her stomach away, and began to die on the sofa. Got worse and worse, and was always raving about Somebody's where she had once been a lodger, and perpetually shrieking that she would cut somebody else's heart out. At last she died on the sofa.

Forster claims that Dickens would have regarded this material as too improbable for treatment as fiction. Certainly, Dickens is once more giving a factual illustration of the oddness of human behaviour. Again the effect shifts in an incongruous manner, this time from interest in a curious case of human motivation to farce and then to the horror of an alcoholic's death.

Along with the themes of the eccentric upper-class female recluse and the sexually frustrated woman who seeks revenge through a perversely educated child, a third idea went to the making of Miss Havisham. The source of this idea, that of the jilted bride for ever fixed in her traumatic wedding pose, can be found in an article Dickens contributed during 1853 to *Household Words:*

> Another very different person who stopped our growth, we associate with Berners Street, Oxford Street; whether she was constantly on parade in that street only, or was ever to be seen elsewhere, we are unable to say. The White Woman is her name. She is dressed entirely in white, with a ghastly white plating round her head and face, inside her white bonnet. She even carries (we hope) a white umbrella. With white boots, we know she picks her way through the winter dirt. She is a conceited old creature, cold and formal in manner, and evidently went simpering mad on personal grounds alone— no doubt because a wealthy Quaker wouldn't marry her. This is her bridal dress. She is always walking up here, on her way to church to marry the false Quaker. We observe in her mincing step and fishy eye that she intends to lead him a sharp life. We stopped growing when we got at the conclusion that the Quaker had had a happy escape of the White Woman.

As in so many of his portraits in the novels, Dickens repeats an epithet. But the repetition of 'white', here, creates no other effect than curiosity at the eccentric behaviour of the woman and suggests monomania which is then explained. Not a trace of sympathy for the mad jilted creature is encouraged. On the contrary, her disagreeable features are stressed and she is dismissed as a ridiculous figure. . . . The material does not create a unified impression but a succession of separate effects. It begins as a picture of eccentricity which whets the reader's curiosity about human behaviour, shifts to a catalogue of disagreeable traits, and ends in a jocular vein. Again, there is the untidiness we might expect to find in a record of real life.

The main interest of all three 'originals' then, lies in the information about human oddity which they convey. The stress is upon facts rather than effects, as we would wish in a good report. Wherever there are effects they remain mild and simple, and the major appeal is to the reader's curiosity. . . . In no case is there an attempt to present a strong unity of effect through a rigorous selection of subject matter. Such effects as there may be are even permitted to clash and weaken each other. What is absent from the material, in fact, is rhetoric . . . , a structure determined by effect and vision.

The 'originals' should be compared with the study of Miss Havisham into which Dickens finally combined and transmuted them. The following description is Pip's (and the reader's) earliest impression of her:

> Whether I should have made out this object so soon, if there had been no fine lady sitting at it, I cannot say. In an arm-chair, with an elbow resting on the table and her head leaning on that hand, sat the strangest lady I have ever seen, or shall ever see.
>
> She was dressed in rich materials—satins, and lace, and silks—all of white. Her shoes were white. And she had a long white veil dependent from her hair, and she had bridal flowers in her hair, but her hair was white. Some jewels sparkled on her neck and on her hands, and some other jewels lay sparkling on the table. Dresses, less splendid than the dress she wore, and half-packed trunks, were scattered about. She had not quite finished dressing, for she had but one shoe on—the other was on the table near her hand—her veil was but half arranged, her watch and chain were not put on, and some lace for her bosom lay with those trinkets, and with her handkerchief, and gloves, and some flowers, and a Prayer-book, all confusedly heaped about the looking-glass.

At first, Miss Havisham is described as if she were any normal well-to-do bride, making the final preparations for her wedding. Only a faint hint that anything is amiss is betrayed by Pip's reference to her strangeness and her white hair. Unlike the White Woman, there is nothing repelling about Miss Havisham so far. Nor is she ridiculous. On the contrary, she is a rather grand lady preparing for a most important public appearance. The richness and splendour of her dress, the brightness of her many jewels, appear to lend her dignity, even a kind of brilliance, which is ironical in view of what is to follow in the next paragraph:

> It was not in the first few moments that I saw all these things, though I saw more of them in the first moments than might be supposed. But, I saw that everything within my view which ought to be white, had been white long ago, and had lost its lustre, and was faded and yellow. I saw that the bride within the bridal dress had withered like the dress, and like the flowers, and had no brightness left but the brightness of her sunken eyes. I saw that the dress had been put upon the rounded figure of a young woman, and that the figure upon which it now hung loose, had shrunk to skin and bone.

All the great expectations of wholesome fulfilment we normally entertain for a bride are suddenly shattered. All the sensuous prospects of young married life and fruition that we associate with her wedding day are skilfully reversed into their opposites. Miss Havisham's pose as a bride turns out to be a bitter ironical burlesque. Behind the appearance is the mocking reality of withered age, sterility, and decay. Dickens uses form with considerable subtlety here. The powerful ironic effect is produced by a reversal which is both a discovery and a peripety. Through the discovery of the truth we are led by Dickens into experiencing the same pattern which Miss Havisham's catastrophe followed. At once, we divine roughly what has happened to her. We relive, in some measure, there-

fore, through that earlier ironic shock, the discovery by Miss Havisham that her great expectations were to come only to dust and decay. Furthermore, the appalling visual signs of her catastrophe begin to waken our pity. The normal ravages of time in the human face and body might have been expected to arouse a certain pity. But there is much more than this here. These are ravages of time set in the perspective of earlier hopes. This is old age seen as defeat, the mocking, humiliating defeat of all the dearest promises that life holds out to the greater part of womankind. Our pity is redoubled. Finally, there is, towards the close of the paragraph, still one more effect, which Dickens proceeds to intensify:

> Once, I had been taken to see some ghastly waxwork at the Fair, representing I know not what impossible personage lying in state. Once, I had been taken to one of our old marsh churches to see a skeleton in the ashes of a rich dress, that had been dug out of a vault under the church pavement. Now, waxwork and skeleton seemed to have dark eyes that moved and looked at me. I should have cried out, if I could.

Dickens is not piling on the horror here for its own sake. It is part of a larger effect. The spectacle which provokes this horror, the living corpse in its bridal shroud, 'Without this arrest of everything, this standing still of all the pale decayed objects, not even the withered bridal dress on the collapsed form could have looked so like grave-clothes, or the long veil so like a shroud', also arouses pity and irony through the defeat which it represents. An image of tragic defeat is, in fact, the final visual impression that Pip carries away with him from this scene:

> Miss Havisham's face . . . had dropped into a watchful AND BROODING expression—most likely when all the things about her had become transfixed—and it looked as if nothing could EVER lift it up again. Her chest had dropped, so that she stooped; and her voice had dropped, so that she spoke low, and with a curious dead lull upon her; ALTOGETHER, she had the appearance of having dropped, (altogether) BODY AND SOUL, WITHIN AND WITHOUT, under the weight of a (blow) CRUSHING BLOW.

Revisions in the manuscript, which stress the overwhelming defeat registered by Miss Havisham's posture, the utter helplessness to which the traumatic shock has reduced her, deliberately aim at winning the reader's sympathy. Yet, even here, the effect is no simple one. The situation which evokes pity is skilfully set in an ironic frame, for the immediate context of this description of defeat is a kind of victory. Immediately before the description, Miss Havisham notes with satisfaction that her plan to involve Pip with Estella and eventually to break his heart is beginning to succeed; he admits to Miss Havisham that he is both smitten with Estella and wounded by her treatment of him. Immediately after the description, Estella beats Pip in a game of cards; significantly, perhaps, the game is 'beggar my neighbour'. In this incident are to be found the roots of a tragic and ironic growth which will spread throughout the novel. Love has become a power game to Miss Havisham and Estella. Love was the cause of proud Miss Havisham's great defeat in life. Through love, she will avenge this defeat. Estella will defeat Pip in this sinister game also. But through her apparent victory, Miss Havisham will sustain a second defeat with its own pathos, irony, and horror. And Estella will only lose in the end.

A comparison between the study of Miss Havisham and the 'originals' at once brings out three striking points of difference. First, the picture of Miss Havisham is much more complex. This complexity does not result simply from combining material from three 'originals'. It is a matter not of addition but of coalescence and transmutation, of a compound not a mixture. The Duchess's neglect of her house simply resulted from her idiosyncrasy as a recluse. But the neglect and decay of Satis House is a parallel to the physical decay of its mistress while both forms of disintegration are outward manifestations of her emotional decay. Furthermore, by establishing a living correspondence between inward and outward decay, Dickens is presenting his vision of a world which is spiritually one, insisting that the spiritual truth about things is what really matters. The ultimate statement of the truth in *Great Expectations* is to be found in the ironic, pathetic, and horrifying symbol of the wedding-cake which has gone rotten. Putrefaction appears to spawn a lower parasitical life which, in its turn, feeds on decay. As a form of the archetypal Life-in-death, Miss Havisham also signifies that, when love dies, something is born quite as active, furtive, and repulsively malevolent as the parasites which feed on the rotting cake. Indeed, the effect created by Dickens's description of the putrefaction and parasitical life is deliberately intensified through revisions in the manuscript:

> Every discernible thing in it (looked as if it was) WAS COVERED WITH DUST AND MOULD, AND dropping to pieces . . . I saw (spiders) SPECKLED-LEGGED SPIDERS WITH BLOTCHY BODIES running home to it, and running out from it.

The promise of love has putrefied into hatred, malice, and revenge.

Again, Dickens develops and transforms the idea of the Duchess's living in the dark. Instead of an addiction to total darkness, Miss Havisham is given an aversion to daylight which she shuts out of her rooms in favour of candlelight. Watches and clocks are stopped at the precise time when she learned that her bridegroom had deserted her. She refuses to acknowledge the days of the week. In turning her back on time and the light of the sun, Miss Havisham is rejecting life and nature. By refusing to accept the goodness of growth, she allows ascendancy to the nightmarish evil of decay. The horror, pathos, and irony aroused by the spectacle of such a condition are clear marks of the tragedy it represents.

Similarly, when Dickens transforms the motivation of the deserted wife into Miss Havisham's master-motive, he complicates his presentation of it. The motivation and the form it takes do remain roughly the same. A woman who has been rejected by a man seeks revenge by corrupting a young girl. She then uses the girl as a weapon against the male who is vulnerable through his love for the girl. In the case of *Great Expectations,* Dickens substitutes the sexual relationships of the girl for the original relationship between the girl and her father and he directs Miss Havisham's spite against the male sex in general instead of the man who had deserted her. These changes make the general design much neater and offer greater possibilities as regards the plotting of the story. But the really important difference is that Miss Havisham's motive, unlike that of the deserted wife, is made to create an effect. We view her plan through a thin veil of irony. Since the viewpoint throughout the novel is Pip's, only an ironic reading can penetrate his earlier naïvety and obtuseness. At first, Miss Hav-

isham's plan is passed off as a kind of sport, a competitive game; there is only the faintest hint of something sinister. But when Dickens finally comes out into the open about it he deliberately draws attention to the irony of hatred masquerading as love:

> "Hear me, Pip! I adopted her to be loved. I bred her and educated her, to be loved. I developed her into what she is, that she might be loved. Love her!"

> She said that word often enough, and there could be no doubt that she meant to say it; but if the often repeated word had been hate instead of love—despair—revenge—dire death—it could not have sounded from her lips more like a curse.

Certainly, the irony distances what might otherwise have appeared melodramatic. The handling of Miss Havisham's motivation in this respect need only be contrasted with the stark treatment of Orlick's motivation to make this point clear. Even more important, however, the irony is dovetailed into the larger effect and vision of the novel since it also draws critical attention to the naïvety, obtuseness, and self-deception out of which Pip's own ironic tragedy grows. In addition, Miss Havisham's motivation is made part of a further pattern of irony for, like the plan of the deserted wife, that of Miss Havisham is made to recoil on her.

A second striking point of comparison is the way in which the heterogeneous material of the 'originals' with its weak and contradictory effects is wrought into an effective unity in the finished portrait. . . . [The] effect is a complex one.

Thirdly, unity and complexity help to explain the extremely powerful effect and vision which the figure of Miss Havisham contributes to *Great Expectations.* What is the nature of this vision, how do the effects help to focus it, and how is it related to the over-all effect and vision of the novel? As a victim of her own self-deception, first about Compeyson and later about life and love, so neatly summed up in her false bridal pose, Miss Havisham is viewed as both an ironic and tragic figure. In her wilful deception of Pip, she in her turn sows the seeds of further ironic tragedy. Dickens's view of Miss Havisham, therefore, belongs to his general vision of life as an ironic tragi-comedy of deception. Such a vision is complex to the point of paradox since it demands that man should enter into the suffering of life's victims even while he stands back and criticizes their folly. Irony, therefore, ensures a proper critical distance from Miss Havisham's delusions and deceptions but pity binds us to her fate, the long agony which will culminate in her remorse, redemption, and the final ordeal of her death by fire. The vision of an ironic tragi-comedy of deception is at the very core of *Great Expectations* and thus explains Miss Havisham's central importance in the book. The frustration of her own great expectations as regards love foreshadows and incites her to engineer the shattering disappointment of Pip's hopes of love. Pip's longing for wealth and status is shown to be motivated by his desire for Estella. True, his burning sense of social inferiority and injustice, which are inflamed by Estella's conduct at their first meeting, are factors in his motivation. The sense of inferiority may partly explain both the submissive role he adopts towards Estella and his compensatory drive towards status. But the fundamental point is that both Pip's sexual and life goals are distorted through his relationship with Estella. That this relationship is the starting-point of his later development is made absolutely clear at their first meeting. The ironic tragedies of Miss Havisham and Pip illustrate the corrupting power of unsatisfied love. The early deprivation of maternal love and the un-loving attitude of his sister are important factors in Pip's de-velopment. Like Miss Havisham, Pip is the victim of the false values which a perverse attitude to love has bred in him, and, if we censure Pip's snobbishness, his social climbing, his pur-suit of idleness and unearned wealth, we also pity him when the ironic blows of fate tear away one delusion after another from his eyes. For, like Miss Havisham, Pip also suffers the traumatic shocks that flesh may be heir to. And, parallel to the almost physical blow which appears to crush Miss Hav-isham at their first interview, we find that inward bleeding wound which Pip feels he has received on learning that Estel-la will marry Bentley Drummle; finally, the kind of horror which complicates the vision of Miss Havisham marks the tragedy as belonging to a special type. There is a very dark side indeed to the world of *Great Expectations,* a side not only represented by the sadistic malice of Mrs. Joe Gargery, Miss Havisham, and Estella or by the murderous assaults of Orlick but also by the cruel, organized, social violence of the public whippings and hangings, the mass sentencings to death, and the bestial savagery of the convict prisons and hulks. Even Pip is not without some responsibility, since his perverse submissiveness to Estella arouses and inflames her sexual cruelty towards him. This dark vision can, I think, be summed up as the negation and inversion of love, with all the horrors that this may imply. The corruption which Miss Havisham embodies is more than her own personal inward state. It is the dark shadow of spiritual corruption which touches Pip and almost the entire world of *Great Expecta-tions.* This is the full meaning of the horror which the rotting wedding breakfast spawns. This is the final ironic tragedy which it represents. (pp. 177-88)

*Harvey Peter Sucksmith, in his* The Narrative Art of Charles Dickens: The Rhetoric of Sympathy and Irony in His Novels, *Oxford at the Clarendon Press, 1970, 374 p.*

**WILLIAM F. AXTON**  (essay date 1972)

[*Axton examines the relationships between the characters in* Great Expectations, *discovering a primary source of evil and guilt in those affiliations where, instead of sharing equally in the partnership, one character exploits another for such reasons as greed and revenge; moreover, he argues that the novel impli-cates the systems of social stratification and criminal justice as mechanisms of such exploitation.*]

The habit of holding great, but unrealistic or unobtainable ex-pectations of life is the source of wrong, evil, and finally of guilt in *Great Expectations.* This is so because those whose expectations have been thwarted commonly turn out of a sense of injustice, to revenge; but this vengeance is directed toward or through the innocent. Or else, those who entertain great expectations are led into condescension, irresponsibili-ty, patronage, timeserving, ingratitude, or the imputation of evil to others. At the heart of these themes and their source is the patron-protégé relationship, a type of the much more fundamental theme of instrumentality—that is, the tendency to create relationships between people based on an inter-change of patronage and dependency, superiority and inferi-ority, *noblesse oblige,* and extorted gratitude, in which each party "expects" something in return that will serve the self. Every human relationship is cankered by its exploitation as an instrument of self-aggrandizement—love, friendship, par-enthood, and other ties of blood, even benevolence: indeed,

it is the expectation of getting something for oneself out of a relationship with another which is finally the source of evil in *Great Expectations,* whether that "something" be revenge, wealth, status, moral ascendency, sadistic pleasure, a sense of superiority, extorted gratitude, or mere condescension. In contrast, an alternative system of radically egalitarian values centered on Joe Gargery, Biddy, and Trabb's boy argues the moral preferability of a mutually disinterested interchange of love and affection as the basis for human relationships, one altogether indifferent to class distinctions and personal ad-vantage or disadvantage, one which substitutes love and af-fection for hatred or obsessive infatuation, forgiveness for re-venge, friendship for patronage, and responsibility for that imputation of evil to others which clears one's own skirts. The essential character of wrongdoing in this novel therefore consists in the betrayal or denial of humane relationship by an inhumane one; and events bring the traitor at last to a real-ization of his wrong and to forgiveness.

These thematic interrelationships are, in typically Dickensian fashion, torturously intricate; but matters will become clearer if we begin at the beginning with the simplest example of the simplest thread, the novel's epitome of frustrate expectations turned to persecution of the innocent, Mrs. Joe, Pip's older sister and unwilling foster mother. For if the death of Pip's parents has left him an orphan, the same event has con-demned his sister to sole care of the little brother in her keep-ing. This responsibility she has discharged only at the—to her—extortionate price of marrying, considerably beneath her station, the gentle but imbecilic and illiterate village blacksmith, Joe Gargery. A dual sense of disappointed expec-tations has thus made her the termagent shrew she is. On one hand, she tasks the boy with blame because she has been forced to "raise him by hand"; on the other, she belabors her husband because her reduced circumstances forced her to marry him, when under more advantageous conditions she might have made a better match. Mrs. Joe is, in short, a woman embittered by the frustration of her social expecta-tions, so that, in adopting the role of martyred wife and moth-er, she persecutes those who love and depend upon her. (pp. 279-80)

Mrs. Joe's bitterness expresses itself in a class-oriented deni-gration of her family, in which the imputation of guilt for her sacrifices to them is the principal weapon. Pip's household takes its tone from his class-conscious sister. She opposes Joe's feeble efforts to become literate, Joe says, "for fear as I might rise." She allows no one but herself to address Pum-blechook as "uncle," although Joe is his nephew. She is pre-occupied with minute differentiations in status. Thus the money Pip makes from odd jobs is put in a strongbox on the mantelpiece and saved, "in order . . . that our superior posi-tion might not be compromised" by the fact of his working. Of the Christmas guests at the forge, only the Hubbles (he is a wheelwright) are the social equals of the Gargerys, and Mrs. Joe panders to Pumblechook's superior wealth and posi-tion throughout the dinner. Later, the project to send Pip to Miss Havisham's is proposed in the hope of material advan-tage; and their fatuous speculations about the boy's prospects particularly infuriate Pip.

In respect to Pip, Mrs. Joe's thwarted expectations issue in a systematic program of blame, extorted gratitude, and physi-cal punishment in which the other members of the Gargery circle, with the exception of Joe, participate. It is this system of employing caste differences as a means of self-aggrandizement, with the corresponding use of imputed guilt, inferiority, or ingratitude as its instruments, that lies at the heart of the theme of **Great Expectations** as it is embodied in the character of Pip. Under the regimen of Mrs. Joe, Pumblechook, Wopsle, and the Hubbles, together with the intervention of Miss Havisham and Magwitch, Pip develops into a textbook case of social inferiority and moral guilt as they operate to generate and reinforce each other in an insecure, crime-haunted, condescending snob.

According to Pip, he had been dealt with by his sister from the time of his birth as a "young offender" who had "insisted on being born, in opposition to the dictates of reason, religion, and morality." During Christmas dinner at the forge he is tasked with ingratitude toward those who have "raised him by hand," and condemned for "all the illnesses I had been guilty of, and all the many acts of sleeplessness I had committed." Years later, he is accosted by Wopsle, taken to Pumblechook's parlor, and made the unwilling butt of a reading of Lillo's play about a traitorous apprentice, *George Barnwell, or, the London Merchant.* Immediately thereafter Pip discovers that his sister has been felled by an unknown assailant. The weapon, a convict's leg-iron filed asunder some time previously, convinces the boy of his unwitting complicity in the crime through his childhood association with the escaped convict, Magwitch.

The point of course is that the oppression Pip has suffered at the hand of his sister and her friends, coupled with his encounter with criminality have created in him a morbidly guilty conscience. His sensitivity and moral timidity are the products of his sister's "capricious and violent coercion," which have bred a "finely perceived and finely felt" sense of "injustice." What Pip later becomes, then, is the result of the subtle interweaving of his sister's incipient snobbery and imputation of blame with his own feeling of injustice, so that he will palm off his own guilty acts on those who are the victims of them while he pursues a condition of life that is beyond both commonness and blame.

Meanwhile, in the immediate context of the assault on his sister, Pip's actual sense of guilt is more complicated than appears at first sight. While "it was horrible to think that I had provided the weapon, however undesignedly," a more troublesome anxiety is the continuing secret of the stolen file, which he is afraid to confess to Joe on the grounds that it would alienate him or, worse, that he "would not believe it, but would assort it with the fabulous dogs and veal cutlets as a monstrous invention." What the young Pip feels guilty about is less the original crime of theft, still less its ultimate issue in the attack on Mrs. Joe; rather it is keeping the secret that betrays the affectionate confidence that has always existed between him and Joe. Pip's earlier lie about his first encounter with Miss Havisham now prompts his reticence; and it is this very "moral timidity" in which his present guilt consists. The mature narrator condemns his younger self for failing to trust in Joe's love, forgiveness, and sense of justice.

It could hardly be otherwise, for his sister's regimen has not only made Pip feel blameworthy, but also bred in the boy a no less morbid sensitivity to his humble station as a blacksmith's apprentice. Hence the discomfiture occasioned by his continuing if tenuous links to the underworld suggest to him complicity in crime as well as shame, his sense of being beneath genteel respectability. These anxieties are fatally intertwined from the first: to be low is to be evil, to be respectable is to be good, morally as well as socially superior to others.

Add to this the sense of injustice he felt as the butt of Mrs. Joe's persecution, and one has the insecure and pretentious snob that Pip becomes with his great expectations. The absolute desirability of wealth and position fostered by his sister, coupled with the taunts of Estella for his coarse hands and boots and his common manners, carry both moral and social overtones. His association with criminality is as much a source of moral as of social anxiety. The "restlessly aspiring discontented" Pip fears that Estella will "find me out, with a black face and hands, at the coarsest part of my work, and . . . exult over me and despise me." Awaiting her arrival in London, he contrasts his "taint of prison and crime" with Estella's distance from all that. The reason he does so lies in the fact that he has made of Estella a symbol of the "innermost life of my life." And yet Pip knows that the condition of life she stands for are beyond reach, for "the air of inaccessibility which her beauty . . . gave her tormented me in the midst of my delight, and at the height of the assurance I felt that our patroness had chosen us for one another."

Knowing that he loves Estella against all reasonable expectations, he also realizes that this knowledge had "no more influence in restraining me, than if I had devoutly believed her to be human perfection." The truth is that, while Estella the person may not be "human perfection," proud, willful, even cruel as she is, what she represents to the helplessly infatuated young man as the culmination of all his "wretched hankerings after money and gentility" is nothing less than human perfection. What Pip pursues in the person of the celestially unreachable Estella is not merely a life freed from the commonness, meanness, and coarseness of the forge and of ordinary life in general. On the contrary, he desires a condition of existence immune to blame, guilt, implication in or responsibility for crime or vice, and indeed free from the usual accountabilities: he seeks a state of total moral freedom, an olympian disengagement like that of the stars symbolized by Estella's name. More to the immediate point, Pip's social ambitions are identical with his moral and emotional goals: a way of life that not only transcends the limited human condition but that denies it. His flight from shame is also a flight from guilt; to be a gentleman is to be irresponsible. Acting upon this premise, Pip commits whatever substantial injustice he can be charged with.

The nature of Pip's real wrongdoing, in contrast to that with which he is charged as a boy, consists in his betrayal of the moral and emotional republic he once shared with Joe and Biddy, out of his sense of the distance imposed by his newly acquired gentility. In a larger sense, Dickens seems to have been saying, genteel respectability subverts the moral democracy of humankind by a moral ascendency based upon social or cultural superiority. The latter is a kind of ethical usurpation: it offers a freedom from reproach as well as a freedom to reproach: unjustice, briefly. (pp. 280-82)

The notion that wealth and position determine the essential quality of people is countered by a strain of radical egalitarianism in the novel most pointedly represented by the audacious figure of Trabb's boy, who steadfastly refuses to acknowledge Pip's rise in station as in any way imposing a distance between them, who satirizes Pip's attempts to gain a moral ascendancy over him by his gentlemanly clothes and manner, and who finally affirms their common citizenship in the republic of mankind by saving Pip's life.

Pip's wrongdoing . . . consists in trying to make Joe and Biddy protégés to his patronage and, when they resist, to condemn them for faults which are really his own. In either case, the methods are interoperative: the assertion of superiority implies an imputation of inferiority both social and moral that is self-aggrandizing to the aggressor. The aim remains irresponsible; it is to clear one's skirts of any personal involvement with one's fellowmen.

The demonstration scene between Biddy and Pip in chapter xix is a memorable one. The previous evening, a Saturday, Pip and Joe have received from Jaggers the news of the boy's "great expectations"; and after church the next day Pip sets out across the marshes in a condescending mood. As he passes the church, feeling "a sublime compassion for the poor creatures who were destined to go there . . . all their lives through. . . . I promised myself I would do something for them one of these days . . . bestowing a dinner of roast-beef and plum-pudding, a pint of ale, and a gallon of condescension, upon everybody in the village." On the same page, however, he is reminded of "my companionship with the fugitive . . . limping through these graves, . . . but my comfort was, that it happened a long time ago, and that he had doubtless been transported a long way off, and that he was dead to me." That is the way of life represented by Pip: such people as Magwitch—read Joe and Biddy equally—are a long way off, a long time ago, and are dead to him.

Then, after ostentatiously pledging loyalty to Joe, he takes Biddy aside to deplore the blacksmith's lack of polish, which he says will "hardly do him justice" when at some later date Pip will "remove Joe to a higher sphere."

> "And don't you think he knows that?" asked Biddy.
>
> It was such a provoking question (for it had never in the most distant manner occurred to me), that I said, snappishly, "Biddy, what do you mean?"
>
> Biddy . . . said, "Have you never considered that he may be proud?"
>
> "Proud?" I repeated, with disdainful emphasis.
>
> . . . . "He may be too proud to let any one take him out of a place that he is competent to fill, and fills well and with respect. To tell the truth, I think he is. . . ."
>
> "Now, Biddy," said I, "I am very sorry to see this in you. I did not expect to see this in you. You are envious, Biddy, and grudging. You are dissatisfied on account of my rise in fortune, and you can't help showing it."

Biddy makes the point: whatever their station, justice is one criterion of a gentleman. Pip's accusation of jealousy of his rise in station serves only to underline the thesis of the novel that status creates the opportunity to impute blame to others when one is himself at fault—or one's genteel class. The bonds of moral obligation between men have been broken, and superiority in caste seems to carry with it the need to assert moral superiority as well; and it is here that injustice enters in.

At the same time, Pip has been raised by the truly gentle man, Joe, to whom he is linked by ties of trust and affection that undercut those of class, and his betrayal of this egalitarian relationship troubles his conscience. Thus he lives "in a state of chronic uneasiness respecting my behaviour to Joe. My conscience was not by any means comfortable about

Biddy. . . . I used to think . . . that I should have been happier and better if I . . . had risen to manhood content to be partners with Joe in the honest old forge." This awareness does not prevent Pip from continuing to behave toward Biddy and Joe in the manner outlined above. Having been recalled to his old home to attend the funeral of his sister, Pip substantially reenacts the earlier scene with Biddy, except that now his guilty conscience about his shabby treatment of his old friends since removal to London becomes a complicating factor. Biddy's doubts of his resolve to see more of Joe in the future prompts a similar display of injured innocence and a mock-pious rejection of the offending party: "what an unkindness, what an injury, what an *injustice,* had Biddy done me" (italics mine). And yet, in his heart of hearts, he knows that Biddy's prophecy of his continuing neglect of Joe is true.

Such, then, is an outline of the process by which having great expectations generates real wrongdoing, the blame for which is displaced on to its victims, and thereby constitutes the essential subversion of the idea of gentle status. We may understand this mechanism better by turning to examine the novel's principal personification of evil incarnate, Dolge Orlick, for it is he who most dramatically illustrates the moral and psychological matrix we have already seen in Pip and Mrs. Joe. . . . Pip must come to an understanding of Orlick as an alter ego representing what evil really is as practiced by himself and by the society envisaged in this novel.

Pip learns this lesson at the limekiln, to which Orlick has lured him. What Pip confronts in the person of Orlick is quintessential evil and hatred motivating revenge against the boy who had been put unjustly ahead of him at the forge because of his special relationship with the master, Joe. It is Orlick's jealousy of Pip's favored position there, once the boy has been apprenticed, that prompts his sullen anger when Joe gives Pip a half-holiday to pay an anniversary visit to Miss Havisham, and leads him to demand the same reward for himself. When Joe grants the request and peace is restored between them, Mrs. Joe intervenes, curses Joe for a fool and Orlick for a rogue, and, when the journeyman in provoked to answer in kind, falls into an hysterical frenzy that forces the gentle blacksmith to give Orlick a beating. In revenge, Orlick attacks her that evening while Joe and Pip are at the Three Jolly Bargemen, and leaves her for dead. Yet at the limekiln he unjustly accuses Pip of committing that crime as part of his long-standing enmity against the journeyman. . . . This is of course only the culminating accusation in a long bill of particulars against Pip for having cost him his post as Miss Havisham's gatekeeper, given him a bad name with Biddy, and vowed to drive him out of the country. Still, at the core of his hatred is the accusation, to which he returns time and again, that "you was always in Old Orlick's way since ever you was a child." He feels that he is the victim of injustice.

Yet in no rational sense can Pip be said to have struck down Mrs. Joe, and in the other matters, as he answers sensibly, he has behaved toward Orlick as Orlick's behavior has merited: "You gave [your bad name] to yourself; you gained it for yourself. I could have done you no harm, if you had done yourself none." Orlick's case against Pip is, in short, patently without foundation in fact, as may be seen from an examination of his position at the forge, from which everything else grows. For Orlick was nothing more than a journeyman blacksmith on weekly wages: that is to say, his situation fell far short of having the dignity of permanence and indeed just missed being that of a casual laborer. And yet, when his master's young brother-in-law, whom he treats as a son, is apprenticed to Joe with every expectation of succeeding in time to the status of a master and partner, Orlick feels that his own hopes of advancement at the forge have been thwarted. His unreasonable sense of injury turns to hatred and revenge.

Similarly, Orlick's accusation that Pip has turned Biddy against him is altogether unjust, as the reader is well aware from the time that the girl first expressed her fear of and aversion to him when he "started up . . . from the ooze (which was quite in his stagnant way)" one day while she and Pip were walking on the marshes. And yet Orlick accuses Pip of "coming betwixt me and a young woman I liked." That Pip cost Orlick his post with Miss Havisham is true enough, but since it comes after his assault on Mrs. Joe he cannot rationally count that as a piece of Pip's conspiracy against him. Indeed, now that Pip has come into his "great expectations" and left the forge, it would seem that Orlick's way there was clear; but he gave Joe his notice.

What gradually emerges from this interview is the strange similarity between Orlick and Pip; for not only do they both habitually blame others for their own faults, but each has expectations of the world which cannot reasonably be fulfilled, and each pursues a young woman who does not love him but whom he thinks is his by right. Thus at the limekiln Orlick becomes a kind of grotesquely exaggerated counterpart of Pip, or at least of that aspect of Pip's character which exhibits the "bad side of human nature"—injustice—generally. As Pip condemns Biddy for his own wrong, so Orlick blames Pip for his crimes, accuses him of responsibility for his own failures, and seeks vengeance on his imagined persecutor; and in so doing, he manages to evade any accounting for his own wrongdoing. The innocent victim of a conspiracy to rob him of his due, like his comic counterpart Mrs. Joe he puts the onus of his frustrate expectations on his victims, the object of his vengeance. Within the moral context of this novel, Mrs. Joe's fate at the hands of Orlick constitutes an instance of supremely poetic justice. Similarly, it is altogether appropriate that Pip's rescue from the limekiln should be engineered by the combined efforts of two gentlemen, Pocket and Startop, and that thorn in his flesh, Trabb's boy, if for no other reason than that the act reaffirms the moral egalitarianism which the new-made gentleman has sought to ignore or deny.

In another sense, however, it is misleading to identify Orlick as the novel's leading personification of evil if that encourages us to overlook the dominant but shadowy figure of the gentleman-as-criminal, Compeyson, the seducer of Miss Havisham and the betrayer of Magwitch; for his presence in the background is required to define the rule played by social status in the generation and perpetuation of injustice and moral irresponsibility. *Great Expectations* proposes that the corrupt values implicit in the existence of a privileged class such as that of the "gentleman," with its assumption of a superiority that separates it from the accountability required of humankind, is the operative premise of injustice in the individual and the society which accepts such standards. This is true particularly insofar as the class represented by Compeyson exploits or neglects those inferior to it and yet at the same time refuses to accept any responsibility for, or relationship with, them. Indeed, that class has created a system of criminal justice calculated to heap with blame and punishment those creatures of its own making. These themes are at the core of Pip's troubled conscience; in Compeyson we see them personified and active as the canker of a social order.

Thus Compeyson's importance to the themes of *Great Expectations* cannot be underestimated. Simply as a device of plot he is crucial in starting the action of the novel and keeping it in motion. His seduction, fleecing, and final abandonment of Miss Havisham prompts her morbid withdrawal from the world. His exploitation and eventual betrayal of his partner in crime, Magwitch, generates the latter's resolve to revenge himself not only against Compeyson, but against the whole class of gentlemen he represents, by creating his own gentleman in the person of Pip. Indeed, it is the presence of Compeyson in the Hulks that determines Magwitch's attempt to escape, during the process of which he first encounters the boy. Finally, it is Compeyson who, fearfully seeking to protect himself against the vengeance of the returned felon—and incidentally scheming to expropriate his fortune—enlists the aid of Orlick (who seeks his own vengeance of Pip) and of the legal authorities to capture Magwitch and have his life in forfeit.

Two points are to be particularly noticed concerning Compeyson. The first is that the wrong he does to others—principally exploitation and betrayal—inspires in them a sense of injustice and a desire for vengeance which grows to transcend the individual and to embrace the entire class he represents. In the prosecution of their revenge, furthermore, Miss Havisham and Magwitch exploit others for their twisted purposes quite as fully, if not as ruthlessly, as Compeyson had done with them; but unlike Compeyson they come at last to realize the injustice they have done to their instruments. The second is that society and its legal institutions conspire with gentlemanly adventurers such as Compeyson to assist them in evading accountability for their crimes—not only the gentleman-criminal himself, but the criminally irresponsible genteel and respectable classes as a whole—by adopting a system of guilt-by-imputation which largely absolves the "gentle" folk from their implication in crime. In short, the system of criminal justice is as vengeful and unjust as Orlick, Miss Havisham, or Magwitch, and in the same way: it displaces its own guilt on to its victims, or on to those whom it has exploited, neglected, or abandoned.

These larger issues are first engaged by Magwitch's account to Pip and Pocket of the trial which sent him and Compeyson to the Hulks. For by playing upon the court's class prejudices, Compeyson contrives to load Magwitch with most of the blame for their crimes, in spite of the fact that Compeyson was the ringleader. The result is that the felon receives a heavy sentence, while the "gentleman" escapes with a light punishment, having been "recommended to mercy on account of good character and bad company, and giving up all the information he could" against Magwitch. (pp. 283-88)

The manifest injustice of the trial is underlined by two other scenes in which Dickens stresses the fact that, by neglect and exploitation, respectable society and its institutions create a criminal class like that represented by Magwitch, and by their legal and penal machinery condemn and punish such creatures in a way that absolves themselves and their class not only from any responsibility for the existence of criminals, but also from any relationship to them at all. For they are either executed en masse or conveniently shipped away to the Antipodes, never to return.

In the first instance we are given, in chapter xlii, Magwitch's poignant account of how a childhood of neglect and persecution by various institutions inevitably led him to the courtroom in which those same authorities, in their legal aspect, try and convict him. As "gentleman" Compeyson puts his own crimes on the shoulders of his confederate and tool, so the class Compeyson represents unburdens itself of responsibility for such creatures as Magwitch through the machinery of the penal code. Later in the novel, when Magwitch is tried as a returned transport and condemned to death along with thirty-two others, the effort of the judge to separate himself, his class, and his society from the criminally guilty standing before him is unmistakably discountenanced, first by the slanting ray of sunlight that links court and condemned alike before a higher, divine tribunal, and second, by the closing invocation of the parable of the Pharisee and the Publican.

That caste, rank, and status, whether conferred by blood relationship, as in the case of Matthew Pocket's wife, Belinda, or by money, as in the case of Pip and Estella, are centrally involved in the novel's complex scheme of injustice, irresponsibility, neglect and exploitation, and revenge which together comprise the constituent elements of its themes, seems indisputable. (pp. 288-89)

Miss Havisham is again at the heart of this theme. . . . As Herbert Pocket relates her story to Pip on their first evening at Barnard's Inn, she was the spoiled daughter of a brewer who had succeeded in achieving genteel status—"I don't know why it should be a crack thing to be a brewer; but it is indisputable that while you cannot possibly be genteel and bake, you may be as genteel as never was and brew. You see it every day." Having lost her mother in childhood and her father in early womanhood, she reaches maturity a proud, self-willed heiress, prey to any fortune hunter. It is then that the adventurer, Compeyson, enters the story at the behest of her half brother, Arthur, her father's son by a secret second marriage to his cook. Upon the latter's death, the son was recognized and introduced into Satis House. But because of his profligacy, Arthur was cut off by his father's will with only a very small share of the family estate, and in consequence "he cherished a deep and mortal grudge" against Miss Havisham for having turned his father against him. As Orlick determines to revenge himself on Pip, whom he conceived to be unjustly standing in his way at the forge, so Arthur Havisham employs Compeyson to gain vengeance against his half sister who was unjustly preferred at Satis House. Using Compeyson to capture his sister's heart, he may then gain control over her fortune and proceed to fleece her, saving the most exquisite part of his revenge for last, when her paramour throws her over on the wedding morning. The "gentleman" uses a "gentleman" to gain revenge on the one whom he blames for a frustration of his expectations that was in fact the consequence of his own vice.

The betrayal of the young heiress, as everyone knows, turns her into a morbid recluse who gradually warps her adopted daughter Estella into an instrument of revenge against the male sex, in the course of which Pip becomes tragically involved. By making Estella into an object of Pip's idolatrous infatuation, like that which Miss Havisham felt for Compeyson, and by encouraging the young man in his erroneous belief that he is Miss Havisham's protégé, secretly elevated to genteel status in order to make him a suitable partner for the celestial Estella, her revenge consists in raising expectations that must be frustrated. The cruelty that she practices upon Pip is only partially motivated by her desire to revenge herself

on the male sex. In part she fosters the illusion of Pip's favor in her eyes in order to torture and frustrate the expectations of her timeserving cousins, Sarah and Camilla Pocket, who dance attendance on her in hopes of sharing largely in her fortune upon her death. Miss Havisham's primary scheme of revenge miscarries in part because Estella comes to hate the self that her foster-mother has made of her and, in perverse revenge upon the woman who has warped her, throws herself away in a masochistic union with the stupid and brutal Bentley Drummle. In part, however, Miss Havisham herself comes to realize and feel remorse for the wreckage she has made of two innocent lives in her keeping, and on her deathbed pleads for forgiveness. The reading of her will, on the other hand, is a triumphant consummation of her scheme of vengeance against her hypocritical Pocket cousins, Sarah and Camilla, who are cut off with a pittance. At the same time, her loyal and disinterested cousin, Matthew Pocket, who alone among her relatives had penetrated the gentlemanly façade of Compeyson and warned her against putting herself so completely in his power—with the result that she turned him out of the house—is rewarded with a handsome legacy. In thus practicing on the greed, envy, and hypocrisy of her cousins, Miss Havisham takes her revenge for having been victimized by Compeyson and yet does justice in the process.

Miss Havisham's life following her abandonment by Compeyson is framed to hide from herself her own fault in the affair, in part by morbidly embracing the condition of a recluse, in part by casting the blame for her unhappiness on to the male sex. Indeed, her principal motivation for withdrawing behind the walls of Satis House and laying it waste seems to have been humiliation, not guilt: having prostrated herself wholly before her lover and having been brought low by his abandonment, she abandons herself to self-pity and vengeance. (pp. 289-91)

But the chain of injustice, vengeance, extorted gratitude, and evaded responsibility is broken significantly when those who have used others for their own twisted purposes come to realize the enormity of their wrong and beg forgiveness of their victims, . . . as Miss Havisham does when she enjoins Pip to "take the pencil and write under my name, 'I forgive her,'" and as Pip does following the illness through which Joe nursed him. Moreover, both Pip and Estella must be brought by suffering to understand their own wrongdoing and seek forgiveness from those who were the victims of their injustice. In Estella's case, the victim is Pip, whom she tormented while he loved her and betrayed by marrying Bentley Drummle.

> "You said to me [once before] . . . 'God bless you, God forgive you!' And if you could say that to me then, you will not hesitate to say that to me now—now, when suffering has been stronger than all other teaching, and has taught me to understand what your heart used to be."

With this, the novel's long circle of injustice, revenge, and forgiveness comes round upon itself.

At the core of this latter theme stands the patron-protégé relationship, inasmuch as it engages the themes of gratitude and thanklessness, obligation and irresponsibility, love and infatuation, gentility and gentleness. *Great Expectations* abounds in patrons and protégés of every shape and description, all eager to use this relationship to gain something for themselves: fraudulent ones like Pumblechook, genuine ones like Magwitch, who began in simple gratitude to the boy who

*A scene from the 1947 film adaptation of* Great Expectations, *showing Estella, Miss Havisham, and Pip.*

once helped him, and those somewhere in between, like Miss Havisham and Mrs. Joe, who are alternately a little of both.

What poisons this relationship is that it is never assumed disinterestedly: it plays upon and perpetuates a system of values that subverts human ones; it exploits or corrupts its recipients; it extorts gratitude from or imputes blame to its victims; and it thrives on and encourages not obligation but irresponsibility, not love but ambition or vengeance, not fulfillment but frustration, not equality but degree and distance, not equity but injustice.

In contrast stand the novel's many instances of genuine and disinterested responsibility for others, like that of Wemmick for his "Aged P"; of friendship that transcends self-interest, like that of Herbert Pocket for Pip; of love that has no other end in view but the welfare of the beloved, like that of Pocket for Clara Barley, of Biddy for Joe, and of Joe for Pip, and hence finds it easy to forgive transgressions because there is nothing to revenge; even, finally, of patronage that conceals itself, like that of Pip toward Pocket. These relationships are unique in the novel in that they are wholly lacking in any instrumental character: they exist for their intrinsic value alone and not as means to some other, selfish end. They have, in short, no great expectations but those of justice. Thus, where other relationships further revenge for wrongs done by another, these forgive and forget; where others impute evil, these compassionate; where others plume the self, these are anonymous and undemanding; where others exploit, neglect, betray, or abandon, these are loyal and responsible; where others promote the differences of rank and status, these level

all to a common moral egalitarianism based on simple gentleness; where others are passionate, obsessed, or infatuated, these are calm, deep, and abiding.

These themes finally precipitate into a single issue, the question of love, and particularly love as it engages the relationship between the self and others, between the lover and the beloved; for the moral tenor of this relationship is determined by the maintenance of the equality, integrity, and identity of the partners: their justice toward one another. The canker at the heart of the emotional relationships in *Great Expectations,* as of its moral and social relationships, is distance and degree, but expressed in this context in terms of domination and abasement—and therefore of justice—self-respect and respect for one's beloved. Once again, Miss Havisham and Magwitch give the key and set the tone for everything else, since each conceives of love or affection in terms of self-abasement. Miss Havisham's morbid conception of love— "blind devotion, unquestioning self-humiliation, utter submission, trust and belief against yourself and against the whole world, giving up your whole heart and soul to the smiter—as I did!"—she communicates to Pip, who as we have already seen prostrates himself before his vision of Estella. Estella, on the other hand, is sufficiently perverse to subject herself to the tender mercies of marriage with Drummle. Through their different but analogous sufferings, both Pip and Estella win through to a human love relationship based upon an equitable interchange of compassionate understanding. Magwitch, meanwhile, while loving his manufactured gentleman, abases himself before Pip because of his "lowness"; indeed, Pip's moral regeneration consists in transcending his patron's sense of inferiority by affirming their equality. Similarly, it was Pip's earlier subversion of the affectionate commonwealth that had existed between him, Joe, and Biddy in the days at the forge which constitutes the substantial wrong he does as a would-be gentleman. It is this very moral identity that Biddy asserts, much to Pip's discomfiture, in the two scenes between them following the young man's "rise in fortune"; and it is the barrier imposed between Joe and Pip by the latter's consciousness of his superior station that denies the equivalence implied by Joe's oft-repeated "Ever the best of friends, Pip!" For what is wrong with love relationships which involve abasement of one partner or the other is, paradoxically, that the act of humiliation carries with it a claim for possession: to be possessed as Pip and Miss Havisham are is to seek to possess, as Pip, Miss Havisham, and Magwitch do in their various ways. This theme accounts for the existence of Jaggers' housekeeper, the tigress Molly, Magwitch's sometime common-law wife and Estella's natural mother, a savage murderess who killed in a paroxysm of possessive jealousy. In contrast, the reader is asked to attend to the gentle and undemanding love of Pocket for Clara Barley and of Joe and Biddy—even their comic counterpart in the persons of Wemmick and Miss Skiffins. By refraining from the desire to possess another, they avoid both possession and being possessed. The principal moral irony of **Great Expectations,** then, is that these gain the only things of any value. Put another way, it consists in the allegation that gentility means gentleness, wherever it is found; and that the latter means justice, equity. (pp. 291-93)

*William F. Axton, "'Great Expectations' Yet Again," in* Dickens Studies Annual, *Vol. 2, 1972, pp. 278-93.*

## A. L. FRENCH (essay date 1974)

[*French considers the ways that characters' actions in* Great Expectations *are determined by their upbringing or by traumatic events in their formative years.*]

**Great Expectations** is . . . full of situations in which parents, or their substitutes, dominate and indeed determine their children—not merely what the children do but also what they are. Pip himself is exposed to four such influences: Joe, Mrs. Joe, Miss Havisham and Magwitch—all of them being pretty unsatisfactory. Herbert Pocket perhaps owes his decency to his having been allowed to 'tumble up' instead of having been 'brought up by hand'; Clara, his fiancée, is waiting, quite openly, for her detestably domineering father to die. And if Pip, when Magwitch comes back, feels like a Frankenstein in reverse—pursued by the creature who has made him—Miss Havisham, before she is burnt to death, realises she has created a monster, Estella, feels 'pity and remorse', and begs Pip's forgiveness. Estella, like Pip, is the victim, or beneficiary, of another's wishes; although in her case there seems little prospect of her being able to free herself from Miss Havisham's influence. About the only normal relationship between a parent and child in the novel is that between Wemmick and the Aged P.: but that exists only behind a raised drawbridge and, besides, the Aged P., being stone deaf, can't really communicate with his son, nor his son with him. The tone of the novel when Walworth sentiments are in question is indulgent, not cynical, but the implication—which Dickens chose not to follow up—is that affection may even depend on *not* communicating. Nor does the novel explore the real problems of having an aged parent, at least in reference to Wemmick, though Old Bill Barley (Clara's rum-and-pepper father) starts some uncomfortable reflections which Dickens couldn't perhaps afford to pursue.

We see the foundations of Pip's nature being laid early in the book: the experience with Magwitch in the churchyard merely plays in an even harsher key the tune he is used to at home, from Mrs. Joe, Pumblechook, and the Hubbles: his life is largely a matter of being threatened, bullied, knocked around, and made to feel ashamed of eating and being alive. Pip himself gives this account of the effect on him of his upbringing:

> My sister's bringing up had made me sensitive. In the little world in which children have their existence whosoever brings them up, there is nothing so finely perceived and so finely felt, as injustice. . . . Within myself, I had sustained, from my babyhood, a perpetual conflict with injustice. I had known, from the time when I could speak, that my sister, in her capricious and violent coercion, was unjust to me. I had cherished a profound conviction that her bringing me up by hand, gave her no right to bring me up by jerks. Through all my punishments, disgraces, fasts and vigils, and other penitential performances, I had nursed this assurance; and to my communing so much with it, in a solitary and unprotected way, I in great part refer the fact that I was morally timid and very sensitive.

Of course, being 'morally timid and very sensitive' is not the only possible reaction to injustice; Pip, if he had been born with a different temperament, could have responded in Magwitch's way to the injustice he met: by becoming 'hardened', getting his own back. But Pip takes the way of submission, shrinking from or flowing round difficulty and violence rather than fronting up to it. That in itself doesn't call for criticism, given that there is no proper way to deal with such a situation; whatever we do with Pip, we are not (usually) meant to use him as an occasion for feeling moral superiority. But perhaps our sympathy with his timidity and sensitivity is put in a slightly different light when we have taken, in the previous chapter, the kind of unaware self-justification that Joe offers him as an explanation of why he doesn't protect him against Mrs. Joe. The whole episode is intensely interesting, but for my present purposes I shall only look at the central passage. Having made Pip feel deeply grateful for having been taken in ('I said to your sister, "there's room for *him* at the forge!" '), Joe goes on to explain why Pip must teach him to read and write 'on the sly': because Mrs. Joe is 'given to government'—she domineers and won't have Joe being a 'rebel'; she is a 'master-mind'. All this seems to suggest that Joe feels his subservience to his wife is not only inevitable, but right: as though a slave should defend his not rebelling on the grounds that his master is wiser. One's sense that these thoughts are questionable becomes stronger when Joe goes on to connect his marriage with his parents':

> I see so much in my poor mother, of a woman drudging and slaving and breaking her honest hart and never getting no peace in her mortal days, that I'm dead afeerd of going wrong in the way of not doing what's right by a woman, and I'd fur rather of the two go wrong the t'other way, and be a little ill-conwenienced myself. I wish it was only me that got put out, Pip; I wish there warn't no Tickler for you, old chap; I wish I could take it all on myself;

> but this is the up-and-down-and-straight on it, Pip,
> and I hope you'll overlook shortcomings.

The suggestion seems to be that he doesn't want to put Mrs. Joe in the position of his mother (his father, we have heard, was a drunk who stopped Joe from going to school and 'hammered' him and his mother), so that the only course of action for Joe is to let her have her way. But obviously, what he is doing is reliving his parents' marriage in his own, except that now it is the man who never gets no peace and the woman who does the hammering: the sexes are reversed but the relationship is the same. And if Joe can believe, nevertheless, that 'my father were that good in his hart', he can also believe—and get Pip to agree—that his wife is 'a fine figure of a woman', a 'mastermind', and so on. Pip's reaction to this self-justification of Joe's is significant: 'Young as I was, I believe that I dated a new admiration of Joe from that night. . . . I had a new sensation of feeling conscious that I was looking up to Joe in my heart'. The older Pip, who is narrating the story, not only renders but apparently also approves this 'new sensation'; at least, I see no sign that he is dubious about it or about Joe. And while Pip, in chapter 8, sees clearly enough that his sister's regime is a matter of 'injustice', he has got from Joe a powerful confirmation of his own tendency to deal with it by not dealing with it and by feeling 'admiration' for the inner voice (as it becomes) which rationalises inaction into a higher courage than action. The only time before Magwitch's return when Pip squares up to things is in the boxing-match with the pale young gentleman; but he can't avoid that and it is, in any case, purely comic.

Pip's sensibility is thus fixed in early life: he is a kisser of rods. And when we ponder what Joe could have seen in Mrs. Joe, to make him want to marry her (loneliness is the explanation he gives, unconvincingly), we might then make a further link: if there's something in Joe that enjoys being dominated, there is no less something in Pip which feels drawn to Estella for the very reason that she ill-treats him. No doubt it's true enough to say, as Mrs. Leavis does [see Leavis entry in Further Reading dated 1970]. that when he first meets her he adores her purely for what she represents; but to go on and claim that he never loves her for what she is, since she is 'unlovable and unloving', and that the whole relationship is clearly seen by Dickens to be merely unrealistic, is to overlook, or at any rate to slight, an important vein of feeling that runs through the whole book. Once Pip has come into his Expectations, after all, Estella can hardly go on representing for him the glamour of wealth, education and social status that he hasn't yet got. In fact, after he has gone up in the world there still remain two painfully conflicting feelings about her, which lead Pip to say rather different things at different times. On his first visit to his home town after removing to London, the clashing emotions come out in the form of a contradiction. First, near the start of the chapter, we have this:

> though [Estella] had taken such strong possession of me, though my fancy and my hope were so set upon her, though her influence on my boyish life and character had been all-powerful, I did not, even that romantic morning, invest her with any attributes save those she possessed. I mention this in this place, of a fixed purpose, because it is the clue by which I am to be followed into my poor labyrinth. According to my experience, the conventional notion of a lover cannot be always true. The unqualified truth is, that when I loved Estella with the love of a man, I loved her simply because I found her irresistible. Once for all; I knew to my sorrow,

often and often, if not always, that I loved her against reason, against promise, against peace, against hope, against happiness, against all discouragement that could be. Once for all; I loved her none the less because I knew it, and it had no more influence in restraining me, than if I had devoutly believed her to be human perfection.

This feeling is the hardest thing in the novel for the modern reader to take, because it looks embarrassingly Victorian; so we tend to whisk it out of sight by calling it 'sentimental' or 'unrealistic', with the implication that Dickens sees it so, as part of his 'keen exposure of Pip's case'. Yet, since Dickens is a nineteenth-century novelist, it would scarcely be surprising if he believed as whole-heartedly as Pip does in the value, or at least the interestingness, of a passion whose distinguishing mark is that it is unreciprocated and wholly unsatisfying (in the normal sense of 'satisfying'). The situation is so common in Victorian fiction as to be conventional; and if the paragraph just quoted stood alone, we would be justified in accusing Dickens of having allowed a cliché to do his novelist's work for him. That his intentions in this book were serious and intelligent is shown, I think, by the fact that the slack rhetoric of this paragraph ('often and often . . .') is countered by what we find a little later in the same chapter, where we get a very different account of Estella's irresistibility:

> Proud and wilful as of old, she had brought those qualities into such subjection to her beauty that it was impossible and out of nature—or I thought so—to separate them from her beauty. Truly it was impossible to dissociate her presence from all those wretched hankerings after money and gentility that had disturbed my boyhood—from all those ill-regulated aspirations that had first made me ashamed of home and Joe—from all those visions that had raised her face in the glowing fire, struck it out of the iron on the anvil, extracted it from the darkness of night to look in at the wooden window of the forge and flit away. In a word, it was impossible for me to separate her, in the past or in the present, from the innermost life of my life.

The partial contradiction between the implication, here, that he loves Estella because he can't escape from his childhood impressions, and the implication, in the passage quoted earlier, that he loves her for her own sake and not for what she represented, certainly testifies that Pip very much wants to believe himself free from early influences. Yet, as soon as he enters Miss Havisham's unearthly domain, those influences re-assert themselves potently: 'I fancied, as I looked at her, that I slipped hopelessly back into the coarse and common boy again'. That is, the relationship remains arrested in the form it first took, when they were both children; and while, in the earlier passage, Pip avows that he didn't invest her 'with any attributes save those she possessed', and that he has come 'to love Estella with the love of a man' (normal sexual love), he very quickly grasps, if not altogether consciously, that he can't break the fixed pattern and that 'the love of a man' merely means superadding sexual love to his other feelings of abject dependence. . . . It is clear that Miss Havisham, having brought Estella up to take revenge on men, is casting Pip in the role of victim, confirming him in the part he has always played; the sort of relationship she wants him to have with Estella is analogous to that between a very small child and a brutal parent. (I presume there is always some kind of infantilism in such self-abasement: Dickens has the insight but not the vocabulary.) And Miss Havisham is pushing—or leading—Pip into this position with something of the authority of a parent as well as a supposed patron.

When that night Pip goes back to the Blue Boar, he lies awake and gives a characteristic emphasis to Miss Havisham's words:

> Far into the night, Miss Havisham's words, 'Love her, love her, love her!' sounded in my ears. I adapted them for my own repetition, and said to my pillow, 'I love her, I love her, I love her!' hundreds of times. Then, a burst of gratitude came upon me, that she should be destined for me, once the blacksmith's boy. Then, I thought if she were, as I feared, by no means rapturously grateful for that destiny yet, when would she begin to be interested in me? When should I awaken the heart within her, that was mute and sleeping now?

What 'love' means to Pip, we have already seen; he is now himself rapturously acquiescing in his destiny of being an innocent Lycius to a Lamia or a 'wretched wight' to Estella's Belle Dame sans Merci. 'Adapting' Miss Havisham's words means he accepts that role while refusing absolutely to see that Estella's being 'by no means rapturously grateful for that destiny' is an intended and inevitable corollary of it; 'yet' contrives to insinuate that, at some time, Estella will be grateful and will be able to return his love in, presumably, the normal adult way—a thought brought out further by Pip's reference to 'awakening' her heart. But Estella herself has warned him, only a few pages before: 'I have no heart'. (At the end of the book we meet an Estella whose heart has apparently been battered into sensibility by Bentley Drummle; there is a parallel with Mrs. Joe's being battered into submissive idiocy—a second childhood—by Orlick, whom she then tries, like a frightened child, to propitiate.) (pp. 148-55)

The remainder of Pip's relationship with Estella follows the groundwork already laid down; it would be surprising if there were any real growth on either side, though both come to understand better why they are what they are. (pp. 155-56)

If the novel works in the way I have been suggesting, we needn't make heavy weather of Pip's farewell to Estella when he hears she is going to marry Bentley Drummle; his claim, for example, that 'you must have done me much more good than harm' is poignant in its absurdity; the book has clearly shown his capacity for feeling and living to have been laid as waste as Satis House. Nor need we have any difficulty in seeing how Miss Havisham is relevant. Far from being an engaging Dickens eccentric, or a 'picturesque convenience' (Mrs. Leavis), or a fairy-tale witch, or an example of the hypertrophy of Dicken's art, her 'case' is only the most striking of the many striking images Dickens finds of emotional arrest. Only this arrest isn't caused in a child by dominant parents, guardians or benefactors; it is a deliberate and conscious adult decision—a way (it is hinted) of ostensibly taking revenge on a world that has let one down, while in fact taking revenge on oneself for one's inadequacy, the inadequacy consisting in having *been* let down. Miss Havisham's self-destructiveness is, I take it, the point of the young Pip's hallucination, towards the end of chapter 8, when he sees her 'hanging . . . by the neck' from 'a great wooden beam' in the deserted brewery, as though she had committed suicide—as, emotionally, she has. We learn from Herbert Pocket that 'she was a spoilt child', whose 'mother died when she was a baby, and [whose] father denied her nothing': a scrap of information that makes it clear why she responds as she does to Compey-

son's jilting her. She stops all life and normal feeling at the very moment in her life when she gets his letter, and proceeds to train Estella to do to men what a man has done to her, as well as training Pip to be to Estella what she has been to Compeyson. If Miss Havisham can only conceive of human relationships in terms of dominating or being dominated, of being a harsh parent or a submissive child, of being the smiter or the smitten, then it is shockingly appropriate that when she begins to see what she has done to those two young lives, she should slip into exactly the opposite role to the one she has been sustaining hitherto and become a pleading child:

> She turned her face to me for the first time since she had averted it, and, to my amazement, I may even add to my terror, dropped on her knees at my feet; with her folded hands raised to me in the manner in which, when her poor heart was young and fresh and whole, they must often have been raised to heaven from her mother's side.

> To see her with her white hair and her worn face kneeling at my feet, gave me a shock through all my frame.

What elsewhere in Dickens might have been a distasteful cliché of remorse ('they must often have been raised to heaven') here comes out as a really painful insight—not only into the Miss Havisham of this particular novel but also into the cliché on which, in earlier books, Dickens had been too ready to depend.

A good deal of *Great Expectations* therefore seems to me to be concerned with the ways in which a person is determined either by his upbringing or by a traumatic experience that happens before his character is fully formed. The novel is defining, long before modern psychology, the ways in which the child is father of the man; and there is a strong impulse in its art to see the man as being exclusively and solely the offspring of the child—to see the characters as altogether determined by their earlier lives and being unable to 'bend the past out of its eternal shape'. In other words, the book is at this level an analysis of psychological and moral determinism, as *Hamlet* (in part) is. Yet there is obviously another drive: Dickens believes, or as a Victorian wants to believe, that the will is to some extent free, that there are possibilities of growth and maturing. A good many critics take this to be the main burden of the novel; present its *rationale* as a more or less naive meliorism; and are therefore unable to account for its depressed and muted tone. And it's true that Dickens does want to believe the Pip who is writing the story to be, on the whole, a better and freer man than he would have been had he been left at the forge or, after leaving it, had not been made to suffer. Similarly, Miss Havisham is shown as winning through, shortly before she is burnt to death, to a genuinely clearer and more humane understanding of what she has done; Magwitch 'softens'; and Estella, at the very end, says that 'suffering has been stronger than all other teaching, and has taught me to understand what your heart used to be. I have been bent and broken, but—I hope—into a better shape', so that in her case the past *has* been unbent, by her being bent. Joe and Herbert Pocket find happiness in marriage; and Wemmick's marrying Miss Skiffins suggests that Walworth sentiments are finally stronger than Little Britain ones.

And there are subtler reasons, too, for thinking that the novel wants to work in this way. Despite the circumstances of Pip's childhood, which if they occurred in real life could properly be called horrific, there is something about the tone and poise of those early chapters which throws the horror sufficiently out of focus for us to be able to feel that it wouldn't have been at all impossible for the boy to grow up a free and independent spirit, despite that start. The thing is delicately done, and it is hard to put one's finger on how Dickens contrives to present the Mrs. Joe ménage and at the same time draw its sting. Perhaps what denatures the little boy's experience is the constant intervention of the middle-aged man's voice, which tends to admit the facts, but in a humorous manner. . . . [This comes out] revealingly, I think, in things like the description of the Christmas dinner at the Gargerys'. Abstracted from the jolly tone that the narrator uses (if that were possible), the moral arm-twisting indulged in by all the adults (except Joe) at Pip's expense is perfectly sickening: Mr. Hubble calls him 'naterally wicious', his sister gives him the worst bits of meat and Mr. Pumblechook draws a sadistic contrast between Pip as he is and Pip as he would have been if he had been born a pig:

> 'Dunstable the butcher would have come up to you as you lay in your straw, and he would have whipped you under his left arm, and with his right he would have tucked up his frock to get a penknife from out of his waistcoatpocket, and he would have shed your blood and had your life'.

This leads straight on to Mrs. Joe's complaining of the trouble Pip has been to her:

> [She] entered on a fearful catalogue of all the illnesses I had been guilty of, and all the acts of sleeplessness I had committed, and all the high places I had tumbled from, and all the low places I had tumbled into, and all the injuries I had done myself, and all the times she had wished me in my grave, and I had contumaciously refused to go there.

By the time we get to the end of this sentence, the syntactical pattern ('all the . . . all the . . .') and the bouncing rhythm have so reduced our grasp of what is being said that we don't notice that Mrs. Joe is publicly—and over Christmas dinner!—wishing Pip were dead. If this happened in real life it would be appalling and unpardonable; but from the novel we take away no more than a sense of unease; the child's reaction is 'placed', almost obliterated, by the narrator's avuncular geniality. Similarly, the horrible scraps of meat that Pip gets appear facetiously as 'those obscure corners of pork of which the pig, when living, had had the least reason to be vain'. A good deal of what happens in the first fifteen or so chapters is muffled in this way: even Pip's sense of guilt, after his sister has been struck down—a guilt that looks at first as though it is going to be deeply revealing about how Pip (we suppose) must have felt towards her—dissolves into a worry whether or not he should tell Joe of the ancient episode of the convict.

It's not altogether surprising, then, that when Pip starts to aspire beyond the dullness of the forge, when he begins to try and make himself different from Joe and Biddy, the kind of cruelty he shows them shouldn't be unforgivably gross: as Mrs. Leavis rightly says, 'few in the circumstances could be confident of showing up better'. Though that is a healthy corrective to the notion of Pip as merely a snob, or merely anything, one wonders if it doesn't inadvertently reveal Dickens's problem. Mrs. Leavis has just claimed that

> Pip himself, the mature recorder of his own exemplary history, does not deal tenderly with himself, recording mercilessly every least attractive im-

pulse, but we should notice that these are mitigated always by generous misgivings, permeated by uneasy self-criticism, and contrary movements of feeling of a self-corrective kind.

The consequence of this mingling of the mean act, the misgiving, and the self-criticism, is that the older Pip, whom we think of as having freed himself from his conditioning, must consequently be only *too* acute about his younger failings. By being concerned to show up his younger self, Pip the narrator puts himself in a position of moral superiority so great that it has the unfortunate effect of reducing the moral significance of his earlier experiences—of making the younger Pip into something too like a butt. The intention is no doubt that the older Pip shall show up the younger one's moral shortcomings; the actual effect is to make the younger Pip show up the older one's moral achievements. This comes out rather embarrassingly in the three chapters (17, 19 and 35) which deal with his relationship with Biddy. The kind of irony we get there at Pip's expense seems to me pretty crude—its crudity matches, in a way the older Pip doesn't realise, the crudeness of his younger self's behaviour. Pip indeed behaves callously and arrogantly to Biddy, but the irony underlines the point so heavily that one starts wondering about its motive: to be that 'merciless' (Mrs. Leavis's word) to oneself is to call for admiration; the self-humiliation is a form of self-inflation. No-one, of course, can quarrel with Dickens's undertaking to show the growth of a moral sensibility, but one may wonder whether he hasn't been tempted to think of the narrating Pip as *finally* mature or (as it were) saved, regenerate. If he is, then he casts the deepest doubts on the insights he himself appears to have about the importance of a human being's childhood.

Yet in an odd way we are invited by the novel to see Pip's improvement as happening, not despite, but because of, his upbringing: there is throughout a strong vein of suggestion that suffering . . . is beneficial, and that the benefit consists in making the beneficiary kinder, sweeter, more tolerant, and in general a member of the Lamb's party rather than the Tyger's. We are to regard Pip as better partly, at least, on the grounds that he has rooted out of himself all the darker impulses and every rationalisation by which people normally defend them. Morally that may have something to be said for it; in a work of fiction, the inevitable result is that the Pip who is better is at the same time less interesting and less recognisably human. Pip's progress is also a kind of regress: as a grown man he has learnt to live the ideal of being a well-behaved little boy.

An analogous fate overtakes some of the other characters. We're obviously meant to think Miss Havisham's remorse and prayer for forgiveness to be a testimony to a sort of Original Virtue: human nature can't be suppressed, and it has its own inward drive towards health, freedom and goodness. What I earlier suggested was a crowning irony—that Miss Havisham in chapter 49 becomes a suppliant child begging forgiveness from her 'father'—may just as easily be seen as a quite unironical implication by Dickens that this is the right way to be good. 'Whosoever shall not receive the kingdom of God as a little child shall in no wise enter therein' (Luke xviii.17) is a text that must have meant a great deal to Dickens; it is the optimistic obverse of Mr. Hubble's 'naterally wicious', but it can lead us into some strange emotional places. Magwitch, too, once he goes to the Barleys' (chapter 46 onwards), turns from a figure who was terrifying to Pip because he told him what to do and made him what he is, into a figure who happily complies with Pip's suggestions: Pip becomes active, in determining how he shall be got out of the country, while Magwitch becomes passive ('softened'). . . . It is not that this development is implausible either in fictional terms or in terms of real life; the problem is rather that Magwitch, by becoming submissive, has lost that very powerful presence which the novel gave him: the nearer he comes to death, the better he gets. Goodness, that is, comes here to be associated with physical weakness; Magwitch's being 'tired out' is the condition of that goodness, but the reader regrets that he has lost the fierce will which made him a man, without having acquired any quality which can seriously be taken to replace it. Thus, he too has broken free from the conditioning imposed on him by his childhood (given to us with great vividness in chapter 42), and has ceased to be a 'warmint', but only at the cost of losing his manhood (he, like Mrs. Joe and Miss Havisham, must be mortally hurt). It is no accident that, on Magwitch's death at the very end of chapter 56, Pip should refer to the Biblical text about the 'two men who went up into the Temple to pray', since in Luke xviii (the parable of the Pharisee and the publican) Christ says that 'he that humbleth himself shall be exalted'—a dictum that occurs only three verses before the remark about the 'little child', quoted above.

But there are, as everyone will point out, characters in *Great Expectations* who are neither shown to have been determined by their childhood nor suggested to have the power to free themselves (in however suspect a way) from that conditioning. Orlick, for example, comes into the novel from nowhere; Dickens produces him without antecedents in the very chapter where Mrs. Joe is struck down. Of Mrs. Joe's own background we know virtually nothing. Bentley Drummle, who appears in chapter 25, is given very little in the way of antecedents: 'He came of rich people down in Somersetshire, who had nursed this combination of qualities ["idle, proud, niggardly, reserved, and suspicious"] until they made the discovery that it was just of age and a blockhead'. Mr. Jaggers, who significantly admires Drummle ('I like the fellow, Pip; he is one of the true sort'), similarly has nothing in the way of family background; and the only personal relationship he is capable of is with Molly, his housekeeper, who turns out to be Estella's mother and Magwitch's wife, so that we see Molly tamed by Jaggers in something of the same way as her daughter is tamed by Drummle. If then Orlick and Drummle—characters whom Pip detests—together with Jaggers, about whom the novel is at worst uneasy, are none of them allowed to give (or are given by the book) any explanation as to their brutal domination of others, we must suppose that there is another element altogether in Dickens's thinking about what makes a man what he is. Hitherto, as we have seen, there is a drive in the novel to see man as the victim of his upbringing, a drive that is qualified by the impulse to see him as to some extent capable of freeing himself. But the thoughts represented by these bad characters are only intelligible if we suppose Dickens to have also believed, with part of his mind, that some people are, in Mr. Hubble's words, 'naterally wicious'; if Dickens felt that some kinds of bad temperaments were not explicable in any terms at all. In other words, despite both his psychological insights and his Victorian meliorism, Dickens couldn't help wondering about Original Sin. His interest in theology as such may have been slight, but it isn't surprising that a man so interested in Shakespeare should have been finally dissatisfied with psychological and social 'explanations' of human behaviour, as well as with the notion that the exercise of free-will can save us. We may well regard these thoughts about sin as the deepest insights of all; but unfortu-

nately the novel doesn't really support us. For apart from Mr. Jaggers and Mrs. Joe, the 'evil' characters are disappointingly unrealised and play a pretty peripheral part in the action. . . . And there is also the difficulty that, if the novelist wants to bring in characters whose very point is that their behaviour is inexplicable, he runs a serious risk of seeming arbitrary when he is writing a novel which is otherwise so rich in its psychological and social explanations. Mrs. Joe is of course treated at greater length and in fuller detail than Orlick or Drummle; but in her case, the problem arises that I mentioned earlier: all her behaviour, from the merely mean and ungracious to the openly pathological (the 'rampages'), is as it were shot slightly out of focus, the sharp lines of the child's remembered perception being ever so subtly blurred by the humorous tones and asides of the mature narrator. . . . [If] the aim of these early pages is to establish Mrs. Joe as a potent and terrifying figure, the humour is at odds with that aim. It is true to say, with Mrs. Leavis, that though Pip's 'sufferings are minimised by the amusement with which the adult Pip recounts his memories, there is sufficient poignancy in the recollections to make them moving as well as vivid'; yet the vividness is like that with which someone growing up during the War now remembers those insecure and frightening years; one jokes about having been cold and hungry: one mythologises it. So that, while Dickens in the early chapters of *Great Expectations* may seem to be doing something like what Gorki attempts in *My Childhood*, he never earns the right to say 'the truth is beyond all commiseration', and is unsure how far he is even trying to earn that right. He has therefore put himself in the uncomfortable position of endorsing, in regard to Mrs. Joe, Orlick and Drummle, the notion of 'nateral wiciousness' which, when applied to Pip or Magwitch or Estella, is felt to be itself vicious.

It's in chapter 48 that Jaggers gives his opinion of Bentley Drummle, who is about to marry Estella: ' "A fellow like our friend the Spider . . . either beats, or cringes. He may cringe and growl, or cringe and not growl; but he either beats or cringes. Ask Wemmick *his* opinion" '. And Wemmick (not the Walworth twin) agrees. Much of the world of *Great Expectations* sorts itself out into these two distasteful categories. One may beat because one has been beaten (Magwitch, Estella), or one may cringe for the same reason (Pip, Molly, Joe); or one may, because beaten, simultaneously beat *and* cringe (Miss Havisham); or one may beat for no apparent reason at all except that one happens to have been born that way (Orlick, Drummle, Mrs. Joe). Dickens was obviously bent on pursuing some highly dismaying insights about the exercise of power—psychological as well as social and financial; but it is quite evident that he badly wanted, at the same time, to believe other things about the possibilities of human nature than that it classified itself only along these lines. The result is that the more attentively we read the book, the less we know whether Dickens really grasped just how dismaying the best things in it are. (pp. 158-68)

*A. L. French, "Beating and Cringing: 'Great Expectations',"* in Essays in Criticism, *Vol. XXIV, No. 2, April, 1974, pp. 147-68.*

**JOHN IRVING** (essay date 1979)

[*An American novelist, short story writer, and essayist, Irving is best known for his popular 1978 novel* The World According to Garp. *In the following excerpt, he praises the sentimentality of Dickens's writings, focusing on* A Christmas Carol *and* Great Expectations.]

[In] the spirit of Christmas, who could fault *A Christmas Carol?* "Who can listen," Thackeray said, "to objections regarding such a book as this? It seems to me a national benefit, and to every man or woman who reads it a personal kindness." It is surprising, however, how many readers reserve Dickens—and hopefulness in general—for Christmas; it seems that what we applaud in Dickens—his kindness, his generosity, his belief in our dignity—is also what we condemn him for (under another name) in the off-Christmas season.

The other name is sentimentality—and to the modern reader, too often when a writer risks being sentimental, the writer is already guilty. But as a writer it is cowardly to so fear sentimentality that one avoids it altogether. It is typical—and forgivable—among student writers to avoid being mush-minded by simply refusing to write about people, or by refusing to subject characters to emotional extremes. A short story about a four-course meal from the point of view of a fork will never be sentimental; it may never matter very much to us, either. A fear of contamination by soap opera haunts the educated writer—and reader—though we both forget that in the hands of a clod, *Madame Bovary* would have been perfect material for daytime television and a contemporary treatment of *The Brothers Karamazov* could be stuck with a campus setting. Dickens took Christmas risks all the year round.

"I must make the most I can out of the book," he said, before beginning *Great Expectations*—"I think [it's] a good name?" he said. Good, indeed, and a title many writers wish were free for them to use, a title many wonderful novels could have had: *The Great Gatsby, To the Lighthouse, The Mayor of Casterbridge, The Sun Also Rises, Moby Dick*—all great expectations, of course.

Yet the hopefulness that makes everyone love *A Christmas Carol* draws fire when Dickens employs it in his best novel; when Christmas is over, Dickens's hopefulness strikes many as mere wishful thinking. Dickens's original ending to *Great Expectations,* that Pip and his impossible love, Estella, should stay apart, is thought to be the proper (and certainly the modern) conclusion—from which Dickens eventually shied away; for such a change of heart and mind, he is accused of selling out. After an early manhood of shallow goals, Pip is meant finally to see the falseness of his values—and of Estella—and he emerges as a sadder though a wiser fellow. Many have expressed how Dickens stretches credulity too far when he leads us to suppose—in his revised ending—that Estella and Pip could be happy ever after; or that anyone can. Of his new ending—where Pip and Estella are reconciled—Dickens himself remarked to a friend: "I have put in a very pretty piece of writing, and I have no doubt the story will be more acceptable through the alteration" [see letter dated 1861]. That Estella would make Pip—or anyone—a rotten wife is not the point; they are linked: happily or unhappily, they belong together.

Biographically, it is difficult to resist the association of Pip's trapped worship of Estella with Dickens's own sad adoration of the young actress, Ellen Ternan. Although the suggestion that Dickens revise the original ending came from his friend Bulwer Lytton, who wished the book to end on a happier note, Edgar Johnson wisely points out that "the changed ending reflected a desperate hope that Dickens could not banish

from within his own heart" [see excerpt dated 1952]. That hope is no last-minute alteration, tacked-on, but simply the culmination of a hope that abides throughout the novel, that Estella might change; after all, Pip changes. The book isn't called *Great Expectations* for nothing. It is not, I think, meant to be an entirely bitter title.

In fact, it is the first ending that is out of character—for Dickens, and for the novel. Pip, upon meeting Estella (after two years of hearing only rumors of her), remarks with a pinched heart: "I was very glad afterwards to have had the interview; for in her face, and in her voice, and in her touch, she gave me the assurance that suffering had been stronger than Miss Havisham's teaching, and had given her a heart to understand what my heart used to be." Although that tone—of self-congratulation and self-pity—is more modern than Dickens's romantic revision, I fail to see how we or our literature would be better for it.

The revised ending reads: "I took her hand in mine, and we went out of the ruined place; and, as the morning mists had risen long ago when I first left the forge, so the evening mists were rising now, and in all the broad expanse of tranquil light they showed to me, I saw no shadow of another parting from her." A very pretty piece of writing, as Dickens noted, but eternally open—still ambiguous (Pip's hopes have been dashed before)—and far more the mirror of the quality of trust in the novel as a whole. It is that hopeful ending that sings with all the rich contradiction we should love Dickens for; it both underlines and undermines everything before it. Pip is basically good, basically gullible; he starts out being human, he learns by error, he keeps on being human. That touching illogic seems not only generous but true.

"When people say that Dickens exaggerates," George Santayana writes, "it seems to me that they can have no eyes and no ears. They probably have only *notions* of what things and people are; they accept them conventionally, at their diplomatic value." And to those who contend that no one was ever so sentimental, or that there was no one ever like Wemmick or Jaggers or Bentley Drummle, to name a few, Santayana says: "The polite world is lying; there *are* such people; we are such people ourselves in our true moments, in our veritable impulses; but we are careful to stifle and hide those moments from ourselves and from the world; to purse and pucker ourselves into the mask of conventional personality; and so simpering, we profess that it is very coarse and inartistic of Dickens to undo our life's work for us in an instant, and remind us of what we are." Santayana is also brilliant at defending Dickens's stylistic excesses; "He mimicks things to the full; he dilates and exhausts and repeats; he wallows," Santayana admits, though he adds, "this faculty, which renders him a consummate comedian, is just what alienated him from a later generation in which people of taste were aesthetes and virtuous people were higher snobs; they wanted a mincing art, and he gave them copious improvisation, they wanted analysis and development, and he gave them absolute comedy."

Christmas—or any other demonstration of giving—is no time for "a mincing art"; we should learn that there is really no good time for such cramped elitism. "God bless us every one!" cried Tiny Tim. But this Christmas, since we're so familiar with *A Christmas Carol*—in its several versions—we might well read *Great Expectations;* it is a book many of us read last when we were in school, when we were too young to appreciate it. For its Christmas spirit—its open-hearted and forgiving qualities, and its feast of language—it is the best of novels by a writer of no mincing art.

And when we writers—in our own work—escape the slur of sentimentality, we should ask ourselves if what we are doing matters. (pp. 3, 96)

John Irving, *"In Defense of Sentimentality,"* in The New York Times Book Review, *November 25, 1979, pp. 3, 96.*

## BERT G. HORNBACK (essay date 1987)

[*Hornback is a noted American educator and Dickens scholar. In the following excerpt from his book-length study of* Great Expectations, *Hornback discusses Pip's education, supporting his belief that learning friendship is one of the novel's most important themes.*]

**Great Expectations** is a novel about learning and knowing—and even Pip's relationship with Estella is more one of learning and knowing than it is a relationship of love, perhaps. From the beginning of the first chapter, when Pip the child "found out for certain" "the identity of things," this has been a novel about Pip's education. (p. 39)

Mary Anne Evans, a younger contemporary of Dickens whose novels appeared under the name George Eliot, wrote in her journal that "Feeling is a sort of knowledge," that "What seems eminently wanted is a closer comparison between the knowledge which we call rational & the experience which we call emotional." On the same subject, she wrote to a friend, "If Art does not enlarge men's sympathies, it does nothing morally." Both of these remarks are pertinent for our study of **Great Expectations** and the theme of education in this novel. First, Pip's early attempts at education are restricted to the learning of "things"—information—and manners; and the more he learns, intellectually, about the things that will "raise" him in "society," the more he forgets of human sympathy. Second, his novel has, as its purpose . . . our education, and the enlargement of our sympathies through an understanding of Pip's story.

Pip's story is . . . a story of freedom, and friendship. Freedom and friendship are the same word, etymologically: they both come into the English language from the same Germanic root, *frei,* which means "to love." The bond that friendship makes, then, frees us: freedom becomes much more clearly a social virtue than we might sometimes try to make it, each of us doing his own thing. Both words tell us that you can't be free by yourself. "Ever the best of friends, Pip" is not Joe's threat to his apprentice; it is his pledge for Pip's freedom. Later, Joe gladly gives up Pip's indentures (those papers that "bind" Pip apprentice to the master blacksmith) because Pip is his friend.

To Pip's surprise, however, his new freedom from the forge and his "great expectations" for the future make him lonely rather than happy: he feels it "very sorrowful and strange," he says, that the "first night of [his] bright fortunes should be the loneliest [he] had ever known." He is sad at the prospect of leaving Joe and the world he knows—but still he wants to leave. It takes Joe, in his natural wisdom, to set this problem straight for Pip, and he does it through reference to the double sense of binding that makes friendship free: "Life," he tells Pip, "is made of ever so many partings welded together."

When we understand what Joe says, we will have understood this novel—and our sympathies will be enlarged. Pip narrator understands it, and what he tells as his story records his struggle toward that understanding.

Pip's first learning, in a formal sense, supposedly takes place at Mr. Wopsle's great-aunt's evening school: "that is to say . . . a ridiculous old woman of limited means and unlimited infirmity . . . used to go to sleep from six to seven every evening, in the society of youth who paid twopence per week each, for the improving opportunity of seeing her do it." Mr. Wopsle's great-aunt also has a granddaughter, Biddy, and with her help Pip sets out upon the hard road of scholarship.

As Pip narrator describes it, this hard road is more remarkable for its impediments and dangers than for milestones marking accomplishments. Learning the alphabet is like struggling in "a bramble-bush," and he is "worried and scratched by every letter"; the numbers are "those thieves, the nine figures, who seemed every evening to do something new to disguise themselves and baffle recognition." The child Pip has already associated himself with Magwitch as a boy "going to rob Mrs. Joe," and thus destined for the Hulks (46), and the narrator has reported Mrs. Joe's treating him as a "young offender . . . to be dealt with according to the outraged majesty of the law" and dressed in clothes that, though not necessarily gray like prisoners' uniforms, are designed "like a kind of Reformatory" to restrain "the free use of [his] limbs." Now the narrator connects his child-self's educational endeavors to Magwitch through the bramble-bush and the thieves: "his" thief, in his difficulties, was "stung by nettles, and torn by briars." Further underlining the connection, Pip narrator reckons the time of his first exhibition of his newly won knowledge by reference to Magwitch's capture: he writes Joe a letter "a full year after our hunt on the marshes." (pp. 39-41)

Pip's letter describes his happiness with Joe and his active affection for him: he will teach Joe, he says, and they will both be glad; and when Pip is apprenticed to Joe, "woT larX." Dickens clusters the themes and movements of the novel around this simple but difficult communication. It takes Pip "an hour or two" to write these few sentences to Joe; the labor underlines their significance. What they say, together with the confidence they elicit from Joe in response, mark this evening as the climax of their "ever the best of friends" relationship. But when Mrs. Joe comes home that evening, she brings not only the bullying Pumblechook but the disruptive news that Pip is to "go and play" at Miss Havisham's the next day.

Magwitch, Joe, friendship, and an innocent desire for learning stand on the one side of Pip's letter; Miss Havisham, Estella, riches, dissatisfaction, frustration, and a newly avaricious attitude toward education stand on the other. Pumblechook takes Pip to Miss Havisham's, and his conversation along the way consists of "nothing but arithmetic." Pip resents Pumblechook's running sums and ignores his questions when he can. But sums are to the point in this new world, more so than in the simple world of the forge which Pip has left behind. Miss Havisham's house is "Satis House," and Satis, as Estella explains, means "enough." The point is not that Pip calculates the worth of what he sees when he enters Miss Havisham's room, but that he recognizes it as worth, as "rich" and "splendid." And as Pip soon discovers, he doesn't know enough, generally, in this new world. He knows but one game, and he doesn't know that one properly: he "calls the knaves, Jacks." And he blames his mistake on Joe, who has "taught" him wrong. At the end of the chapter he has learned that he is "a common labouring boy" with coarse hands and thick boots, who calls picture-cards by the wrong name; and "pondering" these things as he walks home, he laments being "much more ignorant than [he] had considered [him]self last night."

At home, Pip complains to Joe, "I am ignorant and backward. . . . I have learnt next to nothing." The next morning he decides to begin immediately to work against his ignorance and determines "to get out of Biddy everything she knew." He proposes to her that, "wishing to get on in life," he would "be obliged to her if she would impart all her learning" to him.

Biddy's knowledge—in terms of book-learning—is scarcely in advance of Pip's own, and he realizes woefully that "it would take time, to become uncommon under these circumstances." Still, he resolves to try and heads for home that evening with "a large old English D"—which he supposes "to be a design for a buckle"—to practice copying.

Just as Pip's letter to Joe, the first proof of his "uncommon" scholarly accomplishment, was followed by his embarrassment at Miss Havisham's for being "ignorant" and "a common labouring boy," so here his resolve to "become uncommon" is thrown back in his face by his "common" past. On his way home he must stop for Joe at the public house, where he encounters the man with the file, who is acquainted with Magwitch. When Pip goes to bed that night, he thinks not of the two pounds he has received, but of "the guilty coarse and common thing it was, to be on secret terms of conspiracy with convicts."

Whenever Pip has the chance, he confides to Miss Havisham his twin ambitions to learn and to rise. When she inquires "what I had learnt—what I was going to be?" Pip must admit that he is to be apprenticed to Joe; but in the same breath he "enlarge[s] upon [his] knowing nothing and wanting to know everything, in the hope that she might offer some help toward that desirable end." Miss Havisham doesn't help, however; "she seemed," says Pip, "to prefer my being ignorant." What she does undertake for him is to pay for his being apprenticed—"bound"—to Joe.

In a sense Pip's life begins again at this point. Pip narrator is careful to represent this new state of his as the awful product of his "ungracious condition of mind," and to blame no one for it: "How much of [it] may have been my own fault, how much Miss Havisham's, how much my sister's, is now of no moment to me or to any one." "The change," he says, "was made in me"—and the unhappiness this change brings almost overwhelms him. (pp. 41-3)

Pip is still trying to learn, still full of his "desire to be wiser." He grows too big to continue his "education" at the evening school, but not until "Biddy had imparted to me everything she knew." In his "hunger for information" he even tries to use Mr. Wopsle as a teacher, but soon gives that up as worthless. He tries now to teach Joe, as he had promised to do as a child; only he is not happy being apprenticed to Joe, and "woT larX" is no longer a part of his vocabulary or his set of values. He wants "to be a gentleman," and when he tries to teach Joe he does so "to make Joe less ignorant and common, that he might be worthy of my society and less open to Estella's reproach."

But Pip can't catch up with Estella through what he learns on his own or with Biddy's help; Estella is learning, too, "educating for a lady" in France. His opportunity to catch up comes when Lawyer Jaggers appears and announces that Pip has "great expectations," and is to be "brought up a gentleman." His expectations include, as an immediate guarantee for his future, funds for his "education." A gentleman can't be educated in a village, however, or while living at a forge, so Pip must go to London: "the sooner you leave here," Jaggers advises him, "the better."

Pip's special education is arranged, and he is eager to be away. But "the first night of [his] bright fortunes" is curiously "the loneliest [he] had ever known," and the next is no better: "the second night of my bright fortunes [was] as lonely and unsatisfactory as the first." Except for what we know from our own experience of ourselves in similar circumstances, we might call young Pip a slow learner for not realizing the reason for his lonely unhappiness. But it is hard to learn what one doesn't want to know—and that is Pip's difficulty here.

Once settled in London, Pip forgets his painful parting from his old world. For the first time in his life he has a friend his own age, and he has "expectations." Herbert Pocket is both Pip's friend and his teacher, though what registers for Pip character as Herbert's teaching is nothing more than a short course in city manners: "in London it is not the custom to put the knife in the mouth"; "society as a body does not expect one to be so strictly conscientious in emptying one's glass as to turn it bottom upwards with the rim on one's nose"; "my dear Handel . . . a dinner napkin will not go into a tumbler." But Herbert is not just a young man with proper manners and an easy congeniality; for all that he impresses Pip as someone who "would never be very successful or rich," he is a true young gentleman. What Herbert teaches Pip, gently, is the meaning of friendship.

Herbert's father is the professional teacher assigned to Pip in London. It is not clear from the narrative what, if anything, Mr. Pocket proposes to teach Pip or expects him to learn. Since Pip is "not designed for any profession," the "mere rudiments" of an education seem to be all that Mr. Pocket thinks he needs. When Pip narrator speaks of his having "applied [him]self to his education," he fails to mention studying—or learning—anything, though he remembers having "stuck to [his] books."

At the end of his education to be a gentleman, Pip discovers himself "fit for nothing." But this realization is in itself something important for Pip to have come to, as it concludes the charade that he has played of studying to be a gentleman. Pip's realization comes, of course, with the collapse of his dreams and expectations, upon the arrival of Magwitch.

In telling Herbert of his new situation, Pip's most pressing concern is himself, and how he can extricate himself from this terrible and shameful difficulty. Herbert responds by reminding Pip that he has a responsibility to Magwitch: "If you were to renounce this patronage and these favours, I suppose you would do so with some faint hope of one day repaying what you have already had." The responsibility that Herbert argues for, however, is not just pecuniary responsibility:

> And you have, and are bound to have, that tenderness for the life he has risked on your account, that you must save him, if possible, from throwing it away. Then you must get him out of England before you stir a finger to extricate yourself.

Pip has introduced the topic of what he should do about Magwitch's appearance by proposing to "go for a soldier": "And I might have gone, my dear Herbert, but for the prospect of taking counsel with your friendship and affection." This "counsel" of Herbert's is of course much more important to Pip than his advice about knives in the mouth and wine glasses on the nose. It is at once Herbert's counsel and his counsel as a friend that Pip must take.

The Pip who wants to "rise" in life has begun, with that ambition, by learning to disregard his friends. Once Pip determines to rise, he and Joe are no longer the "equals" they had seemed before. Pip forgets his respect for Joe because what Pip respects in his life changes. Whereas on the night before he first went to "play" at Miss Havisham's he felt "conscious" of "looking up to Joe in [his] heart," what the heart looks up to no longer has value for Pip, and he looks up only to the place in "society" toward which he climbs.

Herbert has no expectations, and his "general air" seems to tell young Pip, when first they meet in London, that Herbert "would never be very successful or rich." But despite this severe limitation—or perhaps because, with this limitation, he presents no challenge to Pip—he and Herbert become friends.

Herbert has "not a handsome face," but is "extremely amiable and cheerful." His figure is "a little ungainly," but it looks as if it will "always be light and young." And, most important for our young snob in the making, Herbert is "so communicative" that Pip feels "that reserve on my part would be a bad return unsuited to our years."

So Pip and Herbert become friends, and Herbert begins to teach Pip the value of friendship. The first lesson is candor. Before Pip can begin to feel uncomfortable about having been "brought up as a blacksmith" Herbert chooses a new name for him from that lowly past: "We are so harmonious," Herbert says, "and you have been a blacksmith. . . . There's a charming piece of music by Handel, called the Harmonious Blacksmith." And thus Pip becomes Handel, and Herbert's friend.

The resonance in Pip's new name, of course, is the reminder of Joe, whom Pip has left behind. Joe has always been Pip's friend and promises "ever" to be so. But Pip doesn't want Joe's friendship, now that he is a young gentleman. For all that Joe is a model friend—and a model "Man," as Pip narrator insists on calling him—he is not a teacher of any great or special talent. Pip narrator praises Joe's radiant goodness— "It is not possible to know how far the influence of any amiable honest-hearted duty-doing man flies out into the world"—but that goodness can't teach Pip contentment at the forge, or make him less "ashamed of home." Joe's goodness may have "touched [Pip's] self in going by," but as long as Pip is at the forge, he still works unhappily "against the grain." Joe's friendship—and the promise of larks—can't teach Pip happiness.

Joe's friendship, however, never deserts Pip. "Ever the best of friends" is Joe's promise, and nothing Pip can do will change that, as far as Joe is concerned. When Pip awakens from his delirium, late in the novel, Joe is beside him. Joe is there because he is needed. And laying his head beside Pip's on the pillow, he says, "you and me was ever friends. And when you're well enough to go out for a ride—what larks!"

When Pip and Joe have gone on their ride—Pip with his head

on Joe's shoulder—Joe leaves. His friendship will not impose on Pip's freedom, and Pip is "well enough" to be without him. "Ever the best of friends," is the message he leaves.

That Pip follows Joe, this time, back to the forge proves that Pip has learned something. Before, Pip would have been content to use Joe's help, let him go, and send a barrel of oysters as a thank you. But Pip has no money now, and no expectations except those that he creates out of his own heart.

In his open relationship with Herbert, Pip learns what friendship is. Seeing his younger self with Herbert, Pip narrator says, "I had never felt before what it is to have a friend." Eventually, after Magwitch's capture, Herbert finds it necessary to absent himself from London for a time. "I am very much afraid I must go," he tells Pip, "when you need me most." Pip's answer is clear, and sure: "Herbert, I shall always need you, because I shall always love you; but my need is no greater now, than at another time."

It takes Pip a long time to learn affection. Perhaps this is because he grew up an unwanted child, scourged by Tickler and the "moral goads" of his piously unfeeling elders. Whatever the cause—and again, Pip narrator doesn't try to allocate or assign blame—the painful fact remains that it takes Pip a long, hard time to learn the selflessness which lets him love. Learning "things" sometimes seems to be a better protection against a hostile world than learning affection, and the young Pip is victimized for a long time by this seeming. His best teacher for the difficult lesson of selflessness and love is Herbert. This may be because, being the same age, he and Pip are able to be free and open with each other. It may be because Pip, secure for the moment in his expectations, is for the first time able to think and act generously, and to learn for himself what generosity is. Again, whatever the reason, Pip does learn friendship with Herbert, and learns with him the value of friendship. The most harmonious music in the whole novel is that played by Herbert with his hands in Handel's, on his return from France: "Handel, my dear fellow, how are you, and again how are you, and again how are you?" Pip narrator's memory of those words is like the song which the narrator of *Our Mutual Friend* repeats toward the end of that next Dickens novel: "O 'tis love, 'tis love, 'tis love, that makes the world go round!"

Pip's first chance to practice what he has learned comes with Magwitch's capture. His pledge—"Please God, I will be as true to you, as you have been to me!"—is its test. It rings back through the novel, to that first "memorable" day, with which all this began. (pp. 44-9)

Not all of Pip's lessons are lessons in affection and generosity such as Herbert teaches him, or Joe offers him by his noble example. We have discussed what Pip learns at Satis House of the desirability of what is "rich" and "splendid"; what Pip learns in Little Britain from the well-intentioned Wemmick is not much different, and the lesson of his guardian's example in dealing with life is—in the abstract, at least—not at all unlike Miss Havisham's.

Pip should be suspicious of Wemmick from the very beginning of their acquaintance: when upon leaving the office, Pip puts out his hand, "Mr. Wemmick at first looked at it as if he thought I wanted something." Then Wemmick corrects himself and says to Pip, "To be sure! Yes. You're in the habit of shaking hands?"

Wemmick doesn't shake hands, as a rule: there's nothing to

be gained by such a gesture. And Wemmick's philosophy is one of gain; his "guiding star" is "Get hold of portable property." Such, at any rate, is his public or business philosophy; but "the office is one thing, and private life is another," according to Wemmick, and he purports to conduct his life in Little Britain quite differently from his life at Walworth. At the Castle he is affectionate and gentle, "shaking hands" with his Aged Parent and "stealing his arm around Miss Skiffins's waist." Such conduct is possible for him at Walworth, presumably because the Castle is separated from the rest of the world by a four-foot moat with a plank for a drawbridge: "I hoist it up," Wemmick says, "and cut off the communication." But though Wemmick claims to separate his hard-faced office life from his softened, human life at home, the treasures of the Castle, awkwardly, are bits of "portable property" bequeathed him by his business associates at Newgate.

When Pip mentions to Wemmick that he is "desirous to serve a friend," Wemmick responds "as if his opinion were dead against any fatal weakness of that sort." To Wemmick, serving a friend is a waste of "portable property": one might as well "pitch [his] money into the Thames." Should a man "invest portable property in a friend?" he asks, rhetorically; and he answers, with emphasis, "Certainly he should not."

But that opinion is Wemmick's Little Britain opinion, and presumably, according to the fiction Wemmick has created for himself, his "Walworth sentiments" will be different. When, at the Castle, Pip has made a full representation of his plan for helping Herbert, Wemmick agrees to aid him. His initial response, however, even at Walworth, is skeptical and defensive:

> Wemmick was silent for a little while, and then said with a kind of start, "Well you know, Mr. Pip, I must tell you one thing. This is devilish good of you."
>
> "Say you'll help me to be good then," said I.
>
> "Ecod," replied Wemmick, shaking his head, "that's not my trade."

When Wemmick goes out of his way to warn Pip of Magwitch's being watched, he does so from the Castle. But his thinking is Little Britain thinking, still. At the conclusion of his advice, and in such a friendly Walworth manner that he lets Pip shake his hands and then lays his hands upon Pip's shoulders, Wemmick whispers solemnly, "Avail yourself . . . of his portable property. You don't know what may happen to him. Don't let anything happen to the portable property."

Wemmick's double life is a sham—just as the Castle is. A sentimentally benign interpretation of his character would have him comically schizophrenic, living one life at the office and another at home. That would be bad enough, for Dickens, and a serious lesson for us. But Wemmick is not a model schizophrenic; he is much worse. A close examination of his values makes it clear that Little Britain and Walworth are one world, and in both places the values taught, the lessons offered, are self-defense and portable property. "Every man's business," he says, "is portable property."

At the office Wemmick shuts off his humanity, in order to do his worldly business. At the Castle he shuts out the world— "I cut off the communication," he says, revealingly—and presumes to be human. Pip is almost taken in by this pretense, as a young man. But "you can't shut out the world,"

Dickens says; "you are in it, to be of it." And as for business, and "portable property": we all have an obligation to the world—to "make the best of it"—not just to ourselves. The world, for Dickens, is human business. The proper businessman must learn to love it.

Wemmick has a very limited understanding of the possibilities of human existence; the Aged's notion that "this pretty pleasure-ground . . . and these beautiful works upon it ought to be kept together by the Nation . . . for the people's enjoyment" is a wonderfully ironic and comic response to his son's social conscience. Still, Wemmick is innocent—naive—in his defensiveness, and even generously well-meaning in his acts and advices. Lawyer Jaggers, however, is a sinister and intellectually selfish man. And though he offers his act of "saving" Estella as in some way a justification for his life, that act is the only generously good deed he ever performs. Even this good deed is corrupted by his refusal to involve himself—despite what he must know—in what becomes of Estella as Miss Havisham's ward or adopted daughter.

Jaggers would contest my saying that he "must know." The key to Jaggers's self-defense lies in his refusal to know anything that might involve or incriminate him: and he thinks of involvement in this crazy, dangerous world as though it is necessarily incriminating. Though he has no locks upon his doors, he keeps the world away from him as effectively as Miss Havisham does, with her barred and shuttered windows. Miss Havisham knows the meaning of her shutting out of life—knows that, in the end, she will herself replace the rotted wedding cake upon the bride's table—and she hates it. Jaggers tries to survive by means of his retreat, pretending that his defense against the world is life.

Early in the novel Pip almost makes the mistake of telling Miss Havisham what day it is. She interrupts him: "There, there! I know nothing of the days of the week, I know nothing of the weeks of the year." When Pip returns he says "Today is—" and again she interrupts him: "I don't want to know," she says, impatiently.

In Dickens's world, not to know is dangerous; not to want to know is always wrong. For Miss Havisham, "I don't want to know" is supposedly self-defense. But though her intentional isolation from the living, changing world—her refusal to "know" it any more—may have begun as a hurt creature's self-defense, it becomes her destroyer. Determinedly ignorant of the world, she cuts herself off from everything except her festering hatred for men and her self-pity. Her original ambition for Estella, she says, was "to save her from misery like mine"; but isolated from the world and utterly alienated in her defensiveness, she perverts even this one attempt at human responsibility.

Lawyer Jaggers seems to be quite a different creature. His windows aren't barred—he has no locks on his doors at all— and he walks freely about in the world, secure in his knowledge of it. When he appears in The Three Jolly Bargemen, he badgers the men there with his knowledge. What he claims—parades, enforces—is knowledge not of facts but of character. (pp. 50-3)

But we must not be taken in by Jaggers's knowing so much. He knows what he can make use of, and is careful not to know what might work against him. He values knowledge only for its usefulness to himself, and for the power derivable from such useful knowledge. When approached by his clients, in London, he immediately says to them, "I want to know no more than I know." When Pip tries to speak about Magwitch, Jaggers stops him: "Don't tell me anything; I don't want to know anything; I am not curious." He prides himself on having "adhered to the strict line of fact," on never having made "the least departure from the strict line of fact" in his relationship with Pip.

Like Miss Havisham, Jaggers has known all along that Pip misleads himself as to the source of his fortune—and like Miss Havisham, Jaggers lets Pip continue in his error. Miss Havisham's fostering of Pip's ignorance, his misconception, is understandable though still perverse; the situation merely gives her an opportunity to hurt a male, to enact her pitiful revenge. Jaggers, however, has no reason for wanting Pip to make such an awkward and destructive mistake. His carefully irresponsible complicity in Pip's error is purely perverse. Jaggers is much worse, morally, than Miss Havisham; and whereas at the end of the novel Pip forgives a repentant Miss Havisham, the last he shows us of Jaggers—and Wemmick—they are doing, together, what they have always done.

Jaggers is worse than Miss Havisham because his motivation is so meanly selfish. Jaggers has not been hurt by the world or by any particular falseness practiced upon him. He has never made the mistake of loving someone. Rather, he sees the "evil" of the world, and determines not to be hurt by it. As his defense he chooses control: he has no qualms about committing wrong himself if wrongdoing and injustice will keep him in control of the world around him. Control becomes a passion for Jaggers—his only passion—and an obsession. His pleasure in Pip's error about the identity of his benefactor is the obsessive response of a passionately selfish man.

When Pip presents himself at Jagger's office with the knowledge of who his benefactor is, Jaggers refuses to let Pip "tell" him anything—"I don't want to know anything; I am not curious"—and then refuses to apologize for or to try to excuse or even to acknowledge his participation in Pip's error: "I am not at all responsible for that," he says. When he insists that he has "always adhered to the strict line of fact," he makes, implicitly, a careful distinction between fact and truth. As far as Jaggers "knows," factually and professionally, Magwitch is in Australia; what he knows, in truth—that Magwitch is actually in London—is not to be discussed. Jaggers protects himself; that is his profession, his business. He will not let himself become involved in anyone else's life.

When Pip returns to Little Britain, later, with his knowledge of who Magwitch is, he catches Jaggers off his guard by knowing something more than Jaggers knows. Knowledge, for Jaggers, is a weapon: its only function is self-defense. When Pip knows something he doesn't know, Jaggers is in a dangerous situation.

Before he can talk with Jaggers about Magwitch, Pip has business to transact with him. Pip has authority from Miss Havisham to draw nine hundred pounds from her account, for Herbert. "I am sorry, Pip," says Jaggers, "that we do nothing for *you*." Pip responds that Miss Havisham offered to assist him, but that he declined her offer. "Every man should know his own business," Jaggers replies, and then repeats the observation: "I should *not* have told her No, if I had been you . . . but every man ought to know his own business best."

Knowing one's own business best is in a sense—a perverse, twisted sense—Jaggers's motto. When Pip tells him that Miss Havisham has given him what information she had about Es-

tella, Jaggers responds: "I don't think I should have done so, if I had been Miss Havisham. But *she* ought to know her own business best." Knowledge, for Jaggers, is not something to be given away; it is to Jaggers what "portable property" is to Wemmick. Just as Wemmick says, acquisitively, "Every man's business . . . is portable property," so Jaggers might say, with obsessive defensiveness, "Every man's business is controlling knowledge."

But Pip knows more than Jaggers knows, this time: "I know more of the history of Miss Havisham's adopted child," he says, "than Miss Havisham herself does, sir. I know her mother." Jaggers knows Estella's mother; it is Molly: but he has not previously known that Pip knows this. His response is defensive, noncommittal: "Yes? . . . Yes?" Then Pip presses his advantage: a defensive, determinedly uninvolved, unresponsive man who thinks only in adversarial terms has to be challenged and pursued. "Perhaps I know more of Estella's history than even you do," Pip says; "I know her father too."

Pip has come to Jaggers, not to use his knowledge to gain some advantage for himself or to abuse Jaggers with it. Pip simply presents his knowledge as his knowledge, and asks Jaggers to complete it, to verify if he can the conclusions Pip has drawn from what he knows. Jaggers's first response is to ignore Pip and return to his "business": "Hah! . . . What item was it you were at, Wemmick, when Mr. Pip came in?"

Pip insists, and finally persuades Jaggers to tell him what he knows. Jaggers "put[s] the case"—with the strict qualification, "Mind! I admit nothing"—in his most defensive manner. Telling what he knows is an ordeal for Jaggers, and instead of simply giving Pip information, he "put[s] the case" as though he were on trial. When he has submitted his evidence, he returns to his business with the same words he had used before: "Now, Wemmick . . . what item was it you were at, when Mr. Pip came in?"

What was almost human in Jaggers, as he "put the case," is closed off again. When a poor thief who "seemed to be always in trouble" enters the office "to announce that his eldest daughter [has been] taken up on suspicion of shop-lifting" and makes the mistake of shedding "a tear," Jaggers resumes his usual manner, triumphantly: "Get out of this office," he says; "I'll have no feelings here. Get out."

*Great Expectations* is a novel about Pip's education, and the end or goal of his education is that freedom which is friendship. Jaggers is not free because he cannot comprehend friendship. He is locked into his own defensiveness. He lives by power and control, and does not trust affection. There is no evidence in the novel that Jaggers, like Miss Havisham, has had his affection tricked or abused. He has not been brutalized or otherwise victimized by treachery; there is nothing, thus, to excuse or extenuate his cruelty. Therefore, though Miss Havisham is forgiven, before her death, Jaggers is sent back to his psychologically and symbolically solitary cell. His example—the lesson that he would teach—is rejected.

When Pip goes to Satis House upon learning the identity of his real benefactor, he begins by blaming Miss Havisham for his condition: "I am as unhappy as you can ever have meant me to be," he says. His purpose in speaking to her is not to complain, but that is what he does:

> "But when I fell into the mistake I have so long remained in, at least you led me on?" said I.

"Yes," she returned . . . "I let you go on."

"Was that kind?"

"Who am I . . . who am I, for God's sake, that I should be kind?"

Pip apologizes for this "weak complaint," and she reminds him, cruelly, of the ultimate source of his errors: "You made your own snares."

The Pip who has been so mistaken, and whose mistakes have led him into shameful unkindness, comes to Miss Havisham seeking kindness. The kindness that he seeks, however, is not for himself but for Herbert. She ignores his request when he makes it, but thereafter sends word that he is to come to see her on "a matter of business." His first sense when he sees her this time is that there is "an air of utter loneliness upon her," and he is moved to "pity" her. He stands "compassionating" her as they speak. Miss Havisham, too, is pitying, now, and contrite: "I am not all stone," she says; "But perhaps you can never believe, now, that there is anything human in my heart?" Pip reassures her, and she continues "in an unwonted tone of sympathy." Their mutual sympathy is appropriate; it is something that they both have had to learn, through suffering.

As Pip watches Miss Havisham in her distress, the narrator reviews what Pip "knew," standing there: and though what he "knew" was that she had done wrong, he also "knew," he says, "compassion" for her. Miss Havisham, in her turn, explains to him that she "did not know what [she] had done" until she "saw in [Pip] a looking glass that showed [her] what [she] once felt." As his suffering reminds her of her own, it teaches her both remorse and pity. She speaks, he says, with "an earnest womanly compassion" and with "new affection" for him, as she tells the sordid story of how with her "teachings" and her "lessons" she "stole [Estella's] heart away, and put ice in its place." "If you knew all my story," she concludes, burdened now with guilt, "you would have some compassion for me."

Pip does have pity on Miss Havisham and forgives her. He has learned compassion and affection well enough by now to free Miss Havisham—or to try to, at any rate: she dies repentant, knowing that she has done wrong, saying over and over, "What have I done?" and "When she first came, I meant to save her from misery like mine," and "Take the pencil and write under my name, 'I forgive her!'"

Estella is not saved from misery, of course. Miss Havisham's "teachings" and "lessons" make Estella both miserable herself and the agency for inflicting misery on others. Estella knows her own misery early on, even before she marries Drummle: she is "tired of [her]self" and "tired of the life [she has] led." She does not "comprehend" love as an emotion because her "lessons" have taught her to feel nothing, to be "cold." When Miss Havisham complains that Estella has no affection even for her "mother by adoption," Estella answers with reference to what she has been taught: she has sat as a child, she tells Miss Havisham, "learning your lessons," and has never been "unmindful of your lessons." "Who taught me to be proud?" she asks; "Who praised me when I learned my lesson?" And again: "Who taught me to be hard? . . . Who praised me when I had learned my lesson?" What Miss Havisham has "taught" Estella has made her what she is, she insists; the kindest thing she can do, having been so taught, so "formed," is warn Pip away from her.

At the end of the novel Estella is changed. She, too, can "understand" now, what feelings and affections are: what the "heart" is. She has been "taught," she says, by "suffering," which "has been stronger than all other teaching." When Dickens rewrote the ending of the novel, this notion is the only thing he saved from the first version. In the original ending Pip narrator says: "in her voice, and in her touch, [Estella] gave me the assurance, that suffering had been stronger than Miss Havisham's teaching, and had given her a heart to understand what my heart used to be." Her education is not unlike Miss Havisham's, or Pip's. They all learn through suffering: and what they learn is affection, compassion, friendship.

What Estella learns, having been "bent, broken, but . . . into a better shape," is how to be "friends." Like Miss Havisham, she asks Pip to "forgive" her—just as Pip asks Joe and Biddy to "forgive" him. And then she asks Pip to assure her that they are "friends." That they are friends—"and will continue friends apart"—is the conclusion of the novel.

The real lesson of *Great Expectations* is friendship. Joe has difficulty learning to read and write; he is, by his own admission "so awful dull." But Joe knows what friendship is, and what it means. Affection and sympathy make him "ever the best of friends"—and Joe knows, has "calc'lated," that friendship "lead[s] to larks."

In every Dickens novel except *The Mystery of Edwin Drood*, part of the conclusion involves various good young people getting married, and usually having children. With the exception of Mr. Pickwick, who is an old man at the beginning of his novel and a "retired" old man at the end, and Oliver Twist, who is retired by Dickens at the end of his novel at the ripe old age of eleven, the central character of every Dickens novel up to *A Tale of Two Cities* marries at the end. This marriage generally indicates, in part, the achievement of the central character's growing up, or education; it also signifies Dickens's hope for the future.

At the end of *Little Dorrit,* when Amy Dorrit and Arthur Clennam are married, they "paused for a moment . . . in the autumn morning sun's bright rays, and then went down." The rhetoric of the concluding paragraph of that novel is brilliant—more so, perhaps, than even the sun's bright rays shining on this real world. When Amy and Arthur "went down," they "went down into a modest life of usefulness and happiness"; they "went down" to take care of their children and Amy's sister's poor, neglected children; they "went down" to take care of Amy's worthless brother, too. "They went down," the narrator tells us, to conclude the novel, "into the roaring streets, inseparable and blessed; and as they passed along in sunshine and shade, the noisy and the eager, and the arrogant and the froward and the vain, fretted and chafed, and made their usual uproar." The hope that Dickens expresses here does not change the world directly, or begin it over with a new generation of goodness. Rather, it works *in* the world that exists.

Beginning with *A Tale of Two Cities,* Dickens's central characters don't marry at the ends of their novels. Rather, they learn friendship, and the freedom that friendship means. Joe Gargery articulates the idea best, in *Great Expectations:* "Life," he tells Pip, "is made of ever so many partings welded together." Joe may not be a "scholar," but he is a wise man. And though he is not Pip's most accomplished teacher, he is certainly the best example in the novel of a wise—and educated—man. He and Herbert teach Pip friendship, and the value of friendship. Estella learns its value, too—in part through Pip. In the end, though Estella and Pip do not marry—they "will continue friends apart," Estella says—Joe is the best man, and Pip goes off to make his family with Herbert and Clara and do his business in this world.

Pip learns friendship, and friendship earns him the freedom to love Estella, even though they are apart. Because Pip learns this, and in learning it grows wise, his life is not ruined. Indeed, we can expect—from the book he has written, and what it tells us—that his life will have a happy ending.

And as Pip wrote this book for us, may our lives—we "who read this"—have such happy endings also. (pp. 53-60)

> *Bert G. Hornback, in his* Great Expectations: A Novel of Friendship, *Twayne Publishers, 1987, 152 p.*

---

# FURTHER READING

Brooks, Peter. "Repetition, Repression, and Return: The Plotting of *Great Expectations.*" In his *Reading for the Plot: Design and Intention in Narrative,* pp. 113-42. New York: Alfred A. Knopf, 1984.
Applies Freud's concept of the repetition of repressed memories in examining the plot of *Great Expectations.*

Connolly, Thomas E. "Technique in *Great Expectations.*" *Philological Quarterly* XXXIV, No. 1 (January 1955): 48-55.
Examines structure, narrative technique, and character development in *Great Expectations* "to show the unique position which this novel holds among [Dickens's] works."

Crawford, Iain. "Pip and the Monster: The Joys of Bondage." *Studies in English Literature, 1500-1900: The Nineteenth Century* 28, No. 4 (Autumn 1988): 625-48.
Suggests that *Great Expectations* is in revisionist terms a "misreading" of Mary Wollstonecraft Shelley's *Frankenstein.*

Fielding, K. J. "The Critical Autonomy of *Great Expectations.*" *A Review of English Literature* 2, No. 3 (July 1961): 75-88.
Praises *Great Expectations* for lending itself to diverse critical interpretations. Fielding mainly focuses on studies by Humphry House (see entry in Further Reading below), J. Hillis Miller (see excerpt dated 1958), and Julian Moynahan (see excerpt dated 1960).

———. "*Great Expectations.*" In his *Charles Dickens: A Critical Introduction,* rev. ed., pp. 207-23. Boston: Houghton Mifflin Co., 1964.
General examination of the novel.

Frank, Lawrence. "The House of the Self." In his *Charles Dickens and the Romantic Self,* pp. 151-83. Lincoln: University of Nebraska Press, 1984.
Examines Pip's failed search for "his Romantic self," an original identity not shaped by society, language, or history.

Friedman, Stanley. "Estella's Parentage and Pip's Persistence: The Outcome of *Great Expectations.*" *Studies in the Novel* 19, No. 4 (Winter 1987): 410-21.
Argues that the discovery of Estella's true parents gives Pip hope to continue pursuing her and creates expectations in the reader that they will unite, thus making the revised ending particularly appropriate.

Garis, Robert. "*Great Expectations.*" In his *The Dickens Theatre: A Reassessment of the Novels,* pp. 191-225. Oxford: Clarendon Press, 1965.
Asserts that *Great Expectations* is "Dickens's masterpiece" with respect to both theme and technique as well as a prime example of "the Dickens theatre," where the author, an actor playing the main character's part, is always at center stage.

Gervais, David. "The Prose and Poetry of *Great Expectations.*" In *Dickens Studies Annual: Essays on Victorian Fiction,* Vol. 13, edited by Michael Timko, Fred Kaplan, and Edward Guiliano, pp. 85-114. New York: AMS Press, 1984.
A study of the rhythmic qualities of Dickens's prose in *Great Expectations* that explores whether the novel's poetry conveys the "potential meaning and emotion in the book."

Golding, Robert. "*Great Expectations* to *Edwin Drood.*" In his *Idolects in Dickens: The Major Techniques and Chronological Development,* pp. 172-212. London: Macmillan Press, 1985.
Analyzes the idiomatic languages Dickens creates for each of his characters in *Great Expectations, Our Mutual Friend,* and *The Mystery of Edwin Drood.*

Gordon, Andrew. "Jaggers and the Moral Scheme of *Great Expectations.*" *The Dickensian* 65, No. 357 (January 1969): 3-11.
Examines Jaggers's dramatic and thematic function in the novel.

Halperin, John. "Dickens." In his *Egoism and Self-Discovery in the Victorian Novel: Studies in the Ordeal of Knowledge in the Nineteenth Century,* pp. 81-123. New York: Burt Franklin, Publisher, 1974.
Studies the development of characters from "self-absorption" to "self-knowledge" in three Dickens novels, *Dombey and Son, A Tale of Two Cities,* and *Great Expectations,* considering the latter "Dickens's most single-minded treatment" of this theme.

Hartog, Curt. "The Rape of Miss Havisham." *Studies in the Novel* 14, No. 3 (Fall 1982): 248-65.
A Freudian interpretation arguing that Pip is traumatically prevented from reaching psychosexual maturity by the women around him, who generate violence by denying motherhood.

Hollington, Michael. "The Grotesque and Tragicomedy: *Great Expectations.*" In his *Dickens and the Grotesque,* pp. 216-30. London: Croom Helm, 1984.
Regards tragicomedy and the grotesque as prominent elements in the novel.

House, Humphry. "G. B. S. on *Great Expectations.*" In his *All in Due Time: The Collected Essays and Broadcast Talks of Humphry House,* pp. 201-20. London: Rupert Hart-Davis, 1955.
Analyzes *Great Expectations* using Bernard Shaw's criticism (see excerpt dated 1937) as a starting point.

Jordan, John O. "The Medium of *Great Expectations.*" *Dickens Studies Annual: Essays on Victorian Fiction,* Vol. 11, edited by Michael Timko, Fred Kaplan, and Edward Guiliano, pp. 73-88. New York: AMS Press, 1983.
Identifies the various ways in which the word "medium" applies to the novel, including the spiritual connotations of the character Pip being pursued by ghostly manifestations of his guilt and the narrator Pip's use of language as a medium to control his story.

Leavis, L. R. "The Dramatic Narrator in *Great Expectations.*" *English Studies* 68, No. 3 (June 1987): 236-48.
Analyzes Pip's function as narrator and his attitude toward himself as character.

Leavis, Q. D. "How We Must Read *Great Expectations.*" In *Dickens the Novelist,* by F. R. Leavis and Q. D. Leavis, pp. 277-331. London: Chatto & Windus, 1970.
A sympathetic interpretation of Pip's story, arguing that he acted according to the principles of the society and period to which he belonged. This essay is controversial for its peremptory tone and condemnation of previous critics.

Lettis, Richard, and Morris, William E., eds. *Assessing "Great Expectations"; Materials for Analysis.* San Francisco: Chandler Publishing Co., n.d., 230 p.

Reprints twenty essays on *Great Expectations* from contemporary reviews to the early 1960s in order to help students write research papers. Lettis and Morris include study suggestions and an essay on paper documentation.

Lucas, John. *"Great Expectations."* In his *The Melancholy Man: A Study of Dickens's Novels,* pp. 287-314. 1970. Reprint. Sussex: Harvester Press, 1980.

Analyzes three main points of view in *Great Expectations,* those of the reader, Pip as narrator, and Pip as character.

McMaster, Rowland. *"Great Expectations."* In *The Novel from Sterne to James: Essays on the Relation of Literature to Life,* by Juliet and Rowland McMaster, pp. 71-87. Totowa, New Jersey: Barnes & Noble Books, 1981.

Maintains that Pip's development to maturity follows a Freudian pattern of escaping from parental domination.

Millhauser, Milton. *"Great Expectations: The Three Endings."* In *Dickens Studies Annual,* Vol. 2, edited by Robert B. Partlow, Jr., pp. 267-77. Carbondale: Southern Illinois University Press, 1972.

Contends that the original and revised conclusions of *Great Expectations* are perfunctorily treated by Dickens as a means to tie up the novel's loose ends. Millhauser suggests that Pip's return to the forge and his departure for Egypt serve as more important thematic endings than the two that are so often discussed.

Monod, Sylvère. "Back to the Autobiographical Form." In his *Dickens the Novelist,* pp. 471-88. Norman: University of Oklahoma Press, 1967.

A general discussion of *Great Expectations,* touching upon such topics as the strengths and weaknesses of Dickens's style and the novel's composition, themes, and critical reception.

Morris, Christopher D. "The Bad Faith of Pip's Bad Faith: Deconstructing *Great Expectations."* *ELH* 54, No. 4 (Winter 1987): pp. 941-55.

A deconstructionist interpretation that argues Pip is an unfaithful narrator who "varnishes" over the inherent contradictions in his story, particularly those referring to the development of his conscience.

Nisbet, Ada. "The Autobiographical Matrix of *Great Expectations."* *The Victorian Newsletter,* No. 15 (Spring 1959): 10-13.

Argues that "the novel can be seen to be the record of a brutal self-appraisal which centers on the three obsessive passions of [Dickens's] own life—his passion for social status, his passion for money, and his passion for Ellen Ternan."

Rawlins, Jack P. "Great Expiations: Dickens and the Betrayal of the Child." *SEL* 23, No. 4 (Autumn 1983): 667-83.

Considers Pip both a "victim of society's corruption" and in the end "the single unforgiven source of it" because he becomes his own guilty tormentor.

Rosenberg, Edgar. "A Preface to *Great Expectations:* The Pale Usher Dusts His Lexicons." In *Dickens Studies Annual,* Vol. 2, edited by Robert B. Partlow, Jr., pp. 294-335. Carbondale: Southern Illinois University Press, 1972.

An account of the problems Rosenberg faced while editing a new edition of *Great Expectations.*

Said, Edward W. "Molestation and Authority in Narrative Fiction." In *Aspects of Narrative: Selected Papers from the English Institute,* edited by J. Hillis Miller, pp. 47-68. New York: Columbia University Press, 1971.

Shows how authority, a term describing the ways narratives assert themselves on the reader through the techniques of the novelist, and molestation, the problems that prevent or obstruct authority, function in fiction, using *Great Expectations* as the primary example.

Stone, Harry. *"Great Expectations:* The Fairy-Tale Transformation." In his *Dickens and the Invisible World: Fairy Tales, Fantasy, and Novel-Making,* pp. 298-339. Bloomington: Indiana University Press, 1979.

Finds fairy-tale images (ghosts and magic wands) and patterns (good versus evil) in *Great Expectations* that assist Dickens in ordering chaotic reality and, thus, in conveying meaning to the reader.

Tambling, Jeremy. "Prison-Bound: Dickens and Foucault." *Essays in Criticism* XXXVI, No. 1 (January 1986): 11-31.

Applies ideas posited in Michel Foucault's *Surveiller et punir: Naissance de la prison* (1975; *Discipline and Punish: The Birth of the Prison*) to *Great Expectations,* examining the literal and figurative prisons in the novel.

Thurin, Susan Schoenbauer. "The Seven Deadly Sins in *Great Expectations."* In *Dickens Studies Annual: Essays on Victorian Fiction,* Vol. 15, edited by Michael Timko, Fred Kaplan, and Edward Guiliano, pp. 201-20. New York: AMS Press, 1986.

Argues that the deaths of seven characters, each of whom represents one of the seven deadly sins, renders the novel "a secularized morality play that imparts lessons on establishing oneself in Victorian middle-class life."

Wagenknecht, Edward. *"Great Expectations."* In his *Dickens and the Scandalmongers: Essays in Criticism,* pp. 132-36. Norman: University of Oklahoma Press, 1965.

A general introduction to the novel.

Wilson, Angus. *"Great Expectations."* In his *The World of Charles Dickens,* pp. 268-72. 1970. Reprint. Harmondsworth, England: Penguin Books, 1972.

Briefly touches upon several aspects of the novel, which he considers Dickens's "most completely unified work of art."

Worth, George J. *"Great Expectations": An Annotated Bibliography.* New York: Garland Publishing, 1986, 346 p.

A comprehensive resource on the novel listing editions, adaptations, separately published illustrations, early reviews, criticism, influence studies, and reference aids through 1983.

# Theodor Fontane

## 1819-1898

German novelist, autobiographer, travel writer, poet, and critic.

Fontane is considered the foremost master of the German social novel and is also remembered as a prominent man of letters in nineteenth-century Berlin. Recognized throughout most of his life for his ballads and travel books, it was not until the age of fifty-nine that he began writing the novels for which he has become famous, including *Vor dem Sturm: Roman aus dem Winter 1812 auf 13* (*Before the Storm: A Novel of the Winter of 1812-13*), *Frau Jenny Treibel,* and *Effi Briest.* These works have won praise for Fontane's realistic description, skillful use of dialogue, and ability to portray characters in complex human relationships. In addition, Fontane is regarded as an astute observer, recorder, and critic of nineteenth-century Prussian society; his disdain for the prejudices of its class structure is frequently reflected in the themes of his fiction. Among the subjects common to his novels are marital conflicts caused by external social pressures, complicated love triangles, and adultery. Most of his fictional works fall into the genre of the *Gesellschaftsroman,* or "novel of society," which addresses the interaction of individuals within their social environment. Contemporary critical reaction to Fontane's fiction was generally favorable, yet, among the German public, he was primarily recognized as a writer of patriotic ballads. In the twentieth century, Fontane's novels have received considerable critical attention and his work has been the subject of much scholarly analysis. For his portrayal of contemporary life in Berlin, his realistic characterizations, and his innovative use of dialogue, Fontane is now recognized as an important figure in the history of the modern German novel.

Fontane was born in the small town of Neu-Ruppin, just outside of Berlin, to parents of French Huguenot ancestry. His father, a successful apothecary, was largely responsible for Fontane's early schooling. Their animated study sessions (his father was a steadfast believer in the Socratic method) left a strong impression on the young Fontane, and later, in his autobiography *Meine Kinderjahre,* he called this the most valuable period of his education. In the mid-1830s, Fontane moved to Berlin, where his father had arranged for him to work as an apothecary's assistant. During this time, he began writing poetry and became associated with the celebrated literary club Tunnel über der Spree, establishing friendships with such rising literary figures as Theodor Storm and Paul Heyse. It was at the meetings of "the Tunnel" that Fontane first read his work in public, mostly ballads written on themes from English and Scottish folklore and Prussian history. At the age of thirty, Fontane gave up his career as an apothecary to work as a correspondent for the Prussian Ministry of the Interior. Fontane's first book of poetry, *Gedichte,* was published in 1851, and the following year he was sent to London for a brief period to report on Prussian-Anglo relations. During his stay, he recorded his thoughts and impressions of England, using them as the material for several travel guides, among which *Ein Sommer in London* and *Jenseit des Tweed* (*Across the Tweed*) were his best known. Fontane later wrote

a travel guide to the German countryside, *Wanderungen durch die Mark Brandenburg,* a series of historical and descriptive sketches of the Brandenburg landscape. During the mid-1860s Fontane served as a war correspondent for various Berlin newspapers, and from 1870 to 1890 he was the principal drama critic for the liberal *Vossische Zeitung.* As a reviewer at the Royal Theater, Fontane was one of the first to recognize the talents of Henrik Ibsen and Gerhart Hauptmann.

Fontane maintained a lifelong interest in German politics. Wary of political dogma, he remained open-minded, writing for both conservative and liberal newspapers. Fontane had more fundamental misgivings about Prussian society in general, and when in 1878 he published his first novel, *Vor dem Sturm,* it was in part a veiled indictment of contemporary German life. Over the next two decades, Fontane produced more than a dozen novels, most of which reflect his growing distaste for the snobbery of the German class system and what he felt was the materialism and lack of moral code among the bourgeoisie. Despite his impassioned views, Fontane's novels remained characteristically subtle in their denunciation of society. Many critics attribute his mastery of understatement to the fact that he wrote all of his novels at a relatively advanced age, his life experiences having given him a more objective view of society and the world around him. Fontane, however, never became a passive observer, continuing to embrace new ideas and radical ideologies well into his seventies. Late in life, he grew increasingly sympathetic toward the working class and expressed great interest in the socialist movement then gaining popularity in Germany. His last novel, *Die Likedeeler,* a utopian portrayal of medieval communist society, reflects these changing views but was never completed. Fontane died in Berlin at the age of seventy-nine.

Fontane once wrote: "The task of the modern novel seems to me to be the description of a life, a society, a group of people, as the undistorted reflection of the life we lead." For the most part, Fontane adhered to this declaration of realism, writing the majority of his novels in the then innovative genre of the *Gesellschaftsroman.* His early novels have predominately historical settings while his later writings are largely concerned with contemporary Berlin society. His most important historical novels take place during the early years of the Napoleonic Wars, a period familiar to Fontane through the firsthand recollections of his parents. *Vor dem Sturm* portrays the response of the German people to Napoleon's failed Russian campaign of 1813, an event that prompted much patriotic fervor in Prussia. Fontane wrote that his objective in writing this story was to show "how the great feeling, that was born at that time, found the most diverse people, and how it affected them." Critics believe that in many ways Fontane intended *Vor dem Sturm* to serve as a model for contemporary Berlin society by demonstrating the ability of ordinary people, inspired by "a great idea," to successfully bring about change. Stylistically, Fontane introduced in *Vor dem Sturm* many techniques that were to become characteristic of his later works. These include skillful use of dialogue, rather than complicated plot structure, to advance his storyline and define the personalities of his characters. Fontane also experimented with a detached narrative style in which he relayed the action of the novel through the eyes of one objective reporter. The opening pages of *Vor dem Sturm,* for example, consist of a single narrative voice reporting the action from a fixed spot along the busy Klosterstrasse. Communicating merely external behaviors and appearances, this technique allows no room for the author to make conclusive statements about his characters or cast judgment upon their actions; instead readers make their own subjective interpretation of the work. Many contemporary reviewers criticized this style for its lack of narrative force, disparaging *Vor dem Sturm* for having a weak plot and little or no tension among its characters. Despite this mediocre critical reception, Fontane continued writing fiction. His second major historical novel, *Schach von Wuthenow (A Man of Honor),* is also set in early nineteenth-century Germany, just before the Prussian defeat at the Battle of Jena. The story centers on the actions of Schach, a captain in the highly prestigious Prussian cavalry, who seduces the unattractive daughter of a friend. He immediately deserts her, however, fearing that his peers might ridicule him if he were to marry someone who in society's eyes was unacceptable. Upon discovering that the girl is pregnant with his child, Schach is forced into marriage. He determines that the only "noble" way out of the situation is suicide and shoots himself immediately following the wedding ceremony. Because of his misconceived notions of honor, Schach sacrifices his life to what Fontane calls the "false god" of society. The novel is Fontane's first powerful statement against blind conformity to social convention, a theme that was to dominate his later writings.

Critics now agree that Fontane's greatest achievement was his portrayal of contemporary German society in what have come to be known as his "Berlin novels." Of these, *Frau Jenny Treibel* is one of the most acclaimed. In this novel, Fontane severely denounces the superficiality of the rising middle class. The protagonist, Jenny Treibel, claims to live by high moral standards but is in fact only motivated by money and social position. She embodies the hypocrisy that Fontane believed was at the core of the bourgeois class. With an amused, sometimes satiric tone, Fontane depicts the shallow life-style of the Treibel family, centering the story on Frau Treibel's attempts to marry her son into a family of suitable social status. While *Frau Jenny Treibel* was written with obvious comic undertones, *Effi Briest,* widely regarded as Fontane's greatest social novel, is decidedly tragic. Like *Schach von Wuthenow* and *Frau Jenny Treibel,* it explores the consequences of conforming to the codes of society at the expense of individual happiness. The story focuses on Effi, a middle-class girl whose parents arrange her marriage to an aging baron who will be able to elevate her social standing. Effi soon finds herself unhappy and alone while her husband devotes most of his time to the advancement of his career. She seeks attention from a lively young military man, Major Crampas, and their relationship, though there is no love involved, evolves into an ongoing affair. Effi's husband accidentally discovers his wife's infidelity many years later and, although their marriage is now considered successful and happy, feels compelled by the dictates of society to challenge Crampas to a duel. The confrontation results in Crampas's death and Effi's abandonment. Living as a social outcast, Effi is denied the right to see her daughter and is only permitted back into her parent's house when sickness threatens her life. On her death bed, Effi concedes that, despite all of her misfortunes, her husband "was right in all he did." Critics agree that Fontane's complex psychological portrait of Effi Briest, as well as his ability to record in exacting detail the day to day habits of the characters in this novel, is one of the greatest accomplishments of his literary career. Effi has been the subject of extensive scholarly analysis and is often ranked, along with Gustave Flaubert's Emma Bovary and Leo Tolstoy's Anna Karenina, among the great heroines of nineteenth-century fiction. Critical interest in Fontane's writings has been growing steadily since the nineteenth century. Predominately known as a poet and travel writer during his lifetime, Fontane didn't receive widespread recognition for his fictional works until the early twentieth century. It was during this period that Thomas Mann called *Effi Briest* "one of the six best novels I know," reflecting Fontane's increasing stature as a novelist. With most of his major works becoming available in translation in the latter half of the twentieth century, there developed a new wave of critical analysis. In general, scholars have focused on Fontane's mastery of such literary devices as imagery, leitmotif, and symbol, particularly as they relate to the themes of his novels. Most Fontane scholars now regard him as a significant contributor to the modern novel, categorizing his psychological approach to characterization as an important transition between nineteenth-century poetic realism and the more rigorously analytical approach to realistic fiction adopted by many twentieth-century writers.

## PRINCIPAL WORKS

*Gedichte* (poetry) 1851
*Ein Sommer in London* (travel essay) 1854

*Jenseit des Tweed* (travel essay) 1860
  [*Across the Tweed*, 1965]
*Balladen* (poetry) 1861
*Wanderungen durch die Mark Brandenburg.* 4 vols. (travel essays) 1862-82
*Vor dem Sturm: Roman aus dem Winter 1812 auf 13* (novel) 1878
  [*Before the Storm: A Novel of the Winter of 1812-13,* 1985]
*Grete Minde* (novel) 1880
*Ellernklipp* (novel) 1881
*L'Adultera* (novel) 1882
  [*The Woman Taken in Adultery* published in *The Woman Taken in Adultery and The Poggenpuhl Family,* 1979]
*Schach von Wuthenow* (novel) 1883
  [*A Man of Honor,* 1975]
*Graf Petöfy* (novel) 1884
*Unterm Birnbaum* (novel) 1885
*Cécile* (novel) 1887
*Irrungen, Wirrungen* (novel) 1888
  [*Trials and Tribulations,* 1917]
*Stine* (novel) 1890
  [*Stine* published in *Twelve German Novellas,* 1977]
*Gesammelte Romane und Novellen.* 12 vols. (novels) 1890-91
*Quitt* (novel) 1891
*Unwiederbringlich* (novel) 1891
  [*Beyond Recall,* 1964]
*Frau Jenny Treibel* (novel) 1892
  [*Jenny Treibel,* 1977]
*Meine Kinderjahre* (autobiography) 1894
*Effi Briest* (novel) 1895
  [*Effi Briest* (abridged edition), 1962; (unabridged edition), 1967]
*Die Poggenpuhls* (novel) 1896
  [*The Poggenpuhl Family* published in *The Woman Taken in Adultery and The Poggenpuhl Family,* 1979]
*Der Stechlin* (novel) 1898
*Von Zwanzig bis Dreissig* (autobiography) 1898
*Die Likedeeler* (unfinished novel) 1938
*Sämtliche Werke.* 24 vols. (novels, autobiographies, travel essays, and poetry) 1959-75
*Theodor Fontane: Briefe.* 4 vols. (letters) 1968-71

---

### THE NEW QUARTERLY REVIEW (essay date 1855)

[*In the following review of* Ein Sommer in London, *the anonymous critic accuses Fontane of misrepresenting London society.*]

It is not more than seven years ago that a party of ladies and gentlemen belonging to the higher and most intelligent portion of the German aristocracy, asked us, with great commisseration, if we were not highly gratified at seeing the sun, since the air in England was so thick that we never saw the sky, and the few rays of sun that struggled on the brightest day in summer to pierce the dense atmosphere gave us but a very imperfect idea of a proper sunshine. Oh! it is no use denying it, they cried with one accord, we know better. Do not Shakspeare, Scott, Byron, and Bulwer, all say so? What do you live upon? was the next enquiry, as if they expected a cannibal's reply. You have no *Eier und Milch-speisen,* (delicacies made of eggs and milk) for Herr ——— says in his book

upon London and the English, that the largest and richest families never allow the maid who creeps half asleep up the area steps at 8 o'clock in the morning to take in, for the whole day's provision, more than a gill of milk. This they firmly believed, and persisted in their belief in spite of all our assertions to the contrary, and probably would have remained in ignorance until this day, had not railroads, steamboats, and cheap fares—the revolutions of 1849, the exhibition of 1851, brought them to our shores.

Besides which they have had the advantage of reading Dr. Schlesinger's admirable *Wanderings in and about London,* to which Fontane's **Summer in London** forms an extraordinary and disagreeable contrast, for inasmuch as Dr. Schlesinger was master of his subject, and drew a faithful likeness of London and its inhabitants, Theodor Fontane has misconceived and falsely drawn almost every line of his sketch. He appears to have taken his impressions of England and the English, from a certain low public house in Long Acre, which he used to frequent, and which is the resort of the inferior class of German refugees. Upon this house, and the nightly orgies that take place in it, the author bestows a great portion of his book. Theodor Fontane is a verdant German poet; it is therefore quite in character, that he should make his studies among the low and unrestrained, but that he should see England and the English through such a medium, and paint his picture accordingly, is preposterous in the extreme.

For some time the author lived near Mr. Dickens' residence, in Tavistock Square. He was highly delighted with the neighbourhood, for he assures us that the ladies came out upon the balconies in crowds, doubtless for the pleasure of seeing him.

The cool evening breezes blowing from Mr. Dickens' garden, perhaps inspired him with a wish to inhale a portion of the spirit of the English genius, but as far as we are able to judge from his **Summer in London,** no propitious deity has listened to his prayer.

If this be the German type of a true gentleman, we cannot wonder at the angry and incessant war they wage with the Englishman's sense of this much abused individual, "a true gentleman."

A review of "Ein Sommer in London," in The New Quarterly Review, *Vol. IV, 1855, p. 117.*

---

### THE SATURDAY REVIEW, LONDON (essay date 1861)

[*In the following excerpt from a review of* Jenseit des Tweed, *the anonymous critic describes Fontane's travel guide as "worthless."*]

**The Other Side of the Tweed** [*Jenseit des Tweed*] has been evidently manufactured to meet the demand for mild literary soporifics which railway travelling has created. It may be described as a handbook diluted with sentiment and sunsets. It may be useful to such German readers as have not the industry to work through the admirable handbooks, properly so called, which their country produces; but it can have no sort of recommendation to an English reader, unless he has an abstract preference for being sent to sleep by German instead of English commonplace. It is one of those gentle, harmless, worthless records of the most ordinary incidents of travel, which have been called into existence both by the exigencies of railway bookstalls and by the rigid censorship that careful mothers exercise over their daughters' reading. It is a great thing that we possess a light literature warranted free from romance or novelty; but it is unreasonable to expect that such a literature should be entertaining. Yet it is hard that Scotland should not have been in better hands.

*A review of "The Other Side of the Tweed," in* The Saturday Review, *London, Vol. 11, No. 286, April 20, 1861, p. 406.*

## ROBERT ZIMMERMANN  (essay date 1891)

[*In the following excerpt from a review of* Unwiederbringlich, *Zimmermann praises Fontane's realistic depiction of both character and setting.*]

Berlin—which as metropolis not only of intelligence, but also of the empire, is called on to play the part of an intellectual leader—possesses in Theodor Fontane a novelist whose power of realistic description and incisive style may be designated masterly. His charming picture of Prussian castles on his native sands of the Mark, somewhat unjustly decried, has shown that he turns with affection to his country; while his latest novel, *Unwiederbringlich,* which appeared in Rodenberg's *Deutsche Rundschau,* the worthy German counterpart of the *Revue des Deux Mondes,* proves him to be as much at home on the shores of the Great Belt and in the royal palaces of Copenhagen. The subject of the novel is the inevitable conflict between harsh strength of character in a woman and amiable weakness in a man, when the sex would have led us to expect the very opposite. Suggestive drawing of character and witty dialogue are the excellences of this and his second novel *Quitt.*

*Robert Zimmermann, in a review of "Unwiederbringlich," in* The Athenaeum, *No. 3323, July 4, 1891, p. 23.*

## THE ACADEMY  (essay date 1898)

[*In the following excerpt, the anonymous critic briefly reviews Fontane's literary career.*]

[Fontane] visited England in his youth and brought back a collection of English and Scottish ballads, which he rendered admirably in a German dress. He went through the Franco-Prussian campaign as correspondent for a Berlin newspaper, and, having had the good fortune to be captured by *franc-tireurs,* his letters from the seat of war have an almost historical value. It was in this period, no doubt, that he learned the Bismarck cult, and his wish to see what became of the great Chancellor was fulfilled, for Bismarck died on July 30, and Fontane on September 21. At another time he wandered through the Mark of Brandenburg—the tranquil valley, with its absence of surprises, in the midst of which Berlin has grown, and his volume of *Wanderungen* is a permanent treasure of shrewd and delicate observation. It was not till nearly his sixtieth year that he finally settled in Berlin, and turned his attention to romance. It was a quiet and a natural transition, and his stories, like his adventures, took life not at the flood, but in an "episodal chance." There is a touch of Bourget in his work—if Bourget's ladies had been dressed in flannelette; and Fontane could describe the details of this plain toilette with all the Parisian's refinement. But we doubt if the French master has depicted anything so purely white as the water-lily growing in the mud, whom Fontane has entitled *Stine.* But, above all, Theodor Fontane was a true child of Berlin, with all the Berliner's sense of humour. He disbelieved in perfection, and "thanked God for the sins of others." In his *Reminiscences of My Childhood* he poked a little innocent fun at his mother's imaginary fine relations, and related the "amiable absurdities" of his father without any malice prepense. He looked for impressions rather than sought for expressions, and certain phases of life have never been better delineated. The von Poggenpuhls, for instance, who supported existence on three oil-paintings of heroic ancestors, are a type which lingers in the memory.

*"Three German Novelists," in* The Academy, *No. 1391, December 31, 1898, p. 555.*

## ERNST HEILBORN  (essay date 1899)

[*In the following excerpt, Heilborn reviews two of Fontane's late works,* Der Stechlin *and* Von Zwanzig bis Dreissig, *praising his realistic depiction of human life and emotion.*]

It is impossible to make those of another nation understand what Fontane was and still is to us. He was distinctly a North German, Prussian, even Brandenburg writer, and even in Vienna he attracted little notice. But we loved him, and named him the best among us. He depicted the men whom we know as we see or should wish to see them. He was a distinct realist, but his realism had a subjective character. Thus he followed in his own path. His *Stechlin,* though called a novel, has no claim to that designation. There is an almost complete lack of action. We are received into the ancient and humble seat of Stechlin; we sit on the terrace opposite the old widowed lord of Stechlin, who is a capital talker, like Fontane himself, and listen to his chat. We are associated in the management of his estate. His son, who is captain in the Emperor's regiment of Uhlans, arrives on a visit with a few friends, and we learn that the time has come for him to seek a suitable partner for life. He finds her, too, and there is a happy wedding, followed by a calm, resigned death-bed scene; the old lord of Stechlin is attended to his last home, and the ancient dwelling sees a youthful pair within its walls, who will live in their own fashion on the estate of their ancestors. This exhausts the contents of the book, and as it lacks action there is hardly any composition to speak of. All the same this *Stechlin* is a book of the most intimate charm. No matter whether we are sitting on the terrace at Stechlin, or drawing an easy-chair to the fire in Count Barby's house on the Kronprinzenufer at Berlin, where young Stechlin finds his bride, we still feel at home. These people win our hearts. We can see into their hearts, and we rejoice that we are permitted to do so. We know, too, how they adapt themselves to life, each after his own fashion. More than that, we can figure them in any of the many situations which life may present, no matter how different from those depicted in the story, and know exactly how they would act. We might imagine them as the companions of our own lives, and, in fact, this is just what we do. To read Fontane means to live with his characters. And though the novel be wanting in action, there is no lack of matter. New ideas are constantly arising in the world; Liberals and Socialists are seeking recruits, and their views of life are communicated. Even the old aristocracy of the Mark comes under this influence, adopts these ideas, and coquettes with the fashions of the day. What is its real relation to these new ideas. That is the subject of the novel. This problem is treated in a purely human fashion without any subordinate partisan purpose. In his characteristic fashion, with a touch of gentle irony, old Fontane furnishes a symbolic treatment of this theme. Close to Stechlin Castle lies a peaceful lake of the same name. Whenever there is any volcanic eruption or earthquake in any part of the world, the face of this little Mark lake is troubled, waves begin to rise, a fiery column may even seem to be rising from it. It is the symbol of the aristocracy of the Mark. This aristocracy is forced into sympathy with the doings of the world beyond, but it always settles down to its normal condition.

As in his novel, so in his autobiographical sketches *Von Zwanzig bis Dreissig* (that is, from his twentieth year to his thirtieth), the mere human interest predominates. These memoirs are a piece of purely personal literature. An independent interest attaches to Fontane's account of his youthful years, the association of Berlin authors and critics known as the "Tunnel," and his personal connexion with the revolution of March, 1848. But it attains its real value by his method of regarding persons and things, for old Fontane had a broad and kindly spirit, and the superiority of the man who regards life calmly from the spectator's point of view and recognizes the insignificance of his own existence. Still, future historians will have to use Fontane's memoirs with as much caution as Bismarck's. (pp. 16-17)

*Ernst Heilborn, in a review of "Stechlin," in* The Athenaeum, *No. 3740, July 1, 1899, pp. 16-17.*

## KENNETH HAYENS  (essay date 1920)

[*In the following excerpt, Hayens evaluates possible literary influences on Fontane's writings.*]

[In] Fontane's earlier works the influence of certain groups of novelists cannot be overlooked, however much that influence may differ in degree in particular instances; it will hardly be denied that the existence of so much discursive conversation throughout his novels is traceable to the example of the Young German school, however wrong it would be to consider Fontane as in any sense attached to that school. Yet one can say that as he came at one time under the influence of Alexis he owns ultimate relationship to Scott, and as he came at one time under the influence of the Berlin group of novelists he owns ultimate relationship to the French *feuilletonists*. In respect of those novels [written in the second half of his career], . . . it is not possible to associate Fontane with any group or school of writers. If *L'Adultera* and *Frau Jenny Treibel* do not constitute him an actual member of the group to which Paul Lindau and Fritz Mauthner belonged, much less do *Irrungen, Wirrungen* and *Effi Briest* demand his inclusion in the younger, so-called naturalistic ranks. That insistence on the sensual, not to say animal side of man, which is the most blatant mark of the naturalistic school, is wholly wanting in Fontane. One would not, accordingly, expect to find any real literary relationship between Fontane and the prophet and priest of naturalism, Emile Zola; nor would it appear to exist. It is true, certainly, that the material for *Irrungen, Wirrungen* and *Stine,* more particularly perhaps for the latter, would more readily suggest itself to one acquainted with than to one ignorant of the naturalistic novel. But the attempt to realise how Zola would have used it, say on the basis of *Nana,* will suffice to show how far apart the writers stand. On the other hand, Fontane shows a likeness to Flaubert in the skilful use of small incident and in the masterly sketching of subsidiary characters; to Daudet in the symbolical touches, in the impressionistic rather than detailed descriptions of functions, in the anecdotal rather than strictly

consecutive manner of narration; to the Goncourts in the directness of character introduction, and the faithfulness to deduction from observation. And if in every case differences which counterbalance the likenesses are forthcoming, it does not follow that Fontane drew no inspiration from the Frenchmen. Certainly he is no immediate disciple, even of French realism as a whole; but it is improbable that that realism did not exert some influence upon a novelist who was continually in the process of development.

Considering Fontane's connection with England and his knowledge of the English language, which if one credit the experiences he recounts in *Von Zwanzig bis Dreissig* must have been extensive, it may be thought a little strange that his fiction should not show any signs of having been influenced by the English novelists. And if one recalls how he schooled himself in the English and Scottish ballads, one's surprise is likely to increase. Nevertheless, whatever similarities may be found to exist between his work and that of any English novelist, it is certain that no genuine literary relationships are discoverable. One may add that the danger of drawing conclusions from similarities, even when they are of the most obvious character, has been definitely exposed by Daudet, with reference to Dickens and himself, in the introduction to *Fromont jeune et Risler Aîné.*

It is impossible to proceed with the establishment of any final judgment upon Fontane's work without first reaching a conclusion with regard to the speech of his characters. While some critics are of the opinion that all Fontane's characters speak alike, R. M. Meyer maintains that the distinctions in the speech of characters in fiction have never been more finely drawn. It must be remembered that there are two groups of speakers within which the language of the individual is distinguishable only through the variations of emphasis. The first group consists of those who are so far down the scale of society as to have no employment of genuine interest to them, the second, however, of those at the other end of the scale who affect at least the banishment of everything aggressively individual from their manner of speaking. Between these two groups lie the greater mass of speakers whose language receives an individual colouring in main part as the result of the occupations which are followed. Fontane never takes his characters from those at the bottom of the scale; but he does take them frequently from that group which is averse to any crude assertion of self. While it is true that Fontane does at times achieve that distinction without difference in the speech of characters drawn from this group, it is equally certain that he is not always successful in the attempt. On the other hand, the study of the individual novels has shown clearly that it is wrong to assert that there is no variation in the speech of the characters. As so frequently the truth lies between the two extremes.

Again, it must be borne in mind that, although Fontane is neither prophet nor preacher, his novels contain always a more or less distinct theme or themes. These themes arise of themselves out of his fiction, as they do out of facts, unheralded and unsought. It is thus not surprising that one should feel in some cases that the writer is in company with the reader in recognising their full character, only when the novel reaches its conclusion.

The decision, for such it must have been, not to attempt to draw characters from the working classes, is one to which Fontane faithfully adhered. Nor is this self-limitation in the matter of character-selection, which would appear to be due not so much to a desire on the part of Fontane to restrict the class of character as to hesitancy in dealing with something with which he was only imperfectly acquainted, without a rather peculiar complement. While Fontane remains partial to the introduction of clergymen, he will not extend this partiality to their wives.

Although, as has been seen, Fontane in general is content with very slight plots on which there is no insistence, he has given proof of his ability to construct and work out an ingenious plot in **Unterm Birnbaum.** That he can maintain the reader's interest in the course of the action itself is further demonstrated in **Grete Minde;** while the vivid presentation of incident in the latter novel has its counterpart in **Unwiederbringlich.** Both **Unwiederbringlich** and **Cécile** are enhanced by well considered, clear, and concise passages of description. More frequently than by any of these excellences, however, Fontane's work is marked by the style. At times, as in **Die Poggenpuhls** and **Frau Jenny Treibel,** this will be best described as wonderfully apposite; at other times, as in **Schach von Wuthenow, Grete Minde, Effi Briest, Stine,** it is in every sense admirable. It is, however, his genius in the portrayal of character that of itself claims for Fontane the chief place amongst the German realists of the nineteenth century. The dawn of this power is already discernible in **Vor dem Sturm,** and it shows itself in certain cases even in his poorer work, as in the portrait of Van der Straaten in **L'Adultera.** It runs, indeed, in greater or less degree, throughout the series of Fontane's novels, maintaining itself to the last. Judged by the character-drawing alone, **Unwiederbringlich** might be ranked little below **Effi Briest.** One must apply the test of proportion finally to determine which of the novels should be taken as showing Fontane at his best. These will be found to be **Effi Briest, Schach von Wuthenow, Stine, Grete Minde,** and in a lesser degree **Irrungen, Wirrungen.** (pp. 273-78)

*Kenneth Hayens, in his* Theodor Fontane: A Critical Study, *W. Collins Sons & Co. Ltd., 1920, 282 p.*

## HARVEY W. HEWETT-THAYER    (essay date 1924)

[*In the following excerpt, Hewett-Thayer discusses realism in Fontane's novels, focusing on his representations of human relationships, his method of character portrayal, and his use of symbols and leitmotifs.*]

At first glance perhaps, the chief characteristic of Fontane's novels may seem to be the extraordinary fidelity and completeness with which contemporary life is reproduced. The contemporary background in many of its aspects, the topics of thought forced upon society by external conditions are reflected in the lives and especially in the conversations of his characters. His novels abound in references to that which is even minutely contemporary and local. Sweets are procured "of course" from a well-known confectioner, certain popular restaurants or variety theatres in Berlin are spoken of familiarly; a local pastor in the Mark is compared with a famous court preacher. One might be tempted to condemn Fontane's frequent inclusion of such references as akin to the practice of employing recondite allusion or quotation in order to gain the favour of the initiated by flattering their vanity. The time will come,—is perhaps fast upon us,—when a certain type of reader, irritated by the possibility of anything escaping him, will demand annotated editions of Fontane's stories; for, unfortunately, confectioners die and court preachers as well, and go to their reward; social conditions shift, and familiar

subjects of discussion become remote and academic. Fontane's practice in this respect is, however, quite in keeping with the habit of the intimate *raconteur;* discussion or allusion may, for the initiated, open flood-gates of significant reminiscence, but, take it all in all, neither discussion nor allusion bears any essential relation to the real enjoyment of the story, for Fontane establishes the centre of interest in less transitory things.

Though he sees the world about him with unfailing accuracy and is aware of its problems, Fontane is too genuine an artist, or, in other words, too natural a story-teller, to allow his epic purpose to be deflected into sociological byways. His stories do not, except indirectly, present the effects of a transitory environment on the lives of men and women, nor do they engage in the purposeful depiction of a social order, which may or may not be in need of the physician. Like the surface of a lake his characters mirror the clouds above them, are ruffled by the winds of to-day; their motives are modified by contemporary prejudices. But the lake is not essentially changed by cloud or wind. Fontane is primarily concerned with deeper and more elemental matters; he uses the contemporary and the temporary, but only as a means through which the changeless things are discussed.

In other words, Fontane's stories are not "novels with a purpose," and it may be maintained that a part of Fontane's claim to abiding popularity as a writer of fiction is based on the fact that he did not attach his fortunes to the exposition of a particular class or problem, to any plan for social regeneration. Novels thus conceived, though unquestionably valuable to future historians of social conditions as mines of investigation, begin, in just such measure as the temporary considerations outweigh the permanent and elemental, to recede into the dust of literary archæology. The more ambitious novels of Spielhagen, for example, are conscious efforts to grasp the meaning of restricted periods of German cultural history; social and historical conditions which are just fading into retrospect are held firm for our inspection and illustrated by certain characters chosen to react to such a stimulus as the novelist wishes to describe. Spielhagen's novels have long since begun their pilgrimage to the untroubled top-shelves. The same is largely true of Paul Lindau's stories of Berlin life; the consciousness of the transitional period in the life of the capital led Lindau, and others indeed, to incorporate in fiction certain contemporary phases and tendencies of the life about them. But the later student of social history may find a more trustworthy store of material for the reconstruction of past society in the incidental and the casual than in the purposeful and the schematic. Vision is rarely vouchsafed to those who try overhard to see.

In the last analysis, Fontane is concerned with little less than the personal relationships of one human being to another, relationships that are usually conceived in a very elemental or even primitive sense. The individual will may indeed be in conflict with the world-will as registered in the standardized impulses and inhibitions of organized society, and it may be necessary to lay weight upon certain peculiarities of the social organism which are characteristic of a certain time, yet the novelist, after due recognition of accessory circumstance, pursues his quarry to its lair, the recesses of the soul, where one personality meets and enters into relationship with another personality. Like the great master craftsmen of his trade, he strips man to his elemental nakedness, where human spirit meets human spirit in problems essentially unchanged by time and place since the angel with the flaming sword stood at the gate of paradise.

With unwearying reiteration, then, Fontane seeks concrete expression of certain problems which in one form or another seem inalienable from human living as long as men and women retain those characteristics which make them men and women. In the first place, a large fraction of his work is resolvable, upon analysis, into the formula which has been conveniently called the "triangle." These stories, possessing thus a fundamental similarity of plot, differ nevertheless among themselves, and naturally, for otherwise only one of them would be worth telling. Fontane grapples, for example, with the theme made memorable by the story of Anna Karenina; a woman is married to a man considerably older than herself; it is a marriage of convenience, arranged by others on some other principle than on that mutual attraction which deepens into love,—and, with the addition of a third person, the material for tragedy becomes complete. (pp. 27-30)

Even as the typical substance of Fontane's novels is simple and everyday, so is his method of using it direct and unaffected. His characters meet in everyday ways in the routine of life, the ordinary round of neighbourly visits in town and country, the picnics, the different social affairs, varying in pretension according to the wealth and social position of those concerned,—in other words, at normal work and play. Fontane is particularly fond of the dinner-party as a meeting-place for his men and women; here in conversation they disclose themselves; then afterwards he contrives a continuation of the process by making the prominent characters the subject of discussion after the company has broken up into groups. Thus the novels of Fontane have been called "conversation" novels. This is a strictly realistic method; our opinions of other people are largely formed by what they say or by what is said of them by those who know them, only now and then do people really do anything worth mentioning. Sometimes indeed Fontane may be fairly charged with violating the probabilities both in the length of the discourses which he credits to his characters and the generosity with which he parcels out to them his own morsels of penetrating and sententious wisdom. Other realists, Meredith, for example, have erred even more seriously in this wise.

This natural and indirect method of character portrayal Fontane nearly always prefers to direct analysis. Not only is the realism of the story enhanced through this strictly realistic method, but negatively, that is, through the comparative absence of direct analysis of character, the novel gains in vital interest. To just such a degree as he employs pure analysis, perhaps even the more acute the analysis, the more does the novelist transfer the human interest of the story to the intellect, and distinctly to the detriment of the novel in its total appeal. Our interest in people is a curious and unstable compound of the intellectual and the emotional; it is rarely commanding if it is preponderatingly a matter of the intellect. Fulness of life is not granted to those whose companionships are purely of the mind, in which the heart does not inexplicably have its share. Nor is there any material difference when we seek companionships in books; our use of books supplies simply a vicarious enlargement of our human experience. The persistent analyst tends to exhibit his characters as specimens of his own virtuosity, to learn to know them is perhaps a stimulating intellectual experience, but they are not the men

and women whom we really know, for knowledge is not of the mind alone.

Though Fontane in general seeks his material in normal human experience, according to the realist's creed, one hesitates at times to accept certain passages as reconcilable with the typical practice of the realists. For example, the novelist displays not infrequently,—notably in **Ellernklipp,** an attitude toward external nature which one is accustomed to associate with romantic fiction; nature is presented as an interpreter of the mind of man and links her moods in sympathy with his. But more conspicuous still is Fontane's use of symbols and premonitions, a habit which seems distinctly a survival of romantic story-telling. In one novel after another there is a significant repetition of certain phrases; snatches of song are introduced which are instinct with foreboding and which recur with fateful reminiscence, welding the substance of the story more closely together. This practice of Fontane's has been likened to Wagner's use of the "leitmotiv." Often this "leitmotiv" consists of a single foreshadowing suggestion, interwoven with the substance of happy days. It is often akin to the dramatic irony of classic tragedy, consisting merely of a fateful ambiguity; the words are meant by the speaker in one sense but are clearly or vaguely apprehended by the reader as permitting of another meaning. The novelist plays with words which may or may not be interpreted as presaging the future. He introduces hints to which the reader turns back in memory, even perhaps as the characters themselves recall later the warning guide-post which was unnoted at the time. Fontane understood well that trick by which the reader is brought into a peculiarly sympathetic relationship with the characters of a novel, simply through an identity of memory.

Fontane's employment of this device is usually highly effective. In his first novel, **Vor dem Sturm,** an inscription on a tomb makes a deep impression on the hero, and its enigmatical meaning as applied to his fortunes is disclosed in the unfolding of the story; perhaps at this early stage of Fontane's work,—in view of his literary pedigree,—this inscription is a reminiscence of the prophetic verses in *Guy Mannering.* In **Unwiederbringlich** the "leitmotiv" is a stanza of a pensive, melancholy song; the unhappy countess hears the words in an early chapter, they are stamped on her memory, and she leaves them behind as her only coherent message when she seeks in the sea the rest which the lines seemed to promise. In the pathetic little story of **Grete Minde,** the heroine returns to the church after her father's funeral; the evening glow illumines the interior as with fire, and Grete flees from the building in a kind of nameless terror. At the end of the story, the wanderer, now returned to her old home, looks down from the church tower upon the sea of flames beneath her, the substance of her revenge. Only through remembrance does the reader perceive the significance of the earlier scene. The device as used in **L'Adultera** is certainly less successful: Van der Straaten purchases a reproduction of Tintoretto's picture of the woman taken in sin, and hangs it on the wall, as a kind-of symbolic warning. Hence Fontane's scheme becomes simply a direct announcement of the events which are to follow. The failure of the device is not that such a disclosure robs the story of its hold on the reader; one is not led on in such a novel by the mere desire to learn the outcome of a tangle; one is concerned with the development of the characters and of their relations to one another, and the author is undoubtedly justified in warning us as to what the characters are going to do, in order that we may be the more intent on the main problem, the process by which they are led to it. Though Van der Straaten's act is superbly indicative of his character, suggesting his lack of real refinement, his essential brutality, the very use of the "leitmotiv" seems to partake of his brutality, to be equally crude and bald. But such errors of taste are not common in Fontane.

In spite of our first impressions, Fontane's use of the "leitmotiv" is not really inconsistent with realism. The content of our everyday is fertile in material for foreboding. Indisputably that man has lost his peace of mind, if not his mental and emotional balance, who begins to associate the innocent ambiguities of to-day with a possible interpretation for the morrow. But what is madness for the individual in his normal relationship to his own life, may quite reasonably be within the province of the novelist, even of the realistic novelist. Out of the manifold incidents which make up our days, he simply selects certain elements, ordinarily overlooked and forgotten, which cast their shadows into the future.

Fontane's natural attitude of mind made him receptive to the doctrines of naturalism, when that revolutionary movement was first inaugurated. He expressed, indeed, his sympathy with the propaganda of the naturalists, and commended their purpose, as they enunciated it,—to revitalize literature through a rejection of the artificial and conventional, and especially by the employment in literary work of those scientific methods which had been so long successfully tested in the acquisition of knowledge in natural science. But Fontane was never so enamoured of the new theory as to yield to it his personal devotion; he never became so purely objective in his work as to regard his characters as biological specimens, whose pleasures and pains were only of interest as they might afford material for generalizations on the phenomena of human life. He never denied the sanction of the selective process, and he emphasized the right of the artist to select the beautiful rather than the ugly, for both are a part of life. (pp. 54-9)

The practice of the masters in writing the master novels, infinitely various, of course, would yield a kind of empirical rule, although it would be hard to formulate and might be so inconclusive that it would be of little value when we had laboriously achieved it. But, without endeavouring to forecast the findings of such an effort, there would surely be much to say in favour of the type of novel which carries the novelist along as a kind of "super-cargo"; he is always unobtrusive, but he is always there, and can tell the passengers, not too insistently of course, that the voyage after all has some other purpose than to provide a mere pastime for tourists. It is in this sense perhaps that Fontane is present in his books; the novelist constantly betrays his personal attitude toward the characters to which he has given life: he accompanies their fortunes with evident affection and sympathy, particularly in their loneliness and their shattered happiness; with emotion he tells of wasted and blighted lives, of the perennial enigmas of human living.

Yet Fontane is only indirectly a moralist, and he is, in the stricter sense, not a philosopher at all. Fontane has come to his own conclusions with reference to life; that cannot be gainsaid; some of his estimates of life are easily inferable from his stories, but they are implicit and not explicit. Fontane looked out upon the world with clear penetrating eyes, and he recorded his impressions with unusual fidelity; the material of his novels is made up from his accumulated observations, recreated into life by the power of his imagination. And the novelist's attitude toward life is obtained in the same real-

istic way; it is a deduction, his own deduction, from observed phenomena. In it neither religion nor metaphysics plays any appreciable part. He does not start from the concept of divine order or interest. If he believes in God, it is essentially the God of the pragmatists, coloured perhaps with a tinge of poetic pantheism; for his inspection of human phenomena favours the belief in God as a workable hypothesis,—it would be a still sorrier world without it,—and the mass of things beyond our understanding implies a power beyond ourselves, which, whether or not "it makes for righteousness" or in any way "works together for good," must be more than mere chance. There is no such thing as chance, Fontane says. Fontane's views have the obvious advantages and limitations of his method of acquiring them; the deductive view of life is prone to be more fragmentary than the inductive; it is easier to apply an accepted theory to phenomena than to derive a workable theory from their multiplicity. If then, we may derive from Fontane only fragments of a moral system, scraps of scattered comment which take the form of interpretation or precept, there is at any rate one unifying principle in his attitude, his sympathetic charity for erring humanity. He spreads a robe of kindliness to cover the multitude of our transgressions.

Though Fontane's novels, practically all of them, present certain deviations from accepted moral standards, the novelist neither condemns nor condones; he is indignant neither at the individuals whose lives are blotted with irregularities, nor with the general make-up of society which allows or haply even fosters such delinquency. He does not stamp Frau Pittelkow as a moral coward because she accepts an easier way of existence than to work for the support of herself and her children, nor does he present her as pathetically ignorant of the right pathway, or gloss her fault with false sentiment. The sin of Effi Briest ruined her own chance of happiness, of satisfaction in motherhood, or in social life; it dimmed the sunshine for all who loved her, but Fontane has no word of scorn or condemnation. Even for Frau Jenny Treibel, whose fundamental insincerity of character tends to block the happiness of others, he has an amused and quizzical tolerance. Politics as a branch of ethics absorbed much of Fontane's keenest thinking, and his novels bear constant witness to his interest, but they are utterly void of anything resembling political propaganda. As Fontane is kind to human frailty, he looks in gentle forbearance upon the vagaries, the inconsistencies, the dogmatics of the political enthusiasts. In an election for the Diet, Count Stechlin, the very embodiment of class pride, is defeated by a social democrat; as he drives home in a blistering humour, he finds one of his proletarian opponents lying drunk by the way-side; not only does he take him into his carriage but he supplies a material gift for the future well-being of his foe,—but he excludes remorselessly from his house a young physician who has embraced the principles of social democracy. Politics are to Fontane a quite unclarified branch of moral philosophy; they illustrate admirably the inherent capacity of the human mind for error and inconsequence.

Fontane yields naturally to that fatalistic interpretation of life which tends to characterize those who take a serious view of man's living but who have no steadying influence of religious faith to act as an interpreter of the otherwise incomprehensible. "What happened was only what was destined to happen," expressed or implied, is the underlying and accepted fact for all his occurrences; this is ever on the lips of his characters as upon his own. But fatalism is in Fontane, not the grandiose spectre of the ancients, nor the petty demon of the fate-dramatists; it is rather a kind of reluctant acknowledgment that the interacting forces of character and circumstance bring about inevitable results, that guilt demands an unfailing recompense, that a mistake can never really be rectified. Such a fatalism is the foe of all heroics, of all older forms of heroism. Despite the suffering and pain or renunciation, particularly in Fontane's women, there is little of thrilling martyrdom about it all; martyrdom implies a "cause," even if it is an unworthy one. Such a fatalistic conception of life engenders in lesser minds, the average man with the average vision, an indifferent attitude toward goals and purposes; of many of Fontane's characters one could repeat what is told of the unhappy Crampas: "He enjoys life, but at the same time is indifferent to it. He takes everything as it comes along and yet he knows that there isn't much to it after all."

And yet Fontane does not allow his fatalistic determinism to become a sour or embittered pessimism; he says himself that pessimism is a matter of temperament; his own temperament was sweet and wholesome, and though nature endowed him with a keen vision for man's inadequacies, for the sources and the substance of man's unhappiness, the total result of his observations is not a cheerless waste. "The result of life, however poor it is, is still always better than it really ought to have been," is, even if a little paradoxical, a characteristic bit of his thinking. In the end he does not fill us with uneasiness about the human animal in his upward strivings, he will not with Mephistopheles compare him to a grasshopper,

> That springing flies, and flying springs,
> And in the grass the same old ditty sings.

His findings are, indeed, of a nature to give us pause, but though the happiness which supposedly is the legitimate pursuit of man is really unattainable, "all great happiness is a mere fairy-tale,"—the sum total of human accomplishment in character and in deeds born of character is not discreditable.

But upon the wreckage and the losses Fontane looks with a kind of wistful resignation, which supplies a lyric undertone of melancholy even to his merriment. Fontane's novels are serious if not sombre books; the genial personality of their author, his tenderness, his sympathy with man in his uncertain strivings, even his humour, cannot make them otherwise. His novels, it may be said again, are the expression of keen observation and mature thinking,—the voice of one who has "kept watch o'er man's mortality," and who has attained the relative calm of harboured waters. But it is not the calm of an Olympian serenity; it is, at best, the calm of ripened art, which is as yet incomplete, for it sees only through a glass darkly, but has begun to note the presence of the eternal in the transitory. Thus Fontane is not only a close observer and a recorder of German life during a span of years at the century's end; his stories are records of human experience in qualities which know neither time nor place. In this, it may be, lies their abiding worth. (pp. 61-6)

*Harvey W. Hewett-Thayer, "Theodor Fontane the Realist," in his* The Modern German Novel: A Series of Studies and Appreciations, *Marshall Jones Company, 1924, pp. 26-66.*

## ROSEMARY PARK (essay date 1939)

[*In the following excerpt, Park analyzes the distinctive characteristics of Fontane's fictional heroes and assesses their relation to the themes of his work.*]

Theodor Fontane's novels, not unlike the dramas of Friedrich Hebbel, deal with the conflict between individual desire and social convention. This conflict both for Fontane and for Hebbel ends in the apparent triumph of conventional social demands. In Hebbel's dramas the victory of society is only a seeming one, the defeat of the hero temporary, since the progress of history towards the ideals for which the hero stands will ultimately vindicate him. No such metaphysical principles lie behind Fontane's equivocal victories of convention. Indeed, as we shall see, no fair battle between the opposing forces of convention and individual ever takes place. Fontane's heroes do not choose to fight. Any victory of convention over them is therefore a victory by default, an indecisive, equivocal triumph which determines nothing. Conservative though these *dénouements* appear, Fontane himself can not be termed a conservative, unless analysis of his characters, as well as of the conclusions of his novels, should prove him beyond doubt a praiser of things past.

The underlying theme of Fontane's novels is marriage, either contemplated or already in existence. Fontane treats this particular aspect of the relationship between individual desire and social convention without sensationalism, by subtle nuance and implication. For him the business of literature was always the creation of characters, not the definition or solution of problems. In spite of his theoretical realism, however, Fontane could not help seeing life in patterns. Two constant figures of these patterns are the capable woman and the weak man. The subject matter of the novels and the similarity existing among the women characters on the one hand and the men on the other, makes possible a division of Fontane's characters according to sex without doing violence to the illusive flow of his narrative. The capable women have already been studied. It remains to consider the peculiar qualities of the masculine heroes and their significance for the fundamental theme of the novels.

The common characteristic of all of Fontane's men is their failure in life. Since the subject of the novels is so consistently marriage, life and love are apt to be synonymous, failure in one means failure in the other. Indeed the success of Fontane's heroes may be said to stand in inverse proportion to their importance in the novel. The only indubitably successful male character is Wendelin, the older brother of the Poggenpuhl family. He has established himself by his own resourcefulness; he knows what he wants and how to secure it. Once these facts are set forth, neither author nor reader feels any further concern for him. Less outstandingly successful and so more prominent in Fontane's picture of society are a group of men who achieve an equivocal, temporary success, not primarily through their own efforts but rather due to the complete failure of their rivals. Marcell Weddekopf in *Frau Jenny Treibel* wins Corinna Schmidt, not because he convinces her of her error in judgment or cajoles her back to her senses. Even with the encouragement of her father, he takes no active part in her conversion. Only the abject weakness of his opponent, Leopold Treibel, makes it possible for Marcell to carry off Corinna. (pp. 32-3)

The real male protagonists are more complicated in soul, less ambiguous in their failure. In every case, whether it be Schach von Wuthenow, Graf Petöfy, Graf Holk (*Unwiederbringlich*), Baron von Instetten (*Effi Briest*), these men are forced to make a decision with respect to some demand of conventional society. A cynic might say that it makes little difference which course of action they choose. If these characters conform completely to the pattern of their surroundings, their subsequent lives are proper and barren like Botho's, Leopold's and, to some degree, Instetten's. If they defy the order of their community, they do not experience any deep tragedy or great triumph. A brief interlude of unhappy uncertainty ensues, to be followed by their return to security and convention. Another group of characters submit to the demands of society but with a protest, which is in itself futile. Neither Schach von Wuthenow nor Waldemar, Graf von Haldern, learn by a profound conversion to acknowledge the justice of conventional demands. Since they do not choose to fight, there is no battle and no victory. Their protest remains a mere petulant gesture. Schach's friends remarked that he was afraid: "und so sei er denn aus Furcht vor dem Leben in den Tod gegangen." Victoire, his wife, who had more reason than others to study him, and who was capable of passing judgment, believed that it was not fear of an outrageous fortune which drove him to suicide, but rather the realization that he must fight a battle in which he could not trust himself. He felt himself weak and vain, he was not the man to attempt marriage with Victoire in the face of ridicule. This knowledge undermined his defenses against a hostile world. Schach's creator called him a weak character and it is significant that here, in the first of the social novels, Fontane chose a weak male character as a foil to the resolute, charming Madame Carayon. In *Schach von Wuthenow* Fontane establishes the prototype for many more subtly developed male characters of later novels, all of whom are to fail when consciousness of their own weakness prevents resistance to conventional opposition.

Four years before the appearance of *Schach von Wuthenow* Fontane wrote in private correspondence: "Daß man lebt ist nicht nötig, nur das empfind' ich immer tiefer, wenn man überhaupt lebt, muß man auch leben können." These words condemn Schach, but even more truly do they pass judgment upon Waldemar von Haldern, the hero of the novel *Stine.* When Waldemar loses his heart to Stine Rehbein, he knows that no Haldern tradition approves such an action. When he dies, ironically smiling at the thought that his last hours could be called a bacchanal, he has made no peace with this tradition. He does not submit to conventional demands with the satisfaction of knowing that he has sacrificed his individual happiness in support of a traditional decorum. The old Baron encourages him: "Nur Mut!" and he himself expressly declares: "Ich werde selbstständig handeln." But Stine, the humble seamstress, refuses to help him and alone he cannot claim before the world the hand he seemed to have won. The symbol of his life, in his own words, is the half circle. He does not struggle against the law of his class, because he knows himself to be "hilfebedürftig, versöhnungsbedürftig." He is "eigensinnig" but not obstinate enough to stem the tide of opposition he had raised. "Unser Kranker" says Fontane of him. The other characters are less reserved: "Ein krankes Huhn"; "Er war doch man miesig."

Like Waldemar in his failure, but more favorably judged by the other characters in the novel, is Botho von Rienäcker, hero of the novel *Irrungen Wirrungen.* He plays with the thought of a legal union between himself and the laundress Lene Nimptsch, a union which must eventually be contrary to the traditions of his class. But Botho, like Waldemar von Haldern, knows himself to be a weakling: he is only a "Durchschnittsmensch," not the exceptional or aggressive man to succeed in any battle with convention: "Es liegt nicht in mir, die Welt herauszufordern und ihr und ihren Vorurteilen öffentlich den Krieg zu erklären." He prefers to surrender to tradition, rather than live in defiance of society. Sadly he pushes aside the dream of "Einfachheit, Wahrheit, Natürlichkeit," which life with Lene seemed to promise him. One can live without happiness and even advise others to do the same. In this decision Botho does not bow to an objective power stronger than himself. He yields merely because he is not strong enough to fight.

Comic rather than tragic is the situation in which the young hero of *Frau Jenny Treibel* finds himself. With his tongue in his cheek Fontane lets Frau Jenny Treibel, "geborne Bürstenbinder," the onetime daughter of a grocer, oppose the marriage of her youngest son, Leopold, with Corinna Schmidt, the professor's daughter. Leopold, in her opinion, should aspire to greater social heights. With this conviction Frau Jenny sets about defeating the urbane, ironic males, who are all so amused or overawed by her that they do not attempt a united resistance. Weaker than either Botho or Waldemar, Leopold has no sooner taken the dangerous step of engagement to Corinna than he ponders: "Wenn ich in meine Unentschlossenheit zurückfalle!" Like Botho and Waldemar he, too, considers the possibility of opposition to the established order, or in his case, to his mother's idea of the established order. But like a characteristic Fontane hero, he realizes the futility of such opposition: "Ich weiß, ich bin kein Held." In this unheroic mood he submits to defeat by Frau Jenny, lets Marcell, his rival, carry off Corinna from under his nose, but comforts himself with the saying, long familiar to him as a son of Frau Jenny: "Mensch, ärgere dich nicht, wundere dich bloß!" Even less aggressive than Leopold is the hero of *Mathilde Möhring,* Hugo Großmann. He is so entirely the creation of his competent wife, Mathilde, that his only resistance to her is his death, and even that is so subtle a form of opposition that neither the characters nor society would consider it such. The supineness of all these heroes, their "Milchsuppenschaft" as Frau Jenny called the quality in her own sons, is especially significant because these characters are all young men. Not their experience of life has taught them to conform, but their own lack of vital energy predisposes them to defeat. Fontane can hardly be said to uphold in them the sanctity of established custom. He indicates merely through these characters how ineffectual is the opposition to the existing social code.

The only one of Fontane's characters who actually carries out a contemplated resistance to the traditions of his class is Graf Holk in the novel *Unwiederbringlich.* His opposition is at best halfhearted, for Holk is again a weak character. The two women who knew him best agree in that. At times Holk himself admits the truth of their judgment. Carried away, however, with the idea that he deserved another kind of wife than Christine, he seeks a divorce and appeals to the piquant Ebba Rosenberg to bring him the light and laughter he thought life owed him. Ebba had long ago declared: "Sein Charakter ist noch viel schwächer als sein Herz; sein Charakter ist das recht eigentlich Schwache an ihm. Und was das Schlimmste ist, er weiß es nicht einmal." Holk had neither the wit nor the courage to subdue this woman. He turns back as the two skate together toward the open sea. Even his action toward Christine, his wife, he never fully justifies. Fontane writes of him: "Denn während er sich alles bewiesen zu haben glaubte, war er doch im letzten Winkel seines Herzens von der Nichtstichhaltigkeit seiner Beweise durchdrungen." Christine's brother had warned Graf Holk of the danger which lay in marriage with Christine. But when, partly in disregard of this warning, the marriage results in no great happiness, Holk prefers to discover the reason anywhere but in his own failure. "Christine hat mich von sich weg erkältet." So likewise he blames Ebba Rosenberg for having led him on: "Ich kann nicht erkennen, daß mir eine Pflicht vorlag, den Ernst Ihrer Gefühle zu bezweifeln. . . . Sie sind einfach andern Sinnes geworden." Even his final return to Christine does not proceed from any better knowledge of himself but rather from a desire for comfort. Holk fails to secure happiness with either of the two women he thought he loved, because he never acts with any complete conviction of the righteousness of his cause. In Ebba's words he stands condemned: "Sie sind ein Halber!" His defiance to tradition is as futile as the surrender of Waldemar and Botho. In no case does Fontane portray men who renounce happiness in heroic decisions to support the convention of their society. They find no happiness, not because they are crushed by social demands but because they have not the strength to act as undivided personalities in defiance or in accord with these demands. (pp. 34-7)

In Baron von Instetten, the hero of *Effi Briest,* Fontane portrays the greatest of the older men who with a feeling of inner self-sufficiency marry younger women. Again an apparently successful union results. In the earlier novels, *L'Adultera* and *Graf Petöfy,* the personal defects of the hero are the primary cause for the failure of the marriage. Suddenly aware of the thinness of their marriage relationship, the heroines attempt or are tempted to substitute for it a marriage where more community of spirit shall exist. In *Effi Briest,* however, Effi herself has no intention of separating from her husband, Instetten. She does not consciously take the step which leads to dissolution of the marriage, as Melanie van der Straaten does in *L'Adultera.* It is rather Geert von Instetten who, forced on by the traditional demands of his class, terminates the union. As in the case of younger heroes like Botho von Rienäcker or Waldemar, Graf von Haldern, Instetten is called upon to support a class propriety in which he no longer entirely believes. He does not feel any personal injury so gross that he or Major Crampas must die: "Ich bin ohne jedes Gefühl von Haß oder gar Durst nach Rache." The extent of Instetten's indecision is indicated by his calling a friend into consultation before he actually demands satisfaction from Major Crampas. But once having confessed his inability to act with inner conviction and having admitted the existence of letters addressed to Effi by Major Crampas, he is no longer free to chose his course, either in the eyes of this friend or of the world. "Die Welt ist einmal wie sie ist, und die Dinge verlaufen nicht, wie wir wollen, sondern wie die anderen wollen," says the friend. "Unser Ehrenkultus ist ein Götzendienst, aber wir müssen uns ihm unterwerfen, solange der Götze gilt." To both of these propositions Instetten assents. Effi Briest is sacrificed to the idol. Major Crampas dies at the hands of Instetten, a smile on his lips, which seemed to say: "Instetten, Prinzipienreiterei!" Instetten himself experiences no inner regeneration through his act. . . .

Even in Instetten, the perfect official, doubts persist as to the human validity of the conventional social code. Like the other heroes of Fontane's novels, he is conscious that these standards hamper life and that without them life would be simpler, more vital. He has, however, no mission to institute a new order of society and prefers to be resigned, ironic, conservative. His conservatism, like that of Fontane's other heroes, is not a recognition of the power and sanctity of decorum but rather a mask hiding his weakness and indecision. He might well have written, as Fontane himself did in the same year in which *Effi Briest* appeared: "So lange man die Dinge um einen her wie selbstverständlich ansieht, geht es, aber bei Beginn der Kritik bricht alles zusammen. Die Gesellschaft ist ein Scheusal."

In contrast to the indecision of the heroes of the foreground, Fontane often portrays as secondary characters elderly men who comment ironically on the actions of other characters, but who are still capable of energetic decision in opposition to convention. Old Briest in the novel *Effi Briest* quiets his suspicions as to the validity of conventional standards with his favorite phrase: "Ach, Luise, laß . . . das ist ein zu weites Feld." Nevertheless it is he who in the face of disapproval from friends and neighbors telegraphs to his lonely daughter: "Effi, komm!" In *Stechlin* such a character becomes the hero of the novel. The weak young man, his son, is not omitted from the story but Woldemar is so well bolstered by capable women and understanding clergymen that there can be no real fear for his safety nor profound interest which of the charming young sisters he ultimately marries. The novel consciously directs its gaze toward the past. Old Stechlin is the last of his race in spirit, in spite of the fact that young Woldemar returns with a bride to the ancestral castle. Though he can say: "Unanfechtbare Wahrheiten gibt es überhaupt nicht, und wenn es welche gibt, so sind sie langweilig"; though his creator can write of him that he inclined by nature to put a question mark after everything, nevertheless, old Graf Stechlin knew where he stood. Of his son this is no longer true; "solch unsichere Passagiere wie mein Woldemar," so old Stechlin describes him. His heir can only act from *Pietät,* not from true conviction. The broad humanity of the older men does not promise to live again in the sons. "Er hat einen edel Charakter aber ich weiß nicht, ob er auch einen festen Charakter hat," says the younger Stechlin's sister-in-law of him. These words might have been written of all of Fontane's younger heroes, who without exception, as we have seen, cling to tradition for protection rather than uphold it in clearcut decisions. Even the older men, Instetten, Graf Petöfy, or van der Straaten, see in convention an idol which they tolerate because they have not the strength to destroy it. Only in Stechlin and old Briest, representatives of an older generation, is there the inner strength to defy convention if necessary, or to support it approvingly.

The weakness of Fontane's unheroic heroes, whether they belong to the younger or the older generation, lies in their inability to act as undivided personalities. Perception outruns the power of decision, desire fails before the realistic necessity for achievement. There is a touching similarity in their longing for *Einfachheit, Wahrheit, Natürlichkeit.* But because they lack the strength to revolt and by that means attempt to secure an existence more nearly approaching their modest ideal, they prefer to acknowledge the essential rightness of a traditional decorum. Botho von Rienäcker speaks for all these men when he says: "Was predigt dies Denkmal mir? Jedenfalls das eine, daß das Herkommen unser Tun bestimmt. Wer ihm gehorcht, kann zugrunde gehn, aber er geht besser zugrunde als der, der ihm widerspricht." With inherited keenness of judgment, Fontane's young heroes consider the difficulty of their task and their own abilities. Obliged to concede a discrepancy, they resign their hopes for a new life. Their renunciation, however, proceeds, not from conversion or insight into social structure, but is an admitted manifestation of frustration. Too much knowledge saps their energy.

*Fontane in 1843.*

Unlike Thomas Mann's heroes, Fontane's have not learned to turn this weakness, the preponderance of their knowledge over vital energy, into strength by directing their declining vitality toward art, where they might have found a solace and a weapon. Fontane's heroes are still too fundamentally honest to take this revenge on life. From a more idealistic standpoint we may say, no God has given them the power to tell their suffering. It remains for their sons, if any, to develop that completer, more self-conscious alienation from life which Thomas Mann delights to show in his artists and "marked men," to all of whom has been granted a measure of articulateness.

In further distinction from Mann's heroes, Fontane's are fundamentally without belief. They cannot accept the traditional standards, nor have they discovered the more modern worship of life or vital energy as a *summum bonum.* Mann's heroes, no matter how unwillingly, have by implication at least, recognized the primacy of uncomplicated, vital existence in any scale of values. Fontane's characters, in their indecision, are strangely prophetic of the modern liberal. More fortunate than he, however, they can still allow themselves the luxury of final indecision, of resignation. They can refuse to fight for any cause. They do not deny their moral responsibility and substitute a deterministic theory of heredity and environment to explain their weakness. They simply confess their lack of heroism and sink back into a state of passive frustration, from which they have neither the strength nor the desire to rouse themselves.

Though the heroes of his novels are indeed unheroic, it would be unjust to conclude that Fontane denied the existence of heroism or minimized the influence of heroic personalities on the course of historical development. His early enthusiasm for Prussian history and his ballads alone disprove such an assumption. But in addition to these facts, his private correspondence occasionally demonstrates that Fontane never modified his original admiration for true greatness. "Carlyle hat recht, der Einzelne bestimmt alles, darf alles, wenn er der Mann danach ist. Daran hängt's." Or he writes: "Es muß kommen: das Erscheinen großer Geister muß den Volksgeist umgestalten. Aber dürfen wir darauf rechnen?" Or, "Ein großer Mann, ein Erwecker, ein Licht- und Flammenträger muß die ganze Geschichte 'mal wieder aus ihrer Misere herausreißen." In connection with these utterances, it is noteworthy that Fontane did not see in Bismarck, the *Licht- und Flammenträger* he sought. The figure of the Prince casts at times a giant shadow across the easy flow of conversation in the novels. That he is unique in his ability and good fortune is readily admitted, but the idolatrous worship of the man himself is bitterly condemned. Sceptical of all greatness Fontane confesses himself to be, yet he never professes to deny its existence. If his later novels find no opportunity to portray genuine greatness in the heroes, it is only because the older Fontane writes as a realist whose sole purpose is to evoke from his readers the exclamation: "Ja, das ist das Leben!" Beneath the material glamor of the age of Bismarck, Fontane's keen eye saw the slow crumbling of a *Lebensstil.* In his unheroic heroes the uncertainty of a time of transition reaches timid expression. Only in these characters does Fontane seem to pass judgment on his age, a judgment based upon a critical enthusiasm for true greatness.

Unlike the male characters, Fontane's women do not live consciously between two sets of social ideals. Whether it be Melanie van der Straaten or Mathilde Möhring, all his women decide and *act.* Only Effi Briest does not immediately find security in her lonely thoughts, but even she leaves this message for her husband: "Es liegt mir daran, daß er erfährt . . . wie mir hier klar geworden, daß er in allem recht gehandelt." Some of these women may seem limited in their outlook, or it may be that all women are conventional by nature, as Fontane was once moved to write his wife. Whatever the reason, Fontane's women have become unquestionably the main characters of the novels. For however penetrating his analysis of his times may have been, he was primarily an artist, not a philosopher. He measured his world by purely aesthetic standards. Style, that coincidence of desire and achievement, is the characteristic of all his women, no matter how humble their position in society. Judged even by these aesthetic standards the men are failures. They lack style or, in Kantian terms, *Freiheit in der Erscheinung.* Like aristocratic precursors of Tonio Kröger, they stand between two worlds of thought, at home in neither. Fontane's conservatism, then, resolves itself into the question: Are there men who can break the old standards and create new? and his answer, No! Under these circumstances he delights to point out the human virtues of the old and the artistic value of convention. He appears to recommend to his unheroic heroes an imitation of the past rather than an attempt at originality, because he knows these men to be neither strong enough nor convinced enough to carry through the revolution their desire at times envisaged. His unheroic heroes thus become, against his will, the ancestors of a whole generation of modern literary characters whose subtlety and artistic gifts never completely hide the frustration in their lives. (pp. 39-44)

*Rosemary Park, "Theodor Fontane's Unheroic Heroes," in* The Germanic Review, *Vol. XIV, No. 1, February, 1939, pp. 32-44.*

## VICTOR LANGE (essay date 1945)

[*In the following excerpt, Lange evaluates Fontane's talent as a writer, commending, among other things, his keen observation of human behavior, realistic portrayal of characters, and picturesque style.*]

Fontane's . . . work is of unusual distinction: by seizing upon the narrow, yet decisive, Prussian scene and by the keenness of his observation, he succeeded in bridging the common gulf between the provincial theme and the craftsmanship of a cosmopolitan storyteller. The motivating elements of his work are a lively sense of historical continuity and a quick perception of the speech and gestures by which the people of his world reveal their particular virtues. In the early journalistic writings about his travels to England (1860) and his rambles through the province of Brandenburg (1862 ff.), he developed that ironic and intelligent precision which served him supremely well in his major novels, *Irrungen, Wirrungen, Effi Briest,* and *Der Stechlin.*

Technically, he is the most conspicuous of the leading German novelists of the time. His composition is, in an unromantic sense, picturesque; he enlivens his soberly threaded plots with a pointed anecdote, an epigrammatic turn of phrase, and a surprising detail; his devices of portraiture are never pedantic, but always subtle and gentlemanly. Even though the range of his inventiveness is limited, he creates, by his respect for the significant accidents of life and by his careful use of transparent symbols, masterly accounts of human relationships. If, standing between the middle class and the aristocracy, he was ineffective as a social critic, this failure is due, not to an indifference toward contemporary political issues, but rather to the fact that he was interested almost wholly, and without making the slightest concession to sentimentality, in the behavior of the individual. With all his astonishing skill at analyzing the contemporary world in its frailty, he is not a novelist of ideas; and although it may not be altogether possible to rank Fontane with the best of his English and French contemporaries, he is the only writer of German fiction in the late nineteenth century who could, now and again, have held his own in their company. (pp. 11-13)

*Victor Lange, "Perspectives," in his* Modern German Literature: 1870-1940, *Cornell University Press, 1945, pp. 1-29.*

## ERNST ROSE (essay date 1948)

[*In the following excerpt, Rose discusses ways in which Fontane's advancing age was reflected in the themes of his novels.*]

A good novel cannot be written without an extended experience of the objective world and therefore is usually produced at a relatively mature age. The typical case is that of Sir Walter Scott, who had already been a successful writer of lyrics and ballads when he published his first Waverley novel at forty-three years of age. In the case of Fontane the first novel

appeared when he was fifty-nine years old. He consciously changed his whole life in order to start writing novels.

But the Prussian author . . . was much younger than his years, and thus we cannot discover a philosophy distinctly typical of advanced years in Fontane's first stories. Superficially speaking, they merely continue his previous ballads. The novel *Vor dem Sturm* describes the Prussian state and the Prussian people before the outbreak of the Wars of Liberation. The Novelle *Grete Minde* treats a ballad theme of the sixteenth century, *Ellernklipp* one of the eighteenth. *Schach von Wuthenow* can almost be considered as the prose version of a theme whose poetic version is found in the ballad **"Prinz Louis Ferdinand."** But in the Prussian ballads Fontane does not yet feel the need for covering the vast expanse of time in the slow, methodical manner of the novelist. Later he becomes aware of this need, and the swift-moving ballads become slowly developing novels. This changed sense of time is a clear indication of Fontane's adjustment to the oncoming of old age.

Another characteristic of these first novels is the pessimistic sense of doom that surrounds them. Quite a number of Fontane's early ballads inspire by their optimism and can be described as fresh and defiant. Now we have something different. The later ballads with their Nordic themes indicate a more gloomy outlook on life, and the first novels follow suit. The heroine of *Grete Minde* is a young girl ill-treated by her step-brother's wife, who bears the ominous name Trud (= witch). Things finally come to a passionate scene, and Grete Minde elopes with her lover. They become vagrants. But however justified their rebellion may appear to the reader, it proves fruitless in the end. For Valtin, Grete's common-law husband, dies of pneumonia, and Grete is not even taken back as a servant-girl, while her inheritance is kept from her. In her frantic indignation she sets fire to her native town and dies on the collapsing tower of its church. We are left without hope. The clutches of this witch of a sister-in-law have mercilessly strangled the life of the young woman. And even the retribution meted out to Trud and her husband is more than cruel. Grete Minde takes Trud's son together with her own infant up on the tower, and the helpless father has to watch the destruction of their enemy together with that of their only hope. Similar pessimism pervades *Ellernklipp,* which also centers around an orphan girl. *Schach von Wuthenow* leads over to the septuagenarian Fontane with his more subdued colors. But the later Fontane would not have chosen a topic from history.

These then are the characteristics of his first novels: a preference for historical subjects, continued from his ballad period, but with a different sense of time values, and an accentuation of the negative aspects of life. These characteristics usually apply to men from fifty years of age on, but here occur in a much older man. One may again infer that Fontane's development towards a philosophy typical of old age was unusually slow and protracted. We first find the old Fontane with his definitely senescent outlook upon life in *L'Adultera,* which was published when he was sixty-three years old and appeared one year before *Schach von Wuthenow.* We cannot treat all of the later novels in strictly historical succession, but must divide them into two groups. To the first group belong all of Fontane's Berlin society novels, to the second group belong all the others. In the latter group, which we discuss first, there is still much pessimism reminiscent of *Grete Minde* and *Ellernklipp. Unterm Birnbaum* and *Quitt* likewise treat retribution for acts of crime. But in *Quitt,* retribution is less violent than in *Ellernklipp.* It comes only indirectly and after a long and almost happy interval. Fontane's sense of order and his conviction of the unalterableness of the law of crime and retribution are still satisfied, but the scales between murderer and murdered in the later novel are more evenly balanced. The other two Novellen not dealing with Berlin society are *Graf Petöfy* and *Unwiederbringlich.* Both Novellen are works of secondary quality, and in both the representatives of the old order commit suicide.

But in Fontane's best novels, those taking place in Berlin society, we have a more balanced view and a more courageous acceptance of life. Most, though not all of their heroes cheerfully resign themselves to the inevitable, or, with a certain grim humor, bow to the laws of society, which they often know to be highly questionable, but which have to be respected for lack of better ones. It is this defense or at least acceptance of the social *status quo* which marks Fontane as an old man.

In *L'Adultera* Fontane's view is represented by the elderly Kommerzienrat Van der Straaten, who knows how to adapt himself to new circumstances when his lively and youthful wife deserts him in favor of a younger friend of the house. In *Irrungen Wirrungen,* we find a sober and courageous acceptance of the existing code of values. The young lieutenant of the *Gardes du Corps* and his "girl friend" know from the beginning that their affair will be just a passing one. But they accept its simple joys anyway, and when the necessities of the ruling social order put an end to these, they gracefully renounce. The young lieutenant is not willing "die Welt herauszufordern und ihr und ihren Vorurteilen öffentlich den Krieg zu erklären." And his Lene knows: "Es geschieht nur, was muß."

Cecile, the heroine of a Novelle published in 1887, a year before *Irrungen Wirrungen,* has to pay more heavily for her vagaries. The same can be said about *Stine.* Here, a poor seamstress and a young nobleman fall in love with each other, and the young man proposes to marry her in defiance of all social prejudices. She however submits to these prejudices and declines his proposal. Now the frustrated young nobleman takes poison. He might have protested more actively against a doomed code of morals. Yet Fontane, who never observed a young officer protesting in this way, did not draw one. But into the mouth of the officer's uncle, who acts as the representative of the old order, he put the observation that his social class was sinking.

Fontane hardly thought more of the rising bourgeoisie which is represented by Frau Jenny Treibel, the central figure of the Novelle of that name. She is downright materialistic and has little use for higher values. She might sentimentalize over them, but when it comes to a real decision, she would rather marry a rich manufacturer than a mere high school teacher. A more solid kind of realism may be found in the prosaic heroine of *Mathilde Möhring,* a novel written in 1896, but published only posthumously. She schemes to get her law student, until he simply has to propose to her. She contrives to put him into a suitable position and hold him there. When unfortunately he dies, she likewise arranges everything without too much emotion and becomes a teacher. All her arrangements are hardly inspiring, yet they are thrifty, practical, and to the best interest of both Mathilde's and Hugo's families. Mathilde stands for a somewhat sober and narrow,

but thoroughly decent conception of life, which Fontane admitted as one of the possible attitudes.

Our author may be called a bourgeois at heart. But that also implies an inner decency which does not rush to the defense of prevailing social conceptions where they have become empty shells without honest meaning. The moral attitude in *Effi Briest,* his most famous novel, is progressive, although in assuming it Fontane had to make painful sacrifices. At a tender age the heroine is married to a narrow-minded, pedantic Prussian official who might have been her father. Quite naturally she looks for compensation in another, more interesting man, although she does not exactly adore him either. Long after the affair has ended, Effi's husband discovers his wife's infidelity. He shoots her lover in a duel and divorces Effi. Unforgiving, he even turns her child against her. His former wife is left to pine away and only in her last moments is she supported by her parents. Still, Fontane does not entirely condemn her. For Innstetten, Effi's husband, has upheld the conventions only mechanically, without deep, inner conviction, and Effi has really been sacrificed to an insensible Moloch. She herself, to be sure, in her last message to Innstetten attests to the basic justice of his treatment of her. But this attitude only makes her more pitiable, and we question all the more the rigid verdict of society. When Effi's mother asks who is to be blamed for their daughter's mistake, her father implicitly excuses Effi by saying: "Ach, Luise, laß. . . . das ist ein zu weites Feld." The author interprets Effi's fate as unavoidable under prevailing conditions, but is no longer ready to accept these as ultimate. He notices that the world around him is changing.

The septuagenarian clearly sees the handwriting on the wall. To be sure, *Die Poggenpuhls,* his next-to-the-last novel, merely presents the problem of the place of the noble class in contemporary society and arrives at no clear conclusion. Neither does his farewell novel *Der Stechlin* solve this political and social problem. But with all the human sympathy he masters for the old order he sees it definitely doomed. Fontane's strength of conviction in this matter is shown by the fact that before finally deciding in favor of *Der Stechlin* old Fontane was preoccupied with the plan for a novel *Die Likedeeler.* Its heroes were to be a band of medieval communists, in whose fate the author wanted to treat symbolically the social problem of his own days. But the plan was given up, because the problem of the contemporary noble class was nearer to Fontane's heart.

For now the author has become really old and withdraws into the shell of his ego. *Der Stechlin* clearly shows the typical stylistic characteristics of old age present in all of Fontane's novels since *L'Adultera.* The characters always occupy the center of interest, and the plot in the best of them is of subordinate importance. Fontane nowhere takes a firm political or social stand. His novels are works of balanced observation and contemplation and not novels with a purpose. But what they lack in the eyes of the youthful reader feverishly pressing for action, they make good by honest observation and by a rich human sympathy embracing practically all classes of society, people from fine, old noble families as well as underprivileged yet devoted servant girls. In *Der Stechlin* this same attitude is expressed a bit more personally and more unreservedly. I explicitly agree with Thomas Mann's statement in criticism of Wandrey, that Fontane's last novel does not display a weakening of his poetic power.

Herr von Stechlin is an agreeable old Junker who lives unpretentiously in a simple house which he calls his castle only in jest. His cronies are the parson, the teacher, and the forester of his village, and he does not like to be addressed as "Baron von Stechlin." . . . To be sure, this old country squire does not shirk the duties of his class and assumes the conservative candidacy for his electoral district. But he does not take that too seriously, and good-humoredly accepts the election of his socialist opponent, a simple workingman. Stechlin is even said to have a bit of social democracy in his make-up, and in spite of his conservatism keeps in touch with the revolutions of the period. As the representative of his author he clearly knows that times are changing, and he also knows that it is useless to try to oppose this. But he cannot throw off old allegiances quickly, and thus he witnesses the change with a divided heart, fortifying himself only with the thought that every revolution has its place in the great balance of the universe: "Alles Alte, soweit es Anspruch darauf hat, sollen wir lieben, aber für das Neue sollen wir eigentlich leben. Und vor allem sollen wir, wie der Stechlin uns lehrt, den großen Zusammenhang der Dinge nicht vergessen." It is this deliberate fusing of contrasts and opposites *sub specie aeterni* that makes the style of **Der Stechlin** senescent. This harmony of mood should of course not be interpreted as colorless and monotonous. The characters are merely less individualized and approach the status of symbols. But, as Thomas Mann has emphasized, they still are far from being shadows; Fontane's creativeness did not stop suddenly, as was the case with Anatole France, who published no novel in the last twelve years of his life.

If anything, such an attitude of knowing, courageous resignation is conservative, and the young generation of Fontane's period seems to have made a mistake in hailing him as an ally in their fight for better social conditions. But in retrospect their mistake was perhaps not so great. For in spite of its revolutionary appearance the young generation was more contemplative than active. Historically speaking, it represents the successful late-century adaptation of German Classicism's religion of humanity. The affinity between Theodor Fontane and young Gerhart Hauptmann was not the enthusiasm of a conservative critic for a literary rebel. For even in supposedly revolutionary plays like *Vor Sonnenaufgang* (1889), *Die Weber* (1892), *Der Biberpelz* (1893), young Hauptmann portrayed prevailing conditions and left the audience to its own conclusions. There is a good deal in Richard Hamann's observation that impressionism often foreshadows the end of a cultural epoch, although in 1907 he could hardly have foreseen as yet, how true his observation would prove in regard to the modern German impressionism he then was describing. There was an ominous significance in the fact that the young German writers of the eighties and nineties found themselves best understood and represented by a novelist who embodied a philosophy of mellow senescence. (pp. 256-62)

*Ernst Rose, "Theodor Fontane's Novels and the Spirit of Old Age," in* The Germanic Review, *Vol. XXIII, No. 4, December, 1948, pp. 254-62.*

## ROY PASCAL (essay date 1956)

[*In the following excerpt, Pascal studies the characteristics of Fontane's realism, noting the qualities that distinguish him from other writers of his era.*]

'Realism' is the avowed principle of Fontane's art as a novelist, and it confronted him with a double problem: first, that of the theme—'the description of a life, a society, a group of people as the undistorted reflection of the life we lead'; and second, that of a technique. (p. 207)

[He] did not attempt to give an all-embracing picture of his times. Most of his books centre in the Prussian nobility, to which he was drawn by a predilection of his character, by the circumstances of his life and his studies of the Mark; he frequently justified his choice on the grounds of the historical importance of this class in the shaping and management of modern Germany. Compared with the Junkers, the young bourgeoisie of modern Germany receives slight attention in his novels, and the petty bourgeoisie and simple folk appear only as appurtenances of the higher classes. The industrial working class appears not at all. Yet his preoccupation with the Junkers did not strike his young contemporaries, for all their concern with the problems of industrial Germany, as antiquated. Rather, they acclaimed Fontane as a 'modern'. For he describes the nobility as they were in actuality, without nostalgia or idealisation, and beneath his restricted themes and unassuming tales there lies, one feels, the massive totality of his times, implicit but operative.

There is little invention in Fontane's novels; they are as sober as the Mark landscape and, indeed, might be called repetitive. He seems to be continually reconsidering in them the life around him, and the highest demand he could make on a novel was that we should feel, when reading it, that we are continuing our real life. Nearly all his novels are built round anecdotes he heard. What attracted him to them was their representativeness, their embodiment of the essence of the contemporary situation. While his lesser contemporaries used anecdotal material because of its piquancy, he liked piquancy only because it laid bare important issues usually hidden beneath the surface. When Fontane relied on his invention, as in **Irrungen, Wirrungen** or **Frau Jenny Treibel,** his story is so close to typical, everyday life that it is deficient in sharp dramatic quality.

We can see Fontane's method most clearly in the composition of **Schach von Wuthenow.** The anecdote was presented to him. He inquired carefully whether the incident occurred before or after the Prussian collapse at Jena, so that he could relate it unambiguously to a precise social situation. Then he remoulded the given characters, surrounded them with others partly historical and partly invented, and invented minor incidents, in order to build up the characteristic elements of his theme. All is individual, precise, but all is shaped and ordered by his theme. Even when he describes milieux which have all the characteristics of directly experienced knowledge, for instance Schach's Junker mansion or the church at Tempelhof, this generalising technique prevails, hidden under the illusion of precise concrete detail. Contemporary critics, who found the story far-fetched, praised these milieux for their accuracy and truth; Fontane commented sarcastically that he had never been to the church, that Schach's mansion was a complete invention, while the story was the only true thing about the novel.

All Fontane's works show this combination of the typical with the individual; 'truth to life' means for him both the evocation of sensuous experience, of circumstances, objects and people, and the uncovering of a typical social situation and problem which is embodied in the particular. In his ballads—and he wrote odd ballads right to the end of his life—he fell into romantic attitudes; in his novels he scarcely ever departs from this sober conscientious search for truth, avoiding all idealisation. In them he is nearer the new impressionist school of painters—e.g. Liebermann—than the heroic historical school of his old friend Menzel. He discovered the charm of the city landscape, the suburbs, for instance the charm of the evening lights as his characters sit at an open-air restaurant:

> And it was not long before the lights came on. Not only the restaurant itself was all lit up, but also on the railway-embankment on the other side of the river the various coloured signals appeared, while in midstream, where the tugs were hauling the barges, a sooty red glowed through the cabin windows.
>
> (*Der Stechlin*)

He was aware of the difficulties facing the realistic writer. He could see some of his younger contemporaries being submerged under a mass of trivial material documentation. Exact and crowded description was not his purpose, but description which 'illuminates'. He was actually taken to task for his use of a faulty dialect, especially in the language of the simple Berlin folk in his novels; and one can discover other sorts of factual inaccuracies in his books. But he was unconcerned about these 'errors'. An exact rendering of dialect would have made the books inaccessible to the ordinary reader, he said; an absolutely precise accuracy of description would have been boring and superfluous. It suffices, he wrote, to 'suggest things'. 'I did my level best to describe real life. It just doesn't work. You have to be content if the reader gets the total impression, "Yes, that's life".' And this truthfulness is art, the art he recognised and admired in the modern realists of the younger generation. In a review of Ibsen's *The Wild Duck* he wrote:

> It is the hardest thing in the world (and perhaps the highest too) so to illuminate everyday life that what was just now indifferent and prosaic suddenly moves us with the most entrancing magic of poetry.

This is the formula of his own artistic endeavour.

He was extremely interested in the efforts of his young contemporaries to present, as objectively as possible, the actual and often forbidding reality of their times. It is well known that he acclaimed the purpose of the 'consequent naturalists', Holz and Schlaf, to discard conventional literary expression and present characters in their raw, natural state—'here is the parting of the ways, the divide between old and new'. But in this same article he went on to insist that it was an illusion to believe art is the greater the more the artist is eliminated. Even in the works of Holz and Schlaf, he pointed out, the artist has shaped the material; and it is characteristic that, in Ibsen and Hauptmann, Fontane admired immediately the high artistic skill of their writing. When we read a novel, he wrote, we should feel that there is no difference between real life and this invented life, 'except the difference arising from that intensity, clarity, transparency and roundedness and, consequently, that intensity of feeling, which is the transfiguring task of art'. On another occasion he speaks of the 'tone' of the work of art, which interprets the poet's 'purity of perception' and 'transfigures the ugly'.

Fontane was, then, very conscious of the craftsmanship of writing, of the novel as an art. He never falls into the faults of naturalism, but firmly shapes his story according to his intention; in this respect he is the finest stylist among the German novelists. As his theme demands it, he gently but firmly

leads our attention from character to character, from scene to scene. For instance, at a dinner-party we first hear the talk at one end of the table, then we move to the other, and bit by bit the pieces fit together into a picture of the whole company. His chapters succeed one another like the scenes of a play, as the setting for the decisive stages of the story, intermediate stages being cut out. He is a master of suggestion. Rarely is there any extended description of setting, and never any extended psychological analysis. The moral issues accumulate almost imperceptibly, without melodrama, from a host of slight factors. So his 'scenes' conclude without sound and fury; one can almost speak of a 'fade-out' technique which he often uses to conclude a chapter.

In this artistic arrangement of the story, the jumps in place and time, the varying degree of reticence, the author is clearly enough in evidence. . . . But though he came to agree with Spielhagen that it is better if the author does not appear in person to make comments and give explanations, Fontane was never over-anxious on this score. He knew, of course, that all description of circumstances is 'direct comment', though in Fontane such description is nearly always confined to what the characters themselves or what a chance visitor would observe. More important is explanatory comment, particularly psychological explanations or moral judgements. On the whole Fontane, after the earlier novels, leaves specific comments to his characters themselves. In *Schach von Wuthenow* we have seen that he summarises the 'moral' of the story in letters of two of the characters. This is a somewhat clumsy device, and at other times, too, he is not too happy in his choice of means. For instance, in order to build out the younger Stechlin's character (which throughout remains woefully vague), he gives us a few pages of his diary, the content of which would be most unlikely to be found in an intimate diary. We are disturbed too, in this novel, by a sudden change of focus when the author gives a synopsis of the earlier life of the young man's prospective father-in-law.

In his greatest novel, *Effi Briest,* Fontane actually shows himself less anxious about author's intrusions than in many of the others. From time to time he sums up the characters, as for instance when he comments on Innstetten's predilection for Wagner. When Effi yields to Crampas he tells us, rather unnecessarily, that it was because of her lack of firmness. One intervention, a rather striking one, is worthy of analysis. After Effi falls ill, her doctor says to her: 'Don't bother to write; just send Roswitha'—Roswitha is her old maid whom she had left at Innstetten's and whom the reader has ceased to think about. And the novel continues:

> 'Just send Roswitha', the doctor had said. What, was Roswitha with Effi, then? Indeed she was, and in fact had been there for a long time. . . .

The author does a jack-in-the-box trick, suddenly letting us know something he has been deliberately hiding. And the effect is subtle. At the moment when the isolation of Effi was becoming intolerable, this comforting news is broken, with some of the sturdy cheerfulness of Roswitha herself. It is a case where the author's intrusion is not an admission of failure, but a successful artistic stroke.

In general, however, Fontane follows the practice of his great European contemporaries in that the moral and psychological situation becomes explicit through the situation, behaviour and speech of his characters. Partly because of this, his characters are never too precisely defined, never over-rigid; they have numerous facets which new situations bring into view, and therefore have something of the mobility, ambiguity of real life. Thus we see the industrialist Treibel in jovial, expansive mood at the dinner-party, ironically indulgent to his wife's sentimentalism; we see him conning his chances in politics; and, in case we are tempted to sum him up as an ambitious *parvenu,* we see him immediately talking with humane tolerance with his wife's neurotic lady-companion. He is quite ready to approve the marriage of Corinna with his son but, though he argues with his wife, we can see he really is glad that she insists on the 'honour' of the family. What is this industrialist really? There can be no summing up, he is a bundle of qualities and trends. Above all, Fontane is a master of conversation—a famous talker himself, incidentally. The conversations in his novels, whether involving groups of people at parties or on excursions, or whether intimate *tête-à-têtes* like those between Frau von Carayon and Schach or between Effi's parents, are masterly. Fontane brilliantly catches the fine nuances of characters, in relation to important and trivial subjects, in serious or humorous response to others; the whole character of social life, the subtle interplay of individuality and society, comes to expression in these conversations. They are decisive in establishing the tone of his novels, and usually they are the points at which, hardly noticeably, the characters range themselves round the major issues of the theme.

It is clear that Fontane's whole art, as a novelist, is moral in inspiration. His realism itself has moral roots. All his novels are expositions of moral dilemmas. They are not moral tracts, for though they contain much practical wisdom they leave us in some sense indetermined, aware of the complexity of the issues rather than persuaded of right and wrong. For all his satire, Fontane is far less self-assertive than, for instance, his contemporary George Eliot; he himself, full of misgivings as he was about the trends of his times, was also very sceptical about religious and political schemes of reform. His social contribution was less ambitious:

> If one can't get to grips with the matter through sermons and regulations, all the same I think much is gained if modern humanity comes to some insight into the situation, if it sees itself in a mirror and gets a fright.

In this sense he justified the modern realists who were so decried because of their concern with ugliness and sin. He wrote concerning Ibsen's *The Wild Duck* that, if things might not be improved, it was 'better to stare ugliness in the face than distortion—better sin than hypocrisy'. And it was characteristic of him that he was deeply distrustful of the mystical transfiguration in Hauptmann's *Hanneles Himmelfahrt.*

But his realism is of a different quality from that of the younger realists. He was not altogether won over by the Zola-tradition of delving into the most sordid aspects of the modern world; even in Ibsen and Hauptmann he detected a pessimism which he thought was not justified and which, at any rate, was not his own view of things. In his letters he often expresses the harshest condemnation of contemporary trends—of Junker arrogance, of capitalistic greed and philistinism—but he refused to be downcast by such phenomena, and even found good words for the great industrialists of his time. In spite of all the drawbacks of modern society, he was convinced of the great progress that Germany had made, culturally as well as materially, since his youth, and retained a certain modicum of optimism, putting it down at various

times to his sanguine temperament, to his avid interest in life, to his humanism, above all to his humour. His humour was his refuge and strength, and though occasionally he felt that he could no longer take things humorously, humour makes itself felt in all his works, right to the end, as the expression of his tolerance and trust in man. 'Humour is the best way.' And thus he consistently demanded that art must present the reality of life mildly draped over. The essential fault of the modern realists was, in his opinion, that they lacked 'conciliatoriness, mildness, humour, naturalness'. These are the qualities of his writing, as they also indicate his failings. A self-reliant man of ripe experience, his social satire lacks the bitterness and distortion of more sensitive writers and the sensationalism of the vulgar; but it lacks passion, too, for he looks away from characters tortured by desperate needs, and slips evasively away from conflicts when they grow too harsh. That is why, even in his greatest novel, he fails to reach the stature of Flaubert or Tolstoy. (pp. 207-14)

> *Roy Pascal, "Theodor Fontane (1819-98)," in his* The German Novel: Studies, *Manchester University Press, 1956, pp. 178-214.*

## LILIAN R. FURST (essay date 1959)

[*In the following excerpt, Furst examines Fontane's autobiography* Von Zwanzig bis Dreissig, *noting that while it suffers from what she feels are numerous narrative defects, it is a valuable example of Fontane's "extroverted" writing style.*]

**Von Zwanzig bis Dreissig,** with or rather because of its defects, is an interesting and revealing, though paradoxical document. As its title implies, it sets out to recount Fontane's experiences between the ages of twenty and thirty; but in actual fact this long work covers a far greater span of time, for it both includes happenings of later years and recalls the adolescent period on the brink of which **Meine Kinderjahre** had ended. Thus **Von Zwanzig bis Dreissig** gives a delightful picture of Fontane's happy-go-lucky life in Berlin in his late teens, when he was staying with his quixotic Uncle August and Aunt 'Pinchen', whose startling careers are related in considerable detail. When he looks forward to subsequent years, he usually takes as his cue some personality whose acquaintance he made between twenty and thirty and whose friendship he continued to enjoy later. So in connexion with Julius Faucher of the Leipzig *Lenau-Verein* (1840), Fontane fills some fifty pages with an account of his experiences as a journalist in London many years later, when he would also sometimes meet Faucher. Or again, he traces most minutely the life-histories and fortunes of various friends he made in the *Tunnel,* the famous Berlin literary club to which he belonged in his twenties. Though some of its members, such as Storm and Heyse, became well known, others are hardly more than names to us, and their exploits, eccentricities and family affairs are certainly not of the slightest interest. Here already one of the cardinal defects of this autobiography becomes apparent: its tendency to digression. Fontane himself was by no means unaware of this defect; in the preface he refers to the 'unstatthaften Umfang' of his book, which he regards as 'einen Übelstand'. Moreover, in the course of the narrative, he makes no attempt to camouflage his frequent digressions; on the contrary, he repeatedly mentions his straying from the main theme and resolves to return to it forthwith. . . . As long as Fontane's digressions at least depict his stay in Uncle August's family or show a glimpse of the literary life of the period in the *Tunnel,* they are still admissible in his autobiography on the grounds that they reveal significant details of his milieu and social intercourse. But when he goes on—as he unfortunately does—to include a 'curriculum vitae' of the priest who conducted the service at his wedding or to state whom the various guests present at the *Kreuzzeitung* parties eventually married (to mention only two examples), then we cannot but agree with Fontane's own verdict that the excessive bulk of this work is an 'Übelstand'.

Far more startling and disturbing, however, is the other defect of *Von Zwanzig bis Dreissig*; indeed at first it is difficult to believe that so skilled and experienced a writer as Fontane can be guilty of such a fault. Yet the narrative technique of *Von Zwanzig bis Dreissig* is gauche to the point of amateurishness. Fontane makes no real attempt to tell the story well, to present his material in the best possible manner (hence his tendency to digress and ramble). The key to his narrative technique lies in a word which he himself uses several times: 'berichten'. Instead of vividly telling the story of his experiences and development, he is 'reporting' certain happenings—somewhat dryly at that! (pp. 287-88)

The effect of this extremely clumsy narrative technique is twofold. First, what might well be termed its 'nuisance value': the interspersal of such phrases as 'wie schon erzählt', 'wie schon an anderer Stelle hervorgehoben', . . . 'von dem ich in dem voraufgehenden Abschnitt erzählt habe'—the interspersal of these and similar turns of speech, in which this autobiography abounds, must seem a disconcerting shortcoming in literary craftsmanship, especially to the contemporary reader, conditioned as he is to the slickness of the 'well-made' novel. Such a narrative technique—and this is its other effect—never allows the reader to face the action directly and to watch its progress on his own account. The fault lies not so much in the occasional breaking of the theatrical illusion, as in the failure ever to establish such an illusion convincingly. The narrator is always present, an obtrusive and at times excessively loquacious guide to the countryside. How strange it is to speak of Fontane's failure to create a theatrical illusion and to apply such derogatory adjectives to one of the best and greatest German novelists! *Von Zwanzig bis Dreissig* is, however, a complete contrast to Fontane's novels, at least as far as the narrative technique is concerned. In his novels, especially in the later ones, Fontane proves conclusively that he had mastered the art of story-telling, with brilliant results. The merest glance at his chapter openings and endings, his smooth transitions and the delicate, but precise internal structure of his novels reveals what a superb craftsman he was, and how truly he had perfected the literary technique for which he consciously strove long after he had already collected the actual material for his novels in nearly sixty years of human observation. Yet *Von Zwanzig bis Dreissig* is singularly uncouth in manner. Nor can it be defended either as a youthful work or as a product of incipient senility, since it was written between *Effi Briest* and *Der Stechlin*, Fontane's acknowledged masterpieces. This is a paradox which can be explained only in a wider context: 'ich komme weiterhin auf diesen heiklen Punkt zurück'.

If the narrative technique of *Von Zwanzig bis Dreissig* is a surprise to the 'Fontanite', its 'Weltanschauung' on the other hand is certainly that already familiar from the novels. Perhaps 'Weltanschauung' is not the right word, for Fontane presents, rather than a tightly knit system of thought, a delightful series of scintillating a *dicta,* one of the chief charms of which lies in the forthright, fresh formulation typical of

Fontane. In his pronouncements on the social scene above all, he reveals that insight and penetration that form the foundation of his novels. When characterizing the bourgeois, he formulates the pungent word 'Geldsackgesinnung', a state of mind prevalent also among those 'die gar keinen Geldsack haben, oder einen sehr kleinen'! A particularly illuminating remark in this field, and one which provides an interesting commentary on several of his novels is the following:

> . . . in dem entschiedneren Abschwenken (namentlich auch auf moralischem Gebiet) nach rechts und links hin, erkenne ich den eigentlichen Kulturfortschritt.

In his judgments on individuals too, Fontane shows the same upright, unprejudiced approach, evaluating men not according to their class or outer veneer of virtue, but solely by the criterion of true humanity. So he condemns one of the members of the *Tunnel* on the grounds that he was 'ein Doktrinär und kein Mensch', while he praises another highly because he was

> über alles hinaus, in erster Reihe von Grund aus *human* . . . und in seinem tief eingewurzelten Sinne für das Menschliche, sich mit relativen Nebensächlichkeiten wie Standesunterschiede, Wissens- und Bildungsgrade gar nicht beschäftigte.

This is the same rejection of the rigid, the doctrinaire, the hypocritical and the same appraisal of the genuine goodness of the human heart, irrespective of class distinctions, as in *Irrungen Wirrungen* and *Stine.*

But if *Von Zwanzig bis Dreissig* only presented the same lines of thought as Fontane's novels, and in a poor 'mise-en-scène', to so speak, it would indeed deserve the neglect in which it has hitherto lain. This autobiography does, however, shed new light on Fontane in several respects. First, much can be deduced about his philosophy of art from the many asides on this topic scattered throughout the autobiography. In part, at least, his attitude is rooted in his social observation, in his merciless rejection of certain types as 'inhuman' in the wider sense of the word, and therefore not fit recipients of the artist's subtle gifts:

> Der berühmte Satz 'Kunst sei für alle' ist grundfalsch; Kunst ist umgekehrt für sehr wenige und mitunter ist es mir, als ob es immer weniger würden. Nur das Beefsteak, dem sich leicht folgen lässt, ist in einer steten Machtsteigerung begriffen.

This apparently misanthropic statement is a good example of the working of an artist's defence mechanism against the uncomprehending bluntness of the masses. Moreover, at the time when Fontane was writing, culture had ceased to be the concern of an élite, for literacy had spread downwards and with this tendency, standards of appreciation had fallen sharply, a fall accelerated by the increasing materialism of the latter half of the nineteenth century. No wonder that Fontane mistrusts the democratic concept of 'Art for all' and believes instead that one must gradually raise oneself to an appreciation of the best in literature. Young people should therefore not start by reading Goethe, but wait 'in das Beste hineinzuwachsen'. This then is the basis of his philosophy of art. In addition, he sometimes gives comments which bear more directly on his art: in a dictum such as 'Es soll sich die Dichtung nach dem Leben richten, an das Leben sich anschliessen', the foundations for his realistic art are laid. Likewise in his wholehearted support of Spielhagen's precept of 'finden, nicht erfinden', which he calls 'eine nicht genug zu be-herzigende Wahrheit', adding that 'in der Erzählkunst bedeutet es beinahe alles'. At times, his candour in regard to literary affairs can be both startling and amusing, as when he explains, with characteristics honesty and directness why a 'false' foreign correspondent may produce better and truer reports than one on the spot. For the man in Steglitz-Friedenau who takes his words of wisdom from *The Times* can do just as well as he who undertakes the 'process of repro-duction' in Hampstead or Highgate, and both will certainly do better than the independent eyewitness, since a really pen-etrating vision and the ability for expression are so very rare!

One of the most interesting facets of *Von Zwanzig bis Dreis-sig* is the sketch of Fontane himself that emerges from the narrative. He is revealed as a charming, relaxed character, whose most prominent and endearing traits are modesty and a true sense of humour, which allows him to maintain his eq-uipoise throughout the vicissitudes of his life. In the preface there is already evidence of this combination of modesty and humour when Fontane, after apologizing for the bulkiness of the book, solemnly proclaims this to be his last autobiograph-ical effort: 'So blickt denn der momentan umdrängte Leser wenigstens in eine wolkenlose Zukunft.' And so it goes on throughout. Fontane does not hesitate to quote in full various uncomplimentary remarks made about him; as for the 'gute Worte' on the other hand, 'ich werde mich hüten, sie hier niederzuschreiben'. Similarly, in describing the 'glorious' March 18th, 1848, he candidly admits his own passivity, con-fessing that his deeds were in no way commensurate with his revolutionary feelings. On another occasion, when he has fully exposed the silliness of his conduct, he concludes the ac-count of the incident with the words: 'Alles in allem ein Meisterstück unzulässigster Poetennaivität.'

It is his ability to adopt this modest, humorous, detached atti-tude not only towards himself as a private person but also to-wards himself as an artist that distinguishes Fontane from most other writers. (pp. 289-92)

A genuine modesty, not to say reserve, dictates both the tone and the content of *Von Zwanzig bis Dreissig*. Although this is an autobiography and as such necessarily pivots on the per-son of the writer, nevertheless Fontane is most loath to make himself the centre of interest incessantly throughout. He pre-fers to turn the spotlight away from himself and to fill his ac-count of these years of his life with stories of his friendships. *Von Zwanzig bis Dreissig* is thus a report on this period of Fontane's career (cf. 'berichten') rather than a self-portrait or a narcissistic self-reflection. Nothing could be more alien to Fontane than to hold up a mirror to his own personality and feelings. For the distinguishing feature of this autobiog-raphy is its total lack of exhibitionism, which springs from Fontane's deep-seated hatred of artistic vanity and egocen-tricity. Never does he dramatize himself or his struggles in any way, nor does he ever permit himself self-pitying com-plaints. He speaks quite factually of 'jene Tage, wo mein Beruf und meine Neigung auseinander gingen' (when he was a chemist's apprentice); calmly and quietly he accepts what life brings him without either self-pity or mock heroism.

But, however laudable a quality self-effacement may be, it is not an ideal characteristic for the writer of an autobiography, who must be willing to spotlight and, to a certain extent, to dramatize himself. Thus a personal virtue of Fontane's leads to the defects of *Von Zwanzig bis Dreissig*. As an autobiog-raphy, it is somewhat disappointing because it tells too little about his development in these important years and too much about the careers of his various acquaintances. And the de-fects in technique can be traced not to any inability on Fon-tane's part to tell a story well, but to his reticent disposition, which renders him incapable of turning himself, his own life and feelings into a work of art.

Yet it would be utterly wrong to condemn or neglect *Von Zwanzig bis Dreissig* for these reasons. In spite of Fontane's reticence, this autobiography does add to our knowledge of him, particularly as far as his philosophy of art is concerned. Moreover—and herein lies its real importance—it confirms that Fontane was an essentially objective, extrovert artist, who drew the raw material of his writing from his observa-tion of the outside world rather than from any inner, personal dilemmas. Thus he represents the antithesis of the introvert artists typical of the early twentieth century, the neurotic art-ists, obsessed by the problems of their own ego, constantly dramatizing themselves, filling work upon work with self-analyses, confessions and breast-beating. The latter undoubt-edly write more revealing, more interesting, indeed better au-tobiographies than *Von Zwanzig bis Dreissig,* but in fact all their writings are autobiographies, for they cannot liberate themselves from the tyranny of their own problems and neu-roses. Whereas Fontane, the objective extrovert, though he fails where they succeed—in the field of autobiography—conversely succeeds where they tend to fail: in the epic art of the novel. The very same qualities that make *Von Zwanzig bis Dreissig* a somewhat disappointing autobiography also made Fontane a most charming person and, above all, one of the greatest, if not the greatest, writer of 'Gesellschaftsro-mane' that Germany has ever had. (pp. 293-94)

Lilian R. Furst, "The Autobiography of an Extro-vert: Fontane's 'Von Zwanzig Bis Dreissig'," in Ger-man Life & Letters, n.s. Vol. 12, No. 4, July, 1959, pp. 287-94.

**LAWRENCE O. FRYE** (essay date 1962)

[*In the following excerpt, Frye examines how Fontane uses "unrealistic" devices—fatalistic premonitions, dreams, visions, and leitmotifs—to develop the themes of his novels.*]

Emphasis has most often been given to the historical and so-cial-political ideas in Fontane's novels. Accordingly, his works have been examined mainly for their "realistic" ele-ments, to the neglect or summary dismissal of what does not fall into such a category. Although that which we shall term the unreal cannot always be given the same significance in each work, to minimize the importance of its function is to distort an integral part of Fontane's artistic expression.

The purpose of this paper is not to provide a dictionary of the unreal or "Romantic" elements as they have often been called, nor is it to provide a key to the various sources of Ro-mantic influence. To attempt the latter task would illuminate historically the Romantic tradition in nineteenth-century German literature, but simultaneously it would not focus suf-ficient attention on the needed analysis of Fontane's works. What seems to be more basic is a general examination of the different patterns into which the unreal elements fall and the basic structural purpose they serve; for one of the dominant themes in Fontane, that of unfulfilled love and resignation, is often developed by means of the unreal.

The characteristic which is essential to the idea of the unreal is that some relationship is established between the emotional state of an individual and a sphere which lies beyond the immediate sensuous contact of that individual. This sphere may not be concretely representable (as in a religious experience), or it may assume concrete form: this form, or object, then conveys an impression which suggests more than the object's ordinary significance. In Fontane, a character may often feel unconsciously or intuitively (as in dreams or waking premonitions) a situation or condition which does not actually exist at the moment of feeling. Or, an object or scene may evoke a sensation which has no apparent connection with the object itself.

The appearance of the unreal is most noticeable and consistent in Fontane's first novel *Vor dem Sturm*, and then in the novelle *Grete Minde* and in *Ellernklipp*. These three works are all of an early composition; and all present a story which is not based on contemporary social problems or events: in the first case the action is set in 1812-1813, in the latter two the plots are from chronicles (*Grete Minde* "nach einer altmärkischen Chronik," *Ellernklipp* "nach einem Harzer Kirchenbuch"). *Vor dem Sturm*, although fashioned upon historical events, is constructed around what appears to be a fate theme. Fontane has worked various unreal events into his story in order to bring the fate theme into focus and to lend momentum to the theme's development.

The fate of the von Vitzewitz family has been established by an old curse on the house. The manifestation of this fate then revolves about three main foci in the course of the narrative. Like the Romanticists, Fontane has distilled the theme of his plot in verses interspersed within the novel. The first important verses are appropriately found on a graveyard tombstone:

> Sie sieht nun tausend Lichter,
> Der Engel Angesichter
> Ihr treu zu Diensten stehn;
> Sie schwingt die Siegesfahne
> Auf güldnem Himmelsplane
> Und kann auf Sternen gehn.

These verses, and especially the last line, project the quiet yearning for happiness and serenity which possesses Lewin.

The complement of these verses is found in the poeticized curse on the family, which ends: "Und cine Prinzessin kommt ins Haus." These verses are so woven into the novel that the occurrence of one calls forth the other; for the "Prinzessin" anticipated in the one group of verses is mysteriously linked with the unknown figure envisioned in the lines "Und kann auf Sternen gehn." And it is this figure who can supposedly free the Vitzewitz family from its curse. These verses continue to create a mysterious, foreboding atmosphere until Marie Kniehase suddenly appears at the end of the novel as the anticipated "Princess."

The third focal point for the fate theme is the town of Bohlsdorf. Bohlsdorf is both the initial site of the graveyard verses and later, in the second part of the novel, the place where Lewin has his near fatal fever—the turning point for Lewin's love problems; consequently, it is the place of origin and fulfillment of the verses embodying the fate theme. Other events which reinforce the fate theme also appear: such as the burning of the house wing with the discomforting altar. (Local superstitions are often utilized similarly in the action to reinforce a feeling of foreboding.) These events function as "signs"—events inexplicably foretelling future development.

In *Vor dem Sturm* an end to the curse is signalled by such "signs" although there is no factual basis for such an anticipation. Simultaneously, since the fate of the Vitzewitz family is made dependent on the outcome of the love affairs of the son and daughter, these signs anticipate the realization of love between Marie and the son Lewin.

The underlying fate theme has several effects. One is to create stylistically a unity in the unraveling of the story. But in itself the fate theme gives the impression that the course of events is somehow predetermined by causes lying beyond man's knowledge or control. Seemingly accidental events are woven into a chain, which in itself does not exist in reality, and thus magnified beyond their normal significance. Fontane throughout his works, even when operating without a fate scheme, still has a predilection for anticipating future action by means of this type of magnification.

In *Grete Minde* a similar "fated" development unfolds. However, the action of fate is represented more symbolically than literally—and hence more effectively. The depiction by the wandering players of the *Last Judgement* has a foreboding sense of reality for Grete. Speaking of the players, Grete says: "Aber sie bedeuten 'was, und ich weiß doch nicht, ob es recht ist." And when the young girl appears before the gates of heaven in the play, Grete feels herself personally involved in the scene: "Ihr war, als würde sie selbst vor Gottes Thron gerufen, und ihr Herz schlug und ihre zarte Gestalt zitterte. Was wurd 'aus dem Kind'? . . . 'Unter Engeln sollst du ein Engel sein'." These anticipations become reality when Grete herself plays the same angel in the play after her flight from Tangermünde. Similarly, the feeling that Grete is to depart from the world in which she is not at home is expressed in a comparably foreboding way by the "Domina" when she correctly foresees that in three days upon leaving her, Grete will be dead.

The fate of Hilde in *Ellernklipp* is anticipated in a parallel manner. After sitting on the "Heidenstein," it is prophesied (according to local superstition) that Hilde will suffer a tragic end. The agent through which Hilde's fate is expressed is the Melcher Harms, who foresees that "Ihr Blut ist ihr Los, und den Jungen reißt sie mit hinein. Es geschieht, was muß, und die Wunder, die wir sehen, sind keine Wunder. . . . Ewig und unwandelbar ist das Gesetz." A similar sign of things to come—and again at a time when no real basis for such a sign exists—is signified when Martin and Hilde are sailing their little boats. Martin believes his happiness is linked with Hilde's, but when the boat with his name on it goes aground, he feels a shudder of fear overcome his hopes: "Ach, Hilde, dann ist es ein anderes Schiff, das mit dir fährt."

It becomes apparent that Fontane's conception of fate is not identifiable with an externally determined fate. It is rather a projection of a character's fate as determined by his own conflict with reality. The manner in which Fontane sometimes handles his characters, however, makes it seem *as if* their actions followed a predetermined course. This illusion is also furthered by the use of moments of indistinct anticipation in which the involved characters themselves participate.

Lewin in *Vor dem Sturm* had dreamed during his fever in Bohlsdorf that he was at the altar being happily married to someone who appeared to be Marie. The dream occurs after the unnerving break-up with Kathinka and before Lewin actually realizes he is in love with Marie. The dream thus serves to anticipate a future action, which in reality was unthinkable at the time of the dream, and to give a sense of inevitability to the final happy union. At a less significant point in *Ellernklipp* the servant Joost dreams of the impending death of Hilde's sickly child: "Un weetst, wat ick disse Nacht siehn heww? . . . 'n Sarch wier et . . . Un stunn upp unsen Floor. . . . Een witt Doog leeg dröver, un ick glöw, et wihr de Lütt."

A more important use of the dream within the action of the novel occurs in two places in *Unwiederbringlich.* Holk has turned his attentions to Ebba von Rosenberg, only later to have his hopes for marriage with her thwarted and ridiculed. At the same time, his love for Ebba makes it impossible for him to find happiness with his wife, Charlotte. But even before he has any idea of what might come of his confused affairs, a dream in the Danish castle of Frederiksborg warns Holk and anticipates the sad end to his actions. He dreams that while hanging onto the mast of a storm-wrecked ship, he is being pulled under by Ebba. Before the Ebba episode had even begun, his wife Charlotte had had a similarly foreboding dream as Holk was just departing for the Danish court. Although Charlotte claims dream interpretation is ungodly, she cannot help feeling there is some foreboding truth to her dream: she has seen herself in what seemed to be both a wedding and funeral procession. The dreamt scene later occurs in reality when Holk and Charlotte are unsuccessfully remarried.

Waking visions function in a way analogous to the less frequent dreams. Such visions generally represent a further sense of anticipation and a dissolving of reality before one's eyes. When Hilde in *Ellernklipp* watches her old home burn down, her eyes move from the blackness of the forest, the red of the fire and the white of the snow to the heavens: "Und sie sah hinauf, und die Engel stiegen auf und nieder. Und es war wieder ein Singen und Klingen, und die Wirklichkeit der Dinge schwand ihr hin in Bild und Traum." (pp. 106-10)

Fontane often associates the tendency to envision more than what reality presents with the possession of a vivid imagination. In *Effi Briest* the story of the Chinaman, who supposedly haunts Innstetten's home, constantly frightens Effi. She lives in fear that in one of her lonely moments the Chinaman will suddenly appear before her. This feeling consequently gives her a fright when she and Innstetten are driving past the grave of the Chinaman. Concerning her ignorance of the facts of his story, she says: "So lang' ich es nicht weiß, bin ich, trotz aller guten Vorsätze, doch immer ein Opfer meiner Vorstellungen. Erzähle mir das Wirkliche. Die Wirklichkeit kann mich nicht so quälen wie meine Phantasie." In the same vein she tells the singer Trippelli later: "Wenn ich einen ängstlichen Traum habe, oder wenn ich glaube, über mir hörte ich ein leises Tanzen oder Musizieren, während doch niemand da ist, oder es schleicht wer an meinem Bette vorbei, so bin ich außer mir und kann es tagelang nicht vergessen." Inasmuch as Effi's phantasy lends a reality to what is not real, her anxiety leads her to maintain that "Einbildungen sind das schlimmste, mitunter schlimmer als alles."

Numerous "signs" which do not contribute to a fate theme effect also tend to heighten the feeling of unreality and the subsequent anxiety induced by the imagination. But in some cases there seem to be no real explanations for the occurrence of such phenomena. For example, Effi's fears stem partially from thoughts about the dead Chinaman, who she believes has brushed past her bed one night. Similarly, in *Ellernklipp* Baltzer Bocholt believes he hears the voice of his son calling out "Vater" to him after the father has pushed him over the cliff. It is both an indication of Baltzer's disturbed psychological state and of something more unexplainable when not only Baltzer but others believe later that they hear the same call of "Vater."

Fontane employs other phenomena which in themselves do fall within the realm of normal reality, but which function simultaneously as symbols or motifs. In *Ellernklipp*, Baltzer's body offers more than the usual frightening sight to Hilde because it recalls the effect on Hilde of Maus-Bugisch's limp body earlier in the novel; a frightening anxiety overwhelms Hilde because of this simple association. Analogously, heathen sacrificial and battle stones in both *Grete Minde* and *Effi Briest* cause unexplainable fear and repulsion, perhaps because of their association with death and the fear and anticipation of death they create in the characters.

There are several other phenomena which Fontane uses more commonly to create a foreboding tone. The effect they produce is often reflected in the character who perceives them; but they also serve a more stylistic function in that they may cause their effect independent of the character's reaction to them. For instance, in *Unwiederbringlich* "Romantic" melodies reappear in *leitmotif* fashion to set the tone of the action and to produce their particular effect on Charlotte. These verses have a similar function within this novel as did those in *Vor dem Sturm,* except that the course of events in *Unwiederbringlich* is only fated in a psychological sense. The singing of Uhland's "Des Sängers Fluch" and Waiblinger's "Kirchhof" affects Charlotte's normal composure. What love does not offer her in her marriage to Holk, is offered by the feeling of distance from reality which "Romantic" poetry generates: in place of real happiness, the consuming emotion of melancholy and the desire for peace. Although Charlotte is dispassionate in her normal relations with Holk, these verses so affect her on several occasions that she runs off in emotional turmoil, with the curious desire to commit them to memory. The contrast which these verses provide to her normal, inadequate existence is heightened when the novel closes with the Waiblinger lines left to Holk as an explanation for her suicide.

The graveyard also appears often in Fontane with the same melancholy overtones. Charlotte has one preoccupation aside from her sentimental melodies, and that is to build a "secure" sepulchre for the family. She has a preoccupation with death, one which certainly outweighs her interest in life and its distractions. Likewise, in *Effi Briest* the churchyard hauntingly reappears as a focal point of Effi's wanderings in loneliness. There are frequent suggestions that the churchyard provides not only a natural resting place but also a refuge from the world—both while one is in the world and then, of course, when one has left it. When Baltzer seeks peace from his jealousy in *Ellernklipp,* he seeks the advice of his dead wife in the graveyard; but it is only his suicide which really gives him the peace he had vainly sought.

In *Stine* the cemetery image fuses with another common one, that of the setting sun. Just as the gleam of sunset on Gordon had given Cécile foreboding feelings, so the same impression is created in *Stine* but without verbal acknowledgement. The setting sun accompanies the thought of reality's harshness. In fact, the sunset softens the outlines of objects to a point of indistinctness; in effect, it signals a release from reality's problems and pressures. At one point Stine and her unhappy lover, Waldemar, catch the reflection of the setting sun in a mirror at the window (a mirror which makes things appear smaller, and by this distortion of reality beautifies them). They are completely absorbed in the sun's glow so that a complete unawareness of objects about them prevails. Later, Waldemar notices that the setting sun has illuminated a monument to dead young Amazons. What absorbs him is the fact that this monument lies adjacent to a park with blooming flowers. He finds the contrast of the blooming and the deceased fittingly combined. There is a symbolic representation of death in the midst of life. Such brooding thoughts on death are complemented by Stine's fears that their relationship will come to a tragic end. When it does, the scene is extended in its *leitmotif* manner, in that Stine is magnetically drawn to Waldemar's funeral, which comes to an end as the sun sinks to its rest below the horizon.

Fontane not only uses such scenes to accompany and signify spiritual and physical decline but also to represent the yearning of some of his characters to escape reality. The "yearning theme" provides a counterpart to the "premonition theme" described so far. Both themes tend to represent and be represented by the unreal. There is a yearning to find that which does not exist at a given moment and place; and, as a more specific consequence, a yearning for complete release from worldly bonds. Fontane's women especially partake of this yearning. Cécile is depicted as having been "träumerisch und märchenhaft," "eine Fee in Trauer" in her childhood. Subsequently, in her worldly, adult life she still yearns for the "small" and simple, and for the idyllic—desires which stand in complete contrast to what she does, and is able to, possess. Such desires are characterized by eventual resignation and a tiredness of worldly existence. Without showing the same melancholy character as Cécile, Gordon also reflects in a similar way, upon leaving Berlin and Cécile, that to live is to bury one's hopes.

The idyllic is also the goal of Waldemar in *Stine* and, to some extent, of Lewin in *Vor dem Sturm*. Consequently, their behaviour does not correspond to what is expected of their noble station. While the unpolitically-minded Lewin indulges in reading poetry, Waldemar pictures himself in the blissful scenes of innocence described by Stine. The yearning of Hilde is less specific but even more overwhelming in *Ellernklipp*. Even in her outward expression she transmits mysterious desire. When Baltzer secretly observes her sleeping in the meadow, he feels that "alles drückte Frieden und doch zugleich ein geheimnisvolles Erwarten aus, als schwebe sie, traumgetragen, einem unendlichen Glücke nach." The feeling of unfulfilled longing overcomes Hilde most frequently when she looks out into the evening heavens: "Sie . . . sah hinaus, und eine müde, schmerzlichsüße Sehnsucht überkam sie. Wonach? Wohin? *Dort*hin, wo das Glück war und die Liebe." But there is no real object or person which can satisfy Hilde's need for happiness and love. Her unsatisfied life begins to weary her. Her yearning turns beyond reality. Melcher Harms prophesies: "Und weil sie's auf Erden nicht finden wird, so wird sie's suchen lernen dort oben und wird sich klären und in himmlischer Liebe leben und sterben. Und wird ein Engel sein auf Erden."

In her suffering and "Lebensüberdruß" Hilde discovers that not the bearing of sorrow but the turning of her thoughts to "above" helps. What yearning remains is partially satisfied by the bliss of worldly resignation, and completely by the peace of death. The yearning for other-worldly peace is also the substitute for the lack of worldly peace in *Cécile* and *Unwiederbringlich.* In both cases reality oppresses and exhausts, whereas death provides relief. And in both cases religion— and in *Cécile* a form of Catholicism—is the last expression and hope for this relief. The same process repeats itself in *Effi Briest.* As full of impulsive life as Effi is, there are still echoes of a yearning for peace in her early, monotonous married life and of a resignation which seeks other-worldly solace in her last days.

The complex of dreams, "signs" and yearning for that which is not permits a two-fold interpretation. The one, which is sometimes made, entails a negative interpretation of those characters who indulge in the phantasy which such phenomena accompany and reflect. This aspect is depicted humorously in *Frau Jenny Treibel.* Fontane himself treats ironically the Jenny who pretends to poetic understanding and who, for the sake of the Professor, reminisces in sentiments which the Professor realizes only make up a false shell for the really quite practical, ambitious Jenny.

However, where phantasy is a real part of one's character, there are usually accompanying signs of sickness. Phantasy— with its stimulus, a dissatisfaction with, and inadequacy in, reality—often manifests a spiritual, psychological weakness. This is illustrated, for example, in *Vor dem Sturm* in the contrast between the "Romantic" leanings of Hansen-Grell and Faulstich. While the former finds spiritual strength and an impetus for action in his Hölderlin studies, the latter exemplifies through his attitude towards Novalis the weakness of self-abandonment to the poetic, and the social-political ignorance and inactivity derived from Romanticism. It has consequently been suggested that *Vor dem Sturm* represents a rejection of Romanticism by Fontane. It would seem more accurate to suppose Fontane has rejected only one of the possible dangers of Romanticism—a spiritual weakening, isolation from reality and a resultant indulging in sentimentality. But despite whatever aspects of Romanticism Fontane may have rejected, "Romantic," or unreal, characteristics nevertheless remain an essential—and often artistically too obvious— feature of his novels.

It is in the spirit of being at odds with reality that both Stine and Waldemar are depicted as socially secluded and physically ill. Illness also befalls the other characters who find their lives consist only of earthly weariness and a desire for release from life. It would seem that Fontane is trying to illustrate the need to accept and maintain the existing social and moral order. And to do this would mean to discipline an imagination which dwells in wishes and dreams rather than reality. It is in this vein, for example, that Fontane criticizes the attempt of Holk to see the hand of a higher being instrumental in saving him from the burning Frederiksborg castle, and hence encouraging him to continue pursuing Ebba. Fontane criticizes Holk's imagining such a "sign" because Holk is only deluding himself by attributing his own foolish wishes to higher design. In the same manner Fontane ironically relates the daydream in which Holk describes in detail his future happiness with Ebba—a daydream without any real basis or future fulfillment.

It is important to notice, on the one hand, Fontane's absorption in the problem of the weak, "unrealistic" individual, and his generally consistent manner of describing him. Although Fontane does portray the yearning phantasy as a weakness, he also occupies himself with it sympathetically. And although there are innumerable indications of his dislike for any attempt to disrupt the social order, he nevertheless does not hesitate to criticize it. An unmistakable undercurrent of irony and pessimism runs through his works: irony and pessimism towards a social and spiritual order which binds and destroys the spirit of those passionate and exuberant individuals who end in resignation and unrealistic yearning for a non-existent life.

When Fontane criticizes Holk's belief in a higher "sign," or his idle daydreaming, he does not reject these things in themselves. He recognizes both the imagination which seeks something more idyllic than the existing, and the suggestion that there be something higher (although intangible) than man; for Fontane accuses Holk of ignoring both his inner conscience—which tells him the contrary of his daydreaming—and mistaking the true sign which God (a word Holk avoids using) has given him through the castle fire. Likewise, Fontane does not appear to be trying to dispel the unrealistic, or "Romantic," but to be giving it an essential function within the mundane. It is to represent that portion of life which the realistic and practical cannot offer—even if that portion may lead to self-deception or provide for an unfortunate escape from life. (pp. 110-15)

> Lawrence O. Frye, "The Unreal in Fontane's Novels," in The Germanic Review, Vol. 37, No. 2, March, 1962, pp. 106-15.

**RUDOLF KOESTER** (essay date 1966)

[*In the following excerpt, Koester explores the depiction of suicide in Fontane's novels.*]

Fontane depicts more suicides than any other German writer of his century. In his narrative prose no less than six major characters take their own lives: two women and four men. In *Unwiederbringlich* Christine Holk, after a period of estrangement, is reconciled with her husband; but when she finds that her former marital happiness cannot be recaptured, she grows despondent and drowns herself. The suicide of Cécile (in a narrative of the same name) is the consequence of a duel in which her husband kills one of her admirers for his insulting behaviour towards her. In *Ellernklipp* an ageing game-

*Fontane seated at his desk.*

keeper, Baltzer Bocholt, marries his young foster daughter, after killing his own son in a fit of jealousy over her. Later, overwhelming guilt feelings drive the old man to take his own life. Another marriage between age and youth which ends disastrously is depicted in *Graf Petöfy.* There the ageing Adam Petöfy ends his life when he loses his young bride to a man her own age. For Schach von Wuthenow suicide is an escape from an undesirable marriage, which he entered under pressure. The opposite of this, the frustration of a marriage, causes the death of Waldemar (in *Stine*); this aristocrat kills himself because class barriers block his marriage to a lower-class girl. While the personalities and motivations behind these suicides differ widely, they have one trait in common: all have to do, in one way or another, with an ill-starred man-woman relationship.

At first glance it may seem paradoxical that an author who has come to be known for his avoidance of extremes should feature an extreme act of this kind in so many of his writings. But, then, in Fontane the frequency of suicide does not constitute a lapse in his literary taste; for he carefully avoids an exploitation of this theme for its sensational aspects. No attempt is made to shock the reader by crass detailed descriptions of the suicides. In this sensitive area Fontane proves himself a master of restraint. Except in one instance, the reader is not even allowed to witness the actual moment of suicide. With Adam Petöfy, Christine Holk, and Cécile one learns about the act only after it has taken place; in the case of the two women it is reported in letters. When Schach von Wuthenow and Baltzer Bocholt turn their guns on themselves, no one is in their immediate presence; the fatal shots are only heard. In the case of Baltzer the suicide is so unobtrusive that a careless reader could easily miss it.

In emphasizing Fontane's flair for understatement, I do not mean to imply that the suicides catch the observant reader unprepared. On the contrary, the author by his careful craftsmanship takes pains to plant deliberate hints, such as pregnant phrases of dialogue or subtle images, which foreshadow the impending event. In *Unwiederbringlich,* for example, there is an atmosphere of gloom and death from the very opening. Besides depicting Christine's preoccupation with the restoration of the family tomb, the early chapters reveal her delicate emotional equilibrium, which is upset by the singing of a text by Waiblinger with the significant title, 'Der Kirchhof'. Moreover, a few chapters later, Christine has a foreboding dream, where she sees herself participating in a procession that sometimes has the appearance of a wedding procession and then again that of a funeral cortège. Finally, just before the suicide, Christine's husband makes the prophetic statement:' . . . wir treiben einer Katastrophe zu.'

While in *Unwiederbringlich* Fontane uses the singing of a gloomy song to foreshadow a future calamity, in *Ellernklipp* he utilizes the same device to convey a disastrous event which is taking place as the song is being sung, but off stage, as it were. While a group of young people is marching through the forest singing a popular ballad, 'Er nahm aus seiner Taschen/Ein Messer scharf und spitz . . . ,' their song is interrupted by a shot in the distance. Not knowing that it is Baltzer committing suicide, the group takes up the song again, the text of which serves to relate what has just transpired: 'Ach, reicher Gott vom Himmel,/Wie bitter ist mein Tod.'

In *Cécile* the motif of death is sounded shortly after the opening of the story, when some hotel guests check the register for the name of Gordon-Leslie, Cécile's admirer. It reminds them immediately of Schiller's tragedy. 'Das ist ja der reine "Wallensteins Tod",' one of them says. This is followed by the comment: '. . . da könnt man am Ende noch was erleben.' Here is the first (though still vague) indication of an unhappy ending. But in the very next chapter Fontane becomes more specific, as he introduces the suicide motif itself. On one of her excursions Cécile is impressed by a beautiful villa, which prompts her to remark: 'Wirkt es nicht, als wohne der Friede darin oder, was dasselbe sagt: das Glück.' However, Gordon informs her that its last resident did not attain happiness at all, but took his own life. This mirrors Cécile's own fate: her futile search for happiness and her eventual suicide. Later, on another excursion, Cécile and Gordon pass through a community called Todtenrode. It is significant that the two ride through that ominous place when they are separated from the rest of their party. In this way Fontane subtly segregates the only two characters in the novel who are destined to die. Again, it is probably no accident that later, when he reminisces about Cécile, Gordon realizes that she reminds him of a painting he once saw of Mary Stuart, another figure who suffers a premature (though not suicidal) death. A final cue, preparing the reader for the manner of the heroine's death, is the revelation of how her father died. Through his sister Gordon (and the reader) learns not only of Cécile's own scandalous background, but also that her father died under mysterious circumstances, i.e. he probably committed suicide.

While in *Cécile* the heroine's death is foreshadowed chiefly through her environment and the people in it, in *Stine* the victim's own words provide most of the hints. They reveal a mind preoccupied with death. For instance, when Waldemar surveys the lush scenery outside Stine's window, his remarks indicate his morbid if not moribund personality. He says: 'Das ist nun ein Park und heisst auch so. Aber ist es nicht eigentlich wie ein Kirchhof? Dass alles blüht, das hat der Kirchhof auch. Und der Obelisk sieht aus wie ein Grabstein'. In viewing the obelisk, a memorial to victims of a recent ship disaster, Waldemar recalls that most of the dead were young people and his statement sounds 'fast, wie wenn er sie [die Ertrunkenen] mehr beneide als beklage'. Thus, only about half-way through the novel the perceptive reader, by learning of Waldemar's yearning for death, begins to anticipate the demise of this 'seelenschwindsüchtige Person'. In the penultimate chapter no doubt is left about the impending suicide, as Waldemar sits on a park bench and unconsciously draws semicircles in the sand around the tip of his boot. Reflecting on them, he reveals his awareness of his unfulfilled life and his intention to bring it to an abrupt conclusion:

> 'Unwillkürliches Symbol meiner Tage. Halbkreise!
> Kein Abschluss, keine
> Rundung, kein Vollbringen . . . Halb, halb . . .
> Und wenn ich nun einen
> Querstrich ziehe', und er zog ihn wirklich, 'so hat
> has Halbe freilich seinen
> Abschluss, aber die rechte Rundung kommt nicht
> heraus.'

*Graf Petöfy,* a novel comprising thirty-five chapters, introduces the suicide motif as early as the third chapter. Here Fontane departs from his usual subtlety, resorting to a shock tactic. Adam Petöfy is about to embark on an evening of gay festivity, when his nephew bursts in with the news that one of Adam's friends has just shot himself. Petöfy is stunned for a moment; but when one of the guests makes some trite re-

mark about the senselessness of taking one's own life, he launches out into a spirited defence of suicide. If this seems a crude device for foreshadowing Adam's own fate, Fontane utilizes much more subtle means in the penultimate chapter. It abounds in death images, which are quite effective because they blend in so well with the setting. As the hero takes his last ride through Vienna on a foggy November morning, the people in the streets look to him like 'Schatten' and he is prompted to observe: 'Ist es doch, als ob es ein Unterweltsjahrmarkt wär.' This visual Hades image is supplemented by an audible omen of catastrophe. 'Vom Kasernenhofe her klangen Trommel und Hörner, aber dumpf wie Notsignale'. Next, as Petöfy rides out of the city, nature displays a sight which reinforces the atmosphere of gloom and impending disaster. The hero observes a colony of field mice threatened by drowning in the water from an overflowing drain. They flee their holes by the hundreds, only to fall prey to some waiting crows, who swoop down on the helpless mice. Petöfy reacts with this pregnant remark: 'Überall dasselbe: keine Flucht vor dem, was einmal beschlossen.'

In *Schach von Wuthenow* hints as to the hero's future fate are carefully woven into the fabric of the dialogue and the setting of the story. Some of the devices in this narrative—as in some of the stories discussed above—are so subtle that it seems appropriate at this point to note Benno von Wiese's warning: 'Die Verschleierung symbolisch andeutender Zeichen ins gewollt Triviale oder scheinbar Nebensächliche gelingt Fontane in dieser Erzählung oft so meisterhaft, dass der Interpret, der auf sie hinweist, das Risiko eingeht, sich dem Verdacht auszusetzen, er höre das Gras wachsen.' For example, after seducing Victoire von Carayon, Schach leaves her with the words, 'Bis auf morgen,' when he has no intention of returning the next day. Then, on his wedding day (at the end of which he commits suicide) Schach parts from Victoire uttering the same phrase, 'Bis auf morgen', obviously with the same intention, not to return. A less subtle clue is contained in Fontane's transparent phrasing of the couple's parting embrace: 'Er . . . umarmte sie, wie wenn er Abschied nehmen wolle für immer. . . .'. But even earlier, as Benno von Wiese points out, there are death images, which are inconspicuous because they blend in so well with the setting. For instance, when Schach has fled to his country estate in order to reflect on his dilemma, he cannot fall asleep in his stuffy room because dozens of nocturnal insects have flown in through the open window. As von Wiese says, this could be regarded as 'harmlose Milieuschilderung', but it also points to death. The same applies to two wreaths of everlasting flowers with black and white ribbons which hang in the living-room of Schach's estate. Moreover, at the wedding an aunt claims that on a recent excursion to a local church Victoire picked some violets for Schach, but that she threw them away again and that the bouquet landed on a grave near the church door. This event, the confused aunt alleges, must have a meaning. 'Dieses unverständliche, aber ganz realistisch dargebotene abergläubische Gerede in Tante Marguerites Toast auf das junge Brautpaar dient dem Erzähler zugleich als künstlerisches Mittel, noch einmal leitmotivisch auf jenes Sterben und jenes Grab vorzubereiten, das ja gleich auf die Hochzeit folgen sollte.' In view of the above, I cannot agree with Peters's assertion: 'Der Selbstmord Schachs kommt dem Leser überraschend.'

Concerning Fontane's prose in general Hatfield has aptly observed: '. . . he describes but rarely judges.' This is especially apparent in his portrayal of suicide. When he confronts clergymen with it (as he frequently does), Fontane has a choice opportunity of passing a moral judgment, but he does not do so. . . . [The] fact that Baltzer Bocholt dies by his own hand is glossed over by the clergyman at the funeral. Again, no moral judgment on suicide is given by the minister at Waldemar's funeral. His body is brought home to his family estate, where it is entombed 'an geweihter Stätte'. Not only the local pastor waits at the station for the arrival of the deceased, a high church official comes especially from Berlin to conduct the funeral service. The subject of suicide is not broached. However, in *Cécile* this cannot be avoided because it is the minister, Hofprediger Dórffel, who is charged with informing the heroine's husband of her death. Still, Dörffel's discreet wording contains no judgment of her act. In the case of Adam Petöfy, a Catholic, suicide constitutes a cardinal sin. Yet, 'nachdem seitens der Kirche sein gewaltsamer Tod auf einen Anfall von Melancholie gedeutet worden war,' Pater Fessler presides over Petöfy's funeral, which is carried out with all the pomp and circumstance appropriate to his station. It is evident that Fontane's clergymen, when confronted with suicide, adopt a compassionate attitude.

They refrain from condemning the act as strict adherence to the letter of theological doctrine would require. But, then, Fontane himself viewed orthodox theology with scepticism. It is likely therefore, that his characters reflect the author's own humanity and his sympathy for human frailty. It is likewise possible that within the scope of his narratives Fontane regarded any definitive pronouncement on the subject of suicide 'ein zu weites Feld'.

While in Stifter's prose (where religion still operates as a generally accepted vital part of life) suicide appears as a threat, as temptation, in Fontane the sting is removed; it no longer bears the stigma of immorality. At the same time it is not an indication of character weakness or youthful. 'Weltschmerz', for, with the conspicuous exception of Waldemar, the author portrays individuals with strong (though sometimes misguided) convictions. Nor is it an expression of ethical nihilism on the writer's part. On the contrary, in *Ellernklipp*, which is reminiscent of a 'Schicksalstragödie', Baltzer's suicide satisfies not only the demands of poetic justice, but also those of an ancient ethical law, a tooth for a tooth; his act marks the propitiation of a crime, the murder of his son, and with that he attains peace. For the other characters, too, suicide, though not connected with any crime, is a source of peace, a final, welcome escape from a life no longer livable. This view, while conflicting with certain ethical tenets of Fontane's time, is really not so revolutionary; for all the suicides (except Baltzer) are members of the nobility, who have traditionally looked upon the taking of one's own life as an honourable way out of an intolerable situation. The fact that their actions are 'in character' may explain why there was no significant public reaction against Fontane's frequent portrayal and 'conciliatory' interpretation of suicide.

No doubt, this interpretation is closely allied with Fontane's own outlook on life. As a man without illusions, he resigned himself to the indifference of life with courage and a kind of subdued cheerfulness. 'Das den Dingen scharf ins Gesicht sehn,' he writes, 'ist nur momentan schrecklich; bald gewöhnt man sich nicht nur daran, sondern findet in der gewonnenen Erkenntnis . . . eine nicht geringe Befriedigung.' Like the suicides in the above discussion, Fontane sees in death a source of tranquillity. 'Die höchste Ruhegebung . . . kommt einem aus dem *memento mori*. . . .'

In view of this, the absence of any elegiac tone in the depiction of suicide comes as no surprise. Fontane does not have to steep his works in melancholy and despair. His characters show no self-pity or sentimentality; they face death without loss of dignity. Schach even attains a certain serenity as he anticipates suicide. In going through with the marriage, Schach reasons, he will satisfy his obligation to obey the king, who ordered the marriage, and by taking his own life immediately afterwards he will satisfy his own nature, which rebels against marrying an unattractive woman. When he has reached this resolution, the account says: '. . . er fühlte sich, nach Tagen schweren Druckes, zum ersten Male wieder leicht und frei'.

In analysing Fontane's depiction of suicide, this discussion should not neglect what is probably the most essential element: proper motivation. That the author himself is keenly aware of this requirement can be inferred from his critique of Turgenev's *Virgin Soil*, which is marred, according to Fontane, by the hero's uncalled-for suicide:

> Das macht einen trübseligen Eindruck. Wenn das Sich-tot-Schiessen einen Effekt machen soll, so muss etwas vorhergegangen sein, das diesen Ausgang rechtfertigt oder fordert, fehlt es aber an Ereignissen, die ein Recht haben, mir die Pistole in die Hand zu drücken, so muss ich sie auch nicht aus Katzenjammer in die Hand nehmen.

Fontane carefully shuns the pitfall he describes here. None of his protagonists kills himself in a moment of sudden and unexpected dejection. Here suicide is depicted as an organic reaction of particular personality components subjected to a particular set of circumstances. There is no need to give a detailed reiteration of these elements because they are quite conspicuous in the plot of each story. It requires no special discernment to understand, for example, that Schach, whose whole life is based on the approbation of society and whose vanity demands an attractive wife, cannot go on living when faced with the prospect of being mocked by that society, partly because he is chained to an unattractive woman. Of course, there is more to it than this, but the reader can readily assemble the other pertinent details for himself. This also applies to the other narratives. However, while the immediate cause of each suicide and the chain of events leading up to it are as varied as the respective plots themselves, there is one feature which all of Fontane's suicides have in common: their death can be traced, in one way or another, to a fatal miscalculation about their own character or that of someone close to them, or both.

Lest my earlier statement concerning suicide motivation be taken to imply that Fontane's characters act according to a mechanical formula or rigidly rational pattern, let me emphasize that the author is fully aware of the irrational, unpredictable forces in human behaviour. These unknowns in the human equation are especially evident among the suicides. They do not foresee that they will kill themselves. They seem to be compelled to do so by 'fortuitous events', involvement in which is directly connected (whether they know it or not) with their personalities. (pp. 34-40)

*Rudolf Koester, "Death by Miscalculation: Some Notes on Suicide in Fontane's Prose," in* German Life & Letters, *n.s. Vol. 20, No. 1, October, 1966, pp. 34-42.*

**HENRY HATFIELD**   (essay date 1969)

[*In the following excerpt, Hatfield discusses the political themes in Fontane's* Der Stechlin.]

Often referred to as his "novel of old age," **Der Stechlin** appeared in late 1898, a few months after Fontane's death. Of course none of his narratives was written when he was young, but the tag is not useless. The book deals largely with the declining years and death of Dubslav von Stechlin, with whom Fontane often almost identifies himself; and it is less concerned with action and passion than with reflections on politics, religion, and life in general. Even more than *Die Poggenpuhls,* this is a work in which "how" has largely replaced "what." It is uncharacteristically long—over five hundred pages—and contains so many conversations that it could be called garrulous—although agreeably so. There is a tendency toward duplication: *two* visits to Stechlin's castle are presented at length, and there are *two* wise old men. (Herr von Barby, Stechlin's opposite number, shares many of his attitudes.) While there are many scenes of great verisimilitude, Fontane is less concerned than before with the conventions of realism. Thus Lake Stechlin, we are told, is mysteriously linked to volcanoes all over the world; when there is an eruption in Iceland or Java, a waterspout is formed on its surface. (As will appear, Fontane used this legend for symbolic purposes; such improbabilities no longer disturbed him.) Similarly, the young woman who grasps instinctively the symbolic importance of the lake is given the name of a water nymph—Melusine.

It is not the case that "nothing happens" in the novel. Thus Stechlin's son Woldemar chooses between two sisters, marries, and will carry the family tradition farther. There is no shortage of characters: the friends von Rex and von Czako, who are neatly contrasted, as are Melusine and her sister Armgard von Barby; the usual eccentrics, often with comic names; a *nouveau riche* couple; and many others. Fontane now appears to be less interested than before in preserving distance or neutrality: we are told bluntly that Stechlin's sister dislikes anything which suggests beauty or freedom to her mind. Basically this is a novel of ideas; action as such is subordinated to the themes discussed. Woldemar von Stechlin is a rather dim figure; it is the thinkers and conversationalists—especially Dubslav, the liberal Pastor Lorenzen, and Melusine—whom we remember. The topics of conversation are important in themselves; discourse here is more than a social pastime. Conversely, the manner of talking is rooted in character; we do not have imaginary dialogues carried on by faceless persons.

Before turning to the themes of **Der Stechlin,** we should consider the book's protagonist. Dubslav's views are a mixture of the extremely conservative—he is a Junker after all—with the liberal; the latter prevails. There is something of the eighteenth century about him. Like Fontane, he is basically a skeptic, of the tolerant, not the bitter, sort. If he believes that there are "no indisputable truths," he upholds certain attitudes unswervingly: "Conceit and arrogance . . . were about the only things which infuriated him." His skepticism is very far from nihilism. It is typical that he gives as his reason for not remarrying—he was widowed young—his fear of cutting a ridiculous figure in heaven with two wives. (Actually, he does not believe in the resurrection of the body.) Characteristically, he can admire both Russian czars and the Social Democratic party. If his views are unduly eclectic, his character is winning; although anything but stuffy, he is proud of

belonging to an old if somewhat impoverished family, which he considers quite as good as the Bismarcks or the Hohenzollerns. He seems to be that sort of nobleman who can accept new ideas and social forces gracefully. (His sister incarnates the "know-nothing" type of Junker; Fontane's attitude toward her is made clear early in the story.) Dubslav is a partisan neither of the old nor of the new; the type of aristocracy he represents, Fontane indicates, can form a valuable part of the era which is coming.

When Fontane called **Der Stechlin** political, he was using the term very broadly, to include social behavior and ethics. Thus there is an indissoluble link between politics and religion: Pastor Lorenzen—an old friend of Stechlin and the mentor of his son Woldemar—is deeply concerned with political and especially social matters; his ideas are closer to the intention of the book than are the protagonist's. Just as Fontane can express admiration of Frederick the Great without championing the "good old days," he (and the book) distinguish between healthy forces in the present and those which are sinister or comic. Again, the theme of the new versus the old is central.

When young Woldemar champions the new spirit, Lorenzen replies that men should uphold "the old as long as it functions decently, and the new only as far as necessary." Perhaps he is leaning over backward to avoid offending the others present. Melusine later formulates the matter differently: "We should love everything old insofar as it deserves it, but it is for the new that we should really live." As one would expect, neither liberals nor conservatives have a monopoly of virtue or of Fontane's sympathies. Thus the Social Democratic politican Torgelow is a charlatan, but the party itself is referred to with respect. While Stechlin is delightful, most of his fellow Junkers are rather unprepossessing, and his reactionary sister Adelheid is referred to as "petrified" and "prehistoric." Old Stechlin's philippic against modern tendencies, when he is near death, loses most of its sting because it is basically good-humored. Feeling that his son's generation is unduly catholic in its tastes, he lists its heroes:

> old Wilhelm and Kaiser Friedrich and Bismarck and Moltke, and Mazzini and Garibaldi in between them, very friendly-like, and Marx and Lassalle—at least they were dead—and Bebel and Liebknecht next to them. And then Woldemar says: "Look at Bebel. My political opponent, but a man of character."

Old Stechlin would himself admit that a political opponent could be decent; his point here is that the liberal pantheon is too inclusive, and he is not entirely wrong. To Pastor Lorenzen, the real heroes of the present are the inventors and explorers.

The relations among the various social classes and the tensions within them also appear as elements of the general dialectics of present versus past. Three years before **Der Stechlin** was finished, Fontane wrote to a friend that the book would be concerned with "the contrast between the nobility as it ought to be and as it is." As has been noted, this is not a major theme of the finished novel, but the opposition between the enlightened nobles Stechlin and Barby (and their children) on the one hand and Adelheid's circles on the other is very clear. As usual, servants and other members of the "lower" classes appear in a very favorable light, but in this explicitly political novel, Fontane goes further and speaks of the fourth estate. In one of the book's numerous conversations, the intelligent

Czech Dr. Wrschowitz describes the Berlin population in one lapidary sentence: "Upper class good, lower class very good; middle class not very good." Again, the bourgeoisie could hardly be worse, and the newly ennobled Herr von Gundermann, with his freshly acquired ultraconservative views, is equally unattractive. Unlike the Junker families, the rich burghers show no sense of *noblesse oblige* in dealing with their servants.

A similar dichotomy between old and new appears in religious matters. The likable characters, especially Stechlin, Lorenzen, and Armgard von Barby, are decidedly Christian in their ethics and basic attitudes, though Stechlin is anything but orthodox, and Lorenzen, despite his calling, seems to be even less so. The "party-line" Christians like Adelheid von Stechlin are intolerably intolerant, whereas Armgard, who is not particularly pious, instinctively prefers St. Elizabeth to Queen Elizabeth: helping the poor is the highest ideal, she feels. It is as if socialism were invoked to take the curse off dogmatic Christianity, and Christianity were to perform the same function for doctrinaire socialism. Some sort of Christian socialism, then, would seem to be an integral part of the synthesis to which the book points. When Lorenzen reassures Stechlin that the new Christianity is identical with the old, he recalls the early Christians who "had all things in common" and preserves the novel's Fontanean balance between past and present.

If the term "Christian Socialism" has a somewhat ambiguous ring today, that is largely the fault of Adolf Stoecker, court preacher at Berlin from 1874 to 1889. However sincere Stoecker may have been in his efforts to win back the working classes to Christianity by preaching a highly conservative sort of "social gospel," he is now mainly remembered for his propagation of anti-Semitism. Fontane realized that Lorenzen's social aims would remind his readers of Stoecker's, and he mentions the actual pastor in the novel in order to differentiate between the two types. It is characteristic of Fontane's realism that he brings in a number of contemporary figures from Bismarck down, while he is very careful to preserve the privacy of ordinary citizens. It is also typical that he does not mention Stoecker's anti-Semitism, not (I believe) because the theme was taboo but because it was beneath contempt. He wrote to Friedrich Paulsen that the novel tended to uphold the ideas of Stoecker and the Social-Democratic leader August Bebel in ennobled form, rather than the Prussian ideal. Lorenzen and the other champions of "the new" are not expressly committed to any specific economic or social reforms; their socialism is based on the New Testament, not on the class struggle.

Quite clearly, the symbol of Lake Stechlin is the key to understanding the book's political drift. As will be recalled, when a volcano erupts anywhere in the world, a waterspout is formed; during really great catastrophes, a red rooster also appears. Doubtless, the volcanoes and earthquakes, as in Goethe's *Faust,* symbolize revolutions; it has been plausibly suggested that the red rooster—the Gallic cock?—points to France. In other words, even the most rural, remote parts of Prussia are inextricably linked, like Germany as a whole, to the rest of the world: Adelheid and the other reactionaries are wrong, for no country is immune to change. Although there is something frightening about the lake, what it symbolizes is basically beneficent. Further, the lake preserves its character throughout the centuries—not despite these occasional "revolutions" but because of them.

If this interpretation is correct, the novel must be largely acquitted of any charge of ambivalence. Much of Stechlin's charm derives from the fact that he usually transcends the prejudices of his class. Not that Fontane was or claimed to be an activist. His own attitude recalls that of Professor Schmidt, in *Frau Jenny Treibel,* who tells his daughter that he would join the Social Democrats—if he were not a professor. Yet *Der Stechlin* remains rewarding for its theme as well as its style, for "what" as well as "how." Whether or not one attaches the label "late" to the novel, it has a special character, an appeal of its own. (pp. 28-34)

*Henry Hatfield, "The Renovation of the German Novel: Theodor Fontane," in his* Crisis and Continuity in Modern German Fiction: Ten Essays, *Cornell University Press, 1969, pp. 1-34.*

## E. F. GEORGE (essay date 1971)

[*In the following excerpt, George traces the "illusion-reality" theme in Fontane's novels.*]

Fontane's interest in the illusion-reality theme did not spring from philosophical speculation either in the sense of penetrating into ultimate truth or of the dilemma as to whether experience comes from within or outside ourselves. His interest lay in human nature and how far it can truly express itself within the forms and fashions which society has made inevitable. (p. 68)

Fontane acknowledges . . . an aesthetic value in how things appear, but this he qualifies by relating it to the prevailing outlook, to deeply ingrained modes of thought, and not to any conviction on his part that form should take precedence over content. On the contrary, he came increasingly to fear that pretence and hypocrisy were taking the place of a concern for what is genuine, natural and true. Social prestige, parading in public, the idea that how one appears is more important than what one is—all this, which may be seen as a characteristic stamp of the Wilhelmine Age, was repugnant to Fontane. Posturing of any kind he disliked intensely, even when he found it in Theodor Storm, whom he respected as a true poet while detesting what struck him as Storm's inordinate self-esteem and the pleasure he took in casting himself in a role exalted above others. He was aware that dissembling may take various forms, some of them trivial and comparatively harmless, and others more subtle and insidious and also more damaging in their effects. He saw that the danger lay not only in deceiving others but in deceiving ourselves: indeed, much of his creative writing turns on an awareness of two levels, the situation as it actually is and how it appears when seen through a false perspective. In *Die Poggenpuhls,* for instance, the real circumstances of the family are set against the varying degrees in which they delude themselves about their ability to maintain a social status which belongs to the past.

It would be wrong to say that Fontane's principal aim was identical with Ibsen's, to lay bare the corruption in society, but despite his predominantly hostile criticism of Ibsen's thought he shared the same concern to expose what is deceitful and pure façade, and often his characters, like those of Ibsen, being enclosed within the cramped and suffocating confines of their social position, yearn to be free. But there is this difference, that Fontane was much more sceptical than Ibsen about the degree of freedom and self-determination that it was reasonable to seek or expect in life. His review of

*The Lady from the Sea* makes it clear that he did not believe that freedom was the answer to every human problem or the source from which all benefits flow. He criticises with heavy irony the change in Ellida at the end of the play: this he finds too sudden and not sufficiently motivated to be psychologically convincing. That she should have been given her freedom is not in itself, so he argues, a satisfactory explanation for the abrupt reversal which follows. . . . In his works Fontane demonstrates that to suppose that it is either possible or desirable to free oneself entirely from social pressures and obligations is an illusion.

As early a work as *Grete Minde* gives a striking illustration of this. Grete is tightly enclosed within a world which is foreign to her nature and aspirations. She feels imprisoned and longs to escape, dreaming of a freedom and happiness which are denied to her through the conditions under which she lives. But these dreams are illusions and nothing more, as she discovers when with Valtin she flees from home and encounters a series of crippling misfortunes which end in madness and suicide. Although she suffers monstrous injustice she is shown to be herself substantially at fault in that she rebels and in rebelling cuts away the ground without which she cannot survive. The conclusion is that one must resign oneself to reality, however abhorrent or unjust its demands may be. This is basically what Grete herself comes to realise, even though her thoughts throughout are clothed in religious terms.

For Fontane realities include the circumstances in which we have been brought up, tradition, family, class, financial means and professional status, and the standards which have evolved within the social system. Defiance of these realities or failure to comply with their demands is shown to be imprudent or indeed almost inconceivable without forfeiting all that makes life possible within society, including one's own equanimity and self-respect. Moreover, the judgment which society passes upon us tends in the long run to become identified with the judgment which we pass upon ourselves. At all events the claims of society cannot be ignored, and whether right or wrong they have to be weighed carefully and conscientiously against the evidence of personal conviction.

*Irrungen, Wirrungen* deals with the perplexities which arise when one sets out on a course which diverges from the established, though everchanging pattern of life. Botho and Lene, for as long as their courtship lasts, live in a world unrelated to reality. Lene knows this and unlike Botho makes no attempt to disguise it from herself. She cherishes the illusion, while recognising it as such and knowing that it cannot endure. And when the break finally comes, Botho, in deciding to part from Lene, finally realises that he cannot live on dreams and that if he were to rebel against social demands he would also be rebelling against all that has made him what he is. In *Stine* Waldemar is more deeply committed to a deeper illusion and for this reason cannot survive its destruction. He is by nature prone to indulge in dreams and to interpret what he sees and experiences in the light of his imagination. This Stine recognises as a defect in him. She sees that he is blinded by self-deception and that his proposal to marry her and go to America flies in the face of the facts and could only end in disappointment and misery. . . . That Fontane's plebeian characters neither rebel nor wish to rebel against the social order is indisputable, but to see this as a serious shortcoming while recognising the moral quality shown by Fontane in their being free from illusion is contradictory, since the reluctance to rebel is in itself an integral and perhaps the most essential part of such freedom.

The most striking way in which Fontane signifies illusion is through the presence of moonlight, with all its Romantic associations, and this is contrasted with what the sun represents in terms of candour, happiness and integrity. *Effi Briest* begins with "heller Sonnenschein", an appropriate setting for Effi's childhood innocence and for her buoyant and carefree spirits. Years later, while on holiday in Ems, she enjoys the sunshine once again, until the letter arrives from her parents, with its calamitous news and the warning that she now belongs to those people "die sich um freie Luft und lichte Sonne gebracht haben." The significance of the sun is closely linked to the freedom of fresh air, the constant opening of windows as a means of finding relief from oppression and anxiety. The moon on the other hand points above all to an escape from reality. Under its rays all things appear grotesque and distorted. Whenever it presides over the meeting of lovers, it lends to their surroundings and to the courtship itself a thick layer of phantasy. In *Stine* Waldemar identifies his fate with the setting sun, but his love for Stine and the illusions which accompany it, together with his introspection, neuroticism and obsession with death are all closely interwoven with moonlit scenes. And under the magic and transforming light of the moon a yearning is brought out, a yearning which stretches out for what the world cannot give, a yearning for an ideal which lies beyond the empirical realities of human experience. Lene in *Irrungen, Wirrungen* experiences this when surveying the moonlit landscape at "Hankels Ablage", and under the hypnotic influence of the moon Franziska in *Graf Petöfy* casts her mind back to her home and her childhood, and is filled with a deep yearning which she cannot define but which, whatever else it may be, expresses discontent with reality, both as it is and as it was in the past. All these threads are gathered together in *Mathilde Möhring* when Thilde, recognising that Hugo is weak and frail and that what he needs is more vigour and a sense of practical purpose, tells him: "Ach, Herr Großmann, der Mond ist nichts für Sie, Sie brauchen Sonne . . . Sonne gibt mehr Kraft."

But to Fontane these illusions are not in themselves absurd or without value; on the contrary, they contain a deeper truth in face of which the social realities, even though they dictate to us, are transient, empty and meaningless. In *Meine Kinderjahre* he writes of his mother's scale of values:

> Reich sein, Besitz (am liebsten Landbesitz), alles womöglich unterstützt von den Allüren eines Gesandtschaftsattachés—das war etwas, das schloß Welt und Herzen auf, das war eine wirkliche Macht; das andere war Komödie, Schein, eine Seifenblase, die jeden Augenblick platzen konnte.

But this idea, that wealth, property and prestige are hard facts and all else is unreal and impermanent, Fontane, while conceding its limited validity, found distasteful. In *Irrungen, Wirrungen* he shows that to Botho and Lene their love represents the only true happiness which they can ever know, even though it is fleeting, hemmed in on every side and rarely free from anxiety. Through it, all that is natural and sincere within them finds expression, and in their response to each other they discover a freshness and a depth of feeling beside which the social forms are merely superficial. To Botho the intensity of what he has experienced is such that, as he looks back on it, he is hurt as with a cut from broken glass. Reality for him means a shallow marriage to a shallow wife, whose character is summed up in her ability to talk endlessly without saying anything of consequence, and for Lene it means marriage to a husband, who represents down-to-earth affairs, a point which is neatly summed up in his topics of conversation "von allerlei städtischen Angelegenheiten, von Schulen, Gasanstalten und Kanalisation und mitunter auch von seinen Reisen."

Much of the social system is indicted by Fontane for its inhumanity and for being itself illusory, since it has few enduring values and in most of its aspects represents outward show without inner content. Those who think purely in social terms are shown to have no feeling or to strip themselves of what feeling they possess. In **Stine** Waldemar's stepmother comes into this category; at Waldemar's funeral she is concerned solely with social decorum, feels no grief and takes it amiss when the heartfelt sorrow of Stine threatens to expose her own cold indifference. In **Schach von Wuthenow** society in Prussia is shown to have lost its integrity and respect for the truth, and to be wholly dependent upon semblance and the tokens of social prestige. Schach commits suicide because he knows no values other than social values and because he therefore shares the illusions of the society in which he lives. In **L'Adultera** Melanie is ostracised by a society which is likened to the Pharisees in their condemnation of the adulteress. But it is in **Effi Briest** that Fontane gives us his most powerful indictment of the standards which govern social life. Innstetten's one clear aim is to rise in his profession and thereby in social esteem. This becomes for him an almost neurotic obsession, and all else, including concern for his wife's needs, is ruthlessly subordinated to it. Yet after his duel with Crampas his whole scale of values crumbles and falls to pieces about him. Social honour and advancement, around which his whole life had previously revolved, now reveal themselves to him as an empty illusion. . . . This illusion, to which, as he knows, his marriage has been sacrificed, now disgusts him, and he is left with a view of life which is excessively modest in its demands and expectations. But he also gains an insight into what really matters, the pure and unaffected kindness which is shown to Effi by Roswitha and which puts all else to shame. The last glance from Crampas before he dies tells Innstetten that what he has done is not only absurd but callous and inhumane, no different from the whole code to which he had deferred, a code which works like a machine without soul or feeling. The duel together with what follows, the banishment of Effi, Innstetten recognises as "eine halbe Komödie," a charade which has no real point and no relevance to basic human needs. The cruelty of the code is further stressed through Effi's parents, who for a time consider it their social duty to deny their daughter a sanctuary at home, and thereby to express publicly their condemnation of her misconduct. And that Effi should be deprived of what nature entitles her to, the love of her daughter, is also inhumane.

In Fontane's eyes many features of morality are closely tied to their social context and indeed have no validity unless referred to the social forms out of which they have evolved. But this did not include marriage, which despite occasional doubts he conceived of as having claims more absolute than those of ephemeral social convention. Nevertheless, in his works marriage is shown to have this in common with social pressures, that it imposes a certain discipline and restricts personal freedom, and the figures in his novels who go wrong in their marriages do so at least in part because they find it irksome or are temperamentally unsuited to accept these conditions. Fontane keeps present the thought that marriage

may be regarded as a kind of captivity which frustrates what is natural to the human spirit. The bird in the cage, so frequently a part of Fontane's furnishings, is a reminder of this theme, and Graf Petöfy underlines the symbol when towards the end he thinks of his wife as having been a willing captive, but like a bird which, when the spring comes, cannot resist the impulse to leave its open cage and fly out and away into the free air. But marriage without some measure of personal sacrifice is impossible. This is recognised by the heroine in **Cécile,** whose whole predicament is mirrored in the heart complaint from which she suffers. She has difficulty with her breathing, but this, so Gordon argues, is because she is "eingeschnürt und eingezwängt", and what she needs—"das ist nicht Luft, das ist Licht, Freiheit, Freude." But Cécile, standing firm and rejecting this appeal, acts in the knowledge that, because she is a married woman, such uncurbed freedom must be denied to her.

In discussing Ibsen's *Ghosts* Fontane rejects the view, which he took to be proclaimed in this play, that to marry for money instead of love is bound to have disastrous consequences and that such marriages, being by their nature untruthful pretence, should be dissolved without delay. Fontane argues that history and experience prove the contrary, and he concludes:

> Unter allen Umständen bleibt es mein Kredo, daß, wenn von Uranfang an statt aus Konvenienz und Vorteilserwägung lediglich aus Liebe geheiratet wäre, der Weltbestand um kein Haarbreit besser wäre, als er ist.

This may seem strange coming from an author who so often deplores the defeat of nature in her struggle with social requirements. But Fontane saw that the human heart was more subject to change and caprice and no less fallible in its dictates than human institutions. It became clear to him that what marriage needed, if it was to work out successfully, was good sense and sound judgment, and that love by itself was no adequate substitute for this. The problems of marital friction were known to him from his parents, and in **Meine Kinderjahre** he quotes his father as saying: "Zuneigung ist nicht genug zum Heiraten: Heiraten ist eine Sache für vernünftige Menschen. Ich hatte noch nicht die Jahre, vernünftig zu sein." In the case of his parents not only two temperaments but two different attitudes to life and its purpose came into conflict with each other, a conflict which only perseverance, indulgence and mutual understanding could have resolved.

Of all the instances of adultery depicted by Fontane only that in **L'Adultera** is shown in some measure to justify itself, and even here there are distinct reservations. Melanie insists on divorce, not primarily because she is attracted by the prospect of a new life with her lover, Rubehn, but because her honesty and self-respect demand that she should commit herself openly, in face of the world, to the consequences of what she has done in secret. Having then made her decision, she is shown to have a very heavy burden of sorrow and anguish to endure, even though, somewhat unconvincingly, all turns out well in the end. The happiness which she and Rubehn finally achieve is not presented with full conviction, possibly because it was not within Fontane's power to make an artificial situation ring true. Peter Demetz is certainly right in considering this ending to be "tief unter Fontane's Niveau". All the other cases of adultery are shown to be purely disruptive, nothing good comes of them, and in themselves they fail to bring even temporary satisfaction or relief. Holk in **Un-**

*wiederbringlich* and Effi Briest both feel that marriage has deprived them of the freedom, light and air which their natures crave for, but they are deluded in supposing that this can be remedied through infidelity. Effi is attracted to Crampas because she shares his reckless spirits and because in his contempt for regulations, order and discipline he appeals to her own innate but thwarted sense of freedom: in him she sees the opportunity presented of breaking free from all that oppresses her. But this in itself proves to be an illusion. The spell cast by Crampas holds her captive, and while under this spell she is no less imprisoned than before and no less starved of light and air. Fontane emphasises the sadness, the misgivings and almost, one might say, grief which overcome her during the short period in which she is ensnared. At this stage she has a clear vision of what is happening and a pronounced distaste for the clandestine and fraudulent nature of the whole affair. Holk's adventure is also fraudulent, although he is slow to recognise this. It brings to light all his failings, above all the absurd extent to which he misjudges what is involved and misinterprets his own character and the position which befits him in society: it is an act of folly which covers him in ridicule and wrecks the home to which he really belongs. Both these instances of adultery are pointless in human terms and contain nothing to compensate for the devastating damage which they cause.

Fontane's conception of what is genuine and what is illusory varies in accordance with the different perspectives in which he views life. The answer to him was not as simple and clear-cut as it was to Ibsen, because he had a much greater respect for reality in the sense of what conditions are and how they have evolved. In his review of Ibsen's *Ghosts* he writes:

> Unsere Zustände sind ein historisch Gewordenes, die wir als solche zu respektieren haben. Man modle sie, wo sie der Modlung bedürfen, aber man stülpe sie nicht um.

His twofold attitude to illusion springs from a similar division in his attempt to come to terms with the problem of order and individual freedom. In *Meine Kinderjahre* he speaks of the lively interest with which he followed the Polish insurrection of 1830-1 and of his mixed feelings towards it both at the time of its occurrence and since. His sympathies were brought to bear on the side of the rebels and yet, so he tells us, he always remained conscious of "ein gewisses Engagement zugunsten der geordneten Gewalten." The one is a poetic appeal to which he instinctively responds and the other a commitment based on a careful appraisal of where the real strength and corresponding justification must ultimately lie. In a letter to Georg Friedländer, October 3rd, 1893, Fontane ascribes to himself "einen ganz ausgebildeten Sinn für Tatsächlichkeiten", and he adds: "Ich habe das Leben immer genommen, wie ich's fand und mich ihm unterworfen. Das heißt nach außen hin; in meinem Gemüte nicht." Fontane thoroughly understands the futility of trying to resist or of allowing oneself to be angered and frustrated by what circumstances have decreed. But the practical world, although it has its legitimate claims upon him, wields no absolute authority. Accordingly he submits in his outward behaviour and also in the sense of rendering unto Caesar, but not deep within himself. The values which he affirms are not derived from the powers which reign over society—"Geld, Adel, Offizier, Assessor, Professor"—for which reason these powers call forth his obedience, perhaps in some respects his allegiance, but not his inner assent. The most satisfactory solution to this problem, as Fontane saw it, is outlined in *Quitt,* a novel which is of

more interest for what it aims to do than for what it achieves. Here neither the unconditional freedom and individualism which America represents nor the rigid order and discipline characteristic of Prussia are given unqualified approval: what Fontane commends and in his more optimistic moments may have visualised as a possibility for the future is a compromise between the two, a sense of order which is a reasonable and living reality, which is not inflexible, and which we obey because in doing so we remain true both to ourselves and to others. And it is by this criterion of truth that we can best judge where illusion is to be found and how it can be guarded against. (pp. 68-75)

*E. F. George, "Illusions and Illusory Values in Fontane's Works," in* Forum for Modern Language Studies, *Vol. VII, No. 1, January, 1971, pp. 68-75.*

## A. R. ROBINSON (essay date 1974)

[*In the following excerpt, Robinson discusses Fontane's method of autobiographical writing in* Meine Kinderjahre, *focusing, in particular, on the relationship between this work and his prose fiction.*]

Fontane's approach to autobiographical writing is (subject to the general fallibility of the human memory) unbiased, in so far as he has no ulterior motive in writing of himself, either in *Meine Kinderjahre* or in the subsequent volume dealing with his early manhood. He has no abstruse philosophical theories to promulgate, either as a man or as a writer, nor does he attempt to discover prophetic signs and portents of future greatness in the events of his childhood. As an author whose creative work strove after clarity and a dispassionate recording of events and personalities, he was able to bring a well-balanced mind to the task of self-examination, without feeling the need to colour or distort what he found. There are examples of highlighting, of course, and likewise of toning-down; it would be extremely difficult to remain dispassionate about something so intimate as family relationships. There is possible evidence, for instance, of lingering bitterness in the description of how his mother had once spoilt his Christmas; this may, however, have been simply an outlet for the frustration and petulance of a sick man "writing himself well again", as he puts it, or it may be the momentary flicker of a smouldering resentment that still lurked in the recesses of his mind. In the last resort only the writer himself knows the true significance of what he writes. It can hardly be without some inner meaning, moreover, that in the 185 pages of his childhood memories he barely mentions his brothers and sisters.

Fontane's approach to the work is, typically enough, an anecdotal one. In contrast to, say, Anthony Trollope, whose account of his schooldays is intensely egocentric and self-pitying, Fontane tends from the very start to look outwards at those who surrounded him and made an impact on his life. The first two chapters are dominated by the figures of his parents, presented in detail as finished portraits, not just sketched in as a background to his own life, and they were to recur throughout the pages of *Meine Kinderjahre.* One of them, his father, becomes almost the dominant—and certainly the most memorable—personality of the whole work. Another noticeable deviation from the practice observed in other autobiographies of repute, especially again that of Trollope, is the repeated use of the collective 'we' and 'our' in the titles of the various chapters; "Unsere Übersiedlung nach Swinemünde", "Unser Haus, wie wirs vorfanden", "Unser Haus, wie's wurde", "Wie wir in unserem Haus lebten", "Was wir in Haus und Stadt erlebten", "Was wir in der Welt erlebten", "Wie wir in die Schule gingen und lernten", "Wie wir erzogen wurden—wie wir spielten in Haus und Hof", "Wie wir draußen spielten, an Strom und Strand". Some chapter headings are even less self-centred and point entirely in the direction of others: "Die Stadt, ihre Bewohner und ihre Honoratioren", "Die Schönebergs und die Scherenbergs", "Die Krauses". Occasionally, when the centre of gravity moves closer to the writer, Fontane uses an impersonal title, such as "Allerlei Gewölk" or "Das letzte Halbjahr". Never is a chapter heading prefaced by "ich", while the only example of the singular possessive adjective is at the top of the first chapter, "Meine Eltern", and this heralds the speedy direction of the reader's attention towards the parents rather than their eldest son.

Not only are the small-scale events of childhood and the persons in the immediate vicinity—parents, relations, friends, servants, teachers, townsfolk—introduced by the technique of the anecdote; major political events of the period, including international as well as national occurrences, are treated in similar fashion. The battle of Groß-Görschen, in which Fontane's father had taken part, survives in the mind of his son largely through the miraculous escape of his parent who received a French bullet in his army pack, which saved his life. Characteristically, the son also recalls with dry humour the emphasis placed by his father on the fact that it was a "Seitenschuß" during an attack and not from behind! Similarly the serious outbreak of cholera in eastern Europe during 1831 is seen principally in the context of some ludicrously inadequate measures taken by the Prussian authorities to close the frontiers and station troops at strategic points, such as sea-ports. This meant that Swinemünde received, first, a battalion of the Kaiser Franz Regiment (later to be Fontane's own regiment while a volunteer soldier, though typically he rejects the opportunity of seeing anything symbolic or prophetic in this coincidence), then an artillery unit. Both are recalled principally because of the amusing incidents with which they are associated and his vivid memory of the firing display of the latter, when cannon balls were bounced along the surface of the sea like a game of "ducks and drakes" played with a flat stone on a village pond. Two whole chapters are devoted to local families of note; the Schönebergs and Scherenbergs in one, followed by the Krauses in the next. In each case interest is centred on the members of these families in their own right as well as for the impression they made upon the young boy, and in each instance Fontane's account is liberally strewn with anecdotes, many of a humorous character, such as one might find in most of his novels, but more particularly the first, *Vor dem Sturm,* with its broad outlines and casual pace, and the last and most anecdotal of them all, *Der Stechlin.*

*Meine Kinderjahre* soon reveals a close relationship with more than just the novels. One is constantly reminded of an earlier phase of the novelist's development, namely his authorship of *Wanderungen durch die Mark Brandenburg,* the series of travel books which he wrote during the years between 1861 and 1881, and to which he added a further appendage as late as 1889, only three years before beginning his autobiography. These "Wanderungen" have been defined as a "combination of landscape painting and historical reminiscence, a blending of social and human studies with nature-poetry in prose, of general observation with personal experience". Much of this description could also be applied to Fon-

tane's depiction of his childhood years at Swinemünde. The impressionistic night-ride to Berlin in very early days at Neu-Ruppin and the morning arrival at the home of his grandparents already suggest similar affinities. The inspirational source of Fontane's joy and skill in sketching travel, countryside, houses, furnishings and the like becomes apparent when the reader reaches the description of the young boy's education at home in his early years. This was almost entirely in the hands of his father, whose interests were as one-sided as his pedagogic methods. Nevertheless, Fontane remarks, "so sonderbar diese Stunden waren, so hab ich doch mehr dabei gelernt als bei manchem berühmten Lehrer". It is difficult to say precisely whether history or geography bulked the larger in the young Fontane's arbitrary curriculum, for much of his father's instruction consisted of a blend of these two, his own favourite subjects. The geographical element tended to be punctuated with population statistics, with which Fontane *père* had a life-long obsession, but the history lessons came alive, thanks to the vast store of irrelevant stories possessed by the father, from whom his son inherited a similar propensity. One example, couched in vividly reconstructed dialogue, is the story of Latour d'Auvergne, "le premier grenadier de France", which was not only rehearsed verbally between Fontane and his father in accordance with the latter's "Socratic method", but was imprinted still more firmly on the child's mind by being treated as a miniature drama, in which each of them acted a part.

The descriptive passages of *Meine Kinderjahre* show the author to have been an impartial and accurate observer of both places and people, equally at home in delineating outdoor scenes in the town, around the harbour or in the surrounding countryside, and in providing vivid details of the furnishings, pictures, books and knick-knacks of people's homes, always with a keen eye for the objects that throw light on the personality of the owner. In nearly all his works of prose fiction, he makes the reader aware of background factors; he evokes atmosphere by placing unobtrusive stress on features that blend with, and sometimes influence, the mood of his characters. His skill is seen at its peak in three scenes from the young Fontane's last years in Swinemünde; the first deals with an escapade in the harbour one April morning in 1831, the second relates a near escape from drowning while out in a small boat during the autumn of that year, while the third evokes the dreams of glory that fill a boy's mind as he leads a troop of youngsters on adventure bound—his private army or band of robbers as occasion required.

A sharp ear for the kind of dialogue that lends spice to Fontane's novels had evidently been present from his earliest years. Conversations between father and son are here reproduced effortlessly, despite the lapse of sixty years, and it is clear that they are no mere acts of retrospective creation, for the exchanges have a ring of authenticity. Moreover the personalities of the two participants emerge clearly and are consistent with those revealed through family correspondence and other sources. The same flair for dialogue is evident in the recollection of dinner-parties and various social occasions during the Swinemünde period. Such scenes are utilized in his novels and *Novellen* as a framework for one of his most successful techniques, namely that of characterization through conversation. The reader forms a far more rounded impression of the elder Fontane from his own words than from the direct descriptions contained in the first two chapters. Accounts of the paternal "Socratic method" in action or the last conversation, which should have been a solemn occasion, before Theodor Fontane leaves the parental home, provide an admirable foil for the superb, even though, strictly speaking, irrelevant chapter entitled "Vierzig Jahre später", in which the picture of Louis Henri Fontane is completed in the perspective of old age. For, as his son observes, "wie er ganz zuletzt war, so war er eigentlich". In this "Intermezzo", as the author calls it, devoted entirely to a visit by the middle-aged son to his frail and elderly father, the autobiography reaches its climax. Throughout the work Fontane's father has been an influential figure, but in a very different sense from that described in Edmund Gosse's account of *Father and Son,* which he calls "the record of a struggle between two temperaments". This inserted chapter confirms Louis Henri Fontane's preeminence, and fortunately the autobiographical structure is not destroyed by its intrusion. In the crosscurrent of talk between father and son, just as much is revealed of the latter through the manner in which he treats the episode and the loving tenderness with which he recreates the last meeting with his old father. Throughout **Meine Kinderjahre** it is the father rather than the mother who receives the lion's share of the author's attention, for a closer bond of sympathy had always linked them. Neither parent is viewed exclusively from the emotional viewpoint of the child, and one senses that Fontane is attempting to offer a scrupulously just account. This is not only of importance viewed as sourcematerial for the student of Fontane, but, thanks to the care and skill which has been expended in the process, it is a literary achievement of no mean order. Traces of his father's personality, with its nervous bonhomie, can be discovered in a number of the novel characters, particularly in their style of relaxed, slightly daring conversation at social gatherings when ladies are present. The author was aware of this affinity, summing it up in these words: "Wenn ich entsprechende Szenen in meinen Romanen und kleinen Erzählungen lese, so ist es mir mitunter, als hörte ich meinen Vater sprechen." Vater Briest, Kommerzienrat von Treibel, Onkel Kurt Anton von Osten, van der Straaten and Dubslav von Stechlin are all beneficiaries to some considerable extent from the inheritance ultimately derived from Louis Henri Fontane.

One of the striking facts about the whole of this account of Fontane's childhood is its basic normality. It is not the story of an outsider or a misfit. Misunderstandings there certainly were, particularly with his more austere and rigid mother, whose admirable qualities of character and willpower in a marriage fraught with insecurity he only fully recognizes in later years and openly acknowledges in this work. It is not a mere coincidence that Fontane's women novel-characters are almost all stronger than their men-folk. But the overall pattern of this account of boyhood years is one of predominantly kind treatment, of normal friendships with his own age-group, of healthy games of adventure and typical boyish fantasies. All this is reflected in the pictures of childhood presented in the novels and *Novellen,* where the children generally make satisfactory contact with others, play the usual games of childhood, and learn to accept the rough with the smooth in their relationship with the adult world around them and on which they are for the time being dependent. (pp. 115-19)

Questions of style deserve consideration, both in the context of this work as an autobiography and in connection with its author's characteristic features as a novelist. Echoes from the novels and *Novellen* are unmistakable. There is, for a start, the same tendency throughout **Meine Kinderjahre** to indulge in digression, usually in the form of incidental anecdotes. Re-

peatedly the reader may glimpse Fontane pulling himself up with a jerk as he realizes that he has strayed away from the original topic—but the anecdote is too dear to him to be eliminated. So he adds a perfunctory apology, and leaves the 'offending' passage just where it was. These digressions are legion and the reader would, in many cases, share the author's reluctance to forego them. The whole of chapter 16 is an instance of what Fontane calls "ein Exkurs", but it is the crowning glory of the entire work. In it one may find outstanding examples of Fontane's art of 'characterization through conversation', as he champions his frail and elderly father, now fully aware of the magnitude of his youthful follies and weaknesses. He is seen living alone and in nearpoverty, still generous by inclination and as talkative as ever, tended only by a helper from the village of whom Fontane remarks that she "nach dem Satze lebte: 'Selig sind die Einfältigen', aber einen etwas weitgehenden Gebrauch davon machte." In an easy, flowing style the memories of those years with which the rest of **Meine Kinderjahre** deals are conjured up afresh and viewed in an atmosphere of critical examination mingled with gentle nostalgia, thus lending a new perspective to the autobiography as a whole. Basically the old man has not changed, but merely acquired insight into himself. Even his hunger for 'useful' statistics remains; as they open a bottle of red wine with their lunch he still cannot resist observing that Médoc had a population of about 1,400. But there are gentle undertones of sadness and decay, conveyed with a delicate mastery, hinting softly at the coming end. An acquaintance of Fontane's father during his Swinemünde days, the one who had so prided himself on his vintage Bordeaux, is apparently no more—"Ist nun auch schon zur großen Armee. Alles marschiert ab. . . . Na, ewig kann es nicht dauern." Like Effi Briest, at the end of her loneliness and suffering, the elder Fontane has achieved a deeper insight into the motives of others as well as of himself and pays the same sort of belated compliment to the wife, from whom he is now separated, as that paid by Effi to Innstetten: "Sie hat recht gehabt in allem, in ihren Worten und in ihrem Tun". Masterly, too, in its stylistic restraint is the brief and undramatic parting, despite its betrayal of fears on both sides that it might prove (as it did) to be the final one:

> "Nun lebe wohl, und laß dich noch mal sehen." Er
> sagte das mit bewegter Stimme,
> denn er hatte die Vorahnung, daß dies der Abschied sei.
> "Ich komme wieder, recht bald."
> Er nahm das grüne Käpsel ab und winkte.
> Und ich kam auch bald wieder.
> Es war in den ersten Oktobertagen, und oben auf
> dem Bergrücken, da, wo wir von
> "Poseidons Fichtenhain" gescherzt hatten, ruht er
> nun aus von Lebens Lust und Müh.

The ability to move the reader deeply and convey to him the intensity of unexpressed emotions is, of course, prominent in the prose-works of Fontane's maturity, one of the most memorable examples being the conclusion of chapter 15 in **Irrungen, Wirrungen,** where Lene and Botho part for ever, again without drama or pathos. The playing down of scenes of high emotion, whether of a pleasant or unpleasant kind, is as characteristic of his fiction as it is of this account of his own life. In **Meine Kinderjahre** there are instances of highly disagreeable childhood memories, involving elemental violence; there is the slaughter of the pig in chapter 2 and that of the geese in chapter 9. In neither case is the unpleasantness of the occasion glossed over, and the little that the reader is told is still sufficiently realistic to chill his blood, but Fontane does not linger over the details, preferring to indicate the situation in outline and leave the rest to the power of the human imagination. This technique of "playing down" emotional situations is not, of course, without its dangers. In several of the novels crucial events which represent a turning-point could easily be missed by readers not accustomed to Fontane's style (for example, the seduction of Effi Briest). The absence of intense emotions in *Meine Kinderjahre* forms a striking contrast with Dickens' childhood memories as expressed in *David Copperfield.*

Humour is a vital factor in Fontane's works, and this one is no exception. The author, with his "fehlendem Sinn für Feierlichkeit", could never take himself seriously for long, and his childhood autobiography bubbles with exuberant good humour, directed both at himself and at others. Although written at a time of illness and depression, *Meine Kinderjahre* does not reflect Boethius' view that "there is no greater sorrow than to remember past happiness in days of adversity"—rather the opposite, in fact. Surviving the long passage of the intervening years, the memory of his father's attempts to impress the local "Honoratioren" with his home-made pronunciation of "Lon-DON-derry" ("er erzeugte dadurch eine vollkommene Donnerwirkung"), can still amuse him at seventy-three, as can the incident when Louis Henri Fontane fell victim to the jokes of the Swinemünde "Ressource" and was fully convinced, after a ceremony of grotesque hocus-pocus, that he had been admitted to the ancient craft of Freemasonry! His father's open-handed hospitality, especially at dinners and social evenings, reminded him of the feast of Belshazzar, "insoweit als eine Geisterhand schon den Bankrott des Gastgebers an die Wand schrieb".

By contrast, certain expectations, which could arise if one were to read the autobiography before the works of prose fiction, are not fulfilled in the latter. One might anticipate, for instance, that a writer with such a pronounced French Huguenot background would express this in a variety of ways in his novels and *Novellen,* since it is so emphatically stressed in *Meine Kinderjahre.* Here Fontane has traced his ancestry at length in the first two chapters, taking it back to the original spelling of the family name as "Fontanes". French Christian names predominate until the writer's own generation, when he, too—a fact seldom quoted—was given the first name of "Henri" (which he never used) before the more familiar "Theodor". Thereafter the practice appears to have lapsed. It might therefore have been expected that France and French themes, French characters and French history would play a large part in the novels of a man who had sprung from what, until his generation, had been a very closely-knit French Protestant community in Berlin. But this does not occur, and Theodor Fontane is remembered above all as the poet and novelist of Brandenburg-Prussia, while the most obvious non-German influence on his way of thinking is that of Britain, not France. A few idiosyncrasies, perhaps, in the choice of names for his characters—St. Arnaud, Cécile, Victoire, for instance, may be attributed to the Gallic influences recorded with such detail in his childhood story; in his style, the cool scepticism and detached observation of the society around him may equally well have been a residue of Huguenot settler attitudes, of the 'outsider' in an alien land. These and similar possibilities nonetheless remain a mere drop in the ocean of Fontane's close identification with the Prussia about which he wrote his whole life long in verse and prose and of which he felt himself to be such an integral part.

Another cause for surprise, on reading *Meine Kinderjahre,* is that the influence of his parental and home background is not more strongly in evidence in his creative works than is the case. It has been conceded (even by the author) that his father, particularly in his more expansive moods, has left his mark on a number of the older male characters. One might, if so determined, find traces of his mother's sense of "Representation" in Frau Jenny Treibel as well as her strength of character in so many of his females. Again, in the schoolmaster and clergyman figures of the novel-world echoes may be found of people he met as a child, but one never has the impression that they are ghosts of the past to be exorcized, as one so often does in the case of Dickens.

What is one to make of this account of childhood and how may one evaluate its literary status? Is it, in fact, as it claims to be by virtue of its sub-title, "an autobiographical novel", or is it genuine autobiography? The writer himself helps to dispose of several difficulties in his brief but valuable Foreword, which, in its combination of playful ambiguity and disarming frankness, is so typical of Fontane. Recognizing his weakness for "Anekdotisches" and leisurely "Kleinmalerei", he realized at once that he would have to restrict himself to a limited period of his life. For this purpose he found his childhood years the most suitable and, in a sense, the most logical choice: "to begin with the beginning", as he puts it in one of those recurrent English phrases to be found throughout his writing. Another reason for this choice was an extension of the theory that "the child is father to the man"; he feels that the depiction of his boyhood years might well serve as a symbolical account of his whole life. There was also a secondary intention, namely that of portraying in miniature a bygone era as it was experienced in a small coastal resort on the Baltic during the early decades of the nineteenth century by one family from the French "Kolonie" in Berlin which had made its home there from 1827. The preface concludes with a characteristic Fontane paradox: everything is drawn from life, we are told, but, for the benefit of those liable to quibble about the precise veracity of this or that detail, the work is to be entitled an "autobiographical novel". For such people it may rank as "Dichtung", but Fontane's intention was clearly to offer the reader "Wahrheit".

The years of childhood are presented in chronological order and, despite a tendency towards an episodic approach, the complete work has a structural unity. The appeal to the present-day reader may vary from the intense interest aroused by the father-son relationship and its analysis to relative indifference towards the chapters on the Scherenbergs and Schönebergs, which really belong in style and content to the world of his *Wanderungen durch die Mark Brandenburg.* Perhaps its principal appeal lies in its spontaneity and freshness when describing the interaction of environment and the growing personality, and this is enhanced by an unselfconscious modesty, so typical of the author. Continual preoccupation with how he appears before the world can blunt a man's recollections of how the world then appeared to him. This danger Fontane has instinctively avoided.

A historian will probably turn to an autobiography in order to measure the repercussion of major events on the average man of reasonable education and intelligence. The literary critic, on the other hand, will sift it carefully for clues as to the author's personality which may provide a key to the better understanding of his works. The ordinary reader, however, merely peruses the work for the sake of enjoyment—and that, surely, is its ultimate justification. How far, then, does Fontane's **Meine Kinderjahre** measure up to such expectations? It offers none of the piquancy of a Byronic life-style or the revelations of a famous political figure, but it avoids the ever-present pitfalls of the self-centred writer or public man who insists on believing that his life must be as fascinating to the rest of the world as to himself. Some autobiographies may, it is true, be more eventful, others may have more universal literary merit, but Fontane's, with its warmth, humour and humanity, may fairly claim to be a monument to one who possessed, like his own creation, Dubslav von Stechlin, "das was immer gilt und gelten wird: ein Herz". (pp. 120-24)

*A. R. Robinson, "Recollections in Tranquillity: An Examination of Fontane's 'Autobiographical Novel'," in "Erfahrung und Überlieferung": Festschrift for C. P. Magill, edited by Hinrich Siefken and Alan Robinson, The University of Wales Press, 1974, pp. 113-25.*

## DAVID TURNER (essay date 1978)

[*In the following excerpt, Turner examines how Fontane handled his source materials for* Effi Briest, *showing how he shaped a sensationalistic, excessively romantic story into a psychologically intricate novel.*]

In **Effi Briest,** one of his last novels and published in 1895, Fontane followed a practice he had adopted before in basing his novel on an event from the 'chronique scandaleuse', as told him by the wife of the editor of the *Vossische Zeitung.* Remarkably enough, only a year later, in 1896, the same event was used as the basis of another novel, *Zum Zeitvertreib,* by Friedrich Spielhagen, a writer of society novels, known to Fontane, a man in fact with whom he corresponded about the writing of **Effi Briest.** Direct comparisons between the two novels are tempting, but must be treated with care, since it is unlikely that both writers had equal access to the same information. (We know, for example, that Spielhagen was well enough acquainted with the original 'Effi' to be in correspondence with her.) Nevertheless a few simple points of contrast may be made here, which lead into the important question of treatment. While Fontane's interest is concentrated on the heroine, depicted as little more than a child who after only a few years of marriage drifts into an adulterous affair, Spielhagen makes his heroine a 'femme fatale' and then lays the greater stress on her unfortunate lover, a schoolmaster, who is ruined by the affair. Spielhagen also extracts the maximum of melodrama from his material: the lovers' embrace coincides with the sudden illness of one of the schoolmaster's children; the lovers are trailed by detectives and caught *in flagrante delicto;* and after the duel, in which desire for personal revenge is a strong motive in the wronged husband, the dead schoolmaster's widow physically assaults the heroine who has robbed her of her husband. Fontane, by contrast, with his customary distaste for sensationalism, keeps the emotional temperature cool throughout. Indeed, it is possible to argue that, in a similar way to George Eliot in aspects of *Middlemarch,* Howells in *The Rise of Silas Lapham,* and Galdós in *Fortunata and Jacinta,* he has written his novel *against* the implied pattern of the popular romance or the cheap novel, just as he also did in his earlier masterpiece *A Suitable Match* (*Irrungen, Wirrungen*), where the unfortunate lovers, separated by insuperable class barriers, contemplate in turn the extremes of elopement and suicide, only in the end to reject both and opt for a modicum of happiness in

basically loveless marriages with partners from their own class. Given the basic ingredients of Fontane's source, what may loosely be called the 'romantic' recipe for **Effi Briest** might read something like this:

A beautiful young heroine is forced by tyrannical parents into marriage with a much older man, who soon proves to be a monster. On the arrival of a handsome young officer she falls passionately in love and forms a liaison with him. The affair is discovered by the husband, who takes his revenge by shooting the lover in a duel and banishing his wife, whereupon she falls into deep remorse and spends her remaining years in a convent, while he leaves everything behind and goes off to Africa.

If that should appear an unnecessarily crude and meretricious invention, it is worth recalling that it is probably not so far removed from the sort of novel read by Flaubert's Emma before her marriage. And for that very reason it is a useful means of illustrating how Fontane circumvents the popular clichés, and in such a way as to underline some of the fundamental practices of the Realist novel.

In the first place, Effi's parents are not tyrannical and do not force her into marriage. There is much less blatant compulsion than, for example, Verga depicts in the marriage to which Isabella must submit in *Mastro-Don Gesualdo.* Instead the Briests apply more insidious, though still powerful *social* pressure to a daughter who is still only a child, appealing particularly to her ambition: she will be married before any of her schoolfriends and will therefore be one rung ahead on the climb up the social ladder. Although Effi herself has been sufficiently inculcated with the social attitudes of her parents to accept their view without protest, it is quite clear that there is no personal desire or fulfilment involved. When questioned by her friends about her feelings as a newly-betrothed young woman, she can answer only in the impersonal voice of one who reacts as society expects her to react:

'Is he really Mr. Right?'

'Of course he is. You don't understand, Herta. *Anyone* is Mr. Right. Of course, he's got to have a title and a situation in society and look presentable.'

'And so you're really happy already?'

'When *someone's* been engaged for two hours, *they're* always really happy.'

Effi's marriage to Innstetten, especially its inauspicious start as they tour the cultural shrines of Italy, may remind us of Dorothea's marriage to Casaubon in *Middlemarch.* Yet the similarity is only superficial. For while Dorothea resists the social pressures, which are all against this particular union, and pursues her own ideal in the footsteps of St. Theresa, Effi, on the other hand, emerges as the consenting victim of a social ritual.

Second, Innstetten is no monster. And in his correspondence Fontane had several times to defend him against what he saw as unjust or exaggerated attacks, especially from his female readers. True, like his Tolstoyan counterpart, Karenin, Innstetten is a man of ambition, character, and strict principle and has something of the punctilious schoolmaster about him. Yet Fontane is also careful to portray him as a good master of his servants, to distinguish him from the more reactionary and chauvinistic gentry who seem to dominate life in the neighbourhood of his Pomeranian home, to show him in acts of consideration for Effi, even moments of genuine longing for her return when she is away. The trouble is that he cannot express emotion without embarrassment, reserve, or the fear of somehow damaging his career. It is characteristic of him that he has to be prompted to kiss his wife. The fairest assessment of Innstetten is provided by Effi near the end of the novel in words which are spoken in a spirit of reconciliation, but which nevertheless imply an inescapable indictment: 'He had a great deal of good in his nature and was as fine a man as any one can be who doesn't really love.'

Third, Effi does not fall desperately in love with Major Crampas, but drifts into the affair without real love, more out of dissatisfaction with her marriage, desire for adventure, and, perhaps also, the provocative attraction of a man who is the very opposite of her husband. She knows nothing of that unique passion which so powerfully and repeatedly asserts itself in the adultery of Galdós's Fortunata. And Crampas himself, though something of a ladies' man, is nevertheless older than Innstetten, already married, and is physically deformed as a result of an earlier duel. Altogether it is difficult to visualize him as the dashing young hero.

Fourth and most notable of all, since it represents a significant adaptation of his source, Fontane has introduced a gap of some six years between the adultery and its discovery. A move from the Baltic resort of Kessin to Berlin has provided Effi with a means of breaking off the affair, to the relief of both Crampas and herself; she has put the affair behind her and begun a new life together with Innstetten in the more lively and interesting capital city. These six years of new life not only indicate that, given the appropriate circumstances, her marriage might yet have succeeded tolerably well; they also mean that when Innstetten discovers the tell-tale letters, there can be absolutely no question of jealousy or revenge; indeed he openly admits that he still loves his wife. Instead the duel is fought largely in deference to an abstract principle (honour) embodied in the collective attitude of an abstract entity (society), which ultimately proves stronger than personal desire, stronger too than that other important consideration in the novel, the healing effect of time.

Fifth, as to the question of penitence, the feelings that come closest to this in the heroine are not activated by her banishment, but pre-date the discovery by almost the full six years. They are not, moreover, penitential and lack a truly religious dimension. In a rare, extended passage of psychological analysis the heroine looks back over her affair, but discovers no deep-seated sense of guilt, only the fear of being found out and shame at the pretence she has been forced to keep up. Indeed it is her very lack of a sense of guilt that causes her greatest sorrow, for if all women are like that, it is bad for the world, yet if others feel differently, then she alone is bad. As far as Innstetten's final gesture is concerned, the mention of an escape to Africa is not part of my invention. He does contemplate precisely that, late in the novel, when promotion has come but he is no longer in a position to enjoy it. Yet the important and characteristic point is that this essentially romantic notion is soon set aside; he follows the advice of his friend and stays at his post, content to accept what little happiness comes his way.

At every turn, therefore, Fontane disappoints any 'romantic' expectations the reader might have and presents a more truthful picture of human behaviour. If it is argued that, compared with other great novels, *Effi Briest* is a work lacking in passion, the point may readily be conceded as long as it is

not taken to imply a criticism. Effi marries and commits adultery. Innstetten banishes his wife and shoots her lover—all without passion. yet this is precisely Fontane's insight as a Realist: that in a society such as that of the late nineteenth century in Germany it requires no overwhelming passion to cause great suffering and wreck the lives of individuals—and that includes Innstetten as well as Effi and Crampas. For it is one of the bitterest ironies of the novel that the highest point of his career in social terms—his decoration with the order of the Red Eagle—coincides with his lowest moral and spiritual ebb, the time when he sees his own life as a 'mess', his ambition as folly, society as 'fiddle-faddle', that is to say, when he rejects all that has motivated his action and behaviour hitherto.

In spite of the middle-class orientation of German Realism in general, in spite also of Fontane's own middle-class origins, he tended to draw the characters of his novels mainly from the lower ranks of the nobility, less frequently from the middle classes, and almost never from the working classes. From the social and political point of view he came to regard the Prussian *Junkers* as anachronistic, conceited, and unbearable, but his aesthetic judgement nevertheless pronounced them rewarding material for literary treatment. The main characters of *Effi Briest* are also members of the gentry. Yet for all that they are quite unexceptional and remain completely within our intellectual and sympathetic grasp. Whatever the social background, Fontane's literary preferences lay always with the average man and woman in ordinary situations; and that meant a denial not only of Romantic excesses, but also of the Naturalist excesses he detected in the more degenerate characters of Zola and his German imitator, Max Kretzer, the sort of excesses which, according to Georg Lukács, may be interesting clinically, but lack social typicality.

Representativeness is easier to assert than to prove. And in the case of a novel like *Effi Briest* the sceptical scientific mind would probably require statistics showing the incidence of adultery, divorce, and duelling among the Prussian gentry in the last quarter of the nineteenth century before pronouncing judgement. The literary commentator may nevertheless be forgiven for presuming to argue, without statistics, that Fontane has here written much more than an individual history. In the first place, although the particulars of the novel have to do with adultery, divorce, and duelling, these in their turn raise much wider social issues: the power of convention and taboo, the possibility of individual freedom, the conflict between the natural self and the public persona, the relationship between the sexes and between parents and children. And in the second place, the reaction of Fontane's reading public is evidence that, especially in the depiction of his female characters, he frequently touched a raw nerve. After the publication of *Effi Briest* he had every reason to be alarmed, as he once confessed to being, at the prospect that the original of his heroine might one day pick up the novel and find her own story recorded there; and yet he could also with equal justice describe the whole thing as 'a story of adultery no different from a hundred others'. (pp. 236-41)

If one may describe this work as a social novel, it is in the double sense that it both portrays the day-to-day life of a given social class and casts a critical eye on some of its fundamental weaknesses. On the one hand, therefore, Fontane is content to operate within the conventions of the 'fashionable novel' and reflect the social habits of his day—the pastimes of the gentry, their obligatory dinnerparties, amateur theatricals and musical evenings; the ladies' visits to the watering places and their shopping expeditions to the capital; the treatment of servants, and so forth. His more critical scrutiny, on the other hand, is directed towards the social problems associated with love, sex, and marriage.

Notice particularly how important stages in Effi's fate as a woman are marked and influenced by social attitudes and pressures. From the conversation between the four schoolgirl friends in the opening chapter it is clear that in their world marriage is regarded as the highest aim in life; not to marry is a disgrace. That is why Effi's sudden engagement is not really a surprise and why, incidentally, for much of the rest of the novel her friend Hulda has to maintain the (for the reader) comic pretence that she has a man in the offing, while her mother can barely conceal her annoyance with Effi. Marriage is the subject of a competition, and Effi has won.

After the heroine's marriage and move to Kessin her boredom and dissatisfaction have their roots largely in social causes: the necessity for people in their position to visit the local gentry in all their narrowminded provincialism, and the absences of Innstetten, who, with his concern to make a successful career, cannot refuse invitations to go and see Bismarck. Similarly, it is official duties which, although they lead to promotion, also prevent him from accompanying his wife and Crampas on their horse-rides and so help to throw them closer together.

These causes of unrest Effi voices or at least is aware of. What she does not complain about, presumably because it is accepted as a matter of course in her society, is the way in which the wife is regarded as an extension of, even appendage to the male: the way in which Innstetten sees her as a means of gaining popular support for his election victory or is concerned about the favourable impression she will make at the Ministry in Berlin. And one may interpose that her very silence on this point, together with the fact that she drifts into a liaison, makes it difficult to consider her adultery as an expression of revolt against a patriarchal society in the manner of other novels of adultery.

After the end of the affair and the move to Berlin, why is Effi away from home when Annie has her accident and the letters are discovered in the search for bandages? She is taking a cure to overcome her temporary infertility so that she can provide Innstetten with a male heir. And why does he not accompany her? He is too busy at the office. Finally, after the divorce, why do her parents refuse for so long to receive her back home? Because, writes Effi's mother, that would cut them off from society and they must nail their colours to the mast, that is to say, show the condemnation of her act that society demands. In this unhappy state of ostracism the only ones to show genuine humanity and to give natural expression to their affection for Effi—and it is difficult to see this as anything but a judgement on the society of the day—are her clumsy, plebeian maid, Roswitha, and the dog Rollo.

In the long, important dialogue with his colleague Wüllersdorf that precedes the duel Innstetten says, 'There's no hatred or anything of that sort and I don't want to have blood on my hands merely for the sake of the happiness I've been deprived of, but the *something* which forms society—call it a tyrant if you like—is not concerned with charm or love, or even with how long ago a thing took place. I've no choice, I must do it.' Innstetten's formulation smacks of the more extreme scientific determinism we normally associate with Naturalism, suggesting a conception of man as a creature deprived of free moral choices and subject instead to the influences of his environment. And the whole weight of these influences seems almost to operate like Fate—Atropos in nineteenth-century dress, so to speak. For the debate on the necessity of the duel, which takes in Crampas as well as Innstetten and Wüllersdorf, is framed by the two phrases 'Is it necessary?' and 'It's got to be done,' which in the original German not only answer each other directly, but already possess fatalistic overtones from their use by Beethoven as a motto over the finale of his last string quartet: 'Muss es sein?—Es muss sein.' Taken as a whole, however, the novel speaks with a rather less deterministic, let alone fatalistic voice. The strength of social pressures is clearly exposed, but so also is the often active support they receive from the individual, including Effi herself, who is second only to Innstetten in her ambition. At one point or another most of the characters perceive the folly and fallibility of the social code, and yet they continue to live *as if* they still believed in it. As Wüllersdorf puts it, speaking what might almost be the motto of this society, 'All that high-falutin' talk about "God's judgement" is nonsense, of course, and we don't want any of that, yet our own cult of honour on the other hand is idolatry. But we must submit to it, as long as the idol stands.' What is remarkable here is not only that traditional religious values have been replaced by social factors, but that these receive almost religious veneration even while their vanity is openly acknowledged.

Although the novel therefore acknowledges the importance of external pressures, it does not absolve the characters of blame, ignore their personal guilt: the homage paid by Innstetten to honour rather than affection, for example; his failure to tell Effi of the possibility of his promotion and move to Berlin (which might so easily have saved her from involvement with Crampas); or his excessive pedagogical impulse, revealed most tellingly in that scene where his young daughter is permitted to visit her divorced mother, but can only parrot the words 'Oh yes, if I *may*' (my emphasis); the ambition and lack of resolve in Effi herself; or her parents' promotion of what can scarcely fail to prove a misalliance; their inability to act at decisive moments; their emphasis on conformity and appearances rather than parental affection.

In this world of social reality, of ordinary people and unremarkable events, one thing in particular seems to stand apart from the rest. This is the Chinaman, the ghost that haunts the Innstettens' house at Kessin. J. P. Stern rather disparagingly calls it 'a piece of bric-a-brac left over by poetic Realism.' [see Further Reading] Yet Fontane himself regarded it as crucial to the whole novel. Certainly, it introduces an element of unresolved mystery, but it also acquires an important function on the level of the social, moral, and psychological lives of the characters. Innstetten uses it as a pedagogical weapon to keep his wife on the straight and narrow and also as a status symbol to enhance the interest and reputation of his house—without, however, committing himself as to the actual existence of the ghost. For Effi, on the other hand, it becomes an expression, sometimes even a projection, of her conscience and as such pursues her even after the move to Berlin.

In matters of narrative method Fontane always displayed a keen awareness of the need for accuracy of setting in the widest sense. 'I haven't the effrontery just to write things down without caring whether they are right or not', he wrote to his wife in 1885. Consequently we find many topical references to important political events and personalities; to well-known cultural, religious, and scientific figures of the time; to the popular as well as the serious newspapers. Effi's mother pays a visit to a named eye-specialist of the day; when Effi herself goes on a cure, Fontane sends her to the right spa for her complaints; and of course, as a former dispensing chemist himself, he gives full and accurate details of the medicines prescribed for her by Dr. Rummschüttel.

The locations are of two kinds, the fictional and the real; and it is interesting to observe how the author's method differs accordingly. Effi's home, the manor-house at Hohen-Cremmen, is entirely fictional and so is created by the author in a lengthy and detailed description at the very beginning of the novel, a description whose solidity and homogeneity reflect something of the stable world from which his heroine is soon to be snatched away. Kessin, the Innstetten's home on the Baltic, is also fictional, although here Fontane has borrowed details from the town of Swinemünde, where he lived as a boy. This setting too—town, house, and surrounding countryside—has to be created by description, although his method this time is to reveal the details piecemeal, as the heroine gets to know more of the place. When it comes to the third important location, Berlin, the author is of course faced with a different problem. To most of his readers it is a known quantity. Consequently, though in the sharpest contrast with Flaubert's treatment of the equivalent problem in his *Sentimental Education,* he virtually foregoes all description and contents himself with simply naming streets and districts, parks and public buildings, shops and restaurants, and leaves his readers to complete the mental picture.

In the matter of dialogue just as much as location Fontane was interested in accuracy. Indeed it is generally agreed that he was the first true master of natural dialogue in the German novel. Yet, much as one may admire his ability to use speech as a means of bringing his characters to life, of differentiating them as individuals or members of a particular social class, it must be stressed that this was achieved not by strict phonographic reproduction, but by a mixture of a keen ear and sheer artistry. (pp. 242-46)

*Effi Briest* is a highly organized work of art, which excludes extraneous matter and makes even the most trivial occurrences relate to the central issues. Consider, by way of example, such structural niceties as the way in which the opening chapter contains the germ of the whole novel, with its picture of the tomboy Effi and her love of danger, its anticipation of her fate in the solemn game with the gooseberry skins and the oriental tale of marital infidelity and its dire consequences; the way in which the novel returns to the opening scene at the very end, though with subtle, eloquent differences; the way in which the various settings are used to mark the different phases of Effi's life—the security of home and childhood at Hohen-Cremmen, the desert of married life at Kessin, the shattered hope of a new beginning in Berlin (even the locations seem fragmented in this phase), and the final return to home and a transfigured innocence back in Hohen-Cremmen; the way in which leitmotifs—Effi's striped linen smock, her swing, the plane trees in the garden—are used to link important parts of the novel. Two verbal leitmotifs, however, call for particular comment. The first is the catchphrase associated throughout with Effi's father, 'That is too big a subject' (*'Das ist ein zu weites Feld'*), which has since achieved proverbial status in the German language. It is more than a mere

comic device; it is an expression, on the positive side, of his dislike of hasty, stereotyped, or absolute judgements and, on the negative side, of his inability to act as an individual and his unwillingness to take responsibility—the latter characteristics being important contributory factors in the fate that befalls his daughter. The catch-phrase is significantly absent during the conversation leading up to his decision to call his sick daughter home again, the one point where his supposed independence is put into practice, but it returns once more, a sad reflection on his basic incorrigibility, to round off the entire novel at the very end. The second verbal leitmotif will be completely hidden to readers of the present English version. It is contained in the words that Effi's exuberant friends call to her through the open window at the end of Chapter II, on the day of her engagement, the words which leave such a strong impression on Innstetten's somewhat superstitious mind, yet do not prevent him from going through with the marriage. In the original the identical words ('Effi, komm') are used as the simple message which Briest belatedly telegraphs to his daughter to call her home to Hohen-Cremmen before her death. A better translation to cover both occasions would, I believe, have been 'Come back, Effi'. For on both appearances the phrase is meant to convey the appeal (in the literal and figurative sense) of childhood and home. And we can be sure that the echo was important to Fontane, because he once reported that, as he listened to the story of the original 'Effi', it was the occurrence of this very phrase that first made him resolve to write the novel. (pp. 247-49)

Fontane's first novel, *Vor dem Sturm,* was written under the general stylistic influence of novelists such as Thackeray, Dickens, Scott, and Scott's German follower, Willibald Alexis, writers who were not averse to letting their presence be felt or to making observations behind the backs of their characters. When therefore Fontane saw a review of his novel by a supporter of Spielhagen, who attacked 'the direct appeals to the reader, which jeopardize the poetic illusion', he responded in a letter to his publisher with the words 'sheer nonsense' and enlisted the best English novelists in his defence. None the less his subsequent practice did undergo a change, especially in his novels of modern society. In these works, which also of course include *Effi Briest,* he usually kept his presence as narrator very much in the background and let the story tell itself as much as possible. In later years too, in his correspondence with Spielhagen, he gave general approval to the latter's theory, always, however—in his characteristic manner—reserving the right to make exceptions, leaving a loophole open:

> The intrusion of the narrator is nearly always a bad thing, or at least superfluous. And what is superfluous is wrong. At the same time it won't always be easy to determine where the intrusion begins; the writer in his capacity as writer must after all do and say a great deal, otherwise it won't work, or will be artificial. The only thing is he must avoid making judgements, delivering sermons, trying to be wise and clever.

What we find in *Effi Briest* therefore is a fairly complete withdrawal of the narrator as a discernible personality. He describes locations and events, even summarizes occasionally. For the rest Fontane relies very much on dialogue as a means of narrating events or commenting on them and, more especially, as a means of characterization. He is also able very often to depend on his skill at distinguishing his characters by their manner of speech in order to avoid those editorial allocations 'he said', 'she replied', and so forth. Only very rarely is this pattern of non-intrusion broken, and the effect is inevitably one of surprise. In Chapter XXXII, for example, Fontane rather affectedly asks the rhetorical question, 'Was Roswitha with Effi, then?' in order to introduce a brief flashback of recent happenings. And, perhaps most remarkable of all, near the very end he permits himself a sympathetic sigh: 'Poor Effi, you spent too long looking up at the marvels of the heavens and thinking about them and in the end the night air and the mists rising from the pond stretched her once more on a bed of sickness.'

Although Fontane has virtually renounced the possibility of commenting himself on the events of the novel and the problems facing the characters, *Effi Briest* is by no means without implied comment, even criticism. In the first place, he seems to anticipate some of those many questions which naturally arise from time to time in the reader's mind about the course of the heroine's life as a woman. Would she have done better to resist the general pattern of marriage and choose another role in society? If Innstetten had kept her informed about the move to Berlin and she had never become involved with Crampas, or if her letters had not accidentally been discovered, what would have been the future of her marriage? Would her fate have been worse, or even different, if she had belonged to a different social class? But the answers Fontane provides are not to be found in any overt statements; they are implied rather in those other female portraits of the novel, which together form a series of variations on the theme of woman's role in society.

Effi's own mother is present from the start as an example of the social norm, the woman who has married not for love, but for the security offered by an older man, and who now lives out her life in a prosaic, unremarkable, but tolerably happy marriage, which is essentially the sort of marriage that the heroine's might have become if those letters had not been discovered. In Sidonie von Grasenabb Fontane presents a picture of the unlovely and unloving spinster, who lives out her days in narrow-minded, malicious bigotry. This alternative to the customary marriage, which is perhaps also a warning of the fate that awaits Hulda Niemeyer, is clearly more disagreeable than the prose of marriage. Frau Zwicker, the widow who accompanies Effi on her visit to the spa, exemplifies the woman who is now freed from the constraints of marriage and so can afford to be liberal in her ideas, for example in sexual matters (she is the one who reads Zola's *Nana*); but she has little moral substance and is in any case an exceptional character. This last point also applies to the figure of Mme Tripelli (*alias* Trippel), the daughter of a free-thinking Lutheran clergyman, an emancipated woman and a singer, now associating with a Russian prince. She has a blunt, self-assured manner and brings a welcome breath of fresh air into the novel. But she is acceptable only because she is an exception. She does not represent a role in society that could work for more than a few women. Indeed it is one of the paradoxes of Mme Tripelli that, although she can afford to be a free-thinking individual, she supports strict religious orthodoxy in public matters. In other words, it is permissible for the individual to follow this course by way of exception, but it will not work for society as a complex whole. Among the lower classes the most important variation is provided of course by the story of Roswitha, not only because of the interest it arouses in Effi herself, but because it presents another version of the rejection that follows adultery and its discovery. Here it takes the form of a physical assault with a red-hot iron by her blacksmith-father. But who is to say it is ultimately more cruel than the social ostracism, the spiritual and emotional isolation, imposed by Innstetten and Effi's parents?

In addition to this variation technique Fontane makes skilful use of leitmotifs and symbols, of structural elements altogether in fact, to make his point. Consequently it is never sufficient simply to make the structurally interesting point that he has introduced into Effi's life at Kessin three important male characters, her husband, Major Crampas, and the eccentric, deformed apothecary, Gieshübler. His purpose is to make us aware of his heroine's various needs, which fail to find satisfaction in her marriage. Innstetten answers to her ambition, but is too reserved and too busy; Crampas answers to her love of danger and adventure, but is untrustworthy; and Gieshübler answers to her need for affection and loving consideration, but would be ridiculous if considered as a lover and a social embarrassment if considered as a husband. Again, it is possible to show that Fontane has punctuated his narrative at important phases by reflective dialogues between Effi's parents—one on the day after her marriage, one after a visit of Effi, following the move to Berlin and the break with Crampas, one at the very end after her death. But in that repeated preposition 'after' lies the clue to Fontane's implied criticism. For it is characteristic of the Briests that they are wise *after* the event and fail to act at the right moment. Even the title of the novel is more than merely a reference to the central character. After all, Effi is married in only the fifth out of thirty-six chapters and so for the greater part of the novel is Frau von Innstetten. In the two other nineteenth-century novels that are sometimes compared with this, *Anna Karenina* and *Madame Bovary,* the authors have chosen either the heroine's married name or, with added detachment, her social appellation as a married woman. Fontane, on the other hand, wishes to remind us in his title—as he also does by the cyclical structure of the novel and the simple inscription on his heroine's gravestone—that she was little more than a child who ought not to have been transplanted so young from her native soil at Hohen-Cremmen.

By now it will perhaps be apparent that Fontane's characteristic mode of narration entails not only withdrawal, but also much oblique statement, the use of hints. Since it is a method which relies very much on the attentive, imaginative cooperation of the reader, things can go wrong—and on one notorious occasion did go wrong in a rather elementary matter. Not long after the publication of the novel Fontane received a letter from a puzzled lady reader, inquiring whether adultery had actually taken place. In his reply he could not of course point to a particular spot in the narrative; all he could do was to draw her attention to some of the subsequent details that *implied* the adultery.

Clearly we have here a reflection of the prudery of the times—and the novel provides its own humorous gloss on this prudery in the little incident where Effi's maid, Roswitha, sent to the lending library to borrow books for her mistress, deletes one title from the list on her own initiative, because it includes the word 'trousers.' At the same time it must be remembered that Fontane himself, though by no means a prude, preferred discretion in his novels, not only in sexual matters. Note, for example, the brevity, the understatement of his account of the duel; contrast the elegiac quietness of Effi's death, not actually narrated but reported retrospectively, with the explicit and detailed horror of Emma Bovary's death. Fontane also refrained from prying too closely or too often into the minds of his characters, choosing much of the time to externalize their mental state or to reveal it by means of gesture and speech—the manner of their speech, the things they avoid saying as well as those they do say.

Outstanding instances of externalization are the way in which the heroine's moral and spiritual uncertainty, insidiously undermined by the advances of Crampas, is projected in the image of the Slough, the quicksand through which she must pass in Chapter XXII, and the way in which her renunciation of all participation in life and society and her melancholy reflection on the fleeting association with Crampas are evoked by the picture of her near the end of the novel, as she sits watching the trains pass by and observes 'two plumes of smoke which merged with each other for a moment and then went off separately again to left and right.' As far as the relation between psychology and dialogue is concerned, one must keep in mind one of the shrewdest comments that Frau von Briest makes about her daughter: 'She certainly feels the need to talk now and again but she doesn't feel the need to empty her heart out, and she keeps a lot to herself; she's informative and discreet at the same time, almost secretive.' For an important consequence of this is that the reader must be acutely attentive to the nuances of her speech, to the many unwitting half-revelations: to that illogical but all too understandable request for a fur-coat, for example, which lights up like a flash her subconscious dread of marriage away from home; to those confused expressions of uncertainty at the amateur theatricals directed by Crampas, which betray her fear of his insidious influence on her marital fidelity; to her passionate concern at the plight of some shipwrecked sailors and her excessive relief at their rescue, which give us a brief glimpse of her own anguished sense of moral danger; to the rebuke she gives Roswitha for dallying with the coachman, which is in reality a warning to herself; or to her almost morbid interest in the detailed life-story of her maid, Roswitha, precisely because it mirrors her own painful situation. All of this is part of Fontane's characteristic art of suggestion.

J. P. Stern sees the perennial mode of realism as one of balance, as a middle course between extremes; and J. M. Ritchie describes German Realism in terms of ambivalence. The Realism of *Effi Briest* possesses something of both these qualities. It pays due homage to the given facts of the world and strives for accuracy in their presentation, but it also imposes its own structure and order; its author does not intrude his own personality, yet he is able to make his attitudes felt by less overt means; its subject-matter verges on the sensational, but the treatment is entirely unsensational; it portrays individual fates and at the same time manages to suggest a wide social reality; it presents characters whose attitudes and behaviour are very much influenced by the collective ethos of their environment, but it also reveals their individual responsibility.

The total result of this for the reader, besides aesthetic pleasure, may be a more sympathetic understanding of the human condition, an intensity, even clarity of vision; yet it is also likely to entail some uncertainty of response. The society Fontane portrays is clearly unsatisfactory; its standards are hollow, its conventions are rigid and lifeless and help to cause considerable suffering. 'Would it therefore be better', the reader may well wonder, 'to escape altogether or to fly directly in the teeth of society?' The answer which the novel, through its characters, seems to give is a resigned 'No!'. The advice, as we have seen, is rather to stay where you are and accept what little happiness life may afford you. What, then, is the reader to make of these characters? Are they the only conceivable heroes of such a world? Or are they perhaps just fools?

That is *too* big a subject. (pp. 249-55)

> David Turner, "Theodore Fontane: 'Effi Briest'
> (1895)," in The Monster in the Mirror: Studies in
> Nineteenth-Century Realism, edited by D. A. Wil-
> liams, Oxford University Press, 1978, pp. 234-56.

## HENRY GARLAND    (essay date 1980)

[*In the following excerpt, Garland focuses on Fontane's style in the "Berlin novels," examining his narrative prose, dialogue, use of leitmotifs and symbols, and characterization.*]

**Der Stechlin** raises in acute form the problem of Fontane's relationship to his work, since Dubslav is often taken to be a self-portrait, and in a recent German television version (1975) the actor of the part was made up to resemble Fontane in old age. Some of Dubslav's views echo opinions recorded in Fontane's letters. Yet the old man (who incidentally is portrayed as being ten years younger than Fontane) is not the author disguised as a Junker. It is true of Fontane and of the character he created that they are too honest to masquerade as any one. And Fontane was above obtaining vicarious satisfaction by imagining himself as a member of the aristocracy. Yet a novelist contributes something of himself to every character he creates, and Dubslav certainly has important affinities with his sponsor. He shows divergences which are of equal importance and involve mood, temper, and outlook. The real common ground is a fundamental integrity and impatience with sham.

Caution is always necessary in interpreting characters in the light of views expressed in Fontane's letters. He is not always consistent in his opinions, and no character can be identified with him, though there are rare moments when fiction wears a little thin and the author's voice, prompting his character, is noticeably audible. To read the letters and to read the novels are absorbing, but distinct experiences. Apart from their natural preoccupation with personal relationships the letters reveal Fontane as an acute, original, and outspoken commentator on public affairs, political, social, moral or religious. Once the tingling wires of his creative faculty were activated, his mind drew upon the wide range of his experience and knowledge, organizing it and transmuting it to give it a new coherence and a greater tension. Each novel has, to use a musical metaphor, its distinctive tonality, which it retains, since its diverse parts resemble modulations into related keys. Each of the Berlin novels is a world unto itself, even though all of them are drawn from a limited area and a single century—and most of them from two decades of that century. Of course a great and vigorous capital city can provide endless opportunities for the novelist; Fontane managed also to extract almost the same variety from what many would consider the 'dead' countryside of the March. (pp. 273-74)

Fontane differs from the majority of German novelists of the nineteenth century (and from some of the twentieth) by making the path of his readers easy. Though he is especially prized for his dialogue, at least half the text of most of his novels consists of narrative or descriptive prose. His style is exceptionally easy-paced, fluent, and lucid. He is a master of the crisp short biography, varying, according to the importance of the character from a paragraph to a page or two. In his travel series, the *Wanderungen durch die Mark Brandenburg,* he had perfected a skill in topographical and architectural description. Above all, writing letters may be said to have been his hobby, practised from his twenties onwards. It was this epistolary preoccupation that most of all determined the prose style which, after nearly forty years of constant application, lay ready to hand when he belatedly discovered that he could write novels. Any one who can read German will obtain both profit and pleasure from an anthology of the letters such as that of G. Erler, whether it is by sampling or by reading from cover to cover. Unfortunately they have not been translated; but Fontane as a letter-writer is in the same class as Madame de Sévigné.

From its origin in the informality of personal correspondence and relaxed conversation . . . his style tends towards a partnership. At certain points in *Vor dem Sturm* this contact with the reader appears as a somewhat artificial device; in his subsequent work Fontane does not repeat this attempt to establish an intimate personal rapport except for one remarkable instance in *Effi Briest.* In Chapter 32 he describes Effi's existence in Berlin after the divorce, giving the reader the impression that she is quite on her own; he then unexpectedly lets drop the name Roswitha and thereupon enters into conversation with the reader: 'Then was Roswitha with Effi? Was she no longer in Keithstrasse but in Königgrätzerstrasse? That she was, and had been for a considerable time, in fact just as long as Effi herself had lived there. However much it may seem to be a throwback in technique, this sudden approach to the reader at once wins his heart by the pleasure felt at unexpected good news and the warmth of tone in which the news is announced.

This stylistic episode represents the full—and unique—crystalization of an element which unobtrusively pervades the prose of the novels. The reader is constantly admitted to the author's confidence, but rarely becomes conscious of it. Here and there an alert ear may detect the form of address in a sentence beginning with 'Ja, . . .', such as 'Yes, Dörr was the principal subject of these conversations' in *Irrungen, Wirrungen* or, in *Der Stechlin,* 'Yes, it cheered old Dubslav to see the child.' To this personal tone belongs also the use of 'so' as an opening adverb, to which many have objected; but Fontane's use is ironical, signifying, 'So much for the Polzins' in *Stine* or 'So much for Therese von Poggenpuhl' in *Die Poggenpuhls.* It will be noted that the other sisters, of whom we are expected to approve, are spared this treatment. The speaking voice is also heard without these adjuncts, as when the author says of Schach's orderly Baarsch, 'For he had a diplomatic streak like all peasants' or comments in *Irrungen, Wirrungen,* 'That was neither prudent nor wise of Botho'.

The combination of directness, ease, and crispness in this style makes it exceptionally congenial to the reader. The readability of the novels is further enhanced by their relative brevity and by their division into short chapters, rarely exceeding ten and sometimes no more than two pages. Fontane, as we have seen, tends to construct his novels in 'scenes', which can often be accommodated within the limits of one of his chapters; where necessary he does not hesitate to use a group of chapters, so arranged that each includes a distinct phase of the scene. The chapters themselves are subdivided by spacings, so that a pause or change of tempo is made clear by the typography.

Fontane knew well the importance of making a good start.

*A sketch of Fontane in 1896.*

Each of the Berlin novels specifies the location on its opening page, either directly or casually. Time, too, is fixed, either by sub-title (as in *Schach von Wuthenow*), or by an allusion, or a piece of scene-painting, or by the general context in the introductory paragraphs. None of his openings is dull. He became adept at interweaving topographical with other matters. *L'Adultera* starts with character and biography, but its very first words are name and address. *Irrungen, Wirrungen* blends topography with nostalgia, *Der Stechlin* with mystery. The most original are *Vor dem Sturm, Cécile,* and *Frau Jenny Treibel,* each of which is 'reported' by a local observer. The beginning of *Stine* combines location with Pauline Pittelkow's passion for tidiness and, in the factory workers of Borsig and Schwarzkopff, a reminder of the world of labour.

Fontane was not so uniformly successful with his endings. He tried the sentimental retrospect in *Vor dem Sturm,* the conventional happy ending in *L'Adultera,* the epistolary in *Schach von Wuthenow* and *Cécile,* and the symbolical in *Der Stechlin,* but none of these is wholly satisfactory, not even the last. In *Stine* he comes very close to solving the problem with comment by the landlord and his wife, who constitute a kind of comic chorus. Dialogue is also used for Fontane's three most completely successful endings. In *Irrungen, Wirrungen,* in *Frau Jenny Treibel,* and in *Effi Briest* the final remark caps the work and provides a superb open end.

The Berlin novels are not lacking in sensational action. Within their pages are three suicides, two fatal duels, two adulterous unions, and two liaisons in which both parties are unmarried—seven if we may count minor figures in *Irrungen, Wirrungen* and *Mathilde Möhring.* Yet no one could justifiably describe Fontane as a sensational novelist. He passes over events in a few words, playing down what for some would be a splendid opportunity for writing up. The duel in *Effi Briest* is a classical example: 'the arrangements were quickly completed, and the shots rang out. Crampas fell to the ground.' The discretion informing the sexual episodes is well known. When sensation is in the offing he is always for understatement. It has been suggested that he learned this through his years in England. It is surely an essential feature of his temperament, though one which ought to be congenial to English readers.

The absence of sensationalism goes hand in hand with a neglect of suspense. Yet though he did not use it to keep his readers on tenterhooks Fontane was very conscious of time in his novels. Not only are they placed at an almost exact point of time, their chronology can often be traced with accuracy. His commonest use of time is consecutive; he also developed a technique of simultaneity, which is most obvious in *Frau Jenny Treibel,* and is conspicuous in *Cécile, Effi Briest,* and *Die Poggenpuhls.* Its use permits effects of strong contrast and also produces, especially in the first of these novels, situations of dramatic irony, in which sets of characters are ignorant of each other's actions, though the reader-spectator perceives them all.

Notably in the tragic novels, but also in some others, Fontane uses anticipatory hints to support a sense of inevitability. Such are in *Cécile* the motif of Schiller's *Wallenstein* introduced by the two Berliners and the idyllic-looking mansion which proves to be a house of sudden death; the funeral procession in Chapter 3 of *Stine* likewise foreshadows the end; and in *Effi Briest* the swing in which Effi takes so much pleasure can be interpreted as a sign either of her childlike ignorance of danger or a wish to court it. All of these motifs can be seen in more than one light and can also be disregarded, and this ambivalence is both a feature of Fontane's technique and a symptom of his outlook. Less ambiguous, but of similar purpose is Dubslav von Stechlin's half-jocular reference in Chapter 6 to his shortness of breath which foreshadows his fatal illness; though even here a doubt persists as to whether or not he has grasped the full purport of his own remark. Equally prophetic is Lene's 'Hair binds' in Chapter 11 of *Irrungen, Wirrungen.* More obvious are the symbols, such as the Holy Family and the ghosts in *Vor dem Sturm,* the dust and moths of *Schach von Wuthenow,* the lake in *Der Stechlin* and the masquerades and theatrical symbols of *Irrungen, Wirrungen, Frau Jenny Treibel, Die Poggenpuhls,* and *Mathilde Möhring.* All these objects, allusions and casual remarks contribute to form a pattern which the reader may not consciously distinguish, the effect of which, however, he certainly feels.

Fontane's partiality for anecdotes is well known; in *My Years of Childhood* (*Meine Kinderjahre*) he attributes this to the influence of his father, who haphazardly taught him history and geography by the use of a great range of anecdote. He occasionally includes in his novels stories of this kind, but the pleasure he derived from anecdotes had another and much richer harvest; it is seminal for his work. Several of his novels originate either in episodes told to him or in the printed

equivalent, the newspaper paragraph or *fait divers.* Something of this kind underlies *Schach von Wuthenow, L'Adultera, Effi Briest,* and—to some extent—*Cécile;* it applies also to five of the six 'non-Berlin' novels. A brief well-pointed story was clearly of help in activating his imagination, so that from something of epigrammatic proportions a convincing and vivid fragment of life emerged. In the later novels he seemed to need the anecdote less, though all except *Der Stechlin* and perhaps *Die Poggenpuhls,* can be reduced in the imagination to anecdotal length.

The principal characters in Fontane's novels are usually delineated in two stages: an introduction followed by elaboration. The introduction is a brief biography with equally brief commentary and derives, one cannot help feeling, from his addiction to and skill with anecdotes; the elaboration of this outline takes place through the extensive dialogue, occasionally supplemented by a comment by the narrator. The lesser characters are often portrayed by their speech alone, and it speaks for the high quality of Fontane's dialogue that these minor figures are throughout as lifelike in their brief appearances as those who play the principal parts. It is not perhaps surprising that secondary characters, such as Gieshübler and Roswitha in *Effi Briest* should carry such conviction; but it is truly remarkable that figures such as Christel in *L'Adultera,* General Rossow in *Cécile,* and Uncle Osten in *Irrungen, Wirrungen* should emerge as recognizable individual human beings, whilst in *Effi Briest,* Buddenbrook, Crampas's second in the duel, is caught to the life not by his own speech but by Wüllersdorf's.

Fontane's dialogue is as remarkable for its quality as it is for its quantity and function in the novels. Practice undoubtedly made it more flexible and subtle, but the level was already high in *Vor dem Sturm.* Among the characteristic features of this dialogue is the use of hackneyed quotation (often inaccurate) and of cliché as a means of suggesting a veneer of culture, as with 'Gold ist nur Chimäre' from Meyerbeer's opera *Robert le diable,* a quotation which is used twice, in Chapter 5 of *L'Adultera* and in Chapter 3 of *Frau Jenny Treibel.* A characteristic instance of cliché is Gundermann's reiteration of 'water for the mills of Social Democracy' in Chapter 4 of *Der Stechlin.* The widespread use of quotation is, however, not limited to this function; it occurs as a familiar echo of common speech and even, on occasion, as a hallmark of literacy.

Fontane's dialogue is described, understandably and, I think, justifiably, as 'realistic'; yet the vivid quality which we call lifelike is not achieved by the author acting as a taperecorder or a stenographer. If we examine any page of conversation and consider whether dialogue of this fluency, poise, and appositeness is what Fontane could have consistently or even frequently heard, the answer must, I think, be negative. This is a fuller, richer, more fluent, and more rhythmical speech, quite apart from its lack of hesitations or stumblings, than was actually heard in the streets and houses. In his dialogue Fontane is a poet in that he enables each of his characters to achieve the optimum quality of speech which his or her personality and background will allow. They surpass the actual articulateness of their equivalents in real life. This is as true of Lene Nimptsch, Pauline Pittelkow, or Roswitha as it is of van der Straaten, Herr von Briest, or Dubslav von Stechlin. This essential rightness of speech approximating to everyday language whilst eliminating slovenliness, incoherence, and anacoluthon is an achievement which puts Fontane on the same plane as Jane Austen. The 'poetic' quality of dialogue in the novels is perhaps at its finest in the speech of Dubslav von Stechlin and also, rather unexpectedly, in that of Fontane's father in *Meine Kinderjahre,* especially in Chapter 16, which is headed 'Forty Years Later. An Intermezzo.' But is this really the transcribed speech of Fontane *père*? It no doubt has some resemblance to it. The little work is subtitled 'Auto-biographical *novel*' and in it Fontane is writing at the height of his powers (1892-3) of a meeting which took place in 1867. His affection for his father has led him to give of his best and the resulting speech is perfected, so that it foreshadows—though he did not then know that it would—the phrasing, cadences, and rhythms in which Dubslav von Stechlin expresses himself.

Through the extensive use of dialogue Fontane is able to approach the delineation of character in a way that is both original and fascinating. A character in speaking reveals himself both consciously and unconsciously, and the one revelation may modify the other. Speeches addressed to him may, usually indirectly, modify the picture still further. And what is said of him in his absence will also contribute to the complete picture. It is also open to the narrator at any time to interpolate a comment. All or any of the revelations may contain an element of untruth. Uncertainty or even mystery can result from the use of this technique, and the reader is called upon to interpret the characters. Even in his function as narrator Fontane frequently leaves motives unclear by himself professing uncertainty, using some such phrase as 'either because . . . or because . . .' This subtle and many-faceted manner of writing is bound up with Fontane's 'psychographic' process of creation, which leaves certain areas inaccessible, certain motives obscure. His discretion, his silences, his withdrawals are all aspects of ambivalence, of elusiveness, of an ultimate personal reserve which forbids further disclosure. One finds side by side in the novels, and sometimes in the letters, disbelief in the supernatural and yet a persistent presence of the eerie and ghostly, the affirmation of rationalism and yet an attachment to superstition, the rejection of religion and yet a pervasive influence of religion. The continuing thread of what is taken to be Fontane's outlook is always liable to snap under the tension of inconsistencies. Certainty is unattainable and consequently we are bound to have recourse to interpretation of the novels, of the characters, of the man himself. This is necessary because the *whole* of the evidence is never available.

Though Fontane's personality is less transparent than it might appear at first sight, his moral qualities are not in question. His human sympathy was deep and broad, his tolerance was accorded to all but the self-righteous, the pretentious, the careerists, and the hypocrites; and even in these he could often detect compensating virtues. In the four novels of crime (*Grete Minde, Ellernklipp, Unterm Birnbaum, Quitt* ), none of which is a 'Berlin novel', sympathy is not denied to the criminal. Faulty characters occur in his novels, but evil ones are absent. The unhappiness, the misfortunes, and the tragedies that occur are wrought by circumstances and by good, though often mistaken, intentions; much of the blame attaches to society, yet even society, in his novels, can plead extenuating circumstances.

Fontane never forgets that society is composed of individuals, and his sense of the complexity of human life does not desert him in his treatment of social questions. His original intention in some of his works, for instance *Frau Jenny Treibel,*

was harsh and uncompromising; but as soon as the creative faculty began to operate the sharp edges of criticism were smoothed and softened by human understanding. Righteous indignation sometimes speaks in the letters; it has no place in the novels. The pro and contra in human conflict has never been more *fairly* set out than in Fontane's novels. The following sentences from a letter reflect perfectly his undogmatic and flexible attitude: 'I fully admit that I may be wrong. Much genuine feeling may often be found in odd and dubious relationships.' This attitude may be construed as weakness; in reality it denotes Fontane's willingness to investigate facts and phenomena, his sensitiveness in responding to them, and his unvarying readiness to recognize his own limitations. (pp. 275-83)

*Henry Garland, in his* The Berlin Novels of Theodor Fontane, *Oxford at the Clarendon Press, 1980, 296 p.*

## MARIANNE HIRSCH   (essay date 1983)

[*In the following excerpt, Hirsch explores Effi Briest's character development, comparing her psychological progression with that of such heroines as Johann Wolfgang von Goethe's the Beautiful Soul and George Eliot's Maggie Tulliver.*]

*Effi Briest* is traditionally read not as a novel of development, but as a social novel (*Gesellschaftsroman*), as Fontane's indictment of Prussian morality that lovelessly destroys the adulterous heroine, as his articulation of the conflict between natural and social law. Even though Fontane uses Effi to make a larger social point, her circular progression, culminating in extinction, does articulate a development that follows the paradigm of inner growth and return similar to that of the Beautiful Soul [in Johann Wolfgang von Goethe's *Wilhelm Meister's Apprenticeship*] and Maggie Tulliver [in George Eliot's *The Mill on the Floss*].

Unlike Maggie and the Beautiful Soul, Effi is exceedingly conventional; she values money, nobility, and diversion. Still, at the beginning of the novel, Effi possesses a very special, perhaps exceptional, zest for life, as well as a powerful and active imagination and a passionate nature. Her boyish physical activity is described as a yearning for freedom; she refuses to behave like a lady. She is childlike not only in her joyful play with her friends but also in her powerful attachment to her home, her parents, and her girlfriends. In the novel's first scene, we find Effi, aged sixteen, and her mother sitting in the garden quilting an altar rug: her attachment to home remains, as for Maggie, a kind of religion for Effi.

The marriage proposal she receives on that day constitutes a violent break in this idyll. Again, for Effi, growth is not a gradual process but a violent transformation. The interruption of her childish games recalls Hades' rape of Persephone: as Persephone innocently picks flowers with her friends, he abducts her to the underworld to be his wife and queen. As in the myth, marriage is a form of death in *Effi Briest.* This is symbolically obvious even to her husband, Instetten, as Effi, inside the dark house, is now unable to respond to her girlfriends' sunny call to play: "Come on, Effi!" Instetten's stern, unloving nature, the bleak setting of the distant Kessin where the couple go to live, the "underworld" atmosphere Effi encounters or creates there reinforce the parallel between marriage and death. Effi's marriage contrasts drastically with the dreams of exotic bedroom screens and red lamps that preoccupied her during her engagement. Instead, another dream world emerges, one ruled by fear and disappointment rather than by sensuality. In her imagination, the history of her house takes on ominous proportions, as do the cook's creepy black hen, the uncanny stuffed shark and crocodile in the entry way, and especially the Chinaman who died of a broken heart and is said to haunt the house. Here is the underside of Effi's yearnings for the exotic; yet, terrifying as she finds the spook, she still prefers it to the desperate loneliness and emptiness of her Kessin life that more and more directs her inward.

Effi's affair with Major Crampas is a symptom of her ennui and not of passionate love. She succumbs to him unwillingly, sinking as her carriage sinks into the slough. Her image of a "God's wall" of snow, which protects a poor widow from the fierce enemy she fears, indicates Effi's feeling of helplessness, her desire for protection. Yet the enemy Effi fears is both within and without, in herself as well as in Crampas: "She was strongly affected by all that was mysterious and forbidden." Sexuality itself is described through Crampas's narratives of Heine poems as violent, dangerous, deathly. The protection Effi desires and desperately needs, however, was lost when she was so suddenly separated from her home at a point when she was yet unequipped for the strong conflicts and utter desolation of adult life, unprepared for its static and uneventful sameness.

The parental home, as Effi continues to maintain, comes first for her; even long after her marriage and the birth of her child, it remains the seat of her attachments and the object of her desire, the source of her inner world. As such, it is never superseded by her attachments to either husband, lover, or child. In fact, the inner longing for home motivates all of Effi's behavior. Yet, like Maggie's, Effi's relationship to her home is a problematic one. Her father, like Mr. Tulliver, is loving but highly ineffectual. (Even their expressions of helplessness are similar: Tulliver's "It's a puzzling world" and Briest's "That's *too* big a subject.") Her mother fails to understand her dissatisfactions; in fact, her mother is very much the cause of Effi's premature and mistaken marriage. *She* was initially in love with Instetten and, in suggesting so emphatically that Effi accept his proposal ("and if you don't say no, which I can hardly imagine my clever Effi doing, then by the age of twenty you'll have gone as far as others have at forty. You'll go much further than your mother," she insists that her daughter both live out *her* fantasy and repeat her own decision of marrying a man who is suitable but whom she does not love. Mother and daughter are at the same time similar—Effi maintains that her vitality is her mother's legacy to her—and vastly different—Frau Briest has learned to control her energy by a strict and highly conventional demeanor. Her mother's stern distance and high ambitions leave Effi forever longing for warmth, nurturance, and understanding. She writes numerous frank letters about her fears and loneliness, letters that evoke from her parents no more than a helpless sadness. Effi is thus a Persephone who, lacking Demeter's protection, must fend for herself in the social underworld.

In response to her longings and fears, Effi finds Roswitha, for her the good natural maternal presence, untouched by the unnatural conventions that rule Frau Briest's maternal behavior. Effi meets Roswitha in the cemetery and talks to her about childbirth: acquainted with birth and death, Roswitha has the power to assuage Effi's fears. In hiring Roswitha to be her child's nurse, Effi also hires her to be her own mother:

Effi immediately insists that Roswitha share her bedroom and removes Instetten to another room. Even more significant than this substitution is the playful substitution of Roswitha for Crampas; when Effi goes out walking to meet her lover, she always arranges to meet Roswitha as a pretext. They never meet, of course. In fact, nothing about the meetings between the lovers is revealed but this playful failure to find Roswitha. This ellipsis suggests that Roswitha, or the mother, is the actual object of Effi's desire. Both Instetten and Crampas are mere stand-ins for a much deeper longing for the maternal nurturance of home. Her preoccupation with it keeps Effi eternally confined to an inner landscape.

The misdirected nature of Effi's affair makes its discovery seven years later seem all the more meaningless. Yet, Effi's resulting banishment from marriage, motherhood, and her parental home, followed by her failed attempt to lead an independent life in Berlin, constitutes a second violent break in her development and occasions a gradual and progressive extinction. Imprisoned in her small apartment, devoid of any activity and any company except that of Roswitha, Effi spends most of her days staring at the cemetery outside her window. Society has ostracized her: there is no place for the adulterous woman. When she is almost dead, the only possible step forward is also a step backward: her return to Hohen-Cremmen. Her father's brief telegram, "Come, Effi," recalls her girlfriends' call to childhood games and Demeter's retrieval of Persephone from the underworld. Whereas Persephone's return is cyclical, Effi's is total; the novel's last scenes are almost identical and therefore ironic repetitions of the first. Wearing the same dress, swinging as high as she can, Effi resumes a childlike life in her parental family. At her age, however, that existence can only be fulfilled in death.

On her deathbed Effi confesses that the days of her final feverish illness were her best days. This acknowledged valorization of the inner over the outer life constitutes Effi's most meaningful *Bildung*. As she spends hours gazing at the stars, Effi expresses a longing for a heavenly home, one that precedes and surpasses even Hohen-Cremmen. It is not a longing for Christian redemption, but for a mystical fusion with the night. According to the text, this gazing into the cool night ends up killing her, but her death is described in unequivocally positive terms as a stillness, a feeling of liberation, peace.

Not the active rebellion of Antigone, not the decisive withdrawal of the Beautiful Soul, nor the heroic effort of Maggie, Effi's death is a slow extinction. And yet, it results from the same dislocation, the same cosmic disorder as the other three "deaths." Here, the "lack of harmony" between the inner and the outer life is defined as a disjunction between natural instinct and cultural codes and imperatives. Even the most intimate family relationships are tainted by this conflict: the Briests' confusion between parental love and social disapproval indirectly causes Effi's death.

In this context, Effi's forgiveness of Instetten, who most clearly exemplifies this disjunction, emerges as a device that weakens her own resistance to the values she ends up underwriting. In forgiving Instetten, she recognizes that her own allegiance to natural laws, to home and parents, that her longings for pre-Oedipal symbiosis are regressive and antisocial, and that only Instetten's cold and calculated ambition can serve the advancement of this society. Realizing that she herself has only death to offer, Effi is willing to let him raise their daughter: her influence, like the Beautiful Soul's, is dangerous to children. This recognition, however, is most ironic in relation to Effi's own mother who, subscribing fully to the codes of the Prussian culture, failed to produce a daughter who could survive in it. In letting Effi forgive (Antigone never does), Fontane neutralizes the potentially subversive power of her own spiritual development. This scene clearly demonstrates the novel's primary focus: not Effi herself, but Effi as an example. In this male-authored text, the woman serves as the optimal illustration of social injustice and deterioration.

Effi's death, like that of the other heroines, has been prepared by her "inclination for the invisible," by the inward direction of her life and growth and by her exclusively subjective activity. In this novel, too, female plots are described as static; the conventional romantic *Geschichte,* like that of her mother's youth told by Effi to her friends, is defined by renunciation, self-denial. Effi faces her death with equanimity, convinced, like the man in the anecdote she recounts, that should she be called away from the dinner table prematurely, she would "not really miss anything." If her only active participation is not in the outer but in the inner life, her early death is not an interruption but a culmination. This type of female plot becomes a reversal of the conventional male plot, as female *Bildung* is no longer marked by progress or linear direction, but by circularity and dissolution. In her ability to recover her interrupted past, Effi, like Maggie, is allowed a reversal of the conventional plot, but that reversal is an interruption of plot.

With death as her only possible fulfillment, Effi is clearly a victim; like the ancient pre-Christian victims who were sacrificed on the stones that so horrify her when she visits the Hertasee, Effi is the sacrifical victim of the conflict between "elemental tendencies and established laws." The removal of Effi leaves society intact. (pp. 37-42)

> *Marianne Hirsch, "Spiritual 'Bildung': The Beautiful Soul as Paradigm," in* The Voyage in Fictions of Female Development, *Elizabeth Abel, Marianne Hirsch, Elizabeth Langland, eds., University Press of New England, 1983, pp. 23-48.*

## HILDEGARD EMMEL   (essay date 1984)

[*In the following excerpt, Emmel evaluates Fontane's contribution to the development of the German novel, focusing on the* Zeitroman, Gesellschaftsroman, *and* Eheroman *genres.*]

Theodor Fontane . . . was able to create convincing novels. He was the first to break away from the descriptive style characteristic of the majority of German novels in past decades. Recognizing his contribution, Thomas Mann spoke of an "evaporation of the contents" in Fontane's novels [see Further Reading]. With this evaporation, Fontane's style led into the twentieth century even more decisively than Raabe's. Fontane's novels were a transition and a preparation for modern forms and already contained much of what Thomas Mann, Hermann Broch, and Robert Musil were to express later from a different perspective.

Fontane was already fifty-nine years old when his first novel, *Before the Storm (Vor dem Sturm)*, appeared. Although he had never written a novel before, he had read extensively and had studied the genre for decades, as evidenced by his many essays and letters. In particular, he was interested in the relationship between the historical novel and the *Zeitroman* and wrote significant essays on Sir Walter Scott and Willibald Alexis. He summarized the fruits of his deliberations in question and answer form in his review of Gustav Freytag's *Our Forefathers,* "What is the purpose of the *modern* novel? What *material* should it choose? Is the range of its material unlimited? And if *not,* within what limits of time and space does it have the best chance of proving itself and satisfying the hearts of its readers?" His answer is as follows: "The novel should be a picture of the times in which we live, at least the reflection of a time at whose border we ourselves have stood or of which our parents have spoken." He believed it "characteristic" that even Sir Walter Scott did not begin with *Ivanhoe* (set in 1196), but with *Waverley* (set in 1745), to which he "expressly added the second title *'Tis Sixty Years Since."* Scott was quite correct in feeling that "two generations is approximately the limit which, as a general rule, it is *not* recommendable to exceed." Not until he was successful as a novelist did Scott feel secure enough to delve into the past.

What is striking about Fontane's statements is not his call for the *Zeitroman,* for this was not new at all. Nor was it a new idea that "all narrative literature which has survived over the last 150 years" essentially fulfilled the requirements which Fontane had outlined. He accurately observed that the "great English humorists of this and the former century depicted *their* times; the French novel, in spite of the elder Dumas, is a . . . *Gesellschaftsroman* [novel of manners or society]; Jean Paul, Goethe, yes even Freytag (in *Debit and Credit* ) wrote about *their* world and *their* times." All of this is not of consequence for the history of the German novel, however. Much more striking is the fact that the narrative material of significant novels from the first half of the twentieth century is also rooted in the time period which Fontane defined, a period which the authors had experienced themselves or about which their "parents had spoken." This is the case in *Buddenbrooks* (1901) and *The Magic Mountain* (1924) by Thomas Mann, *The Sleepwalkers* (1931) by Hermann Broch, and *The Man without Qualities* (1932) by Robert Musil. Moreover, it is astonishing that as early as 1875 Fontane set the temporal limits which a novel, insofar as it is a *Zeitroman,* may not exceed even today if it is to have the best chance of "proving itself and satisfying the hearts of its readers." One need only think of the success of Günter Grass's first two novels, *The Tin Drum* (1959) and *Dog Years* (1963), and of other novels after the Second World War which were faced with the task of coming to terms with the events of the preceding decades. The productive results of combining the historical novel and the *Zeitroman*—two forms which were long thought of as separate—became evident in the twentieth century when authors chose as their setting that period on the border of the present which is already historical but is nonetheless part of the reader's personal experience.

If one considers that Fontane had *Before the Storm* in mind for well over a decade before publishing it, then the time setting of the work conforms with his own rule and only seems to have been overstepped a bit due to its delayed completion. *Before the Storm* is a historical novel which tends towards a *Gesellschaftsroman.* It bears the subtitle *Novel from the Winter of 1812-13.* This is the same period Leo Tolstoy dealt with in *War and Peace* (1868-69). *Before the Storm* cannot compare to Tolstoy's great work; the strong wind of history that sweeps through the Russian novel is hardly detectable even as a light breeze in Fontane's *Before the Storm.* Nonetheless, the historical atmosphere directly preceding the Wars of Liberation affects all the characters and determines their lives.

Many scenes in *Before the Storm* take place in Berlin, but the primary setting is the Prussian countryside west of the Oder River between Küstrin and Frankfurt, where the ancestral seat of the family Vitzewitz, Schloss Hohen-Vietz, is located. Noblemen, farmers, and citizens of Brandenburg and, to a lesser extent, Berlin, make up the circle of characters. They are Fontane's primary concern. In an early stage of his work on the novel, he said that "amiable characters" should "entertain the reader, perhaps eventually win his love, but without turmoil and éclat. Stimulating, cheerful, and if possible, witty conversation" was most important to him. Such a statement of purpose was new to the nineteenth century. Indeed, Fontane accomplished his goal, for the book is pleasant reading. Although its plot is not terribly significant, there is a great deal of action. The reader glides from one episode to another, always warmed and impressed by truly amiable characters who demonstrate that they are members of fine society by their self-assured, correct, appropriate conduct in all situations. It is a society which comprises all ages and classes and also gives a place to outsiders.

Two young Polish immigrants, Kathinka von Ladalinski and her brother Tubal, create unrest at Hohen-Vietz. To the older generation they seem to be the right marriage partners for the young members of the Vitzewitz family, Lewin and Renate, and for a while Lewin and Renate agree. They both feel an honest, deep affection for their prospective partners and are willing to wait for their feelings to be reciprocated. Yet their aunt, the Countess Pudalga, describes the true situation in a letter.

> Mais les choses ne se font pas d'après nos volontés. I am sure of the young people from Hohen-Vietz, but not of those from the house of Ladalinski. Kathinka accepts Lewin's homage, but otherwise she is just playing with him; Tubal has some feeling for Renate, qui ne l'aurait pas? But it is nothing more than the admiration evoked by youth and beauty everywhere. So there are difficulties which, I believe, lie in Kathinka's indifference and in Tubal's superficiality of emotion. Et l'un est aussi mauvais que l'autre.

The countess's elegant letter handles the delicate topic with sophistication and is characteristic of Fontane's artistry. In a letter written to Mete Fontane, the author said of his *Gesellschaftsromane*, "My entire attention is focused on allowing the characters to speak as they do in real life. Wittiness (which sounds a bit arrogant) flows most easily from my pen. I am, betraying my French heritage once again, a causeur in speaking and writing; but because I am above all an artist, I know where witty causerie belongs and where it does not." Already in his first novel Fontane lets each person speak in an individual manner. This is the reason he does not need a forceful plot. Conversation replaces the plot and is the substance of the novel. The society and its problems take shape in and from the conversations. Therefore, both historical novel and *Zeitroman* become a *Gesellschaftsroman* which comes to life through the speech, and occasionally the eloquent silence, of its characters.

There are many characters in *Before the Storm.* Researchers like to use Fontane's terms "portrait gallery" and "panoptic" to describe the work. The overwhelming fullness of human life, which captivates the reader, is reminiscent of Balzac, Tolstoy, Dickens, and Thackeray. However, it cannot be said that Fontane was directly influenced by them or that he imitated them. He greatly admired William Makepeace Thack-

eray (1811-1863) and for years preferred him to Dickens; *Vanity Fair* (1847-48) was one of his favorite books. But *Before the Storm* is fundamentally different from *Vanity Fair.* Fontane was not trying to depict *vanitas vanitatum,* but simply wished to present "amiable characters." He believed that art has the responsibility to glorify and transfigure and was convinced that literature has "different laws of truth from history." A novel should "first be judged according to aesthetic principles." He did not want to give ugliness too much space. Though some might feel that Fontane contradicts himself, he personally saw no inconsistency in claiming that the "modern novel should be a picture of the times." As he explained in his review of Freytag's *Our Forefathers, "What is the purpose of a novel?* It should, while avoiding all exaggeration and ugliness, tell a story we *believe."*

Fontane talked about the unique structure of *Before the Storm* in response to criticism from Paul Heyse. He wrote to Heyse that *Before the Storm* is a *Vielheitsroman* (pluralistic novel). In addition to "novels such as *Copperfield,* in which we see a man's life from its beginning," those which "closely examine a multifarious time period instead of an individual" are also legitimate (December 9, 1878). As is so often the case with Fontane's theoretical statements, it seems at first as if this were nothing fundamentally new. But a comparison with Robert Musil's reflections on modern narration in the first volume of his novel *The Man without Qualities* (1930) shows the importance of Fontane's comments; Fontane was already working with concepts similar to Musil's. Fontane knew that readers, as Musil later said, prefer a simple narrative sequence, but unlike Musil he thought that the narrative thread depended on the fact that the novel just has one hero and relates his story alone. Therefore for Fontane narrative problems first emerged when the attempt was made to present a multifarious time period. He conceded to Heyse that "narrations 'with *one* hero'" would always possess greater dramatic interest, but stressed that "the *Vielheitsroman* with all its breadth and retardations, with its masses of portraits and episodes," could nevertheless equal the *Einheitsroman* (unitary novel), if not in its "effect," then in its "artistry." Against the charge that *Before the Storm* was weak in composition, he argued that, quite to the contrary, herein lay its strength. One would hesitate to take issue with this proud defense, for in fact Fontane's *Vielheitsroman*—the term is quite useful—was the most modern nineteenth-century novel to have appeared. The author was right about his book. Other historical novels of the day all fell short of *Before the Storm;* the only work of equal originality was Immermann's *Münchhausen.*

Fontane did not publish another work like it, but instead concentrated on the *Gesellschaftsroman,* a genre that did not yet exist in Germany. *Before the Storm* had already tended in this direction. In the works that followed, Fontane wrote of high society and of good people from the lower classes. In these circles one has a sense for what is, as Goethe would say, "proper" (*das Gehörige*): one behaves with decorum, and there are always a few people, particularly among the lower classes, who are good-hearted. In *Before the Storm* this was taken for granted, for otherwise the characters would not have been amiable. In the series of novels beginning with *L'Adultera,* it is no longer taken for granted but is something special and exceptional. This gives the novels a pointedness, concentration, and emphasis not yet found in *Before the Storm.* With the exception of *Stechlin,* in which many elements from *Before the Storm* recur, they all show a slice of a world that as a whole remains unilluminated. For this reason the form of most of these novels borders on the novella.

The majority of Fontane's *Gesellschaftsromane* are *Eheromane* (novels of marriage). As the basis for his plots he often used actual incidents that he had heard of locally. When reproducing them in novel form, he stressed the underlying social conventions and revealed the social structure within which the marriage partners were confined. The code of honor, general patterns of behavior, and individual reactions provided a plot system which could be varied from case to case by a shift in emphasis. There is no doubt that conditions during the last two decades of the nineteenth century supplied Fontane with rich material, both with respect to actual events as well as to the customs and attitudes which came to prevail as the profile of the young *Kaiserreich* emerged. Of equal importance was Fontane's confrontation with Goethe's *Elective Affinities.* Jürgen Kolbe provided important insights into this relationship and spoke of Fontane's "renewal" of *Elective Affinities.* An evaluation of Fontane's *Eheromane* cannot be based upon the problems of the late nineteenth century alone; his place within the tradition of Goethe's influential novel must also be taken into account.

The artistic merit of *L'Adultera* is controversial, as is the case with most of Fontane's *Eheromane.* Scholars are almost evenly divided between admiration and limited criticism. The simple triangle story is not a piquant story of adultery, nor can this be said of Fontane's other *Eheromane.* If many of his contemporaries saw moral laxity in the work and were scandalized, this only shows how accurately Fontane described his society and how little the critics understood his moral views. The plot is uncomplicated, almost banal. Melanie de Caparoux, well-bred and appealing, the "spoiled child of a rich and fashionable home," was without means after the death of her father and at seventeen married the financier, van der Straaten, a man twenty-five years her senior. Ten years later, when a compatible partner for Melanie appears, a widely traveled, elegant young businessman's son from Frankfurt am Main, she leaves her husband to marry him. Society condemns her and her own children turn away from her, but the pair endures the ostracism. When they come into financial difficulties, Melanie handles herself most impressively; she reduces household expenses and earns money by giving lessons.

This plot, which contains a number of elements later found in *Effi Briest,* is the motivation for what is actually important: the conversations. They develop, as is customary in a *Gesellschaftsroman,* at breakfast, in the drawing room, at formal dinners, on excursions into the country. Peter Demetz speaks of the "follow-up discussions, which (like in Jane Austen's novels) make the just completed social event and its conversations the topic of renewed conversation." Like the plot, the conversations revolve primarily around the main characters, van der Straaten and Melanie, whose manner of speaking—an ironical, impersonal dialogue without warmth—is the cause of their separation. Van der Straaten, "accustomed since his youth to saying and doing whatever he liked," makes use of ambiguous speech to express what society forbids; most of all he enjoys saying things the others consider improper. His provocative behavior is demonstrated to the reader early in the book on the occasion of an evening gathering and is interpreted by the guests in a "follow-up" conversation. Some of the guests feel sorry for Melanie, but others think that van der Straaten is so rich that he can say what

he wants. In addition, his wife receives enough from him that she ought to be able to tolerate him. What Melanie herself feels is revealed by the narrator, who tells us how glad she is to spend the summer outside the city. Van der Straaten only visits her there every third day and "in the days between she enjoyed the happiness of her freedom. . . . She had peace from his expressions of love and unabashedness." Her constant self-control is evident even in her first dialogues with van der Straaten. Later she characterizes the tone of the house as "a little biting, a little ambiguous, and always improper," and says of her husband, "he knows so wonderfully how to say things that injure and expose and humiliate." Her separation from him is a direct result of this. Before leaving she tells him, "I am tired of this despicable lie. . . . I'm not leaving out of guilt, but out of pride" and "in order to restore my self-respect. . . . I want to be able to see clearly and hold my head up again." Van der Straaten's manner of speaking oppresses her, and she frees herself from it. The fact that honest affection for another man brings her to take this step and that she leaves one marriage for another is not forgotten for a moment: the plot is structured around it. Van der Straaten has long been expecting adultery.

*L'Adultera* differs from Fontane's later *Eheromane* in that the main characters' actions are sure and straightforward, the adulterous woman is genuinely committed to another man, and the ending is friendly. Fontane anticipated criticism of the moral issue and hence incorporated his contemporaries' indignation into the novel. Melanie knows she will face gossip and self-righteous condemnation, and Fontane shows how she is ostracized when she begins her new marriage. At the same time he takes her side. Perhaps this is the reason why he elaborated on the story, giving Melanie strength and insight when her second husband has financial problems.

All of Fontane's later *Eheromane* can be viewed under the aspect of the "tragic novel" in the sense of Goethe's *Elective Affinities.* They are similar to Goethe's novel insofar as one partner is always destroyed by the conflicts that arise; they differ in that passions seldom play a role. Fontane's *Eheroman* is a *Gesellschaftsroman,* not a novel of love. Marital problems are treated as societal problems and are deadly serious. Feelings may be dealt with, but they may also be disregarded; since they are related to marriage, they affect the person's position in society. If duels and suicides occur again and again, this shows that the individual sees no escape from the expectations of society. (pp. 170-76)

The cycle of *Eheromane* culminates in Fontane's most famous and widely read work, *Effi Briest.* At the age of seventeen, Effi Briest is wed to her mother's former admirer, Baron von Innstetten, and is taken from the warm atmosphere of her parents' home and her circle of young friends into a gloomy, somewhat eerie governor's residence. Her husband's conduct is proper but insensitive. The young wife is left alone much of the time and must learn to hide her distress from her husband. Her liaison with Major Crampas, more a diversion than a strong emotional attachment, provides her with a brief escape and at the same time causes her great anxiety. She is relieved to end the affair when Innstetten is transferred to Berlin. Seven years later Innstetten discovers letters from Crampas, insists on a duel in which he kills the major, and then abandons Effi. Scorned by society and condemned by her parents, Effi lives with a good-hearted servant in a small Berlin apartment until an elderly doctor persuades her parents to let their sickly daughter return home. She dies there in peaceful contentment.

Effi's story is bound to its times. Both decisive plot elements—Effi's early marriage and Innstetten's reaction to the letters—stem from customs of the day which (here the narrator leaves no doubt) do not make for a sensible ordering of human affairs. Effi's marriage is questionable from the very beginning. The dialogues between mother and daughter before the wedding and between the parents afterward touch on all the delicate points. As soon as Effi is informed by her mother that Baron Innstetten has "asked for her hand," the reader knows that there will be problems. Effi's reaction is, "Asked for my hand? Truly?" Although Frau von Briest emphasizes that it is "not a matter to joke about," the question of the seriousness of the courtship would persist if this were not a *Gesellschaftsroman*. Only within the context of this genre can the almost unbelievable courtship be taken seriously. Like a matchmaker, Frau von Briest reminds her daughter that "if you don't say 'no,' which I can hardly imagine from my smart Effi, then by the time you're twenty you'll already have what others have at forty. You'll surpass your mother by far." Effi has neither the time nor the opportunity to consider her mother's recommendation, nor is she given any further explanation of the situation awaiting her. She is merely consulted one month before the wedding about her wishes for the dowry and ceremony. On this occasion she is also asked whether she loves Innstetten. Effi's answers regarding Innstetten are somewhat unsettling to her parents, or at least this is what they say in their discussion after the wedding. They point out that their daughter is pleasure-loving and ambitious. Since Innstetten is career minded, she should be satisfied. But Frau von Briest suddenly expresses the opinion that this is "only half." Effi's "penchant for play and adventure" will hardly be nourished and Innstetten will not particularly amuse her, nor will he try to help her alleviate boredom. When Effi realizes this, "she will be insulted. And then I don't know what will happen. For as gentle and compliant as she is, she can also be rabid." This is an accurate prophesy of Effi's life with Innstetten. What will happen is already interpreted here by her mother. In addition, Effi had answered the question whether she loved Innstetten very naively. Her father brings this up in the discussion with his wife and says that if Effi doesn't really love him, that "would be bad. For with all his good qualities, he is not the man to easily win her love." This is also an important foreshadowing of later events. Frau von Briest confirms her husband's feelings and admits that she also has her doubts. Upon observing Effi's cool reaction to a letter from Innstetten, her mother felt "her heart sink."

It is characteristic of the novel's style that these questions are discussed in such detail after the wedding, whereas they did not seem to be of importance before hand when the decision was made. Then it was only a question of finding a good match. Of course, after the fact the Briests would have been very pleased to learn that Effi was content in her marriage. Not until after the wedding has taken place do they admit to the importance of her feelings and suddenly see all the potential dangers.

A comparison of the parents' dialogue after the wedding with the conversation between mother and daughter beforehand shows that Frau von Briest does not accurately repeat what her daughter tells her. Moreover, she conceals an important objection to Innstetten raised by Effi as well as her confession

that she is afraid of him. After praising Innstetten, Effi admits, "And I could almost say I am entirely in favor of him, if he only . . . yes, if he were only a little different." According to the pastor, Innstetten is "a man of principles," while Effi says, "and I . . . I have none. You see, Mama, that is something that torments and worries me. He is so kind and good to me and so considerate, but . . . I'm afraid of him." Effi's clairvoyant fear is all too well founded. After her confession, the conversation breaks off; Frau von Briest does not reply. In both dialogues love is respected but fear ignored.

When Effi begins her married life, the story unfolds as has been anticipated in the conversations. It is now only a question of how it will happen. Major Crampas and the "ghost" in the house in Kessin as well as Innstetten's attitude towards the ghost all weave the net in which Effi is caught. She is extremely uncomfortable in her new home; since the first night, when she hears the sound of long curtains being swept across the floor by the wind in the room above her bedroom, she cannot free herself of the feeling that there is something strange all around her. After that night she suggests to her husband that the curtains be shortened or at least the windows closed. Later, when she realizes that she will often be left alone in the house, she requests that they move, for she feels particularly threatened by the ghost of a "Chinaman" who is buried in Kessin and, as Innstetten tells her, lived for a time in the house as a servant and friend of the former owner. In neither case does Innstetten comply with her wishes. His own attitude towards the ghost of the Chinaman remains ambiguous. As opposed to Effi, he does not want to be rid of it or get away from it. Effi's fear does not seem important to him. Later Effi learns from Crampas, who knew Innstetten from his military days, that Innstetten had thought the same way when in the regiment and enjoyed telling ghost stories. Aside from the fact that Innstetten's haunted house is something out of the ordinary which could help him in his career, Crampas believes that he uses it as a way of educating his young wife. Effi calls this "a calculated apparatus of fear" and says, "All warmheartedness was lacking and it almost bordered on cruelty."

Effi's relationship to the major is never described in detail. It is as if the narrator is reporting from a perspective which allows only Effi's reaction to her new experiences to be seen and not the experiences themselves. It is this reaction which is decisive to the narrator. The enchanting and transforming power of the secret liaison changes not only Effi's facial features but her entire person. Innstetten is slow to notice the change: "And how well you look! . . . You used to have something of the spoiled child and now all at once you look like a woman." After the interlude with Crampas has long faded into the past, it comes to light, and Innstetten acts as the "man of principles" Effi had feared when she hardly knew him. Like Botho von Rienäcker in *Trials and Tribulations,* he makes a decision contrary to his own wishes to satisfy society. Yet Innstetten conforms more consciously and resolutely than Botho, who simply sees no other choice and is pressured by the circumstances and his family to abandon the young girl he loves. Innstetten is not pressured by anyone; he renounces Effi merely on principle. He knows that he has a genuine alternative which is actually the only decent course of action: to forgive Effi. But his respect for the concept of society means more to him than his wife whom he still claims to love. Ingrid Mittenzwei sees Innstetten as a failure: "It was not Effi's responsibility to destroy the letters, but Innstetten's—as her husband, not as the baron. He fails because he puts the nobleman above the married man." This is an accurate judgment from a humanitarian standpoint, regardless of whatever else one might say about the social system as a whole. Effi's statement at the end that Innstetten "was right in all he did" can be explained as the forgiveness of a dying woman and as the author's wish to glorify her. Nonetheless, the sharpest comment which can be directed against Innstetten in an *Eheroman* comes from Effi and is her last word on him: "as noble as anyone can be who has no real love."

*Effi Briest* has been compared with the great novels of passion—Gustave Flaubert's (1821-1880) *Madame Bovary* (1857) and Leo Tolstoy's (1828-1910) *Anna Karenina* (1873-76)—and has been criticized for its lack of passion. A comparison with Goethe's *Elective Affinities* could also result in the same criticism. Yet the degree of passion is certainly not a viable criterion for judging a work's quality, but merely serves to characterize it. *Effi Briest* is a genuine *Gesellschaftsroman,* insofar as the views of the society in which it is set are also its primary concern. Society is not the background for the novel's action but the theme itself. Here it is not passion but fear which is the main character's strongest emotion.

Before writing *Effi Briest,* the author had already moved beyond the genre of the *Eheroman* in its narrow sense with *Jenny Treibel (Frau Jenny Treibel)*. Here he expressed his dislike for the bourgeoisie by showing the hypocrisy of a woman who constantly refers to her ideals, but actually is motivated only by greed and family pride. The reader is struck by the severity of Fontane's attack on her. The characters in Frau Treibel's circle are also depicted with scorn. Some are insignificant and weak, some ridiculous and silly, displaying pretentious and dishonest behavior. On the whole the work has more of a plot than Fontane's other novels.

Fontane structured his last two novels, *The Poggenpuhl Family* (*Poggenpuhls*) and *Stechlin,* differently from his previous works. Of *The Poggenpuhl Family* the author said, "The book is not a novel and has no contents. The 'how' must take the place of the 'what,' *The Poggenpuhl Family* is a delicate composition which presents a subtle world. A humanitarian atmosphere pervades all the relationships, in particular between servant and master. In *Stechlin* this atmosphere is largely attributable to the title character, Dubslav von Stechlin, of whom it is stated at the outset, "His finest quality was a deep humanitarianism that came straight from his heart." Everything Dubslav says and does throughout the book can be seen in this light. It is he who gives the work its inner cohesiveness, which has always been poorly understood by critics. Dubslav is not the main character with regard to the plot, nor is he the most active character. Yet from the very beginning he sets the tone by which everything is decided and judged. When Dubslav's son Woldemar describes his fiancée Armgard's family, he speaks of the similarities between his future father-in-law, Count Barby in Berlin, and his own father Dubslav: "the same Bismarck head, the same humane traits, the same friendliness, the same good spirits." They are most similar in "the entire atmosphere of their homes, the liberality." Woldemar says he knows no other man who is "inwardly as free" as his father and has "no trace of selfishness. And this beautiful trait (ah, so rare), the old count has it too."

A character of particular importance is Count Barby's older daughter Melusine. Beautiful and charming, she brings the lightness and joy of her personality to the drawing room conversations. Dubslav is very impressed by her. When her sister

Armgard mentions this to her father after the two sisters have visited Dubslav, Count Barby considers it to be a good sign:

> There are so many people who have a natural hatred for everything charming, because they are so lacking in charm themselves. All narrow and arrogantly stiff individuals . . . all pharisees and would-be greats, all the self-righteous and vain feel injured and hurt by people like Melusine, and if old Stechlin has fallen in love with Melusine, then I already love him for it, because that means he is a good man.

Melusine provides the Barby home with a counterbalance to Dubslav's circle. The fact that the young pair, Armgard and Woldemar, and the other characters do not play a more prominent role has been faulted by critics and scholars. But this is entirely in keeping with the structure of a novel which is not concerned with single characters but with affinities that lie beneath the surface.

Fontane knew that in *Stechlin* he had deviated greatly from the traditional novel form. "In the end an old man dies and two young people marry; that is about all that happens in five hundred pages. There are no entanglements and solutions, no conflicts of the heart or conflicts at all, no tensions or surprises." Various persons "meet and discuss God and the world. Nothing but talk, dialogue . . . Naturally I think this is not only the correct, but indeed the only way to write a *Zeitroman,* yet at the same time I know only too well that the general public thinks otherwise." As with *Before the Storm* twenty years ago, Fontane again characterizes the distinctive quality of his work quite accurately. At that time he spoke of the *Vielheitsroman* (pluralistic novel) and defended it in a letter to Paul Heyse; now he describes the structure of his last novel in much the same way, declaring his procedure to be not only correct but also mandatory in light of his intentions. From his statements it is easy to see how similar the two novels are. It is not surprising that now as before he has no illusions about the limited appeal of his work.

Discerning readers have always appreciated *Stechlin.* In 1920 Thomas Mann said that upon rereading Fontane's late work he was "delighted . . . enchanted!" One word was "constantly on my lips: 'sublime.'" Ten years earlier he had written to Maximilian Harden, "*Effi Briest* is in my judgment still the best German novel since *Elective Affinities.* What else was and is there?" Weighing the quality of one against the other, he explained to Conrad Wandrey, "And there it stands: If *Effi Briest* extends furthest beyond Fontane's epoch in a social-ethical sense, then *Stechlin* does so artistically." (pp. 178-83)

*Hildegard Emmel, "From Heinrich Heine to Thomas Mann," in his* History of the German Novel, *translated by Ellen Summerfield, Wayne State University Press, 1984, pp. 109-94.*

---

## FURTHER READING

Andrews, Wayne. "The Distance of Theodor Fontane." In his *Siegfried's Curse: The German Journey from Nietzsche to Hesse,* pp. 75-102. New York: Atheneum, 1972.

A biographical sketch that examines the influence of Prussian society on Fontane's life and writings.

Avery, George C. "The Chinese Wall: Fontane's Psychograph of Effi Briest." In *Views and Reviews of Modern German Literature: Festschrift for Adolf D. Klarmann,* edited by Karl S. Weimar, pp. 18-38. Munich: Delp Verlag, 1974.
Explores the symbolic function of the Chinese ghost in *Effi Briest.*

Bance, Alan. *Theodor Fontane: The Major Novels.* Angelica Germanica Series 2, edited by Leonard Forster and M. Swales. Cambridge: Cambridge University Press, 1982, 253 p.
A comprehensive study of seven Fontane novels, concentrating on the development of his prose style.

Barry, David T. J. "Threads of Threeness in Fontane's *Irrungen, Wirrungen.*" *The Germanic Review* LXIV, No. 3 (Summer 1989): 99-104.
Traces the recurrent appearance of the number three in *Irrungen, Wirrungen* and discusses its possible significance to the theme of the novel.

Bruford, W. H. "Theodor Fontane: *Frau Jenny Treibel.*" In his *The German Tradition of Self-Cultivation: 'Bildung' from Humboldt to Thomas Mann,* pp. 190-205. London: Cambridge University Press, 1975.
Analyzes the contrast between the social classes in nineteenth-century Prussia as presented in *Frau Jenny Treibel.*

Davis, Arthur L. "Fontane as a Political Thinker." *The Germanic Review* VIII, No. 3 (July 1933): 183-94.
Examines how Fontane's French ancestry and knowledge of history contributed to his highly objective view of German politics.

——. "Fontane and the German Empire." *The Germanic Review* II, No. 4 (October 1936): 258-73.
Documents Fontane's changing political views as reflected in his writings.

Davis, Gabriele A. Wittig. *Novel Associations: Theodor Fontane and George Eliot within the Context of Nineteenth-Century Realism.* Stanford German Studies, vol. 19. New York: Peter Lang, 1983, 170 p.
A "comparative investigation" of the lives and works of Fontane and George Eliot.

Harrigan, Renny. "The Limits of Female Emancipation: A Study of Theodor Fontane's Lower Class Women." *Monatshefte* 70, No. 2 (Summer 1978): 117-28.
A feminist analysis of the portrayal of lower-class women in Fontane's novels.

Howe, Patricia. "The Child as Metaphor in the Novels of Fontane." In *Oxford German Studies,* vol. 10, edited by P. F. Ganz, pp. 121-38. Oxford: Willem A. Meeuws, 1979.
Studies the role of the child in Fontane's novels, examining his use of children as metaphors for society.

——. "Fontane's *Ellernklipp* and the Theme of Adoption." *The Modern Language Review* 79, No. 1 (January 1984): 114-30.
Examines the theme of adoption in the novel *Ellernklipp,* focusing on the complex relationship between its primary characters, Hilde and Bocholt.

Loewen, Harry. "From Prussianism to Mennonitism: Reality and Ideals in Theodor Fontane's Novel *Quitt.*" *Journal of German-American Studies* XV, No. 2 (June 1980): 25-38.
Contrasts nineteenth-century Prussian society with Fontane's utopian Mennonite community in the novel *Quitt.*

Mann, Thomas. "The Old Fontane." In his *Essays of Three Decades,* translated by H. T. Lowe-Porter, pp. 287-306. New York: Alfred A. Knopf, 1948.
A well-known, highly laudatory essay focusing on the latter part of Fontane's literary career which, as Mann describes it, was "a phenomenon of old age returning artistically, intellectually, and morally to youth. . . . "

Remak, Joachim. *The Gentle Critic: Theodor Fontane and German Politics, 1848-98.* Syracuse: Syracuse University Press, 1964, 104 p.
Traces Fontane's interest in German politics, asserting that, as a political critic, he was "gentler" and more objective than many of his contemporaries.

Riechel, Donald C. "*Effi Briest* and the Calendar of Fate." *The Germanic Review* XLVIII, No. 3 (May 1973): 189-211.
Establishes fate as a key element in Fontane's life and writings, addressing, among other things, his use of numerology in *Effi Briest.*

——. " 'Thou com'st in such a questionable shape': Theodor Fontane's *Die Poggenpuhls.*" In *Herkommen und Erneuerung: Essays für Oskar Seidlin,* edited by Gerald Gillespie and Edgar Lohner, pp. 241-55. Tübingen, West Germany: Max Niemeyer Verlag, 1976.
A discussion of the novel *Die Poggenpuhls,* focusing on its critical reception and unconventional form.

Shears, Lambert A. "Theodor Fontane as a Critic of the Novel." *Publications of the Modern Language Association of America* XXXVIII, No. 2 (June 1923): 389-400.
Examines Fontane's efforts as a literary critic, concluding that his lack of formal training in the field is overshadowed by his "discerning skepticism" and sensitivity.

Stern, J. P. M. "*Effi Briest: Madame Bovary: Anna Karenina.*" *The Modern Language Review* LII, No. 3 (July 1957): 363-75.
Discusses how Theodor Fontane, Gustave Flaubert, and Leo Tolstoy created heroines that were contrary to the "normal conventions" of the everyday world.

Subiotto, Frances M. "The Function of Letters in Fontane's *Unwiederbringlich.*" *The Modern Language Review* 65, No. 2 (April 1970): 306-18.
Explores Fontane's use of letters in developing the plot of *Unwiederbringlich.*

Thum, Reinhard H. "Symbol, Motif and Leitmotif in Fontane's *Effi Briest.*" *The Germanic Review* 54, No. 3 (Summer 1979): 115-24.
Shows how Fontane's use of symbol, motif, and leitmotif elevates *Effi Briest* from a simplistic tale of adultery to a complex portrayal of human relationships.

Wolffsohn, Lily. "Theodor Fontane's Child-Life." *Temple Bar* 112, No. 443 (October 1897): 173-85.
A biographical sketch with short synopses of episodes from *Meine Kinderjahre.*

# Stephen Collins Foster

## 1826-1864

American songwriter.

Foster is known as the author of some of the most beloved songs in the history of American music. "Oh! Susanna," "Old Folks at Home," "My Old Kentucky Home," and "Jeanie with the Light Brown Hair" comprise just a few of his best-known works. Their widespread popularity, which has continued unabated from Foster's era to our own, is generally attributed to their simple melodies and heartfelt evocations of contemporary life. Today, Foster is considered one of the first American composers to eschew European models and seek inspiration from his own environment, thereby creating songs that are distinctively American in rhythm and theme.

Foster was born at Lawrenceville, Pennsylvania, near Pittsburgh, the tenth child of Elizabeth and William Foster. In 1832, the family moved to Allegheny, also in western Pennsylvania, where the composer spent much of his life. Sporadically educated at local schools and at home by tutors, Foster received little formal musical instruction. Yet he displayed what his father viewed as "a strange talent for musick" and began writing songs at a young age, publishing his first in 1844. His parents offered little encouragement, however: they considered music an unsuitable occupation and in 1846 sent him to work as a bookkeeper at his brother's business in Cincinnati. But Foster continued writing songs, and his four-year stay there is generally considered the beginning of his greatest creative period. His first major triumph was "Oh! Susanna," which became an anthem for the forty-niners as they made their way westward to search for gold in California. Following this success, Foster was offered contracts by two music publishers, which assured him a steady though modest income. Convinced that he could now make a living by writing music, he left Cincinnati in 1850 and returned to Allegheny, where he married Jane Denny McDowell; their only child was born the following year. The early 1850s proved to be a prolific and successful period for Foster, witnessing the creation of many of his finest songs, including "Gwine to Run All Night" ("Camptown Races"), "Old Folks at Home" ("Way Down upon the Swanee River"), "Massa's in de Cold Ground," "My Old Kentucky Home," "Old Dog Tray," and "Jeanie with the Light Brown Hair." To introduce his compositions to the public he sought out several black minstrel troupes, which were then very popular, and often gave out copies of his songs before they were published and copyrighted. As a consequence, many of his songs were widely distributed in unauthorized versions for which Foster received no royalties, and they were also sometimes published anonymously or credited to others, often to the minstrel troupes that first performed them. One such troupe was the Christy Minstrels. In 1851, Foster granted E. P. Christy, the leader of the troupe, the right to perform his new songs prior to their publication and to bring out what became Foster's most famous song, "Old Folks at Home," under Christy's name. Initially, Foster preferred to publish his minstrel tunes anonymously to avoid public prejudice against that style of music. But he changed his mind when he saw the success of "Old Folks at Home," writing to Christy that "I have

concluded . . . to pursue the Ethiopian [minstrel] business without fear or shame and . . . to establish my name as the best Ethiopian song-writer." Scholars agree that by the mid-1850s Foster had done exactly that.

Yet Foster began to experience a variety of personal and financial problems. Despite contracts with publishers, his earnings proved inadequate for his expenses, and he and his wife went deeper and deeper into debt. In 1857 he began selling his publishers the rights to future royalties on his existing songs, thereby earning enough to cover some current debts but ultimately depriving himself of future income. In 1860, the family moved to New York City to be near Foster's publishers, but the marital problems that had resulted in a temporary separation in 1853-54 resurfaced. Jane and their daughter returned to Pennsylvania the following year, and Foster saw little of his family thereafter. He also began to drink heavily. As his financial difficulties worsened he was forced to write at a frantic pace, turning out about one hundred songs in his last four years. While living alone in New York in 1864, impoverished, alcoholic, and ill, Foster fell on a washbasin and severely cut his neck; he died a few days later.

Foster created over two hundred songs during a twenty-year period. His best-known writings fall roughly into two groups:

sentimental ballads and minstrel tunes. Foster composed over one hundred sentimental ballads, many in a style similar to the traditional Irish and English ballads then popular in America. Such acknowledged favorites as "Jeanie with the Light Brown Hair," "Come Where My Love Lies Dreaming," and "Beautiful Dreamer" belong to this group. Foster's ballads feature simple melodies consisting of a vocal line accompanied usually by piano or guitar; their lyrics often reflect a nostalgic longing for home, a loved one, or the past. Foster repeated these themes in his Ethiopian music, songs that were largely inspired by black life in the antebellum South. This group, which numbers about thirty songs, includes both dialect and nondialect pieces. Some are humorous, like "Oh! Susanna" and "Camptown Races," while others are somber or pathetic, like "Old Folks at Home," "Massa's in de Cold Ground," "My Old Kentucky Home," and "Old Black Joe." These songs were written to be performed on stage and are often more varied in structure than Foster's ballads, incorporating solo parts, multi-voice choral arrangements, and instrumental passages. Although Foster employed different musical styles in his sentimental and minstrel songs, both groups generally feature sincere and compelling emotional themes, poetic lyrics, and simple yet poignant melodies that are easy to sing.

While Foster's songs have always been popular with the public, critical response to his works has been mixed. During the nineteenth century, critics consistently noted Foster's enormous popularity, some attributing his appeal to the intimate connection between his simple lyrics and melodies: as a reviewer for the *Atlantic Monthly* remarked, "Foster thought in tune as he traced in rhyme, and traced in rhyme as he thought in tune." Other early reviewers, however, castigated him for the unrefined subject matter of his minstrel tunes, and many dismissed his work as transient popular entertainment. Some of these attitudes have continued to this day, limiting serious consideration of his poetic and musical achievements. Yet a number of modern critics have attempted to identify the source of Foster's widespread appeal and to define his contribution to American music. Many note that Foster captivated his audience with emotionally evocative depictions of contemporary life that reflected the national mood during the mid-nineteenth century. Foster's articulation of the American experience and his rejection of European models in many of his songs has led some commentators to elevate his works to the status of folk songs. Although the exact nature of his contribution to American folklore continues to be debated, critics today unanimously praise the honesty, simplicity, and pathos of Foster's best melodies. Perhaps Deems Taylor best described their charm, hailing them as "songs that find an eternal echo in our hearts."

## PRINCIPAL WORKS

*"Open Thy Lattice Love" (song) 1844
"Oh! Susanna" (song) 1848
"Old Uncle Ned" (song) 1848
*Songs of the Sable Harmonists* (songs) 1848
"Nelly Was a Lady" (song) 1849
"Summer Longings" (song) 1849
†"Gwine to Run All Night" (song) 1850
"Nelly Bly" (song) 1850
‡"Old Folks at Home" (song) 1851
"Massa's in de Cold Ground" (song) 1852
"My Old Kentucky Home, Good Night" (song) 1853

"Old Dog Tray" (song) 1853
"Ellen Bayne" (song) 1854
"Jeanie with the Light Brown Hair" (song) 1854
"Willie We Have Missed You" (song) 1854
"Come Where My Love Lies Dreaming" (song) 1855
"Comrades, Fill No Glass for Me" (song) 1855
"Hardtimes Come Again No More" (song) 1855
"Gentle Annie" (song) 1856
"Old Black Joe" (song) 1860
"Beautiful Dreamer" (song) 1864
*The Melodies of Stephen C. Foster* (songs) 1909
*Foster Hall Reproductions: Songs, Compositions, and Arrangements by Stephen C. Foster, 1826-1864* (songs) 1933
*Stephen C. Foster's Forgotten Songs* (songs) 1941
*A Treasury of Stephen Foster* (songs) 1946

*The lyrics for this song were written by George P. Morris.

†This song is known as "Camptown Races."

‡This song is also known as "Way Down upon the Swanee River."

---

### ALBANY STATE REGISTER  (essay date 1852)

[*This anonymous critic comments on black minstrel songs, revealing the wide popularity of "Old Folks at Home" during Foster's era. These remarks first appeared in the* Albany State Register *in 1852.*]

We confess to a fondness for negro minstrelsy. There is something in the melodious **"Uncle Ned"** that goes directly to the heart, and makes Italian trills seem tame. . . . God bless that fine old colored gentleman, who we have been so often assured has

> Gone where the good niggers go.

**"Old Folks at Home"** . . . is on everybody's tongue, and consequently in everybody's mouth. Pianos and guitars groan with it, night and day; sentimental young ladies sing it; sentimental young gentlemen warble it in midnight serenades; volatile young "bucks" hum it in the midst of their business and their pleasures; boatmen roar it out stentorially at all times; all the bands play it; amateur flute players agonize over it at every spare moment; the street organs grind it out at every hour; the "singing stars" carol it on the theatrical boards, and at concerts; the chamber maid sweeps and dusts to the measured cadence of **"Old Folks at Home"**; the butcher's boy treats you to a strain or two of it as he hands in the steaks for dinner; the milk-man mixes it up strangely with the harsh ding-dong accompaniment of his tireless bell; there is not a "live darkey," young or old, but can whistle, sing, dance and play it, and throw in "Ben Bolt" for seasoning; indeed at every hour, at every turn, we are forcibly impressed with the interesting fact, that—

> Way down upon de Swanee Ribber
>   Far, far away,
> Dere's whar my heart is turnin' ebber
> Dere's whar de old folks stay.

> *An extract in* Our American Music: Three Hundred Years of It *by John Tasker Howard, third edition, Thomas Y. Crowell Company, 1954, p. 185.*

## JOHN S. DWIGHT   (essay date 1853)

[*Dwight laments the success of "Old Folks at Home." His essay was originally published on 19 November 1853 in the* Journal of Music, *which Dwight edited.*]

We wish to say that such tunes [**"Old Folks at Home"**], although whistled and sung by everybody, are erroneously supposed to have taken a deep hold of the popular mind; that the charm is only *skin-deep;* that they are hummed and whistled *without musical emotion,* whistled "for lack of thought"; that they persevere and haunt the morbidly sensitive nerves of deeply musical persons, so that they too hum and whistle them involuntarily, hating them even while they hum them; that such melodies become catching, idle habits, and are not popular in the sense of musically inspiring, but that such and such a melody *breaks out* every now and then, like a morbid irritation of the skin.

> *John S. Dwight, in an extract in* Our American Music: Three Hundred Years of It *by John Tasker Howard, third edition, Thomas Y. Crowell Company, 1954, p. 185.*

## JOHN B. RUSSELL   (essay date 1857)

[*Russell examines the immense appeal of Foster's songs. His comments were first published in the* Cincinnati Daily Gazette *on 22 January 1857.*]

If popularity is any test of merit, to Stephen E. [*sic*] Foster's Melodies must be assigned a high rank. Probably no man's ideas have been more often repeated, when we consider singing, playing, whistling, etc. His tunes are a perpetual solace to the miner of California, the slave in the cotton fields of the South, and they gladden the tedious watches of the sailor in every sea reached by American or English enterprise. It is hardly too much to assert there is not a family in this country where any musical taste exists, that has not been cheered with the melody of his songs. In fact they are sung all over the civilized world, the seacoast cities of China not excepted. We lately read of an American traveller (Bayard Taylor, we think) teaching **"Uncle Ned"** to the Arabs in Africa and explaining to them, at their request, the meaning of the words in their own dialect. A Paris correspondent of a Boston paper says, on hearing **"Oh, Susannah"** whistled through the streets, he enthusiastically cried out "America for ever!"

Dickens speaks of its popularity in the prisons of England; and a friend who has spent some time in Central America says he has heard the natives amuse themselves by the hour in singing snatches of Foster's early songs which they had caught from the roving Californians. (pp. 127-28)

Like Tom Moore, Haynes Bayley and Mrs. Norton, the poetry of Mr. Foster is wedded to his own melodies. It is this intimate connexion between his poetry and music that gives such a charm to his compositions. His subjects are always simple, and so is his treatment of them; yet they are broad and well defined. It is impossible to conceive of anything better suited to the popular ear than the subject matter of his melodies and words. (p. 129)

> *John B. Russell, in an extract in* Stephen Foster, Youth's Golden Gleam: A Sketch of His Life and Background in Cincinnati, 1846-1850 *by Raymond Walters, Princeton University Press, 1936, pp. 127-29.*

## *LITTELL'S LIVING AGE*   (essay date 1864)

[*In this excerpt from an obituary notice first published in the* New York Evening Post, *the critic admires the sweetness and simplicity of Foster's songs.*]

On the tomb of Donizetti, in the cathedral at Bergamo, is a modest inscription saying that the dead composer was "a finder of many melodies." The simple record—too unpretending for the merits of the Italian composer—will be peculiarly applicable to the late Stephen C. Foster. . . . (p. 333)

His melodies are so sweet, so simple, so unpretending, that few people supposed that he had studied music scientifically, and was familiar with the more classical works of Mozart, Beethoven, and Weber. . . . [He] wrote all the words as well as the music of his songs. These words were in style almost identical with his melodies,—sweet, simple, and no worse in rhyme or rhythm than the majority of popular lyrics. . . .

His later works exhibit greater grace and tenderness than his earlier ones; and had he lived, and taken proper care of his health, he might have obtained the most enviable eminence as a musician. As it is, he had the blessed, heavensent gift of melody, and his compositions, if not his name, are known all over the world. Russians, Italians, Germans, French, and even Egyptians and Chinese, have heard and admired those sweet strains which made Stephen C. Foster pre-eminently the ballad-writer of America. We hope his publishers will make a collection—if not of all—of his best songs and choruses, and publish them in some enduring form; for their popularity will not die with the man whose genial imagination gave them birth. (p. 334)

> *"The Late Stephen C. Foster," in* Littell's Living Age, *Vol. 80, No. 1028, February 13, 1864, pp. 333-34.*

## [ROBERT PEEBLES NEVIN]   (essay date 1867)

[*Nevin briefly describes the characteristics of Foster's minstrel songs and praises their pathos.*]

[The verses of all Foster's negro melodies] are distinguished by a *naïveté* characteristic and appropriate, but consistent at the same time with common sense. Enough of the negro dialect is retained to preserve distinction, but not to offend. The sentiment is given in plain phrase and under homely illustration; but it is a sentiment nevertheless. The melodies are of twin birth literally with the verses, for Foster thought in tune as he traced in rhyme, and traced in rhyme as he thought in tune. Of easy modulation, severely simple in their structure, his airs have yet the graceful proportions, animated with the fervor, unostentatious but all-subduing, of certain of the old hymns (not the chorals) derived from our fathers of a hundred years ago. (p. 614)

In the true estimate of genius, its achievements only approximate the highest standard of excellence as they are representative, or illustrative, of important truth. They are only great as they are good. If Mr. Foster's art embodied no higher idea than the vulgar notion of the negro as a man-monkey,—a thing of tricks and antics,—a funny specimen of superior gorilla,—then it might have proved a tolerable catch-penny affair, and commanded an admiration among boys of various growths until its novelty wore off. But the art in his hands teemed with a nobler significance. It dealt, in its simplicity, with universal sympathies, and taught us all to feel with the slaves the lowly joys and sorrows it celebrated.

May the time be far in the future ere lips fail to move to its music, or hearts to respond to its influence, and may we who owe him so much preserve gratefully the memory of the master, STEPHEN COLLINS FOSTER. (p. 616)

[*Robert Peebles Nevin*], "*Stephen C. Foster and Negro Minstrelsy*," in The Atlantic Monthly, *Vol. XX, No. CXXI, November, 1867, pp. 608-16.*

## FRÉDÉRIC LOUIS RITTER   (essay date 1890)

[*Ritter extols the originality, naiveté, and simplicity of Foster's songs.*]

It is curious to observe the American white man, on the whole indifferent as to the creation of original songs, imitating and appropriating the melodic forms and tonal characteristics of the songs of the colored slave. But not alone are the forms of the melodic material of the slave-songs to be found in the "negro-minstrel" ballads: we also find the quaint, fantastic, often grotesque forms of speech of those songs imitated by the white composer in order to give his ballad a certain *couleur locale,* and to make it more attractive. These ballads have become very popular, especially as sung on the stage of that peculiarly American institution, the negro minstrel performance, and have absorbed the talent of many American ballad-composers; among whom the genial *Stephen C. Foster* was undoubtedly the most naturally gifted and most successful. (p. 437)

Foster was of a gentle, sweet temper, and full of feeling. His love and devotion to his father and mother were conspicuous traits of his character, and when they died his grief was sad to behold. He never could speak of his mother, after her death, without shedding tears. All these natural, noble, and refined qualities made Foster the sweet singer of so many pure songs. His ballads are, with regard to melodic and harmonic treatment, very *naïve* and simple; tonic, dominant, and subdominant are all the harmonic material upon which they rest. But beyond this natural simplicity, a genuinely sweet and extremely pleasing (though at times a little too sentimental) expression is to be found; and a good deal of originality in melodic inventiveness belongs to the Foster ballad, though in some of his later ballads, after he had reached great popularity, the composer often repeated himself. The harmonic accompaniment, for pianoforte or guitar, is extremely simple: but simplicity is here in place; a richer harmonic setting would have interfered with the natural simplicity of these songs. Foster's ballads reflect a gentle, refined spirit; they are the old psalm-tunes idealized and transplanted into their real secular sphere, with a certain Irish strain of pathos superadded. The composer of **"Old Dog Tray," "Old Kentucky Home,"** etc., said *naïvely* and gently what he had to say, without false pretension or bombastic phrases; but his sweet sayings touch the heart and remain in the memory. Numerous were the imitators of his peculiar style, but none possessed Foster's natural æsthetic taste and geniality. He may be called the American people's composer *par excellence.* (pp. 439-40)

*Frédéric Louis Ritter, "The Cultivation of Popular Music," in his* Music in America, *second edition, 1890. Reprint by Burt Franklin, 1972, pp. 421-40.*

## H. T. FINCK   (essay date 1912)

[*Finck argues that Foster's works can rightly be considered folk songs.*]

The standard which excludes the popular songs of our Stephen Foster from the list of real folksongs cannot be accepted as "scientific." Dr. Hugo Riemann, the leading German theorist and lexicographer, defines the word "Volkslied" as "either a song which originated among the people (*i. e.,* the poet and composer of which are no longer known), or one which has been adopted by the people; or, finally, one which is 'volksmässig,' *i. e.,* simple and easily comprehended in melody and harmony." The Foster melodies are included under both the second and the third of these definitions as true folksongs; they have been adopted by the whole American people, and they are always simple in melody and harmony. To exclude them for the reason that their composer happens to be known, is an argument that can be reduced *ad absurdum* by a question: Suppose some antiquarian discovered that certain folksongs dear to the Germans for generations were composed by such and such an individual; would a single person in the whole empire cease to consider them folksongs? And if by some miracle the names of all the originators of these melodies were ascertained, would folksong cease to exist?

Foster wrote his own poems as well as his melodies, and the words and music of such songs as **"Way Down Upon the Suwanee River," "Massa's in the Cold, Cold Ground," "My Old Kentucky Home"** are as closely allied as are the text and the music in Wagner's "Tristan und Isolde." Yet—and here is another point of identity with the originators of true folksongs—he was not a professional musician. Far from it. To save his life he could not have composed a symphony or a so-

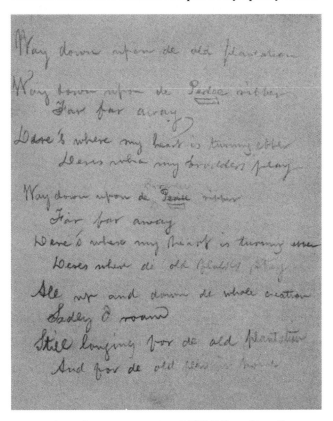

*Original manuscript version of "Old Folks at Home."*

nata, or even a short piece for the pianoforte. His harmonies seldom go beyond the three most elementary chords—tonic, dominant and sub-dominant; and his melodies are so rich and satisfying in themselves that they give pleasure even without harmonies, which bring them under the definition of folksong given by Berlioz. Of musical form Foster took no more thought than a canary. His songs "give voice to the joys, sorrows, hopes and aspirations of a people rather than an individual;" they are songs created by the people—the folk—for he was one of them. If they are not folksongs, what under the sun are they? Some have called them by the German name "volksthümlich," which means conscious imitations of folksongs, like Schulz's "Lieder im Volkston;" but Foster did not consciously imitate the songs of his or any other country; he wrote what he did because his genius was built that way.

Not only are his songs—there are over a hundred and fifty of them—genuine folksongs; they are genuinely American, too.

On this phase of the subject, also, erroneous notions are still widely current. Thousands who sing his songs do not know who wrote them, or care; many other thousands think they are negro plantation songs. Now, Foster did visit the plantations and campmeetings of the black men to catch their idiom; he had to make his living by writing for the "negro-minstrels," who at that time had practically a monopoly of the concert business; yet even those of his poems which he wrote in the negro dialect voice the general feelings of mankind rather than those of a particular race; and as for his melodies, they are as unlike true negro music as a Hungarian rhapsody is unlike a Bellini operatic aria. In every way they betray his own individual genius and that this individual genius was thoroughly American is indicated by the way in which the American people have taken them to heart—infinitely more than they have any imported folksongs. Apart from a national anthem, nothing arouses such intense enthusiasm in an American audience as the singing of one of these American folksongs. Indeed, there is nothing quite like it in any foreign country.

H. T. Finck, "The Position of Stephen Foster in Musical History," in The Etude, Vol. 30, March, 1912, p. 224.

## HAROLD VINCENT MILLIGAN (essay date 1920)

[In this excerpt from the conclusion to his full-length biography, Milligan assesses Foster's strengths and weaknesses as a composer.]

As a composer, Stephen Foster is a paradox. The wonder is that anyone who could write so well, could at the same time write so poorly. Was he a man of mediocre talent, who stumbled almost by accident upon a few nuggets of pure gold in the midst of much of little worth, or was he endowed with a great gift which remained for the most part mute and found expression only in a few brief moments of song?

He had practically no constructive ability. So far as the first impulse of his inspiration could carry him, he went, but no farther. Judged by the standards of musical composition, nearly all of his one-hundred and seventy or more songs are on the same level. These songs were written throughout a period of about twenty years, during which time he neither gained nor lost in the power of expression. His death, at thirty-seven, found him as a composer just about where he had

been at the beginning of his career. Both melody and harmony are of the utmost simplicity. He could neither develop a melody nor vary his harmony. His melodies repeat themselves monotonously, and he was content with a few simple chords and modulations. And yet when his inspiration is of so pure and exalted a nature as it is in "The Old Kentucky Home," or "The Old Folks at Home," the very limitations of his power become virtues, resulting in a simplicity and directness of utterance which no amount of erudition and sophistication could have equalled in sincerity and potency. He put the best of himself into the composition of these songs, and it is because they are the honest expression of real emotion that they found their way directly and at once to the world's heart.

In order to understand Foster's limitations as a musician, it is necessary to realize the conditions of his early environment. For the proper development of artistic expression, an old and well established civilization is necessary. This is especially true of the development of the musician, i. e., the composer, the man who produces music. The other arts, literature, painting, sculpture, and the drama, are more or less imitative and drawn directly from life and experience, but music is esoteric in its nature, and, for its proper expression, demands not only the power and impulse to create, but also initiation into the forms and formulæ of the art itself. This esoteric quality distinguishes music from all other activities of the human spirit, even religious aspiration, which it most closely resembles. (pp. 109-10)

Stephen Foster's career is a good example of what happens when a musical soul is placed in an unmusical environment. Nothing ever takes the place of instinctive and intuitive culture, and this is absorbed unconsciously during the early years of life. No amount of study and industry can develop to its fullest possibilities the talent of one whose childhood is barren of music. Neither poverty, nor the material conditions surrounding his early life, thwarted the development of Stephen Foster's genius. The answer to the riddle is to be found in the mental atmosphere in which he found himself.

There is no evidence that Stephen Foster ever attempted to overcome the deficiencies of his early musical education. On the contrary, he was either content with his achievements or, feeling that the struggle was hopeless, lacked the courage to begin it.

It may be seriously doubted whether greater technical facility would have improved his music or achieved for him a greater name in history. The general average of his work might have been higher, but his best songs might have lost something of the sincerity and naïve charm which are their greatest attribute. Limited as it was, his technical equipment was exactly suited to the production of such a song as "The Old Folks at Home."

It would be futile to compare him with any of the great men of music. The circumstances of his life, the environments of his mind, were so totally different from those surrounding any of the acknowledged masters of the Art, that any speculations of this kind would be idle. He bears some resemblance to Schubert. Who can say what would have been the sum of Franz Schubert's achievements had he been born in Pittsburgh in 1826?

Foster's melodies display a surprising vigor; they abound in wide intervals, the initial phrase frequently extending over an octave, a characteristic said to be indicative of an active temperament and an energetic mind. Intervals of a fourth, a fifth and a sixth are quite common, while the leap of an octave occurs often enough to be noted as a characteristic. Among the melodies in which the octave leap occurs are those of the songs **"Uncle Ned," "Massa's in the Cold, Cold Ground," "The Old Folks at Home," "Come Where My Love Lies Dreaming," "Willie Has Gone to the War," "Nell and I,"** and the Schubertian **"Open Thy Lattice, Love,"** written at sixteen.

The repetitiousness of Foster's melodies is such that one cannot fail to wonder that they exert such an influence upon the listener as they do. Even among the folksongs and the simple tunes to which they can be compared, few are as rudimentary as they. For example, let us analyze **"The Old Folks at Home,"** which, for widespread popularity, is the most successful of his songs. The verse is composed of a four-bar phrase which is repeated four times, twice with a semicadence (dominant seventh), and twice with a tonic cadence. The beginning of the chorus presents a new phrase of four measures, answered by the verse-phrase with the complete cadence. The song is provided with a "prelude" and "postlude" for piano which are nothing but duplicates, an octave higher, of the first two lines of the verse. In other words, we have a ten-line musical verse of which nine lines are identical. The musical material from which the song is made proves to be two four-measure phrases. The harmonic texture is as naïve as the melody. There are no modulations whatever, and only the three primary chords are employed, tonic, dominant (seventh) and subdominant, all of which appear in the root position, except one subdominant chord which is in a second inversion. This is, indeed, music in "words of one syllable," and it is a striking evidence of the beauty and potency of Foster's inspiration that his songs have won the affection of the musically sophisticated, as well as of the unlearned. (pp. 112-14)

Of late years there has been a movement of protest against the use of certain of Foster's songs in the public schools. The agitation reached a climax recently in Boston, where a book of *Forty Best Songs,* compiled for school use, was withdrawn by the Boston School Committee because it contained seven songs by Stephen Foster in which occurred the words "nigger," "darky," and "Massa." It was claimed by the protesting negroes that these words were used as epithets and as terms of reproach, and that their children were jeered at unmercifully as a result of singing the songs. The Pastor of the First African M. E. Church of Boston declared that "The songs **'Old Black Joe,' 'My Old Kentucky Home,'** and **'Massa's in the Cold, Cold, Ground,'** are an insult to the whole colored race." The School Committee agreed to withdraw the book, but their action was severely criticised throughout the country and brought about a discussion of the whole subject of Foster's songs which demonstrated how wide-spread is their popularity and how deep the affection in which they are held.

There may be some cause for complaint against the perpetuation of such a song as **"Oh Susanna,"** in which the negro appears only as a buffoon, a song typifying an attitude toward the negro which has long since died out, but it is difficult to understand how the singing of such songs as **"Old Black Joe"** and **"My Old Kentucky Home"** can humiliate the colored race. On the contrary, it would seem that these songs are a distinct tribute to the colored race, being among the permanent contributions to American literature inspired by the negro, comparable to *Uncle Tom's Cabin* and *Uncle Remus.*

Paul Lawrence Dunbar, the negro poet, makes frequent use of the objectionable words. It is impossible to eliminate from history the story of the Civil War, nor should the younger negroes be allowed to grow up in ignorance of the fact that to secure their freedom the white people of the North fought for four years, gave freely of their lives and treasure, and with their hearts' blood won for the negroes the blessings of life, liberty and the pursuit of happiness. The life of the American people is mirrored in their literature, in which the songs of Foster occupy an exalted and imperishable place.

Stephen Foster touched but one chord in the gamut of human emotions, but he sounded that strain supremely well. His song is of that nostalgia of the soul which is inborn and instinctive to all humanity, a homesickness unaffected by time or space. It is a theme which has always made up a large part of the world's poetry, and will always continue to do so as long as human hearts yearn for love and aspire toward happiness. Among all the poets who have harped the sorrows of Time and Change, no song rings truer than that of Stephen Foster. . . . From the unpromising soil in which he grew, he was able to distill by some strange alchemy of the soul such sweet magic of melody as to win an immortality far beyond his dreaming. These wildflowers of music which blossomed, unwatched and untended, from unsuspected seeds, have found for themselves a spot which is all their own, where they may bloom forever in Fields Elysian. (pp. 114-16)

> *Harold Vincent Milligan, in his* Stephen Collins Foster: A Biography of America's Folk-Song Composer, *G. Schirmer, 1920, 116 p.*

### J. G. BURTNETT   (essay date 1922)

[*In this examination of the national elements in Foster's melodies, Burtnett delineates those aspects of the songwriter's background that contributed to making him the "true interpreter" of black life in mid-nineteenth-century America.*]

Stephen Collins Foster was born in Pittsburgh at noon, July 4, 1826, the day that both Adams and Jefferson passed through the shadows. If in prophetic vision these patriots foresaw the dispute, vindictiveness and ungovernable passion that was to threaten the young Republic and end in bloody fratricidal strife, let us hope that they also foresaw how this human mite was to pluck the white flower of love from our national crown of thorns and immortalize its beauty, not by irrefutable logic, but by the power of verse and song. It is not our purpose, however, to enlarge upon biography further than is necessary to reveal some phase of his personality, or some quality of his work. While it is impossible to trace the beginnings of any life history back through interwoven conditions or generations in order to see at what time Fate said: "I find thee worthy; do this deed for me," yet there are undoubted facts of environment and heredity that certainly influenced the character and the art of this melodist. (p. 322)

[Foster's father] was of pure Celtic stock, a native of Virginia, born and reared in the social and economic conditions that were favorable to slavery and made it flourish. At sixteen, carrying with him the traditions, the manners, and the customs of the land of the Cavalier, he came to Pittsburgh. In an incredibly short time, by industry, cleverness, and a genius for details, he made himself a noted factor in merchant circles. From him the son inherited the Celtic peculiarity of visioning nature and life in its minutest details.

But the father who gave him temperamental traits and the enviable material environment whereby life was not too hard for the artistic temperament to flourish, was not the only source of inherent and acquired excellence. His mother was a woman of rare beauty and noble character. She was descended from English ancestors, long settled on the eastern shore of Maryland, and from a family gifted in music and poetry. Elizabeth Foster, born in affluence, bred amidst unusual opportunities, was always distinguished by deep religious feeling; this so impressed itself upon her children that their wildest mood never carried them beyond its restraint. She was also endowed with rare common sense that drew back from the too unusual or the too unique. Fearing those common extremes, exhibited by people of an artistic temperament, she opposed her son's becoming a professional poet or musician. That her intuitions were justified is proven by the fact that Stephen Foster verified tradition by living the wild, irregular life of genius. That his wayward habits were never so pronounced as to shut out a vision of the noble, the beautiful, and the good is doubtless due to her influence. The pathos and remorse voiced in **"Comrades Fill no Glass for Me"** needs no comment. **"A Dream of My Mother"** and **"Farewell, Sweet Mother"** show that filial love and its teachings held sway in his soul to the last.

At his thirty-eighth year the fires of genius went out; he died in New York City. . . . The solicitude of the mother had sent him to Cincinnati to learn the "ways of trade" with his brother, but nothing could change the direction of his inclinations. In that bustling Ohio City a deeper and closer intimacy with slavery and its attendant institutions was afforded by voyages up and down the Ohio and the Mississippi. Nevertheless, it is a mistake to suppose that Foster's knowledge and interpretation of negro life and character was largely or fundamentally acquired on these trips. The father and mother were both born and bred where the institution of slavery, at least economically, was taken as a matter of course, and where no family was without its negro servant or servants.

That the Foster family brought to their northern home the institutions, the customs, and the manners of their forbears is an unquestioned fact. In the veins of his mulatto nurse mingled the blood of a West-India negro mother and of a French father. This "bound girl" Olivia was an expert dancer and taught the art in "select families." She was accustomed to take the child Stephen to her own church. If we knew only this fact it would tell us how the traditions, the customs, and the feelings of the "Old South" were transmitted to this, and to many other households of early Pittsburgh. In the close domestic relations with negro servants in his own home and the homes of relatives, as well as by observation while associated in business with his brother, we must look for the influences that made Foster the true interpreter of the thoughts and the emotions of a race placed in a unique and never-to-be-repeated relation to another people. No other people ever came into contact with the black race in the same intimacy, the same close touch, and yet with the peculiar aloofness as the southern whites in slavery days. The Southerner had and still retains an understanding of, and an affection for the negro. It cannot be denied that the old master had more personal love and sympathy for the slave than the soldier who fought for the freedom of the black race.

It seems almost an anomaly that the epoch in American history from the time of the landing of the Dutch trader in 1620 to the Civil War, the period so fraught with enmity and ran-

cor, should give birth to a certain kind of song that has not only become an expression of our national life, but is so universal in its nature as to be hummed, thrummed, and sung on the high seas, in every port of the world, and in all civilized lands. Indeed Foster's songs are more widely and far better known than our national hymn. Only such a genius as Foster, for whom the spiritual world flung wide its doors, revealing what was universal, could take slavery—the most contradictory thing in our national life—separate the deformed from the fair and give to his songs a universal appeal, a mystic charm, that finds the point of kindred emotion in all people although untouched by dogma or creed. The greatest artists, masters of the classic strains, like the divine Patti, sang these songs with such fervor and feeling as to bring tears to the eyes of cold audiences. By an impassible gulf, by something akin to sacredness, they are separated from cabaret minstrelsy, rag time, common Coon and Jim Crow songs.

Foster was interpreting a child race, a folk who loved to run the whole gamut of simple emotions,—a folk who loved the warmth of the sunlight and the southern moonshine. He not only saw the well springs of emotion but also caught the peculiar rythm, the harmonic interval, the bewitching cadence of the music in which this race expressed its emotions. The negro race has an inevitable sense of time; to this element of music all things are subservient, words are mere pawns to be scuttled about in any way. This brought into negro music the jerk or catch illustrated in **"Old Uncle Ned"**:

> Hang-up-de-fiddle-and-de-bow,
> Lay-down-de-shobel-and-de-hoe.

This catch found its extreme in the ecstatic shouting of the "Jerusalem Jump," a sort of frenzied religious demonstration that was common on the plantation, and doubtless witnessed by Foster in the church where Olivia took him.

But the perfect artistic sense of Foster did not permit him to use the extreme catch in his music, no more than it permitted extremes in idioms of speech. Just enough of each necessary to reveal the true ethnical element. His American ballads and sentimental songs have a vapory lightness through which the spirit speaks like moonlight. They are marred by no suggestion that is impure and by no sentiment that is unmanly.

Even genius plays on various strings before it finds its keynote. Foster found his real place in art as an interpreter of negro life. But for his genius our national music could in no way be complete. This music immortalizes by its artless art an episode that is irrevocably a part of our national life. His music could not have grown up anywhere else. He saw the wonderful tenderness for the master; the aspiration of the negro to be like his owner, as in **"My Nelly Was a Lady."** **"Swanee River"** sings the whole pathos of the slave snatched from his environment. This song while pre-eminently related to slavery expresses the love of all people for the place of nativity. **"My Old Kentucky Home"** combines the home sentiment with the warm sensuous appeal of nature, the ease, the rest of the body, and the freedom of the heart, while the intense, child-like religion in **"Old Black Joe"** leads one to believe that Stephen Foster foresaw the doom of slavery and the scattering of the black race. Perhaps he visioned a tenantless "cot among de bushes" and a race's final good night to its **"Old Kentucky Home."** "The old order changeth giving place to new," but the sun yet shines and the moon glimmers over the old plantation—fit symbol of the immortality of Foster's genius, personality and art.

In emotional simplicity his masterpieces are folk-songs, in eternal essence they are art songs. Nor is this all, for they have in them the essentials of real national art. They externalize, immortalize slavery as truly as the "Dying Gladiator" tells the story of the arena. (pp. 323-26)

*J. G. Burtnett, "National Elements in Stephen Foster's Art," in* South Atlantic Quarterly, *Vol. 21, No. 4, October, 1922, pp. 322-26.*

## GRACE OVERMYER   (essay date 1926)

[*In this excerpt from an article celebrating the centenary of Foster's birth, Overmyer discusses the uneven quality of his lyrics.*]

A fact which may not be overlooked in appraising the work of Stephen Foster is that with one or two exceptions he wrote the words, as well as the music, of his songs. Prevailingly pathetic in tone, his verse like his music follows a few simple structural patterns and does not venture to depart from them; and, again like his music, most of it seems, in this sophisticated age, quaintly simple in sentiment, but now and then there is a suggestion of true poetry—now and then a bit which causes regret that one who could occasionally write so well did not do so more often. There is that line from one of the most famous of the songs—a line drawn from the nearly inarticulate depths of human emotion:

The day goes by like a shadow o'er the heart.

**"My Old Kentucky Home"** is, indeed, one of the most consistently poetic of the songs, painting in few words happiness and sorrow by deftly simple contrasts:

The sun shines bright in my old Kentucky home
'Tis summer, the darkies are gay.

. . . . .

A few more days for to tote the weary load,
No matter, 'twill never be light.

**"Come Where My Love Lies Dreaming,"** the title of one of the now almost forgotten songs, is a line which has always seemed to us essentially and charmingly poetic, nearly catching some of the finely imaginative *Mid-Summer Night's Dream* spirit. We find to our regret that the rest of the poem does not live up to the quality of the title:

Come where my love lies dreaming,
   Dreaming the happy hours away,
In visions bright redeeming
   The fleeting joys of day.

The little touch of art is only regained in a line of the second stanza:

Come with a lute, come with a lay.

Others of the now forgotten sentimental songs have similarly poetic titles—**"Stay, Summer Breath"**; **"What Must a Fairy's Dream Be."** And in another, less imaginatively entitled **"Voice of By-Gone Days,"** Foster proves himself more than a mere sentimental versifyer, condensing in two lines the baffled mortal query:

Why should the beautiful ever weep,
   Why should the beautiful die?

Inseparable now through long association, Stephen Foster's

words and his music are inseparable also in spirit and in thought, and the pathos of the verses is, by its very lack of subtlety, deep and poignant. That too may be art.

His fingers were long like de cane in
   de brake,
   An' he had no eyes for to see
An' he had no teeth for to eat de
   corncake,
   So he had to let de corn cake be.

(p. 8)

*Grace Overmyer, "One Hundred Years of Stephen Foster," in* The Musical Observer, *New York, Vol. XXV, No. 7, July, 1926, pp. 7-8.*

## *MUSICAL COURIER*   (essay date 1930)

[*This critic argues that the American public's renewed interest in Foster is long overdue.*]

Stephen Collins Foster, "Who set a nation a' singing," is so much a part of the American people that it would seem that the long time it has taken for his own country to recognize his value is carrying out the truth of the old adage that a prophet has no honor in his own country.

There is no corner of America, and one might say of the world, where the strains of **"My Old Kentucky Home"** and **"Suwanee River"** have not been hummed, yet it is often that one meets those who do not know who first put those strains of music on paper. Perhaps this has been due to the fact that the songs are looked upon as "folk songs," things which are supposed to spring "from the people," and yet with a little thought on the subject the realization is apparent that all things have a beginning; the source of some are merely lost in the transmission.

Foster's first claim to the affections of the American people is that he has given us the greatest contribution to our folk-lore. . . .

Stephen Foster's further claim to the affection of Americans is that he sings primarily of the negro, an integral factor of American life, and that his songs were born at the very time when the negro was a paramount subject in the United States. To Stephen Foster's credit is that he revolutionized the art of negro minstrelsy, a strictly American form of entertainment, raising it from the level of coarseness and buffoonery to one of humor and pathos. Stephen Foster is, of course, more popularly known because of his negro contributions, but prior to launching on this career he wrote many songs which well up from the heart of the nation at large, of which an excellent example is the typical **"Nelly Bly."**

It required audacious courage for a youth of western Pennsylvania, a century ago, to announce his intention of becoming a song writer, a hitherto unknown vocation in America. But it was a force within himself which Foster could not have controlled. He was born with a gift, a rare gift, which neither he nor his family recognized for a long time. This is not surprising however, since those were pioneer times, days for the clearing of timbered lands, building roads and canals, establishing trading posts, building homes, churches and schools, rather than strumming on a guitar and writing poetry and melodies. It required a certain willingness to stand aside from the crowd, to be ridiculed by many and pitied by those who were more tolerant, even to the point of being singled out by his father as "possessing a strange talent for musick."

What this strange talent might have developed into had it been nurtured in a musical atmosphere is hard to say, especially when one considers the inherent weaknesses of Foster's character, yet, because of this very weakness do his songs sing of loneliness and nostalgia, and tug at the heart strings. Perhaps if Foster had developed greater technical facility his songs would have lost some of their spontaneous sincerity and their greatest asset, the charm of their naivete.

The simplicity of his songs is no doubt due to the same characteristic in his nature; he hated any sort of show, his sympathies were preferably with the under dog, his feelings were of the most sensitive sort and his emotions easily aroused. . . . But with this sensitiveness he had a great physical courage.

As is seen, Stephen Foster was in many ways a paradox. Perhaps this is the privilege of genius, a title to which he can lay claim because of his ability for the honest expression of real emotion. Such expression is the life blood of art, no matter what its form, and it also happens that Stephen Foster's art had that appeal which is not only American but universal. But because he was American and because the life of the American people is closely woven with the very essence of his songs, does he deserve the consideration which has only recently been accorded him. (p. 34)

*"Pictorial Biography of Stephen Collins Foster," in* Musical Courier, *Vol. 100, No. 12, March 22, 1930, pp. 34-41.*

## CARL HOLLIDAY   (essay date 1930)

[*Denying that Foster's compositions may be properly termed folk songs, Holliday contends that his contemporary success derived from his ability to create melodic, sentimental ballads that satisfied the public's "emotional hunger."*]

Contemporary life seems to have had almost no influence upon Foster's creations. He simply created a dreamland of emotions, now and then with a Southern or plantation background, but more often without it, and built upon this basis an exceedingly simple musical structure. Evidently the prolonged Civil War affected him but little; he composed but four songs dealing with it: **"We're a Million in the Field," "For the Dear Old Flag I'll Die," "Was My Brother in the Battle,"** and **"Stand by the Flag."** His was indeed an individualistic note, not easily attuning itself to great causes or national crises.

Foster has frequently been called the chief "folk-song writer of America." Indeed Elson declares him "as truly the folk-song genius of America as Weber or Silcher has been of Germany" [see Further Reading]. A folk-song, however, is a

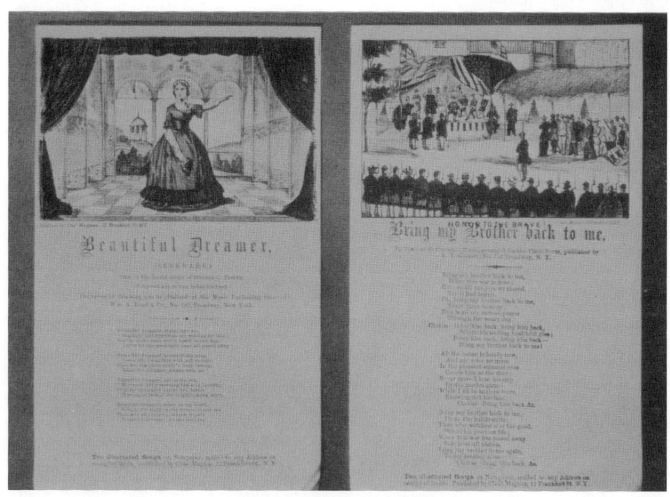

*Broadsides containing the words of Foster's songs.*

song *arising out of a folk,* and Foster's **"Old Kentucky Home," "Swanee River," "Old Black Joe,"** and **"Uncle Ned,"** while using the negro life as a background and a very crude imitation of negro dialect as a medium of expression, are not, either in melody or in thought, an expression of the negro folk of plantation days. The most superficial comparison of Foster's songs with such true negro folk lyrics as "All God's Children Got Wings" and "Swing Low, Sweet Chariot" makes this clear.

He would probably have smiled rather wistfully if some admirer in his own day had called him a creator of folk-songs. He was a producer of sentimental ballads—with a sentiment so true and with a comprehension of the pathos of life so pungent that they rise above the confines of this or that folk or race. They touch those primitive emotions that are *universal.*

He came at a time when the black-face minstrel was monarch of the American stage. The theatres of Nassau and John Streets rang with the applause of "highly respectable audiences," who were enraptured by the singing of such burnt-cork artists as John H. Murphy and "Hunk" Mudge. . . .

Those old-time American audiences were hungry aesthetically, were starving for romance, and when the aforementioned John H. Murphy came forward from among his black-faced brethren and sang "Write Me a Letter from Home" or "Dear Mother, I'll Come Back Again" there were tears aplenty. . . .

Foster came at just the right hour to supply this hunger for a certain broad "happy pity," and he did it with an art that has made his songs popular even in this sophisticated age. He combined a moderate touch of pathos with a bit of melody simple enough for the untrained ear of his day, and the combinations in not a few instances are masterpieces.

It was, and is, *melody* pure and simple that has carried these songs of Foster on the high wave of popularity throughout the years. The accompaniments are totally innocent of any attempt to be ornate; they are obvious and even conventional. Like their hearers, these and other attempts in American lyrical music revealed no ambition to step outside the elemental field of *melody.* (p. 200)

[If] Stephen Foster were living today he would, in all probability, be composing jazz—and making Irving Berlin look to his laurels and royalties. For Foster, like Berlin, was attentive to the emotional hunger of the common folk; he simply expressed for the folk what they were vaguely feeling or longing for. And in so doing he revealed a power in simple melody that places him among the genuine poets in the world of music. His was not the intricacies of modern counterpoint; his audience was not trained up to such intricacies—and he was never very far in advance of his people. Had he lived in a day or a nation of greater musical culture he might have risen to supreme heights as a composer of music for the orchestra; for the basis of works for such large combinations of instruments is easily discovered in some of his so-called plantation songs. As it was, however, he was a pioneer among those who have taught the general public, perhaps unconsciously, the ever growing appreciation for the art of music—the creator of

> Short swallow flights of song that dip
> Their wings in tears and skim away.

(p. 223)

Carl Holliday, "Stephen Collins Foster," in *Overland Monthly and Out West Magazine, Vol. 88, No. 7, July, 1930, pp. 199-200, 223.*

## ROBERT MacGOWAN   (essay date 1932)

[*MacGowan examines the reasons for Foster's widespread appeal, highlighting his ability to understand and articulate the sentiments of all humankind.*]

Everybody understands Foster—or at least thinks he does, which is more to the point—and in this Foster resembles the minstrels of ancient time. Who wrote the precious ballads that tell the sins and sorrows, the struggle and sufferings of our human kind in those dim days? Their names are lost to history, though their works live always. It is not otherwise with Foster. Millions in America who sing his songs daily never heard of their author. It is a magnificent tribute to the genius who gave them birth, for it is the poet's privilege to be quoted as it is the commander's to be obeyed. His songs have entered into the musical diet of mankind. . . . Why? Because he is so human, because he speaks the language of the common people without whom the world cannot do business and poets have no audience; because he voices the universal sentiments of the human heart in his own strange, simple, and ingenuous fashion. Foster is truly America's contribution to minstrelsy.

One is amazed at the variety of his moods, and yet it should be no occasion for surprise, for the poet responds becomingly to every breeze that blows through the heart of nature. True, there is a strain of melancholy in his compositions quite out of keeping with our saxaphone age, but Matthew Arnold has taught us once and for all that great literature is always characterized by 'deep seriousness.' This accounts for his sentimental ballads and his **"Summer Longings."**

> Waiting sad, dejected, weary—waiting for the May
> Spring goes by with wasted warnings, moonlight evenings,
>   sunbright mornings
> Summer comes, yet dark and dreary, life still ebbs away
> Man is ever weary, weary—waiting for the May.

On the other hand his sense of humor balances the pathos that troubles his heart. This is well illustrated in **"Uncle Ned"**—

> He had no wool on de top of his head, On de place where
>   de wool ought to grow.

But

> When old Ned die Massa take it mighty hard,
> De tears run down like rain;
> Old missus turn pale and she look'd berry sad,
> Kase she neber see Old Ned again.

Well, it is all very elemental, but somehow on that account Stephen Foster includes ourselves. Joy and sorrow are strangely mated through the years, and to give life its proper balance is the work of the true interpreter. Foster sings for the world.

But this in itself is not enough to explain his universal acceptance. Many a time one hums a song unconsciously until it becomes obtrusive. Then it is time to investigate. Closer inspection reveals its shallowness and somehow we part company. Any idea must justify its presence. Now the beauty of Foster's simplicity is just this: it can stand closer inspection.

The author is saying something; he is never shallow. And this may account for his slender output; he did not write to catch a market, even if the Christy Minstrels found his product profitable. Foster was a prophet in that he was a seer first. Ruskin has taught us this transvaluation of values. For every hundred who can think, there is only one who can see. Foster looked deep into the tragedy of life, finding it in the lowly type that crooned its songs along the wharves or down in the old plantations. But he did not see merely the hunger of body and soul, the crude dwellings, the ache and anguish of ceaseless toil. He saw a rich content, a patient sublimation of disappointed hopes and fruitless longings in the form of happy comradeship in song and dance and the sacred revel of the home, with its multitudinous offspring and its grinding labors of love. He heard the rollicking chorus of fantastic religion, the warm surrender of life in penitential adoration—the common concern of faith whether in surplice or in rags—and the sweetest sounds that earth can ever hear, the music of cooperation and human brotherhood. He heard it all when other ears were closed, for he was the prophet of a new day, in the far distance still, but coming, just as sure as we live, in a grander and yet more glorious dawn. (pp. 16-20)

Read, sing Foster's songs again in the light of what I have written and perhaps your age will find once more the springs of contentment and brotherhood in those pathetic pictures of human love and longing. The Old Kentucky Home habit exists in spite of its environment, not because of it, and whatever the economic state that can best develop such an inward and spiritual paradise, let it be welcomed. Old Black Joe may not have been so unhappy after all. Life had its compensations, and his soul was nourished with a hope that no money can buy and no brain manufacture. Whether we be rich or poor, there are fundamental cravings of the soul that must be satisfied or life is lived in vain, and Foster knew the secret.

> Gone are the days when my heart was young and gay,
> Gone are the friends from the cotton fields away,
> Gone from the earth to a better land I know,
> I hear their gentle voices calling, "Old Black Joe."
>
> I'm coming, I'm coming, for my head is bending low:
> I hear their gentle voices calling, "Old Black Joe."

When life reaches its great crisis, such gentle voices are wondrously consoling. Such spiritual penetration enriches the years, and age can find no happier comforter when the head is bending low. We are sorely deceived if we attempt to build a civilization without such an ethereal element, even if it be only of the imagination. Men live the best of their lives there anyhow, and it is the business of the poet to remind us of that fact again and yet again. 'The heart aye is the part aye that makes us right or wrong.' Here then is the true Foster, the Foster who lives on in the heart of humanity, the Foster who sang for mankind the joys of the unfettered soul.

Foster was a patriot, too. He lived in a time when literature still drank from the wells of European culture. America was subject then, as now, to an inferiority complex. Of course, there was good and sufficient reason. Across the ocean was the well-cultivated field of the arts. Fashions, feminine and literary, were 'imported.' But the new world was slowly coming into possession of her soul, and Foster played no small part in helping her on. He sang about his own land and his own people in their own tongue. His work is American through and through. No poet in any other land could have produced it then, or could produce it now. It is unmistakably our own. In this also his greatness is supreme, that he could

be so intensely national and yet convey such universal sentiment. Especially is he the poet of the Ohio Valley—not that he sang of her glories—that is still in the future—but that he represents a stage of culture in the making of the west. . . . [Foster's] depth is not metaphysical; there is nothing speculative in his thinking; he is not the product of any school of philosophy—though he may have helped to create one. He would not be Foster if he were. He is a humanist if he is anything, with a smack of the realist thrown in for good measure, and as such he represents the kind of thinking that prevailed during his time. But above all he stood in Pittsburgh at the meeting place of North and South at a time when the rivers carried the large bulk of the traffic. The North was becoming negro conscious, and Foster reflects the movement of melody from the plantations out into the wider world. To what better and more sympathetic hands could such a commission have been entrusted? Out into the far spaces of the earth his sweet music has traveled—a gracious medium for such a philosophy as I have tried to outline in this paper. Foster has given our beloved country the best of advertising, and as patriots we owe him a debt far beyond our ability to repay. (pp. 21-3)

> *Robert MacGowan, in his* The Significance of Stephen Collins Foster, *n.p., 1932, 25 p.*

## FLETCHER HODGES, JR.   (essay date 1938)

*[In addition to contrasting the critical and popular reputations of Foster's songs, Hodges accounts for the success of his best-known compositions.]*

Stephen Foster of Pittsburgh has been in his grave for almost three quarters of a century, yet a score of his best songs live on. Due to their healthy vitality, they have stood the tests of peace and war and time, and have emerged fresh and strong and ever-young. They have become, not only a part of the American heritage, but of the world's heritage. If music can achieve for itself immortality, then our Pittsburgh composer's simple melodies will be heard for all time, in the noble company of the magnificent compositions of Haydn, Beethoven, the other masters, and a few gems of folk song like "Barbara Allen." . . . (p. 79)

It is unnecessary and futile to attempt to justify Foster's past popularity or to defend the present high position he occupies in the realm of music. The American people have taken judgment out of the hands of the critics, who have not always judged Foster accurately. Some of his contemporaries, while admitting that his contributions to negro minstrelsy were amusing, or entertaining, or even the best of their kind, labeled them merely interesting songs that caught the popular fancy for the moment and would soon be forgotten. Their composer was advised to devote himself to "higher types" of music. Others considered **"Old Folks at Home"** and **"My Old Kentucky Home"** grotesque negro songs, and suggested that the sentimental ballad should be Foster's real field of endeavor. Still others, a few Boston and New York classicists anxious to raise the general level of music appreciation in the United States, frankly dismissed the works of Stephen Foster as cheap, coarse, written in poor taste, even as "melodious trash." And thus having disposed of him, they turned their attention to operas and symphonies. But all this meant little to the general public who continued to sing and love his songs, and to adopt them as their own, even as the Forty-Niners took unto themselves Stephen's hearty **"Oh! Susanna,"** made it their marching song across the continent to the gold fields of California, and eventually transformed it into that young state's unofficial anthem. For fifty years after Stephen's death, he was with few exceptions forgotten by critic and professional musician alike, even while his melodies were becoming ever more strongly impressed on the national consciousness. The home and the community instinctively recognized qualities in his music which they valued, even though they may not have analyzed them. Yet the name of Stephen Foster was seldom associated with his works. Therefore, from a purely technical viewpoint, his songs might be considered true folk songs. He himself was rapidly becoming a semimythical figure, whom the mists of time were obscuring with traditions unbased on facts. He might have been lost, altogether, had not the last quarter century witnessed a marked revival of interest in both the music and the life of the composer.

Foster's fame rests chiefly on his four great songs of the South, **"Old Folks at Home," "My Old Kentucky Home," "Massa's in de Cold Ground,"** and **"Old Black Joe."** These beloved plantation melodies were intended to portray one race of people, one section of our country, one period in our history, yet through his genius Foster succeeded in creating songs which have leaped the boundaries of space and time, and express universal thoughts and emotions. The best of his sentimental ballads are still sung to-day: his hauntingly beautiful **"Jeanie with the Light Brown Hair,"** his tender **"Come Where My Love Lies Dreaming"** and **"Beautiful Dreamer"** recall the charm of an age which is past. **"Oh! Susanna"** and **"Camptown Races"** are proof that Foster possessed a sense of humor and occasionally sang in lighter vein. Other songs still heard to-day are **"Old Dog Tray," "Old Uncle Ned," "Nelly was a Lady,"** and **"Nelly Bly."** Altogether, he produced more than two hundred original songs and compositions. About twenty of them, his best works, so combine the qualities of poetry, melody, simplicity, and sincerity, that the resulting songs form a remarkable contribution to the music of our nation and of all mankind. (pp. 80-1)

[Foster] was among our first genuinely American composers, in that his songs were American in theme, rather than imitations of the English and German music of his time. There were other composers in America during his youth, it is true, but most of them lived in the older seaboard cities of Boston, New York, Philadelphia, or Baltimore, where the influence of European-trained teachers was strong. Such men looked across the Atlantic to England and Germany for their inspiration, with the result that they merely composed transplanted English or German music. Not so with Stephen Foster! Born at the meeting place of North and South, East and West, he did not look elsewhere for his inspiration—he found it all about him. And he sang of the America that he knew: the American home, the sentimental emotions underlying the superficial practicality of the American temperament, life on the Ohio and Mississippi rivers, slavery, the slumberous plantation life, the red-hot political campaigns, and southern battlefields. Because he generally knew what he was singing about, and felt it deeply, his best music lives and breathes. (pp. 82-3)

*Fletcher Hodges, Jr., "A Pittsburgh Composer and His Memorial," in* The Western Pennsylvania Historical Magazine, *Vol. 21, No. 2, June, 1938, pp. 77-106.*

**BERNARD DEVOTO** (essay date 1941)

[*An editor of the* Saturday Review of Literature *and longtime contributor to* Harper's Magazine, *DeVoto was a highly controversial literary critic and historian. A man whose thought enraged much of America's literary establishment during the 1930s and 1940s, he was frequently motivated by anger at authors he considered ignorant of American life and history. In the following excerpt from a regular column in* Harper's *entitled "The Easy Chair," DeVoto argues that Foster's songs are guides to understanding American popular culture in both the 1840s and 1940s.*]

Several times during the past year this column has invited you to look at the America of the 1940's through a lens just a century old. That was due in part to the fact that the Easy Chair is writing a book about the 1840's in America, but in greater part to a belief that the decade has much to say to our own, and that whoever understands it can be fairly confident about certain matters that are of the utmost importance in our own time. This month it seems suitable to remind you of [Stephen Collins Foster], a minor musician of the 1840's. . . . (p. 109)

On April 27, 1846, the Virginia Minstrels of Edwin P. Christy played in New York for the first time, at Palmo's Opera House. The date will do as well as any to fix a fact: that the American drama had matured its first native form. For at least four years such companies as Christy's, with such artists as Daddy Rice, Dan Emmett, and Dan Bryant, had been appearing in the full-length, standardized variety-performance in black-face known as the minstrel show. (pp. 109-10)

A Tin Pan Alley had arisen to give the minstrels songs, and the best of the song-smiths was only two years away from the beginning of his service to Christy and the others. In March of '46 a twenty-year-old Pittsburgh youth failed of appointment to West Point, and so at the end of the year he went to keep books in his brother's commission house at Cincinnati. He took with him the manuscripts of three songs, all apparently written in this year and all completely in the minstrel-nigger tradition. One celebrates a lubly cullud gal, Lou'siana Belle. In another an old nigger has no wool on the top of his head in the place whar de wool ought to grow, and you heard your grandfather, as your children's grandchildren will hear theirs, telling the chorus to lay down de shubble and de hoe for poor old Ned has gone whar de good niggers go. And in the third, American pioneering found its *leitmotif* for all time: it was **"Oh! Susanna."**

Stephen Foster himself need not occupy us long. He was different from fifty contemporaries, and his songs were different from theirs only in that an obscure chemistry of genius concentrated an era and a society in him. He was as Bohemian as Edgar Allan Poe, Fitz-James O'Brien, Mayne Reid, or the first period of Walt Whitman. He took no thought of the morrow, could not make a marriage work, lived precariously, accepted the tinsel of the cheapest theater, came to the proper end of pathetic artists—and said perfectly what his people felt. He wrote well over two hundred songs, all potboilers, most of them quite dead now. He took what pleased him—from his friends if research was too troublesome. He repeated himself and his rivals monotonously. And the difference between him and everyone else was that he made a final music. A hundred years after him you need only play the opening bars of **"My Old Kentucky Home"** or **"Old Folks at Home"** to rouse in any American the full nostalgia of things past, or to bind any audience, be they naturalized Czechs or the

Daughters of the American Revolution, South Carolina Consistory, in the unity of a nation that knows itself. Art is mysterious, it is the miraculous and undefined; but if that should chance to be art which a people take most closely to their bosoms and hold there most tenderly and longest, then Stephen Foster is incomparably the greatest American artist.

His music is the America of the Forties, building the nation toward to-day. He dreamed of Jeanie with her light-brown hair, floating like a vapor on the soft summer air. The joys of other days oppressed him, he could not sing to-night, and why should the beautiful ever weep, why should the beautiful die? He supped sorrow with the poor, dreaming of a once happy day, and with the gentle voices gone he had no friend left but Old Dog Tray. The emotion shifts to the period's refined lust, and gone are the cares of life's busy throng, beautiful dreamer, awaken to me; light is the young heart, so come where my love lies dreaming the happy hours away. It changes to a jig and here is Susanna—de buckwheat cake was in her mouth, de tear was in her eye, and he is off to Alabama wid his banjo on his knee. It becomes a buck and wing—de Camptown racetrack five miles long, gwine to run all night, gwine to run all day, he bet his money on de bobtail nag, somebody bet on the bay. But it is surest in that limpid pathos. I cannot work before to-morrow cayse de tear drop flow. Gone are the days when my heart was young and gay, where are the hearts so happy and so free?—I hear their gentle voices calling Old Black Joe. All de world am sad and dreary, ebrywhere I roam, hard times come again no more, the head must bow and the back will have to bend wherever the darky may go—a few more days for to tote the weary load, no matter 'twill never be light, a few more days till we totter on the road, then . . . for Foster and many millions of Americans who have answered with an unmistakable assent to a feeling only started, not expressed, by the music, my old Kentucky home, good-night. He made the Americans members one of another.

Between the America of the 1840's and the America we belong to a century has built a barrier which can be penetrated only with the greatest difficulty. What is called the modern temper has complexities, ambiguities, and tentatives that the Forties did not know. We persuade ourselves that our consciousness is tragic. That may be; certainly the American consciousness of the Forties lacked the sense of tragedy. It had achieved only pathetics. But no one will understand the decade in whose mind that assertion is tinctured with reproof or superiority. . . . The emotions of the Forties were simpler than our own, more limpid, more absolute, and more forthright.

They were an inchoate people between two stages of the endless American process of becoming a nation, with their heads down and their eyes resolutely closed to the desperate realities which a few more years would force them to confront in the deadliest of awakenings. They were a people without unity and with only a spasmodic mutual awareness, at that moment being pulled farther asunder by the centrifugal expansion of the frontier and the equal explosiveness of the developing industry—both of which would turn back again in the nation-making curve, but not for a long while still. A people, at the moment when Foster wrote **"Oh! Susanna,"** going blithely into a war of conquest whose certain results few or none tried to foresee. A people divided by racial differences, sectional cleavages, cultural antipathies, an enormous disparity of assumption, expectation, hope, and philosophy. A peo-

ple united only by equalitarian assumptions, by habits of democratic association, by a political system and tradition which were nearing the deadly test—and by a common readiness and reality of feeling which were shaped by the way they had come out of what they had once been, and which few took conscious thought of. That commonality of feeling, in its simplicity, sincerity, and high potential, was their commonwealth, the great deep in which they were a united people, and it is the one feasible way into them. Stephen Foster caught it at dead center—the maiden's grave under the willows, the old times that come again no more, the Camptown races, Susanna's immortal quickstep, the ready regret, the instantaneous and immortal confidence that was bred in the bone and acknowledged if only half-realized in a joke. A forthright people, with a readiness of sincere tears and an energy that could be neither measured nor stayed. The way to understand them is to steep yourself in Foster's songs.

So let us not casually dismiss him as a folk artist—an idiotic phrase on any man's lips—or as a songsmith from the Tin Pan Alley of popular art. True, he had no Kentucky home and probably had never seen one till after his song was written, and the Swanee River he longed for was the Pedee in the first manuscript. But the songs are not his experience and not so much an American experience as the evocation of one. As that, they are one of the very few crucial things in all our national art. Not in them so much as by way of them the Americans of the Forties and Fifties realized a fact alluded to in Fourth of July oratory but radically contradicted by the flux of everyday life, that they were a nation; that there had come to be a nation on this continent, shaped by the past and held together by the sentiments begotten of that past. They manifested a unity, not of politics nor of social organization nor of economic interest but of immeasurable, indefinable feelings that had grown slowly but had also grown organic. It was a unity that, when Foster wrote, was beginning to be just strong enough. . . . What was it that Lincoln addressed in the American people, speaking to it with such skill and authority that it recognized itself? The nation he brought through the fires of the most terrible years in our history was a unity of feeling. It was a nation hardly to be seen as a map and certainly not to be contained within a formal statement, but a totality of tradition, habit, belief, and of feeling most of all. Foster's songs irradiated moments of its self-recognition— and Lincoln, it will be remembered, was also gifted at the popular art of jokes.

Look for us there to-day. Possibly it is a strange thing to be an American, but the nation is a totality of things felt, the sum and product of what we have come to be out of what we were. Emotions roused by Foster's songs, the flight of a ball toward the outfield thirty years ago, the sound of a locomotive whistle in the night hills, jokes passed at the cigar store in summer twilights—such things are the membrane that incloses us. (pp. 110-12)

*Bernard DeVoto, "Stephen Foster's Songs," in* Harper's Magazine, *Vol. 183, June, 1941, pp. 109-12.*

## DEEMS TAYLOR   (essay date 1946)

[*Taylor searches for the source of Foster's enduring appeal, finding it in his creation of original American folk music.*]

So far as I know, only one song has ever made the Hit Parade eighty-seven years after it was written and seventy-seven

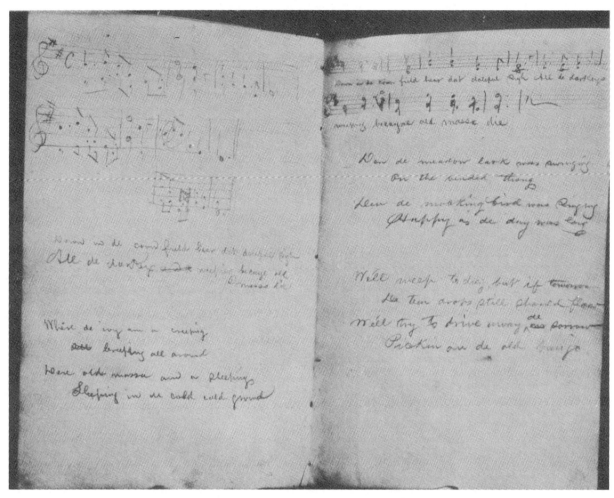

*Manuscript version of "Massa's in de Cold Ground."*

years after the death of its composer. That song is **"Jeanie with the Light Brown Hair,"** by Stephen Collins Foster. In 1940 and '41, when the broadcasters and the American Society of Composers, Authors, and Publishers were feuding, the radio suddenly discovered **"Jeanie."** She was sung, she was played—as a ballad, an aria, a chorus, a fantasy, a ballet, a foxtrot, a swing tune. It is a safe wager that during those two years Foster's ballad had more performances and was heard by more people than in all the years since its creation. The wonder is that it survived such mauling, that it has not departed into Limbo together with "Yes, We Have No Bananas" and the "Hut Sut Song."

Survived it has, for it has in it the stuff of imperishability. Together with a half dozen of Foster's other songs, it will be heard for many generations to come. Just why? What is the peculiar charm about so many of Foster's songs that sets them apart from the works of his contemporaries, that keeps them alive and glowing today? For one thing, they are great tunes, true melodies. In their pristine versions their accompaniments were primitive in harmony and childishly simple in form. The radio and dance bands have brought the harmonies up to date and some of their accompaniments and arrangements are fearsomely sophisticated. No matter. Foster's airs lean upon no accompaniment. Many of them are almost more effective without any accompaniment at all. Also, they are

well within the range of the average, untutored voice, without ever conveying any sense of deliberate limitation. A child can sing them; so can a coloratura. In his own field their creator, who started as a bookkeeper and ended in a free hospital ward, was a genius. (p. 7)

What quality [do Foster's songs have] that gives them such tremendous staying power? After all, other men, in his day, wrote songs that were simple, easy to sing, and easy to remember. Some of them were as popular as his, possibly more so, at the time. What was his secret?

It was, I think, that he helped to fill a gap that had always existed in our musical culture. Technically, we have no folksongs. Our ancestors, coming here from all quarters of the globe, brought with them the folksongs of what had been their native lands. These songs went into the melting pot and emerged, warped and often corrupted. They were recognizable, but they were not, and are not, peculiarly ours. It is ironic that the only race that developed a folksong literature *in this country* is the race that was brought here against its will, and was and has been the most brutally exploited of all—the Negro. The Negro spirituals and Stephen Foster's songs are the nearest to completely indigenous folksongs that we possess.

Nor is it, I think, a coincidence that most of the best of his songs are in Negro dialect and sing the woes of the Negro. A folksong is the speech of primitive people, of simple persons. It is highly improbable that the Russian Ippolitoff-Ivanoff ever heard of Foster. But it is not strange that both the Sirdar's March from the "Caucasian Sketches" and **"Old Black Joe"** start off with the identical phrase. Both are expressions of primitive life. Foster's acquaintance with the Negro may have been superficial, may even have been confined to the phony Negro of darky minstrelsy. Nevertheless, that acquaintance, and his choice of idiom, forced him to think in simple, clear, universal terms. And that thinking produced songs that find an eternal echo in our hearts. (p. 8)

*Deems Taylor, in a foreword to* A Treasury of Stephen Foster, *Random House, 1946, pp. 7-8.*

## JOHN TASKER HOWARD   (essay date 1953)

[*Howard's* Stephen Foster, America's Troubadour, *excerpted below, is a respected, detailed appraisal of Foster's life and work including extensive bibliographic information. In the following extract, drawn from the introductory section, Howard attributes the immortality of Foster's songs to their "distinctively American" yet universal appeal.*]

Many of [Foster's] songs are now more than a century old. They have come to be recognized as a genuine folk expression, even though they were created by a single individual. Foster assimilated the native influences that surrounded him, and gave them an expression that was natural and unaffected, spontaneous and unmanufactured. He wrote for a market, but when he was at his best, the market never soiled his work—it merely gave him a voice that would be understood.

Because the influences that moulded Foster's songs were so basically American his own songs are perhaps the most typically native product that had been produced up to his time. He was not like the composers in seaboard cities who imitated foreign models; he was under the spell of the minstrel shows, the singing of the Negroes who came to Pittsburgh and Cincinnati on the river boats from the South, and of the Negro worshippers in a little church near his childhood home. His songs are distinctively American, and yet the thoughts they express are so basically human that they are sung throughout the world. Foster achieved a nationalistic expression that is at the same time universal in its appeal.

While they have a folk flavor, his songs are not merely a folk expression. They reflect the character and temperament of their composer, and in that sense they are truly an art product. They provide an autobiography of the man who wrote them, in all but a few, both words and music. The finest of the sentimental songs are lyrics of home. With Stephen the love of home and the companionship of parents, brothers, and sisters was his strongest emotion. He was thoroughly miserable when he was away from the friends of his youth. The nonsense songs, **"Oh! Susanna,"** **"De Camptown Races,"** and others of their kind, show a laughing Stephen, sometimes a leader and sometimes led. The man who understands Foster's songs will have no difficulty in understanding Foster.

Stephen Foster's fame rests chiefly on his great songs of the pre-Civil War South. These beloved plantation melodies were intended to portray one race of people, one section of our country, one period in our history, yet through his genius Foster succeeded in creating songs which have leaped the boundaries of space and time, and express universal thoughts and emotions.

The purse that held the thirty-eight cents which were his total assets when he died had one more item in it, a little slip of paper with five penciled words—"Dear friends and gentle hearts." No doubt this was the title of an unwritten song, but whatever its intent, the phrase describes quite perfectly the dear friend and gentle heart who added **"Old Folks at Home"** and a dozen other immortal songs to the world's spiritual riches. (pp. 2-3)

*John Tasker Howard, in his* Stephen Foster, America's Troubadour, *revised edition, Thomas Y. Crowell Company, 1953, 433 p.*

## CARL BODE   (essay date 1959)

[*Bode argues that Foster's lyrics contributed to the popularity of his songs by providing Americans with an escape from three dominant aspects of their national culture: "the dour trio of puritanism, materialism, and competitiveness."*]

"Who writes our songs?" asked the New York *Evening Post* in 1859. Its answer was Stephen Foster. Praising him as the most popular living song writer, the *Post* proceeded to list the reasons for his vogue. They were the "easy, flowing melody, the adherence to plain chords in the accompaniments, and the avoidance of intricacy in the harmony or embarrassing accidentals in the melody." The *Post* was correct. But it failed to go quite far enough in analyzing Foster's music, and it ignored the significance of his lyrics.

The winning charm of the music accounts indeed for most of his appeal. The plaintive, simple airs are easy to remember. Their harmonies consist of the most ordinary tonic, dominant, and subdominant chords; their scope stays well within the range of the ordinary human voice. When a high note does occur, Foster smoothes the singer's approach to it by placing it at a point where the breath is full instead of at the end of a long phrase. The beat is firm and regular, designed for amateurs to follow either in group or solo singing. The lyrics too, if we examine them for the moment as units of sound instead of meaning, contribute to Foster's popularity, for the words making them up are often monosyllables. When polysyllables occur, Foster is apt to separate them musically by a deftly spaced sequence of notes. The consequence of all this calculated simplicity is a flow of melody that asked to be sung. . . . (pp. 25-6)

Yet melody alone was not enough. By itself it could not account for the thousands and thousands of copies of Foster's songs which the American people bought. The lyrics also had their importance. . . . [They] were a part of the changing social pattern of their time. (p. 26)

[The] rise of evangelical religion . . . helped to assure Foster's popularity if only indirectly so. About religion as such he had little to say in his songs; he was no theologian. The moral and ethical values growing out of evangelical religion, however, were those he advocated in his lyrics. The kindly view of human nature, the emphasis on unselfish love, and the willing obedience to evangelical religion's rules of daily conduct appear and reappear.

The appeal of this side of Foster was powerful. But there was more to him than that. He also offered America escape from its still present puritanism, its materialism, and its aggressive competitive spirit. He did this with a fortunate indirectness, especially where puritanism was concerned.

For he led his hearers away from puritanism only after making his proper bow to it. That is, he offered them a gentle, lively never-never land where the escape was from something rather than to something, from care and stern responsibility rather than to lusty living. The main symbol Foster used in his antipuritanism was the Negro, and he used him well. It is true that this began as an accident, for he was simply writing very catchy minstrel songs. Once having his subject, however, he developed it winningly. He pictured the carefree darky in his prime on the old plantation, cutting up with rousing good spirits. The South was the place the darky loved, and if away from it he longed to return:

> We'll put for de souf
> Ah! dat's the place,
> For the steeple chase and de bully hoss race—
> Poker, brag, eucher, seven up and loo,
> Den chime in Niggas, won't you come along too.

When he left the South, he also left his joyous childhood: "The young folks roll on the little cabin floor, All merry, all happy and bright." And he left the peace and tranquillity of old age as well.

Often Foster wove together the feelings of childhood and of age for the sake of artistic contrast. He joined the simple, animal joy that the pickaninnies represented with the tender melancholy of "old folks" close to death. But it was death itself that attracted him most. Death on the plantation was always sad but never stark, regardless of what it might be elsewhere. Usually it contained within it the promise of eternal rest, most often shown as sleep. In **"Old Black Joe"** Foster developed, for his time and place, the perfect popular restatement of an always moving theme, the theme of old age living only for its memories and now ready to make them real again through death.

> Why do I weep when my heart should feel no pain
> Why do I sigh that my friends come not again,
> Grieving for forms
> Now departed long ago?
> I hear their gentle voices calling "Old Black Joe."

When the Civil War began, Foster sided strongly with the North. But before that time, whether he knew it or not, he was making a classic contribution to the myth of the antebellum South. The contented darkies, the kind old massa, and the pillared plantation are standard in his songs. Whether the strain be comic or sad, the moral is that the plantation was a pastoral utopia.

The South could justly be gratified. Foster's lyrics assured it that slavery was basically good and did this, doubtless, with more emotional power than any proslavery lectures, tracts, or treatises coming out at the same time. The North, on the other hand, might have been expected to remonstrate. Yet it failed to. Probably it found in his songs simply the reflection of its own minstrel-inspired idea of what the Negro and the South were really like. If any abolitionists had the wit to see the psychological menace to their cause of Foster's conceptions, they never said so effectively. They failed to remark that not till 1852 did Foster travel through the South. And they neglected to observe that his early views were based chiefly on seeing Negro church services and watching minstrel shows.

Foster invited Americans to escape harmlessly from puritanism, but similarly he invited them to escape from the crude materialism that foreign visitors frequently censured. This materialism was accompanied by an emphasis on the competitive spirit, on aggressiveness. Though aggression suited the frontier more than the eastern seaboard, it could be found everywhere in the United States. It had become even then a leading part of what would someday be called the capitalistic ethic. The combination of materialism and the will to win crowded out the softer emotions. If sentiment played any part in prewar business life, it must have been a small one; and Mark Twain was not the only man to point out that in postwar business it never showed itself at all.

Yet the softer emotions still existed. Men might try to dismiss them as fit for women alone but could not suppress them entirely. The anima, the female element in man as defined by the psychologist Jung, was both their source and their haven. In Foster's music these tender feelings found their most popular expression. It is true that some of his best-loved songs are gay but most of them strike a sad note. It is the note of death, of longing, of farewell, or of nostalgia. For every song with the bounce of **"There's a Good Time Coming"** or **"Camptown Races,"** there are a dozen with the melancholy of **"Summer Longings," "Farewell Old Cottage," "My Hopes Have Departed Forever," "Massa's in de Cold Ground," "Old Memories,"** or **"Under the Willow She's Sleeping."** The melancholy, however, is always muted. Foster never affects a blatant emotionalism.

Even the love so abundant in his lyrics is not reckless nor extreme—any more than . . . it was illicit. It is almost always a man's love and so is directed at either his mother or some beautiful girl. If the composer sings to mother, it is the usual paen (still selling widely today) about those dear gray hairs and gentle eyes. Mother stays loyal when all the rest of the world has abandoned us: **"Mother, Thou'rt Faithful to Me."**

If the composer sings to some other woman, it is to a fragile maiden. She never seems mature nor really nubile, and no hint of sexuality ever lurks in Foster's tender lines about her. Often—and this is the most obvious of retreats from sex but musically quite effective—she is either dead or dying. His favorite metaphor for death, we can recall, is sleep. "Sweetly she sleeps, My Alice fair," Foster will write. One of his favorite devices is to begin the lyrics with the listener thinking that the girl is merely sleeping and then to end by letting him realize that she is really dead. Foster's Annies, his Jeanies, his Lindas turn into lavendered wraiths. And that, it would appear, was the way American men wished them and American women thought they ought to be.

Rich with symbols of escape, Stephen Foster's songs captured the American heart. Turning for a while from the dour trio of puritanism, materialism, and competitiveness, the American listened to Foster's gentle strains. In them the Freudian of today would detect a variety of regressions and projections. He would observe Oedipus complexes, necrophilia, and the "angel theory of childhood," among other things. At the same time even the least speculative among us could notice the escapism represented by distance in time (in three modes: childhood, old age, the "good old days"), distance in space (the South), distance from reality (dreams), and distance from life (death). (pp. 26-9)

*Carl Bode, "Melody en Masse," in his* The Anatomy of American Popular Culture: 1840-1861, *University of California Press, 1959, pp. 19-37.*

## WILFRID MELLERS (essay date 1964)

[*Mellers shows how Foster transformed conventional European ballads into folk song-like compositions through his use of the theme of lost innocence.*]

Foster was born in 1826, near Pittsburgh. . . . That he was brought up in Pittsburgh (and later in Cincinnati) is significant, for Pittsburgh was not New York or Boston, in touch with European culture; it was an urban industrial society—on the edge of a wilderness. This is literally true. As late as 1812 "savages" still "infested" the Alleghenies within two hundred miles of Pittsburgh, which was then a trading post. By the date of Foster's birth it was a town . . . , but though the Indians had gone, the wilderness remained. Here in Pittsburgh, Foster wrote, at first as an amateur, spare-time composer in such leisure as he had from work in office and printing press, quantities of parlour music that was neither better nor worse than the common denominator of taste permitted. His public was polyglot: English, Irish, German, Italian by ancestry, with a heavy leaning towards Puritan heritage.

These urban people no longer sang folk songs, and if Foster ever heard any real folk music it would have been sung by Negroes working on the rivers. The genteel middle-class society, for whom Foster wrote, sang hymns and sentimental parlour songs of a type derived from the ballads of British composers such as Arne and Hook: and played salon pieces for piano in a degenerate rehash of the classical conventions of Europe. A new industrial town was too busy growing to admit to needs for artistic satisfaction. Nobody wanted more from art than a momentary respite from work: so those conventions that were handiest, and most familiar through usage, seemed the best.

But though Foster had no ambition other than to "give the public what it wanted", he knew what those wants were better than did the people themselves. This discovery he made in his "Ethiopian songs": which were based not on real negro spirituals or plantation songs, but on the songs of the Christy

*Foster's pocketbook, found in his clothes at the time of his death. The slip of paper is thought to record lyrics for a new song.*

Minstrel shows. These were an exploitation of the Negro by white men with blackened faces—in an idiom closer to English ballad, march and hymn than to Negro music. . . . The conventionalized form of the Christy show, with its interlocutory figure and two stooges with tambourine and bones, crystallized the white myth of the wide-grinning, white-toothed, red-lipped nigger, lazy and good-for-nothing, yet innocently happy. Foster's genius lay in his revealing how the myth got it both ways, since the Negro, although happy, was also homeless, and therefore sad. The minstrel show took the savagery out of his merriment, making him a harmless figure of fun: while at the same time it related the Negro's homesickness, his sense of oppression, to the frustration and nostalgia inherent in every man, whatever the colour of his skin—and especially in man in a raw industrial society that knew but obscurely where it was going. Indeed the minstrel show as a whole was a presentation, as drama and entertainment, of the Great American Myth: which accounts for its prodigious appeal. It is, however, interesting that the show's positive evocation of the American Hero—who . . . appears as the figure of the Backwoodsman—should . . . be subservient to the American Innocent, as represented by the Comic Negro. Both the Hero and the Anti-Hero are treated facetiously, and the main dramatic items are burlesques of European classics. Significantly Washington Irving loved minstrel shows and had an almost extravagant affection for Foster's songs: which were all based on yearning for the Good Old Days: which mattered because they were true, and were true because they were innocent. But they were not innocent as real folk music is innocent, for they expressed modern man's *consciousness* of loss. This is why the songs are sentimental in no pejorative sense: and is also why the technique of the songs is at once simple and artificial. The ballad is an artefact—made in conventions derived from Europe: English ballad (especially Dibdin); French waltz; Italian opera; all of which had reached, in garbled form, the Pittsburgh parlour. In Foster's finest songs, however, the heartfelt simplicity transforms the artefact into something like folk art. We can see this in three different degrees, in three songs written at various periods of his life.

The first song on which we will comment was one of the last Foster wrote. . . . ["**Beautiful Dreamer**"] is the closest to the American parlour, the furthest from Foster's mythical Ethiopia, of the songs to which we shall refer. Its technique is artificial in that it draws directly on clichés, if not conventions, from European art-music; and its text is a direct statement of the escape-motive. It invokes a "Beautiful Dreamer": presumably a young woman, whom Foster (or you, or I) can awake by song: who will then banish "sounds of the rude world" and disperse "all clouds of sorrow". Musically, it is a rudimentary version of the ballad-style of a composer such as Hook, with an infusion of French waltz in the rhythm and of Italian opera in the arpeggiated accompaniment and in the repetitions of the cadential phase. The tune, like the young woman, has an insidious memorability, perhaps because its symmetrical clauses, with falling arpeggio balanced by rising fifth, never defeat expectation. But there is something a little horrifying about the regularity of the tune's insistence; and this is related to the artificiality of the technique, especially the cadential modulation and the final repetition of the cadence phrase with sobbing grace-note. . . . It is not that the feeling is fundamentally insincere—Foster wrote this song in New York, from a bitter awareness of what Broadway meant, as compared with the provincial Pittsburgh of his early days. It is rather that the feeling is knowingly indulged in: so that it sullies, at the same time as it reveals, the aspirations of the common heart.

One can see how a taint of "commercial" degeneration has crept into this song if one compares it with a dream-song of Foster's Pittsburgh period. Even in the words a difference is discernible: for whereas the words of **"Beautiful Dreamer"** are heavy with cliché, anticipating the moon-June convention of Tin Pan Alley, the words of **"I dream of Jeanie with the light brown hair"** preserve a certain poetic freshness, along with a survival of eighteenth-century elegance:

> I dream of Jeanie with the light brown hair,
> Borne, like a vapor, on the summer air;
> I see her tripping where the bright streams play,
> Happy as the daisies that dance on her way.
> Many were the wild notes her merry voice would pour,
> Many were the blithe birds that warbled them o'er.
> Oh! I dream of Jeanie with the light brown hair,
> Floating, like a vapor, on the soft summer air.

Both the freshness and the elegance communicate themselves to the music. The lovely tune, with its gracefully balanced undulations, is haunting with the simplicity of an Irish or Scots folk-song, and even has a pentatonic flavour. Formally and tonally, of course, the song is artificial, with a modulation to the dominant to make the daisies dance on their way, a brief middle section for her merry voice and the blithe birds, and a little cadenza to take us back to the *da capo,* which ends with the tenderest cadential thirteenth on the word "summer". . . . But the simplicity of the art exactly matches the fragility of the dream; the song resembles an eighteenth-century British arrangement (and urbanization) of a celtic folk-tune, and is superior to the comparable pastoral songs of (say) Arne because the tune is so much more beautiful and memorable. Indeed, **"Jeanie"** is an art-song that has become a part of folk-culture, as no tune by Arne ever could; and this may be in part because the experience is particularized, as well as generalized. The Beautiful Dreamer of the New York song was, one suspects, a concoction of the fancy; Jeanie was a real girl, and Foster's wife, even though she seemed no more tangible than a vapour. **"Jeanie"** may well be so poignant *because* of the disparity between dream and reality. Foster could see his Jeanie as lovely and merry only through a soft summer haze, since in fact their marriage was a failure.

The theme of lost innocence finds direct expression in the Ethiopian songs, including the most famous of them all, **"The Old Folks at Home"**. Vestiges of eighteenth-century elegance have disappeared from this music; the harmony is almost consistently tonic, dominant and subdominant (chromatic passing notes and so on are later, non-Fosterian accretions), and the tune is restricted to five notes. Yet this song has become the apotheosis of the regressive instinct, known and sung all over the habitable world. It owes its obsessive quality to its very rudimentariness: the fourfold repeated phrases make their effect because they are *worth* repeating, for the leaping octave followed by a pentatonic minor third contains an age-old yearning, while the declining cadential phrase brings us safe to the security of Home. . . . The other internationally celebrated Ethiopian song, **"My Old Kentucky Home"**, is hardly less primitive structurally, and melodically employs only six notes. It has nothing to do with genuine Negro music, not even the Westernized forms of the plantation song, and it is not true, never was true, that the sun always shone bright on the old Kentucky home, nor that the birds made music all the day. What is true is the singer's long-

ing for release from weariness. It is this which has preserved the tune's potency throughout a hundred progressively wearier and less innocent years.

Foster's music is a quintessence of the Common Man's nostalgia, his yearning for innocence, his fear of experience. It is pertinent to note that, despite the fabulous appeal of his music, his life was an unsuccess story. If we think of him as one of the progenitors of the American pop-music industry, there is an allegorical appropriateness in the fact that he should have been congenitally mother-tied, a man "to whom Home meant everything, and for whom home was impossible", as his brother Morrison put it. Morrison also tells us that Stephen's love for his mother "amounted to adoration . . . and there is not one reference to Mother in the homely words in which he clothed his ballads that did not come from the heart". Stephen had little general, as well as musical, education because he so frequently refused to leave home and attend school, where "there is too much confusion"; and it is clear from Mrs. Foster's *Recollections* that she encouraged her son to think of the White Cottage as an oasis in the hostile desert of the world:

> The sloping terraced grounds about the Cottage, dressed off with many a rose and dancing flower, laughed gaily on that sweet morning in the bright sunlight. I knew that a happy Home awaited me, with breakfast table laid, and husband kind, and infant footsteps pressing the green sod. . . . Is it that memory of long buried joyous hours comes o'er our spirits like a pleasing Dream, and drapes the loved ones in such Angelic Shapes as makes them seem indeed the favorites of a better world? When Fancy lends her wings to bend my memory back, it seems as if in some sweet dream my happy buoyant steps had been within Eden's walls.

Perhaps it was fortunate that this white-cottage Eden at Lawrenceville had to be sold when Stephen was still a small boy. But he never really escaped its obsessive memory: so that he lost his Jeanie, who might have helped him to grow up; succumbed to the Genteel Tradition; drank himself into ill-health; and died in a New York slum. His degeneration started, moreover, when he ceased to be an amateur song-writer and entered the commercial music racket. Then the Common Heart was overlaid with rhetoric; then other men began to reap material profit from his world-wide popularity. (pp. 245-50)

> *Wilfrid Mellers, "Introductory: Music and Entertainment in Nineteenth-Century America; Stephen Foster, Louis-Moreau Gottschalk and John Philip Sousa," in his* Music in a New Found Land: Themes and Developments in the History of American Music, *Barrie and Rockliff, 1964, pp. 239-61.*

### GILBERT CHASE (essay date 1966)

[*In this excerpt from his survey of American music, Chase argues that Foster's achievement lies in his ability to create minstrel songs, sentimental ballads, and songs that combine these two distinct traditions.*]

Stephen Foster's music may be described as a product of the urbanized frontier. Had he been raised in Boston, New York, or Philadelphia, he would have grown up hearing concerts of music "by the most celebrated European composers"; he would have heard operas, oratorios, symphonies, concertos, and he might have been tempted to try to become a composer in the grand style. He would, in any case, have been entirely an urban, that is to say, a thoroughly Europeanized product, completely cut off from the frontier. In Pittsburgh, and in Cincinnati, he had contact with the frontier, he became a part of the process of Americanization achieved by the frontier. Yet his environment was that of the *urbanized* frontier, which was rapidly ceasing to be a frontier at all as the cities of the then West became more and more Europeanized, aspiring to cultivate the "polite arts" in the same degree as the older cities of the Atlantic seaboard. Stephen Foster's wide appeal lies largely in this cultural dualism of his background, through which he was able to combine the vitality of the frontier and a certain element of primitive simplicity with the genteel tradition of the urban fringe, dominated by sentimentality, conventionalism, and propriety.

To appreciate Stephen Foster's musical output in relation to the cultural context in which it was produced, one needs to go through all of his more than two hundred songs in their original or at least contemporary sheet-music editions, or in nineteenth-century songbooks like *The Love and Sentimental Songster* or *The American Dime Song Book,* to see their illustrated covers with portraits of sentimental maidens and lovers in stilted romantic attitudes, and to realize the overwhelming proportion of merely "pretty" songs that he turned out for the genteel trade. Stephen Foster's preeminence as an American songwriter rests upon some dozen songs, to which may be added another dozen of lesser fame but of evident superiority to the rest of his output or to that of his contemporaries. The "big four" among Foster's songs, the pillars of his universal fame, are **"Old Folks at Home," "My Old Kentucky Home," "Massa's in de Cold Ground,"** and **"Old Black Joe."** Now, these are not the songs that are closest either to the roots of Negro folksong or to the prevailing style of blackface minstrelsy. Neither are they the closest to the genteel tradition of the Europeanized urban fringe. In terms of Foster's songs, they stand midway between **"Oh! Susanna"** or **"Camptown Races"** and **"Come Where My Love Lies Dreaming"** or **"Wilt Thou Be Gone, Love?"** In three of the "big four," the Negro dialect has been eliminated, and in the fourth, **"Massa's in de Cold Ground"** it is somewhat attenuated. Foster himself stated that he intended to make the minstrel melodies or Ethiopian songs palatable to refined tastes, and this is part of the cleaning-up process. Musically, these four songs are in slow tempo: *Moderato con espressione, Poco adagio, Poco lento,* and again *Poco adagio* for **"Old Black Joe."** Above all, *"con espressione"!*—that is an indispensable requirement of the genteel tradition. Compare, for example, such an old-time minstrel song as "Long Time Ago" with **"Old Folks at Home."** The former is really rooted in popular tradition: it is marked Allegro, and the minstrels have their way with it as a comic song. . . . Morris and Horn made a sentimental song out of "Long Time Ago." Their concoction strikes us as ludicrous now because it leans so obviously on a faded tradition. Foster wrote plenty of sentimental songs that seem equally ludicrous—one need only mention **"Willie We Have Missed You"** as an example. But he was not, like Charles Horn, a hopeless victim of the genteel tradition. Like the Ohio and the Missouri flowing into the Mississippi, two traditions converged in the broad stream of Stephen Foster's best music. It is this that gives him his unique position and significance in American music. How thoroughly he was master of both traditions is proved by the fact that he excelled in the pure minstrel song, he excelled in the sentimental ballad, and he excelled in the combination of both types: the

blending of simplicity and pathos with expression and refinement that marks his most famous and most beloved songs.

Stephen Foster's songs may be divided into two broad categories: minstrel songs and nonminstrel songs. Under the latter there are some minor subdivisions, such as religious songs and war songs, which have slight value if any. The best of Foster's Civil War songs is probably **"We Are Coming Father Abraham, 300,000 More,"** published in 1862. As for the "Ethiopian" productions, they fall into two groups: the comic songs and the sentimental songs, the latter represented chiefly by the "big four" already mentioned. Let us glance more closely at a song in each of these groups.

**"Oh! Susanna"** is a typical example of the comic or nonsense minstrel song. The music consists of four nearly identical periods, each divided into two phrases to correspond with the eight lines of the verse. The same period is used for the last two lines of the chorus, so that the only new material occurs in the first portion of the chorus, which also contains the one instance of syncopation, on the word "Susanna." Having said that the melodic periods are nearly identical, it remains merely to remark that the only difference lies in a slight melodic variation of the second phrase. The first period leads to a semicadence on the dominant, the second to a full cadence. The second phrase of the chorus, "do not cry for me," has exactly the same melodic and metrical pattern as the last phrase of the first line. This unity through repetition, with only slight but effective contrasts, is characteristic of Foster's songs. Harold Vincent Milligan, remarking on this trait, wrote: "The repetitiousness of Foster's melodies is such that one cannot fail to wonder that they exert such an influence upon the listener as they do" [see excerpt dated 1920]. But, being such good tunes to begin with, it is precisely through this repetitiousness that they make their unfailing effect. And this, in turn, makes the variation doubly effective when it does occur.

**"Old Folks at Home"** may be taken as an example of the sentimental plantation melody constructed on the same simple basis. As in the case of **"Oh! Susanna,"** the first introduction of new melodic material occurs in the first two lines of the chorus, and again this is followed by a repetition of the main melody. Again we have four successive repetitions of the principal melody, ending twice on a semicadence and twice on a full cadence. Very characteristic is the rhythmical "snap" which dislocates the accent on words having normally a feminine ending, such as "ribber," "ebber," "plantation," and "weary." Except for the first part of the chorus, the melody of **"Old Folks at Home"** uses only the five tones of the pentatonic scale.

While recognizing the element of repetition in Foster's melodies, we should nevertheless bear in mind that slight metrical variations in the melody were, in some cases, introduced for different stanzas, as shown by the original editions. (pp. 297-99)

As regards harmony, Foster stays pretty close to the tonic, dominant, and subdominant. A rare example of the use of secondary chords is to be found in the song **"Ah! May the Red Rose Live Alway."** Modulations are very scarce and confined chiefly to the dominant key, as in **"My Old Kentucky Home"** and **"Old Black Joe."** . . .

[We might observe], according to the dictum of Marius Schneider, that the popularity of a melody depends partly on its degree of simplicity and partly on its conformity "to the melodic type current in a given culture." The melodies of Stephen Foster fulfill these conditions in the highest degree. Simplicity is the essence of his music. His songs conform to melodic types widely current in American folklore. These melodic types and their basic harmonic patterns, in turn, are deeply rooted in age-old folk traditions inherited from Anglo-Celtic civilization transplanted to America. These factors contribute to make Stephen Collins Foster the most beloved composer whom America has produced. (p. 300)

> *Gilbert Chase, "America's Minstrel," in his* America's Music: From the Pilgrims to the Present, *revised edition, McGraw-Hill Book Company, 1966, pp. 283-300.*

## RONALD L. DAVIS (essay date 1976)

[*Davis links the sentimental and nostalgic tone of Foster's songs to the national mood, briefly touching on a few of his best-loved works as illustrations.*]

[Stephen Foster] emerges as the luminary of mid-nineteenth-century American popular songwriters because at his best he was a master at nostalgic expression and projected an honesty that most of his contemporaries lacked. He rose above the hackneyed songsmiths of his day, because he wrote from the heart, infantile though his emotions might be. (p. 61)

His classic **"Old Folks at Home"** appeared in 1851, selling forty thousand copies within the first eleven months. Although Foster wrote the song in a crude, inconsistent Negro dialect, he was dealing with a theme close to his own heart, the love of home.

> All up and down de whole creation,
> Sadly I roam,
> Still longing for de old plantation,
> And for de old folks at home.

The composer merely transferred to the plantation black those same sentiments more genteelly expressed in his parlor ballads, sentiments that Foster, in his reluctance to leave the parental nest, had experienced intimately. Yet while the spirit of **"Old Folks at Home"** was genuine, the immediate setting was distant and artificial. Musically, the strength of **"The Old Folks at Home"** lies in its honest simplicity, which reinforces the theme of lost innocence. (p. 62)

[Despite the difficulties of his last years, Foster] pulled himself together twice, long enough to write the two masterpieces . . . **"Old Black Joe"** and **"Beautiful Dreamer."** Probably composed just before Foster came to New York, **"Old Black Joe"** was the last of his great plantation songs. For a fleeting moment the creative spark returned, and out of the turmoil of his emotions Foster was able to gather a genuine expression of human grief—the grief he felt over the loss of his family and departed youth, intensified by his growing sense of insecurity and failure. "It is not a blackface minstrel who steps forward on the stage to sing **'Old Black Joe,'** Fletcher Hodges contends. "It is Stephen Foster himself, and he sings to us from his very soul."

> Gone are the days when my heart was young and gay,
> Gone are my friends from the cotton fields away;
> Gone from the earth to a better land I know,
> I hear their gentle voices calling "Old Black Joe."

There is no hint of Negro dialect now, for Foster is voicing his own feelings, only faintly disguised in the southern setting.

**"Beautiful Dreamer,"** copyrighted in 1864, represents the last spurt from the composer's dying genius. Evidently he is seeking an escape from the grim realities of the world about him, a dream to eclipse the failure of his life in New York. He longs for the contentment of an earlier moment.

> Sounds of the rude world, heard in the day,
> Lulled by the moonlight, have all passed away.

Trite though some of the lines may be, the piece is musically among his best loved songs. But . . . thc love object is unattainable, since she is asleep, and emerges from the piece as elusive as vapor.

Viewed against the larger picture, Foster's nostalgia was consistent with a greater national longing for the past. Americans, particularly in the more settled East, already were beginning to look back on a "once happy day" of unspoiled forests and virgin lands. Ruin and change followed in the wake of the pioneer, and as industry made its inroads into the Jeffersonian garden, the sense of uneasiness and dislocation grew. In literature Washington Irving expressed resistence to the transition in progress through his legend of Rip Van Winkle. As Lewis Mumford explains, "The old landmarks have gone; the old faces have disappeared; all the outward aspects of life have changed. At the bottom, however, Rip himself has not changed; for he has been drunk and lost in a dream, and . . . he remains, mentally, a boy."

Still too steeped in optimism for gloom, Americans—like Foster—regarded the passing of their innocence with gentle melancholy rather than bitterness, glorifying the old in preference to depreciating the new. Yet in the face of a heightening sectional conflict, the waning of frontier abandon, industry's exaggerated emphasis on materialism, aggressiveness, and a competitive spirit, there was cause for disquietude. Foster offered an urbanizing people a harmless escape from crass commercialism and the confusion of a changing world without denying any of the fundamental principles of the day.

Paradoxically, while Americans of the nineteenth century welcomed an opportunity to respond publicly to cheap sentimentality, they cherished from their Puritan heritage a cultural ideal of exercising restraint in the display of genuine emotions. Rather than violate this convention, or appear womanly, Foster employed the mask of the plantation Negro so much in vogue at the time. His more contrived sentiments he openly exposed in his parlor ballads, but his sincere feelings, those from the heart, he felt obliged to veil behind blackface. Unquestionably his minstrel songs, as a group, represent his most honest writing, once the popular "never-never land" image of the South is scraped aside. Initially he even attempted Negro dialect to disguise the emotional flow more carefully, but the practice dwindled to a trace, then stopped altogether. As his personality disintegrated, the composer seems either to have forgotten or no longer to have possessed the strength to lift the mask before the last plaintive cries from his tormented soul.

Foster's recognition as America's first great songwriter must be viewed against the background of his age, for certainly his songs transcend the banal efforts characteristic of the popular music of the early nineteenth century. At his best Foster clearly rises above the bathos of "The Old Arm Chair" or the contrived tearfulness of "The Blind Orphan Girl," and even at his worst there is little of the oafish overstatement of the topical songs of the period or the hysterical unreality of train wrecks, mountain blizzards, maniacs clawing asylum walls, or eagles snatching babies from mothers' arms. In his masterworks the sentimental predilections of his time are sublimated, allowing honest feeling to issue forth. Like his contemporaries, Foster offers escape, but in mitigated form, within the pale of credibility. His escapism generally comes from distance—distance in time (childhood, old age, the "good old days"), distance in place (the South), distance from reality (dreams), and distance from life (death—although usually softened in metaphor to sleep).

From the shipwreck of his life Foster was able to draw an expression of nostalgia in sympathy with the fears and longings of the urban frontier in which he lived. Far more reflective than philosophical, the composer was able to generalize his own experience into an attitude harmonious with young America's consciousness of vanishing innocence. When more adult personalities attempted to appeal in popular song to the puerile feelings of the burgeoning nation, their efforts as a rule were synthetic and theatrical, since the sentiments they voiced sprang from a designing intellect rather than from the heart. But in his inspired moments Stephen Foster conveyed genuine emotion through pure simplicity, an adolescent spirit serenading an adolescent land. (pp. 63-5)

> *Ronald L. Davis, "Sentimental Songs in Antebellum America," in* Southwest Review, *Vol. 61, No. 1, Winter, 1976, pp. 50-65.*

---

## FURTHER READING

Austin, William W. *"Susanna," "Jeanie," and "The Old Folks at Home": The Songs of Stephen C. Foster from His Time to Ours.* New York: Macmillan Publishing Co., 1975, 420 p.
  An extensive survey that divides Foster's songs into three groups—comic, poetic, and pathetic—and documents the historical and social significance of each group.

Beckwith, John A., and Coope, Geoffrey, eds. *Contemporary American Biography.* New York: Harper & Brothers Publishers, 1941, 347 p.
  Contains biographical sketches on Foster by Sigmund Spaeth, Ted Malone, and Haniel Long.

Elson, Louis C. "The Folk-Music of America." In his *The History of American Music,* pp. 123-39. The History of American Art, edited by John C. Van Dyke. New York: Macmillan Co., 1904.
  A brief history of Foster's life and work.

Foster, Morrison. *My Brother Stephen.* Indianapolis: Privately printed, 1932, 55 p.
  An intimate biographical portrait written by the composer's brother.

Fuld, James J. *A Pictorial Bibliography of the First Editions of Stephen C. Foster.* Philadelphia: Musical Americana, 1957, 181 p.
  A comprehensive listing of the first editions of Foster's songs with reproductions of their title pages.

Gombosi, Otto. "Stephen Foster and 'Gregory Walker'." *The Musical Quarterly* 30, No. 2 (April 1944): 133-46.
  Studies harmonic structure in Foster's songs, finding that one of his favorite bass patterns dates from the sixteenth century.

Hitchcock, Wiley. "Stephen Foster." *HiFi/Stereo Review* 18, No. 1 (January 1967): 47-58.
  A biographical account that surveys both Foster's parlor or sentimental songs and his theatrical or minstrel music.

Hodges, Fletcher, Jr. *Stephen Foster, Democrat.* Pittsburgh: University of Pittsburgh, 1946, 30 p.
  Examines Foster's political views as expressed in his political and war songs.

Howard, John Tasker. "The Literature on Stephen Foster." *Music Library Association Notes* 1, No. 2 (March 1944): 10-15.
  Reviews some of the recent literature on Foster.

————. "Stephen Collins Foster (1826-1864)." In his *Our American Music: Three Hundred Years of It,* pp. 184-98. New York: Thomas Y. Crowell Co., 1954.
  A biographical sketch of Foster.

Jackson, George Pullen. "Stephen Foster's Debt to American Folk-Song." *The Musical Quarterly* 22, No. 2 (April 1936): 154-69.
  Argues that Foster's songs were derivative of a large body of popular spiritual tunes.

Kaufmann, Helen L. "The Sentimental Ballad and Its Foster Father." In her *From Jehovah to Jazz: Music in America from Psalmody to the Present Day,* pp. 89-109. New York: Dodd, Mead & Co., 1937.
  Includes a brief overview of Foster's life and career that emphasizes his devotion to his mother.

Morneweck, Evelyn Foster. *Chronicles of Stephen Foster's Family.* 2 vols. Pittsburgh: University of Pittsburgh Press, 1944.
  A biography of Foster and his family composed primarily of personal reminiscences, written by his niece.

Overmyer, Grace. "Stephen Collins Foster." In her *Famous American Composers,* pp. 35-54. New York: Thomas Y. Crowell Co., 1944.
  Expands on the biographical information presented in her earlier essay on Foster (see excerpt dated 1926).

Pattee, Fred Lewis. "In Minor Key." In his *The Feminine Fifties,* pp. 307-21. New York: D. Appleton-Century Co., 1940.
  In a literary history of the United States during the 1850s, assesses Foster's songs as reflections of the emotionalism that characterized the national mood during this decade.

Walters, Raymond. *Stephen Foster, Youth's Golden Gleam: A Sketch of His Life and Background in Cincinnati, 1846-1850.* Princeton: Princeton University Press, 1936, 160 p.
  A biography of Foster that focuses exclusively on the years he spent in Cincinnati, Ohio.

Whittlesey, Walter R., and Sonneck, O. G. *Catalogue of First Editions of Stephen C. Foster (1826-1864).* Washington, D.C.: Government Printing Office, 1915, 79 p.
  A bibliography, compiled by the staff of the Library of Congress, that describes all the first editions of Foster's songs discovered by 1914.

Wilson, Edmund. "Books: Sidney Lanier and Stephen Foster." *The New Yorker* XXII, No. 44 (14 December 1946): 138, 141-42.
  Reviews a collection of songs entitled *A Treasury of Stephen Foster.* Wilson briefly compares Foster's art, as well as his personal life, to that of Edgar Allan Poe.

# Harriet Martineau

## 1802-1876

English short story writer, autobiographer, novelist, travel writer, essayist, journalist, historian, and biographer.

Martineau was a highly successful and celebrated literary figure in her time. A remarkably prolific writer, she is best known for her didactic stories in which she popularized economic theories, her accounts of her travels in the United States, and her *Autobiography*. Martineau was also an outspoken opponent of slavery and a champion of women's rights, and although her works were largely neglected following her death, her social theory, especially her feminism, has received renewed attention in recent years. Most commentators agree with Gayle Graham Yates's assessment that "her genius lay in her ability to discern new ideas with quick intelligence, to communicate them clearly to the public, and thus to rally, time and again, supporters and advocates of the new viewpoints and causes."

The daughter of a middle-class textile manufacturer, Martineau was born in Norwich. A sickly child, she experienced a progressive hearing loss and was almost totally deaf by the time she was fourteen. Her family was Unitarian, and she grew up in an atmosphere characterized by liberal religious thought and keen interest in intellectual and political matters. Much of Martineau's early education, unusually rigorous for a girl of her day, took place at home, where she was tutored by her older siblings in languages and classics. At the age of sixteen, Martineau enrolled at a school in Bristol run by her aunt, where she met the Reverend Lant Carpenter, a Unitarian minister who introduced her to the doctrine of necessity formulated by David Hartley and Joseph Priestley. Martineau embraced this philosophy, which holds that all action is a consequence of what has preceded it and that human beings have no free will, and later rejected Christian doctrine altogether. In 1820, Martineau made her first attempt at writing: her essay "Female Writers on Practical Divinity" was published in the Unitarian periodical *Monthly Repository* that year. Like many of her later works, this article reflected her interest in the status of women and her desire to teach through writing. Martineau continued to publish articles in the journal for the next several years.

During the mid-1820s, the financial situation of Martineau's family steadily worsened, and her father died in 1826. Since her deafness precluded her being a governess, Martineau supported herself by needlework and writing. After reading Jane Marcet's *Conversations on Political Economy,* she planned a series of stories that would explain economic concepts to the newly literate working class. Her *Illustrations of Political Economy* was a huge success when the initial monthly parts appeared, and in 1832 she moved to London where she became active in literary society. After two years, during which she maintained a gruelling schedule of monthly tales for the *Illustrations* as well as other didactic stories, she planned a trip to the United States.

Starting her journey in 1834, Martineau fulfilled an earlier obligation during the voyage by writing *How to Observe Morals and Manners,* designed as a manual for travellers. She

spent two years in the United States and travelled approximately ten thousand miles, visiting New England, the South, the Midwest, and the Great Lakes region. When Martineau returned to England, she published two books about her trip: *Society in America* and *Retrospect of Western Travel.* In 1839, illness forced her to return early from a European tour, and she retired to Tynemouth, where she lived as an invalid for the next five years. Despite her illness, Martineau continued to write and to stay involved in intellectual and political life. She refused the offer of a government pension, fearing it would jeopardize her objectivity as a writer. Reflecting on her own experiences, she wrote *Life in the Sick-Room,* in which she discussed the psychological effects of long-term physical illness. After several friends recommended she try mesmerism, an early form of hypnotism, she began a course of mesmeric treatment that she believed cured her.

Following her recovery, Martineau did not return to London but built a house at Ambleside in the Lake District, where her neighbors included William Wordsworth and Matthew Arnold. During the late 1840s and early 1850s, Martineau addressed a variety of subjects in her works. In *Letters on the Laws of Man's Nature and Development* and *Eastern Life, Present and Past,* she displayed her increasing estrangement from conventional Christian belief, intensified by a trip to

Egypt and Palestine during 1846 and 1847, and in *The History of England during the Thirty Years' Peace, 1816-46,* a project she took over from her friend, the London publisher Charles Knight, she made an attempt at contemporary history. She also began writing "leaders," or editorials, for the *Daily News* and other journalistic essays as well. Continuing to refine her philosophical and religious thought, she was drawn to the positivism of Auguste Comte, and she undertook the ambitious process of translating and condensing his six-volume *Cours de philosophie positive.* In 1854, she became ill again, and, convinced she was dying, she immediately wrote her autobiography and had it printed and bound, ready for distribution at her death. She lived for more than twenty years, however, and was able to write and receive visitors for much of that time. Martineau died in 1876.

Many of Martineau's works were intended to educate readers and reflected her belief that education would solve political, social, and economic problems. In her first major work, *Illustrations of Political Economy,* she popularized the economic theories of James Mill, Adam Smith, and David Ricardo. Martineau used James Mill's definition of political economy—the production, exchange, distribution, and consumption of wealth—as an outline for the series of stories. Each story describes a particular social problem and the solution effected by applying the appropriate economic concept, then concludes with a summary of the principle involved. Because Martineau was the first to address subjects later used by other Victorian novelists—"A Manchester Strike," for example, focuses on labor unrest and is one of the earliest fictional treatments of industrial life—the series is considered an important antecedent of the English social novel. While the *Illustrations* were praised for their realistic descriptions, Martineau was often criticized for failing to integrate story and theory. She was also attacked for the topics she addressed; many Victorian readers thought the discussion of Malthusian principles and the dangers of overpopulation in "Weal and Woe in Garveloch" inappropriate for a woman writer, especially an unmarried one, and "Demerara," in which Martineau criticized slavery, caused her to be met with hostility when she went to the United States.

Martineau wrote several novels, but critics generally conclude that she never produced a work of superior quality. In *Deerbrook,* her best-known novel, a village doctor is in love with one woman but marries her sister after being convinced that he has compromised her. According to critics, some aspects of the work are effectively done, such as the portrayal of the jealousy between the sisters, but Martineau was not able to sustain the development of a scene without relying on melodramatic formulas. The novel is considered strongest in its depiction of day-to-day village life and in the ironic contrast Martineau draws between the serene appearance of the village and the hypocrisy that constrains the lives of its inhabitants. The themes of *Deerbrook* have been seen by some critics as anticipating similar concerns in the works of other nineteenth-century novelists, including Charlotte Brontë, Charles Dickens, George Eliot, and William Makepeace Thackeray. Martineau was more successful as a fiction writer in *The Playfellow,* a series of four children's stories. "The Crofton Boys," usually regarded as the best story in the series, relates a young boy's experiences at boarding school and has been praised for its sensitive portrayal of a child's psychological development. Gillian Thomas finds this series to be the only work of Martineau's worth reading for "strictly literary merit."

Martineau's travel writings and her contributions to social science methodology are considered by many commentators her most important works. *How to Observe Morals and Manners* has been praised as one of the first systematic guidelines for observing a society and is regarded as an early contribution to the disciplines of anthropology and sociology. Martineau believed that societies should be judged against their own goals and standards, and while she did make some comparisons—contrasting American and British agricultural practices in *Society in America*—she avoided constant references to European customs and achievements in her evaluation of other cultures. *Society in America,* which has been ranked with Alexis de Tocqueville's *De la démocratie en Amérique* as an insightful analysis of early American society, is divided into three sections: politics and government, economics, and cultural life. An outspoken abolitionist and women's rights advocate, Martineau was one of the first commentators to draw an analogy between the status of women and slaves; the chapter "On the Political Non-Existence of Women" is considered an important early document in the women's rights movement. *Retrospect of Western Travel,* a more personal account of her visit to the United States, is organized as a narrative rather than thematically and was generally preferred by English audiences. In *Eastern Life, Present and Past,* Martineau was less judgmental than in the American books and was more reflective about her responses to the places she visited. Visiting the sites of Biblical events, Martineau became convinced that religion should be understood not as divine revelation but as part of the historical development of humanity.

Martineau's religious and philosophical thought found additional expression in *Letters on the Laws of Man's Nature and Development* and her translation and condensation of Comte's *Cours de philosophie positive. Letters,* composed of Martineau's questions to Henry G. Atkinson, an English intellectual who has been described as "a scientific and philosophical dilettante," and his responses, takes the form of meditations on phrenology, mesmerism, and the ordering of the universe. Like many Victorian intellectuals, Martineau reached a type of agnostic humanism by replacing belief in Christian dogma with faith in science and "natural law." She was drawn to Comte's philosophy, which provided a framework in which she was able to organize much of her thought. She believed she had evolved through his hierarchy of intellectual orientations: theological, metaphysical, and positive. According to Yates, Martineau "found better expression for what she already believed in the way Comte said it."

Because her works had often provoked controversy, Martineau felt that she owed society a record of her life. In her *Autobiography,* she recounted her childhood, the development of her writing career, and the evolution of her religious thought. Although her spiritual development has frequently been described as a deconversion, she often used the imagery and language of conventional Christianity to describe her life, which she viewed as a sort of "pilgrim's progress" from ignorance to enlightenment. Martineau also described current events, such as Queen Victoria's coronation, and many of the literary and political figures she knew. While the *Autobiography* was often criticized by her contemporaries for its bluntness, it is recognized today as an important literary and historical document and as a valuable contribution to women's autobiographical writing.

In her obituary, which she wrote in 1855 when she thought

she was dying, Martineau assessed her accomplishments this way: "With small imaginative and suggestive powers, and therefore nothing approaching genius, she could see clearly what she did see, and give a clear expression to what she had to say." Yet, while Martineau is not necessarily regarded as an original thinker, much of her work was innovative: *Illustrations of Political Economy* and *Deerbrook* helped introduce domestic realism into Victorian fiction, her travel writing and *How to Observe Morals and Manners* are early examples of social science methodology, and her views on women's status and her *Autobiography* are important contributions to feminist thought and writing. For these reasons, Martineau is receiving increasing recognition as a Victorian writer and as an early feminist.

(See also *Dictionary of Literary Biography,* Vol. 21: *Victorian Novelists Before 1885* and Vol. 55: *Victorian Prose Writers Before 1867* and *Yesterday's Authors of Books for Children,* Vol. 2.)

## PRINCIPAL WORKS

"Female Writers on Practical Divinity" (essay) 1820; published in journal *Monthly Repository*
*Devotional Exercises, Consisting of Reflections and Prayers for the Use of Young Persons; To Which Is Added a Treatise on the Lord's Supper* (handbook) 1823
*Principle and Practice; or, The Orphan Family* (novel) 1827
*Five Years of Youth; or, Sense and Sentiment* (novel) 1831
*Poor Laws and Paupers Illustrated* (short stories) 1833
*Illustrations of Political Economy* (short stories) 1834
*Illustrations of Taxation* (short stories) 1834
*Society in America* (essay) 1837
*How to Observe Morals and Manners* (handbook) 1838
*Retrospect of Western Travel* (travel essay) 1838
*Deerbrook* (novel) 1839
*The Hour and the Man* (novel) 1841
*The Playfellow* (children's stories) 1841
*Life in the Sick-Room: Essays by an Invalid* (essays) 1844
*Letters on Mesmerism* (essays) 1845
*Forest and Game Law Tales.* 3 vols. (short stories) 1845-46
*Eastern Life, Present and Past* (travel essay) 1848
*The History of England during the Thirty Years' Peace, 1816-46* (history) 1849
*Household Education* (essays) 1849
*Introduction to the History of the Peace, from 1800 to 1815* (history) 1851
*Letters on the Laws of Man's Nature and Development* [with Henry G. Atkinson] (philosophy) 1851
*The Positive Philosophy of Auguste Comte* [translator and adaptor; from *Cours de philosophie positive* by Auguste Comte] (philosophy) 1853
*A Complete Guide to the English Lakes* (handbook) 1855
*The Factory Controversy: A Warning against Meddling Legislation* (essay) 1855
*British Rule in India: A Historical Sketch* (history) 1857
*Suggestions Towards the Future Government of India* (essay) 1858
*England and Her Soldiers* (essay) 1859
*Health, Husbandry and Handicraft* (essays) 1861
*Biographical Sketches* (biography) 1869
*Harriet Martineau's Autobiography, with Memorials by Maria Weston Chapman* (autobiography) 1877

[G. P. SCROPE]   (essay date 1833)

[*In this excerpt from a review of* Illustrations of Political Economy, *Scrope questions the validity and presentation of the economic principles Martineau popularized in the series.*]

Here we have a monthly series of novels on Political Economy—Malthus, M'Culloch, Senior, and Mill, dramatised by a clever female hand. (p. 136)

There is, we admit, much which it is impossible not to admire in Miss Martineau's productions—the praiseworthy intention and benevolent spirit in which they are written,—and the varied knowledge of nature and society, the acute discrimination of character, and remarkable power of entering into, and describing the feelings of the poorer classes, which several of her little narratives evince. But it is equally impossible not to laugh at the absurd trash which is seriously propounded by some of her characters, in dull didactic dialogues, introduced here and there in the most clumsy manner; and what is worst of all, it is quite impossible not to be shocked, nay disgusted, with many of the unfeminine and mischievous doctrines on the principles of social welfare, of which these tales are made the vehicle.

This young lady's work consists of the several chapters of the [*Illustrations of Political Economy*], according to the doctors we have named, rendered into popular stories. Each tale has attached to it the 'principle' it is intended to illustrate; and the readers of each little volume are expected, we suppose, by the time they arrive at the end, to have duly imbibed and digested the substance of these 'principles.' We can only say, if any individual has accomplished this feat, his powers of deglutition and digestion are such as an ostrich might envy. Hear, however, how complacently the fair writer talks of her own doings in her preface:—

> We do not dedicate our series to any particular class of society, because we are sure that all classes bear an equal relation to the science, and we much fear that it is as little familiar to the bulk of one as of another. We should not be so ready to suspect this ignorance, if we did not hear so much of the difficulty of the subject. We trust it will be found that as the leading principles come out in order, one after another, they are so clear, so indisputable, so apparently familiar, that the wonder is when the difficulty is to come.

Miss Martineau has no modest misgivings:—

> She can deep mysteries unriddle
> As easily as thread a needle.

The first story, **'Life in the Wilds,'** is intended to exhibit the elements of wealth, and the advantages of the division and economy of labour. A small body of South African settlers are represented as suddenly stripped, by an incursion of savages, of their whole stock of valuables, including houses, furniture, arms, tools, down to a knife, a hatchet, even a nail;—left, in short, in possession absolutely of nothing but the clothes they had on, the seeds buried in the soil, and their wits. The latter article seems to be monopolized in joint-stock partnership by a Mr. Stone, the chaplain, and Captain Adams. By the advice of these gentlemen the disconsolate colonists set to work to make the best of their position,—shooting game with bows and arrows, seeking caves for houses, carving their meat with flints, and digging the soil with hedge-stakes. All this gives occasion to many lectures from Mr. Stone on the elements of wealth, and the necessity of labouring in some form or other to produce it, and to many experimental proofs of the vast progress that has been made by civilized nations in facilitating, by various contrivances, the labour of production. But to our mind, if we must be candid, *this* chapter of Political Economy has been 'illustrated' long ago in a much more amusing and instructive story than any of Miss Martineau's—*viz.,* Robinson Crusoe—a story which has the advantage of making our little people fully sensible of the value of civilization, with all its hardly-earned blessings, without puzzling their intellects with such unintelligible and fantastical refinements as the following:—

> "I am afraid, Sir," said Hill, "that your doctrine would go far towards doing away the distinction between labour that is *productive* and that which is *unproductive.*" "It is impossible," replied Mr. Stone, "to do away that difference, because it is a difference of fact, which no opinions can alter. It must always be as clear as observation can make it, whether a man's labour *produces* any of the things which constitute wealth. . . . . However industrious or useful they may be, *domestic servants are unproductive labourers.* . . . . Fulton, the currier, *produces* leather out of what was only the hide of a beast; and Harrison *makes* bricks out of what was only clay; Links, the farrier, is *unproductive as a farrier*—but he is also a smith, and *makes* horseshoes and nails, and implements out of what was only a lump of iron. Here he is a labourer *of both kinds.*"—*"That is curious!"*—"And so are you, Mr. Hill. You *make* medicines; but when you give advice, or bleed patients, or shave your customers on a Saturday night, you are an unproductive labourer." [This is curious too.] "And how do you class yourself, my dear?" said Mrs. Stone. "Unproductive in my pulpit and the schoolroom," replied her husband, "and productive when I am *working* in my field." "You have *cleared* up the matter completely, Sir," said Hill.

Only to think of *lectures* on such subjects among a parcel of poor houseless wretches, struggling for existence on the sands of Caffreland!—But to overlook this absurdity,—instead of the wise and wonderful Mr. Stone's having 'cleared up the matter completely,' as the Unitarian chaplain's admirer, Hill, thinks he has done, we are of opinion, that no chaplain, even of the Established Church, could possibly have rendered a plain matter more obscure. If wealth means (and we know no better definition of it) all that is valuable in exchange, then it is obvious that all labour which is bought and sold is productive of wealth. Can there be sillier nonsense than an attempt to draw a broad line of distinction between the labour of the farrier while he is shoeing a horse, and that of the same individual while making the shoe; to call the grazier and the farmer productive—the butcher and the cook unproductive labourers? It seems no labourer is to be called productive who does not '*make*' something! Why, even this silly verbal distinction will not carry Miss Martineau out in her exclusion of domestic servants, (after Malthus,) for a cook makes puddings, and a housemaid makes beds. Miss Martineau quite forgets that, by her own definition, (and she is quite correct in this,) no labour *creates* anything, but only changes the form or the place of natural objects; and is not this done to as good a purpose, that is, as productively, by the cook who roasts a leg of mutton, as by the grazier who fattens it—by the man who fastens the shoe on the horse's foot, as by the man who hammers it into shape on the anvil? Here, as elsewhere, the doctors are only too faithfully dramatised.

Tale the second illustrates the utility of capital, and especially of machinery, in a clever and agreeable manner. '**The Hill and the Valley**' is decidedly, in our opinion, the best of Miss Martineau's productions. We cannot say much for the next; the moral of which is the advantage of the consolidation of small farms into large ones. (pp. 136-38)

'**Demerara,**' the fourth tale, is powerfully written. The picture it contains of slavery, is, however, evidently drawn from imagination and the accounts of the anti-slavery missions, not from observation or the reports of unprejudiced bystanders. For example, a runaway slave is represented as hunted and torn to pieces by blood-hounds! Will Miss Martineau favour us with an authenticated relation of any such occurrence of late years in Demerara, or any of our West Indian colonies? In the summary of 'principles,' at the end of this tale, the injustice of slavery is proved in the following manner:—

> Property is held by conventional, not natural, right. As the agreement to hold man in property never took place between the parties concerned, *i.e.,* is not conventional, man has no right to hold man in property.

If there were no stronger argument against slavery than this, our slave-owners need be under no apprehension of its abolition. Why, by this rule, *what* have we a right to hold in property? The agreement to hold a horse or a house in property 'never took place between the parties concerned,' and, therefore, there can be no property in horses or houses! Or if Miss Martineau means, by 'the parties concerned,' all who have any desire to use horses or houses, let her say where the convention sat, consisting of all these parties, which 'agreed' to make a present to the Marquis of Westminster either of his stud or his streets. Miss Martineau is said to be high authority in the law courts. We would strongly recommend, therefore, the next thief who is tried at the Old Bailey, to plead that 'property is held by conventional not natural right;' and as he, Timothy Tomkins, never agreed that the prosecutor should hold his silk handkerchief in property, he had no more right to it than he, Timothy. It was *nullius in bonis,* and therefore liable to the maxim *capiat qui capere possit.* The theory which derives rights exclusively from a 'social contract' 'entered into by all parties concerned,' is as foolish as it is dangerous. Has Miss Martineau ever read Blackstone? or does she write works on the principles of legislation in total ignorance of all that has been previously written on the same subject?

'**Ella of Garveloch,**' the fifth tale, is improbably, but amusing,—that is to say, if we skip the political economy in it, which consists of sundry long and doleful dialogues on the nature of *rent.* Miss Martineau formally adopts the Ricardo definition of rent as 'that which is paid to the land-owner for the use of the *original indestructible powers of the soil*'; and yet with a droll inconsistency, makes her young she-farmer, Ella, begin by paying rent only for the *house* and *fences* on her occupation, and a further rent at the end of a few years for the *kelp-ground* and *herring-fishery* attached to it; and even the rent she is ultimately charged for the *land* of her little farm, is expressly set down to the account of the vicinity of the sea-shore rendering it capable of fertilization by the refuse weed; so that there is not a single particle of the rent she at any time pays which can be said to arise from 'the original indestructible powers of the soil!' This is *illustrating* a definition in an odd fashion. But thus it is,—when the axioms and definitions of these political economists are tested by an application to facts, they are found not to fit above one in a hundred.

The sixth tale takes up the history of Garveloch (a rocky islet among the Hebrides) at a later period. A fishing company had established a station upon it; a fishing village had been built; and encouraged by the demand for labour thus occasioned, a considerable population had settled there from the neighbouring islands, and was rapidly increasing—herrings and bannocks being a prolific diet. This is a state of things to alarm a Malthusian; and Ella, the Martineau of Garveloch, begins, even when the island is at the zenith of its prosperity, to quake at the anticipation of its over-population. She sees the cultivation of the islands so rapidly improving, that their produce had more than doubled in the last ten years, but she is impressed with the idea that 'all this time the consumers are increasing at a much quicker rate.'

> "Not double in ten years, surely?" "Certainly not; but say twenty, thirty, fifty, a hundred, or any number of years you choose; still as the number of people doubles itself for ever, while the produce of the land does not, *the people must increase faster than the produce.*"

This is rare logic and arithmetic, and not a little curious as natural history. A plain person, now, would have supposed, that if the produce doubled itself in ten, and the people only in a hundred years, the people would not increase *quite* so fast as the produce; seeing that, at the end of the first century, the population would be multiplied but by two, the produce by one thousand and twenty-four! But these are the discoveries of genius! Why does Miss Martineau write, except to correct our mistaken notions, and expound to us the mysteries of the 'principle of population?'

But what follows is yet more surprising in every way:—

> If all the corn that was raised in the islands had been used for seed-corn, instead of nine-tenths of it being eaten; if all the fish had been turned into its market-price on the spot, without any expense of curing, packing, and conveying, this capital would still have doubled itself *much more slowly* than the number of people who were to subsist upon it!

Now, since the corn sown in these islands, by the admission of the author, increases at present ten-fold in a year, it is as clear as arithmetic can make it, that if all were used for seed-corn (under the supposition proposed) it would be necessary, in order that the population should keep up only to the same rate of increase,—and putting the stock of fish out of the question—and supposing nobody to die—that every female should marry at three months old, and have twenty children at a birth! We believe *the herrings* multiply at some such rate; and it seems Miss Martineau thinks herring-fisherwomen must be equally prolific. A little ignorance on these ticklish topics is perhaps not unbecoming a young unmarried lady. But before such a person undertook to write books in favour of 'the preventive check,' she should have informed herself somewhat more accurately upon the laws of human propagation. Poor innocent! She has been puzzling over Mr. Malthus's arithmetical and geometrical ratios, for knowledge which she should have obtained by a simple question or two of her mamma. (pp. 139-41)

The next of these philosophical romances, the **'Manchester Strike,'** contains some well-drawn pictures of the state of the operatives in our manufacturing towns—and some useful lessons to that class, on the mischief and inutility of their 'strikes and turn-outs'—but has its moral marred entirely by the constant reference of the distress that arises from a temporary and local redundancy of hands, to the sinfulness of those weavers who marry without having previously ascertained that there cannot for a generation occur a stagnation of business in the cotton-trade! What?—when masters occasionally advertise throughout the kingdom for 'several thousand fresh hands wanted' at Macclesfield or Manchester—when hordes of Irish are pouring in daily to supply the demand for labour in our great manufacturing districts—are the *natives* of those very districts to be told that it is *their* fault if labour is ever in excess; that *they* have the remedy in their own hands, by refraining from matrimony: and that they neglect their duty to society by taking wives under such circumstances? When it is notorious that in these districts the relative supply and demand for labour often oscillates from one extreme to the other within a year or two—we are to be informed by Miss Martineau, in delicate phrase, that the labourers have the power, and they alone, by more or less of continuence, to adjust the supply of labour exactly at all times to the demand! Are the interests, the existence of millions, to be thus trifled with? Is the destiny of our industrious population to remain in the hands of men who have the imbecility to listen with reverence to such 'principles' as these—or the quackery to pretend to do so?

In another story, **'Cousin Marshall,'** Miss Martineau follows up her grand 'principle' to its legitimate inference, the grievous abomination of poor-laws; and not of poor-laws only, but of charity in every shape,—of anything, in short, which can stand for an instant of time between the poor and that utter destitution,—which this gentle philosopher expects to teach them to keep their numbers within the demand for their labour,—and which, at all events, would *kill them off* down to the desirable limit. If the subject were not too sadly serious, the monomania of these misogamists would be amusing. (pp. 143-44)

It being obvious, that the reformed legislature must have their hands full of Ireland, it was considered fit and proper, that Miss Martineau, as the extra-official ally of the Angleseas and Stanleys, should visit that island. She repaired accordingly, it appears, to Dublin: sojourned in that capital for five or six weeks, seeing of course the Seven Churches, Lady Morgan, and the Vale of Avoca; and returned to Norwich, excellently qualified, not only to beat Miss Edgeworth as a delineator of Irish manners, but to detect and grapple with the difficulties of the economical condition of 'the Green Isle,' in a series of profound lucubrations, the first of which bears the modest epigraph of **'Ireland.'**

In a far corner of the island—hundreds of miles, we believe, from any district that Miss Harriet condescended to inspect—a large population of cottiers is described as settled on the estate of a Mr. Tracey, an absentee. Mr. Rosso, a resident gentleman, owns an adjoining property, which he exerts himself to improve, and by establishing a school and acting as a magistrate, endeavours to render himself as useful to his impoverished neighbours as his means permit. Sullivan, one of the cottiers, while struggling to keep life and soul together, by miserably cultivating his meagre potato-patch, and the little his daughter Dora can add by her spinning, suffers a seizure of his cattle and pigs, and his entire potato-crop;—not for his own rent—that had just been paid by extraordinary effort—but for the arrears due by his immediate landlord—the tenant of some higher link in the chain of Irish subtenantcy. In this condition, all that remains to him of worldly goods—from the bed to the potato-pot and Dora's wheel—all is carried off by a visit from the tithe-proctor, and Sullivan is left alone with four bare walls, and a hungry family. When things are at the worst with an Irishman, it is the moment for a wedding. So thinks Dan, Dora's lover. He has just enough in his pocket to pay the priest's fee, and then they would be all on a footing, and must help one another as well as they could. The marriage takes place early in the morning, that Dan may be in time to bid for the occupation of land, some lots of which were that day to be let by auction, or, as the phrase goes, by cant. The most miserable are of course the hardiest bidders, and Dan carries off his lot in triumph, at a promised rent of *nine* pounds per acre. Luckily for him, the bounty of Mr. Rosso, who is accidentally present at the auction, affords him the means of buying the few tools necessary for his tillage, and a wheel and a stock of flax for his bride. The potatoes they glean out of the furrows left by the last occupant on taking up his crop, serve to support nature; so that, though without bed or furniture, Dan begins the world nearly as well off as his neighbours, and with what he considers a 'dacent prospect' before him. The Sullivans live with him, and they rub on, better than might have been expected, till rent-day comes round. Even for this Dan by great exertion has contrived to prepare—but he is not prepared for what ensues immediately on parting with his money,—an ejectment from the holding he had improved by unremitting toil, under promise of a lease, the signing of which had been delayed by neglect.

Mr. Tracey had written to his agent to say that it was evident to him his property had been much injured by its subdivision, that it was his pleasure no new leases should be granted, and that the process of consolidating the small holdings into large farms should take place without delay, the cottiers who held no leases being ejected from their occupations. These measures are carried into immediate execution by the zealous agent, and the natural consequences ensue. The ejected tenants, rendered desperate by the absence of all possible resource, set fire to their houses and turfstacks—hough all the cattle of the tenants who are brought in to succeed them—and take to the bogs and mountains in a state of rebellion. The family of Mr. Rosso, witnesses to all this desolation, talk it over in a long-winded dialogue, of which we extract a specimen:—

> "Would this were all over, boys! (said Mr. Rosso.) Every case I hear of seems a harder one than the last; and it breaks one's heart to leave them to take their chance. See, from this very point, what melancholy groups of them: aged parents, or helpless children, or weakly women in each! So much for that policy of landlords, by which they first increase the numbers of their tenantry, in order, by force of competition, to let their land high; and then, finding that they have gone too far, take a fit of consolidation, and make no provision for the crowd they called up around them, and now deprive of the means of subsistence. What think you of such policy, Henry?" "I was just thinking, Sir, that it is rather surprising to me that you lift up your voice, on all occasions, against establishing poor-laws in Ireland, while you have such scenes before your eyes."

It is indeed surprising that any one should think it right for *the law*—which *should* have as much regard for a peasant's welfare as a duke's—to place such a frightful power over the lives of millions, without check or restraint of any kind, in the hands of the Squire Traceys. But what is Mr. Rosso's answer to the appeal?

> "If the law could rectify these evils, Henry, I would cry out with as loud a voice as you. It is because I am convinced that *a legal charity* would only aggravate them, that I advocate other methods of rectification. The principle of *growth* is inherent in that system, whether that growth be rapid or slow; and *the destruction of the country in which it is established becomes merely a question of time.*(!) *The only way to get the better of it, is to annihilate it in time;*(!) and this being the case, it is mere folly to call it in for the relief of temporary evils."

And all this vague assumption is to be a sufficient answer to the strong cry of the hungry, the destitute, the desperate cottier—his cry for a legal protection from the sentence of death which his landlord passes on him and his children when he ejects them from their little holding!

Miss Martineau's grand panacea is *education:*—that is, we presume—make the Irish poor read and understand **'Ella of Garveloch,'** &c., and all will be right. We do not probably agree with this lady as to what *education* means—but we are quite as anxious as she can be to see the intellectual condition of the Irish poor elevated. We can, however, by no means believe, that real and immediate relief to the physical sufferings of the peasant is to be anticipated from book-work—*no,* not though 'the preventive check' were made, as Miss Martineau clearly intends it should be made, the primary topic of instruction. Her *secondary* remedies, viz. emigration, and the employment of the now idle cottier in drainages, embankments, making roads, cutting canals, and other comprehensive improvements of the country, we have always advocated as the primary, the true, and the only modes of putting an end to the misery and turbulence of the poor natives, and developing the resources of their country in a way which will make the improvement in their condition permanent. But a principal point on which we differ from Miss Martineau, is her notion that all or any of these works will ever be undertaken *spontaneously* by the Irish landlords. We are confident that such an expectation is hopeless; and that it is absolutely necessary for the legislature to step in, and *compel* such an appropriation of part of their rental to these purposes, as, while it must eventually benefit *them* in an extraordinary degree, by adding to the value of their estates—is an act of bare justice towards the suffering population of those estates. (pp. 144-47)

We hardly think it worth while to remark upon another story, in which this lady is good enough to exemplify the phenomena of money, by supposing a Siberian market carried on very briskly for a whole day upon *five mouse-skins,* as the sole circulating medium—the said mouse-skins, from some unaccountable quality, being ten times as valuable at the end of the day as at the beginning. The mouse-skins are then carried off by the cat, or some traveling fur-traders, we forget which, and the Siberian colonists have recourse to a new kind of money, consisting of *mammoth-bones!* Fancy a pocket-full of mammoth-tusks and tibiæ, with the grinders, we presume, for small change! And this trash is to bring political economy within the comprehension of babes and sucklings!

Our readers have by this time had enough of this damsel. We will only express our sorrow at observing, that in her remaining tales she still continues to harp on 'the necessity of limiting the number of consumers'! Nor is sorrow, perhaps, the word we ought to use. We should be loth to bring a blush unnecessarily upon the cheek of any woman; but may we venture to ask this maiden sage the meaning of the following passage:—

> A parent has a considerable influence over the subsistence-fund of his family, and *an absolute control over the numbers to be supported by that fund.*

Has the young lady picked up this piece of information in her conferences with the Lord Chancellor? or has she been entering into high and lofty communion on such subjects with certain gentlemen of her sect, famous for dropping their gratuitous advice on these matters into areas, for the benefit of the London kitchenmaids? We all remember Moore's 'She Politician.'

> Tis my fortune to know a lean Benthamite spinster,
> A maid who her faith in old Jeremy puts,
> Who talks with a lisp of "the last new Westminster,"
> And hopes you're delighted with "Mill upon Gluts," ¢.

Did Miss Martineau sit for the picture? But no;—such a character is nothing to a *female Malthusian. A woman* who thinks child-bearing a *crime against society!* An *unmarried woman* who declaims against *marriage!! A young woman* who deprecates charity and a provision for the *poor!!!*

Miss Martineau has, we are most willing to acknowledge, talents which might make her an useful and an agreeable writer. But the best advice we can give her is, to burn all the little books she has as yet written, with one or two exceptions;—to abstain from writing any more till she has mastered a better set of 'principles' than the precious stock she has borrowed from her favourite professors; and, in the mean time, to study the works of a lady who, with immeasurably greater abilities in every way, was her predecessor in the line she considers so wholly original—the illustrating by fiction the natural laws of social welfare. Political economy is far more ingeniously as well as justly illustrated in the *Absentee* and *Castle Rackrent,* than in **'Ireland.'** There is not indeed one tale of Miss Edgeworth's but conveys some useful lesson on questions which materially concern the economy of society. But the difference between the two writers is, that the moral of Miss Edgeworth's tales is naturally suggested to the reader by the course of events of which she peruses the narrative; that of Miss Martineau is embodied in elaborate dialogues or most unnatural incidents, with which her stories are interlarded and interrupted, to the utter destruction of the interest of all but detached bits of them. (pp. 150-52)

> [G. P. Scrope], *"Miss Martineau's 'Monthly Novels',"* in The Quarterly Review, *Vol. XLIX, No. XCVII, 1833, pp. 136-52.*

## [BENJAMIN DISRAELI]   (essay date 1837)

[*One of the most distinguished British statesmen of the nineteenth century, Disraeli is considered the originator of the political novel and a significant historian and critic of the English system of government. In the following excerpt from a review of* Society in America, *he disparages Martineau's analysis of American culture and institutions.*]

Miss Martineau has a ready eye for the picturesque, and pos-

sesses considerable descriptive powers. Her style, indeed, especially in the present work [*Society in America*], is somewhat overstrained for her strength, and abounds in solecisms scarcely to be expected from the humblest writer, and which in one of so much pretension are inexcusable and even painful. Miss Martineau tells us, that "the land is being cleared"—"the cows are being milked"—"new houses are being built daily"—an use of the auxiliary verb which we doubt whether Miss Martineau found in America, but rather suspect she derived from some of those cockney authorities to whom, we fear, she is indebted for something even worse than her indifferent grammar. Had Miss Martineau estimated the tether of her talents a little more accurately, had she confined herself to a simple and vivid description of what she witnessed in the new world, and interspersed her far from ordinary powers of picture with those just and shrewd remarks which occasionally figure in her pages, she might have produced a very pleasant and popular work, instead of a very absurd and a somewhat dull one.

Miss Martineau, forsooth, is a very great sage, and seems to have been far more intent on communicating to her English readers her own impracticable schemes for what she esteems the amelioration of her species and the emancipation of her sex, to favouring them with a lively and accurate idea of the life and country of their American neighbours. The parade of what is called philosophy in this book is indeed one of the most preposterous and burlesque exhibitions that we have long met with. The three volumes are primarily divided into four subjects, bearing the comprehensive titles of Politics, Economy, Civilization, and Religion: these portions are again subdivided into some 40 or 50 sections, very often bearing not the slightest connexion with the class from which they branch, when indeed we have been able clearly to comprehend the meaning of that class. Thus, under the very equivocal and not very inviting head of "Economy," nearly a volume is occupied with the most amusing part of the book, a series of rambling sketches, descriptive of the baths and watering-places, stage-waggons and steam-boats, farmhouses, and rural life and lake scenery of the United States; while, under the head of "Civilization," we have a chapter bearing the mysterious, and to us incomprehensible, title of "Utterance," and which, on turning to it, we found to be a very flimsy and superficial sketch of the state of literature in the United States, quite worthy of the most paltry magazine. But still we are compensated for the meagre slipslop thus encountered by the profound spirit of analysis which classes and describes the literature of a country under the apt head of "Utterance!" It is not a course of sober criticism which Miss Martineau requires, so much as to figure as the heroine of a grave farce by Moliere. In default, however, of the profound humour that created *Les Precieuses Ridicules,* we really think that we must recommend her to the ingenious and witty annalist of Little Pedlington, who recently celebrated with so much merriment one of the more obscure professors of modern nonsense. He might make something very diverting of this she apostle and her morbid love of analysis, and extravagant passion for definition. . . .

But with all this love of definition, it is curious that it is impossible from her work to obtain anything like a comprehensive notion of America either physical or moral. Affecting to be universal, it is essentially fragmentary; it is, in fact, only a series of articles, the greater portion of which might have been written without even visiting America at all; like some former lucubrations of this lady "under the immediate superintendence of the Society for the Diffusion of Knowledge," who it seems deemed her a fit instructor to enlighten her fellow-citizens in spite of her grammar.

Volney was the first traveller who broke loose from the trammels of mere narrative, and methodized the fruits of his observation and speculative thought. He brought great powers to a great task; an intellect in which the reasoning and imaginative faculties were happily and equally blended, very considerable learning, a spirit of profound investigation, a fine taste, and the command of a style certainly not excelled in French literature, and which will long remain a model for its picturesque delineation, its unfailing precision, and its transparent lucidness. The country to whose examination Volney applied his new system of travel-writing was admirably adapted to his scheme; the Orient was a tranquil and monotonous region, with a decaying yet deeply-implanted scheme of civilization, with little stirring life to distract the mind from its vast and various memorials of the past, and offering in every light the same strongly-marked characteristics. . . . Recently M. de Tocqueville, a disciple of the school of Volney, applied to America a similar system of moral analysis and material description. In every respect inferior to Volney, he is nevertheless a valuable writer; his style is simple, precise, and graphic; the spirit in which he writes is modest and tolerant; his work has taken its place in our libraries, and is without doubt the only work on America which yet deserves that distinction. But if M. de Tocqueville had equalled in ability M. Volney himself, he would have failed in producing a work which could have occasioned equal satisfaction, or have obtained so lasting a celebrity. The scheme of examination that suits an ancient and decaying country will fail when applied to a new and still unformed society. The analysis of Eastern civilization affords us the moral of an exhausted experiment, while that of the United States must terminate in crude speculations on a method of existence of which the character is perpetually shifting, which has not yet assumed any settled or determined form, and which a true philosopher approaches in a laudable spirit of doubt and hesitation. . . .

Not so Miss Martineau. Amidst the ruins of Baalbec and of Antioch, Volney was not so magisterial and dogmatical as this lady in the streets of New York and of New Orleans. She doubts nothing, she decides upon everything. She explains how everything occurred, and announces how everything must happen. With no learning, and, as we suspect, with very limited reading—with no experience of human nature derived either from books or men, armed only with the absurd axioms of an arbitrary scheme of verbiage which she styles philosophy, and which appears to be a crude mixture of Benthamism, political economy, and sansculotte morality, she hurries over the vast regions of the United States in half the time that Volney spent in Damascus and Aleppo, analyzing, resolving, defining, dividing, subdividing, and mapping out "the morals" of America, to adopt her own favourite jargon, not as they appear to her or to any other chance speculator, but as they ought to figure according to the principles which she imbibed before her visit, and the crude meditation of which probably amused her outward voyage. There is something infinitely ludicrous in the vanity and presumption with which this lady squares the circle of American morals and discovers the longitude of the impending civilization of a new world!

The consequence of this dogmatical arrogance is merely this—that throughout Miss Martineau's three cumbrous vol-

umes her facts and her inferences invariably contradict each other. But this is not surprising, for she found her facts on her arrival, and she brought her inferences with her ready made. We do not doubt the accuracy of her facts, for they always tell against her conclusions; we doubt not, therefore, she may be depended upon. Her first volume commences with a chapter on politics, wherein she delivers herself of an oracular announcement, viz. that the Government of America is the government of the majority, and that "the majority must always be right." This chapter was probably written in London, perchance under the superintendence of the Society for the Diffusion of Useful Knowledge. When Miss Martineau arrives in America she finds that the majority are always wrong; and the whole of her work is a continual struggle between her first principle, which she will not abandon, and her local observations, which she is too honest to suppress. She finds a population absorbed with a morbid desire of wealth, and so reckless and shortsighted in its pursuit, that there is some difficulty in finding in America a man who has not been a bankrupt; she finds in this land of freedom, under the title of public opinion, a tyranny established which renders it impossible for any well-intentioned and independent mind to act according to the dictates of its conscience; she finds the most corrupt and least intelligent press in existence, and a place-hunting population; she finds that the only way to arrive at public appointments is gross bribery and coarse flattery of the coarsest portion of the inhabitants; she finds half the union in a state of social disorganization from a system of slavery which she confesses is infinitely more infamous and heartrending than any that was ever tolerated in our own colonies, and from whose menacing consequences she confesses in despair the only remedy to be for the white population to fly the land; she finds the other portion of the states in a state of impending anarchy from what is styled Jacksonism, and which appears to us to be something very like Jacquerie, or a struggle between property and poverty; she lives in a great city, where on an average there are 365 duels in the year, or one for every day in the twelve months; she acknowledges that throughout the states there is virtually no freedom of the press, and a very guarded intercourse in private life; that no one dares to express his real opinions; that men are executed constantly without trial, and that during her brief residence she knows that not less than four individuals were burnt alive, and probably many more; but that such is the general system of lawlessness and terrorism, that no newspaper dare notice these tremendous incidents: and then Miss Martineau confesses "that many leaders of the democratic party think the people at large less fit to govern themselves wisely than they were five-and-twenty years ago." Yet, notwithstanding all this, Miss Martineau adheres firmly to her first principle, and assures us that "there can be no doubt that the majority must always be in the right," for that is an axiom in politics, and politics she condescendingly informs us, though taking due credit to herself for the profound discovery, are "a part of morals."

[*Benjamin Disraeli*], *"Society in America," in* The Times, *London, May 30, 1837, p. 5.*

### R. H. HORNE   (essay date 1844)

[*Horne provides an appreciative overview of Martineau's works.*]

The list of works published by Harriet Martineau is sufficient of itself to prove her great industry and perseverance in a course once begun. It will be seen that she published early in life, and that the series of her works proceeds with scarcely a break, year by year, onward to the period of her illness. Full as it is, it does not comprehend her numerous contributions to periodical literature, some of which are among the most valuable of her compositions. (p. 229)

From these works, the authoress would doubtless, like all those who have published early in life, gladly expunge some of the earliest. Yet there is not one among them which is out of keeping with the rest. All are written with a moral aim, in some higher, in others lower, but always apparent; all are remarkable for a free, clear, and unaffected style, which in her later productions is admirable from its lucid distinctness and simple force; and the whole taken together evince a continual improvability and progression, an undoubted sign of the possession on the part of the writer, of a mind open to and earnest for truth.

The year 1830 marks an epoch in the mind we are studying: the works from that period assume a higher tone, and have in general a higher aim. The *Traditions of Palestine* was a beautiful conception, executed in a spirit of love and poetry which throws a charm over its pages. The period in which Jesus Christ fulfilled his mission on earth, the people among whom he dwelt, the scenes in which he moved, the emotions he awakened, the thoughts he kindled, all are portrayed in a series of descriptions; while He himself (with that true art which has in this instance been instilled by reverence) is never introduced in person. This little book must kindle pure and holy thoughts wherever it is read.

The three Prize Essays published in this and the following year by the Association of Unitarian Dissenters, to which Miss Martineau belongs, display some of the chief powers of her mind. At this period she began her contributions to the *Monthly Repository;* these were sometimes original essays, tales, or poetry; sometimes reviews of metaphysical or theological works. Among the most excellent we may notice the **"Essays on the Art of Thinking,"** on the **"Religion of Socrates,"** and **"True Worshippers;"** but *above all,* the poem for the month of August, in a series by different authors, entitled **"Songs of the Months."**

All these literary labours were coincident with the design which was afterwards accomplished in the *Illustrations of Political Economy.* She has herself ascribed the original idea of this successful work to the reading of Mrs. Marcet's *Conversations on Political Economy,* which made her perceive that in her own tales entitled the **"Rioters"** and **"The Turn-Out,"** she had written political economy as M. Jourdain spoke prose, without knowing it. The question which thence presented itself, as to why all the doctrines of the science should not be equally well illustrated by fiction, was followed by a resolution to risk the publication of her Tales. (pp. 229-30)

This is not the place for an examination of the doctrines of political economy; nor would any such task be incumbent, even in a lengthened analysis of Miss Martineau's work. The task which she proposed to herself was to illustrate such parts of the fundamental doctrines of the science as lead to important practical results, adopting the doctrines as taught by the highest contemporary authorities. No one will deny the clearness and completeness of her illustration. Her correct interpretation of her authorities is questioned only on one point by a high authority, Mr. John Mill, in his review of her series.

That point is her "unqualified condemnation of the *principle* of the poor-laws." "In this," says the reviewer, "she is decidedly behind the present state of the science." What this principle has effected in the working, is another matter. We should, however, conceive on the evidence of passages in her work on *America,* relating to the competitive system and its necessary results, that she has subsequently abandoned her former views on this subject.

The stories, by means of which she illustrates her main points are generally constructed admirably, and testify to a great power of invention. It was no slight undertaking to contrive an interesting plot bearing on twenty-four doctrines of political economy; six more on taxation; and four more on poor-laws and paupers! But the majority of these stories really are interesting on their own account; some of them deeply so. We need only instance **"Ireland"** as perhaps the finest of all, and add that it was worthily companioned.

The choice of such a class of subjects gave rise to all manner of imputations. The *Quarterly Review,* in especial, while enlarging on what did not appear to it as "feminine," certainly forgot what was gentlemanly [see excerpt by G. P. Scrope dated 1833]. To most dispassionate inquirers, the choice will appear simply an evidence of the possession of a mind keenly alive to perceptions of all outward things; actively benevolent; observant of passing events, and the wants and evils of the age; turning its attention, therefore, to studies bearing on those evils and their remedies; logical rather than creative; hopeful of good, therefore too ready at times to adopt a theory bearing a promise of good; and, having embraced it, clear and acute in working it out. Too unshackled in spirit, too unaffected and simple-minded to be deterred for a moment from putting forth to the world that which she had conceived of truth and wisdom, by any consideration of what this or the other organ might decide on the subject of feminine occupations; but that which she found to do, "doing it with her might."

The work on *America,* written after the tour which Miss Martineau made in that country, is very valuable, as containing an admirably written description by an accurate observer, with a most candid mind and a thirst after the truth. At that period she was possessed of perfect health, and the good spirits natural to her were enhanced by success. The book breathes of cheerfulness and hopefulness. She evidently enjoyed her residence among the Americans, and she has dwelt on their fine institutions, their grand country, their many advantages, as on a favourite theme. Their lighter faults she has touched lightly; their graver errors with a melancholy earnestness. "Their civilization and morals," she says, "fall far below their own principle." This is enough to say. It is better than contrasting them with "European morals and civilization." This is undoubtedly the only philosophical view of the matter; and it is wiser to have faith like Harriet Martineau that the ideal standard set before them will elevate them to itself in time, than to reproach them with the discrepancy. It is no wonder that the subject is puzzling to us, who have outgrown our Institutions, and are obliged to maintain a continual struggle to bring them into something like harmony with our morals and civilization. Her chapters on slavery and its aspects have a solemnity of reprobation. On the other hand, the following passage contains a view of this subject which other nations are too apt to forget, and is a good instance of that clearsightedness and candour which are so characteristic of the writer:—

The nation must not be judged of by that portion whose worldly interests are involved in the maintenance of the anomaly; nor yet by the eight hundred flourishing abolition societies of the north, with all the supporters they have in unassociated individuals. The nation must be judged of as to Slavery by neither of these parties; but by the aspect of the conflict between them. If it be found that the five abolitionists who first met in a little chamber five years ago, to measure their moral strength against this national enormity, have become a host beneath whose assaults the vicious institution is rocking to its foundations, it is time that slavery was ceasing to be a national reproach. Europe now owes to America the justice of regarding her as the country of abolitionism, quite as emphatically as the country of slavery.

This work is as remarkable for its fearless outspoken tone as for its cheerful, hopeful, and candid views of things. Among other subjects on which the opinions of the writer are freely stated, is that of the condition of women. Miss Martineau accuses the American Constitution of inconsistency in withholding from women political and social equality with men. She points out that while it proclaims in theory, the equal rights of all the human race (except the blacks) it excludes one-half of the human race from any political rights whatever; neither providing for their independence as holders of property, nor as controllers of legislation, although their interests are equally concerned in both with those of men. (pp. 231-33)

The *Deerbrook* of Harriet Martineau has not enhanced the reputation of its authoress. The conception involves a moral puzzle, which is always painful. Neither does the catastrophe solve the puzzle. As the hero is made to sacrifice love to a supposed and mistaken view of duty, thus tampering with a great reality for the sake of a shadow, the plot ought to end in a tragedy, instead of in peace after a struggle. *The Hour and the Man,* is a story of deep interest; but fiction has done little for it. In the form of an authentic memoir of its grand subject, the life and death of "Toussaint L'Ouverture," its effect would have been more powerful. Much finer than either of these works of fiction are the tales comprising the series called the *Playfellow,* published within the last two years. These tales, constructed simply, to suit the minds for which they are intended, and founded on the emotions and actions of children, breathe a spirit of noble fortitude, endurance, energy, and self-control, which make them healthy reading for old and young. If they have a fault it is that they are rather wanting in love as an influence, resting more on the teachings of suffering. Among them all **"The Crofton Boys"** is our especial favourite. In all these works there is evinced very great power of description, and frequently a quiet humour. Harriet Martineau is never personal or satirical. *Life in the Sick Room* is published without a name; but that she is the authoress cannot be doubted for a moment by any one who has studied her writings, and far less by any one who has ever held companionship with herself; for it breathes of herself in every thought and word, chastened, purified, and instructed by suffering, and with eyes firmly fixed on the countenance of the Angel of Death, which is to her not terrible, but calm, in pale and solemn beauty. It would also appear, though no name is mentioned, that the friend to whom she dedicates the volume is Elizabeth B. Barrett, the elegant poetess and accomplished scholar, who, like herself, long immured within the four walls of her chamber, yet possesses sympathies alive to beauty and all fine influences, and a spirit expanding into and aspiring towards infinity. The holy teachings of this book are more touching in their wisdom than would be the words of one who came to us "from the dead;" for here the bourne is not passed; the words come indeed from one who has become accustomed to her "footing on the shaking plank over the deep dark river," but who is not too far removed from our sympathies, and has not yet laid aside the conditions of our common nature. (pp. 235-36)

R. H. Horne, "Harriet Martineau and Mrs. Jameson," in his A New Spirit of the Age, edited by R. H. Horne, J. C. Riker, 1844, pp. 227-37.

## HARRIET MARTINEAU   (essay date 1855)

*[In this excerpt from her obituary, which she wrote in 1855 when she thought she was dying, Martineau assesses her career.]*

[Harriet Martineau's] first appearance in print was before she was out of her teens, in a religious periodical. . . . Not only her contributions to the *Monthly Repository,* but her first books were of a religious character, her cast of mind being more decidedly of the religious order than any other during the whole of her life, whatever might be the basis and scope of her ultimate opinions. Her latest opinions were, in her own view, the most religious,—the most congenial with the emotional as well as the rational department of human nature. In her youth she naturally wrote what she had been brought up to believe, and her first work, **Devotional Exercises,** was thoroughly Unitarian. Of this class, and indeed of all her early writings, the only one worth mention is the little volume **Traditions of Palestine,** which first fixed attention upon her, and made her name known in the reviews. There are some even now who prefer that little volume to all her other writings. Before it was out its writer had formed the conception of the very different kind of work which at once and completely opened her career, her **Illustrations of Political Economy.** Her stimulus in all she wrote, from first to last, was simply the need of utterance. This need she had gratified early; and those who knew her best were always aware that she was not ambitious, though she enjoyed success, and had pride enough to have suffered keenly under failure. When, in 1829, she and her sisters lost their small fortunes by the failure of the house in which their money was placed, Harriet continued to write as she had written before, though under the new liability of having no money to spend upon ventures. Without capital, without any literary connections (except the editor of the *Monthly Repository*), without any visible means of accomplishing her object, she resolved to bring out a series of **Illustrations of Political Economy,** confident that the work was at that time (1831) very much needed by the working-classes, to say nothing of other persons who had influence in the community, agitated as it then was by the Reform struggle. . . . The original idea of exhibiting the great natural laws of society by a series of pictures of selected social action was a fortunate one; and her tales initiated a multitude of minds into the conception of what political economy is, and of how it concerns every body living in society. Beyond this, there is no merit of a high order in the work. It did not pretend to offer discoveries, or new applications or elucidations of prior discoveries. It popularized, in a fresh form, some doctrines and many truths long before made public by others. Those were the days of her success in narrative, in fiction. In about ten years from that time she had nearly ceased to write fiction, from simple inability to do it well. On the whole, perhaps, her novel of **Deerbrook** has been the most popular of her works of fiction, though some prefer her history (in the form of a romance) of Toussaint L'Ouverture (**The Hour and the Man**), and others again her story-book for children, written in illness,—**The Playfellow.** But none of her novels or tales have, or ever had, in the eyes of good judges or in her own, any character of permanence. The artistic aim and qualifications were absent; she had no power of dramatic construction; nor the poetic inspiration on the one hand, nor critical cultivation on the other, without which no work of the imagination can be worthy to live. Two or three of her Political Economy Tales, are, perhaps, her best achievement in fiction,—her doctrine furnishing the plot which she was unable to create, and the brevity of space duly restricting the indulgence in detail which injured her longer narratives, and at last warned her to leave off writing them. It was fortunate for her that her own condemnation anticipated that of the public. To the end of her life she was subject to solicitations to write more novels and more tales; but she for the most part remained steady in her refusal. Her three volumes of **Forest and Game Law Tales** and a few stories in *Household Words,* written at the express and earnest request of Mr. Dickens, and with little satisfaction to herself, are her latest efforts in that direction. (pp. 37-9)

After an absence of two years [during which she visited the United States] she returned to England in August, 1836, and early in the next spring she published **Society in America.** Her own opinion of that work changed much for the worse before her death. It was written while she was in the full flow of sympathy with the theoretical American statesmen of that time, who were all *à priori* political philosophers to a greater or less degree like the framers of the Declaration of Independence. Her intercourse with these may be traced in the structure and method of observation of her book, and her companionship with the adorers of Thomas Carlyle in her style. Some constitutional lawyers of the United States have declared that there is no error in her account of the political structure and relations of the Federal and State governments of that country; and the book contains the only account we have of the condition of slavery, and of the country under it, at the time of the rise of the abolition movement. But, on the whole, the book is not a favourable specimen of Harriet Martineau's writings, either in regard to moral or artistic taste. It is full of affectations and preachments, and it marks the highest point of the metaphysical period of her mind. Little as she valued the second work on America—**Retrospect of Western Travel**—which she wrote at the request of her publishers, to bring into use her lighter observations on scenery and manners, it was more creditable to her mood, and perhaps to her powers, than the more ambitious work. (pp. 41-2)

[**The History of England during the Thirty Years' Peace, 1816-46**], the bulkiest of her works and the most laborious, was undertaken at the request of Mr. Charles Knight, who had himself written the first few chapters, then deputed the work to another, and presently found it at a stand. Harriet Martineau had no idea whatever whether she could write history; but, on Mr. Knight's pressing his request, she went to work in August, 1848, and completed the work (after an interval of a few weeks) in the autumn of 1849. The introductory volume was written in 1850, also at Mr. Knight's solicitation. Without taking the chronicle form this history could not, from the nature of the case, be cast in the ultimate form of perfected history. All that can be done with contemporary history is to collect and methodize the greatest amount of reliable facts and distinct impressions, to amass sound material for the veritable historian of a future day,—so consolidating, assimilating, and vivifying the structure as to do for the future writer precisely that which the lapse of time and the oblivion which creeps over all transactions must prevent his doing for himself. This auxiliary usefulness is the aim of Harriet Martineau's history; and she was probably not mistaken in hoping for that much result from her labour. It rendered her a personal service which she had not anticipated. There was an impression abroad of her being a sort of demagogue or dangerous Radical, though it is hard to say which of her writings could have originated such an impression. The history dispelled it thoroughly; and if it proved that she belonged to no party, it showed that it was not because she transcended the extremes of all.

The work which she published on her return from her Eastern travels, which she enjoyed as the guest of Mr. and Mrs. Richard V. Yates, of Liverpool, had shown that she was no longer a Unitarian nor a believer in revelation at all. **Eastern Life, Present and Past,** exhibits the history and generation of the four great faiths—the Egyptian, the Jewish, the Christian, and the Mohammedan—as they appear when their birthplaces are visited in succession. She had passed from the Nile to Sinai; and thence to Jerusalem, Damascus, and Lebanon. The work in which she gave out her views on her return ranks, on the whole, as the best of her writings; and her reputation assumed a new, a graver, and a broader character after its appearance. It was followed in 1851 by a volume which, though not for the most part written by her, was of her procuring and devising. She took the responsibility of the **Letters on the Laws of Man's Nature and Development,** which were for the greater part written by her friend, Mr. Atkinson, in reply to the short letters of her own which occupy a small proportion of the book. This book brought upon its writers, as was inevitable, the imputation of atheism from the multitude who cannot distinguish between the popular and the philosophical sense of the word,—between the disbelief in the popular theology which has caused a long series of religious men to be called atheists, and the disbelief in a First Cause,—a disbelief which is expressly disclaimed in the book. A full account of Harriet Martineau's faith and philosophy will of course be found in her forthcoming **Autobiography,** where it is more in place than here. As to the consequences of such an expression of them, they were somewhat different from what might have been expected. The reception of the volume disclosed some curious social facts, revealing to its authors an altogether unexpected proportion between the receivers and repudiators of dogmatic theology in this country. What is called "the entire periodical press" condemned the book, without, however, in any one case meeting its argument or recognizing its main subject; and yet was it excellently received and widely sympathized with. Every body supposed that its authors would be ruined, excluded from society, stopped in their work, and so forth. But the actual result was that this open avowal of heretical opinion made all the relations of life sounder than they had ever been. As Harriet Martineau declared, it dissolved all false relations and confirmed all true ones. At no time of her life was she more occupied, more prosperous, so cheered by sympathy, or so thoroughly happy, as during the interval between the publication of that book and the close of her labours.

Besides some small works, such as **Guide to the Lakes,** it remained for her to bring out two of more general importance,—her volume on **Household Education,** which is more popular than almost any of her works, and her condensation of Comte's *Positive Philosophy.* The story of the intention and achievement of that work is told in its prefaces. Begun in 1852, it occupied the greater part of the year 1853, and appeared in November of that year. It was her last considerable work; and there is no other, perhaps, which so well manifests the real character of her ability and proper direction of her influence,—as far as each went. Her original power was nothing more than was due to earnestness and intellectual clearness within a certain range. With small imaginative and suggestive powers, and therefore nothing approaching to genius, she could see clearly what she did see, and give a clear expression to what she had to say. In short, she could popularize, while she could neither discover nor invent. She could sympathize in other people's views, and was too facile in doing so; and she could obtain and keep a firm grasp of her own, and, moreover, she could make them understood. The function of her life was to do this, and, in as far as it was done diligently and honestly, her life was of use, however far its achievements may have fallen short of expectations less moderate than her own. Her duties and her business were sufficient for the peace and the desires of her mind. She saw the human race, as she believed, advancing under the law of progress; she enjoyed her share of the experience, and had no ambition for a larger endowment, or reluctance or anxiety about leaving the enjoyment of such as she had. (pp. 46-8)

> *Harriet Martineau, in* Harriet Martineau on Women, *edited by Gayle Graham Yates, Rutgers University Press, 1985, 283 p.*

## HARRIET MARTINEAU   (essay date 1855)

[*In this selection from the first two volumes of her* Autobiography, *completed by Martineau in 1855, she describes her methods of composition and offers her judgment of some of her major works.*]

I suppose I must tell what [my first published] paper was, though I had much rather not; for I am so heartily ashamed of the whole business as never to have looked at the article since the first flutter of it went off. It was [entitled] **"Female Writers on Practical Divinity."** I wrote away, in my abominable scrawl of those days, on foolscap paper, feeling mightily like a fool all the time. I told no one, and carried my expensive packet to the postoffice myself, to pay the postage. I took the letter V for my signature,—I cannot at all remember why. The time was very near the end of the month: I had no definite expectation that I should ever hear any thing of my paper; and certainly did not suppose it could be in the forthcoming number [of the *Monthly Repository*]. That number was sent in before service-time on a Sunday morning. My heart may have been beating when I laid hands on it; but it thumped prodigiously when I saw my article there, and, in the Notices to Correspondents, a request to hear more from V. of Norwich. There is certainly something entirely peculiar in the sensation of seeing one's self in print for the first time:—the lines burn themselves in upon the brain in a way of which black ink is incapable, in any other mode. So I felt that day, when I went about with my secret.—I have said what my eldest brother was to us,—in what reverence we held him. He was just married, and he and his bride asked me to return from chapel with them to tea. After tea he said, 'Come now, we have had plenty of talk; I will read you something;' and he held out his hand for the new *Repository*. After glancing at it, he exclaimed, 'They have got a new hand here.

Listen.' After a paragraph, he repeated, 'Ah! this is a new hand; they have had nothing so good as this for a long while.' (It would be impossible to convey to any who do not know the *Monthly Repository* of that day, how very small a compliment this was.) I was silent, of course. At the end of the first column, he exclaimed about the style, looking at me in some wonder at my being as still as a mouse. Next (and well I remember his tone, and thrill to it still) his words were—'What a fine sentence that is! Why, do you not think so?' I mumbled out, sillily enough, that it did not seem any thing particular. 'Then,' said he, 'you were not listening. I will read it again. There now!' As he still got nothing out of me, he turned round upon me, as we sat side by side on the sofa, with 'Harriet, what is the matter with you? I never knew you so slow to praise any thing before.' I replied, in utter confusion,—'I never could baffle any body. The truth is, that paper is mine.' He made no reply; read on in silence, and spoke no more till I was on my feet to come away. He then laid his hand on my shoulder, and said gravely (calling me 'dear' for the first time) 'Now, dear, leave it to other women to make shirts and darn stockings; and do you devote yourself to this.' I went home in a sort of dream, so that the squares of the pavement seemed to float before my eyes. That evening made me an authoress.

It was not all so glorious, however. I immediately after began to write my first work,—***Devotional Exercises,*** of which I now remember nothing. But I remember my brother's anxious doubting looks, in which I discerned some disappointment, as he read the M.S. I remember his gentle hints about precision and arrangement of ideas, given with the utmost care not to discourage me; and I understood the significance of his praise of the concluding essay . . . praise of the definiteness of object in that essay, which, as he observed, furnished the key to his doubts about the rest of the book, and which he conveyed only from an anxious desire that I should work my way up to the high reputation which he felt I was destined to attain. This just and gentle treatment, contrasting with the early discouragements which had confused my own judgment, affected me inexpressibly. I took these hints to heart in trying my hand at a sort of theologico-metaphysical novel, which I entered upon with a notion of enlightening the world through the same kind of interest as was then excited by Mr. Ward's novel, *Tremaine,* which was making a prodigious noise, and which perfectly enchanted me, except by its bad philosophy. I mightily enjoyed the prospect of this work, as did my mother; and I was flattered by finding that Rachel had higher expectations from it than even my own. But, at the end of half a volume, I became aware that it was excessively dull, and I stopped. Many years afterwards I burned it; and this is the only piece of my work but two (and a review) in my whole career that never was published.

Already I found that it would not do to copy what I wrote; and here (at the outset of this novel) I discontinued the practice for ever,—thus saving an immense amount of time which I humbly think is wasted by other authors. The prevalent doctrine about revision and copying, and especially Miss Edgeworth's account of her method of writing,—scribbling first, then submitting her manuscript to her father, and copying and altering many times over till, (if I remember right) no one paragraph of her *Leonora* stood at last as it did at first,—made me suppose copying and alteration to be indispensable. But I immediately found that there was no use in copying if I did not alter; and that, if ever I did alter, I had to change back again; and I, once for all, committed myself to a single copy. I believe the only writings I ever copied were

*Devotional Exercises,* and my first tale;—a trumpery story called **"Christmas Day."** It seemed clear to me that distinctness and precision must be lost if alterations were made in a different state of mind from that which suggested the first utterance; and I was delighted when, long afterwards, I met with Cobbett's advice;—to know first what you want to say, and then say it in the first words that occur to you. The excellence of Cobbett's style, and the manifest falling off of Miss Edgeworth's after her father's death (so frankly avowed by herself) were strong confirmations of my own experience. I have since, more than once, weakly fallen into mannerism,— now metaphysically elliptical,—now poetically amplified, and even, in one instance, bordering on the Carlylish; but through all this folly, as well as since having a style of my own,—(that is, finding expression by words as easy as breathing air)—I have always used the same method in writing. I have always made sure of what I meant to say, and then written it down without care or anxiety,—glancing at it again only to see if any words were omitted or repeated, and not altering a single phrase in a whole work. I mention this because I think I perceive that great mischief arises from the notion that botching in the second place will compensate for carelessness in the first. I think I perceive that confusion of thought, and cloudiness or affectation in style are produced or aggravated by faulty prepossessions in regard to the method of writing for the press. The mere saving of time and labour in my own case may be regarded as no inconsiderable addition to my term of life.—Some modifications of this doctrine there must of course be in accordance with the strength or weakness of the natural faculty of expression by language: but I speak as strongly as I have just done because I have no reason to believe that the natural aptitude was particularly strong in myself. I believe that such facility as I have enjoyed has been mainly owing to my unconscious preparatory discipline; and especially in the practice of translation from various languages. . . . And, again, after seeing the manuscripts or proof-sheets of many of the chief authors of my own time, I am qualified to say that the most marked mannerists of their day are precisely those whose manuscripts show most erasures, and their proof-sheets most alterations. (pp. 118-23)

It was in the autumn of 1827, I think, that a neighbour lent my sister Mrs. Marcet's *Conversations on Political Economy.* I took up the book, chiefly to see what Political Economy precisely was; and great was my surprise to find that I had been teaching it unawares, in my stories about Machinery and Wages. It struck me at once that the principles of the whole science might be advantageously conveyed in the same way,—not by being smothered up in a story, but by being exhibited in their natural workings in selected passages of social life. It has always appeared very strange to me that so few people seem to have understood this. (p. 138)

As for the method, in regard to the Political Economy Tales, I am not sorry to have an opportunity of putting it on record. When I began, I furnished myself with all the standard works on the subject of what I then took to be a science. I had made a skeleton plan of the course, comprehending the four divisions, Production, Distribution, Exchange and Consumption: and, in order to save my nerves from being overwhelmed with the thought of what I had undertaken, I resolved not to look beyond the department on which I was engaged. The subdivisions arranged themselves as naturally as the primary ones; and when any subject was episodical (as Slave Labour) I announced it as such. Having noted my own leading ideas on the topic before me, I took down my books, and read the

treatment of that particular subject in each of them, making notes of reference on a separate sheet for each book, and restraining myself from glancing even in thought towards the scene and nature of my story till it should be suggested by my collective didactic materials. It was about a morning's work to gather hints by this reading. The next process, occupying an evening, when I had one to spare, or the next morning, was making the Summary of Principles which is found at the end of each number. This was the most laborious part of the work, and that which I certainly considered the most valuable. By this time, I perceived in what part of the world, and among what sort of people, the principles of my number appeared to operate the most manifestly. Such a scene I chose, be it where it might.

The next process was to embody each leading principle in a character: and the mutual operation of these embodied principles supplied the action of the story. It was necessary to have some accessories,—some out-works to the scientific erection; but I limited these as much as possible; and I believe that in every instance, they really were rendered subordinate. An hour or two sufficed for the outline of my story. If the scene was foreign, or in any part of England with which I was not familiar, I sent to the library for books of travel or topography: and the collecting and noting down hints from these finished the second day's work. The third day's toil was the severest. I reduced my materials to chapters, making a copious table of contents for each chapter on a separate sheet, on which I noted down, not only the action of the personages and the features of the scene, but all the political economy which it was their business to convey, whether by exemplification or conversation,—so as to absorb all the materials provided. This was not always completed at one sitting, and it made me sometimes sick with fatigue: but it was usually done in one day. After that, all the rest was easy. I paged my paper; and then the story went off like a letter. I never could decide whether I most enjoyed writing the descriptions, the narrative, or the argumentative or expository conversations. I liked each best while I was about it.

As to the actual writing,—I did it as I write letters, and as I am writing this Memoir,—never altering the expression as it came fresh from my brain. On an average I wrote twelve pages a day,—on large letter paper (quarto, I believe it is called), the page containing thirty-three lines. (pp. 193-95)

While my twelfth number [of the Tales] was printing, I was writing the thirteenth, **"The Charmed Sea,"**—that sea being the Baikal Lake, the scenery Siberian, and the personages exiled Poles. The *Edinburgh Review* charged me with relaxing my Political Economy for the sake of the fiction, in this case,—the reviewer having kept his article open for the appearance of the latest number obtainable before the publication of the review. There was some little mistake about this; the fact being that the bit of doctrine I had to deal with,—the origin of currency,—hardly admitted of any exemplification at all. Wherever the scene had been laid, the doctrine would have been equally impracticable in action, and must have been conveyed mainly by express explanation or colloquial commentary. If any action were practicable at all, it must be in some scene where the people were at the first remove from a state of barter: and the Poles in Siberia, among Mongolian neighbours, were perhaps as good for my purpose as any other personages. Marco Polo's account of the stamped leather currency he met with in his travels determined me in regard to Asiatic scenery, in the first place; and the poet Campbell's appeals to me in behalf of the Poles, before I left Norwich, and the visits of the venerable Niemcewicz, and other Poles and their friends, when I went to London, made me write of the Charmed Sea of Siberia. My reviewer was right as to the want of the due subordination of other interests to that of the science; but he failed to perceive that that particular bit of science was abstract and uninteresting. I took the hint, however; and from that time I was on my guard against making my Series a vehicle for any of the 'causes' of the time. I saw that if my Edinburgh reviewer could not perceive that some portions of doctrine were more susceptible of exemplification than others, such discrimination was not to be expected of the whole public; and I must afford no occasion for being supposed to be forsaking my main object for such temporary interests as came in my way. (pp. 234-36)

In planning my next story, **"Berkeley the Banker,"** I submitted myself to my reviewer's warning, and spared no pains in thoroughly incorporating the doctrine and the tale. I remember that, for two days, I sat over my materials from seven in the morning till two the next morning, with an interval of only twenty minutes for dinner. At the end of my plotting, I found that, after all, I had contrived little but relationships, and that I must trust to the uprising of new involutions in the course of my narrative. I had believed before, and I went on during my whole career of fiction-writing to be more and more thoroughly convinced, that the creating a plot is a task above human faculties. It is indeed evidently the same power as that of prophecy: that is, if all human action is (as we know it to be) the inevitable result of antecedents, all the antecedents must be thoroughly comprehended in order to discover the inevitable catastrophe. A mind which can do this must be, in the nature of things, a prophetic mind, in the strictest sense; and no human mind is that. The only thing to be done, therefore, is to derive the plot from actual life, where the work is achieved for us: and, accordingly, it seems that every perfect plot in fiction is taken bodily from real life. The best we know are so derived. Shakspere's are so: Scott's one perfect plot (the *Bride of Lammermoor*) is so; and if we could know where Boccaccio and other old narrators got theirs, we should certainly find that they took them from their predecessors, or from the life before their eyes. I say this from no mortification at my own utter inability to make a plot. I should say the same, (after equal study of the subject) if I had never tried to write a tale. I see the inequality of this kind of power of contemporary writers; an inequality wholly independent of their merits in other respects; and I see that the writers (often inferior ones) who have the power of making the best plots do it by their greater facility in forming analogous narratives with those of actual experience. They may be, and often are, so inferior as writers of fiction to others who cannot make plots that one is tempted to wish that they and their superiors could be rolled into one, so as to make a perfect novelist or dramatist. For instance, Dickens cannot make a plot,—nor Bulwer,—nor Douglas Jerrold, nor perhaps Thackeray; while Fanny Kemble's forgotten *Francis the First,* written in her teens, contains mines of plot, sufficient to furnish a groundwork for a score of fine fictions. As for me, my incapacity in this direction is so absolute that I always worked under a sense of despair about it. In the ***Hour and the Man,*** for instance, there are prominent personages who have no necessary connexion whatever with the story; and the personages fall out of sight, till at last, my hero is alone in his dungeon, and the story ends with his solitary death. I was not careless, nor unconscious of my inability. It was inability, 'pure and simple.' My only resource therefore was taking sug-

gestion from facts, witnessed by myself, or gathered in any way I could. That tale of **"Berkeley the Banker"** owed its remarkable success, not to my hard work of those two days; but to my taking some facts from the crisis of 1825-6 for the basis of my story. The toil of those two days was not thrown away, because the amalgamation of doctrine and narrative was more complete than it would otherwise have been: but no protraction of the effort would have brought out a really good plot, any more than the most prodigious amount of labour in practising would bring out good music from a performer unendowed with musical faculty. (pp. 237-39)

In choosing the ground of my work, *Society in America,*—(which should have been called, but for the objection of my publishers, *Theory and Practice of Society in America,*) I desired fairness in the first place: and I believed it was most fair to take my stand on the American point of view,—judging American society, in its spirit and methods, by the American tests,—the Declaration of Independence, and the constitutions based upon its principles. It had become a practice so completely established to treat of America in a mode of comparison with Europe, that I had little hope of being at first understood by more than a few. The Americans themselves had been so accustomed to be held up in contrast with Europeans by travellers that they could not get rid of the prepossession, even while reading my book. What praise there was excited vanity, as if such a thing had never been heard of before: and any censure was supposed to be sufficiently answered by evidence that the same evils existed in England. I anticipated this; and that consternation would be excited by some of my republican and other principles. Some of this consternation, and much of the censure followed, with a good deal that I had not conceived of. All this was of little conse-

*Martineau about the time she visited the United States.*

quence, in comparison with the comfort of having done some good, however little, in both countries. The fundamental fault of the book did not become apparent to me for some time after;—its metaphysical framework, and the abstract treatment of what must necessarily be a concrete subject. The fault is not exclusively mine. It rests with the American theory which I had taken for my standpoint: but it was the weakness of an immature mind to choose that method of treatment; just as it was the act of immature politicians to make after the same method the first American constitution,—the one which would not work, and which gave place to the present arrangement. Again, I was infected to a certain degree with the American method of dissertation or preaching; and I was also full of Carlylism, like the friends I had left in the Western world. So that my book, while most carefully true in its facts, had a strong leaning towards the American fashion of theorising; and it was far more useful on the other side of the Atlantic than on this. The order of people here who answer to the existing state of the Americans took the book to heart very earnestly, if I may judge by the letters from strangers which flowed in upon me, even for years after its publication. . . . Suffice it that though I now disapprove the American form and style of the book, not the less standing by my choice of the American point of view, I have never regretted its boldness of speech. I felt a relief in having opened my mind which I would at no time have exchanged for any gain of reputation or fortune. The time had come when, having experienced what might be called the extremes of obscurity and difficulty first, and influence and success afterwards, I could pronounce that there was nothing for which it was worth sacrificing freedom of thought and speech. I enjoyed in addition the consolidation of invaluable friendships in America, and the acquisition of new ones at home. Altogether, I am well pleased that I wrote the book, though I now see how much better it might have been done if I had not been at the metaphysical period of my life when I had to treat of the most metaphysical constitution and people in the world.

Some of the wisest of my friends at home,—and especially, I remember Sydney Smith and Carlyle,—gently offered their criticism on my more abstract American book in the pleasant form of praise of the more concrete one. The ***Retrospect of Western Travel*** was very successful. . . . Readers who thus read for amusement, and skip the politics, liked my second book best: and so did those who, like Carlyle, wisely desire us to see what we can, and tell what we see, without spinning out of ourselves systems and final causes, and all manner of notions which, as self-derived, are no part of our business or proper material in giving an account of an existing nation. (pp. 102-06)

My doctrine about plots in fiction has been given at sufficient length. It follows of course that I looked into real life for mine. (p. 111)

[For the plot of my novel, ***Deerbrook,*** I] came back, after every divergence, to the single fact (as I then believed it) that a friend of our family, whom I had not seen very often, but whom I had revered from my youth up, had been cruelly driven, by a match-making lady, to propose to the sister of the woman he loved,—on private information that the elder had lost her heart to him, and that he had shown her attention enough to warrant it. The marriage was not a very happy one, good as were the persons concerned, in their various ways. I altered the circumstances as much as I could, and drew the character, not of our English but of an American

friend, whose domestic position is altogether different: and lo! it came to my knowledge, years afterwards, that the story of our friend's mischance was not at all true. I was rejoiced to hear it. Not only was I relieved from the fear of hurting a good man's feelings, if he should ever read ***Deerbrook:*** but ***Deerbrook*** was a fiction, after all, in its groundwork.

The process was an anxious one. I could not at all tell whether I was equal to my enterprise. I found in it a relief to many pent-up sufferings, feelings, and convictions: and I can truly say that it was uttered from the heart. (p. 113)

My own judgment of ***Deerbrook*** was for some years more favourable than it is now. The work was faithful in principle and sentiment to the then state of my mind; and that satisfied me for a time. I should now require more of myself, if I were to attempt a novel,—(which I should not do, if I were sure of living another quarter of a century.) I should require more simplicity, and a far more objective character,—not of delineation but of scheme. The laborious portions of meditation, obtruded at intervals, are wholly objectionable in my eyes. Neither morally nor artistically can they be justified. I know the book to have been true to the state of thought and feeling I was then in, which I now regard as imperfect and very far from lofty:—I believe it to have been useful, not only in overcoming a prejudice against the use of middle-class life in fiction, but in a more special application to the discipline of temper; and therefore I am glad I wrote it: but I do not think it would be fair to judge me from it, any later than the time in which it was written. (pp. 115-16)

*Harriet Martineau, in* Harriet Martineau's Autobiography, *3 Vols., second edition, Smith, Elder, & Co., 1877.*

### GEORGE ELIOT (letter date 1877)

[*An English novelist, essayist, poet, editor, short story writer, and translator, Eliot was one of the greatest English novelists of the nineteenth century. She was acquainted with Martineau, and although the two occasionally demonstrated personal differences, Eliot considered Martineau "the only English woman who possesses thoroughly the art of writing." In this excerpt from a letter to a friend, Eliot offers her opinion of Martineau's* Autobiography.]

You must read Harriet Martineau's ***Autobiography.*** While I was ill Mr. Lewes took my office of reader and for the most part read the first two volumes to me. The account of her childhood and early youth is most pathetic and interesting, but . . . as in all books of the kind the charm departs as the life advances, and the writer has to tell of her own triumphs. One regrets continually that she felt it necessary not only to tell of her intercourse with many more or less distinguished persons—which would have been quite pleasant to everybody—but also to pronounce upon their entire merits and demerits, especially when, if she had died as soon [as] she expected, these persons would nearly all have been living to read her gratuitous rudenesses. But I rejoiced profoundly in the conquest of right feeling which determined her to leave the great, sad breach with her once beloved brother in almost total silence, and as I did not read Mrs. Chapman's volume (Mr. Lewes having glanced through it and told me that it was worthless) I was feeling hardly anything about the book but satisfaction in the picture of a life which was on the whole thoroughly virtuous, beneficent and dignified, until I found (what Mr. Lewes had not observed) that this wretched Mrs.

Chapman has been so forsaken of all the good as to enter into details and accusations connected with that very quarrelling which Harriet Martineau had willed to bury in silence. Really there is nothing but imbecility to be pleaded as a reason why Mrs. Chapman's conduct should not be called wicked. Then again, she has published H.M's private letters—at the end of the very book which begins with a solemn protest against any such publication!

Browning observed to me that Miss Martineau's procedure in demanding back her own letters, made it the more reprehensible for her to enter into statements about her relations with others, because her own letters being destroyed there remained no evidence to check her statements. And one cannot help being convinced that her representations are often false, not from any untruthfulness in her but from the extremely self-satisfied point of view with which she regarded her transactions with business acquaintances and her intercourse with friends.

Still, in spite of Mrs. Chapman, I hope the book will do more good than harm. Many of the most interesting little stories in it about herself and others she had told me (and Mr. Atkinson) when I was staying with her, almost in the very same words. But they were all the better for being told in her silvery voice. She was a charming talker, and a perfect lady in her manners as a hostess. It is a comfort to think—looking back on the vile treatment she received from the *Quarterly* and *Frazers,* making people believe that she was a coarseminded, repulsive woman—that such blackguardism in print could not be tolerated now, and that it would hardly enter into anybody's mind to conceive such sentences for any form of outward utterance. (pp. 353-54)

> *George Eliot, in a letter to Mrs. Charles Bray on March 20, 1877, in her* The George Eliot Letters: 1874-1877, Vol. VI, *edited by Gordon S. Haight, Yale University Press, 1955, pp. 353-54.*

## [MARGARET OLIPHANT]   (essay date 1877)

[*Oliphant was a prolific nineteenth-century Scottish novelist, biographer, critic, and historian who contributed regularly to* Blackwood's Edinburgh Magazine. *Here, she criticizes the tone and the emphasis of Martineau's* Autobiography.]

[Harriet Martineau's ***Autobiography***] is not the first portrait of herself which this distinguished writer has given to the world. In the end of last summer, at the time of her death, there appeared in the *Daily News* a short account of her life, character, and works, which we were informed by an editorial note was from her own hand, and upon which the present writer had begun to found an estimate of Miss Martineau's life and labours, when we were stopped by the announcement that another longer and more detailed autobiography was—not only written, but printed, illustrated, and ready for immediate publication. The fact that a woman had thought it fit and becoming to leave her own account of herself in an editor's drawer for some twenty years, ready for the moment when death might overtake her, was of itself a curious evidence of the high weight she attached to it and her anxiety to make the world aware of her own deliberate judgment upon her own character. But there was the quaint excuse for this that Miss Martineau had already described and estimated in the same columns of the *Daily News* a great many important persons in her own generation, and that to her cool judgment and impartial mind it might seem natural that her

own portrait should hang in the same gallery—an idea which many an able portrait-painter before her has carried out without any breach of modesty. And there was nothing in the concise biography of the *Daily News*—which was entirely historical and descriptive, and not even written in the first person—to offend the hearer, who might indeed smile at the serene sense of national importance with which the progress of her life was recorded, but who could scarcely complain of a selfestimate which was on the whole just enough, and claimed for Harriet Martineau no applause beyond that naturally belonging to talent and industry. The limited space prevented at once all undue detail of self-characterisation, and all that disadvantageous contrast of others with herself, which any extended sketch of society is likely to draw an autobiographer into. Had some kind fairy set fire benevolently to the piles of printed paper so easily disposed of in one stage, so indestructible in another, which have now at last made their way into the world, and are unhappily no longer within the reach of burning, the reputation of Miss Martineau would have settled down into that mellow glow of universal acceptance which lasts longer than more special crowns. We might not have known exactly why it was, but we should no less have acknowledged it as having become her property by possession and prescriptive right—which are better title-deeds than any other, at least in the temples of fame.

It takes a long time to reach to this calm of unquestioned, if not very distinctly understood honour; and Miss Martineau had passed like other people through many clouds and discouragements on the way. There can be no doubt that she was during her life, in the earlier portion of her career, as well abused as most political persons were in that lively and plainspoken period. The difference between her and most other women who wrote, was, that her topics, even when treated under the disguise of what we must call fiction, we suppose, since her generation enthusiastically accepted it as such— were almost entirely of a political, or at least politicophilosophical, character; and accordingly, the same means then in vogue to bring down political opponents of all kinds, were used freely upon her. These means have fortunately for the moment gone out of fashion, and notwithstanding the recent creation of gossip-newspapers, will, we trust, continue out of fashion. It is no longer a matter of much value in criticism whether an author is deaf and a Unitarian, or orthodox and possessed of ears as keen as his who heard the grass growing. We cannot go the length of saying yet that it is immaterial whether the writer be man or woman, for on this point it must be allowed all critics are fallible, and there is no female writer existing who is not benevolently or contemptuously reminded of her sex, except, indeed, George Eliot, whose supremacy is characteristically acknowledged by the absence of this favourite accusation. In this respect Harriet Martineau fared a little worse than most people did in her day, as uniting in her own person the characteristic reproaches addressed habitually to literary women and those addressed habitually to political opponents. The conjunction produced some sharp and violent talk and many biting gibes; but, on the other hand, it was conjoined with, according to her own showing, a most superlative and extraordinary fame and influence, which ought to have neutralised the evil. Both had long ago dropped—or so at least it seemed to the younger generation—into dimness, if not into peaceable oblivion. Abuse dies early, and fame requires a more solid foundation than that upon which hers was based, to resist the wear and tear even of five-and-twenty years. And when she died, not yet a year ago, most people were ready to recognise in Miss Martineau an eminent person, who had played a considerable part in her time, though it was beginning to be doubtful in what way she had been so eminent. That she had written much on philosophical and political subjects people were vaguely aware; and she had produced one clever book, **Deerbrook,** and one little story more than clever, the **"Feats on the Fiord,"** and had written many good newspaper biographies and other articles. These things were scarcely enough to account for the tradition of fame which hung about her; but most people have been born or at least have grown up, since the time when the Reviews snarled at the young lady who was a Malthusian, and angry politicians fought over her in abuse or in praise; and we were willing to be respectful and friendly to her memory without entering too closely into the foundation of our faith. For our own part, we avow, we were about to discuss her literary work calmly, on that level of honest mediocrity to which it seemed to belong, with no more notion that she was one of the greatest of national reformers and authorities—in a way the saviour of her country, the inspirer of laws and instructor of lawgivers—than we have of the undeveloped capacities for government of the child at our knee. Whether this was mere ignorance on our part, the reader has now full power of judging; and we will try to put the materials as well as we can before him. There is not one only, but two autobiographies to decide by: one, the concise record of the newspapers; the other, the diffusive narrative which fills two octavo volumes—the slow and gradual accumulation of her later years.

We scarcely remember any one who has taken so much trouble to set himself right with the world. No literary person, poet or prose writer, of Miss Martineau's period, has had so much care for his or her reputation; and even of the statesmen, only her favourite aversion, Lord Brougham, has taken any steps in his own person to make us aware what he thought of himself, and what of his contemporaries. The mass of human creatures, small and great, are content to leave themselves with no better appeal to recollection than the pathos of a tombstone, and no sure foundation than their own works, good or bad, at the mercy or to the kindness of their fellows. And this confidence in the justice, on the whole, of human nature, is not underserved. Posterity, if severe, is often kind; and so, notwithstanding all private spites and enmities, are a man's contemporaries. Even in the private retirement of the poor queen whom he had helped to wrong, there is found a Griffith to do justice to the fallen Wolsey. Death of itself does much by the mere fact of the isolation and separation it brings; and with death comes gentle charity, indulgence, sometimes understanding and sympathy, such as the living were never able to gain.

But all these gentle influences are neutralised, when, almost before the echo of the living voice is over, we are startled by a postscriptal harangue from the tomb. The grave has all the worst qualities of the pulpit, heightened to almost an infinite degree, in so far as the difficulties of reply are increased: for whereas it may be possible to make the occupant of the latter hear reason when he descends from that point of vantage, or at least to let him know our mind on the subject, the inmate of the first is entirely beyond either conviction or compunction—the one irresponsible, unpunishable moral assailant whom neither complaint, nor protest, nor contradiction can touch, and even in whose favour a certain natural human prejudice is always enlisted. There is a natural presumption that what a dying man says must be true, which gives an indescribable sting to posthumous slander. What good could it do

*them* to lie? Their vengeance, if not righteous, is too diabolical to be consistent with our tremulous instinctive apprehension of them, as beings passed into a region where only truth can reign, and all subterfuges, and even defects of vision, must be done away with. Even the most heedless deathbed utterance takes a certain sacredness—and a letter from a dead hand becomes a supplementary testament, holy and binding to all persons of deep feeling. Posthumous books, however, it must be said, have not done much to keep up this good character of the dead. The sense of immunity from all reprisals—the knowledge that all ordinary bonds of affection, of gratitude, of courtesy, are, as it were, abrogated for the benefit of the writer, who can smile in anticipation at the tumult he will cause, while sure of never being brought to book for what he has said, never called upon to substantiate any accusation or account for any spiteful saying—seems often to inspire a malign pleasure; and it is even possible that a distorted sense of the advantages of making known "the truth" may obscure the eyes to all the baseness of confidence betrayed and injured reputation. That this should be the case even in respect to the home, doubly screened by the obscurity of private life and the lapse of time from public knowledge, which a writer may enhance his own character by traducing and exposing, is a wonderful and horrible thought; yet we suppose it is not without precedent. Often enough the experiences of life steal from us our primitive belief in the authorities which were infallible to our early years; and the best of sons and daughters must often perceive the defects of their own education, even the mistakes made in their training—the little injustices and petty wrongs of the nursery, the hasty judgment, or perhaps too great severity, of father or mother—and by perceiving imply a gentle censure. Nothing can be more common than to record our tacit disapproval of the principles on which we were ourselves brought up, by a total change of system in respect to our children—to be by them reversed again in their day, in all probability, in proof of the fact that no human systems are infallible. But this natural sentiment may exist along with the most tender piety and loyalty to the home, which, at its least, is more to us, and at its worst, better than any strange place. When it leads to the desecration of that home, and the holding up of the chief figure in it to deliberate blame and insult, what can any one say? The writer who does this in the safety of declining years, going back over half a century to impress upon our minds an unfavourable estimate of her mother, revolts us by the very key-note thus struck with determined iteration, as the first thing to be insisted upon in the account of her life. That this could be no fault of accident or inadvertence is clearly apparent by the importance which Miss Martineau attached to her autobiography. "From my youth upward," she says, "I have felt that it was one of the duties of my life to write my autobiography:" and she adds, "for thirteen or fourteen years it has been more or less a weight on my mind that the thing was not done." It was thus with the determination of setting herself right in every respect from her childhood up, that this book was written; and the writer brooded over it for the last twenty years of her life; there can be little doubt, in such a case, that everything said was fully meant.

The tone of the autobiography is all the more remarkable in this respect, from the moderation and good sense of the biographies published by Miss Martineau in her lifetime, and concluding with the article upon herself, which, written in 1855, was published only six months ago. In these sketches there is a prevailing sobriety and justice, an absence of rancour even in respect to those whom she might reasonably have considered her enemies, which is worthy of all praise, and which is admirably carried out in the curiously honest self-estimate which concludes them. All is straightforward, moderate, modest, and sensible in those brief histories, spoken as it were face to face with her audience in the light of day. But the very atmosphere is changed when we get to the detailed and elaborate narrative written in her seclusion, in her weakness, when the clouds were already shadowing over her, and which was not intended to be made public until she had, as she believed, entirely ceased and been made an end of, at once and for ever. (pp. 473-76)

In the year 1854, after some interval of partial illness, [Harriet Martineau] went to London for the purpose of consulting a physician, and was informed that she had disease of heart, and might die at any moment. A more solemn intimation could not be made to any one; and Miss Martineau, who had suspected the state of affairs, took it with her usual courage. She dined with a merry family party on the evening of the day and was as gay as any. Then she took all necessary steps for the arrangement of her affairs, and returned home with a certain, not unpleasing solemnity and cheerfulness. It is in this condition that we leave her—for here the *Autobiography* ends. "In sure and certain hope" of a tranquil annihilation, resigning all life or thought of life for ever, she yet lived on for years; and into the record as it approaches the end, there steals a sense of her own specially important and interesting position as a dying person, which is natural enough. Perhaps the consciousness of this pedestal upon which she is standing has, more or less, inflated the self-applauses of the work throughout, and given a heightening touch to all the incidents of the past as they filed before her in a silent round. And there is a certain excuse in this which the reader will be glad to admit. The hopes of another life, the visions with which most of us beguile the twilight darkness, of light and home and heaven beyond, Harriet Martineau had put aside as vain delusions. And it was very comprehensible that her heart within her, having no outlet of this kind, should concentrate all its last efforts on the monument which she meant to leave of herself within "the warm precincts of the cheerful day." This is the kind of everlasting life which Comte teaches his disciples to desire. Perhaps a month may some time be called after her, and her fellow believers date their letters from the 10th day of Harriet Martineau. We can fancy that she would not have disliked this curious kind of fame. As it was, however, she lived more than twenty years after her death-warrant was given out. At once, and to save time, she wrote, it is evident, the little autobiography of the *Daily News,* with all the moderation and good sense which distinguished her biographies of other people; but having thus secured an immediate notice to her mind, set to work in her long leisure to work it out in detail. This curious sense of human importance and dignity which comes upon her when she knows that her days are numbered is very significant, and one of the most touching things in the book.

We will not spoil the effect of this last apology by any reference to the volume of Mrs. Chapman, a muddle of folly, false enthusiasm, and still more false sentimentality from beginning to end. Miss Martineau does not seem to have had much discrimination in the choice of her friends. It is evident that she could swallow a good deal of praise, especially from America; but we think the detailed comparison between herself and Joan of Arc, which seems to her biographer so happy, must have roused the instinct of British laughter in the sensible Harriet. The verdict of the world upon her will not, we

think, be so high. She was a very sensible woman; yet not very much of a woman at all, notwithstanding her innocent and honest love of Berlin wool. She was a very clever writer, with a most useful, serviceable, working faculty, and as little nonsense about her as could be desired. She was kind, friendly, and reasonable, yet hard in her judgments, and intolerant of opposition; more affectionate to those who depended upon and were subject to her, than to those who were independent and liked their own way. Thus her relations to the elder generation seemed all wrong, false, and jarring; while her relations to her inferiors in the succession of life are all sweet and harmonious. This is perhaps not an unusual characteristic of a strong, somewhat harsh, self-sufficing nature, which can acknowledge the loveliness of voluntary services, but kicks at that which has the claim of a right. We cannot but think she has been very much overrated as a writer; and indeed, except in the single fact that her Political Economy stories really met a public need, we find it very difficult to understand on what her great reputation was founded. And unfortunately it will not be increased by her *Autobiography,* where that good sense, which is her strongest point, shows less strong than ever before, without any increase of power or human interest to set the balance right. (pp. 495-96)

[Margaret Oliphant], "Harriet Martineau," in Blackwood's Edinburgh Magazine, Vol. CXXI, No. DCCXXXVIII, April, 1877, pp. 472-96.

## JOHN MORLEY    (essay date 1877)

[*In commentary first published in* Macmillan's Magazine *in May 1877, Morley outlines the strengths and weaknesses of some of Martineau's major works.*]

Harriet Martineau was not of the class of writers, most of them terribly unprofitable, who merely say literary things about social organisation, its institutions, and their improvement. Her feeling about society was less literary than scientific: it was not sentimental, but the business-like quality of a good administrator. She was moved less by pity or by any sense of the pathos and the hardness of the world, than by a sensible and energetic interest in good government and in the rational and convenient ordering of things. Her tales to illustrate the truths of political economy are what might be expected from a writer of this character. They are far from being wanting—many of them—in the genuine interest of good story-telling. They are rapid, definite, and without a trace of either slovenliness or fatigue. We are amazed as we think of the speed and prompt regularity with which they were produced; and the fertile ingenuity with which the pill of political economy is wrapped up in the confectionery of a tale, may stand as a marvel of true cleverness and inventive dexterity. Of course, of imagination or invention in a high sense there is not a trace. Such a quality was not in the gifts of the writer, nor could it in any case have worked within such limitations as those set by the matter and the object of the series. (pp. 182-83)

In the summer of 1836 Miss Martineau returned to England [from the United States], having added this great question [of slavery] to the stock of her foremost objects of interest and concern. Such additions, whether literary or social, are the best kind of refreshment that travel supplies. She published two books on America: one of them abstract and quasi-scientific, *Society in America;* the other, *A Retrospect of Western Travel,* of a lighter and more purely descriptive quality. Their success with the public was moderate, and in after years she condemned them in very plain language, the first of them especially as 'full of affections and preachments.' Their only service, and it was not inconsiderable, was the information which they circulated as to the condition of slavery and of the country under it. We do not suppose that they are worth reading at the present day, except from a historical point of view. But they are really good specimens of a kind of literature which is not abundant, and yet which is of the utmost value—we mean the record of the sociological observation of a country by a competent traveller, who stays long enough in the country, has access to the right persons of all kinds, and will take pains enough to mature his judgments. (pp. 192-93)

But after her American journey Miss Martineau felt a very easily intelligible desire to change the literary field. For many years she had been writing almost entirely about fact: and the constraint of the effort to be always correct, and to bear without solicitude the questioning of her correctness, had become burdensome. She felt the danger of losing nerve and becoming morbidly fearful of criticism on the one hand, and of growing narrow and mechanical about accuracy on the other. 'I longed inexpressibly,' she says, 'for the liberty of fiction, while occasionally doubting whether I had the power to use that freedom as I could have done ten years before.' The product of this new mental phase was *Deerbrook,* which was published in the spring of 1839. *Deerbrook* is a story of an English country village, its petty feuds, its gentilities, its chances and changes of fortune. The influence of Jane Austen's stories is seen in every chapter; but Harriet Martineau had none of the easy flow, the pleasant humour, the light-handed irony of her model, any more than she had the energetic and sustained imaginative power of Charlotte or Emily Brontë. There is playfulness enough in *Deerbrook,* but it is too deliberate to remind us of the crooning involuntary playfulness of *Pride and Prejudice* or *Sense and Sensibility. Deerbrook* is not in the least a story with a moral; it is truly and purely a piece of art; yet we are conscious of the serious spirit of the social reformer as haunting the background, and only surrendering the scene for reasons of its own. On the other hand, there is in *Deerbrook* a gravity of moral reflection that Jane Austen, whether wisely or unwisely, seldom or never attempts. In this respect *Deerbrook* is the distant forerunner of some of George Eliot's most characteristic work. Distant, because George Eliot's moralising is constantly suffused by the broad light of a highly poetic imagination, and this was in no degree among Miss Martineau's gifts. Still there is something above the flat touch of the common didactic in such a page as that in which she describes the case of 'the unamiable—the only order of evil ones who suffer hell without seeing and knowing that it is hell: nay, they are under a heavier curse than even this, they inflict torments second only to their own, with an unconsciousness worthy of spirits of light.' However, when all is said, we may agree that this is one of the books that give a rational person pleasure once, but which we hardly look forward to reading again. (pp. 193-95)

There are few more delightful books of travel than *Eastern Life, Past and Present.* The descriptions are admirably graphic, and they have the attraction of making their effect by a few direct strokes, without any of the wordy elaboration of our modern picturesque. The writer shows a true feeling for nature, and she shows a vigorous sense, which is not merely pretty sentiment, like Chateaubriand's, for the vast historic associations of those old lands and dim cradles of the race.

All is sterling and real; we are aware that the elevated reflection and the meditative stroke are not due to mere composition, but did actually pass through her mind as the suggestive wonders passed before her eyes. And hence there is no jar as we find a little homily on the advantage of being able to iron your own linen on a Nile boat, followed by a lofty page on the mighty pair of solemn figures that gaze as from eternity on time amid the sand at Thebes. The whole, one may say again, is sterling and real, both the elevation and the homeliness. (p. 199)

To [the mid-1850s] belong the Biographic Sketches which she contributed to a London newspaper. They have since been collected in a single volume, now in its fourth edition. They are masterpieces in the style of the vignette. Their conciseness, their clearness in fact, their definiteness in judgment, and above all, the rightly graduated impression of the writer's own personality in the background, make them perfect in their kind. There is no fretting away of the portrait in over-multiplicity of lines and strokes. Here more than anywhere else Miss Martineau shows the true quality of the writer, the true mark of literature, the sense of proportion, the modulated sentence, the compact and suggestive phrase. There is a happy precision, a pithy brevity, a condensed argumentativeness. And this literary skill is made more telling by the writer's own evident interest and sincerity about the real lives and characters of the various conspicuous people with whom she deals. It may be said that she has no subtle insight into the complexities of human nature, and that her philosophy of character is rather too little analytical, too downright, too content with averages of motive, and too external. This is so in a general way, but it does not spoil the charm of these sketches, because the personages concerned, though all of them conspicuous, were for the most part commonplace in motive, though more than commonplace in strength of faculty. Subtle analysis is wholly unreasonable in the case of Miss Martineau herself, and she would probably have been unable to use that difficult instrument in criticising characters less downright and objective than her own. (pp. 208-09)

*John Morley, "Harriet Martineau," in his* Critical Miscellanies, *Vol. III,* Macmillan and Co., Limited, *1886, pp. 175-211.*

## MRS. F. FENWICK MILLER (essay date 1885)

[*Miller comments on Martineau's treatment of the "Woman Question" in her earliest writings.*]

[Harriet Martineau's] first printed essay is interesting because it was the precursor of so long a course of literary work, rather than for itself. Yet it is not without its own interest, and is very far indeed from being the crude, imperfect performance of the ordinary amateur. The subject [and title of the essay] is **"Female Writers of Practical Divinity."** Here are the first words that Harriet Martineau uttered through the press:

> I do not know whether it has been remarked by others as well as myself, that some of the finest and most useful English works on the subject of practical Divinity are by female authors. I suppose it is owing to the peculiar susceptibility of the female mind, and its consequent warmth of feeling, that its productions, when they are really valuable, find a more ready way to the heart than those of the other sex; and it gives me great pleasure to see women

gifted with superior talents applying those talents to promote the cause of religion and virtue.

There is nothing remarkable in the literary form of this first article. . . . [She soon] came to have a style of her own, vivid, stirring, and instinct with a powerful individuality . . . . But in her first paper the style is coldly correct; imitative of good but severe models, and displaying none of the writer's individuality. Two points as regards the matter of the essay are of special interest, and thoroughly characteristic. It is interesting, in the first place, to know that she who was destined to do probably more than any other one woman of her century for the enlargement of the sphere of her sex in the field of letters, should have written her first article on the subject of the capacity of women to teach through their writings. The second point worth noticing is that her idea of "practical Divinity" is simply, good conduct. Theological disputation and dogma do not disturb her pages. Her view of practical Divinity is that it teaches morals; and it is largely because the women to whose writings she draws attention have occupied themselves with the attempt to trace out rules of conduct, that she is interested in their writings, and rejoices in their labors. Indeed, she only alludes once to the opinions on dogmatic theology of the writers whom she quotes, and then she does it only to put aside with scorn the idea that morality and teaching should be rejected because of differences upon points of theology.

Encouraged by the few stately words with which the editor of the *Repository* had received the offer of more contributions, "Discipulus" [Martineau's male pseudonym] continued his literary labors, and the result appeared in a paper [entitled] **"Female Education,"** published in the *Monthly Repository* of February, 1823. This is a noble and powerful appeal for the higher education of girls and the full development of all the powers of our sex. It is written with gentleness and tact, but it courageously asserts and demands much that was strange indeed to the tone of that day, though it has become quite commonplace in ours.

The author (supposed to be a man, be it remembered,) disclaimed any intention of proving that the minds of women were equal to those of men, but only desired to show that what little powers the female intellect might possess should be fully cultivated. Nevertheless, the fact was pointed out that women had seldom had a chance of showing how near they might be able to equal men intellectually, for while the lad was at the higher school and college, preparing his mind for a future, "the girl is probably confined to low pursuits, her aspirings after knowledge are subdued, she is taught to believe that solid information is unbecoming her sex; almost her whole time is expended on low accomplishments, and thus, before she is sensible of her powers, they are checked in their growth and chained down to mean objects, to rise no more; and when the natural consequences of this mode of treatment are seen, all mankind agree that the abilities of women are far inferior to those of men." Having shown reasons to believe that women would take advantage of higher opportunities if such were allowed them, "Discipulus" maintained in detail that the cultivation of their minds would improve them for all the accepted feminine duties of life, charitable, domestic and social, and that the consequent elevation of the female character would react beneficially on the male; cited the works of a cluster of eminent authoresses, as showing that women could think upon "the noblest subjects that can exercise the human mind;" and closed with the following para-

graph, wherein occurred the phrases by which it is shown that our "Discipulus" of twenty is masqueradiing as a man, more decisively even than by the termination of the Latin *nom de guerre:*

> I cannot better conclude than with the hope that these examples of what may be done may excite a noble emulation in *their own* sex, and in *ours* such a conviction of the value of the female mind, as shall overcome *our* long-cherished prejudices, and induce *us* to give *our* earnest endeavors to the promotion of *women's* best interests.

It is most interesting to thus discover that Harriet Martineau's first writings were upon that "woman question" which she lived to see make such wonderful advances, and which she so much forwarded, both by her direct advocacy, and by the indirect influence of the proof which she afforded, that a woman may be a thinker upon high topics and a teacher and leader of men in practical politics, and yet not only be irreproachable in her private life, but even show herself throughout it, in the best sense, truly feminine. (pp. 51-55)

*Mrs. F. Fenwick Miller, in her* Harriet Martineau, *Roberts Brothers, 1885, 304 p.*

## NAROLA ELIZABETH RIVENBURG  (essay date 1932)

[*Rivenburg identifies inconsistencies in Martineau's social and economic thought.*]

Perhaps the greatest tribute and at the same time the most interesting criticism of Harriet Martineau was made by J. S. Mill when he complained that she had reduced the *laissez-faire system* to an absurdity as far as the principle goes by merely carrying it out to all its logical consequences. He says, "The *laissez-faire* doctrine, stated without large qualifications is both unpractical and unscientific; but it does not follow that those who assert it are not, nineteen times out of twenty, practically nearer the truth than those who deny it". By this Mill would suggest that *laissez-faire* might be a good general rule but like most rules it cannot be literally applied to any and every situation. . . . He was obviously working against unlimited *laissez-faire* and hence was alive to the unconscious repudiation of the system suggested by Harriet in her stories. . . . Harriet had come to believe in a cold mechanic universe governed by laws which one must obey or suffer the consequences. She had bowed God out of her universe. None of the softer elements of kindness and altruistic love should have had place in her world. According to her theory every man is actuated by the law of self-interest, a law that governs his every action. Therefore, he is the best judge as to what is for his good and according to these same fundamental laws of the universe his mental characteristics can be assembled as can any machine. By previously controlling the association the child makes, the educator can predetermine and turn out the perfect man according to specifications. Yet through all this ran a strong vein of sincere longing for sympathy and understanding as well as a desire to be of service to her fellowman. She tried in vain to crush out the sensitive romanticism in her own nature. While she consistently urges the self-regarding instinct as the only real motive in everyone, she risks her own reputation by incorporating the unpopular Malthusian doctrine in her stories and she did this because she believed it was her duty to educate her fellowmen with regard to the evils of overpopulation. In this there is a contradiction which she did not fully realize when she makes self-interest central in motivation and still makes equally central the self as subordinate to the good of society. . . . [The] theory of the *identity of interests* does not stand the test of application to specific situations in real life. Harriet's novels exemplify the failure of this dogma although she seemed unconscious of the fact.

In her attitude with regard to women we also see this conflict between her Victorian ideas of propriety and her concept of the place of woman in the economic world. . . . [She] believed that the supreme duty of every woman was to her home. Every girl was to fit herself to be a home maker, to learn all the domestic arts with as much enthusiasm as a painter would learn his technique. Home-making was to be the profession for every woman of every class. It should be her joy and privilege to fit herself to be an intelligent wife and mother. Here we have the typical mid-Victorian position. Alongside of this point of view we find a radical *laissez-faire* attitude that the woman is a person who should be recognized as equal to man in the eyes of the law. She should have the same freedom to hold any position for which she is physically and mentally fitted. She should be left free to compete with men in any field of work. She should be free to marry or to secure a divorce without legal restrictions except as her children may need to be protected. Harriet opposes legislation for women as curtailing their liberty to make their own bargains. But when faced with the actual situation of women employed in the mines where they received less consideration than did the animals, Harriet's humanitarian zeal overcame her economic dogma and she urged for legislation which should delete such a monstrosity in a civilized country.

As a mid-Victorian of this typical Utilitarian brand Harriet also believed that there should be no outside interference between parents and children. According to her self-regarding theory a man would protect the interests of his child as he would his own interest, but when she was faced with the appalling fact of child labor in the factories where children of eight worked from daylight to dark in unventilated rooms her *laissez-faire* economy collided not only with her humanitarian sympathy but also with another Utilitarian dogma, namely every citizen must be educated to know what was for his own good. But there was no chance for education in the monotony of a factory day so here again Harriet is inconsistent with her own *laissez-faire* theory and reluctantly writes in behalf of the factory law limiting the hours of labor for women and children.

She consistently supported the *laissez-faire* policy which protected the interests of the middle class manufacturer at the expense of the masses of the people. Because she optimistically believed in the essentially good intentions of the factory owner toward his employees she failed to see her own inconsistency in admitting the unrestrained selfishness of many who use their power to exploit men to their own advantage. Harriet also exemplifies this same inconsistency when discussing enclosures where she upholds the right of the moneyed stranger to crowd out the simple minded peasants in the supposition that the capitalist could and would use his money more productively on a large piece of land than could the poor and ignorant farmer on his small bits of property. She made no provision for forcing these same capitalists to use their money for the public good instead of for preserving game or for some other equally selfish and unproductive purpose. She believed that public opinion could check such selfish use of power and money. J. S. Mill was quite skeptical lest

public opinion might not function in this way so he advocated legal interference requiring the owners to use their land for public good.

Again when dealing with profits, Harriet let her *laissez-faire* theory blind her to the dangers of this policy. Neither Harriet nor J. S. Mill saw any way to limit profits from soaring to unreasonable heights. Both argued that freedom of capital to move where it could be most advantageously used would take care of this danger but subsequent history has shown their error. Harriet's stories show the hardships of the ignorant masses in toils of a capitalistic power. She sympathized with them but bade them to be still and learn their economic laws; that certain temporary evils were in the nature of demand and supply, wages and profits. To believe that man had anything to do with giving shape to these laws would be rank heresy in Harriet's mind. Humble obedience to these laws were necessary to man's existence and if he didn't exist he was to blame because he had not learned his lessons in time to pass the test.

Harriet was pathetically sure that all the great inventions of machinery must speed production and furnish more material good for everyone, poor as well as rich, and that life was becoming more abundant. If there were some dislocations of labor by too rapid displacement of men by machines it was only a temporary evil, and the final outcome would be progress and a happier generation to come. She could not believe that these "temporary evils" were inherent in the system or that there was anything the matter with the reasoning of the economist who had taught her.

J. S. Mill was not the only person puzzled between individual liberty and the function of government to harmonize individual interests when they happen to clash. Just how free is a man? Just what rights does he have? Harriet would say that he must be allowed to do what he pleases unless he thereby injures another. It is the function of government to see that each man is free to develop his own interest up to the point where it interferes with the greatest good of the greatest number. We have seen how she defends the right of the capitalist to use his money as he deems prudent, but she fails to appreciate his responsibility to use that capital for the good of the greatest number who are his employees.

Another example in which the right of the individual to live his own life may conflict with the good of the community is in the matter of vaccination. She tried to popularize this much needed precaution against small-pox but she has no remedy for the man who has scruples against its use and who after contracting the disease necessarily spreads it among his fellowmen. In this case many men will die because one refuses to be educated, but Harriet claims that after a few have died the rest will learn the value of vaccination. She much prefers to use moral suasion on the unconverted rather than legislation. Her optimism does not allow her to recognize that some lessons may be learned at too high a price and that an uneducated public opinion may need guidance through intelligent legislation. Here we see an example of the fact that Harriet fails to recognize legislation as a means whereby an educated few may direct the opinion of the uneducated masses. Had Harriet been truly consistent in following her economic theories, she would have sided with the South in their struggle for political freedom and for free trade. The majority of the South wished to secede from the Union and to hold slaves. According to Harriet's theory of the majority rule and of *laissez-faire,* the South should not have been coerced by government interference from the Federal Government. On the other hand, the Southerners were aristocrats, while the Northerners were mostly of the middle manufacturing class, to which Harriet herself belonged. Her hatred of slavery as a cruel and inhuman system completely triumphed over what should have been her stand had she been really loyal to her own party. Perhaps this best illustrates the conflict to which Harriet's *laissez-faire* philosophy must expose a conscientious and truly humanitarian person whether living in the Nineteenth Century or in our year of depression in 1932.

In conclusion, we would again remind the reader that Harriet was typical of the Victorian humanitarians who rose in indignant wrath over the evils of the day. She believed she had found the cure-all for these evils in the *laissez-faire* philosophy of Adam Smith and of his successors. Bravely and fearlessly she undertook to apply these principles to every problem as it arose. She seemed unconscious of her own inconsistencies and of the failure of the system which she exemplified in her application of her philosophy to the facts of life. She never realized that her own compromises were a confession of the inadequacy of her *"immutable laws of nature"*. But we believe that Harriet was a genuine missionary to the victims of difficult social conditions of her day. She lived in stirring times, when men had invented machines and believed in machines, and when man thought of himself in terms of a predictable machine. Democracy was a very young and tender plant. The ideals of the brotherhood of man, equal opportunity for men and for women, respect for personality, education of the masses, better relations for the workingman, all these ideas were budding. They were not brand new. The germ of them we find in Plato's *Republic,* but each new generation needs new interpretations and applications. Harriet rose valiantly to each new challenge presented by social injustice. She was surprisingly versatile, but no person can be jack of all knowledge and avoid serious mistakes. However, not every person would have unfailingly tried her best to serve her own generation as did our author, Harriet Martineau. (pp. 100-03)

> *Narola Elizabeth Rivenburg, in her* Harriet Martineau: An Example of Victorian Conflict, *n.p., 1932, 110 p.*

**JOHN CRANSTOUN NEVILL**  (essay date 1943)

> [*Nevill evaluates a number of Martineau's writings and emphasizes her importance as one of the first Victorian women to be involved in intellectual pursuits and public affairs.*]

[Both books Martineau wrote about her American travels], though the focus is slightly distorted by a definite anti-Slavery bias, were well and competently done. In *Society in America* there is no phase of social or political life that is not fitted into the microscope and scientifically and exhaustively examined, and yet in every chapter the reader is made conscious of a praiseworthy desire on the part of the writer to judge American institutions from an American point of view, to be just and impartial—except with regard to the sufferings of the negroes—and Harriet's criticisms, if occasionally a little over-omniscient, are, at any rate, unlike those of the more feminine-minded Mrs. Trollope, entirely free from any taint of personal rancour. As for *A Retrospect of Western Travel,* it is so brisk, observant, and full of entertainment value, and, moreover, it presents so graphic a picture of existence in the rapidly developing days of the middle eighteen-thirties, that

the wonder is that it has not been reprinted over and over again. (pp. 65-6)

Whilst "pondering" her novel, [Martineau] extended the single chapter of *How to Observe Manners and Morals,* which she had written on the voyage out to America, into a full-length volume of two hundred and thirty-eight pages for Charles Knight, and followed it up with a short series of Guides to Service, which included *The Maid of All Work, The House Maid, The Lady's Maid,* and *The Dressmaker.* These were the sort of chatty text-books that Harriet, a born improver, an ardent apostle of method, routine and good example, could fling off the tip of her pen with the greatest of ease. Indeed she showed so detailed an insight into and understanding of the various avocations she depicted—particularly the housemaid's—that a rumour gained ground in the outside world that at an earlier epoch of her history she had been in service herself.

Harriet's earliest difficulty about the novel was the all-important one of finding a suitable theme. Still warmed by the after-glow of her conversion [to the Abolitionist cause] at Boston, she was "completely carried away" by an article on St. Domingo and its coloured governor, Toussaint L'Ouverture, in *The Quarterly Review.* If she chose L'Ouverture as her hero, and made a story out of his romantic rise from obscurity to power and self-fulfilment, here would be an excellent opportunity for combining truth with fiction, plus a discreet admixture of Abolitionist propaganda. Full of hope she sought the advice of one of the most faithful of her confidantes, but the lady was not encouraging—there was apt to be a noticeable drop in the temperature when Harriet rode her latest hobby-horse—and so the project, for the present, was laid aside. Then her eye caught a police report, "very brief, only one short paragraph," which moved her profoundly; yet this, after due reflection, was also abandoned because she felt it would detract from the interest of her tale if "the catastrophe" were known from the start.

Finally, actuated by the curious belief that plots should be taken from real life—Dickens and Thackeray are sharply criticized in the *Autobiography* for relying too much upon their own imaginations—she decided to write up the story (entirely without foundation, as it afterwards transpired) of a friend of her family, "who was cruelly driven by a match-making lady to propose to the sister of the woman he loved"—and the result was *Deerbrook.*

*Deerbrook,* despite some effectively written scenes, must be counted as one of Harriet's comparatively few failures. Its principal defect is that of *Glenvarloch,* namely, that whenever she was called upon to portray the normal relations existing between a man and a woman in love with each other, her instinct and her technique immediately went to pieces. Passion was something wholly outside the range of her personal consciousness, and she had not succeeded in acquiring even a book-consciousness of it from the writings of other people. Pursuing her chosen subject, she makes a country doctor, Hope by name (in love with Margaret Ibbotson), marry her sister, Hester, whom he does not love. Further, after the return from the honeymoon, she sets them up together in a three-cornered establishment where, notwithstanding that the wife, Hester, is of a jealous, possessive disposition, they all continue to live without any violent emotional upheaval. When drama is essential, it comes, not from within the ill-assorted household, but from a purely political disturbance without. Hope votes for the parliamentary candidate who is standing in opposition to the local squire, the village, which has hitherto held the doctor in the highest esteem, turns against him, mobs his house, insults him in the street, and goes elsewhere for its medical treatment. The Hopes are quickly reduced to the last stages of genteel poverty, and—strangest of all lapses on the part of one who claimed to be an expert in economics—although the sisters have an independent income of seventy pounds apiece, they cannot afford to buy gloves, are obliged to dismiss their servants, and their most substantial meal of the day is composed chiefly of potatoes. Hope's rehabilitation by means of a timely epidemic, his belated discovery that he loves Hester after all, and the ultimate engagement of Margaret to a Mr. Philip Enderby, do not materially improve matters, and the reader is left with a feeling that, having in the first place created a strong situation and then run as far away from it as she possibly could, the authoress simply cast about her and seized hold of any incidents that chanced to present themselves, in order to bring her story to a happy end.

As a preliminary exercise, Harriet had re-read a good deal—perhaps too much—of Jane Austen—*Northanger Abbey, Emma,* and *Pride and Prejudice*—recording of the last: "I think it is as clever as before; but Miss Austen seems wonderfully afraid of pathos. I long to try." She did try—and to her own undoing—for Miss Austen, it may be safely prophesied, is likely to remain inimitable to the end of time. *Deerbrook,* however, had a better reception than it deserved. Carlyle dismissed it as "a poor novel"; but Mrs. Gaskell was enthusiastic, Macready impressed by its high-mindedness, and ten years later Charlotte Brontë sent Harriet a copy of *Shirley,* as a grateful return for the pleasure she had derived from reading the book. (pp. 70-3)

[In the spring of 1840, Martineau's] thoughts went back to Toussaint L'Ouverture, whose prison she had seen on her Continental travels, and she decided that she must begin the book she had always meant to write about him, while she had yet sufficient strength left to carry out her purpose. So convinced was she that she was going to die that she wrote the last part of her story first. All through the spring, the summer, and the early autumn she was busily occupied with it, and in the November of that same year it was published as *The Hour and the Man. The Hour and the Man* was an immense advance on *Deerbrook;* the negro element in itself was enough to guarantee this, for Harriet had the wrongs and oppressions of the coloured people passionately at heart; her message of hope to the Abolitionists was not forgotten, and also she was dealing with realities—a free translation of actual history—and not with flimsy make-believe. The book was an unequivocal success. (pp. 75-6)

During the course of her illness she was surrounded by relays of attentive relatives and friends. People she had known in London would break their journeys, when travelling North, so that they might catch a passing glimpse of her, and those who could not get to her themselves sent presents of game and fruit and flowers. And her work still went on. *The Hour and the Man* was succeeded by the four children's stories by which she is best remembered to-day—"Settlers at Home," "The Prince and the Peasant," "Feats on the Fjord," and "The Crofton Boys"—published as the *Play-Fellow* Series. But now her bodily vigour had so far failed her that she believed her career as a writer was over, and that she must lay aside her pen.

For two years she wrote nothing. In the autumn of 1843,

however, she rallied a little, and became fired by an ambition to write a group of essays, to be published anonymously, under the title of *Life in the Sick-Room.* The work was finished in just under seven weeks. Never had she written anything so easily: "It went off like sleep." Out of her own experience, Harriet had much that was fresh, forceful and illuminating to say on the subject of invalidism. The first edition was quickly sold out, its contents everywhere eagerly discussed, and its authorship instantly detected. From the Wordsworth circle, to whom a copy had been sent by Henry Crabb Robinson, it elicited a warm and glowing response; the poet praised it with more than his usual earnestness, Miss Fenwick was prodigal of her praises, and Mrs. Wordsworth is reported to have exclaimed: "I wish I had read exactly such a book as that years ago." On the other hand, Carlyle's reaction was more sardonic, being, in effect: "Harriet Martineau in her sick-room writes as if she were a female Christ, saying, 'Look at me: see how I am suffering!'" And twelve years later Harriet's feelings concerning the essays approximated more nearly to Carlyle's verdict than to that of the Wordsworths. For when writing her *Autobiography,* she deplores "the moaning undertone running through what many people have called the stoicism, and the total inability to distinguish between the metaphysically apparent and the positively true." (pp. 78-80)

She commenced her [*History of the Thirty Years' Peace*], a general survey of the political events of the years 1815 to 1845—with profound misgivings, having been induced by Charles Knight to continue a task which he himself had abandoned after the first volume. She was not by any means certain that she possessed the necessary qualifications for writing history, and she shrank from being compelled to pass judgment upon the motives and actions of statesmen, recently dead or still alive, who, in many instances, had been, and were even now, her friends. But her amazing elasticity of temper did not desert her for long, and in a few weeks she was "in full career" and her work well in hand. By 1st February 1849 the first of the two remaining volumes was ready for the printers, having taken six months to write; and, in another six, the second was completed. This subsequently was augmented by an introductory volume, covering the years from 1800 to 1815.

Harriet's political panorama of the first half of the nineteenth century was a notably impressive spectacle—bathed in the cold clear light of Philosophic Radicalism. *The Athenaeum* said of it: "Miss Martineau has been able to discuss events which may almost be called contemporary as calmly as if she were examining a remote period of antiquity. She has written a history of a rather undignified reign with a dignity that raises even the strifes of forgotten and exploded parties into philosophical importance. . . . There are few living authors who may be so implicitly trusted with the task of writing contemporary history as Miss Martineau. She has spared no pains in investigating the truth, and allowed no fears to prevent her from stating it." Lord Brougham and others accused her of painting her picture in too sombre a tone, but Knight was more than justified in his choice of her, and the *History* remains to this day an invaluable record of the Ministerial convolutions of her times. (pp. 94-5)

The *Positive Philosophy* of Auguste Comte was published towards the end of 1853. It had taken Harriet two years to write and, when completed, formed an admirable companion-piece to her *History of the Thirty Years' Peace.* These two were

...le evidence of its ...ing grandeur & beauty.' While
I stood in the whirl wind, with the crystal roof above me
the thundering floor beneath, & the foaming whirlpool & ...
floor before me, I saw those quiet, studious hours of the
future world when this cataract shall have become a
tradition, & the spot on which I stood shall be the centre of
a wide sea, ~~the habitation~~ a new region of life. This was
seeing world-making. So it was on the Mississ..., when a
sort of scum on the waters betokened the birth place of new
land. All things help in this creation. The cliffs of the
upper Missouri detach their soil, & send it ~~down~~ thousands
of miles down the stream. The river brings it, & deposits it
in continual increase, till a barrier is raised against the
rushing waters themselves. The air brings seeds, & drops them
where they sprout, & strike downwards, so that their roots bind
the soft soil, & enable it to bear the weight of new accretions. The
infant forest, floating, as it appeared, on the ~~tide~~ surface of
the turbid & rapid waters, may reveal no beauty to the
painter; but to the eye of one who loves to watch the
process of world-making, it is full of delight. These
islands are seen in every stage of growth. The cotton
trees, from being like cresses in a pool, rise breast-high; they
they are like thickets, to whose shade the alligator may
retreat; then, like groves that bid the sun good-night ...
~~from be for loft~~ while he is still lighting up the forest,
then like the forest itself, with the wood-cutter's house
within its screen, ~~& wild~~ flowers springing about its stand,
& the wild-vine climbing to meet the night breezes on
its lofty canopy. This was seeing world-making. Here was
strong instigation to the exercise of analysis. ^
~~... ... ... also the progress of ...~~ conventional life:

*Manuscript page of* Society in America.

the outstanding achievements of her career, for the determination of causes and effects, the proper co-ordination of facts, and the marshalling of seemingly disparate particles into neat symmetrical sequences were an occupation for which she was singularly well equipped. In the world of ideas, whenever the normal clarity of her vision was not obscured by the living personalities with which her impulsive affections identified them—Mrs. Chapman and Abolitionism, Mr. Atkinson and "Mesmeric Atheism"—she moved with a sober conscientiousness which illumined, even if it did not always wholly succeed in vitalizing, everything she touched.

Of her capacity there can be no question: she was full of engaging little personal idiosyncrasies, such as lend themselves all too readily to the mischievous modern practice of "debunking"; she had more than her fair share of the moral arrogance inherent in most Victorians, and she could, at times, be narrow and absurdly prejudiced in her attitude towards life; but, like a rock embedded in a superficially changeful sea, the basic mind was there—strong, fearless and, in effect, inflexible. And though she herself be forgotten, and her books disregarded and unread, she was among the first of those nineteenth-century pioneers—Elizabeth Fry, Charlotte Brontë, Florence Nightingale, George Eliot—to mention only a few at random—who by sheer force of character broke through the male police cordon which excluded their sex from any active participation in public affairs, so that there is hardly an intellectual freedom enjoyed by the women of today that does not give back some far-off lingering re-echo of her voice. (pp. 106-07)

> *John Cranstoun Nevill, in his* Harriet Martineau, *Frederick Muller, Ltd., 1943, 128 p.*

## R. K. WEBB (essay date 1960)

[*Webb has published extensive biographical and bibliographic scholarship on Martineau, but some of his conclusions have been questioned by other critics. In this excerpt from his* Harriet Martineau: A Radical Victorian, *he discusses the development of her religious and philosophical thought.*]

Religion, [Martineau] wrote, in its widest sense is "the tendency of human nature to the Infinite", manifested in the pursuit of perfection in any direction; under this canon some "speculative atheists" had been deeply religious men, even though unable to personify their conception of the Infinite. In a narrower sense, religion is "the relation which the highest human sentiments bear towards an infinitely perfect Being". To narrow it further, to provide any system of reward or punishment is to degrade religion into superstition.

So liberal a construction of the claims of religion is characteristically Unitarian and rationalist. Within this liberal commitment, however, Miss Martineau displayed all the signs of an active Christian faith. She remained a devoted reader of the Bible, putting herself through a course of it in America and confiding to her journal in 1837, "Especially let me fill myself full of the gospel. How one thirsts for it, after a busy interval." She continued to look on the necessarian scheme as the dictate of an all-wise Father.

> While the world and life roll on and on, the feeble reason of the child of Providence may be at times overpowered with the vastness of the system amidst which he lives; but his faith will smile upon his fear, rebuke him for averting his eyes, and inspire him with the thought, "Nothing can crush me, for I am made for eternity. I will do, suffer and enjoy, as my Father wills; and let the world and life roll on!" . . . This universal, eternal, filial relation is the only universal and eternal refuge.

Man's probationary state in this world, she told Milnes, was one lighted by an unseen glory, and consciousness of that same unseen glory pervaded *Life in the Sickroom,* which made Maurice comment on the real faith which the book showed.

In 1844 her belief in immortality—she had never believed in bodily resurrection—was still firm. She believed in a future life, she wrote to Bulwer-Lytton, because, under a benignant Providence, any aspiration so natural as to be nearly universal must be true. She believed in the reunion of those whose love was truly great, who had found that intense and pure intellectual sympathy which could survive any change or development of separated persons on earth or in the hereafter. On such a question one had to abandon reason as a guide and reject it as a barrier, relying on the "life of the heart" and the affections. She was writing a letter of condolence, to be sure, but the tone rings true.

Within three years, however, she had abandoned these remnants of theological orthodoxy—the belief in God as a Father (and with it its corollary, the argument from design, on which Priestley had laid such stress), and belief in life after death. Within a further three or four years she had worked out a positive faith to replace the discarded one. She began in other words, to define religion only in its second, narrower sense. At the same time, her loyalty to its broader meaning became more intense, and for that she found new secular and scientific formulations. It was a pilgrimage similar to that made by a great many thoughtful people at about the same time, a dozen years before Darwin made the Victorian crisis of faith obvious. What was involved in her "conversion", and what brought it about?

Some credit must be given to her pushing further the traditional anti-clericalism of Dissent. The bibliolatry so abhorrent to Unitarians seemed increasingly ridiculous, indeed shameful, witness her steady attack on Sabbatarianism. The bigotry, conventionalism, conservatism, and stupidity of the clergy which she had so often attacked as a dissenter, she encountered in very concrete form in the clerical obstructionism she had to face in Tynemouth and Ambleside—and in Dissent as well. The fate of the educational clauses of the Factory Bill of 1843 had its effect. Worse, the timidity of American clergymen (including some Unitarians) in politics and especially in abolitionism had shocked a dissenting conscience prepared to find across the Atlantic all the advantages of a voluntary system; instead she found that "the yeomanry of America, those who are ever in the presence of God's high priest, Nature, and out of the worldly competitions of a society sophisticated with superstition, are perpetually in advance of the rest of the community on the great moral questions of the time, while the clergy are in the rear". Again and again in her later writing she comes back to the theme that churches do not make religion; religion makes churches. She was opposed to church-building programmes and to missionary activity which took attention away from secular reforms that needed doing. She welcomed the shock of the religious census of 1851 because it might lead to an inquiry into the "form of godliness" that was so rapidly superseding Christianity in England.

Policy considerations could hardly in themselves have brought about the change without an intellectual shift. Here she put great emphasis on the Tynemouth period. She was not yet capable of a wide philosophical survey, she recalled, or morally bold enough for deep investigation of things she had always taken for granted. But when the old questions of divine government, future life, and the origin of evil, were raised acutely, she had the leisure for thought and "abundance of material for that kind of meditation which usually serves as an introduction to a higher". There was a succession of deaths among her friends and relatives, many of them carried off in the prime of life by some accidental or violent means; there was, of course, her own suffering. Both burdens reinforced her old contempt for the orthodox solution of ascribing justice to God and mercy to Christ. Long repelled by the necessary consequence of that view—the tyranny and cruelty of God—she took refuge in the conclusion that we cannot understand the scheme of the universe and that no revelation can truly explain such events because men have no faculty for understanding things beyond humanity. It was a rigorous extension of a commonplace of eighteenth-century theology to be found in Priestley and in her own early periodical writing—that only through revelation or in the next world could men understand God's plans. A new concentration on its implications helped to reveal the unsatisfactory nature of these traditional comforts, however closely she may have clung to them as late as 1844. But if the traditional groundings of security were crumbling, at the same time her increasing conviction, in political and social matters, that things were inevitably coming right helped to provide a bridge to a new, and absolutely necessary, security. She concentrated the ferocity of her Priestleyan optimism on this world, not the next.

The final demolition of the old structure of faith was provided by her trip to the East and, more particularly, by the reading and thinking that surrounded it. Egypt had long fascinated her, and, of course, the Holy Land held a very special spot in her affections from the days of Lant Carpenter and the *Traditions of Palestine.* (pp. 284-87)

[*Eastern Life, Present and Past*] is both descriptive and didactic, a book of travels and a torrent of philosophizing. The criticism of this uneasy marriage of types which met the publication of *Eastern Life* in 1848 was partly an expression of discomfort about the unorthodox conclusions, it was also a complaint of real literary substance. There was so much to say. Climbing Sinai or the Pyramids seemed no effort at all, and she was disappointed that the intense heat prevented her climbing Mount Tabor. She was wonderfully excited by the voyage down the Nile, by her amateur archaeology, by her visit to a harem, by the experience on the desert—mirages and all—and by her conviction that the cures and oracles in Egyptian religion were mesmeric. She was incensed by the ignorance and superstition of the Christians she saw and by the degradation of the Holy Places. Above all, in seeing the Holy Land, her Unitarian conception of Jesus as a man and teacher was reinforced. If Jesus had come to England in the nineteenth century, he would have talked about rural cottages and town alleys, robins, dog-roses and brambles; instead he talked of rock and sand, of ravens and lilies of the field—and now she had seen them. His lamentations for the cities of Galilee became as real as if he had cried "Alas! for you, Liverpool—alas! for you, Bristol."

To my apprehension, on the spot, and with the re-cords of his life in my hand, and the recollections of Egypt and of Sinai fresh in my mind, nothing could be simpler than his recorded words, and nothing less like what is superstitiously and irreverently taught, as coming from him, in most of the churches of Christendom.

All this, as an enthusiastic traveller, she had to communicate—not only because she enjoyed it so much, not only for the enjoyment of her readers, but as a guide to those who might follow—hence the recommendations about clothing and travel and wallwashing in the tombs.

The main burden of the book, however, was something else. Did she dare, she wondered, tell what she had discovered? Would it be presumption to declare that she dissented from the statements of authorities like Heeren and Warburton? Would it be rash to say that the theology of almost everybody in the civilized world was baseless, to state it before she knew that her faith was enough for her own self-government and support?

> I know, as well as I ever knew any thing, that for support I really need nothing else than a steady desire to learn the truth and abide by it; and, for self-government, that it is enough to revere my own best nature and capabilities: but it will require a long process of proof before I can be sure that these convictions will avail me, under daily pressure, instead of those by which I have lived all my life.
>
> (pp. 288-89)

Her contentions can be fairly simply stated. She had travelled to Egypt, Sinai, and Palestine, each of which had produced a distinctive faith; and to Syria where all the modern faiths were in conflict. As she looked back on her travels, she was happy that she had taken the countries in that order, for it made more strikingly evident the genetic connection between them that she, along with some leading scholars of the time, believed to exist. In other words, she was making a study in what we would call comparative religion. She was infuriated at other English travelers in Egypt who rejoiced that western Christians had found the true faith in contrast to the barbarism and idolatry they saw in the tombs. There was barbarism and idolatry enough in the Christians to drive her to unfavourable comparisons; moreover, she insisted that religions be judged by their highest exemplars and not by popular credulity. She would ask as fair a consideration for Christianity five thousand years hence, when its existing forms would be forgotten and its principles expanded into something yet unknown. Would these Christians want a gargoyle on a cathedral to be taken as an indication of their idolatry?

Amid the popular superstitions, amid the symbols and myths repeated in one religion after another, she saw something else—the great governing ideas of mankind as a source of unity. In her mesmerized ramblings at Ambleside she had seen a connected series of life-fountains with all the nations worshipping the source—a conception that goes back at least to 1831; the boundary line there between personal God and Ideas is faint enough. Now she saw these "guiding lights of the human intellect" in their proper role. "The great Ideas of Moral Obligation and strict retribution, of the supreme desirableness of moral good, and the eternal 'beauty of holiness', pass from system to system, immortalizing all with which they assimilate, and finally annihilating all else, dispensing the best blessings that men have ever received, and promising an increase of them in all time to come." (pp. 290-91)

In abandoning a personal God and immortality, she let herself be ticketed an infidel. Actually, she never denied a first cause; she denied only that we could ever know its attributes. And her yielding of immortality, though ultimately complete, was gradual: in 1847 she was still willing to allow the possibility of life after death—not as a scriptural promise but as a still hidden phenomenon of nature which some curious mesmeric accounts made one wonder about. She had, however, given up the presumption in favour of it when she came to question the universality of the desire for immortality on which her presumption was based. The rest, culminating in the joyful stoicism of the last chapter of the *Autobiography,* was a matter of course.

To turn from belief to disbelief in these two immense conceptions was not easy; she recalled how unprepared she was at her first meetings with Henry Atkinson in 1845 to take in the boldness of his talk. Consequently, in looking back at her earlier, "selfish" views, even more in looking about her at the beliefs of others, she readily saw the change as a major break. It was in the light of this appearance that she was so critical of her early works and youthful convictions. But she had for years been dependent on only a few dogmatic beliefs, and they were subject to the powerful corrosives of her rationalism and her view of development or juggled with her two definitions of religion. Her vaunted freedom from dogma came from cutting away inherently incompatible survivals in her Unitarian inheritance. Forcing them out left stronger than ever the central intellectual and emotional concepts which Unitarianism had brought to her from the eighteenth century. In the new dispensation she had a firmer because more consistent security. She had become ashamed, she told Atkinson, of the enthusiasm with which she had formerly acquiesced in God's will when she came to find "a much higher ground of patience" in herself. As for morality, never had she felt more desirous of doing right or more discomposed when she realized she had done wrong. With this strength in herself, largely found in Tynemouth, generalized by her Eastern experience and reflections, she was ready to move on. Not in education alone did it remain to be seen what could be done "by a direct appeal to our noble human nature".

A good many years after Miss Martineau's visit to Egypt, Anthony Trollope turned a knowing eye on the broad churchman and wrote movingly about the challenge that the new learning posed: one had to cut the ropes and put out in the little boat, not knowing where one was bound, for the learned man who beckoned had nothing to offer but doubts and a subrisive smile. It is still a compelling statement of the conflict of inevitability and nostalgia, of security no longer tenable and a threatening future. In that sense Harriet Martineau never faced a crisis in her faith, or faced it only for that brief instant when she turned to Atkinson for advice which she would shortly have given herself. She never doubted that she had a faith to substitute, and she was quickly reassured as to its potency. She proclaimed it to the world in 1851 in what surely must be one of the strangest books to carry the name of a reputable writer, *Letters on the Laws of Man's Nature and Development.*

Atkinson's letters make up most of the book, with Miss Martineau confining herself largely to comment and to drawing him out. Atkinson was a man who had a good many projects in the talking stage, and this expression of his views would never have been printed had it not been for Miss Martineau's insistence and her editing. But if most of the words are his, the doctrine is hers as well, for she accepted everything he said with an enthusiasm which is nothing short of embarrassing. "I do not like to say anything after your last letter," she wrote, "I do not like to touch it, or the state of mind it produces in me. Yet it is right to tell you that it does so work upon any one mind as it does upon mine.—What an emancipation it is,—to have escaped from the little enclosure of dogma, and to stand,—far indeed from being wise,—but free to learn!" Or, in a letter bridging two of his windy phrenological accounts of the physiology of the brain: "Now for the cerebrum! Where do you begin?"

Miss Martineau gushed and Atkinson ranted. (pp. 292-94)

And yet, for all the nonsense and inanity, for all the ignorance and constriction of the *Letters,* there was something in what they had to say. The assumption which underlay the jargon and rodomontade was that which Miss Martineau was to find so compelling in Auguste Comte, and which according to John Stuart Mill formed the basis of all scientific advance—that we can know nothing but phenomena and the laws which govern them. Like the scientists, when they were acting as scientists, from Galileo down, Miss Martineau and Atkinson called for the rigid separation of science and theology, put their faith in the former, and presumably asked "how" not "why". However confusedly, they were on the wave of the future, and much of what they said (about free will, for instance) seems commonplace to our psychologically oriented, relativistic age.

One must convict them, however, of failing to understand a good many of their implications. . . . [Although] they were apostles of science, they continually thought in ways and talked in terms borrowed from their old commitments—incessantly moralizing, resolutely teleological. In short, neither of them ever really understood what science was about. Their proudly flaunted new convictions were little more than a change of rhetoric in the preaching of old concerns. (pp. 294-95)

Science, however, was a means to an end. On the positive side there was the zeal for reform and perfection of society.

> From the recognition of universal law, we shall develope a universal love; the disposition and ability to love without offence or ill-feeling towards any. We shall see that no one can be a true friend to us who is not a friend to all. We shall learn that dirt is beauty unformed; that evil is undeveloped good; or rather, that we judge the universal in reference to ourselves, not ourself in reference to the universal.

I do not know what [Atkinson] means by the last clause, but the drift of the whole is clear. And it is easy to see how Atkinson influenced Miss Martineau. He was not her master; there was nothing insincere or diabolical. Both had long held an intense if woolly vision of the future, a future in which alienations from society (their own included) would be undone, yet more, in which every evil of society would dissolve into perfection. The highest prospect for society, she wrote in the thirties, is that all men should live as brothers. That fraternal principle, the ground of Christianity, the inspiration of the poets and philosophers, was beginning to appear in the working of society. Charity was no longer done from mere compassion, but more abstractly, from a spiritual interest in the welfare of other classes. With missions, abolitionism, and care of the unfortunate, the great day had dawned and would soon brighten into noon.

But the most charming and in some ways remarkable expression of this view by Miss Martineau was purely unconscious. In writing *Eastern Life* she recalled the ugly unison singing of the crew on their Nile boat—always in the minor key, man's natural expression until he is taught otherwise.

> I often wished that I could sing loud enough to catch their ear, amidst their clamour, that I might see whether my second would strike them with any sense of harmony: but their overpowering noise made any such attempt hopeless.—We are accustomed to find or make the music which we call spirit-stirring in the major key: but their spirit-stirring music, set up to encourage them at the oar, is all of the same pathetic character as the most doleful, and only somewhat louder and more rapid. They kept time so admirably, and were so prone to singing, that we longed to teach them to substitute harmony for noise, and meaning for mere sensation.

Action, harmony, and didacticism—the three virtues in that paragraph are leitmotifs of her life. (pp. 297-99)

Against such a background of positive if non-theological faith must be seen her enthusiasm for Comte's *Positive Philosophy*. Neither she nor Atkinson knew Comte's work directly at the time of their book, and they came to what knowledge they had through the chapter on him in Lewes's *Biographical History of Philosophy* and the epitome by Comte's disciple Littré. She had no sooner begun to read the work itself in the spring of 1851 than she hit upon the idea of translating it, a scheme which after some consultations became a plan for a free translation and condensation, reducing the six volumes of the original to two. . . . (p. 303)

Miss Martineau was never a true Comtean. . . . She was never able to accept the lunacy of Comte's positive polity, that totalitarian conception of society modelled on Catholicism, with refinements of intellectual dictatorship the Church had never attained, if it had aspired to them. Even to the positive philosophy of the earlier volumes, her allegiance was remarkably spotty.

Much of the terminology and rhetoric she used. The *Autobiography* and her letters are full of references to her own emergence from theological and metaphysical views to positivism. Her interpretation of history sometimes carries a positivist veneer. But it is by no means exclusively Comtean: Comte never drove out the dramatic prospect of the great struggle for opinion which she had derived from Canning, a struggle she conceived in purely English terms. Again, Comte was scornful of political economy, and she was duly scornful when the opportunity offered; but even though she could say that the pretended science was no science at all, she never failed to preach from the gospel of the economists as if they had attained the final truth. Comte's views on the natural subordination of woman and—even though his later religion worshipped woman—on her confinement to her own proper fields were abhorrent to Miss Martineau, so obviously that she never refers to them, even to refute them, in anything I have seen; her whole tone on the subject of women remained utterly alien to Comte's. And . . . with her insular pride in British institutions as well as her traditional devotion to Protestantism and Dissent, she could only be amused or possibly

annoyed by Comte's almost total blindness to the character and contributions of either.

What, then, was it that attracted her, if only some formulations remain? Surely she could borrow Comte's terminology because he offered an entire system which at one point after another struck familiar notes. Both were necessarians; both were phrenologists. Like her, he insisted on the separation of the spiritual and temporal, on the limits of political action, and on the supremacy of the moral over the political. More remarkably, she had anticipated the law of the three stages years before:

> As the aggregate experience of mankind accumulates, truth is developed, and the faculties of the mind approximate to a harmonious action. The imagination becomes more disposed to exercise itself on forms which have truth for their essence, and are therefore immortal, than on those which are inspired with a capricious and transient life. In the infancy of society, the imagination can find the elements of its creations in nature alone; and therefore its action is, for a time, pure. In a more advanced state, its elements are chosen from the dreams of a preceding age, and its illegitimate exercise gives birth to superstition. But the result of a further discipline of the universal mind is to make the imagination again subservient to truth; while the fuller development of truth expands and exalts the imagination.—Higher and purer excitements are at length administered by truth than ever sprang from delusion, however poetical. The thoughts and feelings suggested by the exercise of the abstract powers on real objects are more influential and permanent than any which originate in superstition. The associations which cluster around realities, in themselves insignificant, afford greater variety of excitements than the machinery of pure fiction.

And for years she had been preaching sociology without the name. Here she is in 1832:

> Such then is the state of inquiry among us. Physical science is advancing steadily, and with an accelerating rapidity, under the guidance of philosophical principles. Moral science is lagging behind, blinded, thwarted, led astray by a thousand phantoms of ancient ignorance and error, which would have disappeared long ago, if the dawn of philosophy had not arisen as cloudily upon this region as brightly upon the other.

She was sure that the time would come when moral science would no longer be the province of the uninstructed, but would be confined to the philosophers who would be as important to the "science of society" as Herschel to astronomy and Beaufort to hydrography. Then, instead of imprisoning philosophers for their discoveries, men would gratefully accept their findings, as now they accept the discoveries of physical science. This is not to claim priority or originality for Miss Martineau; it is simply to indicate that Comte's ideas came out of the commonplaces of his time, another example of "what oft was thought, but ne'er so well express'd".

There is, however, another consideration of overriding importance in which the singleness of Comte's view, the fact that he collected all of these currents into one book, plays an important role. Frederic Harrison, at Oxford, was appalled by the conflict of opinions in the fifties. "How can the minds of keen young students retain their calm or any fixity of thought, when week by week they are swept by 'every wind of doctrine'—winds that blow in turn from each quarter of the theological compass, which they 'box' with incessant revolutions." To this dilemma, to the increasingly unsatisfactory answers which orthodox religion gave to mid-Victorian problems, Comte provided a solution which was heightened by a belief in progress and a passion for serving humanity. "I never parted with any belief till I had found its complement," wrote Harrison in 1890; neither did Miss Martineau. "We are living in a remarkable time," she wrote in her preface to the translation,

> when the conflict of opinions renders a firm foundation of knowledge indispensable, not only to our intellectual, moral, and social progress, but to our holding such ground as we have gained from former ages. . . . The supreme dread of every one who cares for the good of nation or race is that men should be adrift for want of an anchorage for their convictions. I believe that no one questions that a very large proportion of our people are now so adrift . . . The work of M. Comte is unquestionably the greatest single effort that has been made to obviate this kind of danger; and my deep persuasion is that it will be found to retrieve a vast amount of wandering, of unsound speculation, of listless or reckless doubt, and of moral uncertainty and depression.

She had built her new faith on the foundations of her old convictions. It was proclaimed partially from the political economy tales to *Eastern Life* and *Household Education,* stated fully in the *Letters,* and then its analogue given the world in her translation of Comte. As for Comte's deficiencies and errors, they were of as little account to her as the dogma of the economists which she later ignored, or the evidential weaknesses of the mesmerists which she shared, or the fuzziness and arrogance of Atkinson which she never saw or misread as Christ-like. Mill, it will be recalled, commented on her reduction of political economy to an absurdity by carrying it out to all its consequences. Such absurdity never mattered to her when something else mattered more. She was, she told Bulwer-Lytton, a hopeless critic. The only books she could read had one quality in common: they were full of earnest thought. "This provided, I become one with the writer so completely as to be unable to rise to any capacity for judging,—or to any right to compare my likings, (otherwise than experimentally), with those of better trained & qualified readers."

It is a pity that her candour about this defect—which explains so much in her career—did not extend to a candour about her early works, or rather that she misapplied her candour, scoffing at them when she might have seen in them the core of everything she did afterwards. I suppose her pride and belief in progress, perhaps even her quest for martyrdom, made that impossible. Whatever the reason, there is no doubt that after all the reading and thinking and talking and writing, after all the enthusiasm and discovery and rejection, she had found herself—a disciple of Priestley and a manufacturer's daughter—and called the treasure philosophy. (pp. 306-09)

> *R. K. Webb, in his* Harriet Martineau: A Radical Victorian, *Columbia University Press, 1960, 385 p.*

**VINETA COLBY**   (essay date 1974)

[*In an excerpt from her survey of the English novel during the first half of the nineteenth century, Colby assesses Martineau's contribution to Victorian fiction.*]

[The] fine line between fiction and parable, between fact and "tale founded on fact," is one that Harriet Martineau crossed very easily. Indeed, it is to her somewhat questionable credit that she erased that line altogether. Her best work of fiction, *Deerbrook,* had its initial inspiration in an incident from real life, told her by the American novelist Catherine Maria Sedgwick (the basis of Miss Sedgwick's story "Old Maids"). Her most ambitious novel, *The Hour and the Man,* was founded on history and conscientiously researched. Her most popular work of fiction bears the forbidding title *Illustrations of Political Economy,* a collection of tales intended to do precisely what, in fact, they did—namely, educate the public in economic theory by demonstrating abstract principles in realistic stories of ordinary life. Tacked to the end of each of the tales is a straight factual summary of the economic principles embodied in the tale. The characters are carefully selected to personify the issues; the plots and dialogues are constructed to advance the lessons as expeditiously as possible. Harriet prepared herself carefully for her work, read widely, travelled to many of the scenes she described, and drew on her childhood memories of her father's manufacturing business in Norwich. Everywhere the tales reflect the ideas of the necessitarian Joseph Priestley and the utilitarians James Mill and Jeremy Bentham. Yet in spite of their solid foundation of research, the *Illustrations* are lively and even, occasionally, entertaining. She was a good story-teller. Recognizing and capitalizing on that talent, she worked so diligently to integrate story and doctrine that she succeeded better than she or her publishers had dared to hope. (pp. 215-16)

[Martineau's novelistic skills] are displayed, modestly but unmistakably, in the *Illustrations.* Like the professional she was, she wrote methodically, with outlines, plans, research. She claimed that she deliberately restrained herself "from glancing even in thought towards the scene and nature of my story till it should be suggested by my collective didactic materials." Not until she had laboriously composed her Summary of Principles did she allow herself to set the scene of the story and select the characters. But once the imaginative element entered, the work began to fly—"the story went off, like a letter." A mysterious power that the necessitarian-utilitarian Harriet Martineau could never quite account for seemed to take over. All human actions, she maintained, had discoverable antecedents. Yet she could not explain fiction making, creating a plot, "a task above human faculties . . . the same power as that of prophecy." At best in her fiction Harriet Martineau achieved only the verisimilitude of good journalism, but that she should have achieved even this much in a work as forbidding as *Illustrations of Political Economy* is a sign of her considerable ability.

Fiction springs out of these tales almost spontaneously. In a letter to W. J. Fox in 1832 she described the rapid pace at which she worked: "Now (in VI) the British Fisheries being established close by (a fact) they rise & multiply, (a fact) till a bad season or two pinches them, (a fact) & then comes an epidemic, (a fact) thins them & helps up the survivors. Here is room for bustle, in contrast to the last, for uncommon scenery & varied incident, & for showing the miseries of the positive check." Facts feed her imagination—"bustle," "uncommon scenery & varied incident"—the story takes form. Unhappily, for the modern reader at least, the professional in Harriet Martineau kept her didactic purpose uppermost. One must dig for the more purely entertaining qualities, but they are there.

They are there precisely—and almost ironically—because she was not striving for literary and aesthetic effects, because both her sympathies and her previous writing experience directed her toward actuality, the strictest observation and recording of fact. After systematic preparation and planning, she wrote swiftly, without revising and polishing. Her mentor was William Cobbett, who had advised: "Know first what you want to say, and then say it in the first words that occur to you." She found expression by words "as easy as breathing air," with generally happy results—a crisp, natural prose making no claims to high literature. She writes engaging passages of description, dialogue, and characterization even in the chilly depths of exposition on political economy.

The social-documentary story was yet unknown, but the vivid sketches of the degradation and demoralization of the poor that emerged in Disraeli (*Sybil*), Dickens, Kingsley, Mrs. Trollope (*Michael Armstrong*), Charlotte Elizabeth, and Mrs. Gaskell are anticipated by Harriet Martineau. Except Dickens, none of these novelists was more skillful at integrating the materials of fact and fiction. (pp. 220-22)

[*Illustrations*] is the fiction of domestic realism. Its heroes are laborers, farmers, merchants, and bankers; its heroines include a "princess of fishwomen" (Ella of Garveloch) and shopkeepers' daughters. On economic disasters hang not only the welfare of the state but the happiness of young lovers. Harriet Martineau shuttles between one and the other without the slightest self-consciousness: "This evening was the brightest of the whole spring in the eyes of Fanny and Melea. The bank had only sustained a loss, instead of being about to break" (**"Berkeley the Banker"**). Teas are prepared by matrons in their best black silk; currant wine is sipped and seed cake is nibbled, while they talk of rising prices, the dangers of banks' issuing more paper money, the effects of the tariff on local trade, and the need for crop diversification.

Since the lives of real people are affected by economic developments and since people do talk a good deal about prices and business, her fundamental approach to realistic domestic fiction can hardly be faulted. When, unfortunately, her characters talk too much (as their author herself often did, to the dismay of many who knew her), when they slip into lecture and polemics, her stories suffer. Admittedly they carry a burden of didactic purpose too heavy for any first-rate work of fiction to bear. (pp. 224-25)

If Harriet Martineau has not quite formulated a "poetics" of the genre, she has at least established its ground-rules. She made her most distinguished contribution to the form, however, not in a work of fiction but in a literally "true romance of human life"—her *Autobiography*. . . . (p. 227)

The *Autobiography* was potentially a first-rate Victorian novel. But even on what she believed was her deathbed, Harriet Martineau was too vigorous, too absorbed in the problems of "History, Politics, Mind," to distill a novel from autobiography. . . . Thus *Deerbrook* remains her only important novel. Measured against the achievement of her successors, it is a very minor one. Yet like so much of Harriet Martineau's work that we tend nowadays to dismiss or to approach patronizingly, it bears study and offers surprises and even occasional rewards of pleasure. Furthermore it repre-

sents a pioneer effort in the sociological novel—the novel that studies individual character as it is shaped by the society in which it lives—the novel of community. (p. 230)

Modest as its conception was, *Deerbrook* did not fail to tackle the serious problems of life. Typical of domestic fiction, its plot lacks all elements of sensationalism. The closest it comes to violence is a village riot in which some windows are broken; the closest to suspense, an episode in which the heroine falls through the ice while skating on the village pond. The life-death cycle is fully treated: babies are born, a child dies of fever, old people die, younger ones struggle for work, for financial security and prestige in the community, and for the purely personal satisfactions of love and marriage. The interest of the novel lies not in the extraordinary events of life but in the complicating of the very ordinary ones. And Harriet Martineau achieves these complications—as did most Victorians in their domestic fiction—by showing the effects of the undisciplined or improperly disciplined imagination on average human life. The problems of the characters in *Deerbrook* are those of the romantic imagination—the confusion of appearance and reality, the chain reactions of human misunderstandings—acted out in a scene of domestic life. The solutions are those of a practical Christian ethic—submission to the will of God and acceptance of the duties and obligations of living in a community with other human beings.

The plot of *Deerbrook* is based on a misunderstanding, a confusion of appearance and reality arising from a man's marriage to a woman whom he does not love. She *thinks* that he loves her; he *thinks* that he loves her sister. Ultimately he discovers that he loves his wife, but a series of potentially tragic misunderstandings has been unleashed. Nothing is quite as it appears because it is human nature to mistake and misinterpret reality. Even the idyllic village of Deerbrook, which so enchants the two city-bred heroines, is not what it seems. The greenery and shrubbery conceal "the timber and coal yards and granaries." Later this same lovely spot is the scene of nasty gossip, mob violence, crop failure, and—surely not without symbolic significance—plague. The inhabitants constantly confuse appearance for reality—from the sensitive hero whose marriage bodes so much evil, the two sweet Ibbotson sisters whose lives become entangled with his, to the malicious village gossip who is so deeply entrapped in her own lies that she comes actually to believe them. Village life itself, as Harriet Martineau observes in her opening chapter, is conducive to day-dreaming and myth-making. As the Grey family awaits the visit of the Ibbotson sisters from Birmingham, "the ladies were evidently in a state of expectation—a state exceedingly trying to people who, living at ease in the country, have rarely anything to expect beyond the days of the week, the newspaper, and their dinners."

When the sisters appear and one of them, Hester, proves to be a beauty, the well-meaning Mrs. Grey leaps to the conclusion that the local doctor Mr. Hope will fall in love with her. The fact is that he has fallen in love with her less striking sister Margaret. But the human failing of hasty judgment and miscalculation, fed by the human ego, which convinces one of the correctness of his errors, is the essence of the appearance-reality conflict: "It is a fact which few but the despisers of their race like to acknowledge, and which those despisers of their race are therefore apt to interpret wrongly, and are enabled to make too much of—that it is perfectly natural,—so natural as to appear necessary,—that when young people first meet, the possibility of their falling in love should occur to all the minds present."

Mrs. Grey goes busily to work as a matchmaker, and when Hope protests that he has no "intentions" regarding Hester, she accuses him of trifling with the girl's affections. Her confusion compounds his. A man of delicate conscience, he reacts with deep concern: "There was nothing to him so abhorrent as giving pain; nothing so intolerable in idea as injuring any human being: and he was now compelled to believe that through some conduct of his own, some imprudence, in a case where imprudence is guilt, he had broken up the peace of a woman whom, though he did not love, he respected and warmly regarded!" He proposes; Hester, who genuinely loves him, accepts; and Margaret innocently rejoices in their supposed bliss. She meanwhile has fallen in love with Philip Enderby, and that romance flourishes until again delusion causes near-disaster. Enderby accidentally discovers that Hope had once loved Margaret. Blinded by this revelation, he misjudges innocent actions, heeds malicious gossip from his sister Mrs. Rowland, and weaves a web of misunderstanding that is almost fatal to the happiness of all.

In every instance the misunderstandings are the result of over-active minds and imaginations. Hope meets the Ibbotson sisters and his fancy immediately begins to churn: "His thoughts already darted forward to the time when the Miss Ibbotsons would be leaving Deerbrook. It was already a heavy thought how dull Deerbrook would be without them. He was already unconsciously looking at every object in and around the familiar place with the eyes of the strangers, speculating on how the whole would appeal to them. In short his mind was full of them." With such impetuosity, it is less incredible that Hope, a man of intelligence and good will, should make his disastrous decision to marry.

Self-delusion follows a natural course for Hope. Self-betrayed, he blames no one but himself. Fortunately, because he is a rational creature, he not only survives, but he spares his wife the pain of ever discovering his secret. After due suffering, he even comes to love her. Philip Enderby, another man of intelligence and good will, sees his errors too and in the end happily marries Margaret. But self-delusion takes a more unnatural and sinister course in his sister Mrs. Rowland, whose malice blinds her to reality. In the hands of a more gifted novelist than Harriet Martineau, Mrs. Rowland might have become a fascinating study in neurotic behavior. Her jealousy of her neighbors the Greys and their friends (hence the Ibbotson sisters and Mr. Hope become her enemies) is unmotivated. Harriet can portray her only as a monster—possessive, domineering, shrill, fanatical. Presumably sane, she is so blinded by jealousy that she creates her own reality. When Philip announces his engagement to Margaret, she simply refuses to accept the fact, announcing: "I shall deny the engagement everywhere." The study of abnormal psychology was outside Harriet's scheme, but she must have been at least dimly aware of the potential depths of Mrs. Rowland's character. Philip, for example, conjectures that his sister's obduracy "comes from internal torture." She persists, however, until her child lies dying of plague, and Hope and his family, the victims of her malice, rally to her aid. They cannot save the child, but in grief and remorse she at last confesses her lies, clearing the way for a happy ending.

Although Harriet Martineau was writing a warning against the snares and delusions of appearance, she was a firm believer in the ideals of love and romance. The domestic love story,

of which ***Deerbrook*** is not only an example but very possibly the archetype, presupposes every bit as noble an idealism as the romances of chivalry, but it is an idealism transferred to the realities of hearth and home. Chivalry had its charms, but its absurdity, its "irrelevance" in the modern world, had been displayed more than two centuries earlier in *Don Quixote*. To cling to its vestiges in sentimentalized courtship and love-making was only to be caught in the metaphysical trap of confusing appearance and reality. Is there a place for romance in nineteenth-century utilitarian society? Philip Enderby raises this question in a playful conversation with Hester and Margaret.

Margaret Ibbotson, although a girl of deep feeling and sensibility, is a realist. She distrusts allegory: "There is a pleasure in making one's way about in a grotto in a garden; but I think there is a much higher one in exploring a cave on the seashore, dim and winding, where you never know that you have come to the end—a much higher pleasure in exploring a life than following out an allegory." She warns of the dangers of making fancies and "mysteries" of human emotions. Philip protests laughingly that she would thereby outlaw courtship: "You surely would not overthrow the whole art of wooing? You would not doom lovers' plots and devices?" Margaret replies that such artifices are demanded only by silly, vain women—"suitable enough five centuries ago" but false to the realities of married life: "But I certainly think those much the wisest and happiest, who look upon the whole affair as the solemn matter that it really is, and who desire to be treated, from the beginning, with the sincerity and seriousness which they will require after they are married." To this her sister Hester echoes: "If the same simplicity and seriousness were common in this as are required in other grave transactions, there would be less of the treachery, delusion, and heartbreaking, which lie heavy upon the souls of many a man and many a woman."

Harriet Martineau's readers might quietly add—"But there would also be fewer love stories." Yet in reviewing the great Victorian love stories that came after ***Deerbrook*** we note how prophetic she was. The passionate heroine who lives only for her love—Catherine Earnshaw, for example—is doomed. The frivolous girls who demand "wooing" and live by false standards of flirtation and vanity are invariably viewed with a cold eye. Charlotte Brontë has no sympathy for Ginevra Fanshawe or Blanche Ingram; George Eliot sees only disaster for Hetty Sorrel and for the man who loves Rosamond Vincy; Dickens gently ridicules Dora Spenlowe; Thackeray is far less gentle with Blanche Amory and Beatrix Esmond. Marriage, the domestic novelist insists, imposes serious demands, and to pretend otherwise is stupid or dishonest. None of these novelists is blind to the charms of love; they simply wish to transpose these from the delusions of myth to the substantial reality of home and daily life. Thus Harriet Martineau—author of a non-fiction work called ***Household Education,*** the subject of which, she wrote, "is important in its bearings on every one's happiness"—celebrates in fiction the simple joys of furnishing a house. If her readers failed to see the romance of domesticity in this, it was not through lack of conviction on her part. She describes the almost sacred nature of the future wife's tasks: "Both the sisters were surprised to find how much pleasure they took in the preparations for this marriage. They could not have believed it, and, but that they were too happy to feel any kind of contempt, they would have despised themselves for it. But such contempt would have been misplaced. All things are according to the ideas and feelings with which they are connected; and if, as old George Herbert says, dusting a room is an act of religious grace when it is done from a feeling of religious duty, furnishing a house is a process of high enjoyment when it is the preparation of a home for happy love."

Hester is furnishing a modest village house, not a rose-covered bower or a fashionable town-house in Mayfair. The reader knows how much rent will be paid, the terms of the lease, how the furniture will be arranged. But the scene is not without its romantic aura—the cool shade and fragrance of the summer garden, the cozy warmth of fireplace and drawn curtains on winter evenings—in short, the domestic intimacies of marriage are given added seriousness and dignity: "Here will they first feel what it is to have a home of their own—where they will first enjoy the privacy of it, the security, the freedom, the consequence in the eyes of others, the sacredness in their own."

This domesticating of the love story, probably the most interesting feature of *Deerbrook,* is also the source of its artistic failure. Perhaps from Victorian reticence or her own sexual innocence (in one of her political economy tales she urges birth control by conjugal abstinence), Harriet Martineau shrinks from acknowledging the real problem of this ill-conceived marriage and focusses instead on the externals of life. Not that she was unaware of the sexual implications of her subject. She dwells at some length on Hope's anguish as he confronts his (on his side) loveless marriage, his terrors that his bride will suspect the truth, or that he will be unable to conceal his feelings for Margaret, who, true to real-life Victorian practice, lives with the couple after their marriage. Returning home from his wedding journey, he spends a sleepless night: "There was no escape. The peace of his wife, of Margaret—his own peace in theirs—depended wholly on the deep secrecy in which he should preserve the mistake he had made. It was a mistake. He could scarcely endure the thought but it was so."

It is a dilemma that Harriet Martineau cannot translate into the easy domestic terms of most of her novel. Impetuous flight, impassioned confrontations, suicides—these are ruled out by the nature of her work. Yet these domestic tensions demand powerful description and penetrating psychological analysis that she is simply incapable of producing. All that she can do is to raise her authorial voice, to use strikingly inappropriate language ("throbbing pulses," "quivering nerves," "wrung hearts"). Hope soliloquizes in the clichés of theatrical melodrama: " 'So this is home!' thought he, as he surveyed the room, filled as it was with tokens of occupation, and appliances of domestic life. 'It is home to be more lonely than ever before—and yet never to be alone with my secret! At my own table, by my own hearth, I cannot look into the faces around me, nor say what I am thinking. In every act and every word I am in danger of disturbing the innocent—even of sullying the pure, and of breaking the bruised reed. . . . I am in bondage every hour that I spend at home. . . . I am guilty; or rather, I have been guilty; and this is my retribution.' "

Happily, both for the author and for her characters, Harriet Martineau does not preserve the fustian mood but quickly slips back into the steadier rhythms and idioms of natural speech. Hope practices his profession, faces crises caused by gossip and the ignorance of the villagers, and eventually overcomes his foes. Meanwhile he achieves self-mastery, encourages Margaret's marriage to Philip, and develops a genuine love for his wife.

The domestic love story portrays lovers, especially after they marry, as solid citizens. Hope's therapy and salvation lie in constructive work, duty, activity in the community, which he serves as a doctor. No man survives in isolation and no couple, however deep their love, can live exclusively in that love. At best they live happily ever after—in a society, with children, relatives, friends, neighbors, and fellow workers. Victorian families were large, but houses (except among the very rich) were small. Lives constantly impinged on one another. School, church, an occupation or profession, were as interesting to readers of novels as the more intimate personal problems of love and marriage. Even the melancholy romantic giants of Victorian fiction operated in some kind of community. (pp. 241-48)

Many novelists before Harriet Martineau had recognized the effects of the social environment on the nature and behavior of their characters, from Moll Flanders' Newgate to Emma Woodhouse's Highbury. But she was one of the first English novelists to create an imaginative community as a setting out of which, almost organically, the characters and their conflicts emerge. Her center is Deerbrook—the community to which people come to meet their destinies. The novel is *about* Deerbrook; the plot concerns people who happen to live in Deerbrook and who have no fictional existence outside of it. The novel begins with a description of Deerbrook and the arrival of the two heroines. It ends with some characters leaving it, but with others who remain behind, recalling the legend (of a stream where deer came to drink) that gave the village its name. In between, like a protagonist, Deerbrook undergoes crises of crop failure, popular discontent and brief rebellion, pestilence, then rebirth—the last chapter is entitled "Deerbrook in Sunshine."

Not being the artist George Eliot was, Harriet Martineau fails to give life to her villagers, although she attempts to use some of their commentary as a chorus. They remain essentially disembodied—a mob, "a multitude of feet and voices." The social cross-sectioning is also lifeless. The baronet and his wife, who encourage the mob violence against Hope because of his political activity, are merely types—snobbish, arrogant people with no real malice but also no personality. Farmers and workmen are colorless and give no sense of the quality of their speech or work. Only those who move within the orbits of the leading characters—the Greys, the Rowlands, old Mrs. Enderby, the servant Morris—have identity, and of these only the children are characterized convincingly. Yet, thanks to her community scheme, Harriet Martineau gives breadth to her novel and makes this pioneering work a model for many later novels. She breaks out of the confines of the purely domestic scene and personal love story, moving freely from the hearth to the marketplace and the village green. Deerbrook is not the complex social web that Middlemarch is, but it has life as a community and its characters achieve through their existence within it a stature that they would not otherwise have had.

But above and beyond their social existence as members of the community of Deerbrook, these characters must also achieve some stature as individuals. Harriet Martineau, like all writers of moral and artistic sensibility, knew that the novel demanded more substance than a mere chronicle of daily routine within a social framework. The noble heroic exploits of the older romantic fiction had inspired noble heroic sentiments. But when heroes and heroines do nothing more noble than accept and adjust to the demands of simple existence in reality, they must still be capable of feeling lofty emotions and of living noble lives. The humble village of Deerbrook must serve as an arena for the display of the Christian virtues, testing morality and courage less dramatically perhaps but just as rigorously as a metropolis like London or Paris, or a battlefield, or the dangerous high seas. Dedicated from her youth to becoming "a forcible and elegant writer on religious and moral subjects," Harriet Martineau carefully developed **Deerbrook**'s theme of romantic delusion versus reality along the lines of homely but profound moral values. The reality that eludes her characters—thereby producing the confusions and misunderstandings that constitute her plot—is ultimately achieved. It is a reality seized happily by the fortunate lovers in the book, who go forth to build new lives. But it is also a reality that demands, for others, sacrifice, resignation, and fortitude.

In the real world of the domestic novel problems do not end with marriage, and marriage itself is not always attainable. As another novelist and schoolteacher Elizabeth Missing Sewell soberly taught her pupils: "Romance says, 'And so they were married and lived happily ever after.' Reality says, 'And so they were married, and entered upon new duties and new cares.'" The only certainty in life is suffering; the only Christian solution is recognition of this condition as part of God's scheme.

No character in **Deerbrook,** in fact few characters in Victorian fiction, more typically represents this spirit of resignation to suffering than Maria Young, friend and confidante of Margaret Ibbotson. Crippled, confined to a dreary existence as a governess, she can remember a happier past when she was pretty and rich and secretly attracted to Philip Enderby. But a carriage accident and the death of her father force her into the sidelines of life, where she must witness the joys of others denied forever to her. Maria is one of the earliest in that long line of suffering governesses, but unlike the rebellious Jane Eyre and Lucy Snowe, who were certainly influenced by her, she has resigned herself to her lot: "Let a governess learn what to expect," she tells Hester; "set her free from a hankering after happiness in her work, and you have a happy governess."

Maria has learned that happiness is a delusion and that its pursuit is futile and dangerous. Yet she does not despair. Not a Christian-martyr type like the characters in Miss Sewell's evangelical novels, Maria is fatalistic and stoical, consoling herself with memory and imagination ("The delight of a happy mood of mind is beyond everything at the time; it sets one above all that can happen; it steeps one in heaven itself") and in service to others. Thus she encourages the courtship of Margaret and Philip: "Her duty then was clearly to give them up to each other with such spirit of self-sacrifice as she might be capable of"). Like Charlotte Brontë's Lucy Snowe, she has observed that there are some who are destined for happiness ("They marry their loves and stand amazed at their own bliss, and are truly the happiest people upon earth, and in the broad road to be the wisest") and others who will know only suffering, yet will transcend their pain ("They rise to the highest above them. Some of these must be content with having learned more or less what life is, and of what it is for, and with reconciling themselves to its objects and condition"). Ultimately Maria voices the primary purpose of the domestic novel: to teach the acceptance of life by displaying

life as it truly is, neither terrible nor glorious, but part of the greater destiny, the Divine plan. She asks why we should demand "that one lot should, in this exceedingly small section of our immortality, be as happy as another; why we cannot each husband our own life and means without wanting to be all equal. Let us bless Heaven for your lot, by all means; but why, in the name of Providence, should mine be like it?"

**Deerbrook** is a modest novel in its scope and in its achievement. Its vision of life is confined to the reality of ordinary people, the world of the petty bourgeois. Yet there is something vastly ambitious in what Harriet Martineau was attempting to do in this book. Fully to appreciate that attempt, one must look ahead to the major works of nineteenth-century English fiction—to *David Copperfield* and *Little Dorrit, The Newcomes,* and *Middlemarch.* All these novels deal mainly with bourgeois society and the struggles of ordinary people in ordinary life; but their authors recognized that in the very nature of human life there is something divine and sublime—and that is love. The special contribution of the Victorian novelist is that he saw love in a new way—not exalted and heightened by romance, but simply and lucidly displayed in the domestic lives of men and women. There are many celebrations of domestic love in nineteenth-century poetry, ranging in quality from grossly sentimental to touching and beautiful—from Patmore's *The Angel in the House* and Clough's *Maria Magno* to Meredith's *Modern Love.* It is in fiction, however, that the values and institutions of bourgeois domesticity—courtship, marriage, children, parents, neighbors—found their most natural expression. The extent of Harriet Martineau's contribution to this discovery is considerable. In **Deerbrook,** a novel that foreshadowed the best work of the great novelists who followed her—Charlotte Brontë, Mrs. Gaskell, Trollope, George Eliot, Dickens, and Thackeray—Harriet Martineau established the domestic love story as a valid literary genre. Equally important, she framed the social microcosm in the English village, bringing together within its modest borders and applying to the lives of its ordinary citizens those concerns of "History, Politics, Mind" that Matthew Arnold summed up as the principal achievement of her career. (pp. 251-56)

> Vineta Colby, "Domestic Devotion and Hearthside Heroism: Harriet Martineau's 'Deerbrook' and the Novel of Community," in her Yesterday's Woman: Domestic Realism in the English Novel, *Princeton University Press, 1974, pp. 210-56.*

## VALERIE KOSSEW PICHANICK (essay date 1980)

[*Pichanick is the author of a respected biography of Martineau and an essay focusing on her feminist thought. In the following excerpt from the biography, she examines Martineau's social theory and religious philosophy as outlined in such works as* Society in America *and* The History of England during the Thirty Years' Peace, 1816-46.]

Martineau realized that it was important to make an objective study of the political and social institutions of a nation before passing judgment upon it. En route to New York [from England in 1834] she had outlined a primitive sociological methodology which was later published as **How to Observe Morals and Manners.** Determined to avoid partiality herself, she advised would-be travelers not to judge foreign lands by their own countries or to censure manners or customs because they were strange or differed from those to which they were used. She had been forewarned by the example of Frances Trollope's *Domestic Manners of the Americans* which was published in 1832. (pp. 74-5)

Mrs. Trollope's prejudices and preconceptions were those of the English establishment. Unlike her contemporary traveler Alexis de Tocqueville, she was appalled rather than impressed by the "equality of condition" which she found among Americans. Harriet Martineau noted with amusement that Americans, still smarting from Frances Trollope's criticisms, had been forewarned before her own arrival not to chew tobacco or praise themselves in her presence "under penalty of being reported in London for these national foibles." In her two American books—*Society in America* (1837) and *Retrospect of Western Travel* (1838)—she was generally careful to avoid Mrs. Trollope's particular aversions even when she observed them, but she could not resist the occasional comment about spitting and complained somewhat pettishly about a disquieting national partiality for rocking chairs. She found it unsettling to watch ladies "vibrating in different directions, and at various velocities"; perhaps there was a relationship between this discomfort and the childhood fear of magic lanterns and terror of rythmic echoes. By and large, however, she bore her experiences with good humor, and unlike Mrs. Trollope, who refused to associate with those she did not consider her social equals, Martineau was conscious of the danger of associating exclusively with those who *were* her social equals and of therefore having only a "partial intercourse with the nation." So although fêted by the famous, she made a point of meeting ordinary Americans too. Over the two year period of her stay in the United States she traveled some ten thousand miles. She journeyed by Mississippi riverboat, by canal barge, by railway, on horseback, and by stage. She lived during that time in private homes as the guest of the illustrious, but she also lived in boardinghouses and met with the common people. She endured with considerable stamina, especially for one so recently in poor health, the rigors of travel: the stranding of her boat on the Lakes, the near-overturning and miring of her carriage, and the endless delays and wearying overnight journeys in creaking, jolting carriages which bumped their unceremonious way along primitive corduroy roads. All the time she meticulously noted her impressions in her journal. Nothing escaped her keen observing eye, but while losing nothing in private conversation, she admitted that her deafness was a handicap and that she missed "the casual conversation of all kinds of people, in the streets, stages, hotels &c." She acknowledged regretfully that "the lights which are thus gathered up by the traveler for himself are far more valuable than the most elaborate accounts of things offered to him with an express design." Nevertheless, she more than compensated visually for her aural deficiency, and her enthusiastic portrait of America in the 1830s is as vibrant today as it was when she wrote it. Where the *Illustrations* had demonstrated the weaknesses of her fictional prose, Martineau's American volumes illustrated her strengths as a journalist. Although conscious of the importance of objectivity, she was more partial than she realized, for she came to the United States armed with expectations. She believed herself to be

> as nearly as possible unprejudiced about America, . . . [but] with a strong disposition to admire democratic institutions, [and] an entire ignorance how far the people of the United States lived up to or fell below their own theory.

Coming from an intensive study of the condition of human happiness in England where the society had not yet shaken

off the burden of ancient aristocratic dominion, she came to America with high hopes that in this new republic at least the people would be living up to the ideals of humanity manifested in their own Declaration of Independence. She therefore arrived with eager preconceptions which could not but have colored her final judgment of the United States and its people. The value of her observations was far from being obscured by her expectations. Martineau achieved maturity as an author in her American books, and her work derived strength from her new independence and stature as an individual.

After her two years among the Americans, Martineau returned home, and in the following year, 1837, she published *Society in America.* She divided the book into three sections: the first dealt with America's political structure, the second with its economy, and the third, "Civilization," with various aspects of its social mores. As a sociological study the work is uneven in quality. Perceptive observations are interspersed with untidy rambling anecdotes and tangential personal reminiscences which, although interesting enough in themselves, detract from the purpose of an objective survey of society. It was unfortunate that Harriet Martineau wrote *Society in America* before she wrote *Retrospect of Western Travel,* published in the following year. If the order of writing had been reversed she would have been less tempted to digress from her expressed aim in *Society in America. Retrospect* professed to be nothing more than a book of travel, and although it was not without some social commentary, it was an unpretentious work with serious considerations clearly subordinated. In its coherence and in its structure *Retrospect of Western Travel* was superior to the earlier work and was considered so by many of her contemporaries. She herself later described it as "more creditable to her mood, and perhaps to her powers, than the more ambitious work." When he read it, even Carlyle was "vehement" in his delight. It captured much of Martineau's infectious enthusiasm, and her most hostile American critics were prepared to concede the excellence of her descriptions. Nevertheless, for the student of nineteenth-century America *Society in America* remains the more important publication. More than half a century after its composition John Morley was to say of it, and of *Retrospect* [see excerpt dated 1877]:

> We do not suppose that they are worth reading at the present day, except from a historical point of view. But they are really good specimens of a kind of literature which is not abundant, and yet which is of the utmost value—we mean the record of the sociological observation of a country by a competent traveller, who stays long enough in the country, has access to the right persons of all kinds, and will take pains enough to mature his judgments. It was a happy idea of O'Connell's to suggest that she should go over to Ireland, and write such an account of that country as she had written of the United States. And we wish at this very hour that some one as competent as Miss Martineau would do what O'Connell wished her to do.

In *Society in America* Martineau proposed to implement the sociological theories which she had outlined in the as yet unpublished *How to Observe Morals and Manners.* But her purpose was also "to compare the existing state of society in America with the principles on which it was professedly founded; thus testing Institutions, Morals, and Manners by an indisputable, instead of an arbitrary standard." She was quite aware of the danger "of not fully apprehending the principles on which society in America is founded; and of erring in the application to these of the facts which came under my notice." Alexis de Tocqueville had just made a similar examination of American institutions and democratic principles in *Democracy in America* which was published in 1835 while Martineau was still abroad. Both writers were therefore simultaneously and independently engaged in studying American society and examining applications of democratic theory in the new republic. But where Tocqueville was concerned primarily with democracy as a practical expedient, Harriet Martineau used the principles of democracy as a criterion of judgment.

> The inalienable right of all the human race to life, liberty, and the pursuit of happiness, must control the economical, as well as the political arrangements of a people; and . . . the law of universal justice must regulate all social intercourse.

When Harriet Martineau came to the United States in 1834 there were twenty-four states and Andrew Jackson was President. She came from the old world to a new one in "the process of world-making." Pioneers were still extending the frontier into the diminishing wilderness and even the eastern cities were still in embryo. It was a causal universe in which history was being created, and Martineau sensed the dramatic importance of the moment.

> The present . . . is an age in which societies of the whole world are daily learning the consequences of what their fathers did, the connexion of cause and effect being too palpable to be disputed.

She perceived America as suspended between the past and the future "with many of the feudal prepossessions of the past mingled with the democratic aspirations which relate to the future." A necessarian and latent Comtean, Martineau believed that a society grew out of the national experience and was therefore infinitely mutable. But the principles of justice upon which the United States had been founded should, she insisted, remain immutable. She expected to find the spirit of 1776 incarnate in America and her expectations were only partially fulfilled. America compared well with England where the individual was exalted in theory but still despised in the mass. There was no "hereditary humbug" in the United States, and "the English insolence of class to class"— except in the reprehensible case of black Americans—had not been reproduced on American soil. For those Americans who considered themselves "Exclusives" because of wealth or family position, Martineau had nothing but contempt. The natural aristocracy of the country, she believed, was to be found "not only in Ball-rooms and bank parlours, but also in fishing-boats, in stores, in college chambers, and behind the plough." Unlike Fanny Trollope who hardly knew how to receive the "uncouth advances" of her poorer neighbors, Harriet Martineau welcomed the leveling effects of republican equality.

To Martineau, furthermore, the United States appeared to exemplify and substantiate the theories of political economy.

> One remarkable effect of democratic institutions is the excellence of the work turned out by those who live under them. In a country where the whole course is open to every one; where, in theory, everything may be obtained by merit, men have the strongest stimulus to exert their powers, and try what they can achieve.

She was nevertheless disquieted by evidence of materialism in American society. Because she wished to deny that the free enterprise system encouraged a "sordid love of gain," she was unhappy to find it, and despite her loyalty to the principle of individual competition she could not ignore that the mercenary spirit existed. She made the precipitous and melancholy discovery that economic laissez faire and individual liberty were not always compatible, for one individual's freedom to achieve too often encroached on the freedom of another. In *Society in America* she therefore amended her old uncritical acceptance of individualism and generously—albeit temporarily and inconsistently—endorsed instead the essential principles of socialism. Despite all her fulminations against Owenism in the *Illustrations,* and particularly in *"For Each and for All,"* in *Society in America* Martineau wrote:

> . . . there is no way of securing perfect social liberty on democratic principles but by community of property.

To those who knew her, her about-face came as a complete surprise. "How long have you been an Owenite?" exclaimed her brother Robert on reading the manuscript of *Society in America.* But Harriet Martineau was neither an Owenite nor a communist. She never endorsed an arbitrary equalization of property, and she never entirely relinquished her faith in the competitive principle. But in America she became aware of the obsessive nature of economic individualism.

> If money, if success, apart from the object, could give happiness, who would be so happy as the merchants of America? In comparison with merchants generally, they are happy: but in comparison with what men were made to be, they are shackled, careworn, and weary as the slave. . . . Are the mechanic and farming classes satisfied? No: not even they . . . there must be something wrong in a system which compels men to devote almost the whole of their waking hours to procure that which, under a different combination of labour, might be obtained at a saving of three-fourths of the time. Whether their thoughts have been expressly turned to this subject or not, almost all the members of society are conscious that *care for their external wants is so engrossing as to absorb almost all other cares; and that they would most thankfully agree to work in their vocation for the community for a short portion of every day, on condition of being spared all future anxiety about their physical necessities.* [emphasis added]

Forgetting momentarily her earlier imprecations against communal societies in a new almost Marxian concern about leisure time, she ignored her previous rationale that communal responsibility enervated initiative, eroded progress, and was the nemesis of personal responsibility and endeavor. Instead, she acknowledged Godwin's claim that "leisure [was] the birth-right of every human being," and she despaired that without "community of property" it could ever be secured to everyone. She conceded that the majority of Americans would be opposed to an equalization of property, but she did not think that they were beyond the pale of reclamation and she hoped that the false steps which they had taken in imitation of the old world could be retraced. She was confident that the time would come when Americans would recognize where their own best interests lay, but for her own society she had no such expectations. She thought the English too mired in the past, and too enmeshed in the intricacies of ancient property claims to easily find their own rescue. It is ironic that two world wars and a century later exactly the converse proved to be true!

Martineau's softened—indeed altered—attitude toward Owenism may have been influenced by her visit to Rapp's communist community at Economy, Pennsylvania, or merely by her disquieting observation that Americans were preoccupied with material success. Although she never fully endorsed either Owenism or communism, Martineau's concession toward socialist theory was significant, especially from one who continued to be numbered among the laissez fairists. For the student of Martineau this comment on individualism and the American economy is the most intriguing aspect of the section in *Society in America* devoted to the American economy, a section otherwise the least impressive part of the three-volume work and that which would have most benefited if *Retrospect of Western Travel* had been written first. Instead of providing a critical commentary on the economic fabric of the United States she gave impressions of the economy as she saw it functioning. She did not consider the geographical ignorance of her English readers and skipped from one part of the country to another with alarming inconsistency. Nor did she adequately consider her economist friends who doubtless would have welcomed a more scientific analysis of the United States economy. But perhaps the reader expecting to find a professional assessment of the American economy expects too much; after all, Martineau herself acknowledged that she was not an economist. (pp. 75-81)

[Even] before the start of the conscious feminist movement, Martineau observed a parallel between the enslavement of blacks and the subjection of women. She noted that both made a mockery of democratic idealism in America, and in *Society in America* she wrote a chapter entitled: "Political Non-Existence of Women," which is a too much neglected early manifesto in the women's rights campaign. To Martineau it seemed intolerable that

> governments in the United States have power to tax women who hold property; to divorce them from their husbands; to fine, imprison, and execute them for certain offences. Whence do these governments derive their powers? They are not "just," as they are not derived from the consent of the women thus governed.

Both in England and in America women's interests were represented by adult male voters. As Martineau pointed out, even supposedly radical thinkers like Thomas Jefferson in the United States and James Mill in England concurred in this opinion. But Martineau for her part would not accept surrogate representation.

> I, for one, do not acquiesce. I declare that whatever obedience I yield to the laws of the society in which I live is a matter between, not the community and myself, but my judgment and my will. Any punishment inflicted on me for the breach of the laws, I should regard as so much gratuitous injury; for to those laws I have never, actually or virtually, assented.

As a little girl growing up in early nineteenth-century England, Harriet Martineau was more educationally advantaged than most. Even so, she was early aware of the limitations of female education and of female prospects. Her first contributions to literature and to the feminist cause . . . were made when James went off to college and a career and left her at home. As a regular reviewer on the *Monthly Repository*

a few years later, her feminism was further reinforced by William Johnson Fox and his like-minded circle. As a female radical in the era of reform, Martineau admitted to a compulsion "to do something with the pen, since no other means of action in politics are in a woman's power." She resented her inferior status and the subjection of women generally and confided to Francis Place, "I would fain treat of Woman . . . for there is much to be said upon it." (pp. 92-3)

Harriet Martineau was never slow to applaud those who acted upon their principles, and never hesitated to do so herself. She had acted on principle when she tackled the awkward matter of birth control in **"Weal and Woe in Garveloch."** She had acted on principle when she accepted the abolitionists' invitation to speak in Boston in 1835. And she was to act on principle again: when she affronted public opinion with her endorsement of mesmerism; when she disavowed the Christian faith in *Letters on the Laws of Man's Nature and Development* (1851); and when she took up the fight against the Contagious Diseases acts in the 1860s. It is thus not surprising to find her, in *Society in America*, acknowledging the courage of female abolitionists who defied the social conventions which would have robbed them of their freedom of speech.

> The incessant outcry about the retiring modesty of the sex proves the opinion of the censors to be, that fidelity to conscience is inconsistent with retiring modesty. If it be so, let modesty succumb.

*1849 portrait of Martineau.*

(p. 95)

The sphere of woman, Martineau concluded, had been narrowly defined for her by man when it ought to have been circumscribed only by her own natural abilities. She opposed female acquiescence to the limits which had been set on woman's social role and political position.

> The truth is that while there is much said about "the sphere of woman," two widely different notions are entertained of what is meant by the phrase. The narrow, and, to the ruling party, the more convenient notion is that sphere appointed by men, and bounded by their ideas of propriety;—a notion from which any and every woman may fairly dissent. The broad and true conception is of a sphere appointed by God, and bounded by the powers which he has bestowed. . . . That woman has power to represent her own interests, no one can deny till she has tried. . . . The principle of the equal rights of both halves of the human race is all we have to do with here.

Like most contemporary feminists, Martineau saw no conflict whatever between homely duties and intellectual or professional attainments. But without denying the importance of domestic accomplishments she nevertheless would not accept that woman's sole aim or her only place was marriage. Unlike Tocqueville, who believed that equality of the sexes would degrade both men and women, and who approved the American application to the sexes of "the great principle of political economy which governs the manufactures of our age, by carefully dividing the duties of man from those of woman in order that the great work of society may be better carried on." Martineau emphatically denied woman's exclusion from any occupation for which she was physically suited. But Tocqueville, while approving the intellectual improvement of women, still believed that they should be restricted to a peculiarly feminine sphere of influence. Most American women would have agreed. . . . But like Mary Wollstonecraft, who described women as "exalted by their inferiority," Martineau saw the seeming elevation of her sex as false and degrading. In America she was affronted by that chivalry, particularly in the South, which seemed to her to substitute condescension for respect.

> I have seen, with heart-sorrow, the kind politeness, and gallantry, so insufficient to the loving heart, with which the wives of the south are treated by their husbands. . . . I know the tone of conversation which is adopted towards women; different in its topics and style from that which any man would dream of offering to any other man.

She denied that there were hardy masculine virtues and different gentle feminine ones, but she recognized that such an opinion existed. There was, she said, a "prevalent persuasion that there are virtues which are peculiarly masculine, and others which are peculiarly feminine," and that such a "separate gospel" for men and women implied higher expectations of morality for women than it did for men and reinforced the existing and insidious double standard.

As a single woman and a successful professional she thought it reprehensible that woman's prospects should be confined to matrimony, especially since marriage, in America as in England, usually concerned itself with status rather than affection. A woman was therefore seldom able to find satisfaction in marriage and was not permitted to seek intellectual, professional, or romantic gratification outside it as her husband

was able to do. As one who enjoyed independence of thought and action, Harriet Martineau could readily understand and sympathize with the limitations and frustrations suffered by those women trapped in unhappy marriages. She did not believe that the marriage vows were indissoluble, and she became, as a consequence, a supporter of and an advocate for divorce, in which, as in other things, she saw and deplored an invidious double standard.

As a critic of marriage, a proponent of divorce, and a supporter of the equally reprehensible demand for women's rights, Martineau stood outside the mainstream. She was known to embrace these unpopular views and therefore received more than one warning to say nothing in *Society in America* regarding the position of women because of "the unacceptableness of the topic." But instead of persuading her to remain silent this implied censorship only challenged her. Martineau was never one to step aside when her duty seemed clear, and opposition only served to fire her determination. She appeared to have rather enjoyed her temerity, and probably derived as much secret satisfaction from the adverse criticism of her opponents as she did from the praise of her supporters. In the weeks prior to publication she had no regrets about her decision, and would have regarded the suppression of her convictions as a "damning sin." Nevertheless she was uneasy as she sat "in the calm, and awaiting the storm of criticism." When the storm eventually burst she was consoled by the warm appreciation of her friends and appeared unaffected by the condemnation of the more hostile elements of the press which she described as "so completely a matter of course, so temporary, and . . . so absurd, that it does not trouble me more or less." (pp. 97-9)

Although refusing to admit the fallibility of the democratic principle, Martineau had indeed to concede the failure of democracy in the United States. She concluded that as long as slaves were exploited, Indians systematically dispossessed, and women subordinated, American democracy would remain a hollow theory, and her attacks on these inequities were nothing less than an admission of this failure. She regretfully acknowledged that "the civilization and morals of Americans fall far below their principles." Even so, she recognized that compared with the English and the Europeans, Americans had made considerable advances: they had achieved self-government and they admitted democratic principle. Despite their subservience to public opinion, their racial and religious intolerance, and the tyrannies of the majority, they made no obeisance to a hereditary aristocracy and she therefore did not doubt their ultimate progress. The mere fact that there were in America those who fought to secure the just exercise of those fundamental truths upon which the nation had been founded was sufficient to sustain her in the conviction that "the national heart" was sound.

Unlike her review articles in the *Monthly Repository* and the ***Illustrations,*** both of which commented upon or explained the ideas of others, *Society in America* was the product of Martineau's own thoughts and experiences. Its philosophical pronouncements were sometimes inconsistent but its factual observations were generally accurate, and its fundamental issues—democracy, abolitionism, and feminism—were essential questions which nineteenth-century America was yet to resolve, and which would continue to preoccupy Martineau in the years ahead. *Society in America* was good journalism and it made a considerable contemporary impact. As a vehicle of reform propaganda it disquieted conservative forces on both sides of the Atlantic, and succeeded in stirring sleeping consciences and publicizing the needs of the hour. It is worth recording Maria Weston Chapman's 1877 assessment of the work in the *Memorials* to Martineau's *Autobiography.*

> *Society in America* is not only by far the best book of travels in that country, in the judgment of the best qualified Americans and Englishmen, but it needs remain of permanent value as a picture of the United States towards the middle of the nineteenth century. . . . Its fairness, its largeness and accuracy, the truth and beauty of its impartial reprehension of all that was bad and its sympathetic admiration of all that was good, are not only universally acknowledged among intellectual Americans at the present time, but they were so at the very period of publication, when moral opposition was at its hottest.

Although an abolitionist, a close friend, and a consequently less than impartial critic, Maria Weston Chapman was essentially correct on at least one count: Harriet Martineau's three-volume work on America "needs remain of permanent value as a picture of the United States towards the middle of the nineteenth century." (pp. 102-03)

• • • • •

As a journalist rather than a historian Martineau was singularly well-suited to chronicling her own times. "There are few living authors," wrote a reviewer in the *Athenaeum,* "who may be so implicitly trusted with the task of writing contemporary [*sic*] history as Miss Martineau." But though the reviewer thought the [*History of England during the Thirty Years' Peace, 1816-1846* ] "as impartial a contemporary history as could be hoped from any pen," to the modern historian Martineau's objectivity is somewhat more questionable. Indeed, her *History of the Peace* becomes important as much for her patently obvious biases as for her contemporaneity. As a political economist looking back on her own era, Martineau had from the outset every expectation of enjoying "not a little writing of the gains we have made in freedom through peace and its attendant influences." Progress through freedom and peace was an essential dogma to the classical political economist, and *History of the Peace,* concluding with the year of Corn Law repeal, was in a sense a celebration of those laissez faire ideals which Harriet Martineau had sought to propagate more than a decade and a half earlier: in *History of the Peace* she was able to provide an epilogue to the *Illustrations of Political Economy.*

Harriet Martineau undeniably wrote about progress, but she was not in Herbert Butterfield's sense a Whig historian. She did not write in the tradition of her contemporary, Thomas Babington Macaulay, who "brought all history to glorify the age of which he was the most honoured child." Because Macaulay in the Whig historical definition was, or appeared to be, content with his age, he was inclined to judge and justify the actions of the past as they related to the evolution of an evidently satisfactory present. He did not believe in limitless progress or all-embracing democracy, and thought that by its extension to the middle class, democracy had gone far enough. He could feel satisfied that by the mid-nineteenth century the ends of progress had been achieved. But in spite of Britain's progress in the direction of liberalization and democratization, and in spite of the implementation of many of the legislative proposals which she had agitated for in the past, Martineau was forced to recognize that her England

was not yet utopia. Though she did not despair of the ultimate vindication of the philosophy she espoused, she was dismayed by the fact that it had thus far produced so little change in the condition of England. As Elie Halévy—using Martineau's *History of the Peace* as a source for his own history of nineteenth-century England—recognized, Harriet Martineau, despite her reputation for being "nothing but a popularizer of orthodox utilitarianism in its most commonplace form," viewed the era which saw the triumph of laissez faire with less than equanimity. For all her middle-class prejudices, she could not be satisfied with the achievements of reform: she could not regard the revolution as complete.

Martineau's earlier optimism had tempered but she did not despair of her society. As a necessarian and an embryonic Comtean she was able to regard her age as a period of "transition": as a part of the evolutionary process, a "partial advance towards the grand slow general advance which we humbly but firmly trust to be the destination of the human race." Her old insistent optimism had lingered as late as 1843.

> We see that large principles are more extensively agreed upon than ever before—. . . . We see that the dreadful sins and woes of society are the results of old causes, and that our generation has the honor of being responsible for their relief. . . . We see that no spot on earth ever before contained such an amount of infallible resources as our own country at this day, so much knowledge, so much sense, so much vigor, foresight, and benevolence, or such an amount of external means.

Eighteen forty-three had been a bountiful year in England: the country had weathered a six-year period of depression; it had already achieved a measure of parliamentary and social reform; under Prime Minister Peel it was headed (Martineau was certain) for the long-sought repeal of the Corn Laws. Then, hard on the heels of this respite from want and worker unrest, had come the disastrous crop failures of 1845, 1846, and 1847; the famine in Ireland; and the Chartist protests and continental revolutions of 1848. Martineau's confidence was shaken. She could no longer be naively optimistic. The prescribed solutions had seemingly failed to achieve the desired results and the question of the condition of England remained unresolved.

> The tremendous Labour Question remains absolutely untouched. . . . If it be true, as some say, that the labourer's life-long toil demands a return, not only of sufficient food, and domestic shelter for his old age, but of intellectual and spiritual culture, what can we say to the working classes? . . . we ought to put ourselves in their place, . . . and then we shall understand how suspicious they must be of promises of unseen and future good [precisely the sort of promises she had made in the *Illustrations*] when it is offered as better than the substantial good which they see others enjoying, and feel to be their due. . . . they will not acquiesce while they see that those who work less are more comfortable; and they are not told why. This is what remains for us to do;—to find out the why, and to make everybody understand it.

Perplexed for an answer, and less than complacent about the condition of contemporary England, Harriet Martineau was nevertheless encouraged by the measurable progress which had been made. For besides expressing her nagging doubts, her *History of the Peace* also reflected a pride in the achievements of the age. Indeed, it mirrored the ambivalence of her own attitude.

The Harriet Martineau who set her hand to the writing of the history of her times was not the inexperienced author of the *Illustrations.* Her professional skills had improved immeasurably, and her attitude had significantly broadened. Even so, the undertaking was formidable and, in her words, *History of the Peace* was "the bulkiest of her works and the most laborious." She wrote it at the request of Charles Knight who, as publisher of the Society for the Diffusion of Useful Knowledge, disseminated informative, reasonably priced publications intended primarily to help the less prosperous members of society improve their lot and their understanding. (pp. 142-44)

The sources for the *History of the Peace* were the *Annual Register,* Hansard, leading political memoirs and biographies, and the most important current journals and newspapers. In it she catalogued the political confrontations and parliamentary proceedings which accompanied the enactment of reform legislation. She wrote about the nation's economic fluctuations. She drew attention to social problems, especially as they affected the working class. She discussed British foreign and imperial policy and commented on the leading personalities of the period. She noted the irreversible phenomena of industrialization and urbanization, and described cotton manufacturing as a "leading social event," for with it had come the dramatic demographic shifting of thousands from the agricultural to the manufacturing sector, and a new balance between town and country. Although noting this process, she did not, unfortunately, investigate its impact on the society. She barely alluded to the urban conditions which so appalled de Tocqueville and Engels.

The original two volumes of the *History of the Peace* dealt with many of the more important questions of the period: it was not simply a narrative. As the reviewer in the *British Quarterly Review* pointed out:

> The tendency of the author is not to tell the *story of England* during the thirty years, but to collect from the records of that story certain political events, and round them to group the rest as best she may.

There are two main focal points in Martineau's *History of the Peace:* the democratization of the old aristocratic legislative process which culminated with the Reform Act of 1832; and the liberalization of the ancient commercial monopolies which culminated with the repeal of the Corn Laws in 1846. For Martineau both events symbolized progress, and her treatment of them was indicative of her attitude toward that progress. But she also recognized the dark descant side to the story: the obtrusive question of Irish unrest and poverty and, closer to home, the nagging question of working-class suffering and working-class protest. (pp. 145-46)

The author of the *Illustrations of Political Economy* is only occasionally recognizable in the *History of the Peace.* Much of the dogmatism and the pedantry evident in the earlier work had given way to doubt, and much of the irrepressible optimism had been tempered by time and disappointment. Martineau had lost her certitude. She no longer felt sure that she knew the prescription for the greatest happiness but she still believed in the principle.

"The greatest happiness of the greatest number" is

not now talked of as the profession of a school: but the idea is in the mind of politicians and shapes their aims. The truest welfare of the largest classes has been the plea for much of our legislation; and especially for the whole grand achievement of free trade. No statesman would now dream of conducting the government on any other avowed principle than consulting the welfare of the greatest number in preference to that of any smaller class.

She was still a laissez fairist but she had come to realize that there were many areas which fell into the public rather than the private sphere. Perhaps the most significant passage in this regard is in *History from the Commencement:*

> Marked advances were made in kindly legislation, meeting with no other opposition than grew out of a wholesome dread of interfering with private arrangements and personal morality by Act of Parliament. No free Legislature in the world has yet ascertained—much less observed—the proper functions and limits of State action and control; and, in England, there is no point of political philosophy on which further enlightenment and agreement are more urgently required at this hour.

She had always supported government control of education and public health. When the railways appeared to be developing into an ominous new source of concentrated power she advocated a large measure of legislative control there too. And, in spite of her original opposition to the Ashleys and Fieldens in earlier years, she was, by the time she wrote the concluding portion of the *History of the Peace* for her American publishers, willing to concede the benefits of the Ten Hours Act, and of the limitations set on the labor of women and children. She had not completely lost faith in the basic humanity of the employer or in the principle of worker independence, but, as always, she was able to rationalize her deviation from earlier dogmatisms. Workers, and especially women and children, she felt, "had to be protected, not so much from the hardness of employers, as from the rapacity of husbands and fathers, and the tyranny of fellow-workmen [in the unions]." Her opposition to factory legislation had been too long and too consistently maintained for her to make an about-face without offering new and compelling reasons, and, as usual, ignoring the ambiguity of her position.

Martineau still believed in educating the people rather than in legislating for them, but she had learned to accept legislation, at least as an interim measure, until the condition of society made such legislation no longer necessary. She still believed in the inevitability of revolutionary political change, but she was not certain what forms these new governmental structures would take, and she was not sure how much they should govern. She regarded socialism and communism as symptoms of societal problems, not as solutions for them. But her opposition to Owenite paternalism had yielded by mid-century to a pragmatic acceptance of "the devices of domestic socialism" which "supplied the necessaries and comforts of life, on a principle independent of alms-giving, to those who could enjoy them only by means of the economy of Association." She confided privately that "we in England cannot now stop short of 'a modified communism.' " But she did not try to predict the forms which the society of the future would take, and she remained moderately optimistic that this society would be a happier one than any which had preceded it.

> The material for working out a better state is before us. . . . We have science brightening around us,

which may teach us to increase infinitely our supply of food. We have labourers everywhere who are as capable as any men above them of domestic solicitude, and who will not be more reckless about a provision for their families than gentlemen are, when once the natural affections of the citizen-parent are allowed free scope. We have now (by the recent repeal of the remnant of the Navigation Laws) complete liberty of commerce. We have now the best heads and hearts occupied about this great question of the Rights of Labour, with impressive warnings presented to us from abroad, that it cannot be neglected under a lighter penalty than ruin to all. Is it possible that the solution should not be found? This solution may probably be the central fact of the next period of British history; and then, better than now, it may be seen that in preparation for it lies the chief interest of the preceding Thirty Years' Peace.

When she came to write the *History from the Commencement* a decade and a half later, she chose to conclude the final volume with the same cautionary paragraphs which had ended the earlier work. "The tremendous labor question," she reiterated, "remains absolutely untouched." She remained as dubious about the true extent of Britain's progress in this area as she had been previously although the reasons for her fear had shifted. In the preface to the American edition she described the condition of British labor as improved and improving but cautioned:

> The ground of fear is that popular liberty is overborne by the Trades Unions of our days. It seems to be so in every country where such combinations can take place; and the anxious questions are the same in all such cases; the questions how to protect the liberties of individual workers against the dictation and tyranny of leaders and pretenders of their own class; and what are the chances of the class becoming informed and enlightened in regard to their legal and constitutional liberties in time to check the spirit of despotism in the few, and animate that of peaceful resistance to oppression in the many. At present, the Trades Unions of the United Kingdom are its greatest apparent danger.

Martineau's *History of the Peace* is as valuable for its commentary on Martineau as for its comments on her era. The style is occasionally brilliant, the essential historical facts are sound, and Martineau's contemporaneity has, perhaps, even more significance today than it had in her own time. *The History of England during the Thirty Years' Peace* ought not to be the neglected work it is. It should be considered a valuable resource for the modern historian of nineteenth-century Britain, and its intrinsic merits ought to be much more widely appreciated. It is not simply a dated historical narrative which has been superseded by more recent and sophisticated scholarship. Martineau's observations were astute, her research was careful, and her opinions and even her prejudices were informed and are informative. The *History of the Peace* has stood the test of time and can still be read with interest and profit a hundred years after its conception. (pp. 166-68)

• • • • •

By the time of her death most of Harriet Martineau's more immediate causes had become facts of British life. Her writings had lost their polemical immediacy and the purpose which had made them important. They now seemed to be little more than heavy-handed didacticism and had become literary works of the second rank already declining into obscurity. It was now only Harriet Martineau's personal reputation, that "generous purpose" and those "large thoughts" which had inspired her work, which still drew applause from a new generation of Englishmen. John Morley, speaking for this new generation, described Martineau's literary performance as having "acquired . . . little of permanent value," yet

> behind the books and opinions was a remarkable personality, a sure eye for social realities, a moral courage that never flinched; a strong judgment within its limits; a vigorous self-reliance both in opinion and act, which yet did not prevent a habit of the most neutral self-judgment; the commonplace virtues of industry and energy devoted to aims too elevated, and too large and generous to be commonplace; a splendid sincerity, a magnificent love of truth. And that all these fine qualities, which would mostly be described as manly, should exist not in a man but a woman, and in a woman who discharged admirably such feminine duties as fell to her, fills up the measure of interest in such a character.

Martineau's personal reputation seemed to have outlived her work. She had apparently become little more than a phenomenon: a woman who in defying the conventions had achieved a stature seldom attained by members of her sex.

But the quality which made Martineau seem almost irrelevant by the time of her death was the very quality which had made her important during her lifetime and which makes her important today: her contemporaneity is for the modern historian her most interesting and enduring feature. Martineau was an astute observer of her own era. She seized upon the vital issues of the day, and with that dispatch and fluency which made her such a considerable journalist, she informed her public. She wrote much as she lived, energetically, simply, and as honestly as she knew how: "Yielding a glad obedience from hour to hour."

Harriet Martineau had grown to maturity as a woman and a writer in a nascent era, and change had always been the imperative order of the day. "If we attempt to frame moral systems," she had written in 1832, "we must make them for the present only. We must provide for their being modified as the condition of society changes, or we shall do more harm than good." She was fully aware that she lived in an age of transition—a positivist could not but be thus aware. As one of the nation's radical reformers she had long heralded change, and being without personal ambition, she would have been pleased rather than otherwise to think that her works had become neglected because their objects had been achieved. Although she had marched ahead of most of her contemporaries, and had often been considered reprehensibly out of line by many of them, she was seldom seriously out of step with the more advanced opinions and trends of her day. She was, as John Stuart Mill had said, "a sign of this country and Time." And it is herein that her immortality resides. (pp. 242-43)

*Valerie Kossew Pichanick, in her* Harriet Martineau: The Woman and Her Work, 1802-76, *The University of Michigan Press, 1980, 301 p.*

**MITZI MYERS** (essay date 1980)

[*Myers traces Martineau's intellectual and philosophical development as outlined in her* Autobiography.]

Conceived as the final act of conscience by a woman who thought herself dying, ***Harriet Martineau's Autobiography*** is the emancipation proclamation of a female philosopher. Characteristically, Martineau is concerned in her life story with demonstrating truths and elucidating principles through a comprehensive factual account. She is presenting the lessons of a life, a life which she rightly sees as having been lived in terms of an organic theme:

> I am more and more sensible, as I recede from the active scenes of life, of the surpassing value of a philosophy which is the natural growth of the experience and study,—perhaps I may be allowed to say,—the progression of a life. While conscious, as I have ever been, of being encompassed by ignorance on every side, I cannot but acknowledge that philosophy has opened my way before me, and given a staff into my hand, and thrown a light upon my path, so as to have long delivered me from doubt and fear. It has moreover been the joy of my life, harmonizing and animating all its details, and making existence itself a festival.

The imagery is significant, for Martineau's autobiography is organized around her stage-by-stage pilgrimage from darkness to enlightenment. It is both a moving psychological study and a didactic success story, delineating in vivid detail the progress of a Victorian woman's mind from the paralysis of childhood fear to the serene freedom of full self-government. Its last sections are resonant with such passages as the one I have quoted. Finding herself at the close of life "under a new heaven and on a new earth," she tries urgently to realize for her readers what it means to have at last "got out of the prison of my own self."

Believing that she might die of heart failure at any moment, Martineau had hastened from her London doctors back home to the Lake District, where she wrote the *Autobiography* at breakneck speed in three months. So convinced was she of imminent death that she had it printed, illustrated, and bound, ready for publication in 1855, but the volumes waited for more than twenty years while Martineau lived on and on. She never altered what she had originally written, for the *Autobiography,* despite its richness as a record of historical personages and events, is basically the story of an internal evolution—the active formation of a self as it responds to outer circumstances and painfully progresses toward an ever-developing inner ideal. The final stage of that self's freedom and self-knowledge once set down, Martineau left external addenda to the care of her close friend, Maria Weston Chapman, the American abolitionist and feminist who compiled the *Memorials* issued with the *Autobiography* in 1877. The *Memorials*—though often criticized for fulsome commentary (forgivable in a feminist determined to demonstrate a woman writer's importance as a statesman and philosopher)—complete Martineau's life history. More importantly, the letters, diaries, and miscellanea with which the volume is crammed supplement and clarify Martineau's own account of her intellectual and moral development. The *Autobiography* and the *Memorials* illuminate at what expense Martineau's always self-assured public image was erected and how late in her life public image and private self fully became one.

Martineau had long felt it a duty, a moral obligation, to tell the story of her life. As an unknown fledgling author from provincial Norwich, by late 1831 she had written her early mentor W. J. Fox, editor of the liberal Unitarian *Monthly Repository* (the chief recipient of most of her apprentice work) that she had made some progress. She kept copious journals in preparation, and she recurred to the project again during her five years of invalidism at Tynemouth in the early forties. Each time she saw her autobiography as a duty, but the reasons behind the duty enlarged with the progress of her mind. The struggling writer in her twenties had the now familiar story of a miserable nineteenth-century childhood to tell. The Tynemouth invalid was the celebrated author of the ***Illustrations of Political Economy*** (1832-34) and many other political works, which had made her the conferee of government officials and significantly influenced reform legislation; a pioneer sociologist and early propagandist for abolition, who had produced six volumes on the theory and practice of American democracy; and a Unitarian reformer and rationalistic feminist with a host of causes to advocate and a most unusual achievement to relate. But the mature woman who finally completed the *Autobiography* was a freethinking philosopher less interested in self-justification and specific political controversies than in the progress of the mind and the future of society. Believing that humanity has no source of guidance from outside this world and that the all-important science of the human mind—the sole basis of our knowledge and action—is yet in its infancy, she presents herself as an experimental example, offering such testimony as she can to benefit that mental science for which she had already endured such a furor from the religious.

Like so many of Martineau's later concerns, her theory of life writing was clearly articulated during her long literary apprenticeship. Martineau's philosophical view of historical evolution and her lifelong interest in the comparative study of cultures led her to see biography and autobiography as of paramount significance. In 1830, she had already formulated an impressive rationale for life writing. Criticizing deception and panegyric, she called for emphasis on "internal machinery" rather than external deeds and insisted on richly detailed verisimilitude and absolute candor, a recipe linking aesthetic realization with educational value. If all the truth cannot be told, we should at least be given nothing but the truth. She recognized the pain that full life-records might give to those connected with the subject, as well as the difficulties inherent in the writer's bias. But the longing "to assist others" with the experience one has gained made the attempt worthwhile.

The author of scores of outspoken biographical sketches (including her own remarkably unsparing obituary), Martineau was thus a champion of biographical candor in a period of reticence. She no doubt foresaw the clamor that would arise over her record of her childhood, her assessments of the public figures she had known, and her advocacy of "atheism" (what we would call agnosticism). But she was determined to tell as much of the truth about herself as she could, cost what it might, and in committing hoards of her private papers to Chapman with liberty to use them as she saw fit, Martineau knew that what she herself did not completely reveal—the extent of her ambivalence toward her mother, her quarrel with her brother James, for example—would be filled in by her friend. The result is a document of remarkable frankness, which is indeed a contribution to that "philosophical research, with a view to truth" which she so much revered. Like her longtime heroine Godiva, Martineau rather relished going naked for a cause; she was always audacious for what she saw as truth.

Indeed, for many, Martineau is the epitome of the woman writer as stern truth-seeker and scientific investigator. R. Glynn Grylls's summary in *Ideas and Beliefs of the Victorians* is typical: "Mary Wollstonecraft has to yield in feminism to Harriet Martineau. Much more prolific in the production of spiritual daughters, it was she who set the standard of the objective outlook and the scientific approach in place of personal rebellion and political passion—and set at the same time an unfortunate standard of personal plainness to which it was a heresy not to conform." It is not hard to caricature Martineau as a cold-blooded, strong-minded spinster, critical of those who, like Wollstonecraft and Eliot, succumbed to illicit love, and to remember her chiefly for her deafness, her eccentricities (e.g., a taste for cigars and gossip), and her strenuous concern with improvement. But it is important to recognize that just as Wollstonecraft's personal rebellion generated a radical ideology based on the rights of humanity, so Martineau's objective outlook and scientific approach were fueled by private misery and revolt, were indeed very much a defensive response to personal pain. Far from being intrinsically objective and deficient in imagination and passion, the young Martineau was immersed in a nightmare world of subjective suffering; the mature woman's final achievement of a serene, distanced view is supremely valuable to her precisely because of its contrast with her starting point.

As a philosophic autobiographer who is also a woman, Martineau's attitude toward her experience is necessarily complex. She sees her life as at once representative and unique. Having learned to make sense of her own tormenting history, she wants not only to explain why and how she personally became a female philosopher—escaping into "the fresh air of Nature . . . after imprisonment in the ghost-people cavern of superstition"—but also to suggest that individual lives can both represent and recapitulate stages in the progress of civilization. She offers her life as an educational model, which she hopes will help her readers comprehend, accept, and transform their own existences: "The age in which I have lived is an infant one in the history of our globe and of Man; and the consequence is, a great waste in the . . . powers of the wisest of us; and, in the case of one so limited in powers, and circumscribed by early unfavorable influences as myself, the waste is something deplorable. But we have only to accept the conditions in which we find ourselves, and to make the best of them." The mature woman can assent to her life as a bit part in the pageant of human evolution and is content to rest her faith on natural facts and the principles that govern them, "the eternal laws of the universe."

Martineau is thus the narrator of a real-life female *Bildungsroman,* in which deplorable waste is converted into intellectual and emotional sustenance. She recognizes the typicality of her experience in an age of cultural transition, but she is also very much aware of its particularities: her infirmities, her gender, her family configuration. However philosophic, her approach to her story is quite different from, say, Mill's dispassionate intellectual analysis of his life. Where Mill is cool and concise, Martineau is garrulous, emotionally emphatic, and novelistically detailed. She understands that concrete domestic circumstances shape our lives as ineluctably as abstract ideas. Her autobiography is very much a portrait of the *woman* as intellectual.

Martineau's retrospective account of her childhood and

youth is dual in perspective. Her narrative stance entails a delicate balancing act. She wants both to recreate what it was like to be that girl and to judge that younger self and the "early unfavorable influences" that impinged upon her from the vantage point of the disinterested philosopher. Because she is a reformer whose optimism assumes that people are wholly the products of secular facts and conditioning, she must realize fully the social mesh that marked her. She shows in this developmental record an unexpectedly acute psychological insight into the strengths and weaknesses of character that evolved under what she likes to call the "discipline of circumstance," always to her much more formidable in effect than express teaching. Her description of her suffering is extraordinarily vivid, but her awareness of what a difficult and provoking child she must have been is no less keen. Although she was always very grateful to her parents for the excellence of her education, both academic and domestic, she wants also to show how parental mishandling of a proud, reserved child irremediably warped her personality—not so much to castigate as to suggest better methods for bringing out the full potentialities of every child. Before she completed the *Autobiography,* Martineau had already drawn largely from her own youth to enforce this self-realization motif in her *Household Education* of 1849, the personal aspects of which had led Charlotte Brontë to write Martineau that reading it "was like meeting her own fetch,—so precisely were the fears and miseries there described the same as her own."

The recognition was mutual. The closest analogue to Martineau's early girlhood, as she herself emphasizes, is *Jane Eyre.* In fact, she notes that she had been taxed with the authorship by some friends and charged by others with having supplied some of the material in the first volume from her childhood. Martineau "was convinced that it was by some friend of my own, who had portions of my childish experience" in mind. (She was sure the unknown author was a woman—or an upholsterer—because of a passage about sewing on brass rings.) What Martineau and Brontë were creating and responding to in their respective works, what many women then and since have identified with, is an archetypal female success story, a passage from imprisonment to freedom. The novel and the autobiography have very different conclusions, but their youthful protagonists are remarkably similar: a plain, keenly intelligent girl, with delicate health, sensitive nerves, a strong will, and sharp, judging eyes. Each hides her fears and self-doubts under a hard, unchildlike exterior, and each can be goaded by injustice into passionate revolt, to the shock and dismay of her persecutors. As artistically as any novelist, Martineau has formed her youthful memories into powerful images of dependence and rebellion, images which both explain the shape of her own search for identity and independence and mirror the contours of every woman's existence in an oppressive society.

Always a rapid writer, Martineau could set down those early memories so deftly because of their long gestation; they had been used and reused in many earlier works and often told to friends, "almost in the very same words," George Eliot noted [see excerpt by Eliot dated 1877]. That first self-image had long since been replaced by a succession of others, but it was burnt into Martineau's brain as the key to what she became. Her estranged brother James and some biographers have disputed the literal accuracy or emotional coloration of her perceptions, but they are unquestionably valid indicators to the evolution of her character. Martineau's terrified responses to her mother's temper, for example, were psychological truths for her, no matter how much James may urge that his memories of Mrs. Martineau differ. Martineau remembered her childhood as "the most tremendous suffering perhaps of human life . . . the misery of concealed doubts and fears, and heavy solitary troubles,—the misery which makes the early years of a shy child a fearful purgatory." Even while stranded on a sickbed for five years in what she thought was a hopeless illness, she could envision nothing worse than her girlhood, which she summarized as "a painful and incessant longing for the future . . . a longing for strength of body and of mind, for independence of action—for an escape, in short, from the conditions of childhood." (pp. 53-9)

Martineau liked to say that her life began with winter, had no spring, and ended with a fruitful summer and autumn, and she carefully divided the **Autobiography** into "periods" (there are six) to mark her strong sense of stage-by-stage progression. She was very much aware of how her childhood had shaped her existence and directed her toward philosophy. In a letter of 1844, she calls herself "a sort of pioneer in the regions of pain, to make the way easier,—or at least more direct to those who come after. . . . what a continued series of disappointments & troubles my life has been, & how directly whatever I have been able to do has arisen out of this. . . . So do we stumble and grope onwards to the clear issues of our lives!" These clear issues are implicit in the earliest periods of the **Autobiography.** Take, for example, her hatred of irresponsible power and her ardor for justice to all deprived classes and races—those "who dared not speak." It is easy to see the future feminist and radical reformer, the "national instructor" as Fox called her, in what she says of herself as a child: "I had a devouring passion for justice;—justice, first to my own precious self, and then to other oppressed people. Justice was precisely what was least understood in our house in regard to servants and children." Always an intensely religious child, she found "my passion for justice baulked there, as much as any where. The duties preached were those of inferiors to superiors, . . . but not a word was ever preached about the justice due from the stronger to the weaker . . . a doctrine of passive obedience which only made me remorseful and miserable. I was abundantly obedient in act . . . but the interior rebellion kept my conscience in a state of perpetual torture." These are of course verbalizations after the fact, orderings of experience already characteristically directed toward social action.

Even more impressive and significantly indicative of the future philosopher's lifelong obsession with facts, laws, principles—the way nature, society, and the human mind work—is the total gestalt of privation and suffering, rendered in painfully concrete symbols of physical and mental oppression. Selected events stand for a whole orientation toward the world, an existential situation in which this infant's experience recapitulates the infancy of the race. Martineau's memories go back to the age of two: she is standing at a threshold trying methodically to reach solid ground—finally she toddles uncertainly. She is perpetually bombarded by sensations of "monstrous" intensity, and perceived facts seem to have no connection with the sensations they inspire. At four, she is frozen with unaccountable horror by a dream of a stag and her mother offering her sugar; prismatic colors dancing on the wall made her heart race all her life, long after she understood how they came there. She was never afraid of ghosts, but "things as I actually saw them were dreadful to me . . . I had scarcely any respite from the terror." Martineau con-

veys with extraordinary clarity the frightful slipperiness and senselessness of experience to a child. (pp. 60-1)

Autobiography, one critic argues, is essentially an "epistemological genre." In no case is this truer than that of Martineau, whose life from early childhood was one long investigation of the origin, nature, methods, and limits of human knowledge. She describes with wry precision her early attempts to get a fix on experience—cutting the Bible up into little tabular rules for life, being overwhelmed with joy when her sister Ellen was born because she could now see the growth of a human mind from the very beginning, absorbing herself wholly in *Paradise Lost* for seven years. When very young, Martineau began what she calls "to take moral charge of myself." She was always in search of principles which would guide her out of the prison of herself, give her the "ease of conscience" and self-respect she pined for, and satisfy her longings for comprehension, sympathy, and justice. She ultimately found "moral relief through intellectual resource," but it was a long, difficult progression. **Household Education** acts as a gloss on this early period of self-making. Embedding the episodes of her childhood in a discursive analysis, Martineau explains how the child proceeds from being the mere recipient of sensation to slowly learning to think for itself: how it becomes aware of itself, searches into the reasons of things, learns it can modify nature, and, more importantly, itself. With her usual deep reverence for human powers, she spells out the relationship between the child's ability to reason and its development of imaginative faculties—its capacity to conceive a moral ideal for itself and gradually advance toward it. It is no accident that six closely reasoned essays on the "Art of Thinking" were among Martineau's earliest publications or that she cites her working out for herself of the necessarian philosophy as the foreshadowing of her release from the constriction of childhood. Thinking, philosophizing, was her salvation, and necessarianism the bedrock of her thought as both Unitarian and agnostic.

Theology was the meat on which the precocious eleven-year-old cut her mental teeth. Wanting desperately to be good, craving heroism (yet another nineteenth-century St. Theresa), she choked over the problem of how creatures could be blamed or rewarded for their conduct if God foreknew everything. It was a dilemma of pressing personal urgency, but she was put off by her eldest brother when she timidly broached it. Having sorted it out on her own a few years later, she felt as if she had been given a key to interpret life's mysteries. Necessarianism must not be confused with fatalism. Because it showed how every event, material or mental, has its causal antecedents, how humans are products but not prisoners of circumstances, the doctrine of necessity offered Martineau both an answer to her own psychological and moral quandaries and a rationale for her future career as didactic educator. People act as they do because of their previous training and environment; the way to amend them is not to pray for providential intervention, but to improve their education, surroundings, and associations. They can never escape their pasts, but they can turn their experience to advantage. By understanding the influences that act upon them, by controlling their own mental set, they can to some extent will themselves into what they want to be. Action is not "free"—divorced from motive and consequence—but proceeds in accordance with general laws, thus ensuring security of results. Instead of feeling that things were arbitrarily and capriciously governed, as under her mother's rule, Martineau started to believe that life does make sense. It was the beginning of her escape from passive subjectivity. Now she could see herself no longer helplessly faulty, but a self-governing individual capable of change: first, personal; later, social. This is the root of Martineau's radical optimism, her belief that "every human being," if all aspects of conditioning could ever be brought into healthy congruence, "might be made perfectly good." Its implications for her feminism, reformism, and views of autobiography are obvious. Martineau speaks of herself as overwhelmed by the vastness of this new conception and the great alteration requisite in her management of herself. She is reborn, a "new creature," henceforth experiencing, she says, a steady growth in self-command, courage, and disinterestedness. Inspired by an encouraging minister to study David Hartley and Joseph Priestley, the necessarian philosophical heroes of her Unitarian heritage, she felt she had taken a giant step toward freedom, though it was a long time before the "last link of [her] chain snapped" and she became "a free rover on the broad, bright breezy common of the universe."

By the time she came to write her autobiography, Martineau saw her Unitarianism as a way station to something better, and she probably underestimated its importance, just as she consistently underrated her earlier works and personae. But while the peculiarities of her faith explain much about the course of her development, they do not, as some critics of her work imply, explain virtually everything. Not all Unitarians were necessarians, nor did all undergo the deconversion experience which is the leitmotif of the *Autobiography.* Martineau was indeed, as R. K. Webb . . . calls her, "Priestley's disciple" [see excerpt dated 1960], inheriting and revitalizing his Enlightenment attitudes, but she was also a young woman with a complex emotional history and a difficult family situation. Even though her sect was in general hospitable toward women's endeavors to use their minds and better their lot, Martineau did not find it easy to reconcile her ambition to develop her intellect and succeed in a public career with her need to live up to her mother's notions of what was proper for a dependent daughter. The Martineau girls were unusually well educated for their day, being expected to support themselves as teachers or governesses if necessary, but Harriet was also supposed to be a wizard at housewifery and to keep her studies strictly under wraps. She stitched mounds of sewing in public, but she also carried on a busy subterranean intellectual life with her then much beloved younger brother James. She was the leader in their eager discussions, but he was the one who went off to college, leaving her so bereft that he suggested she try writing something for publication. Significantly, her first essays discussed women writers and female education; she was working out a justification for her aspirations. She was ecstatic when her eldest brother told her to leave shirts and stockings to other women and devote herself to writing, but she had to juggle both until she was past thirty and finally succeeded in establishing herself in London in an "independent position." For her, these long years from 1819 to November 1832 were a "marked period," the third stage of her progress and a key time of preparation for the following evolution. Because Martineau's life was essentially a working out of basic principles to their farthest conclusions, it is important to understand this period of Unitarian apostleship—what advantages and challenges her heritage offered her and how it contributed to the attitude toward the self which informs the *Autobiography.*

Lax on doctrine and heavy on social activism, Unitarianism was less a set of tenets than a model for the virtuous self's interaction with the world. A denomination of practical phi-

losophers at once idealistic and scientific, Unitarians combined an optimistic belief in the gradual perfectability of man through rational reform with a rigorously intellectual approach to the examination of factual evidence. They were given to investigation of everything, from biblical miracles to the inequities in contemporary society. Dedicated to freedom, intellectual and political, they were vigorously individualistic, yet forever concerned with the good of the whole. They were temperamentally radical and devoted to education as the vehicle of social change. They often struck others as abrasive and egotistical in their contentious pursuit of truth; isolated and persecuted, they saw every day as an occasion for discipline, activity, and quiet heroism. However acidulous Martineau later became about this legacy, it clearly offered the anxious and ambitious young woman a great deal indeed. It furnished her with an order, a pattern for relating to the world into which she could meld her personal experience and needs, and an ethical ideal around which her own aspirations could crystallize: religion for her was always the pursuit of perfection, mutual and self. It provided tools for inquiry— she never tired of talking about the inductive method. It substituted an acceptable, outwardly directed channel for the self-consuming passion and imagination of her youth. Most importantly, it gave her a voice, a persona of energetic reason, serving as a protective shell within which she continued to grow and develop. Carlyle nicely catches the complex flavor of that early self-image: "One of the strangest phenomena," he exclaimed, "a genuine little Poetess, buckramed, swathed like a mummy into Socinian and Political-Economy formulas; and yet verily alive in the inside of that!"

When the Martineaus lost their money and "gentility" in June 1829 and Harriet began to think about a wider and more remunerative audience than the Unitarian constituency of the *Monthly Repository,* she set down a most revealing set of rules for herself. They contain both a demanding program of self-improvement and a rational assessment of her capabilities and chances of succeeding in what she plans. She is determined to please her family, submit to her God, and control her very thoughts. Because circumstances had led her "to think more accurately and read more extensively than some women," she aims to become "a forcible and elegant writer on religious and moral subjects." Her goal is "to consider my own interests as little as possible, and to write with a view to the good of others." She warns herself against "heat and precipitation." It is a description of someone girding for a battle, in which possible enemies lurk within as well as without. But safely inside the combative conventions of her sect which she adopted and later secularized, Martineau could, paradoxically, find an identity—satisfying, if temporary—by losing herself. She escaped her self-consciousness and individual problems by total absorption in her chosen vocation. The *Autobiography* and the *Memorials* abound in accounts of her extreme pleasure in thought and composition, frankly recognizing the emotional compensations she derived from her intellectual mastery, while primarily conveying an urgent sense of vocation, a conviction that she had a mission to perform in the contemporary social crisis. Through writing, duty and self-realization became one, the fervent youthful desire for personal justice and self-government mutating into the effort to help the powerless "who dared not speak" free themselves from the oppressions of a patriarchal society through understanding the forces that acted upon them and gaining control over their own lives. Different from "normal" girls, shaped by the most persecuted and radical of dissenting sects, she would triumphantly turn to use the special knowledge of the outcast, making her own repressed rebellion and rage into a voice that would transform English society. As a Unitarian and political controversialist, Martineau had found something to say which utilized and enlarged her own hard-won experience, and she had found a mode of saying it.

Her strategies succeeded for quite a long time. The astonishing popularity of the political economy tales validated her bent for practical philosophy to her family and the world. She describes strikingly her difficulties in getting a hearing—endlessly trudging muddy streets in search of a publisher, weeping hysterically all night, and rising to write prose of complete self-assurance in the morning. Her characteristic mask—authority, verve, and cool common sense—and her mission sustained her. She might be inwardly nervous about the work she had taken on or riddled with domestic anxiety (her problems with her mother persisted long after she became famous), but the outward display of confident control seldom faltered. She went through an unprecedented lionizing and accomplished an almost incredible amount of work seemingly without turning a hair, but she worried constantly about succumbing to flattery or having her independence co-opted. She saw herself as purely the instrument of ideas whose time had come and her life as an extraordinary plot, which must not be sabotaged by any weakness of her own: "Here I am," she wrote her mother in the first flush of success, "placed in an unparalleled position, left to maintain it by myself, and (believe me) *able* to maintain it; and by God's grace I will come out as the free servant of his truth . . . the ground of my confidence is *principles* and not my own powers." Her letters of the period display a tough-minded management of the anomalies of her situation as a woman and a radical. Recognizing that women could influence politics only through the pen, she strove for an image of such competence that her gender would be irrelevant. She could also use her sex to advantage on occasion, noticing that she could get access to people in power because the radicalism of a woman did not alarm them. Still, she fretted about chinks in her image. Offered the editorship of a magazine, she reflected in her journal that it would set women forward, always a prime object with her, but wondered if she could live up to her standards: "If I do this, I must brace myself up to do and suffer like a man. No more waywardness, precipitation, and reliance upon allowance from others. Undertaking a man's duty, I must brave a man's fate. I must be prudent, indefatigable, serene, good-natured." All contemporary accounts agree that she had already fully demonstrated every "manly" virtue; considering the reputation for dauntless aplomb she had established, hers is a most surprising statement.

Finally, she fell ill from overwork and family problems. Five years were a long time to think. As ever with Martineau, adversity was a strong stimulant to self-discovery. She struggled to convert suffering into strength, to wrest disinterestedness out of the morbid self-concern of invalidism. Freed from her couch by a celebrated mesmeric cure, she was increasingly excited about the possibilities of a wholly secular mental science and dubious about her Unitarianism, which she saw more and more as simply a subjective stage of thought, a mere fact of human history. She felt the deficiencies of her earlier work and her former self; she was ready for a new philosophy, a final self-image. She had outgrown the buttress of religion; realizing that her conventional faith was quite eroded after a studious trip through the biblical lands, Martineau felt very lonely. In 1847, she wrote: "I know, as well as I ever knew any thing, that for support I really need nothing else

than a steady desire to learn the truth and abide by it; and, for self-government, that it is enough to revere my own best nature and capabilities: but it will require a long process of proof before I can be sure that these convictions will avail me, under daily pressure, instead of those by which I have lived all my life." They did. By 1851, she identified her illness as the "turning point," the time "when I got not to care in the least what became of me,—otherwise than morally. *That* is in our own power; & therefore a proper object of care." Advancing from relying on God for support in her life and career to relying on herself, she had at last succeeded in coming to terms with who she was and could speak with her own voice—she was a completed woman.

Looking back, Martineau interpreted her life as a series of escapes from successive traps of subjectivity—the helpless egotism of infancy in which the whole world was contracted to a child's terrified vision, the metaphysical self-centeredness of early maturity which clung to a religion based on a human-oriented universe, a personal God, and a bait of individual immortality. Any "dogmatic faith," she concluded, "compels the best minds and hearts to narrowness and insolence." Martineau's *Autobiography* is firmly organized as a progress away from isolated I-ness, a pilgrimage toward a nurturing truth which would connect her with a larger whole. Its pervading image is that of gradual ascent, from inside a stultifying, paralyzing enclosure up and out to a wide, clear, farseeing view. From that elevation, the philosopher can take in the slow evolution of humanity's past and the endless vista of increasing knowledge and progress which the future would surely bring as diverse human capabilities and the material world were better understood and reverenced as they deserved. Leaving life, placed apart, Martineau described the condition of humanity as infantine, but hopeful because "the one essential requisite of human welfare in all ways is scientific knowledge of human nature," and attention is at last "fully fixed on the nature and mode of development of the human being." She looked forward to the extinction of crippling theologies and social structures, believing that the real "kingdom of Christ" would be manifested "in the new heavens and new earth of the regenerated human mind." Her intellectual sense of growth and change leads, in its own way, to a textual conclusion as ardently romantic as that of *Jane Eyre*.

Martineau was obsessed all her life with the problem of what we can know and what we cannot, and it was an enormous relief to rid herself altogether of a theology which promised gloriously, yet delivered little of the self-respect and serenity she had so long and so urgently desired. To dismiss the soul, to check the nagging, importunate, never-satisfied self, meant for her the beginning of real fulfillment, of seeing herself in a true perspective and being responsible only for what she could actually understand and do. Bringing all she had learned from former stages of her life into a new coherence, she felt wholly free and in control at last. Understanding how she had become what she was, she could accept even her infirmities—her deafness, the early emotional warping that left her fitted only for a single life—as positive advantages. Selecting and creatively fusing the elements of her life into an integrated pattern, Martineau modulates the intensely individualized early periods of the *Autobiography* into a kind of philosophical confession, a history of the mind with larger implications. Though her definitions of truth and philosophy might evolve, she correctly perceived the thematic continuity of her existence and its written record: "My business in life has been to think and learn, and to speak out with absolute freedom what I have thought and learned." Her own thinking mind and this one world were quite enough; she had absolutely no desire for the immortality which she had forfeited to win her freedom: "The real and justifiable and honourable subject of interest to human beings, living and dying, is the welfare of their fellows, surrounding them, or surviving them. About this, I do care, and supremely." It is a noble Nunc Dimittis. (pp. 62-70)

*Mitzi Myers, " 'Harriet Martineau's Autobiography': The Making of a Female Philosopher," in* Women's Autobiography: Essays in Criticism, *edited by Estelle C. Jelinek, Indiana University Press, 1980, pp. 53-70.*

## GILLIAN THOMAS   (essay date 1985)

[*Thomas analyzes Martineau's didactic writings and her journalism.*]

Martineau regarded her own gifts as a writer as essentially fitting her to be a popularizer of existing ideas rather than an original thinker. In her summary of her career which she intended to serve as her obituary, she referred, for example, to her translation and condensation of Comte in the following manner:

> there is no other, perhaps, which so well manifests the real character of her ability and proper direction of her influence,—as far as each went. Her original power was nothing more than was due to earnestness and intellectual clearness within a certain range. With small imaginative and suggestive powers, and therefore nothing approaching to genius, she could see clearly what she did see, and give a clear expression to what she had to say. In short, she could popularize, while she could neither discover nor invent.

In many respects such a description severely underestimates both Martineau's own accomplishments and the rare talents required for successful popularization.

Martineau's writings tend to draw heavily on her personal fund of experiences, and consequently she usually avoids the most serious pitfall for writers who offer advice to their readers, that of meting out suggestions in a patronizing manner. She constantly refers to anecdotes from her own life and thus provides a texture and interest in her writings on practical matters that is often absent from similar works of the period. This autobiographical component evidently afforded her some personal satisfaction. She remarks, for example, in the preface to **Health, Husbandry and Handicraft:** "It can give me nothing but pleasure to join in the endeavour to make useful these results of a long experience and observations of the homely realities of life." This autobiographical element, particularly in **Health, Husbandry and Handicraft** where she dwells on her Ambleside experiences, provides closely observed incidents and commentary on domestic events, which renders the book still lively and interesting to the modern reader. Her description of her poultry yard, for example, is the careful and amused one of the intimate observer: "the favourite aversion of the drake is his own ducklings. He would destroy them every one if we did not separate them from their passionate parent. The whole feathered colony is, at times, so like the Irish quarter of a port town, with its brawls and faction fights, that imprisonment or banishment

is occasionally necessary, on the one hand, and an accidentward for victims on the other."

In many respects the way in which so much of Martineau's popular writing is rooted so directly in her own experience is reminiscent of Cobbett. Their political views, of course, diverged sharply, but it is evident that Martineau admired Cobbett's writing. They both generalize freely from their own experience and express themselves in a trenchant, emphatic manner. While they are both unabashedly opinionated, Cobbett tends to be more choleric and irascible as if he constantly pictures his reader as an imaginary political adversary. Martineau, however, gives the impression of confidently assuming that any rational reader will inevitably be persuaded to agree with her position.

The chapters which make up **Household Education** (1849) had been written by Martineau over a period of several years as separate articles for the *People's Journal*. In **Household Education** she organized them to track the individual's educational needs and experiences from birth through maturity and old age with such titles as "The New Comer," "Intellectual Training," and "Care of the Powers." From a literary point of view, the main interest in her approach lies in the way in which she generalizes from her own subjective experience, framing each of her educational precepts with an anecdote from her own early life realized in minute detail. Thus the thread of her own experience acts as the unifying principle in what would otherwise be a collection of random essays on a common theme.

In many respects, the range of Martineau's journalistic essays provides us with an extensive map of the intellectual landscape of the period. **Household Education** reflects the way in which a larger middle-class population and the extension of formal education, as well as other more complex social and cultural causes, was both prolonging the period of early life defined as "childhood" and helping to create a greater interest in child development. Publication of works on educational theory had been escalating steadily ever since Rousseau's *Emile* (1762) had provoked heated philosophical discussion of the subject in the previous century. Martineau's book was not intended to make a contribution to the philosophical debate about the ideal mode of childrearing, but rather to outline what she saw as sound principles of education and to offer practical advice to parents of all classes. To judge from her passing references in her **Autobiography,** she herself did not regard the book as a major work, although it was to become one of the most frequently reprinted of all her publications.

Compared with much of the extant Victorian material on childrearing and education, Martineau's notions of the ideal family tend to be more egalitarian than the heirarchical authoritarian model presented in many nineteenth-century sources. She stresses throughout that education should be perceived as a process that does not end in adulthood, and that "every member of the family above the yearling infant must be a member of the domestic school of mutual instruction, and must know that he is so." She is emphatic that education or training which is merely imposed is of no value: "Every member of the household,—children, servants, apprentices,—every inmate of the dwelling, must have a share in the family plan, or those who make it are despots and those who are excluded are slaves."

Although, like most Victorians, Martineau clearly expected

young children to develop considerable powers of self-control, she thought that there was little purpose served in trying to develop self-discipline by forcible means: "There is a tyranny in making a lively child sit on a high stool with nothing to do, even though the thing is ordained for its own good; and every child has a keen sense of tyranny. The patience taught by such means cannot be thorough; it cannot be an amiable and cheerful patience, pervading the whole temper." Similarly, she saw no purpose in rigidly censoring a child's reading by providing bowdlerized versions of the classics: "Whatever children do not understand slips through the mind and leaves no trace; and what they do understand of matters of passion is to them divested of mischief. Purified editions of noble books are monuments of wasted labor. . . . "

Martineau was sometimes circumspect about expressing her views on women's rights if she felt that the forum was inappropriate, but in *Household Education* she asserts firmly that girls have the same right to an intellectual education as boys. She is incredulous about the way in which many works on education, which she otherwise admires, complacently and contradictorily argue against education for girls: "we find it taken for granted that girls are not to learn the dead languages and mathematics, because they are not to exercise professions where these attainments are wanted; and a little further on we find it said that the chief reason for boys and young men studying these things is to improve the quality of their minds." Characteristically, she evidently feels that, having exposed the illogicality of her opponents' argument, nothing more need be said on the matter.

In her travel books, Martineau observed that both Arab children in Egypt and the children of settlers in America developed impressive physical competence and grace compared with their English counterparts. In *Household Education* she argues in favor of a program of physical as well as intellectual education, citing, typically, an earnestly presented, but absurdly exaggerated, example:

> Look at the pale student, who lives shut up in his study, never having been trained to use his arms and hands but for dressing and feeding himself, turning over his books, and guiding the pen. Look at his spindles of arms and his thin fingers, and compare them with the brawny limbs of the blacksmith or the hands of the quay-porter, whose grasp is like that of a piece of strong machinery. Compare the feeble and awkward touch of the bookworm, who can hardly button his waistcoat or carry his cup of tea to his mouth, with the power that the modeller, the ivory-carver, and the watch-maker have over their fingers. It is education which has made the difference between these.

The assumption behind all the notions about education presented in Martineau's books is that most children will never attend school. Although more and more children were receiving formal schooling for longer periods as the century progressed, Martineau's assumption was, for most middle-class female children and nearly all the children of working-class parents, substantially correct. Even children who did go to school generally attended either intermittently or for a very short time. The main emphasis of *Household Education,* therefore, is on the education received by children at home, though Martineau takes pains to stress that the home, even with the provision of well-qualified tutors, cannot compete with the school in teaching "book-knowledge."

The central interest of *Household Education,* for the student of Martineau's work, is not so much in her educational theory itself as in the way in which the book clearly served as something of a dress rehearsal for the more systematic personal reminiscence of the *Autobiography.* Many incidents from her own childhood are presented in the first person; others are more or less disguised by third-person narration. In some cases, as in the account she provides of parental insensitivity to the onset of deafness, the third-person disguise may have seemed necessary, both because the account was still painful and because she is portraying her parents' attitude as implicitly tyrannical:

> I have known deafness grow upon a sensitive child so gradually as never to bring the moment when her parents felt impelled to seek her confidence; and the moment therefore never arrived. She became gradually borne down in health and spirits by the pressure of her trouble, her springs of pleasure all poisoned, her temper irritated and rendered morose, her intellectual pride puffed up to an insufferable haughtiness, and her conscience brought by perpetual pain of heart into a state of trembling soreness,—all this, without one word ever being offered to her by any person whatever of sympathy or sorrow about her misfortune.

Yet other incidents less highly charged with feeling or which do not reflect on her parents are also narrated in the third person with a similar "I knew a little girl . . . " formula.

The often heavy-handed prescriptive tone of *Household Education* is effectively leavened by Martineau's use of these accounts. At times these are more or less incidental to the argument, as is the case when she describes the intensity of her own sensory experiences as a child: "I tried to walk round a tree (an elm, I believe), clasping the tree with both arms; and nothing that has happened today is more vivid to me than the feel of the rough bark to the palms of my hands and the entanglement of the grass to my feet. And then at night there was the fearful wonder at the feel of the coarse calico sheets, and at the creaking of the turn-up bedstead when I moved." The intensity of the remembered sensation tends to evoke empathy and effectively prevents the reader from objectifying the child. This is particularly the case when she frankly reveals the idiosyncratic nature of her childhood fears:

> Some of my worst fears in infancy were from lights and shadows. The lamplighter's torch on a winter's afternoon, as he ran along the street, used to cast a gleam, and the shadows of the window-frames on the ceiling; and my blood ran cold at the sight, every day, even though I was on my father's knee, or on the rug in the middle of the circle round the fire. Nothing but compulsion could make me enter our drawing-room before breakfast on a summer morning; and if carried there by the maid, I hid my face in a chair that I might not see what was dancing on the wall. If the sun shone, as it did at that time of day, on the glass lustres on the mantelpiece, fragments of gay color were cast on the wall; and as they danced when the glass drops were shaken, I thought they were alive,—a sort of imps. But as I never told anybody what I felt, these fears could not be met, or charmed away; and I grew up to an age which I will not mention before I could look steadily at prismatic colors dancing on the wall.

From Charlotte Brontë's remarks about her own deeply felt

response to **Household Education** and from its enormous popularity among its contemporary audience, we may surmise that many nineteenth-century readers saw the book as more than merely another text providing educational advice. Like Brontë, many other readers may well have read her account of the needless cruelties inflicted on children in the name of parental discipline and "firmness" with an all-too-familiar sense of their own childhood brought to mind. (pp. 60-6)

The twentieth-century distinction between the status and function of a "writer" and that of a "journalist" was rarely made in the literary world of the nineteenth century. The majority of the writers who are now regarded as significant literary figures had some connection with the journalism of their day. George Eliot, Dickens, and Thackeray, for example, all wrote extensively for periodical publications ranging respectively from the serious-minded *Westminster Review,* to the popular *Household Words,* which was aimed at a middle-class, middlebrow audience, to *Punch,* whose cartoons and comic sketches mirrored the views of an educated middle-class audience. Any writer of the period intending to earn a living solely from writing almost inevitably relied on publication in the periodical press as a financial mainstay. Martineau, who had supported herself and her dependents entirely on the proceeds of her writing ever since the publication of **Illustrations of Political Economy,** was no exception. She published articles in such publications as the *People's Journal,* the *Leader,* the *Edinburgh Review, Cornhill Magazine, Once a Week,* the *Westminster Review,* as well as over sixteen hundred articles in the *Daily News.*

Martineau's articles in the *Daily News* commented on current political events but also gave her an opportunity to discuss the implications of her views on such subjects as the abolition of slavery and the state of women's rights. In both cases she based her explicit arguments largely on economic rather than ethical grounds, even though we may surmise that the impetus for her argument in each case arose from a sense of moral outrage. Many of her discussions of the vicissitudes of the cotton industry stress the folly of relying on the production of slavery and urged the cotton manufacturers to develop sources of supply based on free labor. Similarly, in her articles on women and employment in the *Daily News* and elsewhere, she quoted statistics to show that the vast majority of women who were employed worked strictly because of the necessity of supporting themselves and their dependents. Drawing on police statistics she exposed the extent of physical abuse of women and children and argued that this arose from the way in which both were assigned a subordinate and degraded social role.

Some of Martineau's most interesting journalistic essays were the obituaries she prepared for the *Daily News.* These were collected in **Biographical Sketches** in order to aid her finances when her investments were no longer yielding an adequate income. Her necessarian convictions and Comtean philosophy give her a view of history as evolutionary inevitability, only marginally affected by the activities of individuals. Thus, she tended to portray her contemporaries either as "characters" or as observers and interpreters of historical events rather than as originators of political and social movements. Her sketch of Robert Owen is an interesting case in point. Even allowing for the fact that he had developed views on factory reform in particular and on society in general that were in sharp contrast to Martineau's rigid laissez-faire

*The Knoll, Martineau's home at Ambleside.*

dogma, she devotes amazingly little space to his theory and tends to treat his views as merely idiosyncratic and irrational: "always a gentle bore in regard to his dogmas and his expectations; always palpably right in his descriptions of human misery; always thinking he had proved a thing when he had asserted it, in the force of his own conviction; and always really meaning something more rational than he had actually expressed. It was said by way of mockery that he might live in parallelograms, but he argued in circles; but this is rather too favourable a description of one who did not argue at all, nor know what argument meant." Allowing that Owen's character and manner may well have been much as Martineau describes them, her account is extraordinary in that it ignores the enormous effect Owen had as an early socialist and as a founder of the cooperative movement.

Her ability to characterize her subject succinctly is at its best when she is describing those of little or no significance on the political scene. Her accounts of literary characters are remarkable records of the period. She is particularly fascinated with the lives of figures who had presided over several generations of literary life. She writes an especially warm account of one of the Miss Berrys who had been a notable saloniste from Dr. Johnson's day until her death in 1852. Martineau is especially intrigued with the perspective such a long life must give to the rise and fall of literary fashions and reputation: "The short career of Byron passed before her eyes like a summer storm; and that of Scott constituted a great interest of her life for many years. What an experience—to have studied the period of horrors, represented by Monk Lewis—of conventionalism in Fanny Burney—of metaphysical fiction in Godwin—of historical romance in Scott—and of a new order of fiction in Dickens, which is yet too soon to characterise by a phrase!"

The sketches are also of interest for the light they shed on Martineau's personal evaluation of particular individuals. She does not appear to have felt constrained by the conventional pious hypocrisies of writing an obituary. Her accounts of her old enemies, Croker and Lockhart of the *Quarterly Review,* while by no means deliberately malicious, made no attempt to disguise her acrimony toward them. Rather than producing a vituperative account, she provides an analysis of the causes for both Croker and Lockhart's practice of systematically demolishing reputations as well as the *Quarterly Re-*

*view*'s techniques of character assassination. Despite its obvious bias, the latter is an important record for any scholar who wished to understand the climate that nineteenth-century writers inhabited. She diagnoses Lockhart's behavior as the result of "moral obtuseness" but devotes more attention to Croker whose relish in hatcheting writers in the *Quarterly* was already notorious enough for Macaulay to remark of him: "Croker is a man who would go a hundred miles through sleet and snow, on the top of a coach, in a December night, to search a parish register, for the sake of showing that a man is illegitimate, or a woman older than she says she is." Martineau suggests that Croker's "malignant ulcer of the mind" resulted from his disappointment with his mediocre political career and suggests that this mediocrity itself arose from the want of "heart" that prevented him from making the best use of moderate talents: "It was the heart element that was amiss. A good heart has wonderful efficacy in making moderate talent available. Where heart is absent, the most brilliant abilities fail, as is said in such cases, 'unaccountably.'"

The *Biographical Sketches* are, almost without exception, spirited and eccentric in very much the same manner as the *Autobiography.* Despite their origins in a publication as ephemeral as a daily newspaper, they provide a vital record of a segment of nineteenth-century social and literary life.

Martineau contributed numerous articles to Dickens's popular periodical, *Household Words.* Her contributions fall into two main areas of recurring interest to her: the description of various new industrial processes; and discussions of education, particularly the education of the handicapped, with an analysis of the ways in which the mentally or physically handicapped can best be integrated and accommodated in society at large in such articles as **"Three Graces of Christian Science"** and **"Blindness."** Compared with the maudlin sentimentality that surrounds much nineteenth-century writing on the subject of physical disability, Martineau's treatment of the subject is both frank and sensitive. She gives thoughtful consideration to the minute particulars of overcoming the educational handicaps of the deaf and the blind. She also reflects at length on the difficulties faced by the parents of handicapped children and advises against the self-immolation of parents in the care of a disabled child, advice which ran strictly counter to the popular Victorian view of the crippled, or otherwise disabled, child as an opportunity for meritorious self-sacrifice on the part of its parent: "If it were good that a mother should nurse an infirm child through the day and guard it all the night, that she should devote all her time and all her love, and sacrifice all her pleasures to it, and minister to its wishes every hour of its life,—if it were good that she should do this, it would not be enough. It is not good, and it is not enough." Even more strikingly, under the bald title **"Idiots Again"** she describes a mother's gradual realization that her child is "mentally defective":

> As the weeks pass, however, and still the child takes no notice, a sick misgiving sometimes enters the mother's mind—a dread of she does not know what, but it does not last long. You may trust a mother for finding out charms and promise of some sort or other in her baby—be it what it may. Time goes on; and the singularity is apparent that the baby makes *no response* to anything. He is not deaf . . . His mother longs to feel the clasp of his arms round her neck; but her fondlings receive no return. His arm hangs lax over her shoulder. She

> longs for a look from him, and lays him back in her lap, hoping that they may look into each others' eyes; but he looks at nobody. All his life long nobody will ever meet his eyes, and neither in that way nor in any other way will his mind expressly meet that of anybody else.

What makes such a passage affecting, even to the modern reader who approaches it equipped with a different set of attitudes, is that rather than relying on a deliberately pathetic rendering of a subject which is already full of pathos, Martineau chooses instead a rather cool and patient account of the precise stages of the mother's rationalizations. (pp. 76-80)

Martineau's writings frequently examine the problems of managing a physical disability. Some of her most convincing fiction focuses on the effect of physical disability on individual psychology. The most striking examples are the struggles of Hugh in **"The Crofton Boys"** to overcome his own self-pity after his foot has been amputated, and the sympathetic characterization of Maria Young, the lame governess in ***Deerbrook.*** Many of her articles on educational methods for the deaf or the blind published in *Household Words* and other periodicals offer implicit advice to the handicapped or their families, but in **"Letter to the Deaf"** (1834) and *Life in the Sickroom* (1844) she specifically addresses those who, like herself, are deaf or living the restricted life of an invalid.

**"Letter to the Deaf,"** originally a magazine article, was frequently reprinted as a booklet for deaf readers by charitable or cooperative agencies concerned with the welfare of the deaf. Despite its original issue to the general audience of *Tait's Edinburgh Magazine,* she makes it plain that she is addressing her article to deaf readers only and that she is unconcerned about the reactions "of those who do not belong to our fraternity."

Throughout the essay she argues strongly in favor of the deaf achieving and maintaining as much autonomy as possible and regards the protectiveness of friends and relatives as harmful, "in as far as it encourages us to evade our enemy instead of grappling with it." Anything that prevents the deaf person from fully acknowledging and understanding the nature of his or her deafness is seen as inimical to the necessary demystification of the subject: "Advice must go for nothing with us in a case where nobody is qualified to advise. We must cross-question our physician, and hold him to it till he has told us all. We must destroy the sacredness of the subject, by speaking of it ourselves; not perpetually and sentimentally, but, when occasion arises, boldly, cheerfully, and as a plain matter of fact." She suggests that the deaf inform strangers immediately of their disability in order to avoid confusion and mystery. At the same time she carefully points out that the deaf should not interfere with the ease of communication between those who hear adequately by asking for remarks to be repeated for their benefit.

She outlines the undesirable personality traits that are likely to arise from deafness:

> the persuasion that people are taking advantage of us in what they say,—that they are discussing us, or laughing at us,—that they do not care for us as long as they are merry,—that the friend who takes the pains to talk to us might make us less conspicuous if he would,—the vehement desire that we might be let alone, and the sense of neglect if too long let alone; all these, absurd and wicked fancies

as they are seen to be when fairly set down, have beset us all in our time; have they not?

These distortions of perspective are best combatted, she suggests, by trying, in as far as the degree of deafness permits, to extend the diminished aural faculty by deliberately seeking out such sounds as are audible to the hard of hearing: the street barrel-organ, the rushing of a stream, or "the sough of words without the sense" of a House of Commons debate. She suggests, too, that the deaf combat their natural tendency to shun society and that they develop an active social life to avoid becoming "selfish, or absorbed in what does not concern our day and generation, or nervous, dependant, [*sic*] and helpless in common affairs."

In *Life in the Sickroom* and **"Letter to the Deaf,"** Martineau is primarily interested in the psychological rather than the physical effects of disability. Unlike the earlier article, *Life in the Sickroom* was published anonymously, though there can have been little doubt about its authorship. It, too, is addressed to those in similar situations rather than to a general audience, and she takes advantage of the more lengthy book format to devote ten pages to a dedication to "some fellow-sufferer" whom she hopes could benefit from such a book.

Typically, as well as giving advice on how to combat the oppressiveness of confinement to bed or to a single room, Martineau is eloquent about the ways in which the experience of invalidism can be turned into an opportunity for moral education. For example, she suggests that the restricted life of the sickroom dweller may give an opportunity to develop a more tolerant view of the world.

She constantly warns her readers against the dangers of invalid isolation leading to a distorted subjective view of the world, and to this end advises against the invalid's keeping a diary. She also writes at considerable length about the necessity of an invalid's having a view of the outside world from the sickroom. She writes vividly of the view from her own window, which shows her children flying their kites, lovers and friends walking together, the washerwomen with loads of laundry on their heads, "and the mistress of the garden, bringing up her pails of frothing milk from the cow-house, looks about her with complacency, and comes forth with fresh alacrity to cut the young lettuces which are sent for, for somebody's supper of cold lamb."

Martineau's urging her readers, in both **"Letter to the Deaf "** and *Life in the Sickroom,* to set aside subjectivity and isolation in favor of observation of and participation in the social world echoes one of the most persistent themes of nineteenth-century writing. We find it expounded by Dickens in the broad strokes of *A Christmas Carol* (1843) when Scrooge is converted from miserliness to convivial sociability. George Eliot's exploration of the shift away from self-absorption to empathy with others is much subtler and more complex. She describes the process most eloquently in *Middlemarch* (1872) through the development of Dorothea Brooke from the totally self-absorbed girl who yearns after the life of a Saint Theresa to the woman who, at the end of the novel, watches the dawn workers from her window and feels herself "a part of that involuntary, palpitating life, and could neither look out on it from her luxurious shelter as a mere spectator, nor hide her eyes in a selfish complaining." Martineau's description of invalid life and particularly her essay on the view from her sickroom window has much in common with George Eliot's description of Dorothea Brooke's shift in moral conscious-

ness as she watches the scene from her window. As elsewhere in Victorian literature when this theme occurs, Martineau's exploration of it owes its force to the power of the conflicting impulses of the longing for seclusion and the profound desire to be involved in and to comprehend human society. The moral education which Martineau outlines for her "fellow-sufferers" in her essay for the deaf and in her book for invalids is a programmatic and prescriptive form of the conflict between the two powerful impulses which gives Victorian literature much of its energy and interest. (pp. 83-6)

> *Gillian Thomas, in her* Harriet Martineau, *Twayne Publishers, 1985, 144 p.*

## VALERIE SANDERS    (essay date 1986)

[*In the following excerpt from a study of Martineau's place in the development of the English novel, Sanders discusses Martineau's literary criticism and her ideas regarding the purpose of fiction.*]

1832 was a crucial year, for British politics, for literature, and even for public health. While the Reform Bill was hanging in the balance, and a cholera epidemic killing thousands, Bentham, Goethe, Crabbe and Scott were dying, and several cheap periodicals beginning. One of these was *Tait's Edinburgh Magazine,* for which Harriet Martineau wrote her critique of Scott, in the year of her own real début (since much of her earlier work had appeared anonymously, and was not widely circulated). Her appraisal was divided into two halves: one headed **'Characteristics of the Genius of Scott,'** the other, **'Achievements of the Genius of Scott.'** To William Tait, she explained that their chief purpose was

> to show what Scott had done for *the people,* & how far he has *unconsciously* opened a way for a new species of literature w[hich] shall stand in the same relation to them as he intended his to stand in to the aristocracy. Beautiful & glorious was he! but how much so can only be known when the issues I am endeavouring to anticipate shall become obvious to all.

What were these issues?

In **'Achievements of the Genius of Scott,'** Harriet Martineau argues that moral sciences are best taught by exemplification, and 'unprofessionally': that is, by dramatists and novelists, instead of moralists whose job it is to systematise a science, and present it in dry, abstract terms. Scott's works, she felt, had taught society the importance of benevolent actions and racial tolerance, the right of women to be treated as rational beings, and the evils of fanaticism and priestcraft. But as she indicates in the letter to Tait, she considered that Scott's contribution to the moral code had often been negative, unconscious, or overlooked by himself. He might have done much more; he might have tried to communicate a philosophy which he had thought out, and could illustrate vividly by the interaction of his characters. She had little time for Scott's declaration that works of fiction have no great moral influence: 'we are not bound to estimate his works as lightly as he did,' she reminded her own readers and his. He had taught the next generation the power of fiction as an agent of morals and philosophy: it was now their responsibility to profit from this lesson, and not merely by flat imitation of his style and plots. The 'progression of the age' required appropriate literature to reflect and further it:

If an author of equal genius with Scott were to arise to-morrow, he would not meet with an equal reception; not only because novelty is worn off, but because the serious temper of the times requires a new direction of the genius of the age. Under pressure of difficulty, in the prospect of extensive change, armed with expectation, or filled with determination as the general mind now is, it has not leisure or disposition to receive even its amusements unmixed with what is solid and has a bearing upon its engrossing interests.

Harriet Martineau speaks here as a clear prophet of mid-Victorian high seriousness, the representative of a growing public concern about individual integrity and knowledge, political responsibility (which the 1832 Reform Act was beginning to extend) and the role of every man, woman and child in a changing, interdependent society. Anticipating Bulwer in *England and the English,* she takes up the reviewers' cry for a weightier intellectual content in the novel, and sets a pattern followed, whether consciously or not, by subsequent critics of Scott, including Carlyle, Walter Bagehot and Sir Leslie Stephen. (pp. 10-11)

Harriet Martineau's main argument in her second Scott paper was that a writer could not satisfy the public's appetite for philosophy unless he looked below the aristocratic class for his leading characters; an idea similar to that of the *Fraser's* critic, who denied that any 'silver-fork' novelist could offer an instructive commentary on human affairs. She felt that tastes had changed, to reflect the acceleration of political reform, and that the novelist must, in turn, keep pace with the reader:

> The bulk of the reading public, whether or not on the scent of utility, cannot be interested without a larger share of philosophy, or a graver purpose in fiction, than formerly; and the writer who would effect most for himself and others in this department must take his heroes and heroines from a different class than [sic] any which has yet been adequately represented.

This is the most important point she makes: that the novel must widen its scope dramatically, to bring in all the social groups and individuals that were usually considered unworthy of notice, except as caricatures or incidental figures. Most novelists employ a chorus of peasants or servants, and useful sets of doctors, lawyers or shopkeepers. Scott did this himself, and went further, choosing, for example, Jeanie Deans, as heroine of *The Heart of Midlothian,* and offering many detailed descriptions of poor cottagers and their way of life. Harriet Martineau admired Jeanie, but was still dissatisfied. 'There is not a *character* from humble life in all his library of volumes; nor had he any conception that character is found there,' she complained:

> Faithful butlers and barbers, tricky lady's maids, eccentric falconers and gamekeepers, are not those among whom we should look for the strength of character, the sternness of passion, the practical heroism, the inexhaustible patience, the unassuming self-denial, the unconscious beneficence—in a word, the *true-heartedness* which is to be found in its perfection in humble life. Of all this Walter Scott knew nothing.

Scott, she suggests, regarded strength of soul as the exclusive attribute of the higher classes (the knightly hero, for example); whereas she wanted novelists to show that precisely the same heroic struggles go on in the spirit of an ordinary working man, facing conflicts of another kind. In short, Scott 'knew not that all natural movements of society, that he has found in the higher, exist in the humbler ranks; and all magnified and deepened in proportion as reality prevails over convention, as there is less mixture of the adventitious with the true'. As a statement of literary principles, published when most novelists and readers were still entranced by the glamour of Almack's and the latest levée, this should be seen as a radical plea for greater sympathy, courage, and ambition in the next generation of novelists. Harriet Martineau believed that the poor should be shown experiencing all the passions and finer feelings normally associated with high-born knights and ladies, and that new authors should overrule existing literary conventions, and introduce compassionate portraits of working-class characters into their pictures of contemporary life. A boundless field lay open before anyone who was keen enough to try: 'no less than the whole region of moral science, politics, political economy, social rights and duties.' The widest interests and the richest materials seemed to her untouched: 'for there has yet been no recorder of the poor; at least, none but those who write as mere observers; who describe, but do not dramatise humble life.'

Significantly, the place where she makes a similar statement of the changes she wished to see in modern fiction, is in her own miniature imitation of the fashionable novel. The difference is that Lord and Lady F—, hero and heroine of the story **'For Each and For All'** (1832) are no ordinary pair of frivolous-minded aristocrats, but embodiments of all Harriet Martineau's own theories about feminism, socialism, the treatment of domestic servants, regulation of the labour-market, financial speculation, and the vast areas of unexplored territory still left to the novelist. She gives Lady F— an acting background, based, apparently, on what she knew of Fanny Kemble: at least, wrote Fanny in her memoirs, 'Miss Martineau once told me that she had derived some slight suggestion of the character from me.' She may also have been influenced by Madame de Staël's *Corinne* (1807), which caused a great sensation among early nineteenth-century women readers; but her mockery of the 'silver-fork' school soon shows through:

> Everybody agreed that she was beautiful, and very amiable, and astonishingly simple, and conducting herself with wonderful propriety: and everybody admired the good-natured earl's manner towards her, and wondered whether it was lady Frances's own choice to come with her, and conjectured what Lord F—'s happiness must be to witness his bride's flattering welcome to the rank he had given her.

The parody is perfect, though too soon submerged in long dialogues about co-operation and competition. But at the close of the story, Lord and Lady F— glance ironically at themselves as potential subject-matter for a novel, and conclude that writer and readers must be satisfied without much narrative. The action, they assume, is all internal, reflected in their conversations; but the plot has its surface excitements. Lady F— tears round London in search of moneylenders to help her reckless brother-in-law, Mr Waldie, survive an enormous financial risk, which leaves him 'as rich as Croesus,' but an imbecile, destroyed by brain fever. Indeed, all the *Illustrations* have their share of deaths, drownings, and other high drama: **'Ella of Garveloch'** (1832) ends with the accidental death of Ella's idiot brother, Archie; **'Cousin Marshall'** (1832) opens with an account of a warehouse fire; Dora, in

'Ireland' (1832) is transported as a convict, and Jane in '**The Farrers of Budge Row**' (1834) dies at sea in a reckless bid to evade the income tax man. Harriet Martineau was astute enough to realise that most readers needed some inducement to read on to the Summary of Principles at the end of each number. But she meant to concentrate on the emotional experiences of her characters, who were to struggle with problems central to their existence, and talk about them. Lady F— begins the crucial discussion of artistic principles, which enables Harriet Martineau to end her story with a forceful declaration of her own ideas on the proper function of the novel:

> The true romance of human life lies among the poorer classes; the most rapid vicissitudes, the strongest passions, the most undiluted emotions, the most eloquent deportment, the truest experience are there. These things are marked on their countenances, and displayed by their gestures; and yet these things are almost untouched by our artists; be they dramatists, painters, or novelists.

Like Wordsworth, who had chosen his subjects from 'low and rustic life,' as he explained in his Preface to *Lyrical Ballads,* because the passions were there 'less under restraint, and speak a plainer and more emphatic language,' she suggested that the poor revealed their feelings in a way that was impossible for the self-conscious and brittle rich, trained to conceal their private emotions at public assemblies. Moreover, the daily life of the rich was often monotonous. Lord F— wonders why so many 'painters of life' prefer to show even the fundamental human experiences of birth, marriage and death in aristocratic settings. 'They take Love,' he tells his wife, 'and think it more becoming to describe a Letitia going to the altar with a Lord F—, than a weaver and his thoughtful bride taking possession of their two rooms, after long waiting and anxiety.' Life in its reality, Letitia agrees, cannot be known to those classes who are set above the basic toils; and yet these are the very classes who supply the fine arts with most of their material. Lord F— proposes that the aristocracy should have their sympathies broadened by reading and seeing true images of the classes below them: an idea repeated in the second Scott article. Letitia then summarises:

> Yes; let humble life be shown to them in all its strong and strange varieties; not only in faithful butlers and housekeepers,—in pretty dairy-maids and gossiping barbers. Let us have in books, in pictures, and on the stage, working men and women, in the various periods of their struggles through life.

As in the critique of Scott, Harriet Martineau protests about the peopling of novels with 'stage' peasants, too quirky or decorative to embody much deep-seated feeling.

She could not expect any instant results from her criticisms, except through her own exertions in the remaining political economy stories, and the tales she wrote afterwards. Literary patterns evolve slowly and gradually, as one generation dies away, and the next finds the old tools unsuitable for new uses. But her attack on the fashionable novel, and her plea for new material, seem to anticipate George Eliot's criticisms of literary convention in 'The Natural History of German Life' (1856) and *Adam Bede* (1859). (pp. 12-16)

Though Harriet Martineau's direct influence on other writers is difficult to establish, she took the lead in literary experiments, testing new methods and ideas, and suggesting approaches for other writers to try. Even when she had stopped

writing fiction, she thought of fresh possibilities; was half inclined to emerge from full-time journalism and begin another novel. A letter to Henry Reeve implies that she was stimulated by the shortcomings of other novelists and felt she could do better. 'I sh[ould] very much like to throw myself into the scenery, external & internal, of worky-life,' she admitted: 'I dare say you are aware (it now strikes me) how entirely Mrs. Gaskell fails, except in single portraits & collecting anecdotes. Her personages are a museum of oddities, each one of which has struck her fancy, some time or other.'

This was a criticism more often levelled at Dickens than at Mrs. Gaskell; but in the 1850s, when George Eliot, Charlotte Brontë, Mrs. Gaskell and Dickens were publishing regularly, Harriet Martineau read their novels, and often attacked their concepts of realism, usually through a neutral correspondent. When Mrs. Gaskell's *Life of Charlotte Brontë* appeared, she thought of basing a general critical article on it, partly about biographies, but also indicating

> what sort of knowledge of life, exterior & interior, is requisite for writing good fiction, in all ages, & especially in our own,—glancing at the differences of the same world as shown by CB, Dickens, Thackeray, Mrs. Gaskell, & Miss Austen, in proof of the necessity of very strict self discipline if pretending to exhibit life, or, as the alternative, explaining clearly that it is not actual life that is represented. I think, myself, that immense injury w[ould] have been done by CB's novels, as pictures of life (so vivid through the splendour of her genius!) but for the extreme roughness & coarseness of her people & their doings. With this, the beauty of much of her life contrasts charmingly.

In the event, her article was never published, but this short, informal piece represents her usual stance as a commentator. It shows particularly that she had formed a very decided concept of what, to her, constituted 'realism,' and the difference between vivid delineation and gratuitous, self-indulgent detail that was likely to give offence. Her relationship with Charlotte Brontë which foundered over Harriet Martineau's review of *Villette,* is especially illustrative of this.

The personal background to their disagreement is well known, and summarised in the **Autobiography.** After the two authors had read some of each other's works, and met in London in 1849, they became friendly enough for Charlotte to exact a promise from Harriet that she would give her a frank opinion of *Villette.* Reluctantly, the frank opinion was given, and the brief, affectionate friendship came to an abrupt end. Yet, as Harriet Martineau showed in her review for the *Daily News,* she found only two major faults with the novel, and was not, at the time, among the shocked or prudish critics who shrank from its 'coarseness'. This complaint seems to have been added later, after she had read *The Professor,* and marshalled her ideas for the Mrs. Gaskell article. While many contemporary critics attacked the Brontë novels on religious grounds, Harriet Martineau based much of her criticism on feminist principles, and a growing preoccupation with moral and physical health. She believed that *Villette's* failings were traceable to 'unwholesome influences': namely, the author's morbid condition of mind, and depressing home circumstances:

> We are wont to say, when we read narratives which are made up of the external woes of life, such as may and do happen every day, but are never congregated in one experience—that the author has no

right to make readers so miserable. We do not know whether the right will be admitted in the present case, on the ground of the woes not being external; but certainly we ourselves have felt inclined to rebel against the pain, and, perhaps on account of protraction, are disposed to deny its necessity and truth. With all her subjectivity, 'Currer Bell' here afflicts us with an amount of subjective misery which we may fairly remonstrate against.

She doubted whether so much pain suffered by one person was quite convincing as a reflection of 'true' experience. (pp. 18-20)

Harriet Martineau's second major criticism concerned the portrayal of women in love. 'All the female characters, in all their thoughts and lives,' she complained, 'are full of one thing, or are regarded by the reader in the light of that one thought—love.' It begins with six-year-old Paulina; it ends with the adult Lucy Snowe: all the women need to be loved. But, protested Harriet Martineau, who had got over her own fiancé's premature death, and toured the United States, Egypt and Palestine,

> It is not thus in real life. There are substantial, heartfelt interests for women of all ages, and under ordinary circumstances, quite apart from love: there is an absence of introspection, an unconsciousness, a repose in women's lives—unless under peculiarly unfortunate circumstances—of which we find no admission in this book.

(pp. 20-1)

[Martineau] was baffled by *Wuthering Heights* and *The Tenant of Wildfell Hall,* failing to understand how two young women could have had such experiences as their novels described. They claimed to be presenting life as they knew it. Trying to be tolerant, Harriet Martineau asked readers to remember this claim 'when disposed to pass criticism on the coarseness which to a certain degree pervades the works of all the sisters, and the repulsiveness which makes the tales by Emily and Ann [sic] really horrible to people who have not iron nerves.'

George Eliot's novels also troubled her initially. 'We have been reading "Clerical Scenes," & find them odious,' she told Henry Reeve, excepting only 'Mr Gilfil's Love Story' from the general censure: ' "Janet's Repentance" leads one through moral squalor as bad as Dickens's physical squalor, (in the Marshalsea & elsewhere). I am sure it is bad art in both,—& in all such cases. Plenty of "power",—of satire; but I don't like *coarse* satire.' Repeatedly she associated 'coarseness' with artistic failure. 'I am so struck with the amount of ability w[hich] at present goes into bad art,' she observed in 1861: 'Passing over Dickens,—what a specimen Miss Evans's last year's novel was! Then there is my friend, James Payn, whose short tales are exquisite,—what great & various ability he puts into novels which are downright disagreeable!' 'Miss Evans insists (or did formerly),' she added, 'that, in all the arts, true delineation is good art. This was before a disagreeable picture of a stork killing a toad. Being asked whether men on a raft eating a comrade w[ould] be good in art, she was silent; but repeated her dictum afterwards.' (pp. 21-2)

Why did Harriet Martineau apparently reject a rigorously pursued realist position, having, at the start of her career, so strongly endorsed it? Her criticism of George Eliot generally betrays a sense of offended propriety, though she herself was the author of tales once considered indecent. Some of this

dogmatism must be attributed to her disapproval of George Eliot's relationship with Lewes. She found it hard to accept that a great novel could be written by someone with a morally dubious private life, though she told Reeve that she had disliked 'Miss Evans' even before she had 'any notion of Mr. Lewes.' The Lewes relationship clearly soured her attitude, however, as it did Mrs. Gaskell's. 'I wish—oh *how* I wish Miss Evans had never seen Mr. Lewes,' Mrs. Gaskell lamented; while Harriet Martineau admitted she would be glad to die a year or two sooner, if that would change the authorship of *Adam Bede.* 'I admired her abilities, beyond expression,' she assured Reeve; 'but I did not much respect, or at all *like* her.'

Nevertheless, the artistic principles of George Eliot and Harriet Martineau were closer, on some points at least, than either acknowledge: not only in their shared belief that the fine arts should concentrate on the unromanticised poor for new and valuable material, but also in their sense of authorship as a social responsibility, with the power to educate. Every writer, George Eliot told Edith Simcox in 1878, was '*ipso facto* a teacher,—an educational influence—on his readers— and the lightest poetaster could not escape the weight of attendant responsibility.' Hence her anxiety about the permanent moral damage done to ignorant readers by misleading social novels which offered inaccurate representations of the people. Though her didacticism is far less concentrated than Harriet Martineau's, she still felt that novelists should pay the strictest attention to detail when presenting one social group to another.

It would be wrong to dismiss Harriet Martineau as the narrow-minded prude implied by her later, tight-lipped comments on 'disagreeable' literature, but her withdrawal from her earlier realist position is disappointing, and demands some further explanation. Undoubtedly, age and debility made her less tolerant than she had been; and, so often a harbinger of changing moral tastes, her views became more cautious and conservative as the century moved towards a stricter sense of what made suitable reading for the impressionable young. Yet even in the 1830s when she was still courageously open-minded, and insisted that novels were not to be judged by their fitness for children, there were signs of her later reservations about certain topics and the way they were treated. She draws, at times, a thin, idiosyncratic line between what was acceptable and what was not, excluding Smollett ('it disgusts me so utterly'), but not *Ernest Maltravers,* which one of her friends considered too 'immoral' for her children. She wrote firmly in her journal: 'I object to no real subjects into which pure moral feelings of any kind can enter. Whether they are, when finished, moral or immoral, depends on the way in which they are treated; whether in a spirit of purity and benignity, with foul gusto, or with a mere view to delineation.' Here seems to lie the germ of her subsequent objections to certain kinds of realism in the novel. Strong visual or sensual detail was only permissible, in her view, if it had a moral point to make; not if gratuitously paraded. Knowing that she was open to these changes herself, she defended her account of the baby murder in 'The Town' (1834) by explaining: 'It cannot but cost an effort to write and print what is so very disgusting; but, if we are to issue nothing that may not be misconstrued, we may give up the hope of doing the good that is most wanted.' Ironically, her moral position is very close to George Eliot's in her defence of 'Janet's Repentance'. The medium, the author's attitude, both emphasised, was the crucial factor in determining the overall moral effect of a story.

Provided the author's mind was not irreverent or cynical, the work itself might offer a valuable critique of issues outside the range of normal experience, especially for middle-class women. This remained one of the problematic areas in the realist debate about mid-nineteenth-century fiction.

As she read the latest novels of her near-contemporaries, Harriet Martineau found either that they touched too intimately on real life, or else strayed too far away from it. She condemned Dickens's inaccuracy about the Old and New Poor Laws, feeling that he played the 'sentimental philanthropist' without first making sure of his facts. The characters, conversations and incidents of *Hard Times* seemed to her totally unconvincing: 'Master and man are as unlike life in England, at present, as Ogre and Tom Thumb: and the result of the choice of subject is simply, that the charm of an ideal creation is foregone, while nothing is gained in its stead.' 'Unreal', 'unlike life', are the terms Harriet Martineau uses most frequently in her criticism of Dickens, whose works she sometimes enjoyed (*Pickwick Papers* she considered 'scarcely surpassable in humour'), but only when he kept within safe bounds. She wished his literary talents, diverse and excellent as she judged them, could be exercised 'under the broad open sky of nature, instead of in the most brilliant palace of art. While he tells us a world of things that are natural and even true, his personages are generally, as I suppose is undeniable, profoundly unreal.' George Eliot was to make a similar criticism of Dickens a year later, in 'The Natural History of German Life,' where she acknowledged his ability to render the external traits of his characters, but regretted that he rarely passed 'from the humorous and external to the emotional and tragic, without becoming as transcendent in his unreality as he was a moment before in his artistic truthfulness. Most critics of the 1850s, however, regretted that Dickens had abandoned the purely humorous for the more serious topics covered in *Bleak House* and *Little Dorrit*. Harriet Martineau shared the popular appreciation of his humour, but wished for a greater sense of realism, supported by thorough research of social abuses. There is little suggestion, in her criticism of Dickens, that she really understood or sympathised with his chosen approach to the writing of fiction, or was able to view his social-problem novels without reference to her own specific ideological viewpoint.

At first radical, and then more generally representative of the mid-century, decent, dogmatic middle-class outlook on the arts, Harriet Martineau's literary criticism settled gradually into a comfortable, idiosyncratic pattern. She knew her own likes and dislikes, and no longer wanted to struggle with new novels when she could enjoy her old favourites, Jane Austen and Scott. 'Books are, to me, divided mainly into two classes,' she told Edward Bulwer-Lytton, unashamedly:

> those I cannot read, and those I can:—these last are of innumerable kinds, with the one common quality of earnest thought. This provided, I become one with the writer so completely as to be unable to rise to any capacity of judging,—or to any right to compare my likings, (otherwise than experimentally) with those of better trained & qualified readers.
>
> (pp. 22-5)

From 1830 to 1855 (and later, in unpublished letters), Harriet Martineau devised for herself, and for the guidance of any other novelists who might accept her suggestions, a theory of fiction which preserved a fine balance between too stark a realism on the one hand, and too rosy and flimsy an idealism

on the other. She wanted both to expose the dangerous, and often morally offensive effects of bad legislation (as Dickens was to do, in *Oliver Twist, Bleak House,* and other social-problem novels), while providing examples of men and women who overcome their personal hardships through moral strength and integrity. Her chosen artistic form had to be flexible enough for Hogarthian descents into idleness and ruin, and Smilesian progresses into economic paradise. Her brand of realism had to be tempered so that it was not, in her own eyes, 'bad art': a revelling in sordid detail for its own sake. She could not justify the displaying of vice and misery, whether collective or individual, unless they were the direct result of remediable ills, fitting punishment for moral or economic transgressions, or the way to some higher spiritual reward. On the other hand, she disliked novelists who failed to teach their readers the value of more limited kinds of suffering: self-denial, family duties and hardships, fights gainst superstition, prejudice and other kinds of wrong thinking. She wished that Dickens, for example, had suggested a higher moral to sufferers, that he 'could show us something of the necessity and blessedness of homely and incessant self-discipline,' instead of dwelling on 'the grosser indulgences and commoner beneficence'.

Harriet Martineau's scattered comments on literature, her reviews, her private opinions in letters, and public prefaces in books, point to the narrative of personal trial, imposed by adverse circumstances, as her ideal plot-with-a-purpose, a place where romance and realism might combine most successfully. Such a narrative, she believed, would prove exciting to read, spiritually uplifting, and morally beneficial, besides relevant to the difficult times England was experiencing, socially and politically. 'We have had enough of ambitious intrigues,' she declared in her second Scott article:

> why not now take the magnificent subject, the birth of political principle, whose advent has been heralded so long? What can afford finer moral scenery than the transition state in which society now is! Where are nobler heroes to be found than those who sustain society in the struggle; and what catastrophe so grand as the downfall of bad institutions, and the issues of a process of renovation?

It was inevitable, given her literary principles, that her fiction should be closely tied to contemporary affairs. Her best opportunity to show human passions interacting with crises of national development came when she traced the careers of her political heroes, Canning, Peel, and Lord Durham, in her *History of the Peace;* but she felt that the vast social and legislative reforms of the time were actually outdoing fiction in their popular interest. Scott's novels had done so well, she argued, partly because he had been writing during a lull between the Napoleonic Wars and the great period of scientific advancement which followed shortly afterwards. She suspected the novel was a dying form, now that 'the general middle class public purchases five copies of an expensive work on geology for one of the most popular novels of the time.' The role of literature in society seemed to her to have changed irrevocably. (pp. 26-8)

Content to write no more fiction, she was to spend the rest of her life guiding public opinion on the government of India and Ireland, on American politics, and the Contagious Diseases Acts. By then the English novel was so freighted with 'earnest thought' that novelists were preparing themselves with exhausting factfinding missions. The Preface to Charles

Reade's *Hard Cash,* for example, seems like a parody of Harriet Martineau's regular research programme for each of her *Illustrations:*

> *Hard Cash,* like "The Cloister and the Hearth," is a matter-of-fact Romance—that is, a fiction built on truths; and these truths have been gathered by long, severe, systematic labour, from a multitude of volumes, pamphlets, journals, reports, blue-books, manuscript narratives, letters, and living people, whom I have sought out, examined, and cross examined, to get at the truth on each main topic I have striven to handle.

The very possibility of such a hybrid as the 'matter-of-fact Romance' must be, in part, attributed to the work of Harriet Martineau. Her ideas were inspired, as so often happens in literary history, by frustration with existing forms and practices; cross-fertilised, in this case, by the national enthusiasm for political economy, Utilitarianism and Useful Knowledge. But the relevance of her ideas goes beyond the restricted sphere of influence attainable, as a rule, by mere tract-writers. In theory, at least, her conception of the novel's range and purpose foreshadowed much of George Eliot's thinking (stopping short of her unmodified realism); and prepared the ground, more generally, for Dickens, Kingsley and Mrs. Gaskell. (p. 29)

> *Valerie Sanders, in her* Reason Over Passion: Harriet Martineau and the Victorian Novel, *The Harvester Press, Sussex, 1986, 236 p.*

## DEIRDRE DAVID  (essay date 1987)

[*David examines Martineau's position as a female Victorian intellectual and discusses her social thought.*]

In the characteristically self-opinionated fashion that either charmed or antagonised her literary contemporaries, Harriet Martineau tried to have the last say about her life and work. She wrote her own obituary, which appeared in the *Daily News* on 27 June 1876, two days after her death at the age of 74. Some twenty years earlier she had retired to her Lake District home, stricken with the heart disease she believed would very soon end her life, and never one to waste time, she immediately wrote an autobiography that is enjoyably informative about the Victorian literary world she confidently inhabited and surprisingly moving in its revelations of childhood unhappiness. Deploying the cool tone of the obituary writer, she also wrote a short memoir which answers and anticipates almost all past and future criticism of her life and work. It modestly asserts her successes, efficiently articulates her weaknesses, and performs an astute identification of three aspects of her literary production that succinctly sum up the significance of her work as a woman intellectual in early Victorian England.

No complex motives directed 54 years of virtually uninterrupted writing: 'Her stimulus in all she wrote, from first to last, was simply the need of utterance.' Intellectual and expository gifts are assessed as follows: 'Her original power was nothing more than was due to earnestness and intellectual clearness within a certain range. With small imaginative and suggestive powers, and therefore nothing approaching to genius, she could see clearly what she did see, and give a clear expression to what she had to say. In short she could popularize, while she could neither discover or invent.' And of her four volumes of English history, published between 1849 and

1864 and covering the period from the beginning of the peace in 1815 to the outbreak of the Crimean War in 1853, she says this: 'All that can be done with contemporary history is to collect and methodize the greatest amount of reliable facts and distinct impressions, to amass sound material for the veritable historian of a future day,—so consolidating, assimilating, and vivifying the structure as to do for the future writer precisely that which the lapse of time and the oblivion which creeps over all transactions must prevent his doing for himself. This auxiliary usefulness is the aim of Harriet Martineau's history'. Her performance as intellectual, then, is self-characterised as stemming from a need of utterance, as succeeding in popularisation but not in discovery, and as fulfilling an ancillary role. On the stage of English nineteenth-century intellectual history, she cast herself in a supporting part, one that served to highlight the star turns executed by her more luminous, and for the most part male, contemporaries. (pp. 27-8)

Watching, reading, and deciphering the social, cultural, and political signs of her time constitute the foundation of her career. What she says of her work in writing the volumes of English history, that she had engaged in 'consolidating, assimilating, and vivifying' so as to perform a work of 'auxiliary usefulness', may be said about almost all her writing. Just as 'a need of utterance' and a talent for powerful popularisation are generative marks of her career, so, too, is a mode of ancillary elaboration. In a manner that is both passive and active, her 'need of utterance' found its expression in energetic, vivifying analysis of what she quiescently, if alertly, observed: what she observed was ordered into an extensive literary production that legitimated in one form or another many of the influential political and social ideas of her time. This is not to say she was an officially empowered and self-proclaimed propagandist for the English middle-class values and manners with which she found herself most comfortable. Her elaborative 'auxiliary usefulness' was diffused and unannounced, part of the complex cultural processes whereby hegemonic ideologies are disseminated through institutions such as the press, the church, schools and universities rather than coercively imposed upon society. As she was the first to admit, she popularised and did not discover or invent the social and political theories that frame almost all her writing. Yet in a contradictory pattern I see as central to her significance as a woman intellectual, she lived an extraordinarily active, constructive life devoted to passive observation of a rapidly changing society in whose 'making' she believed she had no part. Either she could not see, or was compelled to disguise such knowledge, that her female work of journalistic popularisation 'made' Victorian England as much as did the male work of banking, business, and politics. This was an England she described as being in a constant state of positive alteration, following a sequence of development that she retrospectively imposed upon her own experience.

In what follows I shall argue that Harriet Martineau's career is defined by her auxiliary usefulness to a male-dominated culture. What is interesting about her is that she embraces her subordinate status, while at the same time aligning it with her forthright, courageous, and life-long feminism. (pp. 30-1)

Occasionally, Martineau's texts betray implicit uneasiness about her chosen career of auxiliary usefulness to powerful authority. In the metaphysical musings that enlace the sociological observations of *Society in America* (published in 1837), for example, she suggests that an individual may be seen in two irreconciliable ways: one, 'as a solitary being, with inherent powers, and an omnipotent will; a creator, a king, an inscrutable mystery'; and two, 'as a being infinitely connected with all other beings with none but derived powers, with a heavenly directed will; a creature, a subject, a transparent medium through which the workings of principles are to be eternally revealed'. Having articulated the familiar riddle of free will, she flatly asserts that both ways of seeing an individual are 'true' and leaves it at that. Never relinquishing her belief in a force outside human control that directs the ameliorative development of human affairs, she most certainly performed more as a subject and transparent medium in her intellectual practice than she did as a solitary and sovereign power. The early Unitarianism may have been succeeded by Comtean positivism, but Martineau's Necessitarian belief that the human will is not autonomous remained unshaken and she adamantly insisted that the 'constitution and action of the human faculty of Will are determined by influences beyond the control of the possessor of the faculty'.

To deny individual sovereignty, however, is not to abdicate from disciplined self-management. Her rigorous exemplification of Carlyle's Gospel of Work, her battle with feelings of rage and inadequacy, her active acquiescence in the laws of positive social change that can be seen, for example, in her schemes for improving lower-class housing and education while she lived in the Lake District, all testify to the fact that although she accepted the idea of eternal, immutable laws at work in the universe which broach no interference from the human will, she also believed that man (and woman) as *agent* of those laws may choose between active compliance or resigned submission. Martineau chose enthusiastic and vital compliance.

As Martineau embraced her function as explicating agent of theories of political economy and transparent medium of cosmic and social principles, her philosophical and religious beliefs became aligned with her particular position as woman intellectual in Victorian culture. As she achieved that alignment between intellectual function and gender, however, she implicitly undermined the male power that governed her intellectual life. In a subversive process that redeems her from an essentially uninteresting endorsement of dominant ideologies, she denies the omnipotence of man's will (and this is undoubtedly male will, for it is a king whose power is an 'inscrutable mystery') and welcomes the advent of man's highest honour in 'becoming as clear a medium as possible for the revelations which are to be made through him. Celebrating the dying of superstitious belief in self-originating power and welcoming the birth of a self-dedication of the human will to inscribed laws and principles, she sanctions a structure of instrumentality conjunctive with that of male intellectual authority and female ratification. However, Martineau's thought implicitly subverts male cultural and social power by declaring independence from outmoded beliefs in an omnipotence enjoyed primarily by men and welcoming dependence on certain laws which control the lives of both women *and* men. Martineau's preoccupation with the commonplace problem of free will, which bothered her from the age of six when she asked her brother James to sort it all out for her (he could not), is inextricable from her sexual politics.

For a woman intellectual of Martineau's social class and time, independence often took the literal form of leaving the patriarchal household in the provinces and moving to London. Ironically in the case of Martineau, however, she left the literal world of the father to devote herself to the intellectual needs of new 'fathers' such as Adam Smith, James Mill, Auguste Comte, and, in that later period of her life when she believed she was cured by mesmerism, Henry Atkinson. In effect, Martineau declares herself independent of patriarchal power and refutes the sovereignty associated with the omnipotent and punitive fathers of the Bible, with the Miltonic fathers of her childhood reading, and with the actual Norwich fathers who prepared their daughters for little more than marriage. Yet her relationship to institutions of power remains fraught with an ambiguity nowhere more arresting than in her polemical attacks upon the subjugation of women.

Harriet Martineau consistently introduced the Woman Question into almost all her writings. Displaying an assertive, vivacious prose and armed with an arsenal of personal observation, her feminist polemics took to the field of sexual politics with a steady aim. Women have risen, she scathingly declares, from a state of slavery (exemplified in the subservience of the Indian squaw which she observed with horrified distaste in America) to the 'highest condition in which they are present seen . . . less than half-educated, precluded from earning a subsistence, except in a very few ill-paid employments, and prohibited from giving or withholding their assent to laws which they are yet bound by penalties to obey . . . the degree of the degradation of women is as good a test as the moralist can adapt for ascertaining the state of domestic morals in any country. However, the feminist politics which Martineau tenaciously inserted into almost all her texts more frequently urge women to educated acceptance rather than angry refutation of their socially inscribed destinies, and the admirable clarity of her splendid indignation is sometimes blurred by the traces of male prescriptions for woman's role and function.

If there was anything more distasteful to Martineau than subjugated and debased womanhood, it was women who whined about their wrongs and rights: she wanted women to be more like herself, or at least as she imagined herself-rational, confident, the intellectual equal of any man, or certainly equal enough to sanction his ideas. Perhaps the most personal statement of her feminism is generated by Mary Wollstonecraft's politics, lamentably based, Martineau believed, on personal misery:

> Women who would improve the condition and chances of their sex, must, I am certain, be not only affectionate and devoted, but rational and dispassionate, with the devotedness of benevolence, and not merely of personal love. But Mary Wollstonecraft was, with all her powers, a poor victim of passion, with no control over her own peace, and no calmness or content except when the needs of her individual nature were satisfied. . . . Nobody can be further than I am from being satisfied with the condition of own sex, under the law and custom of my own country; but I decline all fellowship and co-operation with women of genius or otherwise favourable position, who injure the cause by their personal tendencies. . . . The best friends of that cause are women who are morally as well as intellectually competent to the most serious business of life, and who must be clearly seen to speak from conviction of the truth, and not from personal unhappiness . . . women, like men, can obtain whatever they show themselves fit for. Let them be educated,—let their powers be cultivated, to the extent for which the means are already provided, and all that is wanted or ought to be desired will follow

of course. Whatever a woman proves herself able
to do, society will be thankful to see her do,—just
as if she were a man.

Martineau's feminist programme is dictated by a dualistic
perspective on the sexes that unassailably values male over
female. It is to Mary Wollstonecraft's detriment that she permitted her conventionally female disposition to get the upper
hand and that she behaved just like a woman: a victim of passion, lacking control, obsessed with personal needs and unhappiness, she was essentially unstable when it came to the
'serious business of life'—which, it seems, is conducted best
by those who are analytical, dispassionate, capable of subor-
dinating personal need to 'the truth' (which remains undefined in this attack on feminism weakened by feminity). The
primary meaning of the sortie against Wollstonecraft is, of
course, a distaste for what Martineau perceived as her sexual
enslavement to men. Initially it might seem that Martineau
slyly advocates renunciation of men as a condition of constructive feminism—from the conventional Victorian perspective on women (and that perspective, together with Martineau's genuinely indignant criticism of sexual injustice,
guides this passage), what else could be the source of their
'personal unhappiness' except romantic suffering due to the
presence or absence of a man? Martineau here does not speak
of women's 'personal unhappiness' being caused by denial of
the vote, by the inability to own property in one's own name,
or by the lack of freedom to divorce one's husband. A separate sphere founded on feminist isolationism, however, is not
Martineau's goal: she seems more concerned with justifying
a system of sexual privilege based upon women controlling
negative qualities conventionally associated with their sex so
that they might, through behaving more like men, become
better partners for them—which seems to leave us with one
authentic sex and the other performing as emotional and intellectual transvestite.

Martineau urges the opportunity, through education, for all
women to acquire the power enjoyed by men so they may perform an equal, but not identical, part in the creation and elaboration of English middle-class values. For this is really the
core of Martineau's sexual politics—she wants women to participate in the dominant Victorian discourses of culture and
politics, to contribute to the creation and dissemination of the
beliefs and practices of the most powerful class in English society. But they have to do all this . . . in their own female,
essentialist fashion.

When she was offered the opportunity to edit a new periodical dealing with political economy, she noted in her journal
that an 'awful choice' was before her. If she undertook the
editorship she would have to brace herself to the task and suffer like a man: 'undertaking a man's duty, I must brave a
man's fate'. As it turned out, the advice of her brother James
persuaded her against such bravery and she chose to write a
novel instead, *Deerbrook* published in 1839. Editing a periodical, assuming the authority and responsibility entailed in
dealing with other writers—this is man's work in the public
world (undertaken with some skill, incidentally, by Mary
Ann Evans as unpaid assistant editor of the *Westminster Review*) and in order for a woman to do it she must accept a
man's disappointments as well as his rewards. I am not suggesting that Martineau should have rejected the prevailing
Victorian equation of leadership and masculinity. Rather, I
want to emphasise that Martineau's feminism must be examined within the cultural and social context in which it was articulated, its inconsistencies identified as expressive of the pa-

triarchal values inscribed, revised, and sometimes subverted
in that feminism. Obviously unaware that a mode of intellectual activity structured on imitation (suffer like a man, undertake a man's duty, brave a man's fate, and so on) is inferior
to its model, Martineau cannot be charged with a conscious
belief that women are inferior to men, and to castigate her for
flawed feminist politics would be to indulge in self-serving,
ahistorical criticism; if anything, my aim is to illuminate the
bravery of Martineau's feminism in the context of her legiti-
mating politics. Moreover, Martineau's unconscious articulation of prevailing patriarchal ideas about sex and gender must
testify to the entrenched power of the very beliefs she struggled to revise.

When Martineau travelled to America in August 1834 she received a rude shock. She set out with idealistic expectations
based on her understanding of American democratic principles. Practice did not turn out to match principle and the title
of the last section of her chapter on Morals and Politics, 'The
Political Non-Existence of Women', indicates her displeasure
with what she discovered. Significantly, none of her criticism
of the social and political status of English women is as vividly compelling as her matchless attack on the condition of
women in America. Her polemical emphasis evinces two
seemingly disjunctive views of English women, for while implying that they enjoy a higher degree of freedom, *Society in
America* seems also to afford Martineau the opportunity for
displacement of any uneasiness she may have felt about her
acquiescence in the English social and cultural discipline of
the female sex. It is as if the criticism of American society is
empowered by what Martineau has *not* said about the English treatment of women. The tone of these sections of *Society in America* is pugnaciously interrogative: 'One of the fundamental principles announced in the Declaration of Independence is, that governments derive their just powers from
the consent of the governed. How can the political condition
of women be reconciled with this? Governments in the United States have power to tax women who hold property; to divorce them from their husbands; to fine, imprison, and execute them for certain offences. Whence do these governments
derive their powers? They are not "just", as they are not derived from the consent of the women thus governed'. Perhaps
because Martineau has a text, the Declaration of Independence, by which to measure practice against principle, her
rhetorical mode is belligerently analytical, in contrast, say, to
the manner adopted in the *Autobiography* for examination of
her position as woman intellectual in English society: 'I have
no vote at elections, though I am a tax-paying housekeeper
and responsible citizen; and I regard the disability as an absurdity, seeing that I have for a long course of years influenced public affairs to an extent not professed or attempted
by many men. But I do not see that I could do much good
by personal complaints, which always have some suspicion
or reality of passion in them. I think the better way is for us
all to learn and to try to the utmost what we can do, and thus
to win for ourselves the consideration which alone can secure
us rational treatment'. With no institutionalised, inscribed
ideal before her by which to measure performance, she lapses
into a mild appeal for personal action, couched in the vaguest
of language suggestive of sentimental entreaties for people to
pull together in time of adversity. The attack on American
political practice in regard to women, resting upon direct in-
terrogation of the disparity between inscribed ideal and reality, forces the reader's assent to strongly stated criticism of injustice. In contrast, the passage delineating the absurdity inherent in Martineau's own position, that of professional rec-

ognition with no vote, is vapid, delivered in a style matching the essential powerlessness of her status. Her insipid remedy for sexual injustice is virtually meaningless—'I think the better way is for us all to learn and to try to the utmost what we can do'—and the hope of women 'winning' for themselves what is, by the standards applied to American society, only just, indicates propitiation of male authority, or if not that, a weary resignation to her unjust lot.

Throughout *Society in America* Martineau is an astute reader and analyst of the social panorama, at all times concerned with the 'process of formation' of social structures, revising the narratives of other English travellers to America who 'analyze nothing at all'. Always alert to the ways in which American morality and institutions are mutually determinative, she dissects virtually everything she sees. Despite her polemical appropriation of the Declaration of Independence for the uncompromising criticism of American treatment of women, she is characteristically unconcerned with the origin of morality and institutions, with the genesis of that 'process of formation' central to her social analysis. This is not an enquiry into the origins of American culture and society, nor a search for causes of the lamentable treatment of women: this is an analysis of the way in which social systems, either already formed or in a dynamic process of formation, actually work. As pioneer sociologist, Martineau performs an intellectual function somewhat similar to that enacted by George Eliot as novelist in *Middlemarch*. Each figuratively dissects the social web, traces the fine threads of reticular connection between morality and institution, and—allowing for the obvious differences between Martineau's sometimes hasty exposition and Eliot's finely meditated exploration and between sociological travel narrative and novel—it is possible to see both women performing a function characteristic of much women's intellectual practice in the nineteenth century, a function that inclines more to close observation of society than it does to theoretical speculation about its origin. This is not to say that only women writers in the nineteenth century tend more to descriptive than to speculative social analysis. My point is rather that the cultural authority to theorise about society, rather than merely observe the phenomena which is material for theory (an authority demonstrated, for example, in Mill's 'Civilization' and *On Liberty* or in Carlyle's 'Signs of the Times' and 'Characteristics') is more likely to be exploited by a male than a female writer. (pp. 44-51)

*Society in America* also contains a persuasively argued attack on slavery. Punctuated by sobering details of oppression and rhetorically varied with summaries of arguments both for and against the system, the attack is chillingly effective through the inclusion of moving personal narratives of slaves wrenched from their families and of shocking accounts of violence, including the sexual abuse of slave children; it is also composed with firm authority and a lucid, uncompromising style which indicates the clarity and thoughtfulness of Martineau's strong feelings. The unwavering courage she displayed in speaking her mind wherever she travelled in America, even in venturing to the South where her Abolitionist sentiments had preceded her, finds a stylistic parallel in the trenchant, stirring language.

Exerting a polemical power similar to that displayed in her sections on the treatment of American women, she refers to her chapter title, 'Morals of Slavery', in this way: 'This title is not written down in a spirit of mockery; though there appears to be a mockery somewhere when we contrast slavery

with the principles and the rule which are the test of all American institutions'. Practice is measured against principle, as it was in her attack on the oppression of women, and she discovers that the large moral gap is not only uneconomical and irreligious, but also absurd: 'in matters of economy, the pernicious and the absurd are usually identical'. She advances all possible arguments in favour of slavery that she may demolish them, ridiculing, for example, the slave owner's claim that an 'endearing relation' subsists between master and slave; in her view, it is a relation similar to that pertaining between a man and his horse or a lady and her dog. Always returning to her fundamental position that no man has the right to own another human being and always reiterating her call for 'an immediate and complete surrender of all claims to negro men, women and children as property', Martineau speaks with a confident authority notably absent from the vacillating description of her own unjust English lot.

As long as slaves remain property, rather than being liberated to the economic freedom of selling their labour power, as long as women remain uneducated, rather than being released to the social freedom of exchanging their value as rational wife for economic security, both slave owners and husbands end up with a very poor bargain. Slaves and uneducated women are cheap but worthless commodities. Workers owned as property rather than employed as labour, uneducated women cherished as decoration rather than valued as useful partners, labour treated as capital rather than as a purchasable commodity—all create stagnant economic, cultural, and social systems. Abhorring stasis in any form, Martineau locates the wife of a slave owner in a particularly stagnant position, mired in loathsome privilege. Freed from housework by her husband's status, she is herself a slave to overseeing her house slaves who, owned rather than having freely sold their labour power to domestic service, spend all their time lolling against bedposts and leaning on sofas. The wife of a slave owner exists in a condition of unofficial bondage to her husband, no more than sexual ornament and agent of his pernicious values.

If one considers Martineau's deployment of the metaphor of family for social organisation, then an informing correlative between her calls for women to become rational wives or economically independent employees, for the lower classes to become independent through acquisition of mechanical skills and education, for slaves to become proprietors of their labour as commodity, begins to emerge. The way to social adulthood for women, members of the lower classes, and slaves, is through ambitious individualism. (pp. 59-60)

In writing about the 'subordination of the sex' in *Society in America,* Martineau says that the progression or emancipation of any class usually, if not always, takes place through the efforts of individuals in that class. And so it must be for women: 'All women should inform themselves of the condition of their sex, and of their own position. It must necessarily follow that the noblest of them will, sooner or later, put forth a moral power which shall prostrate cant, and burst asunder the bonds (silken to some, but cold iron to others) of feudal prejudices and usages'. Characteristically employing verbs of action to describe progressivist ideas (the heroic woman will 'put forth a moral power' which will 'prostrate cant', 'burst asunder' degrading bonds), Martineau understands women as a social class, and in more modern terms than she would have employed, sees them as exploited by fathers, husbands and employers. In the most extreme example of female subjugation that she ever saw or could imagine, captive Egyptian women, beyond salvation, hideous in their subjugation, are described as being in a worse position than London slum-dwellers—'a visit to the worst room in the Rookery of St Giles's would have affected me less painfully. There are there at least the elements of a rational life, however perverted'. The English working class is capable of self-improvement through hard work and thrift, or at least so it goes in Martineau's rehearsal of the myth of a sensible ambition that sunders the social and historical constraints she both acknowledges and denies in her discourse as she simultaneously proclaims freedom through ambition and teaches subjugation to evolutionary laws. In much the same way that English and American women, once they become conscious of themselves as a degraded sex, will collect their moral power and break the bonds of 'feudal prejudices and usages', so the working class can overthrow antiquated social structures modelled on the feudal family of landowner and tenant. (pp. 60-1)

A central inconsistency emerges from Martineau's celebration of independence from social parenthood and her sanction of a mythical free market in which, as she puts it, the working classes 'may make their subsistence in any way that they may think best'. Unwilling or unable to recognise that what they thought best may not have accorded with the self-interest of their employers, she fails to see that the worker is both free and not free—a central contradiction of capitalism which, of necessity, remains alien to her understanding. The ambiguities of Martineau's political thinking in [sections of **The History of England during the Thirty Years' Peace 1816-1846**] originate in the ambiguities of the English middle-class politics that it is her apportioned role to sanction as organic intellectual produced by that class, and as the intellectual daughter performing work of auxiliary usefulness for male authority. (p. 65)

Attacking slavery, saluting the spirit of Reform, greeting technological change with sanguine forecasts of improvements all round, Martineau does, indeed, enact dutiful, daughterly work for her political fathers. This filial usefulness is further demonstrated in her ratifications of Western cultural superiority in **Eastern Life, Present and Past**. . . . **Eastern Life** is an important text in Martineau's sustained celebration of English middle-class values.

The very simple model of temporal evolution structuring Martineau's theory of organic political life and of dynamic social change, set forth in her narrative of reform (the past is reconstructed in terms of ameliorative stages leading to a transitional present which will lead to an even better future), is deployed to govern her narrative of Western superiority. Arguing for an enlightened understanding of cultures and religions far different from the British and the Christian, she goes on to propose that nineteenth-century Western Christianity is a more mature expression of man's religious impulse than that practised in ancient Egypt. The liberal plea for religious and cultural toleration stems, in fact, from a confident superiority—a culture that does not feel itself to be superior rarely argues for such toleration. Martineau was a vigorous representative in the Middle East of British womanhood, British imperialism, and British intellectual elaboration of the ideology of progress—in sum, a representative of the British representation of the East. (pp. 69-70)

Her plea for liberal toleration, for seeing with unprejudiced vision, is undeniably attractive, if hardly revolutionary: who would quarrel with her argument that the ignorant Christian

in an Egyptian temple, the proud Mohammedan in a Venetian chapel, and an arrogant Jew in a Quaker meeting house, are all one and the same bigoted thing, or deny that her equation of three forms of religious intolerance seems to imply an equal validity of religious belief and practice? Seeing with Martineau's unprejudiced vision, however, is not quite what it seems. What the Christian sees in Egypt is the 'beauty of the first conceptions formed by men' of religious deities, and while the reader is convinced of Martineau's sincere humanitarianism, there remains the undeniable elevation of nineteenth-century Christianity and British civilisation over all that has preceded it. First is not best in Martineau's thinking. Despite its colourfully documented petition for cultural ecumenism, **Eastern Life** is designed to justify British social, political, and religious systems in the nineteenth century. (p. 72)

Martineau's career as woman intellectual may well be understood in terms of filial relationships. She is very much a daughter of the male economists and politicians who constructed the shapes and ideas of her discourse. She welcomed her own agency, elaboration, and legitimation; and there is no better or more accurate characterisation of her professional life than her own—a career of 'auxiliary usefulness'. . . . Relishing her enactment of popularising services for middle-class Radical ideas, she performed as an organic intellectual: in her own terms, she performed as a dutiful daughter in her family and in her culture, always explicitly enacting work of auxiliary usefulness and always implicitly expressing the tensions and conflicts inherent in the careers of women intellectuals who succeed in what was, in Martineau's time, a man's world. Through a rational programme of disciplined work, she mastered that transgressive self of childhood and subdued a rebellious, feminist womanhood not amenable to subjugation and service. Whatever else one might say about Martineau, that she was bossy, a rigid and narrow thinker—perhaps as R. K. Webb would have it, 'a second-rate mind'—at least she had a mind that people knew about. She used that mind fearlessly to speak the subjugation of women by Victorian patriarchy. If only for that, she deserves admiring recognition.

When she came back from the Middle East, Carlyle wrote to Robert Browning, 'Miss Martineau has been to Jerusalem and is back; called here yesterday, brown as a berry; full of life, loquacity, dogmatism, and various "gospels of the east wind".' Despite Carlyle's patronising tone, I like this image of her—the intellectual woman, full of life, brown from stomping across the Sinai in her sensible boots, wasting no time in setting Carlyle straight about Eastern life. Martineau may have been an auxiliary intellectual, but she is a splendid Victorian, certainly as intelligent as any of her male contemporaries, and, I daresay, twice as energetic and tough minded. (pp. 92-3)

*Deirdre David, in her* Intellectual Women and Victorian Patriarchy: Harriet Martineau, Elizabeth Barrett Browning, George Eliot, *The Macmillan Press Ltd., 1987, 273 p.*

## FURTHER READING

Bosanquet, Theodora. *Harriet Martineau: An Essay in Comprehension.* 1927. Reprint. Saint Clair Shores, Mich.: Scholarly Press, 1971, 256 p.

    A biography in which Bosanquet attempts "to relate Miss Martineau's life and opinions, and her continual, if sometimes eccentric, progress toward the final phase of her remarkable career, to the personal influences which so clearly and powerfully affected her."

Courtney, Janet E. "Harriet Martineau." In her *Freethinkers of the Nineteenth Century,* pp. 198-239. London: Chapman & Hall, 1920.

    A biographical sketch that outlines Martineau's writing career and her intellectual development. Courtney asserts that "Harriet Martineau's place in the history of free thought is fixed, not so much by the positive value of her contribution to nineteenth-century philosophy as by her assertion of a woman's right to think."

Dentler, Robert A. "The American Studies of Harriet Martineau." *Midcontinent American Studies Journal* 3, No. 1 (Spring 1962): 3-12.

    A brief survey of Martineau's writings, focusing on "her style as a field observer (particularly in America), her ethnology of American life and her role as the first English translator of August Comte's *Positive Philosophy.*"

Dobrzycka, Irena. "Harriet Martineau and the English Social Novel." *Acta Philologica,* No. 11 (1980): 29-36.

    Praises the value of the *Illustrations of Political Economy* as literature and maintains that the work was a precursor of the English social novel.

Lipset, Seymour Martin. Introduction to *Society in America,* by Harriet Martineau, pp. 5-42. Gloucester, Mass.: Peter Smith, 1968.

    Analyzes Martineau's views on the United States, comparing them with those of other European commentators and emphasizing the originality and importance of the conceptual framework and the methodology she used in researching and writing *Society in America.*

Martin, Robert B. "Charlotte Brontë and Harriet Martineau." *Nineteenth-Century Fiction* 7, No. 3 (December 1952): 198-201.

    Includes brief explanatory background and the text of a letter written by a relative of Martineau's describing the meeting of Martineau and Brontë.

Pichanick, Valerie Kossew. "An Abominable Submission: Harriet Martineau's Views on the Role and Place of Woman." *Women's Studies* 5, No. 1 (1977): 13-32.

    Summarizes Martineau's attitudes regarding the political, economic, and social position of women in English society.

Pope-Hennessy, Una. "Harriet Martineau." In her *Three English Women in America,* pp. 209-304. London: Ernest Benn Limited, 1929.

    Describes Martineau's experiences during her 1834-36 trip to the United States.

Thomson, Dorothy Lampen. "Harriet Martineau." In her *Adam Smith's Daughters,* pp. 29-42. Jericho, N.Y.: Exposition Publishing, 1973.

    Examines Martineau's economic thought, especially as presented in the *Illustrations of Political Economy.* Thomson also comments on Martineau's purpose in writing the series, calling it "a successful experiment in adult education."

Walters, Margaret. "The Rights and Wrongs of Women: Mary Wollstonecraft, Harriet Martineau, Simone de Beauvoir." In *The Rights and Wrongs of Women,* edited by Juliet Mitchell and Ann Oakley, pp. 304-78. Harmondsworth, England: Penguin Books, 1976.

    Compares the feminist thought and writing of the three figures, all of whom, according to Walters, "belong to the same bourgeois feminist tradition." Walters contends that "though all three use very different vocabularies and concepts, their analysis of women's problems is essentially the same."

Wheatley, Vera. *The Life and Work of Harriet Martineau.* Fair Lawn, N.J.: Essential Books, 1957, 421 p.

    A general biography in which Wheatley remarks of her subject, "there has seldom been a Victorian figure so frequently misrepresented and misunderstood."

Wolff, Robert Lee. "The Novel and the Neurosis: Two Victorian Case Histories." In his *Strange Stories and Other Explorations in Victorian Fiction,* pp. 69-141. Boston: Gambit, 1971.

    Compares Martineau's *Deerbrook* with *Massollan* by Laurence Oliphant, asserting that both writers experienced "a sensational—neurotic—adventure" and that "each one wrote a neglected novel which on examination helps to elucidate the mystery of the author's neurosis."

Yates, Gayle Graham, ed. *Harriet Martineau on Women.* New Brunswick, N.J.: Rutgers University Press, 1985, 283 p.

    Writings by Martineau on women and feminist issues selected and excerpted by Yates, with an introductory essay by Yates on Martineau's place in the development of feminism.

# Joseph Ernest Renan

## 1823-1892

French theologian, historian, philosopher, philologist, autobiographer, dramatist, poet, and critic.

One of the most learned and versatile scholars of his age, Renan was a leading exponent of the progressive, scientific spirit in nineteenth-century critical thought. His works established a new direction for religious history by seeking to uncover the historical and psychological basis of modern religions through a careful consideration of geography, culture, language, political structures, and other factors. Renan's literary output was tremendous, but he is best known for his massive, multi-volume study of the development of Christianity from its Judaic origins to late antiquity, *Histoire des origines du Christianisme* (*The History of the Origins of Christianity*), and particularly for that work's first volume, *Vie de Jésus* (*The Life of Jesus*), an unorthodox interpretation of the New Testament that caused a critical uproar—and gained Renan immediate fame—by its rejection of the divinity of Christ. While the originality and depth of Renan's thought was widely acknowledged during his lifetime, he was also highly regarded as a stylist. Characterized by a playful and ironic scepticism, which critics have termed *renanisme,* Renan's literary style influenced several French authors at the turn of the century.

Renan was born on 28 February 1823 at Tréguier, Côtes-du-Nord, an ancient cathedral town in Brittany. Renan's family was from the petit bourgeoisie and had recently fallen on difficult times. His father, Philibert, a grocer and merchant-seaman, drowned at sea when Renan was five, and although his mother, Magdelaine Féger, continued the grocery concern, the family was left in a state of near poverty. However, Renan succeeded in acquiring a good education at Trégieur because the local clergy, who were regular customers at Madame Renan's shop, saw in her son a promising candidate for the Church. Consequently, he was enrolled in the local Collège ecclésiastique in 1832. Studious and reserved, Renan turned out to be a brilliant pupil, which helped to earn him, in 1838, a scholarship to the seminary of Saint-Nicolas-du-Chardonnet in Paris, where he embarked on an intensive study of classical rhetoric. Renan, however, also read widely on his own. He was particularly impressed by the philosophical writings of Georg Wilhelm Friedrich Hegel, whose theory of historical progress caused him to adopt a more critical attitude towards Catholic doctrines; for a while he even considered abandoning his studies. Nonetheless, he entered the seminary of Saint-Sulpice in October 1843 for a two-year course in theology. Although Renan benefited from his instruction at Saint-Sulpice—he began there the study of philology, which would later prove indispensable to his analysis of Western religions—he also felt increasingly doubtful about his career in the Church. After a long period of internal struggle, he left Saint-Sulpice permanently on 6 October 1845. For the next few years, Renan tutored in Paris at the Collège Stanislas and the Pension Crouzet. He also continued his philological studies and won recognition among his peers in 1847 for an essay he wrote on Semitic languages, which was

later published as *Histoire générale et système comparé des langues Sémitiques.*

The February Revolution of 1848 marked a turning point in Renan's life. Appalled by both the futile violence of the masses and the brutal handling of the uprising by the authorities, Renan responded by writing one of his most important books, *L'avenir de la science* (*The Future of Science*), a critique of contemporary society in which he rejected orthodox religion and affirmed his belief in science and social enlightenment under the leadership of an intellectual aristocracy. However, Renan, sceptical about the reception of such a provocative study, withheld the work from publication until 1890. In 1849, Renan was sent to Italy by Louis Napoleon, soon to be Napoleon III, to catalogue Arabic manuscripts located in various libraries. He returned in 1850 to Paris, where he supported himself by working in the manuscript department at the Bibliothèque Nationale. During the 1850s, Renan enhanced his reputation as a scholar with his doctoral thesis on Islamic philosophy, *Averroès et l'averroïsme,* which was published in 1852, and with two important collections of essays that provided an outline of his ideas on history and philosophy, *Etudes d'histoire religieuse* (*Studies of Religious History and Criticism*) and *Essais de morale et de critique.* In October 1860, Renan was invited to participate in an archaeological expedition to Lebanon, where he was to examine Pho-enecian inscriptions. But he soon displayed greater interest in studying the historic sites in the Holy Land in order to pre-pare for the writing of *The Life of Jesus,* the first draft of which he completed during his trip.

Upon his return to France in 1862, Renan was appointed pro-fessor of Hebraic, Chaldean, and Syrian languages at the Col-lège de France. However, his course was suspended after one day because he offended the conservative authorities with his opening lecture, in which he referred to Jesus merely as "an incomparable man." The controversy caused by this lecture was mild in comparison to the uproar generated by the publi-cation of *The Life of Jesus,* which finally appeared in June 1863. Although the work was an enormous popular success, it was vehemently condemned by religious traditionalists for its rejection of the supernatural aspects of Christianity. De-spite the controversy surrounding *The Life of Jesus,* Napo-leon III offered Renan an appointment to the Bibliothèque Impériale in 1864. This he refused, aligning himself instead with a group of intellectuals and society figures, including Gustave Flaubert and Charles-Augustin Sainte-Beuve, who denounced the Second Empire as philistine and materialistic. Renan returned to the Middle East the same year, where he spent two years in preparation for writing *Les Apôtres* (*The Apostles*), which appeared in 1866. Like the other remaining volumes of *The Origins of Christianity,* it had a more limited popular appeal than *The Life of Jesus,* but was greeted with less hostility by critics.

In 1870, Renan was travelling in Norway with Prince Jérome Napoleon, a member of the Imperial family, when the Fran-co-Prussian war broke out. The conflict, disastrous for France, had a marked effect on Renan, who previously had looked to Germany for intellectual and moral guidance. Renan now largely withdrew from public life. However, after the fall of the Second Empire in 1871, he was reinstated in his chair at the Collège de France, and in 1878, his reputation as a great critic, historian, and scholar firmly established, he was elected to the Académie Française. Renan continued to write prolifically in the eighties. *Souvenirs d'enfance et de jeu-nesse* (*Recollections of My Youth*), the author's memoirs, ap-peared in 1883, and the first volume of *Histoire du peuple d'Israël* (*History of the People of Israel*), his second major reli-gious study, in 1887. Renan's last few years were intellectual-ly fruitful. He worked on a sequel to *Recollections of My Youth, Feuilles détachées,* and continued lecturing at the Col-lège de France. But his health had begun to fail. During a trip from Brittany to Paris in October 1891 he caught pneumonia. By January 1892 he was seriously ill, and he died in Paris on 2 October 1892.

The intellectual basis of Renan's works was drawn from two sources: French positivism and Hegelian philosophy. As an adherent of positivism's progressivist ideology, Renan firmly believed in scientific rationalism, and he consistently applied an objectifying, inductive method to the study of human cul-ture. As a disciple of Hegel, however, Renan was intrigued by the notion of historical perfectibility. Hence the goal of his work was to uncover—through positivist methods of analysis and induction—the processes by which humanity was mov-ing towards a progressively more rational and enlightened state of existence. Renan felt that such processes were most clearly revealed in the evolution of languages and religion. In his first published work, *De l'origine de langage,* for instance, Renan argued that language was neither revealed through di-

vine intervention nor a simple product of the reflective facul-ties, but rather arose from the complexities of social interac-tion. He further developed his philological method in *Histoire générale et système comparé des langues Sémitiques,* in which he provided a comparative analysis of Semitic idioms. Renan adopted a more syncretic critical method in *The Future of Science,* in which he conjectured that history could be divided into three phases: the "mythical" phase, in which knowledge was projected in the form of religious myths, the "analytical" phase, characterized by scientific curiosity and the cold use of reason, and the final "age of synthesis," in which scientific progress would be reconciled with religious sentiment, or, as Renan stated, "where poetry, knowledge, and goodness are identical." In this scheme, science was conceived as a particu-lar historical discipline that would "decode" the inner logic of humanity's earliest myths through the careful application of comparative philology. The two collections of essays that appeared in the fifties elaborated on the basic program of *The Future of Science. Studies in Religious History* suggested the range and complexity of Renan's future endeavors in this field, reviewing the history of religion in the West from classi-cal Greek mythology to nineteenth-century Unitarianism. The subjects addressed in *Essais de morale et de critique*— European politics, Byzantine history, and Celtic poetry, among others—were more diverse, but unified by the com-mon themes of intellectual freedom and social progress. After the Franco-Prussian war, Renan's philosophical works be-came more pessimistic. In *Dialogues et fragments philo-sophiques* (*Philosophical Dialogues and Fragments*), for in-stance, he questioned whether social or intellectual progress was attainable at all, while his "philosophical dramas" of the 1870s and 1880s—which were never intended to be pro-duced—are generally regarded as vehicles for political criti-cism of the Third Republic. This is particularly true of the most notable of the dramas, *Caliban,* a continuation of Wil-liam Shakespeare's *The Tempest.* Here, Renan is cast in the role of Prospero, an alchemist-magician standing for an aris-tocratic social order whose power is overthrown by Caliban, symbol of unrestrained populism. Prospero's subsequent withdrawal from society into a state of idle speculation re-flects Renan's pessimistic view of the modern French state, in which he saw the forces of reaction and democracy en-gaged in a constant, futile struggle.

Critics assert that the importance of Renan's religious histo-ries eclipses that of his other works. *The Origins of Christiani-ty* is indeed Renan's central work. In this series, Renan in-tended to distinguish history from myth, and thus focused his attentions on the original sources and manuscripts of the New Testament. Most importantly, Renan wanted to show how Christianity arose out of a particular set of social and cultural circumstances. Hence, in *The Life of Jesus,* Renan attributed the ready acceptance of Christ's philosophy to its compatibility with the established ethical code of the Jewish people, but denied the supernatural aspects of Christ's life— including the miracles and the resurrection—because he felt they were unverified by actual experience. Jesus succeeded in winning over a large following, Renan explained, due to his charming personality and possession of a kind of innate reli-gious sentiment. Renan's portrait of Jesus was generally posi-tive, however. He was described as "doux, délicieux, char-mant," and the depictions of his journeys in Galilee are con-sidered among the finest examples of Renan's mature, deli-cate literary style that exist. The next two volumes of the se-ries, *The Apostles* and *Saint Paul,* illustrate the transition from Judaism to Christianity in the teachings of the disciples.

In the latter work, Renan expressed his latent hostility towards the dogmatic aspects of Christianity, blaming Saint Paul for misinterpreting Christ and inaugurating the "theological" phase of Christianity. Apart from these early works, two other volumes of the series are considered especially noteworthy. In *L'antechrist (The Antichrist)*, Renan created a memorable portrait of the Roman emperor Nero, whose obsession with Christian martydom and decadent aesthetic vision are extensively analyzed. Renan concluded his study of Christianity's origins with *Marc-Aurèle et la fin du monde antique (Marcus Aurelius)*. Essentially a parallel of Roman philosophy and Judeo-Christian theology, the work presented Marcus Aurelius' *Meditations* as a kind of secular alternative to the Gospels, suggesting that as a man Marcus Aurelius might be superior to Christ. In the *History of the People of Israel*, Renan critiqued the Old Testament in the same manner he analyzed the New in *The Origins of Christianity*. Here, he focused on the contributions of the prophets to Judaism, asserting that in the eighth century B. C., the prophet Isaiah anticipated both the cult of the messiah and the universal, socially progressive ethical code taught by Christ. Apart from his historical writings, Renan is also remembered for his *Recollections of My Youth*, noted for their serene, imagistic style. Tracing his life up until his departure from Saint-Sulpice, Renan described himself in the work as "a failed priest" ("Un prêtre manqué"), but reasserted a fundamental, optimistic theism.

During his lifetime, criticism of Renan's works centered on *The Life of Jesus*. Despite Renan's intentions to simply portray Christ in his historical circumstance, the Church was appalled by his claim that Jesus was entirely human and merely a distinguished prophet; Pope Pius IX called Renan the "European blasphemer," and the work was officially condemned by cardinals and bishops in the churches of France. Many scholars, journalists and academicians, however, praised the originality of Renan's endeavor, as well as the historical accuracy of his portrait of Christ. This dichotomy applies to *The Origins of Christianity* in general: the Church refused to accept Renan's unorthodox interpretations of his subjects, but more liberal commentators praised Renan's literary facility and skill at historical synthesis. Unfortunately, much of this commentary on Renan's religious writings is not available in English translation. Apart from these works, nineteenth-century critics were primarily interested in *Recollections of My Youth*, which they praised for its philosophical insights and poetic, subtly ironic style. In 1883, Henry James, commenting on the work, called Renan "the first writer in France," yet Renan's status as an important intellectual figure gradually declined early in the twentieth century. Some commentators, including the famed anthropologist Albert Schweitzer, pointed out faults and inaccuracies in *The Life of Jesus* overlooked by nineteenth-century critics. However, his works continued to be of interest to certain French writers and critics, especially Anatole France, who acknowledged him as a primary influence on his own writings. In the mid-twentieth century, scholars acknowledged the importance of *The Origins of Christianity*, yet interest in Renan shifted towards the secular concerns of *The Future of Science*. In recent decades, scholars have continued investigating this work, and have also begun to explore Renan's approach to philology. While the topical significance of Renan's works has greatly diminished over time, his social theories and method of studying comparative religions remain of great interest to historians and specialists.

## PRINCIPAL WORKS

*De l'origine du langage*  (philology)  1848
*Averroès et l'averroïsme, essai historique*  (history)  1852
*Histoire générale et système comparé des langues Sémitiques* (philology)  1855
*Etudes d'histoire religieuse*  (history)  1857
  [*Studies of Religious History and Criticism*, 1864]
*Essais de morale et de critique*  (philosophy)  1859
*Histoire des origines du Christianisme*. 8 vols.  (history) 1863-83
  [*The History of the Origins of Christianity*. 7 vols. 1897-1904]
*\*Vie de Jésus*  (history)  1863
  [*The Life of Jesus*, 1864]
*\*Les Apôtres*  (history)  1866
  [*The Apostles*, 1866]
*Questions contemporaines*  (philosophy)  1868
*\*Saint Paul*  (history)  1869
  [*Saint Paul*, 1869]
*La réforme intellectuelle et morale*  (philosophy)  1871
*\*L'antechrist*  (history)  1873
  [*The Antichrist*, 1896]
*Dialogues et fragments philosophiques*  (philosophy)  1876
  [*Philosophical Dialogues and Fragments*, 1883]
*Prière sur l'Acropole*  (prose poetry)  1876
  [*Prayer on the Acropolis*, 1963]
*\*Les Evangiles et la seconde génération chrétienne*  (history) 1877
*Caliban, suite de "La Tempête", drame philosophique* (drama)  [first publication] 1878
  [*Caliban: A Philosophical Drama Continuing "The Tempest" of William Shakespeare*, 1896]
*\*L'église chrétienne*  (history)  1879
*Lectures on the Influence of the Institutions, Thought and Culture of Rome, on Christianity and the Development of the Catholic Church*  (history)  1880
*L'eau de Jouvence, suite de Caliban*  (drama)  [first publication] 1881
*\*Marc-Aurèle et la fin du monde antique*  (history)  1882
  [*Renan's Marcus Aurelius*, 1892]
*Souvenirs d'enfance et de jeunesse*  (memoirs)  1883
  [*Recollections of My Youth*, 1883]
*Nouvelles études d'histoire religieuse*  (history)  1884
  [*Studies in Religious History*, 1886]
*L'abbesse de Jouarre*  (drama)  [first publication] 1886
  [*The Abbess of Jouarre*, 1888]
*Le prêtre de Nemi*  (drama)  [first publication] 1886
*Histoire du peuple d'Israël*. 5 vols.  (history)  1887-93
  [*History of the People of Israel*. 5 vols. 1888-96]
*Drames philosophiques*  (dramas)  1888
†*L'avenir de la science: Pensées de 1848*  (philosophy) 1890
  [*The Future of Science: Ideas of 1848*, 1891]
*Feuilles détachées, faisant suite aux "Souvenirs d'enfance et de jeunesse"*  (memoirs)  1892
*Ernest Renan—Henriette Renan: Lettres intimes, 1842-1845* (letters and memoirs)  1896
  [*Brother and Sister: A Memoir and the Letters of Ernest and Henriette Renan*, 1896]
*The Poetry of the Celtic Races, and Other Studies*  (criticism) 1896
*E. Renan et M. Berthelot: Correspondance, 1847-1892*  (letters)  1898
*Cahiers de jeunesse, 1845-46*  (memoirs)  1906

*Nouveaux cahiers de jeunesse, 1846*   (memoirs)   1907
*Correspondance.* 2 vols.   (letters)   1926-28
*Oeuvres complètes.* 10 vols.   (philosophy, history, memoirs, and dramas)   1947-61

*These works were published as *Histoire des origines du Christianisme* between 1863 and 1883, and were later translated into English and published between 1897 and 1904 in the collection *The History of the Origins of Christianity.*

†This work was written in 1848-49.

---

## THE NORTH AMERICAN REVIEW   (essay date 1860)

[*In the following excerpt from a review of* Essais de morale et de critique, *the commentator emphasizes Renan's originality, integrity, and moderate political tone.*]

Ernest Renan is still a young man, as yet only in his thirty-seventh year; yet he has won fame as an Oriental scholar second only to that of Sylvestre de Sacy. His mastery of the Hebrew, Arabic, and Syriac is so thorough, that he writes familiarly in each of these tongues, and in the whole range of philological research he has few superiors. His command of the French language, too, as the volume before us [*Essais de morale et de critique*] splendidly shows, is quite equal to his command of the Semitic dialects. A more remarkable series of essays, judged by literary merit alone, has not for a long time been issued from the French press. His *Essays on Religious History,* collected and published in 1857, were full of promise, which has been fully verified by this new series. It contains thirteen articles, all of them critical, and six of them on biographical subjects. The characters with whom he deals are De Sacy, the younger, as a representative of the liberal school, Cousin, Augustin Thierry, Lamennais, the Benedictine Luigi Tosti, and Creuzer, the German Professor. Besides these biographical criticisms, there are short discussions on the Revolutions of Italy, the "Secret History" of Procopius, the Arabic "Séances" of Haraïri, the mediæval farce of "Patelin," the French Academy, and the Poetry of the French "World's Fair." The closing article, which is long, elaborate, and full of recondite learning, is on the **"Poetry of the Celtic Races."** It is impossible to praise these articles too highly, whether for candor, insight, originality of view, breadth of scholarship, or beauty of style. Not a page is dull, and no page is without some striking thought. The tone of the volume is that of moderate, but very decided liberalism,—of sympathy with man, while there is due respect for institutions. M. Renan never defends despotism or arbitrary power, though he treats it fairly, and sometimes apologizes for its excesses. He believes in the possibility of human progress, and associates himself rather with Rémusat and Laboulaye than with Montalembert and Lacordaire. His vindication of Lamennais is generous and brave, yet he does not fail to show the weak side of this gifted apostate, and to deplore his spiritual self-destruction. M. Renan believes that it is possible to work within the Church for that end which the Church carries in its very idea. Occasionally, some of his sagacious remarks fail to commend themselves to our moral approbation. We cannot assent to the maxim in the article on Cousin, that "it is an excellent principle, always to act in office as if one's successor might be an enemy." Though not properly a political writer, M. Renan has shown, in these Essays, that he well understands both the Italian and the Turkish questions, and has a reasonable solution to give of the difficulties involved in them. His book has a rare charm for a thoughtful reader. (pp. 263-64)

> *A review of "Essais de morale et de critique," in* The North American Review, *Vol. XC, No. 186, January, 1860, pp. 263-64.*

## HIPPOLYTE TAINE   (essay date 1860-63)

[*Often considered the founder of the sociological school of literary criticism, Taine had a profound impact on the sociological criticism of the nineteenth century and on the development of Marxist critical thought in the twentieth. Taine argued that a work of literature can be totally understood as a product of three influences: race, moment, and milieu. By "race" Taine meant the combined physical traits and specific mental habits of a certain nationality of people, such as the French, the English, and so on. It is unclear for most critics what Taine meant by the term "moment," but it is generally assumed that it is either the sum of race and milieu, or simply the milieu of a particular time. The term "milieu" is the only one of the three that is still useful to critics. It includes, according to Taine's definition, not only the physical environment but also political and social conditions. Taine's formula of "race-moment-milieu" has often been severely criticized, and his emphasis on "milieu" as a major force in matters of art and literature has detracted from his standing in the history of literary criticism. In the following excerpt, Taine records his impressions of Renan and the French chemist Pierre-Eugène-Marcelin Berthelot, indicating Renan's lack of philosophical discipline as well as faults in his method of composing* The Life of Jesus. *Taine's remarks were written sometime between 1860 and 1863.*]

I have seen a good deal of Renan at Chalifer, and he also spent a whole evening with me.

He is, above everything, a passionate, nervous man, beset by his own ideas. He walked up and down my room as if he were in a cage, with the jerky tones and gestures of Invention in full ebullition. There is a great difference between him and Berthelot, who is as quiet as a patient, labouring ox, chewing the cud of his idea and dwelling on it. It is the contrast between Inspiration and Meditation.

Neither of them has the analytical habits of Condillac and of Bertrand, the mathematician. The one ferments slowly and obscurely, the other explodes. Neither of them goes methodically forward, passing from the known to the Unknown.

Renan is perfectly incapable of precise formulæ; he does not go from one precise truth to another, but feels his way as he goes. He has *impressions,* a word which expresses the whole thing. Philosophy and generalizations are but the echo of things within him,; he has no system, but only glimmerings and sensations.

In metaphysics, he is absolutely unstable, entirely lacking in proofs and analysis. Roughly speaking, he is a poetical Kant with no formula, exactly like Carlyle; I read him parts of the *Sartor Resartus,* which he thought admirable. He admits that he only perceives phenomena and their laws, that beyond lies an abyss, an X whence they derive, that we suspect something, very little, of it through the sublime sense of duty; we only know that in that Beyond there is Something sublime which corresponds to the sublimity of our sense of duty. In any case, that Something is not a Person; personality and individuality are only to be met with at the other end of physiology, at the extremity of phenomena and not at their beginning. Therefore there is no Personal God.

As to the soul, he does not believe in personal immortality; he only admits that of works. "My idea, the idea to which I have devoted my life, survives me. I myself survive it, in proportion to the love I have given it and the progress I have made with it."

Nevertheless he leaves a lacuna which only Faith and Symbols can fill, if only with simple allegories and pure presumptions; that is the nature of that supreme X, and of the correlation between a noble soul and that X.

"A Sceptic, who, where his scepticism makes a hole, stops up the hole with his mysticism." Berthelot laughed and called me a man of labels, when I told Renan that this was the definition for him.

For everything else, for psychological, historical and all other facts, he is a pure Positivist; he believes in natural laws only, and absolutely denies all supernatural intervention. (pp. 202-04)

Renan is not a society man; he does not know how to talk with ladies, but only with specialists. He lacks the talent of intriguing, of seizing opportunities. He is, before everything else, a man of one idea, the priest of a God. He prides himself justly enough on this fact.

His process of writing consists in throwing down bits of sentences, paragraph headings, here and there; when he has arrived at the sensation of the whole, he strings it all into one.

He read me a long piece of his *Life of Jesus*. He is writing delicately but arbitrarily; his documents are too uncertain and not accurate enough. He puts together all the gentle and agreeable ideas of Jesus, apart from sad ones, makes of them a charming, mystical pastoral, which he dates from the stay at Nazareth. Then, in another chapter, he gathers every threat, every bitterness, and frames them within the journey to Jerusalem.

Berthelot and I vainly told him that this is putting a novel in the place of a legend; that he spoils those parts which are certain by a mixture of hypotheses; that the clerical party will triumph and pierce him in the weak spot, etc. He will hear nothing, see nothing, but his idea. He tells us that we are not artistic, that a simply positive and dogmatic treatise would have no life about it, that Jesus has lived and must be made to live again, that he does not care if people howl, etc., etc. He is neither cautious nor diplomatic. (pp. 204-05)

> *Hippolyte Taine, "Conversations with Renan and Berthelot," in* Life and Letters of H. Taine: 1853-1870, *translated by Mrs. R. L. Devonshire, Archibald Constable & Co. Ltd., 1904, pp. 202-05.*

## [JOHN BROWN PATON]    (essay date 1862)

[*In the following excerpt from a review of* Histoire générale et système comparé des langues Sémitiques, *Paton commends the clarity of Renan's style and his incorporation of historical and ethnological considerations into his philological method, but disputes his interpretation of important Biblical events as scientific phenomena as well as his views on the historical origins of the Semitic languages.*]

The Hebraists and Biblical scholars of both hemispheres have long wished that some one would do for the Shemitic languages what Bopp has accomplished with so much genius, judgment, and learning on behalf of the 'Comparative Grammar' of the Aryan tongues. It is the aim of M. Renan—though not, we are sorry to say, out of any love for the Scriptures or Christianity—to supply this great desideratum; and in [*Histoire générale et système comparé des langues Sémitiques*] we have the first instalment of the work, which France seeks to set by the side of its famous German prototype. The two philological fields are very dissimilar. Bopp's is enormously larger than Renan's; and its growths present a variety in age, aspect, and organization, such as is not to be found within the narrower borders of its neighbour. And this unlikeness naturally leads to a different mode of treatment on the part of the one writer and the other. In the nature of things, Bopp was compelled to limit himself very much to the scientific analysis and comparison of the languages which came within the sweep of his criticism. History and ethnology,—always important as guides and checks to philological induction,—while never lost sight of, must here remain, for the most part, in the background. They were too vast, too complex, often too dim and intangible, to be successfully used and dealt with. On the other hand, the fewness, the structural sameness, and the lifelong firmness of the Shemitic tongues rendered it an easier task to combine the historical element with the logical in the discussion of them, and so could hardly fail to suggest to the comparative critic the importance of securing the advantages which would come of uniting the two. M. Renan does this; and though the part of his work, which will enable us to put him in the balance with Bopp, is as yet unpublished, this first volume of it, devoted to the history of the Hebrew, Aramæan, Arabic, and their kin, illustrates very strongly the use of the double method, and makes the reader regret continually that the German philologer was not in circumstances to adopt the like plan.

Of its kind, M. Renan's book is a prodigy. It is as graceful, erudite, brilliant, and intensely pagan a book as we ever met with. Nothing can exceed the clearness, piquancy, and general force of the author's style. His sentences flow on like a stream of music. You never doubt his meaning; and his words stand for thoughts. Where other men would be bewildered, Renan sees as by intuition; and where others would go on crutches, he often runs like a giant. His knowledge of his subject is large and accurate; and, when certain conspicuous prejudices do not interfere, his literary judgments are usually sound and sagacious. He is never at a loss for his materials; and his mind turns corners with surprising quickness. At once solid and sparkling, bold and subtle, he wields a magician's wand; and the enchantments of it are mighty. We grieve to add, that he is an utter disbeliever in Divine revelation. The Old Testament languages and literature, of course, occupy a large space in his work; yet, so far as we remember, from one end of it to the other there is not so much as a solitary hint at anything like the idea of the supernatural inspiration of either Moses or the Prophets. On the contrary, the author assumes and teaches throughout, that the entire series of phenomena, to which his thesis leads him, belongs as strictly to the sphere of natural causation, as the motions of the planets or the formation of a coral reef. A writer in the *Times* of January last—we hope not the distinguished scholar to whom the article has been assigned—speaks of M. Renan's scepticism with something like respect, because of its fearlessness of consequences. We do not share this feeling. Fearlessness of consequences may be a virtue; and it may be a vice. It is often only another name for a rampant recklessness, or a blind and portentous inconsideration. Where great interests are at stake, and, above all, such as are involved in belief or disbelief of the historic truth of the Bible, scientific criticism is bound to be eminently regardful of consequences; and in so far as it may incline to doubt, it is only worthy of anything approaching to respect, when its reasonings are marked by the utmost caution, modesty, and devoutness. M. Renan's scepticism has none of these features: it is rash, dogmatic, and self-confident. It is a foregone conclusion with him, that the Old Testament writers did not speak as they were moved by the Holy Ghost; and he not only keeps the handkerchief tight upon his eyes, whenever the facts that meet him threaten his theory, but, as if the discernment and honesty of this province of the world of letters were concentred in himself, he makes no account of those who differ from him, and rides with the satisfaction of a conqueror through the ruin he has caused. . . . At present we content ourselves with expressing the deep regret we feel, that a book of so much beauty, worth, and power, should be marred by an irreligiousness which strikes to the core of many of its literary principles and arguments.

In the preface to his work, after stating the circumstances under which it was originally published, M. Renan proceeds to expound and vindicate the double method which he has followed in the treatment of his subject, showing, in a few luminous and forcible sentences, how halting and dull-sighted theoretical philology must needs be without the helps which history affords her. He then calls attention to the singular fact, that, while the Shemitic tongues were the first to be brought into grammatical and lexical comparison with one another, they have been the last to come under the dissecting knife of the youthful science of comparative language. The lights which the Jewish grammarians of the tenth and eleventh centuries fetched from the Arabic and Aramæan for the illustration of the Hebrew, the polyglott labours of the great Hebraists of the seventeenth century, and even the wild and arbitrary match-making of the school of Schultens, were all so many heralds of the birth of that true inductive system, according to which languages are now judged and compared. Yet another linguistic group has hitherto enjoyed all but the lion's share in the interest of modern philologers; while the Shemitic forms of speech—forms which, because of their constancy and homogeneousness, might have been expected to be the earliest to be scrutinized—remain still, for the most part, unexplained and untouched. M. Renan accounts for this on the principle that, though the boniness of the Hebrew and its fellows renders them an admirable study in philological anatomy, they are too unelastic and inanimate to satisfy the aspirations of science, or give full play to what are presumed to be its functions. In this very circumstance, however, our author finds a reason why the languages in question should not be neglected. Comparative philology is in danger of being intoxicated with its own successes. It needs to be kept within bounds. Here is an element that will help to steady it. If Shemitic speech is less various, less luxuriant, and less lifelike than that of the Aryans, it is also more fixed, more definite, more surely reducible to order and law; and will therefore be likely to foster in the student that sober, wary, and circumspect habit of mind, which well-conducted scientific investigation so strongly calls for. Some of the critical doctrines, which M. Renan lays down in connexion with this point, are worthy of golden letters. We only wish he had shown himself more uniformly loyal to them. Indeed he is quick-sighted enough to see, that his readers will not fail to remark the chasm which divides his precepts and practice; and he deprecates their censure on the ground, that antiquity is often tangled, and that generalities are always open to criticism. How this plea can sustain the cause on behalf of which it is put in, we are at a loss to imagine. To our simple apprehensions it seems as though both the fact and the truth, of which it is made up, form the strongest possible argument in favour of the caution and reserve, which M. Renan at once commends and disregards.

The first of the five books into which the author distributes his work, is devoted to a series of discussions on the general character of the Shemites and their speech, on the primitive geographical domain of the Shemitic tongues, and on the question of the origin of dialects, viewed with special reference to the group of languages here under consideration. In all that is advanced on these subjects, there is much to admire and muse over; much also, which cannot be too little accounted of or too soon forgotten. Were it not for the flies, the apothecary's ointment would be priceless; for the hundred pages which these discussions take up are full of striking thoughts, ingenious arguments, and brilliant generalizations. (pp. 285-88)

Books II., III., and IV., of M. Renan's work, occupying together several hundred pages, are constructed on the same general plan, and treat respectively of the three great divisions of Shemitish speech, historically considered: namely, the Hebrew branch, including the Hebrew proper and the Phœnician;—the Aramæan branch, comprehending, first, the Chaldee of the Scriptures, Targums, and Talmud, with the Syro-Chaldaic and the Samaritan; secondly, the pagan Nabathæan and Tsabian; thirdly, the Syriac;—and last of all, the Arabian branch, embracing the Himyaritic, Ethiopian, and Arabic. Of this whole section of the volume, apart from certain monstrous principles and dogmas similar to those on which we have already animadverted, it becomes us to speak in terms of the highest respect. It is a wonderful product of richly gifted and cultivated mind; and we are at a loss to know whether to admire most the fine philosophical spirit, or the unobtrusive wealth of learning, or the bright, full flow of language, which the reader will find in every part of it. The keensightedness with which M. Renan perceives both the correspondences and the diversities of various types of speech, and the striking and felicitous manner in which he paints them, could hardly be exceeded by Ruskin or De Quincey. On all these accounts we deplore the more deeply the presence of so much which religion and reason must agree to condemn. (p. 303)

[The concluding section of M. Renan's volume] is worthy of its position. It well represents both the strength and the weakness which precede it. Great and little, certain and dubious, true and untrue, walk side by side. A noble philosophy joins hands with a crutched and muscleless theorizing. Historical scepticism, such as will not allow a fragment of tradition to pass its lips, is seen coupled with a scientific credulity, which makes no difficulty of swallowing camels. Here, as in other parts of the book, M. Renan within the circle of profane history is one person, and M. Renan on the ground of Scripture and Revelation is another. We have not full faith in all the positions and arguments of the passages in which he treats of the general laws of the development of the Shemitic languages, and compares these with languages of other families, particularly the Indo-European. We think there is much more fancy than truth in the correspondence which he endeavours to exhibit between the geographical situation of the three great members of the Shemitish family of speech, and their several characters. Neither do we believe that within the historical period there has been any such germination and growth of the Shemitic tongues as he speaks of. 'The Hebrew,' he says, 'would unquestionably have become as rich as the Arabic, if time and other circumstances had favoured;' and in support of the assertion, he points to the Rabbinical dialect. 'The Hebrew called Rabbinical is the proof of this;' only 'the development in this case is in point of fact a chaos.' Exactly. The tendency of the Hebrew to expand and fructify appears in the circumstance that it rotted away. We fear the logic of this will bear no closer examination than the statement immediately following it, that the Hebrew possesses in embryo nearly all the processes, which constitute the wealth of the Arabic. If anything more is meant by the term 'processes' here than what is purely syntactical, the dictum is directly contradicted by the entire history of language. M. Renan goes on to speak of the 'dual' in Hebrew, and of the fuller development of the form in Arabic, as if the latter tongue had set out with the poverty of its brother in this respect, but had traded so well with its little, that it had eventually become much. Who does not know that this flies in the face of universal analogy? Where is the historical development of the dual in Greek or Anglo-Saxon? Yet both languages had a fair field, and ought, on M. Renan's theory, to have borne a plentiful crop of the form in question. In like manner, when we hear our author roundly affirm, with the Tatar languages in sight, that nomadic tribes are eminently conservative of their modes of speech; and again, that 'the Shemitic and Coptic have nothing in common in respect of their dictionary;'— these and the like assertions torment our admiration of him, and render us less disposed than we might be to allow other and less questionable doctrines to pass without challenge. A wary reader, however, who knows where to drop the grain of salt, will derive abundant pleasure and benefit from the study of the paragraphs we speak of. Indeed, it would be hard to pass too high commendation upon them, considered as a whole. The nice philosophical perception, the clear-sighted, manly judgment, the ample and well-sorted-learning, the exquisite literary taste, which show in most parts of them, are above all praise.

We wish we could use the like terms in characterizing the passage on the primitive unity of the Shemites, with which the book ends. We have no objection to M. Renan's holding, if he pleases, that the difference between Solomon and Plato may be explained by their early sires having lived, one on one side of a mountain, the other on the other, and by their having dieted respectively on barley and maize. But when he tells us, that the Aryan race in the beginning was for a long period a worshipper of its own sensations, and continued to be such till the Shemite taught it better; when he states, that intuitively the Shemitish stock 'first disengaged its personality from the external world, and then almost immediately inferred the third term, God, the Creator of the universe; when Adam and Paradise are explained by him, in a transcendental sense, to be logical sequences of the belief of the Shemites in the Divine unity; and when the ridiculous legends of India and Persia are seriously quoted as parallels to the most ancient records of the Books of Moses, we submit that the writer entirely overlooks—what he is bound to make the utmost account of—the grand and hitherto unshaken moral and historical argument for the literal truth of the Pentateuch and of the Scriptures in general, and that science, in speaking thus, is playing the merryandrew where she ought to take her most dignified and reverent air. We have no desire to bar or to fetter scientific

investigation by force of authority. Let the physicist and the historian do their own work in the way that is proper to it. We contend, however, that the basis on which the historical truth of the Bible reposes is a scientific one, and that science is bound to pay respect to science. And the utter disregard of this principle by M. Renan, and by the school to which he belongs, we complain of as a grievous injustice done alike to religion and true knowledge.

We lay down this remarkable volume with mingled feelings of sadness and joy. Genius is not wisdom; and darkness knows how to make friends with daylight. M. Renan has done his generation and mankind a great service by what he has here written; yet his blessing has a curse in it; and we much fear in many cases the curse will eat up the blessing. Pleasure is near neighbour to pain, as Socrates said. It is so in the present instance. Scepticism has achieved its worst within the region of Old Testament history. M. Renan cannot be outdone. We know all that can be said, on this ground, against Moses and the Prophets. We record our honest conviction, when, in view of the results, we express our unaltered faith, that this ancient 'foundation of God standeth sure.' (pp. 316-18)

[*John Brown Paton*], in a review of "Histoire générale et système comparé des langues Sémitiques," in The London Review, *Vol. XVIII, No. XXXVI, July, 1862, pp. 285-318.*

### [JOHN BROWN PATON]   (essay date 1864)

[*In the following excerpt from a review of* The Life of Jesus *that addresses the philosophical and religious context of the work, Paton praises the beauty of Renan's style and the integrity of his scholarship but disputes his rejection of the supernatural elements of Christianity.*]

This book [*Vie de Jésus*] has created deep and wide-spread interest alike on the Continent and in our own country. The theme of the book is one of transcendent importance. Whilst it controverts and repudiates everything supernatural or miraculous in the history of our Lord Jesus Christ, and *tanto magis* His proper Deity, it reconstructs for us His history denuded of His Divine glory, with a most cunningly exquisite grace, in accordance with the stern conditions of the *soi-disant* high criticism of our age. The book is written with that consummate art, delicate poesy, sentiment, and thorough scholarship, which have distinguished the previous productions of M. Renan, and placed him in the first rank of living writers. It is undoubtedly the worthiest and greatest work of a purely infidel cast which has been written this century. Written, moreover, with a warm luxuriousness of style, and a subtle refinement of feeling which is almost feminine, and charms the reader's sensibilities like a perfume, it will insinuate its infidelity into many minds which a hard or flippant dogmatism would revolt. And issued in our country at a time when so many clerical harbingers have been labouring to unsettle the Christian faith of their countrymen, and to prepare the way for this beautiful Avatar of modern infidelity, we do not conceal from ourselves the welcome it will receive, the evil it will work. We purpose accordingly to subject this book to a grave, prolonged, and searching criticism. We do so not only because of the seriousness of the occasion which we deem the publication of this book to present,—M. Renan's authority, the truth imperilled, and the insidiousness of the danger, conspiring to augment its gravity,—but also because this book resumes within itself, and exhibits in a palpable and luminous form, certain tendencies of our age which we desire to signalise to our readers, as without an acquaintance with these tendencies it is impossible to interpret the extraordinary religious phenomena of the present time, and especially to explain either the conception and elaboration of such a work as the **Vie de Jésus** by a scholar like M. Renan, or the *éclat* that has hailed its appearance. The first of these general influences which are flowing like currents over the educated mind of Europe is the result of what is called in France *la renaissance religieuse,* 'the religious revival.' . . . The revival and ascendancy of Ultramontanism in Catholic countries . . . give the most astonishing proof of the new spirit that animates the nineteenth century. The powers of the priesthood are exalted, the churches and confessionals are thronged, a very much deeper feeling of superstitious attachment to the Papal Church and her ministers prevails among the masses of the Catholic countries (with, perhaps, the exception of Italy) than could have been dreamt of last century or in the beginning of this. Now let it be understood that the true explanation of this fact is to be found in the revulsion of the human soul from the blank atheism which the Propaganda of wits and philosophers diffused among the people before and during the French Revolution, and the awakening of the religious sentiment, which may for a time be obscured, but which never can die. Eloquently and truly has Emile Saisset set forth this truth. 'So long as our earthly life never yields us perfect happiness, so long as there is in man, together with his reason which meditates upon the mysteries of eternity, an imagination which can realise them in anticipation, a heart which trembles in presence of the Unknown, and that mysterious and profound disquietude which no reasoning can wholly allay, religion will be the most sublime sentiment of the human heart and the most powerful force in social life. These are truths of all times and places. Let any one, therefore, now carry himself back to the moral state of France after the storms of the Revolution; if he thinks of the venerable religious customs of the people which were violently broken down,—of that religious sentiment which is yet stronger than these customs, crushed by tyranny,—of a clergy, which scepticism had enervated, recovering in the midst of persecutions the virtues of the early Church and the sympathies of the people; if he thinks of the many illusions that had vanished, of the many hopes that were disappointed, of the blood that was shed, of the many unforeseen ills that had fallen, and were now irreparable,—then, reviewing all these causes, I am afraid that this great movement of *la renaissance religieuse* which has left its literary date in the *Génie du Christianisme,* and its political date in the Concordat, can give him no cause of astonishment.

There are two facts connected with this great Catholic revival, as it is vauntingly styled, which have further to be noted. Its influence has not confined itself to the masses of the people in the Catholic countries of Europe: it has given a bias and a tone, which are every day becoming more manifest, to the studies and writings of the scholars of these countries—pre-eminently of France. The indifference and materialism of the Encyclopædists have quite vanished from the highest French literature. With the exception of the well-known work of Michelet, entitled *Du Prêtre, de la Femme, et de la Famille,* and the cold glittering essays of the young and brilliant Taine, we could not point to any writings of living authors, which perpetuate the style of Voltaire and Diderot; and even these exceptions are greatly modified by the higher spirit of the age. Though pantheism colours the speculations of the most re-

nowned writers, yet all of them manifest the reverence and earnestness of a religious sentiment. Some few years ago, religious subjects were tabooed in the *Revue de deux Mondes;* as M. de Pressensé informs us, the editor's refusal to the introduction of such subjects being couched in the words, *'Il n'y a pas d'actualité'* in them. Now scarce a number appears without a brilliant monograph on some distinct religious theme. Studies connected with the religions of mankind, and especially with Christianity, seem to have a fascination for the leading thoughtful writers of France. The names of Guigniaut, Quinet, De Remusat, Maury, Nicolas, Colani, Emile Saisset, Laboulaye, Montegut, Rigault, Jules Simon, Vacherot, and Renan, will immediately suggest to those acquainted with French literature the space and prominence that religious speculations have recently held in that literature, and the distinction of the men who have engaged in them. But the religious sentiment which confessedly animates the writings of such of these distinguished scholars as are Catholics is profoundly Catholic. The difference between a Protestant and a Catholic thinker who have been respectively trained in Protestant and Catholic communities, is not to be estimated by the mere divergence or antagonism of their opinions. It is a generic difference of religious feeling. The associations that have subtly woven themselves around the fibres of their moral nature; the form of religious truth that has occupied and coloured their imagination; the thoughts that have touched and thrilled the sensibilities of their heart;—all these are radically different, and their combined influence goes to produce, even in men who have cast off the dogmatic faith in which they were nurtured, modes of religious sentiment which contrast vividly with each other, and which reveal their immense disparity in every conception they form of religious truth, and the discussion of every problem in religious history. A man whose Protestant training brought his mind into immediate contact with the moral discipline and the spiritual truth of the Bible, and whose worship was directed to the Father through the Son, can never assimilate himself with a man whose first and strongest religious sympathies were wound upon an image of the Holy Virgin, or of the *Saint Cœur,* and whose young imagination was fed by the mystic romances of the *Lives of the Saints.* The difference between the clear breeze of heaven and the warm incense of the oratory, is not greater than the difference between the religious sentiment that may linger in the soul of these men even after the expiring of their faith. We venture to affirm that no Protestant could have written M. Renan's **Vie de Jésus.** But we must study to appreciate the influence of the Catholic training of M. Renan, in order to estimate and criticise his work.

Another tendency in our age is manifested in the growth and pretensions of historical criticism, or, as it sometimes styles itself, *high criticism.* Now we cannot better express the growth and arrogance of this new science than by quoting an introductory passage from M. Renan's article on **'The Critical Historians of Jesus.'**

> [Study] the march of criticism since the Restoration, you will see it, always following the line of its inflexible progress, replace, one after another, the superstitions of an imperfect knowledge by the truer images of the past. A certain regret appears to attend every step that is made along this fatal way; but in truth, there is no one of those gods, who have been dethroned by criticism, who does not also receive from criticism more legitimate titles to adoration. It is at first the false Aristotle of the Arab and of the commentators of the Middle Age,

which falls under the blows of the Hellenists of the fifteenth and sixteenth centuries, and gives place to the authentic and original Aristotle; then it is Plato who, raised up for a while by the scholastic peripateticism, preached at Florence as the Gospel, finds his true titles to glory in descending from the rank of a revealer to that of a philosopher. Then it is Homer, the idol of ancient philology, who now appears to have descended from the pedestal on which he stood three thousand years, and assumes his proper beauty in becoming the impersonal expression of the genius of Greece. Then it is premature history, hitherto accepted with a gross realism, which becomes so much better understood as it is more severely discussed. A courageous march from the letter to the spirit; a difficult interpretation, which substitutes for the legend a reality a thousand times more beautiful, such is the law of modern criticism.

It was inevitable that criticism, in this ardent research into the origins of mankind, should encounter that collection of works, products more or less pure of the Hebrew genius, which, from Genesis to the Apocalypse, form, according to the point of view one takes, either the most honourable of sacred books or the most curious of literatures. To arrest the human spirit on that slope was impossible. However, as orthodoxy was still the law of the exterior life, and even of the most of consciences, it was believers who first essayed biblical criticism. Vain illusion, which proves at least the good faith of those who undertook that work, and the fatality which drags the human spirit, once set on the ways of rationalism, to a rupture with tradition, which at first it avoids.

This march of critical science in history is a phenomenon of high significance. The laws of cautious, inductive investigation which have effected such marvellous discoveries in physical science, have been applied with equal enthusiasm and success to the domain of historical research. Vast treasures have been unearthed from their hiding-places in distant regions, and heaped together for the analysis of the scholar. New mental appliances for the study of human history have been discovered, and rapidly improved; such as comparative ethnology, philology, and mythology. And inductive science, with its rigorous probation, its contempt of prescriptive authority, and its slow tentative processes, has doubtless cleared away much of the legendary mist which hung over the ancient traditions of every land and people, and illumined for us in many places the actual scenes of the early life of man. There is now a science of history. That science allures many of the noblest minds of our time, because of the intrinsic nobleness of the study, which is the study not of matter, but of man; and every European literature is continually enriched by master-works of historical criticism.

There are, moreover, two systems of philosophy which have exercised predominating influence on the intellectual movements of our age, and which combine to place the philosophy of history, based upon historical criticism, as the culminating science which crowns and completes the monument of human knowledge. These are positive philosophy and the ideal pantheism of Hegel. (pp. 457-62)

M. Renan unites in himself, and exhibits in the clearest form, these ruling tendencies of our time. He is a positivist. In his famous article on *The Metaphysics of Religion* by Vacherot, he repudiates and denies altogether the possibility of meta-physics. He repeatedly and most unhesitatingly declares that every fact reported as miraculous is false—that there is no miracle. He affirms that every phenomenon in human history, whether in an individual or in society, is the inevitable result of certain conditions inherent in that individual, or in the society: or, in his own words, the phenomena of history are only the regular development of laws as unalterable as reason and perfection. This doctrine he applies in rigid sincerity to the history and influence of Jesus: 'A more extensive view of the philosophy of history will thus make us understand that the true causes of Jesus are not to be sought outside of humanity, but in the bosom of the moral world; that the laws which have produced Jesus are not exceptional and transitory laws, but the permanent laws of the human consciousness.'

M. Renan is still more pronounced as a pantheist. The hard, irreligious secularism of the positive philosophy would not attract many minds, in this age, when there is so powerful a *renaissance* of religious sentiment felt in society. It is the alliance of pantheism, which allows and fosters a certain self-satisfying religiosity of feeling, with positivism, and their identity in scientific methods, pampering the vanity of the human intellect, as pantheism indulges the proud self-deifying religiousness of the human heart, which fascinate with so strong an allurement men like M. Renan. His pantheism, however, is open and daring, though it might not be detected by an unsuspecting reader of the *Vie de Jésus.* Let our readers peruse these passages, which 'arrange in order God—Providence—Immortality,—so many good old words, perhaps a little gross, (*un peu lourds peut-être,*) which philosophy will interpret in senses more and more refined.' 'Eternal beauty will live for ever in that sublime name, (that of Jesus Christ,) as in all those which humanity has chosen in order to remind itself of what it is, and intoxicate itself with its own image. *This is the living God. This is what we should adore.*' 'The absolute of justice and of reason only manifests itself in humanity: regarded out of humanity, *that absolute is only an abstraction;* regarded in humanity, it is a reality. *The infinite only exists* when invested in a finite form.' 'Religion is the aspiration to the ideal.' 'A man who takes life seriously, and employs his activity in a pursuit with a generous aim, he is the religious man. A frivolous, superficial man, with no high morality, he is the impious man.' Compare with these passages the whole of the article on Feuerbach, in [*Etudes d'histoire Religieuse*]. Respecting immortality, the following are his clearest sentences, which are worthy of Buddhism:—'We affirm that he who will have chosen the good will have been truly wise. He will be immortal; *for his works will live* in the definitive triumph of justice. Whilst the wicked, the fool, and the fribble will wholly die, in the sense that he will leave nothing in the general result of the work of his race; the man devoted to good and beautiful things will participate in the immortality of what he loves. The works of the man of genius and of rectitude will alone escape the universal decay.' . . . In another passage of the *Vie de Jésus,* however, he seems to crave for another immortality than that of his works; the passage is remarkable:—'Those who do not stoop to conceive of man as a being composed of two substances, and who find the theistical dogma of the immortality of the soul in contradiction with physiology, love to rest in the hope of a final reparation, which under an unknown form will satisfy the want of the human heart. Who knows but that the last term of progress, in millions of ages, may bring forth the absolute consciousness of the universe, and in that consciousness the awaking of all that has lived? It is certain that moral and virtuous humanity will yet have its revenge, that one day the sentiment of the honest poor man will judge the world, and on that day the ideal figure of Jesus will be the confusion of the frivolous man, who has not believed in virtue, and of the egotistical man, who has not been able to attain it.'

Now to those who know the tenour of pantheistic speculation, a better creed of pantheism could not be exhibited than in these passages. It is not for us to explain M. Renan's inconsistencies. These are his regulative beliefs, solemnly announced. Yet how replete with a species of religious feeling are all his works! This gives them an exquisite charm. He is drunken, in a sense, like Spinoza, with the Divine. Regarding all high aspirations, all heroism and sacrifice, all religious faith, all forms and productions of beauty, all morality and truth, as but the emanations—the manifestations of the Divinity in man, he expatiates in them with delight and adoration. It is the ideal in man that he worships: but so saintly and fervid are his hymns, so tenderly rich his sentiment, so reverent his homage, that his religiousness is felt to be sincere and profound. And yet to us Protestants it is inexplicable. No German or English pantheist, though devout in temperament, like M. Renan, *could* endure it. It has the false and hectic flush, the sickening odours of Catholic sentiment. M. Renan, though of Jewish extraction, was trained among the Jesuits. Like his compatriot, M. Lamennais, he is a native of Bas-Bretagne, where attachment to Catholic faith is intensely strong; and his early Catholic nurture, which enveloped and saturated his opening mind, still colours and taints his conceptions of all religious truth and history in a manner which makes them, at times, revolting to Protestant thinkers. Hence arises his conception of the character and of the life of Jesus, which, notwithstanding all the adulation he bestows upon Him, is more repugnant to us than the clearer, harsher profanity of our English or even of the French Deists. A womanly amiability of heart, which dispenses with stern integrity, such as Catholicism has divinised in the Virgin Mary, and still more in the worship of the *Saint Cœur,*—and a cruel asceticism,—a Manicheism which despises the good of this life in hope of another, such as Catholicism apotheosizes in its Calendar of the Saints: these two great poles of religious sentiment in the Catholic world still abide as the polar magnets in Renan's soul; around which all religious life centres, and upon which it hangs. That revelation of the righteousness of God in His love, which Protestantism exalts, and by which the highest and inexorable demands of the conscience are satisfied, in harmony with a fulfilment of the heart's wants, has never enlightened M. Renan. His religious sentiment is unhealthy religiousness—unrighteous sentimentality. . . . [It] is this which assures us that, whilst we consider his book the ablest attempt that has been made to construct a hypothesis of the life of Jesus, and the origin of Christianity, as phènomena produced by natural causes, it is an hypothesis which will incense the moral sense of England, and rouse a far deeper indignation than the less plausible and more dogmatic work of Strauss.

Now that we understand the principle of M. Renan, and the atmosphere in which his mind has been formed, we shall be able more intelligently and effectually to criticise his work. It is he—a positivist, a pantheist, and who has been a Catholic—a disciple of the Jesuits—who has now written the *Life of Jesus.* Let us not, however, ignore the splendid qualifications wherewith M. Renan is endowed and equipped for the task he has set himself. His life has been enthusiastically devoted to historical studies, especially to dredge the dark depths of human history, in which the origins of the great

functions of humanity, viz., language, laws, and religions, are buried. His intense curiosity has fixed his mind upon the growth of religions; and to the exploration of this profoundest, most mysterious, but noblest theme, he has made all his other acquisitions instrumental. It is thus he conceives the grandeur and the method of this inquiry: 'The religion of a people, being the most complete expression of its individuality, is, in a sense, more instructive than its history. The religious legend is the proper and exclusive work of the genius of each human family. India, for example, has not left us one line of history, properly so called. Scholars sometimes regret it, and would pay its weight in gold for some chronicle, some table of kings. But in truth we have better than all that; we have its poems, its mythology, its sacred books—we have its soul.' 'Religions hold so deeply to the inmost fibres of human consciousness, that a scientific interpretation of them becomes at a distance almost impossible. Full of life, of meaning, and of truth, for the people who have animated them with their breath, they are nothing more to our eyes than dead letters, sealed hieroglyphics: created by the simultaneous effort of all the faculties acting in the most perfect harmony, they are for us nothing more than an object of curious analysis. To make a history of a religion, it is necessary to believe in it no more; but it is necessary to have believed in it.'

And in his Preface to the **Etudes d'Histoire Religieuse** he thus avows his passion for these studies. He says that, in the volume, he exhibits 'the principal forms which the religious sentiment has assumed in antiquity, the middle age, and modern times. These subjects have an attraction for me which I do not dissemble, and which I cannot resist.' In further preparation for his great work on the origin of Christianity, of which the **Vie de Jésus** is but the first instalment, M. Renan has studied very profoundly all the monuments of the Shemitic race, from which Judaism and Christianity have flowed to the world. His great work on the **General History and Comparative System of the Semitic Languages,** of which hitherto the first part alone has appeared, is a witness of his marvellous industry and aptitude in this field of research. Whatever influences surrounded the cradle of nascent Christianity, and moulded in any way its manifestations, were the outgrowth of Semitic character, which was grandly featured in the Semitic tribe,—Beni Israel,—and of the developments in the heart of the Semitic people at the beginning of our era. It is universally confessed that Western civilisation—that Greek or Roman ideas—made no impression upon the purer life of the Israelites, save to close it up in a deeper seclusion and narrower concentration than in their earlier history. If M. Renan's theory be true, that Christianity was not only influenced in form, but derived in essence from these sentiments of the Semitic people, that it was entirely the product of the inherent conditions of Israelitish society at that time; M. Renan has, more thoroughly perhaps than any other man, comprehended these conditions, and prepared himself to vindicate his theory by scientific evidence. In addition to his extensive labours among the antiquities and extant literatures of Semitic nations, he has, as he informs us in the Introduction of his **Vie de Jésus,** made special study of the Apocryphal Scriptures,—of Philo, Josephus, and the Talmud; the great sources of illumination, apart from the New Testament, upon the religious and mental condition of the Jews at the time of the Lord. Still further, he has spent months in the Holy Land, and gathered into his sympathetic spirit every influence, from climate or scenery, that might quicken or colour the sentiment of Jewish society, or of a solitary and lofty religious genius. If, then, M. Renan fails, as he has irretrievably failed, in establishing his thesis, it is because his thesis is false and undemonstrable. We regard, consequently, M. Renan's work as one of the widest and firmest ramparts built in outer defence of the citadel of Christian faith. If the *Life of Jesus* cannot be restored back to those elements of thought and feeling, hung in solution in his age, and which were only crystallized in him;—if *this product* which exists is not the resultant of these inherent conditions of society in that time and country;—then, with a mighty rebound, the argument drives home the conclusion:—Since it is not a natural product, the effect of natural causes, it is supernatural. Since it is not of man, it is of God.

We need not to inform our readers that M. Renan has a magnificent prose style, and that he knows how, with the certain eye and the fine touch of a perfect artist, to chisel out his conception in statuesque and graceful form. His book is a chef d'œuvre of literary art. Each image, too, that adorns his work is luminously pure as the light of diamonds. What the imagination and grace of a poet could do in order to set off, in the harmony and verisimilitude of truth, M. Renan's ideal *Life of Jesus,* is done here. And more, there breathes throughout the book a monotone of sadness which one cannot but feel to be a refrain from the heart of the critic who avows that he has one special qualification for acting the part of a true critic of the life of Jesus: *he has believed, but believes no more.* Yet the heart lingers tenderly over the wreck of its purest joy. The empty alabaster box has yet the sweet fragrance of the precious ointment clinging about it. This feeling awakens unconscious sympathy in the reader, and conciliates even his judgment in favour of the writer. What a work upon this highest of all human themes—the origin of Christianity—M. Renan, thus gifted and accomplished, might have achieved if his faith had survived! The one fundamental axiom of his book, which he maintains to be the foundation of all criticism, 'that there is no miracle,' travesties the real life of Jesus into an impossible, because unnatural, romance. In the execution of his task, to show how natural causes have produced what is supernatural, he outrages truth and probability at every step, and himself concocts an impossible, because an immoral, miracle in the character of Jesus, in order to dispense with the congruous miracles of mercy as of power which blend in the life and attest the divinity of our Lord. Assuming—for this assumption is the groundwork of the entire work—that the supernatural is false, he has necessarily to erase all that is superatural from the Gospel records and the origin of Christianity. He has, consequently, to show that the spiritual monotheism which gave the ascendancy to Christian truth has its origin in the Semitic races; that it is a Semitic dogma, which Jesus loosened from its root-hold, and winged for universal acceptance; that the legendary stories, as he calls the miraculous narratives, are the deposit of a later age, the offspring of credulous and fervid imaginations; and that the remainder of the Gospel records may be so manipulated and humoured as to be fairly pieced together again after their miraculous portions are shred away, and to exhibit something like the original lineaments of the person of Jesus, before these miraculous glosses daubed and obscured His true image. (pp. 467-74)

Granting [Renan's] fundamental principle, which he reiterates as the foundation of all science, and therefore of criticism and true history,—that a miracle is necessarily false; we frankly avow, that we do know how a more gracious and plausible hypothesis could be framed for explaining by natural law the *facts* that are to be solved,—the existence of the Gospel records, and the stupendous renovation of society

which began with the words of Jesus, and advances, with mightier force to-day than ever, to its completion. But how pitiably paltry and insufficient is this hypothesis! How miraculously incoherent and impossible! How gross its outrages upon reason and true science which it professes to save by abjuring miracles! We admit that man has here done the most that learning, genius, and exquisite tact, could have done, or are likely to do, to vindicate a natural and human origin for the Revelation of Jesus Christ: but the loftiness and splendour of the attempt but reveal the more strikingly that he attempts the impossible, and prove the more exhaustively that a cause infinitely transcending nature is necessary to account for this phenomenon. We repeat that this book is a new and rich contribution to Christian Apologetics. (pp. 486-87)

[*John Brown Paton*], *in a review of "Life of Jesus," in* The London Quarterly Review, *Vol. XXI, No. XLII, January, 1864, pp. 457-510.*

## [G. H. CURTEIS] (essay date 1864)

[*In the following excerpt from a review of* The Life of Jesus, *Curteis acknowledges Renan's erudition and rhetorical skills while deploring his rejection of key Christian doctrines.*]

[No] one can possibly deny that [*The Life of Jesus*] is a book which deserves the trouble of a detailed examination. M. Rénan has long ago amply proved his possession of qualities which constitute literary excellence: a rare subtlety, abundant learning, a full and commanding survey of the field of inquiry, a brilliant imagination, and a fascinating style. What counterspell of mere robust common sense is sufficient to ensure us against such a master of the magic arts of writing as this! When these great powers are brought to bear upon a subject of all others the most deeply and universally interesting,—a subject, too, around which such uncouth heaps of material have been piling for years by the ceaseless coralline industry of innumerable German professors,—who can resist a feeling of relief, that one has arisen at last whose mental grasp is wide enough to take in the whole question at once, and whose imagination is powerful enough to produce shape and beauty—although, we are firmly persuaded, not the true shape, or the highest beauty—out of the chaotic products of modern Biblical criticism?

Accordingly, M. Rénan's volume has obtained a wide circulation and a vast popularity on the continent; not altogether due, as we would fain believe, to its destructive tendencies, but due also to the fact that he has presented a clear and definite conception of the person of Christ to thousands of readers in France and Germany, who were perhaps very imperfectly acquainted with the inimitable truth and beauty of the Gospels. It were better for a man to become acquainted with the life of Christ through the pages of M. Rénan, than not to become acquainted with it at all.

But when we have said this, we have said the utmost we are able to say in praise of the book. Its immediate effects are likely to be deplorable. The French mind, in particular, is so easily dazzled by brilliancy, and so readily captivated by dramatic finish and vivid portraiture, that we fear many of M. Rénan's own countrymen are likely to find 'rest for their souls' in this feeble and distorted version of the Gospel of Christ, and to accept his criterion that truth is attained, 'if one has succeeded in combining the texts in a manner to constitute a logical and probable narrative, where nothing jars or is out of tune.' We in England shall probably be of a different opinion. Englishmen have not so much faith in the laws of dramatic unity, or in the irrefragibility of logic,—whether it be 'the logic of facts' or any other. It seems to them—and herein is their safeguard from many kinds of error—that a thing may easily be too complete to be trustworthy, and too logical to be true. They have an obstinate faith in the existence of an outer world, wherein God works, and wherein the narrow world of human thought and human action lies embraced, as some little solar system lies floating in the teeming spaces of the sky, or some little busy ant-hill forms part of a great country whose policy is dominating the globe. Hence our dislike of centralisation, our craving for free scope, our suspicion of over-completeness,—and our safety (it may be confidently predicted) from any risk of a shaken faith or shattered hopes by means of M. Rénan's 'fifth' and humanitarian 'gospel.' (pp. 574-75)

Before M. Rénan can establish any claim to our confidence or respect, he must be prepared to show that in rejecting the received and direct meaning of the Gospel narrative, he is prepared to substitute for it a system more coherent, more intelligible, more credible. Tried by this test he utterly fails. In spite of the violence and distortion he never scruples to apply to the sacred text, we confidently affirm that his [*Life of Jesus*] is not only incredible, but impossible; and that the thing he would substitute for evangelical history and truth, would not pass current as the production of a secondhand writer of fiction. (p. 581)

The existence of [the] spiritual world is the Christian's firm conviction, and its predominance over everything below it is one of the very elementary principles of his faith. Death is, practically to us all, the great standing mystery of mysteries, and appeals with irresistible fascination to the interests of humanity, down to its very lowest dregs. If the Resurrection of Jesus Christ from death were what M. Rénan supposes it to be—a hallucination of credulity or an invention of enthusiasm—not only is there an end of all faith in those narratives which culminate in this great event, but there is an end likewise of the supreme doctrine of Immortality and of Revelation itself. The attempt to deify a human being by the loftiest attributes of our own imperfect nature can never fill up the infinite chasm between the creature and the Creator. A revelation from above must be supernatural, if it be anything at all. But if the fact of the Resurrection of Christ rest on evidence as direct and conclusive as that which demonstrates any occurrence in history—if for that purpose the ordinary laws of life and death were suspended—then what matters it to contest to the Almighty the manner in which He may think fit to exercise his own omnipotence? We recommend those who may be perplexed or distressed by the perusal of this volume to fix their minds on one simple point—the Resurrection of Jesus: as long as they rest upon that signal event with entire faith and certain knowledge, they retain the key to the whole system of Christianity; for to apply the words of Bishop Butler on a precisely analogous occasion: 'If it be incredible on the anti-miraculous hypothesis that Jesus Christ should have risen from the dead, then the anti-miraculous hypothesis is not true; since the Resurrection of Jesus Christ is a well-authenticated historical fact.' (p. 604)

[*G. H. Curteis*], *"Renan's 'Life of Jesus'," in* The Edinburgh Review, *Vol. CXIX, No. CCXLIV, April, 1864, pp. 574-604.*

## HIPPOLYTE TAINE   (letter date 1869)

[*In the following letter to Renan, Taine comments on* Saint Paul, *the third volume of* The Origins of Christianity, *praising Renan's powers of historical synthesis but questioning the stylistic verisimilitude of his translations.*]

I have just been reading ***Saint Paul.*** I postponed writing to you about it, because I am finishing a tiresome chapter which requires my full attention. We will talk it over. It is wonderful to see what you have drawn from insignificant and scattered little texts to throw light on the Epistles and on the *man.* You have a huge and closely-meshed net which you have thrown over the whole literature of the time. The book is most interesting, living and coherent. I am here without a Greek St. Paul, to meet the only objection which has presented itself to my mind. When I read his writings, he seemed to me, probably because I was accustomed to classical Greek, more jerky in style, more rugged than in your translations—a kind of Victor Hugo; it seemed a continuous crying out, convulsive and concentrated exclamations, an inward storm in the soul of a logician who is also a fanatic. But you yourself say in a note that any literal translation would be unintelligible and that you only kept to the sense and direction of the thought. (pp. 293-94)

*Hippolyte Taine, in a letter to Ernest Renan in June, 1869, in* Life and Letters of H. Taine: 1853-1870, *translated by Mrs. R. L. Devonshire, Archibald Constable & Co. Ltd., 1904, pp. 293-94.*

## [JOHN BROWN PATON]   (essay date 1873)

[*In the following excerpt from a review of* Antichrist, *the fourth volume of* The Origins of Christianity, *Paton comments on Renan's stylistic brilliance, his relation to the German school of Biblical criticism, and his scepticism.*]

Having followed M. Renan's labours on the origin of Christianity from the beginning, we feel bound to continue. As the work goes on, the signs of the author's zeal, diligence, learning and artistic skill, become rather more evident than otherwise; and, alas, the tokens of the same merely critical estimate of our holy religion, uncontrolled by any respect for the supernatural element, appear [in *L'Antechrist*]. We discern the same obvious points of difference between the Frenchman and his German fellow-labourers, and we retain the opinion, formerly expressed, that there are certain qualities of style which make M. Renan's work much more perilous to a certain class of readers than the ponderous German works that have been translated and are in course of translation. Those qualities are more conspicuous than ever; nothing can surpass the dramatic skill, picturesqueness of narration, subtlety of illustration, transparency of diction, and faultless clearness, which appear on every page. (p. 135)

It is a remarkable coincidence that M. Renan has been engaged on this volume, which enters on the first fearful tragedy that Christianity had to do with, during the solemn years of his country's "slow agony." He touchingly vindicates himself from the charge of indulging his "taste for history, the incomparable enjoyment that one experiences in beholding the evolution of the spectacle of humanity," which has "especially fascinated him in this volume," during so frightful a period. With his defence of his patriotism we need not concern ourselves. Nor need we dwell on the many indications noticeable in this work of a silent comparison between the despotism of Rome and the ruin of Jerusalem and the despotism of Imperialism and the ruin of Paris. It is of more importance to note that the calamities of his country seem to have in some degree touched the religious sensibilities of his nature. Not that much value is to be attached to his sentimental tributes to spiritual truth. It is vain for him to allege his profound conviction that religion is not a subjective deception, but has an external reality corresponding to it, and that he who surrenders himself to its inspirations is the truly inspired man. Throughout the entire volume there is no gleam of a simple and real acceptance of the essential verities of Christianity. It is not without a feeling of deep compassion that we say this of one who is devoting year after year of most laborious study to all the documents that record the advent of Christianity on earth. Should his last volume follow in due course, and under the influence of the same tranquil and philosophical indifference to the Divine element of power in the Christian faith, his enormous work will be the most remarkable monument extant of an unbeliever's study of Christianity.

This instalment of the history of the Christian *Origines* is professedly devoted to the relations of Nero, the Antichrist, to the Church. But it is really a series of dissertations on all the scenes, documents, and actions in the development of the later New Testament. There is a sense in which Nero is the centre of the drama; and the unity of the whole is preserved with considerable skill. But we shall not be careful to observe that unity in our miscellaneous observations. To deal with the topic suggested by the title would involve us in interminable controversies concerning Antichrist, which would carry us far beyond the limits of the volume reviewed, as also far beyond our own and our readers' patience. The various subordinate discussions of the volume will suggest some subjects both of interest and importance, especially in connection with the Apocalypse and the three great Apostles. Some of them are set before us in a new light by the brilliant French sceptic; and it is exceedingly profitable to observe, however cursorily, the various currents that set in from every quarter and feebly dash against the firm foundations of the faith. It is, moreover, no small reinforcement of our Christian evidences to note how often these currents tend to neutralise each other's force.

M. Renan's plan requires him to determine the authenticity and value of the materials for this portion of history. And here, as we had occasion to show in the former volume, our author renders us good service as against those who in other respects are his allies. He has no sympathy with the sweeping criticism that robs us, on subjective grounds, of three-fourths of the New Testament Canon; his canons would take from us only one-third. He holds the Epistles to the Philippians and Colossians to have been St. Paul's; and, in defending the latter, makes the following seasonable remarks, which obviously may be turned against his own scepticism as to the books he gives up.

> The interpolations which able critics have thought they discerned in it are not evident. The system of M. Holtzmann, in this respect, is worthy of its learned author; but how dangerous is the method, too much accredited in Germany, which sets up a type *à priori*, which must serve as the absolute criterion for the authenticity of the works of a writer! It cannot be denied that interpolations and supposititious writings were frequent in the first two centuries of Christianity. But to discern between the true and the false, the apocryphal and the authentic, is an impossible task.

But it is to what follows that we would direct particular atten-

tion, as showing how strangely sceptic deals with sceptic, and how effectually M. Renan explodes by one argument both the Tübingen theory and his own. The school of Baur gives up many books because they contain doctrines which do not square with the fixed teaching it assigns to each Apostle. M. Renan would retain these books for the precise reason that they exhibit natural and legitimate variations in doctrine. We stand between both, and adopt the premises of both. They are in our view consistent with each other; while the conclusion from both is to us the same. The Apostles had each a fixed type of doctrine, but each taught it with variations; whether we look at their fixed teachings or their variations; we see in each good argument for the genuineness of these books. But the point is well worthy of consideration; and M. Renan will exhibit it with sufficient clearness.

> The great school of Christian Baur labours under this main defect, that it figures to itself the Jews of the first century as complete characters, nourished by dialectics, and obstinate in their reasoning. Peter, Paul, Jesus Himself, resemble, in the writings of this school, Protestant theologians of a German university, all having one doctrine, and only one, which they always preserve unchanged. Now, what is true is this, that the admirable men who are the heroes of this history, changed, and sometimes contradicted themselves; during their life they had three or four theories; they borrowed occasionally from those of the adversaries against whom at another epoch they would have been most severe and inflexible. These men, looked at from one point of view, were susceptible, personal, irritable; science or rationalism, which gives fixedness to opinions, was quite strange to them. They had, like the Jews in all times, their violent contentions: and yet they made up one very solid body.

Nothing is more certain than this last observation, and nothing so effectually tends to confirm us in the assurance of it as the mutual polemics of the different branches of the destructive school. One sees in the Epistle to the Colossians a deviation from St. Paul's fixed type of doctrine, as if the Apostle must needs exhaust himself in one epistle, reserving no new aspects of the truth for any future emergency. Another retains the Epistle to the Colossians, because it contains so fresh a picture of the versatile Apostle; but then he rejects the Pastoral Epistles for some private reasons of his own. Now, we make bold to affirm that a combination of the arguments used by M. Renan and by Baur would issue in the vindication of every canonical book of the New Testament. But we cannot pursue the subject; suffice that the dissensions of the rival theories set up for the construction of the New Testament furnish a strong body of proofs in favour of the orthodox and traditional view of the canon. . . . M. Renan's position is a rather irregular one. He is honest in his semi-philosophical, semi-poetical, account of the origin of Christianity; and there is no stronger proof of his honesty than the exposure of his own folly in the grotesque theory that he has put forth in this volume. (pp. 135-38)

> [*John Brown Paton*], *in a review of "L'Antechrist,"
> in* The London Quarterly Review, *Vol. XLI, No.
> LXXXI, October, 1873, pp. 135-64.*

## HIPPOLYTE TAINE  (letter date 1876)

[*In the following excerpt from a letter to Renan, Taine applauds the poetic character of* Philosophical Dialogues *and*

Fragments, *yet challenges Renan's Hegelian theory of causality.*]

[***Philosophical Dialogues and Fragments***] is like the music of the spheres! Fortunate you to have so heard it, fortunate you to have found a true method of expressing it. There is much of the spirit of Plato in you, almost the spirit of a poet—in which, perhaps, can the truest philosophy be found.

I should like, however, to discuss one of the two things admitted by you as certitudes, namely, that the world is progressing towards a definite goal, and is working out some mysterious design.

This assertion is most helpful for faith and morals, for consolation and for idealism, but I should place this belief rather among the probabilities than among the certitudes.

There is something, you say, that develops through an impulse from within, through unconscious instinct analogous to the movement of plants towards water or to light, to the blind effort of the embryo to leave the matrix, to the impulse that guides the metamorphoses of insects. Be it so; but what if the mechanism that seems to be the effect of an abstract cause should be, as modern naturalists admit, the (effect) of a working cause? What if Darwin be right? What if organic matter arrives at evolution through the mere fact of adaptation and selection? What if the phenomena you quote only simulate the preconception of a definite design, just as flame seems to incorporate the desire to ascend, and water the reverse?

" . . . Un *nisus* universel pour réaliser un dessein, remplir un moule vivant, produire une unité harmonique, une conscience?" I much fear that this may be but metaphorical language, a convenient solution like Newton's attraction, and possibly you may take it thus yourself. You yourself offer the strongest argument against it by proving that this *nisus* is not universal, by stating that conditions are often more than hostile to it, by quoting the abortion of four millions of cod's eggs for every one that is hatched, by stating that the great pachydermals of Siberia were killed off by the glacial period. In short, I should like to see you analyse coldly and in detail the theory of causation. Whether Darwin's solution be true or not true matters little; another similar procedure might have produced living organization; but to take the question generally, there results from his hypothesis that the accumulated effects of a working cause (adaptation to environment, survival of the fittest) give to the observer an illusion as of an abstract cause.

In this—thanks to the naturalists—metaphysics has advanced during the last twenty years.

Many thanks for the word of encouragement in your preface. I will do my best as long as I have power to think and write, but I cannot venture to apply your fine words to myself: "Je sens en moi quelque chose de jeune et ardent; je veux imaginer quelque chose de nouveau."

You, dear friend, are young, your intellect is in full vigour. Your style has never been freer and more natural; but as to myself, my early vigour has long deserted me! Give us whatever new thing your keen eyes may discover, whether it be of science or of visions! (pp. 163-65)

*Hippolyte Taine, in a letter to Ernest Renan on June 3, 1876, in his* Life and Letters of H. Taine: 1870-1892, *edited and translated by E. Sparvel-Bayly, Archibald Constable & Co. Ltd., 1908, pp. 163-65.*

## HENRY JAMES   (essay date 1876)

[*James was an American-born English novelist, short story writer, critic, and essayist of the late nineteenth and early twentieth centuries. He is regarded as one of the greatest novelists of the English language and is also admired as a lucid and insightful critic. A prominent figure in Europe's cosmopolitan literary society, James was also a frequent contributor to several important American journals, including the* North American Review, *the* Nation, *and the* Atlantic Monthly. *In the following review of* Philosophical Dialogues and Fragments, *James focuses on the dialogues, emphasizing the charm of Renan's style while questioning his intellectual posture. James's review first appeared in the* New York Daily Tribune *on 17 June 1876.*]

M. Ernest Renan has just published a new volume, which will not fail to find its way speedily into the hands of all lovers of good writing. A new volume by Renan is an intellectual feast; if he is not the first of French writers, I don't know who may claim the title. In these ***Dialogues et Fragments Philosophiques,*** indeed, it is the dialogues alone that are new; they occupy but half of the volume, the rest of which is composed of reprinted pieces. The dialogues are a sort of *jeu d'esprit,* but a *jeu d'esprit* of a very superior kind—the recreation of a man of elevated genius. They are prefaced by a few pages breathing a very devoted patriotism, and proving that the author's exorbitant intellectual reveries have not relaxed his sense of the plain duties of citizenship. To win back that esteem which he appears willing to concede that they have in some degree forfeited, he exhorts his fellow-countrymen above all things to work. Let each, he says, surpass himself in his own particular profession, "so that the world may still cry of us, 'These Frenchmen are still the sons of their fathers; eighty years ago Condorcet, in the midst of the Reign of Terror, waiting for death in his hiding-place in the Rue Servandoni, wrote his *Sketch of the Progress of the Human Mind.*'" M. Renan imagines a group of friends, who assemble in a quiet corner of a park of Versailles, to exchange reflections upon the "ensemble de l'Univers." The subject is extensive, and it may well take half a dozen talkers to cover the ground. Three persons, however, take the lead, each one of whom unfolds his particular view of the Cosmos. These three views are classed by M. Renan under the respective heads of "Certainties," "Probabilities," and "Reveries." He disclaims them all as a representation of his own opinions, and says that he has simply entertained himself with imagining what might be urged and argued in each direction. It is probable, however, that if his convictions and feelings are not identical with those of either of his interlocutors, they have a great deal in common with the whole mass of the discussion, and that Philalethes, Theophrastus, and Theoctistes are but names for certain moods of M. Renan's mind. If so, one can only congratulate him upon the extraordinary ingenuity and fertility of his intellect and the entertaining company of his thoughts. These pages are full of good things admirably said, of brilliant and exquisite suggestions, and of happy contributions to human wisdom. Their fault is the fault which for some time has been increasing in M. Renan's writing—a sort of intellectual foppishness, a love of paradox and of distinction for distinction's sake. His great merit has always been his natural distinction, but now, in this same distinction, in the affectation of views which are nothing if not exquisite, views sifted and filtered through an infinite intellectual experience, there is something rather self-conscious and artificial. The reader cannot help wishing that M. Renan might be brought into more immediate contact with general life itself—general life as distinguished from that horizon of pure learning which surrounds the *cabinet de travail* of a Parisian scholar—suspecting that, if this could happen, some of his fine-spun doubts and perplexities would find a very natural solution, and some of his fallacies die a very natural death.

Philalethes, the exponent of M. Renan's "Certainties," is not so certain about some things as his friends might have expected; but his skepticism is narrowed down to a point just fine enough to be graceful. "In fact," he says, "if I had been a priest, I should never have been willing to accept a fee for my mass; I should have been afraid of doing as the shopkeeper who delivers for money an empty bag. Just so I should have had a scruple about drawing a profit from my religious beliefs. I should have been afraid of seeming to distribute false notes and to prevent poor people, by putting them off with dubious hopes, from claiming their portion in this world. These things are substantial enough for us to talk about them, to live by them, to think of them always; but they are not certain enough to enable us to be sure that in pretending to teach them we are not mistaken as to the quality of the goods delivered." Theophrastus, who discourses on "Probabilities," takes, on the whole, a cheerful view of the future—it must be confessed with considerable abatements. He agrees probably in a great measure with Theoctistes, who remarks, "I have never said that the future was cheerful. Who knows whether the truth is not sad?" Theophrastus thinks that the maturity of the world is to arrive by the expansion of science—on condition, indeed, that the mechanical theory of heat succeeds within five or six hundred years in inventing a substitute for coal. If it fails—and the failure is quite probable—"humanity will enter into a sort of mediocrity from which she will hardly have the means to emerge." It must be added that Theophrastus is prepared to see art and beauty (as we have hitherto understood it) disappear; "the day will perhaps come (we already see its dawn) when a great artist, a virtuous man, will be antiquated, almost useless things."

The speculations of Theoctistes, however, are much the most curious. He imagines a development of science so infinite and immeasurable that it will extend our relations beyond the limits of the planet on which we dwell, and he deems the function of this perfected machine to be above all the production of great men. The great men may be so selected and sifted and improved that human perfection may at last concentrate itself in one extremely superior being, who will hold all the universe in cheerful and grateful subordination. This is what Theoctistes calls "God being realized." With these sentiments it is not surprising that he should not expect that God will be realized by a democracy. He gets into deeper water than he can always buffet, but his style is the perfection of expression. I must quote a few lines more. "For myself, I relish the universe through that sort of general sentiment to which we owe it that we are sad in a sad city, gay in a gay city. I enjoy thus the pleasures of those given up to pleasure, the debauchery of the debauchee, the worldliness of the worldling, the holiness of the virtuous man, the meditations of the *savant,* the austerity of the ascetic. By a sort of sweet sympathy I imagine to myself that I am their consciousness. The discoveries of the *savant* are my property; the triumphs of the ambitious are my festival. I should be sorry that anything should be missing in this world; for I have the consciousness of all that it contains. My only displeasure is that the age has fallen so low that it no longer knows how to enjoy. Then I take refuge in the past—in the sixteenth century, in the seventeenth, in antiquity; everything that has been beautiful, amiable,

noble, just, makes a sort of paradise for me. With this I defy misfortune to touch me; I carry with me the charming garden of the variety of my thoughts." This paragraph seems to me magnificent; one would like to have written it. The charm of M. Renan's style is hard to define; it is ethereal as a perfume. It is a style above all things urbane, and, with its exquisite form, is suggestive of moral graces, amenity, delicacy, generosity. Now that Sainte-Beuve is dead, it strikes me as the most perfect vehicle of expression actually in operation in France. The only style to be compared to it is that of Mme. Sand; but for pure quality even this must yield the palm. Mme. Sand's style is, after all (with all respect), a woman's style. (pp. 42-5)

> *Henry James, "Renan's 'Dialogues and Philosophic Fragments',"* in his Literary Reviews and Essays on American, English, and French Literature, *edited by Albert Mordell, Vista House Publishers, 1957, pp. 42-5.*

## WILLIAM JAMES (essay date 1876)

[*An American philosopher of the late nineteenth century, James was the founder of Pragmatism as a philosophical school. In opposition to the tenets of scientific materialism and philosophic idealism, which had prevailed in Western philosophy throughout the eighteenth and nineteenth centuries, James attempted to describe human life as it is actually experienced, instead of formulating models of abstract reality. In the following excerpt from a review of* Philosophical Dialogues and Fragments, *James challenges the internal logic of Renan's philosophical beliefs, focusing on his theory of historical teleology.*]

This last production [*Philosophical Dialogues and Fragments*] of a writer who at one time seemed, to say the least, the most exquisite literary genius of France, is really sad reading for any one who would gladly be assured that that country is robust and fertile still. It seems to us no less than an example of mental ruin—the last expression of a nature in which the seeds of insincerity and foppishness, which existed at the start alongside of splendid powers, have grown up like rank weeds and smothered the better possibilities. The dialogues which form the only new part of the book are simply priggishness rampant, an indescribable unmanliness of tone compounded of a sort of histrionically sentimental self-conceit, and a nerveless and boneless fear of what will become of the universe if "l'homme vulgaire" is allowed to go on. M. Renan's idea of God seems to be that of a power to whom one may successfully go like a tell-tale child and say: "Please, won't you make 'l'homme vulgaire' stop?" As the latter waxes every day more fat and insolent, the belief in God burns dim, and is replaced by the idea of a kind of cold-blooded destiny whose inscrutable and inhuman purposes we are blindly serving, with at most the relief of making piquant guesses and epigrams as we go about our Master and ourselves.

The dialogues are three in number. M. Renan warns us in his preface not to suppose that any of the speakers represents his confirmed opinion; but this, we take it, means not that he has any other set of opinions more confirmed, but that of these opinions, though they are his best, he is still sceptical. The personages are, as he says, the different lobes of his brain, and, though the word philosophic is on the title-page, we may say that never did a brain express itself in a less philosophic guise—visions taking the place of concepts, and vagueness that of definition. In the first paper, it is laid down as certain that the universe is a fatal mechanism, but no less certain that it has a mysterious final purpose, to which, in spite of ourselves, we are made to contribute. Our virtues and our passions alike undo us as individuals, but they help along the ends of nature. . . . (p. 78)

In the second dialogue an attempt is made to guess at the nature of this dark ideal end. It seems to be *consciousness,* self-knowledge on the part of the universe. Nature is a factory of thought; but as thought of a truly *distingué* order is rare, the expense of means is almost infinitely disproportionate to the object. The *savant,* the philosopher, is what, through all her sidereal systems, Nature is seeking to form. The improbability of his appearing in a perfect form on any given planet is compensated by the eternity of time and the infinite number of chances which the stars afford. . . .

In the third dialogue we have apocalyptic visions of the actual course of history through future eternity, of which it may be said that none are cheerful, but that all are imaginative on a vast, vague, and original scale. The terrors of the Commune seem really to have organically affected M. Renan's brain, for the clearest and most reassuring image of the future which he allows us to indulge in is that of a league of savants who (when science has become so difficult as to be quite inaccessible to the mass of vulgarians, and is at the same time possessed of unlimited control of natural forces, by means of terrible machines which only a Cauchy or a Laplace shall be able to use) will keep the world in order by mere terror. "On the day," he says, "in which a few privileged children of reason shall possess the means of *destroying the planet,* their sovereignty will be created. This oligarchy will reign by absolute terror, for the existence of all will be in their hands; one may, in fact, call them gods."

How strange it is that the ultimate resort of every Frenchman, struggling with what he conceives to be an adverse destiny, lies in blowing-up something. Whether it be a Communard with the Hôtel de Ville, or M. Renan's "privilégiés de la raison" with the planet, the principle is identical; and it is truly entertaining to see the representative of culture join hands in this way by a secret affinity with his abhorred and dreaded brother with the petroleum can. Fear, mistrust of time and the persuasive force of what is good, seem to be ingrained in the bones of most of the present generation of Frenchmen; and in different ways the only providence they can believe in is a sort of Marshal MacMahon to protect them from their enemies.

The other papers in the volume show the same qualities and defects—sweetness of diction and delicacy of apprehension in detail, with vagueness, pretension, and deep ignorance of the subject where the subject is the history of philosophic thought. The best excuse one can make for them is that they are but half sincere. But, in a writer of Renan's peculiar pretensions, that is a fatal excuse. In his earlier writings all the suavities and many of the severities of language were employed in painting the distinction between the "âme d'élite," the "esprit honnête," and the common man; how the latter was wedded to superficiality and passive enjoyment, whilst the former found austere "joys of the soul" in the pursuit of wisdom and virtue. These surely imply sincerity. The gifted writer particularly congratulated himself on having preserved the vigor of his soul "dans un pays éteint, en un siécle sans espérance. . . . Consolons nous," he cried, "par nos chimères, par notre noblesse, par notre dédain!" "The true atheist is the frivolous man" is one of his early phrases which

has been often quoted. But already in his **Antichrist,** published after the Commune, he spoke of the summit of wisdom being the persuasion that at bottom all is vanity; and if this book be really half trifling, he would seem practically to have espoused that persuasion—in other words, to have become a frivolous man, or, according to his own definition, an atheist. Indeed, if one were to seek a single phrase which should define the essence of religion, it would be the phrase: all is *not* vanity. The solace and anæsthetic which lies in the conclusion of Ecclesiastes is good for many of us; but M. Renan's ostentatious pretension to an exquisite sort of religious virtue has debarred him from the right to enjoy its comforts. That *esprit vulgaire,* Josh Billings, says that if you have $80,000 at interest, and own the house you live in, it is not much trouble to be a philosopher. M. Renan, after parading before our envious eyes in fine weather the spectacle of a man *savourer*-ing his *dédain* and enjoying the exquisitely voluptuous sensation of tasting his own spiritual pre-eminence, must not take it hard if we insist on a little more courage in him when the wind begins to blow. We do not know any better than he what the Democratic religion which is invading the Western world has in store for us. We dislike the "Commune" as well as he; but it is a fair presumption that the cards of humanity have not all been played out. And meanwhile, since no one has any authoritative information about the final upshot of things, and yet, since all men have a mighty desire to *get on* if they can, it cannot be too often repeated that they will all use the *practical* standard in measuring the excellence of their brother men: not the man of the most delicate sensibility but he who on the whole is the most *helpful* man will be reckoned the best man. The political or spiritual hero will always be the one who, when others crumbled, stood firm till a new order built itself around him; who showed a way out and beyond where others could only see written "no thoroughfare." M. Renan's dandified despair has nothing in common with this type. (p. 79)

*William James, "Renan's Dialogues," in* The Nation, *New York, Vol. XXIII, No. 579, August 3, 1876, pp. 78-9.*

## GEORGE SAINTSBURY   (essay date 1880)

[*Saintsbury was an English literary historian and critic of the late nineteenth and early twentieth centuries. A prolific writer, he composed several histories of English and European literature as well as numerous critical works on individual authors, styles, and periods. In the following excerpt, Saintsbury assesses the literary, historical, and philosophical character of Renan's works, focusing on* The Origins of Christianity.]

The literary and philosophical characteristics of M. Renan (for with matters theological we have nothing to do here) are very strongly marked, and for our time by no means common. In his attitude towards books and men he stands apart from any other school or individual of his own country and of the Continent, though, perhaps, it would not be difficult to name an English critic who, with many points of difference, has some points of agreement with him. To those who simply consider him in the light of an assailant or defender of certain theological or ecclesiastical ideas, these peculiarities are necessarily invisible. Let us see if by keeping these ideas apart they can be made to emerge into view.

It is always interesting and instructive to compare the earliest and the latest work of men of literary distinction. The earliest work of M. Renan's known to me—putting aside mere college exercises—is the article on **"L'Etat des Esprits en 1849;"** the latest, omitting **"L'Egalité Chrétienne"** as a simple continuation of a work planned and moulded twenty years ago, is **Caliban.** Between the enthusiasm of five-and-twenty and the quiet scepticism of fifty-five there is, of course, a good deal of difference; but the main features of the author's mind, and even to some extent of his literary style, are identical enough. There is the same disbelief in religious and political nostrums, the same preference for a somewhat vague elevation and expansion of heart, the same contempt of utilitarianism on the one side, and of the merely æsthetic attitude towards art and literature on the other. Between the youthful appeal of thirty years ago in favour of "la pauvre humanité assise, morne et silencieuse, sur le bord du chemin," and the ingenious parody of Shakespeare, which scandalised some grave and precise democrats the other day, their author has something more than a fair amount of work done to show for the summer and early autumn of his life. I need take no account of works of pure erudition, though the treatise *De l'Origine du Langage* is not unimportant from the general point of view, as it shows, in a comparatively neutral field, the same reluctance to adopt materialist explanations and to admit the all-powerful action of circumstances as distinguished from innate powers, which characterise M. Renan elsewhere. The catalogue of his more properly literary work may be limited to the monograph on Averroes [*Averroés et l'Averroisme*], to the four or five volumes of Essays collected and reprinted under different titles, and to the six volumes of the [*Origines du Christianisme*]. The book on Averroes, except for its connection with the author's Semitic studies, and perhaps also with the general history of free thought and revolt against religious dogma, does not seem to be particularly germane to his tastes. It is, however, an excellent book in its way, and the labour of its preparation must, beyond a doubt, have had an excellent disciplinary effect on M. Renan's style and manner. Inclined as he most undoubtedly is, to be exuberant rather than the reverse, if he had given himself very early to easy literature, which requires much writing, little reading, and no research properly so called, the effect could hardly have failed to be unfavourable. Combining, as the book does, a bibliographic study of considerable complexity, an analysis of an extensive work, and a rapid survey of a long period of subsequent history, the amount of labour which it represents is very far out of proportion to its bulk. There are passages here and there, moreover, which distinctly enough foreshadow the manner and method of the author of the *Vie de Jésus,* such as the section on the curious myth of the *Tres Impostores,* and that describing Petrarch's tribulations with the Venetian Averroists. The scattered essays are naturally much more fertile of light on the character of their author, than a work where the plan and almost the contents were traced out for him by his subject. His various studies in religious history may be taken not so much as sketches for the finished work which was to come, as for protreptic discourses put forward to dispose the public to receive that work with understanding and favour, or else critical appreciations of different forms of the religious spirit. The least happy of these is probably that on Channing, in which the author, true to a bad habit of his countrymen, seems to start with a preconceived archetypal Englishman, or American, for it is much the same to him, and to reason downwards. More interesting still are the papers united under the heading **Questions Contemporaines,** which for the most part exhibit in various forms the ardent desire for an improvement in the higher education of his country, which is one of M. Renan's most honourable charac-

teristics, and which, comparatively young as he is, he has lived to see in several ways fulfilled. Nor can the political sketches entitled **Réforme Intellectuelle et Morale** be omitted if a full estimate is to be formed of their author. The famous correspondence with the author of the *Leben Jesu,* while it perhaps exposes only too clearly the sorrowful chances that await the too faithful believer in sweet reasonableness now as in other days, is at least as valuable as a moral tell-tale as it is honourable to the writer. Two long studies, one having the general title of the book, the other headed **"De la Monarchie Constitutionelle en France,"** exhibit not only such practical political ideas as the author has formed, but also a very favourite notion of his, on which the audiences of his recent lectures have heard him more than once descant, that great moral and intellectual achievements unfit a nation for playing a prominent political part, and that in this order of thought, as in another, it must lose its life to save it. Finally, M. Renan's more purely personal and literary studies show less an ability on his part to put himself in the place of the subjects criticised, than an ability to improve them in the ecclesiastical sense, that is to say, to use their history and peculiarities for the purpose of illustrating his own ethical, religious, and political ideas. Interesting, however, as are these lesser pieces to the student, and to all who care for idiosyncrasy of work as opposed to mere volume and importance of subject, they can hardly be regarded even now, and will almost certainly not be regarded hereafter, as anything more than a vestibule and precinct to the book which has occupied the prime of the author's life, and upon which, beyond all doubt, he would himself prefer to base his chances of fame.

It may be questioned whether any writer ever manifested a more distinct and uniform personality of thought and style than that which M. Renan has maintained through the six volumes of his work, the publication of which has now extended over twenty years. The first impression that the *Vie de Jésus* and its successors produce on critical readers, whether they be orthodox or unorthodox, is in all probability identical. Nothing can, to all appearance, be more hopelessly uncritical and arbitrary than the proceeding. To take a connected narrative and reject such details as happen not to square with preconceived ideas, while admitting the others; to reject a prophecy as obviously false, and take it up next minute as a trustworthy history of the events *à posteriori;* to see in a reported miracle, not an imposture, but an innocent distortion of some ordinary fact—all this seems at first sight to partake decidedly more of the spirit of *Dichtung* than of *Wahrheit.* The historian has also, in common with many other historians of the latter half of the nineteenth century, a most remarkable habit of building up whole characters and histories out of slight personal traits. St. James the Less, if he had foreseen that the callosities on his knees and the gold plate on his forehead would bring him into such trouble, would infallibly have discarded the latter and adopted a cushion to obviate the former. The unfortunate Claudius Lysias may fairly complain of the accusation of "stupidity," founded upon one or two casual allusions which certainly do not bear that sense to all readers; while, on the other hand, Barnabas has to thank M. Renan for favours received in return for a very slight historical consideration. But before long the rough places become tolerably smooth to an intelligent walker. The object of the book as a defence of principles and modes of character which seem to the writer of the first importance to the world, soon makes itself apparent. M. Renan's two wings, as the mediæval allegorists would say, are the abstractions which are called, in the technical terms of theology and morals, spirituality and unction. In his use of both of these there are points which are decidedly less akin to the English temperament . . . than to the softer and more feminine temper which is so largely represented in the average Frenchman. The words of the hymn, "Gentle Jesus, meek and mild," express the attraction which the critic has found on the moral side in the founder of the Christian religion; the words "the kingdom of God" represent his attraction on the purely intellectual side. He has inherited from that religion, or has made up for himself (whichever phrase may be preferred), an ideal of unworldliness, as distinguished from the self-seeking and materialism of modern life, of mild and impartial affection, as opposed to the stormy passions or cold indifference of the individual.

With this *à priori* conception he has started, and it is this that shapes his handling of his work. In the earliest volume the sentimental side of the matter has most play, and it is still most remarkable therein. Without being very cynical, it is permissible to feel the abundance of such adjectives as "délicieux," "charmant," "ravissant," "enivrant," "exquis," to be rather cloying. With *Les Apôtres* things improve from this point of view. The sentimental side of the matter is perforce kept in the background, and the "kingdom of God," the battle of spiritualism against materialism of all sorts, comes more to the front. It is in these later volumes, moreover, that the remarkable art of the writer becomes chiefly manifest. To weave a series of fragmentary notices, many of which his critical method compels him to reject, into a connected narrative, to keep up the contrasted importance of the different parts, and in doing this to keep the double end, the inculcation of spiritualism and of moral beauty, in view, without wearying the reader, is a task of sufficient difficulty in itself. But when it is remembered that to the immense majority of readers the story is already familiar, that they have from earliest youth been taught to expect and welcome it in one form only, and are (supposing other prepossessions absent) as much disposed as children are to resent alteration and addition in a favourite tale, the difficulty becomes immensely complicated. Lastly, when we add to all this that the narrative has perforce to take the shape of something like a perpetual commentary, usually the most arid of literary forms, the hardness of the task is raised to very nearly the highest point, and it is clear that only literary faculty of a very remarkable kind could enable the author to discharge it.

The treatment of the subject is of course to a great extent conditioned by its nature, yet it is at the same time shaped by the idiosyncrasy of the practitioner. Of the fortunes of the Christian Church, from the date of the Crucifixion to the beginning of the third century, no document nor tradition, orthodox or unorthodox, gives any connected survey. On the other hand, an immense body of literature of all kinds, sacred and profane, Jewish, Christian, and Pagan, religious, historical, and philosophical, survives containing the materials, the *pièces* of such a history. A critic of the sober school, whether belonging to the merely dryasdust order or to the product-of-the-circumstances sect, would assuredly find too many gaps to be filled more or less conjecturally to please him. Biographers and historians of this class like a subject upon which the full light of day has been thrown, where there is abundant material, and where the task is little more than one of skilful combination and intelligent interpreting. On the other hand, the merely superficial theoriser would find himself hampered by the multitude of scrappy details, jutting up like the tops of submarine rocks, useless and almost impossible for purposes

of landing and cultivation, but sufficient to render careless navigation exceedingly dangerous. Many an ingenious theory has been upset before now by a troublesome and sterile fact of this kind. But M. Renan happens to combine in remarkably full measure the talent for conjecture and the talent for patient research. The way in which he has followed up in courageous dives the submarine world which connects, or might very conceivably connect, the emerging points of fact or tradition, is a triumph of the combined method. The book has been called, like most other histories where the imagination is strongly represented, though perhaps with greater justice than usual, a romance. It would be fairer to call it a conjectural restoration of history. All conjectural restorations incline to the romantic.

A detail worthy of notice in estimating M. Renan's choice and use of his materials, is his extreme predilection for the apocryphal sacred books, both Jewish and Christian, and especially for the apocryphal apocalypses. Since the alteration of the lectionary and the disuse of the custom of binding up the apocrypha with the Old and New Testaments, it is probable that such of these singular documents as used to be recognised by the Church of England, are unknown even to persons professedly observant of religious matters in this country. Some of them again, such as the book of Enoch and the *Shepherd* of Hermas (which, by the way, is not strictly an apocryphal book), have never among us had even this chance of recognition. As far as literary merits go there can be no doubt that this obsolescence is a great pity. There are not many more delightful books of their class than *The Wisdom of Solomon,* than *Ecclesiasticus,* and than the fourth book of Esdras. To all these "oubliés et dédaignés" M. Renan has given his particular attention, and his analyses of many of them, notably of the *Shepherd* and the fourth book of Esdras, are not merely among the most attractive passages of his book, but are also excellent examples of literary abstracts. There are indeed many points about these books which appeal to such a critic. They are perhaps more saturated than the canonical books with the Semitic spirit, in that excited and recalcitrant form which it assumed in the days immediately preceding and immediately following the Christian era; they are full of vague but poetical imagery; they lend themselves in the most obliging way to the conjectural interpretations in reference to historical events of which M. Renan is so fond. Moreover they are in many cases romantic pictures of more or less private life which supply abundance of local colour as well as of information as to modes of thought. Thus they are the most fertile of quarries to a patient worker in mosaic, the most precious of colour-stores to such a painter as M. Renan, who has set himself to depict on a vast scale the whole spiritual and emotional life and movement of a time such as the first two centuries. (pp. 626-31)

In [the *Origines*] M. Renan must be regarded as one of the class of picturesque historians, a class of writers from whom the world has suffered many things in these last days. But he is a picturesque historian with a great many differences, and almost every one of these differences is in his favour. Eclectic and, to a great extent, imaginative as his method is, he can rarely be accused of actual exaggeration, or of affecting the picturesque for the picturesque's sake. He is not in the habit of basing rhetorical generalisations upon nothing at all, merely to add to the forcible character of his picture. There is a sobriety about him which the weary reader, tired of fireworks, in vain demands from certain historians of the same general character in England. Moreover, his picturesqueness, such as it is, is in the strictest keeping with the general plan and purport of his book, and results logically from the principles which he has set before him. "Que je voudrais," he says somewhere of the author of the *Imitatio Christi,* "être peintre, pour le montrer tel que je le conçois, doux et recueilli, assis en son fauteuil de chêne, dans le beau costume des bénédictins de Mont Cassin." The assumption as to the authorship of the famous book may be matter of argument, but the sentence is the key to all the author's own picturesque passages; they are resorted to simply to show us the person or the scene, such as the historian conceives it, and are thus illuminations, not squibs and crackers let off for the purpose of dazzling and crackling. Sometimes, of course, the subjectivity of view is rather excessive; it is certainly a hard saying when one finds M. Renan pronouncing Ecclesiastes "le seul livre aimable" that the Jewish spirit has ever produced. The Preacher is delightful reading no doubt, but amiable is about the last epithet that one would feel inclined to give him. However, everybody must see with his own eyes, and the most that outsiders can do is to lend spectacles to the short-sighted. M. Renan, if in this particular instance his glasses hardly suit our sight, is usually one of the most serviceable of opticians. With the principle that human nature, due difference being made for varieties of race, is everywhere and at all times pretty much the same—that outward circumstances may modify, but cannot wholly determine its action—that happiness, moral good, and intellectual cultivation are the objects of life, he has made edification and delight equally the objects of his book. He has, indeed, stated his main theory with sufficient clearness in the preface to his ***Essais de Morale et de Critique.*** "Morality is the one thing eminently serious and true, and by itself it suffices to give meaning and direction to life. Impenetrable veils hide from us the secret of this world, whose reality is at once irresistible and oppressive. Philosophy and science will for ever pursue without ever attaining the formula of this Proteus, unlimited by reason, inexpressible in language. But there is one foundation which no doubt can shake, and in which man will ever find a firm ground amidst his uncertainties; good is good and evil is evil. No system is necessary to enable us to hate the one and love the other; and it is in this sense that faith and love, possessing no seeming connection with the intellect, are the true base of moral certainty, and the only means possessed by man of understanding in some slight measure the problem of his origin and destiny."

Some notable failings and dislikes of M. Renan's give us important side-lights on his literary and critical character. One such is his attitude towards the Middle Ages. He has written and read about them more than most people, and it requires some courage to bring a charge of short-coming against the author of ***Averroés,*** and of the excellent discourse on the Art of the Fourteenth Century in France. Yet it is soon tolerably clear to an attentive reader, and perfectly clear to one who has some knowledge of mediæval literature, that M. Renan is out of sympathy with the Ages of Faith. He is even so far out of sympathy with them that he fails altogether to understand them in some important points, which have nothing whatever to do with theology or Church history. We rub our eyes when we come to the statement (in the preface of ***Averroés et l'Averroisme***), that the Middle Ages, "intellectually speaking, represent nothing but gropings after a return to antiquity." It would be safer to affirm the exact contrary. In hardly a single great instance of the intellectual development of the Middle Ages is there any real affinity with the spirit of classicism. With characteristic and uncritical docility they sometimes borrowed classical forms, dressed themselves up

in scraps of classical ore, proposed classical masters as objects of admiration and reverence. But in reality the two are poles asunder. The author of *Roland* is separated from the author of the *Iliad,* the author of *Lancelot du Lac* from the author of the *Odyssey,* Audefroy le Bastard from Horace, Anselm from Aristotle, Villehardouin from Thucydides, by a gulf which no possible "gropings" could traverse. Accordingly, whenever M. Renan deals with the Middle Ages, and especially with scholasticism, he is unsatisfactory, because he is unsympathetic. Nor is the reason of this by any means far to seek; it is not the religious side of the Middle Ages that repels him, but their moral and æsthetic side. He seems to miss in them the sunny aspect which attracts him alike in things eastern and in things Greek. The strong shadows that give the character and, to some persons, the attraction of Gothic architecture, make him shiver. If there is any part of Europe on which during those times he looks with satisfaction it is Spain, Provence, and perhaps Italy—all lands that love to lie in the sun—not his own Brittany and northern France, and England and Germany, with their gloom and their combativeness, and the absence of rose-pink and sky-blue in their pictures. In particular M. Renan has evidently a strong dislike to fighting. For such a master of description his sketch of the Siege of Jerusalem is comparatively tame, and he passes over the Battle of Bedriacum—which still awaits its picturesque historian, though surely no battle of the nations ever better deserved one—with a hasty shudder at its butchery. It may be suspected that M. Renan, patriotic as he is, by no means shares the modern admiration for "l'Epopée Française," and that the *chansons de gestes,* with the ceaseless ring of their assonances, clashing like lance on shield and sword on helmet, seem to him distinctly barbarous. He is more at home in the Arthurian legends, for which any native of Brittany must feel a certain reverence. But on the whole the presence of the warlike spirit, against which he again and again testifies, is too strong in the Middle Ages for M. Renan. He says somewhere, "J'aime le moyen age," but I venture to doubt whether his affection is spontaneous and genuine.

Another interesting point in the critic's mental disposition is his attitude towards philosophy of the more abstract kind. Here again, wherever he has to touch on such matters, an absence of sympathy is apparent—strikingly, for instance, in the account of the gnostic sects in the last volume of the ***Origines.*** To any one who has a weakness for speculation, there is something especially fascinating in the fragmentary notices of Basilides and Valentinus, which have come down to us in the sorriest possible condition in which any such notices could possibly come, involved, that is to say, in the partisan refutations of their adversaries. To these unfortunates M. Renan devotes indeed some admirable pages, but they do not inspire him with half the interest that is excited by, let us say, the *Shepherd* of Hermas, that curious mixture of the devout gallantry of the seventeenth century with the apocalyptic fancies of the second. Not many men have been more in contact with scholastic literature than M. Renan, but here again the fantastic attraction which that literature has for some people seems to exercise no influence over him. He evidently does not feel the magnetism of unbridled logic which sometimes tempts the reader in moments of weakness to devote the rest of his life to *Quæstiones Quodlibetates,* and suchlike ware. His allusions, not merely in his book on Averroes but elsewhere, to scholasticism, are possibly just, but certainly harsh. Its absence of form and colour and human interest seems to repel him. This being so, it is not surprising that he should speak of the later philosophy of Germany with respect indeed, but hardly with affection, and still less with enthusiasm. Hegel certainly cannot have much attraction for one who is proof against Basilides and Erigena and Occam. Even in his handling of Spinoza the dialectic element is kept out of sight in a very singular manner. Some of the contents of the *Dialogues et Fragments Philosophiques* may seem to contradict this view. But the greater part of that curious book appears to me to represent no permanent or deep-rooted convictions of its author. Events had for a moment upset M. Renan's equanimity, and he retired upon philosophy. Moreover, in the study which concludes it (**"La Métaphysique et son Avenir"**) his more habitual attitude towards such questions reappears distinctly enough. Indeed it is in this respect that the practical aspect of M. Renan's mind is most evident. He has his Utopias, no doubt; indeed he is very largely estated in those shadowy regions. But they are on the whole very practical Utopias, and the inhabitants are more occupied with conduct than with speculation, with their duties towards their neighbours than with the contemplation of their own interiors. In the Royaume de Dieu of which he is so fond, it does not appear that Barbara and Celarent will occupy a very high place among the thrones and dominations recognised by the constitution. (pp. 634-37)

If this account of the principles of M. Renan's literary and critical character be correct, it is evident that it stands in striking contrast to two other schools which have between them divided most of the critical talent of France during the last half century. In the first place it is far removed—to the extent, indeed, of complete antipathy—from the purely indifferent criticism of form rather than matter in life and literature which has been so strongly represented during that time. Of such criticism there have of course been many varieties differing with the idiosyncrasy of the critics. The sarcastic and, in a way, severe attitude of Mérimée is not the good-natured and purely apolaustic attitude of Gautier. But in all this school there may be said to be sometimes an impatience, sometimes a dislike, sometimes a simple neglect or omission, of the moral view of questions of literature or conduct. On the other hand M. Renan's progress stands in equally sharp contrast to the still more popular method of Sainte-Beuve, one side of which has been developed to an extent which may fairly be called exaggerated by M. Taine. This latter method consists, it need hardly be said, in treating the man and his work as for the most part an effect and not a cause. Its practitioners, in order to explain their patient, set to work to examine his *milieu* in every possible way, and, at any rate professedly, are content to accept the results of their examination as an explanation. The spirit of the age, the character of the surroundings, the influences of grandfathers and grandmothers, the style of education, living, and so forth, are taken as the data out of which the result is to be got. It would not be true, of course, to say that moral considerations exercise no influence over this class of critic, or that he has no likes or dislikes. But his likes and his dislikes are not ostensibly governed by any *à priori* principles, and are directed less to the individual criticised than to the set of influences which are supposed to have produced him. With M. Renan the case is quite different. He has so much of Cousin in him (of Cousin, of whom he never fails to speak with a somewhat exaggerated respect) that the big words Vrai, Beau, and Bien, or, if it be preferred, the great things which these big words signify, are always present before him. As a man or a book happens to fall in or to fall out with these notions of his, so the man or the book is judged. Nor is he apt to attribute much force to the product-of-the-century theory. An accurate student of

history is never likely to ignore the general tendency of periods. But in the formation of that general tendency M. Renan is willing to allow a great deal more force to the influence, and especially to the moral influence, of individuals than most other critics of the day. It is thus that in his principal work he is continually striving to hold up the personality of the actors clearly to view, even when there is the very smallest evidence of that personality to go upon. In judging personalities, too, he never lets himself be carried away by any fascinations of the paradoxical ultra-literary sort. He has perfectly well exposed the oddities of Nero's character [in *L'antechrist*], but those oddities have not inclined him to be lenient to the implacable, beautiful tyrant. If he is disposed to let Nero off at all gently, it is not because of his grandiose fancies, his unquiet searching after some new and infinite form of evil, but because Poppæa and Acte were to all appearance really attached to him. In this point even Nero falls back into the plane of the things that seem to M. Renan lovely and of good report. Indeed the last words fairly enough describe the character of his general predilections. The affections of all kinds—though M. Renan has an odd craze that family affection is an "égoïsme à plusieurs" very liable to abuse—are the coefficients of human character which he likes best to deal with. In matter of natural beauty he inclines in the same way to the idyllic and pastoral. Even in such points as his views on education and science, the same solicitude for the presence of a human interest of the softer sort manifests itself. He is exceedingly anxious that France should devote herself more than has hitherto been the case to "hautes études." But the hautes études which attract him are not mathematics or abstract philosophy, but comparative philology, critical history, the study of religion, all of them more or less intimately connected with the hopes and fears, the daily life and daily wants of the endless generations behind us. Whatever is abstract, bloodless, and dry, repels him. Despite the **"Lettre à M. Berthelot"** and some other things, I should doubt whether he has much genuine affection for what is commonly called natural science. The touch of materialism, and of inhumanity which often accompanies the pursuit of such science, must necessarily revolt him. Thus in every way such force as M. Renan can exert is a force in the direction of spiritualism, morality, peaceable flows of soul. It may sometimes be difficult to square his apparent views and desires with any accurate estimate of the history of the past, or the probabilities of the future. The pleasant cloudy Utopias which he describes, in which great Pan seems to be alive again, and everybody contributes to the foundation and confirmation of the kingdom of God by inoffensive conduct, pure morality, the absence of uncomfortable striving . . . , and the cultivation of comparative philology and the domestic affections, seem occasionally to be situated in a land that is very far off. It has indeed been observed by the wisdom of the elders that the rainbow rarely touches the ground quite close to the spectator's feet, and that St. Brandan's Isle, and other regions of the blest, have a knack of fleeing before the seeker.

Nevertheless it is impossible to assign any but a beneficial tendency to an influence of this kind at such a time as the present. M. Renan represents in French literature the tradition which his countryman Chateaubriand founded, or borrowed from Rousseau, nearly a century ago, and which was continued to our own days by George Sand—the tendency, that is to say, to rely upon and appeal to the emotions rather than the intellect, to dress up amiable thoughts in gorgeous or elegant language, . . . and to cultivate the beautiful. . . . His taste is as much better than Chateaubriand's as his character, though his imaginative power is considerably less; and he rarely lapses into the merely tawdry or the merely sentimental. His philosophy is a good deal saner and less windy than George Sand's (though, as we have seen, he too has a slight weakness for apocalypses), and he has a good deal more of the practical spirit than the Châtelaine of Nohant. Neither of his forerunners was a very distinguished practitioner of purely literary criticism, nor is M. Renan. His opinions on certain points are too definitely and obtrusively present with him for that, and he does not attain to the absolute catholicity which is the first requisite of the literary critic. It is doubtful whether in this direction he could even get as far as the paradox of Thackeray—"I suppose there is no person who reads but must admire . . . and I say that, great as he is, we should hoot him." The desire to hoot would get the better even of the preliminary admiration in M. Renan's case. But if his value as a critic of literature be unequal, it is still considerable. His remarks on the classical French literature of the seventeenth century are unquestionably the best ever made by a Frenchman, being equally distant from the silly parrot-cry of admiration which is now raised more loudly than ever by the neo-classic school in France, and from the exaggerated depreciation of the *romantique à tous crins.* Yet his real value is not that of a critic of letters so much as that of a critic of life. In face of what, with a fine confusion of language, are sometimes called the positive and sometimes the negative tendencies of the day, tendencies which in any case make for a certain hardness of moral texture, the presence of an authority of this kind, taking up his parable and preaching charity, mutual good-will, the admiration of harmless things, and the cultivation of blameless feelings, ought to be counted as on the whole a healthy influence. It is the business no doubt of the avowedly religious person to perform this same function, and to a great extent he does perform it, but in the case of those who do not agree with him he suffers from the reciprocal conjugation of the historical verb *je suis suspect, tu es suspect,* &c. The extremer political reformer is very much more occupied in furthering his views at any cost, than in taking measures to prevent his own manners or anybody else's from becoming fierce. Ordinary politicians and ordinary men of business have something else to do, and are naturally inclined to look upon the function as by no means a practical one. The quaint sentence of surprised contempt which M. Renan in his essay on Channing devotes to the temperance movement, points out excellently the gulf between the philanthropist of the professional kind and his own larger, if vaguer, philanthropy. To say anything about men of science is as dangerous in these days as it once was to say anything about bishops, but it may at least be hinted that the cultivation of the softer feelings has not hitherto received any very active assistance from them. Last of all comes the class of professed devotees of literature and art; among whom, after a manner, M. Renan himself must be classed. Their attitude towards such a propaganda as his is perhaps not less unfavourable than that of other classes. They have . . . a natural horror of anything like "gush," and they have had so much trouble to keep their own studies clear of the question of moral tendency and influence, that they are apt to look on that question with disfavour. Hence sentiment, as distinguished from passion on one side, business on another, and devotion on a third, has not recently had a good time of it in the world, being regarded by some as a mere counterfeit of something better; by others, as unpractical and womanish; by others, again, as leading to absurdities and slips of taste which should, above all things, be avoided. It is in the gap thus formed that M. Renan has

with sufficient courage taken his stand. His gospel may certainly be said to be a vague gospel, and the enemy may contend that Morgane la Fée is architect and clerk of the works at the buildings which he so industriously edifies with graceful words and at the same time, with a vast quantity of solid learning; but of his literary skill there can be no question, and scarcely less of the admirable character of his intentions in the use to which he puts it.

The concluding volume of [the **Origines**]—to judge not merely from the samples of it given recently in his lectures, but from general probability—should be a fitting close to the whole, and moreover one of its most interesting parts. In Marcus Aurelius M. Renan has found an example of one of those fortunate persons whom, as he himself said in a juvenile work thirty years ago, "la tempête a laissés au milieu du grand océan pacifique, mer sans vagues et sans rivages, où l'on n'a d'autre étoile que la raison, ni d'autre boussole que son cœur." Marcus has not exactly produced this effect upon all his readers, but it will be all the more interesting to see in what manner (though, in truth, it is not very difficult to foresee it) he has produced the effect on M. Renan. In the same volume may probably be expected a development of the eloquent projects of regeneration in which M. Renan has more than once hinted that the Church of Rome might, if she would consider the things that belong unto her peace, be called upon to bear a part. The practical side of this falls out of my plan, but it is certainly not unreasonable to anticipate that it will give us a very satisfactory volume from the literary and philosophical point of view. From the former M. Renan has enriched the world with a great deal of excellent work free from the stiffness and aridity which too often characterise the work of learned writers, possessed of a singular and somewhat feminine charm of suppleness, softness, and colour, but seldom deserving the unfavourable epithets of effeminacy, flaccidity or tawdriness. From the latter he has supplied a distinct want in the thought of the time by advocating charity in the full Pauline sense against egotism, morality against mere æstheticism or mere intellectualism, attention to the spiritual as contrasted with the merely material interests of humanity. I happen (were this of the slightest importance) to differ from his views on a great majority of points, from the life of Christ to the advantages of living in common, and from Marcus Aurelius to Béranger. It has been all the greater pleasure to me to try and appreciate his literary character and position, in what I conceive to be the only spirit allowable for the critic. (pp. 639-43)

*George Saintsbury, "Ernest Renan," in* The Fortnightly Review, *n.s. Vol. XXVII, No. CLXI, May 1, 1880, pp. 625-43.*

**HENRY JAMES**    (essay date 1883)

[*In the following excerpt from a review of* Recollections of My Youth *that originally appeared in the* Atlantic Monthly *in August 1883, James reflects on the qualities of Renan's intellect and personality and also illustrates his virtues as a stylist.*]

There has always been an element of the magical in the style of M. Ernest Renan—an art of saying things in a way to make them beautiful. At the present moment he is the first writer in France; no one has in an equal degree the secret of fairness of expression. His style is fair in both the senses in which we use the word—in that of being temperate and just, and in that of being without a flaw; and these Reminiscences of his younger years [**Recollections of My Youth**], lately collected from the *Revue des Deux Mondes,* are perhaps the most complete revelation of it. His problem here was unusually difficult, and his success has been proportionately brilliant. He proposed to talk uninterruptedly about himself, and yet he proposed—or rather he was naturally disposed—to remain a model of delicacy. M. Renan is the great apostle of the delicate; he upholds this waning fashion on every occasion. His mission is to say delicate things, to plead the cause of intellectual good manners, and he is wonderfully competent to discharge it. No one to-day says such things so well, though in our own language Mr. Matthew Arnold often approaches him. Among his own countrymen, Sainte-Beuve cultivated the same art, and there was nothing too delicate for Sainte-Beuve to attempt to say. But he spoke less simply—his delicacy was always a greater complexity. M. Renan, on the other hand, delivers himself of those truths which he has arrived at through the fineness of his perception and the purity of his taste with a candid confidence, an absence of personal precautions, which leave the image as perfect and as naked as an old Greek statue. It is needless to say that there is nothing crude in M. Renan; but the soft serenity with which, in the presence of a mocking world, he leaves his usual plea for the ideal to any fate that may await it is an example of how extremes may sometimes meet. It is not enough to say of him that he has the courage of his opinions; for that, after all, is a comparatively frequent virtue. He has the resignation; he has the indifference; he has, above all, the good humor. He combines qualities the most diverse, and, lighted up as he is by the interesting confessions of the volume before us, he presents himself as an extraordinary figure. He makes the remark that in his opinion less importance will be attached to talent as the world goes on; what we shall care for will be simply truth. This declaration is singular in many ways, among others in this: that it appears to overlook the fact that one of the great uses of talent will always be to discover truth and present it; and that, being an eminently personal thing, and therefore susceptible of great variety, it can hardly fail to be included in the estimate that the world will continue to make of persons. M. Renan makes light of his own talent—he can well afford to; if he appears to be quite conscious of the degree in which it exists, he minimizes as much as possible the merit that attaches to it. This is a part of that constant play of taste which animates his style, governs his judgments, colors all his thought; for nothing can be in better taste, of course, than to temper the violence with which you happen to strike people. To make your estimate of your own gifts as low as may seem probable is a form of high consideration for others; it corresponds perfectly with that canon of good manners which requires us to take up a moderate space at table. At the feast of existence we may not jostle our neighbors, and to be considerate is for M. Renan an indefeasible necessity. He informs us of this himself; it is true that we had long ago guessed it. He places the fact before us, however, in a relation to other facts, which makes it doubly interesting; he gives us the history of his modesty, his erudition, his amiability, his temperance of appetite, his indifference to gain. The reader will easily perceive the value that must attach to such explanations on the part of a man of M. Renan's intelligence. He finds himself in constant agreement with the author, who does nothing but interpret with extraordinary tact the latent impressions of his critic.

M. Renan carries to such a high point the art of pleasing that we enter without a protest into the pleasantness of the account he gives of himself. He is incapable of evil, learned,

*Renan in 1860, from a painting by his father-in-law, Henry Scheffer.*

happy, cheerful, witty, devoted to the ideal, indifferent to every vulgar aim. He demonstrates all this with such grace, such discretion and good humor, that the operation, exempt from vulgar vanity, from motives of self-interest, M. Renan being at that point of literary eminence where a writer has nothing more to gain, seems to go on in the pure ether of the abstract, among the causes of things and above all questions of relative success. Speaking of his ancestors in Brittany, whom he traces back to the fifth century, simple tillers of the earth and fishers of the sea, he says, with great felicity, "There they led for thirteen hundred years a life of obscurity, saving up their thoughts and sensations into an accumulated capital, which has fallen at last to me. I feel that I think for them and that they live in me. . . . My incapacity to be bad, or even to appear so, comes to me from them." Many men would hesitate to speak so freely of their incapacity to be bad; others, still more of their incapacity to appear so. But M. Renan has polished to such clearness the plate of glass through which he allows us to look at him that we are quite unable to charge him with deceiving us. If we fail to see in him so much good as that, it is simply that our vision is more dim, our intelligence less fine. "I have a strong taste for the people, for the poor. I have been able, alone in my age, to understand Jesus and Francis of Assisi." There is a great serenity in that, and though, detached from the text, it may startle us a little, it will not seem to the reader who meets it in its place to be a boastful note. M. Renan does not indeed mean to say that he has been the only Christian of his time; he means he is not acquainted with any description of the character of Jesus containing as much historic truth as the *Life* he published in 1864. The passage is curious, however, as showing the lengths to which a man of high delicacy may go when he undertakes to be perfectly frank. That, indeed, is the interest of the whole volume. Many of its pages are rare and precious, in that they offer us together certain qualities that are almost never combined. The aristocratic intellect is not prone to confess itself, to take other minds into its confidence. M. Renan believes in a caste of intellectual nobles, and of course does not himself belong to any inferior order. Yet in [this volume] he has alighted from his gilded coach, as it were; he has come down into the streets and walked about with the multitude. He has, in a word, waived the question of privacy—a great question for such a man as M. Renan to waive. When the impersonal becomes personal the change is great, and it is interesting to see that sooner or later it must become so. Naturally, for us English readers, the difference of race renders such a fact more difficult to appreciate; for we have a traditional theory that when it comes to making confidences a Frenchman is capable of almost anything. He is certainly more gracefully egotistic than people of other stock, though he may have more real reserve than his style would indicate. His modesty is individual, his style is generic; he writes in a language which makes everything definite, including confessions and other forms of self-reference. The truth is that he talks better than other people, and that the genius of talk carries him far. There is nothing into which it carries people more naturally than egotism. M. Renan's volume is a prolonged *causerie,* and he has both the privileges and the success of the talker.

There are many things in his composition and many things in his writing; more than we have any hope of describing in their order. "I was not a priest in profession; I was a priest in mind. All my defects are owing to that: they are the defects of the priest." The basis of M. Renan's character and his work is the qualities that led him to study for the priesthood, and the experience of a youth passed in Catholic seminaries. "Le pli était pris—the bent was taken," as he says; in spite of changes, renunciations, a rupture with these early aspirations as complete as it was painful, he has remained indefinably, ineffaceably, clerical. The higher education of a Catholic priest is an education of subtleties, and subtlety is the note, as we say to-day, of M. Renan's view of things. But he is a profane philosopher as well as a product of the seminary, and he is in the bargain a Parisian and a man of letters; so that the groundwork has embroidered itself with many patterns. When we add to this the high scholarship, the artistic feeling, the urbanity, the amenity of temper, that quality of ripeness and completeness, the air of being permeated by civilization, which our author owes to his great experience of human knowledge, to his eminent position in literature and science, to his association with innumerable accomplished and distinguished minds—when we piece these things together we feel that the portrait he has, both by intention and by implication, painted of himself has not wanted an inspiring model. The episode which M. Renan has had mainly to relate in these pages is of course the interruption of his clerical career. He has made the history so suggestive, so interesting, and given such a charm to his narrative, that we have little hesitation in saying that these chapters will rank among the most brilliant he has produced. We are almost ashamed to express ourselves

in this manner, for, as we have said, M. Renan makes very light of literary glory, and cares little for this kind of commendation. Indeed, when we turn to the page in which he gives us the measure of his indifference to successful form we feel almost tempted to blot out what we have written. "I do not share the error of the literary judgments of our time . . . I tried to care for literature for a while only to gratify M. Sainte-Beuve, who had a great deal of influence over me. Since his death I care no longer. I see very well that talent has a value only because the world is childish. If it had a strong enough head it would content itself with truth . . . I have never sought to make use of this inferior quality [literary skill], which has injured me more as a *savant* than it has helped me for itself. I have never in the least rested on it . . . I have always been the least literary of men." The reader may be tempted to ask himself whether these remarks are but a refinement of coquetry; whether a faculty of expression so perfect as M. Renan's was ever a simple accident. He will do well, however, to decide that the writer is sincere, for he speaks from the point of view of a seeker of scientific truth. M. Renan is deeply versed in the achievements of German science: he knows what has been done by scholars who have not sacrificed to the graces, and in the presence of these great examples he would fain persuade himself that he has not, at least consentingly, been guilty of that weakness. In spite of this he will continue to pass for one of the most characteristic children of the race that is preëminent in the art of statement. It is a proof of the richness of his genius that we may derive so much entertainment from those parts of it which he regards as least essential. We do not pretend in this place to speak, with critical or other intention, of the various admirable works which have presented M. Renan to the world as one of the most acute explorers of the mysteries of early Christian history; we take for granted the fact that they have been largely appreciated, and that the writer, as he stands before us here, has the benefit of all the authority which a great task executed in a great manner can confer. But we venture to say that, fascinating, touching, as his style, to whatever applied, never ceases to be, none of the great subjects he has treated has taken a more charming light from the process than these evocations of his own laborious past.

And we say this with a perfect consciousness that the volume before us is after all, in a certain sense, but an elaborate *jeu d'esprit.* M. Renan is a philosopher, but he is a sportive philosopher; he is full of soft irony, of ingenious fancy, of poetic sympathies, of transcendent tastes. He speaks more than once of his natural gayety, and of that quality in members of the Breton race which leads them to move freely in the moral world and to divert themselves with ideas, with sentiments. Half of the ideas, the feelings, that M. Renan expresses in these pages (and they spring from under his pen with wonderful facility) are put forward with a smile which seems a constant admission that he knows that everything that one may say has eventually to be qualified. The qualification may be in one's tact, one's discretion, one's civility, one's desire not to be dogmatic; in other considerations, too numerous for us to mention. M. Renan has a horror of dogmatism; he thinks that one should always leave that to one's opponent, as it is an instrument with which he ends by cutting himself. He has a high conception of generosity, and though his mind contains several very positive convictions, he is of the opinion that there is always a certain grossness in insistence. Two or three curious passages throw light upon this disposition. "Not having amused myself when I was young, and yet having in my character a great deal of irony and gayety, I have been obliged, at the age at which one sees the vanity of every-thing, to become extremely indulgent to foibles with which I had never had to reproach myself: so that various persons, who perhaps have not behaved so well as I, have sometimes found themselves scandalized at my complaisance. In political matters, above all, people of a Puritan turn cannot imagine what I am about; it is the order of things in which I like myself best, and yet ever so many persons think my laxity in this respect extreme. I cannot get it out of my head that it is perhaps, after all, the libertine who is right and who practices the true philosophy of life. From this source have sprung in me certain surprises. Sainte-Beuve, Théophile Gautier, pleased me a little too much. Their affectation of immorality prevented me from seeing how little their philosophy hung together (*le décousu de leur philosophie*)." There is a certain stiffly literal sense in which, of course, these lines are not to be taken; but they are a charming specimen of what one may call delicacy of confession. The great thing is to have been able to afford to write them; on that condition they are delightfully human and charged with the soft irony of which I have spoken—the element to which M. Renan alludes in a passage that occurs shortly after the one I have quoted, and in which he mentions that, "save the small number of persons with whom I recognize an intellectual fraternity, I say to every one what I suppose must give him pleasure." He says that he expresses himself freely only with people "whom I know to be liberated from any opinion, and to be able to take the stand-points of a kindly universal irony." "For the rest," he remarks, "I have sometimes, in my conversation and my correspondence, *d'étranges défaillances*. . . My inanity with people I meet in society exceeds all belief. . . . Devoted on a kind of system to an exaggerated politeness, the politeness of the priest, I try to find out what my interlocutor would like me to say to him. . . . This is the result of a supposition that few men are sufficiently detached from their own ideas not to be wounded if you say something different from what they think." We should not omit to explain that what we have just quoted applies only to M. Renan's conversation and letters. "In my published writings I have been of an absolute sincerity. Not only have I not said anything that I do not think, but, a much more rare and more difficult thing, I have said all that I think." It will be seen that M. Renan tells us a good deal about himself.

His Reminiscences are ushered in by a preface which is one of the happiest pieces of writing that has ever proceeded from his pen, and in which he delivers himself of his opinion on that very striking spectacle, the democratization of the world. He is preëminently a man of general views. Few men have more of them at their command; few men face the occasion for speech with greater serenity, or avail themselves of it with more grace. His prefaces have always been important and eloquent; readers of the first collection of his critical essays, published upwards of thirty years ago, will not have forgotten the enchanting pages that introduced it. We feel a real obligation to quote the opening lines of the preface before us; from the point of view of style they give the key of the rest of the volume. We must add that it is not easy to transport their exquisite rhythm into another tongue. "Among the legends most diffused in Brittany is that of a so-called town of Is, which at an unknown period must have been engulfed by the sea. They show you, in sundry places on the coast, the site of this fabled city, and the fishermen tell you strange stories about it. They assure you that on days of storm the tip of the spires of its churches may be seen in the hollows of the waves; that on days of calm you may hear the sound of its bells come up

from the deeps, intoning the hymn of the day. It seems to me often that I have in the bottom of my heart a city of Is, which still rings bells that persist in gathering to sacred rites the faithful who no longer hear. At times I stop to lend an ear to these trembling vibrations, which appear to me to come from infinite depths, like the voices of another world. On the limits of old age, above all, I have taken pleasure in collecting together such echoes of an Atlantis that has passed away." It may have been that M. Renan wrote these harmonious lines with the same ignorance of what he was about that characterized M. Jourdain; in this case he is only to be congratulated the more. The city of Is represents his early education, his early faith, a state of mind that was peopled with spires and bells, but has long since sunk deep into the sea of time. He explains in some degree the manner in which he has retraced this history, choosing to speak of certain things and to pass in silence over others, and then proceeds, by those transitions through which no one glides so gracefully as he, to sundry charming considerations upon the present state of mankind and the apparent future of our society. We call his reflections charming, because M. Renan's view of life always strikes us as a work of art, and we naturally apply to it the epithets which we should use in speaking of any delightful achievement. As a votary of the ideal, a person who takes little interest in the practical, a distinguished member of that beneficent *noblesse* of intellect of which we have spoken, it would be natural that M. Renan should tend to conservative opinions; and he expresses such opinions, in various later pages, with exquisite humor and point: "In other terms, our great democratic machines exclude the polite man. I have long since given up using the omnibus; the conductors ended by taking me for a passenger of no intentions . . . I was made for a society founded upon respect, in which one is saluted, classified, placed, according to his costume, and has not to protect himself . . . The habit that I found in the East of walking only preceded by a forerunner suited me not ill; for one's modesty receives a lift from the apparatus of force. It is well to have under one's orders a man armed with a scourge which one prevents him from using. I should not be sorry to have the right of life and death, so that I might never put it into practice; and I should be very glad to own a few slaves, in order to be extremely mild with them and make them adore me." There is a certain dandyism of sensibility, if we may be allowed the expression, in that; but the author's perfect good-humor carries it off, as it always carries off the higher flights of his fastidiousness, making them seem simply a formal, a sort of cheerfully hopeless, protest in the name of the ideal. M. Renan is always ready to make the practical concession, and he shows that it is a great thing to have a fine taste, which tells us when to yield as well as when to resist, and points out, moreover, the beauty of passing things by. "One should never write save about what one likes. Forgetfulness and silence are the punishment that we inflict on what we find ugly or common in the walk that we take through life." This discretion helps M. Renan to feel that, though the immense material progress of this century is not favorable to good manners, it is a great mistake to put ourselves in opposition to what our age may be doing. "It does it without us, and probably it is right. The world moves toward a sort of Americanism, which wounds our refined ideas, but which, once the crisis of the present hour is passed, may very well be no worse than the old *régime* for the only thing that matters; that is, the emancipation and the progress of the human mind." And M. Renan develops the idea that, in spite of all that the votaries of disinterested speculation my find wanting in a society exclusively democratic and industrial, and however much they may miss the advantages of belonging to a protected class, their security is greater, on the whole, in the new order of things. "Perhaps some day the general vulgarity will be a condition of the happiness of the elect. The American vulgarity [*sic*] would not burn Giordano Bruno, would not persecute Galileo . . . People of taste live in America, on the condition of not being too exacting." So he terminates with the declaration that the best thing one can do is to accept one's age, if for no other reason than that it is after all a part of the past that one looks back to with regret. "All the centuries of a nation are the leaves of the same book." And in regard to this intelligent resignation, which fortifies itself with curiosity, M. Renan says several excellent things: "There will always be an advantage in having lighted on this planet as late as possible . . . One must never regret that one sees a little better." M. Renan's preface is a proof that he possesses the good spirits which he notes as an ingredient of his character. He is a *raffiné*, and a raffiné with an extraordinary gift of putting his finger on sensitive spots; with a reasoned ideal of the millennium. But a raffiné without bitterness is a very harmless person.

The first chapters of this volume are not the most vivid, though they contain a very interesting picture of the author's birthplace, the little dead town of Tréguier, a gray cluster of convents and churches on the coast of Catholic Brittany. Tréguier was intensely conventual, and the young Renan was, as a matter of course, predestined to the church. "This strange set of circumstances has given me for historic studies those qualities that I may possess. The essence of criticism is to be able to understand states very different from those in which we live. I have seen the primitive world. In Brittany, before 1830, the most distant past was still alive." The specimens which M. Renan gives of this primitive world are less happily sketched than the general picture; the coloring is rather pale; some of the anecdotes—that of the little Noémi, that of the Bonhomme Système—are perhaps slightly wanting in point. He remarks somewhere, in regard to the opposition, about which so much used to be said, between the classic and the romantic, that, though he fully admits the latter he admits it only as subject—not in the least as a possible form. To his mind there is only one form, which is the classic. And in another place he speaks of Flaubert, the novelist—"ce pauvre Flaubert"—as being quite unable to conceive of anything abstract. Putting these things together, we see a certain reason why M. Renan's personal portraits (with the exception of the picture of himself) should be wanting in reality. They are too general, too white; the author, wonderfully at home in the abstract, has rather neglected the concrete. "Ce pauvre Flaubert" would be revenged for M. Renan's allusion, if it were possible to him to read the episode of the Flax-Grinder—revenged (an exquisite revenge for an artist) by simply finding it flat. It is when he comes to dip into his own spiritual history that M. Renan shows himself a masterly narrator. In that region of abstractions, where the most tangible thing was the palpitating conscience, he moves with the firmest step. The chapters on the two seminaries in which he spent the first years of his residence in Paris, Saint Nicholas du Chardonnet and Saint Sulpice, are full of the most acute notation of moral and intellectual conditions. The little Breton seminarist moved too fast, and, to speak briefly, very soon transcended his instructors. He had a passion for science, and his great aptitude for philology promptly defined itself. He traces with singular art the process by which, young, simple, devout, dedicated to the church from his infancy, the object

of maternal and pastoral hopes, he found himself confronted with the fact that he could no longer be a Catholic. He also points out well that it was the rigidity of the Catholic system that made continuance impossible, it being all of one piece, so that dissent as to one point involved rejection of the whole. "It is not my fault if my masters had taught me logic, and by their pitiless argumentations had converted my mind into a steel blade. I took seriously what I had learned—the scholastic philosophy, the rules of the syllogism, theology, Hebrew. I was a good scholar; I can never be damned for that." M. Renan holds, moreover, that little was wasted of his elaborate religious education. "I left their hands [those of the priests] with a moral sentiment so prepared for every test that Parisian levity could afterwards put a surface on this jewel without hurting it. I was so effectually made up for the good, for the true, that it would have been impossible for me to follow any career not directed to the things of the soul. My masters rendered me so unfit for all temporal work that I was stamped with an irrevocable mark for the spiritual life . . . I persist in believing that existence is the most frivolous thing in the world, if one does not conceive it as a great and continual duty." This moral richness, these spiritual aspirations, of M. Renan's, of which we might quote many other examples, pervade all his utterances, even when they are interfused with susceptibilities which strike us at times as those of a dilettante; with refinements of idealism which suggest to us occasionally that they correspond to no possible reality, and even that the natural corrective for this would be that reality, in some of the forms which we children of less analytic race are obliged to make our peace with it, would impose itself a little more absolutely upon our critic. To what extent M. Renan's nature has been reduplicated, as it were, by his intellectual curiosity may be gathered from his belief, recorded in these pages, that he would have gone much further in the exploration of the universe if he had not taken his inspiration from the historical sciences. "Physiology and the natural sciences would have carried me along; and I may certainly say it, the extreme ardor which these vital sciences excited in my mind makes me believe that if I had cultivated them in a consecutive manner I should have arrived at several of the results of Darwin, of which I had had glimpses . . . I was drawn [instead] toward the historical sciences—little conjectural sciences which are pulled down as often as they are set up, and which will be neglected a hundred years hence." We know not what M. Renan may have missed, and we know not what may be the ultimate fate of historical conjecture and of the hapless literary art, in both of which he so brilliantly excels; but what such a volume as these mingled, but on the whole delightful, Reminiscences represents in the way of attainment, suggestion and sympathy is a sum not easily to be calculated. With his extraordinarily composite nature, his much-embracing culture, he is a most discriminating critic of life. Even his affectations are illuminating, for they are either exaggerations of generosity or ingenuities of resignation. (pp. 30-42)

*Henry James, "The Reminiscences of Ernest Renan," in his* Literary Reviews and Essays on American, English, and French Literature, *edited by Albert Mordell, Vista House Publishers, 1957, pp. 30-42.*

**ANDREW LANG**   (essay date 1887)

[*Lang was one of England's most powerful men of letters in the closing decades of the nineteenth century. A proponent of the revival of Romantic fiction, Lang championed the works of H. Rider Haggard, Robert Louis Stevenson, and Rudyard Kipling and was harshly critical of the Naturalistic and Realistic techniques of such novelists as Emile Zola and Henry James. A nostalgic vision of the past colored his work as a translator, poet, and revisionist historian. While most of his writings are seldom read today, he is remembered as the editor of the "color fairy book" series, a twelve-volume collection of fairy tales considered a classic in the genre. In the following excerpt, Lang evaluates the seemingly contradictory worldview presented in Renan's philosophical dramas, focusing on the author's professed "gaiety."]*

"One day," says M. Renan, speaking of the time he spent, when young, at the Seminary of Issy, "one day M. Pinault met me in an alley of the park. I was sitting on a stone bench, and was reading, I remember, Clarke's treatise on *The Existence of God*. I was wrapped up as usual in a thick overcoat. 'Oh, the little treasure!' said M. Pinault, when he came near me. 'How pretty he looks there, all nicely packed. Don't disturb him; he will always be like that; he will read, and read, but when he is called to care for the souls of men, he will be reading still. Warm and snug in his fur coat, he will cry, 'Oh, leave me, leave me alone!' "

In reading M. Renan's later works, those singular and ironic apologues to which he gives more or less of the form of comedies, one is often reminded of M. Pinault's pedagogic taunts. M. Renan is still, in the midst of this cold world, wrapped up in the *houppelande* of a warm content, of a soft success. He "sits like God, holding no form of creed, but contemplating all." Like the Buddha, he seems pleasantly situated, outside the great Wheel of existence, watching it roll on its unknown way into the darkness. He cries to the Nature of Things, "Courage, courage, Nature!" as the old man in the pit, at the first representation of *Les Précieuses Ridicules* cried, "Courage, Molière!" And, like the same old man, M. Renan seems inclined to add to his "Courage, Nature!" his comment, "Voilà la bonne comédie!"

On the whole, with all his ironies and reserves, this appears to be M. Renan's final judgment of the world he contemplates and the long result of time. It is comedy, and not bad comedy after all. "The age I have lived in will probably not seem the greatest, but it will assuredly be considered the most amusing of ages." But perhaps this is a mere "subjective impression," for M. Renan admits that he is "gay," and if he finds the spectacle of the universe amusing, it may be that, like the friend of Mr. Peter Magnus whom Mr. Pickwick envied, he is easily amused. His epoch must share this amiable quality with M. Renan, if it is much amused by some of his apologues, for example, by *L'Eau de Jouvence.*

Whether we agree with M. Renan that life is amusing or not, it is certainly of interest to study the confessions of this considerable writer and learned man. His comedies in prose are almost as much "confessions" as his autobiographical *Souvenirs d'Enfance.* They are veiled statements, *gazés,* as he says, if not of his whole philosophy, at least of certain *nuances de pensée,* some forms and shades of thought, which are familiar to him. "A man writes such things," he says, speaking of his *Souvenirs,* "for the purpose of passing on to others that theory of the universe which he carries about with him." Perhaps it can hardly be said that M. Renan possesses a theory of the universe. If ever he says anything seriously, he returns on it with a sceptical smile, or "half sighing a smile in a yawn as it were." You must not imagine that so clever a man is dull

enough to suppose that things are exactly as he thinks they are at any given moment. Still there be certain ideas, notions, *nuances de pensée,* which return more frequently, and are dwelt on with more favour than the rest. For want of anything more permanent, these fleeting and returning forms and phantoms of thought may be accepted at M. Renan's hands as *la théorie de l'univers qu'il porte en soi.*

It is not often that a man of M. Renan's eminence, a man who has lived his life, and done his "darg" of work, and proved all things, cares to turn round and tell the world exactly what he thinks of it all. M. Renan has this candour, and therefore his later writings are worth the attention of the curious. He has studied all religions; the greatest of them all, Catholicism, he has studied from within as well as from without. He has been initiated in the Great Mysteries; he may truly aver that he "has put his hand in the basket, and eaten out of the tumbrel." . . . And what does it come to, his mystic message . . . ? And first, to drive at practice, what is his theory of duty, of conduct? Why, this is the conclusion: that the world is a very diverting place, that a man should enjoy his youth, that virtue is a "kind of wager we make with ourselves, a personal satisfaction, a thing one may take up as a generous line in life, but as for advising another to do as much!" (*L'Eau de Jouvence,* Acte iii.). This is the sentiment of wise Prospero, M. Renan's favourite sage. Ah, how changed from the wizard of Shakespeare's fancy! "J'imaginais la solidarité d'une humanité centralisée," says M. Renan's Prospero, speaking like a newspaper. How far we have wandered from Shakespeare's "fairy way of writing," when Prospero talks of solidarity, and Ariel of "pre-established harmony!" However, it is with M. Renan's ideas, not with his style, that we are concerned just now. "M'étant peu amusé quand j'étais jeune, j'aime à voir s'amuser les autres," says Prospero. M. Renan constantly returns to this position. He did not "take his whack" himself, when he was young, as Mr. Harry Foker frankly avowed his intention to do, but he still cries, "Whack away, my boy," like the indulgent sire of Pendennis's early friend. This, indeed, was the gist of the advice which M. Renan, not long ago, gave some French students. It is a good-natured attitude without envy. "Les vieillards," says Rochefoucauld, "aiment à donner de bons preceptes, pour se consoler de n'estre plus en estat de donner de mauvais exemples." No one will add that, to console himself for having set a good example, M. Renan offers bad advice. His remarks could not add to the natural tendency to "amuse themselves" which is admired in the young, perhaps especially among the young students of fair France. But he does constantly harp on his *jeunesse chaste,* and he is exceedingly fond of displaying his indulgence and good nature. "All we three," says Prospero, addressing two of his friends, "were sober in our youth, for we had a task to perform. Well, seeing how little we took by that course, can we conscientiously recommend to others, who have no task to perform, the same rules of life? . . . Look at the poor, look at people at large, *allez donc.* They are poor, and you want them to be virtuous into the bargain! You ask too much. After all, their lot is not the worst. It is only the simple hearts that amuse themselves. Now amusement is one way, a second-rate way, but real enough, of attaining the end and aim of life. . . . Why, to deprive ordinary folk of the one joy they have" (the magician means drink), "offer them a paradise they will never have at all."

This is Prospero's way of talking, and it closely resembles the way of M. Renan, who remarks, "J'ai pu, seul en mon siècle, comprendre Jesus et François d'Assise." Why, the Sister of

Mercy at the door, who comes to dun you for a few shillings, and goes and spends the money in the stifling hovels of the sick poor, *she* understands St. Francis as well as M. Renan. This learned man claims a monopoly of Christian intelligence, like that of the old Scotchwoman who remarked that she and her husband John were, to her mind, the Church on earth, "and I'm no that sure o' John!" To have *un goût très vif pour le peuple,* like M. Renan, to have "a taste for the poor," is not quite the same thing as to possess, alone of mankind, the power of understanding our Lord and St. Francis.

But it would show a great lack of humour to take this elderly and erudite butterfly quite seriously. These apologues are "le divertissement d'un ideologue, non une théorie." M. Renan writes these diverting variations on man, on God, and on the soul, in Ischia, while the dew lies on the vines. "The philosophy for these hours of rest is the philosophy of larks" (it is indeed!) "and of grasshoppers, which have never doubted, I presume, that the light of the sun is a capital thing, life a delightful gift, and the earth of living beings a pleasant habitation."

Doubly must we be on our guard against taking the grasshopper's ethics too seriously (the grasshopper is not a burden to M. Renan), because there may be a grain of envy at the bottom of our virtuous indignation. M. Renan, of the sober youth, does not envy youth which is not sober, and this excellent example should encourage youth not to grudge the gaiety of M. Renan's age. It is not the moralist alone who must make allowances for M. Renan's being a merry old gentleman. The people, for whom he has "a very lively taste," might be vexed if they conceived that his **Caliban** is his ideal popular representative. In Milan, under the restoration, when Prospero came to his own again, Caliban wallowed in laziness and liquor. Caliban uttered the popular protest against the lot of the working classes, though it is true he did not work. "Je suis exploité," he says to Ariel; "Plat valet, tu ne vois donc pas qu'être exploité par un autre homme est la chose la plus insupportable? . . . La révolte, en pareil cas, est le plus saint des devoirs." So Caliban does arise in the pride of his manhood, and "Caliban est chef du peuple," for whom M. Renan has *un goût très vif.* However, M. Renan's theory of the future of society must not distract us from his conception (as far as his apologues and **Souvenirs** reveal it) of duty and of conduct. That conception is once more stated, or revealed, or reflected, or hinted at, in his latest drama, **L'Abbesse de Jouarre.** This is the most recent, and infinitely the most popular of M. Renan's recreations, in the character of a philosophical lark or reflective grasshopper. (pp. 50-3)

"I hope," says M. Renan in his preface, "that Idealists, who need no belief in the existence of disembodied souls to make them believe in duty, and who are well aware that ethical nobility does not depend on metaphysical opinions, will be pleased with my Abbess." M. Renan's Abbess, although she did not believe in the immortality of the soul, passed her last night (as she fancied it was) in the arms of a lover condemned to the guillotine. Whatever her own "metaphysical opinions" may have been, she devoted part of her fleeting moments to the general views of her ardent and scientific wooer. Years after *he* was executed, she married some other person. Her lofty and spiritual conception of conduct has therefore so greatly pleased Idealists, "who can believe in duty without believing in immortality," that they have already purchased twenty-one editions of **L'Abbesse de Jouarre.** Thus nobly have they testified, like M. Renan in his preface, to "their

confidence in the persistent cult of the Ideal, and in the perpetuity of the species." The Abbess did her best for both. With all his wit, M. Renan has little of what we call humour in English. Passages of **L'Abbesse de Jouarre** inevitably recall that glorious drama, *The Rovers.* For example, D'Arcy the hero, and the Comte de la Ferté are shut up in prison, and are to be executed next day. D'Arcy consoles La Ferté with the hope that the French troops have won a victory somewhere, and this gallant adhesion to the side of his own country, though she slay him, is the pleasantest aspect of D'Arcy's character. D'Arcy expresses a wish that he could see all the people he has loved, and, at that very moment, to him enters the only woman he ever truly loved, the Abbess, veiled. "La seule femme que j'ai aimée," cries D'Arcy, who promptly goes on to seduce, in her latest moments, the only woman who ever won his heart. This he accomplishes in one act and nineteen pages, replete with the most beautiful sentiments. "A cette heure on n'est pas tenté de faire des phrases," says M. Renan, but the Abbess and D'Arcy, being Idealists, make phrases without the excuse of temptation. French ideas are so extremely unlike ours, without being any the worse for that, and M. Renan's ideas are, perhaps, so peculiarly French, that it is almost impossible for an Englishman to criticise these two acts. M. Renan, for example, is "the only person in his generation who understands Christ," and this is the phrase his D'Arcy makes for the conquest of the Abbess: "Rappelez vous le Christ, qui refusa d'abord le calice, mais ne repoussa pas l'ange consolateur." An English reviewer may pass over all this with the brief remark that he is not enough of an Idealist to criticise it.

The plot of the **Abbesse de Jouarre** is well known to readers of the newspapers, and needs not to be analysed here. The whole second act is a funereal *Oaristys,* or love-dialogue, and it is of death, not wedlock, that the cypresses are murmuring. . . . The ideal moral on which the rigid martyr D'Arcy and his liberal Abbess act, is that of ordinary Epicureanism: "Let us eat and drink and make love, for to-morrow we die." M. Renan gravely asserts, in his preface, that all the world would become an Agapemone, if all the world were under sentence of death to-morrow.

> What Otaheiti is, let England be,

cries the emancipated bard in the *Anti-Jacobin,* adding, in a footnote, "That is, let England adopt the manners of Otaheiti," where, as we know

> Each shepherd clasped with unconcealed delight,
> His yielding fair, within the Captain's sight.

In support of his opinion that were the end of the world certain, "l'amour éclaterait de toutes partes avec une sorte de frénésie," M. Renan quotes the performances of the Primitive Christian Church. He might also quote the excesses which the inhabitants of plague-stricken towns have committed. Other thinkers have rather imagined that in presence of the day of doom men would call upon the mountains to fall and cover them. I prefer the latter hypothesis; but it is certain that when a ship is sinking the crew sometimes break into the stores of rum, and "l'amour de l'eau de vie éclate de toutes partes." This has not hitherto been regarded as a supremely moral state of things, but M. Renan is of another opinion. Talking of his frenzy of love, he exclaims, "On mourrait dans le sentiment de la plus haute adoration, et dans l'acte de prière le plus parfait." Perhaps it is not difficult to explain M.

Renan's position. Everyone remembers Mr. Thackeray's *Age of Wisdom,* with its lesson—

> Forty times over let Michaelmas pass,
> Grizzling hair the brain doth clear—
> Then you know a boy is an ass,
> Then you know the worth of a lass,
> Once you have come to forty year.

But add twenty years more, and the sage of forty may come to a different conclusion. Sixty is often a very enterprising period of life. What says the imitative singer?

> Twenty times more let Michaelmas fleet,
> Then you will be of a different cheer;
> Then you'll propose to each maiden you meet,
> Then you'll go falling in love in the street,
> Once you come to sixty year.

At forty years M. Renan would probably not have written the preface to the **Abbesse de Jouarre;** at sixty, "c'est tout ce qu'il y'a du plus naturel."

We may see this, and yet, like M. Jules Lemaître, fail to see where the moral and the Christianity of it all come in. "Merci," whispers the Abbess in the third act, "merci pour ton acte de maître. Tu m'as rendue plus chrétienne que je ne l'étais," to which "that solemn ass," D'Arcy, replies, "L'amour, en effet, est la revelation de l'infini, le leçon qui nous enseigne le divin." I am not very well read in the amatory literature of the eighteenth century, but D'Arcy seems to me to talk more like Tartuffe than like a contemporary of Dorat and Louvet. However, both he and the Abbess had been great students of Rousseau.

The conclusion of the drama is well known. By some oversight the Abbess does not have her head cut off; she is saved by another admirer, M. La Fresnais. Her attempt to strangle herself is frustrated, and she and her little girl, "the consekens," as the elder Mr. Weller says, "of that manœuvre" in prison, live a retired life. The gallant La Fresnais, however, perseveres in his suit, the Concordat comes in the nick of time, the Abbess's little girl wants to know why she has not a baby brother, and the Abbess, ever ready to oblige, accepts La Fresnais, and in announcing her intention to marry, makes some valuable remarks on the Mysteries of ancient Greece.

"The age," says M. D'Arcy, "has not touched us with its frivolity." Perhaps it may be thought that the frivolity has missed D'Arcy, and concentrated itself on his reviewer. But who can take M. Renan's drama seriously? Life is not what he supposes. A loyal man, a true lover, would respect the last hours of his lady and leave her with God. (pp. 53-6)

The popularity of M. Renan's latest piece may be accounted for, as we have seen, by the prevalence of Ideal views of Duty, and by the Ideal character of the work. But it must also be said that the drama is peopled by serious persons, not mere moralising shadows, and that there are dramatic moments, as when the only woman D'Arcy ever truly loved comes in so pat, or when the door of Julie's cell opens, nobody knows how, and is locked again from the outside by whom nobody knows. If D'Arcy bribed the jailer to shut him up with the Abbess, so as to compromise her character after her death, whether his suit succeeded or not, then D'Arcy's chivalry was all unlike that of M. Feuillet's hero in *Un Jeune Homme Pauvre.* He jumped off the top of a tower, it will be remembered, in which he had been shut up accidentally with the

lady of his heart. Perhaps he was not an Idealist. Other dramatic moments in **L'Abbesse de Jouarre** are the conclusion of the Concordat in time to make two lovers happy, and the discovery that the name of the Abbess is not on the list for instant execution. Naturally these points make the modern play much more popular than, for example, **Le Prêtre de Némi.** Yet that *drame philosophique,* which turns on the adventures of

> The priest who slew the slayer,
> And shall himself be slain,

is really more Voltairean in its satire, and has more emotion beneath its banter of religion and society than any of M. Renan's other plays. His object, he says, was "to develop a thought like the Hebrew idea of the Messiah and his mission, namely, a belief in the final triumph of moral and religious progress." The consequence, he admits, is *un tablêau triste,* a sad picture enough of a world in which the Right wins its way so slowly, and the Wrong can say and do so much for itself. Yet M. Renan thinks this a wholesome book, because it teaches us "not to be dismayed at the instable equilibrium of humanity, for we see the good and the true emerge after all from the hideous fens where croak and crawl the follies, and the horrors, and the sins of the world." M. Renan defends his general theory: "Qui sait si la vérité n'est pas triste?" Then, the question arises, Why is M. Renan gay? for, as M. Jules Lemaître says [see Further Reading]: "M. Renan est gai, très gai, et, qui plus est, d'une gaîté comique." A melancholy smile may well wander over the lips of a philosopher; but there is not much melancholy, as a rule, in *la malice de son sourire.*

The truth about M. Renan is perhaps more easily ascertained than the truth about the universe and the nature of things. He has no fixed theory or philosophy. If he be an optimist, as he seems to be in the preface to the **Prêtre de Némi,** his is a deferred optimism. "Let us leave the fortunes of the planet to be accomplished without troubling ourselves as to their conclusion. Our outcries will make no difference, our ill-humour would be out of place. It is not certain that this earth is not missing her destiny, as probably worlds innumerable have long ago missed theirs. . . . But the Universe knows not discouragement; each check leaves it young, alert, full of illusions. . . . Happy they who shall have had a hand in the great crowning success which will be the coming of God."

If this be optimism, it is "deferred," like some stocks in the market. But if M. Renan clings to this theory—and, optimist or not, it is an intelligent and dignified theory—why does he, in another mood, repeat the gospel of "having your fling"? If we are to be fellow-workers with God and blessed in the work, how can it be also true that there are many ways of working out our salvation, that those who do not "faire leur salut" by virtue or science, may do it by travel or sport, or mere diversion. Yet M. Renan, as we have seen, makes Prospero avow that amusement is a mode of attaining the end of life. This, of course, is a relapse into pure hedonism or Cyrenaicism (if we are to employ the language of the schools), and all idea of working together with God is abandoned.

The same instability, the same incongruity, appears in all M. Renan's ultimate views. He has "a lively taste for the people," and he thinks that the people in France are very probably on the march towards "American vulgarity." When the age of American vulgarity has come, however, *les gens d'esprit* will still be able to exist, "on the condition of not being too exacting." However vulgar the people may be, it will not burn men of science, nor persecute the seekers for truth. "Le but du monde est le développement de l'esprit," which may be developed even in Chicago. But when Socialism is the *régime,* and when we are all obliged to work with our hands, as in the Paradise of a new social creed, what will become of *le développement de l'esprit?* Where will *les gens d'esprit* be then? M. Renan does not face this problem of social democracy. M. Renan not only has no theory of the universe, but he is very well aware that he has none. He admits that in all things, except perhaps in politics, he is a *frondeur.* He is a Celt and a Gascon, a priest, and a philosopher; he is a moralist, and an advocate of the theory of "flings;" he is for collaboration with heaven, and for "making our souls" by way of diversion; he is, in fact, as he says, "a tissue of contradictions, like the *hircocerf* of the scholastic philosophy." He is Jekyll, and he is also Hyde; he is *Pulvis,* and he is *Umbra;* he is Indra, and he is the sacrifice on the altar of Indra. "One half of me seems to be busy in eating the other half, like that fabulous animal which devoured its own paws in mere absence of mind." Thus one of M. Renan's theories of the universe devours another, like the serpent which lives on other serpents, the ophiophagous snake. "I am double," he declares; "sometimes part of me laughs while the other cries." He is like Angeli, the funereal jester of Louis XIII., and the bells ring on his sable cap and black bauble. He is *Jean qui pleure,* and he is *Jean qui rit;* he is Democritus, and he is Heraclitus. "This is the explanation of my gaiety," he remarks. "As there are two men in me, one of them is always satisfied." The explanation would explain melancholy quite as well. "Thus to doubt and thus to mock," says M. Jules Lemaître, "is merely to deny; and this Nihilism, however elegant, should be a mere gulf of blackness and despair. True it may be: festive it is not." But M. Renan finds it festive. Why?

Well, M. Renan is gay because he finds life so amusing. He has been thoroughly successful. His fame is to him what her beauty is to a beautiful lady. He sees it acknowledged and reflected in all men's eyes, and in the eyes of women. He has enjoyed the greatest of all delights, a life of study and discovery. He has had the very prime of these "provisional little historical sciences," at which he throws his pebble, sciences which are certainly provisional, but certainly (if one who peeps wistfully within the gate may pronounce) are also full of pleasantness. He has been at once popular and a scholar, a cup given in like measure to one man only, to Charles Darwin. Now he lays by the oars of his scholarly galley and paddles a light popular *caïque.* Could any life be luckier, any part more diverting? It is natural M. Renan should find the world amusing; it is not necessary, perhaps, that he should toss his jeers at serious things among the crowd. Perhaps they do no great harm; one may doubt whether a single student who would have been sober goes off with Mimi and Musette because he has read M. Renan. Not much is done, for good or evil, by preaching, yet one might prefer from M. Renan a different sort of sermon. He has his responsibilities; some of his works do not leave the world happier than they found it. From some he has taken the living friend and counsellor, and has put in his place a Syrian sentimentalist. Amidst their grief he laughs, but it is as the doomed wooers laughed over their latest supper. M. Renan and Mr. Darwin both did much to destroy the old edifice of faith. But M. Renan picnics smiling among the ruins of his cathedral, listening amiably to the musical bells from the church beneath the sea. Mr. Darwin did not play thus with the hopes and fears which many thought that he had ruined: he did not offer jocose pamphlets on mo-

rality. It is a difference of constitution, of temperament, perhaps of taste. M. Renan, among his other causes of gaiety, has drunk very deep of *L'Eau de Jouvence,* from that singular fountain whose waters slake the Late Youth of Philosophers. Most philosophers, recluses at twenty, begin to amuse themselves at sixty. If they have become fashionable they dine out, and flirt, and have a pleasant St. Martin's summer. This fountain of Late Youth may be too intoxicating; M. Renan had tasted of it freely when he wrote *L'Abbesse de Jouarre.* But all these paper bullets of the brain will drop and be forgotten. The fame of the scholar will endure when the babble about the wit is silent, and *Averröes et l'Averröisme* will outlive *Caliban.*

I had finished this little study of M. Renan's lighter books, and was consoling myself for my failure to take pleasure in them by the thought that they were only "by-works," . . . the distractions of a scholar, when I chanced to pick up a volume by P. Cesare A. de Cara. The name of this volume, very sensible in its general criticism, is *Esáme Critico del Sistema Filologico e Linguistico applicato alla Mitologia e alla Scienza delle Religioni.* Having to do with the science of religion, the learned father encounters M. Renan, and how angrily does he rebuke him! For M. Renan's "ignorance of Hebrew" he refers us to the "excellent article of P. Bourquenoud" somewhere; but who are we to judge between Hebraists? He writes, "Not historical truth, not the connection of ideas, not the establishment of principles, and the severe skill of drawing logical conclusions, but *the art of making phrases,* of producing a twilight of ideas and words, of charming the ear and blinding the intellect, of mixing truth and error, real and false, God and Nature, Nature and human dreams about her,"— these are the arms and arts of M. Renan, according to P. Cesare de Cara.

This is the language of a priest, a learned man I believe, a man of great critical power I am certain, but still a priest, one of the garrison of the old fort that M. Renan has abandoned. But it is a curious thing to note that a young French author, no priest, with no pretence to orthodoxy nor severity, judges M. Renan not, more kindly. "As Macbeth murdered sleep, so M. Renan, twenty times, a hundred times, in each of his books, has murdered joy, has murdered action, has murdered peace of mind and the security of the moral life." This is the verdict of M. Jules Lemaître. The newer generation somehow, shares at least some of the sentiments of Catholics if it does not share their beliefs, and it does not adore M. Renan. (pp. 56-60)

*Andrew Lang, "M. Renan's Later Works," in* The Fortnightly Review, *n.s. Vol. XLI, No. CCLXI, January 1, 1887, pp. 50-60.*

## ANATOLE FRANCE   (essay date 1889)

[*France was a French novelist and critic of the late nineteenth and early twentieth centuries. According to literary historians, France's best work is characterized by clarity, control, perceptive judgment, and the Enlightenment traits of tolerance and justice. Here, France, who acknowledged Renan as a major literary influence, highlights the merits of Renan's historiographical method as revealed in the* Origins of Christianity *and the* History of the People of Israel. *This essay originally appeared in the journal* Le Temps, *and was later published in 1889 in France's* La vie littéraire.]

M. Ernest Renan will give us next week the first volume of

a *Histoire d'Israël,* which will comprise three volumes. This work will form a sort of introduction to his history of the *Origines du Christianisme.*

When it is published, M. Renan will have finished his vast enterprise. He will have investigated the profound sources of the religion which was destined to give sustenance to so many peoples, and which to-day still shares with Buddhism and Islam the empire of souls.

Whatever be the manner in which we approach the obscure beginnings of those great ideas which envelop us on all sides, and in which we are steeped, and whatever account we give of the elaboration of so high an ideal, we must admit that M. Ernest Renan made no mistake regarding the nature and extent of his talents when he directed his mind towards such studies. The subject demanded the rarest and even the most contradictory of intellectual qualities. It required a critical sense always on the alert, a scientific scepticism able to defy all the stratagems of believers and their simplicity, which is mightier still than their stratagems. It required at the same time a vivid feeling for the divine, a secret instinct of the needs of the human soul, and, so to speak, an objective piety. Now this double nature is found in an extraordinarily rich degree in M. Ernest Renan. Without belonging to any religious communion, he has his full share of religious feeling. Though he himself does not believe, he is infinitely apt at seizing all the delicate shades of the popular creeds. I may perhaps be understood when I say that faith does not possess him, but that he possesses faith. Thus happily endowed by nature for his work, he has also prepared himself for it with thoroughness. Born an artist, he has made himself a scholar. His youth was devoted to a fierce labour. For twenty years he studied night and day, and he acquired such a habit of toil that he can accomplish immense tasks in his maturity with all the calm of a contemplative genius. To-day, everything is easy to him, and he renders everything easy to us. In a word, he is an artist, he possesses style—that is to say, he possesses infinite shades of thought.

It must also be said that, if M. Renan was fitted to write about the origins of Christianity, he came at a propitious moment. The work was prepared and men's minds inclined towards the subject. Doubt had been born, and with it curiosity. The philosophy of the eighteenth century had freed men's understandings, and had even penetrated into the Protestant theology. The texts, so long held sacred, had been studied with a great deal of critical ability in France, and with a great deal of knowledge in Germany. M. Renan found the materials for his history ready to his hand. The substance was there; and since he is an artist and a poet he gave to it form and soul.

As a general rule it is imprudent to believe in the novelty of ideas and feelings. Everything has been said and felt long ago, and oftenest we only rediscover the thing which we believe we have found. However, it does seem that the scholars of our own time have a new faculty—that of understanding the past and going back to distant origins. Doubtless in all times man has preserved some remembrances and established some traditions. For a long period he has possessed recorded annals, and it is this, even more than the habit of wearing clothes, which distinguishes him from the beasts. He has rightly said, "Our fathers did this or that." But the differences which there were between himself and them impressed him only slightly. He readily lent the appearance of the present to the most distant past. He was not sensible to the profound differences brought into modes of life by time. He pictured to himself the childhood of the world in the likeness of its maturity. This tendency is strikingly shown in the ancient historians, especially Livy, who makes the rude shepherds of Latium speak as if they were contemporaries of Augustus. It is still more strikingly shown in the art of the Middle Ages, which gave to the Kings of ancient Judea the Hand of Justice and the Crown, decorated with its *fleur de lys,* of the Kings of France. With Descartes the human understanding crossed an abyss. None the less, our seventeenth-century tragedies, although they show a perfect knowledge of abstract man, are based, even in Racine himself, upon the invariability of habits and customs throughout the ages. The eighteenth century, although it concerned itself a great deal with origins, did not hesitate to depict Solon as a sort of Turgot and to invest Semiramis with the royal mantle of Catherine II. It seems that the true image of the past has been revealed to us by the great historical school of our own age. It seems that the sense of origins is a new sense, or at least a sense newly employed by man. The generations that will come after us will perhaps say that we have had a very ridiculous and a very trite view of antiquity; but it is nevertheless certain that in some respects we have created the comparative history of humanity. Fresh sciences such as ethnography, archæology, and philology have had a great share in doing this. The men of antique times are seen by us to-day with a physiognomy, with a character, which may well be true, and which at least approaches truth. And this sense of origins, this divination of a lost past, this knowledge of the childhood of humanity, is possessed in the highest degree by M. Renan. He has shown it in all those parts of his work which border on legend and present primitive scenes which the sun of history has not illumined. With peculiar insight and with perfect tact he has discovered what lay submerged in the twilight of dawn.

M. Renan has had full scope for the use of this art, this gift as I should like to call it, in the history of Israel, a history which we see springing in all its primitive simplicity from childish stories and rustic poems. His travels in the East have furnished him with authentic backgrounds for those pastoral or warlike scenes to which his artist's intelligence gives form and feeling. I do not intend to speak now of his book. I only attempt to indicate the essential qualities of the historian, especially those he has shown in a chapter already familiar, that of Saul and David. I cannot refrain from quoting the portrait M. Renan traces of the first King of Israel. It is an excellent example in support of what I have just said.

> He [Saul] usually dwelt in the district of his birth, Gibeah of Benjamin, called, after him, Gibeah of Saul. There he led a family life without pomp or ceremony, the simple life of a peasant noble, tilling his fields when not at war, and in other respects keeping aloof from all business. His house was of considerable size. At each new moon he held sacrifices and feasts in it, and at these all the officers had special places assigned them. The king sat with his back to the wall. To execute his orders he had *râcim,* 'runners,' similar to the Oriental *chaouch* of modern times. There was nothing else which resembled a court. His proud neighbours, who were, like Abner, more or less his relations, kept him company. It was a sort of nobility, at once rustic and military, which we find at the basis of monarchies that endure.

We are far away from the obscure and noble Saul of tradition. How intelligible and clear the shepherd king has become! And M. Renan's David is still more interesting. How living he seems, with the grace of a young brigand, with the craft of a young chieftain, the ingenuous cruelty, the poetry of a savage. I thought as I read those subtle and vigorous pages how very amusing it is to live in a time like ours, a time when one can compare the little David in a *burnous* of M. Renan with the majestic and pensive David whom the thirteenth-century sculptor shows us, wearing a long white beard, covered by a heavy crown, and holding the prophetic lyre in his hands.

Yes, I said to myself, it is interesting and pleasant to live in a time when both science and poetry find their account, when a broad criticism shows us in marvellous fashion the bud full of the sap of reality as well as the flower of the legend in its full bloom. (pp. 283-88)

> Anatole France, "M. Ernest Renan, Historian of Origins," in his On Life & Letters, first series, *translated by A. W. Evans, John Lane, The Bodley Head, 1911, pp. 283-88.*

**ANATOLE FRANCE** (essay date 1892)

[*Here France reviews* Recollections of My Youth, *commending Renan's poetic sensibility and progressive intellectual stance while disputing his interpretation of the concept of friendship, arguing that it is contradicted by Renan's life and work. Although the original publication date of this essay is unknown, textual evidence indicates that it was written sometime before Renan's death in 1892.*]

With your permission, I will devote the whole of my article this week to the consideration of a single book. The book in question is by M. Ernest Renan, and it is entitled *Souvenirs d'Enfance et de Jeunesse.* I can think of no better, no more delightful, book than this.

There is, about the childhood of gifted men, when they themselves tell the story of it, a charm not easy to define, a blend of sweetness and strength that makes a profound impression on us. Heaven forbid that I should be, in any way, astonished at the interest excited by the early life of great men. But if I wanted thoroughly to explain why the subject is so fascinating, and why it stirs us so deeply, I should say that it is because the childhood of great men bears so striking a resemblance to our own.

Our early years, like theirs, were full of promise. We blossomed forth just as they did; they alone bore fruit. The fruit will be duly stored up in the granary; yet the flower, be it barren, or be it fruitful, leaves behind it the memory of its fragrance. I feel that I must give my blessing to genius, because genius, like lowlier gifts, puts forth, in its earliest stages, its tiny fragile flower. Thus the Christian gives thanks to God for becoming like to a little child. Those who have been endowed with the delightful faculty of portraying life in beautiful colours, have never given a more charming example of that gift than when they have represented their dawning sentiments and the delicious innocence of their childish souls. Rousseau has given us an interesting account of his childhood, despite certain avowals he would have been better advised to withhold. Chateaubriand has revealed to us, with his magic pen, the loneliness, the melancholy and the unappeasable longings that possessed him during his sojourn at Combourg. George Sand never wrote more charmingly than when she told us about the days she passed at her grandmother's side at Nohant. And Dickens, if, as I think, we may recognize

him in the touching pictures he gives us of little David Copperfield, has brought tears to our eyes in portraying for us the good little fellow who, in after years, was destined to grow into the kindliest of men and the most sensitive of writers. And now, Monsieur Ernest Renan comes to us, in his turn, with the story of certain episodes in his life, selected in order to show us the successive stages in the growth of his mind.

Never before, as I think, has so delicate a sensibility been found conjoined with such powerful intellectual gifts; and, as we read the *Souvenirs d'Enfance et de Jeunesse,* we cannot but acknowledge that Monsieur Renan's spirit inhabits those lofty altitudes, where the intellect and the affections are indissolubly united.

"We ought never to write save about the things we love," he himself says in his preface. "Silence and oblivion are the reward we mete out to everything that strikes us as unlovely or ignoble on our journey through life." It is to this kindly and agreeable philosophy that we shall henceforth turn for the secret that underlies all the writings of this remarkable man—a man whom Science has inspired with the loftiest conceptions of beauty and of love. We shall know that, if he has studied the gods, it is, as he has said, to excite love for the divinity that is within us, and to show that this divine quality still lives and will endure for ever, in the heart of man.

Now it is an altogether remarkable thing that this very book—full as it is of the quality of love—contains a passage which has given pain and surprise to many kindly souls.

You already know, without my telling you, the passage to which I refer: it is that in which friendship—at least friendship, as it is ordinarily understood—is accused of being rooted in injustice and error.

> I have not cultivated friendship to any great extent . . . ; I have done little for my friends, and they have done little for me.
>
> I sometimes tell myself what my former instructors were in the habit of inculcating upon me, namely, that friendship is a theft committed to the detriment of Society as a whole, and that, in a higher world, friendship would disappear. Nay, sometimes, when I think of the goodwill that ought to prevail among all men in general, it gives me pain to behold two persons bound together by the ties of an exclusive attachment; I feel as though I must avoid them, as I should avoid those unjust judges who have forfeited their impartiality and their independence. These mutual attachments are, to my mind, like some esoteric society that narrows the mental outlook, contracts the sphere of appreciation, and imposes a heavy chain on our individual freedom.

I do not deny that, coming from such a man, these words ought to be given due weight. Their principle is sound; their birthplace is the seminary; they are capable of producing great effects; it is by taking them to heart that a man becomes a great religious teacher, or a great scientific discoverer. Nevertheless, there is implicit in them a hardness against which, do what I may, I cannot but rebel with the whole instinctive force of my being. Neither the moral grandeur of the solitaries of Port-Royal, nor, what is still more compelling, the intellectual beauty of such a man as Renan, will ever make me believe that it is our duty to shun friendship as containing the germ of concupiscence, or that we should hate it as being a crime against mankind in general. I hold, on the contrary, and shall always hold, that friendship, even when it errs on the side of generosity or of love, is the best thing that man has enriched the earth withal. Yes, I cherish Friendship, even though she fail to hold the scales of justice even. And what do we mean by justice? How can we be just? In the name of whom or what? Cruel and vain is the effort to make the law of love subordinate to the law of justice. Brutus was just when he condemned his sons. I ask Monsieur Renan whether he would care to clasp Brutus by the hand. For my own part, I would far rather kiss the hand of a being steeped in injustice, if only the thought of his children could draw from him tears of love and joy. Let us be unjust, if unjust we must be, but let us love one another; the world is founded not on justice, which takes life, but on love, which multiplies it.

Ah, how well has Christianity understood that the law of mercy is nature's real law, and that the law of justice is but a dream of human arrogance! Consider a mother with her children! Is she merely just towards them? No, she loves them in defiance of the whole world! Were it not so, her little ones could never survive. Nor would it fare well with our friends if we dealt with them according to the dictates of strict justice. Any magistrate is bound to give them justice: we owe them something more. They dwell in our sight, within reach of our hand. For us they sum up and typify the human race. Through them, and them alone, we divine the knowledge of mankind in general. We must never fail in our solicitude for them: for by the services we render them, their hearts are touched; and no such services can affect the beings whom we do not know. I watch over my neighbour; I take an interest in his well-being, such as I certainly do not take in the well-being of a Chinaman.

A Christian psychologist whom I never grow weary of studying—I mean Racine—has ascribed to one of the sweetest and chastest spirits that his genius ever created, the same kind of scruple that visited Monsieur Renan under the heading, "Concerning Private Friendships." Josabeth is afraid of bestowing too much love on little Joas. She says, addressing God, as she thinks of the King who is her child,

Si la chair et le sang, se troublant aujourd'hui,
Ont trop de part aux pleurs que je répands pour lui,
Conserve l'héritier de tes saintes promesses
Et ne punis que moi de toutes mes faiblesses.

[If flesh and blood, growing troubled with care to-day,
Have too large a part in the tears I shed for him,
Keep in safety the inheritor of your holy promises
And punish none but me for the failings that are mine.]

Those scruples of hers came from Port-Royal, just as Monsieur Renan's had their origin at Saint-Sulpice. Both of them, however, are conscious of the promptings of their flesh and blood. It is a beneficent failing, and it does them honour. In vain has Monsieur Renan shut the door of his heart; in vain has he called to mind the stern injunction of the Saint-Sulpicians—"No private friendships." He has grievously failed to observe this law. His whole life, one may say, constitutes a defection from it: for he bestows a generous share of love and affection on his family, on old friends, on the memory of all those companions, grave or gay, who have gone the way to dusty death.

Read his *Souvenirs* once more. Not a page of the book but contains an avowal or a pæan of friendship or of love; of love not for humanity in the abstract, but for some one real and definite, the memory of whose countenance is enshrined with-

in his heart. He exemplifies all the delicacy and reticences of friendship; and I feel that I should be guilty of a sort of intrusion upon the inner sanctuary of his soul were I so much as to record in the pages of a public periodical the names which he is never weary of repeating to himself—the four feminine names on which he has bestowed the glory of immortality. But outside the hallowed circle of his own family, how numerous and charming are the meetings with his fellows, which he so delightfully records! how many hours he lavished on the divine beguilements of friendship! Among the little companions of his childhood there was one little girl—I must make special mention of her—who had a particular fascination for him.

[Her name] was Noémi. She was a little model of goodness and grace. Her eyes were deliciously dreamy, instinct with generosity and intelligence; her hair was adorably fair. She must have been two years older than I, and the way she used to talk to me was a strange mixture of the elder sister and the childish confidante. We got on splendidly together.

Even now I cannot listen to anyone singing *Nous n'irons plus au bois,* or, *Il pleut, il pleut, bergère,* without a little tremor at the heart. Certainly, if it had not been for the fatal bonds that held me in thrall, I should have fallen in love with Noémi two or three years afterwards.

The bonds, as you may readily divine, were theological ones. He bade farewell to Noémi while she was still a child, and he never saw her again. "But," he adds, "I have thought much about her since; and when God gave me a daughter, I called her Noémi."

Where shall we find anything purer and more tender than this friendship and the memory it left behind it.

Of his schoolmasters, too, Monsieur Renan retained an affectionate recollection. Of the good priests of Tréguier he says, "To them I owe whatever good I may have in me." The gratitude he evinces towards the professors at the seminaries of Saint-Nicolas du Chardonnet, Issy and Saint-Sulpice, is profound. "They taught me," he says, "to love truth, to respect reason, and to look seriously upon life."

MM. Olier, Gosselin, Gottofrey, Pinault and Leffir are indebted to their pupil Renan for a fame which they neither expected nor desired, but which, withal, was bestowed on them with an infinite delicacy of touch. I need not here mention Monsieur Berthelot, whom Renan adopted as a brother, and whose friendship, he tells us, was a consolation to him in his days of tribulation. I have said sufficient to show that in a life which lacked nothing in the way of goodness and nobility, "private friendships" were not wanting.

How, then, are we to account for this falling out with friendship which comes to us with such a shock? Is it a remnant of his clerical training? There is no doubt about it. The reserve, which he had acquired as a priest, stood him in good stead as a scholar. Monsieur Renan thus explains and completes the idea he had in mind: "I have never really lived save for the public. They have had the whole of me. There will be no surprise for them after my death. I have reserved nothing for anyone."

Well and good. Certainly there is nothing more laudable, nothing greater, than to labour for the public good. Still, let him say what he will, had it not been for his family, his friends, his gentle counsellors, Monsieur Renan would never have written those pages of real life and dream life, of truth and poetry which make him alike the guide and the enchanter of the finest spirits of his generation. No one could have written in that way unless he had experienced those yearnings of the flesh whereof Josabeth repented, because she had been brought up in the temple.

Like her, Monsieur Renan, too, was brought up within the temple, and this education it was that gives to his *Souvenirs* a character of incomparable originality. His childhood glided calmly by in the little ecclesiastical town of Tréguier. He had a great affection for its lofty steeple, its cloisters, and its tombs; he loved its atmosphere of sombre piety. He was only at his ease in the company of the dead, "beside those knights and noble dames wrapt in calm slumber, with their greyhound at their feet and a great torch of stone in their hand."

The lessons he received there left upon him an abiding impression. They were of a serious nature. Moral conduct was the point on which the good priests of Tréguier chiefly dwelt in their sermons.

> These exhortations had a note of solemnity about them which surprised me. . . . Sometimes we should hear all about Jonathas, who died because he ate a little bit of honey. . . . That set me thinking all kinds of things. What was this little bit of honey that makes people die? . . . What filled me most with wonderment was a certain passage in the life of I know not what holy individual of the seventeenth century, who said women were like to firearms that wound from afar. This completely mystified me. I could make nothing of it. I indulged in the wildest hypotheses in my endeavours to guess how a woman could possibly be like a pistol. Could anything be more puzzling! "Woman wounds from afar." And then again, "You are undone if you touch her." I couldn't make head or tail of it.

Monsieur Renan adds that these examples of saintly ineptitude were invested, in his eyes, with an authoritativeness that moved him to the very depths of his being. Now this review is intended for the consumption of men and women of the world, and I write, here, for women at least as much as for men. Well, then, Madame, how does all this strike you? What say you concerning the sermon of this worthy priest of Tréguier? It is my idea, strictly between ourselves, that you are not at all angry with him, and that M. Renan has good reason to believe that you would be much more annoyed if you were told that you were no wounders of hearts; that you were harmless and to be approached without danger. The most modest and the most austere among you might not wish to rob any man of his peace of mind; but she would like to be able to do so, if she were so inclined. It tickles your vanity to think of all the precautions the Church takes against you. When poor Saint Antony cries, "Avaunt, thou beast!" his terror flatters you. You are enchanted at being more dangerous than you thought you were. You suffer fear to have a free hand because you think that love has nothing to lose by it; and you are perfectly right. Yes, indeed! Let yourselves be feared; love will not lose thereby. As for me personally, I never loved you so much as when I feared you like the werewolf.

The old Breton sermonizes, and his young disciple reminds me of some lines of Corneille, which I will recite to you, just to show you how terribly the Church is afraid of you. They are taken from the *Imitation,* and they run like this:

Fuis avec un grand soin la pratique des femmes;
Ton ennemi par là peut savoir ton défaut.
Recommande en commun aux bontés du Très-Haut,
Celles dont les vertus embellissent les âmes
Et sans en voir jamais qu'avec un prompt adieu,
Aime-les toutes, mais en Dieu.

[Take heed that thou flee the company of women;
By that road thy enemy may find thee vulnerable.
Commend to the mercies of the Most High, in general,
All those whose souls are adorned by virtues
And, never seeing them save to bid them a swift God-
     speed,
Love them all, but in the Lord.]

Ah, my sisters, that is wise counsel indeed; and what blood and tears are in store for those who heed it not! But there! Be ye not troubled. It will never be heeded so long as the breath of life and the light of day caress your lovely form. Be not troubled, my sisters. Till Time shall be no more, men will go on cutting each others' throats for you. Meanwhile, those who pay you the homage of a love which, though fervent indeed, is nevertheless discreet, wholly disinterested; those who bring to your worship an unincarnate passion, enjoy the reward of their piety, for they have visions of you which transcend, in beauty and splendour, the reality itself. After all, theirs is the happier lot. Do you remember that splendid passage at the beginning of volume two of the *Histoire des Origines du Christianisme?* Do you remember how it concludes with the following words: "*Noli tangere?* That is the watchword of those who love greatly." I think that women generally are drawn to M. Renan because they feel that in him they have a gifted friend and an enchanting portraitist.

The *Souvenirs d'Enfance et de Jeunesse* are followed by an epilogue and preceded by a preface which unite the past and the present, and which show us the young man of long ago side by side with the elderly intellectual giant of the present day. He speaks to the world, and the world gives heed—the world, but not the masses. M. Renan will never be a deputy. It is hardly likely that he will get into the Upper House, even by the election of the members of that House, who insist on the candidates' adopting the party programme. Monsieur Renan's ideas are addressed to the aristocracy of the intellect; they come with a disagreeable surprise to narrow-minded politicians, who like to measure other people by their own bushel. Moreover, would he himself be able to evolve any practical policy from his intellectual speculations? I doubt it. In any case, none of the parties would listen to him. They never listen to anybody. They are rich in one thing: their plentiful lack of wit.

In the delightful book we have perused together, and which I close with reluctance, I find this salutary reflection, "The real men of progress are those who begin with a profound respect for the past. All that we do, all that we are, is the outcome of immemorial labour."

If all the gifted souls in the world were to unite in giving utterance to this maxim, would it serve to chasten a single one of our political firebrands? Should we perceive any diminution in the number of those little manuals of citizenship which, in order to make us love our country, picture it to us as plunged in twelve centuries of barbarism, and which take a pleasure in assigning to us for ancestors a stupid peasantry or a cruel and rapacious nobility? No, nothing would be of any avail. The ignorant will go on failing to understand the necessary conditions of social development, and expecting trees without roots to bring forth fruit. (pp. 167-85)

Anatole France, "Essay on Ernest Renan," in his Prefaces, Introductions and Other Uncollected Papers, *translated by J. Lewis May, 1927. Reprint by Kennikat Press, 1970, pp. 165-85.*

## JAMES DARMESTETER  (essay date 1893)

[*In the following excerpt, Darmesteter outlines Renan's theory of scientific and moral progress in* The Future of Science, *arguing that it set the direction for the subsequent development of his philosophy.*]

The last two months of 1848 and the first four months of 1849 were devoted to the compilation of [*The Future of Science*]; it formed a large volume, intended to appear in the same year (it was not published until 1890). . . . It is one of those books which are written only at twenty-five, when one is overflowing with illusions and enthusiasm. It is the enthusiasm of the young man who has had the revelation of a great idea, of science, and who, in the intoxication of the discovery, attributes to it all the nobility of his own soul, adorns it with omnipotence, and believes it capable of satisfying all the aspirations of humanity, of healing all its miseries, and of taking by its pillow the rôle which positive religion can no longer sustain. Insufficiently developed, often difficult in expression, obscure through the plethora of thought in a mind which has not yet learned to sacrifice or reserve a part of its treasures, and which gives itself forth entire, often retarded by those considerations of system, after the German fashion, which require an apparatus of thought too considerable for the substantial residue which they leave,—this book has yet more than the merit of being a curiosity, which M. Renan attributed to it when, forty years later, he took it out of his bureau "to show, entirely natural, but afflicted by a serious brain fever, a young man living solely in his intellect and believing fanatically in truth." This book is, in a certain sense, the most complete one that M. Renan wrote, and it contains, more than simply in germ, the whole Renan whom we know. To be sure, in the course of time, he will lose his illusions as to the omnipotence of science; he will recognize that it cannot found a religion of itself alone; that truth can enlighten and direct only those who have already in themselves a directing principle, either in the innate nobility of their education or in the hereditary habits of virtue impressed upon them by ancestors who believed. He himself will say later that the virtue of skeptical ages is the residuum left by ages of faith: "My life is always governed by a faith which I no longer possess." He will recognize that the dream of Plato is only a dream; that philosophy is not made to rule the world and replace politics; and that it is not possible for science to reconstruct the edifice which was built by the spontaneous forces of nature. The fundamental optimism which penetrates these youthful pages; these unmeasured hopes for the future of humanity, considered as the purposed end of the development of nature and remaining in this semi-Hegelian conception, as it was before in the Catholic conception, the centre of the universe, will make way for a limited optimism which, if we consider things objectively, is only the form that theoretical pessimism takes in a good soul enamored of the beautiful and open to the innocent pleasures of life and knowledge. These pages bear the mark of [the 1848 Revolution] in their democratic aspiration, in their conception of humanity as one single being, as a homogeneous body, all the members of which are capable of

comprehending and realizing the same ideal. It is a far cry from this book to the discouraged pages of the ***Dialogues philosophiques,*** and to that transcendent and cruel vision of progress making the immolation of a lower layer of humanity serve the coming of an elect race which will realize more fully the obscure dream of the hidden God.

Nevertheless, despite the corrections which age is to bring to these theories of youth, all Renan's essential ideas are here already, and it is upon this foundation, laid in his twenty-fifth year, that his whole doctrine was developed. For a long time this great Purana, left unpublished, was a sort of monumental quarry from which he drew, without exhausting it, raw material and polished stones, like those architects who built the Rome of the Popes from the stones of the Coliseum. Some of his most admired pages came from this quarry, and nowhere has he brought out more clearly his conception of the divine:

> Beauty in the moral order, this is religion. This is the reason why a dead and outgrown religion is yet more effective than all purely secular institutions; this the reason why Christianity is still more creative, consoles more sorrows and acts more vigorously upon humanity than all the acquired principles of modern times. The men who will make the future will not be petty men, disputing, reasoning, insulting,—partisans and intriguers, without an ideal. They will be beautiful, they will be amiable, they will be poetic. . . . The word 'God,' being in possession of the respect of humanity, having a long prescription, and having been employed in noble poetry, its suppression would put humanity off the track. Although it is not very univocal, as the scholastics say, it corresponds to an idea sufficiently definite: the *summum* and the *ultimum,* the limit where the soul stops in ascending the ladder of the infinite. . . . Tell the simple to live a life of aspiration after truth and beauty, and these words will have no meaning for them. Tell them to love God, not to offend God, and they will understand you marvelously well. God, providence, the soul,—these are so many good old words, a little awkward, but expressive and respectable, which science will explain, but will not replace to advantage. What is God for humanity if not the transcendent résumé of its supersensible needs, *the category of the ideal* (that is, the form under which we conceive the ideal), as space and time are *the categories of matter,* (that is, the forms under which we conceive matter). All may be reduced to this fact of human nature: Man facing the divine rises out of himself, and is held by a heavenly spell, and his own petty personality is exalted and absorbed? What is this if it is not to adore?

Augustin Thierry, to whom M. Renan read his manuscript, dissuaded him from making his entrance into the literary world with this metaphysical epic in his hands. He advised him to send to the *Revue des Deux-Mondes* and to the *Journal des Debats* articles upon various subjects, in which he could publish by instalments a stock of ideas which, presented in one solid mass, would not have failed to frighten the French public. Thus *The Future of Science,* put forth in sections and in a concrete, illuminated and manageable form entered, little by little, into the intellectual circulation. Yet Renan's apprenticeship to learning was sufficiently advanced for him to be in a condition to begin his scientific career proper. This with such a nature had necessarily to take for its object the study of the human spirit; the great progress realized over the seventeenth and eighteenth centuries, for which the study of the human mind was, above all, a logical analysis and a judgment *a priori,* has never been better expressed than in the closing lines of the preface of his book: "The science of the human mind should, most of all, be the history of the human mind, and this history is possible only through the patient philological study of the works which it has brought forth in different ages." It is this history which formed the object of his research for the rest of his life.

Thus at twenty-five M. Renan was what he was to be later, what he will be always. His philosophy is constructed and his life and his work will be its peaceful and uniform development. External circumstances may alter the form and the expression, but not the essence. The critics, who are absolutely determined that every man shall be placed in a category fixed in advance, and are not at ease until they have furnished each name with a label, like the apothecary with his drugs, have often asked whether M. Renan was a philosopher, a scholar, or a poet. As he was plainly an incomparable writer, they concluded that he was, above all, an artist, and that in philosophy he was a reflection of Germany, and in science an amateur. This shows that they but slightly understood M. Renan. No writer of the century sacrificed less to the delusive and barren idol of "art for art's sake." In France, where the art of expression has always been the supreme gift, as in the time of the Gauls, no one has more profoundly disdained and more decisively assaulted that literary dilettanteism, that love of form courted for itself and not pursued as the sincere expression of an idea which deserves to be expressed, that obstinacy in despising the substance of knowledge and esteeming only style and talent, which, from 1830 to 1860, paralyzed science, gave a fatal blow to serious research, and reduced intellectual culture to pompous and superficial qualities, to the art of making academic phrases. Science, philosophy and art are for him and in him one and the same single thing, the diverse aspects of truth sought, comprehended and expressed.

It is not easy to sum up the work of M. Renan, so diverse is it in its subjects and its forms. In the variety of his studies he resembles more a Greek philosopher than a modern specialist. A specialist in the proper sense of the word he never became. If the philosopher devotes himself to a limited field, this is reasonable because of the impossibility of embracing everything; by right the whole universe belongs to him. Classic antiquity, the Middle Ages, art, contemporary history, politics,—M. Renan invaded all these provinces, and if he devoted twenty years of his life to the history of Christianity it was not solely because his ecclesiastical education predisposed him to it, but most of all because Christianity, with its roots in Judaism, led him through the most vital periods of the human soul, and allowed him to refresh himself from one of the most fruitful sources of the moral life of humanity. (pp. 410-14)

The mistaken judgments passed upon M. Renan are due to the fact that in his work he did not place the emphasis upon the Good but upon the True. Men concluded that for him, therefore, science was the whole of life. The environment in which he was formed was forgotten, an environment in which the moral sense was exquisite and perfect, while the scientific sense was *nil.* He did not have to discover the moral sense, it was the very atmosphere in which he lived. When the scientific sense awoke in him, and he beheld the world and history transfigured by it, he was dazzled, and the influence lasted his life long. He dreamed of making France understand this new revelation; he was the apostle of this gospel of truth and science, but in heart and mind he never attacked what is permanent and divine in the other gospel. Thus he was a complete man, and deserved the disdain of dilettantes morally dead, and of mystics scientifically atonic.

What heritage has M. Renan left to posterity? As a scholar he created religious criticism in France and prepared for universal science that incomparable instrument the *Corpus.* As an author he bequeathed to universal art pages which will endure, and to him may be applied what he said of George Sand: "He had the divine faculty for giving wings to his subject, for producing under the form of fine art the idea which in other hands remained crude and formless." As a philosopher he left behind a mass of ideas which he did not care to assemble in doctrinal shape, but which, nevertheless, constitute a coherent whole. One thing only in this world is certain,—duty. One truth is plain in the course of the world as science reveals it: the world is advancing to a higher, more perfect form of being. The supreme happiness of man is to draw nearer to this God to come, contemplating Him in science, and in action preparing the advent of a humanity nobler, better endowed, and more akin to the ideal Being. (pp. 432-33)

*James Darmesteter, "Ernest Renan," in* The New World, *Vol. II, No. VII, September, 1893, pp. 401-33.*

**LUCIEN LÉVY-BRUHL** (essay date 1899)

[*Bruhl discusses the problems of interpreting Renan's syncretically organized philosophy, which he views as a hybrid of religion and science.*]

Renan possessed, first and foremost, a marvellous gift of style. He at once took rank among classical writers beside the great masters of French prose. He was also a historian. Whatever may be the judgment of posterity regarding the ***Origines du Christianisme*** and the ***Histoire du Peuple d'Israel,*** the undertaking was a great one, and marks an epoch in this sort of study in France. But was Renan really a philosopher? In this field do we find in his numerous books anything beyond maxims, opinions, beautifully expressed, but without any bond of unity and inner coherence? Though he shuns all dialectic display, and is careful never to give demonstrations, is there ever found in his writings a consistent and solid nucleus, a body of principles ensuring the continuity of his thought amidst apparent changes, paradoxes and ironies? Renan himself certainly thought that there was. To this not only his ***Dialogues Philosophiques,*** but his ***Drames Philosophiques,*** and above all, ***L'Avenir de la Science,*** testify expressly. The rest of his productions, also, and even his most special works of technical scholarship, as those on linguistics, had evidently in his mind a philosophical bearing. After the example of his master, Burnouf, he believed that the greatest results could often be obtained from the minutest analysis of details. The philosopher in him always stood at the elbow of the philologist.

Various causes may have rendered him liable to misinterpretation. First, the particular nature of his style; he is fond of delicate shades and tints of meaning, and averse to peremptory and sweeping assertions. He must have seemed often a dilettante, who delighted in toying with ideas; and we cannot deny that he was pleased with his own suppleness. But this suppleness was not incompatible with a serious mind and a respect for truth. We must so completely respect truth, says

Renan, as never to overstate it; and we already overstate truth if we present it without the restrictions, the extenuations, the shades, and even the doubts it implies. "A thoroughly complete work ought to leave no need for a refutation." The reverse of every thought ought to be pointed out, that the reader may see at one glance the two opposite faces of which every truth is composed; though this twofold way of thinking may occasion some uneasiness in readers who are fond of simplicity.

Furthermore, it is true that Renan's philosophy varied, not on the chief points, but in details, and above all, in the tone of expression. Being not only much inclined to take a broad view of the world and of mankind, but also very sensitive to the events he witnessed, Renan felt keenly the shock with which these events reacted on him, as is shown by his works. The revolution of 1848 and the June days, the *coup d'état* which made Napoleon the Third an emperor, the disasters of 1870, the final success of the Republican party in 1878, all in their turn exercised a powerful influence upon Renan's mind, giving it, however, rather a different coloring than a new direction. Finally, last but not least among the reasons which may have caused Renan's philosophy to be misconceived, it is not of a regular, and so to speak, classical type. It is not fashioned in the usual form. Its problems are not proposed or solved in the customary terms. The reason for this is that Renan composed his philosophy for his own use, under the pressure of needs peculiar to himself, such as most other men of his generation did not feel as he did. That he was able to communicate these needs to them is not the least part of his glory.

Like Lamennais and Father Gratry, Renan went from the Roman Catholic Church to philosophy. But there is a wide difference between them and him. Lamennais, after having given his whole strength to attacking, with the Traditionalists, the philosophy of the eighteenth century, went on to develop the social principles he discerned in the Gospel, and to work out the conception of a Christian democracy. In his contest with Rome he did not in the least assail the real essence of faith; and he was justified in entitling one of his most vigourous pamphlets *Paroles d'un Croyant*. Father Gratry thought he had found a philosophical proof of what is taught by religious dogmas, or at least by part of them. His "transcendental method," justified, as he thought, by its analogy with the transcendental method used in mathematics, led him to the much-desired reconciliation of reason and faith. Renan's case is quite different. Born and bred in the Catholic faith, brought up in the thought and hope of becoming a priest, never having conceived any other ambition, and being encouraged therein by his family and by his teachers, he perceived at the age of twenty that his belief was no longer sufficient. He had ceased to be a Roman Catholic, and even, in the strictest sense of the word, to be a Christian. He had to break off all his cherished ties and to give up all his fondest hopes. He had to go back into the world and begin life anew.

In what terms was the philosophical problem to present itself to him? In terms, no doubt, quite different from those which occurred to such men as Maine de Biran, Cousin, or even Auguste Comte. His situation was unique. He wanted a doctrine which would restore to him all that he had lost in losing faith, which would, without having recourse to the supernatural, supply him with an acceptable interpretation of the universe, and at the same time with a certain rule of conduct. Had he examined the whole of the problem—had he begun,

as Descartes did, by temporarily considering as false all that he had hitherto thought and believed—he would have entered upon an undertaking unsuited to his character and perhaps beyond his power. He adopted a less radical solution. Instead of developing his doubt logically, he set limits to it. Of the whole system of belief that had been taught him, he rejected only what he saw clearly to be incompatible with his reason—that is to say, with science and criticism; he kept all the rest, and out of it constructed a doctrine which remained essentially religious. What he could no longer admit was the historical husk of religion, the narrow, one-sided notions, the myth that falls before the blows of criticism, the assumption of a supernatural character in the Christian revelation; whereas he knew that we have here to deal with a phenomenon in all respects similar to that of the appearance of Buddhism, Islamism, etc. But in the very essence of religion, the mystery of divinity, and of man's participation in it, Renan did not cease to believe.

His philosophy must therefore needs be a secularized and rationalized form of his faith. He was sorry for a rupture which grieved his dearest friends, but there was within him neither the anguish of moral upheaval nor an intellectual crisis. "To all these outward revolutions there corresponded no inward revolution. I have learned several things, but I have changed in nowise as to the general system of intellectual and moral life. My habitation has become more spacious, but it still stands on the same ground. I look upon my estrangement from orthodoxy as only a change of opinion concerning an important historical question, a change which does not prevent me from dwelling on the same foundations as before. I accept and preserve all the practical and speculative traditions of my past, intending subsequently to correct them by the logical results of my thoughts and studies."

Thus Renan's philosophy does not stand in opposition to religion, and has no intention of taking its place. Nothing can replace religion. It forms part of the very definition of humanity. Without it man falls to the level of the brute. Had Renan been obliged to choose between positive religion, with its mythical elements, and an abstract system of philosophy, devoid of all religious feeling, he would not have hesitated; he would have chosen the positive religion. But happily this dilemma was not presented. The task of our time, one not impossible of accomplishment, consists precisely in preserving all the essential part of religion in a free and harmonious philosophy. We must, therefore, "transfer religion into the region of the unassailable, beyond special dogmas and supernatural belief." Such a philosophy must also take into account all the elements of intellectual and moral life, which Christianity did not do. It totally neglected what is true and beautiful. It looked upon philosophy, poetry and science as so many vanities. Human nature was thus deprived of some of its most essential members. Among intellectual things, which are all alike holy, a distinction was made between the profane and the sacred. A fatal distinction! Whatever comes from the soul is sacred.

Imagine Malebranche having read Gœthe, Kant, and Hegel, having studied under Burnouf and understood Lamarck's theories. If, instead of looking down upon the history of the human mind as a futile picture of what others have thought, the proud Oratorian had consented to look at the world and at humanity, how much wider his horizon would have become! from how many prejudices he would have freed himself! He would have beheld the endless meanderings of legend and history and the infinite web of divine creations; and though the sight might have bereft him of his narrow faith, it would have given him instead a sense of true theology, which is the science of the world and of humanity, the science of universal development (*Werden*), which leads, under the aspect of worship, to poetry and art, and above all, to morals.

Such a nineteenth-century Malebranche Renan tried to be. (pp. 397-403)

[His] philosophy, or science, as Renan chose to call it, is undoubtedly religious, but it is surely not Christian. It is even in a sense anti-Christian. It renews what Malebranche termed the source of every heathen impiety; it denies creation and defies nature. Jesus, says Renan, will always be my God. But Jesus is no longer the Redeemer of man from original sin. Man's nature has no need of being redeemed, for it is not corrupted, but has its part in the divine work of progress.

Thence come the fluctuations, rather apparent than real, in Renan's moral doctrine, which did not vary in its fundamental views. Now he protests that the morals taught by the Gospel will always be his, that Christian education has made him what he is, that he will be eternally grateful to it, and that it will prevent him from ever falling into low, frivolous habits. Again, he speaks to us most admirably of his master Marcus Aurelius, glorifies his fortitude and his melancholy optimism. Still again, he wonders whether virtue may not be delusion, and runs the risk of scandalising Christian souls by declaring that beauty is quite as good as virtue. But all these sayings may be reconciled without supposing in Renan either a surprising instability of doctrine or a desire to astonish his readers. His conception of morals is, at the same time, natural, like that of Epicurus; rational, like that of Marcus Aurelius, and divine, like that of the Gospel. The comprehensive principles of his philosophy admitted of such a synthesis.

Yet he differs from Christian morals on an important point. Nature is divine. Man, who is one of nature's masterpieces, is not born actually good, but with the possibility of becoming so. All the evil in humanity proceeds from want of culture. Renan here agrees with the philosophers of the eighteenth century and their perfect confidence in human nature. "I, who have a cultivated mind, find no evil in myself, and in all things turn spontaneously to what seems to me most beautiful. Were all men's minds as cultivated as my own, all men, like myself, would be in the happy case of finding it impossible to do wrong. An *educated* man has but to follow the delightful bent of his inner impulse. He might adopt the motto of the Abbey of Thélème, 'Do thou as thou choosest,' for he cannot choose any but beautiful things. A virtuous man is an artist."

Shall we call this pride, or perhaps irony? To be sure, the author of Caliban did not shut his eyes to the fierce and base instincts that survived in the soul of the "improved gorilla." He knew how much time and how many efforts it has taken to accomplish the fragile work of civilisation. But the definition of humanity must be found in the ideal to which it dimly tends, and which some time it is to reach. Christianity was mistaken in making a virtue of humility. The foundation of our morality is the excellence, the perfect autonomy of human nature. We must not, therefore, define goodness as obedience to the will of a superior being. Nor must we impose upon man ascetic observances; to affect abstinence proves that we highly value the things of which we deprive ourselves.

Plato mortified his body less than Dominique Loricat did, and no doubt he was more of a spiritualist.

Likewise, the imperative character of duty should not be too much insisted upon. We obey it, but we see the weakness of the arguments upon which it rests. We obey it, because we have faith in God, because we believe in progress, in good, and in the final victory of what is best, and this without any hope of personal reward. The same privilege of human nature which enables us to be religious—that is, to understand the divine work—also enables us to be moral—that is, to have a share in that work. "There is in man a faculty or a need, a capacity, in short, which is satisfied in our days by morals, and which has always been satisfied, and always will be, by something of the kind. I understand that the word *morals* may in future times become inadequate, and may be replaced by another. For my particular use I prefer to substitute for it the word *æsthetics*. Let us remember that whatever is of the soul is sacred. Greece, which carried the beautiful to its utmost perfection, is as much entitled to the gratitude of men as Judæa, which taught them divine justice."

We cannot here enter, even summarily, into the details of Renan's political and social ideas; to summarise them would be simply equivalent to distorting them. They were among his favourite themes for reflexion; their wealth, their variety, and even their apparent incongruities, are indeed often somewhat puzzling. In order to account for this, we must remember the interest Renan took in contemporaneous events, and his tendency to make the whole of his ideas harmonise with them, though without changing those ideas in essential particulars. Moreover, the general optimism of his philosophy did not make him less clear-sighted, and could not prevent him from being aware alike of the folly of revolutionists and of the selfish absurdity of conservatives. Lastly, he himself confesses that his opinion on very important points became modified with time. In *L'Avenir de la Science,* when full of juvenile enthusiasm, and no doubt under the influence of socialist doctrines, he believed that science would finally enfranchise all mankind; he hoped to see all men rising to the new religion and participating in full consciousness "in the organisation of mankind and of God." Later on, in the *Drames,* and chiefly in the *Dialogues philosophiques,* he understands how chimerical such a hope is; he considers it probable that the ignorant mass will always need to be ruled over by an intelligent aristocracy. He even conceives the idea of a few men holding in their hands, by means of their science, the fate of the globe, and reigning over mankind by the terror they inspire. But such a dream, even to Renan himself, was nothing but a sort of nightmare.

At the end of his life, as he looked back upon his juvenile works, he persuaded himself that upon the whole he had been right, and he remained faithful to his leading ideas. "Progress," he says, "save a few disappointments, has been accomplished in the direction I imagined. Like Hegel, I made the mistake of attributing too positively to mankind a central part in the universe. The development of humanity may possibly be of no more consequence than the moss or lichens growing over a damp surface. But still, in our eyes, the history of mankind preserves its supremacy, since mankind alone, for all we know, constitutes the consciousness of the universe. And even though life should disappear from our small planet before mankind has attained to the full consciousness which is its supreme aim, the attempt baffled here would succeed elsewhere, and the effort toward the realisation of God would not be lost. But for this supreme hope, life would be absurd, and this wretched comedy would not be worth playing. Did I not believe that mankind was summoned to a divine end, I should become an Epicurean, if I could, and if not, I should commit suicide. But virtue will be vindicated in the end."

Renan's philosophy is therefore really a kind of faith. Is it a philosophy as well? This is the question which we proposed in the beginning, and which the reader can now answer. Renan's doctrine certainly does not fulfil the idea once entertained of a philosophical system. Renan himself never thought of constructing one. With respect to metaphysics considered as a science, his attitude was that of a positivist. Every truth, he says, has its starting point in scientific experiment. It issues directly or indirectly from a laboratory or a library, for whatever we learn we learn by studying nature or history. "Philosophy is not a separate science; it is one side of every science. In the great optic pencil of human knowledge it is the central region where the rays meet in one and the same light." No doubt there is room for a logic or a criticism of the human mind, such as Kant attempted, but there is no room for vain and shallow metaphysical speculation.

But while abandoning its ancient dogmatic claims, philosophy is enriched, on the other hand, with the ideas of humanity and progress. The idea of humanity is the great boundary line between old and new philosophies. Carefully examine why the old systems can no longer satisfy you, and you will see that it is because this idea is absent from them. In it there is a whole new system of philosophy. The moment that mankind is considered as a consciousness in process of formation and development, there is a psychology of mankind as well as one of the individual. There is, therefore, a science of the human mind, which is not only the analysis of the machinery of individual understanding, but the very history of the human soul.

This philosophy was prepared by the eighteenth century in France, which clearly conceived the import of history. But in history itself it misapprehended the part of spontaneousness and exaggerated that of reflexion, so that it thoroughly understood nothing but itself. It did not see that primitive epochs were the creative epochs; it tried to explain everything with words of superficial clearness—"credulity," "superstition," "fanaticism"—and above all, it attacked religion in its essence, without seeing that it is as eternal as the human soul. The result was a dry, analytical, negative rationalism, satisfactory neither to the imagination nor to the heart, nor even to reason. A. Comte understood the import of history and the idea of progress. But he did not realise the deep variety of mankind. He was unacquainted with the East and India; he studied only the Western world, and even in this overlooked the details of history. Thence comes the arbitrary, artificial and already decrepit character of his building. Only historical and philological sciences can do as much for the knowledge of humanity as the positive sciences have done for the knowledge of nature. And among those historical and philological sciences the science of religions is that which throws most light upon the past of mankind and the direction of progress. Thus, in writing the *Origines du Christianisme,* Renan thought he was writing the most necessary and philosophical book of the age. (pp. 412-19)

*Lucien Lévy-Bruhl, "Renan and Taine," in his His- tory of Modern Philosophy in France, 1899. Re- print by The Open Court Publishing Company, 1924, pp. 397-435.*

## IRVING BABBITT    (essay date 1902)

[*With Paul Elmer More, Babbitt was one of the founders of the New Humanism (or neo-humanism) movement which arose during the 1920s. The New Humanists were strict moralists who adhered to traditional conservative values in reaction to an age of scientific and artistic self-expression. In regard to literature, they believed that the aesthetic qualities of a work of art should be subordinate to its moral and ethical purpose, and were hence opposed to Naturalism and to any literature, such as Romanticism, that broke with established classical tradition. The author of several books propounding his philosophy, Babbitt was more a theorist than a literary critic; most of the New Humanist criticism was written by More, T. S. Eliot, and—until the mid-1920s—Stuart P. Sherman. The following excerpt originally appeared in 1902 as part of Babbitt's preface to* Recollections of My Youth. *Describing Renan as a "scientist and positivist with a Catholic imagination," Babbitt comments on the success of his historical method in* The Origins of Christianity.]

Renan says that his purpose in his *Souvenirs* is not so much to narrate the incidents of his youth as to trace his intellectual origins and "transmit to others his theory of the world." The intellectual life he has thus recorded, extraordinarily rich in itself, derives an added interest from the fact that it is so largely representative of his age. He speaks in one of his essays of *la pensée délicate, fuyante, insaisissable du xix$^e$ siècle.* These are the very epithets that best describe his own thought. He is a Proteus, whom no one has yet succeeded in binding. It would be possible to do justice to him, says Sainte-Beuve, only in a Platonic dialogue; but who, he adds, could be found to write it? If Renan is thus subtle and many-sided, it is because he embodies so perfectly the spirit of modern criticism. The first step in understanding him is to have clearly in mind the difference between this new critical ideal and the old. The critic's business as once conceived was to judge with reference to a definite standard and then to enforce his decisions by his personal weight and authority. The nature of the reaction against this conception is summed up in a phrase of Carlyle's: "We must see before we begin to oversee." Flexibility of intelligence and breadth of sympathy come more and more to take the place of authority and judgment as the chief virtues of the critic. Mere judging—"the blaming of this or the praising of that," says Renan, "is the mark of a narrow method." If the weakness of the old criticism was its narrowness and dogmatism, the danger of the new is that in its endeavor to embrace the world in a universal sympathy, it should forget the task of judging altogether. Renan would rest his criticism on the "excluding of all exclusiveness," on an intellectual hospitality so vast as to find room for all the contradictory aspects of reality. "Formerly," he says, "every man had a system; he lived and died by it; now we pass successively through all systems, or, better still, understand them all at once." No one was ever more penetrated by the teaching of the Hegelian logic, that a truth, to become true, needs to be completed by its contrary. At first glance he would seem to be a new kind of skeptic, who, instead of doubting everything, affirms everything—which is, of course, only an indirect way of denying the absolute truth of anything. Yet we could fall into no more serious error than to suppose that Renan is a real skeptic. "Woe to the man," he exclaims, "who does not contradict himself at least once a day." But there are some points on which he never contradicts himself, however much they may be overlaid in his later writings by irony and paradox. We can come at these essential affirmations more readily if we turn to that remarkable work of his youth, *L'Avenir de la science,* recollecting that though written in 1848 it did not appear until 1890, with a preface in which Renan avers that at bottom he has not changed in the interval. In the peculiar fervor of the cult it renders to science, the book marks a moment, not in the life of Renan merely, but of the century. We have but to listen to the dithyrambic tones in which he speaks of science to see that he has turned away from the faith of his childhood only to become the priest of another altar: "Science, then, is a religion; science alone in the future will make creeds; science can alone solve for man the everlasting problems the solution of which his nature imperiously demands." After humanity has been scientifically organized, science will proceed to "organize God."

Renan has evidently carried over to science all the mental habits of Catholicism. As Sainte-Beuve remarks, "In France we shall remain Catholics long after we have ceased to be Christians." Renan, indeed, may be best defined as a scientist and positivist with a Catholic imagination. For instance, he arrives at the conception of scientific dogma, of an infallible scientific papacy, of a scientific hell and inquisition, of resurrection and immortality through science, of scientific martyrs. When scientific progress is at stake, he is even ready to resort to the Jesuitical doctrine that the end justifies the means. "Let us learn not to be severe with those who have employed a little trickery and what is usually known as *corruption,* if they really have as their object the greater good of humanity." He promises us that if we imitate him we may hope to be, like himself, sanctified through science: "If all were as cultivated as I, all would be, like me, happily incapable of wrongdoing. Then it would be true to say: ye are gods and sons of the Most High."

Renan thus has a special gift for surrounding science with an atmosphere of religious emotion. Like Lucretius of old, he lends to analysis an imaginative splendor that it does not in itself possess. In this way, he attracts many who would have been repelled by a hard and dry positivism. They can have in reading him the pleasant illusion that, after all, they are making no serious sacrifice in substituting science for religion. "God, Providence, soul," says Renan, "good old words, a bit clumsy, but expressive and respectable, which science will interpret in a sense ever more refined, but will never replace to advantage." In other words, all the terms of the old idealism are to be retained, but by a system of subtle equivocation they are to receive new meanings. Thus a great deal is said about the "soul," but, as used by Renan, it has come to be a sort of function of the brain. "Those will understand me who have once breathed the air of the other world and tasted the nectar of the ideal." When this is taken in connection with the whole passage where it occurs, we discover that "tasting the nectar of the ideal" does not signify much more than reading a certain number of German monographs. Men, he tells us, are immortal,—that is, "in their works," or "in the memory of those who have loved them," or "in the memory of God." Elsewhere we learn that by God he means merely the "category of the ideal." By a further attenuation, the ideal has ceased to be the immediate personal perception of a spiritual order superior to the phenomenal world—of idealism in this sense there is more in one sentence of Emerson than in scores of pages of Renan. It is simply the faith in scientific progress reinforced, as we have seen, in his own case, by a religious sensibility of unusual depth and richness. His creed, as he himself formulates it, is "the cult of the ideal, the negation of the supernatural, the experimental search for truth." In spite of the first article of this creed, Renan is like

other positivists in his extreme distrust of the unaided insight or intuition of the individual. We should note how careful he is to rest his revolt from Catholicism, not on the testimony of the reason or the conscience, but on the outer fact.

The belief was once held, and in France with a firmer assurance than elsewhere, that truth might be attained by abstract reasoning. In Malebranche's dialogue, Théodore and Ariste shut themselves up in their room with drawn curtains so as to consult more effectually the inner oracle, and then start out from this luminous proposition: *Le néant n'a point de propriétés.* Renan, for his part, will be satisfied with nothing less than the entire overthrow of apriorism and metaphysical assumption. He regards "the slightest bit of scientific research" as more to the purpose than "fifty years of metaphysical meditation." To be sure, every man has a right to his philosophy, but this philosophy is only his personal dream of the infinite, and has no objective value apart from the scientific data it happens to contain. Superficial readers of Renan are disconcerted when they learn that nothing he had done gave him so much satisfaction as his **Corpus Inscriptionum Semiticarum,** the most aridly erudite of all his works, the one into which he has put the least of himself, according to ordinary standards. But what, Renan might reply, is a mere dream of the infinite, however artistically expressed, compared with the honor of contributing even a single brick to that edifice of positive knowledge which is being reared by science, and is destined to take the place of the air-palaces of the metaphysicians?

Renan is careful, then, to found his study of man not on introspection, but on the positive evidence of history and language. "There is no science of the individual soul." This one phrase contains the denial of the old religion and psychology; but he offers to substitute for this traditional idea of human nature a definite image of humanity as it is revealed in its past. "The only science of a being in a constant state of development is its history." History, therefore, rises at once into immense importance as the means by which man is to arrive at the necessary truths about his own nature.

Renan himself was so admirably endowed for historical study that in thus exalting it he may be suspected of viewing life too exclusively from the angle of his own special faculty. "All the misfortunes of men," says the dancing-master in Molière, "all the fatal reverses that fill the world's annals, the blunders of statesmen and the shortcomings of great captains arise from not knowing how to dance." We cannot, however, easily overrate the importance of the revolution that took place early in the last century in the manner of understanding history. Renan himself was one of the first to see in this new historical sense the chief acquisition and distinctive originality of the nineteenth century. "History," says Sainte-Beuve, "that general taste and aptitude of our age, falls heir, in effect, to all the other branches of human culture." A few believers in direct vision, like Emerson, protested: "Our age is retrospective. It builds the sepulchres of the fathers. It writes biographies, histories, and criticisms." But in this matter Emerson's voice was that of one crying in the wilderness. The fascination of what he calls "masquerading in the faded wardrobe of the past" has made itself felt more and more, until it has come, in such forms as the historical novel, to appeal to the veriest Philistine.

In itself, this imaginative and sympathetic understanding of the past was worth acquiring, even at the cost of some one-sidedness. The old-fashioned historian had an entirely inadequate notion of the variable element in human nature. He had before him in writing a sort of image of man in the abstract which he supposed to hold good for all particular men "from China to Peru"; he used very similar terms in speaking of Louis XIV and a king of the Merovingian dynasty, and judged them in the main by the same standard. A historian like Renan, on the contrary, uses all his art in bringing out the differences that separate men in time and space. He has little to say about man in general, but he makes us feel the ways in which an Athenian of the time of the Antonines had ceased to resemble an Athenian of the age of Pericles, how the mental attitude of a Greek differed from that of a Jew, in what respects an inhabitant of Rome was unlike an inhabitant of Antioch. "The essence of criticism," he tells us, "is the ability to enter into modes of life different from our own." In this definition he favors once more his own talent, which excels in nothing so much as in seizing and rendering the finest shades of thought and feeling, in making the most subtle distinctions. He has in a high degree what he himself calls "the direct intuition of the sentiments and passions of the past." For this gift of historical divination there is needed, in addition to exact scholarship, a perfect blending of those feminine powers of comprehension and sympathy to which Goethe has paid tribute at the end of the second *Faust*. Renan himself is fond of insisting on this feminine side of his nature. "I have been reared by women and priests. In this fact lies the explanation both of my virtues and my faults. . . . In my manner of feeling I am three-fourths a woman." Elsewhere he ascribes this predominance of feminine traits to the entire Celtic race, and especially to his own branch of it.

With his native aptitude for noting minute changes, Renan was peculiarly fitted to receive the new theories of evolution. The German scholarship and speculation, which he did so much to make known in France, are permeated by this idea of gradual growth and development. The old psychology had studied man from the static point of view; in the philosophy of Renan, even God evolves. For him, the great modern achievement is to "have substituted the category of becoming for the category of being, the conception of the relative for the conception of the absolute, movement for immobility." One who has found, like Renan, how much may be explained by the historical method, is tempted to use it to explain everything. He is curiously loath to grant that a work of art, for example, may be valuable by virtue of its universal human truth, and not simply as the mirror of a particular type of man or civilization. "It is not Homer who is beautiful," he says, "but Homeric life, the phase in the existence of humanity described by Homer." "If the Ossianic hymns of Macpherson were authentic, we should have to place them alongside of Homer; as soon as it is proved that they are by a poet of the eighteenth century, they have only a very trifling value." Renan's historical finesse does not compare favorably here with the vigorous good sense of Dr. Johnson, who remarks characteristically of Ossian: "Sir, a man might write such stuff forever if he would only *abandon* his mind to it."

It would be possible to multiply passages from Renan to show that his attitude towards literature is not primarily literary but historical or philological. He confesses that he valued literature for a time only to please Sainte-Beuve, who had had a great deal of influence upon him. No worse heresy from the point of view of the lover of letters was ever uttered than when Renan said that "literary history is destined to take the place in great part of the direct reading of the works of the human spirit"; or when he declared that he would "exchange

all the beautiful prose of Livy for some of the documents that he had before his eyes in writing his history."

It was Renan's ambition, however, to be something more than a mere historian and philologist. It should be remembered that the second article of his creed is the negation of the supernatural, "that strange disease," as he describes it elsewhere, "that to the shame of civilization has not yet disappeared from humanity." All his early training had turned him towards the study of religion. After his conversion from Catholicism to science, there was superadded the desire to apply his new faith, to prove that the positive methods of history and philology are adequate to explain what has always been held to be wholly beyond them. Religion assumes that there is a realm of mystery into which the ordinary reason is unable to enter. There can be no real triumph for the rationalist until this main assumption of religion is attacked and discredited. It was with all this in mind that Renan wrote when a very young man: "The most important book of the nineteenth century should have as its title 'A Critical History of the Origins of Christianity.' " Renan devoted over thirty years of his own life to the accomplishment of this great task. The result is embodied in the seven volumes of his *Origines du Christianisme,* and the five complementary volumes of his *Histoire du peuple d'Israël.* These works, though not perhaps the most important of the century, are, at all events, the most considerable that have appeared in France for one or two generations.

It is quite beyond the scope of the present study to discuss in detail Renan's treatment of the grave questions that necessarily confront a historian of Christianity. The method of this treatment is evidently borrowed from Germany. He has pressed the French talent for expression into the service of German research, and thrown into general circulation ideas that had previously been the property of a few specialists. German scholars, however, had left to scriptural exegesis at least a semblance of special privilege. Renan's work is significant by the very boldness with which he abolishes the distinction between sacred and profane learning, and puts the narratives of the Old and New Testaments on precisely the same footing as those of Livy and Herodotus. The Bible, instead of being absolutely inspired and all of a piece, thus becomes purely human and historical and bears the impress of all the changing circumstances of time and place. The book of Ecclesiastes was once thought to be the word of God; Renan sees in it only the "philosophy of a disillusioned old bachelor."

It is usual to contrast this historical method of Renan with the irreligion of the eighteenth century, founded entirely on reasoning and often as intolerant in temper as the dogma it attacked. This temper is well exemplified by Voltaire's warfare upon the supernatural, especially by the famous watchword of his crusade upon Catholicism, *Écrasez l'infâme.* The militant atheism of former times was, as has often been remarked, a sort of inverted faith. "There is no God, and Harriet Martineau is his prophet." We can accept the contrast between Renan and this type of disbeliever, provided we remember that Renan's philosophy also carried with it no small share of dogmatic rationalism, and something, too, of the mocking irreverence that in France, at all events, nearly always accompanies it. This element comes to the surface more and more as he grows older. There are even moments when he deserves the epithet his enemies have given him,—that of an "unctuous Voltaire." This flippancy in dealing with religious matters is often amusing enough in itself, but one would have preferred to see a man like Renan follow the counsel of the ancient sage and "not speculate about the highest things in lightness of heart."

We cannot be too careful to distinguish these different elements in a nature as complex as Renan's. He has some points in common with Voltaire, and still more with the critics of Germany. On the other hand, he resembles by his sentimental cult for Christianity a Catholic apologist like Chateaubriand. It was to this last trait that he owed much of his power to influence his own generation. For religion, even after it has lost all effective hold on the reason and character, still lingers in the sensibility. When it has ceased to appeal to us as truth, it continues to appeal to us as beauty. As Renan puts it, "We are offended by the dogmas of Catholicism and delighted by its old churches." We are thrilled with emotion by mediæval architecture, by the poetry of Christian rites and ceremonies, by the odor of incense, or, like Renan himself, by the Canticles to the Virgin. This mood may be termed religiosity, and is not to be confused with real religion, with which it has no necessary connection.

Renan, then, came at the precise moment when men were most divided between this sentimental yearning towards the past and their intellectual acceptance of the new order. The heart refused to acquiesce in the conclusions of the head. This struggle between the head and the heart was especially common towards the middle of the century, so much so that, according to Sainte-Beuve, it had become a fashionable pose.

> Ma raison révoltée
> Essaie en vain de croire et mon cœur de douter.

The religious sentiment had still been strong enough in the case of Chateaubriand and a considerable number of his contemporaries to carry with it the reluctant reason. But fifty years later the balance had turned in favor of the modern spirit, and many men were preparing to bid the religious forms of the past a tender and regretful farewell. Renan is their spokesman when he says that "the belief we have had should never be a bond. We have paid out debt to it when we have carefully wrapped it in the purple shroud in which slumber the gods that are dead." He sets out then in his *Origines* to weave the shroud of Christianity, and to give it—so far as it implies faith in the supernatural—a sympathetic and respectful burial. We have already spoken of the faculty that specially fitted him for this enterprise. No one knew better than he how to gild positivism with religiosity and throw around the operations of the scientific intellect a vague aroma of the infinite. *Il donne aux hommes de sa génération ce qu'ils désirent, des bonbons qui sentent l'infini.* Religion that has thus taken refuge in the sensibility becomes largely a matter of literary and artistic enjoyment. This is evidently so in the case of Chateaubriand, and it is not difficult to detect in Renan the same epicurean flavor. He tells us that he has a "keen relish" for the character of the founder of Christianity. He speaks in another passage of "savoring the delights of the religious sentiment." Perhaps nothing so offends the serious reader of the *Vie de Jésus* as Renan's assumption that the highest praise he can give Jesus is to say that he satisfies the æsthetic sense. He multiplies in speaking of him such adjectives as *doux, beau, exquis, charmant, ravissant, délicieux.* (pp. 257-71)

Renan is not at his best in the *Vie de Jésus.* Some would go even further, and say, in the words of Fleury, that "any one who thinks he can improve on the Gospel narrative does not understand it." Renan chiefly excels in rendering, by his art of delicate shadings, the element of relativity in the records of the past; whereas Jesus, as Arnold expresses it, "is, in the jargon of modern philosophy, an *absolute;* we cannot explain, cannot get behind him and above him, cannot command him." The historical method is most serviceable when it is brought to bear on a work like the Apocalypse, or on an event like the persecution of Nero. But it is not what is needed to make us feel the sheer spiritual elevation of Jesus. It fails as conspicuously as it does when applied by Taine, in his "English Literature," to the eminent personality of Shakespeare. Neither Jesus, nor Shakespeare, it would seem, is to be accounted for by any theory of environment, or by the convergent effect of any number of "influences."

Renan's age resembled our own in that it was extraordinarily strong in its sense of what the individual owes to society, and extraordinarily weak in its sense of what he owes to himself; and so, in obedience to the time-spirit, Renan reduces the mission of Jesus, so far as possible, to sentimental and humanitarian effusions. The masculine religion of the will is almost entirely sacrificed in his narrative to the feminine religion of the heart. But, as Sainte-Beuve remarks, two great families of Christians may be distinguished from the first—on the one hand the "gentle and the tender," and on the other the "resolute and the strong." The traits that were thus separated in the followers were united in the founder. As a result of Renan's failure to recognize this fact, there is a real incoherency in his picture of Jesus. It is not made clear to us how the "delicate and amiable moralist" of Galilee becomes the "sombre giant of the last days."

Renan can scarcely conceal his dislike for Saint Paul, whose interest is evidently centred in the spiritual life of the individual, and who cannot, by any device of historical interpretation, be made into a humanitarian. He calls him the second founder of Christianity, but he has little sympathy for the distinctive features of the Pauline religion, its haunting sense of sin and the stress it lays on the struggle between a lower and a higher self, between a law of the flesh and a law of the spirit. "Wretched man that I am!" exclaims Saint Paul, "who shall deliver me from the body of this death?" Renan, for his part, likes to remind us that he is the fellow countryman of the Breton Pelagius, who taught, in opposition to the orthodox church fathers, the natural goodness of human nature. A Christian (in the old-fashioned sense of the term) would see in all this a proof that Renan was lacking in some of the essentials of the inner life. It is, at all events, a curious example of his determination to view everything from the narrow angle of philology. (pp. 272-74)

Renan's positivism is also well illustrated by his attitude towards miracles. He is nowhere so dogmatic as in the confidence with which he decides what is "natural" and what is "supernatural," and rejects forthwith everything that cannot be properly tested in the laboratory of M. Berthelot. As though, with our infinitesimal fragment of experience, we really knew whether the ordinary "law" may not be at times superseded and held in abeyance by a higher "law"! In the *Vie de Jésus* he occasionally resorts to the theory of pious fraud. Much scandal was caused by his suggestion that Lazarus deliberately planned and acted out the scene of his coming to life with a view to increasing Christ's fame as a thaumaturgist. Elsewhere he inclines rather to see in the miraculous the distortion of some natural incident. For example, the story of the Pentecost and the tongues of fire probably had its origin in the lightning flashes of a violent thunderstorm. Paul, overcome by heat and fatigue, was suffering from cerebral congestion, accompanied by an attack of ophthalmia, and so imagined that he met Jesus on the road to Damascus. The doctrine of the resurrection—one, as Renan says, in which the whole future of Christianity was involved—grew out of a hallucination of Mary Magdalene, etc.

Positivist though he is in all these ways, Renan still retains in his thought many traces of the romanticism he was so careful to banish from his style. Hence an occasional lack of objectivity and inability to get away from himself, a tendency to honor the historical personages whom he admires by ascribing to them his own qualities. He has put many of his own traits into his portraits of Jesus and Marcus Aurelius. He himself inclines more and more to ironical detachment, and is unwilling to think that Jesus could have been denied the same superiority. "Jesus had in the highest degree what we regard as the essential virtue of a distinguished person—I mean the gift of smiling at his own work, of rising superior to it, of not allowing himself to be haunted by it." Renan pursues his romantic dream through the outer circumstance and sometimes subordinates the outer circumstance to it. In his unsuccessful electoral campaign of 1869, only a year before the Franco-Prussian War, he advised a reduction of the army. A real statesman would have sacrificed his humanitarian vision of peace, in case he happened to have one, to the actual danger of war which was already patent to a careful observer. The Celtic race, according to Renan, has ever tended to "take its dreams for realities." "The essential element of the poetical life of the Celt is *adventure*, that is to say, the pursuit of the unknown, the unending quest after the ever-fleeting object of desire." Renan himself has found a relation between these racial traits and his own romanticism and love of intellectual adventure. He arrives at few certainties in his studies on religion, but he makes up for these gaps in our positive information by a surprising fertility in hypothesis. There is something stimulating in the very freedom with which he handles ideas and events, or, as some might say, in his lack of intellectual prudence and sobriety. A person intellectually prudent can only marvel at the boldness with which Renan and Taine launch forth into some subject like Buddhism—vast, obscure, imperfectly known as yet even to the specialist—and reduce it all to a few generalizations as fallacious often as they are plausible. "Nature," says Emerson, "resents generalizing, and insults the philosopher in every moment with a million of fresh particulars." Renan, who has made popular so many ideas on race psychology, especially on the psychology of the Semite, asserts, among other things, that the "desert is monotheistic." Yet the "particulars" that tend to disprove this statement were collected during his own lifetime and embodied in the "Corpus" of which he himself was the founder.

It is instructive to compare Renan's method with that of a real skeptic like Sainte-Beuve, to note Sainte-Beuve's care to select a subject that involves no leap into unknown places, and then the invincible caution with which he advances, exploring every foot of the way. To hear Renan speak of Saint Paul one would imagine that he had known him personally. This "ugly little Jew," as he informs us, "was short of stature, thickset, and bent. He had a small, bald head, oddly set on heavy shoulders. His pale face was almost overgrown by a thick beard; he had an aquiline nose, keen eyes, black eyebrows that met over the forehead." Sainte-Beuve had seen Chateaubriand for a number of years in the drawing-room of Madame Récamier, yet he devotes a special appendix of his work on Chateaubriand to discussing the color of his eyes, and then only to arrive at the melancholy conclusion that we must be resigned to say of Chateaubriand's eyes as of the color of Mary Stuart's hair and so many other things: *Que sais-je?*

But we must not linger so long on these doubtful aspects of Renan's genius as to forget the ways in which he is really eminent. Future historians of Christianity may arrive at conclusions entirely different from his regarding those events in its records that transcend ordinary human experience. They may avoid some of the faults that come from his romanticism and abuse of conjecture. But we can be sure that no student of the Bible will be taken seriously hereafter who is without the sense of historical development; and for imparting this historical sense, Renan is, as we have seen, an incomparable master. (pp. 275-78)

*Irving Babbitt, "Renan," in his* The Masters of Modern French Criticism, *Houghton Mifflin Company, 1912, pp. 257-97.*

## ALBERT SCHWEITZER  (essay date 1906)

[*Schweitzer, a French theologian, philosopher, surgeon, and musicologist, achieved fame in the early twentieth century with the publication of a series of original works on the history of Western civilization and New Testament Criticism. His international literary reputation was firmly established by* Geschichte der Leben-Jesu-Forschung (*1906;* The Quest of the Historical Jesus), *one of the first studies of its kind to emphasize the anthropological and Judaic basis of Jesus' ideas. In the following excerpt from this work, Schweitzer assesses the aesthetic merit and historical method of* The Life of Jesus.]

Like [the German theologian David Friedrich] Strauss, Renan designed his *Life of Jesus* to form part of a complete account of the history and dogma of the early Church. His purpose, however, was purely historical; it was no part of his project to set up, on the basis of the history, a new system of dogma, as Strauss had desired to do. This plan was not only conceived, but carried out. *Les Apôtres* appeared in 1866; *St. Paul* in 1869; *L'Anté-Christ* in 1873; *Les Évangiles* in 1877; *L'Eglise chrétienne* in 1879; *Marc-Aurèle et la fin du monde antique* in 1881. Several of these works were more valuable than the one which opened the series, but for the world Renan continued to be the author of the *Vie de Jésus,* and of that alone.

He planned the work at Gaza, and he dedicated it to his sister Henriette, who died soon after, in Syria, and lies buried at Byblus.

This was the first Life of Jesus for the Catholic world, which had scarcely been touched—the Latin peoples least of all—by the two and a half generations of critical study which had been devoted to the subject. It is true, Strauss's work had been translated into French, but it had made only a passing stir, and that only among a little circle of intellectuals. Now came a writer with the characteristic French mental accent, who gave to the Latin world in a single book the result of the whole process of German criticism.

But Renan's work marked an epoch, not for the Catholic world only, but for general literature. He laid the problem which had hitherto occupied only theologians before the whole cultured world. And not as a problem, but as a question of which he, by means of his historical science and aesthetic power of reviving the past, could provide a solution. He offered his readers a Jesus who was alive, whom he, with his artistic imagination, had met under the blue heaven of Galilee, and whose lineaments his inspired pencil had seized. Men's attention was arrested, and they thought to see Jesus, because Renan had the skill to make them see blue skies, seas of waving corn, distant mountains, gleaming lilies, in a landscape with the Lake of Gennesareth for its centre, and to hear with him in the whispering of the reeds the eternal melody of the Sermon on the Mount.

Yet the aesthetic feeling for nature which gave birth to this *Life of Jesus* was, it must be confessed, neither pure nor profound. It is a standing enigma why French art, which in painting grasps nature with a directness and vigour, with an objectivity in the best sense of the word, such as is scarcely to be found in the art of any other nation, has in poetry treated it in a fashion which scarcely ever goes beyond the lyrical and sentimental, the artificial, the subjective, in the worst sense of the word. Renan is no exception to this rule, any more than Lamartine or Pierre Loti. He looks at the landscape with the eye of a decorative painter seeking a *motif* for a lyrical composition upon which he is engaged. But that was not noticed by the many, because they, after all, were accustomed to have nature dressed up for them, and had had their taste so corrupted by a certain kind of lyricism that they had lost the power of distinguishing between truth and artificiality. Even those who might have noticed it were so astonished and delighted at being shown Jesus in the Galilaean landscape that they were content to yield to the enchantment.

Along with this artificial feeling for nature a good many other things were accepted without question. There is scarcely any other work on the subject which so abounds in lapses of taste—and those of the most distressing kind—as Renan's *Vie de Jésus.* It is Christian art in the worst sense of the term—the art of the wax image. The gentle Jesus, the beautiful Mary, the fair Galilaeans who formed the retinue of the "amiable carpenter," might have been taken over in a body from the shop-window of an ecclesiastical art emporium in the Place St. Sulpice. Nevertheless, there is something magical about the work. It offends and yet it attracts. It will never be quite forgotten, nor is it ever likely to be surpassed in its own line, for nature is not prodigal of masters of style, and rarely is a book so directly born of enthusiasm as that which Renan planned among the Galilaean hills.

The essay on the sources of the Life of Jesus with which it opens is itself a literary masterpiece. With a kind of effortless ease he makes his readers acquainted with the criticism of Strauss, of Baur, of Reuss, of Colani. He does not argue, but simply sets the result vividly before the reader, who finds himself at once at home in the new world of ideas. He avoids any hard or glaring effects; by means of that skilful transition from point to point which Wagner in one of his letters praises as the highest art, everything is surrounded with atmosphere. But how much trickery and illusion there is in this art! In a few strokes he indicates the relation of John to the Synoptists; the dilemma is made clear, it seems as if one horn or the other must be chosen. Then he begins by artful touches to soften down the contrast. The discourses of John are not authentic; the historical Jesus cannot have spoken thus. But what about the statements of fact? Here Renan declares himself convinced by the graphic presentment of the passion story. Touches like "it was night," "they had lighted a fire of coals,"

"the coat was without seam," cannot have been invented. Therefore the Gospel must in some way go back to the disciple whom Jesus loved. It is possible, nay certain, that when as an old man he read the other Gospels, he was displeased by certain inaccuracies, and perhaps vexed that he was given so small a place in the history. He began to dictate a number of things which he had better means of knowing than the others; partly, too, with the purpose of showing that in many cases where Peter only had been mentioned he also had played a part, and indeed the principal part. Sometimes his recollection was quite fresh, sometimes it had been modified by time. When he wrote down the discourses, he had forgotten the Lake of Gennesareth and the winsome words which he had listened to upon its shores. He was now living in quite a different world. The events of the year 70 destroyed his hopes of the return of his Master. His Jewish prejudices fell away, and as he was still young, he adapted himself to the syncretistic, philosophic, gnostic environment amid which he found himself in Ephesus. Thus even Jesus' world of thought took on a new shape for him; although the discourses are perhaps rather to be referred to his school than to himself. But, when all is said, John remains the best biographer. Or, to put it more accurately, while all the Gospels are biographies, they are legendary biographies, even though they come down from the first century. Their texts need interpretation, and the clue to the interpretation can be supplied by aesthetic feeling. They must be subjected to a gentle pressure to bring them together, and make them coalesce into a unity in which all the data are happily combined.

How this is to be done Renan shows later in his description of the death of Jesus. "Suddenly," he says, "Jesus gave a terrible cry in which some thought they heard 'Father, into thy hands I commend my spirit,' but which others, whose thoughts were running on the fulfilment of prophecy, reported as 'It is finished.' "

The authentic sayings of Jesus are more or less self-evidencing. Coming in contact with one of them amid the welter of heterogeneous traditions, you feel a thrill of recognition. They leap forth and take their proper place, where their vivid power becomes apparent. For one who writes the life of Jesus on His native soil, the Gospels are not so much sources of information as incentives to revelation. "I had," Renan avows, "a fifth Gospel before my eyes, mutilated in parts, but still legible, and taking it for my guide I saw behind the narratives of Matthew and Mark, instead of an ideal Being of whom it might be maintained that He had never existed, a glorious human countenance full of life and movement." It is this Jesus of the fifth Gospel that he desires to portray.

In looking at the picture, the reader must not allow the vexed question of miracle to distract him and disturb the proper frame of mind. The author refuses to assert either the possibility or the impossibility of miracle, but speaks only as an historian. "We do not say miracle is impossible, we say only that there has never been a satisfactorily authenticated miracle."

In view of the method of treatment adopted by Renan there can, of course, be no question of an historical plan. He brings in each saying at the point where it seems most appropriate. None of them is passed over, but none of them appears in its historical setting. He shifts individual incidents hither and thither in the most arbitrary fashion. For example, the coming of Jesus' mother to seek Him (in the belief that He is beside Himself ) must belong to the later part of Jesus' life, since it is out of tone with the happy innocence of the earlier period. Certain scenes are transposed from the later period to the earlier, because they are not gloomy enough for the later time. Others again are made the basis of an unwarranted generalisation. It is not enough that Jesus once rode upon an ass while the disciples in the intoxication of joy cast their garments in the way; according to Renan, He constantly rode about, even in Galilee, upon a mule, "that favourite riding-animal of the East, which is so docile and sure-footed and whose great dark eyes, shaded by long lashes, are full of gentleness." Sometimes the disciples surrounded Him with rustic pomp, using their garments by way of carpeting. They laid them upon the mule which carried Him, or spread them before Him on the way.

Scenes of little significance are sometimes elaborately described by Renan while more important ones are barely touched on. "One day, indeed," he remarks in describing the first visit to Jerusalem, "anger seems to have, as the saying goes, overmastered Him; He struck some of the miserable chafferers with the scourge, and overthrew their tables." Such is the incidental fashion in which the cleansing of the temple was brought in. In this way it is possible to smuggle in a miracle without giving any further explanation of it. The miracle at Cana is brought, by means of the following unobtrusive turn of phrase, into the account of the period of success in Galilee. "One of His miracles was done by Jesus for the sole purpose of increasing the happiness of a wedding-party in a little country town." (pp. 180-84)

Renan has not been scrupulous where he ought to have been so. There is a kind of insincerity in the book from beginning to end. Renan professes to depict the Christ of the Fourth Gospel, though he does not believe in the authenticity or the miracles of that Gospel. He professes to write a scientific work, and is always thinking of the great public and how to interest it. He has thus fused together two works of disparate character. The historian finds it hard to forgive him for not going more deeply into the problem of the development in the thought of Jesus, with which he was brought face to face by the emphasis which he laid on eschatology, and for offering in place of a solution the highly-coloured phrases of the novelist.

Nevertheless, this work will always retain a certain interest, both for Frenchmen and for Germans. The German is often so completely fascinated by it as to lose his power of criticism, because he finds in it German thought in a novel and piquant form. Conversely the Frenchman discovers in it, behind the familiar form, which is here handled in such a masterly fashion, ideas belonging to a world which is foreign to him, ideas which he can never completely assimilate, but which yet continually attract him. In this double character of the work lies its imperishable charm.

And its weakness? That it is written by one to whom the New Testament was to the last something foreign, who had not read it from his youth up in the mother-tongue, who was not accustomed to breathe freely in its simple and pure world, but must perfume it with sentimentality in order to feel himself at home in it. (pp. 191-92)

*Albert Schweitzer, "Renan," in his* The Quest of the Historical Jesus: A Critical Study of Its Progress from Reimarus to Wrede, *second edition, translated by W. Montgomery, 1910. Reprint by A. & C. Black, Ltd., 1936, pp. 180-92.*

## ALBERT LEON GUÉRARD   (essay date 1913)

[*Guérard, a French-born American critic, evaluates Renan's integral approach to history in* The Life of Jesus, *accentuating the contradictions inherent in his treatment of Christ.*]

The publication of [*The Life of Jesus*] was an event of national importance, and the bibliography of all the articles, pamphlets, and bulky treatises which, within a single year, appeared in criticism, refutation, or praise of this epoch-making work fills a whole volume. Strauss's *Leben Jesu* had certainly created a great stir, not only among theologians, but in the general public; de Vigny's *Diary* proves that even poets read it and felt its influence, and the fact that it was translated by such writers as Littré in France and George Eliot in England is in itself significant. But German has not the universal and proselytising qualities of French; Germany in 1835 was not so sharply divided as France in 1863 between uncompromising orthodoxy and radical free-thought, engaged in a life-and-death struggle; finally, with all its merits, the book of Strauss lacked what, in spite of all its weaknesses, Renan's possessed so abundantly—life and genius. (p. 235)

The significance of the book, for good or evil, was due to its popular character. By "popular" we mean neither vulgar nor superficial: Renan was an aristocrat and a scholar. His erudition has been challenged: no historian, no scientist is infallible. His beautiful style has created a prejudice against him among the Dryasdusts: but we should take Mommsen's word for it: he was a thorough scholar, *in spite* of his style. His election to the Academy of Inscriptions, his appointment to the College de France, the scientific missions entrusted to him—the highest honours that France could bestow—show in what esteem he was held by his peers in the domain of research. On the basis of scientific investigation, Renan wrote a book which was neither theology nor archæology, but human history, a book which could be "understanded of the people." Therein lay the revolution. An abstruse work for the chosen few would have passed unnoticed and therefore unchallenged: a fifth gospel as accessible in language as the other four seemed to herald a new Reformation.

There are four principal conceptions according to which a Life of Jesus could be written. The first, the only one accepted by the orthodox Churches, is a mere Harmony of the Gospels: of this type, Bossuet's remains as good a model as any; Veuillot's, and, with a veneer of philosophy and scholarship, Father Didon's belong to the same class. The second is mainly philosophical: the *idea* rather than the personality of Christ is its main object. In extreme cases, the personality would be entirely lost sight of, and the Life of Christ would become the study of the formation and development of a myth: such is at least the tendency of Strauss's *Leben Jesu.* A third type, strictly scientific, would have to be, first of all, critical: the discussion and comparison of all existing documents, and principally of the Gospels, would be practically the whole history. At the time of Renan and in France, this work was done piecemeal by the Strasbourg school of liberal Protestants. The first method takes the whole question for granted; in practice, it leads to great difficulties: flagrant contradictions cannot be reconciled without straining common sense and good faith to the breaking point. The second is deductive, but dangerously arbitrary. The third is purely destructive, and therefore inadequate to the treatment of the capital event in the world's history.

Renan adopted a fourth method, which he borrowed from

Michelet, the "integral resurrection of the past." When all authorities have been collected, compared, criticised, a few facts stand out as certain, and the impression of a general trend remains; this, of course, is never indisputable, but it often is highly probable. With these few facts, with this general impression, with sympathy, insight, and a feeling for the laws of life, the historian composes a *plausible* and *artistic* narrative. In other words, he offers us a hypothesis which must take all known facts into account, and at the same time conform to our notions of possibility.

The objections to such a method are obvious. The qualities of insight, imagination, sympathy are not to be despised in a historian; when they are kept under control, when facts are numerous and well-established, these qualities constitute properly genius, and transmute erudition into real history. They are evident in the best and soundest works of Michelet and Carlyle, and are not lacking in the greatest German scholars, Niebuhr, Ranke, Burckhardt, Mommsen. There is not a page of real history, as distinguished from the mechanical compilation of documents, that is not a plausible and artistic hypothesis. But, when facts are few and uncertain, when there is no universal consensus as to their significance, the personality of the author becomes the main element in the book, and the theory defines the historical romance rather than history.

And what is that "standard of possibility" to which the narrative is made to conform? . . . In this particular case we have at least two standards of credibility, that of the orthodox and that of the sceptic. Even among sceptics there are differences: some, like Mérimée and Sainte-Beuve's second friend, refused to admit as possible the moral miracle of Jesus's perfection implied in Renan's history. Renan smiled at Quatremère and Buloz, because the one, although an orthodox Christian, rejected the miracles "difficult to perform," and the other refused an article on Buddhism, for the reason that "there could not be such silly people as your Buddhists." Yet both were guided by their own sense of possibility. Renan's criterion is either individual fancy, or so-called common sense: and neither has any authority in the matter.

Even if we accepted Renan's theory, his book, as a work of art, would not fully satisfy us. Too bold in his rejection of miracles, or too timid in his criticism of the Gospels, he did not take a decided stand, which would have given unity to the character of his hero. In spite of all his "gentle solicitations," the texts which he had accepted as authentic and historical agreed in their report of at least some miracles, which he would not admit. This led him to Euhemerist or rationalist explanations, such as those he had derided in Paulus; and, worse still, he had to fall back, in the case of Lazarus at least, on the Voltairian hypothesis of fraud. This assumption is absolutely in contradiction with his own loving and reverent conception of Jesus. Furthermore, his "young Galilean peasant," without being in any way vulgar, must have been ignorant and narrow-minded: all his greatness was spiritual and moral, not intellectual. Yet Renan ascribes to him his own attitude of half-contemptuous superiority, his transcendental scepticism which smiles at all things, not excluding itself, his many-sided and subtle turn of mind which, whilst enabling him to understand all things, would not permit him to judge or affirm anything. As we cannot even think except in terms of our own experience—actual or virtual—all biographers are liable to draw their heroes after their own likeness. But in this case there is absolute incompatibility between the two

types of mind, between the firm, earnest, direct Teacher who spoke "as one having authority," and the cautious, fastidious, over-cultured critic in whose eyes dogmatism was the one unpardonable sin. Every attempt at *Renanising* Jesus seems a sacrilege to the believer, an impossibility to the historian, and an error of taste to the artist.

Even more striking is the contradiction between the beginning and the end of Jesus's career in Renan's book. A historical character is supposed to develop according to the laws of life. Jesus was no exception, and the most orthodox apologists at present speak freely of His growth, an evolutionary view for which there is Gospel authority. But Renan, although such a great master of fine shading, shows us a glaring contrast instead of a gradual change. He describes, with a charm not wholly free from sentimentality, the "joyous idyll" of Galilee, a happy band of children by the shore of enchanted lakes. Then, with the scantiest transition, we are shown a totally different Jesus, harsh, fanatical, revolutionary, a "sombre giant." In this, and by his own tests of harmony and possibility, Renan has manifestly failed.

The **Life of Jesus** is therefore far from being a perfect book: it is not even Renan's masterpiece. As a work of art, the **Antichrist** has more power, more variety, more dramatic interest; whilst in point of poetical charm, refined humour, and kindly philosophy, the **Souvenirs** stand supreme. Like Zola's *Downfall,* for instance, the book owed its success to its subject, rather than to the perfection of its treatment. Yet, faulty as it is, it remains, not only one of the epoch-making works in French literature, but one of the greatest. There is a blessing for him who dares to wrestle with the angel of the Lord. Renan's portrait of Christ is full of contradictions: yet to thousands of readers it seemed less impossible than the conception of the orthodox. The Empress Eugénie, liberal for once, is reported to have said: "It will do no harm to believers: it will do good to unbelievers." A cause of scandal for many, the **Life of Jesus** was for many more a source of edification. An intense love for truth and goodness, for the ideal as embodied in Christ Jesus, pervades these imperfect and incomplete pages. No man has ever been the worse for reading Renan's **Life of Jesus.** (pp. 237-41)

> *Albert Leon Guérard, "Ernest Renan," in his* French Prophets of Yesterday: A Study of Religious Thought under the Second Empire, 1913. *Reprint by D. Appleton and Company, 1920, pp. 224-55.*

## HILAIRE BELLOC   (essay date 1928)

[*Considered one of England's premier men of letters at the turn of the century, Belloc was a writer of light verse and a forceful essayist. His characteristically truculent stance as a proponent of Roman Catholicism and economic reform, and his equally characteristic clever humor, drew either strong support or harsh attacks from his audience. Closely linked to Belloc's Catholic beliefs was his proposed economic and political program called Distributism, a system of small ownership harking back to Europe's pre-Reformation period and fully described in the controversial 1912 essay* The Servile State. *Because he looked to the past—particularly to the Middle Ages—for his ideals, Belloc has not been widely read by modern readers; his desire to return to the values of an authoritarian epoch, as well as flashes of anti-Semitic comment in his works, have contributed to his eclipse as an important literary figure. Here, Belloc argues that Renan's works are fatally marred by a lack of critical intelligence.*]

The other day I had a piece of rare leisure and went right through Renan's *Reminiscences of his Youth.* I had not read the book for half a lifetime. When I had last seen it I was perhaps too young to weigh it as it should be weighed, but coming back to it after so many years, there returned to me with peculiar force the remark made to me by a Spaniard of profound scholarship and intelligence, 'To-day religion has no opponents worthy of it.'

I say that is a profound remark, and one which every modern man should meditate on, for it illustrates his time. I do not know whether it would be better for us or worse if there were now arrayed against the Christian religion men of the old statute, but at any rate it would be an intellectual pleasure to deal with them, and that intellectual pleasure is denied us.

If there was a man fitted to be a worthy opponent of religion it was Renan, and take him all round he is the worthiest we have had within the last lifetime. He was a famous scholar, an admirable writer: his action was peculiarly forcible because he was trained for the Priesthood, and abandoned his vocation with an effect on his contemporaries comparable to the opposite effect of Newman's conversion in England a lifetime before. Renan puts forward his reasons with what seemed at that time—half a lifetime ago—so clear and cogent a process of thought that he was more responsible than any other man for the sceptical attitude towards Christian truth which prevailed in the last part of his own life. Yet on re-reading this famous and magnificently written piece of prose I was more and more impressed by its intellectual insufficiency.

I know it sounds bold to say this, but it is true. It is not only true that I feel this intellectual insufficiency in the man, but it is true that this intellectual insufficiency was there. Great as he is in scholarship, and much greater in the power of expression, in reasoning power he fails. Many people who read such lines from a pen such as mine, which does not pretend to scholarship, will think them insolent, but those who think so must remember that a truth worth telling is always either a well-worn thing, familiar to all, or a rare startling novelty, and this judgment of mine, though perhaps novel and startling and even, I am afraid to many people, offensive, is true. Renan lacked the intellectual capacity which an opponent of the Church should bring with him into controversy.

The lack of a sufficient intelligence in the discussion of any matter dependent upon the reason commonly shows itself in three ways:

First, by the taking for granted of postulates unexamined: accepted blindly as dogmas without being able to put forward the rational basis of acceptation.

Secondly, by not perceiving the implications of what one affirms to be true.

Thirdly, by not appreciating the extent of the field of discussion.

Now all those three insufficiencies are glaringly evident in Renan's work. He 'bolted whole,' as the phrase goes, sundry superficial judgments which he had read, but which he had not examined.

Next, he affirms things as though they were conclusively proved and certain, without perceiving the contradictions in which they involve him.

Lastly, he misses great areas of the field covered by the discussion upon which he is engaged.

I will give a few examples to establish this criticism. In a passage of the book where he is speaking of Scholasticism, he uses words which I translate almost textually, and which are to this effect, that he was trained as a young candidate for the Priesthood in the developed philosophy of the seventeenth-century theologians, and 'not in the puerile and barbaric scholasticism of the thirteenth century.'

Now that stamps the man at once. To begin with the thirteenth century is the century of St. Thomas. The words apply, and can only apply, to the gigantic and final intellectual work of St. Thomas. Renan admits that he has not read it, or, at any rate, that he had not read it when he abandoned his vocation and his Faith; yet he repeats with regard to it the ignorant, insufficient sentences copied from other men who were equally ignorant. He takes it for granted that something which he has never studied was of a particular character, and that this character is negligible, yet anyone who will spend even a few hours upon the most elementary of St. Thomas's work—say upon the first ten questions of the Summa—will see that those two particular adjectives 'puerile' and 'barbaric' are utterly inapplicable. Anyone is free to say that he differs from St. Thomas in his conclusions, that St. Thomas's reasoning is not convincing. Huxley, for instance, was certainly in that mood when he none the less bore witness to the towering intellectual power of the great Dominican doctor. But no one is free to say that the work is either puerile or barbaric. It is as though a man, having heard vaguely of Gothic architecture but never having seen a Gothic cathedral, having studied only the classical renaissance and the architecture of antiquity, were to say that the Gothic architecture in its highest moment (which by the way was contemporary with St. Thomas) was 'puny' and 'uncalculated.' Or it is as though a man unacquainted with Latin were to call Virgil 'prolix' and 'commonplace.'

And now for an example of Renan's lack of power to perceive the implications of his own statements. He rejects all the miraculous on the plea that a strict sequence of unalterable cause and effect governs the whole universe under an iron unity of law which can never be broken. Therefore the story that Our Lord stilled the tempest by supernatural power may be dismissed with contempt, for we know that every atmospheric movement is the necessary result of certain physical causes which are themselves the result of others, and so on, to the beginning of things—if, indeed, things ever had a beginning.

Renan was not the first man by many millions to say that, and will not be the last by many millions to say it, but he wholly missed the implication of it. The implication is that will is absent from the universe. When I lift up a fork with my hand from the table I am not interrupting the blind sequence of things, but am myself no more than part of this mechanical and material process. For if in any human action upon the universe around us we admit that Will is producing a disturbance, then necessarily and inevitably we must admit that superior Will could make a greater disturbance, and that a Supreme Will creative of the universe could exercise a special influence upon any scale it chose.

But Renan does not act either morally or intellectually upon the implications of his statement. He professes respect for truth, a duty to seek it and to promulgate it, indignation against falsehoods; in a word a moral scheme: but a moral scheme is incompatible with a merely mechanical universe.

Perhaps more striking than either of these first two intellectual faults is his third insufficiency, his inability to grasp the scale of the field in which he was conducting his discussion. He studies the Christian doctrines and the historical process whereby the Church came into being and developed. He studies on the same lines the affirmations of Scripture and especially of the Old Testament. He concludes that it is impossible after such study to believe what Christians believe, but he does not even attempt a survey of the positive grounds upon which they believe. He takes it for granted that there are no such grounds. His argument all through amounts to this: 'If only you knew what I know you would no longer hold your faith for an hour,' yet he had in front of him all the great body of Christian thought, ancient and modern, put forth by centuries of men who were at least his equals in his own department of philology, and his superiors in other departments of the inquiry. He does not meet, he seems actually not to know, the arguments which they have found sufficient; he leaves these arguments aside because (to be honest) he does not know that they exist.

Now a comparison of such insufficiencies points, I say, particularly to unintelligence; and I will conclude by what may seem a rather fantastic test of such unintelligence, but I think a sound one. Renan dates—the whole thing already sounds old-fashioned and outworn. He affected his own generation, but he does not continue to affect succeeding generations as the greater opponents of religion in the past still do, as for instance Voltaire still does, or Spinoza. I have chosen Renan as a particular instance, though his name is now growing unfamiliar to Englishmen, and though his original position is admittedly heavily lowered and is still falling.

I have chosen him because he was in his time the best example of that truth which I repeat, that the Faith has to-day no opponents worthy of itself. We may learn from the fate of Renan's work, I think, what the fate of other men's will be, men far less eloquent. (pp. 107-13)

*Hilaire Belloc, "On Renan," in his* A Conversation with an Angel and Other Essays, *Jonathan Cape, 1928, pp. 107-13.*

*Renan in his study, after the etching by Anders Zorn.*

**ALBERT THIBAUDET**   (essay date 1936)

[*Thibaudet was an early twentieth-century French literary critic and follower of the French philosopher Henri Bergson. His work is considered versatile, well informed, and original. Critics cite his unfinished* Histoire de la littérature française de 1789 à nos jours (*1936; French Literature from 1795 to Our Era*) as his major critical treatise. In this work, excerpted below, Thibaudet classified authors by the generations of 1789, 1820, 1850 (including Renan), 1885, and 1914-18, rather than by literary movements. Here, Thibaudet critically assesses Renan's historical writings, focusing on his philological method and literary style.*]

Renan, a reasonably sure philologist, not overly adventurous, without genius, had a healthy, delicate, subtle idea of science, of the precision instruments that it includes. Now, he remarkably exceeded this idea in his great historical works, in that *Histoire des origines du christianisme* and that *Histoire du peuple d'Israël* that were to remain as his monuments and whose fate has not conformed to either his own expectations or the high evaluation of his contemporaries.

Renan wrote in 1848: "The most important book of the nineteenth century should be called *Histoire critique des origines du christianisme.*" When he began it, he was right in eliminating the essential word, which is "critical," and which, on *La Vie de Jésus,* would have seemed an irony.

No critical work would have enjoyed in 1863 the lightning-like world-wide success of *La Vie de Jésus,* which in six months sold more copies at seven francs than, five years before, *Madame Bovary* had sold at only two francs: sixty thousand.

It was the most popular of Renan's books, and the only popular one. In the domain of timeliness and success it can be compared in its century only with M. de Barante's *Histoire des ducs de Bourgogne* and the *Histoire des Girondins.* It was extracted from the Gospels by a skilled artist as the *Histoire des ducs* had been from Froissart, Chastellain, Monstrelet, and Commines. It resembled the *Girondins* in its store of gold, its azure, its ornamentation, its orientation toward the feminine public (it must not be forgotten that the only two imaginative authors who had any influence on Renan's youth were Lamartine and George Sand). But in addition Renan was a philologist, a Hebraicist, and represented the science of the Institut and the Collège de France with the same authority as Etienne-Marc Quatremère and Jean-Louis Burnouf. His duties gave him the keys to German exegesis, which was discussed in those days without being known and of which virtually nothing had yet reached the great public. And now this famous German exegesis was suddenly flooding in through the bright window of a fresh mind that, moreover, had gone to study on the spot, in an official capacity, the geography of the Gospels, as M. Taine had taken the train to Champagne and described its chalky landscape in order to understand and make others understand *Le Meunier, son fils, et l'ane.* Besides, this was no longer a matter of the negative criticism of the eighteenth century but of a positive life of Jesus. It showed how things might have happened on a human level. It did so in a spirit and for minds that were to convert it into the way in which things very probably had happened, in which "a professor at the Collège de France said" that they had happened—that is, into a rationalist gospel by a member of the Institut, who substituted himself, as was fitting in the century of illuminations, for the credulous gospels attributed to mythical characters. Christianity and its founder were secularized with honor by a great Orléanist mind in an operation analogous to that of 1830, and the last page of *La Vie de Jésus* virtually formulated the postulate of a quasi-divinity as there had been quasi-legitimacy. Immediately translated into many languages, this fifth gospel penetrated everywhere on the heels of the four others: no literary event more suddenly became a world event.

And yet, whatever its popular audience, whatever the influence in depth of the cheap reprint issued in hundreds of thousands of copies by Michel Lévy, the enlightened public on all sides showed an astonished reserve in its greeting to the book of which everyone was talking and that set off as many thousands of family and household battles as the first translations of the Bible had ignited in the sixteenth century.

Although on 24 June 1863, the date of its publication, Sainte-Beuve devoted an enthusiastic, somewhat puffing paragraph to it in *Le Constitutionnel,* it was only two and a half months later that he made it the subject of a *Lundi,* much more reserved and singularly accurate in its foresight. Three friends—or, as Renan was to say, three lobes of his brain—went to visit the critic and told him their opinions under the guise of asking for his. The first was a Catholic, who was not too unhappy, for he declared that "the first effect of this book will be to strengthen and redouble the faith of believers." The second was a skeptic, who found that this Jesus who was no longer God and who was other and more than man had nothing in common with historical, moral, or human reality; the third simply did not like to see such questions raised, was impressed only by what "time has assembled and accumulated round these ancient and ageless establishments," and saw the book as a sin against historical time.

Renan's most famous book has become his most outmoded and unreadable. This is not the case with the volumes of *Les Origines* that followed *La Vie de Jésus* and in which Renan was no longer face to face with a single book to be paraphrased and fictionalized, but rather face to face with the Roman world in which Christianity was preached, that he knew through long voyages and of which, especially in *Saint-Paul* and *Marc-Aurèle,* he provided a lively and suggestive picture. But his documentation has aged too much to be able to delude us today; his psychology of the Apostles, and especially of Saint Paul, seems to us arbitrary and brittle. The once-famous psychology of Nero in *L'Antéchrist* has become for the modern reader as literary a fantasy as Renan's Christ. His Marcus Aurelius, who is the traditional Marcus Aurelius, remains solid and splendid nevertheless, and these final volumes of *Les Origines* undoubtedly will long seem the summit of Renan's historical work.

*L'Histoire de peuple d'Israël* is less celebrated and less read, perhaps wrongly. For twenty years Renan was at the center, almost was the center, of Semitic studies in France; his knowledge of the literary and epigraphic texts was unmatched, and his intuition of the psychology of the Semite was very sure. He understood the men and things of the Old Testament and brought them to life with novelty and genius, while the New Testament and the Gospels crushed and surpassed that literary intelligence devoid of *mystique.*

· · · · ·

In Renan philological criticism and intelligence, both strong and healthy, appear to have done their work separately. The arduous searching out of texts, the study and knowledge of them were irreproachable in him. He assembled and possessed all the materials necessary for a critical history. But this critical history, this history dealing with the accessible part of reality, was always overshot by him with a history of the possible, a picture of the probable, an imaginary reconstruction. For him, according to his own admission, it was a matter of saying: "Here are one or two ways in which it is conceivable that the thing happened." Unfortunately, things have never happened as one might conceive that they could have happened, and between the first and the second of these possibilities it is usually a third one that reality has chosen.

· · · · ·

Nevertheless there remains a considerable and living work and presence of the author of the *Dialogues philosophiques.* The parts of Renan's work that were most famous in his lifetime, *La Vie de Jésus* and the two pages of *La Prière sur l'Acropole,* have lost their light. But they lost it only after a tremendous brilliance. What subsists of Renan, what, though it has no strong influence, still deserves consideration, is his function as a protagonist, his almost Socratic function, at the center of the great dialogues of the nineteenth century, which are still in part the dialogues of the twentieth: dialogue on God, dialogue on religion, dialogue on science, dialogue on the future of mankind, dialogue on capital and culture. On all these points he comported and maintained himself like a modern Montaigne, opening breaches, posing problems, feeding their imponderable drive with gray matter, giving them the vehicle of the lightest, the most diaphanous, the most familiar style, the closest to moving thought that has been written in French since the *Essais.*

· · · · ·

It is notable that this justly famous style of Renan's was a belated style, that he discovered it only on the threshold of his fortieth year, that his fluidity and his simplicity emerged only after long treks through dense, heavy country. There are three styles in Renan. The first is his scholarly-review and Institut style, which for a long time was sluggish and colorless. The second is his studied, Saint-Sulpice style in *La Vie de Jésus,* written with enthusiasm in Syria in one of those "masked balls of the imagination" that Flaubert distrusted and that can no longer be borne. But it seems that, like Flaubert's in his first *Tentation,* Renan's style had sown its wild oats in *La Vie de Jésus.* Beginning with *Les Apôtres,* there appeared a historical style of unequaled limpidity, which found all its transparency and its belated youth in *Marc-Aurèle.* The *Dialogues philosophiques* created a style of thought, the *Souvenirs d'enfance et de jeunesse* a narrative style, both of which, and especially the latter, will always rank among the most exquisite discoveries of the French speech.

Two of the *Drames philosophiques, Caliban* and *Le Prêtre de Némi,* reveal in Renan an animator of ideas, a platonic creator of myths. *Caliban,* a political sequel to Shakespeare's *Tempest* as *Télémaque* is a political sequel to the *Odyssey,* remains perhaps the masterpiece of "marginal" literature, and the symbol drawn by Renan from *The Tempest*—Caliban as the people and Prospero as the aristocracy—is linked to the mythology of the Republic, as *Télémaque,* during the eighteenth century, was linked to the ideology of the monarchy. *Le Prêtre de Némi* presents with a great nobility the difficulties encountered by the advent of reason, common sense, and humanity. The same favorable judgment cannot be made on *L'Eau de Jouvence,* a mediocre sequel to *Caliban,* or on

*L'Abbesse de Jouarre,* a senile error aggravated by a preface no less so.

And yet this word, "senile," when one is dealing with Renan, would have to be taken, perhaps, in no more pejorative a sense than the word, "juvenile." Renan, who came to his literary style only late in life, virtually created a style of intellectual old age in his life and in his thought. This drinker of the water of sacred fountains became an Anacreon of the intelligence under the Republic. His life was complete; his work was finished; his ideas were settled, after having been conquered, but "settled" did not mean "arrested"—they retained a mobility like Montaigne's, a movement of dialogue; the flower of doubt gained this trophy of certainties. Paris recognized itself in this old man who knew the art of conversation, and yet Brittany won him back. He became a Breton again, the Breton of the Celtic Dinner, at the moment when the most irreverent of his disciples, the young Barrès, was beginning to be a man of Lorraine. *Huit Jours chez M. Renan* represents a necessary stage for every reader, even if he be Eugène-Melchior de Vogüé. And all in the style of the eve of a departure, the eve of a reaction that broke out as soon as Renan was dead, the style of a ripe olive about to fall. Of the three great Bretons of the nineteenth century, one did not know how to grow old and went in despair to a pauper's grave. This was Lamennais. But the two others had everything of the style of old age. Chateaubriand, before his tomb of Grand Bey, took its severe, its Doric mode; Renan, before the Pantheon, its Ionic. (pp. 316-20)

*Albert Thibaudet, "Renan," in his* French Literature from 1795 to Our Era, *translated by Charles Lam Markmann, Funk & Wagnalls, 1968, pp. 314-20.*

## EDMUND WILSON (essay date 1940)

[*Wilson is generally considered twentieth-century America's foremost man of letters. A prolific reviewer, creative writer, and social and literary critic endowed with formidable intellectual powers, he exercised his greatest literary influence as the author of* Axel's Castle *(1931), a seminal study of literary symbolism, and as the author of widely read reviews and essays in which he introduced the best works of modern literature to the reading public. In the following excerpt, Wilson contrasts the Romantic concept of history held by the nineteenth-century French nationalist historian Jules Michelet with Renan's view of history, arguing that the latter's relativism determined the philosophical conclusions of* The Origins of Christianity. *Wilson's essay was first published in 1940.*]

"You have that thing which is so rare," Michelet had once said to a younger writer, "that thing which they all [all the literary men] lack: the sense of the people and its sap. In my own case, I feel, as I reread what I have sent you [the first volume of the *History of the Revolution*], how much I still lack myself. . . . My poetry is sometimes obscure, inaccessible to the great number."

The French bourgeoisie, who in the great Revolution had seized power from the feudal aristocracy, had, through all the readjustments of the forms and accouterments of government and in the teeth both of monarchist reaction and of socialist working-class revolt, maintained its position as the dominant class; and, except when spasmodically reawakened by the Royalists, the Bonapartists or the clergy, its revolutionary tradition grew feeble. The word "revolution" was coming to connote working-class interference from below with bour-geois property arrangements. The nineteenth century in France was a great literary period, and a period perhaps comparable, for fiction and history, to the Elizabethan period for poetry or the Italian Renaissance for painting. But this literature, for all the immense range in it of the social imagination, was no longer a revolutionary literature. The enthusiasm for science of the Enlightenment persisted without the political enthusiasm of the Enlightenment; and since the Romantic movement, the conception of the literary art was becoming more elaborate and subtle than the mere eloquence, polish and skill which had distinguished the eighteenth century. And Michelet, for all his attempts to reaffirm, to keep always in the foreground of his activity, the original revolutionary principles, was turning out to be one of the chief ornaments of this highly developed literature. With his novelist's sympathetic insight into different kinds of human beings, his sense of social and moral complexity and his artistic virtuosity, he was to live to be read with delight by people who did not share his opinions.

Nevertheless, he was to pass out of fashion. The writer of an article called *Why Michelet Is No Longer Read* predicted in 1898, on the occasion of the Michelet centenary, that the celebration would not do Michelet justice. Michelet is no longer read, he says, because people no longer understand him. Though he was followed in his day by the whole generation of 1850, he commits for the skeptical young men of the end of the century the supreme sin of being an apostle, a man of passionate feeling and conviction. Michelet created the religion of the Revolution, and the Revolution is not popular today, when the Academicians put it in its place, when persons who would have been nothing without it veil their faces at the thought of the Jacobin Terror, when even those who have nothing against it manage to patronize it. Besides, Michelet attacked the priesthood, and the Church is now treated with respect.

Let us take a last look at him, in Couture's drawing, before passing on to his successors: the Michelet of 1842, with his mask of determined will, which seems always to have been straining, never relaxed—the long plebeian jaw, the self-assertive chin, the set mouth, the fine trenchant nose with its distended and mettlesome nostrils, the eyes deep and sharp, sheltering a sensibility taxed by interior struggle, beneath eyebrows as heavy as wings, which make the creases of perpetual effort.

Now look at Renan and Taine. With Michelet, the man has created the mask. But here it is the profession that has made it: Renan, with his great belly, his pudgy hands, his round and puffy face, his heavily-drooping porcine eyelids—the most intelligent and honest of all the French abbés, but still fundamentally a French abbé; Taine (in Bonnat's portrait), with his spectacles and his myopic-looking eyes, his bald dome, his wilting imperial, his high conversational eyebrows—the most brilliant of all the French professors, but still from tip to toe a French professor. Michelet, the man of an unsettled and a passionate generation, has forged his own personality, created his own trade and established his own place. Renan and Taine, on the other hand, are the members of learned castes. Both, like Michelet, set the search for truth above personal considerations: Renan, who had studied for the priesthood, left the seminary and stripped off his robe as soon as he knew that it was impossible for him to accept the Church's version of history, and the scandal of the *Life of Jesus* cost him his chair at the Collège de France; and the materialistic principles of Taine proved such a stumbling-block to his superiors throughout his academic career that he was finally obliged to give up the idea of teaching. But, though rejected by their professional colleagues, they came before long to be accepted as among the official wise men of their society, a society now temporarily stabilized. Both ended as members of the Academy ("When one is *someone,* why should one want to be *something?*" Gustave Flaubert wondered about Renan)—whereas it is only a few years ago that Michelet and Quinet were finally given burial in the Panthéon.

Both Renan and Taine, of the generation twenty or thirty years younger than Michelet, had felt his influence, and combining, as Michelet had done, immense learning with artistic gifts, were to continue his re-creation of the past. Renan tells us with what excitement he read Michelet's history at school: "The century reached me through the cracks in a broken cement. . . . With amazement I discovered that there were laymen who were serious and learned; I saw that there existed something outside of antiquity and the Church . . . the death of Louis XIV was no longer the end of the world for me. Ideas and feelings appeared that had never had any expression either in antiquity or in the seventeenth century." (pp. 42-5)

The French bourgeois intellectual after 1870 found himself in the singular position of belonging at the same time to a dominant class and a defeated nation, of at the same time enjoying advantages and submitting to humiliation; and this paradox produced curious attitudes. Edmond de Goncourt, in his journal, gives an illuminating picture of Renan during the Franco-Prussian War and the Commune—we see him praising the Germans, to whom in his field he owed so much, in the face of the loud protests of his companions; waving his short arms and quoting Scripture against the prophets of French revenge; maintaining that for the "idealist," the emotion of patriotism had been rendered obsolete by Catholicism, that "the fatherland of the idealists is the country where they are allowed to think." One day when he had been standing at the window watching a regiment pass by amidst the shouts of the crowd, he contemptuously turned away: "There's not a man among them all," he cried, "who is capable of an act of virtue!"

But what did Renan mean by virtue? On what did he base his code? Renan's work, for all his smiling indulgence, has a certain austerity behind it. In what school had this virtue been learned? It was the ecclesiastical discipline which had made him: the sense of duty and the self-sufficiency which contributed to the very moral courage he was to display in opposition to the Church had been derived from his training for the priesthood, from that Catholicism which, as he said, had made patriotism obsolete, but in which he had ceased to believe. It is almost as if virtue were with Renan a mere habit which he has been induced to acquire on false pretenses. Though his devotion had been at first directed to the ends of the Enlightenment, to the scientific criticism of the Scriptures which supplemented the polemics of Voltaire, the Enlightenment itself, as I have indicated, was in a sense on the wane with the attainment by the French bourgeoisie of their social-economic objects; and Renan's virtue came more and more to seem, not like Michelet's, a social engine, but a luminary hung in the void. In a hierarchy of moral merit drawn up in one of his prefaces, he puts the saint at the top of the list and the man of action at the bottom: moral excellence, he says, must always lose something as soon as it enters into practical activity because it must lend itself to the imperfection of the

world. And this conception gave Michelet concern: he rebuked "the disastrous doctrine, which our friend Renan has too much commended, that passive internal freedom, preoccupied with its own salvation, which delivers the world to evil." It is curious to contrast the tone of Renan's speech at the inauguration of a medallion of Michelet, Quinet and Mickiewicz at the Collège de France in 1884 with that of his combative predecessors. Renan's emphasis is all on the importance of the calm pursuit of truth, though the turmoil may be raging around us of those who are forced to make a practical issue of it. But he corrects himself: "No, we are posted in sign of war; peace is not our lot." Yet the relation between the rioter in the street and the scholar in his study seems to have been completely dissolved.

In *The Origins of Christianity,* Renan's attitude toward his own time appears very plainly through his story. In any sense in which it is possible to describe human productions as impartial, this enchanting account of the decline of the ancient world and the rise of the Christian religion may be said to be impartial. The effort toward universal comprehension and justice is one of the most impressive things about Renan. But his very artistic form has its bias, the very fall of his sentences has its bias; and before he has finished his story, he *has* undeniably tipped the scales. In *The Origins of Christianity,* which begins with a volume on Jesus and ends with a volume on Marcus Aurelius, it must be confessed that somehow or other Marcus Aurelius gets the better of it. The *Life of Jesus,* which the Goncourts characterized as "Michelet Fénelonized," has always seemed to me the least successful section. Renan makes Jesus a "charming doctor," tends, in fact, to make him a sort of Renan, and minimizes the symbolic tragedy which was to fascinate and sustain the world. He does better perhaps with Paul, but makes us dislike him. The episode we remember best is Paul's arrival in Athens to preach the Christian gospel and his outcry against the Greek statutes: "O chaste and lovely images," Renan cries out in his turn, "of the true gods and goddesses!—this ugly little Jew has stigmatized you with the name of idols!" And so when Renan comes to the Apocalypse, which he interprets as a radical tract directed against the Roman Empire, he does not fail to put the whole exploit in an ironical light from the beginning by commenting on the extreme inappropriateness of John's having selected the little island of Patmos, more suitable, as Renan remarks, for some delightful classical idyl of the type of *Daphnis and Chloë,* for the forging of his fulminations and the concoction of his esthetic monstrosities. The truth is that the moral earnestness of the Jews, to whose literature Renan has devoted his life, is coming to seem to him unsympathetic. And when we arrive at Marcus Aurelius, Renan's preference for the Graeco-Roman culture as contrasted with the agitation of the Christians unmistakably emerges and has the last word. We can note how, almost imperceptibly, his interest and emphasis have shifted since he published the *Life of Jesus* nearly twenty years before. "Marcus Aurelius and his noble masters," Renan had written then, "have had no enduring effect on the world. Marcus Aurelius leaves behind him delightful books, an execrable son, a dying world. Jesus remains for humanity an inexhaustible principle of moral regeneration. Philosophy, for the majority, is not enough; they must have sainthood." But in the volume on *Marcus Aurelius* (published in 1882) Renan manages to give us the impression that the Romans, through their legal reforms, were tending by themselves and independently of the evangelism of the Christians, to put humanitarian principles into practice. Was Christianity necessary, after all? we are prompted to ask ourselves. Will not a society sufficiently developed arrive at this point of view by itself? Marcus Aurelius has all Jesus' love of virtue and is a Roman gentleman as well; and, ruminating sadly on human affairs as he wages his uncongenial warfare against the forces battering in the Empire, he is presented as the perfect exemplar for the French intellectual world of the period after 1870—disillusioned with its political tradition, resigned to its national defeat, disgusted with contemporary tendencies, but persisting in the individual pursuit of such ends, the private cultivation of such qualities, as still seem to be valuable in themselves. "His [Marcus Aurelius'] virtue was based, like ours, upon reason, upon nature. Saint Louis was a very virtuous man and, according to the ideas of his time, a very great king, because he was a Christian; Marcus Aurelius was the most pious of men, not because he was a pagan, but because he was an emancipated man. He was an honor to human nature, and not to a particular religion. . . . He has achieved the perfect goodness, the absolute indulgence, the indifference tempered with pity and scorn. 'To be resigned, as one passes one's life in the midst of false and unjust men'—that was the sage's program. And he was right. The most solid goodness is that which is based on perfect ennui, on the clear realization that everything in this world is frivolous and without real foundation. . . . Never was there a more legitimate cult, and it is still our cult today." Such a morality is attractive to read about, but it will let down rather than support its generation. What kind of champions can be recruited by a preacher who is obliged to have recourse for his sanctions to the stoicism of Marcus Aurelius?—by one who begins by assuring us that we should value the saint above all men, but ends by recommending as a model a sage who plays the man of action with no conviction of the action's value?

Renan himself was, however, sustained to accomplish his historical work. And *The Origins of Christianity* is a masterpiece—perhaps the greatest of all histories of ideas. What Renan can give us incomparably, what we get out of him so that we never forget it, is the sense of the way in which doctrines, conceptions, symbols, undergo continual transformations at the hands of different persons and races. With a sensitiveness of intelligence and a subtlety of presentation which have never been excelled, he follows the words and the story of Jesus as they pass into varied combinations and with every new combination become themselves something new: the Christianity of the Apostles is no longer the Christianity of Jesus; the Christianity of the Scriptures is modified as it is attracted toward the Greeks or the Jews; the Christianity of the Rome of Nero is something entirely different from the primitive Christianity of Judea. Our ideas are all spun from filaments, infinitely long and mingled, which have to be analyzed with an infinite delicacy.

But note that the emphasis with Renan is thus chiefly upon the relativity of religious and philosophical conceptions. There is a relativity, too, in Michelet—his actors play different roles in different historical situations, according to their personal capacities in relation to varying circumstances; but the dominating values are not in doubt. With Renan, of the later generation, the values themselves are beginning to waver; we find him talking about "the clear realization that everything in this world is frivolous and without real foundation." Note, furthermore, that whereas with Michelet we are in the midst of human happenings, among which the propagation of ideas figures merely as one of many kinds of activity, with Renan we are occupied primarily with ideas, behind

which the rest of human history is merely filled in as a background—it is the frame on which the web has been woven, but what we are concerned with is tracing the web. Renan's function is to take us through the texts of the religion and wisdom of antiquity—even though by a spell of imagination he is creating about us as we read them the social atmosphere of the times in which they were written. Though *The Origins of Christianity* is still Michelet's organic history, it is the history no longer of the man as a whole but of man's formulated ideas. (pp. 47-52)

> Edmund Wilson, "Decline of the Revolutionary Tradition: Renan," in his To the Finland Station: A Study in the Writing and Acting of History, Farrar, Straus and Giroux, 1972, pp. 42-52.

## GEORGE SARTON   (essay date 1948)

> [*George Sarton, a Belgian-born American, is considered one of the twentieth century's most important historians of science. A founder and editor of the journals* Isis *(1912-52) and* Osiris *(1936-56), he also wrote histories of science of the classical age, including* Ancient Science through the Golden Age of Greece *(1952) and* Hellenistic Science and Culture in the Last Three Centuries B.C. *(1959). In the following excerpt, Sarton underscores the strong influence of positivism on Renan's thought, arguing that it determined his conception of the history of modern religion as "the progress of science."*]

The most characteristic trait of Renan's thought is his scientific conception of history and, conversely, his rare understanding of the spirit of positive science. To be sure this was largely due to his constant intercourse with Marcellin Berthelot, but the latter's influence would have been of little avail if Renan had not been fully prepared to receive it. When he exclaims in one of his prefaces to the *Life of Jesus,* "History is a science like chemistry, like geology," there comes to us an echo of their discussions on the subject. Renan, whose sole knowledge was historical, had been suddenly brought face to face with a man whose conceptions and ideals, though strangely similar to his own, were based on an altogether different set of facts. On the other hand Berthelot had probably been led to believe—as most young scientists are—that there was no real knowledge outside the field of the positive or experimental sciences, and we may expect him to have taken pains to impress his theological companion with this conviction. The test of knowledge, he might say, is the ability to foresee, to bring about definite results with certainty. The experimental sciences are the only ones which make such knowledge possible. Of course Renan could not share such an intolerant conception, but he would learn to understand the pure scientific point of view, as no other historian ever did. Thus, after having reviewed the intellectual conditions of Islam, he concludes, "The purpose of mankind is not repose in submissive ignorance, but implacable war against error and struggle against evil. Science is the soul of society for science is reason. . . . It creates military and industrial superiority. It will some day create social superiority; I mean a state of society wherein the full amount of justice compatible with the essence of the universe will be available." Berthelot would have expressed himself exactly in the same way, but he would have stopped there. Renan was not inclined to throw overboard as worthless his own treasure of facts, to the collection of which he had devoted so many years of intense study. He realized keenly that there was an immense field of knowledge to which the methods of positive science could not yet be applied—and maybe could never be; but that was no reason to give up its exploration as hopeless. The duty in every case remained the same: to find as much of the truth as possible. If but little truth could be attained with certainty, it was nevertheless one's duty to find that little. The science of the human mind is essentially historical, for all that we do, all that we know, all that we are is the result of ageless labor and immemorial experience. The best way to understand the development of our mind and to fathom its nature and possibilities is to study the history of mankind—to study it with the same scrupulous accuracy with which the naturalist seeks to unravel the succession of geologic or biologic changes. Renan understood all this very clearly and his philosophy was completed by a vague concept of evolution as a universal law of life.

The idea of evolution was of course in the air, and the tumult and disruptions of 1848 had done much to replace in the popular mind the general notions of tradition and immobility by that of ceaseless change. Dynamical or historical explanations were everywhere substituted for the merely static—for the dogmatic descriptions of an immobile reality. It is interesting to note that Spencer and Darwin were thinking on this very subject at the same time as Renan—it must be admitted with far greater depth—but his contribution is nevertheless of great importance, for it came from the other pole of research.

Renan's scientific attitude is best illustrated by his love of concrete facts and his distrust of premature generalizations. Thus he would say, "Reason alone cannot create truth. . . . The attempt to construct a theory of things by the play of empty formulas is as vain a pretense as that of the weaver who would produce linen without putting any thread in his shuttle," and again, "It is philology or erudition which will provide the thinker with that forest of things (*silva rerum ac sententiarum,* as Cicero puts it), without which philosophy will never be more than a Penelope's weaving always to be recommended." This was partly a revulsion against the theological arguments of his youth, partly a natural impulse intensified by Berthelot's example.

I speak of natural impulse advisedly, for it is obvious that Renan was a born scientist. The fundamental qualities of a true scientist were genuine parts of his substance; the love of truth, of accuracy, and even more the disinterestedness and the courage without which this love is easily stifled at the very time when it is most needed.

This leads us to examine his religion, a subject it is far easier to discuss now than in his own time, when some fanatics went so far as to consider him as a sort of Antichrist. The core of his religion, which was intense, was this very love of truth. One might be tempted to ask, is it possible that religion be based on something else? But it is wiser to ask no such question; for it would oblige us to deny the religion of a large number of people who consider themselves, in perfect good faith, as deeply religious, though they have no idea of truth, no means of recognizing it, no love of it, no use for it. Their religion is irrational, but we cannot say that it is not genuine.

Aside from this love of truth which remained the absorbing passion of his life, Renan had retained from his early education a double imprint; the conviction of the necessity of a moral aristocracy, and the feeling that such aristocracy was essentially one of service, enjoying no privilege but to be what it was and expecting no other, not even the privilege of wide recognition. According to him, the truly inferior men are the great mass of the self-centered, snobbish and stupid people, who have no other motives than the improvement of their position, the furthering of their own petty interests. On the contrary, the true mark of the aristocracy—in which he had placed all his hope of moral progress—is its disinterestedness, its eagerness to devote itself to the community without the thought of any reward. He insisted repeatedly in every one of his writings on the essential importance of such disinterestedness. The purpose of man, as far as we can understand it, is to create intellectual values, that is, to produce beautiful things, to discover and vindicate truth, to increase justice and human solidarity. Every disinterested effort in that direction, however humble, is a positive gain, however small, for the whole world. To put it in the simplest terms, he who takes life earnestly and forgets himself is, to that extent, religious; he who is frivolous, self-complacent, superficial, selfish, is, to that extent, irreligious.

When Renan renounced the taking of the sacred orders to devote himself entirely to scholarly pursuits, the change appeared to the bigots immense, abysmal. Some of them could never forgive him; the boy educated to be a priest, but who had decided at the eleventh hour to follow another road, seemed to them a renegade, a vile traitor; and they hated and despised him accordingly. In fact the change was very small. He was fully convinced that the fullest use he could make of his life was to consecrate it to the quest of truth. He was born a priest, but what else is the true scientist?; he remained a lay priest—a priest of science—to the end of his days. His decision to leave the church affected his beliefs, changed his profession; but it did not alter the texture of his soul; it did not disturb his religion. Well might he say when he edited *The Future of Science* after a thoughtful interval of forty years, "My religion is still the progress of reason, that is, of science." And he added a little further in the same preface, "For us idealists, one single doctrine is true, the transcendent doctrine according to which the purpose of mankind is the creation of a superior conscience or, as they put it in the old days, the greatest glory of God." (pp. 112-15)

*George Sarton, "Ernest Renan," in his* The Life of Science: Essays in the History of Civilization, *Henry Schuman, 1948, pp. 101-15.*

### RICHARD M. CHADBOURNE    (essay date 1957)

[*In the following excerpt, Chadbourne, who has written extensively on Renan, assesses the stylistic and intellectual merits of his philosophical, political, and religious essays.*]

One of the outstanding facts in the history of literature within the last thirty years has been the decline of the essay. Our world at mid-century has not been wanting in able journalists, critics, and scholars. But well-written articles, even those of permanent value, are not necessarily essays. It is merely using the term loosely to assign them to the great tradition which for over three hundred years, from Montaigne to Max Beerbohm, brought joy to our ancestors—the tradition of the brief, highly polished prose work, conveying a view (usually very personal) of almost any conceivable subject and worth rereading again and again. To identify almost any piece of nonfictional prose with the essay, furthermore, is to be unjust to the few who have remembered the tradition and still keep it alive, such true essayists as E. M. Forster or E. B. White, T. S. Eliot or Edmund Wilson. Even in France, where the relation between journalism and literary art has long been close, there are few today who are *essayistes* in quite the same way as, several generations ago, Paul Valéry or Alain or Remy de Gourmont.

To the decline of the essay as a distinct form, many causes have contributed. For many English-speaking readers, the essay has become associated with memories of schoolroom chores, of the forced labor of "themes," those artificial expressions of unreal sentiments. A more universal factor undermining the vitality of the essay has been the growth of specialization, with its accompanying diminution in that general competence, that urbanity, which are the soul of the essay. "The art of the essay," it has been pointed out, "like that of conversation, has declined in the last century because there are too few people who know enough about enough matters to afford an audience for the attractive discussion which is expert without being specialized." Even in France, where, as we have said, there is relatively little consciousness of the essay as a distinct genre, the publisher Kra noted in 1929, without great enthusiasm, that specialization seemed to be a characteristic trait of contemporary essayists. The drought of knowing more and more about less and less has touched the land *par excellence* of broad humane culture.

There are deeper reasons, however, for the essay's weakened hold on readers. One would think that the essay's brevity might have been in its favor. But we suffer not so much from the lack of time to read as from the disinclination to read carefully, and the essay, like the short-story and the poem, fellow exiles from best-seller lists, calls for attentive reading, for a certain amount of pondering and savoring. And it is precisely this willingness to savor subtle works of art, in a spirit of meditation and reflectiveness, that has become increasingly rare today. Perhaps it is significant that the essay began to become unpopular about the time, after the First World War, when, as Schweitzer tells us, the spirit of reflectiveness, the awareness of men as whole beings, individual personalities (an awareness also essential to the health of the essay), began to give way to the spirit of totalitarianism. Man the collective being, the faceless statistic, the thinking machine manipulated by propaganda, is, at least, alien to the very spirit of the essay.

Something of this growing unreflectiveness, in writer and reader alike, was perceived by Virginia Woolf to be the underlying cause of the essay's decline. The eloquent thoughts she recorded on the subject in "The Modern Essay," in 1925, will serve both to enlighten us on the essay in general and to link us up . . . with Renan and his time. Herself a member of a great generation of essayists, which included Max Beerbohm, Lytton Strachey, and John Middleton Murry; one of the last perfectionists, in her *Common Reader,* of that difficult art, she makes perfectly clear the distinction between the true essay and the modern ersatz product. It is the distinction between "the shapely silver drop, that held the sky in it and so many bright little visions of human life," on one hand, and, on the other, "a hold-all, knobbed with luggage packed in a hurry," or, even worse, "journalism embalmed in a book."

Whetting our appetites for the old masters—for Montaigne, Bacon, Addison, Lamb, Hazlitt, Hunt, De Quincey, Carlyle, Ruskin, Arnold, Pater, Newman, Bagehot—Virginia Woolf makes us feel how great an art we are in danger of losing. Of the Victorians in particular, Renan's contemporaries, she writes: "It was worth while to speak out upon serious matters in an essay; and there was nothing absurd in writing as well as one possibly could when, in a month or two, the same pub-

lic which had welcomed the essay in a magazine would carefully read it once more in a book." Now (how much more true this is today than in 1925 when she wrote it!), "a common greyness silvers everything. Beauty and courage are dangerous spirits to battle in a column and a half; and thought, like a brown paper parcel in a waistcoat pocket, has a way of spoiling the symmetry of an article."

The nineteenth-century French essay, with Sainte-Beuve as its brilliant pioneer and Renan as perhaps its most versatile representative, flowed through the same channel from periodical to book, was based upon the same premise of broad culture in writer and reader, and professed the same serious literary aim as its English counterpart, described by Virginia Woolf. But there were important differences. The French product admitted of much less variety in form and content; it tended to be critical in nature, whether it treated of politics, history, or literature—critical and much less personal, at least directly personal, much less whimsical and poetic. However, though less luxuriant than its English cousin, the French critical essay, within these limitations, was capable of great diversity, and few writers proved this as successfully as Renan. Few, indeed, possessed the breadth of interests and the flexible command of French prose which made him so well suited to the task.

In the essay Renan found the happiest means—apart, that is, from the writing of history, which remained closest to his heart—for the expression of his personality. Unlike Montaigne and so many of his disciples, especially his English disciples, unlike the romantics, he disliked speaking freely and directly of himself. The *Cahiers de jeunesse,* that dialogue of the young thinker with himself and himself alone, a dialogue which, as Charles Du Bos pointed out, surpasses even the intimate journal in unstudied frankness, is quite exceptional in his total work. For the *journal intime* as a literary genre, we have seen that he felt only distaste. It stemmed from his natural reticence—despite the *Souvenirs d'enfance et de jeunesse,* more often misleading than revealing, he was a reticent man—and from his training in seventeenth-century *honnêteté,* re-enforced by the lessons of Henriette and Sacy. "*Confessions*" he was not loathe to make, but "*confidences*" . . . he withheld. The critical essay, like history, was beautifully suited to this type of modesty, for it allowed him to give generously of his thought and feeling and yet to keep them within the framework of critical restraint, under the sober control of scholarship.

In some ways his essay work seems narrow in scope. Rarely do the "shapely silver drop," the color and poetry of the world around us, the all-important trivia (in Logan Pearsall Smith's sense) of our lives, find a place in it. Only rarely, as in the **"Souvenirs d'un vieux professeur allemand"** or an occasional *feuille détachée,* does he lend himself to whimsical humor. For a Frenchman, his relative indifference to literary criticism, to questions of art, might almost be called neglect. It is in the *Dialogues philosophiques* and the *Drames philosophiques,* rather than in the essays, that he approaches that spirit of delightfully free and unpredictable reverie we admire in so many essayists. On the other hand, the field of the critical essay, as he explored it, was wonderfully wide and fruitful. Breadth is one of his greatest virtues. And although most of the nineteenth-century essayists possessed this gift, so rare today, few writers anywhere have ever equaled Renan in breadth and solidity of culture. On subjects ranging from ancient Greek myths to the memoirs of Guizot, from the Buddha to the Franco-Prussian War, from Isaiah to the metaphysics of Vacherot, he cast the light of his great learning and intelligence. The results he achieved, though all interesting, are not all equally successful, and some attempt should now be made to arrange them in an ascending hierarchy of excellence.

The philosophical essays, as distinguished from the more brilliant *dialogues* and *drames,* seem to me the least durable. In this perhaps most difficult of all the essay forms, Renan is the inferior of Emerson or Santayana or Bertrand Russell. It was no mean feat to condense the whole of his intellectual drama in the extraordinarily rich and subtle **"Examen de conscience philosophique."** But his philosophical thought in general suffers from evasiveness: instead of coming to grips firmly with his terrible dilemma, with the basic contradiction of his mind, namely, emotional attachment to a religion whose truth his intellect denied, he glossed over the problem with vague phrases, proposing a compromise between positivism and spiritualism which, designed to please scientific as well as religious minds, ended up satisfying neither. This was the price he paid for his faithfulness to eclecticism, for he was its star pupil and the greatest demonstrator of its essential futility.

In his historical essays, on the other hand, he gives us solid meat. He takes his rightful place with Montaigne and Pascal, Montesquieu, Fontenelle, Voltaire, and Sainte-Beuve, as a master of that difficult art, in which the French above all have excelled, the art of *vulgarisation.* Like Saturn devouring and digesting the rocks or, to descend to our human level, like Montesquieu "unraveling the chaos of Ripuarian, Visigothic, and Burgundian laws," he turned highly technical knowledge into nourishment for the common reader. To have extracted the "poetry of history" from his own researches and from those of his contemporaries; to have emerged from communion with dead documents, uncontaminated with pedantry and ready to tell of the living things he had seen—this was no small achievement. One need not accept all his views in order to recognize that in his hands the essay in religious history became a source of artistic pleasure as well as of enlightenment, and this is what makes the *Etudes d'histoire religieuse* a major landmark in the history of the French essay. May scholars who are too faint-hearted to risk being called "popularizers" be encouraged by his example: he practiced this art of humanizing learning with no sacrifice of scholarly integrity. He was, in one and the same man, without split personality, the scholar who taught extremely specialized lessons in Hebrew epigraphy and directed the Corpus Inscriptionum Semiticarum and the sensitive prose artist of *L'histoire du peuple d'Israël.* "Let us not blame him too much," said Alfred Loisy, "for having been a marvelous writer as well as a scholar. There will always be enough learned men who write badly."

On an equally high plane with his explorations of our religious past are his essays in the political problems, conceived in the broad French manner, of his own time. He understood, to recall a haunting phrase of Virginia Woolf's, that "reverence for the dead is vitally connected with understanding of the living." As a political essayist, in the best of the *Questions contemporaines* and *La réforme intellectuelle et morale,* he ranks with Walter Bagehot or Lord Acton. The latter work, in great part a gloomy, violent attack on democracy, is to be admired not least of all for its power to provoke. Its prefascist vision of order was, however, only a temporary aberration of his pessimism in the 1870's. Despite some confusion and in-

consistency, his mature political philosophy may be defined as an intelligent conservatism, a belief in liberal constitutional monarchy which did not exclude the possibility of a future working democracy for France. The point is that his essays abound in historical insight, in shrewd wisdom, and in the sense, not especially common in scholars, of political responsibility and readiness to act if called upon. His greatest tour de force was his ability to place these ephemeral questions in a broad moral and historical context which gives them permanent interest; it was simply not his habit, as he remarked with justifiable pride, to treat any subjects in a narrow manner.

At the summit of Renan's essay work, in my opinion, stands his *Essais de morale et de critique,* with its condemnation of materialism and bureaucracy, of the cult of mediocrity, in the modern world and its affirmation of idealism. Less perceptive than Sainte-Beuve or Taine as a literary critic, Renan nevertheless brought unusual understanding to figures on the margin of literature, seeking to illuminate his own time through the study of such predecessors as Cousin, Thierry, Lamennais, Tosti, Sacy, and, elsewhere, Guizot, Burnouf, Le Clerc. Here he practiced with great skill the traditional French *portrait moral,* delicately but firmly passing judgment upon an older generation, seeking to learn from their virtues and errors. But the most remarkable feature of these essays is the manner in which he lets his thoughts crystallize in rich patterns around the subjects he treats, while never allowing us to lose sight of the subjects themselves. The themes which emerge—critically controlled enthusiasm for life and learning, detached but interested participation in the political life of one's time, reaffirmation of poetic and spiritual values, mediation between past and present—make up one of the strongest messages he has left us. One could argue, without absurdity, that this is his true masterpiece.

For each of the major divisions of his essay work, Renan used a different kind of style, and this is an appropriate point to sum up our scattered observations on that subject. Much of what we say should apply to his style in general, for we have come into contact with an incomplete, but nevertheless very substantial, area of his prose.

That diversity of style is as much a feature of his work as diversity of subject matter has not always been recognized. For too long the misconception has been abroad—with few critics to combat it—that *le style de Renan* is almost exclusively a form of poetic prose. The highly artificial lyricism of the *Prière sur l'Acropole* or of parts of the *Vie de Jésus* has been assumed by many to be his strong point, and the assumption has done more harm than good to his reputation. The fact is that this type of writing is much less characteristic of Renan than it is supposed to be. His style usually lacks the vivid color, the abundance of images and metaphors, and especially the marked, self-conscious rhythms of poetic prose. Like all great prose, it is, at its best, clear and forceful, spontaneous and self-effacing. Poetic feeling was but one of its ingredients. Nor, to continue for a moment this negative approach, can we accept the equally widespread error that Renan was an impeccable model of French prose, a legend which has frightened many readers away and challenged others, Jean-Paul Sartre, for example, to prick the bubble, by exposing "baseness" and "ugliness" everywhere. Much more sensible is Brunetière's sober observation that Renan did not always write correctly or purely and sometimes wrote carelessly.

The vagueness which was one of his permanent weaknesses,

the excessive facility and the bad taste which mar so much of his last work—reflecting, we dare say, the moral slackness of *renanisme* itself, for Renan has taught us the moral significance of style—these are his real faults. Revealing that he was aware of perhaps an even more serious one, which he blamed on certain limitations he found inherent in French prose itself, he declared: "What, indeed, does it mean to write well, as we understand it in France? It means constantly to sacrifice sudden flashes of wit (*saillie*) and often frankness to the moderation (*mesure*) of the language. It means to say at the most half of what we think, and at least a quarter of what we do not think." We certainly need not regret that he refined the crude vigorous metal of his youthful prose into such a marvelously subtle critical instrument. But we may well regret, along with Renan, that the sacrifice of frankness went too far. Above all, we may regret that the subtle critical instrument became an instrument of equivocation.

Once we have squarely recognized these faults, we can proceed to the definition of what is truly beautiful in his style. He wrote in several keys, each with its peculiar excellence, and yet his style as a whole has its distinctive seal. To begin with his diversity, it may be explained in part by the rich variety of influences he absorbed: the lyricism of prose poets like Fénelon and Chateaubriand, the simplicity and restraint of classicism, the austere touch of Port-Royal and Sacy, the polemical vigor of Maistre and of the *Liberté de penser,* the sober descriptive power of Thierry, the learned but graceful precision of scholars like Burnouf. At his best his style represents a fusion of all these influences. He began with the aggressive, frank, often harsh manner of his essays for the *Liberté de penser.* In *L'avenir de la science* he was wild and feverish and verbose in his idealism. Much of this early vigor, restrained and sharpened but still virile, passed into his political essays, which are characterized by an incisive, energetic style, fertile in aphorisms. Here there is none of that "softness" and "uncertainty," that "flaccidity" and "lack of muscle" André Gide complained of in the *Souvenirs d'enfance et de jeunesse* and *L'abbesse de Jouarre.* Renan was of course an adept in what Matthew Arnold called the "Attic style," *"lenis minimèque pertinax"* ("easy and not too violently insisting"), and with him this style of delicate insinuation developed undeniable signs of flabbiness. But he could also be perfectly direct and firm; he could even be violent.

His better-known style, however, is the more subtle one first appearing in the *Averroès* and then in the *Etudes d'histoire religieuse* and the *Essais de morale et de critique.* Impelled by his need to harmonize the conflicting intellectual gifts he had received, to unite them in "parallel existences," and inspired by Cousin's vision of an age of synthesis, he sought to become a microcosm of the manifold talents of humanity itself, blending in his work critical poise and moral and religious fervor, scientific accuracy and poetic feeling. But "poetry" was only one of the strands making up the pattern: "I have a certain reflective and psychological turn of mind which keeps coming back and which prevents me from being abundantly or easily poetic." Except for a few essays like **"Les religions de l'antiquité,"** the poetic element was not particularly sensuous or colorful. Little realism entered into this art. Although a member of the first generation of realists and Parnassians, Renan remained, in esthetics, an anti-realist, a spiritualist.

This brings us to what may well be the most distinctive feature of his style, and the true secret of its greatness, namely, the effect it gives of moral intensity achieved by the most conservative means, of spontaneous grace within a framework of order and harmony. His sentences reflect his compelling drive toward regularity, toward a balanced, harmonious view of life, and yet this *"ensemble harmonieux"* did not exclude a certain underlying unrest, a trembling of irony. It is this which gives moral life to his style, but it is perhaps even more the fact that unlike Flaubert or Walter Pater, he did not cultivate form for its own sake or strain after effect. Naturally, we except the artificial tricks of *renanisme.* At his best, he was a highly conscious artist who happily failed to polish all the spontaneity out of his art.

In 1923, comparing him with Taine and Flaubert and estimating their relative chances of survival as living writers, Albert Thibaudet pointed out how wise Renan was to avoid Taine's more obviously oratorical style and Flaubert's cult of art. The special mark of his style, wrote Thibaudet,

> is that of probity, delicacy, and sobriety. Those who believe that style has a value in itself found little favor with him, and, although Flaubert never expressed his opinion on this score, he must have asked himself in astonishment what one could possibly find to admire in Renan's style. What we admire are precisely those spontaneous aspects of the French language which are most foreign to the willful character of Flaubert's own style.

In singling out Renan's essays for detailed study, I have made no claim that they are necessarily superior to the rest of his work or that they reveal what a French critic might call his *vrai visage.* I have tried to avoid isolating them from his other works. Much of the criticism of Renan, however, has suffered from the failure to take his essays into account at all. In them, on the whole, we discover the strong, affirmative side of his nature also expressed, though with much less artistry, in the ***Cahiers de jeunesse, L'avenir de la science,*** and the correspondence with Berthelot. And this *visage,* in all probability, is a truer one than that of the arch equivocator, the dissolver of our sense of truth and error, which has stuck in the minds of so many readers. In summing up the image that emerges from his essays, let us try to separate the gold from the dross.

The most serious of Renan's flaws, I would say, was a certain lack of forthrightness. One cannot deny that at times he demonstrated admirable courage, as when he made a clean break from Saint-Sulpice or defined his stand at the Collège de France in 1862 or probed the national conscience in his unpopular prophetic essays of the war and postwar years. But the weakness of his religious position, his inability to face up to the consequences of his repudiation of Christianity, weigh heavily against him. He who so dreaded being duped deceived himself—or perhaps did, for this intimate side of his thought is not very well known—into believing he had not in fact repudiated Christianity at all. He is the most outstanding example of the widespread nineteenth-century error, defined and attacked by Santayana, in his *Winds of Doctrine* (1913), as "archeological piety," that vague sentimental clinging to the memory of Christianity, to its historical beauty, when one's reason has rejected it. To modern readers, Renan's religiosity, once considered a virtue, is more likely to appear a most obnoxious vice. Would that he had applied to his own work the critical remark he made of "liberal Catholics," namely, that truth, as Bacon said, is more apt to emerge from error than from confusion—"Malheur au vague! Mieux vaut le faux."

An even more serious manifestation of Renan's lack of straightforwardness, however, was the weakening of his sense of responsibility toward his readers in the last twenty years or so of his life. He had reason enough to be disillusioned, to be skeptical: the promise of the Revolution, the great dream of a free society ordering its fate with the help of scientific and historical knowledge and an inspired reason, the great dream of 1848, had collapsed, owing, he believed, to the naïve bungling of the romantic generation. What we must reproach him for is not that he was disenchanted, but that he assumed a mask of frivolity, the mask of *renanisme,* designed to convince his readers that, however much of an idealist he had once been, he was now a wise old cynic, safely detached from the search for truth, protected forever from the danger of having beliefs. No longer subject to the restraining moral influences of his sister, of Thierry or Sacy, the voice of his conscience drowned out by popular applause, he succeeded only too well, and in more senses than one, in this mystification. It is precisely this self-refutation of his own best side, this pleading against his own deeply moral nature . . . , which must be put down as his gravest failing.

But these defects, however serious, should not be allowed, as has too often happened, to obscure his real virtues. Of the vast number of Renan's critics, there have always been some, though they seem to be in a minority, who have suspected that, despite the conspicuous lapse of the last years, he preserved intact to the end his fundamentally moral and idealistic nature. Even critics who have exaggerated his skepticism have had their moments of insight into this stubbornly affirmative core of his being. Barrès . . . was one of them, and so also, surprisingly, was Anatole France; toward the beginning of his speech canonizing Renan as the saint of skeptics, we find this striking sentence, which seems very much out of place: "Those who believed him to be irresolute and fickle had not taken the trouble to observe the world of his thoughts. It was like the region from which he came, where clouds move swiftly overhead in a troubled sky, but the soil is made of granite, and into it oak trees plunge their deep roots" [see Further Reading].

Lanson called this inner strength *"douce inflexibilité,"* and Du Bos, a critic whose deeply moral nature no one will deny, was drawn to it, for he wrote that beneath the ironic smile, the surface wrinkles of *"dédaigneuse bonhomie,"* "le fond est demeuré, et demeure, inattaqué." It would indeed have been incredible had that quality of *sérieux* which we find in Renan's youth, and which Du Bos calls "peut-être la plus belle et la plus pure de tout le XIXe siècle français," disappeared altogether. That it survived and that it is unmistakably present in the greater part of his essay work, I hope my study has shown.

For one thing, the continuing presence in Renan's work of these deep roots, these "essential affirmations," as Irving Babbitt called them [see excerpt dated 1902], is shown in his persistent philosophical view of the universe as an orderly system of laws (whose "immutability" he in fact exaggerated), moving toward moral perfection with an unconscious striving which it is man's duty to interpret and to render ever more conscious. Naïve much of this may seem, but certainly not fickle. Nor should we forget his stubborn pursuit of historical truth, for, despite his belittling of history as a composite of *"petites sciences conjecturales',"* he devoted his life to it, seeking out the truth about the past, compelled to arrange his materials in some kind of coherent, rational picture, even

if it meant embracing hypotheses which more cautious historians would have kept at a distance.

Du Bos's phrase *"fond inattaqué"* certainly referred also to the moral probity of the private man, the *personne* as distinguished from the *personnage,* the devoted husband and father, the conscientious scholar and teacher, the citizen solicitous for his country's welfare. In a well-established French tradition which goes back to Descartes if not to Montaigne, Renan's skepticism remained a speculative affair hardly touching his practical moral life. Despite his occasional pessimism and grimness, there was no despair, no *acedia,* in him. From his quietly troubled and brilliant youth down to his death in his apartment of the Collège de France, he never, so far as I know, uttered a word in condemnation of life. To the last, it held its inexhaustible interest for him. Beside him, Flaubert, with his prescription of art as medicine against hysteria, perhaps even Taine, for whom work was a "slow and intelligent form of suicide," appear sickly indeed.

He possessed to a remarkable degree a quality which is of great help to any artist, but which is, as an English essayist has reminded us, indispensable to the creator of the essay— gusto. His critical sense strengthened rather than weakened this enthusiasm for life. But because his enthusiasm was intellectual in nature, nourishing itself on learning, more than one critic has misunderstood it. Hippolyte Parigot, for example, apparently insensitive to this kind of sober scholarly emotion, accused Renan of lack of feeling, and also of "egotism." But even if it were true that Renan sacrificed some of his personal warmth in the interests of his pursuit of knowledge (Parigot offers only the incomplete evidence of a certain harshness toward Henriette), he would thereby find himself in the company of many a great creative spirit. Some egotism would seem to be the unavoidable price many great writers must pay in order to give us their works.

Parigot failed to see, furthermore, that it was precisely Renan's immense interest in life which saved him from egotism in the sense of self-centeredness. Renan is one of the great teachers of curiosity, of that curiosity which turns us outward from morbid preoccupation with self toward participation in the world around us. "Assuredly," he once wrote, "we must not speak ill of curiosity." Perhaps the very term which has been used to curse him with—the word "dilettante"—should be rehabilitated as an honorable epithet. If to be a dilettante means to skim the surface of life, to grasp nothing firmly, he was no dilettante. Whatever the spirit of shallower writers who fancied themselves his disciples, his own spirit was to know and to love many things as deeply as our brief existence will allow. This spirit shines with special brightness through his essay work. If this be dilettantism, it may be the antidote we need for too much specialization. We need also, in our age of violent and senseless action, which inculcates the use of things and persons merely as means to ends, something of the contemplative spirit which permeates Renan's essays, something of his interest in, his respect for, things and persons in themselves.

Renan deserves a better fate than has befallen him. He deserves more than to be admired from afar, a curious idol preserved by literary historians. His work, despite many dead branches that need clearing away, is still very much alive. That it is a rich and complex work one would suspect simply from the extraordinary variety of temperaments which it has influenced—dabblers in irony as well as scholars and educators of the utmost probity, frivolous dilettantes as well as serious moralists, critics as different as Matthew Arnold and Jules Lemaître, atheists and heretics, agnostics and converts. In the minds of some he sowed doubt and in the minds of others he awakened a sympathy for Christianity after the long dry spell of uncomprehending rationalism. (pp. 193-210)

We have approached Renan through a sizable and significant aspect of his work, the nine books of essays he produced between the age of thirty-four and his death at sixty-nine. They fall into three main periods: the inartistic, dogmatic faith in science (or historical scholarship) and the equally inartistic combative journalism of the 1840's; the mature critical art, in history, moral and political problems, and philosophy, of the 1850's, 1860's, and early 1870's; the disillusionment and affected frivolity of *renanisme,* from about 1876 to his death in 1892. Like most Frenchmen, Renan the mature artist prized, above all, order and clarity of composition, and this admirable national prejudice caused his essays to lose something in pleasurable unpredictability. He rarely took advantage of the essay's unique privilege of being "a loose sally of the mind," as Doctor Johnson put it, even though it was a Frenchman who had invented this delightful art of disorderly order, with its *"allure poétique, à sauts et à gambades."* His essay structure—often the total architecture of the book—is clear but subtle, firmer than Sainte-Beuve's (whose *causerie* is closer to Montaigne and perhaps to the English essay), but not so rigid and artificial as Taine's. He knew how to relax with *"feuilles légères," "fantaisies sans conséquence,"* but these pieces, though often charming, fail to capture the light, penetrating humor so common in the English essay.

Where Renan was at his best was in ranging out over history and contemporary events, over broad moral and political questions, and to the treatment of these in essay form he gave new authority and new luster. To these varied themes, he adapted his style with great skill, achieving now a rare combination of scholarly accuracy, poetic sensibility, and critical acumen, now a clear, direct, vigorous prose for political argument, now a note of rarefied moral feeling, expressed with the simplest and most sober means. He reveals himself in his essays as a scholar of genius, devoted to the enlightenment of his public, a keen and responsible political observer, an unsuccessful conciliator of religion and positivism, a vague and devious philosopher, a man of unusual moral probity (despite the lapses of *renanisme*)—*"un honnête homme à qui manque la grâce."*

With Montaigne and Sainte-Beuve, in the still largely unexplored territory of the French essay—whose modern luminaries, from Bourget and Gourmont to Alain and Valéry, have not been few—he holds an assured and eminent place. His finest essays—**"L'histoire du peuple d'Israël," "M. Augustin Thierry," "M. de Lamennais"** (indeed, most of the *Essais de morale et de critique*), **"Vingt jours en Sicile," "Examen de conscience philosophique"**—are worthy of the greatest in any language. They have the qualities defined by Virginia Woolf as the special virtues of the essay: the delicate harmony of all their parts, the power of creating a single impression within a variety of perceptions, above all, the power to draw a magic curtain round us.

Renan is not, in my opinion, either in his essays or in his other works, a writer of the very first order; he is a great *second.* Like Ariel, in *L'eau de Jouvence,* he lacked a certain fire; but like Ariel also, he had light and air in abundance. To read his essays is to experience something of Henry James's feeling when he opened Emerson and Goethe, the "sense of moving

in large intellectual space." Du Bos, who was aware of Renan's serious weaknesses, tells us how, one evening, he took up the *Essais de morale et de critique* and read the essay on Lamennais for the first time, and how it led him to rediscover Renan's breadth of vision and his tranquillity, his brightness of outlook. Only the Renan of the end, he wrote, "the only one naturally who 'founded a school,'" failed to satisfy him completely. "Beside him," noted Du Bos, "there are hardly any Frenchmen of the nineteenth century who do not seem at times lacking in intelligence."

It is always gratifying to find our literary judgments confirmed by a sensitive critic. It was his contact with this same beautiful book which first aroused the present writer's interest in Renan's essays and drew him across the barrier of prejudice and misunderstanding surrounding the subject of Renan and into the citadel of his work. He can only hope that he may have persuaded other readers to make a similar journey.

In Virginia Woolf's lament for the passing of the essay's heyday, there was much more than literary antiquarianism. The nineteenth, like all centuries, had its share of errors and absurdities, its own forms of barbarism, and from some of these we may have freed ourselves. But it was also a century of deep humanism, of a humanism which found one of its truest expressions in the essay, conceived as a work of art. In our own age of narrow specialization, of the fear of individualism, of growing unreflectiveness and insensitivity to language, we need the lightness and common sense, the breadth and freedom, the thoughtfulness and eccentricity and polish, of the essay. From the more often wise than foolish voice of Renan, speaking to us in the form of this most modest and perhaps most humane of all the literary arts, we have much to learn. (pp. 210-13)

> *Richard M. Chadbourne, in his* Ernest Renan as an Essayist, *Cornell University Press, 1957, 264 p.*

## FRANÇOIS MAURIAC (essay date 1961)

> [*Mauriac, a French Roman Catholic novelist, playwright, poet, essayist, scenarist, and journalist, won the Nobel Prize for Literature in 1952. His novels, according to one critic, offer us "a theology of the passions—or, more exactly, the opposite of a theology: a demonology." Here, Mauriac upholds Renan's intellectual integrity while speculating on the conflict the author experienced between his sympathy for Christianity and his love of philosophical truth.*]

When I first used to think about Renan, whose inner debate was to become the drama of a whole era, I never imagined a young man as poor as he was obscure. I received my first (and most deserved) slaps from Paul Souday, in 1910, via *le Temps,* for having written in reply to some inquiry, "What a bore that hypocrite Renan is!" Twenty years were to pass by before I discovered that every word in Renan's private papers speaks of feelings I have experienced, torments I have known, temptations against which I have had to struggle.

For the Christian, Renan's drama is that of a man whose love of truth separates him from the truth. Base motives never drove him from God. The Christian virtues never weighed heavily on him, and almost to the end of his life he was modest to the point of frugality. In his heart, a heart that was never closed to God, he accepted the asceticism and mystique of the Catholic Church. In his heart he perceived, heard, and embraced the Lord whom he renounced for reasons of philology. He had the misfortune to base his hope in the love that renews both the face of the earth and the heart of man on two exegetical questions: the Messianic interpretation of a psalm and the authorship of the Pentateuch.

Renan did not actually deny that divine love exists. Like a good Hegelian, he established his position in terms of contradiction. If, as he was convinced, science demonstrates that the impression made on him by a Being whom he has adored and whose name alone still makes him tremble, is utterly meaningless and in no way disproves the reality of nothingness, he did not try to erase its stamp. He left everything up in the air, and he taught his daughter, "It is impossible not to believe in immortality, you know. Believe in it, and don't listen to anyone else, even if they quote me to you."

We know that, from the Christian point of view, the lust of the mind is as fearful as the lust of the flesh. A stream of mortal lava flows from Renan. But I feel awfully far away from the simplicities of my youth, when I could damn a man as lightheartedly as one of Claudel's poems proposes. The mystery of the judgments of God on each of us as individuals is the mystery of mercy itself. The Christian is not forbidden to try to imagine through which fault mercy will seep into a man's destiny; and I, on my part, imagine that in Renan's case it was his devotion to what he believed was the truth, (just as in that of Gide it would be total sincerity, love for the underprivileged, and detachment).

Some one once said, in the course of a casual conversation, that after all we don't know what God thought of Protestants. One of the people present, who was most devout, broke in to say, "Well, I know!" which made the first speaker smile. But then, as he thought about it, he realized that he and almost all Christians, no matter to which of the various sects they belong, share this attitude, although they might not always show it so frankly.

But, actually, we do not know. The theologian has a perfect right to insist that he knows how God judges a heresy but not how He judges the heretic. I have known people who, as they lay dying, steeled themselves to reject the summons of a bliss to which they could have responded deeply but from which their minds withheld assent. Did they say no from scruple? Or from pride, or obstinacy? If it was from scruple, perhaps God loved them still.

"Truth to whatever extreme! Truth at any price!" young Renan cried in the seminary and he was still affirming it as the famous old man whose views so impressed those of the same turn of mind as Lemaître and Anatole France. The image, however, of the man—torn and divided against himself as he was for more than half a century—contradicts these effusions. The smile of the sprightly old skeptic belies his child's soul where God still reigns, and his student's heart that is indelibly marked with the name of Jesus.

"Truth to whatever extreme!" What an admission! The truth cannot be strained or pushed to extremes, but the speculations of historical criticism can be. "Truth at any price?" Yes, even at the price of truth.

And now let us listen attentively to his ceaseless cry as he lay dying: "Have pity on me!" He had once said, "I will pray when I am dying. We pray all the time without realizing it." And he kept repeating, "Have pity on me!" Perhaps in the mind of God a little boy of six, Ernest Psichari, had already

been chosen to atone for the wrong that his grandfather had done. Yes, surely so, but the boy was also chosen to bear witness as a visible sign of the Father's compassion for those who seek Him. The God Renan renounced did not deny him but remained with him and with all his people who had received God's blessing. (pp. 111-14)

*François Mauriac, "And on Writers," in his* Second Thoughts: Reflections on Literature and on Life, *translated by Adrienne Foulke, The World Publishing Company, 1961, pp. 51-140.*

**PETER HEINEGG**   (essay date 1975)

[*Focusing on* The Origins of Christianity, *Heinegg discusses Renan's conflicting attitudes towards the Hellenic and Hebraic sources of Christianity.*]

In the English-speaking world Ernest Renan is a dim figure, remembered at most for his controversial **Life of Jesus** (1863). We have forgotten, if we ever knew, the rest of his massive *oeuvre*. We have, perhaps, a vague notion of his presiding as one of the cultural high priests around the end of the Second Empire and the early decades of the Third Republic, but we don't take kindly to pontifical types anyway. Still, Renan deserves something better than oblivion. He was a superb writer, a gifted historian and scholar who mediated, in the best French manner, between the Academy and educated laymen. And his life, while mostly bookish and uneventful, is an interesting example of a characteristic 19th century dilemma: how to hold on to religion after denying your faith? (p. 120)

Not only his personal style, but his intellectual values as well were largely determined during Renan's seminary years, especially at Saint-Sulpice. In **The Future of Science** (written in 1848, but unpublished till 1890) he gives a full-dress display of his idea of the sacerdotal savant. "ONE THING ALONE IS NECESSARY!" he begins emphatically, the one thing being not the search for the kingdom of God, but the quest for and promotion of the Ideal. He goes on to glorify the life of service to science, by which he means all rational truth, as opposed to revelation. Specifically Renan hymns the praises of history and philology (i.e., his own most pressing concerns). They supply the key to fuller knowledge of the origins of language and thought, and hence aid us to understand man and heighten global self-consciousness. The underlying assumption of the book is the axiom later set forth in the preface to his **Memories:** "The goal of the world is the development of mind." Higher and purer states of mind are Renan's equivalents of grace. The purpose of life is perfection, although Renan is as vague about the meaning of this word as he is about "the Ideal." And not by accident—Renan casts his net far and wide to catch as many connotations, old and new, as possible.

The human spirit, he maintains, passes through three phases: primitive syncretism, rational analysis, and definitive synthesis. The world is now in the age of analysis, and it is the stern but glorious task of the philologist-historian to assemble the raw materials for the great synthetic age which he himself will most likely never see. This scientific vocation (Renan never thought of himself as a littérateur) has a religious aura about it. It is a new and better kind of Holy Orders. Renan redefines the religious man not as someone who assents to dogma, but as anyone who takes life seriously and believes in the sanctity of things, who is not a slave to self-interest and crude pleasures.

At the conclusion of *The Future of Science* Renan bids farewell yet again to the world of his youthful faith. He is full of tender regrets, but firmly dedicated to his secular calling. "Ah, how gladly I would beat my breast, if I had any hope of hearing that dear voice that once made me quiver. But no, there is only inexorable nature. When I seek your fatherly eye, I find nothing but the empty, fathomless socket of infinity. When I seek your heavenly face, I strike against a brazen vault, which sends my love echoing coldly back. Farewell, then, God of my youth! Farewell. Although you deceived me, I love you still!"

One might dismiss this effusive apostrophe (Renan was twenty-five when he wrote it) as the product of a tender mind in radical transition, but over the years Renan went on employing the same involuted language that affirms and negates God in the same breath. In effect, he held on to the concepts, categories, and traditional rhetoric of Christianity, but stretched them to fit his needs.

Renan's priestly dedication never flagged in over forty years of tremendous scholarly toil. Taken as a whole, his life has an extraordinary planned unity to it: he accomplished exactly what he set out to do. *The Future of Science* offers a prospectus of his endeavors. With ingenuous conceit he announces that "the most important book of the 19th century ought to have as its title, *Critical History of the Origins of Christianity.* I envy the man who will accomplish this admirable task, which I shall undertake in my maturity, if death or accidental calamities do not prevent me!" The fates were kind (although in 1861, in Palestine, he almost died from the same malaria that killed Henriette), and Renan's *History of the Origins of Christianity* appeared in seven volumes, from 1863 to 1882. He then set to work on his *History of the People of Israel* (logically prior to the *Origins,* but put off to ensure completion of the more important work). This was finished, in five volumes, just before his death in 1892. In addition to this he founded and contributed to the vast *Corpus Inscriptionum Semiticarum* and wrote innumerable articles on religion and related subjects.

Yet in perusing this enormous achievement, one is struck by a persistent doubt: is this what Renan really wanted to do? Does the body of his work reflect the whole man? More particularly, what do we make of the theme of near-worship of Greek culture that runs through the writings of this great Hebraist?

The *locus classicus* of Renan's Hellenism is the *Prayer on the Acropolis.* The Prayer is both an inspired purple passage and an accurate chart of the vacillations of his religious sensibility. His first reaction on seeing the ruins of Athens (in 1865) was ecstasy. "The impression Athens made on me is by far the strongest I have ever felt. There is one place, and only one, where perfection exists: there." The rest of the world seemed barbarous by comparison. All other religions, all other kinds of art were clumsy and coarse. Suddenly Renan wondered whether his life up until then had been mistaken.

Renan sat for hours in contemplation on the Acropolis, but in the process he became aware of a contradiction in his new-found faith. "The hours that I spent on the sacred hill were hours of prayer. My whole life passed before my eyes like a general confession. But curiously, as I confessed my sins, I came to love them. My resolutions to become classical ended

by hurling me headlong . . . to the opposite pole." Fittingly, he described his most intense Hellenic experience with a Hebraic metaphor. The odd phrase about resolving to become classical refers to Renan's impulse, born of overpowering enthusiasm, to rebuild his life on Hellenism. "The miracle of the Hebrews" which had absorbed all his energies no longer appeared to him so marvelously unique. Indeed, it had been put in the shade by "the miracle of the Greeks." Or had it?

The Prayer, addressed by Renan to the goddess Athena, resembles some of the Christian prayers he composed about the time of his falling away: for all the protestations of love, he ends by saying that he cannot believe. After a lengthy romantic summary of his life before coming to Athens (the unenlightened, but still cherished, past), he breaks out into an impassioned cry: "You alone are young, O Korē; you alone are pure, O Virgin; you alone are sound, O Hygeia; you alone are strong, O Victory;" Again a Hellenic eulogy becomes a Hebraic litany. Renan then vows to become a hermit and consecrate himself to the Virgin Athena. "I shall fasten myself to the stylobate of your temple. I shall forget all discipline but yours. I shall become a stylite on your columns, my cell will stand on your architrave . . . I shall tear from my heart every fiber that is not reason and pure art!"

He goes on in this vein, only to be brought up short by the realization that his conversion will not be easy. "How many difficulties I foresee! How many mental habits I shall have to change! How many charming memories I should have to uproot from my heart! I shall try, but I am not sure of myself. Late have I known thee, perfect beauty." Renan, when the fit has passed, must recognize the chilling fact that reason is not enough, and he admits that "a literature which should be, like yours, healthy in every respect, would nowadays arouse no other feeling but boredom."

But for this later-day St. Augustine the problem is not just that fantasms from his old life come pouring out to tempt him. Above and beyond the clash of Hebraism and Hellenism in the mind of an aging scholar (the Prayer was probably not composed till 1876) hangs the somber suspicion that *all* religion, rational or otherwise, is vain. He ends on this low note: "An immense river of oblivion rolls us down into a nameless chasm. O abyss, you are the only god. . . . Everything here below is but symbol and dream. The gods pass, just as men do, and it is well they are not eternal. The faith one has had ought never be a chain. One pays one's debts to it by wrapping it carefully in the purple shroud where the dead gods sleep."

This passage looks forward to the sense of emptiness that troubled Renan so much after 1870, just as the conflict between his "charming memories" and "reason and pure art" looks back to the crisis of 1845. During the first long period after leaving Saint-Sulpice Renan's secular humanism was qualified by many vestiges of Catholicism. During the second, Renan's faith in "science" was shaken, but once again, despite his deepening disillusionment with every kind of dogma, he clung to the forms which tied him to the past, and cheered him somewhat in the face of his approaching death.

Aside from their role in his personal life, Hebraism and Hellenism interested Renan as a historian of Christian origins. He gave perhaps his most concise assessment of the two principles in an address he delivered in 1877, on the occasion of the Spinoza bicentennial. Even though here he is ostensibly praising Hebraism, the arguments he offers parallel those of the Prayer, which dates the year before. "A miracle in its way, the development of the Jewish people belongs right alongside that other miracle, the development of the Greek people; for, if Greece was the first to realize the ideal of poetry, of science, of philosophy, of art, of profane life, if I may use the expression, the Jewish people have founded the religion of mankind." Evidently the Greeks have the lion's share. But at this juncture we must survey the textual evidence from Renan's first *magnum opus, The Origins.*

In the first volume, the *Life of Jesus,* Renan is anxious to free Jesus from any suspicion of sectarian narrowness. This is *his* Jesus, the human hero whom he still loves, though he has been forced to reject his divinity. Christ is metamorphosed into a sort of Jewish Orpheus. "Some would make Jesus into a wise man, others a patriot, or a humanitarian, or a moralist, or a saint. He was none of these, he was an enchanter." Jesus is the initiator of a new spirit, the creator of the pure feeling, the grand master of those who flee to an ideal paradise from the brutishness of the world; or, as Renan calls him in *The Gospels* (1877), the divine dreamer.

When it comes to assessing the relations between Jesus and Judaism, Renan makes a number of comparisons to support an important distinction: "Jesus emerges from Judaism, but he does so the way Socrates emerged from the schools of the sophists, the way Luther emerged from the Middle Ages, Lamennais from Catholicism, Rousseau from the 18th century." Thus, far from propagating Judaism, Jesus breaks away from it, as the future of Christianity will make clear.

But if the universal qualities of Jesus transcend his Jewish origins and make him a hero of humanity, the same cannot be said of St. Paul. For Renan, Paul plays the role of a well-intentioned villain in the drama of Christian history. In one of the central scenes of the *Origins* Renan depicts Paul on the Acropolis, "that ugly little Jew," insensitive to the immortal beauty all around him. "So many wonders scarcely touched the apostle. He saw the only perfect things that have ever existed or will exist, the Propylaeum, that noble masterpiece, the Parthenon, which crushes every other greatness but its own, the temple of the wingless Victory . . . He saw all that and his faith was not shaken, he felt no thrill. The prejudices of an iconoclastic Jew, impervious to the beauty of the plastic arts, blinded him; he took those incomparable images for idols." Paul's blindness will prove to be the death sentence for these "beautiful, chaste effigies, true gods and true goddesses."

Renan's heroes, especially Christ and Marcus Aurelius, have a tendency to sound like Renan himself, but he hated St. Paul and there is none of that ventriloquism here. Instead, we have an implied reproachful contrast: four years before writing *St. Paul,* Renan had walked around the Acropolis and he had been overwhelmed. But Paul, who saw, not the ruins of the citadel but its full, unshattered splendor, in his fanaticism missed the point and went away unaffected.

Paul, Renan admits, had the foresight to lead the early Church in throwing off the strait-jacket of the Mosaic observance. But his good offices in this matter were offset by his forcing the spontaneous teachings of Jesus into the constricting folds of dogma. Paul never knew Jesus in person, and he never acquired his Master's balance and reserve. The keynote of the "true gentleman, the man of virtue" is that at some stage in his life he suffers an agony in the garden, a moment of despair when he doubts what he used to believe. Paul, on

the contrary, "believed grossly." We would like, Renan says, to imagine a sceptical Paul, worn and discouraged by his trials, trimming his sails a little to the adverse winds of experience. Not a bit, he will have none of "our sweet incredulity."

Paul, then, is the prototype of the rigid theologians who have been the bane of Christianity. Happily, the long centuries of his predominance are drawing to a close. The last page of *St. Paul* sums up Renan's case against him as the disseminator of the worst things in Hebraism, which, as he said in the *Life of Jesus,* contains within itself the extremes of good and evil. "Paul is the father of the subtle Augustine, of the arid Thomas Acquinas, of the grim Calvinist, of the crabbed Jansenist, of the ferocious theology which damns and predestines to damnation." This is contradistinction to Jesus, "the father of all those who seek rest for their souls in dreams." Christianity must abjure this harsh dogmatic heritage. "What makes Christianity live is the little that we know of the words and person of Jesus. The ideal man, the divine poet, the great artist, he alone defies time and revolutions. He alone is seated at the right hand of the Father throughout eternity."

Thus Christianity itself has Hebraic and Hellenic (in the broad sense) sources, represented by Paul and Jesus respectively. Or is it that Hebraism has two aspects, one unbending and doctrinaire, the other charming and childlike? Renan is not clear on this. He flatly contradicts himself in a paragraph of *The Gospels* on the issue of which world the gospel belongs to. He writes, "The style of the gospels . . . has nothing Hellenic about it. Its basis is Hebrew. A right proportion of materialism and spiritualism, or rather an indistinguishable confusion of the soul and the senses, makes that adorable language the very synonym of poetry, the pure garment of moral thinking, something analogous to Greek sculpture."

It seems that the problem here is Renan's use of the term "Hellenic." On the one hand, it refers to Greek culture. On the other, its means a timeless ideal, transcending any local setting. Hence the gospels are purely Hebraic, yet Hellenic too. Renan continually inserts comparisons with Greece in his books on Israel and the Christian Church, because he is working on an esthetic bias. He is attracted to the elements of Hebraism which can be disengaged from their literal context and appreciated on the Hellenic grounds of "reason" and "light." Anything not susceptible to this treatment, like the Pauline corpus, Renan ignores or censures.

The culmination of the *Origins* and a critical reflection on the entire work is the seventh volume, *Marcus Aurelius and the End of the Ancient World* (1882). Marcus Aurelius (121-180 A.D.), one of Renan's most beloved historical personalities, is seen as an alternative to Jesus. Jesus marks the beginning of a world, and the years of his Galilean ministry are presented as a sort of pastoral idyll. Thus Renan describes the gospels as "that delicious mixture of poetry and moral feeling, that narrative floating between dream and reality in a paradise where time has no measure," and again "a fairy palace built entirely of luminous stones." But Marcus Aurelius ("like a Christ who has written his own [gospel]"), marks an end.

Marcus Aurelius is for Renan the finest flower of late antiquity, the repository of Roman political genius, but, even more, of Greek philosophical wisdom. With his death the decay of the Empire sets in, while Christianity ceases to be a struggling sect and prepares to become the religion of the Western world. If Jesus teaches poetic spontaneity of consciousness, childlike rejoicing in the grip of the Spirit, Marcus Aurelius teaches the religion of painstaking self-scrutiny, of disillusionment, of disinterested love of the ideal in a world gone bad.

In this reading of Marcus Aurelius, the emperor borrows a thing or two, anachronistically, from Renan, who was fifty-nine when he wrote the book and considerably less sanguine than in 1848. As H. W. Wardman, possibly Renan's best biographer [see Further Reading], has said: "His portrait of the merciful, sceptical sage, tolerant of all human aberrations except Christianity, is the last, the most moving and convincing of the self-portraits of the *Origins*. . . . Both share in the same philosophy of life. Marcus Aurelius had attained to a state of absolute benevolence, to indifference tempered by piety and disdain." Towards the end of *Marcus Aurelius* Renan tells us the emperor's wisdom was absolute, "that is to say, that his wariness and boredom were boundless." Further on Renan suggests that "bidding farewell to happiness is the beginning of wisdom and the surest means of finding happiness."

Renan sympathizes with Marcus Aurelius' acceptance of the universe with what might be termed high moral ennui, but—a sign of his own increasing epicureanism—he criticizes his inability to enjoy himself. Pessimism must not have the final word. "What he learned was the fairy's kiss at his birth, a very philosophical thing in its own way, I mean the art of yielding to nature, the gaiety which discovers that *abstine et sustine* is not all, and that life might also be summarized in 'smile and take pleasure.' "

Despite this flaw, Marcus Aurelius is superior, in a sense, to Jesus, who had at best a limited grasp of the world outside Israel. In philosophy, science, and politics, Jesus was a child. If Marcus Aurelius' Hellenic stoicism was inadequate by itself, so was Jesus' unlettered Hebraic inspiration. If one side of Renan would have liked to wander the roads of Galilee with Jesus, another side would have liked to be a scholar in the emperor's retinue. He notes with approval that Marcus Aurelius established professorial chairs at Athens for all the sciences, "with handsome salaries."

All through the *Origins* Renan argues for the Hellenes and against the Hebrews. In *The Apostles* (1866), speaking of the Jewish Christians' obtuseness to beauty, he writes, "A system where the Venus de Milo is only an idol is a false or at least a partial system; for beauty is almost as important as goodness and truth." Whatever the "almost" may mean here, Renan is clearly impatient with Nazarene bigotry. His tone is reminiscent of a letter he wrote his mother from the seminary in 1841, in which he says he would gladly spend his life reading the *Odyssey*. This inclination had to be subordinated to the demands of *la science,* but it took its revenge in the judgments he would later pass on Hebraism.

Renan laid down most of these strictures in the first half of his career. In *History . . . of the Semitic Languages* (1855) he spoke of that mythical entity, the Semitic race, to propose that "It has never understood civilization in the sense which we give to that word." Semites, we are told, lack flexibility, finesse, imagination, public spirit, and even "the faculty of laughter." Seven years later, in his lecture on **"The Role of the Semitic Peoples in the History of Civilization,"** which cost him his professorship at the Collège de France, he stated that "The Semitic character is in general hard, narrow, egotistical." (Renan presumably missed the small irony that this,

like everything else he wrote, was being brought before his readers by the publishing house of Calmann-Lévy.) He was still capable of declaring in *St. Paul* (1869) that honor is a meaningless word to the Jews, but by and large he had come to moderate his views. He never completely overcame his prejudice, however. In his last major work, *History of the People of Israel* (1887-93), when he wants to bestow his highest accolade on the *Book of Isaiah,* he cannot help saying, "Isaiah writes like a Greek."

One crucial factor governing the way Renan attacked Hebraism and Hellenism was, assuredly, his own ethical make-up. In fact, the sum of his writings on this theme could be read as a macrocosmic picture of Renan's own mind. For a character as protean as his, for a man who could identify himself with Jesus, Marcus Aurelius, Ecclesiastes, Prospero, and the whole "Celtic race," there is nothing improbable in such allegorizing. This helps to explain much of his slighting of Hebraism. Although he never ceased to credit Israel with laying the foundations of Western morality, Renan himself was an exceptionally placid, well-ordered individual, for whom moral problems scarcely existed. A strong sense of evil, of the sort that made Thomas Arnold brood over the sinfulness of his young charges at Rugby, was utterly foreign to him. As he wrote in 1884, speaking of Henri-Frédéric Amiel, "He asks on several occasions: 'What does M. Renan make of sin?' . . . I really think that I do away with it."

Early in his life he dedicated himself to the "Hellenic ideal" of light, reason, and truth, and he could conceive of no other, less exalted level of existence for himself. As he wrote in *Memories,* "I was made in such a way for the good, for the true, that it would have been impossible for me to follow any career not devoted to the things of the soul." Renan insists that he was incapable of real evil, an exemption he attributes to his Breton ancestry. Even though here and elsewhere he waives any personal credit for this immunity from vice, his bland assumption of unimpeachable probity often sounds naively egotistic. In the preface to *Studies in Religious History* (1857) he writes, "If I was, like so many others, a slave to my desires, if self-interest or vanity guided my steps . . . But, desiring nothing, except to do good . . . "

This *is* egotism, but of the unpretentious, unhypocritical Renanian variety. He did not boast of his virtue so much as he took it for granted. (pp. 123-31)

Trying to unravel the tangled strains of his thought, we can say that Renan was religious in everything but orthodox belief. The vocabulary of religion rolls off his tongue, even though his message is anti-supernatural. He is a priest of Athena—wearing an ephod. But he prizes his incongruous Hebraic garment and refuses to dispense with it. For, as he said in *The Intellectual and Moral Reform of France,* " . . . one can be a Catholic without believing in the infallibility of the pope, and a Christian without believing in the supernatural or the divinity of Jesus Christ." Some pages further on in the same book he proposes that the Church make a special arrangement for "liberal" Catholics like himself who hold to the spirit rather than the letter. Twelve years after this, in 1883, Renan explains that he remained a Christian after deciding against Christianity's claim to absolute truth, because he still had "a lively taste for the gospel ideal and for the founder of Christianity." In reducing religion to taste, Renan is only keeping in step with his age, for, as he said in the preface to *Memories,* religion had irrevocably become a subjective matter. And so he has no qualms about making the fanciful request. "Let them place a kneeler next to my deathbed for the women who might wish to pray for me."

His formal faith, Renan tells us, was destroyed by higher criticism. But, although his faith has vanished, it still inspires him, perhaps as we still perceive the light from an exploded star. The problem with tracing the course of this invisible faith is that Renan's language is so loose. Since theological terms were demonstrably unscientific, he did not scruple to use them with poetic license and calculated ambiguity. Thus he will say airily, "the idea which animates all things—that is God!" Or, "Prayer, or better put, rational speculation, is the purpose of the world." He submits the definition, "To love God, to know God, is to love the beautiful and the good, to know the truth." With the casualness that comes from years of habit he will thank "infinite goodness for having granted me the necessary time and energy to fulfill this difficult program." This kind of language, which might have stuck in the throat of another sensitive nonbeliever, came naturally to Renan, and he spoke it in all his works, from first to last.

On the day in 1844, for example, when he received minor orders, he temporarily lulled his doubts by repeating to himself a verse from Psalm 15 (which is sung during the ceremony), "The Lord is the portion of mine inheritance and of my cup: thou maintainest my lot." The tonsure he now bore could be taken as a symbol of dedication to the intellectual life—just in case there were no God. In any event, the lines *had* fallen in pleasant places for him, and his heritage was a goodly one. Come what might, he would always live in a sphere above the crass self-seeking of the "world." Hellenic thoughts for a Hebraic occasion! This sophistical argument was not just a passing conceit. Renan relished all the double meanings of the psalm, which recurs obsessively in his notebooks. Renan was after all a *breton bretonnant*, a deep-dyed Catholic who would not lightly sever the religious link that bound him to his past and made up so much of his identity.

Renan persisted in his ambivalence till the end. By his inconsistency he created a peculiar but effective consistency. When Émile Littré, the lexicographer, died in 1882, Renan, as director of the French Academy, greeted his successor, Louis Pasteur, with a speech defending positivism and extolling Littré as a secular saint. Yet some days before, Renan had attended the funeral mass for Littré (who converted on his deathbed) and surprised the congregation by loudly chanting the Latin responses. As he said the year before he died, "I'm turning into a priest again. Pardon me, gentlemen." Renan spent a good deal of time translating parts of the Old Testament, but the books he edited, translated, and annotated were *Job*, the *Songs of Songs*, and *Ecclesiastes*—surely a Hellenic selection.

Even his dying moments, according to Henriette Psichari (his granddaughter), were filled with confused images from the two worlds of his thought. "The physiological struggle of a man of robust constitution battling with uremia bars us from considering the disjointed phrases which he murmured from time to time about the mosque and the synagogue as anything but quasi-unconscious reflections of the past. . . . In the same way no conclusions should be drawn from the cry which has given rise to so many comments: Take that sun from over the Acropolis!" *Pace* Mme. Psichari, one may at least conclude that Hebraism and Hellenism, in this hallucinatory guise, were on Renan's mind in his last agony.

Renan was a Benedictine of the Future. When his life was interrupted by the downfall of Christian transcendence, he dexterously replaced it with a scheme of analogous values and went on working in his scholar's cell. Despite occasional spells of wavering and depression, he remained true to his vocation. Nonetheless, in *Scattered Pages,* the last of his works to appear before his death, he left a disturbing question unanswered: "We are living on the shadow of a shadow. What will they live on after us?" Renan's solution of the Hebrew-Hellene conflict, his compromise between faith and reason, was too uniquely his own to be useful as a model. The afterglow of Christianity could by itself shed only a dim light. Such as it was, Renan was grateful for it. (pp. 134-36)

> *Peter Heinegg, "Hebrew or Hellene?: Religious Ambivalence in Renan," in* The Texas Quarterly, *Vol. XVIII, No. 4, Winter, 1975, pp. 120-36.*

## BERNARD M. G. REARDON   (essay date 1985)

[*In the following excerpt, Reardon proposes that Renan's thought must be seen as a dialectic between reason and Romanticism. Contrasting Renan's philosophy with that of the leading exponent of French positivism, Auguste Comte, Reardon asserts that Renan's writing displays less analytical rigor but greater emotional commitment.*]

It is not unusual to regard Ernest Renan as the most eminent of Comte's followers, a status, however, assured to him less perhaps for his attainments as a systematic thinker than for his gifts as a writer, since as a *prosateur* he is among the best of his century. But if he is to be counted as a positivist it must be so with qualification. 'I felt quite irritated', he observes in *Souvenirs d'enfance et de jeunesse,* 'at the idea of Auguste Comte being dignified with the title of a great man for having expressed in bad French what all scientific minds had done for the past two hundred years as clearly as he had done.' I am not now concerned to assess the justice of this judgment on Comte himself, but it is surely not open to doubt that in its substance at least Renan's own philosophy is a positivism not far removed from Comte's. Where he diverges from Comte is in the tone of its presentation and in his coloration of scientific rationalism with a large infusion of Romantic idealism, though not without a significant residue of Catholic sentiment inherited from his childhood and youth. 'I was formed', he tells us, 'by the Church, I owe to it what I am, and I shall never forget it.' No wonder he could say 'Je suis double'—'I was predestined to what I am, a romantic in protest against romanticism . . .' It is evident, then, that behind the *penseur* there is the complex, many-faceted personality of the man. He who, whilst still under training for the Catholic priesthood, decided to reject both Catholicism and Christianity, since he found himself unable to admit the Protestant compromise—something always difficult for a Frenchman—could yet envy German Protestant scholarship its ability to reconcile a spirit deeply religious with that of modern criticism. Catholic supernaturalism, he was convinced, could not be adjusted to the scientific outlook of the nineteenth century, but modern man is still in need of a faith, a need, he believed, that would have to be met with an adequate response. Science, he was confident, could give this—were but science rightly understood. It is easy to remark, therefore, that 'no one knew better than Renan how to gild positivism with religiosity and throw around the operations of the scientific intellect a vague aroma of the infinite' [see excerpt by Irving Babbitt dated 1902]. And indeed in his later years he seemed deliberately to cultivate the *persona* of the sceptical dilettante, elegant, learned and trifling. But his sincerity is not to be questioned when he declared that Catholicism sufficed for all his faculties except the critical reason—if of course critical reason were to have the final word.

Renan's was the dilemma, typically nineteenth-century, of the Romantic traditionalist driven to choose faith *or* knowledge. That his thinking was profoundly influenced by German idealist philosophy, and in particular by Herder and Hegel, is hardly open to question. But the influence was powerfully tempered by scientific rationalism. In that sense too Renan could be said to characterize his age, with romanticism and science as the great mutually confronting forces, always in tension and not seldom in open conflict. He himself was a Romantic at least to the extent that he clearly saw the insufficiency of the Enlightenment concept of human reason. For the eighteenth-century thinkers were preoccupied with what is definable because static—with clear and distinct principles and entities. What was in process, and thus more or less inchoate, they disregarded, a restriction of view fatal to any realistic appraisal of life as we know it. 'The infinite, the developing, escaped them. The mystery of origins, the prodigies of instinct, the spirit that moves the crowds, the spontaneous in all its forms, passed them by.' It was this feeling for the infinite, for the spontaneity of the primitive and the collective, for the continuous flux of historical development, that Renan himself drew from the Romantic idealists. The eighteenth century had on the whole little sense of history, which it failed to understand. Nor could it really appreciate the spirit of religion. On the other hand the speculative bent of the romanticists needed to be curbed. The basic themes and sentiments of romanticism were a reflection of and a response to the needs and aspirations of life as it is lived and not merely analysed, but scientific knowledge had to be assigned its place, with its rightful demands and seemingly unlimited fields of applicability. It could not be thrust aside therefore by the impatience of a soaring imagination only too eager to leave the solid earth. Philosophical idealism required the sobering and even chastening contact of the scientific reason, as indeed Hegel himself had very fully realized. Romanticism had by no means abandoned the rational, but what was wanted was a fusion of the diverse and supple romanticist view of reason—the speculative *Vernunft*—with the factual and positive view, covering the aims and methods of the sciences, both natural and human. A religion purged of its antiquated supernaturalism and conjoined with a science guided and stimulated by philosophy could supply modern man with the spiritual nutriment for which he now looked. Such at any rate was Renan's hope and assurance. (pp. 237-39)

It would be idle to seek in Renan any compact scheme of doctrine. What we have is a series of orientations, a variety of perspectives, a sequence of intellectual explorations. He was always subjective, even in his historical work. But he took learning seriously and had the profoundest respect for the critical spirit. Both characteristics have to be set over against his temperamental aestheticism, not to mention his occasionally intrusive sentimentalism. An individualist who ever chose his own way, he nevertheless made it his principle as a historian and student of the achievements of man in society that, as he stated in *L'Avenir de la science,* the individual is nothing, humanity everything. The paradox here offers a clue to the overall direction of his thinking. Renan always preferred the long and comprehensive view, and he realized that the nature of man is the product of his history, to the knowl-

edge of which 'philology'—a favourite term of his—gives the entry. Through history he had himself found intellectual freedom, glimpsing in it, from the outset of his career, the source from which the constitutive elements of his philosophy would have to be drawn. For the content of philosophy, as he saw it, is basically humanity, not nature. In fact 'philosophy' and *philologie,* according to the *Avenir,* are essentially one, its author meaning by this, so evidently we are to assume, that philosophical method is properly experimental and descriptive. And as he himself is concerned with the human mind in its historical development it was appropriate from his standpoint—given also his personal aptitude for linguistic studies—that philology should present itself as the true science of man; not man in some abstract, eighteenth-century sense as a fixed and definable quantity, but in his perpetual 'becoming', his *devenir,* of which history supplies the record. Philology, as Renan uses the word, a usage akin to that more usually found among German scholars, affords insight into the very nature of the human mind, since it is the science of its most characteristic products; the science, that is, whose function it is to study past civilizations from their languages and documents. As such it is one that calls for imagination, sympathy and intuition, beyond mere classification and analysis, in that it has to penetrate the rational to reach the unconscious. The *esprit de géometrie* will be of no help here: 'enthusiasm' and criticism, Renan says, are far from being mutually exclusive; and he considers philology to be especially profitable the farther back into the past it delves, because it is in the primitive stage of a civilization that the human mind is discovered at its most spontaneous and creative. Hence the importance of *myths* in the process of man's mental development, in that the myth is a form of thought which later reflection will by no means dismiss as childish credulity. Myths rather are 'great divine poems wherein primitive peoples have deposited their dreams of the supersensible world'. In this matter Renan could look to German Romantics like Friedrich Creuzer for informed guidance.

We observe here the significance which Renan, at least in the *Avenir de la science,* attaches to history. He does not see it simply as a record of past events reconstituted by means of such disciplines as archaeology, epigraphy and philology. Its deeper purpose is to recover as far as possible the living mind, the actual ways of thinking, of peoples now long distant from us in time and correspondingly alien in outlook. Nor is this itself only an antiquarian exercise; it is an attempt to understand the human consciousness as such, to comprehend the very nature of man's self-awareness and self-identification. To that extent the future itself may be anticipated. But this of course is to envisage a *philosophy* of history, or at least to suggest the feasibility of some general law of interpretation such as Comte believed he had established. No doubt it would be 'subjective', in being framed from our own point of view in time; but this is inevitable, total objectivity being unattainable by minds that are themselves part of history's ceaseless movement. The simple fact that 'definitive' history is never actually written proves it; the past has constantly to be reassessed, not only because of the possible discovery of new facts but because our angle of vision itself shifts with the years. Were this not the case, were we able to suppose that we ourselves could somehow stand 'outside' the historical in order to appraise it objectively, history would simply fail to yield up its secret. Engagement is necessary for understanding. For when rightly understood history is itself philosophy. On this Renan is quite explicit: 'The history of the human mind', he says, 'is the true philosophy for our time. Each of us is what he is only because of his situation in history.' He goes even further and claims to be able to build a new ethic on man's developing 'consciousness'. Obviously his assumption is that in such development the 'good' is realized. He can even convince himself that true religion is 'intellectual culture'.

The idea underlying Renan's interpretation of history is therefore one of a continuous progress discernible over the ages. Each generation contributes its quota to it, though without as a rule perceiving what actually it has accomplished, much as a weaver at work on a big tapestry is scarcely aware of the complex design he is helping to create. In the *Avenir* Renan ventures to offer his own 'law of the three stages': those, namely, of 'syncretism', which characterizes early times, of 'analysis', or the critical awareness which follows later and which conspicuously distinguishes the modern outlook, destructive as this is of religion and 'poetry', and finally of 'synthesis', a state yet to be reached when the rational and affective aspects of life are once again reconciled in an enlightened harmony. This consummation Renan thinks it not inappropriate to deify, so that God becomes the realization by man of his moral and spiritual ideals. All of which invites comparison with the doctrines of Auguste Comte, whose *Système de politique positive* appeared not long after Renan had drafted his *Avenir de la science.* The younger man's interest in race—a subject on which he dwells at some length—was, it is true, of little concern to Comte, who also sees morality in a less personal light than Renan, his own ethical views . . . depending on his conception of sociology as a science standing in close relation to biology. And Comte quite certainly does not share Renan's sympathy with the life and practice of religion in its existing forms. But there is in the ex-seminarian's philosophical musings an element of positivism more firmly based than its author probably realized.

Of positivism as a system, however, Renan was distinctly critical. It clearly was not congenial to him temperamentally. Comte's mind was utterly prosaic, his prose itself being stiff and laborious, whereas Renan, awake to every nuance of sentiment, was a master of rhetoric. Comte, again, seemed to move only in a world of rigid categories and classificatory schemes such as the other, with all a Romantic's sense of the infinite variety of things, instinctively sheered away from. Renan's love of the vague, the ambivalent, the elusive—admittedly his major weakness as a philosopher—was repelled by the wooden symmetry of Comtist thinking. And of course he had no sympathy with positivist materialism. To him it lacked all spiritual sensitivity, besides being devoid of that romanticist feeling for the infinite which he himself, unbeliever though he was in the 'credal' sense, never forswore. On the contrary, while Comte detested Christianity—as distinct from Catholicism, or at least those aspects of it of which he approved—Renan's nostalgic affection for the religion of his youth was genuine and lasting. His naturally 'clerical' disposition and manner were frequently remarked upon by those who met him personally.

But Renan's attitude to the past generally, and not only the Christian, was emotional. He deeply respected it and believed that really great achievements were possible only to those who themselves felt this respect and looked back to the past for their inspiration. He himself viewed it, with truly Romantic enthusiasm, as a vast epic of humanity which through the imagination of the poet-historian could again be brought to life. Indeed it was because of this continuous possibility of resuscitation that it revealed itself as progressive. So far from

being dead, it was living and ongoing, the experience thus accumulated by humanity producing a 'consciousness' ever fuller, more varied and more perceptive, in which the *divine* becomes increasingly manifest. Such at any rate was the vision of the *Avenir.* With the passing of the years and first-hand encounter with history in its current phase Renan's progressivist faith underwent modification, although it was never lost. His one-time political hopes were not realized, compromises having always to be made. European power-politics—as the Franco-Prussian war so brutally demonstrated—were far from idealistic. Even that new and intellectually revolutionary expression of modern scientific insight, the Darwinian theory, could hardly be said, on a more reflective assessment of it, to encourage the notion that evolution and progress are identical. Nonetheless, whether or not the course of history is also an advance to a brighter future, it is to history and to history alone that man can go if he is to contemplate his true visage. That truth Renan never doubted. Moreover, one lesson history quite certainly teaches is the relativism of the time-process. Every succeeding period is what it is, and is to be appreciated accordingly. It is a mark of the critical historian's tact that he should be able to see the past in the right perspective, as only so can the life and culture of former times be understood, relived and enjoyed afresh. But impartiality implies tolerance. Differences are to be treated with sympathy and not merely condemned, since the yardstick of one age is not necessarily applicable to another. And if the rationale of human existence, as the philosopher discerns it, is to be sought in the overall advance of human consciousness then error, intellectual and moral, also has its place in the educative process. As Renan grew older this sympathetic tolerance of all experience became so settled an attitude as to look like moral indifferentism.

In the *Avenir* the developing nineteenth-century conflict between religion and science is already present as a personal issue for the author himself. The scientific view of life had to be accepted—Renan had relinquished his Catholic allegiance because of his conviction that science and Catholic supernaturalism were incompatible—but he was scarcely less convinced that acceptance of science does not imply the abandonment of religion, provided the word 'religion' be taken in a very broad sense and with a firm apprehension of its poetic connotation. For both science and religion he held to be necessary to our humanity. With the former unquestionably modern man cannot dispense: science he has to recognize to be autonomous, uncircumscribed by anything else. But so comprehensive also is it that it is potentially a religion in itself. Henceforth science alone will create symbols; as science alone can resolve for man the eternal problems whose solution his nature imperiously demands. For it is science which will instruct mankind in the true meaning of life and point forward to its real destiny. Renan's book is in fact a prophetic view of the future of science as fulfilling a religious role, teaching not only the truth about the universe but inculcating that spirit of cosmic awe and *pietas* which ought to accompany such knowledge. 'The true way of worshipping God is to know and to love that which is.' It was a vision and an enthusiasm which was never afterwards really dimmed or weakened. Knowledge, he was always to believe, would 'resolve the enigma of life', explain man to himself and provide him with 'the symbolism which religions used to offer ready made and which he can now no longer accept'. In short, Renan embodied all the nineteenth century's hope for science and confidence in its ultimate capacity for good, even when not only philosophers but scientists themselves were beginning to have their doubts.

But it is science with considerable overtones of religious feeling. Positivism was too abstract, too constricted in outlook, too much wanting in *la poésie* for Renan's willing endorsement. He looked on Comte himself as 'un esprit borné', a perhaps not altogether fair judgment in view of the control which sentiment came to exercise over his later thinking. But Comte, for all his emotionalism, especially where the opposite sex was involved, was no poet, and aesthetic sensibility is little in evidence in positivist doctrine. His Religion of Humanity may display all the outward appurtenances of Catholicism, but it has nothing of its inner spirit. Such could not be said of Renan, who was peculiarly sensitive to visual beauty and with whom an undercurrent of feeling is present even in his purely scholarly work. He was never the dry intellectualist. For him thought was compounded of reason, imagination and emotion; rational demands, in all matters of factual knowledge, were paramount, but could not be divorced from the affective side of life. Aesthetic values especially were as real as any others and their place in man's total apprehension of the truth of the world about him had to be acknowledged. The analytical stage in human thought would properly stress the determining role of the critical intellect, but the previous century had so exaggerated its function as seriously to misrepresent the nature of reason itself and the extent to which it is linked with the emotions—a fatal mistake which romanticism had to repair. For feeling is no mere adjunct of thought, it is of its substance, a truth which in the coming age of 'synthesis' would be fully recognized. And of that synthesis Renan saw his own work, in both history and philosophy, to be the herald. The 'complete' man would be one who is simultaneously poet, philosopher and scholar, as well as a man of virtue; and that not intermittently but continuously, through an intimate penetration of each by the other—the poet in being a philosopher, the philosopher in being a scholar.

But an additional respect in which Renan's attitude to religion differs radically from Comte's, as indeed from that of some Catholic apologists, is that he sees it not as a prop for the social order, or still less a mere sop to the feelings of the common man, but as something inherent in human nature. It is to be cultivated and valued for its own sake, not exploited for purposes which have nothing to do with it. So long as humanity survives, Renan believes, religion will also, as expressing a basic psychological need. No doubt when it aims to be 'objective' and scientific, when it attempts metaphysical demonstrations of the ontic truth of its object, it can only mislead. Both 'natural' theology, professing to lay the intellectual foundations of faith, and 'revealed', which pretends to formal knowledge of the facts of the supernatural order, are unacceptable because they misrepresent what religion essentially is. But this is not to say that intuition and spiritual sensibility, the 'heart', are not means to truth. Consider knowledge as bare 'reasoning' and it is at once deprived of its real significance. The teachings of deism were only a debilitated, sapless theology, without poetry or emotional resonance, while declared atheism is brash and superficial. Mankind needs some sort of religious ideal if life is to have true moral worth and dignity. Thus Renan's conception of religion—albeit a 'religion of science'—is very much more inward than Comte's. For what Comte had in mind was no more than contrived forms of organization and ritual which he imagined would serve the new positivist society in much the same way as Catholic institutions had functioned in the past, whereas

Renan is trying to combine his rational belief in the standpoint and methods of modern science with the ethos of a faith he continues to respect.

This emerges plainly enough in the attitudes the two thinkers adopt towards religious liberty. Comte insists on uniformity: dissent would be banned. Renan, because he sees religion in a strongly personal light, holds freedom to be a right which the state must not infringe. This too is why he, unlike both Comte and Lamennais, is sympathetic to Protestantism, which preserved the spirit of religion while less committed than Catholicism to authority and dogma. Hence his regret that, given the historic religious traditions of France, Protestantism in that country afforded no real option for a Catholic who had relinquished the faith of his upbringing. He could only be a *libre-penseur*. Incidentally, of the 'liberal' Catholicism of his day he entertained a poor opinion, dismissing it as an 'insipid compromise'. But Renan was convinced that life could not be lived in its wholeness unless the needs both of reason and of the heart were satisfied, and each by the other: knowledge and aspiration should go hand in hand. His hopes and expectations for the future were therefore in the creation of a 'scientific philosophy', which would be neither profitless speculation, without any real object, nor an arid and exclusive scientism, but one which, in achieving completeness, would be both 'religious and poetical', since poetry is itself the soul of religion. Any 'scientific' religion that is only a thinly disguised logical system is scarcely to be thought of as religious at all. 'God is the product of the conscience, not of science and metaphysics.'

The great difficulty with Renan is of course his habit of shifting the meaning of his key-terms, the same word being used to denote one thing in one context but something rather different in another. *Philologie,* defined as 'the science of humanity', is a prime example, but so too is *science* itself, which can carry as wide a connotation as simply 'the exercise of the mind in an ordered (*régulier*) way', while as the 'sainte poésie des choses' it can even refer to the 'truth' and 'sincerity' of life. But *philosophie* is equally malleable, as too is *existence.* The persuasiveness of Renan's argument often depends on this semantic sleight-of-hand. At times his use of language reminds one of Newman's, whose own reasoning likewise draws on carefully evoked sentiment when its logic begins to falter; and both writers knew well enough the rhetorical effect of irony. The result is that instead of presenting a clearly stated position with which a critical reader can actively engage we tend to have only insinuations and suggestions, a standpoint adopted for the nonce and then quietly abandoned when discussion takes a new turn. In this respect Renan's elusiveness recalls Montaigne's 'diversity'.

In the strict sense of the word Renan is not a philosopher, any more than Newman was. For like Newman he had no real mental aptitude for metaphysics or at any rate for the particular kind of rigorous thinking that philosophy properly demands. Newman distrusted metaphysical arguments, and his Gallic counterpart, in this at least a Kantian, wrote them off altogether. Renan indeed is ready enough, when he chooses, to equate philosophy with science, but not if by the former is meant *a priori* speculation about the ultraphenomenal, although the distinction between philosophy and metaphysics is not always clearly made by him. Science, he holds, must follow *a posteriori* methods, whereas metaphysics as 'une science première' never gets beyond abstractions. Yet he also believes that science must eventually become philosophy, by so broadening its scope as to include within it a great deal more than the term is designed to convey in positivist usage. For 'what indeed is left', he asks, 'if you deprive science of its philosophical goal?'.

However, as Renan insisted, his own intellectual problems as a seminarist were not of a metaphysical kind but rather 'philological'. He could not avoid pondering the implications of German biblical criticism regarding such matters as the unity, authorship and historicity not only of books of the Old Testament like Genesis, Isaiah and Daniel, but of the gospels themselves. And to the intelligent and thoughtful youth brought up in the straightest Catholic piety the result was profoundly unsettling.

> My initiation into German studies [he afterwards wrote] put me in a completely false situation; for, on the one hand, it showed me the impossibility of an exegesis which made no concessions; and on the other, I saw perfectly well that these gentlemen at Saint-Sulpice were right not to make concessions, since a single admission of error ruins the edifice of absolute truth and brings it down to the level of mere human authorities, where each makes his own choice according to his personal taste. In a divine book, indeed, everything is true, no contradiction must be found there.

Yet the Bible, the very source of divine revelation, with an authority not to be questioned at any point, was discovered to contain too many evidences of its essentially human composition. Renan saw no means of compromise, given his own position. An infallible authority must never be seen to be in error. For if the basis of the church's dogma is detected to be thus insecure what can be said for the security of the superstructure itself? Metaphysical speculations were something that could be argued about, perhaps indefinitely, but philological objections were matters of fact capable of being critically investigated and finally determined.

Renan's views on metaphysics are well set out in a short essay addressed to Adolphe Guéroult, a philosopher of some standing in his day, entitled **'La Métaphysique et son avenir'**, first published in the *Revue des deux mondes,* 15 January 1860. The great speculative systems, culminating in that of Hegel, are, he maintains, things of the past. The sciences, both the natural and the historical, have now replaced all such schemes, and there is no sort of 'preliminary' science which can be accepted as containing in itself all the rest, and which affords a basic knowledge not only of the universe and of man, but even of God. The human spirit will always be prone to speculate on what it cannot actually know; such curiosity is as natural to man as his imaginative and emotional creativity. But for any serious attempt to understand the nature of reality it is to the positive sciences that one must go. 'The glory of philosophy', Renan concludes, 'is not to resolve problems but to pose them.' And he ends his essay in characteristically ironic vein with a prayer of blessing to the 'Heavenly Father' for having in the end remained hidden and a mystery. 'For thus our minds and hearts are free.' Three years later, in the letter to his friend Marcellin Berthelot also published in the *Revue des deux mondes,* he restates his position. 'I formerly denied the existence of metaphysics as a distinct and progressive system; I do not deny it as a body of unchanging concepts in the way that logic is. These sciences teach us nothing, but they serve well to analyse what we do know. In each case they are wholly outside the realm of fact.' Obviously, then, speculation about the infinite, the absolute,

freewill and so on has no status alongside knowledge empirically grounded.

It can hardly be denied that Renan's statements are tantalizingly ambiguous and confusing. Sometimes he approximates philosophy and metaphysics, at others he distinguishes them radically. At one moment he can describe the former as 'the general result of all the sciences', a phrase which has a definitely Comtean ring, while at another he declares that 'to philosophize is to know the universe' and that philosophy's role is to be 'the science of the whole', which seems to bring us close to the traditional view of metaphysics. I suspect that it is impossible to fix Renan's meaning precisely. The nearest we can get to doing so is perhaps to say that although for him the only real knowledge is factual, 'how things actually are', for which of course we have to go to the empirical sciences, he nevertheless wants such knowledge, when *conceived as a whole*—assuming, that is, the possibility of so conceiving it—to be regarded not merely as the sum of its parts but as a 'world-view', a *Weltanschauung,* to the final shaping of which subjective factors, moral and aesthetic, make a vital contribution. But what the logical status of such a 'higher' knowledge would be we are not told. (pp. 245-54)

In Renan the tension between reason and romanticism attains its height. Sentiment and imagination drew him in one direction, science and scholarship in another. Both sides of his nature called out for satisfaction, but any really constructive compromise between them proved difficult, if not impossible. Hence the ambiguities and recurrent inconsistencies of his position. He extols morality, but a morality devoid of any profound sense of obligation and thus of normative strength. He is optimistic about human nature, but mainly because he shrinks from contemplating its darker side. The world he prefers to look out upon is the relatively narrow one of the aesthetic sensibility and cultivated erudition of the *savant.* Of such, he all but says, is the kingdom of heaven (always, of course, on earth). Man's divinity is to be realized in all that a person of his own disposition, hopes and ideals may, not without reason, expect to be achieved with time. He was tolerant, imaginative, learned, at a certain level wise, but egocentric in all he attempted and desired. More contemplative than truly introspective—why Amiel should have written his journal he could not understand—he never, one suspects, established authentic self-identity. He admitted, rather, that he saw himself as 'a tissue of contradictions'. Although even then he has to add: 'I do not complain, since this moral constitution has brought me the liveliest intellectual enjoyment that one can experience.' We may admire his frankness and be ready always to concede the insinuating appeal of his personal and literary style. But if he fails to convince it is because, in the end, he himself lacked convictions. (pp. 265-66)

*Bernard M. G. Reardon, "Ernest Renan and the Religion of Science," in his* Religion in the Age of Romanticism: Studies in Early Nineteenth Century Thought, *Cambridge University Press, 1985, pp. 237-66.*

## FURTHER READING

Arnold, Matthew. "Renan." In his *Essays in Criticism, third series,* pp. 153-79. Boston: Ball Publishing Co., 1910.
> Reviews *La réforme intellectuelle et morale,* comparing Renan's political views on France in the aftermath of the Franco-Prussian war with those held by the conservative English statesman Edmund Burke following the 1789 Revolution.

Bachem, Rose. "Arnold's and Renan's Views on Perfection." *Revue de litterature comparée* XLI, No. 2 (1967): 228-37.
> Compares Matthew Arnold's and Renan's theories of intellectual perfection.

Berthoff, Warner. "Renan on W. E. Channing and American Unitarianism." *New England Quarterly* XXXV, No. 1 (March 1962): 71-92.
> An abridged reprint of Renan's critical remarks on the American writer and Unitarian leader William Ellery Channing, with an introduction by Berthoff.

Bierer, Dora. "Renan and His Interpreters: A Study in French Intellectual Warfare." *Journal of Modern History* XXV, No. 4 (December 1953): 375-89.
> Argues that Renan's views on race, religion, and politics were generally misinterpreted by critics in late nineteenth-century France.

Brandes, Georg. "Ernest Renan." In his *Creative Spirits of the Nineteenth Century,* pp. 205-22. New York: Thomas Y. Crowell Co., Publishers, 1923.
> Contains a first-hand portrait of Renan and three interviews with the author that date from 1870.

Cassirer, Ernst. "Influence of the History of Religion on the Ideal of Historical Knowledge: Strauss, Renan, Fustel de Coulanges." In his *The Problem of Knowledge: Philosophy, Science, and History Since Hegel,* translated by William H. Woglom and Charles W. Hendel, pp. 294-326. New Haven: Yale University Press, 1950.
> Examines the development of biblical criticism from David Friedrich Strauss's *Das Leben Jesu kritisch bearbeitet* (1835-36; *The Life of Jesus Critically Examined* ) to Renan's *The Life of Jesus.*

Chadbourne, Richard M. "Renan, or the Contemptuous Approach to Literature." *Yale French Studies* 2, No. 1 (Spring/Summer 1949): 96-104.
> Distinguishes Renan's value as a literary critic from his hostile attitude toward contemporary writers, arguing that "his contempt for literature paradoxically helped to enhance the value of his criticism."

——. "Renan as Prophet of the European and World Future." *The American Society Legion of Honor Magazine* 22, No. 4 (Winter 1951): 299-309.
> Discusses the prophetic nature of Renan's political commentary in his writings from the period 1870-90.

——. "The Generation of 1848: Four Writers and Their Affinities." *Essays in French Literature* 5 (November 1968): 1-21.
> Probes the genesis of Renan's world view in conjunction with that of Charles Baudelaire, Leconte de Lisle, and Gustave Flaubert.

——. *Ernest Renan.* Twayne's World Authors Series, edited by Sylvia E. Bowman, no. 34. New York: Twayne Publishers, 1968, 178 p.
> The most recent full-length study on Renan available in English. Chadbourne's study contains an extensive annotated bibliography.

Charlton, D. G. "From Positivism to Scientism (2): Ernest Renan." In his *Positivist Thought in France during the Second Empire, 1852-1870,* pp. 86-126. Oxford: Clarendon Press, 1959.
> A detailed analysis of Renan's philosophy, tracing the evolution of his thought from doctrinaire positivism to enlightened scepticism.

Dewey, John. "Ernest Renan." In his *Characters and Events: Popular Essays in Social and Political Philosophy,* Vol. I, edited by Joseph Ratner, pp. 18-30. New York: Henry Holt and Co., 1929.
> Discusses the theory of social progress outlined by Renan in *The Future of Science.*

Flint, Robert. "Renan's Relation to the Comtist Philosophy." In his *Historical Philosophy in France and French Belgium and Switzerland,* pp. 622-27. Edinburgh: William Blackwood and Sons, 1893.
> A brief critical précis of Renan's work distinguishing his methodology from that of the French philosopher Auguste Comte.

France, Anatole. "Address on the Centenary of Ernest Renan." In his *Prefaces, Introductions and Other Uncollected Papers,* translated by J. Lewis May, pp. 207-22. 1927. Reprint. Port Washington, New York: Kennikat Press, 1970.
> A manuscript of a laudatory speech delivered by France at the Trocadéro on the occasion of Renan's centenary.

Gaigalas, Vytas V. *Ernest Renan and His French Catholic Critics.* North Quincy, Mass.: Christopher Publishing House, 1972, 281 p.
> Examines the range of French Catholic criticism on Renan from 1863 to 1963.

Gooch, G. P. "The Jews and the Christian Church." In his *History and Historians in the Nineteenth Century,* rev. ed., pp. 478-501. Boston: Beacon Press, 1959.
> Evaluates Renan's critical approach to Jewish history in *The Origins of Christianity,* claiming that "*The Life of Jesus,* though the most celebrated part of the work, possesses the least value."

Gore, Keith. "Ernest Renan: A Positive Ethics?" *French Studies: A Quarterly Review* XLI, No. 2 (April 1987): 141-54.
> Denies that Renan's philosophy represents any particular doctrine, arguing that it actually evolved through time.

Harding, Joan N. "Renan and Matthew Arnold: Two Saddened Searchers." *Hibbert Journal* LVII, No. 1959 (July 1959): 361-67.
> Draws a series of parallels between Matthew Arnold and Renan, comparing their intellectual endeavors and cultural influences.

Lee, D. C. J. "Renan's *Avenir de la science:* Dialogue for an Absent Christ." *Nineteenth-Century French Studies* IV, Nos. 1,2 (Fall/Winter 1975-76): 67-88.
> An in-depth analysis of *The Future of Science,* stressing the work's hidden complexity and close thematic relation to Renan's other writings.

Lemaître, Jules. "Ernest Renan." In his *Literary Impressions,* translated by A. W. Evans, pp. 80-107. London: Daniel O'Conner, 1921.
> A character study of Renan featuring a report of the author lecturing at the *Collège de France.*

Lewis, Gordon K. "From Faith to Skepticism: A Note on Three Apologetics." *Journal of Politics* 13, No. 2 (May 1951): 164-86.
> Assesses the contest between faith and reason in John Henry Newman's *Apologia pro vita sua* (1864), Blaise Pascal's *Pensées* (1670), and Renan's *Recollections of My Youth.*

Lillie, Elisabeth. "Approaches to Symbolism in the Work of Ernest Renan." *Nineteenth-Century French Studies* 14, Nos. 1,2 (Fall/Winter 1985-86): 110-29.
> Investigates the use of symbolism in Renan's work, seeking to determine the causes for his rejection of Symbolism as a movement.

Mott, Lewis Freeman. *Ernest Renan.* New York: D. Appleton and Co., 1921, 462 p.
> Considered the finest available work in English for biographical accuracy.

Neff, Emery. "History as Art: Renan, Burckhardt, Green." In his *The Poetry of History: The Contribution of Literature and Literary Scholarship to the Writing of History since Voltaire,* pp. 150-88. New York: Columbia University Press, 1947.

    Reviews Renan's principal works, accentuating the importance of his theory of history.

Nicholas, Brian. "Two Nineteenth-Century Utopias: The Influence of Renan's *L'avenir de la science* on Wilde's 'The Soul of Man Under Socialism'." *Modern Language Review* LIX, No. 3 (July 1964): 361-70.

    Uncovers similarities in utopian speculation in selected works of Oscar Wilde and Renan.

O'Neill, Moira. "The Letters of Ernest and Henriette Renan, 1846-1850." *Blackwood's Magazine* CCXV, No. MCCC (February 1924): 186-209.

    Comments on a series of letters exchanged between Renan and his sister Henriette that illuminate the author's personal history during four years in Paris.

Raitt, A. W. "Ernest Renan." In his *Life and Letters in France: The Nineteenth Century,* pp. 92-100. Life and Letters in France, edited by Austin Gill. New York: Charles Scribner's Sons, 1965.

    Assesses the extent to which Renan's thought was influenced by the scientism of the French positivist school.

Said, Edward W. "Renan's Philological Laboratory." In *Art, Politics, and Will: Essays in Honor of Lionel Trilling,* edited by Quentin Anderson, Stephen Donadio, and Steven Marcus, pp. 59-98. New York: Basic Books, 1977.

    A study of Renan's philological method that posits him as "a figure who must be grasped, in short, as a type of cultural *prax-is,* as a style for making discursive statements within what Michel Foucault would call the *archive* of his time."

Smith, Colin. "The Fictionalist Element in Renan's Thought." *French Studies: A Quarterly Review* IX, No. 1 (January 1955): 30-41.

    Argues that with Renan "the idea of conscious pretense, the 'useful lie', becomes an indispensable key to the exploration of his thought."

————. "Renan's Final Cosmology." *Forum for Modern Language Studies* XIV, No. 3 (July 1978): 231-46.

    Analyzes Renan's essay "Examen de conscience philosophique," arguing that it indicates a shift in the author's thinking from determinism to relativism.

Soltau, Roger Henry. "Ernest Renan." In his *French Political Thought in the Nineteenth Century,* pp. 215-30. New York: Russell & Russell, 1959.

    Identifies the various components of Renan's political philosophy, asserting that "it is impossible to class him among those political thinkers of a really creative influence."

Wardman, H. W. *Ernest Renan: A Critical Biography.* London: Athlone Press, 1964, 227 p.

    A study of Renan's life and work emphasizing the cultural background of his age.

————. "Philosophy of History and Revolution in Renan." *French Studies: A Quarterly Review* XXV, No. 1 (January 1971): 15-31.

    Attempts to formulate a coherent doctrine from the various references to a "philosophy of history" scattered throughout Renan's texts.

# Emma Dorothy Eliza Nevitte Southworth

## 1819-1899

American novelist.

Southworth was one of the most popular authors in America during the last half of the nineteenth century. Using the signature E.D.E.N. Southworth, she produced over sixty novels, and is often credited with having the greatest sales of any female writer of her era. In such works as *The Hidden Hand* and *The Deserted Wife,* she appealed to the public's taste with her melodramatic plots and staunch morality. Most often, her stories center on the trials of wronged women and abandoned wives who face great odds but are, without exception, triumphant in the end. Although unpopular with contemporary critics, who attacked her for sensationalism, Southworth amassed a devoted following who read her novels in installment form in such weekly newspapers as the *New York Ledger.* Southworth's tremendous popularity, however, was confined to her lifetime; in the twentieth century her black-and-white themes of good versus evil rapidly became outdated. Although her novels are now largely forgotten, Southworth remains of historical interest as the most famous representative of a group of mid-nineteenth-century American female authors whose writings are gaining renewed recognition among feminist scholars.

Born in Washington, D.C., Southworth was the eldest daughter of Captain Charles Le Compte Nevitte and his second wife, Susannah Wailes, who, at the time of their marriage, was thirty years younger than her husband. Disparity in age between husband and wife later surfaced as a theme in several of Southworth's novels and was openly disapproved of by the author. When Southworth was four, her father died. Two years later, Southworth's mother married Joshua L. Henshaw, who came to Washington, D.C. as a secretary to Daniel Webster and later opened a school there. Educated at her stepfather's school, Southworth became an avid reader and developed a spirited imagination. In 1840, she married Frederick Hamilton Southworth, an inventor from New York. They moved to Prairie du Chien, Wisconsin, but, after three years of marriage, Southworth's husband abandoned her and moved to Brazil. Biographers note that this period in Southworth's life left an indelible impression upon her and probably inspired her obsession with the theme of the deserted wife, which she was to use over and over again in her novels. In 1844, Southworth returned to Washington, D.C. with her two children. She found a job teaching in the public schools, but the small salary of 250 dollars a year barely supported her and her family. Soon, however, she began supplementing her income by submitting short stories to weekly newspapers. The beginning of her career as a novelist is marked by the publication in 1849 of *Retribution; or, The Vale of Shadows: A Tale of Passion,* after which she retired from teaching to devote her time exclusively to writing. During the next forty years, Southworth produced, on the average, over a novel a year and enjoyed enormous commercial success. Early in her career, she established several connections in the literary world, including close friendships with the novelist Harriet Beecher Stowe and the poet John Greenleaf Whittier. From 1857 on, Southworth wrote exclusively for the *New York*

*Ledger.* She established an enduring relationship with its editor, Robert Bonner, who was at once employer, financial advisor, and close family friend. He paid Southworth a lucrative salary and often presented her with generous gifts. In return, Southworth's contributions to the *New York Ledger* are said to have doubled its circulation, making it one of the most successful weekly papers of the time. Southworth was widely read not only in America but also throughout Europe, where many of her novels appeared in German, French, Spanish, and Italian translations. With her widespread popularity came the problem of imitation. Other authors managed to take advantage of Southworth's literary success by writing under such names as S.A. Southworth and Ella Southworth, and the *New York Ledger* frequently had to remind its readers that only the trademark initials, E.D.E.N., were genuine. In 1853, Southworth moved to Prospect Cottage, overlooking the Potomac River in Washington, D.C. It was here that she lived the rest of her life, writing her novels and entertaining a broad circle of friends. Her last work was published just five years before she died at the age of eighty.

Southworth's novels were limited to a handful of themes upon which she repeatedly drew. Her most common storylines revolve around innocent women who, in some way, are wronged by the men in their lives. In *The Hidden Hand,* for example, the heroine, Capitola Le Noir, must escape the villainous Black Donald, an assassin hired by her sinister uncle, Gabriel Le Noir, who is after Capitola's sizable inheritance. The plot focuses on Capitola's struggle to survive alone in a male-dominated society but, like almost all of Southworth's novels, ends with the opportune marriage of the heroine. Critics note that there is no middle ground in Southworth's novels: characters are either innately good or thoroughly evil. This approach is in accord with the didacticism that underscores all of her writing. Southworth, in fact, took her self-appointed role of moralizer very seriously, once stating, while discussing her novel *Ishmael; or, In the Depths,* that she wrote "not only for money and fame but for humanity." In addition to using similar plots and themes throughout her novels, Southworth had favorite settings that surface again and again. The adventures of her characters often take place in the untamed countryside of Virginia and Maryland; dismal mountain roads, murky lakes, and dangerous rocky gorges are the characteristic features of her landscapes. She assigned to these ominous places such names as Devil's Run, Black Pond, and Black Valley. This melodramatic flair is typical of almost all of Southworth's novels. She wrote passionately, using heated language and an outlandish, overblown vocabulary to describe her characters and settings. Southworth had little or no time for revision and frequently used such devices as trapdoors, hidden passages, and underground tunnels to write her way out of seemingly hopeless situations. Only toward the end of her career did Southworth's writing become more sedate, losing much of its didactic tone and fervent sensationalism.

During her lifetime, with few exceptions, Southworth was treated harshly by critics despite her enormous popularity. Many contemporary reviewers believed that her risqué plots (often centering on adultery) and the loose morality of some of her characters exceeded the bounds of decency and decorum. *Retribution* elicited the most favorable reviews of any of her novels. One critic said of this debut work, "It exhibits a power of imagination and delineation not inferior to *Jane Eyre.*" For the most part, however, the complimentary reviews ended with *Retribution.* In the late twentieth century, feminist critics have shown a renewed interest in Southworth's writing, praising her for her portrayal of independent women and for addressing the injustices of a patriarchal society. Southworth is also recognized today as the most prominent member of a group of highly popular nineteenth-century female writers, including Fanny Fern, Caroline Lee Hentz, and Mary Jane Holmes, who, while lacking literary talent (Nathaniel Hawthorne once dubbed them "a damned mob of scribbling women"), were unprecedented in their use of distinctly feminine themes reflecting the thoughts and opinions of contemporary women. In this context, Southworth has gained historical significance for her contribution to the understanding of women's lives in nineteenth-century American society.

## *PRINCIPAL WORKS

*Retribution; or, The Vale of Shadows: A Tale of Passion*
　　(novel)　1849
*The Deserted Wife*　(novel)　1850
*The Mother-in-Law; or, The Isle of Rays*　(novel)　1851
*Shannondale*　(novel)　1851
*The Curse of Clifton: A Tale of Expiation and Redemption*
　　(novel)　1853

*The Missing Bride; or, Miriam the Avenger*　(novel)　1855
*The Hidden Hand*　(novel)　1859
*The Fatal Marriage*　(novel)　1863
*The Maiden Widow*　(novel)　1870
*Ishmael; or, In the Depths*　(novel)　1876
*Self-Raised; or, From the Depths*　(novel)　1876
*The Rejected Bride*　(novel)　1894

*Most of Southworth's novels were first published serially in periodicals.

---

### JOHN GREENLEAF WHITTIER　(essay date 1849)

[*Whittier was an American poet, abolitionist, journalist, and critic whose works are noted for their moral content, simple sentiment, and humanitarianism. As a critic, Whittier is best known for encouraging the idea of American literary nationalism. In the following excerpt from an essay first published in the* Washington National Era *on September 20, 1849, Whittier praises Southworth's ability to write popular, romantic fiction, but warns against the possible moral pitfalls of this genre.*]

Without being liable to the charge of imitation, ***Retribution*** reminds us of *Jane Eyre,* and the later productions of that school. It has their strength and sustained intensity, while it embodies, as they can scarcely be said to do, an important moral lesson. It is well called a ***Tale of Passion.*** Painfully intense, its heat scorches as we read. Some of its scenes are overdrawn; mind and heart revolt and protest against those terrific outbursts of passion, on the part of the beautiful fiend, who drags down, in her fatal embrace, the proud, self-deceived statesman. There are a few feeble passages, and some extravagant ones. But, as a whole, we do not hesitate to say, that it is worthy of a place with Brockden Brown's *Wieland, Arthur Mervyn,* and *Edgar Huntley,* the only American romances with which we can properly compare it. It cannot fail to be widely read, and we doubt not its success will warrant its author in the entire devotion of her extraordinary powers to a department of literature which, under the influence of a well-principled mind, a generous heart, and healthful sympathies, may be made the medium of teaching lessons of virtue and honor, the Christian duty of self-denial, and heroic devotion to the right and the true, but which has been too often the channel through which impure fancies, stimulants to already over-excited passions, enervating the body and poisoning the soul, have been sent forth on their errands of evil. (p. 153)

*John Greenleaf Whittier, " 'Retribution'. . . , by E. D. E. N. Southworth," in his* Whittier on Writers and Writing: The Uncollected Critical Writings of John Greenleaf Whittier, *edited by Edwin Harrison Cady and Harry Hayden Clark, Syracuse University Press, 1950, pp. 152-53.*

### *THE SOUTHERN LITERARY MESSENGER*　(essay date 1850)

[*In this excerpt from an anonymous review of* The Deserted Wife, *the critic attacks the morality of the novel.*]

We have been greatly shocked in reading this publication. Coming before the public with the name of a lady as author, and of the Appletons as publishers, we had supposed that at least it was unexceptionable in tone, and did not offend against the proprieties of life. The caption of "*a choice new American Novel*" had not, indeed, beguiled us into the supposition that anything brilliant had burst upon the world, but we were not prepared to find, under such a passport to our favor, a work of the very worst description of the loose-tunic and guilty-passion school. *Retribution, or the Vale of Shadows* had escaped us, and we became acquainted for the first time, in the pages of *The Deserted Wife,* with the fact that French sentimentalism has so far broken through the barriers of our American *morale,* that one of the "gentler sex" may here fairly lay claim to the doubtful honors of a Dudevant. . . .

[We] very much fear that *The Deserted Wife* will pass, by virtue of its *maternity* and the respectability of its publishers, into the family circles of many houses, where it could never find entrance were its character even suspected by the world. For ourselves, we should not have gone further than the Introduction, to make up our opinion of the work, had not our attention been especially directed to the latter portions, after reading which we can conscientiously say that we should as soon put into the hands of a female friend the *Confessions* of Jean Jacques Rousseau as any volume of our new American novelist.

We are at a loss to conjecture how such a performance should find a vehicle to the public in the press of the Messrs. Appleton. No publishing house in this country has deserved, and, we are glad to think, received a larger share of patronage; and we have been always ready to bear willing testimony to their discretion and good taste. But in the present instance they have committed a *faux pas,* the results of which may not be readily averted. We would advise them in future to have a closer eye to the department of fiction, and particularly to leave such works as *The Deserted Wife* to the presses of Ann Street. Dressed out in a flaming yellow cover, printed with the worst of type on the most execrable of paper, and ornamented with a frontispiece of the warmest of the scenes, it might win a large popularity in the less respectable bookshops, among those congenial issues which are lighting up the road to the pit that is bottomless; but it could never, at all events, find its way to the hearth-stone, and shiver the household gods, of one pure and right-thinking family.

*A review of "The Deserted Wife," in* The Southern Literary Messenger, *Vol. I, No. 11, November, 1850, p. 111.*

### THE SOUTHERN LITERARY MESSENGER (essay date 1851)

[*The following review of* Shannondale *represents a complete condemnation of the novel. The critic ridicules the plot and characters, points out historical inaccuracies in the story, and even objects to the paper on which it is printed.*]

To speak in proper terms of this work might lay us open to the charge of assailing a lady, and we therefore forbear to give it that extended notice which, as an American novel, published by a worthy American house, it might otherwise claim. Merits it has none to demand a moment's consideration. Of all the inanities which, within twelve months past, have issued, like the heads of hydra, from previous critical decapitation, to the delight of milliner girls and the terror of editors, *Shannondale* is beyond all question the most flat, stupid and

absurd. The plot is wretched and made worse, if possible, by palpable anachronisms, the characters "have no character at all," and the style is about midway between the nursery and the boarding school. As an instance of what we have charged concerning the plot, we may content ourselves with saying that the scene opens just after the American Revolution, and a young gentleman is introduced who has graduated at the University of Virginia—an institution, at that time undeveloped in the brain of its illustrious founder, Mr. Jefferson. To fortify ourselves as to the characterless condition of the *dramatis personœ* would demand larger space than we can here devote to the subject, and we spare our readers, in mercy, any quotations, as specimens of the style, referring them to the volume, (which we trust they will not buy,) *passim.* But by far the worst feature of *Shannondale* is its imitation of the French school of fiction, and those yellow covered American novelettes near akin thereunto, in which the hero always falls in love with somebody else's wife, and otherwise conducts himself after a fashion quite *contra bonas mores.* We think it high time that respectable publishers should unite in suppressing this demoralizing sort of literature. The Appletons are responsible for the appearance of a former work by Miss (or Mrs.) Emma D. E. Nevitt Southworth—(a *nom de plume,* we sincerely trust,) which we felt in duty bound to condemn as a novel of the Dudevant stamp [see excerpt dated 1850]. We cannot say as much, even in condemnation, of the present volume, for while we consider it equally vicious in its tendency, it surely lays no claim to any of those striking qualities which render so fascinating the compositions of George Sand. *Shannondale* is very appropriately printed with bad type, on wretched paper, and, but for the name of the publishers, might readily enough be mistaken for one of the free and easy issues of Ann Street. In this respect, observing the unities, it is an improvement on the *Deserted Wife.*

*A review of "Shannondale," in* The Southern Literary Messenger, *Vol. XVII, No. 2, February, 1851, p. 128.*

### THE SOUTHERN LITERARY MESSENGER (essay date 1851)

[*In this review of* The Mother-in-Law, *Southworth is criticized for writing in a highly "Frenchified" style and for misrepresenting Virginia society.*]

This is the "latest and newest" work from the pen of Mrs. Emma D. E. Nevitt Southworth—a lady who has of late, through the agency of the enterprising firm of Appleton & Co., been flooding the United States with the *Deserted Wife, Shannondale,* and other volumes of questionable or rather wholly unquestionable morality.

It is almost impossible to convey a distinct idea of the nature of the immorality we refer to; for with one or two exceptions (a scene for example on a steamboat in *The Deserted Wife,*) there are no positively immoral *passages* in Mrs. Southworth's writings. It is rather in the tone, the coloring, the general moulding of character and feeling that this lady's strong, unfeminine, thoroughly *French* organization betrays itself. We hope she will pardon us if we are in error, but having just run over this her latest and *strongest* work, we have come to the conclusion that the authoress of *The Mother-in-Law* is a diligent and admiring reader of the more exceptionable productions of the present French School of Romance writers. The fault lies not in indelicate *scenes,* but in highly indelicate allusions and incidents of the plot—such as a careful perusal could only make evident.

God forbid, however, that **The Deserted Wife,** etc., should be bought and read to verify our remarks! There could be few greater evils in our estimation, than the introduction of these warm, highly-colored, "artist" productions, (as Mrs. Southworth no doubt would characterize them,) into a Virginia family of young girls and boys. We cannot, and we do not pretend to, deny Mrs. Southworth much talent. Her style though at times altogether too ambitious and diffuse, and in many passages highly Frenchified, is ready and flowing—her characters, if they betray no deep insight into the human heart, are well conceived—and her plots are generally, with the exception of the last half of every volume, good. The plot of the **Mother-in-Law,** the best to be found in any of her works, with a little more care might have been made very striking.

Mrs. Southworth has of late turned her attention to a subject which we advise her, with all respect, to abandon at once. We mean the description of what she conceives to be Virginia Society.

We cannot go into particulars, but will state in a few words our private opinion, "which," as Mr. Poe says, "we now take the liberty of making public," that balder, more exaggerated, more utterly *truthless* representations of the outer or inner life of Virginians, were never thrust upon a bamboozled community. These things will not be regarded here in any other light than as very good jokes, but we do protest with all our strength against the works of Mrs. Southworth being received beyond the borders of Virginia, as truthful delineations in any one particular of life and society in this state.

*A review of "The Mother-in-Law; or, The Isle of Rays," in* The Southern Literary Messenger, *Vol. XVII, No. 6, June, 1851, p. 390.*

### THE SOUTHERN QUARTERLY REVIEW   (essay date 1852)

[*In the following review of* Virginia and Magdalene, *the critic discusses the major shortcomings of Southworth's fiction, asserting that while she possesses some measure of skill as a writer, she fails to improve from novel to novel and would benefit from a more discerning and well-informed approach to her subject matter.*]

Mrs. Southworth does not improve. Her first work, **Retribution,** still remains, in all respects of art, immeasurably her best performance. [In **Virginia and Magdalene** she] writes with mistaken notions of what art requires. She lacks repose; she lacks variety. Her themes and scenes are monotonous; her tastes are reckless; her tone is unwholesome. She is too spasmodic, too extravagant, too much on the stilts: Perpetual heroics will not answer; at all events, will not do in stories of ordinary and domestic life. She must pause, and subdue herself to nature; cast off her false models; turn to the better lights of art; emulate the more natural writers. To do this, her better policy will be to forego the practice of writing for serials. To make effective scenes in a newspaper is one thing; and in this form of publication the gourmand will devour any sort of extravagance in broken doses; but the case alters when the same matter is thrown together into a volume. There it palls upon the taste, and a single scene or sketch suffices for the whole. One stops with "*Ohe! jam satis*"—at the end of the second chapter. We have said this much with the view to

Mrs. Southworth's improvement. She has too much real talent to waste herself in this fashion. Let her recover herself in season, and do justice to her endowments, by a careful study of her material and the laws of art; by a judicious selection of subject, and by a painstaking array of all her forces, before she puts pen to paper. (pp. 541-42)

*A review of "Virginia and Magdalene," in* The Southern Quarterly Review, *Vol. VI, No. XII, October, 1852, pp. 541-42.*

### THE LITERARY WORLD   (essay date 1853)

[*In the following excerpt from an anonymous review of* The Curse of Clifton, *the critic praises Southworth as a romantic writer, likening her style to that of Charlotte Brontë.*]

Whatever faults Mrs. Southworth's books may possess, tameness and a want of originality cannot be ranked among them. On the contrary, her startling positions, vivid scenes, and a pervading intensity in language and plot, remind us forcibly of Miss Bronte; and the **Curse of Clifton,** a combination of the horrible, the ultra-romantic, and the transcendental, might be claimed by her without any injury to her fame.

*A review of "The Curse of Clifton," in* The Literary World, *No. 318, March 5, 1853, p. 188.*

### THE SOUTHERN QUARTERLY REVIEW   (essay date 1853)

[*In this excerpt from an anonymous review of* The Curse of Clifton, *the critic suggests that Southworth moderate and redirect her passionate approach to her materials in order to "rise to an honourable rank among living novelists."*]

**The Curse of Clifton,** is an American Romance, the scene laid in Virginia, from the pen of Mrs. Southworth, a writer who possesses many unquestionable powers, but who has great need to tame her disposition to exaggerate monstrously the features which she attempts to delineate. She is content to do few things naturally, and we are made to sleep on surprises, to sup on horrors, and to sit down at the board with some of the most unmitigated social monsters. This story will find readers and will afford interest; but if the author desires to secure a permanent reputation, she must learn to subdue her paces; to get back to nature; to reform her imagination; to mitigate her rages; to put her passion into straight jackets for a season, and labour to live within the common laws of humanity. Let her but adopt Hamlet's direction to the players, and not tear every thing to tatters, and she may yet rise to a honourable rank among living novelists. She has invention in high degree, enthusiasm, and considerable knowledge of the sterner and wilder passions. (pp. 266-67)

*A review of "The Curse of Clifton," in* The Southern Quarterly Review, *Vol. VIII, No. XV, July, 1853, pp. 266-67.*

### SARAH JOSEPHA HALE   (essay date 1855)

[*In the following excerpt, Hale comments on Southworth's inexperience as a novelist, suggesting that although her works often exceed the limits of good taste, they show great promise.*]

Mrs. Southworth is yet young, both as a woman and an author; but she is a writer of great promise, and we have reason to expect that the future productions of her pen will surpass those works with which she has already favoured the reading community—works showing great powers of the imagination, and strength and depth of feeling, it is true, but also written in a wild and extravagant manner, and occasionally with a freedom of expression that almost borders on impiety. This we are constrained to say, though we feel assured that no one would shrink more reluctantly than the young writer herself from coolly and calmly approaching, with too familiar a hand, the Persons and places held sacred by all the Christian world. She seems carried, by a fervid imagination, in an enthusiasm for depicting character as it is actually found (in which she excels,) beyond the limits prescribed by correct taste or good judgment. In other respects her novels are deeply interesting. They show, in every page, the hand of a writer of unusual genius and ability. In descriptions of Southern life, and of negro character and mode of expression, she is unequalled. She writes evidently from a full heart and an overflowing brain, and sends her works forth to the criticisms of an unimpassioned public without the advantage they would receive from a revision, and careful pruning, in some moment when calmer reflection was in the ascendancy. (p. 794)

> *Sarah Josepha Hale, "Southworth, Emma D. E. Nevitte," in her* Woman's Record, *1855. Reprint by Source Book Press, 1970, pp. 793-96.*

## THE LITERARY WORLD   (essay date 1882)

[*In the following excerpt, the anonymous critic addresses the reasons for Southworth's extraordinary success as a novelist despite her insubstantial plots and mediocre style and widespread hostility toward her works on the part of reviewers.*]

The austere reader, who of course is acquainted with the famous Mrs. Southworth only by hearsay, may object to see her name in a reputable journal of criticism. She is wont to be deprecated in public and devoured much in private, as the continual replenishing of all her books requisite in large libraries sufficiently attests. From 1849, the year of her first successful venture, up to 1872, a complete set of her writings numbers thirty-five volumes, and she has published since. To speak in detail of the productions of this female Lope de Vega is impossible,—indeed it is unnecessary, for her devoted admirers admit that to read one is to read all in substance; and yet they do read all, and little else apparently. How explain her remarkable popularity unless it is posited at once that admiration of this sort is worthless and counts for nothing? But this is unfair and not quite thè truth. Understanding well the craving for what is sensational and morbid in fiction, Mrs. Southworth, by a skillful use of the fascinations of crime, and by a systematic introduction of horror as an element of literary construction, has managed to cater so successfully to certain tastes that she stands easily at the head of this class of the trashy school. In her later work she seems to have regretted her earlier faults, to which she may have been driven by a particularly pathetic experience in authorship. In *Ishmael,* one of her last, she founds her plot upon facts in the life of William Wirt, and has produced a story of no mean merit. It is said that she frankly admits her own failings, but claims that she has been accustomed to draw upon actual life for her material. The fidelity to facts is best shown in her *Widow's Son.* Her style is clear, and she tells her story directly; but the reader must accustom himself to sudden breaks, as when, for instance, in *The Changed Brides,* he finds an interval of four hundred and two pages between one sentence and the next consecutive one. Judged by their popularity Mrs. South-

worth's principal stories are: *The Changed Brides, The Bride's Fate, The Curse of Clifton,* also known under the title of *Fallen Pride,* and *The Gipsey's Prophecy.*

> *"Mrs. Emma D. E. N. Southworth," in* The Literary World, *Vol. XIII, No. 11, June 3, 1882, p. 185.*

## EDNA KENTON   (essay date 1916)

[*In the following excerpt, Kenton surveys Southworth's career, commenting briefly on a representative selection of her most popular novels.*]

> . . . Whence is that knocking?
> How is't with me when every sound appals me?
> . . . I hear a knocking,
> In the south entry! Hark!—more knocking!
>                                         SHAKESPEARE.

Hurricane Hall is a large old family mansion built of dark-red sandstone in one of the loneliest and wildest of the mountain ranges of Virginia.

The estate is surrounded on three sides by a range of steep grey rocks spiked with clumps of dark evergreens, and called from its horseshoe form the Devil's Hoof.

On the fourth side the ground gradually ascends in broken rock and barren soil to the edge of the wild mountain stream known as the Devil's Run.

When storms and floods were high, the loud roaring of the wild mountain gorges and the terrific raging of the torrent over its rocky course gave to this savage locality its ill-omened names of Devil's Hoof, Devil's Run, and Hurricane Hall.

Thus begins *The Hidden Hand,* one of the famous old thrillers of the fifties, the most popular serial, bar none, that ever raced through the breathless pages of the old *New York Ledger.* The setting indicated above for the adventures of Capitola, the Madcap, is characteristically Southworthian in topography, nomenclature and Virginity, and Chapter II: The Masks, bends straight to the heart of a situation that Emma Dorothy Eliza Nevitte Southworth thrilled to from her earliest days of authorship. It is a chapter of mountain robbers and Granny Grewell, the midwife; of a blindfolded journey through forests and winding hills and mysterious passages to an attic where lay a girl whose right hand, head and face were swathed and sewn in black crêpe; of the birth of two babes that stormy night, and the death of one; of the Machiavellian rescue of the living child—Capitola!—by Granny Grewell.

Then pass thirteen years, with the turning of a page, and Capitola is a newsboy—"Her sex a page's dress belied, obscured her charms; but could not hide.—Scott"—on the streets of New York. Here she tells Major Warfield, Old Hurricane of Hurricane Hall, in her artless, girlish way, of her rearing in Rag Alley by Granny Grewell, and Old Hurricane intones, "Ah-h!", recognising in her Capitola Le Noir, heiress to a vast Virginian estate, Hidden House, now in possession of the girl's more than wicked uncle, Colonel Le Noir. Old Hurricane declares himself her guardian, and, though the adventures of Capitola may well be said to have begun before her birth, there is a progressive intensity about them from now on that ranks Mrs. Southworth's imagination high indeed.

When Capitola, for instance, reaches Hurricane Hall, Mrs.

Condiment, the housekeeper (note the Southworthian tendency in names), gives her "the room with the trap-door." A verbal diagram of the room follows, and in a parenthesis Mrs. Southworth explains her particularity here. "The furniture of this room I am particular in describing," she says, "as upon the simple accident of its arrangement depended on two occasions the life and honour of its occupant." Capitola demanded a look at the theatrical property that gave her room its name, and Mrs. Condiment obliged her by lifting a rug and revealing a large drop four feet square, kept in place "by a short iron bolt." "Now, my dear, take care of yourself," cautioned the careful housekeeper, "for this bolt slides very easily, and if while you happened to be walking across this place you were to push the bolt back, the trap-door would drop and you would fall down—Heaven knows where! If that horrible pit has any bottom, it is strewn with human skeletons." (pp. 128-29)

***Ishmael, or, In the Depths,*** and its sequel, ***Self-raised, or, From the Depths,*** are two other serials that our grandmothers wept over, and these two novels should not be left unread by their descendants, male or female. Through intrigue, poverty, plottings, misfortunes, and, for many, many pages, the undeserved stigma of illegitimate birth, Ishmael Worth moves, "a veritable prince among men." He loves Claudia, the proud and haughty daughter of Judge Merlin, of Washington. Claudia loves Ishmael, but can she, the fairest beauty of them all, stoop to wed the base-born son of Norah Worth! Ten times no! (p. 131)

***The Bride's Ordeal,*** as portrayed by Mrs. Southworth, is a psychological one, and begins with the receipt of a heavy packing box, on her wedding morn. Erma, the bride, has it opened, and bends to look within. What was it she saw there? What turned her face so wild and white with horror? What caused her to throw herself across the open box, shrieking: "Cover it up! Cover it up! Oh, my soul! Cover it up from all human sight forever and ever!" Dear reader, unless your own horror forces you to skip to—approximately—page 329 of the sequel, you will not know until many hours have passed. Later on her bridal day, a daguerreotype in her new home tells Erma what she had not known before—that her husband's (supposedly) murdered stepfather had met his (supposed) death at *her father's hands.* "Oh, angels have pity on me!" breathed Erma. "Fate closes around me! Shall I go mad? My husband's murdered father—Gustav Perlemonte! The annals of civilised life do not record such an unnatural marriage!" (p. 134)

Any essay at criticism of the Southworth novels were incomplete without mention at least of ***Fair Play*** and its sequel, ***How He Won Her.*** For these two thrillers dealt with two phases of life then comparatively new to fiction: the foreign missionary field, and the Civil War. Britomarte Conyers, heroine, is one of the early martial young women of fiction, with a "hatred" of men, a "deep mystery" in her life, and a vow to mission work in farther India. She refuses to wed Justin Rosenthal, and embarks; so, unknown to her till they are five days out, does Justin. Thus profoundly does he love her. There is an almighty storm at sea, and, after as many chapters as can be wrenched from the old *Ledger* space, Justin, Britomarte, and for propriety's dear sake, a serving woman, Judith, discover themselves upon a desert isle. . . . Here, for two years they live purely and resignedly, while in America, with all the intensity of "thriller" patriotism, gather the clouds of the Civil War. (p. 135)

The garb of man upon the limbs of woman is always a favourite expedient with Mrs. Southworth. Home again, Britomarte still refuses to marry Justin, who thereupon joins the Northern army. Then follows the tale of Justin and his devoted body servant, Wing, a scrubby little boy who is his aid, and whose daring is beyond the dreams of even of conscience-smitten coward! Also follow battles, guerrilla warfare, abductions of fiery Northern maids by impassioned Southrons, forced marriages, death-bed repentings of wounded Rebels, and the acknowledged discomforts of Libby prison. At last, as Justin lies all but dying on a battle field, his faithful Wing creeps out to find him. Wing asks for a final message to the "one best beloved." "Beyond this field of battle," says Justin solemnly, "there is none to whom I care to send a message." As Wing weeps convulsively, Justin murmurs:

> "Britomarte!"

> "Justin, Justin, my beloved!" exclaimed Britomarte, who we shall no longer call by her assumed name of Wing. . . . "Tell me, Justin, how it was you recognised me from the beginning. I thought I was well disguised, and I am a good actress with almost a Protean power of changing my face, and with a ventriloquist's gift of changing my voice!"

> "Yes, you were well disguised. You had sacrificed your tresses, and had put on a skull cap wig of stiff, short, bristling, flaxen hair, and drawn it tight and low over your forehead. You had shaved off your arched black eyebrows, quite altering the expression of your eyes. You had widened your mouth by two deep lines in the corner. You had put yourself in the uniform of a United States soldier, and you always carried four or five pebbles in your mouth to make you speak thickly. And yet when I saw you in the ranks, in the ugly little raw recruit I recognised my beautiful Britomarte."

Thus spoke the (supposedly) dying man.

And so these thrilling old tales run on! ***The Phantom Wedding, The Fatal Secret, The Spectre Lover, The Beautiful Fiend, The Lost Heiress, The Prince of Darkness, The Curse of Clifton, The Gypsey's Prophecy,*** all bear tribute to the real power of Emma Dorothy Eliza Nevitte Southworth. Her pen, turned to the unfamiliar pastures of Scottish dialect, may have slipped on rolling stones, but set free to browse in the fertile fields of Virginia darkeydom and mountain ranges, it meets with not a single misstep. The tales are told with leisure and curious detail, but in the old *Ledger* days, before "efficiency" became the keynote of the publisher, authors were paid by the line. This is why long recountings are so often interrupted by single-hearted ejaculations, and why paragraphing is a simple matter of sentences, and those of the briefest—as the quoted account of Black Donald's (supposed) demise:

> He laughed aloud.
> She pressed the spring.
> The drop fell.
> The outlaw shot downward.

Awful descriptions are the order of the Southworth pages. Vast mountains and ravines abound. It was indeed an awful pass! A road roughly hewn through the bottom of a deep, tortuous cleft in the mountains, where at some remote period, by some tremendous convulsion of nature, the solid rocks had been rent apart, leaving the ragged edges of the wound hanging at a dizzy height between heaven and earth. It was a wild and beautiful ruin, this Gothic edifice, the Haunted Chapel, through whose graveyard ran a little rill, the offspring of the wild waterfall whose roaring could be heard for miles, and whose foam boiled as if by fire of the gods! The Devil's Staircase, the Devil's Ladder, the Devil's Punch Bowl, the Demon's Drop, the Devil's Dripping Pan, are self-explanatory of the landscapes in which they figure. Disguises, beautiful fiends who murmur "*Ciel!*" or scream "Tout les diables!" the old midwife, the changed children or the stolen darling, the real infant heir to Chateau Dubarry, the faithful negro slaves, and the outlawed band—all these abound, together with jealousies, impassioned love, counterplots, *and delicacy,* without which latter aid to life and love the still-enduring fame of Mrs. E. D. E. N. Southworth could not be. (pp. 136-37)

*Edna Kenton, "Best Sellers of Yesterday," in* The Bookman, *New York, Vol. XLIV, No. 2, October, 1916, pp. 128-37.*

### FRANK LUTHER MOTT  (essay date 1947)

[*In the following excerpt, Mott examines the nature of Southworth's considerable appeal to nineteenth-century readers and discusses the reasons for her decline in popularity.*]

The fact is that Mrs. Southworth was incapable of passionate devotion to an idea. She had her ideals, of course. She believed in God and the Bible; in pity, kindness, and philanthropy; in female virtue and manly devotion; in generous ambition as a key to life. These things did not need thinking out; they were axiomatic, and carried with them certain codes to live by. Illustration of these codes by examples was the formula not only of Mrs. Southworth but of many another successful fictioneer of the time. It is a formula which invites numberless fascinating variations and brings up a constant succession of problems which interest the reader because he (or she; surely most of Mrs. Southworth's readers were she's) has to do the same thing the heroine is doing—apply the code to her own situations and problems. It is a wonderful game, of infinite variety; merely as a new kind of puzzle it has its fascination.

But Mrs. Southworth was a highly successful novelist because of two gifts: she was naturally a good story-teller, and she was a born imitator.

Probably she never set out to imitate anyone. But she read voraciously, and she picked up all the tricks of the popular writers of the day. Her reviewers were always comparing her to other and more famous authors—often favorably. Whittier said that her first novel, **Retribution,** was as good as *Jane Eyre*—better, indeed, because it had a moral [see excerpt dated 1849]. Many compared her humorous passages to those of Dickens, and her work is full of echoes of Scott. **Ishmael,** her best known novel, is reminiscent of *John Halifax, Gentleman.* Her use of minor characters often reminds one of Cooper.

But her imitativeness would not have made her a first-flight best seller without her native gift for telling a story. This was not a talent for structure, in which she was lamentably weak, but a strong feeling for melodramatic incident and an instinct to develop such incidents swiftly and in strong colors. There is something satisfying—to the simple mind, at least—in a villain who is thoroughly evil from his crown to his toes, incapable of a single good impulse. And how gratifying the idea of a hero who is slightly more perfect than King Arthur, St.

*Southworth's home in Georgetown.*

Francis, and Daniel Webster rolled in one! Now take the elaborate moral codes referred to, invent situations in which villain and hero and other simply-typed characters are brought into the puzzles of the codes, supply the familiar fictional reagents such as irresistible passion, a storm or fire, the effects of ancestral sins, murder or other sudden death, insanity—and you have, well, at least the beginning of a Southworth romance. (pp. 138-39)

There is a great reading public today for the black-white novel, and apparently the chief reason Mrs. Southworth has gone out of print in the last decade is that her moral codes and her puzzles are out of fashion. They are indeed almost incomprehensible today. Ishmael, hero of the novel of that name, though half starved, would not take the dollar urged upon him for holding the horses and defending with his fists the property of the man who later became his benefactor. Then after he had been admitted to the bar, he distresses a modern reader because, though he himself is poor as Job's turkey, he insists on turning down fat fees and taking only the cases of the poor and unprotected who can pay him nothing. (p. 139)

The honest inquirer after the reasons for Mrs. Southworth's popularity must forget his own repugnance for her excesses and artificialities. Equipped with the gas-mask of tolerance, he must penetrate into her long and involved romances. He will then be able to discern an indefatigable story-telling talent, a strong feeling for blatant and primitive melodrama, a love for sensational effects in both incidents and characterization, and a faculty for passionate declamation. Add to these things the art of echoing the most respected authors of her day, and add also her good fortune in publishers like Bonner and Peterson; and Mrs. Southworth's success begins to seem less an enigma. It may be said of her, as of so many inferior writers and artists, that she had great gifts, but that they were undisciplined either by the restraints of sense or the subtleties of sensibility. (p. 142)

*Frank Luther Mott, "Mrs. E. D. E. N. Southworth," in his* Golden Multitudes: The Story of Best Sellers in the United States, *The Macmillan Company, 1947, pp. 136-42.*

### MARY NOEL  (essay date 1954)

[*In the following excerpt, Noel examines the character of Ishmael in* Self-Made *(the title under which* Ishmael *and its se-*

*quel,* Self-Raised, *were published serially in the* New York Ledger). Noel *also includes some personal reflections from the author on the "experimental" style of the novel and its possible effect on sales.*]

Ishmael was the culmination of the nineteenth century story-paper hero—the great pure abstract of them all. Mrs. Southworth's *Self-Made* was one of the century's best sellers, ranking second only to *Uncle Tom's Cabin.* It is absurd to wonder how readers or author could find so wooden a character at all "convincing"; for to both readers and author Ishmael was an ideal, not just a character, more or less real, in a book. He was the hero who had been in thousands of story-paper serials, often described by just a few lines. He was this hero built up piece by piece—every bone and sinew of his moral anatomy exhibited and put in place by his painstaking creator. Heroes, of course, all overcame obstacles. So this total hero had to overcome every conceivable obstacle: of poverty, ignorance, isolation, and birth. He couldn't, of course, without shocking nineteenth century sensibilities, actually be a bastard. So he was made to appear to be a bastard. This was easy enough, with the story-paper conventions about inadvertently bigamous marriages. After Ishmael's father had disappeared when his first wife turned up alive, and after the secretly wedded mother had died in childbirth, the hero almost immediately began his upward climb.

By the age of twelve he was taking care of a poverty-stricken aunt who was sick in bed with inflammatory rheumatism. Ishmael did odd jobs for pittances all day long, then came home to get the supper, split the wood, and nurse his dear aunt. The snow fell and eliminated his outdoor jobs. They were hungry. Ishmael walked all day to the village by the devious snow-cleared route to get credit for a quarter of a pound of tea for his complaining aunt. The grocer refused him. Ishmael picked up a pocketbook in the snow on the way back and passed through a heroic moral struggle as to whether or not he should "borrow" any of the ten dollars for his aunt's tea. He said to himself: "I would like to make dear Aunt Hannah happy tonight. But I am sure George Washington would not approve of my taking what don't belong to me for that or any other purpose. And neither would Patrick Henry nor John Hancock."

That settled the matter for Ishmael. He was scolded by his aunt, a right sensible woman who was not quite satisfied with the Patrick Henry and John Hancock argument advanced by young Ishmael. When Aunt Hannah finally burst into tears, Ishmael took down his only treasure, a history of his beloved heroes, went back through the snow to the town, and sold the book at a heartbreakingly low price. With the meager proceeds he bought not only Aunt Hannah's tea, but also paper and stickers with which to post up signs around the countryside advertising the lost pocketbook. At this point Mrs. Southworth simply had to say:

> Do you not love this boy? And will you not forgive me if I have lingered too long over the trials and triumphs of his friendless and heroic boyhood? He who in his feeble childhood resists small temptations, and makes small sacrifices, is very apt in his strong manhood to conquer great difficulties and achieve great successes.

Mrs. Southworth was a little worried in her letters to Bonner [her editor] about this time. She wrote: "This story is different in character to any that I have ever written before, and as such may be considered an experiment. In former stories,

I have catered for what I believed to be the popular taste; but in this I have a higher aim—popular good." At another time she was glad to hear "that the story seemed to be 'taking' well." She had been afraid that her "readers who read for excitement would become impatient of the weary steps by which one self-made boy reached his destiny." She promised to hasten it as much as possible "without hurting the development of the story." Still, she took the equivalent of a whole volume to get Ishmael fairly started on his career as a lawyer. He had only an occasional adventure, such as saving two boys who had been very cruel to him from a fire at the risk of his own life, or getting himself injured by throwing himself in front of two horses running away with a carriage containing the judge's beautiful daughter. All this was going to help out in the end—but it took up only a few pages of a story that was, in the meantime, much devoted to Ishmael's daily schedule. Mrs. Southworth was getting decidedly worried. To reassure her editor she wrote:

> All along I have been divided between my wish to do the story justice, by developing it in harmonious proportion, and my fear of wearying my readers; however, the remaining chapters will be as stirring as the most exacting reader would require. . . . This story, I repeat, is an experiment. I can easily return to my old style, if this should not please the millions.

(pp. 161-63)

"This is certainly the very best work of my life," wrote Mrs. Southworth. She spoke of "the harmonious proportions of the whole work." She turned down Bonner's offer to buy the copyright. She explained:

> I think there is not a fast horse in your stable that is dearer to you than this best work of my heart and hand and brain is to me. I wrote it, not only for money and fame, but for *humanity*. Indeed, I know that the last motive was the stronger inspiration. I wish to see it in permanent book form and I particularly wish to publish it this Centennial year, as it is eminently a National work.

The American public sustained her in this opinion. A modern authority on best sellers places the sales at over two million copies; and he refers to Mrs. Southworth as "the most popular authoress in the annals of American publishing," and to *Ishmael* as the best selling of her books. (p. 164)

> Mary Noel, *"The People's Darlings," in her* Villains Galore: The Heyday of the Popular Story Weekly, *The Macmillan Company, 1954, pp. 157-68.*

### HELEN WAITE PAPASHVILY (essay date 1956)

[*In the following excerpt, Papashvily examines some of the salient features of Southworth's novels, focusing on her common theme of the deserted wife and her role in creating a new ideal for American women through her fictional heroines.*]

[In mid-nineteenth-century America, a] successful writer for women, more than a journalist or storyteller or instructor or reformer, had to be a high priestess in a growing cult.

Among the earliest who assumed this office was Mrs. E. D. E. N. Southworth. For readers nourished on short tales, sketches, homiletic parables, she provided more sophisticated fare in the form of a full-length novel, *Retribution.* It was, despite a hundred faults, a remarkable work for a novice.

The author appeared in the wings and bungled on and off stage like a careless scene shifter. A useless subplot, that might better have been saved for another book, told the story of the beautiful daughter petted and adored until her father's death revealed she had the fatal drop of Negro blood that condemned her to the auction block and a life of shame, a theme other writers borrowed again and again for the next fifty years. (pp. 58-9)

Mrs. Southworth, unlike many of her contemporaries, did not rely on the easy power and long arm of Divine Justice to resolve her plot. Her statement at the beginning of *Retribution* might have served as a symbolic brief in the case of women vs. men:

> There are intangible crimes carrying in themselves the seeds of their own most bitter punishment—the punishment being nothing apart from or opposed to this sin, but simply the evil principle itself, in its final stage of development. In these instances no law may be able to touch the guilty—no upbraidings of conscience torment him—no visible judgement of heaven fall upon him—yet as surely as the plant is produced from the seed will the punishment be evolved from the sin. . . .

(pp. 60-1)

Undoubtedly Mrs. Southworth did possess many of the qualities that make a good storyteller. She was imaginative, impressionable, inventive. "There are incidents enough in any one of your stories," Mrs. Harriet Beecher Stowe once told her, "to supply a half dozen novels." Mrs. Southworth had a strong sense of drama; she delighted in color and motion—in contrasts of scene and character. With her readers she shared a taste for the sensational, the violent, the supernatural, the macabre, the mysterious. She knew how to combine the shock and suspense of the old Gothic novel with the pathos, sentiment and humor Dickens and his imitators had made fashionable.

Unlike the majority of her contemporaries who attributed human depravity to the individual's willful and deliberate choice, Mrs. Southworth perceived that more complex and cumulative factors might be involved in personality development. She could understand the crime motivated by passion or immediate need. Despite some small snobberies—she shared the democratic ideal. She hated injustice and sympathized with its victims, the poor, the illegitimate, the abused child, the mistreated slave, the overworked servant, the neglected orphan and—most of all—the deserted wife.

In public biography and private conversation Mrs. Southworth revealed very little about her own broken marriage, writing only:

> Let me pass over in silence the stormy and disastrous days of my wretched girlhood, days that stamped upon my brow of youth the furrows of fifty years—let me come at once to the time when I found myself broken in spirit, health, and purse—a widow in fate, but not in fact.

In her novels, however, Mrs. Southworth was not so reticent. Over and over in plot, subplot, and incident she introduced the wife deserted for good or evil reasons and destined by fate, coincidence, accident or plan to make her way in the world. (pp. 114-15)

Mrs. Southworth removed [the husband] entirely. This plan had several advantages. A martyred wife deserved and usual-ly won the sympathy and approval of her circle. She had the prestige even a poor marriage conferred, with few of the responsibilities. She had control of her person, her children, her earnings. She had, if she were circumspect, almost complete freedom of action. When her wanderer finally returned, as he always did abject and repentant, she enjoyed a day of justification and glory and a lifetime of moral superiority.

*Retribution*'s heroine died leaving her unfaithful husband to his own guilty conscience, but Mrs. Southworth never made this mistake again. In her second book, *The Deserted Wife*, Hagar was made of stronger stuff. When *her* husband ran away with a pretty, compliant young woman (later rather shockingly discovered to be his long-lost sister), Hagar, penniless and near death, turned to the concert stage to support her three children. There she won honors, ovations and a handsome fortune. At the moment of her greatest triumph her erring husband, permitted a glimpse of her surrounded by adoring crowds and applauded by royalty, sought her out to confess:

> Hagar! I have not one word to say for myself! Not one excuse to offer for my weakness! Not one syllable to breath in palliation of my fault! Hagar, I am bankrupt!

Words the heroine and apparently the writer and her readers longed to hear. For through ninety volumes Mrs. Southworth dreamed, and millions of women dreamed with her, the recurring dream: I loved him; I trusted him; I gave him everything—and for what? I was ignored, scorned, betrayed, rejected, but he will come back and yearn for what he cast so lightly away.

In Mrs. Southworth's novels those husbands who did not desert their wives went off to the wars, the legislature, the far West or some equally remote corner of the world and stayed there until needed for the dramatic reunion in the closing chapter with their respective, and always competent, wives.

When Mrs. Southworth exhausted all possible ways of removing a husband, she sometimes varied the situation by removing the wife—admittedly more difficult to manage without violating custom. In *The Discarded Daughter* the wife had to submit patiently to her husband's rages, threats, physical violence, his seizure of all her property and personal possessions, and not until this monster buried her alive did the long-suffering woman feel justified in leaving him. Short of equal provocation any deserting wife ran the risk of losing the moral advantage.

Mrs. Southworth also had wives abducted by wicked guardians, brigands, or rejected suitors, cast on desert islands, and lost in impenetrable wilderness. In these situations unprotected women exerted over their male companions the same power that enables virgins to tame unicorns. Only husbands, actual or potential, ever attempted to assault females.

Mrs. Southworth introduced another way to be "a wife in name only," the child bride. Economic necessity made early marriage common in the United States. Travelers from abroad noted, with surprise, mothers at fifteen, grandmothers at thirty, often with partners several years their senior. Mrs. Southworth's own mother at fifteen had married a man of forty-five. Frequent childbearing and the hardships of the frontier exacted a severe toll and the graves of four, five, sometimes more, "loving spouses" flanked a patriarch's tomb.

Mrs. Southworth's child brides were the pampered, petted darlings of compliant and undemanding old men—with a comfortable, independent widowhood in reversion. In *The Curse of Clifton,* Mrs. Southworth drew such a couple:

> . . . I am too old for you. Georgia—I know it, alas! too well, now that it is too late—and yet you did not raise the least objection to becoming my wife, Georgia.
>
> Ha! ha! ha! . . . *Objection!* I was but fifteen years of age when you bribed me to your arms with a set of jewels, and a gold mounted work-box! I was a child, delighted with glittering toys! and fond, yes! *very* fond of the grandfatherly old man that poured them into my lap! Did *that* child-fondness deceive you?
>
> It did, it did! . . . Georgia, I am an old man, as you justly said—*quite* an old man. I have not very long to live, and when I die, Georgia, you will still be a very young woman . . . in ten years you will be but twenty-seven, and is it even likely that I shall live so long as that? No! And after my heart is cold, and my head is laid low, Georgia will be a beautiful young widow—ay, and with a rich jointure, too! I shall take care of that!

Readers apparently saw nothing unwholesome in such a match. Mrs. Hale of *Godey's* thought the characters "skillfully drawn and true to nature." *The Curse of Clifton* proved one of Mrs. Southworth's most popular books, and it joined *Uncle Tom's Cabin* and Charles Dickens' *Bleak House* as one of 1852's three best-selling fiction titles. (pp. 115-18)

How readers could retain from week to week, year to year the involved plots and complicated interrelation of the characters in Mrs. Southworth's books is a mystery greater than any she wrote. In *Vivia* double cousins, half sisters, uncles, guardians, brothers, husbands, both first and second, and assorted mothers, step, foster, spurious and long lost, crowded her pages. In this novel the inevitable deserted wife became a nun and her lost husband a Jesuit providing several glimpses, all sympathetic, of convent life, rather a daring novelty in the year of the Know-Nothing party's greatest popularity.

Mrs. Southworth, an Episcopalian with some Swedenborgian views and a romantic interest in Catholicism, never exhibited the patent piety of the other domestic novelists. "Sweet and beautiful and lovely as is the deathbed of a Christian," Mrs. Southworth wrote in *The Hidden Hand,* "we will not linger too long beside it." On this principle her heroines, hastening from adventure to adventure while acknowledging a Divine Being, recognizing His particular protection, relied on themselves.

If they had a theology, it was one rather personally their own. In *Vivia* that young lady was "the medium of animating, sustaining or redeeming life to all within her sphere . . . when once asked the secret of her power she answered boldly, 'Faith'."

She urged her friends:

> "Believe it—believe it! Have faith. By faith you shall remove mountains, cure diseases, cast out devils, raise the dead . . ."

Vivia's "Faith" seemed not so much faith in God or faith in herself as just faith in Faith—a kind of militant optimism, peculiarly American, in which to want and to believe and to expect and to deserve equaled to receive. (pp. 119-20)

In *Capitola* as in *Vivia,* long-lost relatives discovered each other with monotonous regularity. Several complicated subplots arose from the machinations of a villain, Le Noir, who murdered his brother, imprisoned his sister-in-law in a madhouse, abducted their child and its nurse, sold them into slavery, confiscated the estate, mistreated his ward and schemed to have her fiancé dishonored and sentenced to death by a court-martial. All this, understandably, provided action and well-sustained suspense but the book's real attraction was Capitola, a new kind of heroine.

In the early decades of the nineteenth century, when "praise to the face was an open disgrace" and "handsome was as handsome did," authors wasted little beauty on their heroines. It was enough for Charlotte Temple to be "a tall elegant girl" with blue eyes to match her bonnet and a habit of blushing, while in *The Coquette* "agreeable manners and refined talents" made Eliza Wharton the toast of her county. During the forties and early fifties the meek gentle doves who glided through the pages of the novels were drawn to a single pattern—brow and hair smooth, eyes and head drooping, rosebud mouth pursed. (pp. 126-27)

[General] fragility, unfortunately far too common among women of the period, frequently betokened serious physical disorders. America, even well into the nineteenth century, was a notoriously unhealthy place. Fevers, agues, rheumatism, dyspepsia, flux were chronic national complaints. (p. 127)

But the role of the confirmed invalid "enjoying ill health," the cheerful sufferer so common in the English domestic novels who spent a lifetime on the sofa, did not appeal to American women. They would be radiant, vigorous and active, fresh skinned, clear eyed, gay, daring and confident, perpetually young and always beautiful. It was in this new mold Mrs. Southworth cast her Capitola.

> Thick clustering curls of jet black hair fell in tangled disorder around a broad white and smooth forehead, slender and quaintly arched black eyebrows placed about a pair of mischievous dark grey eyes that sparkled beneath the shade of long thick black lashes; a little turned up nose, and red pouting lips completed the character of a countenance full of fun, frolic, spirit and courage.

There had been "romps" in fiction before but Capitola added a new dimension to the role. Introduced to the reader disguised as a boy, in moments of stress she admonished herself: "Now, Cap, my little man, be a woman and don't stick at trifles." Spirited, beautiful, independent, unafraid, she flouted her guardian, "That look used to strike terror in the heart of the enemy. It doesn't into mine!" She fought a duel with a gentleman who slandered her and shot him full of dried peas; she outwitted Le Noir; she foiled the brigand Black Donald and his henchmen sent to kidnap her; she laughed at everyone including herself, thumbed her nose at her enemies, stuffed herself with tarts and "abhorred sentiment."

Her author loved Capitola:

> How glad I am to get back to my little Cap; for I know very well, reader, just as well as if you had told me, that you have been grumbling for two weeks for the want of Cap. But I could not help it,

for to tell the truth, I was pining after her myself which was the reason that I could not do half justice to the scenes of the Mexican war. Well now let us see what Cap has been doing—what oppressors she has punished—victims she has delivered—in a word, what new heroic adventures she has achieved.

(pp. 128-29)

Not every woman, of course, was ready or able to be a Capitola. In the domestic novel and in real life the misunderstood, mistreated martyr still suffered and endured—and turned defeat into moral victory. But the frankness and humor, the assurance and independence of Capitola set a style that never went out of fashion. (pp. 129-30)

*Self-Made* (later published in two volumes as *Ishmael; or, In The Depths* and *Self-Raised; or, From the Depths*) became one of the ten best-selling books of the century. It was similar in many ways to Mrs. Southworth's other novels. There were five deserted wives and a fiendish villain with a villainess to match him; the full quota of long-lost relatives discovered each other; the usual abductions, mysterious disappearances, shipwrecks and runaway horses provided suspense. A large portion of the second volume was set in an English castle unusually well provided with trap doors, secret stairs, sliding panels and underground dungeons.

Although *Self-Made* had all the conventional trappings of her other books, the theme—the rags-to-riches rise of Ishmael from poverty to a position of honor—was new. Mrs. Southworth touched the heart of a people who believed in themselves and their country and she created a folk hero that, thanks to Alger, still survives.

If Capitola served as an ideal for the new woman, Ishmael was the model for the male. He was not only successful but "good." As an infant, before he could talk or walk, he crawled around the floor and helped his aunt by retrieving her thread, and he figuratively never rose from this position. He was obliging, docile and agreeable. He had blue eyes, fair hair, a pale, delicate complexion, an arch smile and he spoke in sweet, modulated tones. His illegitimacy and his lack of money further diminished his power.

When Ishmael educated himself and became a lawyer, as his first case he defended, without a fee, a deserted wife. As he pleaded for her in court "his face grew radiant as the face of an archangel." It seems obvious he shared another attribute of the heavenly beings, neuter gender. Where ladies were concerned he always knew his place—respectful, polite, devoted and quite contented to love from afar without hope of return. Mrs. Southworth in a preface to the book hoped "the youth of every land would take him for a Guiding Star." (pp. 132-33)

The promise Mrs. Southworth showed in *Retribution* she never fulfilled. It may be that, like many writers, she had one, and only one, story to tell, or perhaps if she had been less a woman, less bound by devotion to her family and gratitude to her rescuer, she might have been more an artist.

Mrs. Southworth once said she had never met a person who did not know her work. Fifty years after her death in 1899 her books, many still in print, commanded an audience. (p. 201)

*Helen Waite Papashvily, in her* All the Happy Endings: A Study of the Domestic Novel in America, the Women Who Wrote It, the Women Who Read It, in the Nineteenth Century, *Harper & Brothers Publishers, 1956, 231 p.*

## NINA BAYM (essay date 1978)

[*In the following excerpt, Baym surveys Southworth's career, highlighting how her use of exaggeration and melodramatic devices resulted in a style that is "shamelessly decorative." Baym also notes certain feminist qualities in Southworth's writing and examines her portrayal of men.*]

Between 1849 and 1860, Southworth wrote eighteen novels, and though they are certainly full of faults, not one of them shows a trace of fatigue. It is certain that she enjoyed her career and the recognition it brought her. She cast her own experience into the form of a heroine's triumph, all the more glorious because of the depths from which she had emerged. These are her own words, as culled from autobiographical statements in the *Saturday Evening Post* and republished in John Hart's 1854 edition of *Female Prose Writers of America:*

> Let me pass over in silence the stormy and disastrous days of my wretched girlhood and womanhood—days that stamped upon my brow of youth the furrows of fifty years—let me come at once to the time when I found myself broken in spirit, health, and purse—a widow in fate but not in fact, with my babes looking up to me for a support I could not give them. It was in these darkest days of my *woman's* life, that my *author's* life commenced. . . .
>
> The circumstances under which this, my first novel, was written, and the success that afterwards attended its publication, is [*sic*] a remarkable instance of "sowing in tears and reaping in joy;" for, in addition to that bitterest sorrow with which I may not make you acquainted—that great life-sorrow, I had many minor troubles. My small salary was inadequate to our comfortable support. My school numbered eighty pupils, boys and girls, and I had the whole charge of them myself. Added to this, my little boy fell dangerously ill. . . . It was too much for me. It was too much for any human being. My health broke down. I was attacked with frequent hemorrhage of the lungs. Still I persevered. I did my best by my house, my school, my sick child, and my publisher. . . . This was indeed the very *melee* of the "Battle of Life." I was forced to keep up struggling when I only wished for death and for rest.
>
> But look you how it terminated. The night of storm and darkness came to an end, and morning broke on me at last—a bright glad morning, pioneering a new and happy day of life. First of all, it was in this very tempest of trouble that my "life-sorrow" was, as it were, carried away—or *I* was carried away from brooding over it. Next, my child, contrary to my own opinion and the doctor's, got well. Then my book, written in so much pain, published besides in a newspaper, and, withal, being the *first* work of an obscure and penniless author, was, contrary to all probabilities, accepted by the first publishing house in America, was published and (subsequently) noticed with high favour even by the cautious English reviews. Friends crowded around me—offers for contributions poured upon me. And I, who six months before had been poor, ill, forsaken, slandered, *killed* by sorrow, privation, toil, and

friendliness [*sic* Hart, for friendlessness], found myself born as it were into a new life; found independence, sympathy, friendship, and honour, and an
occupation in which I could delight. All this came
very suddenly, as after a terrible storm, a sun burst.

I quote this passage at length to show that Southworth not
only took pride and pleasure in being rich and famous, but
that she had no fear in saying so and that her popularity did
not suffer for her fearlessness. Southworth was not a moralizing writer and her plots lack the educational organization
characteristic of much fiction of the fifties. But one message
does animate her fiction—do not be afraid. Her fearless heroines, and the fearless author behind them, conveyed this message to many hundreds of thousands of feminine readers.

One should note some characteristic habits of expression and
attitude in the passage quoted above. There is first the avidity
with which Southworth appropriates and employs conventional rhetoric: showing in tears and reaping in joy, the battle
of life, morning after night, sun burst after storm. The intensity that she puts into these platitudes pushes them beyond formula into felt experience; she uses clichés when she uses
them, not to avoid experience but to control it. There is also
her habit of weighting each moment with the passions of a
lifetime; the bitterest sorrow, the great life-sorrow of the second paragraph, becomes "life-sorrow," ironically put in
quotes and swept away in the third. This habit of immersing
her characters and readers in the moment without thereby
committing them to it conveys the sense of character at once
caught up in life and yet detached from it, a sense of resiliency
that need not be purchased by avoiding experience. Finally,
note her ready exaggeration: "furrows of fifty years," "too
much for me," "*killed* by sorrow," "after a terrible storm, a
sun burst." Life comes across as full of excitement, drama,
force, great highs, and great lows, every minute intensely interesting. It is really no wonder that her readers went away
rejoicing and that each of her books exceeded its predecessor
in popularity.

Although Southworth was by no means a great writer or a
great stylist, like the other authors of woman's fiction she certainly had her own style. In her works there is a consistency
of elements such that all—story line, characterization, language, message—reflect her boldness and energy by their pre-
vading ornateness. Southworth is a writer whose work is
shamelessly decorative. A modern reader might interpret all
this embellishment as equivalent to that gushing rhetoric
which is supposed to be particularly feminine. It seems to me
rather to represent the genderless impulse that plain people
have toward exuberant decoration as a counterstatement to
a bare life. In an age of feminine restraint, such exuberance
would be decidedly unladylike—thus Sarah Hale admonished her (in *Woman's Record,* quoted by Hart in the 1854
edition of his anthology) for going "beyond the limits prescribed by correct taste or good judgment." Southworth's
writing constitutes a flamboyant rejection of the expected literary behavior of women writers. Not for her were such feminine values as the spare, the self-effacing, the decorous, the
understated, or the unobtrusive. (pp. 111-14)

Southworth's habit of exaggeration means that none of her
characters can be called realistic, although this same habit
also frequently makes them seem alive. Within the constraints of the woman's formula, her work contains a prolifer-
ation of feminine characterizations. Nothing could be further
from her work than the reductive and tedious male dicho-

tomizing of women into evil-dark and angelic-fair (a polarity
actually rare in most woman's fiction of the period); Southworth's women are all shapes, sizes, and colors, all equally
beautiful. Some of her types are conventional, but others are
thoroughly individual. Contrasting to this prodigality of females, she has only two basic representations of the male,
both unamiable: the tyrannical and hypocritical father or fa-
ther-surrogate and the impetuous, self-centered suitor. (The
popular *Self-Made* featured a paragon hero, but it is an exception to the tenor of her fiction.) In the fourteen novels
from the fifties that form the subject of my analysis, I have
found only one thoroughly good man, the father in *The Lost
Heiress.* Most are of limited intelligence and overwhelming
vanity. There are wicked and scheming women who cause
trouble for the heroines, but these women are subordinate to
the men whose folly licenses their wickedness. The major, repeated, varied story is that of the struggle of good women
against the oppressions and cruelties, covert and blatant, of
men. Among Southworth's favorite situations are daughters
disinherited by jealous or materialistic fathers; hasty, secret,
and disastrous marriages into which inexperienced girls are
forced by importunate suitors; misunderstood wives abused,
harassed, or abandoned by self-righteous but deluded husbands.

After her first couple of novels Southworth settled into a
structural formula. She began with a sequence of terrific
melodrama, in which a child and her mother are separated.
The child is brought up in a "home" that travesties the
ideal—it is patched together out of the fragments of a family
and, far from being a female preserve, is dominated by a male.
He, ruling in what culture supposes to be the woman's
sphere, gives her no room to live or breathe and is nothing
like the culture's ideal of man. The man in the house—
passionate, immature, unreasonable, uncontrolled, and un-
controllable—is rather a rampaging beast than a protector,
provider, or model of the rational will. In his obsession with
property, with fantasies of owning and transferring estates
that often actually belong to the women, he rather deprives
his women of security than provides them with it.

The goal of the heroine in such a situation is far more primitive than "woman's rights"; it is to construct the traditional
sphere that some woman's righters found constraining and
wanted to leave behind. Southworth's women want to make
a place for themselves where men can be distanced and controlled. Given the fact that men have all the advantages at the
outset, the realization of this wish is enormously difficult. Ultimately it called for the transformation of the male so that
he saw woman as a human being entitled to possession of herself, to respectful treatment, rather than an object for use,
pleasure, or exploitation. He will come to see women differently only if he is deeply impressed by the example of a "true
woman," which, to Southworth, is nothing more than a true
human being. When he realizes how he has underestimated
women, man will be so overwhelmed at his previous stupidity
that he will become in a basic sense a new man. This new man
is the embodiment of woman's image of ideal man. Only
when such men exist can there be homes, families, and
woman's place. When woman has her place, it will be time
to decide whether that place is fully satisfying.

Taken one way, these novels imply a glorification of the cult
of domesticity; taken another, they represent a severe criticism, because they show that the defective male nature makes
the ideal of the separate sphere generally unrealizable. But ei-

ther way, woman's need to struggle for her survival and her dignity was the base of Southworth's writing; and if in novel after novel she showed woman gaining this victory, she might be conveying something more than entertainment to her vast feminine readership. Given her popularity in the *Ledger,* which was not a woman's magazine, men must have read her fiction in great numbers too; perhaps her work helped both sexes to look on women more favorably.

Southworth used her formula in a series of ingenious variations. She set most of her fiction in rural Virginia and Maryland and embellished it with highly wrought descriptions of landscape. She set forth the manners of a rude aristocracy and the traditions of a rough society down to poor white and slave. She depicted magnificent plantations and log cabins and the kinds of life lived in each. In her own time she was especially praised for her depictions of slaves, and they do seem strikingly free from stereotype: they are strong-minded, self-respecting, highly verbal, intelligent, versatile people; not rebellious, craven, childlike, or shaped according to pro- or antislavery sentiments; they are beings in every way the equal of the whites, making the best of an abominable situation with wit and grace. (Technically a southerner, Southworth was always against slavery and says so repeatedly in her fiction. Her "best" white characters always free their slaves.)

Her novels are usually several hundred pages long, partly because of the large cast of minor characters, partly from stylistic redundancy, and partly because each work develops the stories of two or more heroines simultaneously. She could veer from absurd melodrama to strong naturalism in a single novel, indeed in a single sentence. A wife is tricked into a convent and into leaving her son to be brought up as her evil sister-in-law's child in *Vivia;* but in the same work the daily routines of a lame young widow trying to run a farm and support herself and three elderly, useless female relatives is followed from crop-planting to credit-forestalling, cooking, and ironing. Southworth did not reject false or purloined wills, forged or intercepted or lost letters, storms, floods, fires, droughts, kidnapings, mock murders, feigned marriages and suicides, carriage accidents, shipwrecks, poisonings. Yet her imagination is too spacious and robust to be called gothic, and similar incidents appear in most of the fiction of her time; she differs from the more realistic authors in the frequency of such melodramatic devices, and from the melodramatists in that she uses them in a spirit of fun rather than of high seriousness. (pp. 115-18)

> *Nina Baym, "E. D. E. N. Southworth and Caroline Lee Hentz," in her* Woman's Fiction: A Guide to Novels by and about Women in America, 1820-1870, *Cornell University Press, 1978, pp. 110-39.*

## ALFRED HABEGGER (essay date 1981)

[*In the following excerpt, Habegger examines what he terms the "radical interpretation of female life" in* The Hidden Hand. *Focusing on the orphan-heroine theme of the novel, Habegger addresses the struggle between the sexes in nineteenth-century America by highlighting the effects of masculinization on the protagonist, Capitola.*]

Except for isolated and aging American women—those uneducated consumers of light literature who have never been properly taught the act of reading—***The Hidden Hand*** hardly exists. No recent study of nineteenth-century American literature mentions it, except for Nina Baym's exhaustive survey

of novels by women, *Woman's Fiction,* which gives the book a very perfunctory nod [see excerpt dated 1978]. The most noteworthy explorer of woman's writing in America, Ann Douglas, has not investigated ***The Hidden Hand.*** Even the recent seven-hundred-page tome by Sandra M. Gilbert and Susan Gubar, *The Madwoman in the Attic: The Woman Writer and the Nineteenth-Century Literary Imagination,* is silent on the novel, though it deals in an original yet classic way with a "crazy" woman who must be hidden away.

Southworth's madwoman in ***The Hidden Hand*** is the usual type—a beautiful and docile woman in white. But her daughter is a jaunty, tomboyish daredevil completely devoid of "sensitive perceptions" and "fine intuitions." This unusual nineteenth-century heroine has, I venture to say, a claim on readers' attention even in 1981: her name is Capitola Black; she confronts the threat of rape; she tricks her minister into thinking she's conducting a liaison with a man; she uses profanity and fights a duel; she acknowledges a "pit" in her name. Southworth's basic and brilliant maneuver, moreover, is to begin the novel with the old gothic machinery—a beautiful blonde victim, a group of malign men, a setting redolent of ancient abuses, sacrifices, and superstitions—and then to subvert the genre by introducing this streetwise and self-reliant female prankster. What's more, the novel has a coherent politics: the madwoman's orphaned daughter overthrows evil men and redresses old wrongs in the name of the Declaration of Independence and the Revolution of 1830. Most important of all, this daughter who would avenge her mother's wrongs and solve the problem of woman's vulnerability to man actually passes for a boy at the beginning of the novel. ***The Hidden Hand*** offers a cross-dressing fantasy that represents a major, mainstream response by author and readers to a felt female weakness. (pp. 198-99)

***The Hidden Hand*** has a very coarse look to it: its people, after all, are stock types who nevertheless speak out of character whenever it suits the author. Yet the book sabotages literary convention in a fine and crazy way, achieving an invigorating anarchic comedy and a thematic coherence rare in popular fiction. Capitola Black is in fact none other than the long-lost twin sister of Huckleberry Finn, our other innocent orphan whose inability to see any sense in social contracts most people take for granted generates a life-giving, liberating comedy. The difference is, Southworth's only good novel constitutes a brilliant, radical interpretation of female life. Her interpretation is not quite the same as the going doctrines one hears from the small and carefully defined groups who call themselves radical feminists today. ***The Hidden Hand*** is, or was, radicalism of the center, not the fringe. The fringe is easy to deal with, but popular radicalism is the one thing the Serious Literature Profession long ago agreed never to countenance.

To grasp the ways in which ***The Hidden Hand*** was both new and old, it is necessary to take a brief look at the central figure in so-called sentimental fiction from Samuel Richardson on: the poor but high-minded young woman who leaves or is torn from her home, then struggles to survive with honor in a world that proves much rougher than she had ever dreamed. Although there is a big difference between "seduction novels" like *Pamela* and *The Coquette* and less scandalous Victorian novels like *The Wide, Wide World* and *The Lamplighter,* both types of fiction told a story about a good orphan-girl who undergoes exemplary trials. This was *the* basic formula for nineteenth-century women readers.

The popularity of the orphan-heroine reflected female aspirations and anxieties of the time. These feelings were a consequence of the process of modernization; ancient agreements as to what women and men were supposed to be and how they were meant to coexist were steadily lapsing. The weakening of male supremacy meant more autonomy for women, but also more insecurity. The dissolution of reciprocal obligations between the sexes made women feel vulnerable in a peculiarly modern way. In the American 1850s, women's aspirations for more freedom had grown to be very strong, but possibly no stronger than their fear of what freedom might expose them to. This mixture of aspiration and fear was embodied in the character of the orphan-heroine, deprived of her home yet determined to do well. As Nina Baym has shown, all but a few of the American-authored women's novels in the decade preceding the publication of *The Hidden Hand* told of a girl or young woman who abruptly learns that she must support herself, then struggles to do so without compromising her extremely high ethical standards. The enormous popularity of *Ruth Hall, 'Lena Rivers, The English Orphans,* **The Curse of Clifton,** *Queechy,* and *Beulah,* along with *The Wide, Wide World* and *The Lamplighter,* cannot be explained by their sentimentality, whatever that now largely useless word implies, but by their symbolic representation of the basic contemporary female struggle. In 1854 Marion Harland wrote a book whose simple title sums up the appeal of women's fiction in the 1850s—*Alone.*

Alone is the word that describes the plight of the infant heroine and her widowed mother at the beginning of **The Hidden Hand,** most of which constitutes an analysis of their opposite ways of surviving solitary exposure. Of the two, the mother has been alone in the worst way throughout her adult life. She was married at the age of fifteen and widowed soon after, though not before becoming pregnant. Her brother-in-law does not want her to give birth to any heirs; and so, when twins are born, a girl and a stillborn boy, the brother-in-law is given the dead baby boy as proof there will be no heirs. Together, the midwife and mother conceal the existence of the baby girl from the evil brother-in-law. Meanwhile he imprisons the young mother in his attic, where she remains for fifteen years. She is pale, beautiful, melancholy, and—anticipating Wilkie Collins's *The Woman in White* by a year—always wears white. Of course, Southworth does not give the reader all of this information at once, but rather seeks to generate the appropriate gothic mystifications and frissons. Chapter Two, for instance, consists of a narration of the birthing scene as remembered by the aged, dying midwife. This midwife does not know or reveal the identity of the unfortunate mother, whose face and right hand (hence the book's title) were swathed with "black crepe" during her labor.

The girl baby gets her mother's name, Capitola, and grows up in New York assuming that she is an orphan. She lives in Rag Alley, the stock location in the 1850s for urban ruffianism, as it was called. Her guardians then vanish, and Capitola finds herself at the age of twelve or so in the same position as her mother before her—all alone, with no means of support. However, life in the big city has taught Capitola to be resourceful, and the girl preserves herself by a stratagem not available to her beautiful, genteel mother: Capitola becomes a boy, and thus brings to life her stillborn male twin. Wearing a cap and pantaloons, she supports herself on the street, chiefly by hawking newspapers but also by performing any approximately honest service. That Capitola's male imperson-

ation was an extreme act may not seem obvious to the modern reader; certainly, it was not obvious to the girl herself. But the extent to which she has violated the acceptable limits of behavior becomes more than clear when a policeman notices her long hair under her cap, realizes that she is a girl in disguise, and arrests her. Testifying in her own defense, Capitola explains that, regardless of her tomboyish nature, she had no choice but to assume a male disguise. It was a matter of survival:

> While all the ragged boys I knew could get little jobs to earn bread, I, because I was a girl, was not allowed to carry a gentleman's parcel, or black his boots, or shovel the snow off a shopkeeper's pavement, or put in coal, or do anything that I could do just as well as they.

Only after becoming a boy could Capitola be "happy and prosperous"—that is, until her long hair betrayed her.

It's clear that the key to Capitola's initial success in life is her readiness to undergo masculinization, a process that shapes her personality as well as her attire. For her, street life in Rag Alley is the sort of test that unsupervised boyhood has often been understood to be in America: it either destroys you or makes a man out of you. Capitola is not destroyed and thus necessarily acquires a number of unwomanly qualities: she is slangy, irreverent, blunt, anti-authoritarian, mischievous, adventurous, active, and wholly self-confident. The big question, of course, is: what will she do when she enters womanhood? How far can a tomboy go once she stops wearing boy's clothes? Nine years earlier Nathaniel Hawthorne had brought out a novel in which a mischievous and disobedient seven-year-old female imp had been "humanized" by developing a capacity for sorrow. Dozens of other novels had been written about girls who learned that the way to become true women was to subdue their wayward impulses, never speak sarcastically, forgive their enemies. In *The Lamplighter* little Gerty achieves "the greatest of earth's victories, a victory over herself." Some of Southworth's earlier novels, **Retribution** and **The Curse of Clifton,** for instance, had also come out strong for victory over oneself. But most of her novels had always shown a strong sympathy for heterodox women, and now, in **The Hidden Hand,** as Southworth works out the problem of Capitola's socialization, the author answers the old question in a new and daring way: the masculinized girl can go just as far as she damn well pleases.

Southworth works out this solution by presenting Capitola with an extreme challenge. The girl is taken from New York's rough freedom and modernity to Appalachian Virginia. This move adds two new threats to her independence—the restrictions of authoritarian aristocracy and the perils of gothic mountain outlawry—and thus promises to force Capitola to become a model young lady. Furthermore, her new protector, Ira Warfield, also known as Old Hurricane, is that familiar type in eighteenth- and nineteenth-century literature—the crusty, good-natured, old-school tyrant. Old Hurricane is a gentleman, a slave-owner, and a former army-officer; all his slaves and servants are in terror of him. Aware of Capitola's real identity, he is determined to make a lady out of her. Hence, although he has saved her from possible imprisonment in New York, he represents another grave threat to her freedom. There can be no doubt that Southworth appreciated this threat: the novel appeared only two years before the Civil War, at a time of bitter sectional hostility, and Southworth, although she was Southern bred, opposed both slavery and secession. (pp. 200-03)

What is so inspiriting and comic about *The Hidden Hand* is that Old Hurricane can't make a dent on his young ward. Every time he attempts to discipline or intimidate her, she overcomes him with a defiant insouciance he simply can't handle. When he learns that she has disobeyed his command never to ride beyond a certain stream, he rages at her: " 'Miss! how *dare* you have the impudence to face me, much less the—the—the assurance!—the effrontery!—the audacity!— the *brass* to speak to me!' " Capitola is not impressed by this style of intimidation, combining outraged fury with a genteel parade of synonyms. A few days later, when her protector returns home after dark, she mocks his fury: " 'Sir, how *dare* you have the impudence to *face* me, much less the—the— the—the brass! the *bronze*! the copper! to speak to me?' " She ridicules his solicitous care: " '*didn't* you know the jeopardy in which you placed yourself by riding out alone at this hour? Suppose three or four great runaway negresses had sprung out of the bushes and—and—and—'. " Old Hurricane soon realizes that there is no controlling a Victorian heroine who laughs at the fate worse than death, and he complains, again resorting to his thesaurus: " 'She is such a wag, such a droll, such a mimic; disobeys me in such a mocking, cajoling, affectionate way!' "

Capitola is surrounded by men who try to lay a hand on her. Back in New York, one of her motives for cross-dressing was a need to elude "bad boys and bad men." In a chapter titled "The Peril and the Pluck of Cap" the heroine encounters the most dreadful terror of ladies—dark ruffians hiding under her bed. Instead of panicking, Capitola steels herself to engineer their capture. Later, she manages to trap and injure the gang-leader himself, Black Donald, whose one desire has

*A portrait of Southworth.*

been to get Capitola. Donald represents a real threat, as his gang is known to have raped "a lone woman and her daughter." In trapping Donald, Capitola achieves her dream, for, like Tom Sawyer, her big fantasy has involved, not romance, but the capture of an infamous outlaw. Capitola also tricks the minister who tries to teach her proper Christian deportment. She actually leads him to believe her seducer is hidden in the closet, then opens the door on a little dog. The most dangerous men in Capitola's life are her villainous relatives, the Le Noirs, father and son. It was Colonel Le Noir who killed her father and has kept her mother secretly imprisoned. He and his son, Craven, now seek Capitola's life. Without fully realizing her danger, she repeatedly outwits and humiliates them. Once, after escaping Craven's clutches, Capitola "put her thumb to the side of her nose, and whirled her fingers into a semi-circle, in a gesture more expressive than elegant." Southworth disowns such decidedly unladylike behavior: "Reader! I do not defend, far less approve, poor Cap! I only tell her story and describe her as I have seen her, leaving her to your charitable interpretation." But in view of the great comic elan with which Capitola turns the tables on a number of stodgy, dangerous, or oppressive men, the author's disclaimer seems happily insincere. (p. 204)

The basic difference between *The Hidden Hand* and all other books by the "damned female scribblers," as Hawthorne called his competitors, shows up in the portrayal of secondary female characters. As a rule, these novels had a beautiful, haughty, generally wicked rival who caused the good heroine no end of heartache. . . . *The Hidden Hand* broke the mold: instead of pairing its forward heroine with a haughty destroyer, the book lines her up with a number of helpless blonde victims.

Beautiful Clara Day is only one among these foils. The scene in which Miss Black and Miss Day exchange clothes, so that the former can save the latter, has an obvious symbolic meaning: to escape victimization, the blonde beauty must dress like the tomboy. Another of the novel's helpless victims is named Marah, Hebrew for *bitter* according to Southworth. Marah is bitter because she has been deserted by a husband who thinks, mistakenly, that she has been unfaithful to him. The wrongly deserted wife is the most emotion-charged figure in Southworth's fiction; in another novel, *The Deserted Wife,* she is named Hagar, after Abraham's rejected concubine, and she eventually triumphs over her husband. Southworth's obsession with this type came from hard experience, as she was abandoned by her husband and forced to go to work to support herself and her child. Similarly, her mother, who at the age of fifteen had married a forty-five year old man, was left a widow before reaching twenty. Southworth saw nothing funny in the situation of the young wife married to an old man. What this situation meant in her novels was nothing less than the entrapment of a girl before she is old enough to understand what's what. Thus, another reason why Marah means bitter is that this woman was only sixteen when she married a man three times her age. Most important of all is the fact that inaugurates the whole cycle of suffering the novel records: Capitola's victimized mother was "scarcely fourteen" when she married a much older man. A concern for victimized young mothers appears everywhere in nineteenth-century literature, often uniting a sweetly self-conscious ultra-feminine sense of sisterhood with a programmatic hatred of men. The unusual thing about *The Hidden Hand* is its pragmatism and lack of animus. If femininity is so weak, Southworth appears to say, let's imagine how things would go if women did what Capitola does and became masculinized.

That Southworth had the daring to make this simple deduction, to consider femininity itself simply a dead end, seems evident in the novel's description of the insane asylum where Capitola's mother is eventually confined. This asylum is the ultimate form of the prison of womanhood: its name is the Calm Retreat; it is "very exclusive, very quiet, very aristocratic"; it looks like a "luxurious country seat." The cells, arranged on either side of a long hall, are actually "small bed rooms." Traverse Rocke, the young man who rescues the mother, associates the inmates, chiefly women, with Marah Rocke and Clara Day: " 'even a looking-glass would be a great benefit to those poor girls, for I remember that even Clara, in her violent grief, and mother in her life-long sorrow, never neglected their looking-glass, and personal appearance.' " The doctor in charge never once doubts the story told him by Colonel Le Noir—that Capitola's mother is a seduced girl who has gone mad. This doctor is a gallant old Frenchman who addresses her with an adroit courtesy that frustrates her attempts to tell the truth about herself. When she insists on being called Madame rather than Mademoiselle, he suavely answers: " 'Ten thousand pardons, Madame! but if Madame will always look so young! so beautiful! can I ever remember that she is a widow?' " It seems fitting that this woman should be released from her gallant old-world jailor and his exclusive insane asylum by a plain and mild young man who has the simplicity to imagine that she may be telling the truth.

If masculinization is the remedy for women, then this good young man, Traverse Rocke, reveals Southworth's remedy for men—desexualization. Traverse is obviously a sissy. Brought up solely by the long-suffering Marah, his great and sufficient virtue is that he understands women and other victims. It takes a milksop to rescue the madwoman for the same reason that it takes a tomboy to triumph over woman's oppressors. The reason is, sex itself is the enemy. Most of the characters belonging to the older generation in the novel seem gorgeously in rut or in estrus, and inevitably sort themselves into oppressors and victims. The younger characters have no serious class, status, or gender divisions. When they pair off at the end, it is evident they will achieve the successful marriages that eluded their parents. Southworth, in fact, goes the whole way: she shows no interest whatever in the romance-aspect of these marriages, though she makes it more than clear at the end that both brides, Capitola and Clara Day, will be sure to keep their husbands in check. Thus, the novel dramatizes in an unusually open way a basic means by which American civilization has enabled women to coexist with a sex that is simultaneously stronger, more aggressive, and more libidinous: the women become men and the men become neuters.

At the very end, however, Southworth doesn't seem to be satisfied by a universe of neutered men. Like modern city-dwelling environmentalists who provide for the preservation of predatory animals in remote enclaves, Southworth allows the most untamed and virile man of all—Black Donald, jailed and condemned to die—to escape just before Capitola marries her trustworthy but unexciting pantywaist. The basic reason why Black Donald must escape is that he is a magnificent man:

> He stood six feet eight inches in his boots, and was stout and muscular in proportion. He had a well-formed, stately head, fine aquiline features, dark complexion, strong, steady dark eyes, and an abundance of long, curling black hair and beard. . . .

In spite of this statuesque appearance, Donald has the same perverse polymorphism as Capitola herself: he disguises himself variously as a slave, Quaker pedlar, and revival preacher. He is said to be "the very demon himself!—he does not *disguise* he *transforms* himself!" . . . Sentenced to death, Black Donald weighs heavily on Capitola, partly because of her principles against taking human life, even more because the outlaw embodies her own wayward freedom, but chiefly because he has the male wildness which she has had to defeat. Her final act, before her marriage, is to convey a file to Donald and provide him with money and a horse.

Like so many of Capitola's actions in the novel, this final deed satisfies justice yet violates the law. This paradox captures the spirit and partly explains the enormous appeal of this wild domestic novel. In Southworth's eyes, law and tradition have an inherent cruelty; only a fantastically unfettered (but good, hence female) individual can do justice and love mercy. *The Hidden Hand* is escapist in every possible sense, especially in dramatizing a glorious revolutionary triumph over ancient disciplines. There can be no doubt that Southworth was aware of her revolutionary theme: she makes it clear that Capitola's grandparents—that is, the parents of the imprisoned mother—"had both perished on the scaffold in the sacred cause of liberty" in France in 1830. Elsewhere, just before the first recounting of the sufferings of Capitola's mother, mention is made of the Declaration of Independence. The story of Capitola is thus, among other things, the story of revolution triumphant after penultimate defeat. The explanation of its final triumph lies not in a disciplined cadre of revolutionaries or in organizations of any kind whatever but in the scrappy and disobedient individual whose only motto is, *Don't tread on me.* This is the book that no student of American literature has ever taken seriously. (pp. 206-09)

*Alfred Habegger, "A Well Hidden Hand," in* Novel: A Forum on Fiction, *Vol. 14, No. 3, Spring, 1981, pp. 197-212.*

**JOANNE DOBSON**   (essay date 1988)

[*In the following excerpt from her introduction to* The Hidden Hand, *Dobson examines Southworth's handling of cultural stereotypes and characterization of women in her novels, focusing on her most popular heroine, Capitola.*]

Like others of her female contemporaries, Southworth . . . has failed to satisfy the cultured of our day, and, until very recently, has appeared in the modern literary arena only as the butt for such dismissive epithets as Herbert Smith's designation of her work as "the veritable archetype of the sentimental." "Perhaps an enlightened readership grows up, sighing," he elaborates, "by weaning itself from the bathos of E. D. E. N. Southworth to cut its teeth on the irony and psychology of Henry James." The fallacies here are widespread in much twentieth-century literary analysis of nineteenth-century women writers. Critics influenced by the precepts of modernist literature tend to favor exclusively a literature that *is* ironic and psychological over one possessing other time-honored qualities of the novel, such as adventure, romance, broad comedy, and—yes—even sentiment. Further, they tend to reduce to one characteristic a body of fiction which, when viewed in its cultural context, can be seen, like South-worth's, to be complex.

With Southworth, as with many of her female contemporaries, the question of literary quality arises immediately. "But is it any good?" is the first question, Jane Tompkins reminds us, elicited by any mention of the long forgotten texts of nineteenth-century women writers. Let me make it clear from the start: Southworth was not Henry James, nor would she have had any desire to be. She had neither the inclination nor the privilege. Her forte was not the mastery of stylistics nor the subtle delineation of human complexities. Rather, it was storytelling. She was a popular novelist of skill and endurance, whose strength lay in her ability to render cultural fantasies vividly, in all their fascinating and self-contradictory complexity. Her strengths and weaknesses had a common derivation in her desire—in fact pressing need—to please the multitude; her popularity was literally her bread and butter. Southworth's attempts to satisfy the cultured, if by cultured we mean the literary elite, are practically inconsequential in any long-range assessment of the significance of her work.

In *The Hidden Hand* Southworth is at her satiric best: a brilliantly comedic popular analyst of cultural stereotypes and expectations. In certain other novels, particularly the early ones, she, in a less light-hearted manner, adeptly and energetically manipulates those same stereotypes and expectations, particularly as they relate to the stunted and deprived lives of women, to create an idiosyncratic and still fascinating melodramatic literary universe. She peoples her novels with displaced and abused women. As her titles envision them, her female protagonists are deserted wives, discarded daughters, lost heiresses, missing brides. Displaced and abused as they are, however, these women are for the most part strong, or able to learn strength. Although Southworth's advocacy for women certainly has feminist implications for modern readers, her books did not campaign for the rights of women in the openly and publicly political manner we usually define as feminist. Rather she felt and recorded a deep personal sense of outrage at the oppressions and deprivations of her own life and the lives of the women she saw around her. Her desire to advocate a dignified humanity for women found expression in a fictional arena that did not aspire to literary realism, as we now define that term, but instead reveled in the innumerable imaginative possibilities made available by an overtly fictive universe.

Such an approach has its pitfalls, however. In Southworth's later work her repeated use of conventional depictions of women for the most part came to lack the vitality—the color and fire—of her early novels. As she grew older, more conventionally religious, and less outraged, she looked back on her earlier, more passionate novels with something like embarrassment. In her seventies she wrote to her daughter Lottie about a visit from a Professor Powers: "He told me the first book he ever read was my *Deserted Wife* which his father a Babtist [sic] minister brought him from Washington. I told him it was a wild story, the work of my younger days. . . . I told him I thought more of my failures in fidelity to the gift and the giver than I did of success."

It is for those "wild stories," however, that we are indebted to Southworth. For if they do not give us a precise and realistic image of women's actual lives in society, they do provide us with a vigorous sense of women's feelings about their existence, and with delightful examples of just what kind of compensatory fantasies served to ease their sense of displacement and loss. Of these fantasies, the heroine of *The Hidden Hand,* Capitola Le Noir, otherwise known as Cap Black, is the most enticing.

An irreverent ruffian in her early teens, Cap describes herself as "a damsel-errant in quest of adventures." Kidnapped as an infant, Cap has spent her childhood years in Rag Alley, a New York City slum, and her early adolescence in fending for herself on the streets. When her guardian finds her there, she is disguised as a boy, selling newspapers and running odd jobs. Cap has been countersocialized, having, like a street boy, "never been taught obedience or been accustomed to subordination." After she is "rescued" and taken back to her ancestral Virginia, she finds a conventional woman's life stultifying: she is "bored to death" she says "decomposing above ground for want of having my blood stirred." So Cap goes out, as the respectable female reader might long to do but could not, "in search of adventures." Needless to say, the little adventurer finds herself involved in many escapades. She rescues damsels in distress, captures bandits, fights duels, all with insouciance and style. (pp. xi-xiii)

Southworth was a popular writer in the most accurate sense of the word. Not only did her work find continual favor with an enormous popular audience, but she herself wrote from the vantage point of the people, always bearing in mind the presence of her audience and their desires and preferences. In 1863, when composing a novel more moralistic than her others, she informed her publisher that although she usually wrote for the popular taste, "in this I have a higher aim—popular good." She assured him, however, "I can easily return to my old style, if this should not please the millions." Conventional pieties, personal passions, and radical departures from gentility intermingle in Southworth's work with an almost confounding sincerity, reflecting not only the author's intimate involvement with the values of her society, but also the complexity and self-contradictions inherent in that culture. She played upon the emotions and fantasies of her audience so very skillfully because in many ways she was one of them. Not self-defined as an artist and not self-consciously transcendent of popular experience, she felt always a profound bond and empathy between herself and her readers. She knew what her audience wanted and she gave it to them. She was a crowd pleaser. If that epithet serves to damn her, she might gladly have considered herself among the damned.

Southworth was not simply a passive recorder of cultural complexities, however. While reflective of popular attitudes, she also reflected upon them. As a talented writer and a woman passionate about the injustices perpetrated upon women in a society that allowed them little other than symbolic power, she inevitably helped shape the popular perception of women's status. Through the skilled manipulation of masculine and feminine stereotypes in her writing, she revealed numerous irreconcilable elements packed within the complex and contradictory concept of gender. Her work focuses almost exclusively on gender and gender relations, and its phenomenal popularity is indicative of the ways in which a culture monitors and modifies itself in this as in other areas. Although I disagree with Alfred Habegger's assertion that *The Hidden Hand* is Southworth's only good novel, his description of the "coherent politics" of this story as a "radicalism of the center, not the fringe" is precise and accurate [see excerpt dated 1981]. Presenting a critique coming from within rather than imposed from without, Southworth bequeaths to us throughout her work a lively record of a nineteenth-century American fascination with the nature and possibilities of gender which enhances the hard data of the historical account.

In an era characterized both by feminist agitation (Southworth's first novel was published in 1849, the year after the first Women's Rights Convention in Seneca Falls) and intensive cultural indoctrination regarding woman's exclusively moral nature, selflessness, and domestic inclinations, the popularity of Capitola, the "damsel-errant," points to just what it was about women that both titillated and terrified the American public. Cap was just one in a long line of powerful Southworth heroines, however. From the mousy to the magnificent, for over forty years Southworth's protagonists defined independence, integrity, and personal strength as central to a woman's existence, and these characteristics flourish with particular intensity in atmospheres specifically hostile to them. (pp. xxi-xxii)

Woman's "power" is the theme that ties together Southworth's enormous oeuvre. From her first novel *Retribution,* she presents an ongoing investigation of an extensive range of strengths and ambitions embodied in a glorious variorum of female characters. Although often polarized into good and evil characters, her women, especially in the early work, do not fit neat patterns. Larger-than-life characters such as the delightfully narcissistic "wild Irish girl" Britannia O'Riley and the amazonian Gertrude Lion, otherwise known as the "Gerfalcon," appear as early as Southworth's third book, *The Mother-in-Law.* The women occasionally have a mythic aura; Gertrude is described as having "the majesty of Juno and the freedom of Diana." The feminist Britomarte Conyers "the man hater, the woman's champion, the marriage renouncer . . . magnificent in the sense of conscious strength, ardor and energy with which she impressed all" is the product of Southworth's later imagination in *Fair Play* and *How He Won Her.* These works, originally published serially in 1865-66 under the title of "Britomarte, The Man Hater," are the two-volume saga of a woman who, "if law and custom had allowed her freer action and a fairer field, . . . would have influenced the progress of humanity and filled a place in history."

More typical are the less flamboyant but nonetheless powerful heroines created in the conventional, altruistic mode. The plain and mild Hester Dent in *Retribution* is a young woman with an abiding sense of integrity and responsibility, whose primary concern, even in the face of death, is the manumission of her slaves. *The Mother-in-Law* continues what is to be an enduring mode of feminine characterization with the unselfish Susan Somerville, introduced as a young woman who "calmly and deeply enjoyed her life in every vein." Susan comforts and supports Louis Stuart-Gordon, the man she deeply loves, through a number of traumatic experiences, even though he is divorced (temporarily as it turns out) from a woman whom he desperately loves. Betrothed to him at last, Susan renounces her claim magnanimously when she realizes Louis still loves his lost wife.

Malevolent women characters also abound. *Retribution* investigates a beautiful woman's abuse of her sexual attractiveness. The first step in the megalomaniacal career of the ambitious Julliette Summers is to steal Hester Dent's husband. Years later, having become the powerful mistress of a grand duke, she ends her life beheaded in a European coup d'état.

For Southworth, the possession and use of power is not inappropriate for women; it is the abuse of power she deplores, particularly as it deprives others of the exercise of free will. In *The Mother-in-Law* she investigates the disastrous effects of a domineering woman's attempts to "gain a life-long ascendancy over the heart and mind of [her daughter]" and force "absolute subjection to her will." Southworth's concern is with the negation of self brought about by a radical and unthinking obedience. The daughter, Louise Armstrong, becomes something less than human in her automated obedience to her mother's will and is immobilized by her mother's power. As a good friend tells her, she has been "confined and fettered so long, that you have lost the use of yourself."

Southworth's enduring concern is the fettering of individuality, and such tampering with personal freedom provides the locus of evil not only for female but for male characters. *The Deserted Wife,* Southworth's second novel, is a close study of the deliberate, calculated attempt of a man to destroy the independence of a high-spirited, passionate woman by marrying her and using her love for him to bring her to a state of humiliation and dependency. "I wish you joy of your automaton!", snaps Hagar Churchill to her new husband, Raymond Withers, who induces a wifely "docility" that, as her comment suggests, is neither profound nor permanent. (pp. xxii-xxiv)

Along with her challenge to restrictive roles for women, Southworth is also interesting for her treatment of black characters. An abolitionist and ardent supporter of the Union during the Civil War, she is nonetheless a Southern writer. Most of her novels are set in the South and they contain many black characters, enslaved and free. Unlike most of her Northern contemporaries, Southworth was well acquainted with black men and women. She is not free from the limiting prejudices of her era however. Many of Southworth's black characters are stereotyped in ways offensive to modern readers, and she also partakes of contemporary notions about Jews. In reading her novels, however, one realizes that her mode of characterization is by and large engendered by stereotype. The vast majority of her characters, male and female, black and white, are stock characters straight from the cultural repertoire. The obsequious manservant Wool and the superstitious maidservant Pitapat in *The Hidden Hand,* for instance, are pure, unredeemed cultural schlock, as is the old Jewish pawnbroker who buys Cap's dresses and ringlets when she decides to "become a boy." With them, as with other black and ethnic characters, she attempts humor through the standard means of humorous names, exaggerated dialect, mispronunciations (Pitapat persistently calls Capitola Miss Caterpillar), facial contortions, and allusion to stereotyped personality traits. These are effects she uses with other minor characters as well; the white housekeeper's name, for instance, is Mrs. Condiment, and she is a tremulous, fainthearted parody of swooning feminine servility.

Southworth's mastery of stereotype allows her—although with race not as often as with gender—subtle and sophisticated manipulations designed to reveal the absurdity of cultural assumptions. In *The Hidden Hand* she twice mocks the contemporary bogeyman of the vicious runaway slave. Out riding alone, against her guardian's explicit orders, Cap meets a sinister fellow—a sinister *white* fellow—with rapacious intentions and disarms him by ingenuously pandering to conventional prejudices; with feigned wide-eyed innocence she pretends to welcome his presence as protection against "runaway negroes and wild beasts." Later when her imperious guardian himself returns from a ride alone, she returns his obsessive worries with a mock scolding in his own idiom: "Didn't you know the jeopardy you placed yourself in riding out alone at this hour? Suppose three or four great runaway negresses had sprung out of the bushes and—and—and—." Here she clearly mocks the culturally pervasive and politically powerful stereotype of the oversexed black male and the helpless Southern belle by reversing the situation to reveal its true nature as an absurd myth of oppression.

As always with Southworth what surprises, delights, and instructs is the redeemed stereotype. To offset Wool and Pitapat, we find such black characters as the proud and self-sufficient Jem Morris in *Ishmael* and *Self-Raised,* the tragic, knowledge-starved Anna in *The Mother-in-Law,* the brilliantly talented singer Erminie in *Retribution,* and the merciful midwife, Nancy Grewell, whose compassion and care save the life of the infant Cap. Further, Southworth's matter-of-fact presentation of the marriage of an attractive interracial couple in *Retribution* displays a strikingly liberal attitude toward intermarriage. Although Southworth does partake in certain ways of the pervasive racism of her era, those black characters who do transcend the realm of the conventional reveal an individuality and authorial warmth congruent with that of her friend Harriet Beecher Stowe and rare among her contemporaries. Southworth's dedication to individual self-realization, especially for women, is a dynamic that overrides all obstacles and gives her a vision of individual freedom at times strangely at odds with the cultural limitations motivating her imagination in other ways. (pp. xxiv-xxvi)

In *The Hidden Hand,* through a conscious and canny manipulation of cultural stereotypes of the masculine and feminine, Southworth presents a sweeping critique of the limiting nature of codified gender roles. Exaggeration, distortion, reversal: these comic strategies are the weapons in her literary arsenal, and aiming at ideals of masterful masculine dominance and sentimental feminine submission, Southworth fires with unrestrained exuberance. It is not through a polished and sophisticated literary style that Southworth's novel succeeds; while at times witty and engaging, the prose of *The Hidden Hand* more often relies on stock phrases and exaggerated descriptive vocabulary. Neither is Southworth's forte the regionalist realism of some of her sister writers. Instead, she relies on a mastery of storytelling. And, ironically, the success of *The Hidden Hand* lies in the author's conscious and maximized exploitation of those aspects of fiction generally perceived by modern critics to be weaknesses rather than strengths. With a lavish hand she employs conventional plot lines (relying often on startling coincidences for resolution), heavy-handed symbolism (exotic birthmarks, for instance, and descriptive names), and, most particularly, well-defined, easily recognized stereotypes. Part of the popular idiom, these conventional literary elements offered Southworth instantly recognizable vehicles of communication with which to reach and manipulate her numerous readers. Also, they provided a means of reminding both author and reader that they too were "safe" in this exploration of gender possibilities, because the realm in which they were operating was a purely literary one.

In a manifestly fictional universe anything can happen. In such a universe, one that flaunts its fictiveness with a farcical combination of adventure, Gothic melodrama and sentimentality, Southworth grants herself the imaginative space to ad-

dress the most tabooed subjects. Couched within a humorous idiom—intended to disarm criticism as well as to heighten her critique—is a message of the highest seriousness. Southworth concentrates on the trivialization of women, and *The Hidden Hand* attacks with ridicule a gender ethos that implicitly suggests women are at the disposal of the men who have authority over them. On the one hand Southworth presents Capitola, a model of female autonomy; on the other she shows incarceration, desperation and sexual oppression as the logical extensions of ideal sentimental feminine docility.

"Cap isn't *sentimental,*" explains her guardian, old Major Ira Warfield (otherwise known as Old Hurricane), to the Rev. Mr. Goodwin, a minister to whom he applies for advice on taming this little hellion he has taken under his wing. "[A]nd if *I* try to be," he continues, "she laughs in my face!" When Southworth conceived Capitola and told her tale in the widely circulated pages of the New York *Ledger,* she was writing at a time when the majority of female literary characters *were* "sentimental"—that is, they were embodiments of the dominant culture's attempt to shape and restrict woman's sphere of activity by defining her as narrowly "moral" in essence, exclusively emotional in constitution, and innately domestic in inclination. As Maria McIntosh stated it in *Woman in America* (1850), woman was to rule "in the little realm of home, our legitimate domain, in the spirit of wisdom and of love." Southworth did not reject this ideology; in fact, she had, in many ways, the utmost respect for it. But she detested the trivialization and exploitation of women which were in actuality a concomitant part of their ideological exaltation. In her creation of Capitola Le Noir—tomboy, adventurer, hero, on the one hand, and fascinating, sexually attractive woman, on the other—Southworth too is laughing in the face of authority. In Cap she skillfully evokes and at the same time reverses the conventions of the sentimental heroine. With doubled effect she taps into a potent cultural mythology, sketching the familiar outlines of the paradigm and simultaneously embodying in that sketch the unique energies of a woman who could not be more unlike her fictional contemporaries. (pp. xxvii-xxviii)

Capitola's freedom of spirit is directly associated with her upbringing outside the boundaries of middle-class society and of gender expectations, an implicit recognition of the stultifying effects upon women of conventional socialization. As a white child raised by a black laundress in the slums of New York City, as a girl who spends her early adolescence disguised as a boy, Cap has achieved a unique sense of herself and her possibilities. Whereas the docility of other, more genteel, women in the novel leads them to victimization at the hands of the masculine villains of the story, Cap triumphs over all: "From childhood she had been inured to danger, and had never suffered harm; therefore, Cap, like the Chevalier Bayard, was 'without fear and without reproach'." (pp. xxix-xxx)

The circumstances of Capitola's early years introduce the major theme of the novel and it is a serious one: the trivialization not only of woman's autonomy, but of woman's very existence, by men. Everyone assumes Cap can be disposed of at will. Her "kidnapping" is really just a benign accidental byproduct of a far worse fate—her uncle Gabriel Le Noir has planned to murder her at birth. At her mother's urging, the black midwife who attends her birth sequesters the infant Cap under her shawl and shows the wicked uncle the body of her still-born brother. The bandit Black Donald, Le Noir's collaborator, is not fooled, but, for profit, sells the midwife and child into slavery. Years later he professes to regret it: "It is so much easier to pinch a baby's nose until it falls asleep, than to stifle a young girl's shrieks and cries." In any case, he shows here no hesitation about "stifling" the life of this girl. On their way South, Cap and Nancy Grewell, the midwife, escape drowning in a shipwreck only because they are considered too inconsequential to be saved and are not taken into the lifeboat, which is later swamped. Cap, however, as she asserts over and over again, learns to take care of herself. She is not a disposable woman. Other women, traditionally socialized to obedient passivity, are not so fortunate. They are exploited economically and sexually: deprived of their rightful fortunes, locked in deserted houses, incarcerated in madhouses, abandoned to poverty, threatened with loveless marriages and with rape, all at the will of the men who control their lives.

An aberrant gender socialization, significantly, is Capitola's salvation. In order to survive the dangers facing a homeless waif in the New York of 1845, Cap switches sex. When we first see her at the age of thirteen, she is thriving on the streets. Disguised as a boy, she appears to be "crown prince and heir-apparent to the 'king of shreds and patches,' " but her countenance is "full of fun, frolic, spirit and courage." She has learned to live from hand to mouth with the confidence born of autonomy, ability, and pride. Cap's masculine socialization—her education on the streets where she works as a newsboy—allows her to develop the saving characteristics of self-reliance, irreverence, and active, rather than passive, courage. (p. xxxi)

As a young girl in nineteenth-century New York Cap is unable to find work. Eventually arrested for the illicit act of saving her life by donning the vestments of masculine privilege, she explains to the Court Recorder her difficulties in finding work as a girl. In its thoroughness, Southworth's delineation of Cap's attempts to support herself stresses the absurdity of contemporary rationales for not employing females. Ingrained habits, false propriety, and a skewed sense of what constitutes masculine dignity combine to doom a healthy and ambitious young girl to death or social parasitism.

This indictment of the economic inequities of a gender-defined society is only one aspect of Southworth's understanding of the deadly dangers facing a female child unaligned with a male protector. As well as starvation and beggary, the pubescent Cap also faces constant sexual peril, and it is this that finally drives her to gender disguise. As she further, and reluctantly, tells the court, she was forced to sleep on the streets:

> "That was a dreadful exposure for a young girl," said the Recorder.
>
> A burning blush flamed up over the young creature's cheek, as she answered:
>
> "Yes, sir, that was the worst of all; that finally drove me to putting on boy's clothes."
>
> "Let us hear all about it."
>
> "Oh, sir, I can't—I—how can I? Well, being always exposed, sleeping out-doors, I was often in danger from bad boys and bad men," said Capitola, and, dropping her head upon her breast, and covering her crimson cheeks with her hands, for the first time she burst into tears and sobbed aloud.

> "Come, come, my little man!—my good little *woman,* I mean—don't take it so to heart! You couldn't help it!" said Old Hurricane, with raindrops glittering even in his own stormy eyes.
>
> Capitola looked up with her whole countenance flashing with spirit, and exclaimed, "Oh! but I took care of myself, sir! I did, indeed, your honor! You musn't, either you or the old gentleman, dare to think but what I did."
>
> "Oh, of course! of course!" said a bystander, laughing.

Stressing the prurient interest of Cap's auditors—the fascinated "Let us hear all about it" of the recorder as well as the cynical mockery of the bystander—Southworth suggests that women are twice violated: once in the actual experience of sexual harassment and then again in the recounting of that experience. Everyone assumes the worst, even Old Hurricane, in whose quick forgiveness lies implicit the assumption of female powerlessness in the face of masculine rapacity. But Cap will allow no one to think she is less than virtuous; even if society has conspired in near irresistible ways to create yet another sexual victim, Cap has "taken care of herself " in this as in all other ways. (pp. xxxii-xxxiii)

The male characters in *The Hidden Hand* are not exclusively brutal. At one end of the spectrum of Southworth's imaginative perception of masculinity there is room for Dr. Day, the kindly physician who befriends Marah Rocke and gives her son Traverse a start on his medical education. There is room for Traverse, who in many ways is an adaptation of the best qualities of true womanhood to the masculine character. And there is room for Herbert Greyson, the noble young hero who, on the rare occasion when Cap actually needs help, shows up to provide it. These men are peripheral to the action of the novel, however. Southworth reserves her best comic shots for the men who cluster on the other end of the spectrum, and whose characteristics range from pathological selfishness to murderous villainy. The autocratic and chronically infuriated Major Warfield, the villainous Gabriel Le Noir and his bumbling lecherous son Craven, and the dreaded bandit Black Donald: these are the men whose actions shape the lives of the female characters and thus determine the flow of the narrative. Masculine rage, greed, and desire are the imperative forces of Southworth's fictional world, and it is against these that she pits Cap's autonomy and city savvy.

In her portrayal of these men, Southworth turns, literally with a vengeance, to stereotype: the bumptious oldster, the sinister villain, the dashing bandit. She works, to delicious effect, with stock characters, tapping into the underside of cultural notions about masculine nature. The wide dissemination of these figures within the culture indicates that, despite the prevailing notion of masculine superiority, strong suspicion existed in the popular mind that masculine character, unchecked by feminine influence or by Christian percepts, is imperious, rapacious, and greedy. Southworth's gleeful exaggeration of the stereotypes serves to highlight the grotesquery of a social system that puts unilateral power in the hands of such monsters. (pp. xxxv-xxxvi)

In her vision of a woman free enough of the bonds of feminine decorum to be totally herself, Southworth must resort to the fantasy world made available by the conventions of popular fiction. In this world, although not in reality, Capitola can be at once "outlaw" and heiress. Cap's author knows that the doubleness of her representation offers a titillating vision to her wide reading public. Nowhere is her delight in that doubleness as insistent as in her occasional mock ingenuous "apologies" for the errant behavior of her unruly protagonist. "Reader, I do not defend, far less approve, poor Cap," she says, "I only tell her story and describe her as I have seen her, leaving her to your charitable interpretation."

And the audience *was* charitable. Constant demands for the story . . . [encouraged the reprinting of the serial] in 1868 and again, in revised form designed to highlight the presence of Capitola, in 1883. After its first publication as a book in 1888, **The Hidden Hand** was in print well into the twentieth-century. In addition, the dramatized version played to crowds in major cities across America. Even in London, which Southworth visited at the time of the initial publication of **The Hidden Hand,** she found Capitola to be the rage; boats and race horses were named after Cap and fashionable women wore "Capitola" hats.

That this pernicious imp so captivated the public imagination indicates that popular culture in the nineteenth century was not as monolithic as modern scholars have tended to think, and that the interests of those cultural arbiters who so narrowly defined woman's nature and role were not uniformly the interests of the populace at large. In the figure of impudent Capitola Le Noir we see clear indication that the dominant ideology of obedient, subordinate womanhood was not unmixed. By mining the popular mood and presenting an attractive and previously unarticulated alternative for the contemporary representation of women, Southworth inevitably influenced imaginative possibilities for gender definition. As much as if she had been a woman's rights activist, she was therefore influential in changing the possibilities of reality for women. A figment of public as well as private fantasy, Capitola represents a figure emergent in the popular imagination, one that was to eventuate as a component of the American flapper of the 1920s and strongly influence the image of the modern self-sufficient woman. To the popular mind the fantasy of a woman who "won't obey . . . except when she likes," who feels that "liberty is too precious a thing to be exchanged for food and clothing," had a healthy fascination. With canny insight into the cultural psyche, Southworth played that fascination for all it was worth. (pp. xl-xli)

*Joanne Dobson, in an introduction to* The Hidden Hand; or, Capitola the Madcap *by E. D. E. N. Southworth, edited by Joanne Dobson, Rutgers University Press, 1988, pp. xi-xli.*

## FURTHER READING

Boyle, Regis Louise. *Mrs. E.D.E.N. Southworth, Novelist.* Washington, D.C.: Catholic University of America Press, 1939, 171 p.

> A doctoral dissertation in which the critic discusses Southworth's life and uses a thematic approach to examine her writings.

Brown, Herbert Ross. "Popular Isms and Ologies" and "Home, Sweet Home." In his *The Sentimental Novel in America, 1789-1860,* pp. 181-200, 281-322. 1940. Reprint. New York: Farrar, Straus and Giroux, Octagon Books, 1975.

> Two chapters, each of which contains commentary on Southworth's writings in relation to popular themes in nineteenth-century sentimental fiction.

Huddleson, Sarah M. "Mrs. E.D.E.N. Southworth and Her Cottage." In *Records of the Columbia Historical Society,* edited by John B. Larner, vol. 23, pp. 52-79. Washington, D.C.: Columbia Historical Society, 1920.

> An informal tribute to Southworth and her writings read before the Columbia Historical Society on 22 April 1919.

Kelley, Mary. *Private Woman, Public Stage: Literary Domesticity in Nineteenth-Century America.* New York: Oxford University Press, 1984, 409 p.

> A study of twelve nineteenth-century female writers, including Southworth, who combined their domestic lives with commercially successful literary careers.

Stoddard, Charles Warren. "Mrs. Emma D. E. N. Southworth at Prospect Cottage." *National Magazine* XXII, No. 2 (May 1905): 179-91.

> Personal recollections of Stoddard's friendship and correspondence with Southworth.

# Nineteenth-Century Literature Criticism

## Cumulative Indexes

## Volumes 1-26

# This Index Includes References to Entries in These Gale Series

## Contemporary Literary Criticism

Presents excerpts of criticism on the works of novelists, poets, dramatists, short story writers, scriptwriters, and other creative writers who are now living or who have died since 1960. Cumulative indexes to authors and nationalities are included, as well as an index to titles discussed in the individual volume.

## Twentieth-Century Literary Criticism

Contains critical excerpts by the most significant commentators on poets, novelists, short story writers, dramatists, and philosophers who died between 1900 and 1960. Cumulative indexes to authors, nationalities, and titles discussed are included in each new volume.

## Nineteenth-Century Literature Criticism

Offers significant passages from criticism on authors who died between 1800 and 1899. Cumulative indexes to authors, nationalities, and titles discussed are included in each new volume.

## Literature Criticism from 1400 to 1800

Compiles significant passages from the most noteworthy criticism on authors of the fifteenth through eighteenth centuries. Cumulative indexes to authors, nationalities, and titles discussed are included in each new volume.

## Classical and Medieval Literature Criticism

Offers excerpts of criticism on the works of world authors from classical antiquity through the fourteenth century. Cumulative indexes to authors, titles, and critics are included in each volume.

## Short Story Criticism

Compiles excerpts of criticism on short fiction by writers of all eras and nationalities. Cumulative indexes to authors, nationalities, and titles discussed are included in each new volume.

## Children's Literature Review

Includes excerpts from reviews, criticism, and commentary on works of authors and illustrators who create books for children. Cumulative indexes to authors, nationalities, and titles discussed are included in each new volume.

## Contemporary Authors Series

Encompasses five related series. *Contemporary Authors* provides biographical and bibliographical information on more than 92,000 writers of fiction, nonfiction, poetry, journalism, drama, motion pictures, and other fields. Each new volume contains sketches on authors not previously covered in the series. *Contemporary Authors New Revision Series* provides completely updated information on active authors covered in previously published volumes of *CA*. Only entries requiring significant change are revised for *CA New Revision Series*. *Contemporary Authors Permanent Series* consists of updated listings for deceased and inactive authors removed from the original volumes 9-36 when these volumes were revised. *Contemporary Authors Autobiography Series* presents specially commissioned autobiographies by leading contemporary writers. *Contemporary Authors Bibliographical Series* contains primary and secondary bibliographies as well as analytical bibliographical essays by authorities on major modern authors.

## Dictionary of Literary Biography

Encompasses three related series. *Dictionary of Literary Biography* furnishes illustrated overviews of authors' lives and works and places them in the larger perspective of literary history. *Dictionary of Literary Biography Documentary Series* illuminates the careers of major figures through a selection of literary documents, including letters, notebook and diary entries, interviews, book reviews, and photographs. *Dictionary of Literary Biography Yearbook* summarizes the past year's literary activity with articles on genres, major prizes, conferences, and other timely subjects and includes updated and new entries on individual authors. A cumulative index to authors and articles is included in each new volume.

## Concise Dictionary of American Literary Biography

A six-volume series that collects revised and updated sketches on major American authors that were originally presented in *Dictionary of Literary Biography*.

## Something about the Author Series

Encompasses three related series. *Something about the Author* contains heavily illustrated biographical sketches on juvenile and young adult authors and illustrators from all eras. *Something about the Author Autobiography Series* presents specially commissioned autobiographies by prominent authors and illustrators of books for children and young adults.

## Yesterday's Authors of Books for Children

Contains heavily illustrated entries on children's writers who died before 1961. Complete in two volumes.

# Literary Criticism Series
# Cumulative Author Index

Author Index

This index lists all author entries in the Gale Literary Criticism Series and includes cross-references to other Gale sources. References in the index are identified as follows:

**AAYA:** *Authors & Artists for Young Adults,* Volumes 1-2
**CAAS:** *Contemporary Authors Autobiography Series,* Volumes 1-10
**CA:** *Contemporary Authors* (original series), Volumes 1-129
**CABS:** *Contemporary Authors Bibliographical Series,* Volumes 1-3
**CANR:** *Contemporary Authors New Revision Series,* Volumes 1-28
**CAP:** *Contemporary Authors Permanent Series,* Volumes 1-2
**CA-R:** *Contemporary Authors* (revised editions), Volumes 1-44
**CDALB:** *Concise Dictionary of American Literary Biography,* Volumes 1-4
**CLC:** *Contemporary Literary Criticism,* Volumes 1-57
**CLR:** *Children's Literature Review,* Volumes 1-20
**CMLC:** *Classical and Medieval Literature Criticism,* Volumes 1-4
**DLB:** *Dictionary of Literary Biography,* Volumes 1-90
**DLB-DS:** *Dictionary of Literary Biography Documentary Series,* Volumes 1-7
**DLB-Y:** *Dictionary of Literary Biography Yearbook,* Volumes 1980-1988
**LC:** *Literature Criticism from 1400 to 1800,* Volumes 1-12
**NCLC:** *Nineteenth-Century Literature Criticism,* Volumes 1-26
**SAAS:** *Something about the Author Autobiography Series,* Volumes 1-8
**SATA:** *Something about the Author,* Volumes 1-57
**SSC:** *Short Story Criticism,* Volumes 1-4
**TCLC:** *Twentieth-Century Literary Criticism,* Volumes 1-35
**YABC:** *Yesterday's Authors of Books for Children,* Volumes 1-2

---

A. E. 1867-1935 . . . . . . . . . . . . . TCLC 3, 10
See also Russell, George William
See also DLB 19

Abbey, Edward 1927-1989 . . . . . . . . CLC 36
See also CANR 2; CA 45-48

Abbott, Lee K., Jr. 19??- . . . . . . . . . . CLC 48

Abe, Kobo 1924- . . . . . . . . . . . CLC 8, 22, 53
See also CANR 24; CA 65-68

Abell, Kjeld 1901-1961 . . . . . . . . . . . . CLC 15
See also obituary CA 111

Abish, Walter 1931- . . . . . . . . . . . . . CLC 22
See also CA 101

Abrahams, Peter (Henry) 1919- . . . . . CLC 4
See also CA 57-60

Abrams, M(eyer) H(oward) 1912- . . . CLC 24
See also CANR 13; CA 57-60; DLB 67

Abse, Dannie 1923- . . . . . . . . . . . . CLC 7, 29
See also CAAS 1; CANR 4; CA 53-56;
DLB 27

Achebe, (Albert) Chinua(lumogu)
1930- . . . . . . . . CLC 1, 3, 5, 7, 11, 26, 51
See also CLR 20; CANR 6, 26; CA 1-4R;
SATA 38, 40

Acker, Kathy 1948- . . . . . . . . . . . . . CLC 45
See also CA 117, 122

Ackroyd, Peter 1949- . . . . . . . . . CLC 34, 52
See also CA 123, 127

Acorn, Milton 1923- . . . . . . . . . . . . CLC 15
See also CA 103; DLB 53

Adamov, Arthur 1908-1970 . . . . . . CLC 4, 25
See also CAP 2; CA 17-18;
obituary CA 25-28R

Adams, Alice (Boyd) 1926- . . . CLC 6, 13, 46
See also CANR 26; CA 81-84; DLB-Y 86

Adams, Douglas (Noel) 1952- . . . . . . CLC 27
See also CA 106; DLB-Y 83

Adams, Henry (Brooks)
1838-1918 . . . . . . . . . . . . . . . . . TCLC 4
See also CA 104; DLB 12, 47

Adams, Richard (George)
1920- . . . . . . . . . . . . . . . . . CLC 4, 5, 18
See also CLR 20; CANR 3; CA 49-52;
SATA 7

Adamson, Joy(-Friederike Victoria)
1910-1980 . . . . . . . . . . . . . . . . . CLC 17
See also CANR 22; CA 69-72;
obituary CA 93-96; SATA 11;
obituary SATA 22

Adcock, (Kareen) Fleur 1934- . . . . . . CLC 41
See also CANR 11; CA 25-28R; DLB 40

Addams, Charles (Samuel)
1912-1988 . . . . . . . . . . . . . . . . . CLC 30
See also CANR 12; CA 61-64;
obituary CA 126

Adler, C(arole) S(chwerdtfeger)
1932- . . . . . . . . . . . . . . . . . . . . CLC 35
See also CANR 19; CA 89-92; SATA 26

Adler, Renata 1938- . . . . . . . . . . . CLC 8, 31
See also CANR 5, 22; CA 49-52

Ady, Endre 1877-1919 . . . . . . . . . . . TCLC 11
See also CA 107

Agee, James 1909-1955 . . . . . . . . TCLC 1, 19
See also CA 108; DLB 2, 26;
CDALB 1941-1968

Agnon, S(hmuel) Y(osef Halevi)
1888-1970 . . . . . . . . . . . . . . CLC 4, 8, 14
See also CAP 2; CA 17-18;
obituary CA 25-28R

Ai 1947- . . . . . . . . . . . . . . . . . . . CLC 4, 14
See also CA 85-88

Aickman, Robert (Fordyce)
1914-1981 . . . . . . . . . . . . . . . . . CLC 57
See also CANR 3; CA 7-8R

Aiken, Conrad (Potter)
1889-1973 . . . . . . . . CLC 1, 3, 5, 10, 52
See also CANR 4; CA 5-8R;
obituary CA 45-48; SATA 3, 30; DLB 9,
45

Aiken, Joan (Delano) 1924- . . . . . . . CLC 35
See also CLR 1; CANR 4; CA 9-12R;
SAAS 1; SATA 2, 30

Bambara, Toni Cade   1939-  . . . . . . . . CLC 19
  See also CA 29-32R; DLB 38

Banim, John   1798-1842 . . . . . . . . NCLC 13

Banim, Michael   1796-1874 . . . . . . NCLC 13

Banks, Iain   1954- . . . . . . . . . . . . . . . CLC 34
  See also CA 123

Banks, Lynne Reid   1929- . . . . . . . . CLC 23
  See also Reid Banks, Lynne

Banks, Russell   1940-  . . . . . . . . . . . . CLC 37
  See also CANR 19; CA 65-68

Banville, John   1945-. . . . . . . . . . . . . CLC 46
  See also CA 117; DLB 14

Banville, Theodore (Faullain) de
  1832-1891 . . . . . . . . . . . . . . . . . NCLC 9

Baraka, Amiri
  1934-  . . . . . . . CLC 1, 2, 3, 5, 10, 14, 33
  See also Baraka, Imamu Amiri; Jones,
    (Everett) LeRoi
  See also DLB 5, 7, 16, 38

Baraka, Imamu Amiri
  1934-  . . . . . . . CLC 1, 2, 3, 5, 10, 14, 33
  See also Baraka, Amiri; Jones, (Everett)
    LeRoi
  See also DLB 5, 7, 16, 38;
    CDALB 1941-1968

Barbellion, W. N. P.   1889-1919 . . . TCLC 24

Barbera, Jack   1945-. . . . . . . . . . . . . CLC 44
  See also CA 110

Barbey d'Aurevilly, Jules Amedee
  1808-1889 . . . . . . . . . . . . . . . . . NCLC 1

Barbusse, Henri   1873-1935 . . . . . . . . TCLC 5
  See also CA 105; DLB 65

Barea, Arturo   1897-1957 . . . . . . . . TCLC 14
  See also CA 111

Barfoot, Joan   1946- . . . . . . . . . . . . . CLC 18
  See also CA 105

Baring, Maurice   1874-1945 . . . . . . . TCLC 8
  See also CA 105; DLB 34

Barker, Clive   1952- . . . . . . . . . . . . . CLC 52
  See also CA 121

Barker, George (Granville)
  1913- . . . . . . . . . . . . . . . . . . CLC 8, 48
  See also CANR 7; CA 9-12R; DLB 20

Barker, Howard   1946-. . . . . . . . . . . . CLC 37
  See also CA 102; DLB 13

Barker, Pat   1943-. . . . . . . . . . . . . . . CLC 32
  See also CA 117, 122

Barlow, Joel   1754-1812 . . . . . . . . . NCLC 23
  See also DLB 37

Barnard, Mary (Ethel)   1909-. . . . . . . CLC 48
  See also CAP 2; CA 21-22

Barnes, Djuna (Chappell)
  1892-1982 . . . CLC 3, 4, 8, 11, 29; SSC 3
  See also CANR 16; CA 9-12R;
    obituary CA 107; DLB 4, 9, 45

Barnes, Julian   1946-. . . . . . . . . . . . . CLC 42
  See also CANR 19; CA 102

Barnes, Peter   1931- . . . . . . . . . . . CLC 5, 56
  See also CA 65-68; DLB 13

Baroja (y Nessi), Pio   1872-1956 . . . . TCLC 8
  See also CA 104

Barondess, Sue K(aufman)   1926-1977
  See Kaufman, Sue
  See also CANR 1; CA 1-4R;
    obituary CA 69-72

Barrett, (Roger) Syd   1946-
  See Pink Floyd

Barrett, William (Christopher)
  1913- . . . . . . . . . . . . . . . . . . . . CLC 27
  See also CANR 11; CA 13-16R

Barrie, (Sir) J(ames) M(atthew)
  1860-1937 . . . . . . . . . . . . . . . . . TCLC 2
  See also CLR 16; YABC 1; CA 104;
    DLB 10

Barrol, Grady   1953-
  See Bograd, Larry

Barry, Philip (James Quinn)
  1896-1949 . . . . . . . . . . . . . . . . TCLC 11
  See also CA 109; DLB 7

Barth, John (Simmons)
  1930- . . . . . . CLC 1, 2, 3, 5, 7, 9, 10, 14,
                                      27, 51
  See also CANR 5, 23; CA 1-4R; CABS 1;
    DLB 2

Barthelme, Donald
  1931-1989 . . . . . CLC 1, 2, 3, 5, 6, 8, 13,
                                 23, 46; SSC 2
  See also CANR 20; CA 21-24R; SATA 7;
    DLB 2; DLB-Y 80

Barthelme, Frederick   1943-. . . . . . . . CLC 36
  See also CA 114, 122; DLB-Y 85

Barthes, Roland   1915-1980 . . . . . . . . CLC 24
  See also obituary CA 97-100

Barzun, Jacques (Martin)   1907- . . . . CLC 51
  See also CANR 22; CA 61-64

Bassani, Giorgio   1916-. . . . . . . . . . . . CLC 9
  See also CA 65-68

Bataille, Georges   1897-1962 . . . . . . . CLC 29
  See also CA 101; obituary CA 89-92

Bates, H(erbert) E(rnest)
  1905-1974 . . . . . . . . . . . . . . . . . CLC 46
  See also CA 93-96; obituary CA 45-48

Baudelaire, Charles   1821-1867 . . . . NCLC 6

Baum, L(yman) Frank   1856-1919 . . . TCLC 7
  See also CLR 15; CA 108; SATA 18;
    DLB 22

Baumbach, Jonathan   1933- . . . . . . CLC 6, 23
  See also CAAS 5; CANR 12; CA 13-16R;
    DLB-Y 80

Bausch, Richard (Carl)   1945- . . . . . CLC 51
  See also CA 101

Baxter, Charles   1947-. . . . . . . . . . . . CLC 45
  See also CA 57-60

Baxter, James K(eir)   1926-1972 . . . . CLC 14
  See also CA 77-80

Bayer, Sylvia   1909-1981
  See Glassco, John

Beagle, Peter S(oyer)   1939-. . . . . . . . CLC 7
  See also CANR 4; CA 9-12R; DLB-Y 80

Beard, Charles A(ustin)
  1874-1948 . . . . . . . . . . . . . . . . TCLC 15
  See also CA 115; SATA 18; DLB 17

Beardsley, Aubrey   1872-1898 . . . . . NCLC 6

Beattie, Ann   1947-. . . . . . . CLC 8, 13, 18, 40
  See also CA 81-84; DLB-Y 82

Beattie, James   1735-1803 . . . . . . NCLC 25

Beauvoir, Simone (Lucie Ernestine Marie
    Bertrand) de
  1908-1986 . . . CLC 1, 2, 4, 8, 14, 31, 44,
                                             50
  See also CA 9-12R; obituary CA 118;
    DLB 72; DLB-Y 86

Becker, Jurek   1937-. . . . . . . . . . . CLC 7, 19
  See also CA 85-88

Becker, Walter   1950-. . . . . . . . . . . . . CLC 26

Beckett, Samuel (Barclay)
  1906-1989 . . . . . CLC 1, 2, 3, 4, 6, 9, 10,
                            11, 14, 18, 29, 57
  See also CA 5-8R; DLB 13, 15

Beckford, William   1760-1844 . . . . NCLC 16
  See also DLB 39

Beckman, Gunnel   1910-. . . . . . . . . . . CLC 26
  See also CANR 15; CA 33-36R; SATA 6

Becque, Henri   1837-1899. . . . . . . . NCLC 3

Beddoes, Thomas Lovell
  1803-1849 . . . . . . . . . . . . . . . . NCLC 3

Beecher, John   1904-1980. . . . . . . . . . CLC 6
  See also CANR 8; CA 5-8R;
    obituary CA 105

Beer, Johann   1655-1700. . . . . . . . . . . LC 5

Beerbohm, (Sir Henry) Max(imilian)
  1872-1956 . . . . . . . . . . . . . . TCLC 1, 24
  See also CA 104; DLB 34

Behan, Brendan
  1923-1964 . . . . . . . . . . CLC 1, 8, 11, 15
  See also CA 73-76; DLB 13

Behn, Aphra   1640?-1689 . . . . . . . . . . . LC 1
  See also DLB 39

Behrman, S(amuel) N(athaniel)
  1893-1973 . . . . . . . . . . . . . . . . . CLC 40
  See also CAP 1; CA 15-16;
    obituary CA 45-48; DLB 7, 44

Beiswanger, George Edwin   1931-
  See Starbuck, George (Edwin)

Belasco, David   1853-1931 . . . . . . . . . TCLC 3
  See also CA 104; DLB 7

Belcheva, Elisaveta   1893-
  See Bagryana, Elisaveta

Belinski, Vissarion Grigoryevich
  1811-1848 . . . . . . . . . . . . . . . . NCLC 5

Belitt, Ben   1911-. . . . . . . . . . obituary CLC 22
  See also CAAS 4; CANR 7; CA 13-16R;
    DLB 5

Bell, Acton   1820-1849
  See Bronte, Anne

Bell, Currer   1816-1855
  See Bronte, Charlotte

Bell, Madison Smartt   1957-. . . . . . . . CLC 41
  See also CA 111

Bell, Marvin (Hartley)   1937-. . . . . CLC 8, 31
  See also CA 21-24R; DLB 5

Bellamy, Edward   1850-1898 . . . . . . NCLC 4
  See also DLB 12

Belloc, (Joseph) Hilaire (Pierre Sebastien
    Rene Swanton)
  1870-1953 . . . . . . . . . . . . . . TCLC 7, 18
  See also YABC 1; CA 106; DLB 19

**Bellow, Saul**
1915-...... **CLC 1, 2, 3, 6, 8, 10, 13, 15, 25, 33, 34**
See also CA 5-8R; CABS 1; DLB 2, 28; DLB-Y 82; DLB-DS 3; CDALB 1941-1968

**Belser, Reimond Karel Maria de** 1929-
See Ruyslinck, Ward

**Bely, Andrey** 1880-1934.......... **TCLC 7**
See also CA 104

**Benary-Isbert, Margot** 1889-1979 ... **CLC 12**
See also CLR 12; CANR 4; CA 5-8R; obituary CA 89-92; SATA 2; obituary SATA 21

**Benavente (y Martinez), Jacinto**
1866-1954 .................. **TCLC 3**
See also CA 106

**Benchley, Peter (Bradford)**
1940- ...................... **CLC 4, 8**
See also CANR 12; CA 17-20R; SATA 3

**Benchley, Robert** 1889-1945 ....... **TCLC 1**
See also CA 105; DLB 11

**Benedikt, Michael** 1935- ........ **CLC 4, 14**
See also CANR 7; CA 13-16R; DLB 5

**Benet, Juan** 1927-................ **CLC 28**

**Benet, Stephen Vincent**
1898-1943 ................... **TCLC 7**
See also YABC 1; CA 104; DLB 4, 48

**Benet, William Rose** 1886-1950 ... **TCLC 28**
See also CA 118; DLB 45

**Benford, Gregory (Albert)** 1941-.... **CLC 52**
See also CANR 12, 24; CA 69-72; DLB-Y 82

**Benn, Gottfried** 1886-1956........ **TCLC 3**
See also CA 106; DLB 56

**Bennett, Alan** 1934-.............. **CLC 45**
See also CA 103

**Bennett, (Enoch) Arnold**
1867-1931 ................ **TCLC 5, 20**
See also CA 106; DLB 10, 34

**Bennett, George Harold** 1930-
See Bennett, Hal
See also CA 97-100

**Bennett, Hal** 1930-................ **CLC 5**
See also Bennett, George Harold
See also DLB 33

**Bennett, Jay** 1912-.............. **CLC 35**
See also CANR 11; CA 69-72; SAAS 4; SATA 27, 41

**Bennett, Louise (Simone)** 1919-..... **CLC 28**
See also Bennett-Coverly, Louise Simone

**Bennett-Coverly, Louise Simone** 1919-
See Bennett, Louise (Simone)
See also CA 97-100

**Benson, E(dward) F(rederic)**
1867-1940 .................. **TCLC 27**
See also CA 114

**Benson, Jackson J.** 1930-......... **CLC 34**
See also CA 25-28R

**Benson, Sally** 1900-1972 .......... **CLC 17**
See also CAP 1; CA 19-20; obituary CA 37-40R; SATA 1, 35; obituary SATA 27

**Benson, Stella** 1892-1933........ **TCLC 17**
See also CA 117; DLB 36

**Bentley, E(dmund) C(lerihew)**
1875-1956 ................. **TCLC 12**
See also CA 108; DLB 70

**Bentley, Eric (Russell)** 1916-....... **CLC 24**
See also CANR 6; CA 5-8R

**Berger, John (Peter)** 1926- ...... **CLC 2, 19**
See also CA 81-84; DLB 14

**Berger, Melvin (H.)** 1927-......... **CLC 12**
See also CANR 4; CA 5-8R; SAAS 2; SATA 5

**Berger, Thomas (Louis)**
1924- .......... **CLC 3, 5, 8, 11, 18, 38**
See also CANR 5; CA 1-4R; DLB 2; DLB-Y 80

**Bergman, (Ernst) Ingmar** 1918-..... **CLC 16**
See also CA 81-84

**Bergson, Henri** 1859-1941 ....... **TCLC 32**

**Bergstein, Eleanor** 1938-.......... **CLC 4**
See also CANR 5; CA 53-56

**Berkoff, Steven** 1937-............. **CLC 56**
See also CA 104

**Bermant, Chaim** 1929-............ **CLC 40**
See also CANR 6; CA 57-60

**Bernanos, (Paul Louis) Georges**
1888-1948 .................. **TCLC 3**
See also CA 104; DLB 72

**Bernhard, Thomas** 1931-1989 .... **CLC 3, 32**
See also CA 85-88

**Berriault, Gina** 1926-............. **CLC 54**
See also CA 116

**Berrigan, Daniel J.** 1921-.......... **CLC 4**
See also CAAS 1; CANR 11; CA 33-36R; DLB 5

**Berrigan, Edmund Joseph Michael, Jr.**
1934-1983
See Berrigan, Ted
See also CANR 14; CA 61-64; obituary CA 110

**Berrigan, Ted** 1934-1983 .......... **CLC 37**
See also Berrigan, Edmund Joseph Michael, Jr.
See also DLB 5

**Berry, Chuck** 1926- .............. **CLC 17**

**Berry, Wendell (Erdman)**
1934- ............. **CLC 4, 6, 8, 27, 46**
See also CA 73-76; DLB 5, 6

**Berryman, John**
1914-1972 ..... **CLC 1, 2, 3, 4, 6, 8, 10, 13, 25**
See also CAP 1; CA 15-16; obituary CA 33-36R; CABS 2; DLB 48; CDALB 1941-1968

**Bertolucci, Bernardo** 1940- ........ **CLC 16**
See also CA 106

**Besant, Annie (Wood)** 1847-1933 ... **TCLC 9**
See also CA 105

**Bessie, Alvah** 1904-1985.......... **CLC 23**
See also CANR 2; CA 5-8R; obituary CA 116; DLB 26

**Beti, Mongo** 1932-................ **CLC 27**
See also Beyidi, Alexandre

**Betjeman, (Sir) John**
1906-1984 ....... **CLC 2, 6, 10, 34, 43**
See also CA 9-12R; obituary CA 112; DLB 20; DLB-Y 84

**Betti, Ugo** 1892-1953 ............ **TCLC 5**
See also CA 104

**Betts, Doris (Waugh)** 1932-.... **CLC 3, 6, 28**
See also CANR 9; CA 13-16R; DLB-Y 82

**Bialik, Chaim Nachman**
1873-1934 ................. **TCLC 25**

**Bidart, Frank** 19??-................ **CLC 33**

**Bienek, Horst** 1930-............. **CLC 7, 11**
See also CA 73-76; DLB 75

**Bierce, Ambrose (Gwinett)**
1842-1914?.................**TCLC 1, 7**
See also CA 104; DLB 11, 12, 23, 71, 74; CDALB 1865-1917

**Billington, Rachel** 1942-........... **CLC 43**
See also CA 33-36R

**Binyon, T(imothy) J(ohn)** 1936- .... **CLC 34**
See also CA 111

**Bioy Casares, Adolfo** 1914-.... **CLC 4, 8, 13**
See also CANR 19; CA 29-32R

**Bird, Robert Montgomery**
1806-1854 ................. **NCLC 1**

**Birdwell, Cleo** 1936-
See DeLillo, Don

**Birney (Alfred) Earle**
1904- .................**CLC 1, 4, 6, 11**
See also CANR 5, 20; CA 1-4R

**Bishop, Elizabeth**
1911-1979 ...... **CLC 1, 4, 9, 13, 15, 32**
See also CANR 26; CA 5-8R; obituary CA 89-92; CABS 2; obituary SATA 24; DLB 5

**Bishop, John** 1935-............... **CLC 10**
See also CA 105

**Bissett, Bill** 1939-................ **CLC 18**
See also CANR 15; CA 69-72; DLB 53

**Bitov, Andrei (Georgievich)** 1937-... **CLC 57**

**Biyidi, Alexandre** 1932-
See Beti, Mongo
See also CA 114, 124

**Bjornson, Bjornstjerne (Martinius)**
1832-1910 .................. **TCLC 7**
See also CA 104

**Blackburn, Paul** 1926-1971 ...... **CLC 9, 43**
See also CA 81-84; obituary CA 33-36R; DLB 16; DLB-Y 81

**Black Elk** 1863-1950 ........... **TCLC 33**

**Blackmore, R(ichard) D(oddridge)**
1825-1900 ................. **TCLC 27**
See also CA 120; DLB 18

**Blackmur, R(ichard) P(almer)**
1904-1965 ................. **CLC 2, 24**
See also CAP 1; CA 11-12; obituary CA 25-28R; DLB 63

**Blackwood, Algernon (Henry)**
1869-1951 .................. **TCLC 5**
See also CA 105

**Blackwood, Caroline** 1931- ....... **CLC 6, 9**
See also CA 85-88; DLB 14

**Blair, Eric Arthur** 1903-1950
See Orwell, George
See also CA 104; SATA 29

**Blais, Marie-Claire**
1939- ............. **CLC 2, 4, 6, 13, 22**
See also CAAS 4; CA 21-24R; DLB 53

**Brand, Millen** 1906-1980 .......... CLC 7
See also CA 21-24R; obituary CA 97-100

**Branden, Barbara** 19??- .......... CLC 44

**Brandes, Georg (Morris Cohen)**
1842-1927 ................. TCLC 10
See also CA 105

**Branley, Franklyn M(ansfield)**
1915- ....................... CLC 21
See also CLR 13; CANR 14; CA 33-36R;
SATA 4

**Brathwaite, Edward** 1930- ......... CLC 11
See also CANR 11; CA 25-28R; DLB 53

**Brautigan, Richard (Gary)**
1935-1984 .... CLC 1, 3, 5, 9, 12, 34, 42
See also CA 53-56; obituary CA 113;
DLB 2, 5; DLB-Y 80, 84

**Brecht, (Eugen) Bertolt (Friedrich)**
1898-1956 .......... TCLC 1, 6, 13, 35
See also CA 104; DLB 56

**Bremer, Fredrika** 1801-1865 ..... NCLC 11

**Brennan, Christopher John**
1870-1932 ................. TCLC 17
See also CA 117

**Brennan, Maeve** 1917- ............. CLC 5
See also CA 81-84

**Brentano, Clemens (Maria)**
1778-1842 ................... NCLC 1

**Brenton, Howard** 1942- ........... CLC 31
See also CA 69-72; DLB 13

**Breslin, James** 1930-
See Breslin, Jimmy
See also CA 73-76

**Breslin, Jimmy** 1930- .......... CLC 4, 43
See also Breslin, James

**Bresson, Robert** 1907- ............ CLC 16
See also CA 110

**Breton, Andre** 1896-1966... CLC 2, 9, 15, 54
See also CAP 2; CA 19-20;
obituary CA 25-28R; DLB 65

**Breytenbach, Breyten** 1939-... CLC 23, 37
See also CA 113

**Bridgers, Sue Ellen** 1942- ......... CLC 26
See also CANR 11; CA 65-68; SAAS 1;
SATA 22; DLB 52

**Bridges, Robert** 1844-1930......... TCLC 1
See also CA 104; DLB 19

**Bridie, James** 1888-1951 .......... TCLC 3
See also Mavor, Osborne Henry
See also DLB 10

**Brin, David** 1950-................. CLC 34
See also CANR 24; CA 102

**Brink, Andre (Philippus)**
1935-.................. CLC 18, 36
See also CA 104

**Brinsmead, H(esba) F(ay)** 1922- .... CLC 21
See also CANR 10; CA 21-24R; SAAS 5;
SATA 18

**Brittain, Vera (Mary)** 1893?-1970... CLC 23
See also CAP 1; CA 15-16;
obituary CA 25-28R

**Broch, Hermann** 1886-1951....... TCLC 20
See also CA 117

**Brock, Rose** 1923-
See Hansen, Joseph

**Brodkey, Harold** 1930-............ CLC 56
See also CA 111

**Brodsky, Iosif Alexandrovich** 1940-
See Brodsky, Joseph (Alexandrovich)
See also CA 41-44R

**Brodsky, Joseph (Alexandrovich)**
1940- ........... CLC 4, 6, 13, 36, 50
See also Brodsky, Iosif Alexandrovich

**Brodsky, Michael (Mark)** 1948- .... CLC 19
See also CANR 18; CA 102

**Bromell, Henry** 1947-............. CLC 5
See also CANR 9; CA 53-56

**Bromfield, Louis (Brucker)**
1896-1956 ................. TCLC 11
See also CA 107; DLB 4, 9

**Broner, E(sther) M(asserman)**
1930-..................... CLC 19
See also CANR 8, 25; CA 17-20R; DLB 28

**Bronk, William** 1918-............. CLC 10
See also CANR 23; CA 89-92

**Bronte, Anne** 1820-1849......... NCLC 4
See also DLB 21

**Bronte, Charlotte** 1816-1855 .... NCLC 3, 8
See also DLB 21

**Bronte, (Jane) Emily** 1818-1848 .. NCLC 16
See also DLB 21, 32

**Brooke, Frances** 1724-1789 ......... LC 6
See also DLB 39

**Brooke, Henry** 1703?-1783 .......... LC 1
See also DLB 39

**Brooke, Rupert (Chawner)**
1887-1915 ................ TCLC 2, 7
See also CA 104; DLB 19

**Brooke-Rose, Christine** 1926-...... CLC 40
See also CA 13-16R; DLB 14

**Brookner, Anita** 1928-...... CLC 32, 34, 51
See also CA 114, 120; DLB-Y 87

**Brooks, Cleanth** 1906-............ CLC 24
See also CA 17-20R; DLB 63

**Brooks, Gwendolyn**
1917-........... CLC 1, 2, 4, 5, 15, 49
See also CANR 1; CA 1-4R; SATA 6;
DLB 5, 76; CDALB 1941-1968

**Brooks, Mel** 1926-.............. CLC 12
See also Kaminsky, Melvin
See also CA 65-68; DLB 26

**Brooks, Peter** 1938-............. CLC 34
See also CANR 1; CA 45-48

**Brooks, Van Wyck** 1886-1963...... CLC 29
See also CANR 6; CA 1-4R; DLB 45, 63

**Brophy, Brigid (Antonia)**
1929-................. CLC 6, 11, 29
See also CAAS 4; CANR 25; CA 5-8R;
DLB 14

**Brosman, Catharine Savage** 1934-.... CLC 9
See also CANR 21; CA 61-64

**Broughton, T(homas) Alan** 1936- ... CLC 19
See also CANR 2, 23; CA 45-48

**Broumas, Olga** 1949-............. CLC 10
See also CANR 20; CA 85-88

**Brown, Charles Brockden**
1771-1810 ................ NCLC 22
See also DLB 37, 59, 73;
CDALB 1640-1865

**Brown, Claude** 1937- ............. CLC 30
See also CA 73-76

**Brown, Dee (Alexander)** 1908- .. CLC 18, 47
See also CAAS 6; CANR 11; CA 13-16R;
SATA 5; DLB-Y 80

**Brown, George Douglas** 1869-1902
See Douglas, George

**Brown, George Mackay** 1921-.... CLC 5, 28
See also CAAS 6; CANR 12; CA 21-24R;
SATA 35; DLB 14, 27

**Brown, Rita Mae** 1944-........ CLC 18, 43
See also CANR 2, 11; CA 45-48

**Brown, Rosellen** 1939-............ CLC 32
See also CANR 14; CA 77-80

**Brown, Sterling A(llen)**
1901-1989 ................ CLC 1, 23
See also CANR 26; CA 85-88; DLB 48, 51,
63

**Brown, William Wells**
1816?-1884.................. NCLC 2
See also DLB 3, 50

**Browne, Jackson** 1950- ........... CLC 21
See also CA 120

**Browning, Elizabeth Barrett**
1806-1861 ............... NCLC 1, 16
See also DLB 32

**Browning, Robert** 1812-1889..... NCLC 19
See also YABC 1; DLB 32

**Browning, Tod** 1882-1962 ........ CLC 16
See also obituary CA 117

**Bruccoli, Matthew J(oseph)** 1931- .. CLC 34
See also CANR 7; CA 9-12R

**Bruce, Lenny** 1925-1966 .......... CLC 21
See also Schneider, Leonard Alfred

**Brunner, John (Kilian Houston)**
1934-..................... CLC 8, 10
See also CANR 2; CA 1-4R

**Brutus, Dennis** 1924-............. CLC 43
See also CANR 2; CA 49-52

**Bryan, C(ourtlandt) D(ixon) B(arnes)**
1936-..................... CLC 29
See also CANR 13; CA 73-76

**Bryant, William Cullen**
1794-1878 ................. NCLC 6
See also DLB 3, 43, 59; CDALB 1640-1865

**Bryusov, Valery (Yakovlevich)**
1873-1924 ................. TCLC 10
See also CA 107

**Buchanan, George** 1506-1582 ........ LC 4

**Buchheim, Lothar-Gunther** 1918-.... CLC 6
See also CA 85-88

**Buchner, (Karl) Georg**
1813-1837 ................. NCLC 26

**Buchwald, Art(hur)** 1925-.......... CLC 33
See also CANR 21; CA 5-8R; SATA 10

**Buck, Pearl S(ydenstricker)**
1892-1973 ............ CLC 7, 11, 18
See also CANR 1; CA 1-4R;
obituary CA 41-44R; SATA 1, 25; DLB 9

**Buckler, Ernest** 1908-1984........ CLC 13
See also CAP 1; CA 11-12;
obituary CA 114; SATA 47

Author Index

Foote, Horton 1916-............. CLC 51
See also CA 73-76; DLB 26

Forbes, Esther 1891-1967......... CLC 12
See also CAP 1; CA 13-14;
obituary CA 25-28R; SATA 2; DLB 22

Forche, Carolyn 1950-............ CLC 25
See also CA 109, 117; DLB 5

Ford, Ford Madox 1873-1939 ... TCLC 1, 15
See also CA 104; DLB 34

Ford, John 1895-1973............. CLC 16
See also obituary CA 45-48

Ford, Richard 1944-.............. CLC 46
See also CANR 11; CA 69-72

Foreman, Richard 1937-.......... CLC 50
See also CA 65-68

Forester, C(ecil) S(cott)
1899-1966 ................... CLC 35
See also CA 73-76; obituary CA 25-28R;
SATA 13

Forman, James D(ouglas) 1932- .... CLC 21
See also CANR 4, 19; CA 9-12R; SATA 8,
21

Fornes, Maria Irene 1930-........ CLC 39
See also CA 25-28R; DLB 7

Forrest, Leon 1937- .............. CLC 4
See also CAAS 7; CA 89-92; DLB 33

Forster, E(dward) M(organ)
1879-1970 .... CLC 1, 2, 3, 4, 9, 10, 13,
15, 22, 45
See also CAP 1; CA 13-14;
obituary CA 25-28R; DLB 34

Forster, John 1812-1876 ........ NCLC 11

Forsyth, Frederick 1938-...... CLC 2, 5, 36
See also CA 85-88

Forten (Grimke), Charlotte L(ottie)
1837-1914 ................... TCLC 16
See also Grimke, Charlotte L(ottie) Forten
See also DLB 50

Foscolo, Ugo 1778-1827.......... NCLC 8

Fosse, Bob 1925-1987............. CLC 20
See also Fosse, Robert Louis

Fosse, Robert Louis 1925-1987
See Bob Fosse
See also CA 110, 123

Foster, Stephen Collins
1826-1864 ................. NCLC 26

Foucault, Michel 1926-1984 .... CLC 31, 34
See also CANR 23; CA 105;
obituary CA 113

Fouque, Friedrich (Heinrich Karl) de La
Motte 1777-1843 .......... NCLC 2

Fournier, Henri Alban 1886-1914
See Alain-Fournier
See also CA 104

Fournier, Pierre 1916-............ CLC 11
See also Gascar, Pierre
See also CANR 16; CA 89-92

Fowles, John (Robert)
1926- .... CLC 1, 2, 3, 4, 6, 9, 10, 15, 33
See also CANR 25; CA 5-8R; SATA 22;
DLB 14

Fox, Paula 1923-................. CLC 2, 8
See also CLR 1; CANR 20; CA 73-76;
SATA 17; DLB 52

Fox, William Price (Jr.) 1926- ..... CLC 22
See also CANR 11; CA 17-20R; DLB 2;
DLB-Y 81

Frame (Clutha), Janet (Paterson)
1924- ................CLC 2, 3, 6, 22
See also Clutha, Janet Paterson Frame

France, Anatole 1844-1924 ....... TCLC 9
See also Thibault, Jacques Anatole Francois

Francis, Claude 19??-............. CLC 50

Francis, Dick 1920- ......... CLC 2, 22, 42
See also CANR 9; CA 5-8R

Francis, Robert (Churchill)
1901-1987 ................... CLC 15
See also CANR 1; CA 1-4R;
obituary CA 123

Frank, Anne 1929-1945 ......... TCLC 17
See also CA 113; SATA 42

Frank, Elizabeth 1945-............ CLC 39
See also CA 121, 126

Franklin, (Stella Maria Sarah) Miles
1879-1954 ................... TCLC 7
See also CA 104

Fraser, Antonia (Pakenham)
1932- ....................... CLC 32
See also CA 85-88; SATA 32

Fraser, George MacDonald 1925-.... CLC 7
See also CANR 2; CA 45-48

Frayn, Michael 1933-...... CLC 3, 7, 31, 47
See also CA 5-8R; DLB 13, 14

Fraze, Candida 19??- ............. CLC 50
See also CA 125

Frazer, Sir James George
1854-1941 .................. TCLC 32
See also CA 118

Frazier, Ian 1951-................ CLC 46

Frederic, Harold 1856-1898...... NCLC 10
See also DLB 12, 23

Fredman, Russell (Bruce) 1929-
See also CLR 20

Fredro, Aleksander 1793-1876..... NCLC 8

Freeling, Nicolas 1927- .......... CLC 38
See also CANR 1, 17; CA 49-52

Freeman, Douglas Southall
1886-1953 .................. TCLC 11
See also CA 109; DLB 17

Freeman, Judith 1946-........... CLC 55

Freeman, Mary (Eleanor) Wilkins
1852-1930 ............ TCLC 9; SSC 1
See also CA 106; DLB 12

Freeman, R(ichard) Austin
1862-1943 .................. TCLC 21
See also CA 113; DLB 70

French, Marilyn 1929-......... CLC 10, 18
See also CANR 3; CA 69-72

Freneau, Philip Morin 1752-1832 .. NCLC 1
See also DLB 37, 43

Friedman, B(ernard) H(arper)
1926- ....................... CLC 7
See also CANR 3; CA 1-4R

Friedman, Bruce Jay 1930-.... CLC 3, 5, 56
See also CANR 25; CA 9-12R; DLB 2, 28

Friel, Brian 1929-.............. CLC 5, 42
See also CA 21-24R; DLB 13

Friis-Baastad, Babbis (Ellinor)
1921-1970 ................... CLC 12
See also CA 17-20R; SATA 7

Frisch, Max (Rudolf)
1911- ........ CLC 3, 9, 14, 18, 32, 44
See also CA 85-88; DLB 69

Fromentin, Eugene (Samuel Auguste)
1820-1876 ................. NCLC 10

Frost, Robert (Lee)
1874-1963 ... CLC 1, 3, 4, 9, 10, 13, 15,
26, 34, 44
See also CA 89-92; SATA 14; DLB 54

Fry, Christopher 1907-....... CLC 2, 10, 14
See also CANR 9; CA 17-20R; DLB 13

Frye, (Herman) Northrop 1912- .... CLC 24
See also CANR 8; CA 5-8R

Fuchs, Daniel 1909-............ CLC 8, 22
See also CAAS 5; CA 81-84; DLB 9, 26, 28

Fuchs, Daniel 1934-.............. CLC 34
See also CANR 14; CA 37-40R

Fuentes, Carlos
1928- ....... CLC 3, 8, 10, 13, 22, 41
See also CANR 10; CA 69-72

Fugard, Athol 1932-... CLC 5, 9, 14, 25, 40
See also CA 85-88

Fugard, Sheila 1932- ............. CLC 48
See also CA 125

Fuller, Charles (H., Jr.) 1939-...... CLC 25
See also CA 108, 112; DLB 38

Fuller, (Sarah) Margaret
1810-1850 ................... NCLC 5
See also Ossoli, Sarah Margaret (Fuller
marchesa d')
See also DLB 1, 59, 73; CDALB 1640-1865

Fuller, Roy (Broadbent) 1912-.... CLC 4, 28
See also CA 5-8R; DLB 15, 20

Fulton, Alice 1952-............... CLC 52
See also CA 116

Furphy, Joseph 1843-1912........ TCLC 25

Futrelle, Jacques 1875-1912 ...... TCLC 19
See also CA 113

Gaboriau, Emile 1835-1873 ...... NCLC 14

Gadda, Carlo Emilio 1893-1973 .... CLC 11
See also CA 89-92

Gaddis, William
1922- CLC 1, 3, 6, 8, 10, 19, 43
See also CAAS 4; CANR 21; CA 17-20R;
DLB 2

Gaines, Ernest J. 1933-...... CLC 3, 11, 18
See also CANR 6, 24; CA 9-12R; DLB 2,
33; DLB-Y 80

Gale, Zona 1874-1938 ........... TCLC 7
See also CA 105; DLB 9

Gallagher, Tess 1943-............. CLC 18
See also CA 106

Gallant, Mavis
1922-........... CLC 7, 18, 38; SSC 5
See also CA 69-72; DLB 53

Gallant, Roy A(rthur) 1924- ....... CLC 17
See also CANR 4; CA 5-8R; SATA 4

Gallico, Paul (William) 1897-1976 ... CLC 2
See also CA 5-8R; obituary CA 69-72;
SATA 13; DLB 9

**Galsworthy, John** 1867-1933 ...... **TCLC 1**
See also CA 104; DLB 10, 34

**Galt, John** 1779-1839 ........... **NCLC 1**

**Galvin, James** 1951- .............. **CLC 38**
See also CANR 26; CA 108

**Gann, Ernest K(ellogg)** 1910- ...... **CLC 23**
See also CANR 1; CA 1-4R

**Garcia Lorca, Federico**
1899-1936 ................ **TCLC 1, 7**
See also CA 104

**Garcia Marquez, Gabriel (Jose)**
1928- .... **CLC 2, 3, 8, 10, 15, 27, 47, 55**
See also CANR 10; CA 33-36R

**Gardam, Jane** 1928- .............. **CLC 43**
See also CLR 12; CANR 2, 18; CA 49-52;
SATA 28, 39; DLB 14

**Gardner, Herb** 1934- ............. **CLC 44**

**Gardner, John (Champlin, Jr.)**
1933-1982 .... **CLC 2, 3, 5, 7, 8, 10, 18,
28, 34**
See also CA 65-68; obituary CA 107;
obituary SATA 31, 40; DLB 2; DLB-Y 82

**Gardner, John (Edmund)** 1926- ..... **CLC 30**
See also CANR 15; CA 103

**Garfield, Leon** 1921- .............. **CLC 12**
See also CA 17-20R; SATA 1, 32

**Garland, (Hannibal) Hamlin**
1860-1940 ................... **TCLC 3**
See also CA 104; DLB 12, 71

**Garneau, Hector (de) Saint Denys**
1912-1943 ................. **TCLC 13**
See also CA 111

**Garner, Alan** 1935- .............. **CLC 17**
See also CLR 20; CANR 15; CA 73-76;
SATA 18

**Garner, Hugh** 1913-1979 ......... **CLC 13**
See also CA 69-72; DLB 68

**Garnett, David** 1892-1981 ......... **CLC 3**
See also CANR 17; CA 5-8R;
obituary CA 103; DLB 34

**Garrett, George (Palmer, Jr.)**
1929- ................. **CLC 3, 11, 51**
See also CAAS 5; CANR 1; CA 1-4R;
DLB 2, 5; DLB-Y 83

**Garrigue, Jean** 1914-1972 ........ **CLC 2, 8**
See also CANR 20; CA 5-8R;
obituary CA 37-40R

**Gary, Romain** 1914-1980 ......... **CLC 25**
See also Kacew, Romain

**Gascar, Pierre** 1916- .............. **CLC 11**
See also Fournier, Pierre

**Gascoyne, David (Emery)** 1916- .... **CLC 45**
See also CANR 10; CA 65-68; DLB 20

**Gaskell, Elizabeth Cleghorn**
1810-1865 ................. **NCLC 5**
See also DLB 21

**Gass, William H(oward)**
1924- ......... **CLC 1, 2, 8, 11, 15, 39**
See also CA 17-20R; DLB 2

**Gautier, Theophile** 1811-1872 ..... **NCLC 1**

**Gaye, Marvin (Pentz)** 1939-1984 ... **CLC 26**
See also obituary CA 112

**Gebler, Carlo (Ernest)** 1954- ...... **CLC 39**
See also CA 119

**Gee, Maggie** 19??- .............. **CLC 57**

**Gee, Maurice (Gough)** 1931- ....... **CLC 29**
See also CA 97-100; SATA 46

**Gelbart, Larry (Simon)** 1923- ...... **CLC 21**
See also CA 73-76

**Gelber, Jack** 1932- ........... **CLC 1, 6, 14**
See also CANR 2; CA 1-4R; DLB 7

**Gellhorn, Martha (Ellis)** 1908- ..... **CLC 14**
See also CA 77-80; DLB-Y 82

**Genet, Jean**
1910-1986 ... **CLC 1, 2, 5, 10, 14, 44, 46**
See also CANR 18; CA 13-16R; DLB 72;
DLB-Y 86

**Gent, Peter** 1942- ................ **CLC 29**
See also CA 89-92; DLB 72; DLB-Y 82

**George, Jean Craighead** 1919- ...... **CLC 35**
See also CLR 1; CA 5-8R; SATA 2;
DLB 52

**George, Stefan (Anton)**
1868-1933 ................ **TCLC 2, 14**
See also CA 104

**Gerhardi, William (Alexander)** 1895-1977
See Gerhardie, William (Alexander)

**Gerhardie, William (Alexander)**
1895-1977 ................... **CLC 5**
See also CANR 18; CA 25-28R;
obituary CA 73-76; DLB 36

**Gertler, T(rudy)** 1946?- ........... **CLC 34**
See also CA 116

**Gessner, Friedrike Victoria** 1910-1980
See Adamson, Joy(-Friederike Victoria)

**Ghelderode, Michel de**
1898-1962 ................ **CLC 6, 11**
See also CA 85-88

**Ghiselin, Brewster** 1903- .......... **CLC 23**
See also CANR 13; CA 13-16R

**Ghose, Zulfikar** 1935- ............. **CLC 42**
See also CA 65-68

**Ghosh, Amitav** 1943- ............. **CLC 44**

**Giacosa, Giuseppe** 1847-1906 ...... **TCLC 7**
See also CA 104

**Gibbon, Lewis Grassic** 1901-1935 ... **TCLC 4**
See also Mitchell, James Leslie

**Gibbons, Kaye** 1960- ............. **CLC 50**

**Gibran, (Gibran) Kahlil**
1883-1931 ................ **TCLC 1, 9**
See also CA 104

**Gibson, William** 1914- ............ **CLC 23**
See also CANR 9; CA 9-12R; DLB 7

**Gibson, William** 1948- ............ **CLC 39**
See also CA 126

**Gide, Andre (Paul Guillaume)**
1869-1951 ................ **TCLC 5, 12**
See also CA 104, 124; DLB 65

**Gifford, Barry (Colby)** 1946- ....... **CLC 34**
See also CANR 9; CA 65-68

**Gilbert, (Sir) W(illiam) S(chwenck)**
1836-1911 ................... **TCLC 3**
See also CA 104; SATA 36

**Gilbreth, Ernestine** 1908-
See Carey, Ernestine Gilbreth

**Gilbreth, Frank B(unker), Jr.**
1911- ...................... **CLC 17**
See also CA 9-12R; SATA 2

**Gilchrist, Ellen** 1935- .......... **CLC 34, 48**
See also CA 113, 116

**Giles, Molly** 1942- .............. **CLC 39**
See also CA 126

**Gilliam, Terry (Vance)** 1940-
See Monty Python
See also CA 108, 113

**Gilliatt, Penelope (Ann Douglass)**
1932- ............... **CLC 2, 10, 13, 53**
See also CA 13-16R; DLB 14

**Gilman, Charlotte (Anna) Perkins (Stetson)**
1860-1935 ................... **TCLC 9**
See also CA 106

**Gilmour, David** 1944-
See Pink Floyd

**Gilroy, Frank D(aniel)** 1925- ........ **CLC 2**
See also CA 81-84; DLB 7

**Ginsberg, Allen**
1926- ......... **CLC 1, 2, 3, 4, 6, 13, 36**
See also CANR 2; CA 1-4R; DLB 5, 16;
CDALB 1941-1968

**Ginzburg, Natalia** 1916- ...... **CLC 5, 11, 54**
See also CA 85-88

**Giono, Jean** 1895-1970 .......... **CLC 4, 11**
See also CANR 2; CA 45-48;
obituary CA 29-32R; DLB 72

**Giovanni, Nikki** 1943- ........ **CLC 2, 4, 19**
See also CLR 6; CAAS 6; CANR 18;
CA 29-32R; SATA 24; DLB 5, 41

**Giovene, Andrea** 1904- ............. **CLC 7**
See also CA 85-88

**Gippius, Zinaida (Nikolayevna)** 1869-1945
See Hippius, Zinaida
See also CA 106

**Giraudoux, (Hippolyte) Jean**
1882-1944 ................ **TCLC 2, 7**
See also CA 104; DLB 65

**Gironella, Jose Maria** 1917- ....... **CLC 11**
See also CA 101

**Gissing, George (Robert)**
1857-1903 ............... **TCLC 3, 24**
See also CA 105; DLB 18

**Gladkov, Fyodor (Vasilyevich)**
1883-1958 ................ **TCLC 27**

**Glanville, Brian (Lester)** 1931- ...... **CLC 6**
See also CANR 3; CA 5-8R; SATA 42;
DLB 15

**Glasgow, Ellen (Anderson Gholson)**
1873?-1945 ................ **TCLC 2, 7**
See also CA 104; DLB 9, 12

**Glassco, John** 1909-1981 ........... **CLC 9**
See also CANR 15; CA 13-16R;
obituary CA 102; DLB 68

**Glasser, Ronald J.** 1940?- ......... **CLC 37**

**Glendinning, Victoria** 1937- ........ **CLC 50**
See also CA 120

**Glissant, Edouard** 1928- .......... **CLC 10**

**Gloag, Julian** 1930- .............. **CLC 40**
See also CANR 10; CA 65-68

**Grendon, Stephen** 1909-1971
See Derleth, August (William)

**Greve, Felix Paul Berthold Friedrich**
1879-1948
See Grove, Frederick Philip
See also CA 104

**Grey, (Pearl) Zane** 1872?-1939 . . . . . TCLC 6
See also CA 104; DLB 9

**Grieg, (Johan) Nordahl (Brun)**
1902-1943 . . . . . . . . . . . . . . . . TCLC 10
See also CA 107

**Grieve, C(hristopher) M(urray)** 1892-1978
See MacDiarmid, Hugh
See also CA 5-8R; obituary CA 85-88

**Griffin, Gerald** 1803-1840 . . . . . . . . NCLC 7

**Griffin, Peter** 1942- . . . . . . . . . . . . . CLC 39

**Griffiths, Trevor** 1935- . . . . . . . . CLC 13, 52
See also CA 97-100; DLB 13

**Grigson, Geoffrey (Edward Harvey)**
1905-1985 . . . . . . . . . . . . . . . . CLC 7, 39
See also CANR 20; CA 25-28R;
obituary CA 118; DLB 27

**Grillparzer, Franz** 1791-1872 . . . . . . NCLC 1

**Grimke, Charlotte L(ottie) Forten** 1837-1914
See Forten (Grimke), Charlotte L(ottie)
See also CA 117, 124

**Grimm, Jakob (Ludwig) Karl**
1785-1863 . . . . . . . . . . . . . . . . . NCLC 3
See also SATA 22

**Grimm, Wilhelm Karl** 1786-1859 . . NCLC 3
See also SATA 22

**Grimmelshausen, Johann Jakob Christoffel**
von 1621-1676 . . . . . . . . . . . . . . . . LC 6

**Grindel, Eugene** 1895-1952
See also CA 104

**Grossman, Vasily (Semenovich)**
1905-1964 . . . . . . . . . . . . . . . . . CLC 41
See also CA 124

**Grove, Frederick Philip**
1879-1948 . . . . . . . . . . . . . . . . . TCLC 4
See also Greve, Felix Paul Berthold
Friedrich

**Grumbach, Doris (Isaac)**
1918- . . . . . . . . . . . . . . . . . . CLC 13, 22
See also CAAS 2; CANR 9; CA 5-8R

**Grundtvig, Nicolai Frederik Severin**
1783-1872 . . . . . . . . . . . . . . . . . NCLC 1

**Grunwald, Lisa** 1959- . . . . . . . . . . . . CLC 44
See also CA 120

**Guare, John** 1938- . . . . . . . . . CLC 8, 14, 29
See also CANR 21; CA 73-76; DLB 7

**Gudjonsson, Halldor Kiljan** 1902-
See Laxness, Halldor (Kiljan)
See also CA 103

**Guest, Barbara** 1920- . . . . . . . . . . . . CLC 34
See also CANR 11; CA 25-28R; DLB 5

**Guest, Judith (Ann)** 1936- . . . . . . . CLC 8, 30
See also CANR 15; CA 77-80

**Guild, Nicholas M.** 1944- . . . . . . . . . CLC 33
See also CA 93-96

**Guillen, Jorge** 1893-1984 . . . . . . . . . . CLC 11
See also CA 89-92; obituary CA 112

**Guillen, Nicolas** 1902-1989 . . . . . . . . CLC 48
See also CA 116, 125

**Guillevic, (Eugene)** 1907- . . . . . . . . . CLC 33
See also CA 93-96

**Gunn, Bill** 1934-1989 . . . . . . . . . . . . . CLC 5
See also Gunn, William Harrison
See also DLB 38

**Gunn, Thom(son William)**
1929- . . . . . . . . . . . . . CLC 3, 6, 18, 32
See also CANR 9; CA 17-20R; DLB 27

**Gunn, William Harrison** 1934-1989
See Gunn, Bill
See also CANR 12, 25; CA 13-16R

**Gurney, A(lbert) R(amsdell), Jr.**
1930- . . . . . . . . . . . . . . CLC 32, 50, 54
See also CA 77-80

**Gurney, Ivor (Bertie)** 1890-1937 . . . TCLC 33

**Gustafson, Ralph (Barker)** 1909- . . . . CLC 36
See also CANR 8; CA 21-24R

**Guthrie, A(lfred) B(ertram), Jr.**
1901- . . . . . . . . . . . . . . . . . . . . CLC 23
See also CA 57-60; DLB 6

**Guthrie, Woodrow Wilson** 1912-1967
See Guthrie, Woody
See also CA 113; obituary CA 93-96

**Guthrie, Woody** 1912-1967 . . . . . . . . CLC 35
See also Guthrie, Woodrow Wilson

**Guy, Rosa (Cuthbert)** 1928- . . . . . CLC 26 13
See also CANR 14; CA 17-20R; SATA 14;
DLB 33

**Haavikko, Paavo (Juhani)**
1931- . . . . . . . . . . . . . . . . . CLC 18, 34
See also CA 106

**Hacker, Marilyn** 1942- . . . . . . . CLC 5, 9, 23
See also CA 77-80

**Haggard, (Sir) H(enry) Rider**
1856-1925 . . . . . . . . . . . . . . . . TCLC 11
See also CA 108; SATA 16; DLB 70

**Haig-Brown, Roderick L(angmere)**
1908-1976 . . . . . . . . . . . . . . . . . CLC 21
See also CANR 4; CA 5-8R;
obituary CA 69-72; SATA 12

**Hailey, Arthur** 1920- . . . . . . . . . . . . . CLC 5
See also CANR 2; CA 1-4R; DLB-Y 82

**Hailey, Elizabeth Forsythe** 1938- . . . CLC 40
See also CAAS 1; CANR 15; CA 93-96

**Haley, Alex (Palmer)** 1921- . . . . . . CLC 8, 12
See also CA 77-80; DLB 38

**Haliburton, Thomas Chandler**
1796-1865 . . . . . . . . . . . . . . . . NCLC 15
See also DLB 11

**Hall, Donald (Andrew, Jr.)**
1928- . . . . . . . . . . . . . . . CLC 1, 13, 37
See also CAAS 7; CANR 2; CA 5-8R;
SATA 23; DLB 5

**Hall, James Norman** 1887-1951 . . . TCLC 23
See also CA 123; SATA 21

**Hall, (Marguerite) Radclyffe**
1886-1943 . . . . . . . . . . . . . . . . TCLC 12
See also CA 110

**Hall, Rodney** 1935- . . . . . . . . . . . . . CLC 51
See also CA 109

**Halpern, Daniel** 1945- . . . . . . . . . . . CLC 14
See also CA 33-36R

**Hamburger, Michael (Peter Leopold)**
1924- . . . . . . . . . . . . . . . . . CLC 5, 14
See also CAAS 4; CANR 2; CA 5-8R;
DLB 27

**Hamill, Pete** 1935- . . . . . . . . . . . . . CLC 10
See also CANR 18; CA 25-28R

**Hamilton, Edmond** 1904-1977 . . . . . . CLC 1
See also CANR 3; CA 1-4R; DLB 8

**Hamilton, Gail** 1911-
See Corcoran, Barbara

**Hamilton, Ian** 1938- . . . . . . . . . . . . . CLC 55
See also CA 106; DLB 40

**Hamilton, Mollie** 1909?-
See Kaye, M(ary) M(argaret)

**Hamilton, (Anthony Walter) Patrick**
1904-1962 . . . . . . . . . . . . . . . . . CLC 51
See also obituary CA 113; DLB 10

**Hamilton, Virginia (Esther)** 1936- . . . CLC 26
See also CLR 1, 11; CANR 20; CA 25-28R;
SATA 4; DLB 33, 52

**Hammett, (Samuel) Dashiell**
1894-1961 . . . . . . . CLC 3, 5, 10, 19, 47
See also CA 81-84

**Hammon, Jupiter** 1711?-1800? . . . . NCLC 5
See also DLB 31, 50

**Hamner, Earl (Henry), Jr.** 1923- . . . CLC 12
See also CA 73-76; DLB 6

**Hampton, Christopher (James)**
1946- . . . . . . . . . . . . . . . . . . . . CLC 4
See also CA 25-28R; DLB 13

**Hamsun, Knut** 1859-1952 . . . . . . TCLC 2, 14
See also Pedersen, Knut

**Handke, Peter** 1942- . . CLC 5, 8, 10, 15, 38
See also CA 77-80

**Hanley, James** 1901-1985 . . . CLC 3, 5, 8, 13
See also CA 73-76; obituary CA 117

**Hannah, Barry** 1942- . . . . . . . . . . CLC 23, 38
See also CA 108, 110; DLB 6

**Hansberry, Lorraine (Vivian)**
1930-1965 . . . . . . . . . . . . . . . . . CLC 17
See also CA 109; obituary CA 25-28R;
DLB 7, 38; CDALB 1941-1968

**Hansen, Joseph** 1923- . . . . . . . . . . . . CLC 38
See also CANR 16; CA 29-32R

**Hansen, Martin** 1909-1955 . . . . . . . TCLC 32

**Hanson, Kenneth O(stlin)** 1922- . . . . CLC 13
See also CANR 7; CA 53-56

**Hardenberg, Friedrich (Leopold Freiherr) von**
1772-1801
See Novalis

**Hardwick, Elizabeth** 1916- . . . . . . . . CLC 13
See also CANR 3; CA 5-8R; DLB 6

**Hardy, Thomas**
1840-1928 . . . TCLC 4, 10, 18, 32; SSC 2
See also CA 104, 123; SATA 25; DLB 18,
19

**Hare, David** 1947- . . . . . . . . . . . . . CLC 29
See also CA 97-100; DLB 13

**Harlan, Louis R(udolph)** 1922- . . . . . CLC 34
See also CANR 25; CA 21-24R

**Harling, Robert** 1951?- . . . . . . . . . . . CLC 53

**Harmon, William (Ruth)** 1938- . . . . . CLC 38
See also CANR 14; CA 33-36R

Author Index

**Longfellow, Henry Wadsworth**
1807-1882 ................ **NCLC 2**
See also SATA 19; DLB 1, 59;
CDALB 1640-1865

**Longley, Michael** 1939-.......... **CLC 29**
See also CA 102; DLB 40

**Lopate, Phillip** 1943- ............. **CLC 29**
See also CA 97-100; DLB-Y 80

**Lopez Portillo (y Pacheco), Jose**
1920- ...................... **CLC 46**

**Lopez y Fuentes, Gregorio**
1897-1966 ................... **CLC 32**

**Lord, Bette Bao** 1938-.......... **CLC 23**
See also CA 107

**Lorde, Audre (Geraldine)** 1934-..... **CLC 18**
See also CANR 16, 26; CA 25-28R;
DLB 41

**Loti, Pierre** 1850-1923 .......... **TCLC 11**
See also Viaud, (Louis Marie) Julien

**Lovecraft, H(oward) P(hillips)**
1890-1937 ........ **TCLC 4, 22; SSC 3**
See also CA 104

**Lovelace, Earl** 1935-.............. **CLC 51**
See also CA 77-80

**Lowell, Amy** 1874-1925 ........ **TCLC 1, 8**
See also CA 104; DLB 54

**Lowell, James Russell** 1819-1891 .. **NCLC 2**
See also DLB 1, 11, 64; CDALB 1640-1865

**Lowell, Robert (Traill Spence, Jr.)**
1917-1977 ... **CLC 1, 2, 3, 4, 5, 8, 9, 11, 15, 37**
See also CANR 26; CA 9-12R;
obituary CA 73-76; CABS 2; DLB 5

**Lowndes, Marie (Adelaide) Belloc**
1868-1947 ................. **TCLC 12**
See also CA 107; DLB 70

**Lowry, (Clarence) Malcolm**
1909-1957 ................. **TCLC 6**
See also CA 105; DLB 15

**Loy, Mina** 1882-1966............. **CLC 28**
See also CA 113; DLB 4, 54

**Lucas, George** 1944-.............. **CLC 16**
See also CA 77-80

**Lucas, Victoria** 1932-1963
See Plath, Sylvia

**Ludlam, Charles** 1943-1987..... **CLC 46, 50**
See also CA 85-88; obituary CA 122

**Ludlum, Robert** 1927- ........ **CLC 22, 43**
See also CANR 25; CA 33-36R; DLB-Y 82

**Ludwig, Otto** 1813-1865.......... **NCLC 4**

**Lugones, Leopoldo** 1874-1938..... **TCLC 15**
See also CA 116

**Lu Hsun** 1881-1936 .............. **TCLC 3**

**Lukacs, Georg** 1885-1971......... **CLC 24**
See also Lukacs, Gyorgy

**Lukacs, Gyorgy** 1885-1971
See Lukacs, Georg
See also CA 101; obituary CA 29-32R

**Luke, Peter (Ambrose Cyprian)**
1919-...................... **CLC 38**
See also CA 81-84; DLB 13

**Lurie (Bishop), Alison**
1926-............... **CLC 4, 5, 18, 39**
See also CANR 2, 17; CA 1-4R; SATA 46;
DLB 2

**Lustig, Arnost** 1926-............. **CLC 56**
See also CA 69-72; SATA 56

**Luther, Martin** 1483-1546.......... **LC 9**

**Luzi, Mario** 1914-............... **CLC 13**
See also CANR 9; CA 61-64

**Lynn, Kenneth S(chuyler)** 1923-.... **CLC 50**
See also CANR 3; CA 1-4R

**Lytle, Andrew (Nelson)** 1902-...... **CLC 22**
See also CA 9-12R; DLB 6

**Lyttelton, George** 1709-1773....... **LC 10**

**Lytton, Edward Bulwer** 1803-1873
See Bulwer-Lytton, (Lord) Edward (George
Earle Lytton)
See also SATA 23

**Maas, Peter** 1929- ............... **CLC 29**
See also CA 93-96

**Macaulay, (Dame Emile) Rose**
1881-1958 ................. **TCLC 7**
See also CA 104; DLB 36

**MacBeth, George (Mann)**
1932-.................... **CLC 2, 5, 9**
See also CA 25-28R; SATA 4; DLB 40

**MacCaig, Norman (Alexander)**
1910-...................... **CLC 36**
See also CANR 3; CA 9-12R; DLB 27

**MacDermot, Thomas H.** 1870-1933
See Redcam, Tom

**MacDiarmid, Hugh**
1892-1978 ............ **CLC 2, 4, 11, 19**
See also Grieve, C(hristopher) M(urray)
See also DLB 20

**Macdonald, Cynthia** 1928-...... **CLC 13, 19**
See also CANR 4; CA 49-52

**MacDonald, George** 1824-1905..... **TCLC 9**
See also CA 106; SATA 33; DLB 18

**MacDonald, John D(ann)**
1916-1986 ............. **CLC 3, 27, 44**
See also CANR 1, 19; CA 1-4R;
obituary CA 121; DLB 8; DLB-Y 86

**Macdonald, (John) Ross**
1915-1983 ...... **CLC 1, 2, 3, 14, 34, 41**
See also Millar, Kenneth

**MacEwen, Gwendolyn (Margaret)**
1941-1987 ................. **CLC 13, 55**
See also CANR 7, 22; CA 9-12R;
obituary CA 124; SATA 50; DLB 53

**Machado (y Ruiz), Antonio**
1875-1939 ................... **TCLC 3**
See also CA 104

**Machado de Assis, (Joaquim Maria)**
1839-1908 ................. **TCLC 10**
See also CA 107

**Machen, Arthur (Llewellyn Jones)**
1863-1947 ................. **TCLC 4**
See also CA 104; DLB 36

**Machiavelli, Niccolo** 1469-1527 ...... **LC 8**

**MacInnes, Colin** 1914-1976...... **CLC 4, 23**
See also CA 69-72; obituary CA 65-68;
DLB 14

**MacInnes, Helen (Clark)**
1907-1985 ................ **CLC 27, 39**
See also CANR 1; CA 1-4R;
obituary CA 65-68, 117; SATA 22, 44

**Macintosh, Elizabeth** 1897-1952
See Tey, Josephine
See also CA 110

**Mackenzie, (Edward Montague) Compton**
1883-1972 ................... **CLC 18**
See also CAP 2; CA 21-22;
obituary CA 37-40R; DLB 34

**Mac Laverty, Bernard** 1942-....... **CLC 31**
See also CA 116, 118

**MacLean, Alistair (Stuart)**
1922-1987.............. **CLC 3, 13, 50**
See also CA 57-60; obituary CA 121;
SATA 23

**MacLeish, Archibald**
1892-1982 .............. **CLC 3, 8, 14**
See also CA 9-12R; obituary CA 106;
DLB 4, 7, 45; DLB-Y 82

**MacLennan, (John) Hugh**
1907-...................... **CLC 2, 14**
See also CA 5-8R

**MacLeod, Alistair** 1936- .......... **CLC 56**
See also CA 123; DLB 60

**MacNeice, (Frederick) Louis**
1907-1963 ............ **CLC 1, 4, 10, 53**
See also CA 85-88; DLB 10, 20

**Macpherson, (Jean) Jay** 1931-...... **CLC 14**
See also CA 5-8R; DLB 53

**MacShane, Frank** 1927-........... **CLC 39**
See also CANR 3; CA 11-12R

**Macumber, Mari** 1896-1966
See Sandoz, Mari (Susette)

**Madach, Imre** 1823-1864........ **NCLC 19**

**Madden, (Jerry) David** 1933- .... **CLC 5, 15**
See also CAAS 3; CANR 4; CA 1-4R;
DLB 6

**Madhubuti, Haki R.** 1942-.......... **CLC 6**
See also Lee, Don L.
See also CANR 24; CA 73-76; DLB 5, 41

**Maeterlinck, Maurice** 1862-1949 ... **TCLC 3**
See also CA 104

**Mafouz, Naguib** 1912-
See Mahfuz, Najib

**Maginn, William** 1794-1842....... **NCLC 8**

**Mahapatra, Jayanta** 1928-........ **CLC 33**
See also CANR 15; CA 73-76

**Mahfuz Najib** 1912-........... **CLC 52, 55**
See also DLB-Y 88

**Mahon, Derek** 1941-.............. **CLC 27**
See also CA 113; DLB 40

**Mailer, Norman**
1923- ...... **CLC 1, 2, 3, 4, 5, 8, 11, 14, 28, 39**
See also CA 9-12R; CABS 1; DLB 2, 16,
28; DLB-Y 80, 83; DLB-DS 3

**Maillet, Antonine** 1929-.......... **CLC 54**
See also CA 115, 120; DLB 60

**Mais, Roger** 1905-1955 .......... **TCLC 8**
See also CA 105

**Maitland, Sara (Louise)** 1950-...... **CLC 49**
See also CANR 13; CA 69-72

Nichols, John (Treadwell) 1940-.... CLC 38
See also CAAS 2; CANR 6; CA 9-12R;
DLB-Y 82

Nichols, Peter (Richard) 1927-... CLC 5, 36
See also CA 104; DLB 13

Nicolas, F.R.E. 1927-
See Freeling, Nicolas

Niedecker, Lorine 1903-1970.... CLC 10, 42
See also CAP 2; CA 25-28; DLB 48

Nietzsche, Friedrich (Wilhelm)
1844-1900 .............. TCLC 10, 18
See also CA 107

Nievo, Ippolito 1831-1861 ....... NCLC 22

Nightingale, Anne Redmon 1943-
See Redmon (Nightingale), Anne
See also CA 103

Nin, Anais 1903-1977... CLC 1, 4, 8, 11, 14
See also CANR 22; CA 13-16R;
obituary CA 69-72; DLB 2, 4

Nissenson, Hugh 1933-.......... CLC 4, 9
See also CA 17-20R; DLB 28

Niven, Larry 1938-............... CLC 8
See also Niven, Laurence Van Cott
See also DLB 8

Niven, Laurence Van Cott 1938-
See Niven, Larry
See also CANR 14; CA 21-24R

Nixon, Agnes Eckhardt 1927-...... CLC 21
See also CA 110

Nkosi, Lewis 1936-.............. CLC 45
See also CA 65-68

Nodier, (Jean) Charles (Emmanuel)
1780-1844 .....,...... NCLC 19

Nordhoff, Charles 1887-1947...... TCLC 23
See also CA 108; SATA 23; DLB 9

Norman, Marsha 1947- .......... CLC 28
See also CA 105; DLB-Y 84

Norris, (Benjamin) Frank(lin)
1870-1902 ................. TCLC 24
See also CA 110; DLB 12, 71;
CDALB 1865-1917

Norris, Leslie 1921-............. CLC 14
See also CANR 14; CAP 1; CA 11-12;
DLB 27

North, Andrew 1912-
See Norton, Andre

North, Christopher 1785-1854
See Wilson, John

Norton, Alice Mary 1912-
See Norton, Andre
See also CANR 2; CA 1-4R; SATA 1, 43

Norton, Andre 1912- ............ CLC 12
See also Norton, Mary Alice
See also DLB 8, 52

Norway, Nevil Shute 1899-1960
See Shute (Norway), Nevil
See also CA 102; obituary CA 93-96

Norwid, Cyprian Kamil
1821-1883 ................ NCLC 17

Nossack, Hans Erich 1901-1978 ..... CLC 6
See also CA 93-96; obituary CA 85-88;
DLB 69

Nova, Craig 1945-............. CLC 7, 31
See also CANR 2; CA 45-48

Novak, Joseph 1933-
See Kosinski, Jerzy (Nikodem)

Novalis 1772-1801 ............. NCLC 13

Nowlan, Alden (Albert) 1933-...... CLC 15
See also CANR 5; CA 9-12R; DLB 53

Noyes, Alfred 1880-1958 ......... TCLC 7
See also CA 104; DLB 20

Nunn, Kem 19??-................ CLC 34

Nye, Robert 1939- ........... CLC 13, 42
See also CA 33-36R; SATA 6; DLB 14

Nyro, Laura 1947- ............. CLC 17

Oates, Joyce Carol
1938-..... CLC 1, 2, 3, 6, 9, 11, 15, 19,
33, 52
See also CANR 25; CA 5-8R; DLB 2, 5;
DLB-Y 81

O'Brien, Darcy 1939-............ CLC 11
See also CANR 8; CA 21-24R

O'Brien, Edna 1932-.... CLC 3, 5, 8, 13, 36
See also CANR 6; CA 1-4R; DLB 14

O'Brien, Fitz-James 1828?-1862.. NCLC 21
See also DLB 74

O'Brien, Flann
1911-1966 ....... CLC 1, 4, 5, 7, 10, 47
See also O Nuallain, Brian

O'Brien, Richard 19??-............ CLC 17
See also CA 124

O'Brien, (William) Tim(othy)
1946-.................. CLC 7, 19, 40
See also CA 85-88; DLB-Y 80

Obstfelder, Sigbjorn 1866-1900.... TCLC 23
See also CA 123

O'Casey, Sean
1880-1964 ......... CLC 1, 5, 9, 11, 15
See also CA 89-92; DLB 10

Ochs, Phil 1940-1976............ CLC 17
See also obituary CA 65-68

O'Connor, Edwin (Greene)
1918-1968 ................. CLC 14
See also CA 93-96; obituary CA 25-28R

O'Connor, (Mary) Flannery
1925-1964 ... CLC 1, 2, 3, 6, 10, 13, 15,
21; SSC 1
See also CANR 3; CA 1-4R; DLB 2;
DLB-Y 80; CDALB 1941-1968

O'Connor, Frank
1903-1966 ........ CLC 14, 23; SSC 5
See also O'Donovan, Michael (John)
See also CA 93-96

O'Dell, Scott 1903-.............. CLC 30
See also CLR 1, 16; CANR 12; CA 61-64;
SATA 12; DLB 52

Odets, Clifford 1906-1963 ...... CLC 2, 28
See also CA 85-88; DLB 7, 26

O'Donovan, Michael (John) 1903-1966
See O'Connor, Frank
See also CA 93-96

Oe, Kenzaburo 1935-.......... CLC 10, 36
See also CA 97-100

O'Faolain, Julia 1932-....... CLC 6, 19, 47
See also CAAS 2; CANR 12; CA 81-84;
DLB 14

O'Faolain, Sean 1900-..... CLC 1, 7, 14, 32
See also CANR 12; CA 61-64; DLB 15

O'Flaherty, Liam 1896-1984 ..... CLC 5, 34
See also CA 101; obituary CA 113; DLB 36;
DLB-Y 84

O'Grady, Standish (James)
1846-1928 ................. TCLC 5
See also CA 104

O'Hara, Frank 1926-1966 ..... CLC 2, 5, 13
See also CA 9-12R; obituary CA 25-28R;
DLB 5, 16

O'Hara, John (Henry)
1905-1970 ...... CLC 1, 2, 3, 6, 11, 42
See also CA 5-8R; obituary CA 25-28R;
DLB 9; DLB-DS 2

O'Hara Family
See Banim, John and Banim, Michael

O'Hehir, Diana 1922-............ CLC 41
See also CA 93-96

Okigbo, Christopher (Ifenayichukwu)
1932-1967 ................. CLC 25
See also CA 77-80

Olds, Sharon 1942-............ CLC 32, 39
See also CANR 18; CA 101

Olesha, Yuri (Karlovich)
1899-1960 ................. CLC 8
See also CA 85-88

Oliphant, Margaret (Oliphant Wilson)
1828-1897 ................. NCLC 11
See also DLB 18

Oliver, Mary 1935-............ CLC 19, 34
See also CANR 9; CA 21-24R; DLB 5

Olivier, (Baron) Laurence (Kerr)
1907- ..................... CLC 20
See also CA 111

Olsen, Tillie 1913- ............. CLC 4, 13
See also CANR 1; CA 1-4R; DLB 28;
DLB-Y 80

Olson, Charles (John)
1910-1970 ..... CLC 1, 2, 5, 6, 9, 11, 29
See also CAP 1; CA 15-16;
obituary CA 25-28R; CABS 2; DLB 5, 16

Olson, Theodore 1937-
See Olson, Toby

Olson, Toby 1937- .............. CLC 28
See also CANR 9; CA 65-68

Ondaatje, (Philip) Michael
1943- ................. CLC 14, 29, 51
See also CA 77-80; DLB 60

Oneal, Elizabeth 1934-
See Oneal, Zibby
See also CA 106; SATA 30

Oneal, Zibby 1934-.............. CLC 30
See also Oneal, Elizabeth

O'Neill, Eugene (Gladstone)
1888-1953 ............. TCLC 1, 6, 27
See also CA 110; DLB 7

Onetti, Juan Carlos 1909-....... CLC 7, 10
See also CA 85-88

O'Nolan, Brian 1911-1966
See O'Brien, Flann

O Nuallain, Brian 1911-1966
See O'Brien, Flann
See also CAP 2; CA 21-22;
obituary CA 25-28R

Remark, Erich Paul 1898-1970
See Remarque, Erich Maria

Remarque, Erich Maria
1898-1970 ................. CLC 21
See also CA 77-80; obituary CA 29-32R;
DLB 56

Remizov, Alexey (Mikhailovich)
1877-1957 ................. TCLC 27
See also CA 125

Renan, Joseph Ernest
1823-1892 ................ NCLC 26

Renard, Jules 1864-1910 ........ TCLC 17
See also CA 117

Renault, Mary 1905-1983 .... CLC 3, 11, 17
See also Challans, Mary
See also DLB-Y 83

Rendell, Ruth 1930- .......... CLC 28, 48
See also Vine, Barbara
See also CA 109

Renoir, Jean 1894-1979 .......... CLC 20
See also obituary CA 85-88

Resnais, Alain 1922- ............ CLC 16

Reverdy, Pierre 1899-1960 ....... CLC 53
See also CA 97-100; obituary CA 89-92

Rexroth, Kenneth
1905-1982 ...... CLC 1, 2, 6, 11, 22, 49
See also CANR 14; CA 5-8R;
obituary CA 107; DLB 16, 48; DLB-Y 82;
CDALB 1941-1968

Reyes, Alfonso 1889-1959 ....... TCLC 33

Reyes y Basoalto, Ricardo Eliecer Neftali
1904-1973
See Neruda, Pablo

Reymont, Wladyslaw Stanislaw
1867-1925 ................. TCLC 5
See also CA 104

Reynolds, Jonathan 1942?- ...... CLC 6, 38
See also CA 65-68

Reynolds, Michael (Shane) 1937- ... CLC 44
See also CANR 9; CA 65-68

Reznikoff, Charles 1894-1976 ....... CLC 9
See also CAP 2; CA 33-36;
obituary CA 61-64; DLB 28, 45

Rezzori, Gregor von 1914- ......... CLC 25
See also CA 122

Rhys, Jean
1890-1979 ...... CLC 2, 4, 6, 14, 19, 51
See also CA 25-28R; obituary CA 85-88;
DLB 36

Ribeiro, Darcy 1922- ............ CLC 34
See also CA 33-36R

Ribeiro, Joao Ubaldo (Osorio Pimentel)
1941- ........................ CLC 10
See also CA 81-84

Ribman, Ronald (Burt) 1932- ....... CLC 7
See also CA 21-24R

Rice, Anne 1941- ................ CLC 41
See also CANR 12; CA 65-68

Rice, Elmer 1892-1967 .......... CLC 7, 49
See also CAP 2; CA 21-22;
obituary CA 25-28R; DLB 4, 7

Rice, Tim 1944- ................. CLC 21
See also CA 103

Rich, Adrienne (Cecile)
1929- ......... CLC 3, 6, 7, 11, 18, 36
See also CANR 20; CA 9-12R; DLB 5, 67

Richard, Keith 1943- ............. CLC 17
See also CA 107

Richards, I(vor) A(rmstrong)
1893-1979 ............. CLC 14, 24
See also CA 41-44R; obituary CA 89-92;
DLB 27

Richards, Keith 1943-
See Richard, Keith
See also CA 107

Richardson, Dorothy (Miller)
1873-1957 .................. TCLC 3
See also CA 104; DLB 36

Richardson, Ethel 1870-1946
See Richardson, Henry Handel
See also CA 105

Richardson, Henry Handel
1870-1946 .................. TCLC 4
See also Richardson, Ethel

Richardson, Samuel 1689-1761 ....... LC 1
See also DLB 39

Richler, Mordecai
1931- .......... CLC 3, 5, 9, 13, 18, 46
See also CA 65-68; SATA 27, 44; DLB 53

Richter, Conrad (Michael)
1890-1968 .................. CLC 30
See also CA 5-8R; obituary CA 25-28R;
SATA 3; DLB 9

Richter, Johann Paul Friedrich 1763-1825
See Jean Paul

Riding, Laura 1901- ............. CLC 3, 7
See also Jackson, Laura (Riding)

Riefenstahl, Berta Helene Amalia
1902- ..................... CLC 16
See also Riefenstahl, Leni
See also CA 108

Riefenstahl, Leni 1902- ........... CLC 16
See also Riefenstahl, Berta Helene Amalia
See also CA 108

Rilke, Rainer Maria
1875-1926 ............. TCLC 1, 6, 19
See also CA 104

Rimbaud, (Jean Nicolas) Arthur
1854-1891 ................. NCLC 4

Ringwood, Gwen(dolyn Margaret) Pharis
1910-1984 ................. CLC 48
See also obituary CA 112

Rio, Michel 19??- ............... CLC 43

Ritsos, Yannis 1909- ........ CLC 6, 13, 31
See also CA 77-80

Ritter, Erika 1948?- ............. CLC 52

Rivera, Jose Eustasio 1889-1928 ... TCLC 35

Rivers, Conrad Kent 1933-1968 ..... CLC 1
See also CA 85-88; DLB 41

Roa Bastos, Augusto 1917- ........ CLC 45

Robbe-Grillet, Alain
1922- ...... CLC 1, 2, 4, 6, 8, 10, 14, 43
See also CA 9-12R

Robbins, Harold 1916- ............ CLC 5
See also CANR 26; CA 73-76

Robbins, Thomas Eugene 1936-
See Robbins, Tom
See also CA 81-84

Robbins, Tom 1936- ............ CLC 9, 32
See also Robbins, Thomas Eugene
See also DLB-Y 80

Robbins, Trina 1938- ............ CLC 21

Roberts, (Sir) Charles G(eorge) D(ouglas)
1860-1943 .................. TCLC 8
See also CA 105; SATA 29

Roberts, Kate 1891-1985 ......... CLC 15
See also CA 107; obituary CA 116

Roberts, Keith (John Kingston)
1935- ..................... CLC 14
See also CA 25-28R

Roberts, Kenneth 1885-1957 ...... TCLC 23
See also CA 109; DLB 9

Roberts, Michele (B.) 1949- ........ CLC 48
See also CA 115

Robinson, Edwin Arlington
1869-1935 .................. TCLC 5
See also CA 104; DLB 54;
CDALB 1865-1917

Robinson, Henry Crabb
1775-1867 ................. NCLC 15

Robinson, Jill 1936- ............. CLC 10
See also CA 102

Robinson, Kim Stanley 19??- ....... CLC 34
See also CA 126

Robinson, Marilynne 1944- ........ CLC 25
See also CA 116

Robinson, Smokey 1940- .......... CLC 21

Robinson, William 1940-
See Robinson, Smokey
See also CA 116

Robison, Mary 1949- ............. CLC 42
See also CA 113, 116

Roddenberry, Gene 1921- ......... CLC 17
See also CANR 110

Rodgers, Mary 1931- ............. CLC 12
See also CLR 20; CANR 8; CA 49-52;
SATA 8

Rodgers, W(illiam) R(obert)
1909-1969 ................... CLC 7
See also CA 85-88; DLB 20

Rodriguez, Claudio 1934- ......... CLC 10

Roethke, Theodore (Huebner)
1908-1963 ..... CLC 1, 3, 8, 11, 19, 46
See also CA 81-84; CABS 2; SAAS 1;
DLB 5; CDALB 1941-1968

Rogers, Sam 1943-
See Shepard, Sam

Rogers, Thomas (Hunton) 1931- .... CLC 57
See also CA 89-92

Rogers, Will(iam Penn Adair)
1879-1935 .................. TCLC 8
See also CA 105; DLB 11

Rogin, Gilbert 1929- ............. CLC 18
See also CANR 15; CA 65-68

Rohan, Koda 1867-1947 .......... TCLC 22
See also CA 121

Rohmer, Eric 1920- ............. CLC 16
See also Scherer, Jean-Marie Maurice

Rohmer, Sax  1883-1959 . . . . . . . . . TCLC 28
  See also Ward, Arthur Henry Sarsfield
  See also CA 108; DLB 70

Roiphe, Anne (Richardson)
  1935- . . . . . . . . . . . . . . . . . . . . . CLC 3, 9
  See also CA 89-92; DLB-Y 80

Rolfe, Frederick (William Serafino Austin
  Lewis Mary) 1860-1913 . . . . . . TCLC 12
  See also CA 107; DLB 34

Rolland, Romain  1866-1944 . . . . . . . TCLC 23
  See also CA 118

Rolvaag, O(le) E(dvart)
  1876-1931 . . . . . . . . . . . . . . . . TCLC 17
  See also CA 117; DLB 9

Romains, Jules  1885-1972 . . . . . . . . . CLC 7
  See also CA 85-88

Romero, Jose Ruben  1890-1952 . . . TCLC 14
  See also CA 114

Ronsard, Pierre de  1524-1585 . . . . . . . LC 6

Rooke, Leon  1934- . . . . . . . . . . . CLC 25, 34
  See also CANR 23; CA 25-28R

Roper, William  1498-1578 . . . . . . . . . LC 10

Rosa, Joao Guimaraes  1908-1967 . . . CLC 23
  See also obituary CA 89-92

Rosen, Richard (Dean)  1949- . . . . . . . CLC 39
  See also CA 77-80

Rosenberg, Isaac  1890-1918 . . . . . . TCLC 12
  See also CA 107; DLB 20

Rosenblatt, Joe  1933- . . . . . . . . . . . . CLC 15
  See also Rosenblatt, Joseph

Rosenblatt, Joseph  1933-
  See Rosenblatt, Joe
  See also CA 89-92

Rosenfeld, Samuel  1896-1963
  See Tzara, Tristan
  See also obituary CA 89-92

Rosenthal, M(acha) L(ouis)  1917- . . . CLC 28
  See also CAAS 6; CANR 4; CA 1-4R;
  DLB 5

Ross, (James) Sinclair  1908- . . . . . . . CLC 13
  See also CA 73-76

Rossetti, Christina Georgina
  1830-1894 . . . . . . . . . . . . . . . . . NCLC 2
  See also SATA 20; DLB 35

Rossetti, Dante Gabriel
  1828-1882 . . . . . . . . . . . . . . . . . NCLC 4
  See also DLB 35

Rossetti, Gabriel Charles Dante  1828-1882
  See Rossetti, Dante Gabriel

Rossner, Judith (Perelman)
  1935- . . . . . . . . . . . . . . . . . CLC 6, 9, 29
  See also CANR 18; CA 17-20R; DLB 6

Rostand, Edmond (Eugene Alexis)
  1868-1918 . . . . . . . . . . . . . . . . . TCLC 6
  See also CA 104, 126

Roth, Henry  1906- . . . . . . . . . . CLC 2, 6, 11
  See also CAP 1; CA 11-12; DLB 28

Roth, Joseph  1894-1939 . . . . . . . . . TCLC 33

Roth, Philip (Milton)
  1933- . . . . . . CLC 1, 2, 3, 4, 6, 9, 15, 22,
                                        31, 47
  See also CANR 1, 22; CA 1-4R; DLB 2, 28;
  DLB-Y 82

Rothenberg, James  1931- . . . . . . . . . CLC 57

Rothenberg, Jerome  1931- . . . . . . . . . CLC 6
  See also CANR 1; CA 45-48; DLB 5

Roumain, Jacques  1907-1944 . . . . . TCLC 19
  See also CA 117

Rourke, Constance (Mayfield)
  1885-1941 . . . . . . . . . . . . . . . . TCLC 12
  See also YABC 1; CA 107

Rousseau, Jean-Baptiste  1671-1741 . . . LC 9

Roussel, Raymond  1877-1933 . . . . TCLC 20
  See also CA 117

Rovit, Earl (Herbert)  1927- . . . . . . . . CLC 7
  See also CANR 12; CA 5-8R

Rowe, Nicholas  1674-1718 . . . . . . . . . . LC 8

Rowson, Susanna Haswell
  1762-1824 . . . . . . . . . . . . . . . . . NCLC 5
  See also DLB 37

Roy, Gabrielle  1909-1983 . . . . . . CLC 10, 14
  See also CANR 5; CA 53-56;
  obituary CA 110; DLB 68

Rozewicz, Tadeusz  1921- . . . . . . . . CLC 9, 23
  See also CA 108

Ruark, Gibbons  1941- . . . . . . . . . . . . CLC 3
  See also CANR 14; CA 33-36R

Rubens, Bernice  192?- . . . . . . . . CLC 19, 31
  See also CA 25-28R; DLB 14

Rudkin, (James) David  1936- . . . . . . CLC 14
  See also CA 89-92; DLB 13

Rudnik, Raphael  1933- . . . . . . . . . . . . CLC 7
  See also CA 29-32R

Ruiz, Jose Martinez  1874-1967
  See Azorin

Rukeyser, Muriel
  1913-1980 . . . . . . . . . . CLC 6, 10, 15, 27
  See also CANR 26; CA 5-8R;
  obituary CA 93-96; obituary SATA 22;
  DLB 48

Rule, Jane (Vance)  1931- . . . . . . . . . . CLC 27
  See also CANR 12; CA 25-28R; DLB 60

Rulfo, Juan  1918-1986 . . . . . . . . . . . . CLC 8
  See also CANR 26; CA 85-88;
  obituary CA 118

Runyon, (Alfred) Damon
  1880-1946 . . . . . . . . . . . . . . . . TCLC 10
  See also CA 107; DLB 11

Rush, Norman  1933- . . . . . . . . . . . . CLC 44
  See also CA 121, 126

Rushdie, (Ahmed) Salman
  1947- . . . . . . . . . . . . . . . CLC 23, 31, 55
  See also CA 108, 111

Rushforth, Peter (Scott)  1945- . . . . . CLC 19
  See also CA 101

Ruskin, John  1819-1900 . . . . . . . . . TCLC 20
  See also CA 114; SATA 24; DLB 55

Russ, Joanna  1937- . . . . . . . . . . . . . CLC 15
  See also CANR 11; CA 25-28R; DLB 8

Russell, George William  1867-1935
  See A. E.
  See also CA 104

Russell, (Henry) Ken(neth Alfred)
  1927- . . . . . . . . . . . . . . . . . . . . . CLC 16
  See also CA 105

Rutherford, Mark  1831-1913 . . . . . . TCLC 25
  See also CA 121; DLB 18

Ruyslinck, Ward  1929- . . . . . . . . . . . CLC 14

Ryan, Cornelius (John)  1920-1974 . . . CLC 7
  See also CA 69-72; obituary CA 53-56

Rybakov, Anatoli  1911?- . . . . . . . CLC 23, 53
  See also CA 126

Ryder, Jonathan  1927-
  See Ludlum, Robert

Ryga, George  1932- . . . . . . . . . . . . . CLC 14
  See also CA 101; obituary CA 124; DLB 60

Séviné, Marquise de Marie de
  Rabutin-Chantal  1626-1696 . . . . . LC 11

Saba, Umberto  1883-1957 . . . . . . . TCLC 33

Sabato, Ernesto  1911- . . . . . . . CLC 10, 23
  See also CA 97-100

Sachs, Marilyn (Stickle)  1927- . . . . . CLC 35
  See also CLR 2; CANR 13; CA 17-20R;
  SAAS 2; SATA 3, 52

Sachs, Nelly  1891-1970 . . . . . . . . . . CLC 14
  See also CAP 2; CA 17-18;
  obituary CA 25-28R

Sackler, Howard (Oliver)
  1929-1982 . . . . . . . . . . . . . . . . . CLC 14
  See also CA 61-64; obituary CA 108; DLB 7

Sade, Donatien Alphonse Francois, Comte de
  1740-1814 . . . . . . . . . . . . . . . . . NCLC 3

Sadoff, Ira  1945- . . . . . . . . . . . . . . . . CLC 9
  See also CANR 5, 21; CA 53-56

Safire, William  1929- . . . . . . . . . . . . CLC 10
  See also CA 17-20R

Sagan, Carl (Edward)  1934- . . . . . . . CLC 30
  See also CANR 11; CA 25-28R

Sagan, Francoise
  1935- . . . . . . . . . . . . CLC 3, 6, 9, 17, 36
  See also Quoirez, Francoise
  See also CANR 6

Sahgal, Nayantara (Pandit)  1927- . . . CLC 41
  See also CANR 11; CA 9-12R

Saint, H(arry) F.  1941- . . . . . . . . . . CLC 50

Sainte-Beuve, Charles Augustin
  1804-1869 . . . . . . . . . . . . . . . . . NCLC 5

Sainte-Marie, Beverly  1941-
  See Sainte-Marie, Buffy
  See also CA 107

Sainte-Marie, Buffy  1941- . . . . . . . . CLC 17
  See also Sainte-Marie, Beverly

Saint-Exupery, Antoine (Jean Baptiste Marie
  Roger) de  1900-1944 . . . . . . . . TCLC 2
  See also CLR 10; CA 108; SATA 20;
  DLB 72

Saintsbury, George  1845-1933 . . . . . TCLC 31
  See also DLB 57

Sait Faik (Abasiyanik)
  1906-1954 . . . . . . . . . . . . . . . . TCLC 23

Saki  1870-1916 . . . . . . . . . . . . . . . . TCLC 3
  See also Munro, H(ector) H(ugh)
  See also CA 104

Salama, Hannu  1936- . . . . . . . . . . . . CLC 18

Salamanca, J(ack) R(ichard)
  1922- . . . . . . . . . . . . . . . . . . CLC 4, 15
  See also CA 25-28R

Salinas, Pedro  1891-1951 . . . . . . . . TCLC 17
  See also CA 117

**Sillitoe, Alan**
1928- .......... CLC 1, 3, 6, 10, 19, 57
See also CAAS 2; CANR 8, 26; CA 9-12R;
DLB 14

**Silone, Ignazio** 1900-1978 ......... CLC 4
See also CAAS 2; CANR 26; CAP 2;
CA 25-28, 11-12R,; obituary CA 81-84

**Silver, Joan Micklin** 1935- ........ CLC 20
See also CA 114, 121

**Silverberg, Robert** 1935- ........... CLC 7
See also CAAS 3; CANR 1, 20; CA 1-4R;
SATA 13; DLB 8

**Silverstein, Alvin** 1933- ........... CLC 17
See also CANR 2; CA 49-52; SATA 8

**Silverstein, Virginia B(arbara Opshelor)**
1937- ..................... CLC 17
See also CANR 2; CA 49-52; SATA 8

**Simak, Clifford D(onald)**
1904-1988 ................ CLC 1, 55
See also CANR 1; CA 1-4R;
obituary CA 125; DLB 8

**Simenon, Georges (Jacques Christian)**
1903-1989 ...... CLC 1, 2, 3, 8, 18, 47
See also CA 85-88; DLB 72

**Simenon, Paul** 1956?-
See The Clash

**Simic, Charles** 1938- ...... CLC 6, 9, 22, 49
See also CAAS 4; CANR 12; CA 29-32R

**Simmons, Charles (Paul)** 1924- ..... CLC 57
See also CA 89-92

**Simmons, Dan** 1948- ............. CLC 44

**Simmons, James (Stewart Alexander)**
1933- ...................... CLC 43
See also CA 105; DLB 40

**Simms, William Gilmore**
1806-1870 ................ NCLC 3
See also DLB 3, 30

**Simon, Carly** 1945- .............. CLC 26
See also CA 105

**Simon, Claude (Henri Eugene)**
1913- ................ CLC 4, 9, 15, 39
See also CA 89-92

**Simon, (Marvin) Neil**
1927- .............. CLC 6, 11, 31, 39
See also CA 21-24R; DLB 7

**Simon, Paul** 1941- ............... CLC 17
See also CA 116

**Simonon, Paul** 1956?-
See The Clash

**Simpson, Louis (Aston Marantz)**
1923- ................CLC 4, 7, 9, 32
See also CAAS 4; CANR 1; CA 1-4R;
DLB 5

**Simpson, Mona (Elizabeth)** 1957-... CLC 44
See also CA 122

**Simpson, N(orman) F(rederick)**
1919- ....................... CLC 29
See also CA 11-14R; DLB 13

**Sinclair, Andrew (Annandale)**
1935- ..................... CLC 2, 14
See also CAAS 5; CANR 14; CA 9-12R;
DLB 14

**Sinclair, Mary Amelia St. Clair** 1865?-1946
See Sinclair, May
See also CA 104

**Sinclair, May** 1865?-1946 ...... TCLC 3, 11
See also Sinclair, Mary Amelia St. Clair
See also DLB 36

**Sinclair, Upton (Beall)**
1878-1968 ............... CLC 1, 11, 15
See also CANR 7; CA 5-8R;
obituary CA 25-28R; SATA 9; DLB 9

**Singer, Isaac Bashevis**
1904- .... CLC 1, 3, 6, 9, 11, 15, 23, 38;
SSC 3
See also CLR 1; CANR 1; CA 1-4R;
SATA 3, 27; DLB 6, 28, 52;
CDALB 1941-1968

**Singer, Israel Joshua** 1893-1944 ... TCLC 33

**Singh, Khushwant** 1915-........... CLC 11
See also CANR 6; CA 9-12R

**Sinyavsky, Andrei (Donatevich)**
1925- ...................... CLC 8
See also CA 85-88

**Sirin, V.**
See Nabokov, Vladimir (Vladimirovich)

**Sissman, L(ouis) E(dward)**
1928-1976 ................ CLC 9, 18
See also CANR 13; CA 21-24R;
obituary CA 65-68; DLB 5

**Sisson, C(harles) H(ubert)** 1914-..... CLC 8
See also CAAS 3; CANR 3; CA 1-4R;
DLB 27

**Sitwell, (Dame) Edith** 1887-1964... CLC 2, 9
See also CA 9-12R; DLB 20

**Sjoewall, Maj** 1935-
See Wahloo, Per
See also CA 61-64, 65-68

**Sjowall, Maj** 1935-
See Wahloo, Per

**Skelton, Robin** 1925- ............. CLC 13
See also CAAS 5; CA 5-8R; DLB 27, 53

**Skolimowski, Jerzy** 1938- ......... CLC 20

**Skolimowski, Yurek** 1938-
See Skolimowski, Jerzy

**Skram, Amalie (Bertha)**
1847-1905 ................ TCLC 25

**Skrine, Mary Nesta** 1904-
See Keane, Molly

**Skvorecky, Josef (Vaclav)**
1924- ................... CLC 15, 39
See also CAAS 1; CANR 10; CA 61-64

**Slade, Bernard** 1930- .......... CLC 11, 46
See also Newbound, Bernard Slade
See also DLB 53

**Slaughter, Carolyn** 1946-.......... CLC 56
See also CA 85-88

**Slaughter, Frank G(ill)** 1908- ...... CLC 29
See also CANR 5; CA 5-8R

**Slavitt, David (R.)** 1935- ........ CLC 5, 14
See also CAAS 3; CA 21-24R; DLB 5, 6

**Slesinger, Tess** 1905-1945 ........ TCLC 10
See also CA 107

**Slessor, Kenneth** 1901-1971........ CLC 14
See also CA 102; obituary CA 89-92

**Slowacki, Juliusz** 1809-1849 ..... NCLC 15

**Smart, Christopher** 1722-1771........ LC 3

**Smart, Elizabeth** 1913-1986........ CLC 54
See also CA 81-84; obituary CA 118

**Smiley, Jane (Graves)** 1949- ....... CLC 53
See also CA 104

**Smith, A(rthur) J(ames) M(arshall)**
1902-1980 ................. CLC 15
See also CANR 4; CA 1-4R;
obituary CA 102

**Smith, Betty (Wehner)** 1896-1972... CLC 19
See also CA 5-8R; obituary CA 33-36R;
SATA 6; DLB-Y 82

**Smith, Cecil Lewis Troughton** 1899-1966
See Forester, C(ecil) S(cott)

**Smith, Charlotte (Turner)**
1749-1806 ................. NCLC 23
See also DLB 39

**Smith, Clark Ashton** 1893-1961 .... CLC 43

**Smith, Dave** 1942- ............ CLC 22, 42
See also Smith, David (Jeddie)
See also CAAS 7; CANR 1; DLB 5

**Smith, David (Jeddie)** 1942-
See Smith, Dave
See also CANR 1; CA 49-52

**Smith, Florence Margaret** 1902-1971
See Smith, Stevie
See also CAP 2; CA 17-18;
obituary CA 29-32R

**Smith, John** 1580?-1631............. LC 9
See also DLB 24, 30

**Smith, Lee** 1944-................. CLC 25
See also CA 114, 119; DLB-Y 83

**Smith, Martin Cruz** 1942-......... CLC 25
See also CANR 6; CA 85-88

**Smith, Martin William** 1942-
See Smith, Martin Cruz

**Smith, Mary-Ann Tirone** 1944-..... CLC 39
See also CA 118

**Smith, Patti** 1946- .............. CLC 12
See also CA 93-96

**Smith, Pauline (Urmson)**
1882-1959 ................ TCLC 25
See also CA 29-32R; SATA 27

**Smith, Rosamond** 1938-
See Oates, Joyce Carol

**Smith, Sara Mahala Redway** 1900-1972
See Benson, Sally

**Smith, Stevie** 1902-1971.... CLC 3, 8, 25, 44
See also Smith, Florence Margaret
See also DLB 20

**Smith, Wilbur (Addison)** 1933-..... CLC 33
See also CANR 7; CA 13-16R

**Smith, William Jay** 1918- ......... CLC 6
See also CA 5-8R; SATA 2; DLB 5

**Smollett, Tobias (George)** 1721-1771 .. LC 2
See also DLB 39

**Snodgrass, W(illiam) D(e Witt)**
1926- ............CLC 2, 6, 10, 18
See also CANR 6; CA 1-4R; DLB 5

**Snow, C(harles) P(ercy)**
1905-1980 ....... CLC 1, 4, 6, 9, 13, 19
See also CA 5-8R; obituary CA 101;
DLB 15

**Snyder, Gary (Sherman)**
1930- .............. CLC 1, 2, 5, 9, 32
See also CA 17-20R; DLB 5, 16

Taylor, Mildred D(elois)   1943- . . . . . CLC 21
See also CLR 9; CANR 25; CA 85-88;
SAAS 5; SATA 15; DLB 52

Taylor, Peter (Hillsman)
1917- . . . . . . . . CLC 1, 4, 18, 37, 44, 50
See also CANR 9; CA 13-16R; DLB-Y 81

Taylor, Robert Lewis   1912- . . . . . . . . CLC 14
See also CANR 3; CA 1-4R; SATA 10

Teasdale, Sara   1884-1933. . . . . . . . . TCLC 4
See also CA 104; SATA 32; DLB 45

Tegner, Esaias   1782-1846. . . . . . . . NCLC 2

Teilhard de Chardin, (Marie Joseph) Pierre
1881-1955 . . . . . . . . . . . . . . . . . . TCLC 9
See also CA 105

Tennant, Emma   1937- . . . . . . . . CLC 13, 52
See also CAAS 9; CANR 10; CA 65-68;
DLB 14

Teran, Lisa St. Aubin de   19??- . . . . . CLC 36

Terkel, Louis   1912-
See Terkel, Studs
See also CANR 18; CA 57-60

Terkel, Studs   1912- . . . . . . . . . . . . . CLC 38
See also Terkel, Louis

Terry, Megan   1932- . . . . . . . . . . . . . CLC 19
See also CA 77-80; DLB 7

Tertz, Abram   1925-
See Sinyavsky, Andrei (Donatevich)

Tesich, Steve   1943?- . . . . . . . . . . . . CLC 40
See also CA 105; DLB-Y 83

Tesich, Stoyan   1943?-
See Tesich, Steve

Teternikov, Fyodor Kuzmich   1863-1927
See Sologub, Fyodor
See also CA 104

Tevis, Walter   1928-1984 . . . . . . . . . CLC 42
See also CA 113

Tey, Josephine   1897-1952 . . . . . . . TCLC 14
See also Mackintosh, Elizabeth

Thackeray, William Makepeace
1811-1863 . . . . . . . . . . . NCLC 5, 14, 22
See also SATA 23; DLB 21, 55

Thakura, Ravindranatha   1861-1941
See Tagore, (Sir) Rabindranath
See also CA 104

Thelwell, Michael (Miles)   1939- . . . . CLC 22
See also CA 101

Theroux, Alexander (Louis)
1939- . . . . . . . . . . . . . . . . . . CLC 2, 25
See also CANR 20; CA 85-88

Theroux, Paul
1941- . . . . . . . . CLC 5, 8, 11, 15, 28, 46
See also CANR 20; CA 33-36R; SATA 44;
DLB 2

Thesen, Sharon   1946- . . . . . . . . . . . CLC 56

Thibault, Jacques Anatole Francois
1844-1924
See France, Anatole
See also CA 106

Thiele, Colin (Milton)   1920- . . . . . . . CLC 17
See also CANR 12; CA 29-32R; SAAS 2;
SATA 14

Thomas, Audrey (Grace)
1935- . . . . . . . . . . . . . . . CLC 7, 13, 37
See also CA 21-24R; DLB 60

Thomas, D(onald) M(ichael)
1935- . . . . . . . . . . . . . . CLC 13, 22, 31
See also CANR 17; CA 61-64; DLB 40

Thomas, Dylan (Marlais)
1914-1953 . . . . . . . . . TCLC 1, 8; SSC 3
See also CA 104, 120; DLB 13, 20

Thomas, Edward (Philip)
1878-1917 . . . . . . . . . . . . . . . TCLC 10
See also CA 106; DLB 19

Thomas, John Peter   1928-
See Thomas, Piri

Thomas, Joyce Carol   1938- . . . . . . . . CLC 35
See also CA 113, 116; SATA 40; DLB 33

Thomas, Lewis   1913- . . . . . . . . . . . . CLC 35
See also CA 85-88

Thomas, Piri   1928- . . . . . . . . . . . . . . CLC 17
See also CA 73-76

Thomas, R(onald) S(tuart)
1913- . . . . . . . . . . . . . . . CLC 6, 13, 48
See also CAAS 4; CA 89-92; DLB 27

Thomas, Ross (Elmore)   1926- . . . . . . CLC 39
See also CANR 22; CA 33-36R

Thompson, Ernest   1860-1946
See Seton, Ernest (Evan) Thompson

Thompson, Francis (Joseph)
1859-1907 . . . . . . . . . . . . . . . . TCLC 4
See also CA 104; DLB 19

Thompson, Hunter S(tockton)
1939- . . . . . . . . . . . . . . . CLC 9, 17, 40
See also CANR 23; CA 17-20R

Thompson, Judith   1954- . . . . . . . . . . CLC 39

Thomson, James   1834-1882 . . . . . . NCLC 18
See also DLB 35

Thoreau, Henry David
1817-1862 . . . . . . . . . . . . . NCLC 7, 21
See also DLB 1; CDALB 1640-1865

Thurber, James (Grover)
1894-1961 . . . . . . CLC 5, 11, 25; SSC 1
See also CANR 17; CA 73-76; SATA 13;
DLB 4, 11, 22

Thurman, Wallace   1902-1934 . . . . . TCLC 6
See also CA 104, 124; DLB 51

Tieck, (Johann) Ludwig
1773-1853 . . . . . . . . . . . . . . . NCLC 5

Tillinghast, Richard   1940- . . . . . . . . CLC 29
See also CANR 26; CA 29-32R

Timrod, Henry   1828-1867 . . . . . . . NCLC 25

Tindall, Gillian   1938- . . . . . . . . . . . . CLC 7
See also CANR 11; CA 21-24R

Tiptree, James, Jr.   1915-1987 . . . CLC 48, 50
See also Sheldon, Alice (Hastings) B(radley)
See also DLB 8

Tocqueville, Alexis (Charles Henri Maurice
Clerel, Comte) de   1805-1859. . NCLC 7

Tolkien, J(ohn) R(onald) R(euel)
1892-1973 . . . . . . CLC 1, 2, 3, 8, 12, 38
See also CAP 2; CA 17-18;
obituary CA 45-48; SATA 2, 32;
obituary SATA 24; DLB 15

Toller, Ernst   1893-1939 . . . . . . . . . TCLC 10
See also CA 107

Tolson, Melvin B(eaunorus)
1900?-1966. . . . . . . . . . . . . . . CLC 36
See also CA 124; obituary CA 89-92;
DLB 48, 124

Tolstoy, (Count) Alexey Nikolayevich
1883-1945 . . . . . . . . . . . . . . . TCLC 18
See also CA 107

Tolstoy, (Count) Leo (Lev Nikolaevich)
1828-1910 . . . . . . . . TCLC 4, 11, 17, 28
See also CA 104, 123; SATA 26

Tomlin, Lily   1939- . . . . . . . . . . . . . . CLC 17

Tomlin, Mary Jean   1939-
See Tomlin, Lily
See also CA 117

Tomlinson, (Alfred) Charles
1927- . . . . . . . . . . . . . CLC 2, 4, 6, 13, 45
See also CA 5-8R; DLB 40

Toole, John Kennedy   1937-1969 . . . . CLC 19
See also CA 104; DLB-Y 81

Toomer, Jean
1894-1967 . . . . . CLC 1, 4, 13, 22; SSC 1
See also CA 85-88; DLB 45, 51

Torrey, E. Fuller   19??- . . . . . . . . . . . CLC 34
See also CA 119

Tournier, Michel   1924- . . . . . . CLC 6, 23, 36
See also CANR 3; CA 49-52; SATA 23

Townshend, Peter (Dennis Blandford)
1945- . . . . . . . . . . . . . . . . . CLC 17, 42
See also CA 107

Tozzi, Federigo   1883-1920. . . . . . . TCLC 31

Trakl, Georg   1887-1914 . . . . . . . . . . TCLC 5
See also CA 104

Transtromer, Tomas (Gosta)
1931- . . . . . . . . . . . . . . . . . . . . CLC 52
See also CA 117

Traven, B.   1890-1969 . . . . . . . . . . CLC 8, 11
See also CAP 2; CA 19-20;
obituary CA 25-28R; DLB 9, 56

Tremain, Rose   1943- . . . . . . . . . . . . CLC 42
See also CA 97-100; DLB 14

Tremblay, Michel   1942- . . . . . . . . . . CLC 29
See also CA 116; DLB 60

Trevanian   1925- . . . . . . . . . . . . . . . CLC 29
See also CA 108

Trevor, William   1928- . . . . . CLC 7, 9, 14, 25
See also Cox, William Trevor
See also DLB 14

Trifonov, Yuri (Valentinovich)
1925-1981 . . . . . . . . . . . . . . . . CLC 45
See also obituary CA 103, 126

Trilling, Lionel   1905-1975 . . . . CLC 9, 11, 24
See also CANR 10; CA 9-12R;
obituary CA 61-64; DLB 28, 63

Trogdon, William   1939-
See Heat Moon, William Least
See also CA 115, 119

Trollope, Anthony   1815-1882 . . . . . NCLC 6
See also SATA 22; DLB 21, 57

Trotsky, Leon (Davidovich)
1879-1940 . . . . . . . . . . . . . . . TCLC 22
See also CA 118

Trotter (Cockburn), Catharine
1679-1749 . . . . . . . . . . . . . . . . . LC 8

# Literary Criticism Series
# Cumulative Topic Index

This index lists all topic entries in the Gale Literary Criticism Series *Contemporary Literary Criticism,* *Literature Criticism from 1400 to 1800, Nineteenth-Century Literature Criticism,* and *Twentieth-Century Literary Criticism.*

# *NCLC* Cumulative Nationality Index

**SWEDISH**

**SWISS**

# Title Index to Volume 26

509

**Title Index**